Encyclopedia of
THE OTTOMAN EMPIRE

Gábor Ágoston
Georgetown University, Washington, D.C.

Bruce Masters
Wesleyan University, Connecticut

An imprint of Infobase Publishing

Encyclopedia of the Ottoman Empire

Facts On File, Inc.
An imprint of Infobase Publishing
132 West 31st Street
New York NY 10001

Library of Congress Cataloging-in-Publication Data

Ágoston, Gábor.
Encyclopedia of the Ottoman Empire / Gábor Ágoston and Bruce Masters.
p. cm.
Includes bibliographical references and index.
ISBN-13: 978-0-8160-6259-1
ISBN-10: 0-8160-6259-5
1. Turkey—History—Ottoman Empire, 1288–1918—Encyclopedias. 2. Turkey—
Civilization—Encyclopedias. I. Masters, Bruce Alan, 1950– I. Title.
DR486.A375 2008
956'.01503—dc22   2008020716

Text design by Joan M. Toro, Erik Lindstrom
Maps by Sholto Ainslie

Printed in the United States of America

VB Hermitage 10 9 8 7 6 5 4 3 2 1

This book is printed on acid-free paper and
contains 30 percent postconsumer recycled content.

CONTENTS

EDITORS AND CONTRIBUTORS

EDITORS

Gábor Ágoston is associate professor at the Department of History of Georgetown University. His research focuses on Ottoman economic and military history from the 15th through 18th centuries, early modern Hungarian history, and on the comparative study of the Ottoman and Habsburg Empires. In addition to his five Hungarian–language books and numerous articles, he is the author of *Guns for the Sultan: Military Power and the Weapons Industry in the Ottoman Empire*.

Bruce Masters is the John Andrus Professor of History at Wesleyan University. He holds a Ph.D. in Near Eastern Studies from the University of Chicago. His publications include *Christians and Jews in the Ottoman Arab World: The Birth of Sectarianism* and *The Origins of Western Economic Dominance in the Middle East: Mercantilism and the Islamic Economy in Aleppo, 1600–1750*.

CONTRIBUTORS

Erhan Afyoncu is assistant professor in the Department of History at Marmara University, Istanbul. He teaches Ottoman political and military history in the 15th through 18th centuries. He has published three books in Turkish, including a guidebook on how to conduct historical research regarding the pre-Tanzimat era.

Zeynep Ahunbay is professor of architecture and head of the Department on Restoration of Monuments at Istanbul Technical University, and former president of ICOMOS Turkey (1999–2005). She teaches Ottoman architectural history and conservation of cultural heritage. She has been involved in the restoration of several war-damaged monuments in the Balkans. She is the author of several books and articles on Ottoman architecture.

Ali Akyıldız teaches at the history department of Marmara University (Istanbul). He has been one of the editors of the new Turkish-language *Encyclopedia of Islam* (TDVİA) since 1997, and was a visiting professor at the universities of London and Tokyo. His Turkish–language publications include two books on the reforms in the Ottoman central government during the Tanzimat and on the introduction of paper money. His book on *Ottoman Securities* was published in both Turkish and English.

Hüseyin Al is board member of the Banking Regulation and Supervision Agency of Turkey. His research interests include the financial history of the Ottoman Empire with particular reference to banks, banking, capital markets, and relation with international money markets in the 19th century. In addition to articles on the above topics, he has published two books in Turkish on international capital and Ottoman finances in 1820–1875 and on Ottoman foreign debts in 1854–1856.

Zeynep Atbaş has been a curator of manuscripts at the Topkapı Palace Museum since 1998. Her research interest concerns Islamic manuscripts and she has published several articles and papers on miniature paintings.

Cemil Aydın is assistant professor at the Department of History, University of North Carolina at Charlotte, where he teaches courses on Middle Eastern and international history. His recent publications include *Politics of Anti-Westernism in Asia: Visions of World Order in Pan–Islamic and Pan–Asian Thought*.

Salih Aynural is professor of history at the Gebze Institute of Technology, Turkey, where he teaches Ottoman economic history. In addition to his articles in Turkish and English on the provisioning of Istanbul, he has published a book in Turkish on the Istanbul mills, millers, and bakers in the 18th and 19th centuries.

Yakup Bektaş is an historian of technology with the Tokyo Institute of Technology. His articles on the history of the Ottoman and American telegraph appeared in *Technology and Culture* and in the *British Journal for the History of Science*.

Bestami S. Bilgiç is assistant professor at the Department of International Relations, Çanakkale Onsekiz Mart University, Turkey. He teaches courses on political history, Balkan history, and Turkish foreign policy. His research field is history and politics of the Balkans. He has published several articles on Turkish-Greek relations in the interwar period.

Ö. Faruk Bölükbaşı is a Ph.D. student at Marmara University, Istanbul. His thesis focuses on the history of the Ottoman Imperial Mint. His book on Ottoman financial administration in the time of Abdülhamid II was published in Turkish.

Günhan Börekçi is a Ph.D. candidate in history at Ohio State University. His dissertation focuses on the Ottoman royal court and favorites during the reign of Sultan Ahmed I (r. 1603–1617). His article on the Janissaries' volley fire tactic appeared in 2006. He is also the co–editor for the publication of Feridun Ahmed Bey's illustrated chronicle on Sultan Süleyman's last campaign in 1566.

İdris Bostan is professor in the Department of History at the University of Istanbul, and an expert on Ottoman maritime history. His publications in Turkish include several monographs on the history of the Ottoman Naval Arsenal (*Tersane-i Amire*), Ottoman sailing and rowing ships, and the Aegean island under Ottoman rule. He is also co–author of *A Short History of the Period of Ottoman Sovereignty of the Aegean Islands*, and *The 1565 Ottoman Malta Campaign Register*.

Palmira Brummett is professor of history and distinguished professor of humanities at the University of Tennessee. She is the author of *Image and Imperialism in the Ottoman Revolutionary Press, 1908–1911*, and *Ottoman Seapower and Levantine Diplomacy in the Age of Discovery*. Her current projects concern the Ottoman Adriatic and early modern mapping, in narrative and image, of Ottoman space and sovereignty.

Mustafa Budak is vice general director of the State Archives of Turkey and director of the Prime Ministry's Ottoman Archives in Istanbul. His fields of research include the history of the Caucasus, the Crimean War, and Turkish foreign policy. In addition to his articles on these subjects, he has published a Turkish-language book on Ottoman foreign policy before the Lausanne Peace Treaty.

Yücel Bulut is assistant professor at the Department of Sociology of Istanbul University. In addition to his Turkish-language book on the history of Orientalism, he has published numerous articles on contemporary Turkish thought and the history of Turkish sociology.

Baki Çakır was a researcher at the Research Center of the Istanbul Municipality, between 1995 and 2000. In addition to his articles on Ottoman financial and institutional history, he has published a book in Turkish on the Ottoman tax farming system in the 16th through 18th centuries.

Coşkun Çakır is associate professor at the University of Istanbul. His research interests include Ottoman economic and social history. He is the author of two Turkish–language books on Ottoman fiscal policy during the Tanzimat era and on a 19th-century Anatolian city.

Vanesa Casanova-Fernandez is a Ph.D. candidate in the Department of History at Georgetown University. Her dissertation examines the construction of ethno-religious identities and hegemonic masculinities on the Spanish-Moroccan frontier in the 17th through 19th centuries.

Tûba Çavdar is assistant professor in the Department of Information Management at Marmara University, Istanbul. Her main field of research is the history of Ottoman libraries and books. Her book on the Rare Book Collection of the Istanbul Chamber of Commerce Library was recently published.

Yüksel Çelik is lecturer in the Department of History at Marmara University, Istanbul, where he teaches courses on Ottoman military history and reforms. His research interests include the Albanian National Awakening and Hüsrev Mehmed Pasha's political and military activities (1756–1855).

Gökhan Çetinsaya is professor of history in the Department of Humanities and Social Sciences at Istanbul Technical University. His main fields of research are modern Turkish political history (19th and 20th centuries), Turkish foreign policy, and the history of the Middle East. He is the author of *Ottoman Administration of Iraq, 1890–1908.*

David Cameron Cuthell Jr. is the executive director of the Institute of Turkish Studies in Washington D.C. and visiting adjunct professor at Columbia and Georgetown Universities. His research focuses on the 19th century immigration of Muslims from the Caucasus and the Crimea and their role in transforming late Ottoman Anatolia.

Géza Dávid is professor and head of department in the Department of Turkish Philology at the University of Budapest. His research interests include Ottoman demographic and administrative history. Several of his articles appeared in his *Studies in Demographic and Administrative History of Ottoman Hungary.* His recent publications include two co-edited books (with Pál Fodor): *Ottomans, Hungarians, and Habsburgs in Central Europe,* and *Ransom Slavery Along the Ottoman Borders.*

Fatmagül Demirel is assistant professor at Yıldız Technical University, Istanbul. Her research interests include legal and cultural history of the late Ottoman period. Her recent publications in Turkish include a monograph on Ottoman censorship under Abdülhamid II (r. 1876–1909).

M. Uğur Derman has studied with the famous calligrapher Necmeddin Okyay. He has published more than 400 articles and encyclopedia entries and numerous books on Ottoman calligraphy and book culture, including *Calligraphy Ottoman* (1990), *Letters in Gold* (1998), and *The Art of Calligraphy in the Islamic Heritage* (1998).

Mehmet Ali Doğan is a Ph.D. candidate at the Middle East Center of the University of Utah, where he studies American missionary activities in the Middle East in the 19th century. He is the co-editor of a forthcoming book on American missionary enterprise in the Middle East in the 19th and 20th centuries.

Kathryn Ebel is academic and administrative director of Georgetown University's McGhee Center for Eastern Mediterranean Studies in Alanya, Turkey. She is a specialist in the cartographic history of the Ottoman Empire, including city views, miniature paintings, and other visual sources for the urban and historical geography of the Ottoman world. Her articles have appeared in *Imago Mundi* and *Türkiye Araştırmaları Literatür Dergisi.* Her forthcoming book is titled *City Views, Imperial Visions: Cartography and the Visual Culture of Urban Space in the Ottoman Empire, 1453–1603.*

Feridun M. Emecen is professor of history at the University of Istanbul. His research and teaching interests include Ottoman chronicles, the history of the early Ottoman state, institutions, and provincial administration, military, and urban history. He is the author of numerous articles, encyclopedia entries and books on early Ottoman history, the conquest of Constantinople, the Jews of Manisa, and the administrative and economic history of Manisa.

Edhem Eldem is professor at the Department of History of Boğaziçi University, Istanbul, and has taught as visiting professor at the University of California at Berkeley and at the École des Hautes Études en Sciences Sociales, Paris. Among his fields of interest are foreign trade in the Levant in the 18th century, Ottoman funerary epigraphy, the development of an urban bourgeoisie in late 19th-century Istanbul, the history of the Imperial Ottoman Bank, and late 19th-century Ottoman first-person narratives and biographies. His publications include: *French Trade in Istanbul in the Eighteenth Century; A History of the Ottoman Bank; The Ottoman City between East and West: Aleppo, Izmir and Istanbul* (with Daniel Goffman and Bruce Masters); and *Death in Istanbul. Death and its Rituals in Ottoman–Islamic Culture.*

Sami Erdem is lecturer at the Divinity Faculty of Marmara University, Istanbul and was a visiting scholar at the University of Jordan in 2005–2006. He has published on the modern history of Islamic and Ottoman law, the Mecelle, the Caliphate, and the modernization of law in the Muslim world. He was the chief editor of the Turkish-language journal *Divan (Journal of Interdisciplinary Studies,* 2003–2007), and the co-editor of the TALİD's (*Turkish Studies Review*) special issue on the history of Turkish law.

Zeynep Tarım Ertuğ is associate professor in the history department at Istanbul University, where she teaches courses on Ottoman cultural history, visual sources, and the Ottoman imperial court. Her research interests include Ottoman manuscripts and miniatures, as well as court ceremony. Her book in Turkish on Ottoman enthronement and funeral ceremonies in the 16th century was published in 1999.

Şeref Etker is consultant pediatric surgeon and urologist at Zeynep-Kamil Hospital in Istanbul. His fields of interests include the medical interaction between the various religious communities in the Ottoman Empire, and modernization of Turkish military medicine. His articles were published in *Studies in Ottoman Science,* among others.

İhsan Fazlıoğlu is associate professor in the faculty of Letters and Arts at Istanbul University. He holds a Ph.D. in philosophy. He is an expert on the history of science and thought in the Ottoman Empire, focusing his research on mathematical science and natural philosophy.

Aleksandar Fotić is associate professor at the Department of History, University of Belgrade. He was visiting professor at the Institute for Mediterranean Studies, Rethymno (Greece) in 2002 and 2004. His research interests include the history of the Ottoman Balkans, the status of non-Muslims, urban culture, and everyday life. In addition to his articles in Serbian and English, he has published a book in Serbian on Mount Athos and Hilandar in the Ottoman Empire (15–17th centuries) and edited one on private life in Serbia at the dawn of modern age.

Mehmet Genç has taught Ottoman economic history at the Universities of Istanbul and Marmara, and more recently at Bilgi University. He is the foremost authority on Ottoman economic history in the 18th century. Several of his studies were collected in his Turkish-language book entitled *State and Economy in the Ottoman Empire*. He is the co-author and co-editor (with Erol Özvar) of a recently published two-volume book on Ottoman financial institutions and budgets.

Ibolya Gerelyes is deputy head of the Department of Archeology at the Hungarian National Museum. She has written numerous articles on Ottoman material culture, archaeology, and architecture. Her edited volumes include: *Süleyman the Magnificent and His Age*; *Archaeology of the Ottoman Period in Hungary* and (with Gyöngyi Kovács) *Turkish Flowers: Studies on Ottoman Art in Hungary*.

John-Paul Ghobrial is a Ph.D. candidate in the Department of History at Princeton University. His dissertation explores the circulation of news and information among Ottoman officials, European merchants and diplomats, and ordinary taxpayers in Istanbul in the latter half of the 17th century.

Rossitsa Gradeva is associate professor at the American University in Bulgaria, and research fellow at the Institute of Balkan Studies, Bulgarian Academy of Sciences. Her research interests include Ottoman provincial administration, application of Islamic law in the Ottoman Empire, status of non–Muslim communities and everyday life in the Ottoman Balkans, the Danube frontier, and the decentralization processes in the pre–Tanzimat era. She has published two volumes of collected essays: *Rumeli under the Ottomans 15th–18th Centuries: Institutions and Communities*, and *War and Peace in Rumeli, 15th to Beginning of 19th Century*.

Molly Greene is a professor in the Department of History at Princeton University, with a joint appointment in the Program in Hellenic Studies. Trained as an Ottoman historian, she has a particular interest in the history of the Greeks under Ottoman rule, as well as the history of the early modern Mediterranean. Her publications include *A Shared World: Christians and Muslims in the Early Modern Mediterranean*.

Feza Günergun is professor of history of science at the University of Istanbul. Her research fields include the introduction of modern sciences to Turkey in the 19th and 20th centuries with a special focus on educational institutions, journals, translations from European texts, biographies of Turkish scholars, as well as historiography of science and history of metrology. She is the editor of *Studies in Ottoman Science*, and numerous books including *Imperialism and Science,* and *Science Technology and Industry in the Ottoman World*.

Eren Jon Alexander Gryskiewicz is a graduate of Georgetown University who has studied at the London School of Economics and Pembroke College, Cambridge. Currently he is an international development consultant based in Washington, DC.

Steven Chase Gummer is a Ph.D. candidate in modern German history at Georgetown University. His dissertation focuses on German foreign policy and the press in the Ottoman Empire from 1875 to 1915. He has written articles on the Ottoman public debt and the German reaction to the Eastern Crisis of 1875–1878.

Emrah Safa Gürkan is a Ph.D. candidate in early modern European history at Georgetown University. His dissertation focuses on the Ottoman-Habsburg rivalry in the Mediterranean in the 16th century.

Gottfried Hagen teaches Turkish (including Ottoman) language and culture at the University of Michigan. His research focuses on Ottoman intellectual history, with a particular interest in geography, historiography, and religion as world interpretation. He is the author of *Ein osmanischer Geograph bei der Arbeit. Die Entstehung und Gedankenwelt von Kātib Čelebis Ğihannümā*, and numerous articles.

Oleksander Halenko is head of the Center for Turkish Studies at the Institute of History of the National Academy of Sciences of Ukraine and assistant professor of history at the University of Kyiv-Mohyla Academy. His research focuses on Turko-Slavic relations and on the history of the northern Black Sea region, including the Ottoman province of Kefe (Caffa), and the Crimean Khanate. His book in progress examines the slave trade in the Black Sea region from its origins to the 18th century.

M. Şükrü Hanioğlu is professor and chair in Near Eastern Studies and director of the Program in Near Eastern Studies at Princeton University. He is a specialist on late Ottoman history, with particular interest in the history of the Committee of Union and Progress and the Young Turk Revolution. His publications include *The Young Turks in Opposition*; *Preparation for a Revolution*; and *A Brief History of the Late Ottoman Empire*.

Colin Heywood taught Ottoman history for 25 years at SOAS, until his retirement in 1999, and was visiting professor at Princeton, Chicago, and Cyprus. He is now an honorary research fellow in the Maritime History Research Centre, University of Hull. He has published a number of articles on diverse aspects of Ottoman history and, more recently, on English and Mediterranean maritime history and on the intellectual legacy of Fernand Braudel. Some of the former have been collected in *Writing Ottoman History: Documents and Interpretations*. He is currently editing *The Levant Voyage of the* Blackham Galley, *1696–8: the Sea Diary of John Looker, Ship's Surgeon* and (with Maria Fusaro) *After Braudel: The 'Northern Invasion' and the Mediterranean Maritime Economy, 1580–1820*.

Ekmeleddin İhsanoğlu is secretary general of the Organisation of the Islamic Conference (OIC). He was the founding chair of the first department of history of science in Turkey at the University of Istanbul (1984–2000), and has taught at Ankara, Exeter, Istanbul, and Munich universities. He is former president of IUHPS, member of Academie Europea and the International Academy of History of Science. He is the holder of the UNESCO Avicenna Medal; Alexandre Koyré Medal of the International Academy of History of Science, and numerous honorary academic titles. He was the founding director general of OIC Research Centre for Islamic History, Art and Culture (IRCICA, 1980–2004). He is the editor and co-author of the 15 volume *Series of History of Ottoman Scientific Literature*; the two-volume *History of the Ottoman State and Civilization*; *Culture and Learning in Islam*; and author of *Science Technology and Learning in the Ottoman Empire*; *Turks in Egypt and their Cultural Heritage*; and *History of the Ottoman University (Darülfünun)*.

Handan İnci is associate professor in the Department of Turkish Language and Literature at Mimar Sinan University, Istanbul. Her research interests include western influences in Turkish literature and the history of Ottoman literature during the Tanzimat era. She has published books in Turkish on the memoirs of Ahmet Midhat Efendi, on Beşir Fuad, and on the Turkish novel.

Mária Ivanics is associate professor and head of the Department of Altaic Studies at the University of Szeged, Hungary. Her research interests include the history and sources of the Golden Horde and the Crimean Khanate. She is the author of a book in Hungarian about the role of the Crimean Tatars in the Habsburg-Ottoman War of 1593–1606 and co-author (with Mirkasym A. Usmanov) of a book in German on the Genghis-name, a 17th–century historical source written in the Volga-Turkic language.

Ahmet Zeki İzgöer is an historian at the Prime Ministry's Ottoman Archives in Istanbul. In addition to his monograph on Ahmed Cevdet Paha, he has edited and published in modern Turkish more than 20 books originally written in Ottoman Turkish, including the memoirs of Cemal Pasha (1913–22), the works of Namik Kemal and Ziya Gökalp, and the Salnames of Diyarbekir.

Maureen Jackson is a Ph.D. candidate at the University of Washington, Department of Comparative Literature. Her areas of interest include Ottoman, Turkish, and Jewish social history, with a focus on Ottoman classical music.

Mustafa Kaçar is professor at the University of Istanbul. His research interests include the history of science and technology in the Ottoman Empire (17th –19th centuries), introduction of modern sciences to Turkey, history of military engineering education, and Ottoman scientific instruments.

Sevtap Kadıoğlu is associate professor in the Department of History of Science at the University of Istanbul. Her research focuses on the modernization of scientific and educational institutions in the Ottoman Empire and on the history of science in Turkey. Her book on the history of Istanbul University's faculty of science (1900–1946) was recently published in Turkish.

Kemal H. Karpat is professor emeritus of history at the University of Wisconsin, Madison. From 1967 through 2003 he was associated as lecturer, researcher, or scholar in residence with several major Turkish universities as well as Montana State University, New York University, Harvard, Princeton, Johns Hopkins, and Paris. He has authored and edited more than 20 books, including his last major work *The Politicization of Islam: Reconstructing Identity, State, Faith, and Community in the Late*

Ottoman State. He is also the editor of the *International Journal of Turkish Studies*, and occasional contributor to Turkish newspapers.

Eugenia Kermeli is a lecturer in the history department at Bilkent University, Ankara. She had also taught at the universities of Manchester and Liverpool. Her primary fields of research are the transition from late Byzantine to early Ottoman institutions, the position of *dhimmi*s in the Ottoman Empire, and Ottoman legal history. She is the co-editor of *Islamic Law: Theory and Practice*. She is currently working on a monograph on parallel systems of justice in the Ottoman Empire.

Markus Koller is associate professor for South Eastern European history at the University of Gießen, Germany. His numerous studies on Ottoman and Balkan history include *Bosnien an der Schwelle zur Neuzeit. Eine Kulturgeschichte der Gewalt (1747–1798)* (2004). He is also the co-editor (with Kemal Karpat) of *Ottoman Bosnia: A History in Peril* and (with Vera Costantini) *Living in the Ottoman Ecumenical Community: Essays in Honour of Suraiya Faroqhi (2008)*.

Dariusz Kołodziejczyk is associate professor at the Institute of History, University of Warsaw. He also holds a position in the Polish Academy of Sciences and was visiting professor at the University of Notre Dame. His research interests include the history of the Ottoman Empire and the Crimean Khanate, international relations in early modern Europe, and multicultural experience of today's Eastern Europe. His publications include *Ottoman-Polish Diplomatic Relations (15th–18th Century)*, and *The Ottoman Survey Register of Podolia (ca. 1681)*.

Orhan Koloğlu is assistant professor at the Press Museum of Istanbul. His fields of research include the history of the late Ottoman Empire and modern Turkey, modernization, political movements, parties and their leaders, and the Ottoman and Turkish press. He has published numerous books in Turkish on the Ottoman and Turkish press, the history of the early Turkish republic, Free Masonry in republican Turkey, as well as biographies of Sultan Abdülhamid II, Kemal Atatürk, and former prime minister Bülent Ecevit.

Elias Kolovos is lecturer in the Department of History and Archaeology at the University of Crete, Greece. He taught as a visiting lecturer at the Ecole Pratique des Hautes Etudes in Paris and at Boğaziçi University in Istanbul. His research interests include Ottoman peasant history, the history of monasteries under Ottoman administration, and insular societies in the Ottoman Empire. He has published a book in Greek on the history of the Aegean island of Andros under Ottoman rule and co-edited *The Ottoman Empire, the Balkans, the Greek Lands*.

Tijana Krstić is assistant professor at Pennsylvania State University, where she teaches Ottoman and Mediterranean history. Her forthcoming book is entitled *Contested Conversions to Islam*, and she is the author of articles on religious politics in the early modern Ottoman Empire that will appear in *Comparative Studies in Society and History* and the *Turkish Studies Association Journal*.

Sadi S. Kucur is assistant professor at the Department of History, Marmara University, Istanbul, where he teaches courses on the Seljuks. His research and publications concern Seljuk institutional, social and economic history, as well as numismatics and epigraphy.

Nenad Moačanin is professor at the Department of History, University of Zagreb. He teaches Croatian history in the context of the history of the western Balkans in the 16th–18th centuries, as well as Ottoman paleography and diplomatics. He has published four books that focus on social and economic history, in particular taxation, demography, and rural economy, including *Town and Country on the Middle Danube, 1526 – 1690*.

Hidayet Y. Nuhoğlu was lecturer at Hacettepe University (1978–82) and Istanbul University (1990–2000) and researcher and assistant director general at IRCICA (Research Centre for Islamic History, Art and Culture) in Istanbul (1980–2000). In addition to his articles he has edited works on Ottoman education and learning and on Ottoman postage stamps.

İlber Ortaylı is professor of history at the universities of Galatasaray (Istanbul) and Bilkent, and head of Topkapı Palace Museum. He is a specialist of 19th century Ottoman and Russian history, especially the history of public administration, urban, diplomatic, cultural, and intellectual history. His articles in English were collected in *Ottoman Studies*, and *Studies on Ottoman Transformation*. He is also the author of numerous Turkish-language books on the 19th-century, post-Tanzimat era provincial administration, the family in the Ottoman Empire, German influences in the Ottoman Empire, westernization, and the Topkapı Palace.

Victor Ostapchuk teaches Ottoman studies at the Department of Near and Middle Eastern Civilizations of the University of Toronto. His interests include the Ottoman Black Sea and the empire's relations with Muscovy, Poland, and Ukraine; Ottoman institutional history; Ottoman historical archaeology; and the history of the Great Eurasian Steppe. In addition to his numerous scholarly articles he is the author of a forthcoming monograph entitled *Warfare and Diplomacy across Sea and Steppe: The Ottoman Black Sea Frontier in the Early Seventeenth Century.*

Erol Özvar is associate professor in the Department of Economics at Marmara University, Istanbul. He is an expert on Ottoman economic and financial history. His publications in Turkish include a monograph on the life long tax farming (*malikane*) system in Ottoman finances and a two-volume book on Ottoman financial institutions and budgets which he co-edited and co-authored with Mehmet Genç.

Sándor Papp is associate professor and chair of department at the Gáspár Károli University of the Hungarian Reformed (Calvinist) Church (Budapest) and associate professor at the University of Szeged, Hungary. His research interests include Ottoman diplomatics and paleography, Ottoman–Hungarian relations, and the history of Ottoman vassal states. He is the author of *Die Verleihungs–, Bekräftigungs– und Vertragsurkunden der Osmanen für Ungarn und Siebenbürgen.*

Şevket Pamuk teaches economic history and political economy at the London School of Economics and Political Science where he directs the chair on contemporary Turkey and at Boğaziçi University, Istanbul. He is the author of *The Ottoman Empire and European Capitalism, Trade, Investment and Production, 1820–1913*; *A Monetary History of the Ottoman Empire*, and *A History of the Middle East Economies in the Twentieth Century* (with Roger Owen). Pamuk was the president of the European Historical Economics Society (2003–2005).

Daniel Panzac was until his retirement director of research at CNRS, University of Provance in Aix-en-Provance, France. A former president of the European Association for Middle East Studies, Professor Panzac is a specialist on Ottoman demographic and maritime history. His many publications include: *Barbary Corsairs: The End of a Legend, 1800–1820*; *La caravane maritime: Marins européens et marchands ottomans en Méditerranée, 1680–1830*; *La peste dans l'Empire ottoman, 1700–1850*; *Quarantaines et lazarets: l'Europe et la peste d'Orient, XVIIe–XXe siècles.*

Maria Pia Pedani is associate professor in the Department of Historical Studies at the University Ca' Foscari of Venice. She is the author of several books in Italian, about Ottoman ambassadors to Venice (*In nome del Gran Signore*), Ottoman documents kept in the Venetian State Archives (*I "Documenti Turchi" dell'Archivio di Stato di Venezia*) and borders between Muslim and European countries (*Dalla frontiera al confine*). Lately she wrote a short history of the Ottoman Empire in Italian and an historical play *The Venetian Sultana*, already performed in Ankara and Istanbul.

Şefik Peksevgen is assistant professor in the Department of History at Yeditepe University, Istanbul. His research interests include political history of the Ottoman Empire in the early modern era, with a special emphasis on building and exercising sovereign power in a comparative perspective.

Christine Philliou is assistant professor in the Department of History at Columbia University. She specializes in the social and political history of the 18th- and 19th-centuries Ottoman Empire and is particularly interested in the role of Phanariots in Ottoman governance. Her forthcoming book is entitled *Biography of an Empire: Ottoman Governance in the Age of Revolution.*

Andrew Robarts is a Ph.D. candidate in Russian and Ottoman history at Georgetown University, where he also received a Master's Degree in foreign service. His dissertation focuses on population movements and the spread of disease between the Ottoman and Russian empires in the late 18th and early 19th centuries. He has published articles on Bulgarian history and the Russian Federation's migration management policies.

Claudia Römer is associate professor and head of the Institute of Oriental Studies, University of Vienna. Her research interests include Ottoman diplomatics; early modern Ottoman social and economic history; Ottoman historical grammar, syntax and stylistics; contact linguistics; and Ottoman proverbs. Apart from articles on these topics, she has published Ottoman documents: (with Anton C. Schaendlinger) *Die Schreiben Süleymans des Prächtigen an Karl V., Ferdinand I. und Maximilian II*; *Die Schreiben Süleymans des Prächtigen an Beamte, Militärbeamte, Vasallen und Richter*; *Osmanische Festungsbesatzungen in Ungarn zur Zeit Murāds III*; and (with Gisela Procházka-Eisl) *Osmanische Beamtenschreiben und Privatbriefe der Zeit Süleymāns des Prächtigen.*

İlhan Şahin is professor at the Kyrgyz–Turkish Manas University, Bishkek (Kyrgyzstan). In addition to his numerous articles in Turkish and English on Ottoman administrative, social and economic history, he has published a book in Turkish on the Yağcı Bedir Yörüks. A selection of his articles on the nomads was published in his *Nomads in the Ottoman Empire.*

Kahraman Şakul is a Ph.D. candidate in Middle East history at Georgetown University. His dissertation focuses on Ottoman-Russian relations in late 18th century. He has published articles on Ottoman military history and the reforms of Sultan Selim III (1789–1807).

Fikret Sarıcaoğlu is assistant professor in the Department of History at Istanbul University. His field of research is the history of Ottoman institutions in the 15th through 17th centuries, historical sources, and the history of Ottoman cartography. He is the author of a Turkish-language book on Abdülhamid I (r. 1774–89).

Mustafa Şentop is associate professor at the Faculty of Law of Marmara University, Istanbul. His field if research is the history of Ottoman and Turkish law. He has published studies on the sharia courts and Ottoman criminal law in the post-Tanzimat era.

Vildan Serdaroğlu has been a researcher at ISAM (Center for Islamic Studies, Istanbul) since 2000. She provides entries on Turkish literature for the new Turkish-language *Encyclopedia of Islam (DVİA)*, teaches Ottoman Turkish, Ottoman literature, and coordinates academic meetings at the center. Her book on the 16th-century divan poet Zati was recently published in Turkish.

Amy Singer is professor of Ottoman history in the Department of Middle Eastern and African History at Tel Aviv University. Her major interests are in socio-economic history, with a particular focus on charity and philanthropy, in particular the large Ottoman public kitchens, and on agrarian history. She is the author of *Charity in Islamic Societies*, and *Constructing Ottoman Beneficence: An Imperial Soup Kitchen in Jerusalem*; and the co-editor of *Feeding People, Feeding Power: Imarets in the Ottoman Empire* (with Nina Ergin and Christoph Neumann), and *Poverty and Charity in Middle Eastern Contexts* (with Michael Bonner and Mine Ener).

Selçuk Akşin Somel is assistant professor of Ottoman history in the Faculty of Arts and Social Sciences at Sabancı University, İstanbul. He is an expert on 19th-century Ottoman education, focusing his research on peripheral populations, gender history, legitimacy and power, and the modernization of central bureaucracy. His recent publications include *The Modernization of Public Education in the Ottoman Empire (1839–1908)*, and *Historical Dictionary of the Ottoman Empire*.

Faruk Tabak was, before his untimely death in February 2008, Nesuhi Ertegün assistant professor of modern Turkish studies in the Edmund A. Walsh School of Foreign Service at Georgetown University. Prior to Georgetown he worked as a research associate at the Fernand Braudel Center for the Study of Economies, Histori-

cal Systems and Civilizations at Binghamton. He is the author of *The Waning of the Mediterranean, 1550–1870: A Geohistorical Approach*, and co-editor of *Landholding and Commercial Agriculture in the Middle East; Informalization: Process and Structure;* and *Allies As Rivals: The U.S., Europe, and Japan in a Changing World–System*.

Judith Tucker is professor of history and director of the Master of Arts in Arab Studies Program at Georgetown University, and editor of the *International Journal of Middle East Studies*. Her research interests focus on the Arab world in the Ottoman period, women in Middle East history, and Islamic law, women, and gender. She is the author of many publications on the history of women and gender in the Arab world, including *Women, Family, and Gender in Islamic Law; In the House of the Law: Gender and Islamic Law in Ottoman Syria and Palestine; Women in Nineteenth-Century Egypt;* and co–author of *Women in the Middle East and North Africa: Restoring Women to History*.

Yunus Uğur is a Ph.D. candidate in the Department of History at Boğaziçi University. His research concentrates on urban historiography and Ottoman urban history. He is also among the editors of a periodical titled *Türkiye Araştırmaları Literatür Dergisi (Turkish Studies Review)* and was a chief editor of its special issue on urban history of Turkey.

Ali Yaycıoğlu is a postdoctoral fellow at Hellenic Studies, Princeton University. His Ph.D. thesis from Harvard is entitled "The Provincial Challenge: Regionalism, Crisis and Integration in the late Ottoman Empire, 1792–1812."

Asiye Kakirman Yıldız is assistant at Marmara University, Istanbul. Her research interests include archives, libraries, and information management. Her book on Hüseyin Hilmi Pasha's collection was published in 2006.

Hüseyin Yılmaz is visiting assistant professor at Stanford University. His research interests include pre-Tanzimat political thought, Ottoman historiography, and constitutionalism in the Ottoman Empire.

Nuh Yılmaz is a Ph.D. candidate in cultural studies at George Mason University, where he teaches aesthetics and critical theory at Art and Visual Technologies as an adjunct professor. His area of expertise includes visual studies, semiotics, non-western picturing practices, and aesthetic theory. He has published articles on contemporary Turkish politics and Islam, and on human rights issues.

İlhami Yurdakul is assistant professor in the Department of History at the University of Harran, Şanlıurfa

(Turkey). His research interests include the history of Ottoman religious institutions and urban history. He is the author of a recent book on the reform of the Ottoman religious institutions and a catalogue of the archives of the office of the Chief Mufti (Şeyhülislamık) in the Ottoman Empire.

Dror Zeevi teaches history of the Middle East at Ben Gurion University of the Negev. He was the first chair of the Middle East Studies Department from 1995 to 1998 and again from 2002 to 2004. He was also among the founders of The Chaim Herzog Center for Middle East Studies and Diplomacy and chaired it from its foundation in 1997 to 2002. From 2006 to 2008 he served as president of the Middle East and Islamic Studies Association of Israel. His research and teaching interests include Ottoman and post-Ottoman society and culture. His most recent book is *Producing Desire: Changing Sexual Discourse in the Ottoman Middle East, 1500–1900.*

Madeline Zilfi is associate professor of history at the University of Maryland, College Park. Her research focuses on Ottoman history of the 18th and 19th centuries, particularly urban society, slavery, religious movements, legal practice, and women and gender. She is the author of *The Politics of Piety: The Ottoman Ulema in the Post–Classical Age*, and editor of *Women in the Ottoman Empire: Middle Eastern Women in the Early Modern Middle East*, and has also written on Islamic revivalism, slavery, divorce, and consumption patterns.

LIST OF ILLUSTRATIONS AND MAPS

Illustrations

Maps

ACKNOWLEDGMENTS

An encyclopedia is by its nature a collaborative work, and this one is no exception—indeed, to a greater extent than we could have imagined when embarking on the project. Initially the editors planned to write the lion's share of the entries for this volume, commissioning only the articles that we did not feel competent to write ourselves. As the process unfolded, however, we ended up commissioning a substantial part of the work, ordering articles from more than 90 colleagues. These submissions were all handled by Gábor Ágoston, who wishes to express his gratitude to the contributors who shared their expertise with us and braved many rounds of revision and clarification.

Our editors at Facts On File, Claudia Schaab (executive editor), Julia Rodas (editor), and Kate O'Halloran (copy editor) rigorously vetted, queried, and edited the text; we wish to thank them for their meticulous work on the volume. Thanks also go to Alexandra Lo Re (editorial assistant); Dale Williams and Sholto Ainslie (map designers), as well as to James Scotto-Lavino and Kerry Casey (desktop designers), who reproduced and sharpened our photos.

Some entries were written originally in Turkish and translated into English. The substantial work involved in re-writing and editing these articles was done with the help of a number of talented graduate and undergraduate students at Georgetown University. Elizabeth Shelton worked the most on these articles, but I also got help from Ben Ellis, and Emrah Safa Gürkan translated two articles from French. As part of Georgetown University's Undergraduate Research Opportunity Program (GUROP), Anoush Varjabedian and Jon Gryskiewicz edited several entries, and Wafa Al-Sayed searched the Library of Congress and other public domain sites for illustrations.

Finally, I wish to thank Kay Ebel and Scott Redford, directors of Georgetown University's McGhee Center for Eastern Mediterranean Studies in Alanya (Turkey), for their collegiality during my stay in Alanya in the spring 2008, when I finished the second round of editing. Most of the photos were taken during our field trips to Bursa, Edirne, Istanbul, Syria and Cyprus. Kay Ebel helped me in selecting the photos and writing the captions, and to get through the last phases of the work.

—Gábor Ágoston

NOTE ON TRANSLITERATION AND SPELLING

Because *The Encyclopedia of the Ottoman Empire* was written with high school and college students in mind, we have tried to minimize reliance upon specialized academic vocabulary as much as possible. However, we do expect our readers to have basic familiarity with commonly used historical terms and geographical names. With regard to foreign words, Facts On File follows the conventions of *Merriam Webster's Dictionary* (MW). Consequently, Ottoman terms and expressions that have entered the English language are found using the spellings indicated in MW. Most such words are Arabic or Persian in origin and will be familiar to students of Islamic civilization. The reader will thus find words like agha, caravansary, fatwa, hammam, madrasa, muezzin, pasha, sharia, and not the Modern Turkish equivalents *ağa, kervansaray, fetva, hamam, medrese, müezzin, paşa* or *şeriat*. Also, since these foreign terms have entered English they are not italicized. We go by this rule even when the term has become part of a proper name (Osman Agha, Osman Pasha, etc.) However, when a term found in MW forms part of a compound Ottoman name or term (e.g. Kemalpaşazade, *kapı ağası, kızlar ağası*) we use the modern Turkish transliteration, for it would be confusing to the reader to see the Anglicized form of these compound phrases without their grammatical inflections in Turkish. This also makes cross-referencing easier for the reader, since such compound phrases are usually given in the modern Turkish transliteration in other reference works and secondary literature.

Those Ottoman terms that are not found in the 11th edition of *Merriam-Webster* are considered by Facts On File to be foreign words, and thus are italicized. In these cases, we use modern Turkish transliteration, even if the word is of Arabic origin (e.g., *darüşşifa*, lit. "the house of healing," that is, hospital) However, proper names of institutions are not italicized (Darülfünun-i Osmani, lit. "The Ottoman House of Sciences," that is, The Ottoman University). We omitted the circumflex above a, i, and u that is used to denote lengthened vowels in words of Arabic or Persian origin. The only exception is the world âlî, (high/tall sublime, exalted etc.), such as in *Dergah-ı Âlî* (Sublime Porte) or Âlî Pasha Mehmed Emin, to differentiate him from the many Ali Pashas. Also, we do not generally use the Turkish capitalized dotted İ for place and personal names that have entered common usage in English (Istanbul, Izmir, Ibrahim), while lesser known names are given in their Turkish orthography (e.g. İzzet). The dot also disappears from words set in small caps (SELIM, NIZAM-I CEDID). Slavic names are transcribed according to MW, as are foreign place names in general. We made, however, exception with some Turkish place names, where the name forms we use are more easily recognizable for those familiar with the geography of present-day Turkey. However, in the case of the Ottoman imperial city we use "Constantinople" and the present-day name of the same city, "Istanbul," interchangeably. With this we hope to dispel a common misbelief according to which the Ottomans renamed the Byzantine capital after they conquered it in 1453. In fact, the Ottomans called their new capital city Kostantiniyye (the Arabic form of Constantinople) on coins and official documents throughout the history of the empire, while the name Istanbul (a corruption of the Greek phrase meaning "to the city") was also widely used in both the official language and by the common people.

Modern Turkish contains letters that differ from standard English orthography or pronunciation as follows:

C, c = "j" as in jet
Ç, ç = "ch" as in cheer
Ğ, ğ = soft "g," lengthens preceding vowel
I, ı = undotted i, similar to the vowel sound in the word "open"
İ, i = "ee" as in see
Ö, ö = as in German, similar to the vowel sound in the word "bird"
Ş, ş = "sh" as in should
Ü, ü = as in German, or in the French "tu"

With regard to words of Arabic origin: the editors have chosen to simplify the highly technical system that is normally used when transcribing Arabic words and names into English. We have done away with the diacritical marks normally used to differentiate long from short vowels or to distinguish aspirated from non-aspirated consonants. The Arabic letters *hamza* and *ayn* are not indicated other than the use of double vowels: aa, ii, uu. These should be pronounced with a pause between the first and second vowel, example *Shii* is prounounced "Shi-i". The consonant clusters "kh" and "gh" represent guttural sounds in Arabic not found in American English. The "kh" is similar to the "ch" in the Scottish word "loch" or the German "Bach." The "gh" is a soft, fricative "g" similar to the "g" sound before back vowels (a, o, u) in Castillian Spanish, example "algo" and in Modern Greek, example "logos."

INTRODUCTION

WHO ARE THE OTTOMANS?

The Ottomans, named after the founder of the dynasty, OSMAN (d. 1324), were one of many Turkic ANATOLIAN EMIRATES or principalities that emerged in the late 13th-century power vacuum caused by the Mongols' obliteration of the empire of the Rum SELJUKS. They were driven out of their central Asian homeland by the Mongols in the 13th century and settled in north-western Asia Minor or Anatolia, in the vicinity of the shrinking Eastern Roman or BYZANTINE EMPIRE shortly before 1300.

The region they settled had previously been ruled by the Seljuks of Rum. Following the victory of the Great Seljuks over the Byzantine army in 1071, a branch of the Great Seljuks established its rule in eastern and central Anatolia, known to them as Rum (i.e., the lands of the Eastern Roman (Rum) Empire) and soon came to be known as the Seljuks of Rum. Under the Rum Seljuks, large numbers of semi-nomadic Turks migrated from Transoxania in Central Asia to eastern and central Anatolia, where the upland pasturelands and warm coastlands offered ideal conditions for the pastoralists' way of life.

The Seljuks brought with them the religion of Islam, and conversion seems to have been widespread from the 11th century onward. At the time the Ottoman Turks arrived in the 13th century, there was still a large population of Greeks and Armenians in Asia Minor, especially in the towns, and relations between Greeks and Turks were closer and inter-marriages more common than usually assumed. Greeks worked in the Seljuk administration in high offices, Turkish troops were often hired by the Byzantine emperors, and fleeing Turkish rulers sought refuge in Byzantium more often than among their Muslim brethren in Syria, Mesopotamia, and Iran.

By the time the Ottoman Turks settled in the Sakarya valley in the vicinity of the Byzantine Empire, the population of western Asia Minor had largely become Turk-ish-speaking and Muslim in religion. The influx of Turkic semi-nomadic peoples or Turkomans into western Anatolia is closely related to the Mongol invasion of the Middle East in the 1240s and 1250s. A western army of the Mongols invaded and defeated the Rum Seljuks in 1243 at Kösedağ, northeast of present-day Sivas in Turkey. In 1258, Hülegü, the brother of the great khan, Möngke Khan, conquered and sacked BAGHDAD, ending the rule of the ABBASID CALIPHATE (750–1258). The Rum Seljuks soon became the vassals of the Ilkhans ("obedient khans"), the descendents of Hülegü, who established their own empire in the vast area stretching from present-day Afghanistan to Turkey. As the Mongols occupied more and more grasslands for their horses in Asia Minor, the Turkomans moved further to western Anatolia and settled in the Seljuk-Byzantine frontier. By the last decades of the 13th century the Ilkhans and their Seljuk vassals lost control over much of Anatolia to these Turkoman peoples. In the ensuing power vacuum, a number of Turkish lords managed to establish themselves as rulers of various principalities, known as *beylik*s or emirates. The Ottomans, who were only one among the numerous principalities, settled in northwestern Anatolia, in the former Byzantine province of Bithynia.

It was a fortunate location for many reasons. In 1261, the Byzantines recaptured Constantinople from the Latins, who had conquered the city in 1204 during the Fourth Crusade, established a Latin Empire in Constantinople (1204–61), divided the former Byzantine territories in the Balkans and the Aegean among themselves, and forced the Byzantine Emperors into exile at Nicaea (present-day Iznik in Turkey). From 1261 onwards, the Byzantines were largely preoccupied with policies aiming at regaining their control in the Balkans, and, in the words of the contemporary Byzantine chronicler Pachymeres (writing circa 1310), "the defenses of the eastern territory were weakened, whilst the Persians (Turks) were emboldened to invade lands which had no means of driving them off." Owing to their location, the Ottomans were best positioned to conquer the eastern territories of the Byzantine Empire. However, the situation was more complex and to view the history of the northwestern Anatolian frontier solely as a clash between Cross (Byzantium) and Crescent (invading Muslim Turks) would be a mistake. The shift in Byzantine policy also offered new opportunities for the Turkish principalities in western Anatolia, for the Byzantines needed allies and mercenaries. The Ottomans, who were perhaps the least significant among the Turkish emirates and thus posed the smallest threat to Byzantine authority around 1300, seemed to be perfect candidates for the job. Indeed, the Ottomans arrived in Europe as the allies of the Byzantines and established their first bridgehead in Europe in Tzympe, southwest of Gallipoli on the European shore of the Dardanelles, in 1352.

Within 50 years, through military conquest, diplomacy, dynastic marriages, and the opportunistic exploitation of the Byzantine civil wars, the third Ottoman ruler MURAD I (r. 1362–89) more than tripled the territories under his direct rule, reaching some 100,000 square miles, evenly distributed in Europe and Asia Minor. His son BAYEZID I (r. 1389–1402), according to some scholars the first Ottoman ruler to use the title sultan ("sovereign," ruler with supreme authority), extended Ottoman control over much of southeastern Europe and Asia Minor, up to the rivers DANUBE and Euphrates, respectively. Alerted by this spectacular Ottoman conquest, Europeans organized a crusade to halt Ottoman advance, but were defeated in 1396. However, Ottoman expansion was stopped by TIMUR or Tamerlane, a skillful and cruel military leader of Mongol decent from Transoxania, who defeated Bayezid at the battle of Ankara (July 28, 1403, see ANKARA, BATTLE OF). Bayezid died in the captivity of Timur, who reduced the Ottoman lands to what they had been at the beginning of Murad I's reign. Fortunately for the Ottomans, however, the basic institutions of the Ottoman state (tax system, revenue and tax surveys, central and provincial bureaucracy and the army) had already taken root and large segments of Ottoman society had vested interests in restoring the power of the House of Osman. Moreover, Bayezid's victorious conquests served as inspiration for his successors who managed to rebuild the state, and half a century later, in 1453, Ottoman armies under Sultan MEHMED II (r. 1444–46, 1451–81) conquered Constantinople (see CONSTANTINOPLE, SIEGE OF), the capital of the thousand-year-old Byzantine Empire. The Ottomans emerged as the undisputed power in southeastern Europe, the eastern Mediterranean, and Asia Minor. Within another 50 years, in the possession of Constantinople that they made their capital and the logistical center of their campaigns, the Ottomans cemented their rule over the Balkans and turned the Black Sea into an "Ottoman lake," although their control of its northern shores was never complete. In 1516–17 Sultan SELIM I (r. 1512–20) defeated the MAMLUK EMPIRE of Egypt and Syria, incorporating their realms into his empire whereas SÜLEYMAN I (r. 1520–66) conquered central HUNGARY and IRAQ. By this time, the Ottoman Empire had become one of the most important empires in Europe and in territories known today as the Middle East.

Although Europeans called the Ottomans "Turks," they considered themselves Osmanlı (Ottomans), followers of Osman, the eponymous founder of the Osmanlı dynasty. In the early decades of the empire's history everyone who followed Osman and joined his band was considered Ottoman, regardless of ethnicity or religion. Later the term referred to the Ottoman ruling elite, also known as askeri ("military," after their main occupation), whereas the taxpaying subject population, Muslims and non-Muslims alike, was known as the reaya, the "flock." While the term "Turk" is not entirely incorrect to denote the Ottomans—for they were originally Turks—one should remember that the descendents of Osman were ethnically mixed due to intermarriages with Byzantine, Serbian, and Bulgarian royal houses and the dynasty's practice to reproduce through non-Muslim slave concubines. More importantly, while superficially Islamized Turks comprised the largest group among the followers of Osman, the early Ottoman society was complex and included members of numerous religions and ethnicities. Members of various Islamic sects, Orthodox Christians, Islamized and/or Turkified Greeks, Armenians and Jews lived and fought alongside the Turks. The population of the empire's Balkan provinces remained largely ethnically Slavic and Orthodox Christian in religion, despite voluntary migration and state organized re-settlements of Turks from Anatolia to the Balkans. In short, it was a multi-ethnic and multi-religious empire ruled by the Osmanlı dynasty from circa 1300 until its demise in World War I. The empire's elites considered themselves Ottoman and used the word Turk as a disparaging term for the uneducated Anatolian subject peasant population. These Ottomans spoke the Ottoman-Turkish language (see LANGUAGE AND SCRIPT) that, with its Arabic and Persian vocabulary, was different from the Anatolian Turkish spoken by the peasants. The Ottomans also produced, supported, and consumed the Ottoman literature that would largely have been unintelligible to the masses. Thus, it is more correct to call this empire Ottoman than Turkish.

WHY STUDY OTTOMAN HISTORY?

The Ottomans built one of the greatest, longest-lived, and most splendid multi-ethnic and multi-religious empires, only to be compared to the better-known other Mediterranean empires of the Romans and Byzantines, the simi-

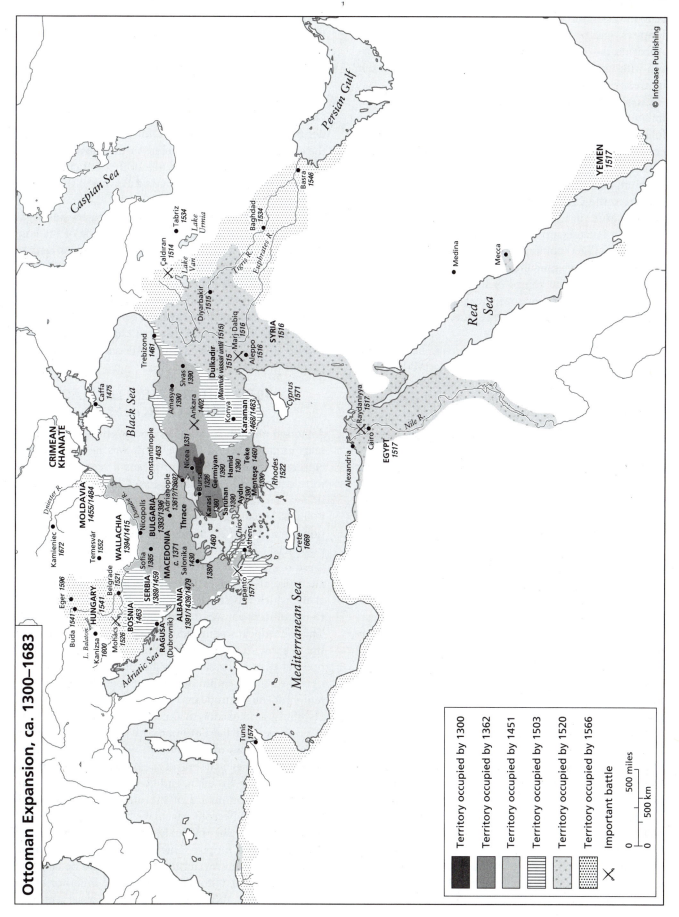

Ottoman Expansion, ca. 1300–1683

© Infobase Publishing

Caspian Sea

Persian Gulf

YEMEN
1517

Basra
1546

Tabriz
1534

Lake
Urmia

Baghdad
1534

Çaldiran
1514

Lake
Van

Tigris R.

Euphrates R.

Red
Sea

Medina

Mecca

Diyarbakir
1515

SYRIA
1516

Marj Dabiq
1516

Trebizond
1461

Dulkadir
(Mamluk vassal until 1515)
1515

Aleppo
1516

Amasya
1390

Sivas
1390

Black Sea

Caffa
1475

CRIMEAN
KHANATE

Ankara
1402

Konya

Karaman
1468/1483

Cyprus
1571

Raydaniyya
1517

Nile R.

Constantinople
1453

Nicea 1331

Bursa
1326

Germiyan
1390

Hamid
1390

Teke
1460

Cairo

EGYPT
1517

Alexandria

MOLDAVIA
1455/1484

Dniester R.

Adrianople
1361?/369?

Bulgaria
1392/1396

Thrace

Karasi
1360

Saruhan
1390

Aydin
1390

Mentese
1390

Rhodes
1522

Kamieniec
1672

WALLACHIA
1394/1415

Danube R.

Nicopolis
1385

MACEDONIA
c. 1371

Chios

Athens

Crete
1669

Temesvár
1552

Sofia
1385

Salonika
1430

1460

1380

Eger 1596

Belgrade
1521

SERBIA
1389/1459

ALBANIA
1391/1439/1479

Lepanto
1571

Buda 1541

HUNGARY
1541

Mohács
1526

BOSNIA
1463

RAGUSA
(Dubrovnik)

L. Balaton

Kanizsa
1600

Adriatic Sea

Mediterranean Sea

Tunis
1574

Legend
- Territory occupied by 1300
- Territory occupied by 1362
- Territory occupied by 1451
- Territory occupied by 1503
- Territory occupied by 1520
- Territory occupied by 1566
- Important battle

500 miles
500 km
0

larly multi-ethnic neighboring Habsburg and Romanov Empires, and to the other great Islamic empires of the Abbasids, Safavids, and the Indian Mughals. In comparison with many of these empires, the Ottomans' record is impressive.

The Ottomans ruled with relative tolerance and flexibility for centuries over a multiplicity of peoples who followed different religions and spoke languages as divers as Turkic, Greek, Slavic, Albanian, Arabic, and Hungarian. At the height of their power, in the 16th century, their empire stretched from Hungary to Yemen, from Algiers to the Crimea and Iraq. They established peace, law, and order in the Balkans and the Middle East, territories that have seen much violence since the breakup of the empire. The Ottomans also brought economic stability and prosperity and cultural flourishing to many parts of their empire. The spread of local fairs and markets, the establishment of new towns (e.g., Sarajevo), and the population increase in the 16th century, are signs of this economic prosperity.

From the conquest of the Byzantine capital city Constantinople in 1453 until its demise during World War I, the Ottoman Empire was an important player in European politics: in the 15th through 17th centuries as the preeminent Islamic empire that threatened Christian Europe on its own territory, later in the 18th and 19th centuries as a weakening empire whose survival was a major factor in the balance of power. The empire's possible partition either by the Great Powers and the empire's neighbors (France, England, Germany, Austria/Austria-Hungary, Russia) or by the emerging nationalist movements became a major concern of international politics, and was known as the "Eastern Question." For the Ottomans it was a "Western Question": How to withstand the pressure of the western Great Powers and Russia, as well as the nationalities supported by them, and how to modernize the empire's military, bureaucracy, and finances to do so.

As for the empire's legacy, the roots of many of the ethnic conflicts we witnessed in the 1990s in the Balkans can only be understood if one studies the wars, voluntary migrations, and state-organized forced resettlements in the Ottoman Balkans that radically changed the ethnic and religious landscape of that region. For instance, the roots of the Serbian-Albanian struggle over Kosovo go back to Ottoman times, and are related to the Ottoman expansion and the ensuing Serbian emigration from and Albanian immigration to Kosovo. The conflicts between Catholic Croats and Orthodox Serbs in Krajina are likewise connected to the region's Ottoman and Habsburg history. Vojna Krajina or the Military Frontier in Croatia was established by the Austrian Habsburgs from the mid-16th century on, in order to halt further Ottoman expansion. In the 16th and 17th centuries, and in the 18th century when the Military Border was reorganized by the Habsburgs following the Ottomans' loss of Hungary, the population of the region became increasingly mixed, with more and more Serbs settling there. This heavy Serbian presence was used by Serb nationalists for territorial claims in the 1990s leading to war between Serbs and Croats. On the other hand, whereas Ottoman borders proved stable for centuries—the border between Turkey and IRAN, for instance is essentially the one established in 1639—border disputes and wars in the Middle East are often results of the artificial borders established by the European Great Powers at the demise of the empire.

Yet despite its world historical importance and legacies, the Ottoman Empire has remained one of the less-studied and less-understood multiethnic empires, leading to many misconceptions and misinterpretations of Ottoman history in the generalist literature and college textbooks. This short introduction intends to acquaint the reader with some of the many labels by which historians tried to describe the essential characteristics of the empire. It is followed by a short overview of the past and present state of Ottoman studies.

WORLD EMPIRE, MERITOCRACY, HEIRS OF ROME?

Although modern sociologists do not consider the Ottoman Empire a world power for it was not a sea-borne empire, for 16th-century Europeans it seemed the most formidable of all empires Western Christianity faced on its own territory. It held this image by virtue of its geopolitical situation, its enormous territory and population, its wealth of economic resources, and a central and provincial administration that was capable of mobilizing these resources to serve the goals of the state. The efficient use of resources formed the base of the Ottoman army, which was considered to be the best and most efficient military known to contemporaneous Europeans. These Europeans admired the territorial immensity and the wealth and power of the sultan, who, in the words of one Venetian ambassador, "is the most powerful."

The sultan's empire was feared and admired by contemporaneous Europeans. Ogier Ghiselin de Busbecq, Habsburg ambassador to the Ottoman capital in 1554–62, commended the Ottomans' meritocracy noting that Ottoman officials owed their offices and dignity to their "personal merits and bravery; no one is distinguished from the rest by his birth, and honor is paid to each man according to the nature of the duty and offices which he discharges." Niccolò Machiavelli (1469–1527) found in the Ottoman Empire many of the virtues associated with the Roman Empire. The French jurist and historian Jean Bodin (1529–96) argued that "it would be far more just to regard the Ottoman sultan as the inheritor of the Roman Empire." While these European observers were certainly influenced by the success of the Ottomans, they also had their own agendas. Busbecq, for instance, seems to have overemphasized the power of the sultan, for he wanted to augment the power of his own ruler, Holy Roman Emperor Charles V, vis-à-vis the Estates, ostensibly in order to better fight the Ottomans. However, these descriptions also reflect realities and the power and ambitions of the Ottomans. Mehmed II's sobriquet ('the Conqueror') and the Roman-Byzantine title of 'Caesar' that he assumed, indicated his ambitions for universal sovereignty and the fact that he considered himself heir of the Roman emperors.

HOLY WARRIORS OR PRAGMATIC RULERS?

The early Ottomans have often been presented as *ghazis*, who were fighting *ghazas* or "Holy Wars against the infidels." However, recent scholarship has demonstrated that the early Ottoman military activity described as GHAZA in Ottoman chronicles were more complex undertakings, sometimes simple raids in which Muslims and Christians joint forces and shared in the booty and in other times "holy wars." The Ottomans also fought numerous campaigns against fellow Muslim Turks, subjugating and annexing the neighboring Turkoman principalities. However, aiming to portray the early Ottomans as "holy warriors," 15th-century Ottoman chroniclers often ignored these conflicts, claiming that the Ottomans acquired the territories of the neighboring Turkic principalities through peaceful means (purchase and/or marriage). When they did mention the wars between the Ottomans and their Muslim Turkic neighbors, Ottoman chroniclers tried to legitimize these conquests by claiming that the Ottomans acted either in self defense or were forced to fight, for the hostile policies of these Turkic principalities hindered the Ottomans' holy wars against the infidels.

This latter explanation was used repeatedly by Ottoman legal scholars to justify Ottoman wars against their Muslim Turkoman neighbors, such as the Karamans and Akkoyunlus (1473). The justification of the wars against the Mamluks was more problematic. The Mamluks followed Sunni Islam, as did the Ottomans, and the descendant of the last Abbasid caliph al-Mustansir resided in CAIRO. The Mamluk sultans were also the protectors of MECCA and Medina and guarantors of the Muslim pilgrimage, the HAJJ. To justify his attack against the Mamluks, Sultan Selim I advanced several pretexts and secured a legal opinion (FATWA) from the Ottoman religious establishment. This accused the Mamluks with oppressing Muslims and justified the war against them with the alleged Mamluk alliance with the SUNNI Ottomans' deadly enemy, the Shii Safavids, who from the early 1500s ruled over what is today IRAN.

Ottoman victory over the Mamluks in 1516–17 and the introduction of Ottoman rule in these Arab lands had major ideological and political consequences. With his conquests, Selim became the master of Mecca and Medina, "the cradle of Islam," as well as of DAMASCUS and Cairo, former seats of the caliphs, the successors of Prophet Muhammad. Sultan Selim I and his successors duly assumed the title of "Servant of the Two Noble Sanctuaries" (Mecca and Medina), and with this the task of protecting and organizing the annual pilgrimage to Mecca, which gave the Ottomans unparalleled prestige and legitimacy in the Muslim world.

This is not to say that the Ottomans did not use the ideology of the "Holy War." In the 1300s, the spirit of the holy war was alive in the Turco-Byzantine frontier. Situated in the vicinity of Byzantium, the seat of eastern Christianity, the Ottomans were strategically positioned to wage such wars, and served as a magnet for the mighty warriors of the Anatolian Turco-Muslim emirates, or principalities. By defeating repeated crusades, conquering Constantinople, and subjugating the Balkan Christian states, the Ottomans emerged as champions of anti-Christian wars. Their successes against the Venetians in the Aegean and the western Balkans under Mehmed II and Bayezid II, and against the Habsburgs in the Mediterranean and Hungary under Süleyman I further enhanced the Ottomans' prestige as holy warriors and defenders of Islam.

In their rivalry against the Habsburgs, Ottoman ideologues and strategists used religion, millenarianism, and universalist visions of empire to strengthen the legitimacy of the sultan within the larger Muslim community. Similarly, Ottoman victories against Habsburg Catholicism and Safavid Shiism formed an integral part of Ottoman propaganda. In the early years of Süleyman's reign, GRAND VIZIER Ibrahim Pasha consciously propagated the sultan's image as the new world conqueror, the successor of Alexander the Great, whereas in his latter years the sultan viewed himself as "lawgiver," or "law abider" (*kanuni*) a just ruler in whose realm justice and order reigned.

In short, the early Ottoman sultans appear as pragmatic rulers whose foreign policy was complex, as was that of their European enemies and allies. There was no iron curtain between the Muslim Ottomans and Christian Europeans, and the Ottomans masterfully exploited the growing political (Habsburg-Valois) and religious (Catholic-Protestant) rivalries in Christian Europe, allying themselves with France and England, against their common enemies, the Catholic Habsburgs.

"GOLDEN AGE" AND "PERIOD OF DECLINE"

Traditional historiography maintains that after the conquest of Constantinople in 1453, the Ottoman sultans embarked upon a centralizing project, which resulted in

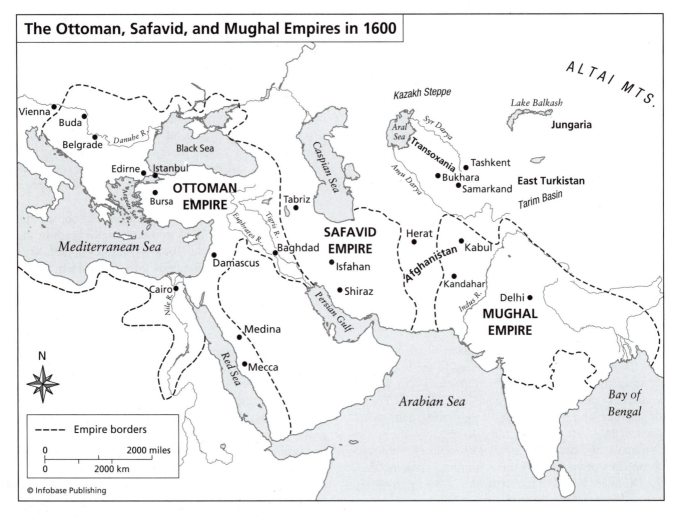

The Ottoman, Safavid, and Mughal Empires in 1600

the establishment of the "classical" absolutist Ottoman state, a patrimonial world empire, with its "peculiar" pre-bendal land tenure system and centralized administration. Under Süleyman I the Ottoman central administration in Istanbul is said to have reached its perfection, increasing its control over the provinces and frontiers. Consequently frontier societies and institutions became similar to those in the core territories of the empire. Almost everything that one may read in general historical works on the empire's central and provincial administration, and on its army, economy, society, and culture, is limited to this one-hundred-year period. Western observers and scholars, from the 16th-century Italian politician and philosopher Niccolò Machiavelli (1469–1527) to the Marxist historian Perry Anderson, have long focused on the idea of "Turkish/Oriental despotism." Recent research, however, has emphasized the limits to centralization, the regional differences, and the continuation of earlier, pre-16th-century Ottoman administrative practices. In recent research, the Ottomans emerge as pragmatic and flexible rulers who accepted local forms of taxation, monetary systems, and economic forms; compromised with and co-opted local elites into their military and bureaucratic systems; and adjusted their military according to new challenges.

Closely connected to the idealized view of the "classical age" is the theory of "Ottoman decline." According to this theory, by the end of the 16th century the Ottoman expansion slowed down, the empire reached its limits and the porous frontiers, that had formerly been the major source of social dynamism, became rigid. Proponents of the decline theory argue that this perceived age of decline was characterized by weak sultans, decentralization, destruction of the classical Ottoman institutions (land tenure system, taxation, revenue surveys, etc.), deterioration of military capabilities, and by the disruption of the "world order" (*nizam-i alem*), to use the expression of the Ottoman literature of advice to princes (*nasihatname*).

In discussing the "classical age" and the "age of decline" students often became victims of their sources. If one looks at the sultanic decrees sent from Constantinople to the provinces during the mid-16th century, the impression gained is one of an Ottoman central government whose will prevailed even in the most remote

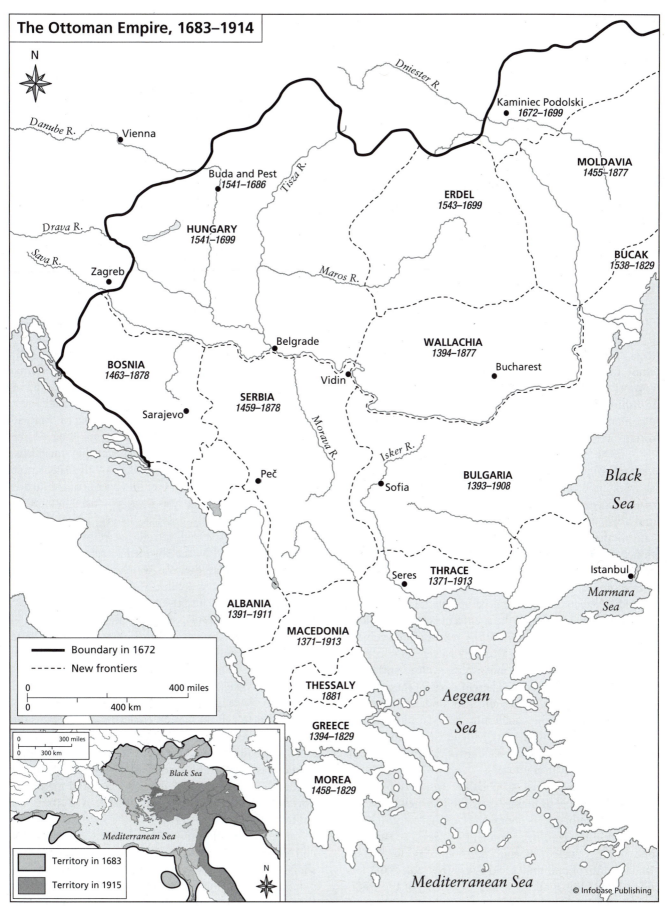

The Ottoman Empire, 1683–1914

N

Danube R.

Vienna

Dniester R.

Kaminiec Podolski
1672–1699

MOLDAVIA
1455–1877

Buda and Pest
1541–1686

Tisza R.

ERDEL
1543–1699

HUNGARY
1541–1699

Drava R.

Maros R.

BÚCAK
1538–1829

Sava R.

Zagreb

Belgrade

WALLACHIA
1394–1877

Bucharest

BOSNIA
1463–1878

Vidin

SERBIA
1459–1878

Sarajevo

Morava R.

Isker R.

*Black
Sea*

Peč

Sofia

BULGARIA
1393–1908

Istanbul

ALBANIA
1391–1911

Seres

THRACE
1371–1913

*Marmara
Sea*

MACEDONIA
1371–1913

*Aegean
Sea*

THESSALY
1881

GREECE
1394–1829

MOREA
1458–1829

*Mediterranean
Sea*

▬▬▬	Boundary in 1672
----	New frontiers

0 ——————— 400 miles
0 ——————— 400 km

0 ——— 300 miles
0 ——— 300 km

Black Sea

Mediterranean Sea

N

�	Territory in 1683
▮	Territory in 1915

© Infobase Publishing

frontier areas. Further, provincial tax registers also suggest that the administrative and taxation system was extremely uniform and efficient. However, one should not forget that the systematic study of this rich material (tens of thousands of sultanic decrees and hundreds of provincial tax registers) has only started in recent years. It is symptomatic that whereas at around 1609 the empire's territories were divided into more than 30 provinces and well over 200 sub-provinces (see ADMINISTRATION, PROVINCIAL), we posses fewer than half a dozen monographs that are devoted to the comprehensive study of individual provinces, and the number of case studies of sub-provinces is similarly limited.

Previous historical reconstructions of Ottoman administrative practices and capabilities are based on random evidence, often from the core provinces of the Balkans and Asia Minor, that have very little to say about regional variations outside the core zones. The minutes of local judicial courts, complaints of provincial authorities, and the communication between the central and local authorities present a different picture and demonstrate the limits to centralization. In these sources local and central government appear to have enjoyed a relationship that was far more complex than the one-sided command-and-execute relationship put forward by historians in the past.

Furthermore, students of the Ottoman Empire have long relied on the so-called literature of advice to princes as works that reveal the economic and social conditions of the "classical era" and that of the "period of decline," and as impartial writings elaborating sincere and selfless reform proposals. However, recent research has questioned the relevance of the Ottoman advice literature in reconstructing the economic and social conditions of the empire; instead it is now accepted that these writings should be treated as political pamphlets, often partisan and biased, that furthered the agenda of certain individuals or special-interest groups, often reflecting the subjective opinions and fears of a narrow elite of intellectuals and bureaucrats who were rooted in traditions and often idealized the "classical era." Therefore, while these political pamphlets are excellent sources for understanding the fears and views of the tradition-bound old bureaucratic elite, they ought to be used with great caution when attempting to reconstruct the nature of the Ottoman state in the 16th and 17th centuries.

Recent Ottomanist scholarship, inspired by such diverse disciplines as literary criticism (Cornell Fleischer, Gabriel Pieterberg); economic (Halil İnalcık, Mehmet Genç, Linda Darling), monetary (Şevket Pamuk), and military history (Gábor Ágoston, Virginia Aksan, Rhoads Murphey); and sociology (Ariel Salzman) has questioned almost all the major arguments of the traditional "decline schools." This literature has emphasized

"transformation" instead of decline with regard to Ottoman institutions and argued that the Ottoman economy, society, and military in the 17th and 18th centuries were flexible and strong institutions. However, none of these new studies was able to satisfactorily explain the decline of the Ottoman military might in the late 18th and 19th century vis-à-vis the empire's two major rivals, Habsburg Austria and Romanov Russia. Ottoman studies and accessibility to primary sources have, in the past two decades or so, improved considerably, and it is hoped that future research will answer many of the remaining questions about the Ottoman empire and its declining military.

OTTOMAN STUDIES IN TURKEY

Turkey has traditionally been the center of Ottoman studies. The Ottoman past is part of the national history of the country, no matter how ambivalent the approach towards the Ottoman past might have been at different times. Turkish historians have both advantages and disadvantages over their foreign colleagues in studying the history of the Ottoman Empire. During the Ottoman Empire, Ottomanist historians were able to rely on a long tradition, accumulated knowledge, access to manuscripts and archival sources, and they did not have to deal with linguistic or paleographical difficulties, for their sources were written in the language and script they themselves used. However, Ottoman historians of the late empire also faced disadvantages. First, they were constrained by tradition. Ottoman history as it was practiced in the 19th-century meant mainly political history, which followed the official chronicle tradition started in the 15th century. The history as told by the chronicles was mainly the history of the Ottoman dynasty, which had very little to say about the complex and colorful society and economy of this multi-national, multi-ethnic, multi-cultural empire (see HISTORIOGRAPHY). Second, though accumulated knowledge was important, the lack of an Arabic letter printing press until 1729, and in fact until the late 18th century (see PRINTING) and private journalism until 1861 (see NEWSPAPERS) hindered the dissemination of accumulated knowledge in books and scholarly journals, and confined it to certain literate circles, whose membership was far smaller than in contemporaneous Europe. Third, since the sources (manuscript chronicles of the Ottoman dynasty and archival sources preserved in the Palace Archives) mainly concerned the dynasty and the central government, the access to and utilization of them was controlled by CENSORSHIP.

The combination of restricted access to manuscripts and archival sources, the sensitiveness of Ottoman censorship, and the lack of Ottoman printing houses had a number of serious consequences. Most importantly, there were no major systematic source publications in the late Ottoman Empire comparable to the multi-volume monumental source collections (*Fontes, Akten, Documenti, Collection, Calendars,* etc.) of European histories published from the mid/late-19th century on. Although some important Ottoman chronicles (*Naima, Silahtar, Peçevi,* etc., *see* COURT CHRONICLES) appeared in this period, these publications were usually based on a single manuscript and cannot be considered critical editions, as their editors made no attempt to compare all the available extant manuscripts or verify authorship. These publications also lacked all the usual features—such as indication of manuscripts versions, later insertions, notes and explanations—of the European *edition critiques* of classical and medieval texts. On the contrary, these early editions of Ottoman chronicles were often abridged and altered according to the expectation of the late-19th-century Ottoman censorship. A well-known example of such tampering with historical texts is the 10-volume description of the empire by the famous 17th-century Ottoman traveler EVLIYA ÇELEBI, in which entire paragraphs and pages, regarded by the censorship as unfavorable and/or critical of the sultan and the Ottoman elite, were omitted. The situation was similar in the field of archival source publications. Except for some pioneers—such as Ahmet Refik who published imperial orders concerning a wide variety of themes (the history of Istanbul, Ottoman mines, various political affairs) from the *mühimme* ("important affairs") collections that contained imperial orders sent to Ottoman provincial governors, judges, vassals, and foreign rulers—there was no large-scale scholarly undertaking comparable to the systematic publication of hundreds of thousands of sources concerning European history in the monumental series of *Diplomataria et Acta* and *Documenti,* among others.

Although ambivalent in its approach toward its Ottoman past, Turkish historiography during the Republican period improved Ottoman studies considerably. Seeking answers for the backwardness of the country, as well as facing the scholarly and political challenges in the successor states of the Balkans and the Middle East, Turkish historiography undertook large-scale scholarly projects initiated and supported by the Turkish Historical Association (TTK), Ministries of Education and Culture, and by some of the main universities.

The TTK, which has its own printing press, published the multi-volume history of the Ottoman Empire and its institutions by İ. H. Uzunçarşılı and E. Z. Karal, a series of shorter concise histories of European states, and some significant source publications. The history departments of the universities of Istanbul and Ankara trained generations of able historians, did important research work, and published their results in newly established scholarly journals. New centers were established, such as the Institute of Ottoman Economic and Social History at the University of Istanbul, where under the leadership of Ö. L. Barkan invaluable source publications (including the Institute's new journal) appeared. Landmark studies concerning the Ottoman land-tenure system, taxation, population movements, and Ottoman economic and social history in general, were also published. Under the sponsorship of the Ministry of Public Education, between 1940 and 1987, the first edition of the *Encyclopedia of Islam* (originally published in Leiden in 1901–39) was not only translated into Turkish but augmented with substantial new material, concerning mainly Ottoman and Turkic history, religion and culture, such that the original 5-volume encyclopedia became a 15-volume handbook.

Although Turkish historiography during the Republican era tried hard to make up for what 19th-century Ottoman historiography had missed, the lack of major source publications, together with the inaccessibility of the Turkish archives, had significant consequences. On one hand, this situation hindered the ability of Turkish historiography to produce basic handbooks, such as state-of-the art concise histories, historical, biographical, and prosopographical dictionaries, chronologies, historical geographies, and histories of Ottoman institutions. On the other hand, it made the incorporation of Ottoman studies into western historiography very difficult. Turkish and non-Turkish Ottomanist historians alike used the bulk of their time during their research in the archives with locating, deciphering, and editing their documents. They had very little energy left over to challenge old and new ideas put forward by Eurocentric and Orientalist historiography, to join in the major trends of western historiography, or to formulate new theories. This situation has changed only during the last couple of decades. In this, certain vital developments concerning higher education, the archives, research and scholarly publication, have played a considerable role.

During the past two decades or so, dozens of new universities have been established in Turkey, many of them privately endowed (*vakıf*) universities. One might have legitimate concerns about the quality of these institutions and their professors. However, the overall outcome of this mushrooming of universities is positive. New centers of Ottoman studies have been established, some by top professors from Istanbul and Ankara who took up jobs voluntarily or were forced to do so for political reasons; others by a younger generation of historians, who collectively trained hundreds of MA and Ph.D. students in Ottoman history. The number of new history journals, source publications, MA and Ph.D. dissertations, and monographs increased substantially. This new generation of graduate students and young historians not only played a crucial role in discovering, classifying, cataloguing, editing, and utilizing manuscript sources of local libraries untouched for centuries, but also initiated important research in the main Ottoman archives in Istanbul and Ankara concerning the social and economic history of their own regions. In addition, they have published important monographs on the functioning of Ottoman administration in the provinces and sub-provinces, including such topics as land tenure, taxation, and population movements.

The role of the top private universities (Bilkent, Koç, Sabancı, Bilgi, Bahçeşehir, Kadir Has, etc.) in particular should be emphasized. These institutions are often run and administered according to American or European standards, and the language of instruction is English, which facilitates their integration into the international scholarly community. History departments are led by prominent Ottoman historians, often brought back or recruited from abroad. Among their faculty members are foreigners and young Turkish colleagues trained in the United States or Europe, who, in addition to Ottoman history, also teach European and comparative history and incorporate Ottoman history into its broader Mediterranean, Middle Eastern, and European context.

ARCHIVES, MANUSCRIPT COLLECTIONS, AND SOURCE PUBLICATIONS

Another breakthrough came in 1988 when Turkey liberalized its regulations concerning archival research, and initiated a large-scale project to classify and catalogue its archives. Although regulations concerning the Topkapı Palace Archives, which belongs to the Ministry of Culture, are still strict and research conditions have for the past couple of decades been legendarily unwelcoming, permission to enter the most important Ottoman archives, the PRIME MINISTRY's OTTOMAN ARCHIVES or Başbakanlık Osmanlı Arşivi (BOA) require only a simple formality, and research is as easy and efficient as in the main European archives. Although not designed for the purposes of archives, the present building near Sultanahmet Square has plenty of space and light compared to the old small building, and a modern and even more spacious archival complex is planned for the coming years. More important is the impressive classification and cataloguing work that started in the late 1980s. Out of the estimated 95 million documents and 360,000 record books (defters) written in the Arabic alphabet in Ottoman Turkish and preserved in the BOA, only 29,578 defters (revenue surveys, population censuses, tax registers, financial account books, etc.,) and about 1.5 million individual documents were catalogued during the entire period from 1908 to 1987. However, from November 1987 to November 1988 a total of 99,000 record books and more than 1.7 million documents were classified and catalogued. The classification and cataloguing work has proceeded with impressive speed and efficiency since then, thanks to some 350 newly hired archivists, trained in the mid-80s.

A related important development is the publication project initiated by the General Directorate of Archives. This project includes the publication of an up-to-date *Guidebook to the Archives*, auxiliary handbooks, and various archival documents. Among the latter, the most important is the publication of several volumes of *mühimme defteris*. These record books contain the shortened copies of imperial orders sent to governors, financial officers and judges of provinces and sub-provinces, to the heads and leading communities of the vassal states, and to the rulers of foreign countries both Muslim and Christian relating to all sorts of military, economic, religious, social, and cultural affairs (military mobilization, taxation, supply of Istanbul and other big cities, center-periphery relationship, the religious communities of the empire, crime and punishment, gender issues and so on). However, despite these major advances there is much work to be done. The entire collection of *mühimme defteris* catalogued so far contains 394 volumes and almost 110,000 pages, out of which less than a dozen volumes have been published in facsimile and in summary transliteration with indexes.

In addition to archival sources, Turkey also houses the richest manuscript collections related to Ottoman history. The total number of Arabic, Turkish, and Persian manuscripts related to all disciplines is estimated at 300,000, of which more than 105,000 volumes are in the seven main Istanbul libraries belonging to the Ministry of Culture. Although some of the major manuscript libraries in Istanbul (Topkapı Palace Library, Süleymaniye Library) have compiled their own catalogues, until recently we knew almost nothing about provincial libraries. As a result of a massive Union Catalogue of Manuscripts in Turkey (Türkiye Yazmaları Toplu Kataloğu/TÜYATOK) project that started in 1978, the National Library (*see* LIBRARIES) published more than 25 volumes and three CD-Roms. These contain the description of more than 126,000 manuscripts, mainly in Turkey, but the third CD-Rom also includes data regarding Turkish manuscripts in the United States and the main European, Balkan, and Middle Eastern collections. In addition, the Research Center for Islamic History, Art and Culture (IRCICA) published several useful catalogues, bibliographical guides and handbooks in English, Turkish and Arabic.

In short, during the past two decades research conditions in Turkey improved considerably and Turkey has become the major center of Ottoman studies in every respect. New universities and research institutes employ an army of young Ottomanists, hundreds of MA and Ph.D. dissertations are written every year, and conferences and symposia organized in Turkey bring the crème of the profession to Turkey. New handbooks, catalogues, and web pages help foreign and Turkish scholars in their research. One impressive achievement of these positive developments in the field in Turkey is the new Turkish *Encyclopedia of Islam*, launched in 1988 by the Turkish Religious Foundation (Türkiye Diyanet Vakfı). The planned 40-volume handbook would contain some 17,000 articles by more than 2,000 Turkish and foreign scholars. The 34 volumes published so far have proved to be an indispensable source for students of Ottoman history.

OTTOMAN STUDIES OUTSIDE TURKEY

In the 15th through late 18th centuries, the Ottomans represented for Christian Europe a major "Islamic threat," prompting Europeans to study the history and religion of "the Turks," as the Ottomans were then and have been since referred to in Europe. By the late 16th century, Europeans produced an impressive corpus of literature on the Ottoman Turks, known as Turcica-literature, that is, works dealing with the history, religion, and culture of the Turks. While these works contain valuable data and observations for the historian of the empire, they were written from a biased perspective and contain misconceptions that have persisted in later European historiography on the Ottomans. The history and nature of Ottoman studies, along with the image of the empire in the various European countries is complex and differs from country to country, reflecting, among other things, the complex relationship that these countries have had with the Ottomans through the centuries. Until the 1920s or so, Turkish and Ottoman studies in Europe were dominated by the German and Austrian history-writing tradition. Most works were published in German, which by the 19th century had become the *lingua franca* of the field. From the early 16th through early 20th centuries, these countries had close contacts with the Ottoman Empire, and thus Turkish/Ottoman studies were very much a state activity. Some of the early students of the empire in Austria and Hungary were government servants, such as the diplomat Josef Hammer von Purgstall, the author of the 10-volume *History of the Ottoman Empire* (*Geschichte des osmanischen Reiches*, Pest, 1827–35). As government servants, they had the opportunity either to collect considerable Ottoman manuscripts, like Hammer, or had access to Ottoman archival sources preserved in European archives.

Their access to primary sources, along with the general positivist mainstream of the late-19th-century German-Austrian-Hungarian historiography and the schooling of these early Ottomanists, explains their *Quellenkundliche* orientation, that is, their focus on source criticism and publication. It is hardly surprising that it was these European Ottomanists who first studied Ottoman manuscripts and archival sources and who first introduced source criticism into the field of Ottoman studies.

In recent years, however, Ottoman studies have been integrated into general historical studies and members of the youngest generation try to keep pace with the major trends of the history profession as a whole. They are especially strong in economic and military history, and there have been successful attempts to incorporate Ottoman history into its European context by applying some of the latest approaches and theories of European historiography, such as those of the War and Society and Frontier Studies.

In France, the emphasis has been on social and economic history, and Ottomanists were influenced by the *Annales* school of history writing, named after the famous French history journal *Annales d'histoire économique et sociale* (1929–to date in different names), which emphasized long-term social and economic trends as opposed to short-term political ones and used the methodology of a wide variety of social sciences. Besides traditional topics, such as French-Ottoman relations, French scholars also produced significant studies concerning the Arab provinces of the empire, and compiled an up-to-date concise history of the Ottoman Empire.

In the United Kingdom, the traditional centers for Ottoman studies have been the School of Oriental and African Studies (SOAS), and the University of Oxford; however, several other universities have at least one Ottomanist historian. In recent years, through its fellowships, conferences and symposia The Skilliter Centre for Ottoman Studies (Newnham College, Cambridge), the only research center devoted purely to Ottoman studies, became a major center for scholars studying the history of the Ottomans in its wider European and Mediterranean context.

Ottoman studies have always been a strong discipline in the successor states of the empire in the Balkans and more recently there is an interest in the history of the Ottomans in the Arab successor states, too. Some of these countries house considerable collections of Ottoman documents. However, the fact that these countries were under Ottoman rule for centuries has proved to be a disadvantage, for Ottoman history was often subject to political and ideological (nationalist, Marxist, etc.) manipulations and distortions. The Ottoman Empire traditionally got bad press in these countries, starting in the era of nationalisms (see NATIONALISM). Unlike Turkish historiography that tended to focus on the "classical" or "golden age" of the empire (circa 1300–1600), historians in the Balkan and Arab successor states studied the 19th century, the era of "Ottoman decline" and "national liberation movements." Whereas Turkish historiography has emphasized the "Pax Ottomanica," that is, the prosperity of the empire, the meritocracy and efficiency of its institutions, the relative religious tolerance of this multi-religious and multi-ethnic empire in an age when most

European monarchs tried to impose religious homogeneity upon their subjects, historians in the successor states stressed the backwardness and oppressive nature of the late empire, and often projected their negative experience onto earlier periods. These one-sided and distorted images have, however, changed in the past two decades, for Ottoman studies had become an international field of study, not least because of the development of the discipline in the United States.

The study of the Ottoman Empire in the United States has been influenced by many of the same trends that shaped Islamic and Middle Eastern studies in general. Most early students of the Ottomans were trained in departments and centers for Near/Middle Eastern studies, often established in the United States by European scholars along European traditions. Ottoman history was thus studied mainly by Turkologists, that is, specialists in the languages and culture of the Turkic peoples who were usually not trained in history, or by historians who used mainly European sources and either did not know Ottoman Turkish or had no access to Ottoman sources for other reasons. Like students of other "Oriental" empires and civilizations, many of these scholars displayed Orientalist and/or Eurocentric bias. This has changed in the past couple of decades due to a new generation of Ottomanists who were trained jointly by history and Middle Eastern departments and thus acquired the skills of the historian along with the necessary languages.

Changes in attitudes toward empires have also played a role. Prior to the 1990s, the political and intellectual left equated "empire" with "imperialism" and "colonialization," while the political and intellectual right also used it in negative terms, characterizing, in the words of President Ronald Reagan, the Soviet Union, the West's main rival, as "evil empire." By the 1990s, however, empires and "imperial endings" had again become fashionable as an object of study, largely brought on by the dissolution of the Soviet empire and the emergence of the United States as the dominant power in international politics. Since then, many have likened the United States's (temporarily) unrivaled power to that of the Romans and of other past empires. Many study the history of ancient empires in order to search for lessons as to how these empires ruled and dominated international politics in the past.

The Balkan wars of the 1990s as well as the religious and ethnic conflicts in the Middle East have dramatically increased interest in the history of the Ottoman Empire, which ruled these regions for centuries. Nevertheless, scholarship on the history of the Ottomans continues to lag behind that of other empires. Not counting popular histories, there are only half a dozen scholarly histories of the empire written in the past decade by Ottomanists, and most cover only parts of the empire's 600-year history. Historical dictionaries, encyclopedias, and other handbooks are also rare.

The present volume is the first and only English-language *Encyclopedia of the Ottoman Empire*. Its intended readership is high school and college students who are taking courses in Middle Eastern, Balkan/eastern European, and/or world history. Keeping our readership in mind we tried to create larger headings in English, instead of having separate entries on a myriad of Ottoman Turkish terms. Thus, for instance, the reader will not find separate entries on *vilayet/eyalet/beylerbeylik*, *sancak*, *nahiye*, *kaza*, that is, on terms used to denote administrative units in the empire; instead there is a longer article on Ottoman provincial administration (*see* ADMINISTRATION, PROVINCIAL). Similarly, instead of having entries on the various terms related to the Ottoman land tenure system, we chose to commission a longer essay on agriculture. Readers interested in special Ottoman terms are referred to the detailed index that will direct them to entries where they are discussed. Given that this is the first encyclopedia of its kind we hope that graduate students and our colleagues will also find our encyclopedia a useful handbook.

—Gábor Ágoston, Georgetown University

ENTRIES A TO Z

A

Abbas I (Shah Abbas the Great) (b. 1571–d. 1629) (r. 1587–1629) *outstanding shah of Safavid Persia* When Abbas became the Shii shah (ruler) of Safavid Persia (present-day IRAN), approximately half of his country was occupied by the Safavids' traditional Sunni enemies, the Ottomans and the Shaybanid Uzbeks. In order to avoid conflict on two fronts, Abbas concluded a humiliating peace treaty with the Ottomans in 1590, ceding all recent Ottoman conquests in western and northern Iran to Istanbul, including the first Safavid capital, Tabriz. With his western border secured through peace, Abbas turned against the Uzbek Turks. By 1603, through successive wars, Abbas had reconquered the provinces of Khurasan and Sistan, thus stabilizing his eastern frontier. Turning his attention westward, the shah now challenged the Ottomans, whose resources were tied up by the long Hungarian War (1593–1606) (*see* HUNGARY) and the CELALI REVOLTS in Anatolia. Abbas not only managed to retake substantial amounts of former Safavid territory, he also conquered BAGHDAD and Diyarbakır, albeit only temporarily.

Abbas's military achievements were partly due to, and went hand in hand with, his military, administrative, and financial reforms. By establishing an independent standing army, answerable to and paid by the shah, he considerably curbed the influence of the KIZILBAŞ Turkoman tribes and their emirs (chieftains), who had in the past composed the bulk of the Safavid army. Like that of the Ottoman Empire, Abbas's new army was based on military slaves or *ghulams,* recruited, in this case, from among Circassians, Armenians, and Georgians. Abbas's permanent army is said to have included a personal bodyguard of 3,000 men, a cavalry force of 10,000 men, an artillery corps of 12,000 men with 500 cannons,

and 12,000 infantrymen armed with muskets. In order to pay these soldiers from the central treasury, the shah increased royal revenues by converting the military fiefs of the Turkoman chieftains into crown lands. In so doing Abbas further weakened the power of the Kızılbaş emirs. He also brought many of the empire's autonomous and semiautonomous regions under direct royal control. By the end of Abbas's reign, some half of the provinces of Persia, traditionally controlled by the Kızılbaş chieftains, were administered by the military commanders of the new *ghulam,* answerable and loyal only to the shah.

Shah Abbas also realized the economic and political significance of Armenians and other religious minorities (Jews, Zoroastrians, and Hindus) living in Iran. To take advantage of the commercial expertise of Armenians and other Christian minorities, such as JACOBITES and Chaldeans, the shah created separate town quarters for them, supported their trade, and protected them. He also allowed various Roman Catholic orders (Carmelites and Capuchins) to settle and work in Iran. He hoped that his tolerance toward his non-Muslim subjects and the Catholic religious orders would enable him to form alliances with various European Christian powers against the Ottomans and Uzbeks, his Sufi neighbors and adversaries. Although in 1621 he ordered the forcible conversion of many Armenians, in general Persia's Christian population prospered under him. According to historian Roger Savory, the shah's "grand experiment in the creation of a multicultural state, based on religious tolerance" elevated Persia "to unprecedented heights of economic prosperity and artistic achievement."

The remarkable flourishing of Persian arts and culture under his rule was especially visible in Isfahan, which the shah made his new capital. Isfahan's main square (Maidan-i Naghsh-i Jahan) is a remarkable example of imperial urban planning and construction. One of the largest city squares in the world and listed as one of UNESCO's World Heritage Sites, the square is surrounded by the Royal Palace, mosques, colleges or madrasas, shops, markets, caravansaries, and public bathhouses, many of which were built during Abbas's reign. The monumental entrance of the Royal Palace, the Âlî Qapu or Exalted Gate, was meant to rival the Imperial Gate (Bab-ı Hümayun) of the Ottoman sultans' TOPKAPI PALACE. The English traveler and Byzantinist Robert Byron (d. 1941) compared the Sheikh Lotfollah Mosque on the square to Versailles, Vienna's Schönbrunn, Venice's Doge's Palace, or Rome's St. Peter, remarking that "All are rich; but none so rich" as Isfahan's Lotfollah Mosque. The Royal Maidan, with its shops and bazaars, became a commercial and economic hub of the city. To further strengthen the city's economic life, Abbas forcefully resettled thousands of Armenian, Persian, and Turkish artisans and merchants from Julfa in ARMENIA and Tabriz in Azerbaijan, creating two new town quarters. He also invited European merchants and experts to his realm.

While Abbas's rule restored Safavid Persia's former status in the region, curtailed Kızılbaş factionalism, and cemented royal authority with regard to the nomadic tribes, the shah's dynastic policy ultimately weakened Persia. Before Abbas, royal princes were sent to the provinces as governors, where they acquired useful administrative and military skills. Fearing rebellion and coups from within the royal family, Abbas ended this practice and kept the princes in his HAREM. Consequently, most shahs after Abbas lacked the experience and skills necessary to govern well. However, Abbas's economic, administrative, and military reforms strengthened Safavid royal authority, resulting in another century of royal power despite inferior rulers.

Gábor Ágoston

See also HUNGARY; QAJARS.

Further reading: Charles Melville, ed., *Safavid Persia: The History and Politics of an Islamic Society* (London: I. B. Tauris, 1996); Eskandar Beg Monshi, *History of Shah Abbas the Great*, 2 vols., trans. Roger M. Savory (Boulder, Colo.: Westview, 1978); David Morgan, *Medieval Persia, 1040–1797* (London: Longman, 1988); Roger Savory, *Iran under the Safavids* (Cambridge: Cambridge University Press, 1980); Roger M. Savory, "Relations between the Safavid State and Its Non-Muslim Minorities." *Islam and Christian-Muslim Relations* 14, no. 4 (2003): 435–58.

Abbas Hilmi (b. 1875–d. 1944) (r. 1892–1914) *last khedive of Egypt*   After 1841, when Sultan MAHMUD II (r. 1808–1839) made MEHMED ALI hereditary governor of EGYPT, the political status of Egypt was complicated. It was still technically an Ottoman province but its governors, who later held the title of KHEDIVE (viceroy), enjoyed complete independence of action. Further complicating the situation, Great Britain occupied the country in 1882 and declared it a British protectorate, all the while asserting that the khedive governed Egypt as an Ottoman province. When the reigning khedive, TAWFIQ, died in 1892, his son Abbas was only 17 years old and legally could not ascend the throne. But LORD CROMER, Egypt's unofficial British governor, stepped in to suggest that according to the Muslim lunar calendar Abbas was, in fact, already 18. Legality aside, Abbas Hilmi assumed the title of khedive and received an imperial patent from Ottoman sultan ABDÜLHAMID II (r. 1876–1909) confirming his office. Cromer's intervention in his enthronement was emblematic of the troubled relationship that Abbas had with his country's British occupiers. While he owed his throne to the British, he sought to establish his own independent course, especially when promoting Egyptian sovereignty over the recently conquered territory of Sudan. In 1894 Abbas clashed with Lord Kitchener, the British commander of the Egyptian army in the Sudan, and demanded his resignation. Again Lord Cromer intervened, and Kitchener remained in his post.

For the rest of his reign, Abbas Hilmi looked for allies who might get the British out of Egypt and thus help establish him as sole ruler of the country. Initially he contacted the French and the Ottomans for help; when neither seemed willing to take on the British over the question of who rightly governed Egypt, Abbas Hilmi turned to the Egyptian nationalists who were agitating for British withdrawal. Abbas supported several nationalist newspapers and for a time was a political ally of MUSTAFA KAMIL (1874–1908), who became the founder of the National Party. He also consistently supported the Ottoman sultan Abdülhamid II as the champion of Muslim countries' resistance to European imperialism. But with the sultan's fall from power in 1909, Abbas Hilmi developed a grander scheme that would designate him caliph of a revived Arab-Muslim empire.

The khedives often spent their summers in Turkish Istanbul, and Abbas Hilmi chose do so in the summer of 1914. When the Ottoman Empire entered WORLD WAR I (1914–18) as an ally of Germany on October 29, 1914, Abbas did not immediately return to Egypt, thus raising British concerns about his intentions and loyalties. When the khedive finally returned to Cairo in December, the British quickly acted by declaring unilaterally on December 18, 1914 that Egypt was independent of the Ottoman Empire, but still a British protectorate. The next day the British deposed Abbas Hilmi in favor of his uncle, Husayn Kamil (1853–1917), who was given the title sultan of Egypt. Egypt's place as a part of the Ottoman Empire had come abruptly to an end.

Bruce Masters

Further reading: Afaf Lutfi al-Sayyid Marsot, *Egypt and Cromer: A Study in Anglo-Egyptian Relations* (New York: Praeger, 1969).

Abbasid Caliphate   The ABBASID CALIPHATE ruled much of the Muslim world from 750 C.E. until 1258. Many Muslims consider it to have been the Golden Age of Islam, a period when the visual arts, sciences, mathematics, and literature flourished. The Abbasid family came to power in a revolution that brought down the Umayyad Caliphate, which had ruled the Islamic Empire since the death of the fourth caliph, Ali, in 661. The new dynasty traced its origins to Abbas (d. 653), the uncle of the Prophet Muhammad (570–632), and sought to make a clean break with its predecessors by building a new city to serve as their capital in 762. The Abbasids called the city Madinat al-Salam (City of Peace), but everyone else called it BAGHDAD, after a village that previously existed on the site, and that was the name that stuck. By the late ninth century its population is estimated to have reached half a million, making it one of the largest cities in the world in that era. The population declined in the following centuries as the power of the dynasty diminished, but Baghdad remained one of the most important centers for the study and production of philosophy, religious studies, mathematics and science in the Muslim world, attracting scholars, philosophers, and poets from across North Africa and the Middle East.

When the Abbasid family came to power some Muslims hoped that they would take a more forceful role in making the caliphate a religious, as well as a political, office. The people in this group had favored one of the surviving descendants of Ali, the Prophet Muhammad's son-in-law and the father of the Prophet's only grandchildren, to be the caliph. This faction believed that only someone from the Prophet Muhammad's direct line should rule as caliph, but many acquiesced to the rule of a family descended at least from the Prophet Muhammad's more extended relations. Besides the question of who should serve as Muhammad's successor or caliph, there was also the question of what the office of the caliphate should entail. The debate was between those who wanted a more spiritual caliph and those who wanted a merely administrative one. The Abbasids offered a compromise whereby they promised to rule according to Islamic law but would make no claim to spiritual authority for themselves. As long as they did so, the religious scholars would recognize the legitimacy of their rule. Western historians have coined the term the Abbasid Compromise to refer to the agreement. It provided a balance between religious and secular authority that all subsequent states embracing SUNNI ISLAM would follow until the modern era. This was in contrast to the SHIA ISLAM model of government, which envisioned the caliph also as the imam, a spiritual leader and model for the world's Muslims, thereby giving the office both political and religious authority.

At the height of its power in the early ninth century, the Abbasid state controlled territories stretching from Morocco to the borders of China; however, it weakened over time. By the 11th century it had lost control over most of its territory to local Muslim dynasties. According to Muslim political theory as it developed during this period, the world's Muslims should acknowledge one political ruler, the caliph. Due to the strength of that ideal, most of these independent Sunni Muslim rulers, who emerged as the power of the Abbasids declined, maintained a nominal allegiance to the caliph. The alternative for such a ruler was to declare that he was the caliph (or, with Shii Muslims, the imam), something no Sunni leader would do as long the Abbasid family survived. Thus even as its actual power diminished, the Abbasid Caliphate remained a potent symbol for political unity. That dream came to an end with the destruction of Baghdad and the murder of the last reigning caliph, al-Mustasim, by the Mongols in 1258.

For the sultans who ruled the Ottoman Empire beginning in the early 14th century, the Abbasid Caliphate served as a model for good government as it had been the last strong, centralized Sunni Muslim state. The Ottomans chose as their official interpretation of Islamic law the Hanafi school favored by the Abbasid state. Political treatises written by scholars in the Hanafi tradition, such as those of Abu Yusuf (d. 798) and al-Mawardi (d. 1058), served as the basis of Ottoman legal and political theory. The Ottomans also consciously modeled many of their state's political and religious institutions after those of the Abbasids. In the 17th century, Ottoman court historians began to include an account that the last surviving descendant of the Abbasid line, the Caliph al-Mutawakkil, handed his robe of office as caliph to Sultan SELIM I (r. 1512–20) after his conquest of EGYPT in 1517. Although no contemporary accounts recorded such a transfer, the story became the justification for the Ottoman sultan's claim to be caliph of all Muslims during the 19th century.

Bruce Masters

Further reading: Selim Deringil, *The Well-Protected Domains: Ideology and the Legitimation of Power in the Ottoman Empire, 1876–1909* (London: I.B. Tauris, 1998); Hugh Kennedy, *When Baghdad Ruled the Muslim World: The Rise and Fall of Islam's Greatest Dynasty* (Cambridge, Mass.: Da Capo, 2006).

Abd al-Qadir al-Jazairi (Abd el-Kader) (b. 1808–d. 1883) *Algerian resistance fighter, intellectual, and emir of Mascara* Abd al-Qadir "the Algerian" was a warrior, statesman, and religious philosopher. He was born in a village near Oran in present-day Algeria. His family had been prominent in the Qadiriyya Order of Sufism, which followed the teachings of Abd al-Qadir Ghilani (d. 1165), for more than a century. Raised within that tradition, Abd al-Qadir went on the hajj in 1826–27 with his father, Muhy al-Din, leader of the Qadiriyya Order in the region. Together they visited Cairo, Damascus, and Baghdad. In each place, Abd al-Qadir held extensive discussions with various scholars representing different Sufi traditions from whom he gained a wide knowledge of Islam's philosophical and mystical traditions.

He was transformed from religious scholar to warrior with the French invasion of Algeria in 1830. Initially, Abd al-Qadir's father led the Algerian resistance, but the leadership of both his Sufi order and the resistance soon passed to the son. Abd al-Qadir fought a guerrilla campaign against French occupation, encouraging the various Berber tribes in the Algerian mountains to participate in the struggle. It was a cruel war in which tens of thousands Algerians died either directly from the fighting or as a result of the famine that followed the French destruction of Algerian croplands and orchards. In the end, French power prevailed, and Abd al-Qadir surrendered in 1847. He was taken to France and lived there under minimum-security house arrest until 1852. In France, he observed and appreciated the material progress the West was making due to their embrace of scientific rationalism, but he was also drawn further into the study of the writings of ibn al-Arabi, the great 13th-century Sufi intellectual.

When he was released from house arrest Abd al-Qadir went first to Istanbul, then traveled throughout the Ottoman Empire. He finally settled in Damascus in 1855. Abd al-Qadir brought with him a fairly large group of Algerian exiles, and he established an intellectual salon in his home where Muslim scholars could meet and discuss various Sufi texts.

Abd al-Qadir again gained the attention of the West during the anti-Christian Damascus Riots in 1860. When the riot started, Abd al-Qadir sent his armed Algerian retainers into the Christian quarter to residents to safety, even giving refuge to several hundred in his own house. In gratitude, the French government bestowed upon him a medal for bravery, an irony that was not lost on Abd al-Qadir. After this incident, there was much wishful speculation in the West that he might emerge as the "King of the Arabs" in a state independent of Ottoman control. But Abd al-Qadir turned his attention instead to the study of the works of ibn al-Arabi and to questions of how to adapt Islamic laws to the modern age, producing a large body of essays on both topics. After his death, Abd al-Qadir's sons buried him next to ibn al-Arabi's grave.

Bruce Masters

Further reading: Itzchak Weismann, *A Taste of Modernity: Sufism, Salafiyya, and Arabism in Late Ottoman Damascus* (Leiden: Brill, 2001).

Abduh, Muhammad (b. 1849–d. 1905) *Egyptian judge and religious scholar, a founder of Islamic modernism* Muhammad Abduh was one of the leading figures in the Salafiyya, the Islamic reform movement that sought to adapt Islamic law to meet the needs of the modern world. Abduh was born in a village in the Egyptian delta. After receiving a traditional education there, he went to al-Azhar, the central mosque of Cairo, for further study. There Abduh met political philosopher Jamal al-Din al-Afghani and became one of his students. Al-Afghani introduced Abduh to the study of Islamic and Western philosophy that would have a profound impact on all his future writings. After graduation, Abduh began to teach at al-Azhar, but he also contributed articles to Egypt's burgeoning secular press, which led to frequent clashes with the government of the khedive. After Colonel Urabi's revolt in 1882 and the British occupation of Egypt, Abduh's writings ultimately led to his exile. Joining al-Afghani in Paris, Abduh helped publish the protest newspaper *Al-Urwah al-wuthqa* (The firm grip). He also met with British and French intellectuals to discuss what had become the two main issues of his intellectual inquiry: how to respond to colonialism, and the compatibility of Islamic religious belief with ideas of science and progress that had grown out of the European Enlightenment.

Abduh returned to Egypt in 1888, largely through the intercession of the British, and was appointed a judge in the Muslim court system. In 1899 he became the chief Muslim jurist, or mufti, of Egypt, a position he held until his death in 1905. As the principal legal authority in Egypt, Abduh's judicial rulings (fatwa) helped shape the country's legislative and educational bodies. Among his many writings were a commentary on the Quran and a treatise on the unity of God (*Risalat al-tawhid*). In all his work, Abduh stressed two points: that it is possible to be both Muslim and modern, and that true modernity requires religious belief. In other words, Abduh saw Islam as providing a necessary moral balance to a modernity that stresses the importance of worldly material success.

Abduh's writings sought to prove that Islam was not inherently hostile to technological and intellectual innovations coming from the West. Rather, Abduh argued that Muslims must return to the underlying principles of

Islam and not rely on the exterior traditions of ritual and practice that had developed over the centuries. Abduh wrote that if Muslims truly understood what God had said to them in the Quran, they would adapt to a modern world and still remain comfortably Muslim. In Abduh's view, there was no inherent clash of civilizations between the West and Islam. Rather, he saw both civilizations as needing to seek a balance between material progress and spiritual goals. With his teaching and writing, Abduh influenced a whole generation of Islamic scholars in both Egypt and Syria.

Bruce Masters

Further reading: Albert Hourani, *Arabic Thought in the Liberal Age, 1798–1939* (Cambridge: Cambridge University Press, 1983).

Abdülaziz (b. 1830–d. 1876) (r. 1861–1876) *Ottoman sultan and caliph, ruled during second phase of the Tanzimat* Abdülaziz was the son of sultan MAHMUD II (r. 1808–39) and Pertevniyal Valide Sultan. He was born on February 8, 1830, in Istanbul and came to the throne upon the death of his elder brother, Sultan ABDÜLMECID (r. 1839–61) on June 25, 1861. He ruled the Ottoman Empire from 1861 until shortly before his death in 1876. One of his 13 children, Abdülmecid, became the last Ottoman caliph (1922–24), but he never ruled as sultan.

Abdülaziz was well educated thanks to his elder brother Abdülmecid. In addition to Arabic and Persian, he studied French and was interested in MUSIC, CALLIGRAPHY, and poetry. Unlike his brother, Abdülaziz was physically strong and tall; he was a good archer and hunter, and a brilliant wrestler.

His brother, Abdülmecid, had initiated a period of reform known as the TANZIMAT (Reorganization) that aimed to modernize the institutions of the Ottoman Empire. In the first decade of Abdülaziz's rule, statesmen such as MEHMED EMIN ÂLÎ PASHA and FUAD PASHA continued to direct reform measures in central and provincial administration, law, finances, EDUCATION, and the military. These reforms included the introduction of the Provincial Law Code (1864) and the establishment of the Audit Department (1862), the State Council (1868), and the Justice Ministry (1868). Abdülaziz focused his energies on the creation of a powerful armada and the construction of important railroads in Anatolia.

Despite the fact that Abdülaziz, together with Âlî Pasha and Fuad Pasha, promoted a universalizing political approach called OTTOMANISM as an ideological measure to combat separatism, the empire saw the increasing autonomy of SERBIA and EGYPT, as well as significant political events such as the Revolt of the Montenegrins (1862), the unification of the principalities of WALLACHIA and MOLDAVIA into Romania (1866), and the recognition of the Bulgarians as a separate religious community or MILLET (1870).

Abdülaziz visited Egypt in 1863, and was the only Ottoman sultan who also made state visits to European countries. Receiving his first invitation from Napoleon III in 1867, Abdülaziz initially went to Paris to attend the Paris Exhibition, where he met the king and queen. Other heads of state followed with their own invitations and the sultan's trip expanded to 46 days as he traveled to London to meet the Prince of Wales, Edward II, and Queen Victoria of England; he later visited King Leopold II in Brussels, the king and queen of Prussia in Koblenz, and the emperor of Austria-Hungary in Vienna.

As Abdülaziz traveled, a group called the YOUNG OTTOMANS was at home forming an opposition against the bureaucratic domination of Âlî Pasha and Fuad Pasha. Following the death of Âlî Pasha in 1871, Grand Vizier Mahmud Nedim Pasha encouraged Abdülaziz to rule as an autocrat, but the lack of effective political forces to help control the sultan led to general administrative and political chaos. By 1875, this resulted in the bankruptcy of the state. When Mahmud Nedim Pasha failed to suppress the revolts in BOSNIA AND HERZEGOVINA (1875) and in BULGARIA (1876), MIDHAT PASHA, one of the most influential and powerful politicians of the later Tanzimat era and a staunch advocate for constitutional reform, together with the heads of the army and the religious establishment (ULEMA), organized a coup d'état, which led to the deposition of Abdülaziz (May 30, 1876) in favor of his nephew MURAD V (r. 1876). On June 4, 1876, Abdülaziz was found dead in his room, but whether he was assassinated or died of natural causes remains a subject of debate.

Selçuk Akşin Somel

Further reading: Roderic H. Davison, *Reform in the Ottoman Empire, 1856–1876* (Princeton, N.J.: Princeton University Press, 1963); Caroline Finkel, *Osman's Dream: The Story of the Ottoman Empire, 1300–1923* (London: John Murray, 2005); Stanford J. Shaw and Ezel K. Shaw, *History of the Ottoman Empire and Modern Turkey*, 2 vols. (Cambridge: Cambridge University Press, 1977).

Abdülhamid I (b. 1725–d. 1789) (r. 1774–1789) *Ottoman sultan and caliph* Abdülhamid I was the son of Sultan AHMED III (r. 1703–30) and the concubine Şermi Rabia Kadın. After spending most of his life in the seclusion of the palace, he succeeded to the throne at the relatively advanced age of 49. He was the oldest male member of an Ottoman dynasty endangered by the lack of princes. Abdülhamid compensated for his comparatively advanced age by presenting himself as a saintly figure. Making his grand viziers the primary authority in running the government, he acted more as an advisor and arbitrator than as an absolutist sultan.

Abdülhamid came to power near the close of the devastating RUSSO-OTTOMAN WAR of 1768–74, and his reign was characterized by an ongoing threat from Russian military and political forces. The TREATY OF KÜÇÜK KAYNARCA, signed with RUSSIA on July 21, 1774, ended the war, but set disastrous terms for the Ottomans, declaring the Crimea, formerly an Ottoman and Muslim vassal principality that had guarded the Ottoman Empire against Russian expansion, an independent polity. Beginning with the treaty, the Russian menace continued throughout Abdülhamid's time in power with the steady advance of Russia into the Crimea.

Two political factions arose in direct response to this threat. A hawkish faction was headed by Grand Admiral Cezayirli ("Algerian") Gazi Hasan Pasha and Koca Yusuf Pasha, a future grand vizier (1787–90). Gazi Hasan Pasha became a hero and grand admiral of the Ottoman NAVY after a 1770 naval disaster when he expelled the Russians—who had set the Ottoman navy ablaze at Çesme, near Izmir—from the island of Lemnos, a strategic point from which the Russians could have threatened the Ottoman capital. Koca Yusuf Pasha propounded an aggressive stance against the belligerent Russia that had annexed the independent Crimea in 1783 and penetrated the CAUCA-SUS. A rival faction, headed by Grand Vizier Halil Hamid Pasha (1782–85), argued for a more cautious diplomatic stance, pointing to both the need for military reform and the empire's economic instability. This approach was effectively silenced, however, when Halil Hamid Pasha was beheaded after rumors suggested he was plotting for the succession of the future SELIM III (r. 1789–1807), Abdülhamid's nephew.

As the war party rose in power, the Ottoman Empire went to war with the Habsburg and Russian empires (1787–92) (see RUSSO-OTTOMAN WARS) in the hope of recovering the Crimea. Hasan Pasha also organized punitive expeditions to SYRIA and EGYPT to put down local rebellions. However, the total destabilization of the social-economic life of the empire and the continued disruption of administration that resulted from the earlier Russo-Ottoman War limited the success of such measures.

Despite disagreement over foreign policy, the necessity for military reforms along the Western model was universally recognized. Halil Hamid Pasha paid special attention to strengthening the Ottoman fortresses along the Russian frontier and in the Caucasus and worked with the French military mission to strengthen fortresses along the Turkish Straits (Bosporus and Dardanelles) and the Gallipoli Peninsula. Halil Hamid Pasha also undertook the modernization of the technical branches of the Ottoman army such as the Corps of Cannoneers, Corps of Bombardiers, and Corps of Miners, and enlarged the Corps of Rapid-fire Artillerymen organized by Baron de Tott in 1772. The opening of the Imperial Naval Engineering School (Mühendishane-i Bahri-i Hümayun) and the School of Fortification (Istihkam Mektebi) for the education of trained officers, as well as the reinstatement of the printing house founded by Ibrahim Müteferrika in the 1730s, should be counted among the achievements of Abdülhamid's reign.

Abdülhamid also acted as the benefactor and supervisor of the city of Istanbul when it was ravaged by a series of fires in 1777, 1782, 1784, and 1787. He oversaw the provisioning of the city and founded the Beylerbeyi and Emirgan mosques on the Bosporus, as well as sponsoring public institutions and charities such as libraries, schools, soup kitchens, and fountains. His Hamidiye Library was the first sultanic library founded for its own sake outside of a mosque complex with an independent administration and was frequented by the Orientalists and foreign travelers of the time.

Abdülhamid kept at least seven concubines who bore him as many as 24 children, including 10 sons. One of these, the celebrated Sultan MAHMUD II (r. 1808–39), laid the groundwork for the important TANZI-MAT reform period that began in 1839. Beginning with Mahmud II, the last three generations of the House of Osman descended from Abdülhamid. Abdülhamid died of a stroke when reading the news regarding the Russian capture of ÖZI on the right bank of the estuary of the Dnieper River in the Russo-Ottoman War of 1787–92. He was succeeded by his nephew, SELIM III (r. 1789–1807).

Kahraman Şakul

Further reading: Caroline Finkel, *Osman's Dream: The Story of the Ottoman Empire, 1300–1923* (London: John Murray, 2005), 372–400.

Abdülhamid II (b. 1842–d. 1918) (r. 1876–1909) *Ottoman sultan and caliph* Born to ABDÜLMECID I (r. 1839–61) and Tir-i Müjgan Kadın, Abdülhamid II came to power at a time of political upheaval. He succeeded his brother MURAD V (r. 1876), who reigned briefly after their uncle ABDÜLAZIZ (r. 1861–76) was deposed in the coup d'état of May 30, 1876, a political emergency that arose out of the administrative chaos of the early 1870s, the agricultural crisis of 1873–74, and the general inability of the Ottoman government to contain revolts in the Balkans (1875–76). Unable to cope with the stress of the throne, the liberal Murad was forced to give way to his more autocratic younger brother, Abdülhamid, whose reign was characterized by an ongoing sense of threat in response to strong modernizing influences and widespread revolutionary movements throughout the Ottoman Empire and greater Europe.

Abdülhamid II   7

Abdülhamid's education did not reflect the modernist developments of the 1850s. In fact, his instruction barely exceeded the level of primary-school education. However, this meager schooling was supplemented by practical experience of the world when he accompanied his uncle, Sultan Abdülaziz, on a European tour from June 21 to August 7, 1867. During this trip the young Abdülhamid observed material progress in France, Great Britain, Prussia, and Austria. Also, as a youth, Abdülhamid engaged in successful agricultural ventures on the outskirts of Istanbul.

Assuming the throne when his brother stepped down in 1876, Abdülhamid was largely indebted to MIDHAT PASHA who had masterminded the deposing of the preceding sultans. Although Midhat Pasha originally envisaged a constitutional monarchy arising from these changes in rule, the new sultan opposed a liberal system. Abdülhamid did approve the introduction of a CONSTITUTION and a PARLIAMENT, but he forced Midhat Pasha to change the original liberal document into an authoritarian one. The constitution was promulgated by the sultan on December 23, 1876. The parliament convened for only two periods, in 1877 and 1878. On February 13, 1878, the sultan dissolved the parliament and restored autocracy.

The limited constitutional reforms urged by Midhat Pasha failed in part because of Abdülhamid's autocratic preferences but also as a result of military defeat in the Russo-Ottoman War of 1877–78 (see RUSSO-OTTOMAN WARS). When the war came to an end by the Treaty of San Stefano (Yeşilköy) on March 3, 1878, the terms of the treaty ended Ottoman presence in the Balkans and established Russian predominance over southeastern Europe and the Turkish Straits (Bosporus and Dardanelles). This radical shift in European power balances was opposed by the rest of the great powers, leading to a new peace settlement at the Congress of Berlin (June 13 through July 13, 1878, see RUSSO-OTTOMAN WARS), during which Ottoman presence in ALBANIA and Macedonia was restored, despite territorial losses in Europe and Anatolia.

Other international events during Abdülhamid's reign also contributed to a sense on the part of the Ottoman ruling elite that the empire was under immediate threat of dissolution and partition. The Russo-Ottoman War proved that the Ottoman Empire as a political entity did not possess a viable future. Separatist activities by Bulgarians, Armenians, and Greeks, and even by Muslim groups such as Albanians, Arabs, and Kurds, posed an enormous threat to the fragile stability of the empire. In 1897 CRETE acquired autonomy, and in 1903 Russia and Austria-Hungary forced the Sublime Porte to apply reforms in Macedonia.

Contributing to the political difficulties of Abdülhamid's reign were the bankrupt condition of state finances and the masses of Muslim refugees from the Balkans and

Sultan Abdülhamid II (1876–1909) was long portrayed in Ottoman historiography as an autocratic and bloodthirsty ruler, but in fact his reign and his personality were complex and contradictory. Although he used censorship, repression, and other means of autocratic rule, he also continued the modernizing efforts begun in the Tanzimat period. *(Art Resource / HIP)*

the CAUCASUS who posed a major problem for integration. Other significant political challenges included the French occupation of TUNISIA (1881), the Greek annexation of Thessaly (1881), the British invasion of EGYPT (1882), and the Bulgarian annexation of Eastern Rumelia (1885), all of which were either nominally or directly part of the Ottoman Empire, as well as the Greek aspirations on Crete that led to the Greco-Ottoman War of 1897.

Abdülhamid did not want to risk the existence of the empire. For Abdülhamid, stability could only be assured by authoritarian measures such as personal rule, police surveillance, CENSORSHIP, prohibition of public and private gatherings, and restrictions on mobility. Abdülhamid promoted networks of patronage to keep tribal leaders in remote provinces under his personal control and he also used the ideology of Islamism as a tool of control, stressing the notion of being both the secular ruler of all Ottoman subjects (sultan) and the religious head (caliph) of all Muslims everywhere. Propagating SUNNI ISLAM as the true form of belief was instrumental in legitimizing central authority among different Muslim subjects. Islamism was also used as a diplomatic tool to intimidate colonial powers with substantial Muslim populations, such as ENGLAND, FRANCE, and RUSSIA.

Despite Abdülhamid's efforts to exert control, authoritarian measures did not stop separatist movements in the Balkans; Abdülhamid's regime played Bulgarian guerrilla bands against the Greek ones and thus tried to keep control in Macedonia. In Anatolia, Abdülhamid mobilized Kurdish tribes against Armenian guerrillas. In August, 1894, the Armenians staged an armed revolt; this led to the notorious Armenian massacres.

The brutality of these events, international intervention on behalf of the Armenians, the fear of the disintegration of the empire, and the corrupt character of the regime ultimately triggered opposition against the sultan by a dissident group known as the YOUNG TURKS. One Young Turk organization, the COMMITTEE OF UNION AND PROGRESS, succeeded in infiltrating the military elite, leading to revolt in Macedonia and forcing Abdülhamid to restore the constitution (July 4–24, 1908). Under the new regime, Abdülhamid acted as a consti-

Built by the then governor and named after the ruling sultan Abdülhamid II, the Hamidiye covered market provided a new major commercial axis for the city, and served as a way to appropriate the heart of Damascus with a conspicuously modern Ottoman structure. *(Photo by Gábor Ágoston)*

tutional monarch; however, the principal political parties distrusted him. When a reactionary rebellion broke out in Istanbul (April 13–24, 1909), Abdülhamid was accused of being behind it. This incident led to his being deposed on April 27, 1909. Abdülhamid and his family were exiled to Salonika. During the First Balkan War (1912–13) (*see* BALKAN WARS) he was transferred back to Istanbul (October 1912) to spend the rest of his life at the Beylerbeyi Palace.

Although Abdülhamid's regime was characterized by his authoritarian policies and actions, the sultan also encouraged infrastructural and cultural modernization. Under Abdülhamid's rule, Ottoman bureaucracy acquired rational and institutional features where admission into the civil service as well as promotion processes were arranged through objective criteria such as exams and rules. Abdülhamid created government schools for boys and girls throughout the empire, undertook railway construction with the support of foreign capital, began to connect distant provinces to the capital, and extended TELEGRAPH lines to enable administrative surveillance from Albania down to YEMEN. During his reign, the judicial system was reformed. There was also a significant expansion in the availability of literature. New translations were made from Western literature, there was an increase in book printing, and Ottoman poetry and prose acquired worldly and individualistic traits. These changes had a profound impact on young people resulted in the emergence of a Western-oriented generation who were dissatisfied with the autocracy and demanded a constitutional monarchy. The opposition of the Young Turks came mainly from this generation. Abdülhamid's modernizing efforts ultimately laid the foundation for modern Turkey; the founders of the Turkish republic were educated at schools founded by Abdülhamid.

Abdülhamid kept at least five concubines and had four daughters and seven sons, but none played any significant political role. He was succeeded by his younger brother, MEHMED V (r. 1909–18).

Selçuk Akşin Somel

See also ARMENIA; CENSORSHIP; NATIONALISM; PAN-ISLAMISM; RAILROADS, YOUNG OTTOMANS; YOUNG TURKS.

Further reading: Engin D. Akarlı, "The Problem of External Pressures, Power Struggles and Budgetary Deficits in Ottoman Politics under Abdülhamid II (1876–1909)." (Ph.D. diss., Princeton University, 1976); Selim Deringil, *The Well-Protected Domains: Ideology and the Legitimation of Power in the Ottoman Empire, 1876–1909* (London: I.B. Tauris, 1998); François Georgeon, *Abdülhamid II: Le Sultan Calife (1876–1909)* (Paris: Fayard, 2003); Joan Haslip, *The Sultan: The Life of Abdul Hamid* (London: Cassell, 1958).

Abdülmecid (b. 1823–d. 1861) (r. 1839–1861) *Ottoman sultan and caliph* The son of Mahmud II (r. 1808–39) and Bezmi Alem Valide Sultan, Abdülmecid was born in April 1823 in Istanbul and succeeded his father upon his death on July 1, 1839. Starting at the age of 16, Abdülmecid reigned over the Ottoman Empire for 22 years between 1839 and 1861. He died of tuberculosis on June 25, 1861, at the age of 39.

Abdülmecid was well educated and was raised as a Western prince. He was fluent and literate in Arabic, Persian, and French, was an accomplished calligrapher, and had connections with the Mevlevi Order of dervishes. He was an avid reader of European literature and enjoyed Western classical music as well as Western dress and finery. The physically frail Abdülmecid was polite, passionate, and just; he was also extravagant and addicted to entertainment. His numerous concubines bore him 37 children, five of whom—Murad V (r. 1876), Abdülhamid II (r. 1876–1909), Mehmed V (r. 1909–1918), and Mehmed VI (r. 1918–1922)—would later reign.

Abdülmecid met with many internal and external challenges. Of these the most significant were the Egypt question—that is, the contention around Mehmed Ali Pasha's recognition as hereditary ruler of Egypt by the Great Powers (1840); the Crimean War (1854–56); the Imperial Rescript of Reform, which was promulgated on February 28, 1856; and a number of revolts and crises in the Balkans and Syria and Lebanon (1845, 1861).

Two remarkable reform efforts were announced during his reign: the Tanzimat reforms and the Imperial Rescript. The first was an important step in the westernization process. This ferman, or decree, granted equality before the law to all Ottoman subjects regardless of religion or ethnicity. The latter gave important privileges to non-Muslims, although this came about only after England, France, and Russia intervened in the internal policy of the Ottoman State.

Other state innovations during Abdülmecid's reign spanned the administrative, legal, economic, financial, and educational fields. In 1840 the Ottoman Postal Ministry was founded, followed in 1857 by the Education Ministry. The Modern Municipality Organization was established in Istanbul in 1855, while the Penal Code (1840), Law of Commerce (1850), and Land Law (1858) were imported from the West. Sultan Abdülmecid established schools of teaching (1847), agriculture (1847), forestry (1859), and political science (1859). The first privately owned Turkish newspaper in the empire, *Ceride-i Havadis* (Journal of news), began publishing in 1840 during Abdülmecid's reign (*see* Newspapers). The Ottoman economy also saw significant change during this period with the empire issuing its first banknotes being issued in 1839 and incurring its first external debt in 1854.

During his reign, Abdülmecid worked with a number of forceful pashas, of whom Mustafa Reşid Pasha was the most important; in fact, the proclamation of Tanzimat was a project under Mustafa Reşid Pasha's auspices. However, Mehmed Amin Âlî Pasha and Fuad Pasha became more active in reformation in the 1850s.

Despite the many reforms introduced during this era, Abdülmecid's reign was still one of the most turbulent periods in Ottoman history. When he died in 1861, leaving the throne to his older brother, Abdülaziz (r. 1861–1876), the Ottoman state was struggling with internal and external problems and was in financial crisis.

Coşkun Çakır

Further reading: Caroline Finkel, *Osman's Dream: The Story of the Ottoman Empire, 1300–1923* (London: John Murray, 2005); Stanford J. Shaw and Ezel K. Shaw, *History of the Ottoman Empire and Modern Turkey,* 2 vols. (Cambridge: Cambridge University Press, 1977).

accession *See* ENTHRONEMENT AND ACCESSION CEREMONY.

Acre (*Heb.*: Akko; *Turk.*: Akka) Acre today is a sleepy fishing port on the northern coast of Israel. In the Crusades period (1095–1291), the city was the most important crusader-held port in the eastern Mediterranean. But with its conquest by the Mamluk Empire, Acre declined, with Beirut replacing it as the leading port of the Levantine trade. Conquered by the Ottomans in 1516, Acre remained a relatively unimportant port until the 18th century. Its rise in that century was linked to the careers of two men who controlled northern Palestine and southern Lebanon, Zahir al-Umar (d. 1775) and Cezzar Ahmed Pasha (d. 1804). Zahir al-Umar slowly built a base of power in the Galilee region of present-day northern Israel, starting in 1725, by creating alliances with various clans in the region. In 1743 he took Acre, which at the time probably had only a few hundred inhabitants. He fortified the site and moved his base of operations there. Under his patronage, Acre became a major port for the export of cotton and tobacco to France. In 1775, with Egyptian forces advancing, Zahir al-Umar, now an old man, fled the city, thus undermining his authority with his own men. When he fell from his horse on his return to Acre, they beheaded him.

In the aftermath of the Egyptian invasion of Syria in 1775, when Cezzar Ahmed Pasha received the governorship of Sidon, in present-day Lebanon, he wasted no time in moving his base of operations to Acre. There he completed the city walls, built a large Ottoman-style mosque, a caravansary, and a covered market. Although local chroniclers recorded his reign as tyrannical, Acre's economy flourished under Cezzar Ahmed's rule, and the population of the city may have reached 30,000. Acre's moment of fame came in 1798 when its walls resisted a siege by NAPOLEON BONAPARTE. Although a more obvious reason for the French retreat to EGYPT was an outbreak of plague, Cezzar Ahmed was able to claim to the sultan that he had saved the empire with Acre's city walls. After his death in 1804, Acre's fortunes went into a steep decline. By the mid-19th century, although its walls remained intact, the population of the city had dropped to a few thousand as Beirut and HAIFA grew into the area's major commercial ports.

Bruce Masters

Further reading: Thomas Philipp, *Acre: The Rise and Fall of a Palestinian City, 1730–1831* (New York: Columbia University Press, 2001).

administration, central   While the picture of the Ottoman Empire as a super-centralized form of "Oriental despotism" is hardly tenable in light of new research, by the mid-15th century the Ottomans had attained a degree of centralization unmatched in contemporary Europe. The Ottoman sultan's power was not unchallenged, however, and he delegated a good deal of authority to his viziers and other high executives of his empire. His power over the ruling elite also changed over time along with the empire's central institutions. These changes and the evolution of the Ottoman central institutions in turn reflected both the periodic strengthening and weakening of the sultan's authority and the results of the ruler's negotiation with different elite groups of the empire.

THE EARLIEST RULERS

The first rulers of the Ottoman Empire, OSMAN I (r. ?–1324) and ORHAN I (r. 1324–62), were merely beys, or military leaders, and shared this title with the other rulers of the ANATOLIAN EMIRATES as well as with the frontier lords of the expanding Ottoman polity. The flowery titles that appear on 14th-century Ottoman dedicatory inscriptions, such as "sultan of ghazis and of the fighters of the faith," were not unique to the Ottoman rulers and can be seen in other Turkoman emirates. They suggest, however, Ottoman claims and aspirations to a more prominent status within Anatolia and the Ottoman polity rather than actual realities of fluctuating power relations.

The extensive conquests of BAYEZID I (r. 1389–1402) increased the prestige of the Ottoman ruler. However, under MEHMED I (r. 1413–21) and MURAD II (r. 1421–44, 1446–51), Turkish frontier lords, such as the Evrenosoğulları and Mihaloğulları, regained much of their power, due largely to the role they played in reestablishing Ottoman control over the Balkans, which had

been lost after the BATTLE OF ANKARA and the ensuing civil war of 1402–13. Another powerful Anatolian Turkish clan, the Çandarlı family, had acted for more than a century as the sultans' chief ministers and judicial heads (KADIASKER). They amassed great wealth and enjoyed high status within the Ottoman governing elite, often challenging the sultans' decisions. For example, Çandarlı Halil Pasha, GRAND VIZIER or chief minister under Murad II and MEHMED II (r. 1444–46; 1451–81), fiercely opposed the new sultan's plans to conquer Constantinople and was thus executed after the conquest.

THE DIVAN-I HÜMAYUN

Çandarlı Halil Pasha's downfall signaled major transformations in the Ottoman governing elite. By appointing grand viziers from among the sultan's *kuls* or slaves of Christian origin, Mehmed II considerably strengthened the sultan's position, for the former depended on and owed absolute loyalty to the ruler. Empowered by his success in the conquest of Constantinople, Mehmed II also set out to create a centralized state apparatus, appropriate to the empire he envisioned. Mehmed II gave a definite shape to the institutions of his predecessors by defining the authority and hierarchical interrelationships of the various ministers and their offices in his famous law code or *kanunname*, although only part of it was compiled under his reign.

From the earliest times, Ottoman sultans were assisted by an informal advisory body of lords and state officials. Out of this body, the divan or state council emerged as a formal government organ. Known usually as Divan-ı Hümayun or Imperial Council, the Divan was originally a court of justice and appeals that performed the most important task of a near eastern ruler, that of dispensing justice. At the same time, the Divan acted as the supreme organ of government and, in wartime, served as a high command. Until Mehmed II, the sultans personally presided at the Divan's meetings, which usually took place near the gate of the sultan's palace. Thus the terms *kapı* or gate (of the palace) and *dergah-ı âlî* or Sublime Porte came to denote the Ottoman government. However, during the first 150 years of the institution, which saw almost incessant campaigns, the Divan met wherever the sultan was.

In accordance with his policy of royal seclusion, Mehmed II is said to have stopped personally attending the meetings of the Divan around 1475. While BAYEZID II (r. 1481–1512) seems to have attended the meetings, later sultans kept to the practice introduced by Mehmed II. However, following their meetings, the council members, in a set order, personally reported to the sultan about their deliberations and asked for the sovereign's approval. "Lying was mortal," noted the 16th-century French diplomat and linguist Guillaume Postel, because the sultan was "often listening at a window overlooking the said Chamber [of the Divan] without being seen or noticed." Most attribute the creation of this famous window to SÜLEYMAN I (r. 1520–66), although some credit it to Mehmed II.

In the absence of the sultan, the grand vizier presided over the council. According to Mehmed II's law code, the "grand vizier is the head of the viziers and commanders. He is greater than all men; he is in all matters the Sultan's absolute deputy." Under Mehmed II and the two sultans who followed him, it was rare for Muslim Turks to become viziers. Out of the 15 grand viziers who held the post between 1453 and 1516, only three were freeborn Muslim Turks; four came from the DEVŞIRME or child levy system and were trained in the PALACE SCHOOL, while the rest were former members of the Byzantine and Balkan aristocracies and either became Ottomans voluntarily or were taken as captives

The members of the Divan represented the three major groups of the Ottoman ruling class or *askeri:* the "men of the sword" or the military, "the men of the religious sciences" (*ilm*) known as the ULEMA or the religious establishment, and "the men of the pen" or bureaucrats. Each member of the Divan was responsible for a distinct branch of government: politics and the military, the judiciary, and the empire's finances. The representatives of these branches acted independently in their departments and were responsible directly to the sultan. However, the grand vizier, in his capacity as supreme deputy of the sultan, had authority over the various office holders, and in all important decisions the heads of the individual departments needed the consent of their colleagues. Not even the grand vizier could act independently of the other members of the council. These checks and balances, and the necessity of consultation—an old Islamic principle of governance—functioned to prevent the chief executives of the empire from monopolizing power.

In the council, the military was represented by the grand vizier, other viziers whose number grew over time, and the governor (*beylerbeyi)* of Rumelia, originally the commander of the empire's provincial cavalry troops (*timar*-holding *sipahis*). Acknowledging the increasing importance of the imperial navy, Süleyman I appointed Grand Admiral Hayreddin BARBAROSSA to the council. Henceforward the *kapudan pasha* or admiral of the Ottoman navy also had the right to attend the Divan. From the latter half of the 16th century the agha or commander of the sultan's elite infantry, the Janissaries, was also allowed to take part in the council's meetings.

The KADIASKERS or military judges spoke for the religious establishment or ulema in the council. Unlike the viziers, they were Muslims and often Turks and were graduates of the religious colleges (madrasas). As heads of the Ottoman judiciary, they assisted the sultan and the grand

The palace of Ibrahim Pasha, the favorite grand vizier of Süleyman I, occupied a prime location on the Hippodrome of Istanbul. The Hippodrome was the main ceremonial space of the Ottoman capital, situated proximate to the Aya Sofya and the Topkapı Palace. The palace's prime location signaled the importance and influence of Ibrahim Pasha. *(Photo by Gábor Ágoston)*

vizier in matters related to jurisdiction. The first military judge was appointed by MURAD I (r. 1362–1389). He was joined by a second judge in the last years of Mehmed II's reign, and, after the conquest of SYRIA and EGYPT in 1516–17, by a third judge, whose office was soon abolished due to personal rivalry between the grand vizier and the appointee. Besides being the supreme judges of Rumelia and Anatolia, the two *kadıaskers* also supervised the judges (KADI) and college professors of the empire.

The third group of the ruling class, the bureaucracy, was represented by the treasurers or finance ministers (*defterdar*) in the Divan. The number of *defterdars* also grew over time. Under Mehmed II in the 15th century, there was one; in 1526, two; after 1539, three; and from 1587, four. They were responsible for the royal revenues of Rumelia, Anatolia, Istanbul, and the northwestern coast of the Black Sea. The rising number of *defterdars* reflected the growing importance of the treasury in an empire that faced repeated financial crises from the end of the 16th century. The *nişancı*, head of the Ottoman chancery, was

The Divanhane was the meeting place of the imperial council. The Tower of Justice, which was visible from all parts of the city, served to remind both the council members and the subjects of the presence of the sultan and the importance of justice as a principle of Ottoman governance. *(Photo by Gábor Ágoston)*

also a council member. He was responsible for authenticating all imperial documents by affixing the sultan's monogram or TUĞRA, thus ensuring that all orders and letters issued from the Divan conformed to Ottoman laws and chancery practice. All laws, formulated by secretaries, were checked by the chancellor. Then the *nişancı* and the grand vizier presented them to the sultan for approval. The *nişancı* also supervised the Divan's archives (*defterhane*), which housed all the provincial cadastral or revenue surveys and tax registers, classified in alphabetical order by province, as well as other official documents regarding fiefs (*timar*) and lands of religious endowments (*WAQFS*). The clerks of the *defterhane* stood ready during the Divan's meetings so that registers could be consulted promptly if needed.

The clerks of the Divan, perhaps some 110 in the 1530s, worked under the supervision of the REISÜLKÜTTAB or chief of the clerks. The latter's position grew over time and gradually overshadowed that of the chief chancellor. By the 17th century, foreign ambassadors mention the *reisülküttab* as a quasi foreign minister. The success

of *reisülküttab* Rami Mehmed Pasha at the TREATY OF KARLOWITZ further enhanced the position. By this time, however, the council, as it was shaped by Mehmed II, had lost its importance to the office of the grand vizier, which was known as Bab-ı Asafi and, from the 18th century onward, as Bab-ı Âli. Both terms referred to the gate of the grand vizier and were known in Europe as the Sublime Porte, the Ottoman government.

A PATRIMONIAL SYSTEM

Although the Ottoman Empire is often described as a meritocracy, it remained an essentially patrimonial system until the reforms of the TANZIMAT in the 19th century. Besides merit and career service, family ties, clientship, and, above all, loyalty to the sultan were instrumental in attaining and holding the highest offices of the state. This was further complicated by the fact that all high executives of the empire, including the grand vizier, were the sultan's *kuls* or slaves and their position was precarious, subject to the sovereign's will, power politics, and factionalism.

In theory, the sultans ruled with almost absolute power. In reality, however, the sultans' power varied greatly in different periods. From the late 16th through the mid-17th century the queen mothers and the wives of the sultans, backed and often used by court factions and the military, wielded considerable influence through their protégés. In the mid-17th century, actual power passed to the grand viziers; the KÖPRÜLÜ FAMILY of grand viziers attained unparalleled power from 1656 to 1691. With some notable exceptions, most of the sultans until the late 18th century reigned rather than ruled. Sultanic authority was limited and often undermined by competing court factions. In the 18th century sultanic authority was further limited as an emerging network of pasha and vizierial households and their protégés gained power in the royal court. Although MAHMUD II (r. 1808–39) and ABDÜLHAMID II (r. 1876–1909) reasserted sultanic power for a time, during the Tanzimat era (1839–76) the powerful grand viziers returned to their prominent role in the administration of the empire.

Until the 19th-century reforms, the Ottoman government, unlike the governments of modern nation-states, was small, employing no more than 1,500 clerks. Its tasks were limited to a few key areas: defense of the empire, maintenance of law and order, resource mobilization and management, and supply of the capital and the army. Functions associated with government in modern nation-states such as education, healthcare, and welfare were handled by the empire's religious and ethnic communities and by religious and professional organizations (pious foundations, guilds, and so forth). The Ottoman Empire had a less efficient and less centralized government than those of Joseph II's Austria, Frederick the

Great's Prussia, or even Catherine the Great's Russia, let alone France or England.

THE TANZIMAT ERA

Modernization and rationalization of the Ottoman government occurred under Mahmud II and the Tanzimat, which created councils and ministries according to European models. This period saw the institution of many new ministries: the Ministry of Religious Foundations (1826), the Ministry of the Interior (1836), the Ministry of Foreign Affairs (1836), the Ministry of Finance (1838), the Ministry of Commerce (1839), the Ministry of Postal Services (1840), the Ministry of Education (1857), and the Ministry of Justice (1868). Of all these newly established offices, it was the Ministry of Foreign Affairs that gained the greatest influence. Its rise was partly due to the growing significance of diplomacy in the face of diminishing Ottoman military capabilities and the rapid development of Great Power politics, but it was also due to the expertise of the ministers and their staff, knowledge of European languages, societies, economies, and government policies, all vital information for modernizing the empire.

In addition to this transition to ministerial governance, the other important development in the government administration of the era was the creation of consultative councils and assemblies. Of these, the Supreme Council for Judicial Ordinances (Meclis-i Vala-yı Ahkam-ı Adliye) was the most significant. Although not an elected body, the council was vested with a semi-legislative authority and thus played a crucial role in reforming the Ottoman legal system and central bureaucracy. By 1868 it evolved into a Council of State (Şura-yı Devlet). Another significant administrative reform was the opening of the first Ottoman PARLIAMENT in March 1877. Although it failed in its legislative functions, the parliament proved a surprisingly effective forum for government criticism. It was suspended less than a year later, in February 1878, by its reluctant founder, Abdülhamid II, and reopened only in 1909.

ERA OF CENTRALIZATION

Despite the failure of his parliamentary experiment, Abdülhamid II continued many of the reforms of the Tanzimat, albeit in a characteristically autocratic fashion. Abdülhamid II's government—greatly expanded and aided by modern technologies such as the electric TELEGRAPH and RAILROADS—achieved a degree of centralization and efficacy never before seen in Ottoman history. By 1908 the number of government officials had risen to 35,000, compared to the 18th-century bureaucracy of 1,500. Most of these new government officials were professional bureaucrats, educated in specialized schools.

The overland telegraph reached Fao on the Persian Gulf by 1865 and under Abdülhamid II, who established a telegraph station in his Yıldız Palace, it connected all the provincial centers with the central government. The sultan's domestic surveillance system, feared by many, also relied heavily on the new technology. Although the Ottoman railroad system was modest in comparison to European railway networks—in 1911 its total length was 4,030 miles, compared to Austria-Hungary's 14,218 miles and Russia's 42,516 miles—it enabled Istanbul to redeploy soldiers quickly to troubled or rebellious regions. Increasingly, however lack of cash and growing Ottoman DEBT—which, from the establishment of the PUBLIC DEBT ADMINISTRATION in 1881, came under foreign control—hindered further modernization and undercut the authority of the Ottoman government. The new technologies proved to be a double edged sword, which the sultan's domestic and foreign enemies used effectively to topple him.

Gábor Ágoston

See also COMMITTEE OF UNION AND PROGRESS; CONSTITUTION; PARLIAMENT; RAILROADS; REISÜLKÜTTAB; TANZIMAT; TELEGRAPH.

Further reading: Carter V. Findley, *Bureaucratic Reform in the Ottoman Empire: The Sublime Porte, 1789–1922* (Princeton, N.J: Princeton University Press, 1980); Carter V. Findley, *Ottoman Civil Officialdom: A Social History* (Princeton, N.J.: Princeton University Press, 1988); Colin Imber, *The Ottoman Empire, 1300–1650: The Structure of Power* (Houndmills, Basingstoke, UK: Palgrave Macmillan, 2002); Halil İnalcık, *The Ottoman Empire: The Classical Age, 1300–1600* (London: Weidenfeld & Nicolson, 1973); Leslie Peirce, *The Imperial Harem: Women and Sovereignty in the Ottoman Empire* (Oxford: Oxford University Press, 1993); Erik J. Zürcher, *Turkey: A Modern History* (London: I.B. Tauris, 2004).

administration, provincial   Despite ongoing scholarship, the origins of Ottoman provincial administration continue to remain somewhat obscure, especially since the early development of this system included a shift from a nomadic to a more settled way of life, reducing the likelihood that written records would have been kept or securely preserved. At first, as is typical of a seminomadic tribal community, leadership remained in family hands. The first quasi provincial governor was a son of ORHAN I (r. 1324–62), who was vested with much greater authority than his later counterparts. Other offspring of Orhan were sent to govern smaller territorial units.

EVOLUTION OF PROVINCIAL ADMINISTRATION

As the early Ottomans came to develop a more settled agricultural lifestyle, the style of governance also developed into one that understood itself increasingly in geographic terms as opposed to the tribal divisions of leadership that attend a nomadic culture. At this stage of development, the creation of larger and smaller administrative units became a necessity.

The largest entity was the province—*vilayet* or *beylerbeylik*,—which was divided into several subprovinces or districts called *sancaks* (in Arabic, *liwa)*. Sancaks were made up of even smaller units called *nahiyes*. Both this system of division and its nomenclature arise from a combined Turkish and Arabic background in which military commanders, called beys in Turkish or emirs in Arabic, received a standard, or *sancak*, from the sovereign as a symbol of power. Ottoman district governors thus came to be called *sancakbeyi* (in Arabic, *amir al-liwa*). Eventually the area under their control was also called a *sancak*. The first *sancakbeyi* was probably appointed near the end of the reign of Orhan or during the reign of MURAD I (1362–89). By the time of Sultan BAYEZID I (1389–1402), appointing these provincial administrators had became a common practice.

Further expansion and institutionalization led to the need for another level of management, senior administrators to oversee the *sancakbeyi*. This is the origin of the *beylerbeyi* literally, the bey (commander) of the *sancakbeyi*. The *beylerbeyi* ruled over a larger province known as a *vilayet*. It is thought that the first *beylerbeyi*, or governorship, was founded in Rumelia (the European parts of the empire), and administration of this region thus ultimately became the most prestigious position of provincial leadership. Next came the formation of the *vilayet* of Anatolia in 1393. This is how the classical Ottoman system of provincial administration emerged and functioned until the end of the 16th century and in a somewhat changed form through the late 18th to early 19th century.

In the 1520s, there were six to eight *vilayets* altogether and approximately 90 *sancaks*. By around 1570 these numbers had increased to 24 *vilayets* with more than 250 *sancaks*. Structural changes within the Ottoman Empire increased the importance of the *beylerbeyis* and the number of *vilayets* continued to multiply, reaching approximately 35 by the beginning of the 17th century. At the same time, the prestige of the *sancakbeyi's* post began to sink. This was no doubt due in part to the burgeoning number of *beylerbeyis* and the consequent development, beginning in the 1590s, of a related office of secondary importance, the *muhafız* pasha (defender pasha). In certain areas the prebends or *hases*—benefits formerly allotted to *sancakbeyis* were assigned instead to the more senior *beylerbeyis* in the form of an allowance (*arpalık*); this was often done even when the official receiving the benefits was temporarily dismissed.

As the territory of the empire grew under SELIM I (r. 1512–20) and SÜLEYMAN I (r. 1520–66), not only did the number of *sancaks* and *vilayets* increase, but the forms and conventions for incorporating newly conquered frontier zones became more eclectic. New formats of provincial governing structure began to emerge, depending on local traditions, distance from the Ottoman capital, and the degree of pacification of the conquered lands. As well as the administrative units in the Anatolian core provinces and Ottoman-controlled European lands, four further subtypes can be distinguished in the eastern regions from the 1530s: the *ocaklık*, the *yurtluks*, the *hükümet sancağıs*, and the *salyaneli*. In the *ocaklık*, which prevailed in conquered lands occupied by certain Turkoman and Kurdish groups, the traditional tribal chief remained as bey but income from the land in the form of prebends or *timars* was granted to outsiders, imperial tax registers (*tahrirs*) were prepared, and the bey was obligated to support the sultan with troops and military leadership in times of war. The *yurtluks* were similar in form except that the post of bey did not automatically pass from father to son. In the *hükümet sancağıs*, also formed mainly on Turkoman and Kurdish tribal territories, traditional local leadership was maintained on a hereditary basis without the introduction of prebends and tax registers. Nevertheless, joining imperial campaigns was obligatory. Finally, in the *salyaneli* districts, no prebends whatsoever were granted, incomes were collected merely for the treasury, and governors sent from Istanbul were paid in cash from the moneys collected.

The most important consideration in assigning provincial leaders was their loyalty to the Ottoman house. The specific obligations and responsibilities of the *beylerbeyis* were not clearly defined and an individual appointed to a provincial or district governor post probably received fairly laconic instructions. Equally indefinite was the length of the commission, with some appointments lasting mere days while others extended over a decade. In general, *beylerbeyis* were replaced more often than the *sancakbeyis*.

The provincial ruling class in the empire were identified as *ümera* (the plural of *emir*) and included both the *beylerbeyis* and the *sancakbeyis*. In the 16th century, the *ümera* were usually renegades from a variety of ethnic and cultural backgrounds, whereas in earlier periods they would have been either of Turkish origin or from local families. The *ümera* came largely from the Ottoman DEVŞIRME or child-levy system, which collected non-Muslim children from subject peoples on the frontiers of the empire and cultivated the most talented with education and training. After years of labor and schooling, often in positions of political importance and trust, the most able and most unconditionally faithful of these young men were selected for positions of governance. Of course, ability was not the only criterion; the decisive factor in selection was often patronage, with certain candidates pushed into the foreground by the various groups in power or by their high-ranking fathers.

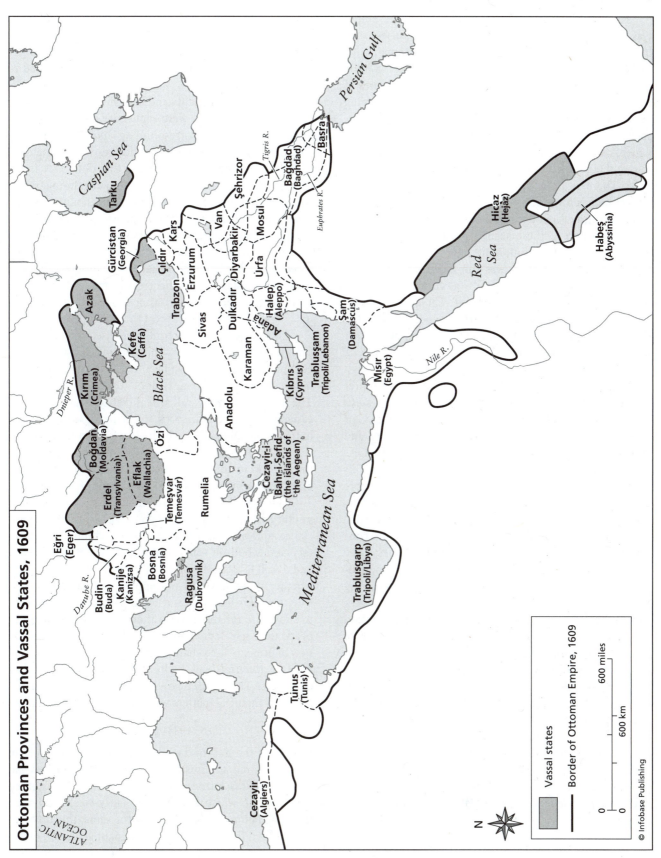

Ottoman Provinces and Vassal States, 1609

ATLANTIC OCEAN

Danube R.

Eğri (Eger)

Budin (Buda)

Kanije (Kanizsa)

Bosna (Bosnia)

Ragusa (Dubrovnik)

Rumelia

Temeşvar (Temesvár)

Erdel (Transylvania)

Eflak (Wallachia)

Bogdan (Moldavia)

Özi

Dnieper R.

Kırım (Crimea)

Azak

Kefe (Caffa)

Black Sea

Trabzon

Gürcistan (Georgia)

Çıldır

Kars

Erzurum

Van

Sivas

Anadolu

Karaman

Dulkadir

Adana

Halep (Aleppo)

Diyarbakır

Urfa

Mosul

Şehrizor

Bağdad (Baghdad)

Tigris R.

Basra

Persian Gulf

Euphrates R.

Şam (Damascus)

Hicaz (Hejaz)

Red Sea

Habeş (Abyssinia)

Nile R.

Mısır (Egypt)

Trablusşam (Tripoli/Lebanon)

Kıbrıs (Cyprus)

Cezayir-i Bahr-i-Sefid (the islands of the Aegean)

Mediterranean Sea

Trablusgarp (Tripoli/Libya)

Tunus (Tunis)

Cezayir (Algiers)

Caspian Sea

Tarku

N

Vassal states

Border of Ottoman Empire, 1609

600 miles

600 km

0

0

© Infobase Publishing

Contributing to the *ümera's* loyalty to the sultan was the fact that, in the 15th and 16th centuries, they belonged to the best paid segment of the Ottoman elite; in the earlier years of the empire, their annual income often exceeded even the remarkably elevated incomes of later years, when *beylerbeyis* are documented as receiving between 800,000 and 1.2 million akçe a year. *Sancakbeyis* started with incomes between 150,000 and 200,000 akçe, which could be relatively quickly augmented, depending on their valor, to produce incomes as high as 600,000 akçe. There is little evidence that these income levels altered between the 1580s and the 17th century, creating an opportunity for abuse and arbitrariness.

In addition to these secular positions of provincial governance, another important figure in the Ottoman provincial administration was the KADI, who generally came from a Muslim family and was educated in a religious school. The *kadıs* served at different levels, depending on their income, which varied depending on the importance of the place to which they were appointed. A juridical district (*kaza*) could encompass a whole *sancak* or one or more *nahiyes*. *Kadıs*, especially those in high ranks, had assistants called *naibs*. While the *ümera* represented the state and Ottoman secular law (*kanun*), *kadıs* were exponents of religious ideology and the SHARIA, or sacred law. These two spheres were complementary, and their agents had some control over each other's activities.

The term *kadı* is usually translated as *judge*, but this is a simplification since holders of the office had more complex responsibilities in this period. They acted as public notaries issuing various documents and certificates. They supervised and authenticated accounts concerning *mukataa* (state) revenues or WAQF incomes. They were also charged with tasks related to military maneuvers such as recruiting craftsmen for the army, repairing roads, and securing provisions. Furthermore, they occasionally sent reports to the ruler on the general situation in the region, public feelings, and the performance of their high-ranking colleagues.

From the 16th century onward, local financial matters were directed on a *vilayet* level, with the *defterdar* or *mal defterdarı* (treasurer) charged to collect state revenues from each territory. The *defterdar* was responsible in turn for disbursing these funds, primarily for military purposes, such as pay for garrison soldiers. He was assisted by two other officials, the *defter kethüdası*, who handled *has* grants and *ziamet* grants (large land grants), and the *timar defterdarı*, who dealt with ordinary *timar* allotments.

THE PROVINCIAL COUNCIL

A typical *vilayet* was directed by a divan, or council, which consisted of the presiding governor, the *sancakbeyis* and their deputies (*miralays* or *alaybeyis*), the *defterdar,* and the *defter kethüdası.* The council probably functioned in a similar way to the imperial *divan* in Istanbul, although assembling less frequently and rarely in full number. It is not known if *kadıs* were invited to the council meetings.

Historical documents indicate that, in the frontier zones, imperial orders were sent more often to the *beylerbeyis* than to the corresponding *kadıs,* while in the core provinces, more numerous decrees were dispatched to the *kadıs.* The chief reason for this difference is the level of consolidation. Where Ottoman administration was rooted more deeply, everyday responsibilities usually came into the *kadıs'* sphere of responsibility. On the other hand, military and diplomatic affairs—which fell into the provincial governor's sphere of responsibility—predominated in the border areas. Because of their great distance from the capital, pashas necessarily made decisions in such matters without consulting the court, often taking unsuccessful measures that cost them their lives.

Court decrees often contained useless generalities, even if the matter raised by the local officials was of special interest or could have been decided using the pertinent *defters* preserved next door to the imperial divan. The overcentralized and bureaucratized state found it easier to refer the issue back to the lower level, alluding to the *kanun* and sharia, which were to be taken into consideration. Repeated orders suggest that the *ümera* and the *kadıs* were not always obedient tools of the sovereign, often employing more or less open forms of sabotage.

The *sancakbeyis'* sphere of activity included both military and civil matters. As commanders of the provincial cavalry or *timariot sipahis,* they had numerous military duties both in war and during times of peace. They had to call to arms the *sipahis* and their retinues, to judge whether those who did not appear had acceptable reasons for their absence, and to find appropriate persons to substitute for them while they were on campaign. In peace they sent letters and registers (*defters*) requesting new allotments for valiant soldiers or an increase in revenue for *timariots* who had excelled in the battlefield or elsewhere. The district governors' civil duties included legal and financial matters with issues of public security.

THE 19TH CENTURY

In 1840, at the start of the TANZIMAT, or Ottoman reform period, the old administrative system was abolished and a new one was introduced. The aim was to strengthen state control, which had become fairly weak. Although the designation *sancak* remained the same, this unit was now headed by a *muhassıl*, or lieutenant governor, rather than by a *sancakbeyi* and the territorial extension was occasionally altered. Smaller provincial units were now called by the name used to designate juridical districts, *kaza,* and were governed by *müdürs.* The smallest units, the *nahiyes,* were directed by *muhtars.* Completely novel advisory councils (*meclises*) were formed on provincial, district, and *kaza* levels from representatives of the government and the principal subject groups, including religious minorities.

Since this first attempt at reorganization did not prove to be efficient enough, further changes were introduced in 1841. Military commanders (*müşirs*) governed the provinces, the office of *muhassıl* was abolished, and *kaymakams* administered the lower-level units. Local notables, or AYAN, were appointed as *müdürs,* responsible for financial affairs. In several places, instead of permanent councils, informal advisory bodies were set up. Where the practice of permanent councils survived, members were appointed by the *kaymakam.* Similar consultative bodies were established around the *müşirs.* The modifications proved beneficial and several economic projects were realized. The CRIMEAN WAR (1854–56), however, had unfavorable effects on the process, since financial resources were lacking and many of the old type administrators returned.

A new provincial regulation was issued in 1858 that did not alter the former structure but gave full authority to the governors. A cadastral department within the Ministry of Finance helped the government learn more about the real property of the subject population and its value.

After a transition period that began in 1860, when more important governorships were renamed as *mutasarrıflık* and their leaders became particularly well-paid officials, the 1864 Reform Law gave the final shape to late Ottoman provincial administration. It prescribed the creation of large units (*vilayets*) of approximately equal size. The governor's range of authority was increased again. He controlled social, financial, security, and political affairs, could deal with questions of public interest (such as education and communication), and had several other prerogatives. He supervised his direct subordinates in the hierarchy, the *mutasarrıfs* at the *sancak* level. Other functionaries (provincial accountant, public works supervisors, and so forth) were sent from the capital and answered to their superiors in Istanbul. The governor's coordinating organization, the *idare meclisi* (administrative council), could not interfere in judicial matters. Such matters were discussed before three different courts, one of them still headed by *kadıs.* The chief consultative body of a *vilayet* was the Provincial General Council, whose members (two Muslims and two non-Muslims in each *sancak*) were elected. The assembly had the right to make proposals to the center in various areas, such as public welfare and tax collection.

Géza Dávid

Further reading: Gábor Ágoston, "A Flexible Empire: Authority and its Limits on the Ottoman Frontiers." *International Journal of Turkish Studies* 9, no. 1–2 (2003): 15–31; Roderic H. Davison, *Reform in the Ottoman Empire, 1856–1876* (New York: Gordian, 1973); Géza Dávid, "Administration in Ottoman Europe," in *Studies in Demographic and Administrative History of Ottoman Hungary* (Istanbul: Isis, 1997), 187–204; Metin I. Kunt, *The Sultan's Servants: The Transformation of Ottoman Provincial Government, 1550–1650* (New York: Columbia University Press, 1983).

Adrianople *See* EDIRNE.

Adrianople, Treaty of *See* EDIRNE, TREATY OF.

Adriatic Sea The Adriatic Sea, known to the Ottomans as the Gulf of Venice, is the large body of water located on the eastern side of Italy that separates the Apennine peninsula from the Balkan peninsula. The Ottomans began to recognize the strategic significance of the Adriatic Sea in the first half of the 15th century, since it was the sea that separated them from their main rival in the region, the Republic of VENICE. In that period, the region of DALMATIA, on the Adriatic coast, was Venetian, except for the republic of Dubrovnik (RAGUSA), which began to pay tribute to the Ottoman sultan in 1442. In 1479 the Ottomans took the Adriatic port city of Vlorë (Valona, Avlonya), in ALBANIA; MEHMED II (r. 1444–46; 1451–81) gave it to his admiral, Gedik Ahmed Pasha, when the Ottomans launched a campaign against southern Italy, attacking Otranto during the summer of 1480. The key of the Adriatic was considered to be the Venetian island of Corfu (Korfuz), which was besieged by the Ottomans in 1537 and again in 1716.

In the second half of the 16th century the Adriatic began to be ravaged by pirates, above all the Christian USKOKS, who lived in Senj and were protected by the Austrian Habsburgs. Their presence marred the relations between Venice and the Ottoman Empire. They were often wrongly considered subjects of the Venetian Republic, and Ottoman merchants held Venice responsible for the losses they suffered at the hands of the Uskoks. The Ottomans threatened to send their NAVY into the Adriatic, but Venice never allowed it. Eventually, Ottoman subjects began to attack Venetian ships in retaliation and Ottoman pirates began to ravage the Adriatic. The Habsburg-Venetian War of 1615–1617 put an end to the Uskok activity.

Ottoman pirates along the Adriatic included both Christians and Muslims from Albania and GREECE, using small boats that could easily find shelter along the rocky coast. Maghreb *levends,* or privateers, also made some expeditions. They were organized in huge convoys of galleys and vessels and looked for the help of Ottoman subjects. The latter, especially Albanians, learned the Maghrebians' tactics and began to attack ships disguised as Maghreb levends. In 1573, because of the Mediterranean piracy, the *sancakbeyi* (provincial governor) of Klis (Clissa), Ali, together with a Jew named Daniel Rodriguez, pushed the Venetians to create a new transit port in Split as the final land destination of a new commercial route between Venice and ISTANBUL. In 1590 the Adriatic seaport of Split became a free port and Bosnian merchants began to take the place of those of Ragusa in the Balkan trade.

The TREATY OF KARLOWITZ in 1699 established that all merchant ships could freely sail in the Adriatic Sea. In 1701 the Ottomans and the Venetians agreed about freedom of navigation in the Gulf of Lepanto and in the waters between the island of Santa Maura (Aya-Mavra) and the mainland. In 1719, after the Treaty of Passarowitz, Emperor Charles IV declared Trieste and Fiume free ports, and in 1732 Pope Clement XII created another free port in Ancon. Venice had to accept that it was not the only naval power in the region, even if, at the middle of the 18th century, Ottoman documents still recognized its sovereignty on the Adriatic Sea.

Maria Pia Pedani

See also CORSAIRS AND PIRATES.

Further reading: Maria Pia Pedani, "The Ottoman Empire and the Gulf of Venice (15th–16th c.)," in *CIÉPO XIV. Sempozyumu Bildirileri*, edited by Tuncer Baykara (Ankara: Türk Tarih Kurumu, 2004), 585–600; Maria Pia Pedani, "Beyond the Frontier: The Ottoman-Venetian Border in the Adriatic Context from the Sixteenth to the Eighteenth Centuries," in *Zones of Fracture in Modern Europe, Baltic Countries-Balkans-Northern Italy*, edited by Almut Bues (Wiesbaden: Harrassowitz Verlag, 2005), 45–60.

al-Afghani, Jamal al-Din (b. 1838–d. 1897) *Muslim political activist and philosopher* Jamal al-Din al-Afghani was perhaps the most important Muslim political philosopher and activist of the late 19th century. Most scholars believe that despite his use of the name al-Afghani, "the Afghan," he was actually born in Iran. But as he spent much of his life in EGYPT and the Ottoman Empire, it would have been convenient for him, as a Persian speaker, to identify himself as Afghan. Many Afghans spoke Persian, but were practitioners of SUNNI ISLAM; in contrast, all the Persian speakers in Iran belonged to the SHIA ISLAM sect. If he were an Afghan, al-Afghani would have been free to preach in Sunni religious schools in Cairo and Istanbul, something that would not have been permitted if he were identified as a Shii. The supposition that al-Afghani had Shii origins is further strengthened by the fact that he studied as a youth in KARBALA, the Shii holy city in Iraq, as well as later in India where both Shii and Sunni religious schools flourished.

Al-Afghani settled in Egypt in 1871 where he was the teacher of a number of young men who had studied the Islamic sciences at AL-AZHAR, the leading institution of higher study in the Arabic-speaking Sunni world during the Ottoman period. Among his students there was religious scholar and Islamic modernist MUHAMMAD ABDUH (1849–1905). In Egypt, al-Afghani taught his own brand of Islam, one heavily influenced by the Shii traditions of philosophy and by SUFISM. But more importantly, he drew his students' attention to the dangers of European imperialism that threatened Muslims around the globe. Al-Afghani emphasized the need for unity among Muslims, regardless of sect, to resist European schemes for political domination of traditional Islamic homelands. This politicized view of Islam caught the attention of the Egyptian authorities and they expelled him from the country in 1878.

Although al-Afghani went first to India upon his expulsion from al-Azhar, by 1884 he was established in Paris, where he was joined by his former student, Abduh. Together they published an Arabic-language newspaper, *al-Urwa al-wuthqa* (The firm grip) that had a profound effect on Muslim intellectuals everywhere. During his stay in Paris and later in London, al-Afghani engaged many European intellectuals in discussions about Islam's future and the role of Western imperialism in the world. As a result, he was highly influential in shaping views on both of these issues for a generation of western European policymakers.

Al-Afghani's importance lies in the fact that he was the first Muslim thinker to see political developments in the Muslim world from a global perspective. Everywhere he looked, he saw that independent Muslim states were falling under European control. In order to resist that process, he wrote that Muslims had to reverse the decline and decay that had infected their civilization. Adopting the concept of "civilization" as late 19th-century French authors defined the term, he asserted that Islam was a civilization, and not merely a religion, as it had a rich culture that was more than simply a set of religious beliefs. In order to revitalize that civilization, al-Afghani argued that Muslims had to return to the study of rational philosophy and to embrace science and technology as had their ancestors. Only then would Muslims reclaim the glories that Islamic civilization had known when it flourished in the Abbasid period (750–1256). Al-Afghani wrote that once that revivification of Islamic civilization had occurred, then Muslims could stand united as the equals of Europeans and resist their imperialist plans. Few of his contemporaries embraced his nationalistic, pan-Islamic vision, but his insistence on the use of individual reason had a great influence on the next generation of Muslim thinkers of the SALAFIYYA.

As al-Afghani grew increasingly wary of growing European imperial ambitions in the Muslim world, he wanted to do something concrete to galvanize Muslim resistance. In 1885, following his work with Abduh in Paris, al-Afghani returned to Iran where he organized popular demonstrations against Nasir al-Din Shah's treaties with European powers. In response, the shah ordered his deportation in 1891 and al-Afghani spent the last years of his life as a guest of ABDÜLHAMID II (r. 1876–1909) in ISTANBUL. There he received a wary welcome from the sultan who, after the assassination of Shah Nasir al-Din in 1896, placed al-Afghani under house arrest until his death in 1897.

Bruce Masters

See also ABDUH, MUHAMMAD; SALAFIYYA.

Further reading: Nikki Keddie, *An Islamic Response to Imperialism: Political and Religious Writings of Sayyid Jamal al-Din "al-Afghani"* (Berkeley: University of California Press, 1983).

Africa *See* NORTH AFRICA.

agriculture The linchpin and trademark of Ottoman agriculture was the small holding peasantry (*reaya*). The imperial seat of power in Istanbul owed its legitimacy to its ability to safeguard the peasantry from the encroachments of notables, and to forestall competing claims over the empire's immense agricultural surplus. As in other imperial powers, forces that undermined the central authority gained strength at times and disturbed this social balance to the benefit of the notables, but not for long. Attempts by local potentates to establish labor systems such as SLAVERY or serfdom at the expense of the peasantry proved ineffectual. The continuity of the empire's agricultural structure was not solely due to the potentates' inability to establish such an order, but may be attributed to a range of factors including geographic, imperial, historical, social, and topographic issues.

The essential features of Ottoman agriculture were derived in large part from the geographical and ecological attributes of the lands the empire occupied. With its broad territory—from Oran, Algeria, in the west to BAGHDAD, IRAQ, in the east; from the Nile Valley in the south to the northern reaches of the BLACK SEA—the empire took root and flourished in the "lands of Rum"—the land of the Romans. This referred not only to the Eastern Roman or BYZANTINE EMPIRE but also to the territory arrayed around the Mediterranean Sea. The lands that surrounded the Mediterranean basin were principally semi-arid in character, fit for dry farming, or raising crops without irrigation in areas that receive little rainfall. The Ottoman Empire's agrarian structures resembled those of the Roman and Byzantine empires that previously occupied the same territory.

Providentially for the house of Osman, the birth and territorial expansion of the *beylik* or principality and, later, the empire took place precisely when the feudal world on its occidental frontiers was in its terminal decline and a manorial revenue crisis was exacting a heavy toll on the serfs. The Byzantine countryside, had fallen into the hands of large landholders. The widespread discontent created by a tightening in the stranglehold of landlords on their serfs hastened Ottoman expansion on both shores of the Bosporus. The increase in the exploitation of the Balkan peasantry was thus broken by their incorporation into the Ottoman realm, rendering these agricultural producers subject to the demands of a strong imperial center instead.

THE *ÇIFT-HANE* SYSTEM

The foundation of Ottoman dry-farming agriculture was, like that of its predecessors, putting peasant households under the yoke—enshrined as *hane* in the Ottoman fiscal records. They worked land that could be ploughed by a pair of oxen, referred to as *çift*. Despite some changes—developments that at times favored local rulers, the institution of long-term and life-term TAX-FARMING arrangements (*iltizam/muqataa* and *malikane*), and the growing lure of commercial opportunities in the 16th and the 19th centuries—small-holding peasantry did not experience large-scale alienation from their lands, and remained the keystone of the empire's agrarian order. This does not mean that there were no changes in the status of the peasantry or in the rights of the peasants to the land. However, they were not enough to fundamentally alter the Ottoman agrarian system. This helped the Sublime Porte consolidate its rule from early on.

Rural households were expected to mobilize their family labor along with draft animals (usually a pair of oxen or, in marshy regions, water buffalo) to cultivate the land placed at their disposal. This land was state-owned (*miri*), but peasant households held an inalienable right to its use, so plots allotted to them could not be sold, endowed, donated, or mortgaged. Nor could the plots be devoted to raising crops other than bread grains. Land that was not ploughed, such as vineyards and orchards, was freehold. The state had the right of eminent domain over village commons—pastures, in particular—as well as over woodlands and wastelands (*mevat* lands), which were all placed under the authority of the *sipahi*, or landholder. If and when wastelands were improved, full ownership rights went to the person who made the improvements, and it was the duty of the *sipahi* to prevent attempts to encroach on village commons. At the end of the 16th century, an impressive 87 percent of the Ottoman soil was within the eminent domain.

Unlike feudal lords, the *sipahi*, resided in the village alongside the peasants. Their power was not absolute and was kept in check by the power of the KADI. The *sipahi* had no specific rights (including hereditary) to land or peasant labor unless stipulated by law. Also, the prebendal system, which constricted the ability of the *sipahis* to act independently of the imperial bureaucracy, had little in common with vassalic feudalism.

THE PREBENDAL SYSTEM

Initially the *çift-hane* system was securely embedded in the prebendal or *timar* regime in which the *sipahi*, or cavalry, were allocated *timar*, or landed estates (called *ziamet* or *has* if the units were larger). Under this system, in the 15th and 16th centuries, the *sipahi* collected and kept the *öşür*, or tithe, and related land taxes—usually half in kind and half in money—as compensation for the military service the *sipahi* was assigned to render. The requirements for military service and supply were determined in proportion to the annual value of the *timar*-holdings, which ranged from 1,000 akçe to 20,000 akçe. These *timariots*, or *timar*-holders, did not play any role in the organization of rural production.

The collection of the tithe and taxes by the *sipahis* as state functionaries prevented the rise of competing claims to the empire's huge agricultural surplus, thus giving the imperial bureaucracy greater protection against contenders to the throne or other outside forces. Whenever the political balance between the central authority and local rulers, tax farmers, or provincial governors remained in favor of the central authority, rural taxes were collected directly. This was the case from the 1450s to the 1650s, when the empire's territorial expansion was at its height. In the mid-19th century, with the implementation of TANZIMAT reforms, state functionaries were once again given the task of collecting rural taxes and supplanted the tax farmer (*mültezim*).

Conversely, when the balance tipped away from the central authority, the Sublime Porte lost its monopoly over the collection of taxes. His privilege conferred upon the highest bidder, who was known as a tax farmer (*see* TAX FARMING). Unlike the *sipahi*, the tax farmer was not burdened with military obligations. This was the case during the 17th and 18th centuries, when notables (or AYANS) gained strength as tax farmers and provincial governors, and in the late 19th century, when the Anglo-French Public Debt Administration (*see* DEBT AND PUBLIC DEPT ADMINISTRATION) took over the function of collecting taxes on certain crops to ensure the repayment of Ottoman state loans.

Given the size of the revenues that accrued from the *timar* holdings of the empire the direct appropriation of rural surplus by the imperial bureaucracy carried enormous weight in the perpetuation of the Sublime Porte's imperium over its territorial holdings. Under SÜLEYMAN I (r. 1520–66), who enjoyed a revenue twice that

of Charles V, it reached 8 to 10 million gold ducats and comprised two-thirds of the imperial budget. Later, as a result in part of the steady erosion of the *timar* system, the percentage fell to 40 percent in the mid-18th century.

FARM SIZE

The size of the peasant farmland, or *çiftlik*, was determined based on the nature and quality of the soil. In the 15th and 16th centuries, when cadastral surveys were conducted, farm sizes ranged from 60 to 80 *dönüms* (roughly 15–20 acres) in the most fertile regions, 80 to 100 *dönüms* (20–25 acres) in lands of average fertility, and 100 to 150 *dönüms* (25–40 acres) in poor lands. Depending on the fertility of the soil, 3 to 4 acres was required to support a person.

When population pressure on land intensified, the size of the plots declined correspondingly. This was the case at the end of the 16th century when in certain parts of Anatolia the size of family plots fell to about 7 acres. On the other hand, population shifts led to an increase in holding size due to depopulation. This was the case during the Great Flight after the CELALI REVOLTS. This also occurred during the 17th and 18th centuries, when a shift of the world economy from the Mediterranean to the shores of the North and Baltic seas led to a decline in the demand for Ottoman grain, and vast stretches of agricultural land were abandoned. By the mid-19th century, due to the increasing demand for wheat and cotton in the British empire, family plots had once again returned in size to the range stipulated in the land surveys of the 16th century—15–20 acres.

CROP DIVERSITY

The inalienable right of peasant households to arable land and the resulting number of small producers dictated the mix of crops grown in the Ottoman dominions. In certain provinces of the empire, especially those inland, an overwhelming proportion of the total production—sometimes close to 90 percent—was cereal grains. In locations that were thinly populated, grain production was combined with livestock husbandry. In areas of low population density, livestock breeding in zones of low demographic density made up one-third of the gross agricultural product, whereas in densely settled regions, it made up about one-tenth. In coastal regions, a greater mix of crops was sowed, from cotton and rice to fruit and vegetables.

Of the cereal crops grown, wheat was the most popular, and constituted at least half of all agricultural output. Yields, as in most areas of the Mediterranean, were between 3 and 4 bushels of grain for every bushel planted, rarely reaching 6 bushels for every bushel planted. Grain production per capita in most parts of the Ottoman Empire far surpassed the 550 pounds (250 kg.) per person level that was the norm in France or Spain in the 16th and 17th centuries. Each household paid 20 to 30 percent of their total agricultural production as *öşür* and related agricultural taxes. Allowing for the share of seed earmarked for the following sowing season, some 50 to 65 percent of rural produce remained in the household for sustenance and as a saleable product; on average, close to one-fourth of the gross agricultural product was available for commercial use. Judging by the vibrancy of markets and fairs in the 16th, 18th, and 19th centuries, it is not difficult to conclude that a significant portion of the surplus found its way into local markets.

LAND AVAILABILITY

The strength and survival of the peasantry was primarily due to the relative abundance of land. The land-to-labor ratio was favorable to the latter. Labor was not sparse enough to require coerced labor systems. The easy availability of land placed a premium on labor, hence the longevity of small peasantry. Even after the new land legislation of 1858—which opened up new land to cultivation by codifying rights over cultivated land, giving peasant families titles to their plots, and hastening large-scale sedentarization—only a tiny portion of the empire's land surface was sown with crops. The relatively limited size of the coastal and inland plains and the mountainous nature of most regions of the empire were partly accountable for this. However, even with the population growth of the 19th century, in most provinces, land under cultivation did not exceed 10 percent of the total land surface; in fact, in certain provinces, the ratio hovered around 4 to 5 percent.

The relative abundance of land gave the peasantry many benefits. One of these benefits was the ability to tap into the resources not only of their own village but also of nearby lands by establishing satellite settlements, or reserve fields, known as *mezraas*. The land surveys of the 16th century reveal that at times the proportion of the *mezraas* to the villages was close to 60 percent. In the mid-16th century, the expansive Ottoman realm was inhabited by more than 550,000 enumerated rural settlements, both village and *mezraa*. Whenever rural order was disturbed, the number of reserve fields and satellite settlements increased: at times, the number of *mezraas* was two to three times greater than the number of villages. By 1800, for example, about half the Anatolian population had come to depend on various types of temporary settlements. The spatial order described above could only be preserved by geographic mobility, short- and long-distance. Spatial mobility became so much a part of the order of things that it was even sanctioned by law, much to the chagrin of *timariots* whose interests were best served by tying the *reaya* to the land. Peasants wandered from one village to another and found everywhere large tracts to cultivate. It is sometimes argued that the peasants' ability to move around was the underlying reason for the lack of large-scale rural rebellions in the Ottoman Empire.

The pace of land reclamation increased after the 1850s, during the mid-Victorian boom when Britain's need for wheat imports increased. In 1858, the new Land Code made land transferable. This new law boosted market relations and brought more land under cultivation. In SYRIA, for instance, an enormous amount of land that had been infrequently used in the past was brought into regular cultivation between 1850 and 1950, and hundreds of places developed from hamlets to sizeable villages. Excluding the Jazirah to the northeast of the Euphrates River about 6.2 million acres of new land were ploughed up and about 2,000 villages were established on this newly-won land; the figures for Transjordan were 100,000 acres and 300 villages. In fact, two-thirds of today's villages and nine-tenths of the cultivated parts of inner Anatolia date back to the second half of the 19th century.

The wheat trade picked up beginning in the 1850s with the repeal of the Corn Laws in England, and land bonification followed suit. The opening up of new arable land was made possible by acquiring rights over large swathes of wastelands, lands left idle during the slowdown in agricultural growth during the 17th and 18th centuries. This is how most of the large estates came into being in the 19th century, almost surreptitiously, since this type of expansion did not entail uprooting the *reaya*.

Forcible dispossession of peasants and the formation of large-scale commercial agriculture took place in the empire's distant provinces under French or British colonial rule. It was not by coincidence that the greatest increase in trade along the shores of the Mediterranean took place in EGYPT, ALGIERS (present-day Algeria), and TUNIS (present-day Tunisia) after they were colonized. Large-scale commercial agriculture, which flourished on waste or colonial lands, lost its force with the emergence of temperate regions as the new granaries of the world economy. Small-holding peasantry managed to survive into the 20th century.

Faruk Tabak

Further reading: Haim Gerber, *Social Origins of the Modern Middle East* (Boulder, Colo.: L. Rienner, 1987); Halil İnalcık "The Ottoman State: Economy and Society, 1300–1600," in *An Economic and Social History of the Ottoman Empire*, edited by Halil İnalcık and Donald Quataert (Cambridge: Cambridge University Press, 1994), especially 103–178; Çağlar Keyder, "Small Peasant Ownership in Turkey: Historical Formation and Present Structure." *Review: A Journal of the Fernand Braudel Center* 7, no. 1 (1983): 53–107. Bruce McGowan, *Economic Life in Ottoman Europe: Taxation, Trade and the Struggle for Land, 1600–1800* (Cambridge: Cambridge University Press, 1981).

ahdname (ahitname) This Ottoman term means letter of contract or treaty; it comes from the Arabic *ahd* (contract, agreement, oath) and the Persian *name* (letter, document), and is often translated as CAPITULATIONS. All kinds of documents providing privileges, irrespective of their type, were called *ahdname* in Ottoman Turkish; these included travel documents, agreements between Ottoman vassal rulers, and letters of privilege or protection issued by provincial Ottoman authorities for a community. At the beginning of the 19th century the term *tasdikname* began to replace the word *ahdname*. Historically, the first letters of contract date back to the 12th century when Christian countries and Muslim powers used them to conclude agreements. The earliest surviving examples were contracts issued to protect the financial and personal safety of Christian foreigners traveling in Muslim territories of the empire.

Three types of *ahdnames* were issued in the Ottoman Empire.

1. The first type, known as capitulations in western Europe, were commercial contracts issued unilaterally by the Ottoman government as letters of privilege in the form of a letter of appointment. Such documents were first given to Venetian merchants and later served as a model for agreements with France, England, the Netherlands, and other states that asked for a privilege for their commercial activity from the Ottoman government.
2. *Name-i hümayun,* or imperial letters, were issued to countries situated directly on the borders of the Ottoman Empire. *Name-i hümayun* were bilateral agreements to settle armed conflict and were issued primarily to the rulers of HUNGARY, the Habsburg Empire, and POLAND.
3. Unilateral *ahdnames* were issued to some countries when they acknowledged Ottoman supremacy. For example, Christian countries that became vassal states of the Ottoman Empire had two different types of status. They were either part of the Ottoman Empire (and thus belonged to the DAR AL-ISLAM) and their inhabitants enjoyed DHIMMI status (as non-Muslim subjects of a state governed by Islamic law), or they had a contractual relationship with the Sublime Porte, or Ottoman administration, and were considered part of the empire in a political but not in a legal sense (DAR AL-HARB). Beginning in the 14th century, Christian vassal states—such as the BYZANTINE EMPIRE, RAGUSA, WALLACHIA, MOLDAVIA, and HUNGARY, TRANSYLVANIA, and Kartli—were given such *ahdnames*. The Ottoman sultans also used a diploma of appointment, or *berat-i hümayun,* to confirm the governance of vassal-state rulers, including the *voievods* of Moldavia

and Wallachia and the princes of Transylvania. Hungarian estates that rebelled against the Habsburg Empire and gave fealty to the Ottoman Empire were also given *ahdnames* on many occasions up to the first half of the 18th century.

Sándor Papp

Ahmed I (b. 1590–d. 1617) (r. 1603–1617) *Ottoman sultan and caliph*   The son of Sultan MEHMED III (r. 1595–1603) and the concubine Handan Sultan, Ahmed I was born in Manisa in western Turkey when his father, as a prince, was governing the province of Saruhan. Following his succession in 1595, Mehmed III transferred his family to the TOPKAPI PALACE in ISTANBUL. In 1603, Mehmed III ordered the execution of his oldest son Mahmud, who was accused of plotting for the throne. Ahmed and his mentally weak younger brother, MUSTAFA I (r. 1617–18, 1622–23), the only two surviving princes, both remained confined in the palace. When Mehmed III died later in the same year, a faction in the inner palace decided that Ahmed should succeed his father as sultan before any vizier or government leader had been consulted. This was an unusual succession; in several respects, it constitutes a watershed in early modern Ottoman history.

Unlike his grandfather, MURAD III (r. 1574–95), and his father, who both ordered the execution of their surviving brothers at the time of succession, Ahmed did not opt for this long-established practice of royal fratricide, and until the end of his reign he kept Mustafa alive and confined in the palace. The reasons behind his decision remain uncertain, but by doing so, he eventually altered the Ottoman succession patterns. When Ahmed died in 1617, he was survived by both his brother and several sons, the eldest being the 13-year-old future OSMAN II (r. 1618–22); both his brother and his oldest son were entitled to rule. This was a situation unprecedented in Ottoman history. A court faction secured the enthronement of Mustafa I instead of Osman, thus further solidifying the end of royal fratricide and giving way to a new principle of seniority in succession practices.

Ahmed was barely 14 years old when he ascended to the throne. Except for the short first reign of MEHMED II (r. 1444–46; 1451–81) in the mid-15th century, the Ottomans had never had such a young and inexperienced ruler. Ahmed's father was the last Ottoman sultan to serve as a provincial governor, thus acquiring training for the sultanate as well as establishing his own household that would form the nucleus of his government at his accession. Ahmed lacked this crucial background. He was the first Ottoman sultan to come to the throne from the inner compounds of the palace. His enthronement thus marked both the end of the tradition of having princes govern provinces and the end of succession wars among rival princes. With Ahmed's reign, dynastic succession, power struggles, and patronage networks shifted from a larger setting, which included the provincial princely households, to a narrower domain consisting of the Topkapı Palace and Istanbul.

In this new political setting, young Ahmed found himself contending for power in a court and imperial government divided by factionalism and favoritism. Ahmed thus needed some guidance in the business of rule. Although there was no institutionalized tradition of regency in Ottoman dynastic establishment, Ahmed's mother and, more importantly, Mustafa Efendi, his preceptor since early childhood, appear to have acted as de facto regents in his early reign. One of Ahmed's first acts was to remove his grandmother, Safiye Sultan, from politics by confining her to the Old Palace in January 1604. Safiye was one of the prime movers of politics under Mehmed III and was the main target of three major military rebellions between 1600 and 1603. Her immediate expulsion from the palace, which was followed by new appointments in the palace administration, indicates that Ahmed and his regents were trying not only to neutralize the factors behind recent unrest in the capital, but also to reconfigure the power relations within the court and the royal household.

Both Handan Sultan and Mustafa Efendi, until their deaths in 1605 and 1607 (or 1608) respectively, were the sultan's chief mentors and guardians, guiding the inexperienced ruler in selecting, promoting, and controlling his viziers. Men chosen by these regents, rather than by Ahmed, often attained positions of power during this early period. Derviş Pasha, a protégé of Handan, quickly rose to the grand vizierate. Handan's death, however, deprived Derviş of his chief royal patron and led to the dissolution of his own faction in the government. Ahmed had him executed in 1606 after he had held the grand vizierate for only a few months. Until 1607, Mustafa Efendi had a more profound influence on the young sultan. His decisions to dismiss or execute several prominent members of his government testify to this.

Ahmed's reign also saw the solidification of the role of favorites in the Ottoman political establishment. Given the increased invisibility and inaccessibility of the Ottoman sultan during this period, a favorite who managed to enter the sultan's quarters was able to consolidate his power against all challengers. In this context, El-Hac Mustafa Agha, who held the office of chief eunuch throughout Ahmed's reign, became the royal favorite par excellence. Mustafa Agha enjoyed exclusive access to Ahmed since he was the highest authority in the royal palace. Thanks to his position, he was not only able to attain enormous power and to control almost all petitions and information addressed to the sultan, but he was also able to distribute wealth, power, and patronage both in the sultan's name and in his own. Empowered by Ahmed, Mustafa Agha and his men acted as intermediaries in the management of imperial affairs and in practical politics.

Ahmed inherited from his father an empire being challenged on both international and domestic fronts. By the time Ahmed took the throne, the Ottomans were waging wars on three fronts: against the Habsburgs in Hungary, against the Safavids in the east, and against the Celali rebels in Anatolia (see CELALI REVOLTS). Ahmed's new grand vizier, Lala Mehmed Pasha (1604–06), the most experienced commander of the Hungarian Wars (1593–1606), captured several Hungarian fortresses (Vac, Pest, and Esztergom), and the Ottomans ended the long war by concluding the Treaty of Zsitvatorok, which left most of the conquered territories in Ottoman hands. However, on the eastern front, the Safavid shah, ABBAS I (r. 1587–1629), had regained all the territory lost to the Ottomans during the war of 1578–90. Although the newly appointed grand vizier Nasuh Pasha (1611–14) signed a peace treaty with the Safavids in 1611 that fixed the demarcation of the frontier once agreed upon by the Treaty of Amasya in 1555, hostilities resumed just four years later. Ahmed was more successful, however, with the Celali revolts; by 1610 the sultan's troops, under the command of his grand vizier Kuyucu Murad Pasha (1606–11), had eliminated the threat of the Celalis.

In such troubled times, Ahmed tried to cultivate the image of a warrior-sultan. He made an early attempt to lead the army personally against the Celali rebels in 1605, but this quickly became a fiasco; when he reached BURSA, Ahmed fell ill, and immediately returned to Istanbul. He gradually occupied himself more with courtly pleasures—riding, hunting, and martial arts—and he undertook major hunting expeditions around Istanbul and Edirne. Ahmed was more successful in representing himself as a pious sultan as well as in imitating his illustrious warrior ancestors, particularly his great-grandfather, SÜLEYMAN I (r. 1520–66). Ahmed was the first sultan after Süleyman to construct a monumental imperial mosque complex in Istanbul. The construction of this mosque (1609–16), which stylistically resembles that of Süleyman, came after the successful wars against the Celalis, suggesting that it should be considered a celebration of these recent military achievements as well as a symbol of Ahmed's piety.

Ahmed's attempts to emulate Süleyman were not limited to the construction of monumental architecture. Like Süleyman I, Ahmed promulgated a law code of his own; imitating Süleyman's piety, he ordered the restoration and the lavish ornamentation of the Kaaba; Ahmed redesigned his imperial seal following the norms set by Süleyman; he constructed a garden at the Dolmabahçe Palace where Süleyman once had one; as a poet and a patron of the arts he asked for new editions and translations of literary works previously commissioned by Süleyman. However, Ahmed's mimicking of his great-grandfather did not change the reality: He was a sultan of a different time, and his reign saw the crystallization of a new political, social, and economic dynamic in the early modern Ottoman imperial establishment.

Günhan Börekçi

See also CELALI REVOLTS; COURT AND FAVORITES; MEHMED III; MUSTAFA I; SÜLEYMAN I.

Further reading: Nebahat Avcıoğlu, "Ahmed I and the Allegories of Tyranny in the Frontispiece to George Sandys' *Relation of a Journey.*" *Muqarnas* 18 (2001): 203–26; Caroline Finkel, *Osman's Dream: The Story of the Ottoman Empire, 1300–1923* (London: John Murray, 2005), 152–195; Leslie Peirce, *The Imperial Harem: Women and Sovereignty in the Ottoman Empire* (Oxford: Oxford University Press, 1993); Baki Tezcan, "Searching for Osman: A Reassessment of the Deposition of The Ottoman Sultan Osman II (1618–1622)." (Ph.D. diss., Princeton University, 2001), 84–194.

Ahmed II (b. 1643–d. 1695) (r. 1691–1695) *Ottoman sultan and caliph* Born to Sultan IBRAHIM I (r. 1640–48) and Muazzez Sultan on February 25, 1643, Ahmed II succeeded his brother, Sultan SÜLEYMAN II (r. 1687–91), on June 23, 1691 in EDIRNE. During his short reign, Sultan Ahmed II devoted most of his attention to the wars against the Habsburgs and related foreign policy, governmental and economic issues. Of these, the most important were the tax reforms and the introduction of the lifelong tax farm system (*malikane*) (*see* TAX FARMING). Ahmed's reign witnessed major military defeats against the Austrian Habsburgs in the long Hungarian war of 1683–99, several devastating fires in ISTANBUL, and the emergence of AYAN, or local magnates, which further weakened the central government's hold over the provinces.

Among the most important features of Ahmed's reign was his reliance on Köprülüzade Fazıl Mustafa Pasha. Following his accession to the throne, Sultan Ahmed II confirmed Köprülüzade Fazıl Mustafa Pasha in his office as grand vizier. In office from 1689, Fazıl Mustafa Pasha was from the famous KÖPRÜLÜ FAMILY of grand viziers, and like most of his Köprülü predecessors in the same office, was an able administrator and military commander. Like his father Köprülü Mehmed Pasha (grand vizier 1656–61) before him, he ordered the removal and execution of dozens of corrupt state officials of the previous regime and replaced them with men loyal to himself. He overhauled the tax system by adjusting it to the capabilities of the taxpayers affected by the latest wars. He also reformed troop mobilization and increased the pool of conscripts available for the army by drafting

tribesmen in the Balkans and Anatolia. In October 1690 he recaptured BELGRADE (northern Serbia), a key fortress that commanded the confluence of the rivers Danube and Sava; in Ottoman hands since 1521, the fortress had been conquered by the Habsburgs in 1688.

Fazıl Mustafa Pasha's victory at Belgrade was a major military achievement that gave the Ottomans hope that the military debacles of the 1680s—which had led to the loss of HUNGARY and TRANSYLVANIA, an Ottoman vassal principality ruled by pro-Istanbul Hungarian princes—could be reversed. However, Ottoman success proved ephemeral. On August 19, 1691, Fazıl Mustafa Pasha suffered a devastating defeat at Slankamen (northwest of Belgrade) at the hands of Ludwig Wilhelm von Baden, the Habsburg commander in chief in Hungary, fittingly nicknamed "Türkenlouis" (Louis the Turk) for his splendid victories against the Ottomans. In the confrontation, recognized by contemporaries as "the bloodiest battle of the century," the Ottomans suffered heavy losses: 20,000 men, including the grand vizier. With him, the sultan lost his most capable military commander and the last member of the Köprülü family, who for the previous half century had been instrumental in strengthening the Ottoman military.

Under Fazıl Mustafa Pasha's successors, the Ottomans suffered further defeats. In June 1692 the Habsburgs conquered Várad (Oradea, Romania), the seat of an Ottoman governor (*beylerbeyi*) since 1660. Although the best Habsburg forces were elsewhere, fighting French invaders along the German Rhine—part of the Holy Roman Empire, ruled by the Austrian Habsburgs—the Ottomans were unable to regain their Hungarian possessions. In 1694 they tried to recapture Várad, but to no avail. On January 12, 1695, they gave up the fortress of Gyula, the center of an Ottoman *sancak* or subprovince since 1566. With the fall of Gyula, the only territory still in Ottoman hands in Hungary was to the east of the River Tisza and to the south of the river Maros, with its center at Temesvár. Three weeks later, on February 6, 1695, Ahmed II died in Edirne.

Gábor Ágoston

See also AUSTRIA; HUNGARY.

Further reading: Caroline Finkel, *Osman's Dream: The Story of the Ottoman Empire, 1300–1923* (London: John Murray, 2005), 312–15; Michael Hochendlinger, *Austria's Wars of Emergence: War, State and Society in the Habsburg Monarchy, 1683–1797* (London: Longman, 2003), 157–64.

Ahmed III (b. 1673–d. 1736) (r. 1703–1730) *Ottoman sultan and caliph* The son of Sultan MEHMED IV (r. 1648–87) and Rabia Emetullah Gülnuş Sultan, Ahmed III succeeded his brother MUSTAFA II (r. 1695–1703) after the Edirne Incident (August 21, 1703), a mutiny

and popular uprising in ISTANBUL that led to the deposing of Mustafa II. Restoration of order in Istanbul and wars with RUSSIA, VENICE, and the Habsburgs occupied the first phase of Ahmed's reign (1703–1718), while the later phase (1718–30) was characterized as the so-called Tulip Era, a time of extravagance, conspicuous consumption, and cultural borrowings from both East and West that ended with another major uprising in Istanbul, the Patrona Halil Rebellion of 1730. When the two subsequent sultans—MAHMUD I (r. 1730–54) and OSMAN III (r. 1754–57), both sons of Ahmed's brother, Mustafa II—died childless, the dynasty continued from the line of Ahmed III through his sons MUSTAFA III (r. 1757–74) and ABDÜLHAMID I (r. 1774–89).

Ahmed III took active measures to impose his authority in Istanbul, moving the court there from Edirne in compliance with the rebels of 1703. He focused his attention on cracking down on those implicated in the Edirne Incident and on building peaceful relations with the empire's neighbors. Therefore, he took no advantage of the War of the Spanish Succession (1703–14) and the Great Northern War (1700–21)—which tied up the armies and resources of Habsburg Austria and Russia, respectively—to recover the territories lost to the Habsburgs and Russians as a result of the TREATY OF KARLOWITZ (1699) and the Treaty of Istanbul (1700). Nevertheless, during this time, the Ottomans were involved in a series of wars on the western front when King Charles XII of Sweden, who was defeated by Peter the Great in the Battle of Poltava (1709) of the Great Northern War, took refuge with the Ottomans. War with Russia broke out when Russia invaded Ottoman territory to pursue Charles. Peter the Great was completely surrounded by Ottoman forces in the Battle of Pruth (1711). However, Grand Vizier Baltacı Mehmed Pasha, without confidence in the fighting quality of the Janissaries, agreed to make peace with the Russians on lenient terms, such as ceding AZAK to the Ottomans. In 1715 the Ottomans managed to recover the whole Morea (Peloponnese) from Venice through coordinated operations of the army and navy. Alarmed by Ottoman successes, the Habsburgs declared war on the Ottomans in 1716, which led to the destruction of the Ottoman army at Peterwardein and the loss of Belgrade by the Treaty of Passarowitz (July 21, 1718); this also marked the beginning of the Tulip Era.

Coined by a 20th-century Turkish historian, the phrase "Tulip Era" (sometimes, "the Age of the Tulip") meant the Ottoman cultural renaissance, or the birth of a neoclassical style in arts, despite its negative connotations in Turkish historiography as an age of frivolity and extravagance tailored to divert people from the decline of the state. The main theme of Turkish modernization—the conflict between "the modernizers" (the ruling elite) and "the conservatives" (the religious establishment or ULEMA and the JANISSARIES)—finds its roots in the Patrona Halil Rebellion that ended the Tulip Era.

After 1718, the sultan promoted various construction projects, including fountains, playgrounds, palaces, pavilions, and gardens along the Golden Horn and the Bosporus inspired by the example of the palace and pleasure grounds at Versailles. The plans for palaces and gardens were brought by the Ottoman ambassador to Paris, Yirmisekiz Çelebizade Mehmed Efendi, who was sent there to observe diplomacy, military arts, and high culture in Europe. More than 120 such palaces were constructed under Ahmed. This era, nevertheless, was more a revival of interest in classical Islamic culture than westernization. The sultan, himself a poet and an accomplished calligrapher, established at least five libraries—the Sultan Ahmed Library in the TOPKAPI PALACE (1718) being the most significant—prohibited the export of rare manuscripts, and founded a bureau for the translation of Arabic and Persian works to be published by the first Turkish printing house, established in Istanbul

The gravestone of Yirmisekiz Çelebi Mehmed Efendi, who served as Ahmed III's ambassador to Paris in 1720 and returned to Istanbul with plans of gardens and palaces that influenced the development of the city during this era. *(Photo by Gábor Ágoston)*

by the Hungarian convert, Ibrahim Müteferrika, in 1727. Grand Vizier Ibrahim Pasha and his wife Fatma Sultan opened a madrasa for teaching Persian and SUFISM, which had disappeared from most school curricula more than a century earlier. Active state patronage revived the imperial arts such as miniature painting and poetry as seen in the works of Levni the painter and Nedim, the celebrated poet of the age, who popularized the elaborate Ottoman poetry and MUSIC of the high culture by drawing his themes and forms from Turkish folk culture and by using simple Turkish. The decline in the manufacture of porcelain and earthenware CERAMICS in Izmid and Kütayha was reversed, owing to the demand for ceramics for the new palaces in Istanbul. The founding of a textile mill, the building of a dam in the capital, and the construction of the gorgeous Sultan Ahmed fountain in front of the Topkapı Palace (1728) are among the accomplishments of this era.

Like Louis XIV of France, the sultan and Ibrahim Pasha tried to serve as models for emulation for the Istanbul elite through competitions of tulip breeding, palace building, and festivities. A growing number of secular celebrations (royal births—31 in total—circumcisions of princes, betrothals and weddings of princesses, military victories, and so forth) set the pattern of consumption. While such celebrations had previously been for the elite, they were now intended for the wider public. They were accompanied by a growing level of tolerance for nonconformity, including—to the dismay of the religious establishment—the increased visibility of women on public occasions. Notably, political execution was almost nonexistent in this era. Presumably, the new forms of cultural expression had something to do with the growing trade with France—500 merchant vessels reached Istanbul annually—which may have created a new class of people in the capital who could afford a grander lifestyle. However, Grand Vizier Ibrahim Pasha's nepotism and fiscal measures, as well as defeats at the eastern front—wars with Iran flared up after the Ottoman-Russian treaty that partitioned Iran's western provinces (June 23, 1724)— all prepared the groundwork for the Patrona Halil Rebellion that resulted in the execution of Ibrahim and the abdication of Ahmed III. While the rebels destroyed palaces and playgrounds, they left untouched such innovations as the Turkish press and the new corps of firemen, suggesting that the widespread resentment stemmed not from reforms, but from the extravagance of the court.

Kahraman Şakul

Further reading: Anthony D. Alderson, *The Structure of the Ottoman Dynasty* (Oxford: Clarendon, 1956); Ekmeleddin İhsanoğlu, ed., *History of the Ottoman State, Society, and Civilisation,* vol. 2 (Istanbul: Ircica, 2001), 630–634; Rhoads Murphey, "Westernisation in the Eighteenth-Century Ottoman Empire: How Far, How Fast?" *Byzantine and Modern Greek Studies* 23 (1999): 116–139; Robert Olson, "The Esnaf and the Patrona Halil Rebellion of 1730: A Realignment in Ottoman Politics?" *Journal of the Economic and Social History of the Orient* 17, no. 3 (1974): 329–344; Donald Quataert, *The Ottoman Empire, 1700–1922* (Cambridge: Cambridge University Press, 2000); Madeline C. Zilfi, "Women and Society in the Tulip Era, 1718–1730," in *Women, the Family, and Divorce Laws in Islamic History,* edited by Amira El Azhary Sonbol (Syracuse, NY: Syracuse University Press, 1996), 290–303.

Ahmed Cevdet Pasha (b. 1823–d. 1895) *prominent Ottoman writer and statesman*   Born in Lovec, Bulgaria on March 27, 1823, Ahmed Cevdet Pasha came to Istanbul in 1839 to study literature, mathematics, Persian, French, and SUFISM. His long career in Ottoman government began in 1844 when he was appointed judge (*kadı*) of Premedi. In 1850 he was appointed as a member of the Council for Educational Reforms; one year later he became a member of the Ottoman Academy of Sciences (Encümen-i Danış). In 1853 he was commissioned to record Ottoman history between 1774 and 1826 and, as a result of his successful work, was appointed official historiographer in 1855. He performed significant services in regions of Rumelia and Anatolia during the era of the TANZIMAT reforms.

After serving two years as governor of Aleppo (in present-day Syria), Cevdet Pasha was appointed minister of justice in 1868. During his tenure, he helped establish modern courts and codify relevant laws and regulations. For example, he drafted the MECELLE, a law book based on canonical jurisprudence of the Hanafi school of Islam, and became the president of the Grand Council for the Mecelle. In 1872 he served as a member of the Council of State (Şura-yı Devlet), an advisory and judicial body, and the next year he served simultaneously as the Ottoman minister of religious foundations and the minister of national education. During this period, major steps were taken toward modernizing education during this period; new curricula were established for schools (he personally wrote three course books), and educational institutions were rearranged. While serving as the minister of justice and during his presidency of the Supreme Court of Judicial Ordinances (Divan-ı Ahkam-ı Adliye), Cevdet Pasha participated in the establishment of legal organizations, including the School of Law (1880) where he also taught. His last government post was as a member of the High Councils for Reforms (Mecalis-i Aliye). He died on May 26, 1895, in Istanbul.

Cevdet Pasha's significant impact on Turkish cultural and political life was not limited to his bureaucratic work. He was also a leading linguist, historian, legal professional, and educator. He wrote in plain Turkish, aiming both to simplify the Turkish language and to demonstrate its usefulness for science. As a historian, he introduced a new dimension and interpretive style to classical Ottoman history, writing with a unique logic and methodology. He wrote many well-known historical texts, including *Tarih-i Cevdet* (History of Cevdet) and *Kırım ve Kafkas Tarihçesi* (History of the Crimea and the Caucasus). Cevdet Pasha is, however, best remembered for his role as a statesman and legal professional during the Tanzimat era. He is particularly noted for his accomplishments during this time: his membership in the Metn-i Metin Commission, which was established for the preparation of the Ottoman Civil Code in 1855, and his membership in the High Council for Reforms in 1857. Furthermore, Cevdet Pasha helped prepare the statutes on criminal law (1858) and land law (1858), as well as the Düstur, another law compilation.

Cevdet Pasha was an advocate of measured westernization and modernization. He sought to build a bridge between the traditionalist-conservative reformists and the advocates of westernizing influence, including those who sought to reconcile scientific advancement with Islamic teachings. Cevdet Pasha believed that the political unity and ruling institutions of the Ottoman Empire, including the caliphate and sultanate, could be preserved according to Ottoman tradition and doctrine. His broad influence and extended career mark him as one of the most significant statesmen and scientists of 19th-century Turkish history.

Yüksel Çelik

Further reading: Beşir Atalay, "Ottoman State and Ahmed Cevdet Pasha's History," in *The Great Ottoman-Turkish Civilization,* vol. 3, edited by Kemal Çiçek (Ankara: Yeni Türkiye, 2000), 389–404; Richard L. Chambers, "The Education of a Nineteenth-Century Ottoman Alim Ahmed Cevdet Paşa." *International Journal of Middle Eastern Studies* 4 (1973): 440–464; Hulusi Yavuz, "Ahmed Cevdet Paşa and the Ulema of His Time" *İslam Tetkikleri Enstitüsü Dergisi* 7, no. 3–4 (1979): 178–198.

Ahmed Pasha, Cezzar See CEZZAR AHMED PASHA.

Akkoyunlu See ANATOLIAN EMIRATES.

Alawi Alawi is a name that was shared by two different, heterodox Muslim sects in the Ottoman Empire. One community, often called by the alternative designation Nusayris, was found almost exclusively in the Mediterranean range of coastal mountains in present-day Syria and the Turkish province of Hatay. The other sect is more commonly known by the Turkish spelling of the name, Alevi. Its members could be—and are—found across

wide sections of central and eastern Anatolia. In the Ottoman period, the authorities condemned both sects as heretical under the generic label of KIZILBAŞ, after the followers of Shah Ismail Safavi. In reality, that identification was only valid for the Alevis of Anatolia, who do claim to be the spiritual descendants of Shah Ismail.

The confusion arose, in part, because both groups hold that Ali, who was both the son-in-law and first cousin of the Prophet Muhammad, is the spiritual source of their faith, and because much of their belief systems is esoteric and not to be shared with outsiders. Not knowing what their actual doctrines were led the Ottoman SUNNI Muslim authorities to suppose that they were, in fact, both part of the same dissenting sect. The Ottomans thus treated both as potential rebels against the sultan's authority and condemned them as heretics. In addition to their reverence for Ali, the adherents of both faiths understand the Quran to be of lesser importance to them as a moral guide than the teachings of their saints (*pirs* in Turkish and Kurdish, *walis* in Arabic), which have been orally transmitted through the generations.

Beyond those similarities, however, there are significant differences between the theological beliefs of the two sects. The Alawis of Syria, for example, share with the DRUZES, another sect that is seen as an offshoot from orthodox Islam, the belief in reincarnation and the transmigration of souls. They also hold, according to some authorities, that the prophets venerated by Islam are valid but that another sacred personage (the *mana* or meaning) who embodied the spiritual truth of the prophetic message accompanied each of those prophets and is the proper object of veneration. In the case of Muhammad, his *mana* was Ali, while that of Jesus was John the Baptist, and the *mana* of the Prophet Moses was his brother Aaron.

The Alevis of Anatolia have abandoned their original messianic fervor that Shah Ismail would return as Mahdi—that is, the "rightly guided one" who Muslims believe will come at the end of time, ready to initiate God's justice on earth with a sword—for a quieter theology grounded in the mystical poetry of Anatolian folk bards such as Yunus Emre and Pir Sultan Abdal. Thus music is an important component of their religious ceremonies. Both Alawis and Alevis permit women a much more active role in their religious ceremonies than do Sunni Muslims. Both traditions are also highly influenced by rural folk practices and beliefs that may predate the coming of Islam. Before the modern period, neither tradition produced scholars to represent their belief systems to the outside world. It was easy, therefore, for the Sunni religious leadership in the Ottoman period to present a negative, and often misleading, interpretations of their beliefs. As folk traditions, the Ottoman religious authorities found reason to condemn both Alawis and Alevis as "heretical." But at the same time, it was almost impossible for those authorities to extirpate them from the hearts and minds of believers, and they remain vibrant traditions today. In the 20th century, both groups have sought to establish that their beliefs are well within the mainstream traditions of SHIA ISLAM and that they are not the heretical sects that the Ottoman authorities once claimed they were.

Bruce Masters

Further reading: David Shankland, *The Alevis in Turkey: The Emergence of a Secular Islamic Tradition* (London: Routledge Curzon, 2003).

Albania The Ottoman conquest of the Albanian territories was a process that started in the 14th century when competing Albanian noble families fell back on Ottoman military support to stand up against their opponents. However, the sultan began to strengthen his influence in that part of the Balkan peninsula by forcing a large number of these local noble families to acknowledge his suzerainty. In addition, he forced them to become his vassals, requiring them to send their sons as hostages to the palace in EDIRNE. The final stage of this process took place after the BATTLE OF KOSOVO (1389), when the victory of the Ottoman army under the command of MURAD I (r. 1362–1389) weakened Serbia as a political and military power in the Balkans. It was the conquest of Skopje (1391) that finally enabled the Ottomans to bring the Albanian territories under their control. The process was disrupted by TIMUR's defeat of BAYEZID I (r. 1389–1402) in the 1402 BATTLE OF ANKARA, but the consolidation of Ottoman rule under Sultan MEHMED I (r. 1413–1421) reestablished the dominant position of the Ottomans with the 1417 conquest of Valona (present-day Vlorë) and Berat. In 1431 the Ottomans established an administrative unit called the Albanian *sancak* (*sancak-i Arvanid*) made up of the western areas of southern and middle Albania, effectively dividing the country into Ottoman and Venetian spheres of control; local lords continued to dominate the northeastern mountainous country. In the following decades, uprisings broke out in southern Albania where Georg (Gjergj) Arianiti offered resistance against Ottoman military forces between 1432 and 1439.

The most famous uprising was led by Georg (Gjergj) Kastriota (called Skanderbeg), who had spent his youth at the sultan's palace as a hostage, had converted to Islam, and presumably was appointed to different posts in the Ottoman administration in Albania. In 1443 he rose up against the Ottomans and convened an assembly of the Albanian nobility for the purpose of organizing military resistance against the Ottomans. In 1450 and 1460, respectively, the sultans MURAD II (r. 1421–1444, 1446–51) and MEHMED II (r. 1444–46; 1451–81) besieged the fortress of Kruja without success. The military conflict ended with the death of Skanderbeg (1468) when the territories hitherto controlled by him fell under Venetian rule. However, the Ottoman armies soon conquered the towns of Kruja (in 1478) and Shkodra (in 1479). By the peace treaty of 1479, VENICE had to abandon its possessions in Albania to the Ottoman Empire. However, Venice sustained its rule in the Albanian seaport of Durres, which came under Ottoman control in 1501. The integration of Albanian territories into the Ottoman Empire began a social and economic transformation. The Ottomans introduced the *timar* system of land ownership, and the irregular process of Islamization also began. The CONVERSION to Islam, which reached its peak in the 17th and 18th centuries, allowed Albanians to advance into the political, military, and cultural elite of the empire. With this change, a large number of Albanians became senior officials in the Ottoman administration; between the 15th and 17th centuries, 25 grand viziers came from an Albanian background. Dervishes, or members of mystical brotherhoods, played a significant role in the spread of Islam by enabling the incorporation of pagan and local non-Muslim beliefs into popular Islam, thus making the conversion more palatable to the new Muslims. The BEKTAŞI ORDER of dervishes gained a strong influence on Islam in the region, and Albania became an important stronghold of this mystical movement. In the early stages of Islamization, many converts declared themselves Muslims without having been completely integrated into the Ottoman-Muslim religious and social world. These Albanians claimed that they lived according to the rules of Islam; however, they also continued to practice Christian rituals. These Crypto-Christians (Muslims who secretly practiced Christianity) lived in areas that were removed from the Ottoman administrative centers. Churchgoing and the baptism of Muslim children were indicators of this widespread religious syncretism.

In times of war between Christian powers and the Ottomans there were many uprisings in Albania. In the 16th century western European powers that waged war against the Ottoman Empire wanted to integrate Christian Albanians into their military and political strategies. During the Cyprus War (1570–73), the Venetians successfully incited the Christian population in some northern Albanian territories into a rebellion. In the 16th and 17th centuries, these rebellions did not seriously endanger Ottoman rule. However, as the 18th century progressed, Ottoman authorities faced increasing difficulties in maintaining their control over this area.

This was also the period when local notables known as AYAN began to extend their power in many parts of the Ottoman Empire. In northern and middle Albania, one of these *ayan* families, the Bushattliu (Mehmed Pasha 1757–75, Kara Mahmud Pasha 1778–96, Mustafa

Pasha 1811–31), established its own power structure. In southern Albania, in Epirus, the Tepedelenli family, represented by ALI PASHA OF JANINA (ca. 1744–1822) also established its own power structure. Sultan MAHMUD II (1808–39) strengthened efforts to eliminate these local rulers. Ottoman military forces besieged Ali Pasha in Janina and forced him to surrender in 1822. In 1831 Mustafa Pasha Bushattliu was defeated but he was pardoned and appointed governor of another Ottoman province.

The efforts to weaken the position of the *ayan* preceded the reforms known as the TANZIMAT (1839–76), which addressed the tax, judicial, and military systems. These reform attempts met with heavy opposition from the Muslim and Christian Albanian population. The tribes in northern Albania that had hitherto enjoyed a semiautonomous status feared that they would lose their privileges. Attempts by the Ottoman administration to recruit troops in Albania led to the outbreak of a riot. The Tanzimat period came to an end when SERBIA and Montenegro declared war on the Ottoman Empire in 1876. The Treaty of San Stefano (1878) provided for the independence of Serbia, Montenegro, and Romania and for the formation of an autonomous Bulgarian principality. This agreement met with disapproval from AUSTRIA and ENGLAND, which wished to limit Russian influence in southeastern Europe. The Congress of Berlin revised the controversial terms of the Treaty of San Stefano (1878): Montenegro, Serbia, and Romania became independent states; Montenegro received the areas of Plav-Gusinje and Bar; Serbia got the districts of Kursumlje and Vranje; and AUSTRIA was entitled to occupy BOSNIA AND HERZEGOVINA and to station troops in the *sancak* (district) of Novi Pazar.

Since these newly created Balkan states included territories where Albanians lived, shortly after the Treaty of San Stefano the Albanians began to organize resistance against these cessions of territory. Dedicated to Albanian NATIONALISM, this resistance was spearheaded by a "central committee for defending the rights of the Albanian nation," which was founded by Albanians living in ISTANBUL. On June 10, 1878, this committee convened an assembly in Prizren that set up the League of Prizren (Lidhja e Prizrenit), which asserted the following goals: no cession of territories to Serbia, Montenegro, and GREECE; return of all Albanian territories occupied by Montenegro and Serbia; Albanian representation at the Congress of Berlin; and Albanian autonomy within the Ottoman Empire. Most of these demands were in the interest of the Ottoman government; however, the demand for Albanian autonomy increased the tensions between the League of Prizren and the Ottoman government in Istanbul. The league began to put the government under pressure by taking over local administration,

as they did in Kosovo in 1881. The Ottoman government responded by restoring its authority by force of arms.

Even though the league could not accomplish its goals, it did usher in a period of national revival. Albanian organizations both in Istanbul and outside the Ottoman Empire took a leading role in the Albanian national movement, which focused on culture and education. At the head of the Istanbul Society was Sami Frashëri, whose book *Shqipëria: Ç'ka qenë, ç'është e ç'do të bëhetë* (Albania: what it was, what it is, what it will be), stands as a manifesto of the Albanian national movement. In 1881, the Istanbul Society was outlawed in the Ottoman Empire. However, it transferred its seat to Bucharest, which became a center for Albanian emigration and culture in the Balkan peninsula. Albanian organizations were founded in other cities as well; they were primarily engaged in distributing Albanian publications and opening Albanian schools. To suppress awakening Albanian nationalism, the Ottoman authorities closed Albanian schools in 1903 and banned Albanian publications. This policy of CENSORSHIP, the introduction of new taxes, and ongoing border conflicts with neighboring states, sparked local riots. The majority of the Albanian political leaders strove for autonomy whereas a minority spoke out in favor of independence. When the YOUNG TURKS (an Ottoman political opposition group)came to power in 1908, Albanian political leaders hoped that the government would accept their demands for Albanian autonomy. However, the Young Turks intended instead to strengthen the centralization of the empire and to integrate Albania into the "Ottoman Nation." This political controversy did not calm the situation in Albania, and as a result, the area was shaken by unrest until the First Balkan War in 1912 when the Balkan coalition (Serbia, BULGARIA, Montenegro, and Greece) declared war on the Ottoman Empire. The military forces of the sultan were defeated and shortly after the outbreak of the military conflict large parts of Albania were occupied by troops of the coalition. Ottoman rule in Albania collapsed and an Albanian national congress, which convened in Valona, proclaimed Albanian independence on November 28, 1912.

Markus Koller

Further reading: Kristo Frashëri, *The History of Albania (A Brief Survey)* (Tirana 1964); Stavro Skendi, *The Albanian National Awakening, 1878-1912* (Princeton, N.J.: Princeton University Press, 1967); Machiel Kiel, *Ottoman Architecture in Albania, 1385-1912* (Istanbul: Research Centre for Islamic History, Art and Culture, 1990).

Alemdar Mustafa Pasha (Alemdar Bayraktar) (b. 1765–d. 1808) *ayan of Ruşçuk, first grand vizier of Sultan Mahmud II (1808-1839)*   Thought to have been born in Ruşçuk (present-day Ruse, Bulgaria) as the son of a soldier from the elite Ottoman JANISSARIES, Alemdar Mustafa Pasha began his official career in the Janissary corps. At that time he came to be called Alemdar (Arabic) or Bayraktar (Turkish), meaning "standard-bearer," and probably referring to the position he held in the corps. After the war of 1787–91, Alemdar Mustafa Pasha left the Janissary corps and engaged in large-scale cattle-dealing and agriculture. He also became the closest assistant of Ismail Ağa Tirseniklioğlu, the uncontested leader of Ruse and one of the most powerful magnates in Rumelia, the European parts of the empire. Mustafa proved to be a talented military commander who repulsed the bands of OSMAN PAZVANTOĞLU, a Vidin-based quasi-independent ruler in northwestern Bulgaria and northeastern Serbia, and a fierce opponent of the New Order, or NIZAM-I CEDID reforms initiated by SELIM III (r. 1789–1807). As a reward, Tirseniklioğlu appointed Mustafa the *ayan* of the adjacent territory of Razgrad in 1803. After the death of his patron in August 1806, Alemdar Mustafa inherited his position and stretched his authority over much of present-day eastern Bulgaria, taking over leadership of the opposition to the Nizam-ı Cedid in Rumelia. However, as with earlier disobedient provincial strongmen, Alemdar Mustafa Pasha was soon co-opted by the Istanbul government. He won several battles against the Russians in the Russo-Ottoman War of 1806–12 (see RUSSO-OTTOMAN WARS). In return for his services, he was granted the rank of vizier, and was made commander in chief of the Danube front and governor or *vali* of Silistra.

Although he had earlier opposed the sultan's reform program, with his increasing ties to the Ottoman leadership, he came to realize the need for modernization of the Ottoman army. Following the Janissary revolt led by Kabakçı Mustafa on May 29, 1807 against Sultan Selim and his Nizam-ı Cedid reforms, some of the most prominent supporters of the deposed sultan found asylum with Alemdar Mustafa Pasha, who became the central figure of a secret committee for the restoration of the deposed sultan and the continuation of the reform process.

On July 28, 1808, at the head of an impressive military force, Alemdar Mustafa Pasha broke into the palace. He could not, however, save the sultan, who was killed by the men of the new sultan, MUSTAFA VI (r. 1807–08), whom the rebels put on the throne. Alemdar Mustafa Pasha deposed the new sultan and enthroned Mustafa's reform-minded brother, MAHMUD II (r. 1808–39). Alemdar Mustafa Pasha became Sultan Mahmud's omnipotent grand vizier, the first provincial notable or *ayan* to rise to this post. Probably the most significant act of Alemdar Mustafa Pasha in this capacity was the preparation of the Document of Agreement (Sened-i Ittifak) on October 7, 1808. Discussed in the presence of many of the *ayan* from Rumelia and Anatolia who were invited to the capital especially for this purpose, the Document of Agreement aimed at securing provincial support for the new sultan and grand vizier, and for the planned military reforms. Other measures undertaken by Alemdar Mustafa are related to the New Segbans, the restoration of a modernized military unit instituted by Selim III. Realizing that he first needed peace to introduce this restoration, Alemdar Mustafa started talks with RUSSIA and ENGLAND. His iron hand, however, soon united the dispersed opposition. Another mutiny of the Janissaries broke out on November 14, 1808, against the new sultan and his grand vizier and their plans to establish new modernized military units and to reform the Janissary corps. Meanwhile, Alemdar had been left with a limited military force as he had dispatched his own troops back to Ruse to protect both his own positions in the region and the Ottoman frontier in the continuing war with Russia. Alemdar was killed in the revolt and the new corps was disbanded. Sultan Mahmud II, however, succeeded in keeping the throne, having ordered the killing of Mustafa IV, the only other male of the Ottoman dynasty.

Rossitsa Gradeva

See also OSMAN PAZVANTOĞLU.

Further reading: Caroline Finkel, *Osman's Dream: The Story of the Ottoman Empire, 1300–1923* (London: John Murray, 2005), 419–23; Stanford Shaw, *Between Old and New: The Ottoman Empire under Sultan Selim III, 1789–1807* (Cambridge, Mass.: Harvard University Press, 1971), 347–49, 353–56, 360–64, 396–405.

Aleppo (Alep; *Ar.*: Halab; *Turk.*: Halep)   The northern Syrian city of Aleppo was the capital of a province bearing the same name existing for most of its history (from 1534 until 1918) under Ottoman rule. During the 17th and 18th centuries, Aleppo was the third largest city of the Ottoman Empire in terms of population, surpassed only by ISTANBUL and CAIRO. From the 16th until the 18th century, Aleppo served as one of the principal commercial centers of the empire. It was a place where merchants from western Europe met the caravans coming from Iran and those bringing Indian goods from BASRA, a port city on the Persian Gulf. In the 19th century, that trade was largely diverted to steamships and the city's international commercial importance declined. The city remained, however, an important commercial and political center for a region encompassing northern SYRIA and southeastern Anatolia until WORLD WAR I (1914–18).

Sultan SELIM I (r. 1512–20) captured the city of Aleppo from its former MAMLUK governors in 1516 after defeating the Mamluks at the Battle of Marj Dabiq. The inhabitants of the city were apparently not sorry to see their former rulers depart and offered Selim and his army three days of feasting to celebrate his entry into their city.

The Ayyubid citadel of Aleppo served as the official residence of the Ottoman governor and his military force. *(Photo by Gábor Ágoston)*

In the immediate aftermath of the Ottoman conquest, the city was placed under the administration of the governor of DAMASCUS. But by 1534, the city had become completely independent of Damascus, its southern rival. Although two of its governors instituted major rebellions that threatened Ottoman rule in northern Syria, in 1606 and again in 1657, Aleppo's political history was relatively quiet in the Ottoman centuries.

Aleppo had already become a major trade center in which European merchants could buy Asian commodities in the 15th century, the last century of Mamluk rule, but its role as a commercial hub continued to increase under the Ottomans. The Ottomans provided increased security for that trade in the 16th century and Ottoman governors of the city invested in its commercial infrastructure by constructing mosques and then building markets and caravansaries (hostels for visiting merchants) as WAQFS, or pious foundations, to support their upkeep. As a result, the commercial heart of Aleppo

almost doubled in size. Its interlocking maze of covered market streets was one of the largest in the Ottoman Empire. By the middle of the 16th century, Aleppo had displaced Damascus as the principal market for pepper coming to the Mediterranean region from India. This is reflected by the fact that the LEVANT COMPANY of London, a joint-trading company founded to monopolize England's trade with the Ottoman Empire that received a charter from Elizabeth I in 1581, never attempted to settle a factor, or agent, in Damascus, despite having had permission to do so. Aleppo served as the company's headquarters until the late 18th century

Ironically. by the time the Levant Company established its factors in Aleppo, the pepper trade that had attracted its interests in the first place was in precipitous decline. The price of transporting the spice by caravan simply could not compete with that of shipping it directly from India to western Europe by sail. That commercial void was quickly filled, however, by the arrival of Iranian silk in the city. The silk of Iran became the leading export of Aleppo from the end of the 16th century until 1730, although locally grown cotton and silk were also important as export items to the West. In exchange, English merchants, and to a lesser extent the Dutch and French, brought silver coins and woolen broadcloth. This provided a major boost to England's nascent clothing industry, providing a major export market and bringing in raw materials for the local luxury clothing market.

The prosperity that Aleppo experienced in the 16th and 17th centuries started to fade as silk production in Iran went into decline with the fall of the Safavid dynasty in 1722. By mid-century, caravans were no longing bringing silk from Iran to Aleppo, and local Syrian production was insufficient to provide for Europe's demands. European merchants left Aleppo and the city went into an economic decline that was not reversed until the mid-19th century when locally produced cotton and tobacco became the principal commodities of interest to the Europeans.

The economic decline of the city in the 18th century paralleled an increasingly troubled political climate, as the Ottoman central government was no longer able to control the various political factions in the city. These factions formed their own gangs of underemployed young men who increasingly turned to violence to press their demands for protection fees. Mob violence remained a constant feature of political life in Aleppo until the occupation of the city by the Egyptian army, led by IBRAHIM PASHA, in 1831.

The restoration of Aleppo to Ottoman rule in 1841 saw the implementation of significant changes by the central government, including conscription for the new army and new taxes. New Ottoman reforms also included the granting of greater freedoms to the empire's non-Muslim minorities, but Muslim resentment regarding these freedoms only added to rising political instability, and the protest over the impending draft developed into an assault on the city's prosperous Christian quarters on October 17, 1850. The mob attacked all the city's churches and hundreds of Christian homes. At least 20 Christians were killed and many more were wounded before Muslim AYAN, or notables in the city, stepped in to prevent further harm. The rioters held the city until November 5, when an Ottoman army bombarded the quarters of the city to which the rioters had fled. The British consul in the city estimated that 1,000 people died in the assault and reported that the quarters from which the rioters had come were reduced to smoldering ruins. After 1850, Aleppo remained politically calm, emerging again as the major trading center of northern Syria by the 1870s, although politically and culturally it was increasingly eclipsed by Damascus. In the aftermath of WORLD WAR I, the city was occupied by troops loyal to Prince Faysal's Arab Kingdom, but in July 1920 Aleppo was occupied without resistance by French forces.

Bruce Masters

See also TRADE.

Further reading: Abraham Marcus, *The Middle East on the Eve of Modernity: Aleppo in the Eighteenth Century* (New York: Columbia University Press, 1989); Bruce Masters, *The Origins of Western Economic Dominance in the Middle East: Mercantilism and the Islamic Economy in Aleppo, 1600–1750* (New York: New York University Press, 1988).

Alevi   *See* ALAWI.

Alexandrette (Alexandretta; *Ar.*: al-Iskandariyya; *Turk.*: Iskenderun)   European merchants developed the port city of Alexandrette, in present-day Turkey, in the early 17th century to serve as an outlet for the goods they purchased in the city of ALEPPO. As Aleppo became increasingly important as a trade emporium in the silk trade between Iran and western Europe in the latter half of the 16th century, European merchants sought to find an alternative to the port of TRIPOLI, in what is today northern LEBANON. Tripoli was at least eight days travel by CARAVAN from Aleppo and was controlled by the Turkoman Sayfa family who were notorious for extorting bribes from Europeans traveling through their territory. The Europeans decided that the natural harbor available at Alexandrette, which could be reached by caravan from Aleppo in three or four days, was preferable to the expensive route through Safya territory. Another advantage was that the region was ruled directly by the governor of Aleppo, thus reducing required customs duties. The fact that the city's proposed location was also a malarial swamp did not seem to figure into their considerations.

The English and French ambassadors in ISTANBUL began to lobby for a customs station at Alexandrette in 1590, but some European merchants had already started to offload their goods there illegally. The Ottomans acceded to their requests in 1593, and by the middle of the 17th century a small European city had grown up around the drained swamps. Initially, the powerful Sayfa family opposed the port and sought, through bribes, to reverse the decision establishing a customs station at Alexandrette. But by 1612, with the family's fall from the sultan's approval, all opposition to European plans for the city ended. Alexandrette was the first of the "colonial" port cities in the eastern Mediterranean that would eventually grow to include Izmir, BEIRUT, and ALEXANDRIA. All four cities grew largely due to European interest in exploiting the markets of the Ottoman Empire.

Reflecting its debt to European merchant capital, Alexandrette's architecture more closely resembles the cities of the European Mediterranean than the architectural styles of interior Syrian cities such as Aleppo and DAMASCUS. Alexandrette remained a major Syrian commercial center through the 19th century, although its fortunes were partially eclipsed as Aleppo's trade declined and Beirut emerged as the leading port of the Syrian coast.

Bruce Masters

See also TRADE.

Alexandria (*Ar.*: al-Iskandariyya, *Turk.*: Iskenderiye) From its conquest by the Ottomans in 1517 until the beginning of the 19th century, the Egyptian port city of Alexandria remained a commercial backwater, overshadowed by the more significant port cities of Rashid (Rosetta) and Dumyat (Damiette), on the two main channels of the Nile River as it reaches the Mediterranean Sea. But as larger European ships began to dominate Egypt's trade, the smaller harbors of Rashid and Dumyat proved incapable of handling them. Endowed with deeper anchorage than its rivals, Alexandria soon became the most important commercial port of Egypt.

The population of Alexandria was estimated at only 5,000 in 1806 but its population had risen to well over 200,000 by 1882, reflecting the city's increasing role in the Egyptian cotton export boom of the 19th century. By the end of the century, the population of Alexandria was a cosmopolitan mix. In addition to native Egyptians, there were large communities of Greeks, Syrian Christians, Italians, and Maltese. There was also a significant Jewish population consisting both of Arabic-speaking Jews and new Ashkenazi immigrants who been drawn by the city's commerce and industry. Ethnic tensions among these various communities erupted in violence on June 11, 1882, when several hundred Egyptians and approximately 50 Europeans were killed.

Although the Egyptian army restored order two days later, because the events occurred during Colonel AHMAD URABI's army rebellion in CAIRO, the British tied the riot to the rebellion and insisted that the Colonel be dismissed. When the paralyzed Egyptian government did not respond swiftly to the British ultimatum, the British navy, in apparent retaliation for the riot, bombarded the city on July 11, killing hundreds of Alexandrian residents before occupying the city. Alexandria continued to grow after the British occupation and threatened to overtake Cairo both in terms of population and commercial importance.

Bruce Masters

See also EGYPT; URABI, AHMAD.

Further reading: Michael Reimer, *Colonial Bridgehead: Government in Alexandria, 1807–1882* (Boulder, Colo.: Westview, 1997).

Algiers (*Ar.*: al-Jazair; *Fr.*: Alger; *Turk.*: Cezayir) The port city of Algiers, which is the present-day capital of Algeria, is located on the Mediterranean coast and served as the leading stronghold of Ottoman naval power in the western Mediterranean in the 16th and 17th centuries. In 1492, after SPAIN conquered the Muslim kingdom of Granada in the Andalusia region of present-day Spain, the Spanish began to seize ports along the North African coast. In response, the Ottomans sought to reverse these Spanish victories, allying themselves with brothers Uruc and Hayreddin Barbarossa (*see* BARBAROSSA BROTHERS), who were raiding Christian shipping in the western Mediterranean Sea as independent CORSAIRS. By 1525, Hayreddin Barbarossa had established the port of Algiers as his base of operations and was recognized as governor by the Ottomans who dispatched a garrison of JANISSARIES to serve at his disposal. Sultan SÜLEYMAN I (r. 1520–66) further granted him the title of *beylerbeyi,* or governor, giving Barbarossa authority over two other North African outposts: TUNIS and TRIPOLI.

Prior to this, Algiers had been a minor port, but under Barbarossa's governance it emerged as the center of Muslim piracy in the Mediterranean. The city's population grew rapidly as adventurers from Anatolia, Muslim refugees from Spain, and "renegades" (Christians who had converted to Islam to profit from piracy) came to the city seeking their fortune. By the end of the 16th century, the total population is estimated to have reached 60,000.

Until 1587, the person holding the governorship of Algiers had also been the *reis,* or admiral, of the Ottoman corsair fleet, but in that year the two positions were separated and a regular Ottoman military commander with the title of pasha was sent from the capital to serve as governor. Real power in the city remained vested in the office of *reis,* however.

Within the military garrison in Algiers, there was tension between the corsairs, who were largely either North Africans or "renegades" by origin, and the Turkish-speaking Janissaries sent out from the capital. In the period between 1659 and 1671, the Janissaries seized power from weak governors and controlled Algiers, but when direct Ottoman rule returned, the *reis* of the corsairs reasserted his authority. He named the *dey* (a term thought to be derived from the Turkish *dayı,* or uncle, but which came to mean simply "governor") to head the Janissary garrison in the city. The persons holding that office were then routinely appointed as governors of the province of Algiers by the sultan.

In 1711, Sökeli Ali Bey eliminated all his Janissary rivals and thus attained the rank of *dey.* Although he, too, dutifully swore to rule in accordance with the command of Sultan AHMED III (r. 1703–30), the promotion of Sökeli Ali signaled the end of direct Ottoman control over the city. While there was no declaration of independence and no end to nominal Ottoman sovereignty, Sökeli Ali and his descendants ruled Algiers more or less independently until the French assumed control in 1830. Because they were in intense competition with their counterparts in Tunis and Tripoli, Algerian corsairs continued to rely on the Ottoman sultan to authorize their piracy, but despite their dependence on nominal approval from ISTANBUL, Ottoman influence in the region remained tenuous. For instance, in 1718, when the Ottomans agreed to end Muslim privateering against Austrian shipping with the Treaty of Passarowitz, the *dey* in Algiers refused to comply and was branded a rebel by the ŞEYHÜLISLAM, the chief Muslim judge of the empire, in Istanbul. Algerians were barred from the HAJJ as long as they persisted in rebellion and, with greater commercial impact, they were prohibited from recruiting Turkish soldiers and sailors in Anatolia. The standoff ended in 1732, when war with Spain forced Sultan MAHMUD I to re-embrace his wayward subjects. For three quarters of a century after this, Algerian corsairs continued to raid Christian ships, including Austrian vessels, with impunity.

As the 18th century came to an end, Algiers was drawn more closely into the French economic orbit. Wheat from the Algerian hinterland supplied FRANCE during the British blockade of the European continent, imposed during the French Revolutionary and Napoleonic periods(1789–1815). Two Jewish families, the Bakri and Bushnaq families, who largely monopolized the grain trade, grew rich in partnership with the *dey,* incurring a huge debt from French creditors in the process. Pierre Deval, the French consul in Algiers, entered into an extended quarrel with the *dey* over payment of this debt and for other French losses in the 1820s. Years of frustration exploded on April 29, 1827, when the *dey* hit Consul Deval in the face with his flyswatter. That incident escalated into French demands for an apology and monetary compensation. Not satisfied, the French government ordered the occupation of Algiers in 1830, and Algeria was annexed to the French Empire.

Bruce Masters

See also ABD AL-QADIR AL-JAZAIRI.

Further reading: William Spencer, *Algiers in the Age of the Corsairs* (Norman: University of Oklahoma Press, 1976).

Ali Emiri Efendi (b. 1857–d. 1924) *scholar, founder of the Turkish National Library* The son of Seyyid Mehmed Şerif and the grandson of poet Saim Seyyid Mehmed Emiri Çelebi, Ali Emiri was born in Diyarbakır in southeastern Turkey in 1857. After completing his primary education, Ali Emiri studied Persian and Arabic in Diyarbakır and in the nearby city of Mardin. During this period, he wrote poetry in the classical Ottoman style. Ali Emiri's writing, both published and unpublished, is extensive. He published reviews in important journals of his time including the *Osmanlı Tarih ve Edebiyat Mecmuası* (Journal of Ottoman history and literature), and *Tarih ve Edebiyat* (History and literature). His literary scholarship, his poetry, and his *Tezkire,* or collection of short biographies of the poets of various provinces and regions of his time, had a significant impact on the world of Turkish literature. Also, through his work as a member of the Ottoman Archives Classification Commission, classifying thousands of documents that are known today as the Ali Emiri Collection, Ali Emiri made an important contribution to scholarship in the field. After retiring in 1908, he moved to ISTANBUL.

Ali Emiri collected books while he traveled throughout Ottoman territory in the course of his official duties as a financial bureaucrat and inspector Although he spent all his earnings amassing a substantial library, Ali Emiri also borrowed and copied any book he was unable to purchase. Collecting was the passion of his life; he never married, and he retired early in order to devote more his time to this work. Ali Emiri's collection contains approximately 16,000 volumes, of which 8,800 are manuscripts and 7,200 are printed. Among the most valuable works are Kaşgarlı Mahmud's famous first dictionary of the Turkish language, the *Divan-ı Lügati't-Türk,* written between 1072 and 1074 C.E., as well as handwritten works by the 17th-century French playwright Molière and texts of the Turkish-Islamic world on language, literature, history, philosophy, and art. The French government offered to buy the whole library in order to obtain Molière's works; Ali Emiri turned down the offer, saying that he had collected the works for the Turkish nation. Ali Emiri endowed his collection to the Library of the Nation, founded in Istanbul on April 17, 1916, as part of the Feyzullah Efendi madrasa. The books that Ali Emiri endowed to the library were recorded and classified by language and subject. Turkish newspapers and journals in Arabic script and 46 edicts of various Ottoman sultans are found in the Ali Emiri section of the collection. Despite his painstaking efforts as a scholar and collector, Ali Emiri did not wish to have the library named after himself as benefactor; rather, he wanted it to be clearly identified as belonging to the state. The Library of the Nation was open to the public from 1962–93, during which time the books of the Carullah Efendi Library, the Hekimoglu Ali Pasha Library, the Pertev Pasha Library, and the Reşid Efendi Library were transferred to the Süleymaniye Library, the other major collection of manuscripts in Istanbul. In 1993 the Library of the Nation became a research library and adopted the Dewey decimal classification system. In 1999 the Marmara Earthquake caused serious damage to the library building and the collection was temporarily transferred to the Beyazıt Devlet Library.

Asiye Kakirman Yıldız

Further reading: Fahir İz, "Ali Emiri," in *Encyclopaedia of Islam,* 2nd ed., vol. 12 (supplement) (Leiden: Brill, 1960–), 63.

Ali Kuşçu (Qushji, Abu al-Qasim Ala al-Din Ali ibn Muhammad Qushji-zade) (b. ?–d. 1474) *Timurid philosopher, mathematician, and astronomer* Ali Kuşçu was a TIMURID philosopher, mathematician, and astronomer who produced original studies in both observational and theoretical astronomy. He broke new scientific ground by rejecting the principles of Aristotelian physics and metaphysics, thus laying the ground for a new physics. Although he followed a long line of Islamic astronomers by asserting that the earth is in motion, he did not depend on Aristotle's philosophical concepts to prove his assertion. Ali Kuşçu also contributed to the preparation of a pioneering astronomical handbook, *Zij,* under the auspices of the scholarly Timurid sultan Ulugh Beg (c. 1393 or 1394–1449) at the Samarkand Observatory. Near the end of his life, Ali Kuşçu emigrated to Istanbul at the invitation of Sultan MEHMED II (r. 1444–46; 1451–81) where his teaching and writings had an enormous impact on future generations of scholars.

Born in Samarkand, in present-day Uzbekistan, probably in the early 15th century, Kuşçu was the son of Ulugh Beg's falconer, whence his Turkish name Kuşçu-zade, "the son of the falconer." He took courses in linguistics, mathematics, astronomy, and other sciences taught by Ulugh Beg and other scholars in his circle. In 1420 Kuşçu moved to Kirman in what is now central Iran. In Kirman, Kuşçu studied astronomy and mathematics with the scholar Molla Cami (1414–92). Upon his return to Samarkand around 1428, Kuşçu presented Ulugh Beg with a monograph, *Hall ishkal al-qamar* (The solution of the question related to the moon). Sources say that Ulugh Beg referred to Kuşçu as "my virtuous son." Indeed, after the death of Kadızade, Ulugh Beg and Kuşçu's teacher and the second director of the Samarkand Observatory, Ulugh Beg commissioned Kuşçu to administer the Samarkand Observatory, which was instrumental in the preparation of Ulugh Beg's *Zij.* Kuşçu contributed to the preparation and correction of the handbook, but to what extent and at what stage is unclear. Later, Kuşçu criticized the *Zij* in his own *Commentary* on Ulugh Beg's astronomical handbook. In addition to his contributions to the *Zij,* Kuşçu wrote nine works on astronomy, two in Persian and seven in Arabic. Some of them are original contributions while others are textbooks.

After Ulugh Beg's death in 1449 Kuşçu, together with his family and students, spent a considerable time in Herat, Afghanistan, where he wrote his commentary to *Sharh al-Tajrid* by renowned scholar and astronomer Nasir al-Din al-Tusi (1201–74), which he presented to the Timurid Sultan Abu Said. In his commentary Kuşçu spells out the philosophical principles underlying his concept of existence, nature, knowledge, and language. After Abu Said's 1459 defeat by Uzun Hasan, the ruler of the Akkoyunlu Turkoman confederation, Kuşçu moved to Tabriz, Iran, where he was welcomed by Uzun Hasan. It is said that Kuşçu was sent to Istanbul to settle a dispute between Uzun Hasan and Mehmed II. After accomplishing the mission, Kuşçu returned to Tabriz. However, around 1472, Kuşçu, together with his family and students, left permanently for Istanbul either on his own initiative or because of an invitation from Sultan Mehmed.

When Kuşçu and his entourage approached Istanbul, Sultan Mehmed sent a group of scholars to welcome them. Sources say that in as they crossed the Bosporus to Istanbul, a discussion arose about the causes of its ebb and flow. Upon arriving in Istanbul, Kuşçu presented his mathematical work *al-Muhammadiyya fi al-hisab* (Treatise on arithmetic) to the sultan, which was named in Mehmed's honor. He wrote four additional books on mathematics, one in Persian and three in Arabic. His *Risala dar ilm al-hisab* (Treatise on the science of arithmetic), written in Persian during his stay in Central Asia (along with his extended Arabic version of this work, *al-Muhammadiyya fi al-hisab*), was taught as a mid-level textbook in Ottoman madrasas. In these works, in accordance with the principles he had outlined in the *Sharh al-Tajrid,* he tried to free mathematics from Hermetic-Pythagorean mysticism. As a result, Ottoman mathematics focused on practical applications, rather than on traditional areas such as the theory of numbers.

Kuşçu spent the remaining two to three years of his life in Istanbul. He first taught in the Sahn-i Seman madrasa, founded by Sultan Mehmed; then he was made head of the Ayasofya Madrasa. In this brief period, Kuşçu taught and influenced a large number of students who were to have an enormous impact on future generations of Ottoman scholars. He died in 1474 and was buried in the cemetery of the Eyyüb mosque.

Kuşçu, especially when compared with his contemporaries, was a remarkable polymath who excelled in a variety of disciplines, including language and literature, philosophy, theology, mathematics, and astronomy. He wrote books, textbooks, or short monographs in all these fields. His commentaries often became more popular than the original texts, and themselves were the subject of numerous commentaries. Thousands of copies of his works are extant today. Kuşçu's views were debated for centuries after his death, and he exerted a profound influence on Ottoman thought and scientific inquiry, in particular through the madrasas or colleges and their curriculum. His influence also extended to Central Asia and Iran, and it has been argued that he may well have had an influence, either directly or indirectly, on early modern European science, which bear a striking resemblance to some of his ideas.

İhsan Fazlıoğlu

Further reading: İhsan Fazlıoğlu, "Qushji," in *Biographical Encyclopaedia of Astronomers*, edited by Thomas Hockey (New York: Springer, 2007) II: 946–948; David Pingree, "Indian Reception of Muslim Versions of Ptolemaic Astronomy," in *Tradition, Transmission, Transformation: Proceedings of Two Conferences on Pre-modern Science Held at the University of Oklahoma*, edited by F. Jamil Ragep and Sally P. Ragep (Leiden: E. J. Brill, 1996), 471–485; F. Jamil Ragep, "Tūsī and Copernicus: The Earth's Motion in Context." *Science in Context* 14 (2001): 145–163; F. Jamil Ragep, "Freeing Astronomy from Philosophy: An Aspect of Islamic Influence on Science." *Osiris* 16 (2001): 49–71; F. Jamil Ragep, "Ali Qushji and Regiomontanus: Eccentric Transformations and Copernican Revolutions." *Journal History of Astronomy* 36 (2005): 359–371; George Saliba, "Al-Qūshjī's Reform of the Ptolemaic Model for Mercury." *Arabic Sciences and Philosophy* 3 (1993): 161–203.

Âlî Pasha, Mehmed Emin (b. 1815–d. 1871) *Ottoman statesman and grand vizier* Âlî Pasha was one of the most outstanding statesmen of the Tanzimat reform period of the 19th century. He was born in Istanbul on March 15, 1815 and was originally named Mehmed Emin. The son of a small shop owner in the Egyptian Market (Mısır Çarşısı), Âlî Pasha eventually became grand vizier five times and foreign minister eight times.

Language study was the original means for the advancement of Mehmed Emin's career. Three years after beginning primary school, Mehmed Emin began to study Arabic. In 1833, with his formal schooling complete, he was appointed to the Translation Bureau (Terceme Odası) where he studied French for two years. Concurrently he mastered the official Ottoman writing style and handling of bureaucratic affairs. In doing so, he gained the confidence and favor of Mustafa Reşid Pasha, an important statesman and diplomat of the Tanzimat period. With Reşid Pasha's help, Mehmed Emin's advancement was greatly expedited, leading to several important diplomatic and bureaucratic positions: second clerk at the Vienna embassy (1835), interpreter to the Imperial Council (1837), chargé d'affaires in London (1838), undersecretary of the Ministry of Foreign Affairs (1840), ambassador to London (1841), and member of the Supreme Council for Judicial Ordinances (Meclis-i Vala-yı Ahkam-ı Adliye, 1844). During his time working for the Ottoman administration he was nicknamed Âlî ("tall"), most likely in ironic reference to his short stature. His real name was soon forgotten, and he was referred to as Âlî Efendi from that point on. In 1846, Mustafa Reşid Pasha became the grand vizier, and Âlî Efendi was appointed minister of foreign affairs. Two years later, in 1848, he was honored with the title pasha. Although Âlî Pasha lost his position as minister of foreign affairs with the dismissal of Reşid Pasha, within the same year (1848), both returned to their former posts. In 1852 Reşid Pasha was again dismissed; however, this time Âlî Pasha was appointed grand vizier.

During his first term as grand vizier, he tried to form his own work team, appointing his close friend Fuad Pasha as minister of foreign affairs. However, Âlî Pasha was dismissed before the end of the year. In 1853 he was appointed provincial governor of Izmir. The following year, 1854, he was appointed governor of Hüdavendigar (also known as Bursa). Still in 1854, he was made the head of the newly founded Council of the Tanzimat and reinstated as the minister of foreign affairs while Reşid Pasha began his fourth term as grand vizier.

Following the outbreak of the Crimean War in 1853, Âlî Pasha was sent to Vienna for negotiations. In 1855 he was appointed grand vizier for the second time. The following year he was sent to Paris as the Ottoman representative at the Paris peace conference, ultimately signing the Treaty of Paris of 1856 that ended the Crimean War. However, he was dismissed from office on the grounds that he failed to represent the interests of the empire during the Paris peace conference. The death of Reşid Pasha in 1858 led to Âlî Pasha's elevation to grand vizier once again, but he was dismissed a year later, discharged on this occasion for failing to solve the empire's economic crises as well as openly criticizing the extravagance of the palace. Despite this censure, he was once again appointed the head of the Council of the Tanzimat, which was followed in 1861 by his sixth term as minister of foreign affairs.

In 1861, following the enthronement of Sultan Abdülaziz (r. 1861–76), Âlî Pasha was made grand vizier for the fourth time. He was dismissed after only four months and was made minister of foreign affairs for the seventh time, this time remaining in office for six years. In 1867 Âlî Pasha began his fifth term as grand vizier, but was criticized this time for what his rivals viewed as soft international policies.

Despite the fact that he was under constant criticism, Âlî Pasha remained aware of the empire's flaws and of the ever-changing dynamic of European international power politics. Accordingly, he advocated compromise in international relations, and supported domestic reforms. Âlî Pasha was a statesman who firmly observed state principles and etiquette, and who was appreciated by his contemporaries in Europe. Following the death of Fuad Pasha in 1869, Âlî Pasha again took over the Ministry of

Foreign Affairs as well as the grand vizierate, in which he served until his death on September 7, 1871. He is buried in the Süleymaniye Cemetery in Istanbul.

İlhami Yurdakul

Further reading: Butrus Abu-Manneh, "The Roots of the Ascendancy of Âli and Fu'ad Paşas at the Porte (1855–1871)," *Tanzimat'ın 150. Yıldönümü Sempozyumu,* Ankara 1994, 135–144; Roderic H. Davison, *Reform in the Ottoman Empire, 1856–1876* (Princeton, N.J.: Princeton University Press, 1963).

Ali Pasha of Janina (Tepedelenli Ali Pasha) (b. ca. 1744–d. 1822) *governor of Janina, quasi-independent ruler of much of the southwestern Ottoman Balkans*   Known as Ali Pasha of Janina the future governor of Janina (Ionnina, Yanina), Ali Pasha was born in Tepedelen (Tepelenë, southern Albania) or a nearby village into a family that had started gaining importance in the late 17th century. Having lost his father rather early, Ali Pasha was forced to affirm his position in local politics first as a bandit chieftain. By 1784 he had managed to establish himself as a power recognized by the Ottoman government. His political flair and successes against his rivals earned him the post of governor or *mutasarrıf* of Delvine and Janina. During this next phase in his rise, until 1812, which marked the peak of his territorial expansion, Ali Pasha controlled the continental provinces south of the Durrës-Bitola-Salonika line except for Attica, with southern ALBANIA and Epirus as the core of his possessions.

In an attempt to use him as a counterbalance to other powerful notables, or AYAN, in the region, the Ottoman government gave Ali Pasha additional areas of control. In 1785 he was appointed governor of Trikkala; in 1786 he was made guardian of the mountain passes, that is, chief of police forces consisting of Christian militia and Albanian Muslim irregulars; and in 1802, for a year, he was appointed governor of Rumelia. Ali Pasha's sons were also appointed to powerful positions. Muhtar Pasha was given Karlıeli and Euboea (Eğriboz) in 1792, and Avlonya in 1810; and Veli Pasha was granted Morea (Peloponnese) in 1807. At the same time Ali Pasha continued to pursue his goals, independent of the central authority in Istanbul, conquering lands from France, seizing power from Albanian notables, and taking control from Ottoman officials and from the semiautonomous tribes of Souli and Himara in the mountainous areas of Thessaly, Greece, and present-day southern Albania.

Ali Pasha's decline was precipitated by the policy of centralization undertaken by Sultan MAHMUD II (r. 1808–39) and the changes in international relations after the fall of NAPOLEON BONAPARTE. One of the few powerful Balkan notables still preserving his autonomy, in 1820 Ali Pasha was ordered to withdraw from all territories outside Janina. Ali Pasha tried to negotiate with ISTANBUL, at the same time establishing contacts with RUSSIA and with members of PHILIKI HETAIRIA, a Greek political group, which was preparing to rise up against the Ottomans. In the winter of 1820, after talks with the central government broke down, the Ottoman troops besieged Janina, engaging most of the Ottoman forces in Europe, and ultimately contributing to the success of the Greek revolt (*see* GREEK WAR OF INDEPENDENCE) and the establishment of the first independent successor state in the Balkans. Ali Pasha surrendered in January 1822 and was assassinated soon after.

Ali Pasha showed admirable diplomatic and military talents, using to his advantage the opportunities created by the emergence of the EASTERN QUESTION, the French revolutionary wars, and the weakened Ottoman central authority. Gradually, he built up a quasi-state and an enormous financial empire based on large land estates, customs duties, extortion, and confiscation. At the same time, until 1820, Ali Pasha never openly defied Ottoman central authority and regularly submitted the taxes due from his provinces.

Ali Pasha pursued an independent foreign policy, flirting with the powers involved in the region's politics. Within his domain, he seems to have ensured relative security, which earned him widespread support among his subjects, especially the upper strata of Greek Christians and, to a certain degree, among Albanian villagers. Christians served in his military forces, occupied administrative positions in his government, and assisted him in his diplomatic contacts with the Christian powers. He allowed limited freedom of religious beliefs, even permitting the construction of new churches. During Ali Pasha's rule, Janina became one of the major centers of Greek scholarship.

One of the most popular figures of his time and a protagonist in works by a number of European writers, including Lord Byron, Alexandre Dumas, Victor Hugo, and Mór Jókai, Ali Pasha became the subject of many historical myths. Some of them were forged by himself, others—especially ones related to his supposed struggle for the establishment of an independent Albanian state—came into being much later.

Rossitsa Gradeva

Further reading: Nathalie Clayer, "The Myth of Ali Pasha and the Bektashis or the Construction of an Albanian Bektashi National History," in *Albanian Identities: Myth and History,* edited by Stephanie Schwandner-Sievers and Bernd Fischer (London: Hurst, 2002), 127–133; Katherine E. Fleming, *The Muslim Bonaparte: Diplomacy and Orientalism in Ali Pasha's Greece* (Princeton, N.J.: Princeton University Press, 1999); Stanford Shaw, *Between Old and New: The Ottoman Empire under Sultan Selim III,*

1789–1807 (Cambridge, Mass.: Harvard University Press, 1971), 228–30, 298–301, and passim.

aliya Aliya is a pilgrimage for JEWS; the term has been used to refer to a temporary or permanent return to the ancient Jewish homeland. The term derives from the Hebrew word for "ascent," but as going to JERUSALEM involved traveling uphill, it also came to be understood as a spiritually uplifting experience for the pilgrims; going to Jerusalem for Jews involved an ascent both of the body and the spirit. Originally, aliya referred only to a Jewish religious pilgrimage to Jerusalem, but once ZIONISM developed as an ideology, the word took on a new meaning of immigration of Jews to Palestine, whether they were going for spiritual reasons or not.

In the last decades of the 19th century, aliya became a significant way in which Jews in the Russian Empire could escape persecution. Some would emigrate to the Americas and others would join the revolutionary movements that were seeking to overthrow the czar's regime. But still others sought a return to Palestine, or Eretz Yisrael (the Land of Israel), where Jews could create new lives. People who believed in that solution to the problems of persecution and anti-Semitism formed a network of organizations in different Russian cities in the 1880s known as Hovevei Tzion (Lovers of Zion) to encourage emigration from Russia and settlement in PALESTINE, then a part of the Ottoman Empire. Starting in 1882, some of the idealists of the group moved to Palestine.

Unlike earlier Jewish pilgrims to Palestine who had settled in the holy cities such Jerusalem, Hebron, Safed, and Tiberias, the new arrivals sought to create Jewish agricultural settlements such as those founded at Rishon le-Zion and Zikhron Yaqov on the coastal plain of what is today Israel, between the cities of HAIFA and Tel Aviv. By 1891, the new settlers had founded eight settlements with a population of over 2,000. Although their numbers were small, they served as the pioneers of a movement for a return to Zion that would gain strength as the 20th century progressed. Later generations would label that group of early pioneers the First Aliya.

The Second Aliya began in 1904 and lasted until 1914, when the outbreak of WORLD WAR I put an end to it. Unlike its predecessor, the Second Aliya was relatively well organized and was financed by the newly formed World Zionist Congress and the Jewish National Fund. The immigrants of this wave were ideologically committed to building a new society for Jews that they believed should be based in socialism and hard work. To promote those ideals, they established collective farms known as *kibbutzim.* Within those settlements, all members of the collective shared the land and the work; this was in contrast with the agricultural settlements of the First Aliya,

called *moshavim,* where the land was privately held. Not all who came in the Second Aliya embraced that view of a return to the soil, however. In 1909, Jewish immigrants founded Tel Aviv on the Mediterranean seacoast north of the old port city of Jaffa to serve as the first modern, and wholly Jewish, city in Palestine.

The total number who participated in the Second Aliya was probably only about 10,000, some of whom subsequently left Palestine during World War I. But those who stayed included many who founded and led the new State of Israel after its creation in 1948. Furthermore, the ideology that the majority had embraced, Labor Zionism, would serve as the ideological foundation of many of the early institutions in Israel.

Bruce Masters

Further reading: Amos Elon, *The Israelis: Founders and Sons* (New York: Holt, Rinehart, and Winston, 1971).

Alliance Israélite Universelle The DAMASCUS INCIDENT of 1840, in which prominent Jews were arrested and tortured by ruling Egyptian authorities in DAMASCUS, awakened concern among the JEWS of western Europe for the safety of their coreligionists in the Muslim world. In 1860 a group of wealthy French Jews formed the Alliance Israélite Universelle for what they called the "regeneration" of the Jews of the East, as they viewed the Jews of the Middle East and North Africa as being mired in tradition. Jews elsewhere in Europe responded enthusiastically to their appeal and the membership of the Alliance rose from 850 in 1861 to more than 30,000 members in 1885. The Alliance captured the imagination of large numbers of middle-class Jewish people, as well as the elite, and these groups were willing to make contributions to fund the Alliance's modernist educational mission. This paternalistic mission toward the Jews of the Ottoman Empire sought to spread a French vision of "modernity" that included schools offering secular subjects such as the sciences, French literature, and history.

The Alliance's success in convincing students to choose their modern Jewish approach to education, as opposed to a Christian school or a traditional Jewish religious school (*heder*), varied from city to city. One of the problems was that the Jewish communities in Ottoman lands had not benefited to the same extent as Christian communities from the empire's growing integration into a capitalist world economy. Many of the Jews of the empire were still traditionalist in their outlook and wary of contact with outsiders, even Jewish outsiders. Another difficulty was that Christian schools were seen as offering ties to the Western powers.

Despite the pull of tradition and the prestige of the Christian-sponsored alternatives, the Alliance could claim substantial success in its mission "to bring light to the Jews of the East." This was especially true in western Anatolia and the Balkans. There were 115 Alliance schools scattered throughout the Ottoman Empire at the start of WORLD WAR I when it was estimated that roughly 35 percent of school-age Jewish children in the empire were attending Alliance schools.

French was the primary language of instruction in the Alliance schools in Anatolia, the Balkans, BEIRUT, EGYPT, and NORTH AFRICA; Arabic was used along with French in Alliance schools in IRAQ and Damascus. Given that linguistic orientation, it has been suggested that although the schools helped prepare students to face the economic and social transformation of their societies, they did little to help integrate them politically into the wider Muslim community in which they lived. Rather, they served to create a cultural bond between students and the West, which fostered emigration. (The same critique is also valid for Christian missionary schools.)

While the children of the Jewish and Muslim elite might attend Christian schools, and Christian and Muslim students could on occasion be found in an Alliance-sponsored school, education remained largely sectarian in the Ottoman Empire. Non-Muslims generally avoided the government schools and Muslim clergy strenuously tried to prevent their flock from attending Christian or Jewish schools. On one level the schools founded by Jewish and Christian organizations, headquartered outside the empire, were a success. By the start of the First World War, Jews and Christians in the Ottoman Empire enjoyed much higher rates of literacy than did their Muslim neighbors.

Bruce Masters

See also JEWS; MISSIONARIES.

Further reading: Aron Rodrigue, *French Jews, Turkish Jews: The Alliance Israélite Universelle and the Politics of Jewish Schooling in Turkey, 1860–1925* (Bloomington: Indiana University Press, 1990).

al-Wahhab, Muhammad *See* IBN ABD AL-WAHHAB, MUHAMMAD.

American Board of Commissioners for Foreign Missions Congregationalist ministers from Massachusetts and Connecticut in the United States formed the Board of Commissioners for Foreign Missions in Boston in 1810 to spread their brand of evangelical Christianity around the globe. The word "American" was added later to create the initials ABCFM. It would become the principal American Protestant missionary enterprise in the Ottoman Empire. The initial goal of the mission to the empire was the conversion of the JEWS of the Holy Land and the first mission station was established in JERUSALEM. However, Ottoman Jews proved resistant to the Protestant version of Christianity. Faced with indifference or open hostility in Jerusalem, ABCFM moved their operations to BEIRUT in 1823, and began to proselytize among local Christians there. They justified this targeting of their "brothers and sisters in Christ" by characterizing them as being "nominal Christians" in need of the "true Gospel." The Americans met immediate opposition from local church hierarchies—especially the MARONITES, a Uniate Catholic sect (*see* UNIATES) that was prominent in what is today LEBANON—who banned their flocks from having any contact with the Americans. Catholic pressure led the Ottoman government, or Sublime Porte, to ban the import of Bibles printed in Arabic from Europe, just as Orthodox pressure had led to a similar banning of imported religious books by Roman Catholics almost exactly a century before. An additional irony lay in the fact that the Bibles the Protestant missionaries were handing out were simply reprints of the Arabic translation of the Bible that Rome had produced in 1671, minus the Apocrypha. To get around the ban, the Board moved their press from MALTA to Beirut in 1834, establishing what would later become an important source for printed Arabic books, both religious and secular, in the 19th century.

After settling in Beirut, the ABCFM embarked on an ambitious program to establish mission stations throughout the Ottoman Empire. In addition to promoting their own version of Christianity, these stations offered schools and medical clinics. By the middle of the 19th century, the directors of the ABCFM realized that actual conversion to Protestantism was proceeding at a slow pace and made a conscious decision to increase their efforts in education in the hope that the example of the American missionaries would convince the young men and women of the Ottoman Empire to accept that their version of Christianity. To further that plan, the Board approved the opening of Robert College, today Boğaziçi University, in Istanbul in 1863, and the Syrian Protestant College, later the American University, in Beirut in 1866.

ABCFM missionaries continued to try to win converts to Protestantism and had some limited success among the Armenians of central and southern Anatolia. But with Protestants in the Ottoman Empire only numbering in the tens of thousands, or less than even one percent of the Empire's Christians at the start of WORLD WAR I, it was the secular education provided by the ABCFM that was ultimately its legacy to the peoples of the former Ottoman Empire.

Bruce Masters

See also MISSIONARIES.

Further reading: Adnan Abu-Ghazaleh, *American Missions in Syria* (Brattleboro, Vt.: Amana Books, 1990); Ussama Makdisi, "Reclaiming the Land of the Bible: Missionaries,

Secularism, and Evangelical Modernism." *The American Historical Review* 102 (1997): 680–713.

amir al-hajj The *amir al-hajj* was the official responsible for the supply of water and fodder for the animals of those making the annual pilgrimage, or HAJJ, to MECCA and for the military escort of the pilgrims. In the 15th through the 17th centuries the man holding the post was often a local military officer with political and economic ties to the BEDOUINS, although occasionally an Ottoman official from ISTANBUL would be appointed to the post. In the 18th century, however, the person holding the post of governor of DAMASCUS took on the role as Bedouin raids against the hajj CARAVAN became more frequent and devastating. Protecting the hajj became the major responsibility of the city's governors and their ability to carry it out was the most important criterion for determining whether they had governed well. The political success of the AL-AZM FAMILY of Damascus was due in no small part to their success at maintaining the security of the hajj in their capacity of as the *amir al-hajj*. In the 19th century, with the decline of the Bedouin threat after the restoration of Ottoman rule to SYRIA, the post became an honorary one that was usually filled by a notable from Damascus.

Bruce Masters

Anatolian emirates Anatolian emirates or *beyliks* is the term commonly used to refer to the semi-independent Turkoman principalities that emerged in Anatolia (present-day Turkey) after the Rum SELJUK Empire collapsed toward the end of the 13th century. Before the emergence of the Ottomans around 1300, the Rum Seljuks established the strongest and most important Turkish state in Asia Minor in the 1070s. However, in 1243, at the Battle of Kösedağ (near present-day Erzincan in Turkey) the Rum Seljuks were defeated by the Mongols, who invaded Persia and Asia Minor. Following this defeat, the Seljuks became the vassals of the Ilkhanid Mongol State, based in Persia. In the ensuing power vacuum, several semi-independent Turkoman principalities emerged in Anatolia, of which the Ottomans were but one. Other Turkoman principalities in Anatolia included the Danishmendid, Saltukid, Mengujekid, and Artukid emirates, in the central and eastern parts of Anatolia. These political bodies bordered the eastern edge of the BYZANTINE EMPIRE. Combined with the Seljuks and the immigration of Turkic tribes into the Anatolian mainland, they spread Turkish and Islamic influence in Anatolia. Unlike the Seljuks, whose language of administration was Persian, the Karamanids and other Anatolian Turkish emirates adopted spoken Turkish as their formal literary language. The Turkish language achieved widespread use in these principalities and reached its highest sophistication during the Ottoman era.

THE KARAMANIDS (C. 1256–1483)

The oldest and most powerful of these Turkoman emirates was that of the Karamanids. Established in Ermenak around 1256, it also became the fiercest rival of the emerging Ottoman state. The Karamanid principality had also been a constant threat to Mongol-Seljukid domination in central Anatolia, and after the disintegration of the Seljukid dynasty the Karamanids took over the central territories of the former Seljukid administration, including its capital city, Konya. They proclaimed themselves the sole inheritors of Seljukid power and, during their confrontation with the Ottomans, they continued to claim suzerainty over other Turkoman principalities. They resisted Ottoman growth by forming alliances with Venice and the Papacy in Europe, and the Akkoyunlu or White Sheep Turkoman confederation (1340–1514) in the east who expanded their dominance over eastern Anatolia, Azerbaijan, and Iraq at the peak of their political power in the 15th century. Despite these attempts, the Karamanid principality was eventually incorporated into the Ottoman Empire during the reign of MEHMED II (r. 1444–46; 1451–81), although the last known Karaman bey ruled until 1483. Local resistance to Ottoman suzerainty persisted until the beginning of the 16th century.

EMIRATES ALONG THE BLACK SEA COAST

In the last decade of the 12th century, Emir Hüsameddin Çoban, one of the leading Seljukid *uç* beys or frontier commanders, founded the Çobanoğulları emirate in Kastamonu. After the empire of Trebizond—an offshoot of the Byzantine Empire founded in 1204 after European crusaders captured Constantinople—occupied Sinop in 1266, the Çobanoğulları emirate became one of the most powerful principalities on the Byzantine frontier. During the period 1277–1322 Sinop and its surrounding area remained under the control of Pervaneoğulları, another local emirate in the region, which later occupied Bafra and Samsun and organized naval campaigns in the Black Sea. In 1292 Kastamonu came under the control of the Candaroğulları principality (also known as Isfendiyaroğulları). Due to its close relations with the Ottomans, the Candaroğulları principality survived until 1462.

Many other small principalities of Turkoman origin also came into being. Among these the Taceddinoğulları principality (1348–1428), founded in close proximity to the Trebizond Empire, expanded over the territory from Bafra-Ordu to Niksar. There were also some other peripheral principalities supposedly bound to Taceddinoğulları that eventually acted for their own benefit.

EMIRATES IN WESTERN ANATOLIA

The emirate of Ladik, also known as the Inançoğulları, which formed in the Denizli-Honaz region of the western Anatolian border lands, was another early Turkoman principality. Mehmed Bey, the Turkoman chieftain of the region, declared sovereignty in 1261 after rebelling against the Seljukid ruler Keykavus II (r. 1246–62). The resulting emirate lasted until 1368.

In the second half of the 13th century the Beyşehir-Seydişehir region saw the rise of the Eşrefoğulları, who disputed Karaman rule in and around Konya, although unsuccessfully. They captured the town of Bolvadin in 1320.

In the neighboring region of Isparta, the principality of Hamidoğulları was founded around 1301. Following the flight of the region's Mongol governor to the MAMLUK EMPIRE, the principality became independent and seized many of the surrounding territories. This suzerainty did not last, however, and the Hamidoğulları lands were eventually divided between the Ottomans and the Karamanids. The Tekeoğulları principality, the last of the western borderland principalities, was established in Antalya at the beginning of the 13th century and was ruled by a branch of the Hamidoğulları family.

"TOWN-PRINCIPALITIES" IN CENTRAL ANATOLIA

Despite the continued presence of Seljukid-Mongol rule in central Asia Minor during the 14th century, several autonomous towns came into existence, including Amasya, Tokat, and Sivas. With the death of the Ilkhanid ruler Ebu Said in 1335, administration of Asia Minor was entrusted to his former governor Eretna Bey, originally an Uighur Turk, who eventually declared himself independent and sought the protection of the Mamluks, the Ilkhanids' major rival in the region. He captured the area around Sivas-Kayseri. During the rule of his son, Mehmed Bey, the emirs bound to the emirate of Eretna grew stronger.

In 1381 Kadı Burhaneddin (d. 1398), a judge (kadı) in Kayseri who was also appointed vizier to represent the emirate of Eretna in that town, brought an end to Eretna's domination of Sivas and established his own government. Kadı Burhaneddin also captured Amasya and Tokat, extending his influence to the eastern shores of northeastern Anatolia. His principality staved off interference in central Anatolia from both the Akkoyunlus and the Ottomans until it collapsed with his death in 1398.

EMIRATES IN EASTERN ANATOLIA

In the eastern and southern parts of Asia Minor the Karakoyunlus, a Turkoman confederation (1380–1468) based in Azerbaijan and Iraq, were the dominant force until they were succeeded by a rival Turkoman confederation, the Akkoyunlus, who ruled over much of eastern Anatolia and Azerbaijan from their capital in Diyarbakır.

In Maraş the powerful Dulkadiroğulları (1339–1521) managed to survive for almost two centuries despite being surrounded by the Ottomans, Mamluks, and Akkoyunlus. Early in the state's history, the Dulkadiroğulları accepted a loosely affiliated vassal status with the Ottomans; they were fully incorporated into the Ottoman Empire around 1530.

The neighboring Ramazanoğulları principality, an emirate in ancient Cilicia in southeastern Asia Minor with its capital in Adana, also showed impressive longevity. Despite being at the frontier zone between the Ottomans and the Mamluks, it managed to survive until the Mamluks were conquered by the Ottomans in 1516–17. However, even after this date, members of the dynasty governed the territory as hereditary governors until 1608, when Adana became a regular Ottoman province.

MARITIME TURKISH PRINCIPALITIES IN WESTERN ANATOLIA

The Turkoman emirates in western Anatolia, including the Ottomans, were maritime principalities active in the Aegean Sea. Initially, the Germiyanoğulları principality (1300–1428) was the supreme force in the region. This principality was established by Turkomans in Kütahya who had immigrated to the western border because of Mongol pressure in the second half of the 13th century.

The coastal principalities of the Karasioğulları (1300–1360), Saruhanoğulları (1300–1415), Aydınoğulları (1308–1425), and Menteşeoğulları (1280–1424) were havens for pillaging in the Aegean Sea. Motivated by wealth and by GHAZA or holy war raiders launched naval attacks on the Aegean islands, the Greek mainland, the Peloponnesian peninsula, the Thrace district, and even the Balkans. At the same time, they also established commercial links with the Byzantine Empire and the maritime Italian city-states from which they benefited greatly.

The oldest of these four principalities was the Menteşeoğulları, founded in 1280 in Muğla in southwestern Turkey, along the Aegean coast. It was composed of Turkish settlers under the leadership of Menteşe Bey. The other three principalities—the Karasioğulları, Saruhanoğulları, and Aydınoğulları—appeared around the same time.

The Karasioğulları principality, centered in Balıkesir-Bergama, was founded by Karasi Bey. Karasi Bey was the son of Kalem Bey, an attendant of Yakub Bey of the Germiyanoğulları principality. The Karasioğulları principality was known for its naval activities in the waters close to the Byzantine center. Karasid mariners operated primarily along the southern edge of the Marmara coast and in the shallows of the Gallipoli peninsula. The Karasioğulları principality was the first of the four to accept Ottoman hegemony, and in 1360 the integration of the principality into the Ottoman state was complete. The Ottoman administration welcomed the Karasid mariners for they possessed a wealth of nautical knowledge as well as being familiar with the Balkan region upon which the Ottomans subsequently launched campaigns.

The Saruhanoğulları principality was established in Magnesia around 1310 and stretched seaward to the Menemen-Phokia line. It was founded by Saruhan Bey, who seems to have been a Turkoman chieftain; however, his personal history remains somewhat obscure. Saruhanoğulları sailed mainly in the Thrace region and occasionally entered into alliances with the Byzantines. The Saruhanoğulları principality lasted until the turn of the 15th century when it was absorbed as a *sancak* or subprovince of the Ottoman state.

The Aydınoğulları principality, which often acted in concert with the Saruhanoğulları, was founded in the region containing Aydın, Tyre, and Smyrna by Mehmed Bey (d. 1334), the son of Aydın. The former served Yakub Bey of the Germiyanoğulları principality as the the subaşı (commander). This principality gained impressive notoriety due to its naval campaigns that struck as far as the Peloponnesian shores. Individual mariners also managed to claim a modicum of fame. Most notably, Umur Bey (d. 1348), a *ghazi* or warrior for the Islamic faith, secured lasting fame in the Turkish maritime tradition. He is credited with having raided as far as Chios, the Peloponnesian peninsula, Thrace, Salonika, and even Macedonia as a Byzantine ally. Following his death, the Aydınoğulları eventually declined until they too fell under Ottoman control (1425–1426).

The Ottoman principality was formed around the Sakarya River in Bitinia (present-day western Turkey), and was initially a meager and unnoticed political entity. Encircled by the much more powerful principalities of Germiyanoğulları and Candaroğulları, the Ottoman emirate showed few initial signs of success. This anonymity lasted only as long as it took for the Ottomans to create a political relationship with the Byzantine Empire. The strategic importance of their location helped the Ottomans develop quickly and extend their influence over the surrounding principalities. The conquests of Bursa in 1326, Nikaia in 1331, and Nicomedia in 1337 brought the Ottomans closer to the heart of the Byzantine Empire. Following the occupation of the Marmara coast, they possessed a starting point from which they launched military operations into Thrace. The Ottoman entrance into Europe marked the beginning of the end for the Anatolian emirates. Shortly thereafter, the political unity present under the Seljukid throne was reestablished under the Ottoman state.

Feridun M. Emecen

Further reading: Clifford Edmund Bosworth, *The Islamic Dynasties: A Chronological and Genealogical Handbook* (Edinburgh: Edinburgh University Press, 1967), 129–140; Claude Cahen, "Note pour des Turkomans d'Asia mineure au XIIIᵉ siècle." *Journal Asiatique* 239 (1952): 335–354; Claude Cahen, *Pre-Ottoman Turkey* (London: Sidgwick & Jackson, 1968); Feridun Emecen, *İlk Osmanlılar ve Batı Anadolu Beylikler Dünyası* (Istanbul Kitabevi 2003); Halil İnalcık, "The Rise of the Turcoman Maritime Principalities in Anatolia, Byzantium and Crusades." *Byzantinische Forschungen* 11 (1985): 179–217; Speros Vryonis, *The Decline of Medieval Hellenism in Asia Minor and the Process of Islamization from the Eleventh through the Fifteenth Century* (Berkeley: University of California Press, 1986); Paul Wittek, *The Rise of the Ottoman Empire* (London: Royal Asiatic Society, 1938).

Anaza Confederation   The Anaza was a confederation of loosely related Bedouin tribes that starting moving from Najd in Arabia into the Syrian Desert in the late 17th century, displacing the Mawali Bedouins who had previously been the dominant tribe along the borders of the Ottoman Empire. This migration continued well into the 19th century. It is not certain what set this migration in motion, but due to the weakness of the Ottoman central government at that time, it went largely unopposed. Once the Anaza tribes dominated the open desert, they began to attack both the villages in the steppe lands on the desert's edge and caravans crossing this territory. The results were disastrous for trade, communications, and agricultural production

Increasingly subject to attack, by the end of the 18th century peasants abandoned as many as a third of the villages they had occupied at the start of the 17th century. In an attempt to reclaim land for agricultural production and to stem the depredations of the Anaza, the Ottoman government attempted various schemes to settle migrants from other parts of the empire into the steppe lands of the desert. In 1870, the Ottoman state created a new province at Dayr al-Zor along the Euphrates River in Syria to serve as an anchor for development of the region and to control the Bedouins. As the power of the central state grew in the 19th century, the level of destruction caused by raids from the Anaza Confederation diminished, although the possibility of Bedouin attacks on smaller caravans remained a possibility until the end of the empire.

Bruce Masters

See also al-Azm family; Bedouins.

Anglo-Ottoman Convention (1838)   In the 1830s, the Ottoman Empire was teetering on the verge of political collapse. The sultan's forces had not been able to stop Ibrahim Pasha's advance on Istanbul in 1832 using military means, and the Ottomans had to ask for British diplomatic help to secure a withdrawal to SYRIA of the Egyptian forces. The Ottoman government realized that British support was the only way to survive and so they agreed to a commercial treaty, filled with provisions that the British had been demanding for over a decade. Historians have labeled that agreement the Anglo-Ottoman Convention of 1838. British industry was already well established by this period, and British capitalists sought free-trade agreements that would allow them to sell their manufactured goods abroad at low tariffs while acquiring raw materials abroad, unhindered by export controls.

The agreement abolished all Ottoman state monopolies in foreign trade, prohibited the ban on exports of any commodity, and allowed British merchants to settle anywhere in the Ottoman Empire. While it actually raised duties on imports and exports slightly, the agreement abolished internal tariffs on British merchants moving goods between Ottoman provinces. Those internal tariffs remained in effect for Ottoman merchants and for merchants from other European nations. That inequity had long-ranging effects, as other European countries later followed England's lead and received similar treaties. Non-Muslim Ottoman merchants sought to get around the discriminatory clauses of such agreements by gaining protection from European powers. This eventually put Ottoman Muslim merchants at a distinct disadvantage as they found themselves continuing to pay taxes from which their competitors were exempt. The treaty also ended the Ottoman Empire's ability to set tariffs unilaterally as it had to negotiate any future changes in customs duties with Great Britain.

There has been much debate among historians over the impact of this early free trade treaty on Ottoman handicraft production. Nonetheless, by the end of the 19th century, cheap British manufactured goods had replaced many of the items formerly produced in Ottoman workshops. Furthermore, the trade balance between the Ottoman Empire and the West was overwhelmingly in the latter's favor, leading to the empire's default on its foreign loans in 1876.

Bruce Masters

See also ALEXANDRIA.

Further reading: Şevket Pamuk, *The Ottoman Empire and European Capitalism, 1820–1913: Trade, Investment, and Production* (Cambridge: Cambridge University Press, 1987).

Ankara, Battle of   Fought near Ankara (present-day capital of Turkey) on July 28, 1402, this was a decisive battle between the Ottoman Sultan BAYEZID I (r. 1389–1402) and TIMUR, a cruel and skillful military leader of Mongol descent from Transoxania (present-day Uzbekistan) and founder (r. 1370–1405) of the Timurid Empire in Central Asia and Iran. Timur's victory in this battle

significantly altered the power balance in the region, for Sultan Bayezid died in Timur's captivity in March 1403 and the very existence of the Ottoman state was threatened. However, under sultans MEHMED I (r. 1413–21) and MURAD II (r. 1421–44, 1446–51), the Ottomans managed to rebuild their state and reassert their rule over much of their former territories. Half a century after the devastating Battle of Ankara, Ottoman armies under MEHMED II (r. 1444–46; 1451–81) conquered Constantinople (*see* CONSTANTINOPLE, CONQUEST OF), the seat of the BYZANTINE EMPIRE, and emerged as the dominant power in southeastern Europe and Asia Minor.

When, in the late 1390s, Bayezid I extended his rule over eastern Anatolia, the clash between the Ottomans and Timur became unavoidable. Timur claimed descent from Genghis Khan (r. 1206–27), the founder of the Mongol Empire, and thus considered himself the ruler of all territories once controlled by the Ilkhanid Mongols, including Seljuk-Ilkhanid Anatolia. Timur thus demanded that Bayezid accepted him as suzerain. In open defiance, Bayezid turned to the head of SUNNI ISLAM, the caliph in CAIRO, and requested the title of "sultan of Rum," used by the Rum SELJUKS, whom the Ottomans considered their ancestors. The Turkoman principalities of eastern Anatolia and Azerbaijan tried to maneuver between Bayezid and Timur, giving ample pretext for each ruler to attack the other. The Karakoyunlu (Black Sheep) Turkoman confederation (1380–1468), who were in the process of extending their rule from the region of Lake Van (eastern Turkey) to Azerbaijan, sided with Bayezid. Their rivals, the Akkoyunlu (White Sheep) Turkoman confederation (1378–1508)—whose territories in eastern Anatolia including their capital in Diyarbakır were threatened by the Ottomans' eastward expansion—appealed to Timur. The latter responded by launching a campaign against the Ottomans and their allies.

After conquering ALEPPO, DAMASCUS, and BAGHDAD (1400–01), Timur left his winter headquarters in the CAUCASUS for Anatolia in early summer 1402. He marched into Asia Minor to recapture the disputed fortress of Kemah, which controlled the upper EUPHRATES RIVER and had recently been seized by Bayezid. The fortress fell within 10 days and Timur continued to Sivas in northern Anatolia, which had been seized by the Ottomans in 1398. Here the Ottoman envoys rejected Timur's demands to surrender the captive sultan of Baghdad and the chief of the Karakoyunlu Turkomans, both of whom had sided with Bayezid against Timur and found refuge with the Ottomans. Timur's army advanced to Ankara and laid siege to the castle there. The siege was lifted when scouts brought news of the approaching Ottoman army.

The ensuing battle between Timur and the Ottoman army took place at Çubukovası (Çubuk Plain), northeast of Ankara, on Friday, July 28, 1402. Figures regarding the size of the opposing armies vary from several hundred thousand to the rather far-fetched 1.6 million. Reliable modern estimates put the number of men in Timur's army at 140,000 and in Bayezid's army at 85,000. Among those in Timur's army were the rulers of the Turkoman principalities of western Anatolia (Germiyanoğulları, Aydınoğulları, Menteşeoğulları, Saruhanoğulları) whose lands had been conquered by Bayezid. Many of their former subjects, however, were in Bayezid's camp, along with the Ottoman sultan's vassals in the Balkans, including Stephen Lazarević of SERBIA.

Apart from their numerical inferiority and exhaustion, another factor that significantly weakened the Ottomans was their lack of fresh water resources, a major drawback in the hot Anatolian summer. Most accounts agree that Timur destroyed the wells situated around Ankara. Modern scholarship has suggested that Timur had also diverted the Çubuk Creek that flowed on the Çubuk Plain by constructing a diversion dam and an off-stream reservoir south of the town of Çubuk, denying drinking water to the Ottoman fighting forces and their horses on the day of the battle.

The battle started around nine in the morning of July 28 and lasted until late evening. Despite all their disadvantages, the Ottomans fought successfully for a while. When, however, the Kara (Black) Tatars on the Ottoman left wing, in a treacherous agreement with Timur, attacked the Ottomans' back, and when the cavalrymen from the recently subjugated emirates deserted, Sultan Bayezid's fate was sealed. He fought bravely with his JANISSARIES and Serbian vassals until he was defeated and captured.

Ottoman domains in eastern and central Anatolia, recently seized by Bayezid from the Anatolian Turkoman principalities, were restored by the victor to their former lords. A bitter fight started among Bayezid's sons over the remaining Ottoman realms, and a decade of interregnum and civil war almost led to the downfall of the Ottoman sultanate. Fortunately for the Ottomans, however, basic institutions of state—such as the Ottoman land tenure system and the structures of central and provincial administration—had already taken root, and large segments of Ottoman society had vested interests in restoring the power of the House of Osman.

Gábor Ágoston

See also ANATOLIAN EMIRATES.

Further reading: Ahmad Ibn Muhammad (Ibn Arabshah), *Tamerlane, or Timur the Great Amir,* trans. John Herne Sanders (London: Luzac & Co, 1936); Colin Imber, *The Ottoman Empire, 1300–1481* (Istanbul: Isis, 1990); David Morgan, *Medieval Persia, 1040–1797* (London: Longman, 1988).

Antioch (*Ar.:* **Antaqiyya;** *Turk.:* **Antakya**) Antioch is today in southern Turkey near the Syrian border. It was an

important city in the BYZANTINE EMPIRE and it became the capital of a crusader state in the 12th century. However, under the MAMLUK EMPIRE (1260–1516), it lost most of it former population and was reduced to fewer than 1,000 inhabitants. At some time during the Mamluk period, the Orthodox patriarch of Antioch, who had formerly been resident in the city, moved his place of residence to DAMASCUS while continuing to hold the title "patriarch of Antioch and all of the East." In the Ottoman period, the town's fortunes revived a little as it provided an important stop for the mule CARAVANS traveling between ALEPPO and its port of ALEXANDRETTE. It was approximately two days from Antioch to either location. Due to its location in the hills, European merchants resident in Aleppo often used Antioch as a summer resort to get away from the heat of Aleppo's summers. They also thought Antioch had "healthier air," and fled there during the periodic outbreaks of bubonic PLAGUE that afflicted Aleppo.

Bruce Masters

Antun, Farah (b. 1874–d. 1922) *Arab intellectual and author* Farah Antun was a Christian Arab journalist and novelist. He was born in TRIPOLI in the area that is LEBANON today, but spent most of his adult life in CAIRO and New York. Perhaps his most famous work was a study of the medieval Islamic philosopher ibn Rushd, which was published in Cairo in 1903. He presented the philosopher as a modern humanist who understood religion as a metaphor for a moral code by which humans should live, and informed people about how they should treat one another. The book explicated Antun's own view of the world in which science provides the necessary tools for living and constructing a just society, all the while ascribing his views to ibn Rushd. Under the guise of appealing to an ancient authority, Antun was attempting to introduce in Arabic the positivist French philosophy of the late 19th century using a Muslim pedigree.

Antun argued that religion and science should each have their separate spheres and that political states should not privilege one religion over another. Religious leaders, he wrote, often used religion as a way of misleading people for their own ends and of promoting hatred. His opinions were obviously shaped by his status as a Christian in a region where the majority of the population was Muslim and that had recently experienced sectarian violence directed at his religious community. Antun sought to make common ground with modernist Muslim thinkers who were seeking to adapt Western political and scientific thought to Islam. He had been friends with both MUHAMMAD ABDUH and MUHAMMAD RASHID RIDA, two of the most prominent Muslim "modernists." However, the publication of Antun's book ended these relationships as the two felt that Antun was distorting the ideas of ibn Rushd, who was viewed as one of the greatest Muslim thinkers of the medieval period.

Antun did not give up on his hopes for sectarian harmony, however. In 1904 he published a novel, *New Jerusalem,* which he set in the period following the Muslim conquest of Jerusalem in the seventh century C.E. In it, he highlighted the tolerance the Muslim rulers showed toward their non-Muslim subjects.

Antun left Cairo in 1904 for New York, where he contributed articles to the Arabic-language newspaper *al-Huda.* he returned to Cairo after the YOUNG TURK Revolution of 1908 because he believed that the best hope for Syria's future lay in the Ottoman Empire and felt he could accomplish more from a base in Cairo than from New York. It is unclear why he did not return then to his homeland, however, and he died in Cairo in 1922.

Bruce Masters

See also NAHDA.

Arabistan (the Arabic-speaking lands)

Arabistan in Turkish today refers to the Arabian peninsula that is, the part of southwest Asia south of the Syrian Desert that includes Saudi Arabia, YEMEN, Oman, the United Arab Emirates, Qatar, and KUWAIT. Because the word "Arab" in both Ottoman Turkish and Arabic meant simply BEDOUIN for most of the Ottoman period, Arabistan literally means "the country of the Bedouins." However, the Ottomans saw this territory as beginning somewhere south of the Taurus Mountains and including much of what is today SYRIA in addition to the Arabian peninsula. The 17th-century Ottoman traveler Evliya Çelebi called the town Gaziantep in present-day TURKEY "the bride of Arabistan," implying that the territories to the south of that city comprised Arabistan. The Ottomans never included the territory that is Iraq today as Arabistan, although Persian-language sources, such as the chronicles of Shah ABBAS I (r. 1587–1629), did so. So there was not a clear connection between the geographical appellation and those who spoke Arabic. In Arabic, there was no equivalent geographical expression to correspond to the Ottoman Arabistan. The term gained official currency in 1832 when the Egyptian forces that occupied what is today Syria named the province they created there Arabistan. When the Ottomans reorganized their army during the TANZIMAT reform period after 1839 the army that was garrisoned in DAMASCUS was called the "Army of Arabistan," although the province itself was renamed Suriye or Syria By the end of the Ottoman period, however, the geographical boundaries of Arabistan had shrunk, and it referred only to the Arabian peninsula, as it does today.

Bruce Masters

Arab Revolt (1916)

The Arab Revolt was the name given by the British to the rebellion led by FAYSAL IBN HUSAYN AL-HASHIMI against the Ottoman Empire during WORLD WAR I. The uprising was the culmination of British efforts to find a Muslim leader who could counter the claim of Sultan MEHMED V (r. 1909–1918), as caliph, that the empire was fighting a jihad in World War I against the Allied Powers on behalf of all the Muslim peoples of the world. In reality, few Muslims outside the Ottoman Empire took the sultan's claim to the CALIPHATE seriously, as the Ottoman family was not descended from the Prophet Muhammad's clan of the Banu Hashim (*see* ASHRAF). According to Muslim political and religious traditions, only a member of the Banu Hashim could rightfully claim the title of caliph, and by definition that person would have to be an Arab. But the Allied Powers—ENGLAND, RUSSIA, FRANCE, and Italy—all had Muslim populations within their empires and were afraid of the possible influence the sultan's call to jihad might have on their Muslim subjects, perhaps leading them to rebel. To neutralize that potential threat, the British sought a Muslim leader with sufficient international recognition from the world's Muslims who could proclaim a counter-jihad against Mehmed and his German allies.

The British decided that the best choice for such a leader was HUSAYN AL-HASHIMI, the SHARIF OF MECCA. The British reasoned that Husayn had excellent credentials to rally Muslim support around the world because he was the governor of Islam's holiest city and, crucially, he was a member of the clan of the Banu Hashim. Based on conversations that Husayn's son, Abdullah, had with British officials in CAIRO in the autumn of 1914, British military planners were convinced that Husayn would cooperate in return for British support, following the defeat of the Ottoman Empire, for Husayn's claim to rule an Arab kingdom, the proposed boundaries of which were left vague. The British war against the Ottoman Empire went badly in 1915 with their expeditionary forces stalled at both Gallipoli, at the juncture of the Aegean Sea and the Sea of Marmara, and in southern IRAQ. They hoped that a revolt in Arabia would weaken Ottoman defenses at a time when they were planning an invasion of the empire from EGYPT.

Between July 1915 and March 1916, letters between Emir Husayn and Sir Henry McMahon, the British High Commissioner in Cairo, set out British promises of support to establish an independent Arab kingdom in the postwar settlement if Husayn would declare a revolt against the sultan from MECCA (*see* HUSAYN-MCMAHON CORRESPONDENCE). In the end, it was FAYSAL IBN HUSAYN AL-HASHIMI, Husayn's eldest son, who declared the revolt in June 1916. By this means, if the revolt failed, his father would still be technically a loyal subject of the Ottomans. Faysal's army quickly took MECCA and JEDDAH because most of the BEDOUIN tribes of the HEJAZ, today the western region of Saudi Arabia, joined his call to rebellion. The garrison at MEDINA, supplied as it was by the HEJAZ RAILROAD, held out against the rebels. The Ottomans were not fooled by the tactic of using Faysal to lead the rebellion. In July 1916 the sultan declared Husayn a rebel and named Ali Haydar al-Hashimi, a distant cousin of Husayn's, governor of Mecca. However, Ali Haydar was unable to reach Mecca and remained an Ottoman puppet, trapped in Medina for the rest of the war.

Most of those rallying to Faysal's call for a revolt were Bedouin tribesmen who were looking for religiously sanctioned plunder, but a significant number of officers from Iraq who believed in the Arab nationalist cause deserted the Ottoman army and added their strategic skills to the rebellion. There were also British advisers, the most famous of whom was T.E. LAWRENCE, better known as Lawrence of Arabia. The Arab Army, as it was now being called in the Western press, took the Red Sea port of Aqaba in July 1917, thereby providing a forward base that could be supplied with arms by the British navy. That came at a time when the British advance into PALESTINE had stalled at GAZA. The American journalist Lowell Thomas did much to publicize the revolt, focusing on the personality of Lawrence. The reading public in both the United Kingdom and the United States found that a war fought in the desert by Bedouins riding camels and supposedly led by an eccentric Englishman was an antidote to the dreary accounts of trench warfare on the western front in France. The revolt thereby gained media attention that far outweighed its actual strategic contribution to the war.

In the fall of 1917, the British were finally able to take Gaza and move into Palestine, occupying JERUSALEM before Christmas. Spurring the Arab Revolt northward toward DAMASCUS, the British government announced the Balfour Declaration in November 1917, around the same time that the Soviet revolutionaries published the secret SYKES-PICOT AGREEMENT. The Balfour Declaration promised British support for the creation of a Jewish homeland in Palestine after the war ended, while the Sykes-Picot agreement proposed the partition of the northern part of what was supposed to have been Emir Husayn's Arab kingdom into British and French zones of control. The publication of these two documents set off shock waves among the Arabs as they realized what the British aims in the postwar Middle East really were.

It then became a race between the British forces advancing along the coast and the Arab Army moving north from the desert to see who would reach Damascus first. The British had promised that, when a postwar settlement was made, all territories taken by the Arab Army would remain in Arab hands, and the Arab rebels desperately wanted Damascus to serve as the capital of the new

Arab kingdom. They believed that if they took the city it would be theirs. Which army actually entered Damascus first on October 1, 1918, is still a matter of debate, as there were apparently advance units of each in the city on that day. But Faysal arrived in the city on October 3, declaring that he was liberating the city in his father's name, and was greeted as a liberator by the city's population. Later that month, his army rode into the northern Syrian city of ALEPPO. The Arab Revolt had come to an end.

Bruce Masters

Further reading: C. Ernest Dawn, *From Ottomanism to Arabism* (Urbana: University of Illinois Press, 1973).

architecture   During the six centuries of Ottoman rule, architecture was one of the major fields of cultural activity. In the early years, Ottoman architecture had connections with Iranian and central Asian building traditions. As the state expanded to include the former territory of the BYZANTINE EMPIRE, the Balkans, the Near East, and EGYPT, it acquired a multiethnic character; the building techniques, types, and decorative vocabulary of the newly conquered lands were incorporated into Ottoman architecture.

The Ottomans constructed a wide range of building types, including religious buildings (mosques, convents), guesthouses (*tabhanes*), schools (madrasas and *mektebs*, or primary schools), libraries, commercial buildings (*arastas*, *bedestans*, caravansaries), hospitals (*darüşşifas*), BATHHOUSES (*hammams*), water conveyance systems, fountains, *sebils* (small kiosks with attendants who dispensed water), bridges, and military buildings (castles, barracks, powder houses). The chief architect controlled and regulated the major projects in the capital and the regions. The norms set at his office were disseminated to the provinces by other court architects, resulting in a unified and distinctly Ottoman style that can be seen even today across the vast territory once governed by the Ottomans, including BULGARIA, BOSNIA-HERZEGOVINA, SERBIA, GREECE, ALBANIA, SYRIA, Jordan, and EGYPT.

Many of the public works—such as schools, hospitals, fountains, public kitchens, and caravansaries on the intercity roads—provided free service to the people. Economically, such services were dependent on WAQFS or pious foundations initiated by benefactors. The sultans and their families, high-level officials, and other well-to-do citizens donated money and property to establish and run these charitable institutions.

The imprint of Ottoman planning and architecture can be seen on many towns and buildings in the cities of the former Ottoman Empire. The most striking element is usually a domed mosque, surrounded by or grouped together with other buildings to form a complex or *kül-*

liye that incorporated educational and other public facilities such as a fountain, hospice, bath, the tomb of the founder, and a cemetery with old cypress trees.

Mosque designs were very important in the development of Ottoman architecture. The early mosques were single-domed or timber-roofed structures. As the economic means of the state increased, the size of the mosques increased and their designs became more sophisticated, incorporating elements such as semidomes, arcaded courtyards, double porticos, and side galleries.

The Ottomans had great respect for the dead (*see* DEATH AND FUNERARY CULTURE). The simplest form of Ottoman burial was a grave with two vertical stones marking the head and the foot. Men's headstones were decorated with the headgear of the deceased person, indicating his rank or affiliation. Inscriptions and verses on the tombstone provided information about the person and the date of his death. Women's gravestones were usually decorated with flowers. Funerary buildings (*türbes*) could be very refined and monumental, reflecting the status of the deceased person. Modest tombs took the form of canopies resting on four or more columns or piers. A more developed form is the polygonal tomb covered by a dome; the octagonal plan was the most common.

Madrasas were the high school and university buildings in the Ottoman system. They were usually one story tall, with a spacious courtyard surrounded by arcades and cells for students. The classes were conducted in a large room, usually covered by a dome. The number of students in a madrasa was specified in the foundation deed of the *waqf*. Imperial foundations of Mehmed II and Süleyman the Magnificent included several madrasas in their programs (*see* EDUCATION).

Hospitals were usually founded by the imperial family and their number was rather limited. The Bayezid complex in EDIRNE (built in 1484–1488) has a mental hospital with an interesting layout. According to EVLIYA ÇELEBI, who visited the establishment in the mid-17th century, there were musical performances for the sick to ease their suffering. The perfume of the flowers from the surrounding garden was also a relief to patients.

To be clean for ritual prayers is a religious requirement for Muslims. Bathhouses or *hammams* were located in both the commercial and residential quarters of towns. *Hammams* were an important part of the social life of towns. The main parts of a Turkish bath are the dressing hall, tepidarium, hot section, and stoke, which included the water tank and the furnace to warm the bath and the water. The entrance hall was a big room with a pool at its center. People used the raised stone sofas along the walls to place their belongings and to rest after a bath.

In Ottoman towns, commercial and industrial activities were arranged around the marketplace. There were *arastas*, streets lined with shops of the same guild. In most cases the craftsmen produced and sold their work in the same place. If the town was large and prosperous, its commercial center was complemented by a *bedestan,* a closed market building with a long domed or vaulted hall and external shops, which was used to store and sell valuable goods such as silk, jewelry, and expensive handicrafts. *Bedestans* had thick walls to protect the goods stored in them from theft and fire. Only very large cities, such as ISTANBUL, had more than one *bedestan*. Public fountains also played an important role in the cityscape of Istanbul. Supported by the *waqfs, sebils* served water to thirsty pedestrians free of charge; some even served sweet drinks on certain holidays.

Ottoman houses were usually two stories high, with a garden secluded from the street by high walls. The men's part of the house was called the *selamlık*. It had a separate entrance and a room where male guests were received. The harem or women's section was reserved for the private life of the family. Kitchen and storage areas were located on the ground level, close to the courtyard or garden, which often had fruit trees and lots of greenery. The upper stories usually projected from the masonry walls of the ground floor with bays, which provided a fine view over the street or the landscape.

Amasya, Konya, and Manisa (all in present-day TURKEY) were towns ruled by Ottoman crown princes as governors before their accession to the throne. After the princes became sultans they made generous donations to the cities, embellishing them with beautiful monuments. In Amasya, the complex of BAYEZID II (r. 1481–1512), with its spacious mosque, madrasa, and public kitchen, is a good example illustrating this relationship. The Selimiye Complex in Konya and the Muradiye Complex in Manisa are two other examples.

THE EARLY PERIOD: 13TH–15TH CENTURIES

The Ottoman state was founded in Söğüt, a small, inland settlement in northwestern Anatolia, at the end of the 13th century. Iznik (ancient Nicaea) became the first capital, and several important early Ottoman monuments—Yeşil Cami (Green Mosque), Nilüfer Hatun Imaret, Süleyman Pasha Madrasa, several tombs, Ismail Bey Hammam, and Büyük Hammam—still stand in this small town.

The Ottomans extended their territory in the region, seizing BURSA (northwestern Turkey) in 1326. Originally, the town was surrounded by Hellenistic walls, but after becoming the Ottoman capital, it developed outside the citadel. The production of silk and velvet, as well as the movement of CARAVANS loaded with goods, provided for a lively economic life. A vast area surrounding the Ulu Cami (Great Mosque, built in 1396–1399, at the order of Sultan BAYEZID I, r. 1389–1402) was developed into a busy commercial center with spacious inns, a large *bedestan*, and streets lined with shops.

In the early period, during the 14th and early 15th centuries, mosques were usually combined with hospices (*tabhane*) or guest rooms, arranged along an inverted T-plan, so that the additional buildings form wings of the inverted "T"; the mosque of Orhan Bey (r. 1324–62) in Bursa is the first of this type. The influence of Byzantine masonry construction techniques—using brick and stone courses—is evident in most of the early Ottoman buildings in Bursa. The complex of Hüdavendigar, near the Çekirge district, has a spectacular position, overlooking the Bursa plain. The mosque and the madrasa are combined in a single building, which makes this monument unique in Ottoman architecture.

The first Ottoman sultans were buried in Bursa. The graveyard next to Muradiye Mosque in Bursa contains several interesting tombs from the early Ottoman period. The tomb of Sultan Çelebi Mehmed (r. 1413–21) in Bursa is one of the most impressive. Skilled craftsmen from Iran and Central Asia were involved in the glazed tile decoration and delicate wood carving of the monuments within the Yeşil Complex, including the tomb, mosque, and madrasa.

In 1361, MURAD I (r. 1362–89) took Adrianople, a strategic point on the road linking Constantinople (Istanbul) to the Balkans. This ancient garrison town became the new Ottoman capital, known in Turkish as EDIRNE, and the city expanded outside the walls, including a new commercial center, religious buildings, and residential quarters. An imperial palace, several mosques, a *bedestan*, numerous beautiful public baths, and bridges remain from the 14th and 15th centuries.

Interesting architectural ideas were developed and put into practice in Edirne. With its 72-foot (24-meter) diameter dome, the Üç Şerefeli (three-balconied) Mosque (built in 1438–47) is regarded as an important benchmark in the development of Ottoman mosques. For the first time in Ottoman architecture, an arcaded courtyard was erected. After the Üç Şerefeli Mosque, spacious courtyards with an ablution fountain in the middle were integrated into imperial mosque compositions. Another novelty was the increase in the number of minarets and their balconies (*şerefes*). The Üç Şerefeli Mosque is the first Ottoman mosque with four minarets. The architect devoted special attention to each minaret, decorating the shafts with different kinds of fluting or patterns in red stone, which give it a fanciful appearance. The tallest shaft, with a chevron pattern and three balconies, stands out in the silhouette of Edirne.

The Ottomans built castles and towers at strategic points in their territory. Their first castle on the Bosporus—Anadolu Hisarı (Anatolian castle)—was built during the reign of Bayezid I as a frontier stronghold. Before the siege of Constantinople, Rumeli Hisarı (European Fortress) was built across from Anadolu Hisarı to control sea traffic up and down the Bosporus.

AFTER THE CONQUEST OF CONSTANTINOPLE

The CONQUEST OF CONSTANTINOPLE in 1453 by the young sultan MEHMED II, known as Fatih or the Conqueror (r. 1444–46, 1451–81), accelerated the development of Ottoman architecture. Mehmed made Constantinople, later known as ISTANBUL, his new capital, and the repopulation and reconstruction of the deserted city demanded careful planning. Several grand projects were accomplished in the second half of the 15th century. The most significant of these included the new administrative center of the Ottoman Empire, the TOPKAPI PALACE; the FATIH MOSQUE COMPLEX, a university with eight colleges; the Seven Towers (Yedikule) fort, a treasury; the Eyüp building complex, covered bazaars or *bedestans*; and the Tophane, or the Imperial Cannon Foundry. Starting with Mehmed II, the Ottoman sultans were buried in Istanbul.

The Selimiye mosque in Edirne is considered the masterwork of the 16th-century Ottoman imperial architect Sinan. The mosque and its complex were built with spoils of the conquest of Cyprus (1571) to commemorate that victory. (*Photo by Zeynep Ahunbay*)

Another masterpiece of the architect Sinan, the Süleymaniye mosque and building complex dominates one of the highest hills of imperial Istanbul, shaping the skyline of the city. *(Photo by Zeynep Ahunbay)*

Ottoman architects were inspired by HAGIA SOPHIA, a grand Byzantine monument from the sixth century, and they attempted to match its beauty and scale in the design of their mosques. The first Fatih Mosque, which was destroyed in the earthquake of 1766, was a domed structure, with a semidome in the southeast direction. The combination of a dome with an increasing number of semidomes became a hallmark design of the mosques built in Istanbul in later centuries, including the Bayezid Mosque (commissioned by Bayezid II), the Şehzade Mosque, the Süleymaniye Mosque (commissioned by SÜLEYMAN I, r. 1520–66), the Sultan Ahmed Mosque (commissioned by AHMED I, r. 1603–1617), and the Yeni Cami, or New Mosque. The central dome and cascading semidomes of these mosques create a space of perfect harmony in the interior. The exteriors and interiors of the mosques were decorated with white and colored marbles, delicate stone carving, CALLIGRAPHY, bright Iznik tiles (*see*

CERAMICS), elaborate colored glass, mother-of-pearl inlay, and colorful paintwork.

Ottoman palace architecture is best exemplified by the Topkapı Palace in Istanbul. The 15th-century palace was modified in the course of the following centuries by additions and renovations. The location of the palace is exceptional, as it has a commanding view of the Bosporus and the Golden Horn. The palace grounds were surrounded by high walls. The original design consisted of three consecutive courtyards; the degree of privacy increased as one proceeded from the exterior toward the inner parts.

THE CLASSICAL PERIOD: THE 16TH AND 17TH CENTURIES

Many important buildings in Istanbul and other parts of the empire were built during the 16th century. Strongly supported by economic and political power, the building activity of the period reflects a remarkably high level in design and craftsmanship. Stylistically, the architecture of the 16th and 17th centuries is considered the classical period of Ottoman architecture.

SINAN

The classical period of Ottoman architecture is best represented by Sinan (1489–1588), the empire's chief architect between 1539 and 1588. The mosque complexes of Süleymaniye in Istanbul and Damascus; the bridges of Büyükçekmece near Istanbul; and the bridge of Sokollu Mehmed Pasha at Višegrad (Bosnia), crossing the River Drina, are just a few examples of his extensive work across the large territory commanded by the Ottomans.

Among Sinan's most extensive projects in Istanbul are the Süleymaniye and Atik Valide Sultan mosque complexes. The Süleymaniye Mosque contributes much to the skyline of Istanbul with its high domed structure overlooking the Golden Horn. The complex incorporates almost all the religious, educational, and charity institutions that were active in the 16th century, as well as the tomb of Süleyman I the Magnificent and his wife, Hurrem. Both are octagonal in plan but the sultan's tomb is larger and surrounded by an ambulatory (covered walkway), and its facade was fully covered by marble.

Sinan's responsibilities included engineering tasks such as facilitating Istanbul's supply of fresh water. He built long aqueducts to cross the valleys between the water springs and the city. Uzun Kemer, Maglova, and Egri Kemer are three of the two-story aqueducts that were part of the Kırkçeşme water conveyance system, which provided water to many fountains in the city.

He also constructed bridges over lakes and rivers to transport travelers, commercial goods, and military campaigns. The Uzunköprü bridge over the Ergene River in the Thracian part of Turkey is one of the most spectacular long bridges over a wide river. Mostar (in Bosnia and Herzegovina) is known for its single arched bridge over the River Neretva. The bridge was largely destroyed during the war in 1993; reconstruction was completed in 2004. To further strengthen these stone bridges, their piers were strengthened by abutments, allowing them to withstand strong currents. The middle of the bridge usually included inscription panels and a small loggia for the sultan or vizier to inspect the army as the soldiers marched by. The Büyükçekmece bridge, near Istanbul, was built between 1565 and 1568 on a lagoon near the Sea of Marmara. The bridge is 2,080 feet (635 m) long and consists of four separate bridges resting on small islands built in the lake.

CARAVANSARIES

Caravansaries located on roads between cities were *waqf* buildings that served travelers free of charge. The central part of the hall was reserved for animals and goods. High benches served as sitting and resting places for travelers who would warm themselves at night by the fireplaces along the walls. These stopping points were safe places, protected and maintained by the staff of religious endowments to offer travelers a secure place to rest at night during their travel from one city to another. The inn was usually connected to a small mosque, a covered bazaar, or rows of shops and a bath, offering merchants the opportunity to perform their religious duties, exchange goods, and take a bath to refresh themselves.

Caravansaries in city centers, which are also called *hans*, were commercial buildings, where tradesmen had their offices, shops, and storage places. These buildings were rented and their revenue was used to run *waqfs*. They were named according to the goods that were sold in them, such as Koza Han (cocoon market) and Pirinç Han (rice market) in Bursa. *Hans* were usually two-story buildings with arcades surrounding one or more spacious courtyards. The Rüstem Pasha Caravansary in Edirne is a good example of a 16th-century caravansary with two courtyards.

The power of the Ottomans started to decline at the end of the 16th century and thus the architectural activity slowed down in the 17th century. Sultan Ahmed Mosque (built 1609–17), also known as the Blue Mosque, is one of the major imperial projects in Istanbul from this time period. Architect Sedefkar Mehmed Aga (d. 1622) designed a grand complex that included the tomb of Ahmed I, a madrasa, a public kitchen, shops, and several houses for rent. The mosque is the only one in Istanbul that has six minarets. It is the first Ottoman mosque with a royal apartment (*hünkar kasrı*) next to the northeast corner of the mosque. A similar pavilion was built by Turhan Valide Sultan next to the Yeni Cami in the second half of the 17th century.

The best known single-arched bridge over the Neretva River at Mostar was built during the reign of Süleyman I and destroyed during the Yugoslav war in 1993. *(Photo by Zeynep Ahunbay)*

Before the 17th century, books were kept in mosques and madrasas, with a librarian in charge of the collection. The Köprülü Library is the earliest library building in Istanbul. Interest in books and libraries continued and many other libraries were constructed in the 18th century, some within madrasa complexes (e.g., Feyzullah Efendi, Damad Ibrahim Pasha in Istanbul), others as the nucleus of small building complexes incorporating a school, a *sebil*, a fountain, and the lodging of the librarian (e.g., Ragip Pasha in Istanbul).

THE 18TH AND 19TH CENTURIES

The early 18th century is known as the Tulip Period, when rococo influences are visible in Ottoman architecture as a result of contacts with Italy and FRANCE, and the period between 1730 and the 19th century is called the baroque period in Ottoman architecture. The Nuruosmaniye Mosque is the first grand mosque built in the baroque style in Istanbul. It is a single-domed mosque with heavily articulated arches supporting the dome. The form of the courtyard is unique in Ottoman architecture with its elliptical plan. The sultan's lodge, a library, a soup kitchen (*imaret*), public fountains (*sebil*), and the tomb of the founder (sponsor of the complex) complete the set of buildings.

As in many European countries, neo-classical, neo-baroque, and neo-Gothic styles dominated the architectural sphere of the 19th century. European architects and engineers who were invited to design modern schools, hospitals, or barracks introduced European architectural types and styles to Turkey. Thus it is possible to see many 19th-century European-style buildings in Istanbul and other parts of the empire. The end of the 19th century also saw an Ottoman revival called Nationalist Architecture, which was adopted by foreign and native architects such as A. Vallaury, R. D'Aronco, Kemalettin Bey, and Vedat Tek. Art Nouveau style was introduced to Istanbul at the turn of the 20th century by architects such as R. D'Aronco, who worked for ABDÜLHAMID II (r. 1876–1909), designing several pavilions for him in the Yıldız Palace compound. Thus the final years of the Ottoman Empire show a mixture of Ottoman revival and Art Nouveau styles. The Nationalist style continued for some time even after the establishment of the Turkish Republic in the 1920s.

Zeynep Ahunbay

Further reading: Godfrey Goodwin, *A History of Ottoman Architecture* (London: Thames & Hudson, 1971); Dogan Kuban, *Sinan's Art and Selimiye* (Istanbul: Economic and Social History Foundation, 1997); Aptullah Kuran, *Sinan: The Grand Old Master of Ottoman Architecture* (Washington, D.C.: Institute of Turkish Studies, 1987); Gülru Necipoglu, *The Age of Sinan: Architectural Culture in the Ottoman Empire* (Princeton, N.J.: Princeton University Press, 2005).

archives *See* PRIME MINISTRY'S OTTOMAN ARCHIVES.

Armenia (*Arm.*: Hayasdan; *bib.*: Minni; *Turk.*: Ermenistan) The mountainous region that is today shared between the Republic of Armenia and TURKEY emerged as the Kingdom of Armenia in the first century B.C.E. For much of its history after the founding of the kingdom, Armenia existed in a delicate balance on the borders of more powerful empires. In the first three centuries of the Common Era, the kingdom was an ally of the Romans against the Persian Empire. In the early fourth century C.E., the Armenian king Trdat (Tiridates) became a Christian and Armenia became the first political state to establish Christianity as its official religion. With the emergence of the Eastern Roman Empire (also known as the BYZANTINE EMPIRE) under the leadership of Constantine (d. 337 C.E.), the Kingdom of Armenia was sometimes its ally against Sassanian Persia. Later, in the seventh century C.E., Armenia served as a buffer between the ABBASID CALIPHATE and the Byzantines, with its nobles sometimes allied with the Muslims (as was the case in the eighth century) and sometimes with the Byzantines (as was the case in the 11th century), in a delicate balancing act between two more powerful neighbors.

Despite the wars, Armenia emerged as a kingdom with a distinct culture of its own. Its language was written in a unique alphabet. Although the Armenians were Christian, their understanding of Christ's nature—that he was primarily divine and only secondarily human—was at odds with that of the Orthodox Christian faith, which held that Christ was equally divine and human. That combination of a distinctive faith and an idiosyncratic language, tied to a particular geographic location, gave Armenians a strong sense of their own unique ethnic identity that persevered even after their kingdom fell to the Turks in the 11th century.

After their historic homeland was divided between the Ottoman and Safavid empires in the early 16th century, Armenian merchants traded and established communities in most of the cities of the Middle East and in places as far away as India, East Asia, and Europe. These trading communities thrived in the 17th and 18th centuries, providing the Armenian commercial elite with cosmopolitan connections, although during most of the Ottoman period, the overwhelming majority of the Armenians were peasant farmers in the mountain valleys of the eastern Ottoman Empire or in the western territories of the Safavid Empire in Iran.

For pre-modern Armenians, whether they were villagers or traders in distant lands, their identity as a people was vested in their communion with the ARMENIAN APOSTOLIC CHURCH. But that identity was more than simply being Christians, as Armenians were the only people who belonged to their Church and it recognized no ecclesiastical authority above their own catholicos, the Armenian equivalent of a bishop, whose see is in

Etchmiadzin, near present-day Yerevan, the capital of the Republic of Armenia. That position was challenged, however, with the establishment of the office of the Armenian patriarch in Istanbul by MEHMED II (r. 1444–46; 1451–81) in the 15th century. In subsequent centuries, the men holding that office asserted their spiritual authority over all the Armenians living in the Ottoman Empire.

Before the 19th century, Armenian political life in the Ottoman Empire was vested in the Armenian MILLET, or religious community, with its leader, the Armenian patriarch of Istanbul. Starting with Mehmed II, the Ottoman sultans had established that the patriarchs of the Orthodox Christian Church and the Armenian Apostolic Church would be the representatives of the Orthodox peoples and Armenians respectively and would be free to organize much of the internal workings of their respective communities. With that authority, the two church hierarchies were able to administer the schools, clergy, family law, and even taxes of their respective communities throughout the Ottoman Empire. The Armenian *millet* served to cement the sense of a shared identity among Armenians by creating a political identity that transcended the specific location in which they lived and that linked them to other Armenians throughout the empire.

In the late 18th century Armenian merchants and bankers, known as *amiras*, began to use their wealth to buy influence among Ottoman officials so as to place those sympathetic to their interests in the post of patriarch. The rise of a secular leadership among the Armenians was further aided by changes in the *millet* system resulting from the Ottoman empire's TANZIMAT reforms in the 19th century. Under the reforms, new laws were enacted outlining the institutions of internal governance for each *millet* that would replace the Church hierarchies. These allowed for greater lay participation and reduced the power of the clergy. The *millets* continued to administer schools for the community, and Armenian children attended schools that emphasized the language, history, and culture of their community. As a result of these schools, many Armenians whose parents spoke either Turkish or Arabic as their first language switched to Armenian as their daily language. Additionally, many Armenian parents enrolled children in schools run by Catholic or Protestant missionaries, where the language of instruction was also Armenian. As a result, the Armenian population was proportionately the best educated in the Ottoman Empire and Armenians were often the bearers of new technologies, such as photography and mechanics, to provincial towns throughout the empire.

Although their society was traditionally dominated by agriculture, beginning in the 18th century, Ottoman Armenians migrated out of their mountain villages at a much higher rate than did their Muslim neighbors, and by the late 19th century, Armenians formed a minority population in most Ottoman cities. Nevertheless, the majority of the Armenian population remained concentrated in the six northeastern provinces of the Ottoman empire: Van, Bitlis, Diyarbakır, Erzurum, Mamuret el-Aziz, and Sivas. In 1876, Russia invaded the empire with the specific goal of seizing this region, known as the Six Provinces. That ambition failed, but Russia did annex the province of Kars in the northeastern corner of the Ottoman Empire. The Treaty of Berlin of 1878, which further delineated the conditions set by the Treaty of San Stefano, put the Ottoman Empire on notice that the Western powers were particularly concerned about the political and economic conditions of Armenians living in the Six Provinces. The "Armenian Question," whether the Armenians should be granted an independent state or remain within the Ottoman Empire, was becoming highly politicized and very volatile. The situation was further complicated by a new militancy on the part of the Kurdish tribes to assert their control over lands that Armenian peasants were farming.

Faced with the realities of the decline of the Ottoman Empire, Armenian intellectuals began to dream of political alternatives to the empire. One group, known as the Hnchak (Bell) after the name of their newspaper, called for the creation of an independent socialist republic in Ottoman Armenia. Another, the Dashnaktsutiun (organization) or Dashnaks, called for a state that would be more nationalist in its orientation. Both parties held as their ultimate goal the secession of the Six Provinces from the empire. Both the Dashnaks and the Hnchaks gained support among some Armenian subjects of the sultan, but the majority of the intellectuals of that community continued to support the continuation of the Ottoman Empire. Rather than independence, they sought a return of the constitution that had been suspended in 1878 and the greater participation of Armenians in the political affairs of the Ottoman state.

Nevertheless, citing the potential threat posed by Armenian nationalists, Sultan ABDÜLHAMID II (r. 1876–1909) authorized the recruitment of Kurdish tribesmen into a cavalry militia known as the HAMIDIYE in the 1890s. This tipped the balance of power in the east by aligning the Ottoman state with the KURDS. Further exacerbating religious tensions, the Ottoman state settled Muslim refugees from the Balkans and the Caucasus in the eastern provinces. These had grievances against their former Christian neighbors who had driven them into exile and they did not distinguish between the Christians of their old homelands and their new Christian neighbors. In 1893, the situation in eastern Anatolia exploded. There were clashes in the spring between armed Armenian peasants and their Muslim neighbors in the province of Maraş in southeastern Anatolia. Rumors spread among the Muslim population as far from the trouble as

Aleppo that the Armenians were going to rise in rebellion as the Greeks had done in the 1820s.

That summer, Kurdish tribesmen descended upon an Armenian village in the Sasun region and plundered it, killing a number of villagers. When the Armenian villagers retaliated by killing Kurds, the authorities punished them but not the Kurds who had initiated the violence. Armenian villagers across southeastern Anatolia responded by declaring that they would not pay their taxes until they were protected. The governor of Bitlis declared the Armenians in rebellion and gave the Hamidiye militia a free hand to loot and plunder. The Hamidiye perpetuated a series of massacres on the Armenians from 1894 until 1896 that the Ottoman state did little to control. It may even have encouraged the violence by issuing statements that implied that the Armenian population was disloyal. Finally, European pressure forced the Ottoman army to intervene and rein in the Hamidiye. This was done, but relations between Kurds and Armenians remained tense.

Many Armenians welcomed the Young Turk Revolution of 1908 as they hoped it would mean the restoration of the Ottoman constitution. The Socialist Armenian Hnchak Party even made common cause with the COMMITTEE OF UNION AND PROGRESS. But in the attempted counter-coup against the new regime in 1909, riots directed at the Armenians in the province of Adana in southeastern Anatolia left thousands dead. During the BALKAN WARS, the ideology of the YOUNG TURKS became increasingly Turkish nationalist in its orientation. Its leadership distrusted the Christian minorities of the empire, fearing that their ultimate political goals involved the empire's dismemberment.

The tensions between the ethnic and religious communities accelerated with the outbreak of WORLD WAR I. After a failed Ottoman attempt to liberate Kars province from the Russians, the Russian army moved into eastern Anatolia in the winter of 1915. The Ottoman government was convinced that Ottoman Armenians had aided the Russian advance; whether some had, in fact, done so is disputed by historians. In addition, there were cases of armed Armenian resistance to conscription in the region that had been racked by the Hamidiye raids 20 years before as the Armenians feared, with some justification, that conscripts would simply be led off and executed. Saying that they could not trust the Armenian population near the front, the Ottoman authorities ordered their deportation to the Syrian Desert in April 1915. Whether or not they planned the extermination of the Armenian population of eastern Anatolia with that order is also still debated. But it is clear that as a result of the deportations, which were extended to Armenians living far from the battlefields, at least a million people were uprooted, and most of those were either murdered or died along the path of exile to the Syrian Desert. Thousands more died in the relocation camps from disease and famine. In the aftermath of the war, perhaps only a few thousand Armenians still lived in the mountains of eastern Anatolia that had been part of the Armenian homeland for at least 2,000 years.

Bruce Masters

See also ARMENIAN APOSTOLIC CHURCH; ARMENIAN MASSACRES.

Further reading: Ronald Grigor Suny, *Looking Toward Ararat: Armenia in Modern History* (Bloomington: Indiana University Press, 1993); Christopher Walker, *Armenia: The Survival of a Nation* (London: Croom Helm, 1980).

Armenian Apostolic Church   The Armenian Apostolic Church, sometimes referred to as the Gregorian Armenian Church by Western scholars, serves as the national church of the Armenian people. Independent of either the Roman Catholic Church or the Orthodox Church, Armenians claim that their Church is the oldest established national church in the world, dating from the conversion of the Armenian King Trdat (Tiridates) III in the early third century C.E. Because the king reportedly accepted Christianity through the mission of Saint Gregory the Illuminator (also known as Gregory of Nyssa), the Armenian Church is sometimes called the Gregorian Armenian Church. Members of the Church prefer "Apostolic," however, as they say that St. Gregory was a true apostle of Christ who converted their ancestors through the Holy Spirit; thus to call the church "Gregorian" is to elevate the man above his mission.

The principal theological difference between the Armenian Church and its Roman Catholic and Orthodox counterparts lies in the Armenian Church's rejection of the doctrine of the nature of Christ established with the Council of Chalcedon in 451 C.E. This council elaborated the belief that Christ had two natures, human and divine, which coexisted in one being. The clergy of the Armenian Church chose to emphasize Christ's divine nature, while not denying his humanity. The dominant Christian tradition, represented by the Orthodox and Catholic churches, labeled that diminution of Christ's humanity as heresy and those who believed in it as heretics. The relationship between the Armenian Church and the Orthodox Church of Constantinople was often troubled, especially in the seventh century when the Kingdom of Armenia came under direct Byzantine rule and Armenian Church leaders were persecuted by the Orthodox clergy.

Although the Kingdom of Armenia lost its independence after the Turkish victory at Manzikert in 1071, the Seljuk and those Turkish dynasties that ruled Anatolia after them accorded the Armenian Church equal status with the Orthodox Church. Equality between the two churches also informed the Ottoman treatment of the Armenian Church. According to Armenian tradition, not long after the CONQUEST OF CONSTANTINOPLE in 1453, Sultan MEHMED II (r. 1444–46; 1451–81) invited the Armenian bishop Hovakim of BURSA to come to his new capital in ISTANBUL to be the head of the Armenian Church in his domains. He had similarly raised the Greek Orthodox monk Gennadios to head the Orthodox Church. Although it is not certain that this event actually happened, that version of the past became the foundation myth for the Armenian MILLET.

It is clear that, from the reign of Sultan Mehmed II onward, the Ottoman sultans considered the two churches as legitimate and equal. Over the following centuries, the two churches and the communities that they served were called by the Ottomans the Orthodox, or Greek, *millet,* and the Armenian *millet,* from the Turkish word for "people" or "nation." Each church was headed by a patriarch living in the capital who was confirmed in his position of spiritual authority over all the Orthodox Christians or Armenians in the empire by an imperial decree from the sultan. This innovation was contrary to the Armenian religious tradition that granted several high-ranking clergymen the title of catholicos, roughly the equivalent of a bishop in the Roman Catholic Church, with all of them being equal in the Church hierarchy in terms of their spiritual authority.

By the 18th century, the Armenian patriarch of Istanbul had achieved the equivalent status of the ecumenical patriarch of the Orthodox Church, and complaints about clergy from throughout the empire were routinely forwarded to him for action. He also came to represent the numerically smaller NESTORIAN and Jacobite Christian communities of the empire. In the second half of the 18th century, the office of the Armenian patriarchate was under the control of prominent Armenian merchants and tax farmers in Istanbul, known collectively as the *amiras.* The dominance of secular notables encouraged the establishment of schools, under the management of the Armenian *millet,* which taught a curriculum that was increasingly influenced by Western learning.

The Armenian patriarchs suffered further erosions of their authority when lay members of the community took advantage of new imperial regulations governing *millets* in the TANZIMAT period and promulgated a national constitution for the Armenian *millet* in 1863. The constitution provided that the patriarch was the chief executive of the *millet* but that he was to be elected by a general assembly, to be composed of both laity and clergy. Further limiting his former powers, the assembly could impeach the patriarch and remove him from office if charges against him were proven true. The constitution further provided for the formation of two national councils, one responsible for the spiritual affairs of the community and the other responsible for temporal matters. The former consisted entirely of clergy and the latter of laity. The constitution also established provincial assemblies and executive councils. This reform left the patriarch as the spiritual head of the Armenian Apostolic Church and the Armenian *millet* but it also introduced a liberal, more democratic and representative system in which ordinary Armenians could participate.

The relationship between the Armenian Church and the Ottoman state began to deteriorate after the Treaty of Berlin in 1878, when the status of Armenians within the empire became an international issue. In response to international pressure and the violent actions of a few Armenian nationalists, Sultan ABDÜLHAMID II (r. 1876–1909) became increasingly convinced that the Armenian community was disloyal. His perception was enforced by the growth of the Armenian Nationalist Dashnak Party, which sought independence for Armenia from both the Ottoman and Russian empires, although only a tiny minority of his Armenian subjects embraced the party's ideology. The overthrow of the sultan in 1908 brought some hope that the relationship between the state and the church would improve, but with the rise of the COMMITTEE OF UNION AND PROGRESS regime in Istanbul that became less and less likely.

Bruce Masters

Further reading: Kevork Bardakjian, "The Rise of the Armenian Patriarchate of Constantinople," in *Christians and Jews in the Ottoman Empire,* vol. 1, edited by Benjamin Braude and Bernard Lewis (New York: Holmes & Meier, 1982), 89–100; Avedis Sanjian, *The Armenian Communities in Syria under Ottoman Dominion* (Cambridge, Mass.: Harvard University Press, 1965).

Armenian Massacres (Armenian Genocide) The term Armenian Massacres refers to the massive deportation and execution of ethnic Armenians within Ottoman-controlled territories in 1915. Although the precise circumstances of these events and the total number of dead are hotly contested by scholars from opposing political camps, even the most conservative estimates place Armenian losses at approximately half a million. The higher figure given by Armenian scholars is one and a half million dead. The elimination of Armenian civilians as part of this process was well documented by accounts written by diplomats and missionaries from neutral nations who were present at the scene of the deportations.

This episode started in April 1915 during WORLD WAR I, after the Ottoman suffered a major defeat at the hands of RUSSIA. Ottoman authorities ordered the deportation of Armenians from eastern Anatolia to the Syrian Desert. This drastic step was taken because of reports that Armenian nationalists had aided the Russian invasion of Ottoman territory; according to some sources, this led Ottoman leaders in Istanbul to fear that all Armenians might prove disloyal in the case of further Russian advances. The process started with the limited deportation of men of military age, many of whom were summarily executed. As Armenians came to fear that conscription would lead simply to the execution of those drafted, armed Armenian resistance to the conscription broke out in Zeytun, near Maraş, and later in Van, and the Ottoman authorities used this resistance as an excuse to order the wholesale deportation of Armenian civilians from other provinces in the line of a possible Russian advance. The order for deportations soon expanded to include the entire Armenian population of the eastern provinces of the Ottoman Empire, perhaps a million people. The area affected included towns in central and southeastern Anatolia that were hundreds of miles from the front lines, a fact that has led many to conclude that Ottoman authorities had embarked on a genocidal policy of "ethnic cleansing" so that no Armenians would remain in eastern or central Anatolia.

The expulsion of the Armenians was often accompanied by rape, plunder, and murder; many more of the deportees were killed, or died of hunger and exposure, en route to internment camps near Dayr al-Zor, a town on the Euphrates River in present-day Syria. Many thousands of others died of starvation and disease in the concentration camps established there.

Survivors and their descendants have argued that what happened was clearly genocide, a deliberate and coordinated government plan to eliminate the Armenians as a people, and have sought official recognition of this analysis by various international bodies, including the U.S. Congress. This view has gained the support of many in the international community, including the lower house of the French parliament, which passed a law defining the denial of an Armenian genocide as a crime. The government of Turkey, however, argues that there was no deliberate plan on the part of the Ottoman authorities to eliminate the Armenians as a people. As evidence, they cite the fact that deportation orders were not extended to Armenian populations in western Anatolian cities such as Izmir, Bursa, or Istanbul. Moreover, some scholars point to the fact that there was a high number of Muslim deaths in eastern Anatolia during these years, suggesting the possibility that Armenian deaths were due, at least in part, to civil conflict and to the war-related disease and famine that also killed many thousands of Muslims. What is not contested, however, is that the Armenians, who were the descendants of a people who had lived in eastern Anatolia for more than 2,000 years, had disappeared from their ancestral homeland.

A consensus on the causes and severity of the deportations may never be possible. Turkish authorities have not allowed independent scholars to examine the wartime archives, and the intentions of the Ottoman government in ordering the deportations remain debated. There is little doubt as to the impact the massacres had on the survivors. The memory of this event has remained a crucial aspect of Armenian national identity until the present, with many Armenians claiming that there can be no reconciliation with the Turkish Republic until it acknowledges that an act of genocide occurred.

Bruce Masters

Further reading: Donald E. Miller and Lorna Touryan Miller, *Survivors: An Oral History of the Armenian Genocide* (Berkeley: University of California Press, 1993); Justin McCarthy, *The Ottoman Peoples and the End of Empire* (London: Arnold Publishers, 2001); Richard Hovannisian, ed., *The Armenian Genocide* (New York: St. Martin's, 1992).

army *See* FIREARMS; JANISSARIES; MILITARY; MILITARY SLAVERY; WARFARE.

arsenal *See* TERSANE-I AMIRE.

arts *See* ARCHITECTURE; CALLIGRAPHY; CERAMICS; ILLUSTRATED MANUSCRIPTS AND MINIATURE PAINTINGS; LITERATURE; MUSIC.

artillery *See* FIREARMS; MILITARY ORGANIZATION.

ashraf (sadah) In Islam, all believers are held to be equal before God, with no group privileged above any other. However, those believers who can trace their descent back to the Prophet are given special recognition. Collectively, those descendants are known as the *ashraf,* or in Iraq as *sadah,* with an individual known as a sharif or *sayyid,* a term that can also be used as an honorific title added to the person's name, for example, Sharif Ali. The male members of the *ashraf* are allowed to wear green turbans (although few do so today), the only class of persons who could do so, and they were exempt under Ottoman law from certain taxes. Uniquely in a patriarchal society, the lineage could pass to a child from either mother or father, a necessity in that the Prophet Muhammad had no male heirs who reached maturity; thus all those who claim *ashraf* status must ultimately claim it from his daughters. Ottoman governors and judges stationed in Arab cities in the 17th and 18th centuries often sought to marry daughters of sharif families so that their sons might inherit the honor from their mothers. As the title of sharif or *sayyid* carried considerable social prestige, wealthy individuals often made the claim that they were entitled to it, even when there was no genealogical evidence to support the claim. As a result, there was a great deal of skepticism among Muslims who did not carry the title about the claims of those who did.

In cities where there were sizeable communities of *ashraf,* the group would select a marshal (*nakibüleşraf).* He sat in the provincial divan (cabinet) and advised the governor along with the chief judge, treasurer, and other leading officials of the city. In theory, the *nakibüleşraf* in Istanbul appointed the men who held the office in the provincial centers. In reality, he usually offered nominal approval of the names forwarded to him from the provinces because the local *ashraf* typically rejected nominees from the capital. The office of *nakibüleşraf* could have a great deal of political influence. In Jerusalem and Aleppo, the *nakibüleşraf* marshaled his reputed kinsmen into the streets to threaten and even topple the governors of the city at several different times in the 18th century. The Tanzimat reforms of the 19th century ended the political power of the *nakibüleşraf,* but the men holding that position continued to exercise great moral authority until the end of the Ottoman Empire.

Bruce Masters

Further reading: Herbert Bodman, *Political Factions in Aleppo, 1760–1826* (Chapel Hill: University of North Carolina Press, 1963).

Assyrians *See* Nestorians.

astronomy *See* sciences.

Atatürk, Kemal (Mustafa Kemal) (b. 1881–d. 1938) *first president of the Republic of Turkey* There is a certain irony involved with the inclusion of Mustafa Kemal, better known as Atatürk, in this *Encyclopedia of the Ottoman Empire,* for more than any other individual or group, it was Atatürk who was instrumental in transforming the remains of the Ottoman Empire into the modern Turkish state, and today, Atatürk and his legacy are synonymous with the creation of the modern Republic of Turkey. Atatürk and his reforms brought about one of the most dramatic social, cultural, and historic breaks in human history. In short, Atatürk brought about an almost complete effacement of the Ottoman Empire, inventing a modern Turkey that eradicated Ottoman political and social systems and Ottoman literature and culture, effectively erasing the historical memory of the Ottomans in the culture of modern Turks.

One of the best-known photographs of the founder of modern Turkey, Mustafa Kemal Atatürk, shows him in European dress with a *kalpak*-style military hat. *(Library of Congress)*

Although Atatürk was instrumental in ending the Ottoman Empire, it should be remembered that he was nevertheless a child of late Ottoman society and as such was shaped by its social, educational, and cultural surroundings. He was, above all things, a brilliant officer and field commander whose worldview was shaped in large part by the Ottoman state and the Ottoman military. And it is fitting to remember that Atatürk, the man who led the creation of the modern Turkish state, a modern secular democracy with its capital located in Anatolian Ankara, drew his last breath in Dolmabahçe Palace, the last of the palaces of the Ottoman sultans in Istanbul. In order to better understand this irony as well as the magnitude of Atatürk's achievement, three aspects of his life need to be examined: the late Ottoman world he came from; his transformation of this world from empire to nation; and the enduring legacy of the modern Republic of Turkey.

AN OTTOMAN OFFICER

Atatürk's origins lay firmly within the context of late Ottoman society and in many respects exemplified the aims of the 19th-century reformers of the TANZIMAT period. Atatürk was born Mustafa, the son of Ali Riza, a minor Ottoman official employed as a customs inspector, and his wife Zübeyde. As was the case with most Ottoman subjects, no precise date is given for his birth. The entry of the Muslim calendar year of 1296 indicates he was born sometime between March 1880 and March 1881. In keeping with Turkish customs of the time, the child was only given one name, Mustafa, meaning the chosen. The place of his birth, SALONIKA now in Greece, was a quintessential late Ottoman city whose small-town Thracian origins had been transformed by the 15th-century immigration of Iberian Jews after expulsions by the Spanish crown. By the late 19th century, Salonika was a thriving commercial center with a diverse population of Turks, Greeks, Jews, and Levantines, among others. It was also located where the rising forces of nationalism were beginning to test the cohesion of the empire.

Atatürk's education reflected many of the transformations going on in the empire at the time, in particular the movement away from religious schools to a more modern schooling employing a secular and scientifically based curriculum. These were the *rüştiye* and *idadiye* schools promoted under the rule of ABDÜLHAMID II (r. 1876–1909). For a brief time the young Mustafa was enrolled in a religious school with a traditional curriculum centered on the Quran. However, his father appears to have won a family battle, and the child was moved to a private school and then on to the Salonika *mülki rüştiye* (civil preparatory school) sometime after his father's death. When this did not prove satisfactory, Atatürk is said to have secretly sat for the military school entrance exam and in 1891 entered the Salonika military academy prep school. It was here that a teacher gave him his second name, Kemal, meaning "perfect" or "perfection," perhaps reflecting an early recognition of a talent that was to manifest itself to the world at a later date. His new name most likely also served to distinguish him from other Mustafas in his class.

In the years following Atatürk's graduation from military school, the young officer was exposed to both the continuous external threats to the empire, in the form of hostile European powers, and to the growing fissures within Ottoman lands represented by the rising tide of nationalist consciousness within the empire among the non-Muslim populations such as Greeks and Armenians. During this period leading up to WORLD WAR I, the Ottoman military was confronted with invasions or uprisings in YEMEN, LIBYA, and the Balkans. For the Ottoman army, and especially its junior staff, the weakness of the Ottomans in the face of indigenous nationalist movements or European powers was painfully obvious. Although the empire had long faced the hostility of the West and Russia, the rising nationalist strength in the Balkans was a new and difficult challenge.

During the first decade of the 20th century, Atatürk's home town of Salonika became a hotbed of reformist politics, the most notable reformist group being the COMMITTEE OF UNION AND PROGRESS (CUP). Atatürk, while a member of the CUP, was never within the inner circle, a fact that annoyed the ambitious young man, but later served to free him from the taint of the CUP. His role in the overthrow of Abdülhamid II, an act undertaken by the CUP, was therefore minimal, yet this did not stand in the way of his advancement. The outbreak of war with Italy following the Italian invasion of Ottoman Libya in 1911 marked the beginning of his rapid rise to power. In that campaign, Atatürk first had to evade the British forces occupying EGYPT on his way to Libya. Once there, he had to work in nontraditional military situations that demanded initiative and improvisation. The Ottoman defeat in the war against the Italians in Libya was followed by war in the Balkans against the Bulgarians. This continual state of war reached a climax with the outbreak of World War I. During World War I, Atatürk was sent to fight at the Anafartlar lines in Gallipoli, was given commands along the Caucasus front, and was finally placed in command of the Ottoman 7th Army in SYRIA.

With the end of World War I came the utter defeat of the Ottoman Empire by the Allied Powers and the collapse of its government. The Allied Powers carved out zones of occupation in the former Ottoman territories, with the French taking the southeastern coastal region of Cilicia, the Italians taking the south-central and western coastal regions, and the British, ever mindful of maritime supremacy, occupying the straits of the Bosporus and the Dardanelles. To make matters worse, the sultan and the Ottoman government were reduced to taking orders from the occupying Allied powers who were intent on the complete reduction of any remaining power. In fact, had the Allies been able to fully carry out their plans, modern Turkey would have amounted to a landlocked, rump state in northeastern Anatolia.

At the same time, the end of the war found Atatürk an ambitious, undefeated military commander. He moved back to the Ottoman capital of Istanbul to face the challenge of preventing the annihilation of Ottoman Turkish life as he knew it. Istanbul had been occupied by the victorious powers, the leaders of the CUP had fled, and the Ottoman government itself had been reduced to the status of a puppet, controlled by the European victors. As Atatürk was known to the Allied Powers not only as a skilled military commander but also now as a staunch Turkish nationalist and thus a threat to the occupying powers, it was only a matter of time before a warrant was issued for his arrest. Fortunately for Atatürk, news of the impending arrest reached him in time for him to secure an appointment as inspector of the Third Army in Anatolia, giving him the opportunity to leave occupied Istanbul and seek shelter in the heartland away from the reach of the Allied Powers. His timing could not have been better. On May 15, 1919, the Greek army landed at IZMIR on the Aegean coast of Turkey, the first step in an attempt to wrest most of western Anatolia from the remains of the Ottoman Empire and attach it to a greater Greek Republic. On May 16, Atatürk slipped away from Istanbul, setting out for Samsun on the Black Sea coast on the steamship *Bandirma* and from there into the relatively safe haven of central Anatolia.

A TURKISH NATIONALIST

For the next four years, Atatürk was to play the leading role in orchestrating the creation of the modern Turkish Republic. Given that the state lacked political legitimacy, military power, and financial resources, Atatürk's success in constructing a Turkish republic is something of a miracle. The first dilemma Atatürk faced on arriving in Anatolia was that of his own questionable authority among the remnant of Ottoman army forces stationed there. Although, in his role as inspector of the Third Army, Atatürk was the senior commanding officer, he was still subordinate to orders emanating from the defeated Ottoman army command in Istanbul, which was now in the control of the Allied Powers. By July 1919, Atatürk had left Samsun and the reach of the occupying British forces for the relative safety of Amasya. Here he met with other Ottoman military commanders and set forth a proclamation of resistance. However, the danger of being ordered back to Istanbul or risk being branded as a rebel forced Atatürk to take an even greater personal risk: resigning from the Ottoman military. In this respect Atatürk gambled on the friendship and loyalty of General Kazim Karabekir, commanding officer of the Ottoman Third Army in Anatolia This was a defining moment in the history of the Turkish Republic, for had Karabekir elected to clap Atatürk in irons and ship him back to Istanbul, the story might have ended here.

Instead, Karabekir gave his support to Atatürk, who now traveled to Erzurum, in mountainous eastern Anatolia where he helped form the first Turkish Nationalist Congress and was elected its chairman. A second congress was held in September at Sivas, a city in central Anatolia and at a distance from the reach of the occupying powers. Here, Atatürk was made the leader of the executive committee formally charged with resisting the occupying European powers. During this period, Atatürk was forced to play a delicate game, balancing these resistance activities against the demands made for his arrest by the Allied-controlled government in Istanbul. Using a core of Ottoman army officers and playing a deft game of diplomacy, the nationalist cause, led by Atatürk, was able to mount an effective, low-profile resistance against the occupying French, British, and Italian forces, as well as against the invading Greeks. Further complicating the nationalist efforts was an almost total lack of funds and the need to keep competing resistance organizations, such as remnants of the disgraced CUP, at bay.

In December 1919 Atatürk moved to Ankara and began setting up what was to be the new capital of Turkey. In doing so, Atatürk placed this new Turkish capital in the center of what was to become the new nation of Turkey, well out of the immediate reach of the Allied powers. During this time, events taking place in Istanbul and Izmir were to aid in the rapid consolidation of Atatürk's leadership in the nationalist resistance to the occupation. The first event was the effective collapse of the legitimacy of the Istanbul government, which was now widely viewed as the puppet of the occupiers, especially the British. The second was the unchecked and continuing attack into western Anatolia by the Greek army that had landed earlier at Izmir These events served to underscore the fact that by 1920, under Atatürk's leadership, the Ankara nationalists had become the only meaningful source of resistance.

At first, the situation seemed hopeless. Greek victories as well as the Allied takeover of power in Istanbul made it clear that the Ottoman government was not able to defend itself. Added to this were Armenian military victories in eastern Anatolia and the French occupation of the city Urfa, ancient Edessa, in southeastern Anatolia. Capping this moment of political crisis was the one-sided TREATY OF SÈVRES, signed by the Allied Powers and the Istanbul government on August 10, 1920, a document that, had it become reality, would have virtually eradicated Ottoman Turkish society and reduced any successor state to a largely landlocked country in northeastern Anatolia.

As bad as 1920 proved for both the Ottomans and the nationalists, 1921 proved to be a year of triumph for Atatürk and the nationalists in Ankara. A December 1920 Turkish victory over Armenians forces in the east was followed by the Treaty of Gümrü. Far more important was the victory of Atatürk's close friend Ismet Pasha over the Greek army in western Anatolia along the banks of the Sakarya River at Inönü. Ismet Pasha's second victory in April brought the Greek offensive to a standstill. In early August Atatürk's role as chief architect of the resistance was recognized with his election as commander in chief of the army. At the same time he received the honorific *ghazi* or "religious warrior."

By the month's end, the final Greek offensive in the Sakarya region had been reversed. Success soon followed success; by October the eastern front had been secured through a treaty with Russia and the French had agreed to withdraw in the south. Military consolidation in the field found parallels in the political realm. One of Atatürk's most trusted lieutenants, Rauf (Orbay) Pasha, became prime minister of the Grand National Assembly in Ankara. The pace of the nationalist consolidation of power increased in 1922 with the defeat and evacuation of the Greek army from Asia Minor and the evacuation of Greek forces from Izmir. An armistice agreement between the Allied Powers, the Greeks, and the new Turkish government was signed at the port of Mudanya in October. Most important was the removal of any Ottoman challenge to nationalist legitimacy, which came with the flight from Istanbul of the last Ottoman sultan, MEHMED VI (r. 1918–1922), aboard a British warship. This was followed by the decision of the national government in Ankara on November 1, 1922 to abolish the sultanate, thereby ending more than six centuries of Ottoman political and religious rule. This astonishing reversal of fortunes was confirmed the following year with the successful negotiations of the new Turkish government under the leadership of Atatürk's trusted lieutenant Ismet (Inönü) Pasha. By October the Allied Powers evacuated both Istanbul and the straits of the Bosporus and the Dardanelles, leaving Atatürk's government in Ankara as the uncontested sovereign power. On October 29, 1923, the Republic of Turkey was proclaimed by Parliament, with Atatürk elected president and Ismet (Inönü) Pasha elected prime minister.

ARCHITECT OF REFORM

Despite Atatürk's unparalleled military and political success during the preceding decade, he was not content to rest on his laurels. Turkey was still surrounded by hostile powers and was in a state of serious political and economic crisis. Millions of former Ottoman subjects—Turks, Greeks and Armenians—were dead. Millions more, mostly the surviving Greeks and Armenians, had fled Turkey or left under population exchange agreements, leaving the fabric of the new Turkish Republic in tatters. Beyond this there was the weight of the Ottoman legacy, with its past glories and failures, bearing down on the Republic. Atatürk's answer to this dilemma was to look to the future and never turn back. Most notable in this policy were the decisions of early 1924 to abolish the caliphate, or the leadership of Sunni Islam, a role played by the Ottoman sultan since the early 16th century. This was soon followed by the closing of religious schools. With the stroke of a pen Atatürk removed the legal and legitimating power of Islam from the modern Turkish Republic.

In doing so, Atatürk set the modern republic on a road that embraced a new secular ideal and turned its back on the past and its religious institutions. New civil and criminal codes were passed in 1926, ending the centuries of religious law or SHARIA. Muslim organizations were suppressed and dervish lodges closed. With these actions, the new government demonstrated its willingness to back its reforms with force if called to so.

While Atatürk's reforms suppressed many of the historical, cultural, and religious influences of the Ottomans and Islam, further reforms were aimed at broadening the enfranchisement of the citizenry and the institutionalization of their legal rights within the republic. Perhaps nowhere was this more in evidence than in the advancement of legal rights for women. In the new Turkish civil code of 1926, women were for the first time granted full and equal rights as citizens, the beginning of a deliberate civil program of women's emancipation to which Atatürk demonstrated a wholehearted commitment, albeit with some seemingly incongruent results. Thus Atatürk's agenda included the voting rights that came in 1926, the selection of a national beauty queen in 1929, and the appointment of women judges in 1930.

Beyond these reforms were a series of laws designed to force modernization through external appearances. These included the Hat Law of 1925, an act that banned the Ottoman fez and replaced it with the brimmed hats common in the West. The aim here was to break the links between status and dress, a longstanding Ottoman practice, as well as to remove outward symbols of religious affiliation such as the fez. These reforms extended to all aspects of daily life in the republic. In Ottoman society individuals were, for the most part, known by one name—for example, Ali, Mehmed, or Emine. This was all to change in 1934 when Atatürk—then still Mustafa Kemal—pushed for a law requiring everyone to have a surname. Mustafa Kemal took the name Atatürk, meaning "father of the Turks," for himself; no one else has been allowed to take the name since that time.

The most radical reforms enacted during Atatürk's time, however, were those that served to build a historical and cultural barrier between the youth of Turkey and their Ottoman forebears in an effort to turn Turkey irreversibly westward and toward the ideals of the Enlightenment. None was more powerful than the adoption in 1928 of the modern Turkish alphabet to replace the far more complex Ottoman Arabic script that was the official writing used by the imperial administration. This reform, coupled with the development of national schools and a national curriculum, served to move the greater part of the Turkish population past the barrier of illiteracy that was commonplace during the Ottoman period. An unfortunate result of this reform was that Turkish children from the 1930s onward were unable to read their parents' and grandparents' writing as the modern modified Roman script had complete replaced the ancient, cursive, modified Arabic script. To further reinforce this divide, a special organization, the Dil Kurumu or Language Institute, was established in 1932. The goal of the institute was to promote "pure" Turkish in place of the Arabic or Persian words found within Ottoman Turkish. The result was a radical reordering of the language, at the expense of much that had existed before in literature and poetry. Young Turkish citizens not only could not read their parents' letters or books, they could not understand the many words of Persian of Arabic origin that were now supplanted by officially approved neologisms of ostensibly Turkish origin.

The results of Atatürk's reforms as seen from the perspective of today's modern republic are nothing short of astonishing. While Turks today are virtually all Muslim, the public sphere of Turkey is staunchly secular in sharp contrast to the Ottoman system of *millets* or religiously defined communities. Turkey's political and economic orientation for the past 70 years has been, for the great part, Western. In contrast to its Muslim neighbors of Iran, Iraq and Syria, Turkey enjoys almost universal literacy among the young, a strong economy despite a lack of oil reserves, and a political system that has made the transition from early autocratic rule to a functioning democracy. The price of these reforms has at times been difficult to bear, for both the reformers and the general population. For Atatürk, the price was high. His enormous charisma, clarity of vision, and drive left him with few close friends. His penchant for late-night debates fuelled with liberal quantities of *rakı,* his favorite drink, took a terrible toll, and by the late 1930s it was obvious that his health was failing. On November 10, 1938, at 9:05 in the morning, Mustafa Kemal, Atatürk, died in the last palace of the Ottoman sultans. Today the palace is one of the great tourist attractions in Istanbul as is Atatürk's tomb in Ankara, the final resting place of Turkey's most revered citizen.

David Cameron Cuthell Jr.

Further reading: Lord Kinross, *Atatürk: A Biography of Mustafa Kemal, Father of Modern Turkey* (New York: Morrow, 1965); A. L. Macfie, *Atatürk* (London: Longman, 1994); Andrew Mango, *Atatürk: The Biography of the Founder of Modern Turkey* (Woodstock, N.Y.: Overlook Press, 2000); Vamık D. Volkan and Norman Itzkowitz, *The Immortal Atatürk: A Psychobiography* (Chicago: University of Chicago Press, 1984).

Auspicious Incident (Vaka-i Hayriiye, the beneficial event, the blessed affair) The Auspicious Incident refers to the formal abolition of the JANISSARIES on June 17, 1826. The Janissaries had long ceased to be a military force. By the 18th century, many of them had become tax-exempt shop-owners while continuing to receive military pay. The disastrous defeats inflicted by RUSSIA and the Habsburgs in the late 18th century convinced the Ottomans of the need for a disciplined army

organized along Western lines. However, any Western-inspired military reform ultimately threatened the whole traditional Ottoman system, challenging the vested interests of the Janissaries as well as the religious leadership or ULEMA. In the face of this potential threat, a Janissary-ulema coalition had gradually come into being as early as the Patrona Halil Rebellion (1730) and enjoyed popular support from the Muslim inhabitants of Istanbul as the sole protectors of the traditional system. As a result, attempted reforms to the traditional system proved abortive, such as attempts to introduce military training on a regular basis in the Janissary corps and to restrict the selling of Janissary pay certificates. Nevertheless, even attempts at reform frustrated the Janissaries, bureaucrats, and ulema because the proposed reforms challenged traditional privileges.

It was the GREEK WAR OF INDEPENDENCE (1821–26) that became the decisive factor in altering public attitudes toward the corrupt Janissary system. The Muslim population expressed resentment against the Janissaries because they continued their traditionally close relations with the Greeks, despite the onset of open hostilities. Moreover, the humiliation of the Janissaries by these rebels formed a stark contrast with the performance of the modern Muslim Egyptian army in the same confrontation. Thus the Muslim population of ISTANBUL became convinced of the necessity of Western military reforms and began to regard such reforms as conforming with religious propriety. With this shift in attitude, the public did not rally behind the Janissaries when they again revolted against a military reform project in 1826.

A series of related events culminated in the Auspicious Incident. The first was the promulgation of a new reform project on May 29, 1826, with a view to reforming the Janissaries from within by setting up a modern military unit (Eşkenci), composed of the ablest members of the corps in Istanbul. Next, the Janissaries began an uprising by symbolically overturning their regimental soup cauldrons in Et Meydanı (the Meat Quarter) on June 15, in defiance of the sultan. In response, the sultan unfurled the sacred standard of the Prophet in declaration of jihad against the rebels; this was followed by the bombardment of the Janissary barracks by the loyal technical corps. That same day, June 15, the masses of Istanbul rose up against the Janissaries, resulting altogether in the deaths of approximately 6,000 Janissaries. The following day, June 16, the decision was made to abolish the Janissary corps; on June 17, the sultan promulgated its formal abolition.

It is not clear when MAHMUD II (r. 1808–39) actually decided to abolish the Janissaries. While he is said to have played with this idea as early as 1812, immediately after the Russo-Ottoman War of 1806–12 (*see* RUSSO-OTTOMAN WARS), real change in policy toward the Janissaries came in 1823 with the removal of some influential bureaucrats who enjoyed Janissary support. Cautioned by the mistakes of his uncle SELIM III (r. 1789–1807) in the Kabakçı Mustafa Revolt of 1808 (see SELIM III and NIZAM-I CEDID), Mahmud II pursued a policy of winning over the traditional supporters of the Janissaries: the low-ranking ulema (through politics of piety), the technical corps (by bribing and coercion), and the people of Istanbul.

The degree of harshness in the Auspicious Incident stunned many contemporaries and historians, who likened it to the destruction of the Streltsy army by Peter the Great in Russia. Roughly 6,000 Janissaries perished in the bombardment of the barracks and the ensuing melee. Hundreds of Janissaries were formally executed following summary courts, some 20,000 more were sent into exile in Anatolia. The convents of the BEKTAŞI ORDER of dervishes were the next to be suppressed, because the Janissaries were traditionally Bektaşis. Mahmud II confiscated the properties of the Bektaşi Order and passed some of them over to more orthodox orders such as the NAQSHIBANDIYYA ORDER of dervishes, which had given the sultan substantial support against the Janissaries. Mahmud is even said to have ordered the destruction of the Janissary muster rolls and tombstones (though this latter has proved to be untrue), completely effacing the traditional Janissary establishment.

While Mahmud may have staged the military reform to provoke the rebellious Janissaries, the spontaneity of the events, rather than Mahmud's intention, accounts for the violence in Istanbul. Liquidation of the Janissaries stationed in the provinces proved less violent, with most of these troops simply dissolving into civilian society. After the abolition, Mahmud II allowed pensions to loyal Janissaries and lifetime salaries to the holders of Janissary payroll tickets. The Bektaşi purge was meant to destroy the organizational structure of the order, but as a belief system it has continued to survive even to the present

While the Auspicious Incident paved the way for the modernizing reforms of the TANZIMAT by eliminating the most resolute opponents of reform, it also meant a rupture between the sultan and the urban class of Muslim artisans, the ex-Janissaries, who subsequently refused to wear the fez, which became the symbol of Mahmud's absolute authority. The history of Ottoman modernization must thus accommodate the contradictory representations of "Mahmud the Great" and "Mahmud the Infidel."

Kahraman Şakul

Further reading: Butrus Abu-Manneh, *Studies on Islam and the Ottoman Empire in the 19th Century, 1826–1876* (Istanbul: Isis, 2001), 66–69; Caroline Finkel, *Osman's Dream: The Story of the Ottoman Empire, 1300–1923* (London: John Murray, 2005), 432–446; Avigdor Levy, "The Military Policy of Sultan Mahmud II, 1808–1839." (Ph.D. diss., Harvard University, 1968); Avigdor Levy, "The Ottoman Ulema and the Military Reforms of Sultan Mahmud II." *Asian and African Studies* 7 (1971): 13–39; Howard A. Reed, "The Destruction of the Janissaries by Mahmud II in June, 1826." (Ph.D. diss., Princeton University, 1951); Stanford J. Shaw and Ezel K. Shaw, *History of the Ottoman Empire and Modern Turkey,* vol. 2 (Cambridge: Cambridge University Press, 1977), 19–24.

Austria (*Ger.*: **Österreich**; *Turk.*: **Nemçe, Avusturya**) Ruled by the Habsburgs from 1282 through 1918, the present-day central European country of Austria had a long common history with the Ottomans, which can be divided into two distinctively different phases. The first phase can be described as the era of "Turkish menace," which lasted from the mid-15th century through the mid-18th century and was characterized by Ottoman raids, continual Austro-Ottoman wars, and the defense of Austria. The second phase lasted from the mid-18th century until the dissolution of the two empires after WORLD WAR I. The first decades of this era saw three Austro-Ottoman wars. The 19th century was characterized by similar external and internal threats for both empires (Russian expansionism in the Balkans for the Ottomans, and nationalist and Pan-Slavist movements for Austria) that significantly influenced Austrian policy regarding the Ottoman Empire and its Balkan domains.

OTTOMAN ADVANCE AND THE CREATION OF THE AUSTRIAN HABSBURG MONARCHY

Intermittent Ottoman raids reached the southern parts of Austria (Carniola and Styria) between 1408 and 1426. More serious ones followed between 1469 and 1493, forcing the Austrians to enact several laws to strengthen the country's defenses and armed forces. The belief that none of the countries of Central Europe was capable of withstanding Ottoman assaults was used to justify the creation of dynastic unions in the region by which two or more of the crowns of Austria, HUNGARY, Bohemia (the Czech lands), POLAND, and Lithuania were united for shorter or longer periods. While several ruling houses tried to join the crowns and resources of Central Europe, it was the Habsburgs who succeeded in uniting the crowns of Austria, Hungary, and Bohemia by 1526. Their success was due to their dynastic treaties and marriages, as well as to the Ottomans' victory against the Hungarians in 1526.

The 1515 Habsburg-Jagiello Treaty concluded between Holy Roman Emperor Maximilian I (r. 1496–1519) and Uladislaus II Jagiello, king of Hungary and Bohemia (r. 1490–1516), stipulated that if one dynasty died out, the other would inherit its lands. The treaty was later strengthened by the double marriage of Maximilian's grandson and granddaughter (Ferdinand and Mary) to the daughter and son of King Uladislaus (Anna and Louis). When at the BATTLE OF MOHÁCS (1526), Sultan SÜLEYMAN I (r. 1520–66) killed Louis II of Jagiello, king of Hungary and Bohemia (r. 1516–26), the Bohemian and Hungarian estates elected as their king Maximilian's grandson, Ferdinand of Austria, the younger brother of Holy Roman Emperor Charles V (r. 1519–56).

With his election, Ferdinand laid the foundations of the Danubian Habsburg monarchy. However, Ferdinand's rule in Hungary was challenged by János (John) Szapolyai, also elected king of Hungary (r. 1526–40), whom the Ottomans supported as their vassal. Despite intense diplomacy and campaigning, Ferdinand failed to unseat his rival. When King János died in 1540 and Ferdinand's troops besieged Hungary's capital, BUDA, Sultan Süleyman decided to conquer Buda and central Hungary in 1541. This led to the tripartite division of the country. Of the three parts, the Austrian Habsburgs ruled the western and northern parts (royal Hungary), which served as a buffer zone between Austria and the Ottomans from 1541 through 1699. Central Hungary became a new Ottoman province, while the eastern parts evolved into a new polity, the Ottoman client principality of TRANSYLVANIA.

DEFENSE OF AUSTRIA AND ITS CONSEQUENCES

The Ottoman threat not only promoted the establishment of a new political entity, the Austrian or Danubian Habsburg monarchy, but it also urged the Habsburgs to modernize their military, finances, and government, and to reorganize the collapsed Hungarian defense system. The main office of military administration was the Viennese Aulic War Council or the Austrian Habsburg Ministry of War (Wiener Hofkriegsrat, 1556–1848), whose jurisdiction extended to the whole monarchy, including the Military Border (Militärgrenze) built in Croatia and Hungary. This new defense line stretched some 650 miles from the ADRIATIC SEA to Upper Hungary (present-day Slovakia) and was made up of more than 120 large and small fortresses and watchtowers. Since Vienna lay only about 80 miles from the major Ottoman garrisons in Hungary, the Habsburgs rebuilt and modernized the key fortresses of their Croatian and Hungarian Military Border according to the latest standards of fortress building. In the 1570s and 1580s, some 22,000 soldiers guarded the border, of whom 15 percent were German, Italian, and Spanish mercenaries stationed in the key fortresses, while the rest were Hungarians, Serbs, and Croats.

The Aulic War Council was responsible for the manning, building, and maintenance of border fortresses, warehouses, and arsenals, as well as for the recruitment, armament, and the supply of field troops. However, it had limited financial authority, and depended on the Court Chamber or Ministry of Finance (Hofkammer), set up by Ferdinand I (1527), and to a lesser degree on the Hungarian Chamber, which administered royal revenues (crown lands, tolls, customs, coinage, and mines) from the king's Hungarian domains.

While the Ottoman threat aided Austrian state centralization, it also limited the power of the monarchs and helped the Austrian and Hungarian estates to guard their centuries-old privileges and their relative religious freedom. The latter was especially important, for by the middle of the 16th century many of the estates chose either the Lutheran or the Calvinist reform churches, whereas the Habsburgs remained Catholic. The rulers of Austria (who, after the abdication of Charles V (1556) also held the title of Holy Roman Emperor) in their endeavors to maintain their anti-Ottoman garrisons, were dependent on the "Turkish aid" (Türkenhilfe) and various other taxes, authorized by the Imperial Diet and the Austrian, Bohemian, and Hungarian estates. Thus, the estates possessed considerable leverage with their ruler. The Lutheran estates of Inner Austria (an administrative unit made up of Styria, Carinthia, and Carniola), for instance, had their former privileges confirmed in 1578, in return for their service along the Croatian strip of the Military Border.

Although the Ottomans launched numerous campaigns against the Austrian Habsburgs (1529, 1532, 1541, 1543, 1551–52, 1566, 1663–64) and the two empires waged two exhausting wars (1593–1606 and 1683–99), the Ottomans failed to conquer Austria. Vienna itself withstood two Ottoman sieges in 1529 and 1683 (see VIENNA, SIEGES OF). The latter siege triggered an international anti-Ottoman coalition war (1683–99), led by Austria. By the conclusion of the TREATY OF KARLOWITZ (1699) that ended the war, most of Hungary was in Austrian hands, making Austria the strongest central European power.

AUSTRIA'S LAST TURKISH WARS

Habsburg-Ottoman relations remained relatively calm following the Treaty of Karlowitz, while both empires waged wars on other fronts. However, Sultan AHMED III's (1703–1730) recent conquests in the Morea (Peloponnese) and CRETE in the first years of the Venetian-Ottoman war of 1714–18 soon dragged Austria into war. On the suggestion of Prince Eugene of Savoy (1663–1736), imperial field marshal and president of the Aulic War Council, the Habsburgs concluded a defensive alliance with Venice in 1716, which led to Istanbul's declaration of war against Vienna.

In Austria's Turkish war of 1716–18, Eugene defeated the Ottomans (1716) and took BELGRADE (1717). The Treaty of Passarowitz (Požarevac, 1718) reflected these victories: Istanbul surrendered to Austria the Banat of

Temesvár, that is, the only remaining Ottoman territory in southern Hungary across the "natural" Danube border, as well as parts of northern Serbia and western Wallachia.

However, Austria lost Belgrade and parts of Wallachia to Istanbul in the humiliating Treaty of Belgrade (1739) that concluded Austria's Turkish war of 1737–39, fought in coalition with Russia. During the war, Austria was alarmed by Russia's ambitions and advance in the Balkans that would in the future also influence its relationship with both Russia and the Ottomans.

By the mid-18th century the fear of the "Turkish menace" of the previous centuries had been transformed into an interest in everything Turkish. Until the end of the century, the Austro-Ottoman relationship was characterized mainly by diplomatic and trade contacts, rather than war, mainly due to Austria's European wars and commitments.

Following the death of Holy Roman Emperor Charles VI (r. 1711–40), his daughter and declared heiress to all his Habsburg kingdoms, Maria Theresa, had to defend her inheritance in a series of wars (1740–48, 1756–63, and 1778–79), mainly against Frederick the Great of Prussia (r. 1740–86). Although Maria Theresa secured Austria, Hungary, and Bohemia (r. 1740–80) and her husband and son were both elected Holy Roman Emperor (Francis I, r. 1745–65, and Joseph II, r. 1765–90, respectively), she lost Silesia (present-day southwestern Poland) to Prussia. The loss of Silesia, and the fact that Prussia replaced Austria as the new leader of the German states, directed Vienna's attention yet again to the Balkans.

After Czarina Catherine II of Russia (r. 1762–96) shared with Emperor Joseph II her "Greek Project" that envisioned the partition of the Ottoman Empire, it was clear to the emperor that Austria had to be part of Russia's next Turkish war if Vienna was to check Russian advance in the Balkans and share in the Turkish spoils. In 1783, Austria backed Russia's annexation of the Crimea—a former Ottoman client state (1474–1774) that was declared "independent" after the humiliating Ottoman defeat in the RUSSO-OTTOMAN WAR OF 1768–74—but came away empty-handed, profiting only modestly from the opening of all Turkish seas for Austrian shipping.

When, after numerous Russian provocations, Istanbul declared war against Russia in August 1787, Austria joined its ally, hoping for the reestablishment of the 1718 border and substantial territorial gains in Serbia and Bosnia. However, the war brought only modest reward at enormous cost: 33,000 dead and 172,000 sick and wounded between June 1788 and May 1789, and major destruction in the recently colonized Banat during the devastating Ottoman raids in the autumn of 1788. Weakened by unrest in the Netherlands and Hungary and threatened by the possibility of a Prussian attack, Vienna

was willing to end the war at all costs. The TREATY OF SVISHTOV (August 4, 1791) reestablished the prewar situation, granting only minor border adjustments to Austria.

AUSTRIAN FOREIGN POLICY AND THE OTTOMANS IN THE 19TH CENTURY

In the three decades following the Congress of Vienna (1815) that reshaped Europe after the Napoleonic Wars (1803–15), Austria played a vital role in European politics. This was due to the skillful diplomacy of Prince Klemens von Metternich, Vienna's omnipotent foreign minister, who acted as the chief arbiter of post-Napoleonic Europe while in office (1809–48). Through various alliances and conferences, Metternich and his European counterparts attempted to deal with Europe as an organic whole for the first time in history and managed to maintain the precarious balance of power among the leading European powers. Austria also led the German Confederation (1815–66) that replaced the defunct Holy Roman Empire. During these decades, Austria also witnessed sustained industrialization and massive investments in infrastructure: pig iron, coal, and textile production grew especially quickly, and by 1848, the monarchy's railroad system had more than 1,000 miles of track. However, the Metternich system proved unable to cope with the social consequences of industrial development, the growing tide of nationalism and democratic-liberal movements, and the EASTERN QUESTION. The Metternich system was overthrown by the European revolutions of 1848 that rose up against the regime's oppressive policies, characterized by domestic surveillance and censorship and by the suppression of liberal and nationalist movements.

The revolutions in the Austrian, Hungarian, and Italian parts of the monarchy were all put down and it seemed that the neoabsolutist governments (1848–59) managed to restore the old regime under Franz Joseph II (r. 1848–1916). However, the problems and foreign policy concerns that Vienna faced during the revolutions would occupy Austria in the decades to come.

Austria's neutrality during the CRIMEAN WAR (1853–56) that pitted the Ottoman Empire, FRANCE, and ENGLAND against Russia, understandably alienated St. Petersburg, which had helped Vienna suppress the Hungarian revolution and war of independence of 1848–49. With the establishment of a unified Italy in 1861, Austria lost its Italian domains. By 1866, Austria had lost its leading position among the German states to Prussia. The latter's ascendancy in German politics became even more obvious with the establishment of the unified German Empire in 1871, whose founder and first chancellor (1871–90) was Otto von Bismarck, Prussia's prime minister (1862–73, 1873–90). The loss of the

Italian possessions and the establishment of the German Empire turned Vienna's attention to its eastern domains and neighbors.

Vienna's 1867 compromise (Ausgleich) with the Hungarian ruling estates transformed the Austrian monarchy into the Austro-Hungarian monarchy (1867–1918). Russian expansionism in the Balkans and fear of Pan-Slavism (a movement to advance the cultural and political unity of all Slavs) as well as nationalist and separatists movements among their Slav peoples brought the Ottoman and Austro-Hungarian empires closer. Austria-Hungary considered the preservation of the Ottoman Empire and the status quo in the Balkans as a must in order to contain Russian advances in the region. Under Gyula Andrássy's foreign ministry (1871–79), Austria-Hungary allied itself with Germany and Russia for just those reasons: to restrain Russia in the Balkans and, if the partition of Istanbul's Balkan territories became unavoidable, to share in the Turkish spoils. Partition, though, was not seen as desirable, for it would further complicate the monarchy's problems with its Slav subjects. Thus, during the Bosnian and Serbian uprisings (1875), Austria and Germany convinced Russia to give up (at least temporarily) her plans regarding the partition of the Ottoman Balkans. However, during the Serbian uprising in 1877, Russia declared war on the Ottomans and was instrumental in creating Greater Bulgaria, which many saw as St. Petersburg's client state in the Balkans. With England's and Germany's support at the Congress of Berlin (July 1878), Andrássy managed to substantially reduce Bulgaria's territories. The Congress guaranteed Serbia's independence, forced Russia to content itself with Bessarabia (territories between the Dniester and Prut rivers, mostly in present-day Moldova), and allowed Austria to occupy BOSNIA AND HERZEGOVINA, which, however, remained under nominal Ottoman rule. Andrássy's last act in office was the Dual Alliance with Germany (1879), which assured mutual support in case of a Russian attack. Vienna's dependence on its stronger German ally would dominate, and significantly limit, Austro-Hungarian foreign policy during the remaining years of the monarchy.

Although in the 1880s and 1890s Germany and Austria-Hungary managed to include Russia, Serbia, and Italy into their various alliance systems, by the early 1900s relations with Russia and Serbia became tense. Fearing that Serbian expansionist policies and Ottoman reforms made by the new YOUNG TURK government would undermine Austrian positions in Bosnia-Herzegovina, Austria-Hungary annexed Bosnia and Herzegovina in 1908, provoking opposition from Serbia and Russia. It was, again, German backing for Austria-Hungary (plus financial compensation to Istanbul from Vienna) that persuaded Russia, Serbia, and the Ottoman Empire to accept the annexation and settle the Bosnian crisis (1909).

Since the Bosnian crisis, the pro-war party in Vienna considered confrontation with Serbia inevitable and argued for a preventive war. When, on June 28, 1914, in Sarajevo, a Bosnian nationalist assassinated Archduke Francis Ferdinand, the heir of Franz Joseph, the Viennese foreign office held Serbia responsible for the assassination. The Austrian ultimatum was unacceptable, and Vienna declared war on Belgrade (July 28, 1914). In the ensuing war (*see* WORLD WAR I), Austria-Hungary and the Ottomans fought as allies, and both empires perished.

Gábor Ágoston

See also BOSNIA AND HERZEGOVINA; HUNGARY; RUSSIA; WORLD WAR I.

Further reading: Michael Hochendlinger, *Austria's Wars of Emergence: War, State and Society in the Habsburg Monarchy, 1683–1797* (London: Longman, 2003); Steven Beller, *A Concise History of Austria* (Cambridge: Cambridge University Press, 2007).

ayan   Ayan is the plural of the Arabic word *ayn*, meaning "something or someone that is selected or special." The term was used differently by different communities within the Ottoman Empire. The singular is not used in Arabic to refer to an individual, but in its plural form, it was used by Arabic speakers from the 16th through the early 19th centuries to refer collectively to the secular leadership of a town or city, as opposed to the ulema or religious authorities. An individual might be called "one of the *ayan*" in the chronicles written in the 18th century, but never "an *ayan*." The *ayan* included among their ranks wealthy merchants, heads of Janissary garrisons, leaders of important craft guilds, those who had bought the right to collect taxes for the government in Istanbul, and those who supervised the distribution of wealth generated by, and the maintenance of, pious endowments (WAQFS). Among Arabic speakers of the Ottoman Empire, the term *ayan* was reserved solely for those notables who were Muslims.

In Ottoman Turkish, the word *ayan* was most often applied to an individual who was recognized as a civic leader in a town or village or, after the 17th century, to a provincial notable, as contrasted with Ottoman officials appointed from Istanbul. Such men had their own armed forces to support them and enjoyed varying degrees of autonomy from the central government in provincial administration.

The difference in meaning that the same word could have in the two languages points to the varying roles that local people carved out for themselves in the Ottoman Empire beginning in the 18th century. In most of the Arab provinces, civil authority devolved to collective civic bodies composed of men representing contending extended families or interest groups. Such coalitions were usually unstable, due to personal rivalries within a given city, and only rarely did one person emerge as an unchallenged political boss. By contrast, in both Anatolia and the Balkans, individuals could amass wealth as tax collectors and hire their own private armies to secure their political and economic positions, often challenging, or even replacing, the provincial governors.

ANATOLIA AND THE BALKANS

In the 15th and 16th centuries in Anatolia and the Balkans, the term *ayan* was used generically to denote a distinguished person regardless of his position or background. In contrast to Arabic, it could be used to refer to a single person. From the 17th century onward, the term *ayan* and *ayan-ı vilayet* (provincial notable) came to signify exclusively a leader of a provincial community. In the Ottoman provincial governance, many administrative functions, including management of tax collection and allocation, supervision of public expenditures and security, were carried out with the active participation of, and in negotiation with, community leaders. Throughout the 18th century, as a result of structural transformation in the Ottoman provincial governance and fiscal system, the central authority allowed broader and more formal participation of such local leaders in the provincial administration.

The devolution of power to local people in the 18th century facilitated the rise of "*ayan*-ship" as a formal office at the district (*kaza*) level. From the late 17th century, the assessing of lump-sum taxation on various rural communities became an increasingly common practice in the absence of updated tax registers and the proliferation of inefficient or corrupt tax collectors. Furthermore, the provincial governors and deputy governors imposed extraordinary tax claims to finance their military campaigns and their growing retinues of armed men. Under these circumstances, local communities came to negotiate their taxes with the agents of the central government and imperial governors, through their community leaders, the *ayan*.

By the mid 18th century, in several regions of Rumelia and Anatolia (the empire's European and Asian possessions, respectively), the title of *ayan* (or *kocabaşı* if the individual were a Christian) came to mean a notable of a district who was elected by the community itself or had at least received the unanimous consent of the community to negotiate in its name and to manage the collection and allocation of taxes. Increasingly, the *ayan* came to control almost all aspects of the district governance, including not only taxation but also security, the provisioning of the district in times of famine, and the maintenance of public buildings. As many provincial districts,

which were formerly governed by judges (*kadıs*), came to be governed by the *ayan,* the judges who were appointed from the capital, like other imperial agents, were marginalized and their jurisdiction was limited solely to judiciary and notary, rather than administrative, functions.

In the second half of the 18th century, the central authority initiated reforms to increase its control over the provinces and to reorganize the relations among the governors or deputy governors, the *ayans,* and the communities. Between 1762 and 1792, the central government tried to initiate several regulations for the elections and appointment of the district *ayans.* Nevertheless, the central government did not impose any of these either systematically or universally, and in most cases the election process was left to local community practice. The central government also intended to regularize the allocation process of provincial taxes and other public expenditures of the districts. The process and pace of reform was hindered by the Russo-Ottoman war of 1787–1792 (*see* RUSSO-OTTOMAN WARS). During the war, almost all administrative functions, from provisioning to military recruitment, came under the control of the provincial leaders who acted as deputy governors or district *ayans,* making the central government entirely dependent on their active collaboration. By the end of the war, several provincial notables had consolidated their power in their respective regions and evolved into regional powerholders. The most powerful of them had expanded their territories, established large autonomous polities, and challenged the integrity of the empire.

Between 1792 and 1812, much of the Ottoman Empire in the Balkans and Anatolia was partitioned among these power brokers. In the Balkans, these included OSMAN PAZVANTOĞLU in Vidin, BULGARIA; Ismail Bey in Serres, GREECE; Tepedelenli Ali Pasha in the Epirus, Greece; Tirskiniklioğlu Ismail Agha in Rusçuk (Ruse), BULGARIA. In Anatolia, they included the Karaosmanoğlu family in western Anatolia, the Cabbaroğlu family in central Anatolia, the Canikli Family in northeastern Anatolia, the Tekelioğlu family in Antalya, and the Menemencioğlu and Kozanoğlu families in Cilicia. These individuals or families established autonomous control over vast territories, erected palaces, monopolized tax sources, and recruited personal armies. They developed strategies for transmitting wealth and status within their households or families. Most of them were vigorously engaged in the shifting, and often treacherous, political life that marked the court in the last years of the reign of Sultan SELIM III (r. 1789–1807) and at the start of the reign of Sultan MAHMUD II (r. 1808–1839).

These power-holders were simultaneously warlords, local leaders, governors, landlords, fiscal agents, and business entrepreneurs. In fact, the Ottoman central authority neither totally recognized nor explicitly rejected their claims to local authority. It rather preferred to negotiate with them and sought to develop strategies to keep them loyal to the empire without making any concessions regarding the nominal sovereignty of the Ottoman sultan. On the other hand, while some of the provincial power-holders were ready to be incorporated into the imperial establishment, albeit on their own terms, others challenged the imperial system and became outlaws. When the central government failed to suppress a rebel, it was often ready to pardon him and even grant him an honorary title in an attempt to reintegrate him into the imperial elite. As rebellion became a means of negotiation for the *ayan,* the boundaries between loyalty and treason, legality and illegality, came to be blurred.

The challenge of the provincial power-holders in the late 18th and early 19th centuries did not result in a disintegration of the empire. On the contrary, during the constitutional crisis between 1807 and 1808, many provincial magnates, instead of seeking independence, created alliances with different factions of the central government. Toward the end of 1808, after the coup led by ALEMDAR MUSTAFA PASHA, the *ayan* of Ruse (Rusçuk), Bulgaria, the leading provincial power-holders were summoned for a general assembly. During the assembly the magnates agreed to remain loyal to the sultan, while Sultan Mahmud II agreed to recognize the claims of the magnates as legitimate rulers of the Ottoman provinces. A document called the Document of Agreement (Sened-i Ittifak), was signed between the sultan, the provincial magnates, and the dignitaries of the central government in 1808.

During the rest of the 19th century, although the role of the local leaders continued in Ottoman politics, they were never again as powerful as they were in the late 18th and early 19th centuries. As the Ottoman Empire was transformed into a modern state, the provincial leaders were forced by the growing strength of the revived Ottoman army to abandon their earlier claims. They were demilitarized and forced to adapt to the new rules of provincial politics. While some were able to integrate into the imperial elite as bureaucrats, soldiers, or politicians, those who resisted the modern state were gradually suppressed and eliminated.

ARAB PROVINCES

During the 18th century, Ottoman rule was as tenuous in the Arab provinces as it was in the Balkans and Anatolia. The devolution of political power into the hands of local people who could ensure both the flow of revenue to Istanbul and order in the countryside accelerated as the central government's ability for direct rule weakened. But with the exception of CEZZAR AHMED PASHA in ACRE, none of the prominent political actors who emerged in that century could directly challenge the authority of the central government. Rather, they had to work within the framework of imperial rule, obtaining governorships only as long as their relations with the sultans were good. Arabic-speaking chroniclers in the lands that would become SYRIA and IRAQ labeled as *ayan* their contemporaries who played such mediating roles between the authorities in the capital and the military forces on hand in their native cities. Included among these notables were men from well-established scholarly families, leading merchants, and commanders of military units raised locally in the provinces.

However, that being said, only those *ayan* families who gained their prominence from military service rose to positions of political dominance, receiving appointments as governors from the sultans, in their respective cities. A distinction should therefore be made between those who held influence through their wealth or religious authority and those who held it by virtue of the sword. Nevertheless, as members of prominent Muslim families from all three categories intermarried, there were often overlapping identities and loyalties. Not every Arab city witnessed the rise of a single prominent family from among the "notable" families who jostled for power. This was definitely the case for JERUSALEM and ALEPPO. In both of these cities, a relatively small number of families—generally fewer than 10—were recognized by the rest of the population as being their respective city's notables, but none was able to seize power for itself at the expense of the others. In cities where a single family did emerge, such as the JALILI FAMILY in MOSUL or the AL-AZM FAMILY in DAMASCUS, its members were able to provide security in an age that was increasingly characterized by political turmoil.

Unlike the case of the Balkans and Anatolia, the Ottoman central state did not reassert itself forcefully in the Arab provinces during the reign of Sultan Mahmud II, and *ayan* politics continued well into the 1820s. But with the occupation of what is today Syria, Lebanon, and Israel by the Egyptian Army led by IBRAHIM PASHA in 1831, the authority of a strong centralized state was restored. As a result, the *ayan* families of the region resented the Egyptian occupation and welcomed the return of the Ottoman army in 1840–41. In the decades that followed, many of these families were able to reassert their leadership roles in their respective cities, for example, by winning provincial and mayoral elections, and they remained prominent in their respective cities' politics through the end of the empire

Ali Yaycıoğlu and Bruce Masters

Further reading: Fikret Adanır, "Semi-autonomous Forces in the Balkans and Anatolia," in *The Cambridge History of Turkey*, vol. 3, *The Later Ottoman Empire, 1603–1839*, edited by Suraiya Faroqhi (Cambridge: Cambridge University Press, 2006), 157–185; Bruce Masters, "Semi-autonomous Forces in the Arab Provinces," in *The Cambridge History of Turkey*, vol. 3, *The Later Ottoman Empire,*

1603–1839, edited by Suraiya Faroqhi (Cambridge: Cambridge University Press, 2006), 186–206.

Ayasofya   *See* HAGIA SOPHIA.

Azak (Azof, Azov, Tana)   Located at the mouth of the Don River at the northeastern corner of the Sea of Azov, the town and fortress of Azak was known as Tana before its conquest by the Ottomans in 1475. In the wake of the Mongol conquest, in the 14th century, Italian traders, first Genoese and then Venetians, formed colonies in Tana. During this period it served as an important stop on the east-west silk and spice route. In addition, furs and other products from the north traveled into the BLACK SEA region via Azak.

After the Ottoman conquest, Azak became a *kaza* (district) and eventually a *sancak* (subprovince) in the province of CAFFA. While Tana had lost its importance as an entrepôt of the long-distance east-west trade even before the Ottoman takeover, the city remained an important conduit of regional trade between Muscovy and the steppes to the south, and the Black Sea region along with ISTANBUL. Aside from furs and food products (mainly caviar-bearing fish), Azak had a slave market, though it was of lesser importance than that of Caffa.

By the second half of the 16th century, Azak had gained crucial strategic importance for defense of the Sea of Azov and the Black Sea as a result of the escalating number of raids by the Don COSSACKS who by the 17th century, along with the Ukrainian Cossacks, were raiding all shores of the Black Sea. In 1637 the fortress did in fact fall to the Cossacks. It was occupied until 1642 when, for lack of support from the czar, the Cossacks were forced to withdraw, but not before demolishing much of the fortress. This began a long period of shifts in political and military control over this stronghold. Czar Peter I was unsuccessful in his attempt to recapture Azak in 1695, but succeeded in the following year, only to return it to the Ottomans after the signing of the Treaty of Prut in 1711. In 1736 Azak was again taken by the Russian Empire. According to the Treaty of Belgrade (1739) between the Ottoman Empire and AUSTRIA, its walls were destroyed, thereby ending its strategic importance.

Victor Ostapchuk

al-Azhar   Al-Azhar is the name of the central mosque in CAIRO and the university that is attached to it. The university became the leading institution of higher study in the Arabic-speaking Sunni world in the Ottoman period in the 17th and 18th centuries. The scholar who headed that institution held the title of Sheikh al-Azhar and was the leading Muslim legal authority in EGYPT from the 18th century until the present day.

The Fatimid dynasty that ruled Egypt from 969 until 1171 founded the mosque and school in 970 c.e. to be a center of learning for the Ismaili branch of SHIA ISLAM. But with the conquest of Cairo by the Sunni Ayyubid dynasty in the 12th century, the university became a center of Sunni thought and learning. It did not, however, reach prominence as the pre-eminent center of learning for SUNNI ISLAM in the Arabic-speaking world until the Ottoman period. From the 17th century onward, scholars at the university began to assert their interpretation of Islamic law against what was then the current authoritative source on the subject, the Muslim schools of ISTANBUL.

Students enrolled in al-Azhar often numbered more than 1,000 in any given class year. These students were housed in resident hostels (*riwaq*) representing their different geographical origins: North African, Egyptian, Syrian, and Anatolian. Compared to the traditional Ottoman religious schools in Istanbul, Rumelia, and Anatolia, the classes and the teaching at al-Azhar were less hierarchical,

Students eating lunch in the courtyard of al-Azhar University in 1891. During the Ottoman period, al-Azhar became a major center of Sunni Muslim education, attracting students from the Arabic-Speaking provinces of the Ottoman Empire but also from North and West Africa. *(Photograph by Maison Bonfils, courtesy of the University of Pennsylvania Museum, Philadelphia)*

and a tutorial system prevailed with individual students and teachers setting out the curriculum to be studied.

During the 18th century, al-Azhar was the premier cultural institution of the region with influence extending far beyond the boundaries of the Egyptian province. Although the dominant legal tradition taught at the university was that of the Shafii school of law, which had been favored during the period of the MAMLUK EMPIRE (1260–1517), teachers in the Hanafi tradition, the school of law favored by the Ottomans, were also available for students from Syria, as the majority of Muslims in their homeland had shifted their adherence from the Shafii school to that favored by the sultans. The writings of Muslim reformers such as MUHAMMAD IBN ABD AL-WAHHAB, who sought to purge Islam of practices such as SUFISM that he felt were un-Islamic, were also circulated and studied beginning in the late 18th century.

But as a uniquely Egyptian institution that was staffed largely by local scholars, al-Azhar often became the focus of discontent and urban unrest directed at Ottoman authorities or their Mamluk surrogates as its teachers were viewed by ordinary Egyptians as their natural leaders against a foreign oppressor. In the riots that developed out of these confrontations in the 18th century, students often took the lead in bloody clashes between the urban mobs and the Ottoman military sent to restore order.

The monopoly that al-Azhar exercised in the educational life of Egypt went unchallenged until 1872, when the Egyptian governor, or KHEDIVE, established Dar al-Ulum College to train teachers for new state schools. Although many early students of the college were in fact graduates of al-Azhar, middle-class and upper-class Egyptians increasingly considered a secular education, especially one that emphasized science, as preferable to that being offered at al-Azhar. Due in part to the increasing defection of this student base to the secular college, MUHAMMAD ABDUH created the Administrative Council for al-Azhar to promulgate new curricula, establish texts to be taught, oversee examinations, and to build a centralized library (1895). In 1908, the Egyptian government founded the National University, which would eventually come to be known as Cairo University, to provide an opportunity for completely secular education. In particular, its mission was to offer courses in the sciences and medicine that were missing from the curriculum at al-Azhar. In response, al-Azhar added a medical facility. Other departments that specialized in the natural and physical sciences were added later.

Bruce Masters

Further reading: Bayard Dodge, *Al-Azhar: A Millennium of Muslim Learning* (Washington, D.C.: Middle East Institute, 1961).

al-Azm family   The Azms were an AYAN, or notable, family who provided the governors of the province of DAMASCUS for most of the 18th century. The family came to this position of prominence when Sultan AHMED III (r. 1703–30), to preserve the security of the hajj whose pilgrims were increasingly under attack, broke with two centuries of tradition and appointed a Syrian-born military commander, Ismail Pasha al-Azm, to serve as governor of Damascus, instead of naming a career Ottoman military officer from ISTANBUL. Ismail Pasha had formerly proved himself invaluable as governor of the province of TRIPOLI from where he had commanded the *jarda*, the military escort that was sent out with provisions to meet pilgrims returning from the HAJJ and then to escort them to Damascus. Faced with growing insecurity in the Syrian Desert, the sultan calculated that a local man might understand the BEDOUINS better than someone from the capital as he would know their customs and local tribal politics.

Despite the claims of Arab nationalist historians that the family was Arab, Ismail Pasha al-Azm was from a family whose ethnic origins are uncertain. Whatever their origins, the family had developed strong local ties. Al-Azms had served as tax farmers, collecting imperial taxes levied on the peasants in the region surrounding the central Syrian towns of HAMA and Maarra in the 17th century. From those rather humble origins, the family's wealth and influence grew as it provided governors for the provinces of Damascus, Tripoli, and even briefly ALEPPO, between 1725 and 1783. Asad Pasha al-Azm, who ruled Damascus from 1743 until 1757, enjoyed an unprecedented longevity in his post due to his skill at balancing local and imperial concerns, as the governors of the city who preceded him had only held the office for a year or two at the longest.

Despite the family's success in dominating the political life of Syria, they served as governors only as long as they could effectively balance contending military forces in the provinces they governed. More importantly, they remained in office for only as long as those with influence among the various political factions at court in Istanbul suffered them to do so. Asad Pasha's downfall came after he incurred the enmity of the Kızlar Ağası, the chief eunuch of the sultan's HAREM, a powerful figure in that age of politically weak sultans. Asad was transferred to the governorship of Aleppo in 1757. The following year he was summoned to Istanbul where he was executed on charges of abuse of his office and corruption. Despite this seeming disgrace, the family continued to play a significant role in the politics of Syria as they still served as governors for all of Syria's provinces (Aleppo, Tripoli, and Sidon, as well as Damascus) at one time or another in the second half of the 18th century. But no other individual would reach a position of power or wealth comparable to the one that Asad Pasha al-Azm had enjoyed.

Because Damascus had grown accustomed to governors with very short tenures and no interest in the people or the city as anything other than a source of cash to purchase the next appointment, having one family with vested interest in the city's well-being was a real relief. Although the Azm governors proved no less greedy, they used some of their wealth to support the construction of new public buildings and private mansions that helped boost civic pride. The construction of madrasas and caravansaries by the al-Azms greatly altered the physical face of their adopted city and boosted the city's economic and cultural fortunes. Chronicles written in their lifetimes depicted members of the al-Azm family as local heroes whose justice, generosity, and religiosity were praised in contrast with the rapacity of most of the governors coming from Istanbul.

Bruce Masters

Further reading: Abd al-Karim Rafeq, *The Province of Damascus, 1723–1783* (Beirut: American University in Beirut Press, 1966).

B

Baban family   The Babans were a Kurdish family who, in the 18th and 19th centuries, dominated the political life of the province of Shahrizor, in present-day Iraqi Kurdistan. The members of the Baban clan were able to keep their position by a delicate balancing act that provided the Ottoman Empire with security along its Iranian border but retained Baban autonomy from central government control. The first member of the clan to gain control of the province of Shahrizor and its capital, Kirkuk, was Sulayman Beg, who saw his family as the natural rivals of the Kurdish princes of Ardalan, a dynasty that dominated the mountainous region on the Iranian side of the border. The *mirs*, or princes, of Ardalan controlled the Iranian portions of Kurdistan from the border town of Sanandaj, now in IRAN, and frequently claimed the loyalty of the Kurdish clans on the Ottoman side of the frontier. To establish his authority over the frequently rebellious Kurdish clans in the region of Shahrizor, Sulayman Beg invaded Iran in 1694 and defeated his rival, the *mir* of Ardalan. When the Iranian army came to the defense of the house of Ardalan and defeated Sulayman Beg's tribal irregulars, he fled back across the Ottoman frontier. The Ottomans considered the invasion to have been reckless as it endangered the peace between Iran and the empire. At the same time, however, they recognized the family's usefulness as a buffer to any future Iranian invasion. So rather than punishing him for his folly, Sultan MUSTAFA II (r. 1695–1703) assigned Sulayman the *sancak,* or district, of Baban to be his fief. The district was named after the family and included the town of Kirkuk.

The Baban family's relations with Ottoman officials in IRAQ was often strained, but the Ottomans' need for the Baban clan's Kurdish irregular troops outweighed Istanbul's desire to unseat them. Enjoying almost full autonomy, the family established Kirkuk as their capital, and erected religious buildings there to commemorate their rule. It was from this time that KURDS in Iraq began to view Kirkuk as their natural capital. This persisted even after the Babans moved their administration to the new town of Sulaymaniya, named after the dynasty's founder, in the late 18th century. The Ottoman governor of BAGHDAD finally felt secure enough to crush the power of the Babans in 1850, hoping to gain greater central control in southern Kurdistan. Instead, the fall of the house of Baban led to a deteriorating political climate as various clans contended with each other to fill the political vacuum. The result was anarchy in the region that was only ended with the rise of another Kurdish clan, the Barzinji family, at the beginning of the 20th century.

Bruce Masters

Further reading: David MacDowall, *A Modern History of the Kurds,* 2nd ed. (London: Tauris, 2000).

Baghdad   (*Turk.*: **Bağdat**)   Baghdad served as the capital of a province with the same name that included the fertile plain between the Tigris and EUPHRATES rivers in what is today central IRAQ. The city was founded as the capital of the empire of the ABBASID CALIPHATE (750–1258) At the height of that dynasty's prestige in the ninth and tenth centuries, Baghdad was one of the largest cities in the world and a center of Islamic culture where advances were made in medicine, mathematics, and technology. But Baghdad's fortunes fell after its complete destruction in 1258 at the hands of the Mongol general Hülegü, who sought to obliterate all signs of the fallen dynasty.

Baghdad played a pivotal role in the struggle between the Sunni Ottoman Empire and Shii IRAN from the 16th through the 18th centuries. The territory that would become present-day Iraq was crucial to both empires. As a border territory, Baghdad occupied a strategic central location from which a much larger region could be controlled; also, whoever held Baghdad could control river traffic on the Tigris and Euphrates rivers, which were then major trade routes between India and the Mediterranean Sea. Baghdad was also an essential garrison city, strategically placed to stop the northward raids of BEDOUINS from the Arabian Peninsula. In addition, a number of Shii holy places were located in or near the city. Recognizing its strategic importance, ISMAIL I (r. 1501–24), the founder of the Shii Safavid dynasty in Iran, took the city in 1508 from the Akkoyunlu Turkomans. Ismail I, also known as Shah Ismail, sought to replace all other interpretations of Islam with SHIA ISLAM. He considered any Muslims who would not accept his leadership in both matters of faith and political affairs to be guilty of the sin of disbelief and thus eligible for execution. In an act that shocked the Sunni world, he destroyed the graves of the Abbasid caliphs and the revered legal scholar Abu Hanifa (d. 767), founder of the Hanafi school of law, which the Ottoman state followed as its legal guide. Shah Ismail ordered the tombs destroyed because he viewed their construction as acts of heresy. Further demonstrating his contempt for SUNNI ISLAM, he killed large numbers of the city's Sunni residents as heretics. Because his vision of Islam did not give minority religions the protected status that was recognized by the Ottoman Empire, he also had many of the city's Jews and Christians killed as infidels. To give Baghdad a physical symbol of its place in the Shii sacred geography, he began construction of a large mosque complex over the grave of Musa al-Kadhim (d. 799), the seventh imam according to the Shia, in a suburb to the north of the city in what is today the urban district of Kadhimiyya.

The recovery of Baghdad for Sunni Islam remained a priority for the Ottoman sultans but it was not until 1534 that SÜLEYMAN I (r. 1520–66) was able to capture the city. Süleyman was quick to restore the tomb of Abu Hanifa whose body was, according to Sunni accounts, discovered in the rubble of the shrine perfectly preserved. In stark contrast to the violent aggression displayed by Shah Ismail, Süleyman also contributed funds for the completion of the mosque of Musa Kadhim and for the repair of various Shii endowments in NAJAF, in southern Iraq. Although Ottoman rule would establish the Sunni interpretation of Islam as the politically dominant one, the Ottomans continued to permit Shii belief and practice in the city. Ottoman tolerance of non-Muslims also led to the growth of the Jewish community in the city as Jewish refugees persecuted by the Iranian shahs found their way to the city in the 16th through the 18th centuries. By the end of the Ottoman period in 1918, Jews comprised almost half the city's population. Similarly, the Ottomans allowed Roman Catholic missionaries to take up residence in Baghdad in the 17th century, and the city also became a major center for Uniate Chaldean Catholics.

The Iranians again occupied Baghdad in 1623. Although the Ottomans would send armies against Baghdad in 1626 and 1630, it was not until 1638 that the city was finally returned to Ottoman rule. In 1639 Sultan MURAD IV (r. 1623–40) and the Iranian Shah Safi (r. 1629–42) agreed to the Treaty of Zuhab, which awarded Baghdad to the Ottomans and settled the frontier until the Safavid dynasty collapsed in the 1720s. The end of hostilities between the Ottomans and the Safavids did not usher in a period of total tranquility for the province, however, as the ambitions of the city's governors put them on a collision course with the governors of BASRA, in southern Iraq. At the same time the Bedouin became increasingly restive with the arrival of the SHAMMAR BEDOUIN confederation who settled in the western desert and harassed traffic to and from Baghdad. Troubles with Iran flared again, too, when NADIR SHAH (r. 1736–47), who had seized power in Iran in 1729, besieged Baghdad in 1733. In 1775 another adventurer, KARIM KHAN ZAND, ruler of Iran from 1753–1779, sought to advance his ambitions by invading Iraq. In both instances the governors of the city were able to hold out until Ottoman relief forces arrived.

The greater province of Baghdad also provided a continuing problem for the Ottoman sultans in the 18th century. Faced with Bedouin unrest and the persistent threat of Iranian invasion after the collapse of the Safavid dynasty, the Ottoman sultans needed strong men with local interests to hold the province for the empire. The first of these was Hasan Pasha, an Ottoman official appointed to the governorship from Istanbul who held off both Bedouins and Kurds and won the approval of Sultan AHMED III (r. 1703–30). Enjoying that support, Hasan Pasha remained as governor for an unprecedented 18-year term, from 1704 until his death in 1722. His son Ahmed succeeded him and governed from 1723 to 1747. Both men started their careers in the Ottoman military and had no previous connection to Baghdad, but their length of service in the city gave them the opportunity to recruit MAMLUKS, military slaves, into their households. These men were typically Georgian slaves, whom the two Ottoman governors emancipated and brought into their extended households. This practice was unusual in Istanbul but followed the cultural norms established by the royal court in Iran.

Uniquely, women of the governor's family played a pivotal role in the process of choosing successors to head the household that dominated Baghdad politics until

1831. Ahmed Pasha had no sons; his daughter, Adile, succeeded in having her husband, Süleyman—a former mamluk of her father—named governor in 1747. As was the case of mamluk households in Cairo, the former master of a mamluk often gave him important responsibilities in running the household and strengthened that relationship through marriage of his kin to his former slave. Süleyman ruled until his death in 1762. His successor was another mamluk from the household who was married to Adile's younger sister, Ayşe. Although this was unusual in Ottoman families, it became a regular practice when the daughters of the household produced no male heirs. For the following decades, most of Baghdad's governors were mamluks from the ruling household, many of them married to female descendants of the founding household.

The fortunes of the mamluks ended as the Ottomans sought to restore authority in Iraq after the fall of SYRIA to the Egyptian army under IBRAHIM PASHA in 1831; the male members of the household were executed. From that year until 1869, when the Ottoman reformer MIDHAT PASHA (d. 1884) was appointed to the post, regular Ottoman army commanders were appointed to the city as governors. Midhat was an enthusiastic supporter of the TANZIMAT reforms. He sought to implement a modernized form of government in Baghdad that would include a salaried bureaucracy and consultative councils made up of prominent local men, based on the model he had previously introduced as governor of the DANUBE PROVINCE. In particular he sought to put into effect the Ottoman Land Law of 1858 whose intent was to give title, or formal ownership, of the land to those who worked it. In Iraq, however, the tribal chieftains ended up with the title of the land. The reforms that were meant to weaken tribal leaders' hold over their kinsmen in fact strengthened it. The decades between 1880 and 1910 witnessed the intensification of rivalries among the Bedouin tribes in Iraq. Although Ottoman officials were usually appointed as the provincial governors the tribes retained their autonomy, if not outright independence, everywhere except within the city of Baghdad itself.

During the last decades of Ottoman rule in Baghdad, the city modernized at a much slower pace than the empire's European provinces or Syria. At the start of WORLD WAR I, for example, railroad tracks only ran from Baghdad to Samarra, a distance of just 70 miles; there was no rail connection to any seaport. Trade, largely directed to India, lagged behind that of the Syrian provinces. But things were changing even in Baghdad. The Euphrates and Tigris Steam Navigation Company, founded in 1861 by the Lynch family of Great Britain, helped open the region to international trade. The company's central role in commerce in what would become Iraq also pointed to increased British interests in the country, fueling ambitions among some bureaucrats in the India Office to dream of adding the province of Baghdad to the British Empire.

With the start of World War I in 1914, British troops occupied the port of Basra in southern Iraq. In 1915, a British military force moved north in an attempt to take Baghdad, but was stalled by a stiff defense mounted by the Ottoman Army in the Iraqi marshes near the town of Kut al Amara, about halfway between Basra and Baghdad. Cut off from supplies, the British soldiers surrendered in April 1916. A second drive was mounted from Basra in December 1916; on March 11, 1917, the British Army occupied Baghdad. After the end of World War I in 1918, the Allied Powers created the new country of Iraq, with Baghdad as its capital. The newly created League of Nations assigned Iraq to Great Britain as a mandate in 1920. Mandates were a new political invention of the League, with a status between a colony and an independent state. The British were recognized by the League of Nations as being in control of Iraq but they were "mandated" to help guide the country towards independence in the future. Fierce resistance on the part of the Iraqis in 1920 to the continuation of British occupation forced the British to rethink their options, however. In 1922, Iraq was proclaimed a kingdom under British protection and most British forces were withdrawn. Iraq gained full independence in 1932.

Bruce Masters

Further reading: Stephen Longrigg, *Four Centuries of Modern Iraq* (Oxford: Clarendon, 1925); Tom Nieuwenhuis, *Politics and Society in Early Modern Iraq: Mamluk Pashas, Tribal Shaykhs and Local Rule Between 1802 and 1831* (The Hague: Martinus Nijhoff, 1982).

bailo   A *bailo* was a representative of the Republic of Venice and head of a Venetian community abroad, including the Ottoman Empire. The *bailo* made justice for his countrymen, collected taxes and customs, oversaw Venetian trade, and was an official contact for local authorities. The word *bailo* (plural *baili*) comes from the Latin *baiulus* (porter) and was first used in Latin translations of Arabic documents during the 12th century. At first the word referred only to Muslim officials, but from the 13th century onward the term was used to designate a Venetian official specifically since Venice appointed *baili* to govern its eastern colonies and lands, including Negroponte, Patras, Tenedos, Tyre, TRIPOLI in Syria, ACRE, Trabzon, ARMENIA, CYPRUS, Corfu, Durazzo, Nauplia, ALEPPO, Koron, and Modon. Around 1265, Venice assigned a *bailo* to the BYZANTINE EMPIRE, replacing an official who had been designated as *podestà* (from the Latin for "power"). The office of the *bailo* was maintained when, in 1453, the Ottomans conquered Constantinople and made it their capital.

The *bailo*'s appointment usually lasted two years, but in Constantinople (later, Istanbul), he typically served for three years. He had a chancellery and was assisted by a council made up of the most important members of the colony (Council of Twelve). The *bailo* was obliged to send Venice information not only about politics and colonial affairs but also about the prices and quantity of the goods sold in local markets. A *bailo* was more important than a consul. Although they shared some functions, if both lived in the same foreign country, the *bailo* was the direct superior of the consul.

By the end of the 15th century most Venetian *baili* had become either consuls (when they ruled over Venetian subjects in foreign countries) or governors (when ruled on Venetian lands and colonies), and the position of the *baili* in foreign countries was assumed by resident ambassadors. In 1575 a Venetian law recognized that the *bailo* in Istanbul had to be considered as a resident ambassador. In 1670 the *bailo* was considered responsible for all the Venetian consuls in the Ottoman Empire. The *bailo* in Istanbul began to deal more and more with the highest Ottoman authorities, even if extraordinary ambassadors or lower-ranking diplomatic envoys were also assigned to the city. When a *bailo* came back to Venice he had to deliver a detailed report or country study (RELAZIONE).

The office of *bailo* in Istanbul was usually much desired by Venetian noblemen because it was the only important position abroad that was profitable, not expensive. It was given to experienced diplomats who often went on to become doges, or Venetian rulers. Hostilities between Venice and the Ottoman Empire put the *bailo* in a difficult situation. Sultan MEHMED II (r. 1444–46; 1451–81) executed the last *bailo* in the Byzantine Empire, Girolamo Minotto (1453), because Minotto had assisted the besieged Byzantines in their defense against the Ottomans. Other *baili*, including Paolo Barbarigo, Nicolò Giustinian, Jacopo Canal, and Giovanni Soranzo, were imprisoned either in the Rumeli Hisarı, the European Castle outside Istanbul along the Bosporus, in the Castle of Abydos on the Hellespont, or even in their own houses.

In 1454 Mehmed gave the Venetian *baili* the house that had belonged to the community from the Italian city of Ancona. In the 16th century the *baili* lived either in Istanbul proper or in the Jewish quarter, but they also had a house in the GALATA district. About 1527 the *baili* established a household on the upper part of the Galata Hill in a place called *le vigne di Pera* (the vineyards of Pera). This eventually became their primary residence; it is the present-day Italian consulate in Istanbul. The office of *bailo* disappeared in 1797, with the end of the Venetian Republic.

Maria Pia Pedani

Further reading: Eric R. Dursteler, "The Bailo in Constantinople: Crisis and Career in Venice's Early Modern Diplomatic Corps." *Mediterranean Historical Review* 16, no. 1 (Dec. 2001): 1–30; Maria Pia Pedani, "Elenco degli inviati diplomatici veneziani presso i sovrani ottomani." *Electronic Journal of Oriental Studies* 5, no. 4 (2002): 1–54; Donald E. Queller, *Early Venetian Legislation on Ambassadors* (Genève: Droz, 1966).

Balkan wars   The Balkan wars were a series of military conflicts in southeastern Europe between the autumn of 1912 and the summer of 1913. In the First Balkan War (October 1912–May 1913), an alliance of Balkan states fought the declining Ottoman Empire; the war ended with the signing of the TREATY OF BUCHAREST (September 1913). In the Second Balkan War (June–September 1913), BULGARIA confronted a coalition of SERBIA, Montenegro, GREECE, Romania, and the Ottoman Empire; it ended with the signing of the Treaty of Istanbul (September 1913). The Balkan wars were a consequence of the emerging NATIONALISM of the Balkan states, which led them to try to overcome intra-Balkan rivalries, expel the Ottomans, and share the Balkan territories among themselves.

The First Balkan War began in October 1912 when Montenegro declared war on the Ottoman Empire. The other Balkan states—Serbia, Bulgaria, and Greece—followed suit, each attacking the Ottomans, sometimes separately, sometimes as a combined force. The major battles took place in Thrace between the Bulgarians and the Ottomans. The Ottomans were defeated badly and retreated behind Çatalca, the last defense line before ISTANBUL. The Bulgarians also besieged the key Ottoman city of EDIRNE. While Bulgaria was busy in Thrace, the Serbians and Greeks attacked Ottoman strongholds in western Macedonia and ALBANIA. Meanwhile, the Montenegrins and Serbians attacked Shkodra (Işkodra, northern Albania) and the Greeks attempted to take Janina (Yannina, northwestern Greece). Although the Bulgarians and the Greeks raced for SALONIKA, the Greeks arrived first and claimed this most important Macedonian town. In two months, the Ottomans had lost almost all their European territories.

Due to heavy losses, the Ottoman government resigned. A new government was formed and asked the Great Powers (Germany, Italy, Austria-Hungary, Britain, France, and Russia) to intervene and help establish a ceasefire. A conference was convened in London in December 1912. According to the conference, the lands that were occupied by the Balkan states remained in their hands. Only the region to the east of the Midye-Enez line would be left to the Ottomans. However, a military coup in the Ottoman capital in January 1913 installed a new government that did not consent to the Bulgarian takeover of Edirne. Frustrated by the new Ottoman attitude, the Bulgarians attacked Edirne and captured the city in March. In the same month, the Greeks took Janina, and in the following month Shkodra also fell into their hands. As a result, Istanbul remained the only Ottoman-controlled domain in Europe. An agreement was finally reached in May 1913 by which the Midye-Enez line was accepted as the new Ottoman border. The Ottomans renounced all claims in Thrace and Macedonia and recognized the annexation of CRETE by the Greeks. In the meantime, Albania became independent.

Although the Ottomans were largely expelled from Europe, the Balkan states could not agree on the subsequent division of territories. Serbia and Greece, especially, felt bitter about large Bulgarian gains. Concerned about a potentially injurious Greek-Serbian alliance, Bulgaria waged a surprise attack on Greece and Serbia in June 1913. Immediately after the Bulgarian attack, Romania and Montenegro joined Greece and Serbia. Together, these forces inflicted heavy damages on Bulgaria, which was forced to retreat. Taking advantage of Bulgaria's precarious situation, the Ottomans then occupied eastern Thrace and retook Edirne in July.

After the Second Balkan War, the treaties of Bucharest (August 1913) and Istanbul (September 1913) were signed, with Serbia and Greece gaining the most by these agreements. Serbia took northern Macedonia and divided the *sancak,* or province, of Novi Pazar with Montenegro. Greece obtained a large Macedonian territory, including Salonika; it also acquired Epirus and Janina. Albania's independence was recognized. The Ottoman Empire and Romania, too, gained territories. Edirne was given back to the Ottomans, while southern Dobruja passed to Romania.

The Balkan wars were the first in the 20th century where armies motivated by strong nationalist ideologies fought to the limits of moral, physical, and material exhaustion. The Balkan wars also provide striking early examples of trench warfare (especially in Thrace), as well as effective early use of machine guns. Airplanes were also used, albeit to a limited degree; they were used mostly for reconnaissance purposes, although some towns were bombarded from the air. These wars did not affect only the military; civilian populations also met with brutal treatment, many being displaced, killed, tortured, and raped.

From an Ottoman perspective, the Balkan wars were the first to be fought for and with all Ottomans. The Ottoman government mobilized the entire population regardless of religious and gender differences. Using mass propaganda, it adopted a vague secular Ottoman ideology around which it tried to rally the "whole nation." However, when the wars were lost, differences among Ottoman citizens (especially religious differences) became so apparent that the ruling elite had to give up the discourse of secular Ottomanism. With the loss of its Christian-inhabited territories, the reduced empire saw a dramatic influx of Muslim refugees (around 420,000) to Ottoman Thrace and Anatolia, significantly altering the demographic configuration of the empire. The Ottoman Empire became predominantly Muslim, with a noticeable emphasis on a Turkish identity. Although official commitment to Muslim Ottomanness continued until 1918, a strong Turkish nationalism began to make itself felt in the capital and in Anatolia. A shift in identity from Muslim to Turkish began to emerge, especially after the desertion of Muslim Albanians in the Balkans. Furthermore, in government circles, discussion of a homeland for Turks began to come to the fore. This new discourse reached its zenith with Mustafa Kemal (*see* ATATÜRK), a former Ottoman military commander who established the modern Turkish state in October 1923.

Another legacy of the Balkan wars for the Ottomans and modern Turks was the Turkish military's tendency to interfere with civilian politics. The YOUNG TURKS, an Ottoman political group, had carried out a revolution in 1908 and placed civilians of their choice in power, but that was not an outright military coup. Five years later Enver Pasha, a prominent leader of the Young Turks, stormed the Sublime Porte when the government was in session in January 1913 and compelled the government to resign. After the government resigned, Enver Pasha took the reins of government in Istanbul. This military coup, known as the Bab-ı Âli Baskını (Storming of the Sublime Porte) in Turkish historiography, set a precedent for future military interventions in Turkey (in 1960, 1971, and 1980).

After the Balkan wars, Ottoman pride was severely hurt, for the empire was badly defeated by the relatively small Balkan states that were formerly its vassals. To regain the newly independent Balkan territories, which had been under Ottoman control for the previous 500 years, the Ottomans were eager to fight again if the opportunity arose. The Ottoman urgency to regain these lands was one motivating factor in the empire's willingness to enter WORLD WAR I.

Bestami S. Bilgiç

Further reading: Richard C. Hall, *The Balkan Wars, 1912–1913: Prelude to the First World War* (London: Routledge, 2000); Eyal Ginio, "Mobilizing the Ottoman Nation during the Balkan Wars (1912–1913): Awakening from the Ottoman Dream." *War in History* 12, no. 2 (December 2005): 156–177; Barbara Jelavich, *History of the Balkans,* vol. 2, *Twentieth Century* (Cambridge: Cambridge University Press, 1983).

Baltalımanı, Treaty of   *See* ANGLO-OTTOMAN CONVENTION.

banks and banking   Interest-bearing financial operations were technically forbidden by the Ottoman government because of Islamic religious law (SHARIA). Modern banking in the Ottoman Empire came into existence in the second half of the 19th century. Before that, some individuals, such as moneylenders, and some institutions, such as WAQFS (pious foundations), were granted special permission to operate as financial intermediaries. They mainly conducted activities such as financing international trade, foreign exchange, and lending. Issuing currency and determining interest rates were controlled by the government. Attempts to establish modern banks and modern banking date back as far as 1839, but these attempts were realized for the first time in 1843 with the establishment of the Smyrna Bank. Most of the banks established in the second half of the 19th century were owned by foreign capitalists or non-Muslim minorities whose financial dealings were less restricted by sharia. Banks with national capital were established in the beginning of the 20th century.

PRE-MODERN BANKING

Before modern economic institutions, the Ottomans employed cash *waqfs* to serve a number of financial purposes. *Waqfs* were historically pious foundations with endowments in the form of land or buildings, the income from which was used for religious or charitable purposes. Ottoman religious and legal scholars, however, adopted the view of the Hanafi school of law and decided that money could also be endowed, which provided opportunity for the development of cash *waqfs*. The cash *waqfs* that thus developed were major institutions that functioned as financial intermediaries. Interest on moneys so endowed accumulated by the granting of loans at a rate determined by the state. The interest income thus derived was then granted for the spending of the charitable *waqf*. These cash *waqfs* spent interest income on social activities such as CHARITY, public works, EDUCATION, and the abolition of SLAVERY and polygamy. Similar financial institutions such as "common funds" and "artisan funds," which were formed by the JANISSARIES and by artisans for vocational solidarity, operated small-scale credit institutions by granting loans to members at the rate determined by the government.

In the period prior to modern banking and the initiation of foreign DEBT in the 19th century, non-Muslim *sarrafs* (originally, money changers) and bankers were the primary financial intermediaries in the Ottoman Empire. Greeks, Armenians, Jews, and Levantines were the main non-Muslim groups engaged in banking activities. *Sarrafs* and bankers, operating mainly in the GALATA district of Istanbul, concentrated primarily in such business as financing trade, foreign exchange, lending, TAX FARMING, and financing tax farmers. Greeks largely specialized in financing international trade, Jews and Armenians were primarily interested in financing the Palace and govern-

ment agencies, as well as mint administration and foreign exchange transactions. These financial agents filled the financial needs that arose out of the expanding foreign trade with Europe, inconsistencies in the money market, transactions in different moneys in the market, and the straitened financial circumstances of the empire.

Usurers who lent money at high interest also served as financial intermediaries before the modern banking era. Usurers profited from the hard conditions faced by peasants by lending money at rates above those set by the state. As a result, they faced prosecution and heavy penalties, such as exile to Cyprus. Usury increased when the central authority was weak, but later lost ground due to increasing competition from non-Muslim money changers and bankers.

MODERN BANKING

Modernization and REFORM campaigns that began at the end of the 18th century in the Ottoman Empire initially applied to the military During the 19th century they expanded into administrative and financial areas. These ideas were first declared in 1839 in the Imperial Rescript of Gülhane (TANZIMAT). The Imperial Rescript of 1856 recognized the existence of banks in a modern sense for the first time in the Ottoman Empire. These financial reforms were driven by four primary needs: to stabilize exchange rates; to withdraw debased coins and standardize coin currency; to withdraw unstable *kaime* (paper money); and to establish a state bank to control the issue and circulation of paper money and provide stability in the money markets. Government reform efforts, borrowing requirements, and increasing international trade, particularly with European countries, accelerated the process of establishing modern banks.

The first failed attempt to establish a modern bank in the Ottoman Empire was promoted by English businessmen in 1836. A second attempt in 1840 to establish a bank to be named the General Bank of Constantinople was also unsuccessful. The first successful attempt came with the Smyrna Bank, established by foreign merchants (English, French, Austrian, Dutch, Russian, American, Italian, Danish, Spanish, and Greek) under the Swedish Consulate in Izmir in 1843. This bank was established by merchants exporting agricultural products to Europe in order to diminish their dependence on other merchants and bankers. However, the government closed the Smyrna Bank the same year it opened for operating without permission. In the view of the English, the reason for the bank's closure was opposition from local merchants and bankers.

The Bank of Constantinople, established in 1849, is thought to be the first successful modern bank established in the Ottoman Empire. More than a commercial bank, the Bank of Constantinople functioned as a foreign exchange stabilization fund for European currencies. Losses the bank suffered from this role were to be compensated by the empire. According to the exchange stability agreement introduced in June 1843, the French and Austrian merchants Alyon (or Alléon) and Baltacı (or Baltazzi) committed to the implementation of a parity of 1 pound (£) sterling = 110 Ottoman piastres (modern Turkish kuruş) in order to protect importers against risks from devaluation of the local currency. To compensate Alyon and Baltacı for their losses, the Ottoman government gave the tribute of Egypt as security, but as government debt to the bank increased, the losses were not repaid, and the bank went out of business in 1852.

STATE BANK PROJECTS

Before the Bank of Constantinople was closed, a project to establish a state bank under the name of the Ottoman Bank could not be implemented due to the Ottoman government's straitened financial circumstances and the ongoing expense of the CRIMEAN WAR (1853–56). However, such attempts accelerated after the war, and the Imperial Rescript of 1856 emphasized the importance of banks in the empire and encouraged their establishment. Two bank licenses were granted to foreigners in 1856, only one of which was realized. Despite having been granted a license, the establishment of the Bank Oriental was not successful. However, the Ottoman Bank was established by English capitalists with capital of £500,000 (equivalent to about $52 million in 2007 U.S. dollars). Established on a small scale in 1856, the Ottoman Bank became an imperial bank by 1863. It grew in spite of the difficulties it faced due to a disorderly money market and political agitations in the empire. In the face of the demand from French capitalists to establish banks, the Ottoman government allowed them to join the English capitalists in the Ottoman Bank, thus bringing together capitalists of the two nations in 1863. The Ottoman government also extended the role and official status of the bank, changing its name from the Ottoman Bank to the Imperial Ottoman Bank. Along with its regular commercial banking activities, the Imperial Ottoman Bank would execute the treasury operations with its empire-wide branch network, undertake internal and external debt services, approve a credit line of £500,000 to the Ottoman treasury, and discount the *serghis* (a kind of treasury bond) of the Ministry of Finance. The operations of the bank were exempt from all kind of taxes and took commissions of £20,000 (about 2.1 million in 2007 U.S. dollars) annually in return for services to the state. The bank also had the exclusive privilege to issue banknotes. The Ottoman government itself would not issue banknotes and this privilege was not granted to any other financial institution. The privilege was initially given for 30 years, to be exercised under the supervision of the Ottoman

government, and was thereafter extended. According to an 1866 regulation, the income reserved for the repayment of foreign debt would be invested in this bank and the debt would be paid directly from the bank. In 1875 the Imperial Ottoman Bank became a true state bank with new privileges that granted it the authority to pay for government expenditures and collect government incomes, in addition to issuing banknotes. Furthermore, it would perform the duties of purchase and sale of treasury bills and other documents issued on behalf of the government. The bank was successful in eliminating the instability in the Ottoman money market and played an important role in economic life by investing in infrastructure and financing trade.

The French started controlling the bank around 1875 when English capital decreased. Although the bank had some struggles with the Ottoman government during the wars at the beginning of the 20th century, such as the Balkan Wars and World War I, it continued to exercise its privileges until the TREATY OF LAUSANNE was signed in 1923. At this time, with the establishment of the Central Bank of the Republic of Turkey, banknotes issued by the Imperial Ottoman Bank were recalled, a process that was completed in 1948. The Imperial Ottoman Bank turned into a commercial bank after losing its privileges and continued its operations with French capital until 1996. In this year, Doguş Group (backed by Turkish capital) bought the bank, and its commercial life ended when it merged with Garanti Bank in 2001.

FOREIGN BANKS

Although many banks with foreign capital were established in the Ottoman Empire, most of them failed. Most of these banks were formed with the intent of lending to the Ottoman government. Although there were efforts to modernize the government and to improve public finances, these reform efforts were ineffective. In addition to ongoing financial difficulties, the outbreak of the Crimean War precipitated a spate of external borrowing that quickly spiraled out of control. Foreign banks then came to Istanbul to provide financing to the Ottoman Empire. Among these were the Société Générale de l'Empire Ottoman (1864), Crédit Général Ottoman (1868), the Banque Austro-Ottomane (1871), the Crédit Austro-Turque (1872), the Bank of Constantinople (1872, this bank is different from the Bank of Constantinople that was established in 1849 mentioned earlier), and the Société Ottomane de Change et de Valeurs (1872). The existing bankers in the empire, and the Galata bankers in particular, were the primary financiers of the government before the advent of these foreign banks. The Galata bankers either formed partnerships with other foreign banks or merged with each other to be able to compete with newly forming foreign banks. Many banks were established to lend to the government until 1875, when the Ottoman government declared a moratorium on its debt payments.

Other foreign banks were founded to finance commerce between the Ottoman Empire and the founders' home countries. The Ottoman Empire exported raw materials to western European countries and imported industrial goods from them. This led some foreign banks, such as the German banks that were founded in the early 20th century, to finance these trade activities. Even though Germany opened to world markets later than England and France, it surpassed these countries by making rapid progress in its relations with the Ottoman Empire. The first German bank to be established on Ottoman soil, the Deutsche-Palestina Bank, opened in Jerusalem in 1899. The Deutsche Orient Bank, founded in 1906, was established to finance infrastructure in all regions of the Ottoman Empire. The Deutsche Bank was the most important representative of German interests in the Ottoman Empire and contributed to projects such as the Berlin-Baghdad Railroad and the irrigation of the Konya and Adana plains. Austria, Italy, Holland, the United States, Russia, Romania, Hungary, and Greece also founded banks in Ottoman Empire.

NATIONAL BANKING MOVEMENTS

Until the second constitutional monarchy period in 1878, most of the players in the Ottoman banking sector were foreign banks and financial institutions established by non-Muslim minorities. There were a few exceptions. For instance, agricultural cooperatives or *memleket sandıkları* were formed under the leadership of Grand Vizier MID-HAT PASHA in the DANUBE PROVINCE in 1863 to provide low-interest loans to the agricultural sector. These cooperatives were later expanded into other parts of the country later and finally transformed into the Agricultural Bank (Ziraat Bankası) in 1888. The Agricultural Bank is one of the few banks that survived to the period of the Turkish Republic and is still active today. The Emniyet Sandığı, which was also founded under the leadership of Midhat Pasha in 1868, was a savings fund that stayed in business until the 1980s. The Orphans Fund (Eytam Sandıkları) was formed under sharia courts and functioned as an authorized credit institution.

The idea of a national economy gained popularity after the COMMITTEE OF UNION AND PROGRESS (the CUP or Ittihat ve Terakki) was established by the YOUNG TURKS in 1906. This concept worked against the idea of a state bank owned by foreign capital. During the BALKAN WARS (1912–13), the Imperial Ottoman Bank was unwilling to extend credit to the government even though it was itself a state bank. As a result, the CUP government moved to create a central bank with national capital. These early attempts to establish a central bank failed with the onset of WORLD WAR I in 1914. In 1917,

toward the end of the war, the National Credit Bank (Itibar-ı Umumi Bankası) was established to serve as a central bank. Designed to take over the roles of the Imperial Ottoman Bank, the National Credit Bank became a central bank when the Ottoman Empire collapsed in 1923. In 1927 the National Credit Bank merged with Iş Bank (established in 1924). The founders of the state that emerged from the ashes of the Ottoman Empire also subscribed to the idea of a national economy, paving the way for a modern banking system controlled by national capital in the new Turkish Republic.

Hüseyin Al

Further reading: Christopher Clay, *Gold for the Sultan: Western Bankers and Ottoman Finance, 1856–1881* (New York: I.B. Tauris, 2000); Edhem Eldem, *A History of the Ottoman Bank* (Istanbul: Ottoman Bank Archives and Research Centre/Economic and Social History Foundation of Turkey, 1999); André Autheman, *The Imperial Ottoman Bank,* trans. J. A. Underwood (Istanbul: Ottoman Bank Archives and Research Centre, 2002); Şevket Pamuk, "The Evolution of Financial Institutions in the Ottoman Empire, 1600–1914." *Financial History Review* 11, no. 1 (June 2004): 7–32.

Barbarossa brothers The Greek Barbarossa (meaning "red beard") brothers, Uruc (Aruj) and Hayreddin (Khair ad-Din), are among the most renowned and successful CORSAIRS, or pirates, of all time. Greek converts to Islam who hailed originally from the island of Mytilene (or Lesbos) in the eastern Aegean, the brothers are a prime example of how Greek maritime skill and knowledge were transmitted to the Ottomans through religious conversion. While many Greeks served in the Ottoman NAVY, the Barbarossa brothers are the most famous of these because they rose so high in the Ottoman naval hierarchy and because they were instrumental in extending the empire's borders to North Africa. They began their association with the Ottomans around 1500, engaging in piracy off the southern and western shores of Anatolia under the patronage of Korkud, one of the sons of Sultan BAYEZID II (r. 1481–1512). Korkud's execution in 1513 forced the brothers to flee the eastern Mediterranean and they went all the way to NORTH AFRICA. This turned out to be a fateful choice, because their presence there paved the way for the extension of the Ottoman Empire to North Africa in the 1520s.

Given that they had to flee, the western Mediterranean was attractive to the Barbarossa brothers because ongoing religiously motivated hostilities between SPAIN and the tiny kingdoms of North Africa meant new opportunities for naval exploits. With their defeat of the Kingdom of Granada in 1492, Spanish armies had effectively ended any form of Muslim political control in the Iberian peninsula, thus completing the age-old Spanish dream of extending Christian sovereignty over the entire area and ridding the peninsula of Islam. Now Spain threatened the Muslim rulers of North Africa and those rulers, along with thousands of Muslim refugees from Spain, were calling for Ottoman assistance. The Ottoman sultans were initially unwilling to involve themselves in such faraway endeavors. Thus the Barbarossa brothers sailed out on their own to assist the North Africans and continue their own piratical activities, with the Spanish as their new target. With their superior naval ability, which prevented Spain from conquering North Africa as well, the brothers' support of local North African leadership quickly turned into domination. In 1516 Uruc captured ALGIERS, forcing the ruler to flee.

At this point the interests of the Ottoman government and the Barbarossa brothers were once again in synch. The brothers were looking for political support and the Ottomans were more than willing to take advantage of the situation and extend their rule to North Africa. The Ottoman government quickly appointed Uruc governor of Algiers and chief sea governor of the western Mediterranean. A steady stream of military support now flowed from Istanbul to the North African cities. When Uruc was killed in 1518 fighting the Spanish, his brother, Hayreddin, stepped in to continue the defense of North Africa against Spain. After taking TUNIS for the Ottomans in 1531, Hayreddin was made admiral in chief of the Ottoman navy in 1533. In that capacity he went on to future exploits, including the 1538 defeat of the Spanish navy at Preveza (in present-day Greece), a tremendous victory that secured the eastern Mediterranean for the Ottoman Empire.

Molly Greene

See also ALGIERS; CORSAIRS; SPAIN.

Further reading: Andrew Hess, *The Forgotten Frontier: a History of the Sixteenth Century Ibero-African Frontier* (Chicago: University of Chicago Press, 1978); Godfrey Fisher, *Barbary Legend: War, Trade and Piracy in North Africa 1415–1830* (Oxford: Clarendon Press, 1957); Colin Imber, *The Ottoman Empire, 1300–1650: The Structure of Power* (New York: Palgrave Macmillan, 2002).

Barbary states The Barbary states or, more poetically, the Barbary coast (perhaps because Ottoman control beyond the coastline was limited), was the term that came to be applied in Europe to the Ottoman Empire's North African provinces. These provinces, corresponding roughly to the present-day states of ALGERIA, Tunisia, and LIBYA, were added to the empire in the early 16th century. In the 19th century they all came under more or less formal European, and particularly French, control. For the average European, the Barbary states were synonymous with Muslim piracy of the most heinous and brutal kind.

For several centuries the horror stories of European sailors and sea captains captured and sold into "white slavery" in NORTH AFRICA found a wide and sympathetic audience in Europe. However, violence at sea was widely practiced on both the Christian and the Muslim sides of the Mediterranean divide. The tiny island of MALTA, home to the piratical KNIGHTS OF ST. JOHN, was the capital of Christian piracy, while ALGIERS, TUNIS, and TRIPOLI were the leading Muslim pirate cities. The North Africans also supplied the Ottomans with some of the empire's best sailors and admirals and their high level of maritime skill, at a time when Europeans were trying to conquer the world's seas, also excited fear and loathing in Europe.

The North African orientation toward the sea was grounded in both geography and history. Just beyond a narrow coastal strip of fertile soil, the desert looms. For urban elites, much more profit was to be had in raiding the rich shipping of the Mediterranean than in trying to extract resources from the inhospitable hinterland. Moreover, the Ottoman provinces of North Africa came into being as the frontline in the battle to contain Spanish power in the Mediterranean. With the surrender of the Muslim state of Granada in 1492, the Spanish "reconquest" (*reconquista*) of the Iberian peninsula was complete. There were well-founded fears that Spain would try and cross the narrow strip of water separating Africa and Europe and assault the Muslim establishment on the African continent. Muslim sailors, adventurers, and pirates of all stripes flocked to North Africa to join the battle against this threatened Christian encroachment. At the same time England was locked in an ongoing war with Spain and many footloose Englishmen also settled in the North African port cities and made a living out of raiding the long Spanish coastline. In fact, the term "Barbary pirates" initially referred to English, rather than Muslim, adventurers in North Africa. This swashbuckling heritage continued even when the threat from Spain had receded by the 17th century. By that point the English corsair population was no longer as prominent but a tradition of European emigration to Algiers, Tunis, and Libya to pursue the life of a pirate—often including conversion to Islam—continued. Some of the most famous Barbary pirates were of European, particularly Italian, origin.

Molly Greene

Basra (Busra, Busrah, Bussora, Bussorah; *Ar.:* al-Basra) The port of Basra was both a major commercial center for almost all the trade between the Ottoman Empire and India and the administrative center for a province of the same name. In 1534, when Sultan SÜLEYMAN I (r. 1520–66) defeated the Iranians and assumed control of BAGHDAD, Rashid al-Mughamis, the Bedouin emir who then controlled Basra, submitted to Ottoman rule without a fight; an Ottoman governor was appointed by 1546. Throughout the 16th century, Basra served as Ottoman naval base for expeditions to the Indian Ocean in an attempt to counter the threat posed by the Portuguese navy to Muslim shipping between India and the Middle East.

Basra was, however, a difficult port to hold. It was linked to the Persian Gulf to the south by the Shatt al Arab waterway, which was relatively narrow and not easily defensible. Further complicating its position, Basra was on the border of a hostile Safavid IRAN, open to Portuguese naval attack, and surrounded by the openly hostile Muntafiq Bedouin confederation whose tribesmen could hide in the vastness of the neighboring marshes when pursued by the Ottoman army.

In 1596 a local man named Afrasiyab, of whose origins little is known, was able to buy his elevation to the post of provincial governor. With a skillful balancing of Portuguese and Iranian interests and interventions in local city politics, he and his descendants ruled the city until 1668, surviving both the Iranian seizure of Baghdad in 1623 and the Ottoman return to that city in 1638. The governors of Afrasiyab's line acknowledged the Ottoman sultans as their sovereigns but otherwise ruled the city as if they were independent governors.

When direct Ottoman control was again restored to Basra in 1668 in the form of an Ottoman governor who arrived in the city from Istanbul, it remained a remote and difficult place to control. Throughout much of the rest of the 17th century, the paramount sheikhs of the Muntafiq often threatened the city's security by harassing the caravans coming to and going from the city, and even attacking European ships coming up the narrow Shatt al Arab from the Persian Gulf. It was not until 1701 that Hasan Pasha, then governor of Baghdad, secured the city and restored Ottoman authority to the province after establishing a stronger Ottoman military garrison in Basra. Shortly, thereafter, as a political expediency, and in recognition of the power that the governors of Baghdad wielded, the Ottoman sultan simply added Basra to the province of Baghdad. It remained a political dependency of that city until 1878.

During the 18th century, Basra became an increasingly important trade nexus between India and YEMEN to its south, and the rest of the Ottoman Empire and Iran to its north. It also provided the hub for a large regional market that extended from southwestern Iran in the east to the oases of the eastern Arabian Peninsula in the west. Although the bulk of the trade passing through Basra was in transit to somewhere else, the region surrounding the city was famous both for its dates and for its Arabian horses; the latter were shipped primarily to India. During the second half of the 19th century, horses from Basra were an important import of the British raj in India, both for lei-

sure riding and for the cavalry. Basra's commerce made it a desirable target for neighboring Iran and the city suffered sieges by NADIR SHAH, the military strongman who effectively ruled Iran from 1729 until his death in 1747. Nadir Shah attempted to take the city several times between 1733 and 1736 and again in 1743. But the swamps surrounding the city served to defeat most attackers. The city's luck ran out, however, in 1775, when KARIM KHAN ZAND, ruler of Iran from 1753 until 1779, laid siege to the city. Basra surrendered to Zand's Iranian forces in 1776 and Iran then ruled the city for three more years until Zand's death.

Following the Iranian occupation, Ottoman rule returned once again to Basra. But the city's trading fortunes went into steep decline and the number of factors, or agents, of the East India Company, which had been the major European trading presence in the city, was sharply reduced. There was a revival of the city's fortunes in the second half of the 19th century as trade between the Persian Gulf and India revived. As an indication of that revival, Basra again became the capital of an independent Ottoman province in 1878, severing its dependence on the province of Baghdad. Basra's commercial connections to India led some British colonial planners to hope that it would be incorporated into the British Empire. When WORLD WAR I began in 1914, British troops quickly occupied the port and it served as the base for British military operations in IRAQ during the war.

Bruce Masters

Further reading: Thabit Abdullah, *Merchants, Mamluks, and Murder: The Political Economy of Trade in Eighteenth Century Basra* (Albany: State University of New York Press, 2001); Hala Fattah, *The Politics of Regional Trade in Iraq, Arabia and the Gulf, 1745–1900* (Albany: State University of New York Press, 1997).

Başbakanlık Osmanlı Arşivi *See* PRIME MINISTRY'S OTTOMAN ARCHIVES.

bathhouse A key resource of any Muslim city was its public baths. Public baths were a part of the urban culture and infrastructure that Muslim states such as the ABBASID CALIPHATE (750–1258) or the Ottoman Empire had inherited from their Byzantine and Roman predecessors. A city was not considered to be a proper city by Muslim travelers in the pre-modern period unless it had a mosque, a market, and a bathhouse (in Ottoman Turkish, hammam). In fact, most Ottoman cities had a public bathhouse in every neighborhood. The baths provided not only an opportunity for cleanliness but also a public space for relaxation and entertainment. This was especially true for women, as men were allowed to socialize in the COFFEEHOUSES and public markets. Muslim women of the upper classes were not supposed to leave their homes except to go to the public baths. Even though most upper-class homes had their own bath, women from those families used the excuse of going to the bathhouses to socialize with other women. As the social custom of strict gender segregation prevented women from going to coffeehouses, women could find an opportunity to get away from their ordinary routine in the baths to meet with friends, drink coffee, and be entertained by female performers. In many neighborhoods, there were separate bathhouses for women. Where there were no separate bathhouses for women, the bathhouses designated different days for men and women.

Men used the baths for many of the same reasons as women, but unlike visits to coffeehouses, there was no hint of impropriety for those who went to the baths to socialize. The baths were also places where representatives from differing social classes were welcome as long as they had the price of admission. Although no class distinction was made between various male patrons of the bathhouses, the same could not be said of differences in religion. In some places, Muslim jurists required non-Muslim men to use the baths on different days of the week than Muslim patrons lest the distinctions between the religious communities become blurred. The jurists also worried about illicit activities that might occur in bathhouses as these places provided the opportunity for the blurring of class distinctions as well as those of religion. As was the case with women's use of the bathhouses, men saw them as places to socialize, although it was not common for bathhouses catering to males to provide entertainment. After all, such entertainments were available to men in the coffeehouses, but unlike the coffeehouses, bathhouses themselves were never an object of condemnation by the community's moral guides, the Muslim religious authorities. Although some bathhouses had private owners, most were funded by pious endowments (WAQFS), as Islamic tradition prescribed cleanliness as a virtue for believers.

Water was brought to the baths by the same system that brought it to wealthier private homes. This usually involved a system of aqueducts that brought water into the cities from external sources, such as mountain streams. The water was brought to a central location within the city from which a system of clay pipes, laid beneath the streets, brought it to those lucky enough to have direct access to it. For the poorer classes, most neighborhoods had fountains fed by aqueducts or in some cases by individual wells that could be tapped beneath the city's streets. The other major requirement for the bathhouses was heat. In most Ottoman cities, this was supplied by the guild of street sweepers who cleaned the city's marketplaces and removed the rubbish, which was then burned in furnaces beneath the bathhouses. In this way, bathhouses not only provided the means for personal hygiene, they promoted civic cleanliness as well.

All European visitors to the Ottoman Empire were impressed by the bathhouses and every account by a contemporary traveler includes extensive notes about them. Of particular interest to historians is the account of Lady Montagu, an English noblewoman who visited ISTANBUL in 1717–18. In her letters home, she described in great detail the role of the bathhouses in Ottoman women's and provided a woman's view of Ottoman culture.

Bruce Masters

Further reading: Lady Mary Montagu, *The Complete Letters of Lady Mary Wortley Montagu*, 3 vols. (Oxford: Clarendon, 1965–67).

Bayezid I (Yıldırım, or Thunderbolt) (b. 1354–d. 1403) (r. 1389–1402) *Ottoman sultan* Known as Yıldırım, or Thunderbolt, Bayezid I was born in 1354 to Sultan MURAD I (r. 1362–89) and Gülçiçek Hatun. His reign was characterized by constant fighting in Anatolia and the Balkans, and Bayezid extended the Ottoman realms to the DANUBE RIVER in the northwest and to the EUPHRATES RIVER in the east. He was ultimately checked by TIMUR, a military leader of Mongol descent from Transoxania in Central Asia, who defeated Bayezid at the BATTLE OF ANKARA (July 28, 1402). Bayezid died while being held captive by Timur, who reduced the Ottoman lands to what they had been at the beginning of Murad I's reign. However, Bayezid's conquests served as inspiration for his successors, who managed to rebuild the empire, and half a century later Ottoman armies under Sultan MEHMED II (r. 1444–46; 1451–81) would succeed in the CONQUEST OF CONSTANTINOPLE, the seat of the BYZANTINE EMPIRE, emerging as the dominant power in southeastern Europe and Asia Minor.

Bayezid began his political career in about 1381 when he married the daughter of the emir of the Germiyanoğulları emirate, a Turkoman maritime principality in western Asia Minor. With the dowry from this marriage, the Ottomans acquired parts of the Germianid lands. Bayezid was appointed prince-governor of Kütahya, the former center of the ANATOLIAN EMIRATE, and was entrusted with the task of guarding the Ottoman domains from the east.

This meant fighting against the Karamans, the strongest of the Anatolian Turkoman emirates, who considered themselves heirs to the SELJUKS of Rum, the former rulers of Asia Minor, and who thus refused to acknowledge Ottoman suzerainty. The Karamans' firm stance against Ottoman expansion in Asia Minor also suggested that dynastic marriages, used extensively by the Ottomans to win over possible rival Turkoman emirs and to subjugate Balkan Christian rulers, did not always work.

For example, Alaeddin Bey (r. 1361–98) of Karaman had married Bayezid's sister, but the marriage did not make him a subservient vassal. When, in 1386, Alaeddin Bey captured further territories that the Ottomans claimed as their own, Sultan Murad I decided to take military action. In the resulting battle, fought in late 1386 at Frenk Yazısı near Ankara, Bayezid earned his sobriquet Yıldırım or "Thunderbolt" for his valor as a fighter. Thanks to his Ottoman wife, Alaeddin Bey escaped the confrontation with minimal damage and loss of territory, but the Karaman challenge did not disappear until the late 15th century, when their territory was finally incorporated into the Ottoman Empire.

Upon the death of Murad in the BATTLE OF KOSOVO (June 15, 1389), Bayezid was recognized as the new sultan; he had his only living brother, Yakub, killed to forestall a possible contest for the throne. The Battle of Kosovo had strengthened Ottoman positions in the Balkans. When the Serbian prince Lazar was killed in the battle, Lazar's son, Stephen Lazarević, became an Ottoman vassal and was forced to wed his sister, Olivera, to the new sultan. However, this Ottoman victory also put HUNGARY on its guard since the victory at Kosovo meant that this most important regional power would for the first time be sharing a border with the Ottomans. The battle also heartened the Anatolian Turkoman emirates who used the absence of Ottoman troops in Anatolia to recapture several of their former territories. During his swift campaign in the winter of 1389–90, Bayezid annexed the western Anatolian emirates of Aydın, Saruhan, Germiyan, Menteşe, and Hamid. He then turned against Karaman and laid siege to Konya, the capital of Karaman in present-day south-central Turkey. However, Bayezid's former ally, Çandaroğlu Süleyman Bey of the Black Sea coastal emirate of Kastamonu, made an agreement with Kadı Burhaneddin Ahmed of Sivas against Bayezid. The sultan thus was forced to give up the siege of Konya and turn against them. In 1392, Bayezid defeated and killed Süleyman Bey and annexed his territories. The smaller rulers of the region, including the ruler of Amasya (south-southwest of the Black Sea coastal city of Samsun), also accepted Ottoman suzerainty. However, the dispute with Kadı Burhaneddin was not resolved until 1398.

Ottoman campaigns in Anatolia emboldened the sultan's more distant Christian rivals. The Byzantines, recently reduced to vassalage and forced to fight alongside Bayezid in Anatolia, tried to solve their internal disputes in the hope that, if they were united and received help from the western Christian states, they might stop Ottoman encroachment into their territories. However, this policy provoked a long-lasting Ottoman siege and blockade of the Byzantine capital, Constantinople (1394–1402). To control navigation along the Bosporus, Bayezid ordered the construction of a castle at the narrowest point of the strait, less than three miles north of Constantinople on the Asian shore. Known today as Anadolu Hisarı or the Asian castle, the fort played an important role during the Ottoman CONQUEST OF CONSTANTINOPLE in 1453. Despite these actions, however, Bayezid did not succeed in seizing Constantinople, for he had to abandon the siege to fight on fronts in Europe and Asia Minor.

While Bayezid was fighting against his Muslim and Turkoman enemies in Anatolia, his frontier lords continued their raids in the Balkans, which in turn provoked HUNGARY to take countermeasures. The Ottomans raided southern Hungary periodically from 1390 onward, and Ottoman and Hungarian forces clashed in 1392 when the Hungarians crossed the DANUBE RIVER, the country's natural southern border. In 1393 Bayezid conquered Turnovo, annexing Czar Ivan Shishman's (r. 1371–95) Danubian BULGARIA and sending Shishman to Nikopol on the Danube as his vassal. Alerted by Bayezid's recent victories along Hungary's southern borders, King Sigismund of Luxembourg (r. 1387–1437) extended Hungary's influence to northern Serbia, parts of Bosnia, and the Romanian principalities of WALLACHIA and MOLDAVIA, as part of a new defense policy against the Ottomans that aimed at creating Hungarian client-states between Hungary and the Ottomans. In the autumn of 1394, Bayezid entered Wallachia and deposed its pro-Hungarian ruler, Mircea (r. 1386–1418), replacing him with his own vassal, Vlad (r. 1394–97). In the spring of 1395, the Ottomans raided southern Hungary again, and in June captured Nikopol and executed Czar Shishman. King Sigismund, in his turn, marched into Wallachia and reinstated his protégé, Mircea (July–August 1395), whose position, however, remained shaky. By the summer of 1396, King Sigismund, who had been planning a crusade since 1392, had amassed an international army to move against the Ottomans. The crusade was promoted by King Sigismund, the pope, the Duke of Burgundy, and some French nobles. It had been urged by the Byzantine Emperor Manuel II Palaiologos (r. 1391–1425), whose capital was under Ottoman blockade and whose envoys visited Hungary in January 1396, seeking help against the Ottomans. Some 30,000–35,000 crusaders from Hungary, Wallachia, France, and Burgundy reached Nikopol by September and besieged it. However, the crusaders lacked siege artillery and were soon surprised by Bayezid's relief army of 40–45,000 men. In the ensuing battle on September 25 (according to some European sources, September 28) at Nikopol, the sultan defeated the crusaders, due partly to the French vanguard's premature attack and partly to some 5,000 Serbian heavy cavalry in Bayezid's army who, toward the end of the battle attacked the Hungarians, already weakened by the sultan's Anatolian light cavalry. King Sigismund barely escaped the battle, reaching Constantinople by boat via the Danube and the Black Sea. In Constantinople he met Byzantine

Emperor Manuel, returning home via the ADRIATIC SEA aboard Venetian ships. Following the battle, Bayezid took Vidin from Czar Ivan Stratsimir (r. 1365–96), who had allied himself with the crusaders, ending the last independent Bulgarian czardom.

The next two years saw Bayezid again in Anatolia, defeating and killing his two most powerful enemies in the region, Alaeddin Bey of Karaman and Kadı Burhaneddin of Sivas, and incorporating their lands to his realms. Byzantine support for the anti-Ottoman crusade provoked the tightening of the Ottoman blockade of Constantinople. The small relief army led by Jean Boucicaut, marshal of France, that reached the Byzantine capital via the Bosporus was not sufficient to save the city. Emperor Manuel decided to travel personally to western Europe to seek more substantial military and financial aid. By the time he returned home in 1403, his city was saved, not due to western assistance but because of Timur's decisive victory over Bayezid.

Timur claimed suzerainty over all Anatolian emirs on account of his descent from Genghis Khan, whose Ilkhanid successors ruled over Asia Minor in the second half of the 13th century. Bayezid, on the other hand, considered himself heir of the Seljuk Turks, the rulers of Anatolia from the late 11th through the early 14th century. From his capital in Samarkand, Timur's army, dominated by expert Chaghatay cavalry archers, overran the territories of the Golden Horde in southern RUSSIA, northern India, Persia, SYRIA, and eastern Anatolia. When, in the late 1390s, Bayezid extended his rule over eastern Anatolia, the clash between the two rulers became unavoidable.

The contest between Timur and Bayezid took place on July 28, 1402 near Ankara, and ended with Timur's victory. Bayezid was captured; Timur restored to their former lords territories in eastern Anatolia that had been recently seized by Bayezid. A bitter fight began among Bayezid's sons over the remaining Ottoman realms. In the words of one European eyewitness, Ruy Gonzales de Clavijo, "Bayezid died miserably in March 1403, and Constantinople for the next half century was thus spared to Christendom." Fortunately for the Ottomans, however, basic institutions of the Ottoman state (including the tax system, the central and provincial ADMINISTRATION, and the army) had already taken root, and large segments of Ottoman society had a vested interest in restoring the power of the House of Osman.

Gábor Ágoston

Further reading: John W Barker, *Manuel II Palaeologus (1391–1425): A Study in Late Byzantine Statesmanship* (New Brunswick, N.J.: Rutgers University Press, 1969); Caroline Finkel, *Osman's Dream: The Story of the Ottoman Empire, 1300–1923* (London: John Murray, 2005); Colin Imber, *The Ottoman Empire, 1300–1481* (Istanbul: Isis, 1990); Halil İnalcık, "Bayazid (Bayezid) I," in *Encyclopaedia of Islam*, edited by P. Bearman, Th. Bianquis, C. E. Bosworth, E. van Donzel, and W. P. Heinrichs. Brill, 2007. Brill Online. Online edition (by subscription), viewed 1 March 2007: http://www.brillonline.nl/subscriber/entry?entry=islam_SIM-1302

Bayezid II (b. 1448—d. 1512) (r. 1481–1512) *Ottoman sultan*   The son of Sultan MEHMED II (r. 1444–46; 1451–81) and Gülbahar Hatun, Bayezid II spent the first part of his reign in the shadow of a possible crusade by his European rivals. The second half of Bayezid's reign witnessed important world political developments that shaped both his rule and the future of the Ottoman Empire: the expulsion of Iberian JEWS to whom Bayezid offered a new home in his domains, Portuguese expansion in the Indian Ocean, and, most importantly, the emergence of a new enemy, Safavid Persia (*see* IRAN). Bayezid proved unable to deal effectively with the Safavids and their KIZILBAŞ followers in eastern Asia Minor. This failure cost him his sultanate, for on April 24, 1512 he was deposed by his son SELIM I (r. 1512–20), who followed a more belligerent policy against the new enemy, and thus was favored by the very JANISSARIES who had initially secured the throne for Bayezid.

In 1456, the seven-year-old Bayezid was sent as prince-governor to Amasya in central Anatolia. During his tenure as governor, the maturing Bayezid distinguished himself as the guardian of the empire's eastern borders. He participated in the 1473 campaign against Uzun Hasan (r. 1453–78) of the Akkoyunlu (White Sheep) Turkoman confederation that ruled over eastern Anatolia and Azerbaijan. The campaign ended with the crushing defeat of Uzun Hasan, although both Hasan and his son carried on the fight against the Ottomans until Selim I incorporated their lands into his empire.

Despite his services along the empire's eastern frontiers, Bayezid's behavior was not approved of by his father Mehmed or by Mehmed's grand vizier, Karamani Mehmed Pasha (in office in 1476–81). In fact, the grand vizier favored the advancement of Bayezid's younger brother CEM (b. 1459–d. 1495), the prince-governor of Karaman (in south-central Turkey). Bayezid, in turn, defied his father on several occasions, and Bayezid's provincial court became a safe haven for those who disagreed with Sultan Mehmed's policy of centralization and his penchant for confiscating privately held lands.

ACCESSION TO THE THRONE

When Mehmed II died on May 3, 1481, Grand Vizier Mehmed Pasha sent word to both Cem and Bayezid, hoping that since Cem in Konya was closer to ISTANBUL than Bayezid in Amasya, the grand vizier's favorite would be first to claim the throne. However, Mehmed Pasha's enemies, supported by the JANISSARIES, intercepted his messenger to Cem, assassinated the grand vizier, and proclaimed Bayezid's eleven-year-old son Korkud regent. When Bayezid reached Istanbul, he was enthroned by the Imperial Council on May 22. Prince Cem went to the old Ottoman capital, BURSA, where he formally set himself up as Bayezid's rival by proclaiming himself sultan. Defeated by Bayezid in 1481 and 1482, Cem first sought the protection of the Ottomans' rivals, the MAMLUK EMPIRE in CAIRO, then turned to another traditional enemy, the piratical Christian KNIGHTS OF ST. JOHN of RHODES. However, in September 1482, unbeknownst to Cem, Bayezid had struck a deal with the Knights, who had promised to keep Cem in confinement in their castles in France; for this Bayezid paid them 45,000 gold ducats annually. Cem spent the rest of his life in exile in France and Italy as hostage of the Knights and the papacy; he died on February 25, 1495, in Naples. Because Cem became a pawn for numerous European crusading plans (none of which materialized), Bayezid wisely pursued a cautious policy with regard to Europe.

Following Cem's exile in 1482, Kasım, the claimant to the Karaman emirate who had supported Cem during his military campaigns against Bayezid in 1481 and 1482, made a deal with Bayezid and accepted the sultan as his overlord. In return, he was rewarded with the Ottoman governorship of the province of İçil (Cilicia). When Kasım died in 1483, the former emirate of Karaman was incorporated into the Ottoman Empire, although Karaman pretenders challenged the government in Istanbul for another generation or so.

The allegiance of the Ramazanoğlu and Dulkadıroğlu emirs southeast and east of the Taurus Mountains in the buffer zone between the Ottomans and the Mamluks was also unreliable, and the two empires fought an inconclusive six-year war (1485–91) over these territories. During the war, Mamluk armies and their Anatolian Turkoman supporters besieged Ottoman castles as far as Kayseri in the province of Karaman, and reestablished their hold over Adana, the center of the Ramazanoğlu emirate. This territory was eventually incorporated into the Ottoman Empire after Sultan Selim I's victory over the Mamluks in 1516–17, although the Ramazanoğlus governed their ancestral lands as hereditary governors of Istanbul for almost another century, and Adana would become a regular Ottoman province only in 1608.

CAMPAIGNS IN MOLDAVIA

Bayezid was more successful in reasserting his suzerainty over MOLDAVIA (roughly present-day eastern Romania and Moldova), a reluctant Ottoman vassal state from the mid-15th century, whose ruler, Stephen the Great (r. 1457–1504), had stood up against Mehmed II, repeatedly attacking the neighboring Ottoman vassal principality, WALLACHIA, to the south of Moldavia. In order to secure his northern frontier and to punish Stephen, who

rejected Bayezid's demand for tribute, the sultan personally led his army against Moldavia in 1484. With the help of his Wallachian and CRIMEAN TATAR vassals, Bayezid captured Kilia and Cetatea Alba (Akkerman, present-day Belgorod-Dnestrovsky in southwestern Ukraine), two strategically important castles that guarded the Danube delta and the mouth of the Dniester River, respectively. He forced Stephen to pay tribute to Istanbul as an acknowledgement of Moldavia's subject, or client, status.

Following Cem's death, Bayezid's hands were freed with regard to his western rivals and enemies. In the 1499–1503 Venetian-Ottoman War, Bayezid tried to clear the eastern ADRIATIC SEA of his Venetian rivals. In late August 1499, the sultan fought successfully in the Battle of Lepanto (present-day Navpaktos in southern Greece), and ordered the construction of two forts to guard the entrance of the Corinthian Gulf separating mainland Greece from the Peloponnese. The next year Modon, Navarino, and Koron on the southwestern coast of the Peloponnese, known then as the Morea, fell to the Ottomans. The Venetians briefly recaptured Navarino in 1500–01. However, according to the treaty of 1503, Venice only kept control of the islands of Cephalonia and Zante along the western coast of the Morea, and Monemvasia on the southeastern end of the same peninsula. Venice also had to pay an annual tribute of 10,000 gold pieces to the sultan. In the same war, Venice also lost some of her outposts on the Albanian coast of the Adriatic, of which Durazzo (Durrës in western Albania) was the most important.

During the Venetian-Ottoman War, Bayezid considerably strengthened Ottoman naval power. In the winter of 1500–01 alone, he ordered the construction of no fewer than 50 heavy galleys and 200 galleys with large cannon. Starting in the autumn of 1502, Bayezid initiated the total reorganization of the Ottoman NAVY, which was only partly due to the war against Venice, with whom peace negotiations were already underway. The work was part of a larger naval strategy that transformed the Ottomans, originally a land-based empire, into a formidable naval power that would, within a generation, become the undisputed master of the eastern Mediterranean. The reformed Ottoman navy would also become instrumental in halting Portuguese expansion in the Red Sea and the Persian Gulf and in the conquest of Mamluk Egypt.

In the early 16th century, however, Bayezid faced a more dangerous enemy to the east of his empire. In 1501 ISMAIL I, the leader of a militant Shii religious group and son of the former head of the Safaviyya (Safavid) religious order, took Tabriz (in northwestern Iran) and declared himself shah, or ruler, of Iran. The leadership of Shah Ismail was backed particularly by followers among the KIZILBAŞ or "Redheads," so named for their 12-tasseled red hats that symbolized the Imami or Twelver branch of SHIA ISLAM. These followers in IRAN, Azerbaijan, and eastern Anatolia saw in Shah Ismail the reincarnation of Imam Ali, Prophet Muhammad's cousin and son-in-law and the founder of the minority Shii branch of Islam; many others hoped that Ismail was the long-awaited hidden imam who would bring justice to the world. Shah Ismail was an unpopular figure, however, among the Ottomans, because his belligerent policy against SUNNI ISLAM, his persecution of Sunni Muslims in his realms, and his propagandists' proselytization in the eastern provinces of the Ottoman Empire ran counter to Ottoman culture and undermined Ottoman political authority. Bayezid, however, seemed reluctant to deal with the threat, which led to further disagreement between the sultan and his son Selim, the prince-governor of Trabzon on the Black Sea coast in northeastern Anatolia, who argued for a more aggressive anti-Safavid policy.

The Safavids regularly encroached on Ottoman territories. In 1507 they marched against the Dulkadırs, whose emir was Selim's father-in-law. In 1510 a Safavid army, led by Shah Ismail's brother, threatened Trabzon. When Selim retaliated for the 1507 incursion with his own raids into Safavid territory and defeated the Safavid army in 1510, this was interpreted in Istanbul as insubordination. Frustrated by his aging father's inactivity against the Safavids, and concerned about a possible succession fight with his two elder brothers (princes Ahmed—the sultan's favorite—and Korkud), Selim decided to act preemptively. Since both Ahmed's seat in Amasya and Korkud's seat in Antalya, were closer to Istanbul than Selim's court in Trabzon, Selim demanded a new governorship closer to Istanbul. When rumor spread that Bayezid was about to abdicate in favor of Prince Ahmed, Selim traveled to CAFFA, which was governed by his own son, the future SÜLEYMAN I the Magnificent (r. 1520–66). Thence Selim crossed into the Balkans. In March 1511, with his army of 3,000, he reached the former Ottoman capital of EDIRNE, where Bayezid had been residing since the 1509 Istanbul earthquake. In the meantime, a major Kızılbaş revolt broke out in Teke in southwestern Anatolia, led by a holy man known in Ottoman sources as Şahkulu ("the slave of the shah"). The rebels defeated the imperial forces sent against them under the command of Prince Korkud and marched against Bursa. At that point, Bayezid yielded to Selim's demands, appointing him prince-governor of the Danubian province of Semendire (Smederevo on the Danube in Serbia). However, Selim did not trust his father. When he learned that the grand vizier planned to bring Prince Ahmed to the throne, Selim decided to seize the throne. However, on August 3, 1511 Selim was defeated by Bayezid's army near Çorlu, between Edirne and Istanbul, and fled to Caffa.

When he heard about the battle between his father and his brother, Prince Ahmed went to Istanbul, hoping that Bayezid would abdicate in his favor. However, the JANISSARIES supported Selim and blocked Ahmed from entering the capital. Frustrated, Ahmed left for Anatolia, hoping to return with his Anatolian supporters. In the meantime, yet another Kızılbaş rebellion broke out around Tokat in northcentral Anatolia. Yielding to pressure from the Janissaries, Bayezid invited Selim to Istanbul, appointing him commander in chief of the army. Selim arrived in Istanbul in April 1512. With the support of the Janissaries he deposed his father and was proclaimed sultan on April 24. It was the first time that the Janissaries orchestrated the abdication of a sultan. The deposed sultan died on June 10, 1512, on his way to Dimetoka, his birthplace in Thrace.

Gábor Ágoston

See also SELIM I.

Further reading: Palmira Brummet, *Ottoman Seapower and Levantine Diplomacy in the Age of Discovery* (Albany: State University of New York Press, 1994); Caroline Finkel, *Osman's Dream: The Story of the Ottoman Empire, 1300–1923* (London: John Murray, 2005); Shai Har-El, *Struggle for Domination in the Middle East: The Ottoman-Mamluk War, 1485–91* (Leiden: Brill, 1995); Halil İnalcık, "Selīm I," in *Encyclopaedia of Islam,* edited by P. Bearman, Th. Bianquis, C. E. Bosworth, E. van Donzel, and W. P. Heinrichs. Brill, 2007. Brill Online. Online edition (by subscription), viewed 8 March 2007: http://www.brillonline.nl/subscriber/entry?entry=islam_COM-1015.

Bayrakdar Mustafa Pasha   *See* ALEMDAR MUSTAFA PASHA.

bazaar   *See* GRAND BAZAAR; MARKETS.

bedestan   *See* GRAND BAZAAR; MARKETS.

Bedouins   *Bedouin,* derived from the Arabic word *Badawiyyin* meaning "those who live in the desert," is the term used to label the nomadic, Arabic-speaking tribes who inhabit the desert regions of south-west Asia and North Africa. The origins of the Bedouin date to the first millennium B.C.E. when the camel was first domesticated. The camel, unlike the horse, could store large amounts of water in its stomach and could live in the desert for days without having to drink. This gave to those who mastered them the ability to use the desert as a transportation route and to seek refuge in it from their enemies. One of the persistent problems that the Ottomans faced in their attempts to maintain their hold over the Arab provinces of EGYPT, BAGHDAD, BASRA, MOSUL,

Damascus, and Aleppo was the defiant, often belligerent, behavior of the Bedouins. From the initial Ottoman conquest of these regions in the first half of the 16th century until the 20th century, technology limited travel in the deserts of North Africa and the Middle East. Only the Bedouins, who knew how to handle camels and navigate the routes through the seemingly uniform desert, had the ability to travel in these areas. Therefore the settled peoples of the region, who consisted mostly of Arabic-speaking peasants, and the Bedouins had a sometimes mutually symbiotic relationship. The townsmen needed the Bedouins to handle and guide the caravans that the region's trade depended upon, and the Bedouins needed the towns for grain and most of the material goods—such as cloth, steel weapons, saddles—that they consumed. But the Bedouins were also a law unto themselves, and their relationship with the peasants who tried to make a living from the plains of Syria or in the fertile valleys of the Nile, Euphrates, and Tigris rivers could turn deadly. Heavily armed and well versed in the highly mobile tactics of desert warfare, the Bedouins were virtually undefeatable on their own ground. As raiding offered an easy source of income, whenever the Ottoman state grew too weak to maintain garrisons on its desert borders (as was the case in much of the 17th and 18th centuries), Bedouin tribes could make life unbearable for the peasant farmers of the region, while also making caravan travel a risky proposition.

The core of the Bedouin social and political life was the tribe, or *qabila*. Although a tribe might number tens of thousands of tents, each one usually consisting of one nuclear family, all members of a tribe would claim descent from a common ancestor. Each tribe was, in effect, a very large extended family. Within a tribe were smaller units of more closely related families known as *ashira*, or clans. Members of a clan usually married within the clan, with first-cousin marriages being the most socially prized. This created a strong bond of solidarity within a particular clan that was not as apparent within a tribe. Clans were often in conflict with one another and blood feuds were relatively common. The tribe's stability was based on the ability of its leaders to hold the clans together. This did not always work, and new tribes might form through the union of various clans that had formerly belonged to different tribes. In such cases, a new lineage would be created, or even forged, whereby all the clans that currently constituted the tribe shared a common founding father.

The economy of a Bedouin tribe was based on its herds of camels, goats, and horses. The Bedouins were nomadic in that they had no fixed place of settlement but tribes were keenly aware of boundaries of the territory (*dirah*) that they considered theirs. The boundaries were determined by the location of wells, whose water was solely the property of the tribe who controlled it, or

This photograph taken in the 1880s shows the sons of the tribal chieftain Ali Diyab of the Mawali Bedouin who inhabited the Syrian Desert and were the sometime allies of the Ottomans against the more troublesome Anaza Confederation. *(Photograph by Maison Bonfils, courtesy of the University of Pennsylvania Museum, Philadelphia)*

by natural features such as mountains or dry riverbeds (*wadi*). The Bedouins subsisted almost entirely on the meat of their camels and goats and products made from their herds' milk. Only a very few tribes engaged in any form of agriculture and so the rest had to barter with settled peoples for the wheat flour and dates that supplemented their diet. Beyond animal husbandry, the Bedouins raised money by hiring themselves out as guides or guards for caravans or, alternatively, by extracting protection money from those same caravans or from the peasant farmers who lived on the edges of the desert. Outright banditry was also an element of the Bedouin economy.

The head of a Bedouin tribe held the title of sheikh. Within a tribe, one clan would typically hold the title of *ahl al-bayt*, the "people of the house," and its male members were eligible for the position of tribal sheikh. The tradition within the Bedouins tribes was not one of primogeniture so if there were no one candidate on whom the clan leaders agreed, when a ruling sheikh died or became incapacitated, cousins might battle each other for the title.

The confederation of tribes, a feature common to the last two centuries of Ottoman rule in the Arab lands, was even more unstable than a tribe itself, as the confederation consisted of several tribes, all of whose sheikhs considered themselves the equal of any other in the confederation. The WAHHABIS, followers of an extremist form of Islam, represented an exception to this rule. As the tribes within that confederation were brought together on the basis of religious ideology rather than being united for defense as was the usual case, they conceded the role of *ahl al-bayt*, or political leader of the confederacy, to the family who traced itself back to one of the founders of the confederation, MUHAMMAD IBN ABD AL-SAUD. But as the checkered history of the House of Saud illustrates, with its moments of defeat as well as triumph, even the bond of religious ideology was not sufficiently strong to hold an extended tribal confederation together permanently.

As the political bonds of a confederation and even within some tribes were tenuous at best, the typical Ottoman policy when confronted with problems caused by Bedouins was to seek to bribe clans or even contestants from the *ahl al-bayt* to work for the state. This worked rather effectively in the 16th and 17th centuries. But as the central government's control over the desert borderlands weakened, new tribal confederations emerged to challenge Ottoman control over the Fertile Crescent, the Tigris-Euphrates river valleys and the coastal strip along the Mediterranean Sea. The Ottoman army of the 19th century, with its modern European weapons and training, proved as ineffective against the Bedouins as its predecessors had been. The Bedouins adapted to rifle technology as quickly as did the Ottoman army, and artillery was only effective against Bedouin charges at fixed points of defense such as military garrisons or fortified towns. In the open desert, the Bedouins continued to hold the tactical advantage, and an uneasy stalemate developed between the Ottomans and various tribal confederations in different points along the desert frontier. The Egyptian campaigns against the Wahhabis in 1811–1813 and 1816–1818, and the campaign of MIDHAT PASHA in 1871, illustrated this stalemate between the Bedouin tribes and the modernizing armies of either Egypt or the Ottoman Empire. The tribes could no longer threaten towns that were garrisoned, but the new Ottoman and Egyptian armies did not have the resources to control the desert directly.

Ottoman policy in the second half of the 19th century was to encourage the settlement of the borderlands by a peasantry who would be militarily strong enough to fend off Bedouin attacks. In earlier centuries, a similar thinking had led the Ottomans to encourage the settlement of the nomadic Turkoman tribes along the EUPHRATES RIVER frontier. This had not had the desired results, however, as many of the Turkoman tribesmen also began extorting money from caravans. In the late 19th century, the Ottomans were more successful with the settlement of refugee Muslim farmers from the Caucasus Mountains along the desert frontier in what is today Syria and Jordan. Although these settlers were collectively known as Circassians, this group included not only Circassians (Adige) but also other Muslim peoples of the Caucasus—including Chechens and the Ingush—who had fled into the Ottoman Empire following the Russian conquest of their homeland.

In addition, Bedouin tribes were encouraged by large gifts to settle down on agricultural land and become peasants. This program was most effective with the few remaining Christian Bedouin tribes who settled in the towns of Karak and Maan, in present-day Jordan. The settlement projects served to stabilize the frontier in the late Ottoman period near the turn of the 20th century, but the larger tribal confederations remained a potential source of disorder. This was demonstrated in 1916 with the call by FAYSAL AL-HASHIMI for an ARAB REVOLT. With the exception of some Arab deserters from the Ottoman Army, the forces that responded to the call were entirely Bedouins who subsequently fought the Ottoman army to a standstill using the same tactics as their ancestors.

Bruce Masters

Further reading: Norman Lewis, *Nomads and Settlers in Syria and Jordan, 1800–1980* (Cambridge: Cambridge University Press, 1987); Eugene Rogan, *Frontiers of the State in the Late Ottoman Empire: Transjordan, 1850–1921* (Cambridge: Cambridge University Press, 1999).

Beirut (Beyrut; *Ar.*: Bayrut; *Fr.*: Beyrouth; *Turk.*: Beyrut)   Today the capital of LEBANON, the city of Beirut experienced remarkable changes in fortune during the Ottoman period. It served as a center of learning, and especially law, in the Roman Empire, but after its conquest by the Muslims in the eighth century C.E., its economic fortunes declined as other port cities along the Syrian and Lebanese coasts flourished. In the 15th century, trade between DAMASCUS, the capital of present-day SYRIA, and southern Europe increased with the export of luxury goods that had reached Damascus by caravan from Asia. Some of these goods were then brought to Beirut by caravan and shipped to Europe in European boats.

After its conquest by the Ottomans in 1516, Beirut continued to serve as the port of Damascus. But international trade shifted away from that city at the start of the 17th century as caravans from the east shifted northward to the city of ALEPPO due to increasingly violent attacks by the BEDOUINS. With that shift, Asian goods no longer appeared in Beirut's markets, and its importance began to diminish. From then until the start of the 19th century, Beirut was overshadowed by Lebanon's other port cities, TRIPOLI and Sidon. But in the 19th century, French commercial interests encouraged the growth of

Beirut in the 1880s, photographed from the campus of the Syrian Protestant College. The Syrian Protestant College founded by American missionaries in 1866 would later be renamed The American University in Beirut. By the time this photograph was taken Beirut had already become one of the busiest ports in the eastern Mediterranean. *(Photograph by Maison Bonfils, courtesy of the University of Pennsylvania Museum, Philadelphia)*

a silk industry in Lebanon, drawing peasants from the mountains into the coastal cities to work in the silk-reeling factories that were established by French investors. That, in turn, led to the burgeoning of Beirut's population. It was transformed, over the course of the 19th century, from an overgrown village with 6,000 to 7,000 inhabitants in 1800 to the most important commercial port of the eastern Mediterranean basin between IZMIR and ALEXANDRIA, with a population of over 100,000 in 1900. European shipping companies began to visit Beirut regularly; by 1907, it handled 11 percent of the Ottoman Empire's international trade.

The Ottomans were slow to capitalize on this growth, but in 1840 the governor of the province of Sidon moved his residence to Beirut, and in 1864 the city was added to the newly constituted province of Suriyye with Damascus as its capital. In 1888, long after most European powers had established major consular representation in the city,

the Ottomans created a new province that included northern PALESTINE and coastal Lebanon, with Beirut as its capital. The leading American MISSIONARY organization in the Ottoman Empire, the AMERICAN BOARD OF COMMISSIONERS FOR FOREIGN MISSIONS, established its headquarters in Beirut in 1834, and in 1866 founded the Syrian Protestant College to which a medical school was added in 1884. The Jesuits followed suit and moved their seminary of Saint Joseph from Ghazir in the Lebanese mountains to Beirut in 1870. In 1881 the Vatican elevated Saint Joseph to university status. In 1888, again following the lead of the Protestants, the university opened a medical school. In the last decades of the 19th century, Beirut became the major publishing center in the Arab provinces of the Ottoman Empire, and intellectuals there played an important role in the Arab cultural renaissance known as the NAHDA.

However, not all those who lived in Beirut embraced a cultural identity as Arabs. In the second half of the

19th century, some MARONITE Catholic intellectuals in Beirut began to articulate the theory that there was a distinct Lebanese identity and culture. Until then, most of those who lived in Beirut and the surrounding countryside would have viewed themselves as Syrians. That was how most immigrants from Beirut arriving in the United States in the years between 1880 and 1914 described themselves to American immigration officials. But the proponents of a distinct Lebanon argued that unlike the Syrians, who were Arabs, the Lebanese were actually descendants of the ancient Phoenicians, even though they spoke Arabic. Whereas Syria's people were predominantly Muslim, the majority of the people of Lebanon were Christian. Lebanon was therefore, the Lebanese nationalists argued, distinct from its neighbors, and should be a separate country with Beirut as its capital. The French government supported those who promoted a separate Lebanon as they felt this could create a state in the Middle East whose interests would be close to those of France. In 1920, in the aftermath of WORLD WAR I, the League of Nations created Lebanon as a separate nation from Syria, with Beirut as its capital. The country was then awarded to France as a Mandate, a status somewhere between colony and independence.

Bruce Masters

Further reading: Leila Fawaz, *Merchants and Migrants in Nineteenth-Century Beirut* (Cambridge, Mass.: Harvard University Press, 1983); Jens Hanssen, *Fin de Siècle Beirut: The Making of an Ottoman Provincial Capital* (Oxford: Clarendon, 2005).

Bektaşi Order   The Bektaşi order is a sect of SUFISM that was popular among the peasants of Anatolia (present-day Turkey) and in the Balkans from the founding of the Ottoman Empire until its demise. It still retains some popularity among Albanian Muslims. The order, however, had little appeal for Muslim intellectuals and other urban Sunnis who viewed it as a religion for peasants with beliefs verging on heresy. The Bektaşi Order was perhaps most famous for being the interpretation of Islam that was embraced by the JANISSARIES. That relationship between members of the order and officers of the Janissary corps gave the group a political dimension as well as a spiritual one.

The origins of the order are shrouded in legend but the founder is said to have been Hajji Bektaş, a mystic who came to Anatolia in the 13th century from northwestern IRAN. The order's cosmology and practices were highly unorthodox for Sunni Muslims as they blended elements of Islam with pre-Islamic Turkish shamanism, a belief system that holds that all living things, human, animal, or vegetable, share a common soul and can be communicated with by shamans. The fusion of the two

traditions had great appeal for the nomadic Turkoman tribesmen who were migrating into Anatolia in the centuries of the Crusades (12th through the 14th centuries). Missionaries from the order helped speed the conversion of these tribes to Islam by placing Muslim religious figures such as Muhammad and Ali into shamanistic legends and by presenting apparent acts magic similar to those worked by the shamans. This syncretism between the old religion and the new made the transition from one belief system to another seamless for the tribesmen.

In the late 14th century, members of the order began serving as chaplains and spiritual guides to the Janissary corps, and by the 16th century it was established practice that all members of those elite military units were inducted into the order as the founder of the order, Hajji Bektaş, was viewed as the guiding spirit of the Janissaries, not unlike a patron saint in Christian belief. So while not all adherents to Bektaşi Sufism were Janissaries, all Janissaries were expected to take vows of obedience to the Bektaşi sheikhs, or spiritual guides. That connection lasted until 1826 when the Janissary corps was suppressed and disbanded in the AUSPICIOUS INCIDENT.

Orthodox Muslims consider the beliefs of the Bektaşi Order to be extreme, even heretical. The Bektaşis consume wine, allow dancing in their services, and permit unveiled women to attend, and participate in, their religious services, all of which scandalized more mainstream Muslims. Bektaşis believe in a trinity that consists of God, the Prophet Muhammad, and Ali. They celebrate all the mourning days of SHIA ISLAM and when pressed, members of the order claim that they are, in fact, Shia. The Bektaşi Order also adapted the symbolic cosmology of Hurufism a practice in Sufism in which individual letters of the Arabic alphabet have numerical values that allow for the multiple readings of a text. Using this numerology, the Bektaşis interpret verses of the Quran in ways that practitioners of Sunni Islam often find objectionable. The Bektaşi beliefs, and especially the centrality of the figure of Ali in their cosmology, were similar to those of the KIZILBAŞ, whom the Ottoman religious authorities declared to be heretics liable to execution. The Bektaşis' connection to the powerful Janissaries was perhaps the only reason the order did not face persecution from the Ottoman authorities.

The Bektaşi Order also has practices that resemble those of Christianity. They offer communion of bread and wine in their religious services and encourage celibacy for those men and women who reside in their lodges (*tekke*) Historians have suggested that just as the Bektaşis blended shamanistic practices to appeal to the Turkoman tribesmen, these elements were added to appeal Christian peasants in Anatolia and the Balkans. In point of fact, these Bektaşi practices did have wide appeal to Christians in the empire and scholars credit the conversion of many Christians in the Balkans to Islam to the missionary work of the Bektaşis. The Order provided former Christians with the political benefits of becoming Muslim while allowing them to participate in religious ceremonies that seemed similar to those of their former faith.

After the abolition of the Janissary corps in 1826, the Ottoman government closed many of the Bektaşi *tekkes* as the order was seen as being too close to the Janissaries, but it did not outlaw the order altogether. That leniency was undoubtedly based on their understanding of the grass roots popularity of the order among the peasants. There was a Bektaşi revival in the Ottoman Balkan provinces in the late 19th century among the Albanians and Bosniaks as the political situation in the empire deteriorated and many Muslims sought spiritual solace from familiar traditions that had survived in the villages of the empire, despite the distaste that the urban Sunni elite had shown for the order. The government of the newly formed Turkish Republic banned the Bektaşi Order, along with all other Sufi orders, in 1925 as Mustafa Kemal felt that the orders offered a potential political threat to his new regime and because they represented a "superstitious past" from which he sought to free the new Turkish republic. The Bektaşi Order was also banned again in the 1960s by the Communist regime of Enver Hoxha in Albania, where before the ban approximately a third of the country's population considered themselves to be Bektaşis. Since the fall of Communism in Albania and Yugoslavia, there has again been a revival of the order in the Balkans, marked by the reopening of some of the *tekkes* and the public celebration of Bektaşi feast days and commemorations.

Bruce Masters

See also SUFISM.

Further reading: John Birge, *The Bektashi Order of Dervishes* (London: Luzac, 1965); Frances Trix, *Spiritual Discourse: Learning with an Islamic Master* (Philadelphia: University of Pennsylvania Press, 1993).

Belgrade (*Serbo-Croat.*: **Beograd**) Belgrade is the capital city of the present-day Balkan state of SERBIA, the biggest and best fortified city in that part of the Balkans. In Ottoman documents it was also written as Aşağı Belgrad and Tuna Belgrad, among other names to distinguish it from several other cities of the same name. Due to its strategic importance as a fortress and its desirable position on the imperial highway to ISTANBUL, Belgrade was a hotly contested site and the Ottomans laid two unsuccessful sieges to the city(1440; 1456) before it was finally taken in 1521. It then became the seat of the Ottoman district governor (or *sancakbeyi*) of Smederevo (the nearest fortress and the capital of the Serbian despotate).

While there are no reliable population data, estimates identify Belgrade as one of the largest Ottoman cities in the Balkans, with up to 10,000 inhabitants by the end of the 16th century and as many as 50,000 by the middle of the 17th century. The city was used as a fortress, as safe winter quarters for the army, and as a storage, military, and food-manufacturing center. Because of its geographical position—on the imperial highway and at the meeting point of the two largest rivers in the region, the Sava and the DANUBE—Belgrade played a key role in communications and in commerce (an important focal point of international trade). With the immigration of Ottoman Muslims and the establishment of Ottoman religious endowments or WAQFS, Belgrade gradually assumed the character of an Eastern city, boasting numerous mosques with tall minarets. During the Ottoman-Habsburg wars Belgrade was taken three times by the Austrian army (1688–90; 1717–39; 1789–91) but was ultimately restored to Ottoman control. Under Austrian rule, there was an effort to erase all Muslim symbols that characterized Ottoman governance, and heavy bombardment during numerous sieges, from both sides, damaged the city to such an extent that it took decades to rebuild. Due to the general economic crisis in the second half of the 18th century, Belgrade's Ottoman governors did not manage to restore the city to its former splendor.

In the early 19th century, Belgrade increasingly became the focus of Serbian nationalist attention. With the first Serbian insurrection against Ottoman rule (1804–13), Serbian nationalists captured the city and declared it the capital of the territory they controlled (1806). The city remained in their control until the Ottomans put down the uprising in 1813. During the first half of the century, the city had a joint Serbian and Ottoman civil government, with an Ottoman garrison in the fortress. After another Ottoman-Serbian conflict in 1862, and following intense diplomatic effort, the last Ottoman garrison left Belgrade in 1867. Fearing that they would be without protection in a Christian-controlled Serbia, the remaining Muslim population of Belgrade also left with the Ottoman army.

Belgrade continued to develop rapidly as the capital of the newly independent Serbian state. Only a few traces of the long period of Ottoman rule still remain, most notably the fortress complex, a mosque and *türbe* (mausoleum). However, many place names within the city (for example Kalemegdan, Dorćol, Terazije, and Topčider) still recall its Ottoman past.

Aleksandar Fotić

beylerbeyi   *See* ADMINISTRATION, PROVINCIAL.

Black Sea   The Black Sea region, the margins of which cover the Balkans and Anatolia, also includes the northwestern frontiers of the Ottoman Empire, areas of present-day Moldavia, Ukraine, Russia, and Georgia. The Ottomans were the first power since antiquity to gain effective control of all shores of the Black Sea and the only power ever to hold the region for three centuries. Thus arose the term "Ottoman lake" to refer to the Black Sea.

The Black Sea's strategic importance was the result of two main factors. First, because it was an extension of the Mediterranean Sea and the western terminus of the Great Eurasian Steppe, stretching from Mongolia to UKRAINE, the Black Sea was the meeting point of the Mediterranean powers and the great steppe empires, such as the Old Turks and the Mongols. In addition, the region itself was extremely rich in resources such as foodstuffs and raw materials and provided excellent access to regions in Ukraine and Russia where large numbers of people could be captured for the Ottoman slave market.

Whenever there was a strong power in the Bosporus area, Black Sea trade could be controlled by that power; when there was no such power, trade would flow freely through the straits of the Bosporus and Dardanelles into the Mediterranean Sea and follow the laws of supply and demand. Since antiquity, the northern ports of the Black Sea were important in the supply of grain for either the Mediterranean or whatever power held the straits. When the BYZANTINE EMPIRE was strong, prices could be kept low in Constantinople and the shipment of grain to the Mediterranean could be limited or even prevented. The flourishing of the Venetian and Genoese trade colonies around the Black Sea (*see* CAFFA and AZAK) in the 14th century was in large part based on the decline of Byzantine power. Conversely, with the Ottoman CONQUEST OF CONSTANTINOPLE, the Italian commercial empire in the Black Sea was essentially ended and Ottoman control of the sea was only a matter of time. In 1454, only a year after the fall of Constantinople, MEHMED II (r. 1444–46; 1451–81) sent a fleet of 56 ships under the command of the *kapudan pasha* (admiral) into the Black Sea to notify powers in the region of the Sublime Porte's newly enhanced power and strategic position. The importance of the Black Sea in Ottoman imperial consciousness can be seen in the fact that, after the conquest of Constantinople, Mehmed took the title "Sovereign of the Two Lands (i.e., Rumelia and Anatolia) and of the Two Seas (i.e., the Mediterranean Sea and the Black Sea)." Effective control of the Black Sea was gained by the Ottomans during and immediately after Mehmed's reign: Amasra in 1459, Sinop and Trabzon (Trebizond) in 1461, Caffa and Azak (and other points on the southern Crimean shore and shore of the Sea of Azov) in 1475, and Kilia and Akkerman in 1484. With the latter conquest, which gave the Ottomans control of trade flowing into the Black Sea from the DANUBE and Dniester rivers, economic control of the sea was achieved. Effective political control of all shores was achieved by SÜLEYMAN I (r. 1520–66) with

the capture in 1538 of Bender, upstream from Akkerman, and Özi, at the mouth of the Dnieper River.

With their entry into the Black Sea, the Ottomans faced two potential serious rivals—the principality of MOLDAVIA and the Crimean Khanate (see CRIMEAN TATARS); a third rival, the Empire of Trabzon, headed by scions of the Byzantine Commene dynasty, was eliminated by Mehmed II in 1461. Moldavia proved a formidable opponent especially thanks to the military skills of Stephen the Great (1457–1504), in particular his use of terrain and guerrilla tactics. However, it was enough for the Ottomans to seize the strategic ports of Kilia and Akkerman in 1484 to seal the economic and political fate of Moldavia and turn it into a vassal state.

The Crimean Khanate, which not only controlled the Crimean peninsula but also much of the steppes to the north, was a potentially more dangerous foe if the Ottomans were to attempt to take direct control of its territory. Rather than become involved in difficult operations in the vast and arid Black Sea steppes, the Ottomans used limited force and shrewd diplomacy. Taking advantage of a conflict between the khanate and the Genoese in Caffa in 1475, the Ottoman fleet not only eliminated the Genoese colonies but also managed to establish a mutually advantageous relationship with the Crimean Khanate. In exchange for Ottoman protection and subsidies, the khanate controlled the Black Sea steppes, averting possible threats from their northern neighbors, the Polish-Lithuanian Commonwealth and RUSSIA. There was a strong mutually beneficial commercial basis for the Ottoman-Crimean suzerain-vassal relationship, the basis of which was the supply of slaves for the huge Ottoman market from the Crimean Tatars as a result their annual raids for captives in the Ukrainian lands of the commonwealth and in southern Russia.

A significant aspect of the Ottoman entry into the Black Sea region was that, through the use of astute diplomacy, the Ottomans were able to avoid difficult and potentially futile wars of conquest in the steppe lands to the north and to gain control of the region while keeping a free hand to engage in conquests in central Europe, the Mediterranean, eastern Anatolia, and beyond. On the few occasions when the Ottomans attempted to abandon their traditional defensive stance in this region and engage in attempts to expand north of the seaboard (the Don-Volga campaign of 1569, the Khotin campaign of 1621, the Podolian and Çehrin (Chyhyryn) campaigns of the 1670s), it became clear that such undertakings did not justify the efforts. With the Black Sea a so-called "Ottoman lake," with the northern powers kept at a distance by the Crimean Khanate and the vastness of the steppe buffer zone, the Ottomans possessed an ideal situation in the region—a vast supply of raw materials, foodstuffs, and slaves was available for the benefit of the

Porte. The rapid rise of Istanbul toward becoming the largest city in Europe by the 16th century would probably not have been possible without such a rich reservoir.

However the "Ottoman lake" metaphor breaks down for the end of the 16th and first half of the 17th century as a result of the devastating sea raids by first the Ukrainian and then the Russian COSSACKS. The former were mostly based on the Dnieper River and were known as the Zaporozhian Cossacks (see UKRAINE); the latter were based on the Don River and consequently were known as the Don Cossacks. In their seaworthy longboats the Cossacks first raided settlements and fortresses on the northern seaboard, then those on the western seaboard, and eventually, by the 1610s, all shores of the Black Sea, including even the suburbs of Istanbul on the Bosporus. Even major towns with formidable fortresses such as Kefe, Kilia, Akkerman, Varna, Sinop, and Trabzon were repeatedly attacked and plundered. Ottoman commercial and naval shipping could no longer operate with impunity. With these sudden devastating attacks, what was once a safe heartland was transformed into dangerous frontier zone. Until about the middle of the 17th century, when Ottoman defenses managed to adapt and the Ukrainian Cossacks became engaged in wars with Poland-Lithuania, there was no question of the sea being an "Ottoman lake."

With the rise and expansion of the Russian Empire in the 18th century, the Ottomans faced a struggle over possession of the Black Sea region. Thus an unprecedented program of fortress-building and reconstruction based on artillery-resistant earthen bastions was undertaken. However, by the end of the century, the northern seaboard was lost to Russia, the Crimean Khanate was eliminated, and the entire Crimea was conquered in 1783, including the Ottoman enclave on its southern shore.

Victor Ostapchuk

Further reading: Halil İnalcık, "The Question of the Closing of the Black Sea under the Ottomans." *Αρχεĩον Πόντου* 35 (1979) [Athens]: 74–110; Victor Ostapchuk, "The Human Landscape of the Ottoman Black Sea in the Face of the Cossack Naval Raids." *Oriente Moderno,* n.s., 20 (2001): 23–95; Charles King, *The Black Sea: A History* (Oxford: Oxford University Press, 2004).

Boğdan   *See* MOLDAVIA.

Bosnia and Herzegovina (Bosna i Hercegovina, Bosnia and Hercegovina, Bosnia-Hercegovina) The process of the Ottoman conquest of the Balkan territories of Bosnia and Herzegovina began in 1386, when Ottoman troops looted Hum (Herzegovina), and lasted until 1592, when the town of Bihać fell under the rule of Sultan MURAD III (r. 1574–95). But 1463 is regarded as the year in which the Bosnian kingdom fell to the Ottomans, for it was at this time that Ottoman military forces occupied central Bosnia and killed the last Bosnian king Stjepan Tomašević (r. 1461–1463). After the conquest, the Ottomans established their administrative system in the Bosnian lands by founding the Bosnian (1463) and Herzegovinian (1470) *sancaks* (Ottoman provincial districts), soon after establishing *sancaks* for the nearby territories of Zvornik (1481–81), Klis (1537), and Bihać (before 1620). The Bosnian province (*eyalet-i Bosna*), formed in 1520, included these units in addition to territories of historical Slavonia, DALMATIA, and CROATIA. The first political center of the province was the present-day capital of Sarajevo. From 1553 to 1639, the city of Banja Luka was the main administrative center in the Bosnian province. Sarajevo then regained its former role and kept this position until 1699 when the seat of the Bosnian governors was transferred to the town of Travnik, where it remained until 1832.

RELIGION IN BOSNIA

Pre-Ottoman Bosnia had a fractious ecclesiastical history. Orthodox Christians lived mainly in Herzegovina and some parts of eastern Bosnia. In Bosnia proper, two other churches existed, the Bosnian Church and the Catholic Church. Neither was exclusively supported by the Bosnian rulers and neither had a proper territorial system of parish churches and parish priests. However, shortly after the Ottoman conquest, the ethnic and denominational structure of Bosnia and Herzegovina changed. Orthodox Christian livestock breeders called VLACHS settled in the basin of the river Neretva as well as in northeastern and northwestern Bosnia.

In central Bosnia, under Ottoman influence, conversion to Islam started in the 1480s. This process continued in other regions—principally western Herzegovina, northeastern Bosnia, and northwestern Bosnia—and reached its peak in the 16th century. As a result, by the beginning of the 17th century the majority of the Bosnian population was Muslim. Intensive Islamization resulted from different factors, including a weak Christian ecclesiastical structure, economic conditions, the DEVŞIRME (conscription of boys to serve as Ottoman JANISSARIES and palace staff), and Ottoman-Muslim urbanization. *Poturs,* or converts to Islam who continued to practice their Christian rituals and were incompletely integrated into the Ottoman-Muslim world, were emblematic of the syncretic-crypto-Christianity that prevailed in Ottoman Bosnia. By the end of the 16th century the number of *poturs* in Bosnia was marginal and the term *potur* was primarily used as a pejorative for the Muslim rural population.

THE 17TH CENTURY

The withdrawal of the Ottoman Empire from the Balkan Peninsula began with the defeat at Vienna (1683) and the war against the Holy League (AUSTRIA, POLAND, VENICE, RUSSIA). In 1697, Austrian troops under the command of prince Eugene of Savoy captured Sarajevo. This war ended with the TREATY OF KARLOWITZ (1699), which forced the Ottoman Empire to accept the loss of Hungarian, Croatian, and Dalmatian territories. Moreover, during and after the military conflict, waves of Muslim refugees poured into the Bosnian province. The Ottoman Empire attempted to regain the lost areas. However, after Austrian troops defeated the Ottoman army in the 1716 Battle of Petrovaradin, the sultan had to accept the terms of the Treaty of Passarowitz (1718). According to the clauses of this treaty, the Habsburgs gained a strip of the Bosnian *eyalet* (province) south of the River Sava.

In 1737 Austrian troops again invaded the province and were defeated at the town of Banja Luka in northern Bosnia. According to the Treaty of Belgrade (1739) the Habsburgs were forced to withdraw from the territories south of the river Sava, with the exception of one fortress. The Treaty of Belgrade established a border between the Habsburgs and the Ottomans along the northern frontier of present-day Bosnia-Herzegovina.

Another war with the Habsburgs broke out in 1788 when Austrian troops again invaded the Ottoman province of Bosnia. This war is known as the Dubica War in Bosnian history because the wasted efforts of the Habsburgs to conquer the crucial fortress of Dubica symbolized the failure of this military campaign. One year later, Habsburg military forces overran most of Bosnia and pushed deep into SERBIA. In 1791 the diplomatic pressure of other European powers forced AUSTRIA to concede its territorial gains. In return, Sultan SELIM III (r. 1789–1807) granted the Austrian emperor official status as the protector of the Christians living in the Ottoman Empire.

After the territorial losses agreed to under the TREATY OF KARLOWITZ, Bosnia became a border province of the Ottoman Empire. Especially after the war against the Holy League (1683–99), the Ottoman authorities needed the support of local notables (AYAN) to buttress state administrative functions. In contrast to other Ottoman provinces, in Bosnia local notables were not only *ayans* but also *kapudans*. *Kapudans* appeared at the northern frontier of the *eyalet* in the 16th century and had policing as well as military functions. Over the course of the following 200 years the *kapudan* institution spread over the whole of the province and the *kapudans*, who treated their office as hereditary, played a significant role as commanders of troops and tax farmers. In many cases the possession of a tax farm was the main basis of their political power and social prestige.

The new geopolitical position of Bosnia did not immediately cause tensions between Muslims and Christians. In time, however, it led to a growing fear on the part of Bosnian Muslims about their future and engendered a loss of confidence in the ability of the sultan to defend the border against Christian powers. In addition to other factors, such as epidemics or loss of lives due to war, these fears apparently influenced the demographic development of Ottoman Bosnia. Even though these figures must be treated with caution, it appears that between 1732 and 1787 the Bosnian population grew from 340,000 to 600,000, and historical sources make it clear that the greatest population growth occurred among Christians. In Ottoman Bosnia the number of Catholics increased by 163 percent and the number of Orthodox Christians increased by 124 percent. In comparison, the Muslim population grew by a meager 34 percent.

THE 18TH CENTURY

In the 18th century, the daily life of Christians and Muslims in Bosnia and Herzegovina was divided into two different worlds: a segregated private life, where each religious group lived according to its particular tradition or religious rules; and a business life where Christians and Muslims came together. An increasing number of Muslim merchants had been engaged in trade with Dalmatian and Italian port cities since the late 1500s. However, in the 18th century, Orthodox Christian traders gained in importance. The main stimulus for the development of an Orthodox trading class was the arrival of merchants from the southeastern Balkan territories.

At the same time, a large number of merchants and craftsmen joined the Janissaries. Their goal was to enjoy the social prestige and tax privileges that derived from membership in the Janissary corps. These local Janissaries (*yamak*) often waited in vain for their pay; this contributed greatly to the unrest that shook the province in the middle of the 18th century. The loss of tax exemptions enjoyed by parts of the urban population, heavy tax burdens, and the abuse of power by Ottoman officials paved the way for the outbreak of these riots.

The social and economic life in Bosnian cities such as Sarajevo and Mostar was increasingly dominated by the Janissaries. They formed a privileged social institution to which most Muslim townsmen belonged. In 1826, Sultan MAHMUD II (r. 1808–39) was able to abolish the Janissaries, which had been a powerful opposition to military reforms in the Ottoman Empire. The reaction in Bosnia to this abolition, known as the AUSPICIOUS INCIDENT, was outrage. In 1827 the sultan dispatched military units to eliminate the remaining Janissaries in Sarajevo.

Despite the elimination of the Janissaries in Bosnia, the Western-style training methods and uniforms of the new army stirred up resentments in Bosnia. Local notables used this resentment for their own political purposes. In 1831, Bosnian *kapudan* Husein Gradaščević, with a small local detachment, occupied the town of

Travnik in Central Bosniaand forced the Ottoman vizier to take off his modern uniform and put on traditional dress. Around the same time, an uprising broke out in the north of the nearby Balkan territory of ALBANIA and Husein Gradaščević led his troops into Kosovo, ostensibly to join the army of the Ottoman grand vizier. Once there, the Bosnian notables presented a list of demands to the grand vizier that included administrative autonomy; an end to the military reforms in Bosnia; the appointment of a Bosnian bey (Ottoman honorary title) or *kapudan* to the viziership of Bosnia; and the immediate appointment of Husein Gradaščević to this post. Exploiting the rivalry between the Bosnian beys and *kapudans*, the grand vizier succeeded in detaching the Herzegovinian *kapudans*, led by Ali Agha Rizvanbegović, from Gradaščević's forces. This move enabled the grand vizier to crush the revolt of Husein Gradaščević, who subsequently escaped to AUSTRIA. Gradaščević was ultimately pardoned and died in ISTANBUL in 1833. For his efforts Ali Agha Rizvanbegović was awarded a reconstituted Herzegovina which was separated from the Bosnian *eyalet* and given to Rizvanbegović to rule.

THE 19TH CENTURY

Ottoman reforms undertaken before the TANZIMAT reform period in the 19th century, such as the abolishment of the *timar* system (landholding system), did not significantly affect Ottoman Bosnia. Rather, Bosnia-specific reforms, such as the 1835 replacement of the institution of *kapudans* with *mütesellims* (Ottoman officials) appointed by the governor, had a much more significant impact. Many *kapudans* and *ayans* were appointed as *mütesellims*, even though they were not allowed to command their own troops and the offices were not hereditary. Resistance on the part of some *kapudans* to this reform continued until 1850. The Tanzimat reforms met with opposition in Bosnia, especially from Muslim landowners. This resistance was broken by the Bosnian governor Ömer Pasha Latas (1850–52).

In the 19th century, religious life in Bosnia was characterized by increasing tensions between Christians and Muslims. This development was a result of different processes that had their origins both within and outside the Bosnian *eyalet*. Bosnian Muslims felt more and more disadvantaged in comparison to Christians, whose interests were promoted by the governments and consular officials of RUSSIA and Austria—the protecting powers of Orthodox and Catholic Christians, respectively, in Bosnia. In this period, numerous western European Christian organizations constructed monasteries and opened schools in Bosnia.

This religious situation was further complicated by the influence of Croatian and Serbian national ideologies. The progenitors of these ideologies interpreted the ethnic origin of the Bosnian population to suit their own political purposes, mainly the annexation of Bosnia. Serbian intellectuals, such as Vuk Karadžić, declared that the ethnic origin of the Bosnian and Dalmatian population was Serbian. Representatives of the Croatian national ideology, such as Ante Starčević and Eugen Kvaternik, identified the Bosnians as Croats.

The final collapse of Ottoman rule in the 1870s in Bosnia and Herzegovina, however, was more a product of economic and political conditions than of religious conflicts. In 1875, after a bad harvest, Christian peasants in the Nevesinje district of Herzegovina fled into the mountains to avoid paying taxes and to escape violent measures often employed by local tax collectors. Peasant riots also broke out in northern Bosnia for similar reasons. In response, the Bosnian governor mobilized an army in Herzegovina to suppress the rebellion.

Additionally, some beys employed irregular troops (*başıbozuks*) against the rebels. In 1876 hundreds of villages were burned down and at least 5,000 peasants were killed. In the same year, nearby Serbia and Montenegro declared war on the Ottoman Empire. Despite Ottoman battlefield victories, Russian intervention forced sultan ABDÜLHAMID II (r. 1876–1909) to sign an armistice that prevented the reestablishment of Ottoman rule in Serbia. In the Russo-Ottoman war of 1877–78, the Russian army reached the gates of Istanbul. The subsequent Treaty of San Stefano was rejected by the European powers. The Congress of Berlin (June 13–July 13, 1878) awarded to the Habsburgs the right to occupy and administer Bosnia and Herzegovina. Bosnia, however, remained nominally under Ottoman suzerainty. On July 24, 1878, Austrian troops crossed the River Sava and, after defeating the Bosnian military, conquered Sarajevo on August 19, 1878.

Markus Koller

Further reading: Noel Malcolm, *Bosnia: A Short History* (New York: New York University Press, 1994); Markus Koller and Kemal Karpat, eds., *Ottoman Bosnia: A History in Peril* (Madison: University of Wisconsin Press, 2004); Michael Hickok, *Ottoman Military Administration in Eighteenth-Century Bosnia* (Leiden: Brill, 1997).

Brankovič family   The reputation of the noble Serbian Brankovič family was formally established in the late 14th century with the rise of Vuk Brankovič (d. 1397) to the top of the Serbian nobility; the infamous BATTLE OF KOSOVO (1389), in which both Serbs and Ottomans met with heavy losses, took place on his lands (Vilayet-i Vılk or "The region of Vuk"). Although Vuk Brankovič's eventual capitulation to Ottoman rule has given rise to a Serbian folk tradition accusing him of traitorous activity during the battle, it is well established that Brankovič held out against the Ottomans until 1392 when he became a vassal of Sultan BAYEZID I (r. 1389–1402). Fighting for the Ottomans, Brankovič's son

Djuradj took part in the BATTLE OF ANKARA in 1402 as a vassal. Under Ottoman rule, he later became the despot, or ruler, of vassal SERBIA (1427–39, 1444–56). As confirmation of his vassal state, Branković's daughter Mara, in Ottoman documents known as Despine Hatun, was married to Sultan MURAD II (r. 1421–1444, 1446–51) in 1435, while Branković's son Stefan was taken hostage. Branković's sons Stefan and Grgur were blinded in 1441, at the time of the Ottoman-Hungarian war. Djuradj was first succeeded by his son Lazar (r. 1456–58) and later by Stefan (r. 1458–59), both of whom also ruled as vassal despots. Despot Vuk Grgurević, Grgur's illegitimate son, entered the service of Matthias, the king of Hungary, in 1464, becoming his main prop in the defense of the Hungarian-Ottoman border. Several other descendants of the family, ending with Jovan (1496–1502), received the title of despot from the Hungarian king, along with certain landholdings in southern Hungary.

Aleksandar Fotić

Britain   *See* ENGLAND.

Bucharest, Treaty of (1812)

This treaty, signed in the Wallachian capital of Bucharest on May 28, 1812 and ratified on July 5, 1812, ended the RUSSO-OTTOMAN WAR of 1806–12. Stiff Ottoman military resistance along a fortified line south of the DANUBE RIVER, together with the gathering threat, from 1806 onward, of a French invasion of RUSSIA, allowed the Ottomans to play for time in their diplomatic negotiations with the Russians. In 1812, faced with the impending French invasion, the Russians reluctantly agreed to accept a slice of land between the Dniester and Prut rivers in eastern MOLDAVIA as compensation for Russian losses in the war. Bessarabia, as this territory was subsequently named, constituted the only piece of land to change hands as a result of the Russo-Ottoman War of 1806–12. The acquisition of Bessarabia did, however, afford the Russian Empire access to the Danubian estuary via the Kilia Canal. The Russian Empire was now both a BLACK SEA and Danubian power. The Treaty of Bucharest also formally granted control over western Georgia to the Russians. The new Ottoman sultan, MAHMUD II (r. 1808–39), was not pleased with the outcome of negotiations at Bucharest, and the Ottoman negotiators were beheaded on their return to Istanbul.

The Serbs suffered the most from the Treaty of Bucharest. While most of the articles in the treaty were concerned with defining the nature of Russian and Ottoman relations in the Danubian principalities of WALLACHIA and Moldavia, one article of the treaty (Article Eight) allowed the Ottoman Empire a free hand to suppress a rebellion in its Serbian province. This rebellion had broken out in 1804 and had been sustained by Russian diplomatic and military support. The Ottoman army reoccupied BELGRADE, from which it had been forced to retreat in 1806, and SERBIA was subsequently restored to Ottoman control.

The combination of a series of internal political crises and six years of off-and-on warfare with the Russians had drained the Ottoman Empire of its financial and military resources. The Treaty of Bucharest thus granted Mahmud II the time and space needed to establish his rule and heal the divisions in the Ottoman polity that had been exacerbated by the war. Principally, Mahmud II was afforded the opportunity to reassert his authority over wayward Ottoman provinces in the Balkans. From 1814–20 Thrace, Macedonia, the Danubian region, and most of Wallachia were restored to centralized Ottoman control.

Andrew Robarts

Further reading: Barbara Jelavich, *History of the Balkans*, vol. 1, *Eighteenth and Nineteenth Centuries* (Cambridge: Cambridge University Press, 1983); Paul Robert Magosci, *Historical Atlas of East Central Europe* (Seattle: University of Washington Press, 1993); Alan Palmer, *Russia in War and Peace* (New York: Macmillan Company, 1972).

Buda (*Ger.:* Ofen; *Turk.:* Budin, Budun)

One of the capital cities of medieval HUNGARY, Buda became the center of an Ottoman province (*vilayet*) between 1541 and 1686, and has formed a part of the city Budapest since 1873. The area of present-day Budapest was inhabited as early as the first millennium B.C.E. Originally built by the Romans in the first century C.E. and named Aquincum, it became the provincial capital of Lower Pannonia province in 106 C.E. However, there was no continuity between the Roman town and the medieval Hungarian town. When the Huns occupied Pannonia in 433, Aquincum lost its urban character. The Magyars or Hungarians who moved into the Carpathian basin (present-day Hungary) in the late ninth century soon realized its strategic location along the RIVER DANUBE. Óbuda or "old Buda" is mentioned in 1241 as *medium regni*, that is, the center of the (Hungarian) kingdom. After the Mongol invasion of 1241–42 that destroyed most unwalled towns, King Béla IV (r. 1235–70) founded a fortified town, aptly named Budavár (the Castle of Buda), on today's Castle Hill, which soon became the political and commercial center of the kingdom and a royal seat.

After the Hungarian defeat at the hands of the Ottomans at the BATTLE OF MOHÁCS (August 29, 1526), in which King Louis II (r. 1516–26) of Hungary died, SÜLEYMAN I (the Magnificent, r. 1520–66) entered Buda on November 26, 1526. The sultan soon left Hungary but returned in 1529 to take Buda from the army of Ferdinand I of Habsburg, elected king of Hungary (r. 1526–64). Süleyman gave the city to John I of Szapolyai, also elected king of Hungary (r. 1526–40), who became his vassal. When king John I of Szapolyai died, he left an infant son (John Sigismund), and this led to a new Habsburg attack. At that point, the sultan found it expedient to capture the political center of Hungary. While Süleyman invited the child, his mother, and his retinue to his tent, the Janissaries took the strategic points of the Buda castle. Süleyman promised to return the town to John Sigismund once he came of age; however, in the meantime, he created a new Ottoman *vilayet* and appointed Süleyman Pasha, perhaps of Hungarian origin, as its first governor, or *beylerbeyi*.

The Habsburgs attempted several times to regain Buda from the Ottomans. In 1542, Joachim of Brandenburg led a large army but was unable to achieve success. Similar efforts were made during the Long War (1593–1606), in 1598, 1602, and 1603, but all three attempts failed. However, on September 2, 1686 the united forces of the Holy League, commanded by Charles of Lorraine (1643–90), defeated the defenders headed by Vizier Abdurrahman Pasha, who died in battle.

The population of Buda probably exceeded 10,000 at the end of the 15th century. Five registers still extant from the Ottoman period—from 1546, 1559, 1562, 1580, and 1590—detail the changes in the size of the population of the three main groups, Christians, Jews, and Gypsies. The number of Christian heads of families fell by nearly half in 45 years—indicating that Christians, almost all of whom were Hungarian in origin, felt the need to move to more secure places during the Ottoman period. In contrast, the size of the two other communities, Jews and Gypsies, increased significantly during that same time period—although with ups and downs—suggesting that these two groups managed to coexist more successfully with Buda's new lords. Muslim civilians are not listed in these registers, but it seems reasonable to postulate a growth among them. Paid Muslim soldiers were quite numerous in the beginning—they are listed as numbering almost 3,000 in 1543—but their number decreased to some 1,600 men in 1568. Based on the above figures and tendencies, the total population of Buda can be estimated at 7,000–7,500

The tomb of the Bektashi dervish Gül Baba, said to have died during the Ottoman conquest of Buda (1541), was the most frequented Muslim pilgrimage site in Hungary. *(Photo by Gábor Ágoston)*

throughout the 16th century, with occasional divergences. Due to the almost complete lack of 17th-century data, it is difficult to follow later developments. Indirect proofs suggest that there was no basic change in the number of inhabitants until 1686, although the ethnic composition must have shifted in favor of Muslims.

Agricultural cultivation within the walls of Buda was very limited. The slopes of the Gellért hill as well as Margaret Island, an island in the middle of the Danube near central Buda, were favorable for vine-growing. But the largest amount of wine was produced in nearby (Buda) Örs, approximately 25,000 gallons (100,000 liters) in 1562. Ottoman tax registers do not list specific agricultural products other than wine, but the total tax revenue was quite high: 603 akçe per household in 1562 and 585 akçe in 1580, the equivalent of the value of two oxen.

The town preserved its importance as a center of local and transit trade. Some 310 shops, storehouses, and commercial buildings were referred to in 1562, while four markets and one covered bazaar are mentioned 100 years later. Ottoman customs-books indicate that the main import goods were textiles of various origin and quality, knives, and caps. Clothes and spices arrived from other territories of the Ottoman Empire. When Habsburg Vienna faced shortages of wheat, it was exported there from Ottoman-held southern Hungary on ships via Buda. By the second half of the 16th century about 40 percent of the trade was conducted by Muslim merchants and about 30 percent each by Christian Hungarians and Jews. No sources are available for the 17th century, but Muslim manufacturing probably increased during that time period. Only a few Ottoman monuments are still extant in Buda, including four baths, the *türbe* (mausoleum) of a famous 16th-century Bektashi dervish called Gül Baba, some bastions of the city walls, remnants of a mosque, and a few other, less significant, buildings.

When the province (*vilayet*) of Buda was created in 1541 the areas surrounding the city had not yet been secured and thus the relatively distant subprovinces, or *sancak*s, of Semendire (Szendrő), Alacahisar (Kruševac), Vulçıtrın (Vučtrn), İzvornik (Zvornik), and Pojega (Pozsega) were assigned to the new *vilayet*. As the Ottomans secured more land, the number of subprovinces near Buda increased. In 1568, the realm of the governor included 20 *sancak*s. This territory was significantly reduced in size with the establishment of the provinces of Eger (1596) and Kanizsa (1600), the first of which received four *sancak*s, the latter three *sancak*s formerly under the control of the governor of Buda; however, the reduced size did not affect the prestige of Buda. In 1623 governors of Buda received the rank of vizier and the neighboring Ottoman provinces were subordinated to it.

Seventy-five *beylerbeyi*s served in Buda during the Ottoman period, some of them more than once. Sokollu

Mustafa Pasha served for the longest period (1566–78); others, such as Sufi Sinan in 1595, Deli Derviş in 1622, and Hüseyn in 1631 and 1634, enjoyed the confidence of the sultan for a few days only. For a while in the 17th century the governor's term was limited to a single lunar year. The annual income of the governors of Buda from their military fiefs ranged from 800,000 and 1,200,000 akçe in the 16th century, assuring them an extremely high standard of living. Because of their location near the borders, the governors of Buda made several attempts to enlarge the territory under Ottoman rule, were active in diplomatic matters with the Habsburgs, and organized taxation, spying, and the provisioning of the imperial army while operating in the *vilayet*.

Géza Dávid

Further reading: Lajos Fekete, *Buda and Pest Under Turkish Rule = Studia Turco-Hungarica III* (Budapest: Eötvös Loránd University, 1976); Győző Gerő, *Turkish Monuments in Hungary* (Budapest: Corvina, 1976).

budgets While there is still some debate among historians as to the appropriate use of the term, the documents that contain the annual income and expenditure figures of the Ottoman central treasury are typically called "budgets" in modern studies. Ottoman budgets of the 16th century covered one full year beginning on Newruz, the Ottoman New Year's Day of March 21. The budgets of the 17th and 18th centuries, on the other hand, were calculated on the basis of the lunar calendar. Budgets usually included only those accounts of revenue assigned to meet the expenditures of the central treasury. Furthermore, Ottoman budgets did not reflect all the revenues and expenditures of the state. Two important sectors excluded from the budget were the *timar* sector—landed estates allocated to the cavalry—and the *waqf* sector—endowments of land or other property, usually set up for a beneficent purposes. The Ottoman budgets can be divided roughly into three formal sections: revenues; expenses, and surplus or deficit.

REVENUES

During the early modern period, the revenues (called *asl-ı mal*, *fil-asl-ı mal*, or *el-irad* in the sources) of the Ottoman budgets consisted of three major categories: poll taxes (JIZYA), extraordinary wartime taxes (*avarız*), and revenues from fiscal units administered as tax farms (MUKATAA). The *jizya* was the poll tax extracted either as gold or silver currency from healthy non-Muslim males with an occupation. The bulk of this tax income was transferred to the central treasury. The exemption from poll taxes in return for certain services was quite rare, and the transfer of poll taxes to a bureau other than the central treasury was exceptional. Poll taxes were never included within the *timar* system and given to fief-holders. Separate poll-tax registers provide an important source of information regarding changes in the empire's non-Muslim population and its capacity to pay taxes. Revenues from the poll tax constituted the greater part of total budget income with ratios varying from 23 to 48 percent of the total budget during the 17th and 18th centuries.

Avarız, or extraordinary wartime taxes, could be imposed only by the state and if in financial straits. When determining the size of these special taxes, the estimated capacity of the people was taken into consideration. This tax could be included neither within the *timar* sector nor within WAQF administration.

The budgets included almost all of the revenues collected from these two important sources, *jizya* and *avarız.* However, their position within the budget changed substantially over the centuries. After 1690, the *jizya* taxes were listed separately from other revenues in the budgets. Although the *avarız* taxes had always been a separate tax unit in the budgets, they were not collected regularly in the 17th century. Starting in the 18th century, however, *avarız* taxes began to be collected on a regular annual basis (*mukarrer*). The office responsible for the collection of the *avarız* taxes, notwithstanding its strict dependency on the central treasury, was flexible enough to allow the collection of the taxes as property or services, in addition to cash. Thus the figures seen in the budgets, which only registered cash revenues, reflect only a fraction of the revenues from this tax source. In the 17th and 18th centuries revenues from the *avarız* taxes constituted some 9 to 20 percent of the total revenues of the central treasury.

The third type of Ottoman state revenues registered in the budgets came from *mukataas* or fiscal units administered as tax farms. This sort of revenue, greatly diverse in kind, comprised mostly indirect taxes levied on all kinds of economic activities. Unlike the poll tax and the *avarız, mukataas* could be allocated to *timar*-holders and *waqfs,* although the most profitable *mukataas* remained under the administration of the state treasury. Still, the proportion assigned to the central treasury was limited, although it increased over time, both as a result of the growing use of cash in the economy and the proportional but gradual dwindling of the *timar* revenues. The share of the *mukataa* revenues in the budget ranged from 24 to 57 percent during the 17th and 18th centuries.

Starting in the middle of the 17th century, state revenues came to be used as a source for domestic loans, in addition to the short-term loans provided by wealthy merchants and statesmen. The failure of the state to balance the budget, however, indicates that the state abstained from increasing the tax burden of the subjects above a certain limit. The state seems to have preferred to postpone its own payments rather than to increase its revenues.

EXPENDITURES

The second section of the Ottoman budgets contained an inventory of expenditures (*el-mesarifat*), which was far more detailed than the revenues section. The expenditures were divided into subsections: *el-mevacibat,* which listed salaries of state officials and soldiers; *et-teslimat* (deliveries); *el-ihracat* (disbursements); *el-adat* (customary expenses), *el-mübayaa* (purchases), and *et-tasaddukat* (alms).

The principal category of expenditure in the budgets was salaries (*el-mevacibat*). In addition to the salaries of state officials and troops of the standing army, this section listed payments to military commanders, servants of the royal palace, artisans and tradesmen working for the palace, the royal kitchen, the imperial arsenal, and the imperial stables. In the 17th and 18th centuries these salaries amounted to 45 to 70 percent of the total expenditure of the budget. Wars were the main reason for the increase of troops' salaries and the total expenditure.

The second category of expenditure, deliveries (*et-teslimat*), was assigned to the provisioning of the palace, and it also paid part of the needs of the imperial cannon foundry, arsenal, and stables. These expenditures amounted to 30 percent of the total expenditures in the 16th century, but by the middle of the 17th century this had dropped to 15 percent.

The third principal category of expenditure of Ottoman budgets was disbursements (*el-ihracat*). This included subsidies to the Holy Places of Mecca and Medina, travel allowances, ceremonial expenses, stationery expenses of the treasury, the purchase of honorary robes given to members of the ruling class, expenses related to the restoration of royal palaces, expenses related to the imperial courier system, and so forth. These expenses rose from 10 percent of the total budget to 30 percent in the early part of the 16th century and later varied between 5 and 15 percent. By 1700 this proportion had decreased further, only to rise again after about 1704. The proportion doubled by 1787.

Another entry item of expenditure, called *hases* (large fiefs set aside for high dignitaries) and *salyane* (yearly allowances), covered the sums paid to the central and provincial ruling elite including viziers, governors, the mothers of the reigning sultans, as well as payments made to the admirals of the navy, the Crimean khans and princes, and the Circassian princes. The proportion of these expenses within the total budget varied between 5 and 15 percent in the second half of the 17th century and the first half of the 18th century.

REVENUES AND EXPENDITURES NOT REPRESENTED IN THE BUDGETS

The Ottoman budgets do not reflect all of the revenues and expenditures of the state. Except for the budget of

1527–1528, when *timar*s amounted to some 42 percent of state revenues, the *timar* sector was excluded from the Ottoman budget. To determine its exact contribution to state revenues in other times further research is needed. However, in general, this sector expanded until the beginning or middle of the 17th century, both in terms of amount of revenue and number of estate holders. From that time onward, however, the number of *timar*s declined, although at a slow pace. Nevertheless, the share of *timar* revenue within the state's total budget decreased rapidly, because other revenue sources grew. By the end of the 17th century, *timar* revenues constituted only 25 percent of the total budget. The *timar* sector further declined in the 18th century, but *timar*s survived until the TANZIMAT.

Another important sector excluded from the budget is that of the *waqf*, which made up 12 percent of the state revenues in the first quarter of the 16th century, when it was at its peak. Revenue from the *waqf* sector decreased steadily after that, even though the number of endowments increased.

The central bureaucracy, the judiciary, and the majority of provincial office-holders were not assigned salaries from the central treasury, and thus their payments were not reflected in the budgets. Some of them were paid through *timar*s, while others, although entitled to various fees, had to turn to other sources never included in the budgets. The expenses of tax collection and the profits of the tax farmers did not appear in the budgets either. New sources of revenue (e.g., *kalemiye* [office fees], *imdad-ı hazariye* [emergency taxes for peacetime], and *imdad-ı seferiye* [emergency taxes for wartime]) for the central and provincial high-ranking officials, starting with the last decades of the 18th century, were also excluded from the budget. The ratio of these revenues to the budget can be estimated at around 10 percent.

In 1775 the state developed a new type of tax farming called *esham* (shares), a form of long-term domestic borrowing similar to a bond issue, in which the state borrowed money by estimating the income of a particular revenue. The interest income of the *esham* holders, however, was excluded from the budget. About half of the *mukataa* (tax farming) revenues, some 46 percent of the revenues of the budget in the 1760s, was paid to the holders either as profit or as interest.

Although *avarız* taxes, whose significance increased considerably within the state revenues after the end of the 16th century, were included within the state revenues, the monetary equivalent of supplies and services provided by people in return for exemption from *avarız*—which included, among others, building and maintaining state buildings, bridges, and roads, and the production of salt, saltpeter, timber, wood, and pitch—was not reflected in the figures. To estimate the market value of these services, further studies are needed.

Considering the many types of state revenue that were excluded from the budget it is likely that the state revenues represented in the budgets did not exceed 25 to 40 percent of the actual revenues. Applying the rate of 10 percent as the average share states have in national income to the Ottoman example, Ottoman budgets represented between 2.5 and 4 percent of national income.

From the second half of the 18th century on, separate treasuries of various military and financial institutions were established, indicating that the classical age of Ottoman budgetary and financial history had come to an end. The new era, which lasted until the Tanzimat, is called the multi-budgetary era in Ottoman financial history. During this period of 50 to 60 years no general budgets were generated, indicating a crisis in Ottoman finances. This epoch ended with the centralization of Ottoman finances during the Tanzimat that led to the establishment of the first budget based on Western models.

THE IMPORTANCE OF OTTOMAN BUDGETS

Incomplete as they were, Ottoman budgets provide the modern researcher with valuable information and data regarding state finances. In the 16th century, annual revenues of the Ottoman budgets averaged 132 tons of silver (3,000,000 Venetian ducats), while the average annual expenditure is estimated at about 118 tons of silver (about 2,680,000 ducats).

In 1592 the budget showed a deficit for the first time. By 1608, state expenditures had increased by 116 percent over the first quarter of the 16th century. The rate of increase in revenues, however, was 89 percent. Although financial data from this period is incomplete, other documents and reports of the 17th century confirm the budget crisis.

Although the Ottoman central treasury expanded in terms of both revenue and expenditure between the first quarter of the 16th century and the end of the 18th century, revenues did not keep up with expenditures. Another era characterized by treasury deficits began in 1648 and ended in 1670. This second era coincided with the long siege of CRETE. The third period of budget deficits began in the year of the second SIEGE OF VIENNA (1683) and lasted until the TREATY OF KARLOW-ITZ (1699). The first half of the 18th century brought an end to the budgetary crises as Ottoman treasury revenues began to increase considerably faster than expenditures. In the second half of the 18th century, however, aggravated by wars, the treasury entered another period of growing budget deficits.

Erol Özvar

See also AGRICULTURE; MONEY; TAX FARMING.

Further reading: Ömer L. Barkan, "The Price Revolution of the Sixteenth Century: A Turning Point in the Economic History of the Near East." *International Journal of*

Middle Eastern Studies 6 (1975): 3–28; Linda T. Darling, *Revenue-Raising and Legitimacy: Tax Collection and Finance Administration in the Ottoman Empire, 1560–1660* (Leiden: Brill, 1996); Suraiya Faroqhi, "Othmānli: Social and Economic History," in *Encyclopaedia of Islam*, 2nd ed., vol. 8 (Leiden: Brill, 1960–), 202–210; Halil İnalcik, "Military and Fiscal Transformation in the Ottoman Empire, 1600–1700." *Archivum Ottomanicum* 6 (1980): 283–337; Mehmet Genç and Erol Özvar, *Osmanlı Maliyesi: Kurumlar ve Bütçeler*, 2 vols. (Istanbul: Osmanlı Bankası Arşiv ve Araştırma Merkezi, 2006); Sevket Pamuk, *A Monetary History of the Ottoman Empire* (Cambridge: Cambridge University Press, 2000); Halil Sahillioglu, "The Income and Expenditures of the Ottoman Treasury Between 1683 and 1749." *Revue d'Historie Maghrebine* 12 (1978): 143–172; Halil İnalcık, "State Revenues and Expenditures," in Halil İnalcık and Donald Quataert, *An Economic and Social History of the Ottoman Empire, 1300–1914* (Cambridge: Cambridge University Press, 1994), 55–102; Ariel Salzmann, "An Ancien Regime Revisited: Privatization and Political Economy in the Eighteenth Century Ottoman Empire." *Politics and Society* 21, no.4 (1993): 393–424.

Bulgaria Bulgaria is a state in the Balkan peninsula the territory of which formed an integral part of the core Ottoman provinces for nearly five centuries. During the first centuries of Ottoman rule (from the late 14th century), Bulgaria served, along with other central Balkan areas, as a vast laboratory where most Ottoman administrative, economic, and military institutions took shape. The strategic, historic, and economic importance of these lands as the gateway to Istanbul, as the first administrative units to emerge within the Ottoman system, and as a major source of revenue for the Ottoman treasury was reflected by the prestigious positions of the governors of this region, especially those of Rumelia, who ranked first among their peers. During the 19th century Ottoman REFORM period, most reforms were tested first on a provincial level in this region, and the long period of Ottoman domination has left a lasting imprint on Bulgaria's post-Liberation (1878) political life and on its foreign and domestic policies, as well as influencing Bulgaria's long-term demographic makeup, cultural institutions, and linguistic composition.

BEFORE THE OTTOMANS

Bulgaria draws its name from the Bulgar people, probably of Turkic origin, who formed a political and military alliance with the Slavic tribal union in what is present-day northern Bulgaria. The state became internationally recognized after a successful war with the BYZANTINE EMPIRE in 681. Christianity was adopted from the Byzantines as the state religion in 864 and since then Bulgaria has belonged to the Orthodox Christian world. Shortly thereafter, the Bulgarians adopted the Cyrillic alphabet, which then spread to other Slavic countries. The so-called First Bulgarian Empire reached its political and cultural zenith in the late ninth and early tenth centuries, immediately followed by a period of fragmentation and political weakening when it was conquered by the Byzantines. After a century and a half, in 1186, the independent Bulgarian state was restored and steadily expanded until the mid-13th century, with another peak of cultural efflorescence during the late 13th and 14th centuries. On the eve of its conquest by the Ottomans, the territorially reduced Bulgarian czardom split further into the czardoms of Turnovo and Vidin, and a principality in what is present-day northeastern Bulgaria.

THE OTTOMAN CONQUEST

The Bulgarians were among the first Balkanites to come under Ottoman rule. The Turnovo czardom was taken in 1395 and Vidin was conquered the following year, in retaliation for its ruler's support for the crusaders' campaign that same year. During the first three centuries after the Ottoman conquest, the Bulgarian lands remained in relative peace, with the exception of the decade after the BATTLE OF ANKARA (1402), the last crusader campaign of 1443–44, and the Long Hungarian War (1593–1606). The first real disruption of the regime came with the war against the Holy League (1683–99), when the Habsburg armies reached deep into the Balkans, occupying parts of the territories that make up present-day SERBIA, Bulgaria, and Macedonia. From the second half of the 18th century, with the emergence of the EASTERN QUESTION, Russia developed plans for territorial expansion and political influence south of the Danube; consequently, Bulgaria increasingly became the focus of military and diplomatic activities.

OTTOMAN ADMINISTRATION AND ECONOMY

With the advent of Ottoman control, Bulgaria also experienced a number of significant cultural and political changes. The independent Bulgarian Patriarchate of the Orthodox Church was abolished. The classic Ottoman landholding system was introduced into Bulgarian territories to support the feudal cavalry. In administrative terms, Bulgaria was initially included in the vast province of Rumelia, but in the late 16th century a new Ottoman province was established so that the Ottomans could repel increasingly intense attacks by the COSSACKS. The new province stretched along the BLACK SEA encompassing the territory of present-day eastern Bulgaria, northern Dobruja, and southern Ukraine (with centers in Özı/Ochakov, Ukraine; and Silistra, Bulgaria). The provinces and their subdivisions often followed the political and administrative borders from the pre-conquest period.

Until the Ottoman Reform or TANZIMAT period (1839–76), the territories of administrative units fluctuated, reflecting the changing strategies of the Ottomans in their domestic and foreign policy, the emergence of new threats in the region, and the rise of powerful notables, or AYAN.

After the Ottoman conquest the majority of the local population was given the status of DHIMMI, or non-Muslim taxpaying subjects, while part of the Bulgarian aristocracy integrated into the Ottoman military system as Christian cavalrymen. Being *dhimmi* allowed Bulgarians a limited religious and legal autonomy within the Ecumenical Patriarchate, the Ohrid Archbishopric and the Peć (Ipek) Patriarchate; being taxpayers, the *dhimmi* were subjected to the regular tax regime within the prebend landholding system, with some regional variations. A significant number of the *dhimmi* provided special services to the state, receiving tax concessions in return. They served as paramilitary and security forces, as but-

ter producers, as suppliers of rice and sheep, as miners, as salt producers, and as builders. The Bulgarian lands thus became a major source of meat, wool, rice, wheat, timber, and iron for the palace, the Ottoman capital, and the army.

The pacification of the region after the turmoil of the conquest stimulated the development of urban settlements, especially those situated along important trade and communication arteries. Some had existed in the pre-Ottoman era, others came into being after the conquest or grew from villages as a result of route changes or the rise of the strategic importance of one or another region.

Bulgarian populated lands were integrated into trade networks on several levels: local, regional, empire-wide, and international. Local crafts and trade in the towns functioned within the *esnaf* (guild) system, which survived in many places until the end of the 19th century. In the towns, which were usually also administrative cen-

Banebashi or Molla mosque, still standing in the center of Sofia, is the only Muslim prayer house in the town. Attributed to the school of Mimar Sinan, it was constructed, together with a primary school (*mekteb*) and a library, around 1570-71 as part of the *vakıf* of the kadı Seyfullah Efendi. *(Photo by Rossitsa Gradeva)*

ters and seats of garrisons, a majority of inhabitants were Muslim. The architecture and general outlook of urban settlements were dominated by traditional Islamic structures, which reflected various aspects of the Islamic religion, culture, education, and lifestyle in general. These buildings included mosques, dervish lodges, colleges and primary schools, libraries, covered bazaars, soup kitchens, public baths, and fountains, typically supported by pious foundations called *WAQFS*.

DEMOGRAPHIC CHANGES AND POPULATION MOVEMENTS

While the Bulgarian lands were never an ethnically homogeneous region, the Ottoman conquest brought significant demographic changes, especially with the emergence of a significant Muslim community. The Ottoman conquest triggered colonization by Muslims from Asia Minor and by Tatars from the north, motivating migrations and conversion to Islam among the local population. The central authority focused on colonization along with conquest, creating settlements of Muslims in an effort to strengthen its grip on the newly conquered lands and to release some of the pressure of unruly groups (KIZILBAŞ and various semi-nomadic groups of cattle-breeders) that were in Anatolia. It was relatively intensive during the first century and a half of Ottoman rule in the Balkans and affected primarily the territory of modern European Turkey, the eastern parts of Bulgaria, northern Greece, and Macedonia.

During the late 18th and 19th centuries, Tatars and Circassians from Russia were resettled in Bulgaria as part of international agreements between the two empires. During the 15th century, groups of Bulgarians were sent into Anatolia and ALBANIA, whereas in the 16th century Albanians were resettled in dozens of villages in various parts of Bulgaria. Throughout the period of Ottoman rule, voluntary migrations brought Arabs, Kurds, Serbs, and Greeks, craftsmen and traders, to many towns in the Bulgarian lands. At the same time, Bulgarians expanded their businesses and settled in the Ottoman cities of ISTANBUL, IZMIR, and ALEXANDRIA.

Perhaps the most significant change brought about by Ottoman rule was the gradual conversion of local people to Islam. Having begun with the conquest, the process of conversion gained momentum from the late 16th century onward and reached its peak in the 17th and 18th centuries. One of the ways that this outcome was achieved was by the Ottoman levy of young boys from the 15th to the 17th centuries. This institution involved a system of conscription, called *DEVŞIRME*, of boys from Balkan Christian families, who were removed from the territory, converted to Islam, and trained to serve the sultan in the JANISSARIES and in the palace. Although Balkan historiographies usually associate conversion to Islam mainly with application of force it seems that for the majority of converts the change of the faith resulted from a personal choice triggered by a range of considerations, including an interest in improving social and economic standing. Some new converts were linguistically assimilated into the Turkish-speaking communities established as part of the colonization. However, in the regions where the Turkish element was weak, the converts tended to preserve their language and remained a distinct separate group, called Pomaks.

The persecutions of Jews in Catholic Europe brought several waves of Jewish settlers to the Balkan towns between the late 14th century and the beginning of the 16th century. They joined small Jewish groups that had been living in medieval Bulgaria. By the end of the 16th century, Jewish communities had become an economically important and conspicuous component of the population of all towns in the territory of Bulgaria. In the 17th century, Armenians from the eastern parts of the Ottoman state also began to settle in the Bulgarian lands, moving westward mainly as part of an international trading network serving the Silk Road.

Throughout the Ottoman period, from the 15th century until the mid-19th century, especially as a result of wars between the Ottomans and their Christian neighbors, there were waves of emigration of larger or smaller groups of Christians: during the first centuries mainly toward WALLACHIA, at the end of the 17th–18th centuries toward the Habsburg realm, and from the late 18th century toward Russia, where Bulgarian emigrants settled in Bessarabia, UKRAINE, and the Crimea.

THE 18TH AND 19TH CENTURIES

In the last quarter of the 18th century a large part of the territories populated by Bulgarians was divided among local notables known as *ayan,* some of whom had established hereditary rule over their dependent regions; OSMAN PAZVANTOĞLU in Vidin and Ismail Tirseniklioglu and ALEMDAR MUSTAFA PASHA in Rusçuk (Ruse) are the best known of these. The last decades of the 18th century and the first decades of the 19th century have remained in the historical memory of Bulgarians as a time of chaos in which the real presence of the Ottoman government was reduced to mere islands besieged by bandits. Under Sultan MAHMUD II (r. 1808–39), the central Ottoman authority gradually restored its hold in the region. And during the rest of the 19th century, Bulgarian territories were usually included in the model provinces where the reforms of the TANZIMAT were first applied with the purpose of removing some of the major abuses and corrupt practices in their administration, the most significant case being that of the DANUBE PROVINCE, founded in 1864.

The late 18th and 19th centuries were a period in which international, regional, and local trade and crafts (especially textile related) developed rapidly in the Bulgarian lands, leading to the emergence of a relatively significant group of wealthy Bulgarians. A period called the BULGARIAN NATIONAL AWAKENING corresponds to this transition to modernity and the formation of the Bulgarian nation. For Bulgarians, it was a time of gradual identification as an entity separate from the rest of the Orthodox Christian community (especially the Greeks), rapid expansion of modern secular education and culture, struggle for the establishment of an autocephalous Bulgarian ecclesiastical hierarchy, and for political emancipation. A combination of circumstances triggered a major crisis in international relations and led to the Russo-Ottoman War of 1877–78 (see RUSSO-OTTOMAN WARS) in which the Ottomans were completely routed. Among these circumstances were the suppression of the Bosnian rising of 1875, the Serbo-Montenegro-Ottoman war, and the so-called "Bulgarian atrocities" that occurred after the defeat of the Bulgarian April Uprising of 1876.

LIBERATION AND POST-LIBERATION PERIOD

The military successes of Russia in the Russo-Ottoman War of 1877–78 were crowned with the preliminary Treaty of San Stefano (March 3, 1878), which established a Great Bulgaria made up of all predominantly Bulgarian territories. The Treaty of San Stefano was revised by the Berlin Congress of July 1, 1878 to this effect: Danubian Bulgaria and the district of Sofia came to form a tributary to the Ottoman Empire, the Principality of Bulgaria with its capital city in Sofia; southern Bulgaria formed the autonomous province of Eastern Rumelia; parts of western Bulgaria were given to Serbia; and northern Dobruja was given to Romania. Macedonia and the Rhodopes were left under direct Ottoman rule. The Great National Assembly of the Principality of Bulgaria elected its first prince, Alexander Batemberg, and also adopted its first constitution (1879).

The unification of all parts controlled by the Ottomans dominated Bulgarian foreign policy throughout its subsequent history. In 1885 the Principality of Bulgaria and Eastern Rumelia unified. Bulgaria supported the struggles of revolutionaries in Macedonia and Thrace that peaked with uprisings in 1903. Taking advantage of the YOUNG TURK Revolution crisis, the second Bulgarian prince, Ferdinand of Saxe-Coburg Gotha, declared Bulgaria's independence from the Ottoman Empire in 1908. In 1912, Bulgaria participated in the Balkan alliance declaring war on the Ottoman Empire with the ultimate goal of partitioning Ottoman possessions in Europe. The next year, these Balkan allies turned against one another, engaging in a bloody conflict for the former Ottoman provinces. In this conflict, the Ottoman Empire was able to recover part of the territories that had been taken by Bulgaria. During WORLD WAR I, Bulgaria and the Ottoman Empire together joined the Central Axis powers, and Bulgarian and Ottoman troops fought together against Russia; both losing substantially from the peace treaties negotiated in the wake of this major conflict.

The Ottoman rule that lasted more than 500 years left Bulgaria with demographic, economic, social, and cultural legacies that are still visible today.

Rossitsa Gradeva

Further reading: Richard Crampton, *A Concise History of Bulgaria* (Cambridge: Cambridge University Press, 1997); Rossitsa Gradeva, *Rumeli under the Ottomans, 15th–18th Centuries: Institutions and Communities* (Istanbul: Isis, 2004); Dennis Hupchik, *The Bulgarians in the Seventeenth Century: Slavic Orthodox Society and Culture under Ottoman Rule* (Jefferson, N.C.: McFarland & Company, 1993); Halil İnalcik, "Bulgaria," in *Encyclopaedia of Islam*, vol. 1, CD-ROM edition, edited by Bernard Lewis, Charles Pellat, et al. (Leiden: Brill, 2001), 1302a–1304b; Machiel Kiel, *Art and Society in Bulgaria in the Turkish Period* (Assen/ Maastricht: Van Gorcum, 1985).

Bulgarian National Awakening (Bulgarian National Revival)

This term was coined to describe processes taking place in Bulgarian society under Ottoman rule in the late 18th and 19th centuries, corresponding to the transition to modernity and the formation of the Bulgarian nation. In socioeconomic terms this was a period in which international, regional, and local trade and crafts (especially textile related) developed rapidly in the Bulgarian lands. A relatively significant group of wealthy Bulgarians emerged who had accumulated considerable capital that they invested in entrepreneurial activities, larger-scale land estates, and trade. In the context of Ottoman REFORM, this group was also increasingly involved in self-government at both the central and provincial levels.

For Bulgarians, it was a time of gradual identification as an entity separate from the rest of the Orthodox community, especially from the Greeks, rapid expansion of modern lay education and culture, struggle for the establishment of an autocephalous Bulgarian ecclesiastical hierarchy, and struggle for political emancipation. A kind of national program was drawn in the *Slavo-Bulgarian History* written by Father Paissii of Hilandar (1762), which became a guidebook for generations of Bulgarians and whose postulates were adopted by the leaders of the Bulgarian national movement.

One of the major aspects of the period was the establishment (especially from the 1820s onward) of Bulgarian educational institutions, the adoption of contemporary teaching methods and textbooks, the development of modern Bulgarian literary language and literature, book publishing, the emergence of a Bulgarian press with its main centers in ISTANBUL, Bucharest, Vienna (first newspaper, 1846–47), and IZMIR (first journal, 1844–46). By the beginning of the 1870s, more than 1,600 Bulgarian-language schools had been founded. Public reading rooms, which served as centers of cultural activities, were established in towns and many villages, and these hosted the first amateur theatre performances in the emerging nation. In 1869 the Bulgarian Book Society, the precursor of the Bulgarian Academy of Sciences, was founded in Braila, Romania.

The most significant focus of this movement was establishing a national ecclesiastical hierarchy. This struggle went through several dramatic stages, with Bulgarians finally declaring their secession from the Ecumenical Patriarchate (1860) and the establishment of an exarchate (the relevant *ferman* of the Ottoman sultan was issued in 1870, the first exarch was elected in 1871).

Chronologically last came the armed struggle for national liberation. Bulgarians had taken part in the liberation wars of Serbs and Greeks. In 1841 (Nish) and 1850 (Vidin), in protest against the remnants of the share-cropping system on large land estates and the abuses of local Muslim landlords, Bulgarians rose up against the Ottoman regime. But it was only after the CRIMEAN WAR (1853–56) that a true Bulgarian revolutionary movement emerged, going through several stages of organization and ideological evolution.

The first to draw coherent plans for the military and political strategy for Bulgarian liberation was Georgi Rakovski, who tried to take advantage of the strained relations between SERBIA and the Ottomans and to establish the first Bulgarian political centre in BELGRADE (1862). Later in the 1860s the center of political and revolutionary activities moved to Bucharest, where several emigrant organizations functioned, defending different views regarding ways to achieve liberation. These ranged from closely following the Russian policy in the region through plans for a dualist Ottoman-Bulgarian state to revolutionary struggle.

The peak in the latter was reached with the foundation in 1869 of the Bulgarian Revolutionary Central Committee in Bucharest led by Liuben Karavelov, and with an internal organization led by Vassil Levski. These two groups cooperated closely to encourage a general uprising. These preparations culminated in the April Uprising of 1876. Together with the Bosnian rising and the Serbo-Montenegro-Ottoman war, the suppression of the Bulgarian April Uprising (1876)—the culmination of the Bulgarian revolutionary struggles—triggered a major crisis in international relations and led to the Russo-Ottoman war of 1877–78 (*see* RUSSO-OTTOMAN WARS) in which the Ottomans were completely routed.

Following the peace treaties of San Stefano (March 3, 1878) and of Berlin (July 1, 1878), Bulgarians achieved partial liberation with the establishment of the Principality of Bulgaria, a tributary to the Ottoman Empire.

Rossitsa Gradeva

Further reading: James Franklin Clarke, *The Pen and the Sword: Studies in Bulgarian History,* edited by Dennis Hupchik (Boulder, Colo.: East European Monographs; distributed by Columbia University, 1988); Rumen Daskalov, *The Making of a Nation in the Balkans: Historiography of the Bulgarian Revival* (Budapest: Central European University, 2004).

Bulgarian Orthodox Church   This term is used to describe the ecclesiastical hierarchy associated in different periods with Bulgarian statehood and Bulgarians. Since the official introduction of Christianity in the country in 864, and after the split between the Eastern and the Western churches (the Great Schism in 1054), the Bulgarian Church has adhered to Orthodox Christianity; shortly after its foundation, Bulgarian was adopted as the language of its books and services. In the Eastern Orthodox world, where the principle of caesaropapism (a political system in which an emperor or king seeks to exercise, along with the temporal authority, control over the church in his domain) dominated, rulers usually aspired to have an autocephalous ("self-headed") ecclesiastical hierarchy. Thus historically the Bulgarian Orthodox Church is the church most connected with Bulgarian statehood.

Christianity was adopted as the state religion of Bulgaria in 864 by an act of Khan Boris-Michael I (r. 867–889). The Bulgarian Orthodox Church rose to the rank of a patriarchate during the zenith of the first Bulgarian czardom (927) until the Byzantine conquest of Bulgaria (1018), when Emperor Basil II (r. 976–1025) instituted as its direct successor the Ohrid Archbishopric. In the course of time the Ohrid archbishopric evolved into a regional church without direct association with any of the local states. The restored Bulgarian Church was granted the rank of patriarchate again during the second Bulgarian czardom (1235). On both occasions the Byzantine emperor granted the patriarchate as an act of political concession that was disapproved of by the Ecumenical Patriarchate in Constantinople (*see* ISTANBUL), the dominant church in the Orthodox world. Due to the developing fragmentation of the Bulgarian state shortly before the Ottoman conquest in the 14th century, the Bulgarian Patriarchate, despite its high prestige as a cultural and religious center, consisted of only three eparchies (dioceses).

Between 1393 (the fall of Turnovo, the seat of the Bulgarian patriarch, to the Ottomans) and 1438, the patriarchate disappeared. It fell for a combination of reasons, the most important of which was the dissolution of

Bulgarian statehood. Most of the dioceses populated by Bulgarians were folded into the Ecumenical Patriarchate, a process that had started before the conquest. The Greek language gradually infiltrated the service and Greek-speaking clergy usually headed the dioceses inhabited by a predominantly Bulgarian population. Other dioceses were attached to the Ohrid archbishopric, which survived the conquest.

During the second half of the 15th century and the first half of the 16th century the Ohrid archbishopric expanded to encompass present-day Macedonia, parts of northern GREECE and southern ALBANIA, western Bulgaria, SERBIA, WALLACHIA and MOLDAVIA, and Orthodox parishes in Italy. Until its demise in 1767 it included nine metropolitanates and five bishoprics mainly on the territory of present-day Macedonia, northern Greece, and southern Albania. In 1557 the Ottomans reinstituted the Serbian Peć Patriarchate, which until its abolition in 1766 also contained Bulgarian eparchies. The two Slavic churches were closed down at the instigation of the Ecumenical Patriarchate for financial reasons and as a result of political conflicts.

The struggle for a national ecclesiastical hierarchy, the result of the incompatibility of the ecumenical aspirations of the Church and the emerging Bulgarian nationalism, developed into the most important aspect of the movement for the recognition of a Bulgarian nation within the Orthodox community of the Ottoman Empire. The leaders of this struggle took advantage of the reform acts of the TANZIMAT to submit their demands to the Sublime Porte and the Ecumenical Patriarchate. These demands included church services in Bulgarian, Bulgarian-speaking high clergy, the establishment of a national church, and a form of political autonomy.

An initial success was achieved following the issuance of a decree permitting the construction of a Bulgarian church in Istanbul in 1849. The Bulgarian municipality surrounding the church gradually began to act as an all-Bulgarian representative body communicating with the Ottoman authority and the Ecumenical Patriarchate. In 1860, the refusal of the patriarchate to respond to the Bulgarian demands resulted in the radical step of replacing, during the Easter service, the name of the ecumenical patriarch with that of the ruling sultan. This step amounted to declaring the emergence of an autocephalous Bulgarian Orthodox Church. This event was followed by actions to expel high Greek clergy, the assumption of ecclesiastical and educational affairs by the municipalities, and the recognition of a Bulgarian bishop as the head of the religious hierarchy.

In time, the question of the Bulgarian Church entered the realm of international relations. Several plans to resolve the issue were rejected by the patriarchate, strongly supported by Russia. Finally, in 1870, the sultan issued a decree authorizing the establishment of a Bulgarian exarchate. This exarchate was recognized as the legal representative of Bulgarians in the Ottoman Empire. In 1871 Antim I was elected to be the first Bulgarian exarch. Antim I remained in this position until 1877. The diocese of the exarchate included eparchies in present-day Bulgaria, eastern Serbia (Niš and Pirot), and parts of Macedonia (around Veles). Plovdiv, Varna, and villages on the Black Sea Coast, where the presence of other Orthodox ethnicities was strong, were excluded from the exarchate diocese. Other municipalities were allowed to join the exarchate if more than two-thirds of the local Christians expressed their desire, through voting, to join the exarchate. For example, in 1877 Ohrid and Skopje voted to join the exarchate. In 1872 the Ecumenical Patriarchate declared the exarchate schismatic. This schism lasted until 1945.

After the Russo-Ottoman war of 1877–78 (*see* RUSSO-OTTOMAN WARS) and the ensuing Congress of Berlin, the Bulgarian Orthodox Church was divided into two parts. One part was headed by the Holy Synod and an exarchate deputy in Sofia. This part included the vassal Bulgarian principality and, after 1885, Eastern Rumelia. The other part, led by the exarch in Istanbul, was an Ottoman institution entirely subsidized by the Bulgarian principality's budget. The exarchate lost its eparchies in territories subsequently ceded to Romania and Serbia. By the time of the BALKAN WARS—despite the problems created by revolutionary struggles, the uprising of 1903, and the confrontations resulting from Greek and Serbian propaganda (especially in the bitterly contested Macedonia)—the voting provision provided for in the decree of 1870 allowed the exarchate to expand. It now included eparchies in present-day Macedonia, northern GREECE, and European Turkey. In these Ottoman territories the exarchate supported Bulgarian-language education and church services. After the Second Balkan War the exarchate was forced to move to Bulgaria, leaving a representative in the Ottoman capital to defend the interests of Bulgarians remaining under Ottoman rule. This exarchate was closed in 1945. In 1953 the Bulgarian Orthodox Church again became a patriarchate.

Established with political goals in mind, the fate of the Bulgarian Orthodox Church closely paralleled—and was, indeed, dependent on—the Bulgarian state. During the 1850s to 1870s, the establishment of a Bulgarian hierarchy was part of the nationalist agenda. Even in the Bulgarian principality, however, the Church was treated as a second-rate institution. It was subjected to strict control by the civil authority, which saw its role mainly in the achievement of the national ideal.

Rossitsa Gradeva

Further reading: Zïna Markova, "Russia and the Bulgarian-Greek Church Question in the Seventies of the 19th

Century." *Etudes Historiques* 11 (1983): 159–197; Thomas Meininger, *Ignatiev and the Establishment of the Bulgarian Exarchate, 1864–1872: A Study in Personal Diplomacy* (Madison: University of Wisconsin, 1970); Theodore H. Papadopoullos, *Studies and Documents Relating to the History of the Greek Church and People Under Turkish Domination* (Aldershot, UK: Variorum, 1990).

Bulutkapan Ali Bey *See* QAZDAGHLI HOUSEHOLD.

Bursa (Brusa, Brussa; *Gk.*: Prousa) Located in present-day northwestern Turkey, Bursa was founded in the 200s B.C.E. by the king of Bithynia, Prusias I. It grew in size and importance during the BYZANTINE EMPIRE and was the capital of the Ottoman Empire from 1326 until the early 15th century. Today, it is still one of the five largest cities in Turkey, with an estimated population of 1.4 million. Because of its fertile lands and location at the crossroads between the Balkans and Anatolia, Bursa has played a significant economic, political, and cultural role through the ages. The city's history is reflected in its Bithynian, Byzantian, Ottoman, and Turkish architecture, and many religious and commercial buildings attest to its significance.

Archaeological records date the first settlement of the site to about 5,000 years ago. Prusias I ordered the building of a new city atop a previous settlement and named the city Prusa. The city prospered in Byzantine times, especially after Emperor Justinian I (r. 527–65) had a palace built there. Arabs and then Turks made several military campaigns to conquer it, with the Seljuk Turks succeeding at the end of the 11th century. However, beginning with the First Crusade in 1096, Bursa switched hands several times until the Ottomans finally captured the city from the Byzantine Empire in 1326 after a six-year siege by ORHAN GHAZI (r. 1324–62). After the conquest, some Greeks stayed, although their income and the volume of trade declined. The Ottomans first settled within the castle and then, through the construction of *külliyes* (building complex that typically included a mosque and public structures and spaces such as schools, hospitals, soup kitchens, marketplaces, and lodging for travelers), expanded rapidly outward.

Orhan built a palace for himself at the Tophane and made Bursa his capital city where he minted his first silver coin. He also encouraged urban growth through the construction of buildings such as *imaret*s (building complexes including a public kitchen), mosques, BATHHOUSES (hammams), and *han*s or caravansaries. During the reigns of subsequent sultans, new religious and commercial centers, the foci of city life, were built in the form of endowments (WAQFS) by various sultans, high officials, and

The Great Mosque of Bursa was built during the reign of Bayezid I (1389-1402) as part of an effort to develop and Ottomanize the recently conquered city. Built outside the Byzantine city walls, the mosque provided a space for congregational worship and a hub for the new commercial heart of the Ottoman city. *(Photo by Gábor Ágoston)*

wealthy citizens, including the Ulucami or Great Mosque built during the reign of BAYEZID I (r. 1389–1402). Some women from the royal family—such as Gülçiçek Hatun, mother of Bayezid I, and Hundi Hatun, his sister—also contributed to this development by building colleges (madrasas). The significant mosques of Orhan, MURAD I (r. 1362–89), Bayezid I, Yeşil, and Emir Sultan, as well as many *medrese*s, *han*s, *bedestan*s, bazaars, and caravansaries, were built in Bursa up until the middle of the 14th century, and attested to the city's economic well-being.

Many travelers noted during the 15th century that Bursa had become one of the most important cities in the region within a century after its conquest by the Ottomans. However, TIMUR's victory over Bayezid I in 1402 and Bursa's subsequent sacking crippled the city. Shortly thereafter, EDIRNE replaced Bursa as the capital of the Ottoman Empire.

In the early years of the 15th century, MEHMED I (r. 1413–21) and MURAD II (r. 1421–44, 1446–51) rebuilt the city and revived its earlier prosperity. Patronage was not limited to the sultans. Many of Bursa's newly founded districts bear the names of pashas who built *imarets*, including Fadullah Pasha, Ivaz Pasha, and Umur Beg. The city's boundaries were delineated by Orhan's buildings in the north, Murad I's *imarets* in the west, Bayezid I's *imarets* in the east.

During the reign of MEHMED II (r. 1444–1446, 1451–1481), Bursa grew economically through the silk and spice trades. And although ISTANBUL was then the capital city of the empire, Bursa kept its status as the launching point for the sultans' eastern campaigns. In the 16th century Bursa was one of 30 judicial districts (*kazas*) of the subprovince (*liva* or *sancak*) of Hüdavendigar. The city preserved its administrative position with small changes until the end of the Ottoman Empire. In the 19th century, new buildings such as a theater, municipal buildings, and industrial units began to reshape the city. Bursa was occupied by Greece from 1920 until 1922. Thereafter it served as an important trade, agricultural, industrial, and cultural center for the modern Turkish Republic.

French author Bertrandon de La Broquère mentions that, in 1432, there were 1,000 houses (approximately 5,000 people) in the castle. According to the *avarız* (tax) registers, there were 6,456 households (more than 32,000 people) in 1487 and 6,351 households in 1530. By the 1570s, the city's population exceeded 60,000 (12,852 households). Also, *tahrir* (property) surveys show that Bursa was divided into around 152 quarters in the early 16th and 168 quarters in the late 16th century. These figures indicate fast population growth, possibly a result of a concurrent general population increase in the Ottoman Empire.

The number of non-Muslims (DHIMMI) in the early 16th century was around 1,000, including 400 Christians and 600 Jews; but in the latter part of the century this number reached 4,500, of whom 3,000 were Christian and 1,500 Jewish. Non-Muslims lived outside the castle. Sir George Wheler (1651–1724), a clergyman and scholar who visited the city at the end of the 17th century, recorded that there were more than 12,000 Jews along with some Armenians and Romanians living in the city.

The city's population continued to grow during the 18th and 19th centuries, although the earthquake of 1855 led to a population decline. Nevertheless, in the second half of the 19th century, Armenian migration from the east and refugees from the Russo-Ottoman War of 1877–78 (*see* RUSSO-OTTOMAN WARS) led to a rapid increase in the population of the city. These migrants also established several new villages and quarters, raising the population to approximately 80,000, of whom 6,000 were Greeks, 11,000 were Armenians, and 3,000 were Jews.

Besides its fertile lands and abundant water sources, Bursa's economic significance was due to the fact that it served as a trading center between the Ottoman dominions and SYRIA and EGYPT in the spice trade of the 15th and 16th centuries. Spices for Istanbul, the Balkans, and the northern countries were transported through Bursa. The main routes of the spice trade were the Syria-Bursa caravan route, the sea route from Bursa (via Mudanya port) to Antalya and Alexandria, and the Alexandria-Chios-Istanbul route.

The silk trade with IRAN played an even greater role in the international trade activities of the city. Until 1512, when the Ottomans and Safavids came into conflict, Iranian silk was transferred to Bursa and from there exported to European countries. When the Silk Road began to shift between 1599 and 1628, Aleppo and Izmir replaced Bursa as pivotal points in the silk trade. Bursa continued, however, to produce silk locally until the 19th century, when the development of steam power in the production of silk made and maintained the fame of Bursa's silks.

Yunus Uğur

Further reading: Haim Gerber, *Economy and Society in an Ottoman City: Bursa, 1600–1700* (Jerusalem: The Hebrew University, 1988); Leila Erder, "The Making of Industrial Bursa. Economic Activity and Population in Turkish City 1835–1975" (Ph.D. diss., Michigan University, 1976); Engin Özendeş, *The First Ottoman Capital: Bursa* (Istanbul: Yapı Endüstri Merkezi Yay, 1999); Halil İnalcık, "Bursa," in *Encyclopaedia of Islam*, 2nd ed., vol. 1 (Leiden: Brill, 1960–), 1333–36; Murad Çızakça, "Cash Waqfs of Bursa, 1555–1823." *Journal of the Economic and Social History of the Orient* 38, no. 3 (1995) 313–54; Suraiya Faroqhi, *Making a Living in the Ottoman Lands, 1480 to 1820* (Istanbul: ISIS, 1995).

Büyük Süleyman Pasha (d. 1801) (r. 1780–1801) *governor of Baghdad*   Büyük Süleyman, or "Big" Süleyman, was a product of the great MAMLUK household that dominated the political life of BAGHDAD in the 18th century. Like most of the males in the Mamluk household that provided the city's governors, Büyük Süleyman was born a Georgian Christian but was bought as a slave while still a boy and was raised as a Muslim within the Ottoman Turkish culture of the governor's household. He was initially made governor of BASRA, Iraq's port city, which in the 18th century was a dependency of Baghdad. In that capacity, he mounted a spirited defense of the city against the forces of the Iranian despot, KARIM KHAN ZAND in 1776. But his efforts ultimately failed and he was held as a captive of the Persians in Shiraz, Zand's capital, until Karim Khan's death in 1779. Upon his return to IRAQ, Süleyman was granted the governorship of Basra and that of Baghdad a year later. He ruled in Baghdad until his death in 1802.

Historians consider his reign to be the high point of Mamluk rule in Baghdad. Although his reign was peaceful for the city itself, he faced considerable problems from an unusual alliance in 1788 between the Muntafiq BEDOUINS, the confederation that dominated the region around Basra, and the Kurdish *mir*, or prince, of SHAHR-IZOR, the province comprising Iraqi Kurdistan. Given the fact that the two groups were of different ethnic origins and separated from each other by several hundred miles of Ottoman-controlled territory, it was unusual that they would act in concert, but Süleyman was able to defeat both. Nevertheless, Bedouin incursions, mounted first by the more powerful SHAMMAR confederation and then by the WAHHABIS, threatened the trade routes and the prosperity of his city. In 1798 he organized a campaign with more than 10,000 troops against the Wahhabis and advanced against towns they held in the al-Ahsa region in the northeast of the Arabian peninsula. The campaign ended in a stalemate and a truce. But the Wahhabis broke that truce with their raid on KARBALA, the Shii holy city in southern Iraq, not long before Süleyman's death in 1801.

After his death, there was a struggle among the males of the governor's household over who would succeed him. Ali Kahya, his steward and agha of Baghdad's JANIS-SARIES, won this struggle, but was assassinated in 1807, to be succeeded by Süleyman's son Küçük Süleyman, or "Little" Süleyman. The Jews and Christians of Baghdad remembered Büyük Süleyman Pasha as a just and honorable man. This was undoubtedly due, in no small part, to the fact that governors before and after him used their office to extort large sums from both communities. Muslim chroniclers, in contrast, saw his reign as less than noble as, like his predecessors, he continued the practice of extracting illegal taxes from Muslim merchants and other tradesmen. Further endearing him to the Chaldean Catholics in the city, during his reign, European Catholic priests were free to offer sacraments openly in Baghdad to any who would take them, as Büyük Süleyman was remarkably tolerant of all the religiously diverse subjects of his province.

Bruce Masters

Further reading: Stephen Longrigg, *Four Centuries of Modern Iraq* (Oxford: Clarendon, 1925).

Byzantine Empire The Byzantine Empire is said to have come into being when the city of Constantinople (ISTANBUL) was founded in 324 C.E. and to have ended when the same city fell to the Ottoman Turks in 1453. During these eleven centuries the empire underwent profound transformations; hence it is customary to divide Byzantine history into at least three major periods: the Early Period, from its founding to about the middle of the seventh century; the Middle Period, up to the conquest of Asia Minor by Turks in the 1070s; and the Late Period, up to 1453, when the empire fell to the Ottomans. These divisions facilitate understanding the shifting borders and new actors in the area covered roughly by the Balkans, Asia Minor, Anatolia, SYRIA, PALESTINE, and EGYPT.

The fight for control of the fertile crescent was an enduring one, first between the Persians and the Byzantines and then between the Arabs and the Byzantines during the Early Period. With the settlement of SELJUK TURKS in the region, this conflict was transformed into a semi-permanent conflict between neighbors during the Middle Period. In the Late Period, after the sack of Constantinople in 1204 by VENICE and knights from the Christian West, known as Latins, the empire was partitioned and the Latin kingdoms assumed control of much former Byzantine territory.

At different points in the long history of the empire the polyglot (Slavic, Greek, Syriac, Coptic, Aramaic, Armenian, Latin) and multiethnic (Bulgarians, Serbs, Croats, Albanians, Greeks, Armenians, Syrians, Egyptians, JEWS) empire had been in grave danger. After the mid-seventh century the Byzantine Empire was a medium sized regional state based in Constantinople and fighting a battle for survival. However, even the disasters of the seventh century did not overturn the Byzantine faith that they were the new Israelites, a Chosen People, ruled by a Christ-loving emperor who dwelt in the God-guarded city. Their belief that failures and defeats were allowed by God as a punishment for sin and that repentance would allow them to be spared was the motivating power behind their recovery and victories in the 11th century. In Byzantine political ideology, as long as the empire retained its three elements—the emperor, the patriarch, and the city (Constantinople)—it continued to exist. Territorial losses were considered to be ephemeral.

Byzantium in the 11th and 12th centuries underwent explosive demographic, urban, and economic growth, which led to competition and discord with its population, and finally to military defeat at the hands of outsiders. In both cultural and political history, the loss of most of Anatolia and the rise of the Comneni dynasty to the Byzantine throne in 1081 marked a new stage. Once more the political decline of Byzantium from an unrivaled superpower to merely the strongest of several strong states subtly changed the cultural mood, and unquestioned self-assurance of Byzantine dominance gave way to a more defensive sense of superiority. The ecclesiastical schism between Rome and Constantinople in 1054 manifested the political and ideological division between East and West that was used to legitimize the attack on the Byzantine Empire after the Fourth Crusade.

The resilience of Byzantine political ideology and culture was tested while the empire was in exile following the events of the fourth crusade and three successive states—

the Despotate of Epirus (northwest of Greece and south of Albania), the Empire of Nicaea (Iznik, Turkey), and the Empire of Trabzon (Trebizond)—claimed to be the legitimate successor states. The reconquest of Constantinople from the Latins in 1261 amounted to a symbolic imperial rebirth. Soon, however, the Byzantine treasury was emptied as its territories shrank to a small part of northwestern Anatolia in the east and Thrace in the west.

Lack of resources, the constant threat of another crusade organized by the West to revive Constantinople as a Latin kingdom, as well as ideological and theological quarrels, prevented Byzantine society from focusing on its eastern borders. By 1320, Byzantium's eastern front had grown unstable but the Ottomans were not yet acknowledged as a true political threat. According to the Byzantines, the Ottoman nomads represented nothing more than the next wave of tribal movement into Anatolia. They were to painfully find out that these nomads had come to stay. The history of the relations between the Byzantines and Ottoman Turks is characterized by periods of conflict and cooperation and may be divided into three main periods: the Byzantines and the Ottomans as adversaries between 1302 and 1341, as cautious allies from 1341 to 1347, and the Byzantines as Ottoman vassals from 1354 to 1453.

BYZANTINE-OTTOMAN ANTAGONISM, 1302–41

The Ottoman emirate was one among many established in former Byzantine Anatolia. The Ottomans, named after their founder OSMAN I (r. c. 1281–1324?), were situated in northwestern Asia Minor, on the Byzantine frontier along the Sangarios River in eastern Bithynia (the Sakarya River in present-day Turkey). Many myths and legends were invented to supply Osman with a long and glorious pedigree; he was, after all, the founder of a dynasty that would inherit the universal Byzantine Empire and "terrorize" western Europe in the 15th and 16th centuries.

Osman, upon the death of his father Ertoğrul in 1288, slowly advanced into the Byzantine province of Bithynia, raiding the upper valley of the Sangarios River as well as the territory between the Byzantine cities of BURSA and Nicaea (Iznik). In July 1302, Osman defeated a Byzantine army at Bapheus near Nicomedia (Izmit). Shortly thereafter he occupied the fortress of Melangeia, or Yenişehir, and made it his base for future operations. It lay between Bursa and Nicaea and so controlled the overland route from Constantinople to Bithynia.

These victories were the direct result of the empire's neglect of the eastern front. Emperor Michael VII Palaiologos (r. 1261–82) had weakened the Byzantine defense of Anatolia by dismantling the frontier defense troops since he was suspicious of their loyalty and by imposing heavy taxation on the local peasants. At the same time, Turkish raids in the Anatolian countryside increased the general state of insecurity. When the emperor's son Andronikos II Palaiologos (r. 1282–1341) came to power he had to renounce the Union of Lyons (1274), an effort to lift the 1054 schism between Orthodox and Catholics, accepted by his father and proclaim the restoration of Christian Orthodoxy, disband the Byzantine navy due to the effects of the economic depression, and negotiate a commercial war between Venice and Genoa fought over the body of Constantinople (1296–1302). On the eastern front neither the Alans employed as mercenaries nor the Catalan Company—a professional mercenary group employed by the emperor to replace them—ended the Ottoman-imposed isolation of Byzantine cities in Bithynia. Local dignitaries and bishops were instrumental in defending the cities against the Turks.

Twice the Ottomans were in grave danger from Byzantine forces. In 1304 the Catalan Company sent by the Byzantines challenged Osman's emirate. However, the dismemberment of the company by the Byzantines when they proved to be more destructive than the Ottomans opened the way for the return of Osman who in 1307 captured fortresses around Nicaea, isolating the city. The Mongol army sent by the khan Öldjaitu to the relief of Nicaea in 1307 was somewhat successful in clearing out the Ottomans from the district. But as soon as Mongol army had passed, Osman conquered the surrounding territory up to the Sea of Marmara, isolating the cities of Nicaea, Bursa, and Nicomedia from each other and from Constantinople.

The fight for the possession of these cities was long and bitter, but their defense was mainly in their own hands. The Byzantine emperor could not spare much thought for the defense of Asia Minor. The empire was financially exhausted by the depredations of the Catalans and their aftermath. For some years, it was as much as it could do to defeat a handful of Turks raiding different Byzantine regions next to the sea in Europe, let alone trying to muster an army to defeat the Ottomans in Asia. The continuous flood of refugees from former Byzantine lands to the capital was a constant reminder of the frontier situation.

A more energetic or resourceful emperor might have been able to resist more ably, but Andronikos II was past his prime. The aging emperor had intended that his eldest son Michael IX, the child of his first wife Anne of Hungary, should succeed to the throne. However, Michael died before coming to the throne; because Michael's son Andronikos had his brother Manuel killed in 1320, Andronikos II disinherited his grandson instead of proclaiming him co-emperor, thus creating a dangerous power vacuum. The younger generation of aristocracy, led by Andronikos' friend Kantakouzenos, used the announcement of increased taxation by Andronikos II as a pretext to rebel. The civil war lasted from 1320 until 1327; eventually the emperor abdicated in favor of his grandson.

During these crucial years, Osman steadily enlarged his principality by overrunning the region between Sangarios and the Bosporus up to the shore of the Black Sea. The conquest of Bursa in 1326 came as a surprise to the Byzantines. It became the first Ottoman capital and was adorned with mosques and endowments. Osman's son, ORHAN (r. 1324–62), after conquering Bursa, directed his activities against Nicaea and Nicomedia, which had been isolated for some years.

Although the Byzantine Empire was in decline, the Ottomans, as the smallest of the Anatolian Turkish emirates, must yet be credited with an outstanding military and strategic performance. Their geographical proximity to the Byzantine capital is stressed by historians as one of the reasons the Ottomans were more successful in building an empire than other Turkish principalities in Anatolia. Historical circumstances and strong leadership also account for their rapid expansion. The pattern of early conquests reveals strategic planning by Osman and his son Orhan. The conquest of the countryside surrounding large and prosperous Byzantine cities in Bithynia not only cut off their supply routes and destroyed their economy but also intimidated their populations. Ottomanists have stressed the ghazi spirit, the attitude of the religious warrior (see GHAZA), as a driving force for the early Ottomans; to wage war against the infidels was the religious duty of Muslims. A contemporary source, the Destan of Umur Pasha, the emir of Aydın, demonstrates that war and conquest were the lifeblood of the ghazi warriors, and as Ottoman territory bordered Byzantium, the Ottomans had plentiful prospects for holy war. As the Ottomans continued their offensive wars against the Byzantines, their numbers swelled with other tribal Turks seeking a life of valor and booty. The main reason for Ottoman success, however, was the development of stable and permanent institutions of government that transformed a tribal polity into a workable state.

The Ottomans utilized all human resources in their emirate and quickly learned skills in bureaucracy and diplomacy. As a result, the Ottomans occasionally made peace with the infidel Byzantines and in some cases even cooperated with them as allies. They also did not slaughter every Christian in their path; rather, they encouraged the Christian inhabitants of the countryside and the towns to join them. Islamic law and tradition declared that enemies who surrendered on demand should be treated with tolerance. The Christians of Bithynia were obliged to pay the haraç, or capitation tax, for the privilege of being tolerated, but this was no more burdensome than the taxes they had paid to the Byzantine government, which had neglected their interests. Once they had made the decision to surrender or defect, the Byzantine population resigned to their fate. The political inducements were often strong, for the Ottomans wanted to increase their numbers; indeed a band of Catalans even joined them in 1304. Some Christians converted to Islam upon joining the Ottomans; however, this was not demanded. Many local Christians even participated in Ottoman raids against Byzantium.

The Byzantine Emperor Andronikos III (r. 1328–41), with the aid of his trusted friend John Kantakouzenos, was determined at least to make the effort to stave off the Ottoman advance along the Gulf of Nicomedia toward Constantinople. The resulting Battle of Pelekanon in June 1329 between the Ottoman and Byzantine forces was nothing more than a series of skirmishes. The Ottoman mounted archers and Orhan's strategy of avoiding a pitched battle with the Byzantine army created panic in the Byzantine camp. After the emperor fled, the fate of his forces was sealed. This battle was the first direct encounter between a Byzantine emperor and an Ottoman emir. From this point onward, the collapse of Byzantine resistance in Bithynia was rapid and total. Nicaea surrendered to Orhan on March 2, 1331. Nicomedia held out until 1337.

Long before the fall of Nicomedia, in August 1333, the emperor crossed over to Asia Minor on the pretext of relieving Nicomedia. But instead of fighting, he invited Orhan to discuss the terms of a treaty. This was the first diplomatic encounter between the Byzantine emperor and the Ottoman emir. The emperor agreed to pay an annual tribute of 12,000 hyperpyra (Byzantine gold coins), approximately one fifth of the annual state budget, to retain possession of the few remaining Byzantine territories in Bithynia.

The Ottomans set such a good example as pacific conquerors that they won the confidence of many former Byzantine subjects. For example, when Nicaea fell, Orhan allowed all who wanted to leave the city to depart freely, taking with them their holy relics, but few availed themselves of the chance. No reprisals were taken against those who had resisted, and the city was left to manage its internal affairs under its own municipal government. By 1336, Orhan had also taken over the emirate of Karasi, extending his domain along the southern shore of the Sea of Marmara. In the 14th century the Venetians and the Genoese possessed many territories formerly belonging to the Byzantines. Their prime concern was the preservation of these territories rather than cooperation with the Byzantine emperors against the Ottomans. Andronikos III and Kantakouzenos were convinced that they might more effectively enter into agreement with competing Turkic emirs. The long friendship between Kantakouzenos and Umur of Aydın was in fact a defensive alliance against the Ottomans. Umur was eager to provide the emperor with soldiers to fight battles in Europe in return for payment and booty. In 1336 Umur lent his ships for the recovery of the island of Lesbos in the Aegean from the Genoese.

BYZANTINES AND OTTOMANS AS CAUTIOUS ALLIES, 1341–47

During the second civil war in Byzantium between 1341 and 1347, the relationship between the Ottomans and Byzantines altered from adversaries to cautious allies. After the death of Andronikos III in 1341, Kantakouzenos was deprived of the regency of the young emperor John V Palaiologos, son of Andronikos; his experience and skills as diplomat and administrator were a threat to the young Empress Anna of Savoy, mother of John V. Kantakouzenos eventually proclaimed himself the emperor in 1341. Once more the bitter struggle for the Byzantine throne transformed into a regional struggle, with SERBIA and BULGARIA changing sides in the civil conflict and supporting one of the candidates to the Byzantine throne against the other according to their interest. After 1345, Kantakouzenos' friend Umur, who had greatly advanced his cause in Thrace with the support of troops, was less able to offer the same generous help, for the league of Western powers sponsored by Pope Clement VI had finally succeeded in destroying his fleet and seizing the harbor of Smyrna in October 1344. Kantakouzenos thus made contact with Orhan in 1345 and in 1346 he gave his second daughter Theodora in marriage to Orhan, a man in his sixties. Contemporary moralists threw their hands up in horror at this apparent sacrifice of a princess to a barbarian chieftain. The groom did not appear but sent his soldiers to receive the bride. The Ottoman troops supplied by Orhan completed the work left unfinished by the soldiers of Umur, and on the night of February 2, 1347, John Kantakouzenos was admitted in Constantinople. The emperor had to apologize in his memoirs for the unprecedented devastation the Ottoman troops inflicted in Thrace. Unlike Umur, the Ottomans departed Thrace at their will, carrying great numbers of booty and slaves. And the Byzantines were left to mourn the losses.

Booty was not, however, the only Ottoman gain. The forces commanded by Orhan's son, Süleyman Pasha, were not merely obeying their Byzantine allies. They came to know the life of the land and to make themselves at home on European territory. In the dispute between John V, the successor of Kantakouzenos, and his son Matthew in the summer of 1354, Süleyman provided Matthew with soldiers. It was during this campaign that the Ottomans acquired their first possession in Europe. Süleyman refused to evacuate the fortress of Tzympe near Gallipoli and while negotiations for the return of the city between Kantakouzenos and Orhan were still in progress, he occupied Gallipoli when its population abandoned it after a devastating earthquake in March 1354.

BYZANTIUM AS VASSAL OF THE TURKS, 1354–1453

The life of John V Palaiologos (r. 1354–91), who ascended to the throne after the abdication of John Katakouzenos, was a difficult one. The Byzantines still had hopes of another crusade organized by the pope to deliver the Balkan lands from the Ottomans, who had renewed their expansion into Europe. Meanwhile, Sultan MURAD I (r. 1362–89), who succeeded Orhan to the Ottoman throne, consolidated his power in Anatolia before launching his attacks in Thrace. In 1361 before coming to his throne, he took Adrianople, the second largest city of Byzantium. In 1365 John V, pressured by the Ottomans in Thrace, took the unprecedented step of leaving his capital to pay a visit to the Hungarian king Louis the Great (r. 1342–82) and plead for help. His hopes for help were betrayed. The Hungarian king mistrusted the emperor and obliged him to leave his son Manuel as hostage. On his way back to Constantinople, John himself was taken hostage by the Bulgarians near Vidin and his son Andronikos seemed in no hurry to intervene on his father's behalf. He was eventually saved by his cousin Amadeo of Savoy who launched an attack on the Bulgarians and forced them to release the emperor in the winter of 1366. John V this time was persuaded to travel to Rome to seek support for organizing a crusade against the Ottomans. He agreed to convert to Catholicism in return for manpower and money. His five-month stay in Rome had little result, however, and on his way back the Venetians reminded the emperor of his debts. The crown jewels were already pawned in Venice during the second civil war. As he was unable to honor his debt, in return he consented to make over the island of Tenedos to the Venetians and thus regain the jewels as well as some much-needed cash. However once more his son Andronikos, prompted by the Genoese, left his father without money or credit as hostage to the Venetians. John eventually made his way back in 1371, weary and disenchanted.

In the meantime Murad's success in the Maritsa Valley in Bulgaria prompted Serbia, Bosnia, and Hungary in 1371 to unite against the sultan, though to no avail. Evrenos Bey and Hayreddin Pasha, the grand vizier of Murad, forced many Balkan lords to submit to Ottoman supremacy as vassals. Murad colonized newly conquered territories and changed the army by introducing the JANISSARIES, a corps of young Christians who converted to Islam and were trained to become his private soldiers. After Murad's death in 1839 at the BATTLE OF KOSOVO, BAYEZID I (r. 1389–1402) continued to weaken Byzantine resistance by setting one member of the ruling family against the other. This initiated the third phase in Byzantine-Ottoman relations, when the Byzantines became Ottoman vassals.

The emperor Manuel II (r. 1391–1402), who was at Bursa when he heard the news of his father's death, slipped out of the sultan's camp by night and hurried to Constantinople to claim his throne. He describes in his letters the misery he experienced while serving the Ottomans in Anatolia. Bayezid's phychological warfare against his Christian vassals lords was a great success. Thus, the crusade at Nicopolis in 1396 headed by King Sigismund of

Hungary seemed to be the last chance of the Byzantines. The assistance of the Byzantines to the crusaders in Nikopol (Bulgaria) in 1394 was answered by a full-scale siege of Constantinople by the Ottomans. Eventually, when TIMUR (founder of the Timurid Empire) defeated Bayezid in 1402 at the BATTLE OF ANKARA, this victory was perceived by the Balkan states as a sign of divine grace. The news reached Emperor Manuel in Paris on a desperate mission to awaken the western powers to the Ottoman threat.

While the Ottoman struggle for the throne was raging, the Byzantines managed to attain short-lived gains. In 1403 the city of Salonika was restored alongside with some Aegean islands and a long stretch of the Black Sea coast from Constantinople to Varna (Bulgaria). During the period known as the Ottoman Interregnum (1402–13) the Byzantines managed to become involved in the Ottoman civil wars by supporting one candidate over the other. The triumph of Mehmed I (1413–20) was due to the support of Byzantium and local *gazha* frontier leaders. However, Mehmed's successor, MURAD II (r. 1421–44 and 1446–51), was not as willing to tolerate Byzantine interference. Byzantine support to Mustafa, the Ottoman pretender to the throne, enraged Sultan Murad II and led to the besieging of Constantinople in 1422. When Emperor Manuel died in 1425, his empire was reduced to the environs of Constantinople, SALONIKA, and Morea (Peloponnese, Greece). His son John VIII (1425–48) was convinced that help would only come from the West. In 1430 the conquest of Janina in Epirus and of Salonika convinced the Byzantines that their appeal to the Western world to save Constantinople might be answered this time as the Ottomans were dangerously approaching Italy. The Union of Churches achieved in the Council of Ferrara-Florence (1438–39) did result in a long-awaited crusade. Sultan Murad, however, defeated the crusaders at Varna in 1444 and at Kosovo in 1448.

In Constantinople, the unpopularity of the Union of Churches among devoted Eastern Christians complicated matters for the Byzantine Empire; an anti-Union party capitalized on the defeats to stress the spiritual and physical isolation of the Byzantines from the Western world. Constantine XI (r. 1448–1453), brother of the late emperor John VIII, found a devastated and divided city when he entered Constantinople on March 12, 1449. In February 1451 Sultan Murad II died at EDIRNE. He had resigned six years earlier in favor of his son MEHMED II (r. 1444–46; 1451–81), but had come out of his retirement to take revenge on the Hungarians and the Byzantines. Known as "the Conqueror," Mehmed II was 19 years old in 1451 and the Byzantines were slow to recognize that so young and inexperienced a ruler presented them with a danger more formidable than any sultan before.

The Byzantines were not alone in underestimating the strength of Mehmed II. His treaties with János (John) Hunyadi, governor of HUNGARY, and with George BRANKOVIĆ of Serbia, and the goodwill he expressed to the KNIGHTS OF ST. JOHN of RHODES and to the Genoese lords of Chios and Lesbos, fostered the illusion in the West that no harm could come while the Ottoman Empire was in the hands of one so young. Former emirs shared this illusion and organized a rebellion in Asia in 1451. The revolt was crushed as soon as Mehmed arrived. The Byzantine emperor suggested that a grandson of the late Prince Süleyman, called Orhan, who lived in exile at Constantinople was a pretender to the Ottoman throne. Mehmed II's response was the construction of a castle on the European shore of the Bosporus. Rumeli Hisarı, as it came to be known, was completed in four months. According to Byzantine chronicles the Byzantines watching the work from their walls now felt that all the prophecies about the end of their world and the coming of the Antichrist were about to be fulfilled.

Omens and prophecies about the ultimate fate of the city had been heard for many years. It was widely believed that the end of the world would come in 1492, the year 7000 after the creation, which meant that there were still 40 years left. The first bombardment of the walls by cannons—including a gigantic cannon built by the Hungarian engineer Orban—began on April 6, 1453, and continued daily. After three Genoese broke through the siege, bringing supplies and weapons to the city, Mehmed knew that he must find a way to get part of his fleet into the Golden Horn. The final attack on the city began in the early hours of Tuesday, May 29, and by the afternoon the sultan entered the city, replacing the carcass of the Eastern Roman Empire with a new polity.

The Ottomans achieved what many neighboring forces—including the Bulgarians, the Serbs, the Hungarians, and the Holy Roman Emperor—had been dreaming of: the conquest of Constantinople, capital of the Byzantine Empire. Even if Constantinople was a mere ghost of its former glorious past, depopulated, impoverished, and in disarray, it was still a strong symbol and a strategic gateway to the West. It immediately became apparent that the Ottomans intended to replace the old empire with an empire of their own. Mehmed II reconstructed and repopulated Constantinople, renaming it Istanbul, and making it the new Ottoman capital, which it would remain until the fall of the Ottoman Empire at the beginning of the 20th century.

Eugenia Kermeli

Further reading: Halil İnalcık, *The Ottoman Empire: The Classical Age, 1300–1600* (London: Weidenfeld & Nicolson, 1973); Halil İnalcık and Donald Quataert, *An Economic and Social History of the Ottoman Empire, 1300–1914* (Cambridge: Cambridge University Press, 1994); Colin Imber, *The Ottoman Empire, 1300–1650: The Structure of Power* (Houndmills, Basingstoke, UK: Palgrave Macmillan, 2002); David Nicol, *The Last Centuries of Byzantium, 1261–1453* (Cambridge: Cambridge University Press, 1993); Warren T. Treadgold, *A History of the Byzantine State and Society* (Stanford, Calif.: Stanford University Press, 1997).

C

Caffa (Feodosiya; *anc.***: Theodosia, Feodosia;** *Ital.***: Kaffa;** *Ottoman and Tatar***: Kefe)** Known today as Ukrainian Feodosiya (sometimes Theodosia), the city of Caffa was a key Black Sea port town and administrative center of the Ottoman Empire, located on the southern coast of the Crimean peninsula. The origin of this town goes back to the sixth century B.C.E. when Theodosia, one of many Greek trading colonies in the northern Black Sea region, was founded.

In the second half of the 13th century, with the rise of the Mongol Empire's trans-Eurasian trade system, a town and fortress named Caffa, which housed a Genoese trading colony, came into being. After the conquest of Constantinople (1453), the expansionist policy of Sultan Mehmed II (r. 1444–46; 1451–81) made it only a matter of time before the Ottomans moved into the Black Sea and effectively eliminated the many Genoese and Venetian coastal emporia. In 1475, the Ottoman fleet took Caffa along with the entire southern coast of the Crimea, as well as Taman, across the strait of Kerch, and Azak, at the mouth of the Don River. These lands were turned into a new Ottoman province (originally a *sancak*, eventually a *beylerbeylik*). The existing polity of the Crimean Khanate (*see* Crimean Tatars) became a vassal of the Ottoman Empire, which, while subject to Ottoman rule, was allowed to continue governing the rest of the Crimean peninsula and the steppe lands to the north.

Under the Ottomans, Caffa continued its earlier role as a major trade emporium. Although long-distance trade had declined, regional trade grew, and Caffa and its Black Sea steppe and Caucasian hinterlands became a major supplier of a vital commodities for the vast Istan-bul market: grain, clarified butter, fish, timber, leather goods, and above all, slaves captured by the Tatars in Ukraine and southern Russia in almost yearly raids. In addition, furs and hunting birds imported from the northern reaches of Russia were important luxury items, especially for the sultan's court.

In 1783, the Crimean Khanate fell to the Russian Empire, bringing Caffa under Russian dominion; at this time, the original name of the city, Feodosia, was restored.

Victor Ostapchuk

Further reading: Halil İnalcık, "Kefe," in *Encyclopaedia of Islam*, 2nd ed., vol. 4, eds. C. E. Bosworth, E. van Donzel, B. Lewis, Ch. Pellat (Leiden: Brill, 1960–), 868–70.

Cairo (*Ar.***: al-Qahira;** *Turk.***: Kahire)** From the time of its conquest by Ottoman Sultan Selim I (r. 1512–20) in 1517, until it fell to Napoleon Bonaparte in 1798, Cairo served as the capital of the Ottoman province of Egypt. With a population of between 200,000 and 300,000 inhabitants, it was the second-largest city in the Ottoman empire, after Istanbul. It was also the richest city in the empire, providing Istanbul with revenues that surpassed those of any other province. Ottoman visitors to Cairo were overwhelmed by its size, the diversity of the goods that could be obtained there, and the grandeur of its mosques. In the 16th and 17th centuries Cairo was a center for the lucrative pepper trade from the Indies and for the import of slaves and gold from sub-Saharan Africa. Cairo also traded in the produce of Egypt's fertile delta, such as rice, cotton, sugar, and indigo, all of which

Taken in the 1880s, this photo shows a street in the ibn Tulun quarter of Cairo. Traditionally, the houses in Cairo were several stories high and were made of mud brick with stone facades on the ground floor. The wooden window projections on the upper floors, known as *mashrabiyya*, allowed the women of the house to watch the street action without being seen. *(Photograph by Maison Bonfils, courtesy of the University of Pennsylvania Museum, Philadelphia)*

were eagerly sought by consumers throughout the empire and beyond. By the 17th century the pepper trade had fallen off as European traders began to trade directly with the Indies. Its place was taken by coffee, as both western Europeans and Ottomans soon acquired a strong liking for the beverage.

Egypt's wealth encouraged Muslim adventurers from the Balkans and Anatolia to migrate to Cairo in search of employment. The recruitment of Muslim mercenaries by provincial governors was an empire-wide phenomenon in the 17th century, but in Cairo, prominent Ottoman officials formed households modeled after those of the former rulers of Egypt's MAM-LUK EMPIRE and brought these men into them. Rather than simply being employees, these men often married daughters or sisters of the official's family and carried on the household name after the death of the original founder. Even if they did not actually marry into the household, the men recruited into it pledged their loyalty to the head of the household as if they were actual kin. In addition to these free-born Muslims, the

heads of the household continued to purchase male slaves, MAMLUKS, who were also added to the retinue of the household. Even after their defeat, the Mamluks retained prestige in Cairo for their military prowess and chivalry, and the founders of some of the city's more successful households often fostered the myth that they were of Mamluk origin, even when they were not For that reason historians have called these households in Cairo "neo-Mamluks" as they adopted the traditions, titles, and even dress of the former Mamluk rulers of Egypt, whether or not they actually descended from the earlier Mamluks.

The military of Egypt in the late 17th was plagued by bloody competition between factions aligned with two of Cairo's neo-Mamluk households, the Fiqariyya and the Qasimiyya. Within these broadly based confederations were smaller individual households who might contend with each other as much as the neo-Mamluks did with rivals from outside their confederation. Between the two factions stood the city's governor, who was appointed by Istanbul. This produced an unstable power triangle in Cairo that periodically collapsed into days of street violence between the contending factions. Within this shifting power balance a household founded by Mustafa Qazdaghli, a member of the JANISSARIES who had himself been a client in the Fiqariyya household, emerged as the dominant power by the middle of the 18th century. The AL-QAZDAGHLI HOUSEHOLD, like those that preceded it, was made up of a mixture of Mamluks and Janissary officers and their retainers who controlled rural tax farms and customs offices. They also dabbled in trade and offered protection to wealthy merchants in a combination of legal and illegal activities, such as extortion and smuggling.

Despite the political turbulence of Cairo's political life in the 17th and 18th centuries, Egypt's prosperity created economic opportunities for the city's civilian population. It would seem that most of its inhabitants simply tried to stay out of the Mamluks' way. With its AL-AZHAR university, Cairo was a center for Muslim learning within the Arabic-speaking world, and its intellectual life seems to have been little touched by Mamluk violence. Although the city was hit by recurring plague epidemics, Cairo's population grew during the Ottoman centuries as its opportunities and wealth continued to draw migrants from throughout the Mediterranean region.

The reign of the Mamluks in Cairo ended with the French occupation of the city in 1798. Napoleon Bonaparte had hoped to use Egypt as a base to invade the Ottoman Empire, but his army stalled at the siege of ACRE, and the French army withdrew in 1801. At this point the city descended into chaos as the Mamluks once again sought to establish their control. MEHMED ALI emerged from the struggle for power as the city's military strongman and in 1805 Ottoman Sultan MAHMUD II (r. 1808–1839) recognized him as governor of Cairo. From that point on, Cairo served as Mehmed Ali's base of power and as the capital of what was, in effect, an independent Egypt. Under his rule, Cairo changed very little physically, but Egypt's center of commerce shifted to ALEXANDRIA.

Mehmed Ali's descendants transformed Cairo by draining the surrounding marshes so that new Western-style neighborhoods could be added. A railroad linking the city to Alexandria was completed in 1858, and with the opening of the SUEZ CANAL, the city once again developed a commercial heart to compete with Alexandria. The pace of modernization increased after the British occupation in 1882. By 1914 Cairo consisted of two very separate cities: the old city, where the architecture and street plans were little changed from what they had been in the Mamluk period, and the new, westernized city, with wide boulevards, tramway lines, street lamps, and all the other technology of an industrialized city.

Bruce Masters

Further reading: Nelly Hanna, *In Praise of Books: A Cultural History of Cairo's Middle Class, Sixteenth to Eighteenth Centuries* (Syracuse, N.Y.: Syracuse University Press, 2003); André Raymond, *Cairo* (Cambridge, Mass.: Harvard University Press, 2000).

caliphate When the Prophet Muhammad died in 632 C.E., the Muslim community chose as his successor Abu Bakr, the Prophet's father-in-law and one of his first converts. While it was understood that he lacked any prophetic abilities, Abu Bakr was nevertheless chosen to head the political community that the Prophet had founded. As this was a new office, the Muslims were hesitant to use older titles such as king or sheikh, and so they called him simply Khalifat Rasul Allah, the "successor to the Prophet of God." That title was eventually shortened to khalifa, or caliph in its English form. From that time until the 13th century, this title was used for the political leader of the Muslim community.

The function and succession of the caliph led to a split within Islam and the rival traditions of SUNNI ISLAM and SHIA ISLAM. The Sunni tradition held that any male member of the Prophet's tribe, the Quraysh, could rightfully be caliph if he were of sound mind and body. They held that the caliph's only religious function was leading the Friday prayer, and that the articulation and implementation of Islamic law, SHARIA, should be left to the religious scholars, or ULEMA. The Shii tradition held the view that the caliph must have special insight into Holy Law and its interpretation that they called *ilm*, literally "knowledge," but by which they meant a specialized esoteric knowledge that only the descendants of Ali pos-

sessed. Therefore, for them, the caliph had to be one of those descendants, whom they called the imam, a title used by Sunnis to mean the person who led the community in its Friday prayers.

Although the Muslim theory of government held that all Muslims had to owe their political allegiance to the caliph, over time independent Muslim states arose. The Muslim legal scholars ruled that these were legal as long as they minted coins in the reigning caliph's name and read his name aloud during the Friday prayers. With this diminution of the office the caliph had become the symbolic, rather than actual, head of the Muslim community. Even this function was deemed unnecessary, however, with the murder of the last universally recognized caliph of the Abbasid line, al-Mustasim, at the hands of the Mongols in 1258.

The question of the caliphate re-emerged with the Ottoman dynasty. According to Ottoman court historians of the 17th century, Sultan SELIM I (r. 1512–20) received the cloak of the caliphate—a symbol of the authority of the office in much the same way a crown symbolized the monarchy in Europe—from the last descendant of the Abbasids when he conquered CAIRO in 1517. However, no contemporary accounts of the conquest of EGYPT mention this transfer of authority. Before the 17th century, the sultans had simply stated that their legitimacy rested on their adherence to the Holy Law, their continuation of the jihad against Europe, and their role as protector of the HAJJ and Arabia's two holy cities, MECCA and MEDINA. The first diplomatic recognition that the sultan might also be caliph came in the TREATY OF KÜÇÜK KAYNARCA in 1774, which ceded the Crimea to Russia. Catherine the Great, the empress of Russia (r. 1762–96), recognized that the Ottoman sultan still exercised "spiritual sovereignty" over her new Muslim Tatar subjects even while she exercised political sovereignty over them. Subsequent losses of Ottoman territory in Bosnia, ALGERIA, and TUNIS saw similar proclamations by the European powers that the Ottoman sultan remained the spiritual guide to their Muslim subjects, in much the same way that they recognized the spiritual authority of the pope over their Catholic subjects.

The appropriation of the tile of caliph by the Ottomans was bitterly rejected by most Sunni legal scholars outside Istanbul, as the Ottomans were not descended from the Prophet's tribe, the Quraysh. For Sunnis, this qualification remained an absolute requirement if a political ruler was to claim the title of caliph. Their opposition did not present a problem until 1876, when the Ottoman Constitution provided a clause stating that the Ottoman sultan was the caliph. Thus legitimated, ABDÜLHAMID II (r. 1876–1909) began to use the title and to make the claim that he spoke for the world's Muslims.

Arabic-speaking Muslim scholars almost universally rejected that claim. Some, such as 19th-century Muslim reformist MUHAMMAD ABDUH, said that Muslims should unite behind the sultan as the last independent Muslim ruler; however, he did not concede that the sultan was also the caliph. The claim that the sultan was also caliph seems to have resonated mostly in Muslim territories that were under direct European colonial rule. This created a fear among the British Empire's governing authorities that the sultan's claim to the caliphate might lead their Muslim subjects into insurrection. This fear led the British to try to cultivate an alternative Muslim authority, the Hashimi family, whose pedigree as descendants of the Prophet Muhammad's clan was more authentic than that of the sultans and who might offer support should Britain and the Ottoman Empire go to war. When Mustafa Kemal (later known as KEMAL ATATÜRK) officially abolished the caliphate in 1924, the largest protest of his action came from British India.

Bruce Masters

Further reading: Kemal Karpat, *The Politicization of Islam: Reconstructing Identity, State, Faith, and Community in the Late Ottoman Empire* (Oxford: Oxford University Press, 2001).

calligraphy Islamic calligraphy (*hüsn-i hat*) is a form of writing elevated to the stature of art. The Arabic script was barely developed and little used before the time of Prophet Muhammad; within a century, as a vehicle for the transmission of the Quran, it evolved into a stunning art form. Its role as a sacred form of communication gives this art its character and importance, and explains its function in the art forms of the Muslim world, including book arts, architectural decoration, metalwork, ceramics, glass, and textiles.

The dynastic rulers of the Muslim world, with their capitals as cultural centers in such diverse locations as DAMASCUS, BAGHDAD, Cordoba, CAIRO, Konya, Samarkand, Herat, and Tabriz, were attracted by the art of calligraphy and patronized its practitioners. During the Ottoman period, calligraphy reached its zenith, and Turkish calligraphy, as it became known, established its own distinct character. The Ottomans practiced calligraphy over a period of nearly 500 years, attaining the highest level of expertise in the 19th and 20th centuries. These calligraphic productions, which also displayed the national characteristics of the Ottoman Turks, increased dramatically as time progressed.

STYLES OF CALLIGRAPHY

The development of Islamic calligraphy benefited from a general use of paper in the Muslim world from the ninth century. In the 10th century the proportions of the letters began to be codified. Numerous types of script developed according to their uses including for the Quran, official correspondence, letters, or scholarly work.

In the city of Baghdad, first the center of the ABBASID CALIPHATE (750–1258) and later of Ilkhanid (1256–1353) power, Arabs gradually perfected calligraphy until it reached its ultimate form in the style of master calligrapher Yakut al-Mustasimi (known as Yakut), who died around 1298, at a time when the Ottoman state was in its infancy. Nevertheless Yakut al-Mustasimi's students spread his style through the wider Islamic world. The six basic styles of calligraphy (*aklam-i sitte*), whose rules were regularized by Yakut, replaced the Kufic script that had previously dominated calligraphic practice. The six scripts are *sülüs, nesih, muhakkak, reyhani, tevki,* and *rıka*. *Sülüs* and *nesih* became the dominant styles after the mid-15th century, and *tevki* and *rıka* were replaced by the styles *divani* and *celi divani* around the same time. *Muhakkak* and *reyhani* were phased out by the end of the 17th century.

The calligraphic form of *celi*, which can be applied to any of the calligraphic scripts, is a large-scale and monumental version of the script. Designed to be read from afar, *celi* was used for decorative panels of inscriptions applied to religious buildings as well as to civilian architectural constructions.

sülüs Often called "the mother of writing," *sülüs*, along with *muhakkak*, attracted the interest of calligraphers from the early years and served as a master style from which many styles later derived.

nesih A clear and very legible script, *nesih* is often partnered with *sülüs*. *Nesih* became the book script, and was often used for the Quran.

muhakkak A regular and highly legible script, *muhakkak* in its *celi* form is often used to write the *besmele*, "In the name of God, the Beneficent, the Merciful."

reyhani Based on *muhakkak*, but smaller, *reyhani* is written with a single pen. (Calligraphers used different sizes of pen for the script, the vowels, and markings while writing *muhakkak* and *sülüs*.)

tevki Based on *sülüs* but smaller and more compact, *tevki*, along with *rıka*, was used as the official script of state and administration in the early Ottoman period.

rıka A smaller form of *tevki* was used as the official script of the early Ottoman state and administration as well as for calligrapher's certificates and signatures and other formal documents.

talik In addition to the *aklam-i sitte*, the calligraphic script of *talik* was also favored by the Ottomans. In the *talik* form no room is given to the vowel and reading signs (*hareke*), and the script is written in a pure and unadulterated form, which makes it very compatible with the writing of Turkish. The *talik* form of writing originated in IRAN, and was applied to a very broad field. Aside from calligraphic panels, the script was also used for the writing of *divans* (collections of poems) and canonical and judicial rulings. The script underwent a number of changes as a result of its extensive application and gave way to a new form known as *neshtalik*, which replaced the old *talik* script completely. From the second half of the 15th century onwards, the *talik* script became widespread. Its finer form (*hurde, hafi*) in particular came to be widely used in writing books as well as in the Ottoman dominions. *Talik* underwent a number of important changes and modifications in a short period of time and eventually gave rise to the official Ottoman script of *divani*.

divani   From the 16th century onward the *divani* script, embellished with diacritical signs and in its further developed form, was assigned for use in high-level official correspondence and was referred to as *celi divani*. These two scripts were reserved for official use only; nonofficial use was strictly prohibited. The use of the scripts of *divani* and *celi divani* was taught only in the Imperial Council (Divan-ı Hümayun). These two scripts were at their peak during the 19th and 20th centuries. These comparatively complicated scripts, recognizable by the upward movement toward the end of lines, were deliberately chosen for official matters so as to avoid easy reading and falsification of documents, ensuring the safety of official correspondence.

The calligraphic form called TUĞRA, containing the names of the ruling sultan and his father together with the prayer "*el-muzaffer daima*" (always victorious), was placed at the top of every official written order. The earliest example of a *tuğra* dates back to the reign of ORHAN GAZI (r. 1324–62). The most striking examples of illuminated *tuğras* were produced during the 15th and 16th centuries. However, in time, the purity of the form of a *tuğra* was lost and, toward the end of the 18th century, the search for new relational proportions in the layout of *tuğras* began.

Because handwriting tends to differ from person to person, in the 19th century it was resolved to regularize the practice of calligraphy. This new form of regularized handwriting was known as *rıka*. The application of this script to official documents was called "the *rıka* of the Sublime Porte (Ottoman government)." The calligrapher İzzet Efendi (1841–1903) practiced *rıka* according to a very strict set of rules, ultimately giving his own name to the form *İzzet Efendi rıkası*.

DEVELOPMENT OF TURKISH CALLIGRAPHY

Calligraphic examples from the period of Sultan MEHMED I (r. 1413–1421) demonstrate that the Yakut style was also being practiced in the Ottoman dominions of Anatolia and Rumelia. In addition to BURSA and EDIRNE, certain provincial areas such as Amasya had also become centers of calligraphic learning and education. Soon after Sultan MEHMED II (r. 1444–46; 1451–1481) conquered Constantinople in 1453 (*see* CONQUEST OF CONSTANTINOPLE), the city developed into the cultural and artistic center of the Muslim world. Today ISTANBUL remains at the forefront of excellence in the art of calligraphy. Sultan Mehmed II is known to have supported the fine arts in general and the art of writing in particular. The calligraphic genius Şeyh Hamdullah lived during his reign and a number of books written by him, and still extant today, were donated to the Palace Library by Mehmed's son Prince Bayezid, the future Sultan BAYEZID II (r. 1481–1512). Furthermore, several of the magnificent monuments erected after the conquest of Constantinople were decorated with inscriptions in *celi sülüs* made by two master calligraphers active in Mehmed's day, Yahya Sofi (d. 1477) and his son Ali Sofi (d.?).

Sultan Bayezid II and his son Prince Korkut (1467–1513) were both taught by Şeyh Hamdullah, who is considered the spiritual founder (*pir*) of Turkish calligraphy. After Prince Bayezid's ascension to the throne in 1481, Şeyh Hamdullah moved to Istanbul where he sought to create the most perfect examples of calligraphy in the Yakut style. Elaborating upon examples of Yakut's work available in the treasury of the official imperial residence, the TOPKAPI PALACE, he created an original new style. Among the six basic scripts of the *aklam-i sitte* perfected by Şeyh Hamdullah and his pupils, *sülüs* and *nesih* became the preeminent vehicles for calligraphic practice. *Tevki* was replaced by the script types *divani* and *celi divani*. The Hamdullah style was transferred to younger generations through his pupils. The calligrapher Hafız Osman (1642–1698) further developed the Hamdullah style; as a result, the six scripts went through a second phase of purification and became known as the "style of Hafız Osman." This new style slowly replaced the style of Şeyh Hamdullah.

The script form of *celi sülüs* did not undergo progressive development until Mustafa Rakım (1758–1826) improved the script toward the end of the 18th century. In the hands of Mustafa Rakım's pupils, the calligraphic form of *celi sülüs* reached its pinnacle. The style was practiced well into the Republican period, the last famous calligraphers of this style remaining active until the 1960s

Calligraphic page by Hafız Osman (1642-1698), one of the most important Ottoman calligraphers *(Bildarchiv Preussischer Kulturbesitz / Art Resource, NY)*

and 1970s. Mustafa Rakım also reformed the calligraphic shape of the *tuğra*. The *tuğra* of Sultan SELIM III (r. 1789–1807) was the first to undergo a serious revision, which was further developed in the *tuğra* of MAHMUD II (r. 1808–1839). The *tuğra* found its definitive shape in the era of ABDÜLHAMID II (r. 1876–1909), in the hands of Sami Efendi (1838–1912).

In the 19th century, two incomparable calligraphers, *kadıasker* Mustafa İzzet Efendi (1801–1876) and Mehmed Şevki Efendi (1829–1887), were the most important representatives of two very different schools of calligraphic practice. Both elaborated upon the work of Hafız Osman and produced samples in *sülüs*, *nesih*, and *rıka*.

THE CRAFT OF CALLIGRAPHY

Manuscripts surviving from the Ottoman period can take the form of books, such as *mushaf*s or *divan*s, but can also come in the shape of so-called *murakkaa*s. A *murakkaa* is a collection of *kıta*s (small original works) that are hinged together on their edges, executed in one or two scripts, on one side only, with illuminated margins on the *recto* side only, and approximately the same size as a book.

Large-scale panels, executed in *celi sülüs* and *celi talik,* were used for the interior decoration of many public and private buildings. Hafız Osman devised a calligraphic composition called *hilye* toward the end of the 17th century. A *hilye* contains the description of the Prophet's physical and moral characteristics, and from the 19th century onward this form also began to be executed on a large scale.

Calligraphers plied their trade on hand-crafted paper which, after being dyed in various colors, was sealed and polished according to a special method called *ahar.* They used an ink produced from soot and gum arabic pounded in a mortar. Other inks were also available such as pure gold ink (*altın mürekkebi*), produced from crushed gold leaf, as well as red and yellow inks.

TEACHING OF CALLIGRAPHY

Calligraphy was taught in Ottoman educational institutions, such as *mektebs, madrasas,* the PALACE SCHOOL, and the Imperial Council. But the best way to learn the art of writing was to attend individual tutorials at a calligraphic master's house. These lessons were given without any form of material remuneration. At the beginning of the 20th century, the Ottoman government decided to institute an academy for the instruction of calligraphy. The minister of Pious Foundations and the şeyhülislam (chief Muslim judge of the empire), Mustafa Hayri Efendi (1867–1922), founded this academy, the Madrasatül-Hattatin. In 1915 the historical building of the Yusuf Agha Sibyan Mektebi (today the building houses the Ministry of Education's press office) in Istanbul's Cağaloğlu district was converted into the Madrasatül-Hattatin. In addition to calligraphy, various arts related to book and paper production were taught, as well as illumination, binding, marbling (ebru), and miniature painting. After the abolition of madrasas in 1925, the school took the name Hattat Mektebi. A great number of graduates of this crucible of artistic culture continued practicing their trade in this school, which discontinued its activities with the introduction of the new Turkish alphabet in December 1928.

Calligraphic instruction was based upon the observance of a strict discipline, according to a master-apprentice system. It was a process that continued from generation to generation. Pupils were able to complete their instruction only after years of practice, receiving a written permit (icazet) to practice the trade of calligraphy at the end of their instruction. The art and practice of calligraphy was a closed world, and therefore, able to withstand the westernizing influences that impacted other Ottoman arts. This isolation resulted in Ottoman calligraphers of the 20th century practicing at a high level of expertise unhampered by Western styles.

M. Uğur Derman

See also LANGUAGE AND SCRIPT.

Further reading: M. Uğur Derman, *Letters in Gold: Ottoman Calligraphy from the Sakıp Sabancı Collection, Istanbul* (New York: Metropolitan Museum of Art, 1998); M. Uğur Derman and Nihad M. Çetin, *The Art of Calligraphy in the Islamic Heritage* (Istanbul: IRCICA, 1998).

cannon   *See* FIREARMS.

capitulations   Capitulations, known in Ottoman Turkish as AHDNAME, were special dispensations for trade, usually in the form of lower tariffs, issued to Europeans by Ottoman sultans seeking potential allies against their rivals, the Venetians. The first capitulations were granted to the French in 1535 by Sultan SÜLEYMAN I (r. 1520–66). Similar treaties with the Netherlands, ENGLAND, VENICE, and Austria followed. By the end of the 18th century almost every European nation held a capitulatory treaty.

These treaties permitted European merchants to reside in specified Ottoman cities and to conduct trade with minimal tariffs and interference. The resident Europeans were not subject to the *jizya* (the head tax on non-Muslim males), nor were they compelled to abide by Islamic law in issues of family law. They were, however, enjoined by the earliest treaties to conduct their business according to the precepts of Holy Law and to take all commercial disputes involving Ottoman subjects, Muslim and non-Muslim alike, to the SHARIA courts.

For the first century and a half of their existence, the capitulations merely established that Europeans could live in the Ottoman Empire but provided few other advantages. That changed as the balance of military power began to shift in Europe's favor. With the introduction of commercial treaties with France in 1673 and with England in 1675, Sultan MEHMED IV (r. 1648–87) gave Europeans the right to take any commercial dispute worth over 4,000 akçe (a relatively small sum—less than the price of a donkey) to ISTANBUL where their ambassador would be present, thus circumventing the authority of the Islamic courts. These treaties also permitted the Europeans to designate Ottoman subjects as translators (DRAGOMAN). While that in itself was not new, the treaties explicitly gave the translators rights comparable to those the Europeans enjoyed, including the payment of the same nominal customs duties as their European patrons. The treaties also exempted dragomans from paying the *jizya*, as if they were Europeans. Since Muslim legal scholars had ruled that it was immoral for Muslims to learn the language of infidel foreigners, all the translators employed by Europeans—and enjoying these special privileges—were non-Muslims; this led to significant discontent. But even while the treaties gave the translators advantages not enjoyed by other Ottoman subjects, they asserted that the translators were to remain the sultan's subjects. This was important to the Ottoman framers of the treaties as a way to assert Ottoman sovereignty and to demonstrate that the translators should remember who ultimately held authority over them.

The Anglo-Ottoman Treaty of 1675 also gave dragomans the right held by English merchants to take any commercial dispute with ordinary Ottoman subjects to Istanbul for adjudication. There the case would be heard in the presence of the ambassador of the country who had issued the dragoman's *berat*, or patent of office. Muslim merchants fiercely contested this concession, saying it gave their non-Muslim competitors a legal advantage over them. Having extended this right to those who were still legally Ottoman subjects, Ottoman judges and bureaucrats consistently tried to limit the commercial activities of the dragomans to ensure that the privilege was not abused.

Many critics of the capitulations point to their wholesale abuse for either monetary or political gain by the European consuls who illegally obtained far more *berats* than they were entitled to, and to the rift they created between Muslim and non-Muslim merchants. The Ottoman bureaucrats were well aware of these potential inequities. They used two approaches to counter the wide-scale abuse: banning dragomans from trade, and enforcing the limit on the number of individuals who could legitimately be employed by a European consul. In 1808 the Ottomans negotiated a secret treaty with Great Britain designed to win the Ottoman Empire's neutrality in Britain's war with NAPOLEON BONAPARTE. The one point that the Ottomans insisted on was that those holding patents as translators for the British would not engage in freelance commerce on their own. However, the treaty was never ratified by the British Parliament. The issue of Ottoman subjects holding rights under the capitulations did not go away even with the far-reaching provisions of the ANGLO-OTTOMAN CONVENTION OF 1838. Again, the Ottoman representatives protested that while they were willing to open their empire to free trade with Britain, they steadfastly opposed the extension of Britain's right to name Ottoman subjects as translators, which effectively made them honorary Britons. By the end of the Ottoman Empire, thousands of Ottoman subjects enjoyed exemptions from some Ottoman taxation and legal regulations because of their status under the capitulations. The YOUNG TURK regime unilaterally declared the capitulations defunct during WORLD WAR I, but the Europeans did not recognize their abolition until the establishment of the Turkish Republic in 1923.

Bruce Masters

See also LEVANT COMPANY.

Further reading: Maurits van den Boogert, *The Capitulations and the Ottoman Legal System: Qadis, Consuls, and Beratlıs in the 18th Century* (Leiden: Brill, 2005).

caravan   Caravans were organized trains of pack animals used to carry cargo overland in the Ottoman Empire. Much of the interior of the empire was either mountainous terrain or desert, and travelers needed the security of numbers as protection against the numerous bandits and tribal raiders who plagued the trade routes. Although the Romans had constructed a network of roads that crisscrossed the eastern regions of their empire, these had been largely neglected over the succeeding centuries, and wagons were rarely used to transport commodities in the Ottoman Empire. In Anatolia and the Balkans, the animal of choice was the mule or donkey, although camels were also used; in the Arab provinces, it was almost exclusively the camel.

The size of the caravans depended in large part on where they were traveling. The danger to travelers in Anatolia and the Balkans was from bandits, so caravans traveling there were smaller, often consisting of no more than a dozen or more animals and a small contingent of armed men. Caravans crossing the desert either to Arabia or from the Mediterranean to the cities of Iraq were much larger, as the BEDOUIN tribes could mount raiding parties consisting of hundreds of warriors. It was not unusual for caravans to and from Iraq to consist of more than 1,000 camels and 100 merchants with their armed escorts. The caravan of the annual HAJJ, or pilgrimage to MECCA, often consisted of several thousand camels and 10,000 pilgrims.

Throughout the Ottoman centuries, the high cost of transporting goods by caravan determined what the animals carried. It was not profitable to transport bulky commodities such as grain or building materials, so each region of the empire had to be largely self-sufficient in these. Rather the caravans most commonly carried luxury commodities such as cloth, spices, coffee, raw silk, and European manufactured goods.

Each caravan had a master who was chosen by the merchants traveling in the caravan. The master was usually a merchant who had traveled the route before and, in the case of the desert caravans, who had good relations with the Bedouins. The caravan master enforced law and order on the caravans, which often suffered theft and even murder from within the caravan while it was en route; however, he could not dispense justice on his own, but was required by the Ottoman authorities to turn over any suspects to a Muslim court once he reached a city.

Along the desert routes, the Bedouins played a symbiotic role with the caravans. They owned and rented the camels to the merchants, and they provided the guides who led the caravans across hostile terrain. But they were also the leading threat to the safety of the caravans. The Ottomans dealt with this problem by providing bribes to the larger tribes so that they would not attack the caravans and would patrol the desert routes against less cooperative tribes. Individual caravan masters would also give gifts to the tribesmen they encountered on the way. This informal system of protection occasionally broke down with disastrous results.

Despite the risks, caravans continued to supply most intercity commerce in the Ottoman Empire throughout the 19th century. It was only with the construction of railroads at the end of that century that alternative methods of transport began to threaten their continued profitability. Caravans finally disappeared only after the fall of the Ottoman Empire in the early 20th century, as trucks became more easily available and a system of roads was once again put in place.

Bruce Masters

Further reading: Bruce Masters, *The Origins of Western Economic Dominance in the Middle East: Mercantilism and the Islamic Economy in Aleppo, 1600–1750* (New York: New York University Press, 1988); Douglas Carruthers, ed., *The*

Desert Route to India: Being the Journals of Four Travellers by the Great Desert Caravan Route between Aleppo and Basra, 1745–1751 (London: The Hakluyt Society, 1929).

caravansary (han, khan) In order to promote the CARAVAN trade, Ottoman authorities maintained a network of fortified hostels along the major trade and pilgrimage routes. These were usually placed at intervals of about 20 miles, that being the distance a caravan could travel in a day. Similar structures were also built in the major commercial cities to house traveling merchants. In the latter case, each structure was maintained as a pious foundation, or WAQF, to support some worthy cause such as the maintenance of a mosque. European travelers called such structures caravansaries, although their name in Arabic was *khan* or in Ottoman Turkish *han*.

Whether constructed along caravan routes or in cities, most caravansaries had a similar architectural plan. Invariably built of stone, they consisted of a two-story rectangle or square built around an open courtyard in which there was a fountain. Many also had a small mosque in the corner of the structure facing MECCA. Storage rooms on the ground floor provided space for the merchants to store their goods and stable their animals, while the merchants themselves occupied apartments on the upper floor. On the open road, these accommodations were generally free of charge, as the Ottoman state paid for their construction and maintenance; in the cities, rent was paid to an employee of the *waqf* who managed the everyday running of the hostel.

European merchants often used the caravansaries in the cities as their permanent residence, and many caravansaries became known locally by the name of the country from which the merchants living there came. Caravansaries also housed Catholic MISSIONARIES as they began to enter the Ottoman Empire in the 17th and 18th centuries, and several had chapels that were added to the interior of the structure. These were supposedly for the private use of the missionaries, who received diplomatic status through the protection of the French ambassador in Istanbul. But local converts to Catholicism from Orthodox Christianity or the Eastern-rite churches would use them at times when Catholic rites in their own churches were forbidden (*see* UNIATES).

Bruce Masters

Carlowitz, Treaty of *See* KARLOWITZ, TREATY OF.

cartography There are no maps from the early days of the Ottomans; only after the middle of the 15th century do the first examples of Ottoman maps appear. They date to the reign of Sultan MEHMED II (1444–46; 1451–81) and are linked to a growing Ottoman-Venetian rivalry. After the Ottoman CONQUEST OF CONSTANTINOPLE, Sultan Mehmed the Conqueror ordered cartographer Georgios Amirutzes of Trabzon to translate Ptolemaus's *Geographiae* and to make a world map by combining his translation with earlier Arabic translations. Ottoman cartographical terminology was based upon terms from European cartography and from Islamic literature. The words *harta* and *hartı* in Anatolian Turkish, meaning map, were most likely developed by renowned Ottoman mariners Piri Reis (d. 1554) and Seydi Ali Reis (d. 1562).

WORLD AND NAUTICAL MAPS

The well-known 17th-century Ottoman traveler EVLIYA ÇELEBI mentions a cartography community called *esnaf-ı haritaciyan* that consisted of eight shops and 15 men, experts in a number of languages including Latin. They made maps by using works such as the famous *Atlas Minor* (1607) prepared by Gerard Mercator (1512–94) and Jodocus Hondius (1563–1612), and sold them to sailors. The Ottomans, especially Ottoman sailors, were encouraged by rewards to draw maps. The oldest navigation chart, or portolan, was drawn in about 1413–14 by Ahmed b. Suleyman et-Tanci (d. after 1414) and includes the Black Sea, the European and African coasts of the Atlantic Ocean, and the British Isles. Another portolan, from 1461, drawn by Ibrahim of Tunis (d. after 1461), a physician in Trablusgarb (LIBYA), depicts the Mediterranean, the Aegean, and the Black Sea as well as the western European shores. The portolan of Hacı Ebul-Hasan (d. after 1560), possibly dating from the reign of Sultan SÜLEYMAN I (r. 1520–66) and preserved in the TOPKAPI PALACE Museum, shows Ottoman lands in three continents—Asia, Europe, and Africa.

Piri Reis (d. 1554), admiral of the Ottoman imperial fleet, is the most famous representative of Ottoman cartography and his work *Kitab-ı Bahriyye* is a masterpiece. In this work, begun under the protection of his uncle, Kemal Reis (d. 1510), Piri Reis writes of his experiences and observations of the seas. He explains each map's definition as well as its omens, giving detailed information about some of the big seas and islands. Piri Reis shows portolans for each port that he mentions and marks the important buildings. The eminent Ottoman scholar and author KATIB ÇELEBI (d. 1657) in his recently discovered *Müntehab-ı Bahriyye* not only used the *Kitab-ı Bahriyye* but also updated its information and maps by making use of a few Western sources while enhancing Piri Reis's prose and adding new charts.

The interest in the famous first world map of Piri Reis has not subsided since its discovery in 1929. Today, only one sheet of this map is extant, dated from 1513.

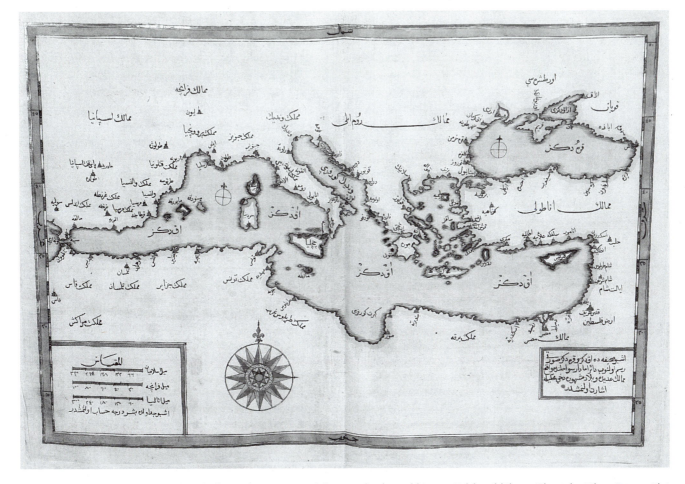

Map of the Mediterranean and the Black Sea from Katip Çelebi's work of naval history *Tuhfetü'l-kibar*. *(Photo by Fikret Sarıcaoğlu)*

In 1517 the map was presented to Sultan SELIM I (r. 1512–20) in CAIRO. It shows the Atlantic Ocean, Spain, FRANCE, the eastern part of America, the Florida coast, and the Antilles. In addition to place names, the map notes the date of discovery, shows the conquered territories of the Atlantic Ocean, and speaks of how the chart was drawn. These notes link Piri Reis's work to some 20 Eastern or Western maps he used as references, including Christopher Columbus' map of 1498.

Another map drawn by Piri Reis, housed in the Topkapı Palace Museum Library, shows the North Atlantic and the deserted coasts of North and Central America around 1528–29. The map, drawn in Gelibolu (Gallipoli), was probably presented to Süleyman the Magnificent, becoming his second world map, identifying such places as the Yucatán, Cuba, Haiti, Florida, and North America.

Hacı Ahmed of Tunis created a heart-shaped world map (1559–60) using maps drawn by J. Warner (1514) and Orontius Finaeus (1531), translating them into Turkish and combining them. This document also contained a map of the firmament including stars and mythological figures.

A nautical cartographer and respected captain, Ali Macar Reis (d. after 1567) finished his own work, *Atlas*, in 1567. This atlas contains seven maps depicting areas from the Black Sea and the Sea of Marmara to the Atlantic coasts and British Isles. It also includes a world map. A similar atlas, *Atlas-ı hümayun* (Imperial atlas), contains nine maps and was completed in 1570. A third atlas, the work of Walters Deniz, includes eight maps. Another Ottoman cartographer, Mehmed Reis of Menemen, drew a map of the Aegean Sea (1590–91). This map, compiled in Turkish, covers the region from Avlona (Vlorë in Albania) to Fethiye on the southwestern coast of Anatolia. *Deniz Kitabı*, drawn by cartographer Seyyid Nuh, dates from 1648–50 and includes 204 nautical charts of the Black Sea and Mediterranean ports, including defensive structure such as castles. Ancient world maps familiar to the Ottomans came via the classical geography books of renowned Muslim geographers Istahri, Idrisi, and Ibnul-Verdi.

MILITARY MAPS

Ottoman military maps were first drawn to show the status of sieges and new international borders after peace treaties. The first military map, assumed to have Venetian

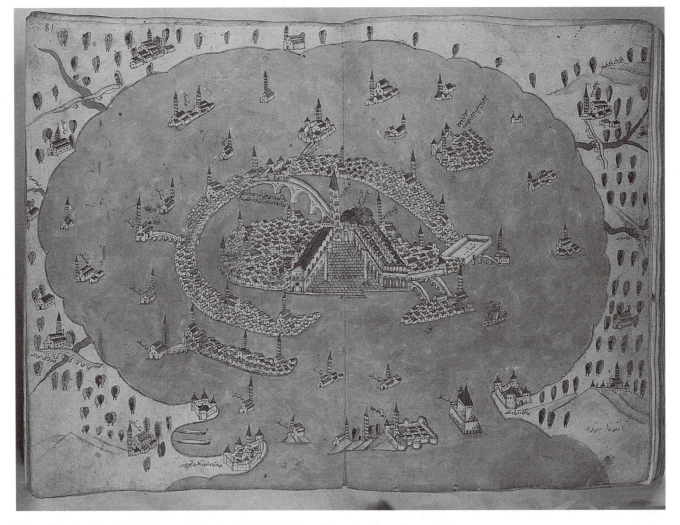

Map of Venice from Piri Reis's nautical atlas *Kitab-i Bahriye*. *(Photo by Fikret Sarıcaoğlu)*

origins, was completed before 1496 by Kulaguz Ilyas of Morea for Sultan BAYEZID II (1481–1512). Another map, that of the Sea of Azov and Crimea, was created between 1495 and 1506. It was drawn especially for the Ottoman fleet and depicted castles around Kiev. Many other maps depict military expeditions, sieges, and battlefields, including those of BELGRADE (1521), MALTA (1565), Szigetvár (in southern HUNGARY, 1566), Vienna (1683), and Prut (1711), as well as the 1736–39 Ottoman-Austrian-Russian wars, the retrieval of Adakale in 1738, ÖZI (1788), Corfu and ALEXANDRIA (1799), and the 1831 siege of BAGHDAD.

TRANSLATIONS AND PRINTING

In the course of the wars of the second half of the 18th century, the Ottomans translated, revised, and edited many European maps according to their military needs. Ressam Mustafa's many translations include a Black Sea and Crimea map that was translated under the control of M. Yorgaki and dates to the war in 1773.

Katib Çelebi, one of the first Ottoman cartographical translators, wrote *Cihannüma*, which depicted continental and territorial maps. The translation of the *Atlas minor* prepared by Mercator and Hondius served as a reference for this work. Katib Çelebi, who defined *atlas* as "a geography book," made this kind of translated book popular for many years. The definition of *atlas* in Ottoman literature later changed to "a set of maps." The geographer Ebubekir Efendi (d. 1691) translated 11 volumes of Wilhelm and Joan Bleau's *Atlas major* in nine volumes that included 242 maps.

The works of Ibrahim Müteferrika (d. 1747), the founder of the first official Ottoman printing house, form the backbone of Ottoman cartography. These efforts had an important place in the history of cartography not only for Ottomans but also for the world. His maps depict the Sea of Marmara (1720), the Black Sea (1724–25), the Ottoman countries and Asia, Persia (1729–30), and EGYPT (1730). His main work, *Cihannüma* (1732), added new maps and filled in the gaps in Katib Çelebi's earlier work. This impressive and important volume included 27 maps and 13 diagrams, and had a total of 40 plates. Maps were the first Muslim documents to be printed (beginning with the printing house of Ibrahim Müteferrika in 1727), and were the first printed works in the Ottoman world.

Ottoman cartography includes a number of continental or territorial maps but they are without much detail. These include maps of eastern Anatolia, western Persia, and the Caucasus (1723–1724). Kostantin Kamner (d. after 1813), a former translator in Morea, also made this kind of map. Some of his works include maps of ISTANBUL, the Bosporus, and the strait of Çanakkale (1813).

After 1797, translated maps and atlases were printed under the control of Müderris Abdurrahman in the MÜHENDISHANE Printing House where a printing press for maps was kept ready. Ottoman statesman Mahmud

Raif Efendi's (d. 1807) translation and adaptation of four sheets of Asia, Europe, Africa, and America from J. B. Bourguignon d'Anville's *Atlas Generale* were published in 1797, followed in 1801 by the portolans of the Mediterranean, the Black Sea, and the Sea of Marmara. Resmi Mustafa Agha's translation of William Faden's *General Atlas* was published in 1803 as *Cedid Atlas Tercümesi*; it is the greatest work of the printing house and contains 24 colored sheets and, although it contains some errors, is respected as the first complete Turkish atlas to be published.

At the beginning of the 19th century, the publication of translated maps and atlases by the Ottomans increased under the leadership of European experts and Turkish officers educated in Europe. While the publication of translated or copied maps continued, some territorial

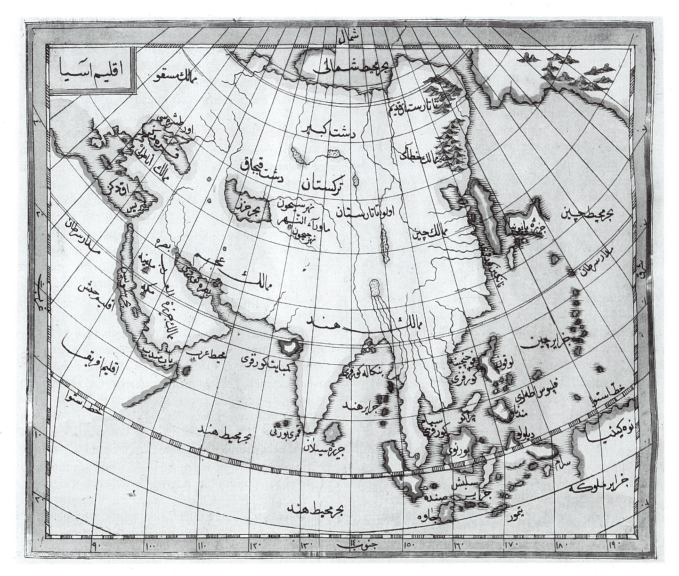

Map of Asia from Katip Çelebi's world geography *Cihannüma*, which was edited and published in 1732 by Ibrahim Müteferrika, the founder of the Ottoman Arabic-letter printing press. *(Photo by Fikret Sarıcaoğlu)*

maps were also drawn in the first official cartographical organization of the Ottoman Empire, the General Staff, in 1860. In 1880 the fifth department of Erkan-ı harb was assigned to deal with cartography matters. Finally, in 1895, a commission of cartography was formed. In the final years of the 19th century, cartography came to be an official profession, and the Ottoman Chamber of Cartography was founded in 1909.

Fikret Sarıcaoğlu

Further reading: Ahmet T. Karamustafa, "Introduction to Ottoman Cartography, Military, Administrative, and Scholarly Maps and Plans," in *The History of Cartography*, vol. 2, Bk. 1, *Cartography in the Traditional Islamic and South Asian Societies*, edited by J. B. Harley and D. Woodward (Chicago: University of Chicago Press, 1992), 206–227; Svat Soucek, *Piri Reis and Turkish Mapmaking after Columbus: The Khalili Portolan Atlas* (London: The Nour Foundation, 1996), 115–120, 128–132.

Caucasus (Caucasia; *Russ.*: Kavkaz; *Turk.*: Kafkasya)

The Caucasus is a mountainous region surrounded by the Caspian Sea in the east, the Black Sea and the Sea of Azov in the west, the Manych and Kuma rivers and the Russian plains in the north, and Anatolia in the south. The Caucasus is thus a natural frontier separating Asia and Europe. Moreover, the Caucasus has historically had strategic importance as a result of the waterways that stretch between, and link, the Caspian Sea, the Black Sea, and the Sea of Azov. The Euphrates and Tigris basins also connect these waterways to the Indian Ocean.

Despite the strategic benefit of the Caucasus, the Ottoman Empire did not view the area as militarily or politically important until the second half of the 16th century. The first half of this century was mostly spent struggling against the Safavid dynasty of Iran. The emergence of Muscovite Russia as a political power in the second half of the 16th century was the catalyst for Ottoman interest in the Caucasus region. Before this time, the Ottoman Empire had dismissed Russia as unworthy of serious attention. However, Russia occupied the cities of Kazan (1552) and Astrakhan (1556), then gained access to the Caspian Sea by seizing control of the Volga region. The introduction of Russian influence into the northern Caucasus was keenly observed by the Ottoman Empire, which now faced three hostile fronts: Russia, Europe, and Iran.

Preventing the Russian advance quickly became an important Ottoman objective. One project intended to further this was the construction of a canal between the Don and Volga rivers to control the northern Caucasus while maintaining military and commercial connections. Additionally, the canal would give the Ottoman Empire strategic control over the conduits to Central Asia and Iran. In 1569 the canal's construction began under the direction of Grand Vizier Sokollu Mehmed Pasha. However, the canal was never completed due to interference from the Crimean khan Devlet Giray who, although an Ottoman vassal, was partially under Russian influence.

Following the failed canal project, Ottoman concern about the Caucasus continued to grow. Nevertheless, the Ottoman Empire remained the main source of political and military power in the Caucasus during the latter half of the 16th century, conquering parts of present-day Georgia, Azerbaijan, and Dagestan in the Ottoman-Safavid War of 1578–90. However, most of these gains were retaken by Shah Abbas I (r. 1587–1629) in 1603.

While the first half of the 17th century saw Europe enmeshed in the Thirty Years War (1618–48), the Ottomans were attempting to contain a series of dangerous internal rebellions known as the Celali revolts. The Safavids took advantage of these revolts in Anatolia and retook Baghdad and Yerevan, the capital of present-day Armenia, maintaining control of these two areas until 1635.

The enthronement of Czar Peter I of Russia (r. 1682–1725) marked the beginning of a new period in the Caucasus for the Ottomans. Peter quickly began an aggressive policy to gain access to warmer waters. His first attempt targeted the Black Sea and resulted in the capture of Azak in 1696. Following his defeat at the River Prut on the eastern boundary of Romania in 1711, Peter turned his attention to the Caucasus. Despite Ottoman attempts at control, the Caucasus and Iran were dealing with political turmoil. Encouraged by this unrest, Peter decided to organize a military campaign in the Caucasus. His fleet set off from the Caspian Sea port of Astrakhan on June 15, 1722; by the end of the campaign Russia occupied the eastern part of the Caucasus at Derbend (in Dagestan on the Caspian Sea) and Baku (capital of present-day Azerbaijan).

To counter the Russian advance, in May 1722 the Ottomans moved to occupy several Iranian cities near the Ottoman border. In October of the same year the Ottomans occupied Tbilisi on the Kura River, the capital of present-day Georgia. Two years later, both Nakhichevan on the Aras River in the southern Caucasus and Yerevan came under Ottoman control. The Ottoman conquests in the Caucasus were completed with the taking of Lori, northeast of Tbilisi, in August 1725 and Gyandzha a major city in present-day Azerbaijan in September 1725.

On June 24, 1724, the Ottomans and Russians signed the Treaty of Istanbul, effectively splitting Iranian land holdings in two. The lands north of the Kura and Aras rivers were ceded to Russia. The western Iranian lands and the Azerbaijan lands were left to the Ottomans. By signing this treaty, the Russians had stretched their presence to the southern Caucasus.

Iran, however, was not content to allow the parceling out of its lands. The emergence of the Iranian leader NADIR SHAH (r. 1736–47) forced the Ottomans to deal simultaneously with both Iran and Russia. Nadir Shah began his reign by ending the Russian occupation of the Caucasus and connecting Dagestan to Iran. He succeeded in conquering Tbilisi, Yerevan, and Gyandzha. Despite these successes, Nadir Shah's death in 1747 marked the return of Ottoman influence to the southern Caucasus. The Ottomans took advantage of this new Iranian political turmoil and focused on attracting Caucasian Muslims to the Ottoman cause against Russia. As a result, Ottoman influence in the southern Caucasus lasted until 1760.

The RUSSO-OTTOMAN WAR OF 1768–74 gave Russian Empress Catherine II (r. 1762–96) the opportunity for a new military expedition to the Caucasus and the Crimea. Russia's purpose was to end the Ottomans' legal claim to the Caucasus. The Crimean Khanate, an Ottoman client state, became independent in 1774 with the TREATY OF KÜÇÜK KAYNARCA and was eventually annexed to Russia in 1783. The Treaty of Küçük Kaynarca also specified the Kuban' River as the new Ottoman-Russian frontier. Russia was not satisfied with this border and moved to gain control of the southern Caucasus as well. In July of 1783, Georgia was connected to Russia by Catherine II through an agreement with the Georgian king Irakli Khan II.

The new Russian action in the Caucasus renewed Ottoman interest in the region. The loss of the Crimea was especially significant because the area had been under Ottoman control from 1475. Not surprisingly, Russian forces attempted to entrench themselves in the area by establishing defense lines in the northern Caucasus. These lines were fortified and extended to connect Russian Georgia. Further Russian attacks on Dagestan and Azerbaijan began to threaten the security of Anatolia and, as a result, the Ottomans were forced to seek a means to halt the Russian advance. The Ottoman response to the threat was to appoint Ferah Ali Pasha to the Soğucak Armed Guard in 1780. Ferah Ali Pasha began to actively spread Islam among the Circassian tribes; as a result the Circassian tribes accepted Islam and fought against Russia in the Russo-Ottoman War of 1787–92 (see RUSSO-OTTOMAN WARS).

In 1785, the emergence of Sheikh Mansur in the Caucasus changed the historical course of the region. Sheikh Mansur was originally a Chechen, but he worked to unite all the Caucasian tribes for jihad. Sheikh Mansur fought against Russia in the Caucasus and played an important role in the Russo-Ottoman War of 1787–92. The Russian attack on Anapa in 1788–89 was unsuccessful due to fierce Circassian resistance. The TREATY OF JASSY in 1792 brought an end to the war, re-establishing the Kuban' River as the Ottoman-Russian frontier. However, the treaty forced the Ottoman Empire to accept Russian superiority in the Caucasus over both the region and its tribes.

One final attempt to dislodge the Russians from the Caucasus was made late in the 18th century. The Iranian ruler Agha Muhammed Khan (r. 1779–97) made a feeble effort to undermine Russian power in the region, but any territorial gains were quickly recaptured by Russia by 1796 and were subsequently held firmly under Russian control.

During the early 19th century the Russians, unlike the Ottomans, were active in the Caucasus. Especially after the Russian annexation of parts of Georgia in 1801, Russian expansion in the Caucasus continued. The first Russian decision was to appoint General Tsitsianof as the general governor of the Caucasus. Tsitsianof was originally Georgian; under his guidance, a new colonial administration was created. General Tsitsianof began by trying to connect the Azerbaijan khanates through various agreements. In 1804, during the Russo-Persian war of 1804–13, the Russians defeated Javad Khan of Gyandzha Khanate and annexed his khanate. Three years later, Baku came under the control of the Russians. In 10 years, Russia strengthened its presence in the southern Caucasus and expanded from the Black Sea to the Caspian Sea. Despite the Russian approach however, the Ottoman Empire showed little interest in the events of the southern Caucasus before 1806.

In 1806 the Ottomans began to show a renewed interest in the Caucasus and as a result the Ottoman Empire clashed with Russia in the Russo-Ottoman War of 1806–12. Russia was occupying Poti, Kemhal, and Sukhumi on the eastern coast of the Black Sea. To counter the Russian force the Ottomans tried to use Circassians, Abkhaz, and other tribes. The hostilities were ended by the TREATY OF BUCHAREST, signed by the Ottoman Empire and Russia in 1812. The terms of the accord forced Russia to abandon conquered Ottoman areas. However, Russia crushed the Iranian army in the same year and forced the signing of the Gülistan Agreement in 1813. Through this victory over Iran, Russia obtained Derbend, Baku, Shirvan, Karabakh Kuban, Lenkeran, and a part of Talish in central Caucasus. These concessions cost Iran all claims on Dagestan, Georgia, Imeretia, and Abkhazia. Russia appointed General Aleksey Petrovich Yermolov soon after as the supreme head of the Russian Caucasian Army and became the sole ruler of the northern Caucasus from 1818–21.

Disturbed by Russian superiority in the Caucasus, Iran united with Dagestan to challenge Russia in 1826. Iran was once again defeated and was forced to sign the Turkmenchai Treaty in 1828. According to this treaty, the Yerevan and Nakhichevan khanates, including the southern banks of the Aras River, were ceded to Russia.

The Ottomans quickly attacked Russia in 1828, hoping to halt the Russian advance on the Caucasus-Anatolia frontier. Russia, however, was again successful, taking Kars, Akhaltsikhe, and the Bayazid provinces, as well as nine fortresses. Russian presence and power in the southern Caucasus was firmly secured, and the newly captured areas soon became the launching points for military raids against Anatolia. The Ottoman Empire and Russia signed the TREATY OF EDIRNE on September 14, 1829, in which the Ottomans renounced all sovereignty rights over the entirety of the Caucasus.

The Russo-Ottoman War of 1828–29 was a turning point in the Ottoman-Russian power struggle in the Caucasus. The Ottoman Empire had been defeated by Russia, and Russia had become the sole military and political power in the Caucasus. However, other foreign powers began to take an interest in the affairs of the region. ENGLAND was concerned about Russian power in the Caucasus as a possible threat to the security of commercial routes between Turkistan and India. Britain also showed interest in the signing of the TREATY OF HÜNKAR ISKELESI between the Ottoman Empire and Russia in 1833. Following the signing of this treaty, Britain was forced to change its policy on what was termed the EASTERN QUESTION, and began discussions with FRANCE about appropriate action. France showed similar concern about the effect of the Russian presence and "the question of the Turkish straits."

During the mid-19th century, a new religious leader emerged as an opponent to Russia. Sheikh Shamil was of Dagestani origin and sought the independence of the Caucasus. In order to achieve this goal, Sheikh Shamil called on all Caucasian tribes to unite and rise up against the Russians. The Ottoman Empire followed Sheikh Shamil's struggle against Russia, but due to fears of Russian reprisal, the Ottomans could not materially support his independence movement. From the beginning of the independence movement in 1834, Sheikh Shamil repeatedly sent requests to ISTANBUL for aid. The Ottomans never responded with physical assistance. However, as caliph, the Ottoman sultan provided moral support and credibility for Sheikh Shamil, allowing him to achieve several key victories against the Russians and to stop their southward advance.

The CRIMEAN WAR of 1853–56, which is accepted as the first modern world war, increased hopes for independence in the Caucasus. When Ottoman-Russian relations were cut off at the end of May 1853, Sheikh Shamil acted to prevent the concentration of Russian troops in Dagestan or the surrounding areas between June and October, 1853. The Ottomans were pleased with Shamil's activities against Russia in Dagestan. The outbreak of the Crimean War on October 4, 1853 once again brought Ottoman attention to the Caucasus. In response, Ottoman Sultan ABDÜLMECID (r. 1839–61) sent a decree dated October 9, 1853 to Sheikh Shamil and summoned him to jihad. Sheikh Shamil responded in a letter dated December 13, 1853. In this letter, Shamil informed the sultan that if a military force were to advance on Tbilisi, the Russians could be expelled from the Caucasus. His strategic advice was dismissed by Istanbul, but Shamil entered the Kaheti region of Georgia for a joint operation with the Ottoman army in July, 1854. Although one Ottoman army was in the Ozurgeti region of Georgia, Shamil failed to locate them and retreated to Dagestan, where he remained until the conclusion of the war. The Treaty of Paris, signed by Britain, France, the Ottoman Empire, and Russia on March 30, 1856, ended the Crimean War. As a result of the treaty, Kars was ceded to the Ottoman Empire. With the threat of war behind her, Russia increased attacks against Shamil, who finally surrendered to Russia in 1859. Following his surrender, tens of thousands of Caucasians fleeing Russian oppression immigrated to the Ottoman Empire.

The Caucasus again saw fighting between the Ottomans and Russia during the 1877–78 Ottoman-Russian War. The war started on April 24, 1877 as the Russian army moved to occupy the cities of Kars and Ardahan in northeastern Anatolia. Russian troops occupied Kars by November 19, 1877. The Russians continued their advance toward the city of Erzurum in northeastern Anatolia, but harsh winter conditions hampered the movement of both the Ottoman and Russian armies from December 1877 to January 1878. As the cold weather receded, neither the Ottoman defense nor the resistance of the local population was enough to prevent the Russians from occupying Erzurum on February 8, 1878.

With their military operations in the western Caucasus, especially Abkhazia, the Ottomans forced the Russians to maintain an important reserve force in Riyon and around the Black Sea between April and August 1877. Despite the numerical superiority of the Ottomans at the beginning of the war, the Russians claimed victory at the city of Batumi on the Black Sea coast. The Ottoman NAVY then fled Sukhumi (the capital of Abkhazia, on the Black Sea) toward the end of August 1877 and Russia claimed victory in the western Caucasus. The Treaty of Berlin was signed on July 13, 1878, officially ending the war and giving Ardahan, Kars, and Batumi to the Russians. Erzurum however, was returned to the Ottomans.

At the beginning of WORLD WAR I, the Ottoman Empire allied itself with GERMANY. The Ottoman view, as championed by statesmen such as Enver Pasha, was that if Germany could remove the Russian presence, the empire could seize enormous political and military influence over the Caucasus and Central Asia. Enver Pasha considered the Caucasus a top priority and went as far as to order General Fuad Pasha to incite the Circassians to rebel against the Russians. The war started on October 29, 1914, with attacks on the Ukrainian seaports of Odessa and Sevastopol by two Ottoman warships under the command of Admiral Suchon. The Russian army was quick to retaliate and crossed the Ottoman frontier on November 1, 1914. There the Russian army met the Ottoman Third Army, responsible for the Anatolian-Caucasian front. The invading Russian forces advanced upon Pasinler and Eleshkirt where they were repulsed and driven back between November 6 and 12, 1914. On November 17, 1914, Ottoman units defeated Russian forces once more.

The most noteworthy battle on the Anatolian-Caucasian front was the Sarikamış operation. Between December 22 1914 and January 3 1915 Ottoman forces led by Enver Pasha moved to the offensive. They were finally defeated by the Russians. The defeat of the Ottoman force was the beginning of the Ottoman decline on the front. In the spring of the same year, Russian forces took advantage of the Ottoman weakness and captured Van, Muş, and Bitlis in eastern Anatolia, all of which were recaptured by the Ottoman Third Army in the summer.

The Russian offensive continued in early 1916 as Russian troops captured a number of strategic cities in eastern Anatolia: Erzurum on February 16; Bitlis and Muş on March 3; Rize on March 8; Trabzon, Bayburd and Gümüşhane on April 18; Erzincan on July 25; and finally Van. The Russian presence in these occupied cities continued until 1918 when Russia pulled out of Anatolia as a result of the Bolshevik Revolution. Russia signed an armistice with the Ottoman Empire on December 18, 1917. Immediately following the signing, the Ottomans began military operations in eastern Anatolia. The First Caucasian Army Corps of the Ottomans, under the command of Kazim Karabekir Pasha, captured many of the Russian-held cities and villages within two months. Ottoman forces finally entered Batumi on April 14. The terms of the Treaty of Brest-Litovsk, signed on March 3, 1918, required Russia to return the so-called Three Cities (Evliye-i Selâse)—Kars, Ardahan, and Batumi—to Ottoman control.

Following the Treaty of Brest-Litovsk, the Ottoman Empire was again an important power in the Caucasus. The Caucasus Islamic Army under the command of Nuri Pasha captured Baku from the British on September 15, 1918. With the signing of the Moudros Armistice, however, Ottoman superiority in the Caucasus finally ended. British forces took Baku on November 17 and Batumi on December 24. The final withdrawal of Ottoman troops occurred in January of 1919, permanently ending the Ottoman presence in the Caucasus.

Mustafa Budak

Further reading: W. E. D. Allen and P. P. Muratov, *Caucasian Battlefields: A History of the Wars on the Turco-Caucasian Border, 1828–1921* (Cambridge: Cambridge University Press, 1953); Abdurakhman Avtorkhanov and Marie Broxup, eds., *The North Caucasus Barrier: The Russian Advance towards the Muslim World* (New York: St. Martin's, 1992); John F Baddeley, *The Russian Conquest of the Caucasus* (New York: Russell & Russell, 1968 [reprint of the 1908 edition]); Thomas M. Barrett, *At the Edge of Empire: The Terek Cossacks and the North Caucasus Frontier, 1700–1860* (Boulder, Colo.: Westview, 1999); Moshe Gammer, *Muslim Resistance to the Tsar: Shamil and the Conquest of Chechnia and Daghestan* (London: F. Cass, 1994); Robert D. Kaplan, *Eastward to Tartary: Travels in the Balkans, the Middle East, and the Caucasus* (New York: Random House, 2000); Firouzeh Mostashari, *On the Religious Frontier: Tsarist Russia and Islam in the Caucasus* (London: I. B. Tauris, 2006).

Celali revolts   Although the phrase Celali revolts has been widely adopted by modern scholars to identify a series of rural Anatolian rebellions against the Ottoman state in the 16th and 17th centuries following the death of Sultan SÜLEYMAN I (r. 1520–66) in 1566, the term is probably a misnomer. The misunderstanding begins with Ottoman court historians of the 17th century who referred to the rebellions as Celali revolts after a certain Sheikh Celal, a follower of Shah ISMAIL I (r. 1487–1524) who raised a popular rebellion against the Ottoman state in 1519. Although his rebellion was simply a continuation of a more general unrest among the Turkoman tribes of central and eastern Turkey that had given rise to the KIZILBAŞ movement, Ottoman historians sought to distinguish him from the earlier movement by characterizing him as a mere bandit. The term Celali revolts was then used more widely by Ottoman officials and court historians to dismiss many subsequent rebellions as peasant banditry, even when these uprisings were clearly of a more political nature.

Historians differ over the reasons for the Celali rebellions. Some cite evidence of severe economic and social pressure in rural Turkey caused by half a century of robust population growth. Others point to the economic upheaval caused by the influx of cheap silver from the Americas; the drop in the real value of silver destabilized prices and led to rapid inflation. Another factor that contributed to destabilization in the countryside was the proliferation of muskets among the peasants and the inability of graduates from the state-run religious schools, or madrasas, to find employment. In fact, all these factors probably contributed to the unrest. Another contributing factor was the need of the Ottoman state to recruit extra men into the military to supplement the standing army of the JANISSARIES. These armed men, known as *levends*, were often former peasants who lacked the discipline of the professional army. By sanctioning their acquisition of firearms, the Ottoman state helped transform popular unrest in rural Anatolia into armed rebellion.

After the Ottoman victory over the Habsburgs at Mezőkeresztes in HUNGARY in 1596, several thousand *levends* deserted the battlefield and fled to Anatolia. There they rallied discontented peasants under the leadership of Karayazıcı Abdülhalim, an unemployed scribe. Sultan MEHMED III (r. 1595–1603) was unable to muster troops to suppress the rebellion because the governor of Karaman, who was sent to destroy the rebels, simply switched sides. The Ottoman state finally had to buy Karayazıcı off by giving him his own governorship in 1600 while it raised troops to defeat him in 1601. That proved to be a standard strategy by which the sultans sought to control the Celali leaders. They would simply buy the rebels' loyalty until such time as they could destroy them.

Perhaps the most famous of the Celali rebels was the Kurdish leader JANBULAD ALI PASHA, although his army consisted of his kinsmen rather than disgruntled peasants with muskets. The JANBULAD FAMILY had long been the chieftains of the Kurdish tribes who inhabited a mountainous area known as Kürt Dağı or "Mountain of the Kurds," which today is split between TURKEY and SYRIA. Janbulad Ali's uncle Husayn had served as governor of ALEPPO but fell out of favor with the GRAND VIZIER and was executed in 1605. Janbulad Ali raised the clan standard to avenge his uncle. Although some *levends* from Anatolia eventually joined his rebellion, the bulk of Ali's army was made up of Kurds. In another move that distinguished his revolt from other so-called Celali revolts, Janbulad Ali sought the military support of the Ottomans' long-standing rival power, Venice. He boasted to its representatives that he would establish himself as the independent sultan of Syria. In an attempt to buy time, Sultan AHMED I (r. 1603–1617) appointed Janbulad Ali as Aleppo's governor in 1605, while simultaneously raising an army to crush him. The two armies met in 1607 and the Janbulad forces were defeated. Janbulad Ali surrendered soon afterward and was appointed to a post in remote WALLACHIA, in present-day Romania. As was the case earlier with Karayazıcı, the Ottoman authorities sought to buy Janbulad Ali's loyalty until a time when they felt they could remove him permanently without a violent reaction from his kinsmen. That opportunity came in 1610 when Janbulad Ali was executed for treason in BELGRADE.

Abaza Mehmed Pasha raised the last of the major Celali revolts in 1623. Abaza Mehmed was the governor of the eastern province of Erzurum, today in northeastern Turkey, who became enraged by the murder of Sultan OSMAN II (r. 1618–22) at the hands of JANISSARIES in the previous year. Not trusting anyone connected to the corps, he began to expel the Janissaries from his province. Those actions led to his dismissal by the newly enthroned Sultan MUSTAFA I (r. 1617–18, 1622–23), who was indebted to the Janissaries for putting him on the throne. Unwilling to accept the orders of a sultan whom he considered illegitimate, Abaza Mehmed organized an army of discontented peasants and marched on Ankara. His successes created panic in ISTANBUL and led to the replacement of Sultan Mustafa by MURAD IV (r. 1623–40), who was then only 11 years old. Despite the change in sultans, Abaza Mehmed continued his rebellion until 1628, when he was offered the governorship of Bosnia. He was finally executed for his rebellion in 1634.

Over the next quarter of a century, other rebellions were mounted by provincial governors, most notably that of Abaza Hasan Pasha between 1657 and 1659. But none threatened the empire as directly as had those of Janbulad Ali and Abaza Mehmed because they failed to mobilize popular support for their cause among the peasants.

The examples of these two revolt leaders illustrate that the various rebellions that are collectively known as the Celali revolts had little in common with each other in terms of their origins. But once they were underway, peasants, unemployed religious students, and army deserters formed the ranks of the rebels. Large-scale looting and plundering of villages and provincial towns were also hallmarks of all the rebellions. The frequency of these revolts and the difficulty that the central government faced in suppressing them point to the growing inability of the Istanbul leadership to control the empire's provinces in the decades following the death of Sultan Süleyman. The instability in the countryside led to the migration of peasants away from their villages to the relative safety of walled cities. While there had been population pressure in the rural areas in the 16th century, the 17th century witnessed the abandonment of farms and villages and an accompanying shortage of rural labor. In the absence of a strong central government, local leaders—provincial notable families known as AYAN—raised their own armies to secure the countryside and to collect tax revenues for the central government.

Bruce Masters

Further reading: Karen Barkey, *Bandits and Bureaucrats: The Ottoman Route to State Centralization* (Ithaca, N.Y.: Cornell University Press, 1994); William Griswold, *The Great Anatolian Rebellion, 1000–1020/1591–1611* (Berlin: Klaus Schwarz, 1983).

Cem (Djem, Jem) (b. 1459–d. 1495) *famous pretender to the Ottoman throne*   Born to Sultan MEHMED II (r. 1444–46; 1451–81) and Çiçek Hatun in 1459, Cem was appointed prince-governor of Kastamonu on the Black Sea in north-central Anatolia in 1469. During his father's 1473 campaign against Uzun Hasan (r. 1453–78) of the Akkoyunlu (White Sheep) Turkoman confederation that ruled over eastern Anatolia and Azerbaijan, Cem was sent to the former Ottoman capital EDIRNE (in European Turkey) to guard the empire's European frontiers. After not hearing from his father for 40 days, Cem started to act as sultan. Although upon his return Mehmed II forgave his son, the sultan executed his tutors, who were behind Cem's acts. In 1474, Cem replaced his deceased brother Mustafa as prince-governor of Karaman, and left for his new seat in Konya.

When Mehmed II died on May 3, 1481, Grand Vizier Karamani Mehmed Pasha (in office in 1476–81), who favored Cem, sent word to both Cem and his elder brother Bayezid, hoping that Cem would arrive first because Konya was closer to ISTANBUL than Bayezid's governorship in Amasya (in central Anatolia). However, the grand vizier's enemies, supported by the JANISSARIES, intercepted the messenger sent to Cem, killed the grand vizier, and proclaimed Bayezid's 11-year-old son Korkud regent. Korkud had been living in Istanbul along with Cem's son who was being kept close to the throne as a form of insurance against a possible coup d'état. Bayezid reached Istanbul on May 21 and was made sultan the next day by the Imperial Council. In the meantime, Prince Cem reached the old Ottoman capital of BURSA, where he proclaimed himself sultan. Bayezid rejected Cem's suggestion to divide the empire and defeated him on June 20 at Yenişehir, east of Bursa.

Cem fled to Konya, whence he retreated to Adana, the gateway to the Cilician (Çukurova) plain southeast of the Taurus Mountains, seat of the Ramazanoğlu Turkoman emirate, a client of the MAMLUK EMPIRE of EGYPT and SYRIA. Cem reached the Mamluk capital of CAIRO in late September. With the help of the Mamluks and a scion of the now-extinguished Karaman emirs, Cem returned to Anatolia in the spring and summer of 1482 and laid siege to Konya. However, his supporters were defeated again by Bayezid, who rejected Cem's repeated suggestion to divide the empire. In the hope that he could cross to Rumelia—the European part of the Ottoman Empire—by sea, Cem arrived in RHODES, home of the KNIGHTS OF ST. JOHN, whose Grand Master Pierre d'Aubusson he knew from his years as prince-governor in Konya. However, by September 1482, Bayezid had struck a deal with the Knights, who promised to keep Cem in indefinite confinement in their castles in FRANCE; in return, they were rewarded with a yearly payment of 45,000 gold ducats from the sultan. Thus started Prince Cem's miserable adventures as Europe's pawn.

Cem spent the next seven years in France. Both Pope Innocent VIII (r. 1484–92) and King Matthias Corvinus of HUNGARY (r. 1458–90) wanted to recruit him for their planned anti-Ottoman crusades. So did the Mamluk Sultan Qayitbay (r. 1468–96), who went to war with the Ottomans from 1485 through 1491 over the Cilician plain and the Turkoman emirate of Dulkadır with its cen-

Brother of Bayezid II and pretender to the Ottoman throne, Cem Sultan died in exile in France in 1495. In 1499 his body was brought back to the Ottoman household's ancestral burial grounds in Bursa. *(Photo by Gábor Ágoston)*

ters in Elbistan and Maraş, east of the Taurus Mountains in Anatolia. By March 1489, Cem was in Rome and the pope started a new round of negotiations with the proponents of crusade. However, King Matthias Corvinus died within a year (April 1490), the Mamluks concluded their own treaty with Bayezid (1491), and Pope Innocent died in 1492.

In 1494, for a short time, Cem was again the focus of international politics. King Charles VIII of France (r. 1483–98), who invaded Italy, forced the new pope, Alexander (r. 1492–1503), to hand Cem over to him. Although Bayezid feared that the French might take him into the Balkans, Cem died in Naples shortly after being handed over to the French on February 25, 1495. It was not until April 1499 that Bayezid managed to acquire his brother's corpse for burial in Bursa. Thus ended the saga of the most famous pretender to the Ottoman throne, whose ambitions and very identity became a threat to the integrity of the Ottoman Empire.

Gábor Ágoston

Further reading: Halil İnalcık, "Djem," in *Encyclopaedia of Islam*, edited by P. Bearman, Th. Bianquis, C. E. Bosworth,

E. van Donzel, and W. P. Heinrichs. Brill, 2007. Brill Online. Online edition (by subscription), viewed 6 March 2007: http://www.brillonline.nl/subscriber/entry?entry=islam_SIM-2062; Roderick Conway Morris, *Jem: Memoirs of an Ottoman Secret Agent* (New York: St. Martin's Press, 1988); Nicolas Vatin, *Sultan Djem: Un prince ottoman dans l'Europe du XVe siècle d'après deux sources contemporaines: Vâki`ât-i Sultân Cem, Oeuvres de Guillaume Caoursin* (Ankara: Impr. de la Société turque d'histoire, 1997).

censorship PRINTING entered the Ottoman Empire with the arrival in 1492 of Spanish JEWS, who went on to establish printing presses not only in ISTANBUL but also in other cities such as SALONIKA, EDIRNE, and IZMIR. By the beginning of the 17th century, printing facilities were well established and were being operated by non-Muslims in Istanbul and in cities throughout the empire. Censorship, the monitoring and control of printed material, went hand-in-hand with the emergence of printing technology, and censorship grew and expanded as rapidly as printing itself. The first form of censorship prohibited the printing of works in Turkish and Arabic but allowed the printing of works in Spanish, Hebrew, Greek, and Latin. Provided that they did not use Arabic letters or publish religiously provocative material, the authorities did not interfere with the activities of non Muslim publishers. When the printing and publishing of works in Arabic and Turkish began in the first half of the 18th century, however, problems arose, leading to stricter regulation.

CENSORSHIP OF BOOKS

Ibrahim Müteferrika, a Hungarian convert to Islam, who founded the first Arabic-letter printing press in the 18th century was the first Ottoman to petition to print works in Ottoman Turkish, presenting his request to the GRAND VIZIER, IBRAHIM PASHA. In his petition, Müteferrika underlined the necessity of printing works in Turkish and requested permission to publish not only religious works, such as *tafsir* (commentaries on the Quran), *hadith* (stories from the life of the Prophet), and Muslim canonical law, but also general works, such as dictionaries, histories, and books on medicine. When he realized that his request was not being viewed favorably, Müteferrika petitioned the grand vizier to obtain a FATWA or religious ruling from the şeyhülislam, the chief religious official of the empire, and a decree from Sultan AHMED III (r. 1703–30), granting permission for the printing of works in Turkish using the Arabic alphabet. Despite protests from those who favored the status quo and who viewed this enterprise as a harbinger of fundamental social change, the şeyhülislam, Abdullah Efendi, issued a fatwa declaring that there was no religious objection to Müteferrika's proposal. As a result of the sultan's decree of July

5, 1727, the first Turkish printing press was established. At first, the printing of religious works was forbidden, and Müteferrika published scientific and technical material only. It was not until 1803 that the ban on printing religious material was lifted.

In the intervening years, other state-sponsored facilities were established for printing books and journals approved by the authorities. No great need was felt for legal regulations governing printing or publishing at this point because no private enterprise was involved, but in later years, as private enterprise began to grow, changes to the law were made to allow for state control. The first such regulation, the Printing Regulation (Matbaa Nizamnamesi) of February 8, 1857, was the first form of book censorship. According to this regulation, works being considered for printing had to be approved by the Meclis-i Maarif, an office under the Ministry of Education. Copies of books and journals printed without permission or considered damaging to the public were collected by the police, the printers responsible were fined, and their facilities were closed.

During the reign of ABDÜLHAMID II (r. 1876–1909), specialized new institutions were established for the purpose of censorship and control. The Telif ve Tercüme Dairesi, a government body that handled copyright and translation, was established for this purpose, but on December 30, 1881 it was replaced by the Council of Inspection (Encümen-i Teftiş ve Muayene). The function of the latter was not only to inspect books and journals before they were printed, but also to examine their contents. It also had the authority to control and inspect the contents of books in libraries. After the Council of Inspection's examination, the Ministry of Education issued a printing license for each individual work. Approval for the printing of religious works was sought from the office of the şeyhülislam; the military granted approval for military works. On average, between five and ten books in languages such as Turkish, Arabic, French, Greek, and Armenian were presented daily to the Council of Inspection for examination and approval.

In 1892 another commission, the Commission for the Investigation of Written Works (Tetkik-i Muellefat Komisyonu), was established and affiliated with the Ministry of Education. This new commission consisted of five members whose task was to review for the second time books in Turkish, Arabic, Persian, as well as Turkish plays that had come from the Council of Inspection. While a book was under examination, discussion was forbidden between the book's publisher and members of the Council. The report prepared for the five-member committee included the names of the books or plays concerned, a summary of their content, the proprietor's name, a note of how many copies were being requested, and the decision made after the first examination. That the books could only be printed following these two examinations shows the government's strictness on censorship.

The works of many famous writers failed to pass the censorship boards during this period, including those of Montesquieu, Voltaire, Rousseau, and Racine. The work of Turkish writers such as Namik Kemal, Ziya Pasha, Ali Suavi, and Abdülhak Hamid also did not pass the censorship board's review because their works were generally critical of state power. Censorship also seriously affected the content of school textbooks, with some important subjects simply being excluded. For example, the text approved for teaching the history of the Ottoman Empire included nothing more than a chronology of the sultans. Although Mizancı Murad, a famous journalist, mentioned important movements and events, such as the French Revolution, in his book written for high schools in 1890, it was a dangerous undertaking at this time to write about contemporary international events, and little correct information was presented in the classroom on major events in human history. In works concerning Russia, the emphasis was solely on its aggressive foreign policy, while books regarding France elaborated on little other than the wars of Napoleon Bonaparte.

Stamps on the cover of a book indicated Ministry of Education approval; any books lacking this stamp were seized for being printed without the required permission. Books printed without approval were seized whenever and wherever they were found, including on printer's premises or in bookshops. In Istanbul, the collected books were sent to the Ministry of Education for burning; in rural areas they were collected and burned locally. In 1902, a May burning held in the Çemberlitaş Bathhouse, a building next to the Ministry of Education, destroyed 29,681 items, including those of the celebrated Turkish authors noted above.

NEWSPAPER CENSORSHIP

Censorship of newspapers began on December 31, 1864, when the first regulation governing the news press was enacted, and remained in force until 1909. According to this regulation, in order to publish a newspaper, an Ottoman citizen was required to apply to the Ministry of Education and a foreigner was required to apply to the Ministry of Foreign Affairs. Inspections followed to determine if the applicant would be allowed to do so. With each new edition, a copy bearing the signature of the owner or editor in chief had to be sent to the Press Directorate in Istanbul or to the local governor in the province in which it was being published. The Press Regulation stated all points to be taken into account when preparing the newspaper for publishing. Fines or imprisonment were the penalties for publishing news that disturbed the peace, endangered state security, or portrayed the sultan, grand vizier, government, or any foreign allied state in a negative light. Newspapers ignoring these regulations were either temporarily or permanently closed.

The reign of Abdülhamid II marked the period of most severe censorship. Before publication, newspapers were censored by officials at the Press Directorate, which at the time was divided into domestic and foreign departments. The former monitored the content of domestic newspapers, while the latter inspected foreign papers for negative press on the Ottoman Empire, reported this to the government, and took any measures considered necessary. Officials at the Press Directorate combed newspapers for what they deemed unsuitable or damaging language or content. This unsuitable content was then removed prior to the newspaper's release. Papers were forbidden to use words such as "strike," "assassination," "revolution," "anarchy," "republic," "freedom," or even to refer to these concepts.

Indeed, during the reign of Abdülhamid II, in all areas of life up to and including political debate, newspapers were little more than official organs of the state. Those seeking permission to produce a newspaper first had to inform the authorities of the political line they would be following. The Press Directorate gave priority to newspapers that chose not to include political news when granting permission for publication, while those papers covering politics were not allowed defame the government. Individuals planning to publish papers were required to guarantee this preferential treatment and were expected to refrain from spreading rumor or speculation concerning civil servants, publishing unsuitable extracts from foreign newspapers, or broadcasting any information on military matters or preparations. Newspapers that ignored these stipulations were closed down, either temporarily or permanently. For example, following the July 10, 1894 earthquake, the newspaper Sabah (Morning) was closed for printing that the Military College had been destroyed in the tremors, resulting in 22 injuries and three deaths. Sultan Abdülhamid II not only shut down Sabah but also ordered other newspapers to publish news contradicting the story's veracity. Following Sabah's closure, other newspapers published only approved news concerning damage and casualties caused by the earthquake. Today this decision renders it almost impossible to determine, with any certainty, the numbers killed and the damage done by this natural disaster.

Fear of fines and closure during the reign of Abdülhamid II reign meant that news of even the most mundane variety was carefully and cautiously prepared. In particular, news that revealed weakness on the part of the state was subject to extreme censorship, leading to the closure of many newspapers. Thus the domestic press was entirely under state control, while the foreign press was strictly monitored. Ottoman ambassadors throughout Europe were responsible for immediately telegraphing to the sultan's palace any news items derogatory to the empire. In response, letters contradicting these news items were written and the newspapers concerned were sued. In order to ensure that such foreign press did not enter the empire, strict controls were put in place at customs and in post offices. Abdülhamid II even personally inspected publications for objectionable items on political or religious grounds. Lists of all newspapers seized by officials at customs and post offices were presented to the palace, including the name and number of the newspaper, its place of origin and language, and the reasons for its seizure.

However, despite all these controls, foreign publications got through by various means. Often they were smuggled among packages of publications not forbidden or sent to foreign post offices between book covers. Since the authorities had no means of exercising direct control over foreign-run post offices or embassies, there was no great difficulty involved in smuggling banned publications into the empire by these methods. The entry and distribution of such publications to the wider population was therefore conducted mainly by foreign residents within the empire.

A subject of particular concern and fear for Abdülhamid II was how domestic events were reflected in the foreign press, and his overriding anxiety about this issue meant that financial payments were made to foreign newspapers and reporters attached to them to ensure that no negative reports of the empire appeared. Unfortunately, this method failed, and indeed led to increasing numbers of damaging news items, with some newspapers even exploiting the situation to blackmail the empire.

Although censorship was officially lifted on July 23, 1908, the new Press Law, which came into effect the following year (on July 29, 1909), continued to impose severe restrictions on the press.

Fatmagül Demirel

Further reading: Donald J. Cioeta, "Ottoman Censorship in Lebanon and Syria, 1876–1908." *International Journal of Middle East Studies* 10, no. 2 (1979): 167–86; Fatmagül Demirel, *II. Abdülhamid Döneminde Sansür* (İstanbul: Bağlam Yayınları, 2007); Johann Strauss, "Printing and Publishing in a Multi-Ethnic Society," in *Late Ottoman Society: The Intellectual Legacy*, edited by Elisabeth Özdalga (London: Routledge Curzon, 2005), 225–253; İpek Yosmaoğlu, "Chasing the Printed World: Press Censorship in the Ottoman Empire, 1876–1913." *Turkish Studies Association Journal* 27, no. 1–2 (2003): 15–50.

ceramics Ceramics may be defined as vessels and other items made from clay and heated to a high temperature to create a durable, watertight material. These are often glazed and embellished. Ceramics was one of the most important and highly developed branches of art in the Islamic word. Ottoman ceramists produced a range of products that display a distinctive aesthetic evolution. Key to the development of Ottoman ceramics were the workshops at Iznik (Nicaea). These underwent a quality change in the late 15th century following the settlement there of ceramic masters from Tabriz, who may have arrived via EDIRNE. Instead of the rough red-clay vessels with a monochrome glaze that these workshops had hitherto produced, there now appeared vessels made from fine white clay rich in silica and embellished with painted motifs beneath a colorless and transparent glaze.

A major reason for the choice of Iznik as a supplier of ceramic products to the sultan's court was that it lay nearer to the capital, ISTANBUL, than did Kütahya, another major center of ceramic production. From the last quarter of the 15th century onward, increasingly close links were established between the Iznik potters and the TOPKAPI PALACE's *nakkaşhane* (painters' workshop), which was established by Sultan MEHMED II (r. 1444–46; 1451–81). This studio played a singular role in the development of classic Ottoman art. The stylistic trends and decorative motifs worked out by the select team of highly trained masters working there were used not only in ceramics but also in almost every branch of the arts. The styles developed in the *nakkaşhane* can be seen in Iznik products from the beginning of the 16th century.

CERAMIC WALL TILES

The embellishment of the exterior and interior surfaces of buildings has a long tradition in Islamic art. The earliest architectural relics from the Samarra palace of the caliphs of BAGHDAD date from the first half of the ninth century. The origins of Ottoman wall tile production can be traced to a number of factors. Along with continuing local traditions, Seljuk buildings covered with wall tiles clearly had an effect. Nevertheless, new types of wall tile appeared during the first half of the 15th century in the territories of Anatolia, SYRIA, and EGYPT. This was in all likelihood occasioned by the release and dispersion in 1411 of the master ceramists gathered together in Samarkand (now in Uzbekistan) by TIMUR (r. 1370–1405). The work of these masters is connected with the so-called international Timurid style, which features motifs adopted from Chinese and Islamic art and which is evident on the wall tiles of 12 structures from the first half of the 15th century spread across Anatolia, Syria, and Egypt.

Under Sultan MEHMED I (r. 1413–21), work began on the Yeşil (green) Cami and Türbe in BURSA, the first Ottoman capital. The head of the team that made the tile coverings for these two structures (which were finished in 1424) was Ali ibn Ilyas, a Bursa man who had spent some years in Timur's capital, Samarkand. The Yeşil Cami and Türbe exhibit close kinship with a number of buildings in Samarkand. Another factor was the appearance in Bursa at this time of masters from Tabriz. The ceramists who made the tiles for the Yeşil Cami describe themselves—in the inscription above the mihrab (a niche or blind arch in the wall of a mosque indicating the direction of MECCA)—as coming from the city of Tabriz. It is in the meeting of these two elements in Bursa that Ottoman tile manufacturing has its origins. From the first decades of the 15th century, itinerant Tabriz potters played a significant role in wall tile production in Anatolia, Syria, and Egypt.

From Bursa, the Ottoman capital moved to Edirne, and the technique, shape, and motifs of the tiles on the mosque built there in 1435 for Sultan MURAD II (r. 1421–44; 1446–51) show a close kinship with those from Persian workshops. Featuring motifs of Chinese origin painted in blue and black beneath the glaze, the hexagonal tiles on this mosque can be linked with tiles on the mausoleum in DAMASCUS that were made by Tabriz masters for the Mamluk governor (Ghars ad-Din Khalil al Tawrizi) in 1430. The use of a white-colored clay rich in silica was likewise a technological innovation of Persian origin. The tiles on Edirne's Üç Şerefeli Cami (1438–48) can be linked to work by a group of these same masters. The year 1500 saw Tabriz masters already well established at Iznik.

IZNIK CERAMICS

During the first half of the 16th century, Iznik and Kütahya seem to have been equally important as centers of ceramic arts, but Iznik's proximity to Istanbul and its close contacts with the court workshops there resulted in its pulling ahead of Kütahya to become the most important ceramic workshop in the empire. The work of the respective centers is usually identified by scholars on the basis of the features of two important pieces produced in Kütahya: a spouted jug from 1510 and a flask made in 1529. The decoration, now known as the Abraham of Kütahya style, features ornamental motifs of stylized lotus buds and lotus flowers on branches with meandering tendrils and long leaves that frequently end in a sharp point. To this pattern are often added cloud motifs adopted from Chinese art. The Kütahya flask is in the Tuğrakeş spiralis style (formerly called the Golden Horn style), which takes its name from the sultan's ornamented TUĞRA, or monogram, and is decorated in a style reminiscent of the tuğra's ornamentation. The tuğra itself contained the words "Ever Victorious"; on it artists embellished the name of the monarch, the name of his father, and the background of the letters with finely drawn meandering tendrils supplied with tiny leaves and flowers.

By the early 1500s, Iznik had already become the main supplier of ceramics to the ruling house. For example, the tiles for the reconstruction in the 1510s of the Şehzade (Prince) Mustafa and Şehzade Mahmud tombs (türbes) in Bursa were made in Iznik, as were those for the Yeni Valide Mosque (1522–23) at Manisa (20 miles northeast of IZMIR) and the Çoban Mustafa Pasha türbe (1528–29) at Gebze (southeast of Istanbul on the northeastern coast of the Sea of Marmara). Other examples of Iznik work are the tile panels—painted in the famous Persian saz style—that embellish the facade of the Topkapı Palace's Sünnet or Circumcision Room.

From the late 15th century onward, data indicate that Iznik products were used at the Topkapı Palace itself. Two are mentioned in a treasury inventory from 1496, and 11 feature in a treasury inventory from 1505. In 1582 Sultan MURAD III (r. 1574–95) organized a huge celebration to which many European ambassadors were invited. At a banquet held during the festivities, approximately 1,000 Iznik vessels were used. It was, perhaps, no coincidence that the fashion in Europe for Iznik ceramics began soon after these celebrations. By way of Venetian and Genoese traders, Iznik items reached not only Italy, but also GERMANY and ENGLAND. Plates made in Iznik and embellished with European coats of arms make reference to customers in Italy and DALMATIA. Especially favored were jugs, which were supplied with metal covers made in European workshops. One such cover (now in the city of Halle, Germany) once belonged to Elector Johann Friedrich of Brandenburg. Although the jug itself has been lost or destroyed, the inscription on the remaining cover proudly proclaims that it was made in Nicaea (now Iznik) and was brought to Halle in 1582.

From the 1560s onward, Iznik ceramics production felt the impact of Kara Memi, head of the nakkaşhane at that time. It was he who worked out the so-called four flowers style, which featured the tulip, the carnation, the rose, and the hyacinth. The plum blossom was added later. The finest pieces in this style recall the mood of gardens in bloom. In some cases the flowers were arranged in a symmetrical picture; other pieces depicted a garden through which wind was blowing, with stems bending this way and that, and with some of them broken. Of course, nakkaşhane motifs used earlier did not disappear entirely. The so-called saz style, which originated in Persia, lived on for many decades; indeed, it was often used in combination with the four flowers style.

In the covering of surfaces, designs consisting of a number of different tiles were executed (tile panels). The technological innovations developed at this time were just as important. Traditional blue and white painting on the Chinese pattern beneath a colorless glaze now gave way to more vivid coloration. The greatest example of technical bravura was the use of bole red in relief-like application. On pieces made during the second half of the 16th century, the use of cobalt blue, bole red, turquoise, and dark green was characteristic. The background was white or cobalt blue.

The finest creations of the classic era of Iznik ceramics production from this period are to be seen on the most important Istanbul buildings of the second half of the century: the Süleymaniye Mosque (1557), the tombs of Sultan SÜLEYMAN I (r. 1520–66) and his wife Hurrem Sultan (1566 and 1558 respectively), the mosque of Rüstem Pasha (1561), and the Selimiye Mosque in EDIRNE (1569–75).

DAMASCUS CERAMICS

As a result of building operations begun there in the 1550s (the heyday of Iznik production), ceramic art in Damascus underwent significant development. The local pottery industry received a powerful boost when a team of potters led by Abdullah Tabrizi chose to work in ALEPPO and Damascus following completion of the repairs to the Dome of the Rock in Jerusalem, in which stencils had been used extensively. This technique was then employed on the tile panels on the Great Mosque in Aleppo as well as on a number of Ottoman edifices in Damascus. These include a complex of buildings named after Sultan Süleyman—the Takya al-Sulaymaniya (1554–60)—and the madrasa (1566–67) erected by Sultan SELIM II (r. 1566–74).

After this, however, a series of tile coverings was made using a new technique: the underglaze painting technique developed in Iznik. Initially, the stock of motifs on these tiles followed classic Ottoman examples, but from the end of the century onward the Damascus masters, having broken with the Iznik originals, introduced a looser, freer manner of depiction, one that often showed living creatures, among them birds and fish. Nevertheless, from a technological standpoint, these masters were never able to match the brilliant green and the relief-like bole red characteristic of Iznik products. The colors used on Damascus tiles continued to be blue, turquoise, manganese purple, and flat green.

After the end of the 16th century, a fundamental change took place. The last major wall tile order from a ruler was for 20,000 tiles for the Sultan Ahmed Mosque (1609–1616) in Istanbul. During the 17th century, output at Iznik fell off. Characteristic of this new age was the covering of a given surface with tiles that were all the same and not with tile panels made up of different tiles. Technical execution, too, became less exacting: the brilliant glaze of the classic period became shabby and the earlier variety of colors disappeared, yielding place to blue and turquoise. Nevertheless, in the first half of the 17th century important creations were still being made. Examples are the Topkapı Palace's Revan Pavilion (1635) and Baghdad Pavilion (1637–1639). Visiting Iznik in 1648, the much-quoted Ottoman traveler and writer EVLIYA ÇELEBI mentioned that just nine workshops were in operation. This contrasts with the 300 active a century earlier. According to some, output remained steady in the first half of this century, although quality declined, with simplification taking place on the artistic and technological levels alike.

In 1724, with the help of masters brought from Iznik, the Tekfursaray ceramics workshop was founded in Istanbul. However, despite every effort to prevent it, the leading role in ceramics production passed not to Istanbul but to Iznik's old rival, Kütahya.

Ibolya Gerelyes

Further reading John Carswell, "Ceramics," in *Tulips, Arabesques and Turbans: Decorative Arts from the Ottoman Empire,* edited by Yanni Petsopoulos (New York: Abbeville, 1982), 73–121; John Carswell, *İznik Pottery* (London: British Museum Press, 1998); Nurhan Atasoy, Julian Raby, and Yanni Petsopoulos, *İznik, the Pottery of Ottoman Turkey* (London: Alexandria, 1994).

Cezzar Ahmed Pasha (Cezzar Ahmet Pasha; Djezzar Pasha) (d. 1804) (r. 1777–1804) *warlord and governor of Acre*   Cezzar Ahmed Pasha was a Bosnian adventurer who became the dominant political personality in SYRIA in the last quarter of the 18th century. His greatest triumph was in 1799 when, from his fortress in the town of ACRE, he stalled the advance of NAPOLEON BONAPARTE. Ahmed left his native Bosnia and, like many other young Muslim men, sought his fortune in EGYPT, where wealth and opportunity abounded. There he gained employment as a hired gun in the household of Bulutkapan Ali Bey in the 1760s. In that role, he dealt ruthlessly with the BEDOUINS of the Libyan Desert who were in rebellion over taxes imposed upon them by his master Ali Bey. It was they who gave him his nickname, Cezzar (the Butcher), for the execution of dozens of Bedouin tribesmen.

In the political vacuum created after the death in 1775 of ZAHIR AL-UMAR, the chieftain of the Ziyadina clan who had dominated what is today northern Israel for almost half a century, Cezzar Ahmed sought to ingratiate himself to Sultan ABDÜLHAMID I (r. 1774–1789) by reasserting the sultan's authority in the port city of Acre. He was rewarded in 1777 with the governorship of the Lebanese province of Sidon, a position he held until his death. Although the authorities in ISTANBUL feared that he aimed to establish his autonomy from the empire, as his former master in Egypt had done, Cezzar Ahmed was able to secure the governorship of DAMASCUS at several different times, with his longest tenure in that office lasting from 1790 until 1795. Through his abilities to defeat the rebellious DRUZE and Shii clans of southern LEBANON, and by providing local security and enabling the uninterrupted flow of taxes to Istanbul, Cezzar Ahmed simply made himself too valuable for Istanbul to remove. Nonetheless, the Ottoman government remained wary and tried to remove him from power whenever possible. Sensing his vulnerability, Cezzar Ahmed chose to remain in heavily fortified Acre even when he held the governorship of Damascus, and did not take up permanent residence in that city.

In a century when locally prominent families, the AYAN, dominated the politics of Syria, Cezzar Ahmed was a consummate outsider, being a non-Arab without a large extended family to support him. Having lived in Egypt and risen through the ranks in a Mamluk household there, he sought to replicate a similar patron-client relationship in Acre with his own MAMLUKS, who remained subordinate to him and under his direct command, while sometimes holding governorships in Tyre and TRIPOLI.

Learning from the mistakes of Zahir al-Umar, Cezzar Ahmed was careful to keep himself in good graces with the sultan and his court. His two main rivals for control of southern Syria were the AL-AZM FAMILY, whose members frequently filled the governorship of Damascus, and the SHIHAB FAMILY in the Lebanese mountains. Although the two families often worked together against his rising political power, Cezzar Ahmed usually held the upper hand due to his wealth and his phalanx of hired men.

Cezzar Ahmed's moment in the international spotlight came in 1799 when he was able to withstand the siege of Acre by Napoleon Bonaparte, albeit aided by an outbreak of PLAGUE that decimated the French ranks. Napoleon's forces had quickly dispatched the Mamluks in Egypt the year before, and the French general had assumed that the Ottoman Empire would offer no stiffer resistance. But Cezzar Ahmed's stubborn refusal to surrender, added to the harassment his forces were suffering from the British fleet in the eastern Mediterranean, forced Napoleon to reconsider his plans for empire in the Middle East, and he returned to Egypt. Napoleon left Egypt not long after his less-than-triumphant campaign in Syria, but his forces stayed on to occupy the country until 1801 when a combined British-Ottoman force secured their surrender.

Bruce Masters

Further reading: Thomas Philipp, *Acre: The Rise and Fall of a Palestinian City, 1730–1831* (New York: Columbia University Press, 2001).

Chaldeans *See* NESTORIANS.

charity Charity touched most people in the Ottoman Empire, as either donors or recipients, whether in the form of small individual acts of spontaneous generosity, regular distributions at holidays or celebrations, or through the social services offered by a public foundation (*WAQF*). Considered equally as charity were alms given to beggars, food distributed irrespective of economic need on festivals or to mark particular celebrations, or the shelter afforded by a mosque or Sufi convent. Almost any occasion, sacred or secular, might be accompanied by the beneficent distribution of money, food, clothing, or other benefits. Yet while charity appears to have been a universal practice in the Ottoman Empire, each action acquired social, cultural, and political meaning within the context of its specific occasion and the individual donor and recipient involved.

The religious traditions of Muslims, who made up the majority of Ottoman subjects, as well as those of the Jewish and Christian minorities, encouraged beneficence to the weak and the poor. Giving alms (*zakat*) is required of all Muslims who possess more than the minimum necessary for subsistence, and the Quran repeatedly reminds believers that prayer and almsgiving are fundamental aspects of belief. Alms are due from money earned in order to remove the taint of profit from the sum remaining. In addition, voluntary giving (*sadaqah*) is recommended emphatically as a way for believers to approach God and to atone for transgressions in the hopes of reaching Paradise after death. Traditions about the Prophet Muhammad (*hadith*) make it clear that anyone, even the poor, can give charity, if only by offering a blessing.

Charitable practice as advocated by Muslim belief and religious texts was reinforced for the Ottomans through other traditions. Philanthropic donations by the Christian rulers of the BYZANTINE EMPIRE, which preceded the Ottomans in Anatolia, supported a variety of charitable good works including hospices for travelers, hospitals, and facilities for the elderly and orphans, and these institutions left an influential imprint in the central Ottoman lands. Following in the tradition of the Byzantines, the Muslim Seljuk rulers of Anatolia (*see* SELJUKS) established charitable endowments that sustained immense khans or caravansarays along the trade routes, as well as mosques, colleges or madrasas, and hospitals in Ottoman cities. Long-standing habits of generous hospitality were a legacy of the Turkic nomadic predecessors of the Ottomans, as well as the contemporary practice of Kurdish, Turkoman, and Arab tribes within the empire. In 14th-century Anatolia, the North African traveler Ibn Battuta noted (and enjoyed) the competition between *ahis* (guild-like brotherhoods) for the privilege of hosting travelers in their towns.

Under the Ottomans, distributions of material goods as well as favors of protection and promotion created widespread patronage networks of power and interdependence throughout the empire. Together, sincere faith, impulses to hospitality, and patronage deriving from political, economic, or social motivations all inspired similar kinds of actions, overlapping both materially and symbolically, which could be labeled "charity," depending on the circumstances and on the different perspectives of donors, recipients, and observers. Individual donations of money, food, clothing, or shelter were probably the most prevalent forms of charity among the Ottomans, as in most societies. Such acts, however, left few and unsystematic traces and are largely impossible to recover or to quantify historically. References to individual generosity, mostly of noteworthy persons such as sultans, imperial women, and high-ranking officials, are scattered throughout the chronicle accounts of Ottoman historians. From them can be derived a representative if incomplete catalog of charitable institutions and deeds. For example, the 15th-century Ottoman historian Aşıkpaşazade lists the works of the early sultans. He claims that Sultan ORHAN (r. 1324–62) built the first Ottoman public kitchen in Iznik (Nicaea, in northwestern Anatolia), adding the anecdote—possibly true, possibly a literary topos—that Orhan lit the first fire with his own hands. A contemporary biography of the late 16th-century imperial architect Mehmed Agha offered a portrait of private beneficence. Mehmed Agha's biographer praised the generous and unpublicized contributions of his patron, which were mostly in the form of small gifts to the needy people and regularly feeding a variety of people from his own kitchen.

Endowments, or *waqfs*, were often the most prominent and visible form of charity, established according to specific conditions under Muslim law (SHARIA). Large and small property owners could make endowments by donating some kind of freehold property, the income from which would sustain a defined purpose. Revenues derived from the property—such as taxes on agricultural lands, rents from houses, shops, or bathhouses, or cash loaned out at interest (a unique feature of Ottoman endowments)—were directed to support specified institutions or beneficiaries, such as mosques, schools, hospitals, hospices, public kitchens, roadside fountains, fortresses, bridges, birdfeeders, neighborhood tax-paying funds, dowry funds, and private family foundations. All were established and sustained with the intention that they last for eternity; in reality, some of them functioned for hundreds of years, while others were defunct within a generation. Revenue-producing properties might include as little as one room in a house or as much as the extensive agricultural lands, urban markets, and dwellings needed to sustain a mosque and all its subsidiary buildings and activities. Any purpose, as long as it did not contradict basic Muslim principles, was a legitimate beneficiary of an endowment. Thus Christians and JEWS also made endowments according to Muslim law that supported community services such as soup kitchens or schools, although they could not make endowments for churches or synagogues.

The great mosque complexes in the imperial capitals of BURSA, EDIRNE, and ISTANBUL, as well as those in smaller cities and towns, were all established as charitable endowments. Each mosque complex formed the nucleus of an urban neighborhood or town. They established spaces for ritual and social services and the money to pay their staff, offered clean water, and were often planted with shade trees and a garden. The endowed revenues of such complexes might be periodically reinforced by direct imperial contributions of cash or the endowment of additional properties. The Süleymaniye mosque complex in the center of the old city of Istanbul epitomizes such complexes, containing a huge congregational mosque (*cami*), colleges (madrasas) for each of the four Muslim schools of law, a primary school (*mekteb*), public kitchen (*imaret*), hospice (*tabhane*), hospital (*bimarhane*) with a medical school, public toilets, and the tombs of the founder, Sultan SÜLEYMAN I (r. 1520–66), and his wife Hurrem Sultan (d. 1558). Thousands of people could pray together inside the mosque, while the public kitchen fed over 1,000 persons daily including the staff of the complex, the students and teachers in the schools, poor people from the neighborhood, and travelers. Education was free for those who qualified for admission, while the hospital took no fees from patients, although people able to afford a private doctor were usually treated at home.

Unlike informal donations, endowments generated extensive written and material records as testimony of charitable practice, making them accessible subjects of historical study. Foundation deeds, account ledgers, imperial orders, and the records of local judicial proceedings all preserve myriad details (if not always systematic histories) of the establishment and management of thousands of endowments around the empire. From these it becomes clear that the founders were men and women from every part of the property-owning classes, urban and rural alike, and that the endowments were integral to the local economies as employers, consumers, suppliers, borrowers, and sources of small loans.

Endowments, and charitable endeavors in general, offered women an important means to participate in public political and social spheres. The mothers, wives, and sisters of sultans as well as many other property-owning women made endowments in their own names and supported the same kinds of institutions already mentioned. Kösem Sultan (d. 1651), the mother of sultans MURAD IV (r. 1623–40) and IBRAHIM I (r. 1640–48), endowed a large CARAVANSARY that included a mosque in the central commercial area of Istanbul. Turhan Sultan, mother of Sultan MEHMED IV (r. 1648–87), endowed two fortresses at the entrance to the Dardanelles as well as the large Yeni Cami mosque in Eminönü, Istanbul.

Making endowments enabled individuals to channel funds toward purposes they chose from a range of goals permitted by sharia, mostly considered as contributing to public welfare (*maslaha*) broadly defined. For sultans and their households, the *waqfs* were an important and highly visible means of establishing legitimacy and reinforcing popular support by demonstrating strength, prosperity, and a commitment to the public welfare of Ottoman subjects. Imperial women were important in getting this message out, with the advantage that their efforts might not be misinterpreted as publicizing their own personal strength at the expense of the sultan's, as might happen with a prince of the dynasty.

All charity, however, contained some message about the status of both giver and recipient, no matter what their initial social standing in relation to one another might be. The contrast between endowment making and more discreet forms of charity, such as those of Mehmed Agha, may reflect the character of the donor. Endowments provided other advantages to their founders, such as the ability to preserve the unity of property and moneys that would otherwise one day be divided according to Muslim laws of inheritance, or the possibility of protecting wealth from confiscation, a not uncommon risk among holders of high office. Charitable acts in general were performed for a variety of reasons: to attain Paradise after death, to intercede on behalf of those who had died, to ward off calamity, to promote recovery from illness, to celebrate festivals, or to mark noteworthy events.

Beneficence took many forms, which are most easily reconstructed from what we know of the lives of the wealthy. Not surprisingly, the distributions of the sultans on the occasion of celebrations such as the circumcision of an Ottoman prince or the wedding of an imperial daughter (and perhaps those of some high-ranking dignitaries) inspired written and sometimes illustrated accounts. At these festivities, banquets were offered for high-ranking officials and the poor alike. Together with the princes, the sultans sponsored the circumcisions of hundreds of poor boys, offering them new clothing and a gift of money. Distributions of coins took place as part of the imperial procession to and from mosques where the sultans attended Friday noon prayers. The return of the victorious army from campaign was another occasion for distributing largesse. Women from the imperial household had their own beneficent projects. For example, the queen mother Kösem Sultan annually sent money to be distributed to the poor of MECCA and MEDINA, as well as going out incognito in Istanbul to arrange the release from prison of debtors and criminals by paying what was required.

The historical record of the Ottomans contains much more evidence for voluntary giving than for the canonical obligation to give alms. References to almsgiving in discussions of Muslim law or in formal legal opinions (fatwa) make it clear that Ottoman Muslims were aware of the obligation, yet the overall impression is that payment was a matter of individual action and conscience, not regulated formally by any state apparatus.

Sufis—Muslim mystics also called dervishes—were prominent beneficiaries of charitable donations in the Ottoman Empire. Many of the Sufi orders (see SUFISM) encouraged their adherents to give up material possessions and sustain themselves exclusively from the donations of patrons, including Ottoman sultans as well as people of more modest means. For this reason, the Sufis were also referred to regularly as fakir (poor). Some orders had well-endowed zaviyes (convents or lodges) that could feed and host the needy as well as their adherents, while also providing space for Sufi ceremonies and teaching. Thus Sufis were often both recipients and benefactors, distributing the revenues of their zaviyes and their begging to the needy.

For most of the Ottoman era, charity was an individual practice, no matter how large or small the donation. Through the reign of ABDÜLHAMID II (r. 1876–1909), sultans continued to use charitable donations as a means to legitimate their rule, reinforcing the idea of the sultan as provider and protector of all his subjects, inspired by religious obligation as well as imperial tradition. Only in the later 19th century does the repertoire of charitable practice change substantially. As well as continuing to build mosques and sponsor mass circumcision ceremonies for tens of thousands of boys, Abdülhamid II also established a large orphanage in Istanbul. Both circumcisions and the orphanage were advertised as adhering to modern methods for the benefit of the children as well as society as a whole.

Beneficent associations also appeared, among the first of which was the Ottoman Red Crescent Society. The society began its activities in the wake of the brutally destructive CRIMEAN WAR, but grew only in fits and starts until the turn of the century. The Young Turk Revolution of 1908 (see YOUNG TURKS) provided further impetus to replace imperial endeavors with state-sponsored efforts and institutions, although these were soon overwhelmed by the humanitarian challenges of the BALKAN WARS and WORLD WAR I, forcing the reopening of institutions such as public kitchens and providing the impetus for new kinds of charitable associations such as the Children's Protection Society.

Charity in the Ottoman Empire was far from uniform, as practices varied according to local conditions and customs. The charitable impulse, whether the result of religious faith or personal self-interest, was the major form of emergency relief and welfare sustenance for those who slipped below the level of independent subsistence, for whatever reason. Moreover, many charitable or philanthropic endeavors in the Ottoman Empire, as in the contemporary world, benefited people of means as well as those described as poor or destitute, particularly in large public endowments such as mosques and fountains.

Nor was charity without its critics. For example, the late 16th-century bureaucrat and intellectual, Mustafa Ali, railed against sultans who made charitable endowments without earning the means to do so (because endowments were supposed to be based on personal wealth and not from the state treasury). Others questioned the sincerity of people who made endowments that served only their families. Charity exploited economic strength to create and maintain social and political hierarchies. Even modest neighborhood distributions ultimately reinforced positions of relative power and weakness. Exclusion from beneficent distributions was a clear signal of truly marginal or outsider status. Yet the manifold forms of charity supported by Ottoman culture were also constructive and flexible, producing some of the empire's most glorious monuments.

Amy Singer

Further reading: Michael Bonner, Mine Ener, and Amy Singer, eds., *Poverty and Charity in Middle Eastern Contexts* (Albany: State University of New York Press, 2003); Leslie Peirce, *The Imperial Harem: Women and Sovereignty in the Ottoman Empire* (New York: Oxford University Press, 1993); Amy Singer, *Constructing Ottoman Beneficence: An Imperial Soup Kitchen in Jerusalem* (Albany: State University of New York Press, 2002); T. H. Weir and A. Zysow, "*Sadaka*," in *Encyclopaedia of Islam*, 2nd ed., vol. 8 (Leiden: Brill, 1960–) 708–16; A. Zysow, "*Zakāt*," in *Encyclopaedia of Islam*, 2nd ed., vol. 11 (Leiden: Brill, 1960–), 406–22; Rudolph Peters et al., "*Wakf*," in *Encyclopaedia of Islam*, 2nd ed., vol. 11 (Leiden: Brill, 1960–), 59–99.

Christians *See* ARMENIAN APOSTOLIC CHURCH; BULGARIAN ORTHODOX CHURCH; COPTS; GREEK ORTHODOX CHURCH; JACOBITES; MARONITES; missionaries; NESTORIANS; SERBIAN ORTHODOX CHURCH.

cizye *See* JIZYA.

coffee/coffeehouses Sometime in the 15th century, the people of YEMEN discovered that the beans of the coffee plant could be roasted, ground, and boiled in water to produce a stimulating drink. Ethiopians claim that the happy accident occurred in their country first, but it was from Yemen that coffee beans were first exported out of the Red Sea region, and that country was associated with its production in the Ottoman geographical imagination. According to Muslim tradition, the first people to use the drink were Sufis seeking to stay up all night to prolong their *dhikr*, the ritual of invoking God. Once discovered, the custom of coffee drinking quickly spread to the holy city of MECCA. From there, returning pilgrims carried it

to the Egyptian cities of CAIRO and DAMASCUS, and by the middle of the 16th century, to the center of the Ottoman empire in ISTANBUL. From that point on, coffee was an empire-wide phenomenon, and an addiction that was indulged by sultans and commoners alike.

The spread of coffee drinking and coffeehouses did not go unopposed, however. Muslim legal scholars (ULEMA) were initially uncertain as to whether the drink, which was clearly a stimulant, was legal. To some, it seemed that it strayed into the category of alcoholic drinks or narcotics, both of which Islamic law forbids the faithful to imbibe. In addition, coffeehouses became gathering places for unsavory types and were viewed with suspicion as providing the setting for immoral and seditious behavior. The use of tobacco, which was entering the Ottoman Empire at roughly the same time, also raised eyebrows. Sultan MURAD IV (r. 1623–40) outlawed both coffeehouses and the smoking of tobacco in 1633, but that action had no long-lasting effect on his subjects' consumption of either substance.

By the middle of the 17th century, coffeehouses were found in every Ottoman city, and even some villages boasted of having one. Although there was a long-established tradition of taverns in the Ottoman Empire, because they were owned and operated by Christians, Muslims were suspicious of them as places of immorality. The proliferation of coffeehouses thus created a social space for Muslim men that had previously been lacking, although their appearance did not diminish the appeal of taverns to those less concerned with religious propriety. The 17th-century Ottoman travel author, EVLIYA ÇELEBI, described coffeehouses in major cities, including some that could serve up to 1,000 patrons at a time. In addition to providing coffee and tobacco, usually consumed in water pipes (*nargiles*), coffeehouses were used as artistic venues by storytellers, puppeteers, and musicians who provided entertainment to the customers. As the authorities had feared, coffeehouses did provide a forum for public political discussions and for the circulation of rumors, some of them seditious. Coffeehouses were also frequently the starting point for urban protests and riots.

Yemen enjoyed a monopoly on coffee production, bringing the region immense wealth and making its chief port, Mocha, a household name in the West. Cairo, on the other hand, served as the center for the coffee TRADE and the profits gained from this trade did much to enhance its commercial position in the eastern Mediterranean. But by the early 18th century Europeans had managed to introduce coffee plants, smuggled out of Ethiopia, into their colonies in the Caribbean Sea; by the end of the century, beans from the Americas began to displace those from Yemen, even in the markets of the Ottoman Empire. Indeed, by the end of the 19th century,

Brazil had become as synonymous with coffee in many dialects of Arabic as Mocha had once been in the languages of the West. The popularity of coffeehouses did not, however, abate.

Bruce Masters

Further reading: Ralph Hattox, *Coffee and Coffeehouses: The Origins of a Social Beverage in the Medieval Near East* (Seattle: University of Washington Press, 1985).

commerce *See* TRADE.

Committee of Union and Progress Originally founded as a student organization, the revolutionary political group known as the Ottoman Committee of Union and Progress (CUP) would go through many incarnations and divisions between its inception on June 2, 1889 and its demise in 1926. During this period, the CUP embraced a variety of political ideals, but generally inclined toward secularization, westernization, Turkism, and centralization. The founders of modern TURKEY, including the first three presidents serving from 1923 to 1960, were former CUP members.

The CUP was originally founded as a student organization at the Royal Medical Academy in ISTANBUL during the reign of Sultan ABDÜLHAMID II (1876–1909). The founders initially named their organization the Ottoman Union Committee (İttihad-ı Osmanî Cemiyeti). Colleges in the Ottoman capital were hotbeds of anti-regime activity during this period, and the organization quickly gained popularity among students in the Royal Military Academy and in the Royal School of Administration. After a series of meetings held in various places, the organization's leaders, known as the YOUNG TURKS, prepared bylaws for the society. Starting in 1893, despite various arrests at colleges and other strong measures taken by the government against the organization, the committee leaders succeeded in recruiting influential members of the ULEMA and bureaucrats and transformed their organization into a serious clandestine political society. In 1895, leaders of the committee contacted Ahmed Rıza, a notable opponent of the regime who had taken refuge in Paris. After long negotiations, Ahmed Rıza joined the committee as its leader in Europe. As a devoted adherent of positivism he asked the founders to rename the organization Order and Progress, adopting the motto of famed French positivist thinker Auguste Comte (1798–1857). The founders insisted on keeping the term "union" and thus the committee settled on the name Ottoman Union and Progress. In 1895, the organization published its regulations and initiated two journals, *Meşveret* and *Mechveret Supplément Français*, in Paris.

In 1895–96, the CUP established an influential branch controlled by ulema in CAIRO as well as a network in BULGARIA and Romania and many branches throughout the empire. During the same period, supporters of two leaders of the committee, Ahmed Rıza and Mehmed Murad (Mizancı), entered into a bitter power struggle that resulted in Ahmed Rıza's expulsion from the organization. The failure of a coup attempt initiated by the Istanbul center in 1896, the breakdown of the Syrian network of the organization in 1897, and the peace campaign of the sultan, who was trying to cash in on the Ottoman victory over Greeks, brought about a near collapse of the organization in July 1897. Many leaders of the CUP returned to the empire in response to the sultan's promise of general reforms and political amnesty. Opposition activities were continued, however, by Ahmed Rıza, his followers, and many doctors who escaped from the locations within the empire to which they had been banished. Between 1897 and 1899, a group led by medical doctors and Ahmed Rıza fought over the control of the committee, and in the end Ahmed Rıza and his faction won control of major branches within the organization, while the positivist Young Turk leader and his followers worked almost independently in Paris.

In 1899 many leading Ottoman bureaucrats, led by Damad Mahmud Pasha, one of the brothers-in-law of the sultan, and İsmail Kemal, a former governor, joined the organization. This produced a committee that worked as an umbrella organization of loosely affiliated groups. Some of the factions within the CUP went as far as forming semi-independent societies under its umbrella. There were six major factions within the organization during this period. Ahmed Rıza led the first faction, advocating a constitution and parliament for all Ottomans, as well as positivism as the prospective ideology of a reformed Ottoman state. The second faction, led by pro-British former high-ranking statesmen, tried to secure foreign intervention to change the regime in the empire. A third faction consisted of medical doctors and college students who promoted a scientist program. A fourth faction, called the activists, advanced anarchist ideas and praised bloodshed in various journals and appeals. A fifth faction was composed of those ulema who became members of the committee and had a religious agenda. Finally the Balkan network established by teachers and artisans adopted a more conservative agenda compared to those promoted by branches in Europe.

The Congress of Ottoman Liberals that convened in Paris in 1902 marked the end of the CUP organization. The majority group that emerged at this congress established a new committee called the Ottoman Freedom-lovers Society and strove to carry out a coup with the help of the British. The minority group composed of the followers of Ahmed Rıza and the activists formed a new organization but decided not to use the title CUP for their new committee. In 1903 some members of the old organization claimed ownership of the CUP, albeit for a brief period.

In late 1905 a leading Young Turk, Dr. Bahaeddin Şakir, attempted to reorganize the alliance between the activists and the followers of Ahmed Rıza. After lengthy negotiations he transformed the alliance into an activist organization under the name of the Ottoman Committee of Progress and Union (CPU), thereby reclaiming the organization. The committee soon established branches in CRETE, CYPRUS, Bulgaria, Romania, and the Caucasus, as well as a host of branches and cells throughout the empire. In September 1907 the CPU merged with the Ottoman Freedom-lovers Society that had been established by officials and officers in SALONIKA. Both parties agreed to use the name CPU for the new partnership organization. Following the merger, the former CPU center in Paris became the external headquarters and the Ottoman Freedom Society became the internal headquarters of the new organization. The merger provided many new branches and cells in the European provinces. By early 1908 the CPU had approximately 2,000 members in these provinces, an overwhelming number of them officers in the military.

The CPU started its revolutionary activity in June 1908, and on July 23 and 24, the sultan issued an imperial decree ordering the reopening of the Chamber of Deputies. Immediately after this, the organization reverted to its former name, and until the elections held in December and the convening of the chamber, the restored CUP worked as the de facto executive government of the Ottoman state, forming a *comité de salut public*, and served as the major political power broker in the empire. In the meantime, hundreds of CUP branches were established by local leaders. The landslide victory of the CUP in the December elections led to its control of legislature.

By 1910, the number of CUP branches across the empire had multiplied from 83 on the eve of the revolution to 360, while individual membership grew from roughly 2,250 to 850,000; although the CUP had clearly become a mass organization, the extent of central control over this unwieldy structure was debatable. In any case, the provincial appendages of the CUP were largely cut off from the process of policy formulation at the center, and a central committee made all major decisions. As a rule, decisions were made collectively, and shared interest in thwarting individual control of the organization ensured that this practice continued. Certain figures did rise to prominence within the CUP, however. The most important of these were the policy makers and organizers Talat Pasha, Dr. Bahaeddin Şakir, and Dr. Nâzım; military leaders Enver Pasha and Cemal Pasha; organizer of

guilds and cooperatives Kara Kemal Bey; and party ideologue Ziya GÖKALP.

The transformation of the CUP from a clandestine revolutionary committee to a major political power brought about significant changes in its organization. In 1909 the organization was divided into two bodies: the committee (*cemiyet*) and the parliamentary group supporting it, called the party (*fırka*). There was little substance to this distinction, however, as the committee nominated all deputies and senators in its parliamentary faction. In 1913 the CUP expanded its definition of the party to include the committee itself as well as the organization's press organs.

In theory, the General Congress of the CUP constituted the highest decision-making body of the organization. The congress, which met annually, was made up of the members of the central committee, deputies and senators who were CUP members (between 1911 and 1913, only their representatives attended), representatives of the local organizations and clubs, general inspectors, and editors of the committee's official NEWSPAPERS; it appointed the central committee members and revised organizational regulations. In practice, the supreme decision-making organ of the CUP was the central committee—a board of between 7 and 12 individuals (the number fluctuated) that issued directives to the formal institutions of state: the cabinet, the military, and the bureaucracy.

Beneath the central committee lay an elaborately structured hierarchy designed to inflate the organization and create the illusion of mass participation, as well as to promote the entrenchment of the CUP. The central committee presided over a number of special branches that dealt with organizational matters in various sectors. These included special branches devoted to subjects such as women, ulema, provincial centers, local and district centers, and military and civil clubs. In 1913 the CUP was restructured. The general congress was preserved and all deputies and senators were again allowed to attend annual meetings. But in addition, a general assembly was created to coordinate the two main policy aspects of CUP activity: its actions as the supreme governing organization of the state, and its parliamentary activity through party representatives in the chamber of deputies and senate.

The CUP refrained from forming cabinets until 1913, despite providing ministers for key portfolios such as the Ministry of the Interior and the Ministry of Finance. However, with the exception of a brief period between July 1912 and January 1913, the CUP played a decisive role in politics and worked as a parallel government. Following the assassination of Grand Vizier Mahmud Şevket Pasha on June 11, 1913, the CUP also established full control over the government and bureaucracy and, in fact, established one-party rule that lasted until October 1918.

The last CUP General Congress was held in November 1918 and resolved on the abolition of the CUP and the establishment of a new political party named the Renovation Party (Teceddüt Fırkası). In the meantime, major CUP leaders fled abroad. The Ottoman government closed down the Renovation Party in May 1919. The CUP network within the empire nevertheless played a significant role in the organization of the Turkish War of Independence between 1919 and 1922. Although the surviving CUP leaders attempted to revitalize the organization after the nationalist victory and the establishment of the Turkish Republic, the trials of 1926 that followed an attempt to assassinate Mustafa KEMAL ATATÜRK resulted in the complete liquidation of the CUP.

M. Şükrü Hanioğlu

Further reading: M. Şükrü Hanioğlu, *Preparation for a Revolution: The Young Turks, 1902–1908* (New York: Oxford University Press, 2001); M. Şükrü Hanioğlu, *The Young Turks in Opposition* (New York: Oxford University Press, 1995); Erik Jan Zürcher, *The Unionist Factor: The Rôle of the Committee of Union and Progress in the Turkish Nationalist Movement, 1905–1926* (Leiden: Brill, 1984).

concubine *See* HAREM.

condominium Although contemporary Ottoman and European sources suggest that the Ottoman sultans governed as absolute monarchs during the empire's "golden age," from about the 1450s through 1600, in fact, Ottoman power was always limited and a number of factors—the military force of the sultan's opponents, geography, and the strength of pre-Ottoman elites in conquered lands—often forced ISTANBUL into political compromise. One element of this compromise was the sharing of authority between Ottoman rulers and the conquered elite. Known as condominium or joint rule, such a practice was especially visible in the early decades of Ottoman governance and in the frontier provinces, and extended to many aspects of government institutions, including land tenure, taxation, administration, and the judiciary.

In the 15th century the Ottoman government was careful to take account of local balances of power and attempted to win over local secular and religious leaders. Ottoman sultans tried to integrate cooperative groups and individuals belonging to the previous social elites into the privileged Ottoman ruling class (*askeri*). This is borne out by the presence of Christian *timar*-holder *sipahis* or Ottoman "landlords" and various privileged auxiliary military units (*voynuks*, MARTOLOS) both in the Balkans and in the territory of the former Empire of Trebizond (1204–1461), one of the three successor states of the BYZANTINE EMPIRE with its capital in Trabzon

(Trebizond), established after the crusaders temporarily occupied Constantinople in 1204. In many places, old forms of property ownership were adopted and retained. The empire also accommodated the previous systems of agriculture and mining, and it adopted certain forms of taxation and coinage. Similarly, the continuation of pre-Ottoman local communal organizations, and the activity of their leaders (*knezes* and *primikürs*) are well documented in SERBIA, BULGARIA, and GREECE.

The same pragmatism can be seen in eastern Anatolia in the early 16th century. Here, the first Ottoman provincial tax codes (*kanunname*) were often exact copies of the tax regulations that had been introduced by the Akkoyunlus, Dulkadırs, and the Egyptian Mamluks, lords of eastern and southeastern Anatolia before the Ottomans. These pre-Ottoman tax codes, as well as the special regulations that the Ottomans applied to the nomadic Turkoman tribes, preserved pre-Ottoman tribal customs, which often contradicted the Ottoman secular law, or *kanun*. Replacing these regulations with Ottoman tax codes took decades and there remained territories where double taxation was the rule rather than the exception.

The Ottomans were also forced to compromise in their conquest east of the Black Sea in territories of the present-day Caucasian country of Georgia. Following the conquest of these territories, Istanbul left members of the former Georgian ruling families at the head of the newly established Georgian *sancaks* or subprovinces. In some cases, families whose members were still Christians received these territories as family estates. Only later did they convert to Islam, probably in order to ensure that they could keep their lands for themselves and their posterity. In 1578, when the Ottomans established a new province in the region, they appointed the former Georgian prince, Minuchir (who in the meantime had converted to Islam and had taken the name Mustafa) as its first governor or *beylerbeyi*. Together with his brother, who had been given the *sancak* of Oltu (near Erzurum, northeastern Turkey), Minuchir was awarded an Ottoman military fief (*has*). With some exceptions, the new province was administered by the Georgian princes of Samtskhe as hereditary district governors or beys until the mid-18th century. In the Georgian areas of Guria, Imeretia, Mingrelia Svaneti, and Abkhazia, which are mountainous and were thus more difficult to conquer, the Ottomans wisely permitted the rule of vassal Georgian princes, who recognized the authority of the sultan by paying symbolic (though often irregular) tributes.

In the 16th and 17th century in HUNGARY, the military balance of power between the Ottomans and the Habsburgs and the armed strength of the Hungarian garrisons also led to joint rule and taxation. A single village had both an Ottoman and a Hungarian landlord and paid taxes to both. Taxes to the Hungarian landlords were collected more regularly, while state taxes (paid to the fiercely adversarial Habsburg kings of Hungary) and taxes for the Hungarian Catholic and Protestant churches could be collected from only two-thirds of the Ottoman-held territories in the 16th century and from only half of it in the 17th century.

As well as taxation, the condominium also extended to jurisdiction and administration. Whereas in the handful of Ottoman garrison towns in Hungary the KADIS or Ottoman judges administered justice, in the more numerous Hungarian market towns that had no Ottoman garrison, the tasks of maintaining law and order, preventing and investigating crime, and passing judgment remained the prerogatives of the local Hungarian authorities. Towns in Ottoman Hungary obtained the right to impose and administer the death penalty. The municipal magistrates administered the disputes of guilds and artisans as well as matters of probate. They also imposed and collected fines. Although the Ottomans initially rejected the idea that the Hungarian estates might collect taxes and administer justice in Ottoman-held areas, the military balance of power and, above all, the armed strength of the Hungarian border soldiers made this a day-to-day practice over time.

As can be seen in Georgia and Hungary, Istanbul attempted to win over the members of the pre-Ottoman Christian elite and to establish its rule through negotiation, cooperation, and co-optation rather than by force. In eastern Anatolia and in Hungary the Ottoman sultans accepted the condominium, double taxation, and shared judicial jurisdiction. Although the representatives of ISTANBUL, Ottoman judges and *sipahis*, were nearly ubiquitous, when conducting daily business, the Ottoman government had to rely on local authorities, village headmen, "elders," or provincial notables known as AYAN. In Hungary these local authorities were called *bírós* (judge); in the Arab lands, they were known as *rais al-fallahin* (head of the peasants) or *sheikh al-qarya* (elder of the village). In 16th-century Syria-Palestine, the *rais al-fallahin* and the leaders of the Jewish community in Jerusalem (*sheikh al-yahud*), presumably both pre-Ottoman institutions that went back to Egypt's MAMLUK EMPIRE (1250–1517), were essential in administering the day-to-day affairs of the local communities.

When neither the Ottoman authorities nor the indigenous local elites could maintain law and order and provide security and safety for villagers from bandits, robbers, and soldiers, villagers formed their own militias and self-defense organizations. These militia groups—called gatherings of peasants (*parasztvármegye*) in Hungary and *zapis* in territories inhibited by Slavic peoples—provided for villagers' self-defense. In Anatolia, such self-defense organizations were known as *il-erleri*, that is, "the bachelors of the province." Members of such groups were young men from the villages who elected their own leaders (*yiğitbaşı*). Their task was to ensure public order and security in the villages and the surrounding areas.

Apart from geographical constraints and limits arising from overextension, the existing presence of residual powers of this kind from the Habsburg and Safavid Empires constituted the main obstacles to Ottoman central administration in its frontier territories.

Gábor Ágoston

See also ADMINISTRATION, PROVINCIAL.

Further reading: Gábor Ágoston, "A Flexible Empire: Authority and Its Limits on the Ottoman Frontiers." *International Journal of Turkish Studies* 9, no. 1–2 (2003): 15–31; Géza Dávid, "Administration in Ottoman Europe," in *Süleyman the Magnificent and His Age: The Ottoman Empire in the Early Modern World*, edited by Metin Kunt and Christine Woodhead (London: Longman, 1995), 71–90; Amy Singer, *Palestinian Peasants and Ottoman Officials: Rural Administration Around Sixteenth-Century Jerusalem* (Cambridge: Cambridge University Press, 1994).

Congress of Berlin   *See* ENGLAND.

Constantinople   *See* ISTANBUL.

Constantinople, conquest of   The 1453 Ottoman conquest of Constantinople, until that time the capital of the BYZANTINE EMPIRE, was a major historical moment for the peoples of the Balkans, Asia Minor, the Mediterranean, and the BLACK SEA, and affected their lives for centuries to come. To the Byzantines, it meant the end of their 1,000-year-old empire and the symbolic defeat of Christianity. To the Ottomans, it brought military, geopolitical, and economic rewards, as well as political and psychological prestige in both the Muslim and Christian worlds. The conquest eliminated a hostile wedge that had separated the sultan's European and Asian provinces, known as Rumelia and Anatolia. It gave the Ottomans an ideal logistical center for further campaigns against Europe and a commanding position over the trade routes between Asia and Europe, the Black Sea and the Mediterranean. It silenced the opposition of those who had suggested that the plans of MEHMED II (r. 1444–46; 1451–81) to capture Constantinople would trigger yet another Christian crusade against the Ottomans. The conquest strengthened the position of the young Ottoman sultan, who was henceforth known as "Fatih," or "the Conqueror." After the conquest, Mehmed II established the imperial capital in the city. He then used his improved position to embark on a remarkable restructuring of the Ottoman elite and state institutions. Many have argued that the centralized and patrimonial empire that contemporary Ottoman and European observers described in the late 15th and early 16th centuries was born in 1453.

The conquest of Constantinople may be understood as having begun with the second accession of Mehmed II to the Ottoman throne in 1451, for it was at this time that the Ottoman conciliatory policy regarding the Byzantine Empire and Christian Europe practiced in previous decades ended, and the new sultan revived the Ottoman warrior tradition. His first target was the seat of the Byzantine Empire. Constantinople not only separated the sultan's European and Asian provinces, its emperor, Constantine XI Palaiologos (r. 1448–53), also played a crucial role in organizing anti-Ottoman Christian alliances and crusades.

To assume control over the Straits, Mehmed had a fortress built at the narrowest point of the Bosporus. Rumeli Hisarı or the European castle stood opposite Anadolu Hisarı or the Anatolian castle, which had been erected by Sultan BAYEZID I (r. 1389–1402) during the first and prolonged Ottoman siege of Constantinople between 1394 and 1402. With their cannons deployed on the walls of the two castles, the Ottomans sealed off Byzantium, depriving it of reinforcements and supplies.

The Ottomans constructed approximately 16 large and 60 light galleys, 20 horse-ships, and several smaller vessels in their arsenal at Gallipoli (Gelibolu, on the Gallipoli Peninsula in southern European Turkey). The sultan's army of 80,000 to 100,000 men was assembled at EDIRNE, which was then the Ottoman capital. In the Edirne foundry some 60 new guns of various calibers were cast by the sultan's Turkish and European cannon founders. The largest cannon that the Hungarian master Orban made for the sultan fired stone balls weighing 1,300 lbs. (600 kg). It was transported to Constantinople by 60 oxen and 200 men.

For the city's defense, the emperor had some 8,000 Greeks and 2,000 foreigners at his disposal along with some 30,000 to 40,000 civilians. They were joined by some 700 experienced soldiers of the Genoese Giovanni Giustiniani Longo, a celebrated expert in siege warfare and defense. From the south and east Constantinople was protected by the Sea of Marmara, while the Golden Horn, an inlet of the Bosporus, guarded the city's northern side. On April 2, in order to deny the Ottoman fleet access into the Golden Horn, where the walls of the city were the weakest, the Byzantines stretched a boom across the entrance of the harbor. The same day the advance forces of the sultan appeared near the city's western landward walls.

On April 5, Sultan Mehmed II arrived with the rest of his troops and erected his tent opposite the Gate of Saint Romanos, along the western walls of the city. A contemporary account reported that in the first weeks "onslaughts, attacks, bombardment, and general warfare were continuous," but the city stood firm. Ottoman shipboard artillery was ineffective against the tall Christian galleys defending Constantinople from the harbor. According to Mehmed II's Greek chronicler, Kritovoulos, Mehmed, a keen student of military technology, urged his cannon-makers to make a different type of cannon that could fire its shot "to a great height, so that when it came down it would hit the ship." Designed by the sultan, the new weapon, soon to be known as the mortar, sank a Christian ship in the harbor.

On the morning of April 23, the Byzantines noticed with terror that some 70 to 80 smaller Ottoman ships had been lowered into the Golden Horn. Using sheep and ox tallow as lubricants, the Ottomans transported their smaller ships from the Bosporus on rollers along the land route that connected the so called Double Columns (the Beşiktaş and Kabataş districts of the city), with Eyüb. Sultan Mehmed's ingenious maneuver was a serious blow for the Byzantines, who now had to allocate men and resources to defend the walls along the Golden Horn. Ottoman assaults and bombardments continued. Food supplies and ammunition in the besieged city were running low. When it was learned that neither relief forces nor the promised Venetian armada would arrive, the defenders lost hope.

On May 29, shortly after midnight, the last assault began. While the Ottoman shipboard artillery stormed the walls along the Sea of Marmara and the Golden Horn, the army attacked the landward walls. The sultan first sent his irregulars and volunteers against the walls, but the defenders, commanded by the emperor and Giustiniani, drove them back. These were followed by more experienced and disciplined troops, who, according to one eyewitness account, attacked "like lions," but they too were forced to withdraw. At the break of dawn, Mehmed ordered his elite JANISSARIES against the walls. In the midst of the fight Giustiniani was badly wounded and was taken to the harbor to a Genoese ship. Not seeing their general, Giustiniani's men lost their spirit and the Janissaries took advantage of the confusion to force their way through the breaches opened by the constant bombardment. Last seen near the Gate of Saint Romanos, Constantine Palaiologos, the last emperor of the Romans, died as a common soldier, fighting the enemy. Riding on horseback, Sultan Mehmed II entered the city through the very same gate, known to the Ottomans as Topkapı (literally, "cannon gate"). The sultan granted a three-day plunder to his troops. After the plunder, however, Mehmed entrusted the newly appointed Ottoman governor of Constantinople with the reconstruction and repopulation of the city.

Gábor Ágoston

Further reading: Franz Babinger, *Mehmed the Conqueror and His Time*, translated by Ralph Manheim, edited by William C. Hickman (Princeton, N.J.: Princeton University Press,

1992); Kritovoulos, *History of Mehmed the Conqueror*, translated by Charles T. Riggs (Princeton, N.J.: Princeton University Press, 1954); Donald M. Nicol, *The Immortal Emperor: The Life and Legend of Constantine Palaiologos, Last Emperor of the Romans* (Cambridge: Cambridge University Press, 1994); Steven Runciman, *The Fall of Constantinople, 1453* (Cambridge: Cambridge University Press, 1965).

constitution/Constitutional Periods   A constitution is a written document that establishes the basic political and administrative principles of a state and determines the power and duties of governments. Before the 19th century, there was no single document that defined the Ottoman imperial system. Theoretically, the sultan was the only source of legislative and executive power. Sultanic decrees were called KANUN, and at each sultanic ACCESSION AND ENTHRONEMENT, previous *kanuns* became null and void. The only legal limitation on sultanic legislation and execution was Islamic law or SHARIA, which concerns itself primarily with private and criminal law. Thus, until the TANZIMAT reform era (1839–76), the Ottoman Empire did not embrace constitutional government. The 19th century, however, witnessed growing political and social demands. The provincial notables (AYAN) forced MAHMUD II (r. 1808–39) to accept the Sened-i İttifak (Deed of Agreement) in 1808, which sought to restrict the sultan's authority in PROVINCIAL ADMINISTRATION while maintaining the interests of the *ayan*. The two most significant imperial edicts of the Tanzimat—the Imperial Rescript of Gülhane (1839) and the Imperial Rescript of Reforms (1856)—included legal and administrative regulations as an answer to the general discontent concerning arbitrary rule, lack of basic individual rights, and discrimination against non-Muslims. Despite the constitutional character of these documents, they did not define the Ottoman state as a whole and failed to stipulate the powers, limitations, and duties of the government.

On the other hand, separatist developments in peripheral provinces led to increasing autonomy for some populations and prepared the way for a formal constitutional structure. The first constitution within the Ottoman imperial realm was promulgated in WALLACHIA and MOLDAVIA in 1831, followed by SERBIA in 1835. In 1861 the North African region of Tunisia adopted the first constitution of the Islamic world.

The YOUNG OTTOMANS were the first in the empire to publicly advocate a constitution that would limit the absolute rule of the sultan by creating a representative parliament. Reformist statesmen of the period, such as MIDHAT PASHA (1822–83), considered the introduction of a constitutional regime as a way to guarantee the territorial integrity of the empire. The administrative, agricultural, and political upheaval of the early 1870s, combined with the Balkan revolts of 1875–76, created an international crisis, and Midhat Pasha organized a putsch on May 30, 1876. As a result, Sultan ABDÜLAZIZ (r. 1861–76) was dethroned in favor of his more liberal-minded nephew, MURAD V (r. 1876). However, when Murad became unable to rule, he was replaced by his more authoritarian brother, ABDÜLHAMID II (r. 1876–1909). The new sultan, unsympathetic to liberalism, forced Midhat Pasha to change the original constitution into an authoritarian document. The text of this eviscerated constitution, know as Kanun-i Esasi, or Fundamental Law, was inspired by the Belgian constitution of 1831 and the Prussian constitution of 1850. According to this constitution, members of the government were directly appointed by the ruler. The government was thus responsible to the sultan and not to the PARLIAMENT, which could not initiate laws but could merely discuss proposed laws. The sultan also had the absolute right to convene or dissolve the parliament. Making full use of this right, on February 13, 1878, when the most recent of the RUSSO-OTTOMAN WARS ended in Ottoman defeat, Abdülhamid used his power to dissolve the parliament; however, the constitution technically remained in force.

With the Young Turk Revolution of July 24, 1908, Abdülhamid was forced to reconvene the parliament. Abdülhamid was deposed on August 21, 1909, and the authoritarian stipulations of 1876 were amended. These amendments restricted the powers of the sultan, and the parliament became a politically sovereign institution. Ironically, the COMMITTEE OF UNION AND PROGRESS (CUP), the Young Turk government, ultimately fell into many of the same authoritarian patterns that they had originally protested against, gradually restricting political freedom and engineering new constitutional amendments that restored some of the autocratic stipulations of 1876. The constitution of 1876 remained in force until Istanbul was occupied by the Allied Powers on March 16, 1920 at the close of WORLD WAR I.

The phrase "Constitutional Period" refers specifically to the two periods when the constitution of 1876 was in full force. The First Constitutional Period began in December 1876 and lasted until February 1878. During this period Grand Vizier Midhat Pasha was dismissed and expelled from the empire. In April 1877 Russia declared war on the Ottomans. This constitutional period ended with an Ottoman military defeat and the dissolution of the parliament by Abdülhamid II.

The Second Constitutional Period began with the Young Turk Revolution in July 1908 and ended with the Allied occupation of Istanbul in 1920) On July 24, 1908, Abdülhamid conceded to reopening the parliament. Following a reactionary rebellion in April 1909, the sultan was deposed in favor of his brother MEHMED V (r.

1909–18). Between 1908 and January 1913, the increasing power of the Committee of Union and Progress did much to quell opposition, but party politics was still possible. When the BALKAN WARS (1912–13) provided an opportunity, the CUP staged a military coup in January 1913. Although the constitution and parliament continued to function, the regime in fact became a military dictatorship under Talât Pasha, Enver Pasha, and Cemal Pasha. The CUP regime led the Ottoman Empire into WORLD WAR I on the side of the Central Powers (Germany, Austria-Hungary, and Bulgaria). When the Ottomans capitulated on October 31, 1918, the three leaders left the empire. The new sultan MEHMED VI (r. 1918–22), an adversary of the CUP, dissolved the parliament on November 23, 1918. However, the Anatolian movement, which opposed Allied plans to partition the empire, forced the sultan to permit general elections. The last parliament in Istanbul met on January 12, 1920 and dissolved itself on March 18, 1920 upon the Allied occupation of the Ottoman capital.

Selçuk Akşin Somel

See also YOUNG OTTOMANS.

Further reading: Feroz Ahmad, *The Young Turks: The Committee of Union and Progress in Turkish Politics, 1908–1914* (Oxford: Clarendon, 1969); Robert Devereux, *The First Ottoman Constitutional Period: A Study of the Midhat Constitution and Parliament* (Baltimore, Md.: Johns Hopkins Press, 1963); Sabine Prätor, *Der arabische Faktor in der jungtürkischen Politik: eine Studie zum osmanischen Parlament der II. Konstitution, 1908–1918* (Berlin: Klaus Schwarz, 1993).

contraband (*memnu eşya, memnu olan meta, merces prohibitae, merces inlicitae, memnuat*)   Since the Middle Ages, rival Christian and Muslim states forbade the export of weaponry and other contraband, or prohibited goods, to each other. These embargoed goods included guns, metal, timber suitable for building fortresses and ships, canvas, horses and other draught animals, servants, and food. Although the popes repeatedly forbade the export of these commodities to the Islamic world, threatening individuals and nations who broke the embargo with excommunication and anathema, there were always European MERCHANTS who were eager to make a profit by supplying prohibited goods to Muslims.

Until the late 18th century, the Ottomans were self-sufficient in the production of FIREARMS and ammunition. However, during protracted wars from the late 16th century onward, they welcomed supplies of gunpowder and hand-held firearms or their firing mechanisms, which were brought to the empire by English and Dutch merchants. The Ottomans also imported tin, the only mineral they lacked domestically, from England.

Following medieval Islamic practice, the Ottomans also forbade the export of weapons and other strategic materials, declaring them *memnu eşya* or *memnu olan meta*, prohibited goods. Molla Hüsrev, the famous grand mufti or jurist of Sultan MEHMED II (r. 1444–46; 1451–81), regarded arms, horses, and iron as prohibited goods even in peacetime, since these commodities could be used for war against Muslims. Prohibitions were incorporated into the peace treaties concluded with Christian states as well as into the passports issued to foreign travelers. Not even merchants of Ottoman vassal states were allowed to import prohibited goods from the sultan's realms.

Ottoman lists of contraband included grains, arms, gunpowder, saltpeter and sulfur (essential ingredients of gunpowder), copper, iron, and lead (metals used for making cannons and projectiles), cotton, cotton yarn, different kinds of leather, canvas, tallow, pitch, and horses. Imperial orders containing long lists of prohibited goods were especially common during prolonged wars in the 16th and 17th centuries. However, judging from the number of repeated decrees, the Ottoman authorities, like their Christian adversaries, failed to suppress the contraband TRADE. Smuggling was undertaken mainly in the winter months, when the Ottoman NAVY was at the Istanbul Arsenal and could not enforce the regulations and stop foreign and Ottoman vessels from engaging in contraband trade. Some of the friendly nations who enjoyed trade privileges through the CAPITULATIONS or special trade agreements, however, were granted the right to import prohibited goods such as cotton, cotton yarn, leather, and beeswax. In return, the empire was able to secure the import of lead, tin, iron, and steel, strategic metals for the war industry, from these countries.

Gábor Ágoston

Further reading: Gábor Ágoston, "Merces Prohibitae: The Anglo-Ottoman Trade in War Materials and the Dependence Theory." *Oriente Moderno* n.s., 20 (2001): 177–192.

conversion   The extent and timing of conversion to Islam in different parts of the Ottoman Empire were dictated by the local conditions in a region before the arrival of the Ottomans and the nature of the region's conquest and incorporation into the Ottoman Empire. Anatolia experienced extensive conversion to Islam of the local population during the early Seljuk period, before the establishment of the Ottoman state, beginning after the Battle of Manzikert in 1071 and with the influx of Turkoman tribes into the region. Reliable sources on the progress of conversion in Anatolia are scarce before the mid-15th century, when it appears from the Ottoman census records that the process was about 85 percent complete. However, areas such as the region of Trabzon on the BLACK SEA (conquered in 1461) witnessed the beginning of the process comparatively late, as conversions to Islam continued to occur in this primarily Christian region well into the 16th and 17th centuries, when the process had been mostly completed in the rest of Anatolia.

The process of conversion to Islam in the Balkans is much better documented. Recent research with Ottoman census records suggests that conversion to Islam in the Balkans was minimal in the 14th and early 15th centuries, increased slightly in the late 15th century, and rose steadily throughout the 16th century, peaking in the mid-17th century only to slow down and come to an almost complete stop by the end of the 18th century. However, significant regional differences exist. For example, the region of Thrace (conquered by the Ottomans in the mid-14th century) saw extensive colonization by Muslims from Anatolia but also a steady rise in local conversions over the centuries. Conversely, Bosnia, conquered in the mid-15th century, witnessed only a limited Muslim colonization but experienced a rapid and extensive process of conversion of the local population to Islam (almost 100 percent in Sarajevo) that was already complete by the end of the 16th century. Scholars are still investigating the nature of the religious dynamic in medieval Bosnia before the Ottoman conquest that made this collective acceptance of Islam possible. By contrast, another majority Muslim area, ALBANIA, which was conquered gradually over the course of the 15th century, saw a significant onset of conversion to Islam only in the second half of the 17th century, presumably due to increase of both the *jizya* and the so-called urgent (*avarız*) taxes in the region, as well as due to significant population shifts.

Nevertheless, some common factors are observable across the region. Existing sources, such as the 15th-century Ottoman census records, suggest that the earliest converts to Islam in the Balkans came from the ranks of the Balkan nobility and military elite that could supply the Ottomans with the manpower and know-how needed to administer the region. Although conversion was not a prerequisite for joining the Ottomans and obtaining a fief (*timar*) from the sultan, over time these local converts to Ottoman governance also became converts to Islam—a process that could take several generations to be fully completed. For example, Ottoman census records dating to 1432 suggest that some Christian *timar*-holders in the district of Arvanid (Albania) had sons who converted to Islam but shared their fief with their Christian siblings.

These voluntary cross-overs of the Balkan military elite were nevertheless insufficient for the growing Ottoman need for manpower. Thus, starting in the late 14th century, the Ottomans institutionalized a levy of children (DEVŞIRME) from among their Balkan Christian subjects that was supposed to supply the Ottoman polity with able soldiers and administrators. As a part of their education, *devşirme* children underwent compulsory conversion to Islam, which is the only documented forced form of conversion organized by the Ottoman state. Although it dominates the Balkan nationalist historiography as the supposed principal Ottoman method of conversion, the *devşirme*, which was discontinued by the mid-17th century, represents a numerically limited phenomenon in the context of conversion to Islam in the Balkans.

Likewise, despite established theories that emphasize "external" agents of conversion, such as proselytizing Sufi mystics or an invasive Ottoman state, both Christian and Muslim sources of different types and time periods suggest that FAMILY and social networks were the most important contexts of religious change and that agents of conversion were usually the people a convert-to-be was familiar with. Among these sources are a number of Orthodox Christian neomartyrologies that describe the suffering and death of Christians who converted to Islam but later reneged and faced trial and execution by Ottoman authorities. Although these accounts are written from an Orthodox perspective, they clearly demonstrate that many converts hailed from religiously mixed households in which one or both parent's conversion to Islam resulted in conversion of their adolescent children, as dictated by Islamic law. At the same time, converts' petitions to the Ottoman imperial council from the 17th and 18th centuries, seeking money for the new clothes that they were entitled to as converts according to Islamic custom, demonstrate that families often converted collectively. Moreover, intermarriage represented an important avenue for women to convert to Islam. Islamic law allowed Muslim men to marry Jewish and Christian women, and although a non-Muslim wife was not legally obliged to convert, many women in interfaith marriages opted for conversion nevertheless. Single women, typically widows with children in need of sustenance and women seeking divorce and custody of their children, also appear in the Ottoman court records. As the SHARIA forbids a union between a non-Muslim man and a Muslim woman, the refusal of the husband to convert to Islam resulted in a quick divorce and the wife's gaining custody over the couple's children. Ottoman sources suggest that, in the 17th century, women throughout the Ottoman Empire increasingly resorted to this strategy.

Kinship networks often overlapped with professional networks, which were another important avenue of conversion. In the Balkans, both neomartyrologies and Ottoman court records suggest that a single young male moving from the countryside to the city in search of work and suitable social and patronage networks was the most likely candidate for conversion. As numerous records in the registers of important imperial affairs (*mühimme defterleri*) show, conversion often followed apprenticeship to a Muslim craftsman or coming to work for a relative who embraced Islam and established a successful business in a city.

Conversion to Islam was a social phenomenon that entailed an interplay of individual, family, communal, and Ottoman institutional initiatives and motives. The process was also influenced by the overall balance of power between the Ottomans and surrounding Christian states. In the late 18th century, the process of conversion seemingly came to a halt with the increasing influence of Western powers and Russia on Ottoman affairs. As these Christian powers extended protection to Ottoman Christian subjects in the 19th century, the Ottomans were pressured into turning a blind eye to the re-conversion of many of their subjects from Islam to Christianity, an action punishable by death according to Islamic law and one that had been strictly punished in previous centuries.

Tijana Krstić

Further reading: Eyal Ginio, "Childhood, Mental Capacity and Conversion to Islam in the Ottoman State." *Byzantine and Modern Greek Studies* 25 (2001): 90–119; Anton Minkov, *Conversion to Islam in the Balkans: Kisve Bahasi Petitions and Ottoman Social Life, 1670–1730* (Leiden: Brill, 2004); Antonina Zhelyazkova, "Islamization in the Balkans as a Historiographical Problem: The Southeast-European Perspective," in *The Ottomans and the Balkans*, edited by S. Faroqhi and F. Adanır (Leiden: Brill, 2002).

Copts Copts are Christians who are indigenous to EGYPT. Both the English designation Copt and the Arabic *qibti* derive from the Greek *aigyptikos*, "Egyptian," and attest to the community's claim to antiquity. The Coptic language is descended from Ancient Egyptian, although it is written with a modified Greek alphabet rather than hieroglyphs. Although no longer a living language, Coptic has continued to serve as the liturgical language of the Coptic Church. While adhering to most of the theology and liturgical practice of the larger Orthodox Christian group from which it derives, the Coptic Church is spiritually and politically independent of the Orthodox patriarch, having parted from the parent church at the Council of Chalcedon in 451. It was that church council that established the theological principle that Jesus Christ was one person in whom two natures, divine and human, were permanently united, but unmixed, a concept with which many disagreed. The Copts accepted the belief that Christ had two natures, but they held that these were fused together through the mystery of the incarnation, an idea the Orthodox Church condemns as the Monophysite heresy. Regarding the Copts of Egypt as heretics, the Byzantine authorities persecuted them, forcing many to flee to Ethiopia, where the Coptic Church is still strong. In revenge for that persecution, some Copts aided the Mus-

lim Arab conquest of Egypt in the 7th century, after which their church was left in peace for several centuries.

That peace was broken, however, and the Copts suffered repeated persecution from Muslim authorities in Egypt, first under the Fatimid Caliph al-Hakim (r. 996–1021) and then under the MAMLUK EMPIRE (1260–1517), because the Mamluks viewed the local Christians as potential allies of their crusader enemies. For this reason, the Mamluks imposed severe restrictions on the Copts' practice of religion and involvement in commerce. They also sought to impose a dress code by which Coptic Christians and Jews would be distinguished from their Muslim neighbors.

Although the Copts probably made up the majority of Egypt's population in the 11th century, by the time of the Ottoman conquest of Egypt in 1517, they had been reduced to only 10 to 15 percent of the total population. Under the Ottomans, the Copts were tolerated, although they received no official recognition from the Ottoman sultans as a MILLET, or recognized religious community. But this seems to have been simply because their patriarch (the head of the church) did not seek that status from the Ottoman sultans. Although Copts were found in every region of Egypt in the Ottoman period, their percentage of the total population was higher in rural Upper Egypt than it was in either CAIRO or the villages of the Nile Delta.

The fortunes of the Copts took a dramatic turn when NAPOLEON BONAPARTE occupied Egypt in 1798. Many of the country's Muslims saw the Copts as natural allies of the French because both were Christian, even if Napoleon proclaimed that he was at heart a Muslim. As a result, anti-French anger in Egypt was often channeled into aggression toward the Copts. In the riots of 1798 in Cairo, Copts, as well as the more prosperous Syrian MELKITE Catholic merchants and Europeans, were targets of Muslim unrest. Under French occupation, however, several Copts served with distinction in the treasury, a niche they had previously occupied in the Ottoman administration, and in the Egyptian military units formed as auxiliaries to the French army.

The Copts again were targeted for Muslim retaliation for their perceived collaboration with the French occupiers when the French forces withdrew from Egypt in 1801. However, under the reign of Egyptian ruler MEHMED ALI (r. 1805–49), the Coptic community enjoyed relief from some of the discrimination they had suffered in the past. Mehmed Ali had a good relationship with Peter VII, the patriarch of the Coptic Church from 1809 to 1859, and granted him the right to build new churches for the first time since the Muslims conquered Egypt. When the Egyptian khedive Said (r. 1854–63) subjected the Copts to the military draft in 1858, the Coptic patriarch Cyril IV intervened to have them exempted in return for a special tax, not unlike the JIZYA, the head tax on non-Muslim men, they had previously paid the state. Cyril was also active in helping the Coptic Church reform itself by building new schools for the community and establishing a printing press. He also undertook the construction of St. Mark's Cathedral in Cairo, which remains the see, or seat, of the patriarchate.

In the second half of the 19th century, the Coptic church hierarchy felt pressure from both Protestant and Catholic MISSIONARIES seeking to win their parishioners over to what seemed to the Coptic clergy as heretical interpretations of Christianity. The presence of these European and American missionaries in Egypt prompted calls for reform among an increasingly educated laity. Influenced by the reforms in the *millet* system that were taking shape in the Ottoman Empire in the period of the TANZIMAT reforms (1839–76), the Coptic laity pushed their clergy to accept a religious council (*majlis al-milli*) to supervise the financial and civil affairs of the Coptic community. The Egyptian ruler, Khedive ISMAIL (r. 1863–79), endorsed the establishment of such a council in 1874 and established that the Coptic laity would directly elect the members of the assembly that would supervise institutions of the community, such as schools and religious endowments. The first assembly met in November 1874, but it was bitterly resented and resisted by Patriarch Cyril V (r. 1875–1927), who worked to block the assembly's reforms in education and local administration of church properties. As a result, the laity and the clergy were often at odds over the assembly's functions and prerogatives until the patriarch's death.

Economically and politically, the Coptic community prospered under the reign of Mehmed Ali and his descendants, with one member of the Coptic community, Butrus Ghali, even achieving the post of prime minister under Khedive ABBAS HILMI (r. 1892–1914). Ghali later served as Egypt's minister of justice and in 1905 presided over the trial of the Egyptians charged in the DINSHAWAY INCIDENT (1906), in which a number of Egyptian nationals were wrongly executed following a fracas with British troops. Ghali was assassinated in 1910 for his role in the decision that went against the Muslim peasants. His death highlighted a growing sense in the Coptic community that the Copts were a minority facing discrimination by the Muslim majority, a view that was frequently expressed in Coptic newspapers. The Coptic bishops of Upper Egypt, the region where Copts are most numerous, convened a General Congress of Coptic clergy and laity in 1910, which among other things called for an end to religious discrimination in government employment, the right of Copts to receive their own religious instruction in the government schools, and that Sunday, as well as Friday, be a government holiday. With the advent of the Egyp-

tian nationalist movement at the turn of the century, nationalist leader MUSTAFA KAMIL (1874–1908) tried to assuage Coptic fears that independence for Egypt would mean Muslim domination over non-Muslims, but tensions in the nationalist movement over the place of religion in an independent Egypt remained present throughout WORLD WAR I.

Bruce Masters

Further reading: Otto Meinardus, *Two Thousand Years of Coptic Christianity* (Cairo: American University in Cairo Press, 1999).

corsairs and pirates   Pirates and piracy are terms that are familiar to modern audiences. Piracy, most simply defined as violence at sea, has been practiced throughout history, and the Mediterranean has had its share. The stony soil and aridity of the region have always encouraged poorer inhabitants to try their luck at sea, and the many islands scattered across the eastern Mediterranean have provided safe harbor and concealment. But piracy is not just the story of outlaws. The Ottomans, like many states before and after them, drew on the knowledge and skills of pirates when they first reached the shores of the Mediterranean in the mid-14th century. With little maritime knowledge and no proper NAVY as yet, the Ottoman sultans engaged pirates, mostly Greeks, to carry out raids against various enemies (who were, of course, doing the same thing). Among these was Hayreddin Barbarossa, a Greek convert from the island of Mytilene and one of the famed BARBAROSSA BROTHERS, who began as a raider for the Ottomans; he eventually took the fight to the western Mediterranean and rose through the Ottoman ranks to become admiral in chief of the Ottoman navy in 1533.

In most parts of the world, when a pirate fought on behalf of a state he was known as a privateer. In the Mediterranean there was the less familiar figure of the corsair. The corsair, who fought a battle known as the *corso*, is somewhere between a pirate and a privateer. Both *corso* and corsair are terms that originated in Italy but that were adopted across the Mediterranean. They draw our attention to, and are a reflection of, certain realities distinctive to the region. It is not an accident that the words corsair and *corso* first came into use in the 12th century, when the antagonism between Christianity and Islam had been given new life by the First Crusade. The term corsair has a religious connotation; to be a Christian corsair was to be a warrior engaged in the eternal battle against Islam, while for the Muslim corsair it was just the opposite. In addition, because this war between Christianity and Islam was perennial, at least in the minds of its combatants, so too was the phenomenon of the corsair. In other words, corsairing was not limited to periods of declared war between, for example, the Islamic Ottoman

Empire and Catholic Habsburg Spain, but was a permanent feature of Mediterranean life. Finally, corsairs often had a closer association with the state than was seen in other parts of the world, where their activity would look suspiciously like mere piracy.

In the 16th century, when conventional navies, on both the Ottoman and the Spanish side, engaged in a number of large-scale battles at sea, corsairs were submerged into the organized fighting forces of internationally recognized states. But toward the end of the century the Ottomans and the Spanish concluded a truce and both turned their attention elsewhere. Left to their own devices, and now bereft of the material opportunities that warfare had provided, corsairs emerged on either side of the religious divide. And not only corsairs, but veritable corsairing states—that is to say, states that were organized for, and lived off the profits of, raiding at sea. This is why the 17th century is known as the Age of the Corsair in the Mediterranean.

The most notorious Christian corsairs were the KNIGHTS OF ST. JOHN on the island of MALTA. On the Muslim side, the three North African corsair states of ALGIERS, TRIPOLI, and TUNIS (so named after their major cities) became infamous raiders of Christian shipping. The relationship of these three states to the Ottoman Empire was exceedingly ambiguous. The Ottomans certainly benefited from North African maritime skill, and more than one Ottoman admiral had risen from the ranks of the corsairs. However, in the 17th century the corsairs became a nuisance to established governments because they routinely preyed on the shipping of countries, such as FRANCE or ENGLAND, that were officially at peace with the Ottoman sultan. These attacks would then provoke complaints by the English or French ambassador in Istanbul. The Ottomans, however, never managed to rein in the North Africans.

The ability of the corsairs to terrorize peaceful commercial shipping in the name of either Islam or Christianity was due to the inability of larger states to impose order at sea. Over time, as the navies of the northern European powers—the French and the English in particular—grew in strength, they were able to rein in the corsairs, and the 18th century saw a marked lessening in such activity. Corsair raids flared up again, however, during the chaos of the Napoleonic Wars at the beginning of the 19th century. Although both Christians and Muslims had always engaged in maritime violence, France was able to selectively highlight North African corsairing as a justification for the invasion of Algeria in 1830, an action that would lead to 130 years of occupation. Significantly, the European rhetoric at the time insisted that the Algerians were pirates, avoiding, for the most part, the term *corsair*, which was always much more ambiguous. The place of the corsair has been enshrined in Western literature by the widely read English Romantic poem "The Corsair," written by George Gordon, Lord Byron, in 1814.

Molly Greene

Further reading: Peter Earle, *Corsairs of Malta and Barbary* (London: Sidgwick and Jackson, 1970); G. Fisher, *Barbary Legend: War, Trade and Piracy in North Africa, 1415–1830* (Oxford: Clarendon, 1957); Victor Mallia-Milanes, ed., *Hospitaller Malta, 1530–1798: Studies on Early Modern Malta and the Order of St. John of Jerusalem* (Msida, Malta: Mireva Publications, 1993).

Cossacks The term Cossacks is a loose appellation for military groups of varied ethnic composition, organization, allegiance, and social standing who lived in the Eurasian steppe. Due to their involvement in east European politics, the Ottomans developed diverse relations with those Cossacks located in the northern BLACK SEA steppe (the Pontic steppe), in particular with the Cossacks in UKRAINE, also known in Ottoman sources as Dnieper Cossacks (Özi kazakları), as they constituted a largely independent political power from the 16th through the 18th centuries.

The origins of the Cossacks are obscure. Though not generally accepted by linguists, it has been suggested that the word *cossack* is derived from the root *kaz*, "to flee, to escape," and means "outcast, vagabond, adventurer." Initially it referred to exiled or breakaway tribesmen (the traditional component of the nomadic polity and the provenance of the name of the Kazak people). In the early 14th century it was interpreted as "guard," which posits Cossacks of that time as trained military slaves (similar to the JANISSARIES). Mongols of the Golden Horde employed them for guarding and maintaining roads, postal stations, and fortresses. Some military units of the Crimean Tatar khans (*see* CRIMEAN TATARS) and tribal leaders, the successors to the Golden Horde in the 15th and the 16th centuries, were also composed of troops called Cossacks. This name entered Ottoman usage as the name for raiders (*akıncı*) positioned around the Ottoman fortresses of Akkerman (at the mouth of the Dniester River) and AZAK (at the mouth of the Don River). Following the outbreak of hostilities between Ottomans and Cossack units in Ukraine and on the lower Don, the name *kazak* ceased to be applied to Ottoman subjects. From the 16th through the 19th centuries, the Ottomans also used the term *kazak* to refer to male slaves of east European origin.

The Ukrainian Cossacks evolved from the military population that the Grand Duchy of Lithuania maintained in the steppe areas that had been taken from the Golden Horde in the second half of the 14th century. Taking advantage of weak governmental control in the border zone these military settlers, now formally serfs of the state, expanded their economic activities in the steppe. As well as hunting and fishing, they engaged in pastoralism and agriculture. The increased demand in western European markets for foodstuffs stimulated this colonizing movement, drawing Slavs (sometimes fugitive serfs) from inner areas and attracting Turkic nomads to cooperate with the newcomers. Political anarchy also offered the possibility for plundering the pastoralists and merchants, thus facilitating the formation of military bands. A net of rivers and streams in this segment of the steppe, which was particularly dense along the middle course of the river Dnieper, below its cataracts, provided the nascent militarist community with excellent refuge. Another name for the Cossacks, Zaporozhians—men from beyond the cataracts—derives from this geographical reference point.

Polish, Lithuanian, and Ruthenian magnates and gentry were also established on the steppe, usually with their retinue (who were also called Cossacks). It was due to the initiative of one of them, Prince Dmytro Vyshnevec'ky (known in Ottoman documents as Dimitraş), that Cossacks built their first permanent fortified camp (sich) on an island in the Dnieper in about 1557. This was the turning point in the process of Cossack consolidation, as after this time such camps turned into headquarter where offices such as the court, treasury, arsenal, and military barracks were located.

The military exploits of the Ukrainian Cossacks began around the end of the 15th century with ambushes and the interception of merchant caravans along the Dnieper. Cossacks also stole cattle and horses from nomadic shepherds and commandeered cattle and horses from Ottoman subjects in Akkerman. Early Cossack land raids were focused on Ottoman and Crimean fortresses (Özi, Akkerman, and Bender) on the northern Black Sea littoral. They also raided into the Principality of MOLDA-VIA, an Ottoman vassal or satellite state. It is believed that Cossack naval raids started in the 1570s. These raids were focused on Rumelia (the European parts of the Ottoman Empire) and the Crimea. The first raid across the Black Sea (against Sinop and Trabzon) is reliably dated to 1614. Raids on the southern shores of the Black Sea reached their zenith in the 1620s. These raids involved up to 300 longboats called *chaikas* and reached the outskirts of Istanbul. The Cossacks engaged in a major naval battle with the Ottoman fleet near Kara-Harman in 1625.

Although these early Cossack exploits were essentially a form of piracy, they quickly developed into a factor in international politics. Beginning in the 1540s Cossack military activity caused tension between the Porte and the kings of Poland. In 1589 a Cossack attack on the Crimea even compelled Elizabeth I of England (r. 1558–1603) to intercede on behalf of Poland in its negotiations with the Porte. Czar Ivan IV (r. 1533–84) of Muscovy was the first foreign ruler to hire Cossacks.

In 1558–62 a unit led by Prince Dmytro Vyshnevec'ky attacked the Ottoman fortress of Azak. The Cossacks also made alliances with Muslim rulers, including alliances with the Crimean khans Mehmed Giray III (r. 1610, 1623–27) in 1624–28 and Inayat Giray (r. 1635–37). At times even the Ottomans sought the assistance of Cossack mercenaries. In 1648 plans were developed to hire Cossacks as marines, to be deployed in a war against Venice. In exchange, the Ottomans dangled the prospect of granting the Cossacks navigation and trading privileges on the Black Sea. The Russian Empire, which ultimately won the allegiance of the Ukrainian Cossacks, employed them militarily against the Crimean Tatars and Ottomans.

Unlike pirates, Cossacks developed the elements of state organization. Oriented economically toward the Polish-Lithuanian Commonwealth, the Cossacks' social and political ambitions hinged on their relationship to this state. From the Polish king the Cossacks received state rights similar to those held by Polish gentry (*szlachta*). An ongoing conflict with the Polish kings concerning the Cossacks' status intensified in 1620 when Cossacks supported the Orthodox cause in Ukraine against the Union of Greek Orthodox and Catholic churches of Poland (1596). Until this point indifferent to religion, the Cossacks were transformed into a pillar of the Orthodox Church. This conflict, in addition to serious political and social upheavals, resulted in a major Cossack revolt against their Polish sovereigns in 1648–54.

During this revolt the Cossacks were allied with the Crimean khan Islam Giray III (r. 1644–54). The Crimean khan's support contributed to the rebels' success. In the ensuing civil war some Cossack factions accepted Ottoman suzerainty, which dragged the Ottomans into wars with POLAND (1672–99) and Muscovy (1676–81). Between 1672 and 1699, the Ottomans occupied parts of western Ukraine, which they organized as a new Ottoman province (*vilayet*) around the capital in KAMANIÇE. The Ottomans looked to the Cossacks as potential allies against growing Muscovite pressure in the steppe and recognized the Cossacks as a separate ethnic and political entity (a tribe or *taife*). Following an alliance between Sweden and the Cossacks in the early 18th century, the Ottomans granted protection to Cossacks fleeing reprisals from Peter I of Russia.

The Cossacks organized their own administration in Ukraine, called the Zaporozhian Host (*ordu*). In an imitation of the Ottoman and Crimean pattern, it was divided into regiments and hundreds. The Zaporozhian Host issued its own legislation and currency and had an elected head of state, or hetman. The Russian government appointed the last hetman in 1750 and abolished this office in 1764. As an autonomous military and political power, the Ukrainian Cossacks survived for only a few years. After the TREATY OF KÜÇÜK KAYNARCA (1774), Czarina Catherine II (r. 1762–96) ordered the disbanding of the Zaporozhian Host and the destruction of its capital, Sich. From 1775 until 1828 the Ottomans permitted Cossack refugees to settle in the Danube delta as a military corps.

Following the disbanding of the Zaporozhian Host, the Russian government used the remaining Cossacks of Ukraine, organized around several Cossack hosts, as military servitors against the Ottoman Empire. These hosts were located on the Yuzhny Bug River (the Bug Cossack Host, 1785–98, 1803–17), between the Dnieper and Dniester rivers (the Black Sea Cossack Host, 1788–1860), and on the northern shore of the Sea of Azov (the Azov Cossack Host, 1832–66). In 1792 the Black Sea Cossacks were partly transferred to the basin of the Kuban' River in the northern CAUCASUS, where they formed the Kuban' Cossack Host. All officers in these hosts were appointed by the government. Cossacks were assigned to specially designed settlements, and their service was rewarded with conditional land grants. At this point, these Cossacks could be described as privileged military settlers.

The Don Cossacks (Ten Kazakları in Ottoman) emerged at the end of the 16th century in the basins of the Don and Seversky Donets rivers. Their composition and organization were similar to the Ukrainian Cossacks except for the notable absence of upper class representatives in their ranks. In fact the Don Cossacks were farmers and freebooters who found a comfortable refuge in this neutral zone and showed less inclination that the Zaporozhian Host to cooperate with any government. Moscow provided a potential economic partner for the Don Cossacks, but the distance between Muscovy and the territory of the Don Cossacks frustrated attempts to build trade connections.

The military activity of the Don Cossacks was limited to raids on Ottoman fortresses and piracy on the Black and Azov seas. The most memorable episode in the history of the Don Cossacks was their seizure and control of Azak from 1637 to 1642. This exploit, however, was not of any long-term political importance. The Don Cossacks continued their piratical activity on the Black Sea in the second half of the 17th century. Again, these raids were devoid of any political agenda and were in contravention to appeals from the Ukrainian hetman to participate in peaceful commerce with the Ottomans. The Muscovite czars used Don Cossacks as guards for embassies to the Ottoman Empire. The Don Cossacks were generously paid for their services. Russian attempts to impose a formal service obligation on the Don Cossacks in return for social and economic privileges were strenuously resisted. In time, Muscovy was able, following the suppression of Cossack raids by regular army units, to impose a tributary status on the Don Cossacks. In the 1670s Muscovy forced the Don Cossacks to swear an oath of loyalty to the czar, abolished their self-government, and effectively impeded the influx of fugitive serfs into the Don Cossack host. The bloody pacification of the Cossacks in 1708 resulted in thousands of deaths. Some Don Cossacks, led by Ignat Nekrasov, fled to the south toward the Kuban' River. These fugitives later formed the nucleus for a military unit known as Nekrasovites that settled in Ottoman territory in the Danube delta. By the end of the 18th century the Russian government had succeeded in transforming the remaining Don Cossacks into loyal military settlers. The Don Cossacks, at this point, were no longer an object of Ottoman foreign policy.

Oleksandr Halenko

Further reading: John Uhre, *The Cossacks* (London: Constable, 1999); Gilles Veinstein, "Early Ottoman Appellations for the Cossacks." *Harvard Ukrainian Studies* 23 (1999): 33–44; Serhii Plokhiy, *The Cossacks and Religion in Early Modern Ukraine* (Oxford: Oxford University Press, 2001); Victor Ostapchuk, "The Human Landscape of the Ottoman Black Sea in the Face of the Cossack Naval Raids." *Oriente Moderno*, n.s., 20 (2001): 23–95; Mykhaylo Hrushevsky, *History of Ukraine-Rus'*, vol. 7–9 (Edmonton and Toronto: Canadian Institute of Ukrainian Studies Press, 1997–2005).

courier network *See* MENZIL/MENZILHANE.

court and favorites In the early modern period (1500–1800), a particular type of court developed in most empires of the world. On the way to the formation of modern nation-states, royal courts were the primary setting for politics, and court favorites were among the leading actors on the political stage. The Ottoman Empire was no exception in terms of the position and functions of the court and favorites. The Ottoman court defined not only a princely residence but also a larger matrix of political, social, economic, cultural, and religious relations that converged in the sultan's household. Like any pre-modern ruler, the Ottoman sultan was personally the source of secular authority and the principal dispenser of offices, patronage, and power. Hence the Ottoman court was the prime locus of decision making, the major house for preferment, and the main spatial setting for daily rituals of rule. Overall, it fulfilled a series of multiple and sometimes opposing functions. While it enclosed the sultan and thus limited access to his person to a favored entourage, it also served as a means of connecting the Ottoman ruler to the larger political universe that lay beyond the palace gates.

The Ottoman court and favorites began to emerge in the mid-16th century with the consolidation of royal power that was coterminous with the centralization of the bureaucracy and the sedentarization of Ottoman imperial rule. A defining feature of the early modern court, this sedentarization was realized with the creation of a permanent imperial seat in ISTANBUL'S TOPKAPI PALACE, a residence that outshone those of all former Ottoman sultans. The majesty of this new palatial residence and its inhabitants was guaranteed and accentuated by elaborately tailored rituals of ceremony, power, and hierarchy. The major consequence of these developments was the emergence of a new type of sultan who tried to rule the empire from seclusion, both physical and ceremonial. At the same time, two interrelated factors became crucial for both building and holding political power in this new setting: controlling the points of access to the person of the sultan, and establishing privacy with the sultan and with other powerful figures of the court.

THE EARLY OTTOMAN ERA: 1300–1450

The first 150 years of Ottoman rule was characterized by frequent military campaigns, which demanded a ruler and political-military elite to be constantly on the move. During this formative period, the itinerant character of the Ottoman political body also required direct involvement and leadership from the sultans. Although there were capital cities—first BURSA (1326) and then EDIRNE (c. 1360)—that accommodated the royal household, the court of the sultan was not sedentary and moved to new locations that were dependent on military conquests and territorial expansion in the 14th century. Thus, between 1300 and 1450, the itinerancy of the Ottoman ruling body hindered the development of a permanent seat for court and favorites.

AFTER THE CONQUEST OF CONSTANTINOPLE: 1450–1550

The Ottoman CONQUEST OF CONSTANTINOPLE in 1453 was a turning point in the making of the empire and court. From this point until the end of the reign of Sultan SÜLEYMAN I (r. 1520–66) came a period of imperial maturation. During this era, the sultans consolidated their imperial-dynastic sovereignty through networks of legitimization by a fully grown bureaucracy and law-making efficacy. The conquest of Constantinople gave the Ottomans a permanent capital city. The construction of the Topkapı Palace in the new capital, or the New Palace as it was called by the Ottomans, began with the initiative of Sultan MEHMED II (r. 1444–46; 1451–81) immediately after the takeover of the city. Although the initial layout of the palace was shaped during Mehmed's reign, successive sultans rebuilt and added sections to the palace. Its construction was rather a process, corresponding to the aspirations of the expanding empire, and it had to be adjusted according to changing conditions. The establishment of the Topkapı Palace as the ultimate residence

of the sultans, together with the increasing seclusion of the sultans in the inner compounds of the palace, were the determining factors for the making of the Ottoman court in the period between 1450 and 1550.

Although the sultans of this period still spent most of their reigns on battlefields, a less visible sultan gradually emerged as part of the new definition of sultanic imagery. The initial signs of royal seclusion and dignity can be found in some of Mehmed II's new practices, which also found their way into his law codes. Perhaps the most significant of these practices was that, beginning with Mehmed II, the sultans ceased to attend the meetings of the Imperial Council.

Constant victories resulting in further territorial expansions during the 15th and first half of the 16th century created a well-fed self-importance and overconfidence among the Ottoman ruling elite. This self-confidence, especially during the reign of Süleyman I, cultivated an appetite for the world domination. The Ottoman sultans' dignity grew, and a well-regulated ceremonial procedure set down the rules of behavior to deal with the sultan. This was manifested in the increasing seclusion of the sultans. The sultans' retinue also grew enormously, and with the reign of Süleyman, the court ceremonial and the fabricated aura surrounding the sultan became more solemn. Süleyman I took another crucial step toward the making of the court. He transferred all members of his royal household from the Old Palace to the new one, and the sultan's household and the business of rule were thus entwined in the Topkapı Palace. The accommodation of the bureaucracy, imperial government, and royal household under the same roof was the most important last step for the making of the Ottoman court as the central stage for power politics between 1450 and 1550.

THE EMERGENCE OF THE OTTOMAN COURT: 1540–1600

The next period marked the emergence of the court as the nerve center of political struggles and practical politics. The emergence of the Ottoman court as the new political setting dictated specific rules for both building and practicing power. The sultans of the latter half of the 16th century ruled within the mechanisms and relations dictated by these rules of court politics. The basic imposition of this new political framework was to create agencies to bridge the gap between the ruler, the court, and the outside world. The main agents who bridged this gap were the favorites. Thus the rise of the favorites as agents of power politics was a direct consequence of the emergence of the Ottoman court.

Although SELIM II (r. 1566–1574) was the first Ottoman sultan whose reign began in this new political setting, the overwhelming control of the grand vizier

Sokollu Mehmed Pasha over the business of rule throughout his reign delayed the true emergence of favorites until the beginning of the reign of Sultan MURAD III (r. 1574–1595). The assassination of Sokollu Mehmed Pasha in 1579, during the fifth year of Murad III's reign, marks the beginning of favorites as a new power elite within the Ottoman political order.

It is challenging to delineate the borders of the Ottoman court in terms of its social, political, and economic interactions with society as a whole. However, one of the most important parameters for understanding how power was built and practiced tin court politics was the concept of access. Since access to the court and access from the court to the outside world were strictly controlled in the Ottoman political order, anyone contending for power in the court—including the sultans—needed to establish a communication network within and outside of the court. Therefore the favorites were not only the inevitable outcome of the changes in the Ottoman political setting, they were also deliberate creations of power contenders at court. In fact, we observe the first examples of such creations in the reign of Murad III.

Of the anti-Sokollu factionalism under Murad III's first years, Şemsi Pasha was one of the first examples of such creations. The main reason for bringing Şemsi Pasha from his retirement to the court of Murad III was his well-known animosity to Sokollu Mehmed Pasha, and with the power invested in him as a favorite, he worked hard to divert the flow of the business of rule toward the sultan. However, the first proper example of created royal favorites was Doğancı Mehmed Pasha, the governor of Rumelia, whose status as favorite was officially granted by an imperial decree in 1584. The extraordinary privileges given to Mehmed Pasha by Murad III bypassed the well-established patterns of the hierarchical order and cut through the jurisdictions of the different offices of the bureaucracy.

A more accurate picture of court politics includes a number of power foci and a multiple set of relations among them. While some favorites were deliberate creations, others were engendered and gained unprecedented power as a result of their control over the points of access to the court and politics of privacy. The most illustrious examples of these new power elites were the queen mothers and chief eunuchs of the palace. After Murad III moved his mother, Nur Banu Sultan, to the Topkapı Palace, the queen mother became one of the most important power contenders of the court. Successors of Nur Banu Sultan, such as Safiye Sultan, the mother of Sultan MEHMED III (r. 1595–1603) or Kösem Sultan, the mother of Sultan MURAD IV (r. 1623–1640) and Sultan IBRAHIM (r. 1640–1648), were prime examples of queen mothers who concentrated immense power in their hands through their own networks of favorites and protégés.

THE TOPKAPI PALACE AND ISTANBUL: 1600–1700

The reign of Sultan AHMED I (r. 1603–1617) constitutes another watershed in the development of the court and the roles played by the favorites in the Ottoman imperial establishment. He was the first sultan in Ottoman history to come to the throne from the inner compounds of the palace without having first served in a province as governor. This lack of experience, which was designed to prepare the princes for a future sultanate, prevented Ahmed from establishing his own retinue that would form the nucleus of his government and court when he came to the throne. Overall, with Ahmed's reign, dynastic succession, power struggles, and patronage networks within the Ottoman political body shifted from a larger setting, which once included the provincial princely households, to a narrower domain consisting of the Topkapı Palace and Istanbul.

Ahmed's reign witnessed the crystallization of the crucial roles played by the favorites. Given the increased invisibility and inaccessibility of the Ottoman sultan during this period, a favorite who managed to enter the sultan's quarters consolidated his power against challengers. In this context, El-Hac Mustafa Agha, who held the office of chief eunuch throughout Ahmed I's reign, became the royal favorite par excellence. Especially after the untimely death of Ahmed's mother Handan Sultan in 1605, Mustafa Agha enjoyed exclusive access to Ahmed since he was now the highest authority in the royal palace. Thanks to his position, he was not only able to attain enormous power and to control almost all petitions and information addressed to the sultan, he also distributed wealth, power and patronage both in the sultan's name and in his own name. It was during the first half of the 17th century that the position and function of the chief eunuch of the palace within court politics were solidly entrenched, and until the end of the 18th century, several chief eunuchs, such as El-Hac Beşir Agha, exercised great power over imperial politics.

However, while the Ottoman court continued to serve as the nerve center of politics until the end of the 17th century, it also remained a contested domain for power struggles in which various factions and patron-client relations limited, and thus often undermined, both the sovereign authority of the sultan and the standing of his favorites. During this period various factions among members of the government, the army, and the religious establishment often allied and worked against the Ottoman rulers and their male and female favorites. Such united factions within the court and the larger political body often managed to make and unmake sultans such as MUSTAFA I (r. 1617–18, 1622–23) and MEHMED IV (r. 1648–87). These factions even led to the first two regicides in Ottoman history: sultans

Osman II (r. 1618–1622) and Ibrahim I (r. 1640–48) were murdered in 1622 and 1648, respectively. Many favorites too lost their lives in the midst of such tumults and as part of the power struggles in the court.

Overall, the early modern Ottoman courtly practice, with embedded royal favorites and constant factionalism, belied the rhetoric of "absolute" and "arbitrary" sultanic power.

Günhan Börekçi-Şefik Peksevgen

Further reading: Cornell Fleischer, *Bureaucrat and Intellectual in the Ottoman Empire: The Historian Mustafa Âli (1541–1600)* (Princeton, N.J.: Princeton University Press, 1986); Gülrü Necipoğlu, *Architecture, Ceremonial, and Power: The Topkapı Palace in the Fifteenth and Sixteenth Centuries* (Cambridge, Mass.: MIT Press, 1991); Leslie Peirce, *The Imperial Harem: Women and Sovereignty in the Ottoman Empire* (Oxford: Oxford University Press, 1993); Caroline Finkel, *Osman's Dream: The Story of the Ottoman Empire, 1300–1923* (London: John Murray, 2005); Baki Tezcan, "Searching for Osman: A Reassessment of the Deposition of The Ottoman Sultan Osman II (1618–1622)" (Ph.D. diss., Princeton University, 2001).

court chronicles   The Ottoman court chronicles (*şehname* or *vakanüvis*) are the official accounts of Ottoman imperial history as recorded by the sultan's court chronicler. Ottoman court HISTORIOGRAPHY produced works inspired by classical Islamic historiography. In this concept of historiography, which developed in the Islamic world prior to the Ottoman period, the chronicler tries to confirm oral traditions by identifying written sources close to the events. Following the traditions developed during the period of classical Islam (Umayyad and Abbasid periods), the chronicler narrates events year by year, and at the end of each year gives a biography of the sheikhs, viziers, poets, and other important people who died during that year. Ottoman historiography was also strongly influenced by Ibn Khaldun (b. 1332–d. 1406), one of the most original philosophers of Arabic history. Compared with Persian historiography, the language used in Ottoman historiography is rather plain.

The writing of *şehname*, the earlier type of chronicle composed in a poetic form, began in the reign of Mehmed II (r. 1444–46, 1451–81) when the sultan appointed Şehdi to record all historical events in the epic style; however, this first attempt was left uncompleted. An even earlier history of this kind, written during the reign of Murad II (r. 1421–44, 1446–51), was *Menakib-name-i Yahşi Fakih*, however, this work is no longer extant.

The most important early court chronicles were written by Idris-i Bidlisi (d. 1520) and Kemalpaşazade (b. 1469–d. 1534) on the order of Bayezid II (r. 1481–1512). Elaborately written in Persian, Idris-i Bidlisi's work, *Heşt Bihişt*, discusses the first eight Ottoman sultans and is modeled on the histories of Wassaf (b. 1265–d 1334) and Djuwayni (b. 1226–d. 1286). Kemalpaşazade's 10-volume chronicle, which covers the first 10 sultans, marks a turning point in Ottoman historiography; unlike earlier chroniclers, the writer did not relate a string of unrelated events, but rather tied events together in a continuous and connected chain.

Another important development in the genre took place under Selim I (r. 1512–20) when, for the first time, a history was produced based on the reign of a single ruler. This text, *The Book of Selim* (*Selim-name*), is the most important source of history for this period. As the empire became firmly established, and with the *Selim-name* and the *Süleyman-name* (written after the ascension of Süleyman I, r. 1520–66, in 1520), the number of chronicles continued to increase as did the number of histories of military campaigns. Under Süleyman I, the post of court chronicler (*şehnameci*) was for the first time made official and the first court chronicler of this period, Arifi Fethullah Çelebi (d. 1561), completed the half-written history left by Şehdi in the mid-15th century.

Early in the history of the practice, the court historian was identified as the *şehnameci* (writer of *şehname* or poetical history). The most famous Ottoman *şehnameci* was Seyyid Lokman who served as court historian for almost 27 years, writing many works before his death at the beginning of the 17th century. The next official *şehnameci*, Talikizade Mehmed Subhi, wrote three *şehnames* while in his post. Talikizade was removed from office in 1601 and replaced with Hasan Hükmi, but despite holding the post for 10 years, Hasan Hükmi did not produce any writing. After that, the office was left vacant.

The court historian or court chronicler ultimately came to be called *vakanüvis*, written originally as *vekayinüvis*, meaning "one who records events." Although the title of *vakanüvis* was used in the 16th century, the appearance of the *vakanüvislik* as a post connected to the royal court did not occur until the beginning of the 18th century with the appointment of Mustafa Naima (b. 1655–d. 1716), who wrote histories covering the period 1574 to 1660. Abdurrahman Abdi Pasha (d. 1692), who wrote the history of the reign of Mehmed IV (r. 1648–87), is sometimes identified as the first *vakanüvis*, but this claim is not generally accepted. Beginning in 1735, the appointment of a *vakanüvis* became standard practice. Although there are significant differences between the posts of the *şehnameci* of the early 17th century and the *vakanüvis*, the later position was essentially a continuation of the earlier one; the *şehnamecilik* and the *vakanüvislik* reflect different periods of official historiography.

The next *vakanüvis* appointed was Şefik Mehmed Efendi (d. 1715), who described the 1703 uprising in EDIRNE that led to the abdication of MUSTAFA II (r. 1695–1703) in the rich and complex language that was to become characteristic of Ottoman documents. Later commentaries illuminate some of the complexities of this text. Picking up the official record from the point at which Naima left off in 1660 was religious scholar Mehmed Raşid (d. 1735), who was appointed *vakanüvis* in 1714. Raşid was commissioned by the acting grand vizier, Nevşehirli Ibrahim Pasha, to record the events from where Naima left off to the ascension of AHMED III (r. 1703–1730) in 1703. After completing this first volume, Raşid's second volume described the events between 1703 and 1718, while the third volume narrated events that took place under Grand Vizier Nevşehirli Ibrahim Pasha (1718–22). Although the works of Naima and Raşid seem to be continuous, there is a small gap between them. Raşid continued in this position until his appointment to the judgeship of ALEPPO in June, 1723. The next *vakanüvis*, Küçük Çelebizade Asım (d. 1760), who was from an academic background like his predecessor, wrote a history that recorded events from between 1722 and 1728. This work was printed as an appendix to Raşid's history.

Asım was succeeded by Rami Paşazade Refet Abdullah Beyefendi (d. 1744), who became *vakanüvis* in 1725; Sami Mustafa Efendi (d. 1734), who had a bureaucratic background and was *vakanüvis* from 1730 to 1731; Şakir Efendi (d. 1742); and Subhi Mehmed Efendi (d. 1769), also from a bureaucratic background, who acted as *vakanüvis* from 1739 to 1743. Subhi Mehmed Efendi wrote about his own period and the preceding one, and his work was printed together with the histories written by Şakir and Sami as *Tarih-i Sami ve Şakir ve Subhi* (The History of Sami and Şakir and Subhi). İzzi Süleyman Efendi (d. 1755), who succeeded Subhi Mehmed Efendi, wrote *Tarih-i İzzi* (History of İzzi), printed in two volumes. His history, like those by most subsequent *vakanüvis*, chronicles the years of his tenure, 1744 to 1752. Seyyid Mehmed Hakim (d. 1770), *vakanüvis* from 1753 through 1766, wrote *Tarih-i Hakim*, which is in manuscript form. His successor was Çeşmizade Mustafa Reşid Efendi (d. 1770), who held the post from 1766 to 1768. His *Tarih-i Çeşmizade* was one of the sources for the history later written by Vasıf.

The *vakanüvises* Musazade Mehmed Ubeydullah Efendi (d. 1782), Esseyyid Hasan Behceti Efendi (18th century), and Ömer Efendizade Süleyman Efendi (d. 1807) did not publish individual works, but their writing was used as a source for *Tarih-i Vasıf*, written by *vakanüvis* Ahmed Vasıf Efendi (d. 1806).

Vasıf also compiled and used as a source the work of his immediate predecessor, Enveri Sadullah (b. 1736–d. 1794). Enveri was appointed *vakanüvis* five times (1769–74, 1776–83, 1787–91, 1791–93 and finally in 1794). The work he prepared, in three parts, is known by his name: *Tarih-i Enveri*.

Ahmed Vasıf Efendi was the most famous of the *vakanüvises*. He was appointed four times (1783–1787, 1791–1792, 1793–1794 and finally in 1799–1806). Vasıf recorded the events that occurred during his time as *vakanüvis* while also completing and rewriting the works of his predecessors (Hakim, Çeşmizade, Musazade, Hasan Behceti, Ömer Efendizade Süleyman, Enveri, Edib, Nuri). He completed writing the history of the empire from 1753 through 1804, with only a few years missing. Of his work, *Tarih-i Vasıf* (History of Vasıf), the volume covering 1752 through 1774 was printed twice; he himself published the volume that chronicled the years 1782–1787, which was the heftiest part of his *History* and the one he wrote first. However, a significant part of his *History*, the sections that discuss the events of 1775–79 and 1789–1804, are still in manuscript form.

When Vasıf was sent to Spain as ambassador in 1787, Teşrifati Hasan Efendi (d. 1797) was appointed in his place as *vakanüvis*. Hasan Efendi recorded events from the time Vasıf left the post. Mehmed Emin Edib Efendi (d. 1802) chronicled events from 1788 through 1792 as deputy *vakanüvis*; his work is known as *Tarih-i Edib*. Vakanüvis Halil Nuri's (d. 1799) six-volume history describes the events of 1794–99, including the various military reforms and other regulations. Mehmed Pertev Efendi (d. 1807), who came to the post on Vasıf's death in 1806, spent two years as *vakanüvis* but did not leave any individual works. He was succeeded by Es-Seyyid Ömer Amir Bey (d. 1815), who was removed from office three and a half months later because he did not carry out his duties. Mütercim Ahmed Asım (d. 1819), appointed in 1807, covered the time period 1803 to 1808, including the first four months of the reign of MAHMUD II (r. 1808–39). After presenting his work to the sultan, he made changes to his own copy, including criticism of some people who had passed away.

Asım was succeeded by Şanizade Mehmed Ataullah (d. 1826), who combined Asım's rough draft with his own chronicle of the years 1808 through 1821 in his four-volume *Tarih-i Şanizade* (History of Şanizade). Sahaflar Şehyizade Mehmed Esad Efendi (b. 1789–d. 1848) was appointed on 29 September 1825. The work that he wrote, *Tarih-i Esad*, covers events from October 1821 to July 1826 and consists of two volumes. Although Esad Efendi remained *vakanüvis* until his death on 11 January 1848, he was unable to compile his notes concerning the period after 1826 into book form due to the number of additional important duties he had to carry out. Recai Mehmed Şakir Efendi (b. 1804–d. 1874), and later Akıf Paşazade Nail Mehmed Bey (d. 1855), although acting as *vakanüvis*, did not leave any written histories.

After the death of Nail Bey, AHMED CEVDET PASHA (b. 1823–d. 1895), the prominent Ottoman writer and statesman of the TANZIMAT or reform era who was to become the greatest Ottoman historian, was appointed to the post. Commissioned to record events from 1774 to 1826, Cevdet Pasha studied documents and histories, interviewed contemporary leaders, and used other contemporary sources to produce *Tarih-i Cevdet*, a 12-volume work. Cevdet Pasha did not just describe events; he was careful to take into account the relationship of cause and effect and occasionally compared Ottoman history with European history.

Cevdet Pasha also kept notes on the period during which he acted as *vakanüvis* (February 19, 1855–January 12, 1866), and when his appointment came to an end upon his acceptance of the post of governor of Aleppo, he gave the work, known as *Tezakir*, to the historian who succeeded him, Ahmed Lütfi Efendi (b. 1816–d. 1907). Using the notes of Cevdet Pasha and Esad Efendi, the official gazette of the time *Takvim-i Vekayi*, and his own observations, Lütfi Efendi wrote a 15-volume history, *Vakanüvis Ahmed Lütfi Efendi Tarihi*, covering events from 1826 through 1868.

For two years after the death of Lütfi Efendi in 1907, no *vakanüvis* was appointed. Abdurrahman Şeref (b. 1853–d. 1925) was appointed to the post on May 18, 1909. The last *vakanüvis*, Abdurrahman Şeref, carried out his duties until the abolition of the sultanate in 1922. The history he wrote, *Vakanüvis Abdurrahman Şeref Efendi Tarihi*, includes the reasons for the proclamation of the Second Constitutional Monarchy (see CONSTITUTION AND CONSTITUTIONAL PERIODS) and the removal of ABDÜLHAMID II from the throne, and one month of the reign of Sultan MEHMED V (r. 1909–18).

Erhan Afyoncu

See also LITERATURE.

Further reading: Robert Charles Bond, "The Office of the Ottoman Court Historian or Vak'anüvis, 1714–1922." (Ph.D. diss., University of California, 2004); Cornell H. Fleischer, *Bureaucrat and Intellectual in the Ottoman Empire: The Historian Mustafa Ali, 1541–1600* (Princeton, N.J.: Princeton University Press, 1986); *Historians of the Middle East,* edited by B. Lewis and P. M. Holt (Oxford University, 1962); Jan Schmidt, *Pure Water for Thirsty Muslims: A Study of Mustafa Âli of Gallipolis Künhü'l-Ahbar* (Leiden: Het Oosters Institut, 1991); Lewis V. Thomas, *A Study of Naima,* edited by Norman Itzkowitz (New York University Press, 1972); Christine Woodhead, "An Experiment in Official Historiography: The Post of Şehnâmeci in the Ottoman Empire, 1555–1605." *Wiener Zeitschrift für die Kunde des Morgenlandes* 75 (1983), 157–182; Christine Woodhead, "Tar'ikh," in *Encyclopaedia of Islam,* 2nd ed., vol. 10 (Leiden: Brill, 1960–), 290–295.

court of law (*mahkama; mahkeme*)   Although some changes were made, the Ottoman justice system evolved from and reflected the structure of the justice systems of previous Islamic states. Until the TANZIMAT reform period of 1839–76, only one type of court existed in the Ottoman Empire. In keeping with Islamic law, or SHARIA, this court had only one judge or KADI, trained in an imperial madrasa, and although it was possible to appeal a judgment, there was no regular multi-staged court structure. In practice, however, the Divan or Imperial Council, the Friday Court, and the court of the KADIASKER, the top judicial official in the empire, accepted and discussed appeals.

Ottoman judicial opinions were the sole purview of judges, although they had assistants. The most important assistant was the clerk (*katib*). Another assistant, the *naib*, assisted the *kadı* in judging, took depositions during investigations out of court, and judged in the *kadı's* stead if he was absent. In some courts, a vice-kadı (*kassam*) was in charge of the dividing up of inheritances. *Kadıs* made decisions in their court regardless of the views of jurisconsults or muftis. Although the Ottoman court system provided for trial observers, they merely watched the trial and did not give any opinions. Because they did not participate in the judging process their role should not be confused with that played by the jury in some Western judicial systems.

In small settlements, courthouses were not distinct structures. The judge presided either in a part of his house or in the mosque. Judgments were usually reached after one hearing, although certain trials required further investigation and a second hearing.

The Ottoman court also expanded its role depending on the need of the individual community. Where notary publics and municipalities did not exist, some transactions of purchases or marriages were finalized in court. Municipal duties—such as giving zoning permits, protecting the environment, the administration of religious foundations, and the protection of orphans and infants—were also sometimes handled by the court. All the works and transactions performed by the courts were recorded in court records or registers (*sicil*). These inventories help to illuminate the activities of the Ottoman courts and contain valuable information regarding the social life, gender relations, and other aspects of the communities under the courts' jurisdiction.

After the Tanzimat period, the Ottoman judicial system underwent significant changes. New courts were established, the Western system of assembled judges was introduced, and a two-stage judicial appeal system was adopted. After various trials, two main court structures were formed. One was the classical Ottoman court, which continued to exist as sharia courts (*şeriyye mahkemesi*). The other was a new court, or the *nizamiye mahkemesi*.

Mustafa Şentop

Further reading: Colin Imber, *Ebu's-su'ud: The Islamic Legal Tradition* (Stanford, Calif.: Stanford University Press, 1997); Halil İnalcık, "Mahkama," in *Encyclopaedia of Islam*, 2nd ed., vol. 6 (Leiden: Brill, 1960–); Ronald C. Jennings, *Studies on Ottoman Social History in the Sixteenth and Seventeenth Century: Women, Zimmis and Sharia Courts in Kayseri, Cyprus and Trabzon* (Istanbul: Isis, 1999); Galal Nahal, *The Judicial Administration of Ottoman Egypt in the Seventeenth Century* (Minneapolis: Bibliotheca Islamica, 1979); Martin Shapiro, *Courts: A Comparative and Political Analysis* (Chicago: University of Chicago Press, 1981).

covered market *See* GRAND BAZAAR; MARKET.

Cretan War (1645–1669) The Cretan War refers to a conflict between the Ottomans and the Venetians between 1645 and 1669 for the possession of the large island of CRETE. Today a possession of GREECE, Crete is situated at the intersection of important sea routes in the eastern Mediterranean and was one of the last significant conquests of the Ottoman Empire, taken only a few decades before the Ottoman retreat from central Europe began. Until it fell to Ottoman control, the island had been under Venetian rule from the time of the Fourth Crusade in 1204.

The Ottomans began the war in 1645, exploiting a favorable international situation: the end of their long war against Safavid Persia (1624–39) in Asia and the continuation of the Thirty Years' War (1618–48) that involved many of the European powers. At the same time, internal changes at the court of Ottoman Sultan IBRAHIM I (r. 1640–48), which came to be dominated by a war party under the leadership of the sultan's favorites Cinci Hüseyin Hoca and Silahdar Yusuf Agha, also favored a campaign against Venetian Crete. The provocation for the beginning of the Ottoman campaign was a Maltese pirate attack in the vicinity of Crete against a ship carrying a number of Ottoman notables from ISTANBUL to EGYPT in the autumn of 1644. The Ottomans accused the Venetians of Crete of having given harbor to Maltese pirates, and the following summer an Ottoman army under Silahdar Yusuf, promoted to the rank of pasha and appointed grand admiral, landed in western Crete with the Ottoman galley fleet.

During the first years of the campaign, the Ottoman army managed to conquer the two major fortified cities on the western part of the island (1645: Chania, 1646: Rethymno), as well as most of the countryside. They declared the island an Ottoman province (*eyalet*) and, in 1651, promulgated a special law code (*kanunname*) and completed a detailed property survey (*tahrir*) of Crete. However, the commander of the invading army, Deli Hüseyin Pasha, was unable to conquer the capital city of Venetian Crete, Candia (Ottoman Kandiye, present-day Iráklion), a fortress specially designed to withstand the increasing firepower of 17th-century warfare. The inability of the Ottoman army to capture Candia was also a result of Venice's successful strategy of blockading the Dardanelles with its fleet, thus preventing the regular re-supply of men and ammunition from Istanbul to the Cretan expedition. Between 1648 and 1656, the Ottoman fleet was often prevented from coming out of the Dardanelles, and the fleet was defeated in two major encounters: first in 1651 in the waters of Naxos and then in 1656 at the entrance of the Dardanelles.

Even when the Ottomans managed to lift the Venetian blockade of the Straits in 1657 thanks to the efforts of Grand Vizier Köprülü Mehmed Pasha (1656–61) (*see* KÖPRÜLÜ FAMILY), the necessary reinforcements for the siege of Candia, which had started in 1647, were not dispatched. The war in Crete was no longer a priority for Köprülü Mehmed Pasha, who was busy punishing Prince György Rákóczi II of TRANSYLVANIA for undertaking an unauthorized campaign against Poland, and suppressing the rebellion of an Ottoman provincial governor, Abaza Hasan Pasha, in Anatolia. The Ottoman position in Crete was seriously endangered and, in 1660, an allied French-Venetian fleet successfully pillaged the environs of Candia and the Ottoman camp outside the city.

It was only after the Treaty of Vasvár (1664), following an unsuccessful Ottoman campaign against Habsburg HUNGARY and AUSTRIA, that Grand Vizier Köprülü Fazıl Ahmed Pasha (1661–76), son of Köprülü Mehmed Pasha, decided to renew the attempt to conquer Candia. At the head of a large expedition, the grand vizier arrived on the island of Crete in the autumn of 1666. This time, the Venetians obtained little support from western Europe. A French force that arrived in the spring of 1669 sailed back home after a short period of fighting. The commander of the Venetians, Francesco Morosini, had no alternative but to surrender the keys of the town, "the most beautiful crown to adorn the head of the Most Serene Republic" according to the Venetians, in September 1669. According to the peace that was then concluded, the Venetians left Candia and abandoned all their possessions in Crete. The island fortresses of Souda, Granbousa, and Spinalonga remained under Venetian rule until they were conquered by the Ottomans in 1715. Köprülü Fazıl Ahmed Pasha stayed on the island for a short time to oversee the implementation of the peace as well as the Ottomanization and Islamization of Crete. A new and innovative law code (*kanunname-i cedit*) was promulgated for the Ottoman province of Crete and a new property survey, or *tahrir*, was carried out throughout the island. During and after the Cretan War, voluntarily CONVERSION to Islam resulted in the formation of an important Muslim community on the island, which nonetheless continued to be dominated by the Orthodox Christian majority.

Elias Kolovos

Further reading: Irene Bierman, "The Ottomanization of Crete," in *The Ottoman City and its Parts: Urban Structure and Social Order*, edited by Irene A. Bierman, Rifa'at A. Abou-El-Haj, and Donald Preziosi (New Rochelle, N.Y.: A.D. Caratzas, 1991), 53–75; Molly Greene, *A Shared World: Christians and Muslims in the Early Modern Mediterranean* (Princeton, N.J.: Princeton University Press, 2000); Kenneth M. Setton, *Venice, Austria, and the Turks in the Seventeenth Century* (Philadelphia: The American Historical Society, 1991).

Crete (Candia; *Gk.*: Kriti; *Turk.*: Girit)   After the Ottoman conquest of CYPRUS in 1570, Crete was the only eastern Mediterranean island of any importance that remained in Venetian hands. Aside from the general desire to control as much territory as possible, Venetian possession of Crete was a particular problem for the Ottomans because it lay directly in the main sea lane that connected ISTANBUL, the imperial capital, to its important province of EGYPT. Egypt was the breadbasket of the Ottoman Empire, much as it had been for previous empires, and maintaining the link was a vital concern. The issue was compounded by the fact that the 17th century saw a huge upsurge in Christian piracy in the eastern Mediterranean. Given the maritime technology of the time, pirates depended upon ready access to ports of refuge where they could take shelter and replenish their water supply. The southern coast of Crete offered such a safe harbor. Desperate to avoid war with the Ottomans, the Venetians did their best to chase pirates away, but at that point VENICE was in decline and no longer enjoyed the resources that would have allowed it to adequately guard its extensive coastline in Crete. Predictably, then, it was an attack by pirates known as the KNIGHTS OF ST. JOHN on Ottoman shipping in 1644 that set off the long (1645–1669) Ottoman-Venetian War of Candia (*see* CRETAN WAR), Candia being the Venetian term for both the island of Crete and its capital city, today's Iráklion. The war was immensely costly for the Ottomans but they managed finally to prevail and 500 years of Venetian rule on the island came to an end.

The conquest of the island was the first major Ottoman territorial acquisition in 100 years, coming about long after the age of Ottoman expansion had ended. Therefore, the organization and incorporation of the island into the empire was somewhat irregular. The outright grant of large blocks of territory to imperial elites, and high levels of CONVERSION to Islam amongst the indigenous (Orthodox Christian) population, were perhaps the two most striking anomalies. Crete was the only Greek island where large numbers of the local population chose to become Muslim. The reasons for this are still unclear but two factors must have been quite important. First, the Orthodox Cretans had endured half a millennium of religious persecution under the Catholic Venetians and this had certainly weakened the religious leadership on the island. Second, by the time the sultan's army arrived on the island's shores in 1645, Ottoman methods of warfare had changed dramatically from previous centuries. The long war was marked by extensive recruitment of the islanders and this close contact with the Ottoman military must have also encouraged conversion to Islam. Whatever the reasons, the mixed population of Christians and Muslims made the age of nationalism a particularly bloody one in Crete.

After the GREEK WAR OF INDEPENDENCE (1821–30), the Greeks of Crete, which was not included in the borders of the new state, rose up repeatedly to demand union with GREECE. This was opposed by the island's Muslim population and the 19th century was marked by a downward spiral of violence, as Christian and Muslim Cretans repeatedly clashed and the Ottoman authorities responded with severe measures against the Christian population. Although the Ottomans were able to prevail militarily against the Christians, they did not succeed on the world diplomatic stage. The Ottoman Empire was now called "the sick man of Europe" and it was Europe that decided, ultimately, which pieces of the dying empire were going to be given away to newly founded states such as Greece. In the end, European pressure forced the Ottomans to cede Crete to Greece in 1912.

Molly Greene

Further reading: Molly Greene, *A Shared World: Christians and Muslims in the Early Modern Mediterranean* (Princeton, N.J.: Princeton University Press, 2000).

Crimea   *See* CRIMEAN TATARS; CRIMEAN WAR.

Crimean Khanate   *See* CRIMEAN TATARS.

Crimean Tatars   A Turkic-speaking ethnic group that founded a khanate in the Crimea and on the grassy steppes above the BLACK SEA in the first half of the 15th century, the Crimean Tatars played an important role in Ottoman history. The Tatars, also known as Mongols, originally arrived on the Crimean peninsula along with the Kipchak Turkic tribes. The Kipchak tribes, along with the other local Turkic and Indo-European inhabitants (Greeks, Alans, Goths, Armenians) of the region, had a major impact on the development of the Tatars who swept in around 1238–39. Under Mongol-Tatar domination, the Crimea was an independent unit, both economically and militarily. In the 1440s Hajji Giray (r. 1426–56), a descendant of Genghis Khan's grandson Toka Temür, created a self-governing khanate with the support of the grand duke of Lithuania and the Crimean Tatar clans. Militarily, the Crimea relied on the inexhaustible human resources of the steppe. Economically, it depended on the peninsula's strong agricultural and pastoral resources and the taxes paid by the Genoese trading colonies on the southern coast of the Crimea.

Following the death of Hajji Giray in 1466, the Ottomans became embroiled in the struggle for succession. Backed by the Ottomans, Hajji Giray's younger son, Mengli Giray (r. 1466–74, 1475–76, 1478–1514), seized power by defeating his brother, Nurdevlet (r. 1466, 1474–75, 1476–78), who was supported by the khan of the Tatar Great Horde and the Genoese. The Ottomans took advantage of the distraction caused by the struggle for power, eliminating the peninsula's Italian commercial colonies and annexing the southern coast of the Crimea that became an Ottoman subprovince, the *sancak* of CAFFA.

The accession of Ottoman-supported Mengli Giray linked the Crimea and the Ottoman Empire on the basis of mutual interest. The Tatars became vassals of ISTANBUL but remained generally independent in terms of their internal and foreign affairs. The election of new khans, for example, was conducted by the four ruling Tatar tribes, and the results of the elections were generally accepted and acknowledged by the Ottoman sultans. However, the Tatar khans were required to send members of their families to Istanbul as hostages as an act of loyalty to the Ottoman court. As a result, the Crimean Tatars enjoyed the protection of the sultan, and the Ottomans relied on Tatar subsidiary troops during their campaigns against eastern Europe.

THE 16TH CENTURY

During the first half of the 16th century the Crimean Khanate was a typical nomadic empire, and as such it had several basic goals: restoring the political cohesiveness experienced under Mongol rule, subduing rebellious clans, and collecting taxes originally paid to the Golden Horde by Poland-Lithuania and the Grand Duke of Muscovy (RUSSIA). The legitimacy of the khan was ensured by his ancestral connection to Genghis Khan. Moreover, the names of the khans were mentioned in the *hutbe* (the Friday sermon in Islam). The final legitimizing tactic utilized by the ruling Tatars was the practice of minting coins (*sikke*) bearing the names of the khans.

The administration of the Crimean Khanate was firmly steeped in tradition. The classical division of center, right, and left wings was common, including the khan, his brothers, and often times his sons atop the hierarchy. The leaders of each wing were titled *kalga* or *nureddin*. Due to the fact that Tatar succession was not defined, the militarily experienced *kalgas* and *nureddins* were well placed to gain the throne. However, power in the Crimea was not achieved through possession of the throne alone. As a ruler, the khan did not hold total power and was forced to seek the support of the Karachi beys of the four ruling Tatar clans: Shirin, Barin, Argin, and Kipchak. Only through the support of the Karachi beys and Ottoman confirmation could power in the Crimea be maintained.

The bulk of the Crimean military strength came from the four ruling clans. The khan also had access to additional manpower in the form of members of the Giray dynasty and their escorts as well as their personal *tüfenkçi* (musketeers), numbering approximately 500 men. Additionally, from 1532 on, the Ottoman Empire provided the khan with a small, fully funded artillery and army. Crimean military campaigns were also commonly joined by nomadic hordes seeking plunder, but their military value was not significant.

Income for the Crimean Khanate came from three main areas: taxes paid by neighboring states, revenues of the khanate, and subsidies paid by the Ottoman government or Sublime Porte. During the 16th century the Crimean khans were paid a regular tribute (*tiyiş*) by the Polish king and the Muscovite czar consisting of cash, costly textiles, and fur. Most of the land of the khanate was commonly owned by the ruling clans and was cultivated by free farmers and slaves. The bulk of the khans' income came from trade in goods and salt. However, a substantial portion also stemmed from plunder, the most lucrative part of which was the slave trade. As an additional supplement, the Porte paid an annuity (*salyane*) to the khan, as well as the *kalga* and *nureddin*, and provided a cash subsidy for military expenses.

The reigns of the two most important Tatar khans of the 16th century, Sahib Giray (1532–1551) and Devlet Giray (r. 1551–77), were marked by competition against Muscovy (known later as Russia). Although the Giray dynasty established khans in both Kazan and Astrakhan on the Volga River, by the middle of the century the Muscovite czar, Ivan IV, had annexed both khanates to his empire. Hoping to get Astrakhan back, the Ottomans attempted to build a canal between the Volga and the Don rivers in 1569, but the plan failed. In response, Devlet Giray launched a campaign against Moscow in 1571 and burned the city. He failed, however, to retake the two Muslim khanates. Having been forced out of the area originally held by the Golden Horde, the Tatars sought closer relations with the Ottomans. During the period from 1578 to 1590, Tatars fought for the Ottomans in the Persian War, and from 1591 to 1606 Crimean troops also participated in Ottoman campaigns against the Habsburgs in Hungary.

THE 17TH CENTURY

During the 17th century the prestige of the khans declined as a result of increased submission to the Ottoman Empire. The sultan's name was recited before that of the khan in the *hutbes*, and the Sublime Porte often dismissed the khans, exiling the former rulers to the island of RHODES in the southeastern Aegean Sea. The Karachi beys managed to maintain their influence throughout the khanate's existence. However, the election of the khan became more and more of a formality.

The Crimean Khanate was plagued by internal strife during this period as well, facing dissension on the part of the Nogay Tatars, the COSSACKS, and the Kalmyks. The Nogays came under Crimean suzerainty after the Volga region fell into Russian hands. The khan offered them Budjak, the southern part of Bessarabia (in the Odessa province of present-day UKRAINE), but the Nogays preferred the idea of Ottoman suzerainty. The struggle for control led to many bloody conflicts between the khans and their Nogay subjects seeking to break away in the first half of the 17th century. The Cossacks, moreover, were a continual threat to the Crimea from about the middle of the 16th century. Using light, quick riverboats, the Cossacks would descend the Dnieper River attacking settlements, ransacking merchants, and taking prisoners. Moreover, both the Polish-Lithuanian Commonwealth and Muscovy utilized the Cossacks as a shield to deflect Tatar raids. The Buddhist Kalmyks, speakers of a Mongolian language, settled on the lower Volga during the beginning of the 17th century. Originally, the Kalmyks were in the service of the czar, and they served a similar function as the Cossacks.

The Tatars were active militarily in the second half of the 17th century. During the uprising against the Polish-Lithuanian Commonwealth led by the Ukrainian hetman Bohdan Khmelnytsky, the Crimean khan, Islam Giray III (r. 1644–54), was a key ally of the Cossacks. On the other hand, Islam Giray's successor (and predecessor) Mehmed Giray IV (r. 1641–44, 1654–66) mediated between the Commonwealth and the Cossacks. The Tatar khan also joined the Northern War for hegemony over the Polish lands bordering Baltic Sea. After Ukraine joined Russia (1654) the Tatars backed the hetmans who were against Russia. In 1672, the khan Selim Giray (r. 1671–78, 1684–91) participated in the occupation of the southeastern borderlands of the Commonwealth (Podolia). In 1683 the Tatars, led by Murad Giray (1678–83), were defeated outside Vienna (*see* VIENNA, SIEGES OF) while fighting on the Ottoman side, but during the second reign of Selim Giray his Tatars continued to support the Ottoman army against the advancing Habsburg troops until the TREATY OF KARLOWITZ in 1699.

THE 18TH CENTURY

By the early 18th century, the Crimean administration was beginning to encounter some serious problems. The Treaty of Istanbul in 1700 declared that the Polish king and the Russian czar would no longer pay tribute to the Crimean khans; it also left the castle of AZAK, which had been occupied by the Don Cossacks, in Russian hands. Pillaging and taking prisoners became more difficult for career soldiers as a result of the treaties. The decline in these acts of freebooting caused a severe economic crisis in the Crimea, and the poorly armed Tatar army was no longer able to repulse Russian attacks. The result of this military ineffectiveness was that, in 1736, Russian General Münnich reached the Crimean capital of Bakhchisarai and burned it. Administrative reform and political compromise became inevitable for the Crimean Tatars. Shahin Giray (r. 1777–83), who had been educated in Europe, set these changes in motion with the support of the Russians. These reforms however, were too extreme for Tatar society and provoked resistance among the religious leaders (ULEMA).

With the end of the RUSSO-OTTOMAN WAR OF 1768–74, the TREATY OF KÜÇÜK KAYNARCA declared the "independence" of the Crimean Khanate. However, this new independence was short-lived as Russia annexed the Crimea in 1783, organizing a new province called Tavrida. Following the Russian annexation, vast numbers of Tatars migrated to Ottoman territories. A second huge wave of migration took place following the CRIMEAN WAR (1853–56). During the early part of the 20th century, a movement to reform the Tatar society and language, led by Ismail Gaspıralı (1851–1914), arose. In 1917 the Crimea became independent for a brief period; in 1944 the Soviet government deported the native Tatars to Uzbekistan, wrongly accusing them of collaborating with Nazi Germany. Approximately half of the Tatar population died as a result of Soviet deportation, and it was only in 1989 that the Tatars were permitted to return to the Crimea. Today significant Tatar communities can be found in Turkey, Romania, Bulgaria, Germany, and the United States.

Mária Ivanics

Further reading: L. J. D. Collins, "The Military Organization and Tactics of the Crimean Tatars during the Sixteenth and Seventeenth Centuries," in *War, Technology and Society in the Middle East,* edited by V. J. Parry and M. E. Yapp (London: Oxford University Press, 1975), 257–276; Alan W. Fisher, *The Crimean Tatars* (Stanford, Calif.: Hoover Institution Publications, 1978); Halil İnalcık, "The Khan and the Tribal Aristocracy: The Crimean Khanate under Sahib Giray I." *Harvard Ukrainian Studies* 3–4 (1979–1980): 445–466; Mária Ivanics, "The Role of the Crimean Tatars in the Habsburg-Ottoman War (1595–1606)," in *The Great Ottoman-Turkish Civilization,* vol.

1, *Politics*, edited by Güler Eren, Ercüment Kuran, Nejat Göyünç, İlber Ortaylı, and Kemal Çiçek (Ankara: Yeni Türkiye, 2000), 302–310; Uli Schamiloglu, "The Qaraçi Beys of the Later Golden Horde: Notes on the Organization of the Mongol World Empire." *Archivum Eurasiae Medii Aevi* 4 (1984): 283–297.

Crimean War (1853–1856) The outbreak of this war, the only general European conflict in the period between 1815 and 1914, resulted from a combination of Russian diplomatic and military aggression against the Ottoman Empire and concomitant British fears concerning a potential recalibration of the balance of power in the BLACK SEA region to the benefit of RUSSIA. Following the TREATY OF HÜNKAR ISKELESI (1833)—a Russo-Ottoman defensive alliance that significantly increased Russian diplomatic influence in the Ottoman Empire—British foreign policy in the Balkans and the Near East centered on maintaining the territorial integrity of the Ottoman Empire and resisting any forward moves by the Russian Empire.

In step with a series of wars fought between the Ottoman and Russian empires over the preceding century, in the Crimean War, Ottoman and Russian troops engaged in military conflict in the Balkans and along the Russo-Ottoman frontier in eastern Anatolia (along the present-day Turkish border with Georgia, ARMENIA, and IRAN). However, the Crimean Peninsula in the north-central Black Sea region constituted the main theater of the conflict between the Russians and the Anglo-French forces. Not surprisingly, given the heavy casualties suffered in this theater of the war, the conflict for control of the Black Sea region is remembered as the Crimean War.

The outbreak of the Crimean War signaled the unraveling of the post-Napoleonic Concert of Europe—a diplomatic system instituted at the Congress of Vienna in 1815 that aimed to prevent warfare between the so-called Great Powers of Europe. The diplomatic blunderings that resulted in the Crimean War originated in a dispute between Orthodox Russia and Catholic FRANCE concerning rights over Christian religious sites and populations in JERUSALEM. Ottoman backing of the French position in this diplomatic confrontation resulted in the dispatch in February 1853 of a Russian mission to ISTANBUL led by Prince Alexander Menshikov. During his negotiations with the Ottoman Sublime Porte or government, Menshikov not only argued for the assertion of Russian rights over Orthodox Christian sites in the Holy Land but also demanded Ottoman recognition of Russian rights to speak on behalf of the 12 million Orthodox subjects of the Ottoman Empire. Beginning with the TREATY OF KÜÇÜK KAYNARCA (1774), Russian government officials had increasingly asserted their presumed right and responsibility to protect the interests of their Orthodox co-religionists in the Ottoman Empire. Most of the Ottoman Empire's Orthodox subjects lived in the Balkans.

1853: THE WAR BEGINS

Presented as an ultimatum during Menshikov's February 1853 mission to Istanbul, Russian demands concerning the Orthodox population of the Ottoman Empire were rejected by the Ottoman Sultan ABDÜLMECID I (r. 1839 –61). In response, the Russian army in early July 1853 moved across the Prut River and took up positions in MOLDAVIA (in present-day Romania). This move constituted an act of war as Moldavia, despite its status as a Russian protectorate, was under nominal Ottoman suzerainty. With British and French warships en route to Istanbul, and believing that they could count on further British and French support, the Ottoman Empire declared war on the Russian Empire in October 1853. The Ottoman army, preparing for war with the Russians, crossed the DANUBE RIVER and moved forward out of eastern Anatolia into the southern CAUCASUS.

In the winter of 1853, the Ottoman Black Sea fleet was harbored in Sinop. This north Anatolian port lay only 100 miles across the Black Sea from Sevastopol—the headquarters of the Russian Black Sea fleet on the southwestern tip of the Crimean Peninsula. Destined to be the focal point of military conflict in the Crimean War, Sevastopol in the mid-19th century was a well-fortified port city with a population of roughly 50,000. In the early morning of November 30, six Russian ships of the line, under the command of Admiral Pavel Nakhimov, launched an attack on Sinop using exploding shell projectiles. Within one hour the entire Ottoman Black Sea fleet had been sunk. The town of Sinop was torched and the commander of the Ottoman Black Sea fleet, Osman Pasha, was taken captive.

The Russian bombardment of Sinop, which intensified the increasing Russo-phobia of British and French public opinion (a new factor in European foreign policy decision making), internationalized the 1853 Russo-Ottoman conflict. On March 28, 1854, following another round of ineffective diplomacy, the British and French declared war on Russia. The opening move in this phase of the war was an Allied bombardment of Russian positions in the eastern Baltic Sea. While this theater remained somewhat peripheral to the main proceedings in the Black Sea region, the Allied threat in the Baltic served to pin down 200,000 Russian troops in the north.

1854: THE SIEGE OF SILISTRA

In order to take advantage of weather conditions conducive to mid-19th-century warfare, Russian campaigns in the Balkans were generally restricted to the period between spring and autumn. In the spring of 1854, the

Russian army opened their campaign by sending two army corps, a combined total of 50,000 troops under the command of Prince Paskevich, across the Danube River at the key crossings of Galatz and Tulcea. In mid-April these Russian troops proceeded to lay siege to the Ottoman fortress town of Silistra on the southern bank of the river. Under the leadership of the capable Ottoman commander Omer Pasha, Silistra was well defended by a 12,000-strong Ottoman army, composed mostly of Egyptian and Albanian troops. Sustained Ottoman resistance at Silistra allowed British and French troops to build up a significant army in the Bulgarian Black Sea port of Varna.

This buildup of Allied troop strength in the Balkans, coupled with an Allied naval bombardment of the important Russian Black Sea port city of Odessa, compelled the Russian army to break off the siege of Silistra and to retreat back across the Prut (which forms the present-day border between Romania and the Republic of Moldova) into Russia proper. Following the Russian retreat, Czar Nicholas I acceded to a joint Austrian-Ottoman military occupation of the Danubian principalities. The Russian retreat and the Austrian-Ottoman occupation of the principalities effectively ended the Danubian phase of the Crimean War.

In the southern Caucasus, forward Ottoman movements in the autumn and winter of 1853 were easily checked by experienced Russian troops, and the Russians seized the initiative in this theater of the Crimean War. A Russian victory in late July 1854 near Bayazid (close to the present-day Turkish border with Iran) opened the way for a Russian advance in strength toward the key eastern Anatolian Ottoman cities of Kars, Erzurum, and Trebizond. A decisive victory by 20,000 Russian troops over 40,000 Ottoman troops at Kurudere near Kars in August closed the 1854 campaign season.

1855: KARS, BALACLAVA, AND SEVASTOPOL

In preparation for an anticipated Russian offensive in the spring of 1855, the 12,000-strong Ottoman army in Kars was reorganized and placed under the overall operational command of a British officer, William Fenwick Williams. In June 1855, the Russian army of the Caucasus, under the command of General Muraviev, appeared before Kars fully prepared for a protracted siege. Despite the fact that the Ottoman troops had not been paid for two years, the defenders of Kars performed admirably, especially the English-trained Ottoman artillery commander Tahir Pasha. A dwindling food supply and the ravages of disease (cholera and typhus), however, forced Williams in December 1855 to surrender Kars to Muraviev.

Rather than stand down their troops following the Russian retreat from the principalities in June 1854, the British and French command decided to strike at the

heart of Russian strength in the Black Sea region—the fortress port of Sevastopol on the Crimean Peninsula. On September 14, 1854, the bulk of the Allied army, composed primarily of French and British troops, landed in Eupatoria on the western shore of the Crimean Peninsula. Moving toward Sevastopol, the Allies scored a victory on the Alma River and, following two major battles (Balaklava and Inkerman), settled in for a siege of Sevastopol. At the height of the Crimean conflict, the Allies maintained an army of almost 140,000 troops on the Crimean Peninsula. Russian military personnel in Sevastopol numbered roughly 100,000. Following an 11-month siege, on September 10, 1855, Sevastopol fell to the Allies. The final siege and occupation of the port city resulted in 24,000 dead.

Although Ottoman troops did provide significant labor and logistical support to the Allied war effort, Ottoman military contributions to the Crimean campaign and the siege of Sevastopol were minor compared to those of the French and British. Some 7,000 Ottoman troops participated in the landings at Eupatoria and for the balance of the campaign were employed primarily to harass Russian supply lines and to screen any Russian attempts to relieve the siege.

THE END OF THE WAR AND THE AFTERMATH

The fall of Sevastopol, Allied bombardments of the key Russian Black Sea ports of Kerch (May 1855) and Kinburun (October 1855), and an Austrian threat to enter the war on the Allied side compelled the Russian czar Alexander II, who had ascended to the Russian throne following Nicholas I's death on March 2, 1855, to agree to negotiations to end the war. Overall, 800,000 soldiers died in the Crimean War. If not for the improvements in the provision of medical relief efforts by Russian and Allied medical personnel, overall casualty totals for the war (from both fighting and disease) would have been still higher. The British nurse Florence Nightingale, who organized medical relief services in Scutari (present-day Üsküdar) near Istanbul, and the Russian doctor N. I. Pirogov, working in Sevastopol, pioneered the provisioning of medical relief services during the Crimean War.

Significant refugee movements accompanied the cessation of fighting. For instance, the CRIMEAN TATARS, charged by Czar Alexander II with collaborating with Allied forces on the Crimean Peninsula during the war, were put under significant pressure to leave the Russian Empire. Russian officials accused Crimean Tatars of acting as a fifth column and disrupting Russian supply lines during the fighting on the Crimean Peninsula. Many Crimean Tatars were victims of Russian oppression and violence and fled for safety to the Ottoman Empire. In the period 1856–60 an estimated 100,000 Crimean Tatars left the Russian Empire and sought refuge in

Ottoman ports along the northern Anatolian coast and in Istanbul.

Following the Crimean War, on February 18, 1856, Sultan Abdülmecid introduced the second phase of the TANZIMAT period by issuing what is conventionally known as the Imperial Rescript of Reforms (Islahat Ferman), launching a far-reaching reform program for the empire. Although the initiatives unveiled in this edict built upon ongoing reform efforts dating as far back to the pre-Tanzimat reign of Sultan SELIM III (1789–1807), the Reform Edict of 1856 was enacted under considerable pressure from Allied diplomats in Istanbul. Key provisions in the edict included assurances of equal treatment for non-Muslim populations in the Ottoman Empire in the areas of education, justice, religion, and taxation.

1856: THE TREATY OF PARIS

The Treaty of Paris, signed on March 29, 1856, ended the Crimean War. On balance, the terms of the Treaty of Paris, insofar as they crippled the Russian Empire, were advantageous to the Ottoman Empire. Territorially, the Russians were forced to relinquish their control over Kars, the Danubian delta, and southern Bessarabia. In return, the Allies gave up their occupation of the Crimean Peninsula. The lower course of the Danube River was internationalized for commerce. The Danubian principalities remained under Ottoman sovereignty, albeit with increased autonomy backed by a joint European guarantee. The Black Sea was demilitarized and neither the Russians nor the Ottomans were allowed to harbor warships along the shores of the sea. Additionally, the Russians and Ottomans agreed to destroy all their coastal fortifications on the Black Sea. All previous Russo-Ottoman bilateral treaties (e.g., the TREATY OF KÜÇÜK KAYNARCA, TREATY OF EDIRNE, and TREATY OF HÜNKAR ISKELESI) were annulled and the Russians agreed to renounce any rights of protection over Orthodox populations in the Ottoman Empire. The Ottoman Empire was termed an equal member of the Concert of Europe and the Allied powers agreed to guarantee the territorial integrity of the Ottoman Empire. In Article 9 of the Treaty of Paris, the signatories agreed to adhere to the principle of non-intervention in the domestic affairs of the Ottoman Empire.

Andrew Robarts

Further reading: Roderic Davison, "Ottoman Diplomacy and Its Legacy," in *Imperial Legacy: The Ottoman Imprint on the Balkans and the Middle East*, edited by L. Carl Brown (New York: Columbia University Press, 1996); Caroline Finkel, *Osman's Dream: The Story of the Ottoman Empire* (New York: Basic Books, 2006); David Goldfrank, *The Origins of the Crimean War* (New York: Longman Publishing, 1994); Charles King, *The Black Sea: A History* (Oxford: Oxford University Press, 2004).

Croatia (*Croat.*: Hrvatska; *Turk.*: Hırvatistan) Today, Croatia is a state in southeastern Europe or in the western Balkans, with Zagreb as its capital. Its territory is about 22,000 square miles (55,000 square km), and the country has slightly more than 4 million inhabitants. The country's borders differ substantially from those of the early Middle Ages: there was no clearly defined border to the east, and the control of Croatian rulers and nobles extended some 60 miles (100 km) to the northwest and about 120 miles (200 km) to the south, into present-day BOSNIA-HERZEGOVINA.

The origins of the Croatian people are not very clear. It is possible that the area was first inhabited by peoples of Iranian or even Turkic origin. Regardless of their origin, they were quickly Slavicized. The Slavs migrated from present-day southeastern POLAND and western UKRAINE westward to Bohemia, then southward sometime around 600 C.E., although some historians argue that this migration occurred in the late eighth century. Some Slavs moved into the area between Carinthia and Montenegro, but most settled between eastern Istria and the mouth of the river Cetina. In the Adriatic hinterland they merged with the already established Slavs and many speakers of local vernaculars pertaining to the just emerging family of Romance languages. The Slavic population of northwestern Croatia had some elements of political organization, but the area frequently changed hands between Croatian, Frankish, and Hungarian rulers until the late 11th or early 12th century, when the Hungarian kings gained lasting control over Croatia. These political ties to HUNGARY continued for the next 600 years or more, through the rule of the Habsburg dynasty that began in 1526, and until the close of WORLD WAR I in 1918, when Croatia entered the Yugoslav period, which ended in 1991–92.

Although fairly autonomous, Croatia was part of the Hungarian kingdom and thus political relations between Croatia and the Ottoman Empire were mainly confined to interactions with local authorities, such as correspondence about and negotiations of borderland issues.

Despite the fact that formal political relations were limited, the Ottoman Empire was nevertheless an important presence for the peoples of Croatia, especially after the early 15th century when the continued expansion of the Muslim Ottomans began to be perceived as a threat to the Catholic population of northwestern Croatia and central Bosnia. After the fall of Bosnia to the Ottomans in 1463, Ottoman expansion continued in the southern areas (Herzegovina and the coastland up to the river Cetina), yet in other places it could not break the defense system set up by King Matthias Corvinus of Hungary (r. 1458–90). A new wave of Ottoman conquests began in 1521 and lasted until 1552, at the end of which the Ottomans had conquered a good portion of present-day Croatia, including territories between the rivers Drava and

Sava. For approximately the next 150 years, due mainly to the fact that the Habsburgs (*see* AUSTRIA) had established an efficient defense system in Hungary and Croatia, the borders in the north and south stabilized. The border was, in effect, a strip of no-man's-land running between Koprivnica and Virovitica near the river Drava to Sisak, then westward to a point near the present-day town Karlovac, then southward to the Plitvice lakes, and in the southwest to the Adriatic; in DALMATIA the Venetian-held territory was reduced to small enclaves around the principal towns.

However, east of the Habsburg border in the central region of Croatia, between the rivers Una and Kupa, Bosnian *ghazis* or Muslim warriors (*see* GHAZA) were still making gains against Croatian nobles, who were fighting without Habsburg support. The situation changed in 1593 when the Croatians broke the offensive power of the Bosnian troops with lasting consequences in a battle at Sisak, on the confluence of the rivers Sava and Kupa. In 1606, at the Ottoman-Habsburg Treaty of Zsitvatorok that ended the war of 1593–1601 between the two empires, the Croatians made some further territorial gains, but from 1699 to 1718 Croatia's surface almost doubled as a result of the treaties of KARLOWITZ and Passarowitz that ended the Long War of 1684–99 between the Ottomans and Habsburgs. However, it took some time to negotiate clear lines of control and actual change came slowly. The jurisdiction of the Croatian autonomous administration in the northern parts of the reconquered lands down to the river DANUBE was extended in 1745, while the rest was integrated in 1871 and 1881, after the Habsburg Military Border was abolished.

The century and a half of Ottoman rule in parts of present-day Croatia (from the mid-16th century until the peace of KARLOWITZ in 1699) brought substantial change to the area, but it also allowed economic and social continuity. The vast majority of the Croatian nobility and clergy either left the Ottoman-controlled territories or perished. A great number of peasants followed their masters into more secure parts of Croatia, western Hungary, or Austria. Their abandoned lands were occupied primarily by pastoralist or semi-pastoralist VLACHS from the south or southeast, especially the Ottoman *sancak* of Herzegovina. In many places Catholic priests were replaced by Serbian Orthodox priests or even Protestant preachers, and later by Bosnian Franciscans. The latter had become active in the Adriatic hinterland shortly after the Ottoman conquest of the mid 16th century, moving into Slavonia after the Treaty of Zsitvatorok (1606). Other than freed slaves, few people in rural areas converted to Islam.

On the other hand, continuity persisted in some important segments of the economy and society. In the Adriatic hinterland pastoralism and trade in dairy prod-ucts continued as the main source of income, with perhaps an increase in cattle breeding and some additional income from auxiliary military engagement. The basic social unit of clan and large extended family remained unchanged and towns remained about the same size as before the Ottoman conquest; towns were mainly dwelling places for small or medium-size garrisons made up of peasant soldiers. In the land between the rivers Sava, Drava, and Danube, however, towns such as Ilok, Osijek, and Požega became quite prosperous due to increased commercial activities and craftsmanship; some reached a population of 1,000 to 2,000 taxpayers (which corresponds to 5,000 to 10,000 inhabitants). Nonetheless, according to 17th-century Ottoman travel author EVLIYA ÇELEBI, the level of cultural achievement remained low.

The withdrawal of the Ottomans had perhaps an even greater impact than the earlier raids, war, and direct rule. It triggered deep political changes in Croatia and led to the modern ethnic, cultural, and national identity of its people. The previously loosely connected Croats, Slavonians, and Catholic Bosnians eventually merged into a new Croatian people.

Nenad Moačanin

See also ADRIATIC SEA; HAYDUK; RAGUSA; USKOKS; VENICE.

Further reading: Ivo Goldstein, *Croatia: A History* (Montreal: McGill University Press, 1999); Nenad Moačanin, *Turska Hrvatska* (Zagreb: Matica Hrvatska, 1999); Nenad Moačanin, "Croatia and Bosnia: An 'Eternal' Movement from Integration to Dissolution and Back," in *Zones of Fracture in Modern Europe: The Baltic Countries, the Balkans, and Northern Italy,* edited by Almut Bues (Wiesbaden: Harrassowitz Verlag, 2005), 99–107.

Cromer, Lord (b. 1841–d. 1917) *British high commissioner for Egypt* Evelyn Baring, Lord Cromer after 1891, served as Great Britain's diplomatic adviser to the government of the KHEDIVE and the de facto British governor of EGYPT from 1883 until 1907. His first contact with Egypt came in 1879, when he was Great Britain's choice to serve on the Dual Control Commission set up by Britain and France to manage Egypt's foreign debt and national budget. After the British occupation of Egypt in 1882, Baring was appointed to be Britain's consul-general in CAIRO in 1883. Although he was technically only Her Majesty's diplomatic representative in Egypt, in fact, his role was much more than that. The first test of his power came soon after his arrival. The Egyptian army was facing a losing battle against the forces of Muhammad Ahmad (1844–85), who had assumed the title of Mahdi, in Sudan, and Baring ordered them to retreat. When Khedive TAWFIQ balked at the order, as he viewed Sudan as properly belonging to Egypt, Baring produced a cable from London saying that henceforth his advice must be followed. Policy makers in London were still uncertain as to what Britain's future role in Egypt should be and some sought a withdrawal of British troops from the country. Baring lobbied strenuously for a permanent British military occupation of Egypt, arguing that control of Egypt was vital to the maintenance of the British Empire in India. His view triumphed in Her Majesty's Foreign and Colonial Offices by 1889.

When Khedive Tawfiq died in 1892, Lord Cromer engineered the accession of Tawfiq's underage son, ABBAS HILMI, to the office of khedive. But having done so, Cromer clashed with the young khedive on several issues. On each occasion, however, Cromer won out, demonstrating that he was in fact the real power in Cairo despite his simple diplomatic title. At the same time, Egyptian nationalists, led by MUSTAFA KAMIL, increasingly challenged both Cromer's position as de facto governor-general and the right of British troops to remain in the country at the start of the 20th century. Taking advantage of the explosive growth of NEWSPAPERS, Egyptian nationalists were able to mobilize public opinion and large public demonstrations following the DINSHAWAY INCIDENT in 1906 in which a number of Egyptian nationals were wrongly executed following a scuffle with British troops. Cromer shortly thereafter announced his retirement and returned to England.

Bruce Masters

Further reading: Roger Owen, *Lord Cromer: Victorian Imperialist, Edwardian Proconsul* (Oxford: Oxford University Press, 2004).

cuisine The imperial court of the Ottoman Empire had a major influence on cultural styles throughout the Middle East and the Balkans. In no field of cultural production was this more apparent than in cuisine. The peoples who now inhabit the former Ottoman Empire are extremely proud of their culinary traditions and each claims that its national cuisine is indigenous. An outside observer cannot fail to notice, however, that they are remarkably the same, with only small regional variations. The pastry known as baklava, for instance, is made in SERBIA with apples and layered thin sheets of pastry dough, while that of Greece is made with honey and walnuts and that of SYRIA, pronounced locally as *baqlawa*, is made with sugar-water syrup and pistachios. Many of the dishes produced in the different nations that once composed the empire have the same name, usually a local variation of a Turkish word. These similarities point to the existence of a court cuisine that emanated from the capital in ISTANBUL and was carried to the provincial centers by the officials assigned there who wished to replicate the imperial style in their own localities.

As in all pre-modern empires, there was a major difference between the cuisine of the palace and that of the countryside. Rice, for example, was the mainstay of the imperial kitchens, while peasants in Anatolia and Syria ate boiled cracked wheat (bulgur). Olive oil was used by the elite while peasants inland from the Mediterranean coast used animal fats: butter in the Balkans, sheep fat in Anatolia and the Arab provinces. According to accounts of European travelers to the empire, most peasant diets were healthy in that they consisted almost entirely of vegetables, beans, and grain products, supplemented with cheese and yogurt. Preserved vegetables, either dried or pickled, were a mainstay of winter diets. Despite their healthiness, meals were also monotonous, with meat usually being available only on feast days. Peasant families ate communally out of one bowl and usually with their hands or perhaps a spoon. There were no tables or chairs and so a special mat was often placed on the floor to serve as a table.

By contrast, the elite ate elaborate meals consisting of numerous dishes (*mezze* in Turkish, *mezedhes* in Greek, *mazza* in Arabic) that would be eaten in a leisurely manner. These ranged from simple salads and pureed vegetables and beans to complex combinations of vegetables and meat in various types of sauces. The main course always consisted of meat. Like the poor, the wealthy did not use dinnerware or tables and chairs until the end of the empire when Western dining fashions became a cultural fad in the empire. Muslims, whether religious or not, generally did not drink wine with their meals. But the less religious among them drank a distilled alcoholic drink flavored with anise (*rakı* in Turkish, *ouzo* in Greek, *araq* in Arabic). Ottoman Christians, however, both produced and consumed wine in many parts of the empire. In all the religious traditions of the empire, men and women of the upper classes ate separately. After dinner, COFFEE was invariably served.

Bruce Masters

Further reading: Sami Zubaida and Richard Tapper, eds., *Culinary Cultures of the Middle East* (London: I.B. Tauris, 1994).

currency *See* BANKS AND BANKING; MONEY AND MONETARY SYSTEMS.

Cyprus (*Gk.*: **Kipros, Kypros;** *Turk.*: **Kıbrıs**) In 1565, after a costly and bloody siege, the Ottomans gave up on their attempt to take the island of MALTA from the KNIGHTS OF ST. JOHN. This defeat is important to understanding their successful conquest of Cyprus just five years later. Until 1565, the Ottomans had enjoyed a string of victories in the Mediterranean, both east and west, a record that encouraged them to think that they might

Famagusta was the principle port of Cyprus when the island was conquered by the Ottomans from the Venetians in 1571. The largest medieval cathedral on the island, the Gothic cathedral of St. Nicholas, was converted into a mosque by the Ottomans. *(Photo by Gábor Ágoston)*

attain hegemonic power over the entire sea. After the failure at Malta, the empire gave up its pan-Mediterranean dreams in favor of the more modest policy of consolidating its hold on the eastern half of the sea. The successful attack on Venetian-held Cyprus in 1570 was the first fruit of this new strategy.

Besides having the general goal of eliminating Christian sovereignty in the eastern Mediterranean, Sultan SELIM II (r. 1566–74) had many reasons to be unhappy with Venetian control of Cyprus. About a month after the start of the war, an Ottoman messenger handed the Venetian doge a list of complaints. Among other things, these complaints alleged that Christian corsairs (*see* CORSAIRS AND PIRATES) interfering with Ottoman authority had been supported with food and water in Cyprus in the summer of 1569 and had then gone on to destroy two Ottoman ships, killing all aboard; in the autumn of that year, another Ottoman ship was plundered off the Egyptian coast by corsairs who had previously stopped on the island. Other complaints touched on areas of Ottoman-Venetian relations not connected to Cyprus, but the fact remained that the island sat on one of the main routes connecting ISTANBUL to its vital Arab provinces, particularly EGYPT. Ships proceeded along the Anatolian coast, then cut between RHODES and the mainland, calling at Famagusta (on the eastern coast of Cyprus), BEIRUT, and Sidon before going to Egypt.

The Ottoman fleet reached the Cypriot coast in July 1570. The fortified cities of the island fell one by one, and by August of the following year the Ottomans were masters of the island. From the beginning, the Ottomans presented the conflict as a war against the "Franks" (Westerners, in this case the Venetians), not against the Orthodox Christian peasantry who formed the vast majority of the island's population. To that end, the conquerors were quick to apply the policy of *istimalet* or leniency that had also characterized their earlier conquests in the Balkans. Peasants were thus freed from the JIZYA (tax applied to non-Muslims) for one year and the tax in crops was reduced for the vast majority of the peasantry from the one-third required by the Venetians to one-fifth. The forced labor required by the former Venetian masters of the island was also abolished.

Istanbul's decision to settle a large Turkish Muslim population on the island would have great consequences for the modern history of Cyprus. For in the age of decolonization that began after World War II, the Muslim population of Cyprus (which had become a British colony in 1878) contended fiercely against the island's Greek Orthodox majority which had launched an armed struggle for union with GREECE, since this was obviously not an attractive political outcome for the island's Muslim citizens. Independence, a sort of compromise solution, was granted in 1960, but the conflicting aims of Greek and Turkish nationalism have continued to trouble the island to the present day.

Molly Greene

Further reading: Ronald Jennings, *Christians and Muslims in Cyprus and the Mediterranean World, 1571–1640* (New York,: New York University Press, 1993).

D

Dalmatia (*Serbo-Croat.*: Dalmacija) Dalmatia is a historic coastal region of Croatia, situated in the Balkans between the ADRIATIC SEA, BOSNIA AND HERZEGOVINA, and the southern slopes of Mount Velebit. The coastal islands from Rab in the north as far as Korcula in the south are also considered to belong to the region. The area around Dubrovnik is sometimes considered to be a part of Dalmatia too. The name Dalmatia is derived from the name of the Roman province that covered nearly the whole of the western Balkans. In the medieval period, under Byzantine, Croatian, Hungarian, and Venetian control, Dalmatia shrank to just a few coastal towns and islands. From the beginning of the 15th-century VENICE became the exclusive master of the coast. From the end of that century until 1537, Ottoman expansion in the Balkans forced Croatian nobles and Hungarian troops to withdraw from the hinterland, leaving a thin strip of land between Ottoman lands and Venetian possessions. During the CRETAN WAR (1645–69), the Ottomans lost some territory to the Venetians, and in 1699 and 1717 Venice was able to push its borders far inland. This "greater" Dalmatia was taken over by AUSTRIA after the end of the Republic of Venice in 1797.

The territory under Ottoman control to the west of the River Krka belonged to the *sancak* or subprovince of Kırka. The region from there to the mouth of the Cetina River (near present-day Split) was part of the subprovince of Klis. The remainder of the territory was part of the subprovince of Herzegovina (Hersek). Most of the population was made up of VLACH colonists: the Orthodox population lived in the north, while the rest was Catholic. In the towns (usually more fortified places than urban centers) plus in some fertile places (along the river Cetina) there were Muslims. These Muslims were mostly converts of local origin. In the south most of the population were simple taxpayers, while in other regions some were ordinary Ottoman peasants (*reayas*) and others were taxpayers under the command of their Ottoman *sipahis* or landlords. Near the coast there were also some prosperous WAQF lands.

There were always sharp differences between way of life near the coast, which was more urban and practiced an intensive Mediterranean-style agriculture, and the hinterland, which was more rural and practiced Balkan-style pastoralism. These differences became accentuated during the two centuries of Venetian-Ottoman cohabitation and conflict. Pastoralism made great progress, Ottoman wheat was exchanged for salt, and landings at Zadar, Šibenik, and Split were opened, mainly to serve the needs of Bosnian traders. However, population movements and popular uprisings, such as the HAYDUK and USKOK raids, frequently underminded the military, political, and economic activities of the Venetian and Ottoman authorities. Much of what is known as south Slavic oral heroic epic originated in Dalmatia and neighboring parts of Bosnia-Herzegovina during the long Cretan War.

Nenad Moačanin

Damascus (*Ar.*: Dimashq, al-Sham; *Fr.*: Damas; *Turk.*: Şam) Syria's present-day capital of Damascus also served as capital city of a province of the same name for most of the Ottoman period. The province included most of what is today southern and central SYRIA, LEBANON, Jordan, Israel, and the Palestinian territories, but not northern Syria. Damascus lays claim to being the oldest

After the riot of 1860, wealthy Damascenes moved out of their old-style courtyard houses in the walled city to the suburban quarter of Salihiyya where houses in the late Ottoman style were constructed along paved streets. This photo dates from the 1880s. *(Photograph by Maison Bonfils, courtesy of the University of Pennsylvania Museum, Philadelphia)*

continually inhabited city in the world; it had served as the capital of the early Islamic Umayyad Dynasty (661–750). As such its capture by Sultan SELIM I (r. 1512–20) in 1516 added to the prestige of the Ottoman ruling dynasty. Additionally, the city served as one of the two major starting points (the other being CAIRO) for the HAJJ, the annual pilgrimage to MECCA in which thousands from throughout the Muslim world participated.

Damascus had served as the administrative center of Syria under the MAMLUK EMPIRE that ruled both EGYPT and Syria between 1260 and 1517, and the initial Ottoman policy toward the province was to leave the Mamluk administration more or less in place. Sultan Selim appointed as the province's governor Janbirdi al-Ghazzali, a Mamluk who had betrayed the last Mamluk sultan, Qansuh al-Ghawri, by switching to the Ottoman side before the crucial Battle of Marj al-Dabiq in 1516. With the death of Selim in 1520, however, Janbirdi al-Ghazzali rose in rebellion against Selim's son, SÜLEYMAN I (r.

1520–66). The rebellion was quickly suppressed and the Ottoman general allowed his troops to sack the city in retaliation for its rebellion. From that date, loyal Ottoman officials appointed from ISTANBUL would govern the city for the next two centuries.

Although Damascus was the capital of a fertile province that produced significant revenues for the state, its importance in the Ottoman period was largely linked to its position as an important starting point for the hajj. Because the sultans understood that Damascus held religious significance as the official starting point for the hajj, they sought to impress the pilgrims who would gather in the city with the majesty of the House of Osman by building a mosque complex that might rival the eighth-century Umayyad cathedral mosque that had served as the city's main mosque. Sultan Süleyman placed the imprint of his dynasty on Damascus with the construction of the magnificent Takiyya al-Sulaimaniyya mosque on the banks of the Barada River, outside the city walls. Designed in 1554

The Umayyad mosque is the central landmark of Damascus and one of the oldest surviving mosques in the world. After the old Umayyad capital became an Ottoman provincial center, the Ottomans made renovations to the structure, including the addition of minaret caps in the style of Istanbul, thus marking the city architecturally as an Ottoman possession. *(Photo by Gábor Ágoston)*

by the famed architect Sinan, it was known as the Taki-yya in reference to the Sufi hostel (*tekke* or *zawiyya*) that was established in its courtyard chambers. Sultan Selim II (r. 1566–74) added the Madrasa Salimiyya to his father's mosque and the complex thereafter served as the starting point for the annual pilgrimage to Mecca.

The first century of Ottoman rule brought prosperity to Damascus. The population in both the city and its rural hinterlands grew. This was due in no small part to the peace that the Ottomans were able to effect with the Bedouin tribes who refrained from attacking either the CARAVANS, carrying trade to the city, or the villagers in the fertile oasis, the Ghuta, that lay to its south and supplied the city with most of its fruits and vegetables. But trade with Europe went into a steep decline in the early 16th century as overland trade routes moved north to ALEPPO to avoid BEDOUIN raids and European merchants who had been in Damascus in the late Mamluk period and the early years of Ottoman rule withdrew from the city. In their absence, the people of Damascus acquired a reputation among Europeans as religiously conservative and hostile to outsiders. In the centuries following the departure of the European merchants, the Damascenes themselves would boast that they had never allowed Franks (western Europeans) to live among them, but that was clearly not the case.

The peace that the Ottomans had brokered with the Bedouin tribes broke down in the early 18th century as a new and more aggressive Bedouin ANAZA CONFEDERATION moved out of Arabia into the Syrian Desert. The Anaza proved far less tractable than their predecessors, the MAWALI, had been. They forced caravans coming from Iraq to abandon the trans-desert route to Damascus in favor of one following the EUPHRATES RIVER to Aleppo, as the latter route could be more easily garrisoned. There was, however, no alternative for the hajj route, and the sultan's prestige suffered as the flow of pilgrims to Arabia was disrupted. To preserve the security of the hajj, Sultan AHMED III (r. 1703–30) broke with two centuries of tradition and in 1725 appointed a local man, Ismail Pasha al-Azm, as governor of Damascus.

Ismail Pasha al-Azm was the first of several highly effective governors from the AL-AZM FAMILY whose ethnic origins are uncertain but who had served as tax farmers in central Syria. The Azm family dominated political life in southern Syria for much of the 18th century, with family members serving as governors of the provinces of Damascus and Tripoli on and off from 1725 through 1783. Asad Pasha al-Azm, who ruled Damascus from 1743 until 1757, enjoyed an unprecedented longevity in the position, as the governors of the city who preceded him had held the office for a year or two at most.

In the 19th century, Damascus was the site of two infamous incidents that involved the city's non-Muslim minorities and that drew the critical attention of western Europeans to the city: the DAMASCUS INCIDENT of 1840 and the DAMASCUS RIOTS of 1860. Both were connected with a return of centralized Ottoman control over the province during the TANZIMAT reform period and with a shift in the city's economic identity as Syria increasingly became a producer of raw materials for the world market and a consumer of imported manufactured goods. This led to the displacement of many who had worked in the handicraft sector and to the enrichment of a few who were able to gain control of lucrative farmlands.

In the aftermath of the riots, the province was reorganized into the province of Syria in 1864, but substantial reforms to the province's political and economic infrastructure did not occur until the Ottoman reformer, MIDHAT PASHA, was appointed as governor in 1878. Although his appointment was intended as an exile, Midhat Pasha threw himself into the task of modernizing the province in his brief two-year term. These modernizations included construction of a road connecting the city to its port at BEIRUT, the further development of the province's network of telegraph lines, the construction of new government schools, and the establishment of a public library. In the second half of the 19th century, wealthy residents of the city began to construct new houses in suburbs such as al-Salahiyya, outside the city walls, using the style prevalent in the city.

Throughout the remainder of the Ottoman period, progress in building modern urban infrastructure and industries was slower in Damascus than in the coastal cities of Syria, where local merchants and foreign capitalists took the lead in importing new technologies and fashions. As a result Damascus earned the reputation of being resistant to rapid westernization. The reputation was not entirely deserved, however, as the city was home to a number of Muslim scholars belonging to the SALAFIYYA movement who probed the possibility of reforming Islam to meet the demands of the modern age. Damascus also emerged as a center of a growing new national consciousness among Arab intellectuals that scholars have named Arabism.

Arabism included a broad spectrum of ideologies that ranged from a simple pride in Arab culture and history to outright calls for the end of the Ottoman Empire and its replacement by a properly Arab kingdom. The latter goal gained popularity after the COMMITTEE OF UNION AND PROGRESS strengthened its control in Istanbul in 1909 and attempted to impose Turkish as the only language of government and as the exclusive medium of instruction in government schools. After WORLD WAR I began in 1914, Cemal Pasha was appointed governor of Syria, where he ruled with a heavy hand, arresting and executing those he believed to be in the Arabist political camp. The city's garrison surrendered to Australian forces on October 1, 1918, while Bedouin forces riding for the Arab Army took the city center.

Damascus was the object of intense political bargaining as FAYSAL AL-HASHIMI sought to establish the city as the capital of his Arab Kingdom. An Arab national congress met in the city in 1919 and declared Faysal its king in 1920. But the European powers did not recognize the kingdom's independence. In July 1920, French forces moved into Syria and defeated the nationalists at Khan Maysalun, a CARAVANSARY just outside Damascus. Facing no further opposition, the French entered the city on July 25, 1920, and proclaimed it the capital of their mandated territory.

Bruce Masters

Further reading: Karl Barbir, *Ottoman Rule in Damascus, 1708–1758* (Princeton, N.J.: Princeton University Press, 1980); Philip Khoury, *Urban Notables and Arab Nationalism: The Politics of Damascus, 1860–1920* (Cambridge: Cambridge University Press, 1983).

Damascus Incident In the middle of the 19th century, Christian and Jewish merchants in Damascus were locked in fierce competition for control of the fast-growing trade with western Europe. Muslim merchants preferred not to deal directly with European merchants, concentrating on the overland trade to Iraq; this left the profitable trade with Europe in the hands of non-Muslims. The Egyptian occupation of Syria in 1831 had opened Damascus to European merchants for the first time in more than two centuries. The tensions between Christians and Jews came to a head in 1840 when a Roman Catholic priest and his servant were reported missing after having last been seen in the Jewish quarter of Damascus. Some in the Christian community charged that the two had been abducted and murdered by Jews so that their blood might be used in a Passover ritual. The Egyptian military governor, IBRAHIM PASHA, levied fines and arrested several prominent members of the Jewish community; those arrested were tortured to confess to the reputed abduction or to name those who had committed it. The incident ushered in a period of heightened tensions between Christian and Jewish communities throughout Syria.

When the reputed bones of the priest were discovered, six members of the Jewish community of Damascus—including three prominent and very wealthy Jewish merchants—were arrested on murder charges. Other Jews were arrested when the reputed bones of the servant were uncovered. In the end, four men died as a result of torture endured while in prison, while the remainder were released only after a prolonged period of negotiations, accompanied by bribes liberally extended to many in the governor's palace. This incident became known as the "Damascus Affair" in Europe where it served to galvanize newly emancipated Jews in western Europe to concern over the fate of their co-religionists in an Ottoman Empire that seemed to be on the verge of collapse. It also made evident the prevalence of anti-Semitism in France where the popular press played up the lurid side of the case.

Bruce Masters

Further reading: Jonathan Frankel, *The Damascus Affair: "Ritual Murder," Politics and the Jews in 1840* (Cambridge: Cambridge University Press, 1997).

Damascus Riots The 1860 Lebanese Civil War between Christians and Druzes heightened the animosity between Christians and Muslims throughout Syria that had been building since the 1856 proclamation of equality among all the Ottoman sultan's subjects, regardless of religious community. During the summer of 1860, with rumors of the ongoing civil war in Lebanon helping convince each community that the other would soon attack, Christians and Jews in Damascus became radically polarized. In July, a group of Muslim teenagers were arrested for painting crosses on the doors of Christian homes. As Ottoman soldiers took the youths away, a mob quickly formed to release them. Having secured their freedom, the mob moved on to loot houses in the Christian quarter of the city. The looting soon escalated into the full-scale sacking and burning of the Christian quarter, including the killing of any Christians encountered by the mob. In the midst of the rioting, Abd al-Qadir al-Jazairi and his Algerian retainers did much to protect Christians, escorting many to safety in the city's citadel. The Ottoman garrison in the city, by contrast, did little to contain the violence.

In the aftermath of the riots, France sent an expeditionary force to Lebanon and the Ottoman army restored order in Damascus. It was not clear how many Christians had been killed. Estimates of the dead ranged from a few hundred to ten thousand. The actual total was impossible to determine since many Christians fled Damascus after the riots and never returned. The Ottoman authorities executed a number of Muslims for the crimes and exiled many more, including some of the city's prominent Muslim religious leaders. The Christian quarter was completely destroyed in the riot. The Christians complained that the Ottoman government had not responded quickly enough to prevent the outburst and was not just in providing compensation for their losses. Although the Christian quarter was rebuilt within a decade, the memory of the riots continued to haunt Christians of the city for at least another generation.

Bruce Masters

Further reading: Leila Fawaz, *An Occasion for War: Civil Conflict in Lebanon and Damascus in 1860* (Berkeley: University of California Press, 1994).

Danube Province (*Bulg.*: Dunav; *Ger.*: Donau; *Hung.*: Duna; *Rom.*: Dunarea; *Russ.*: Dunay; *Turk.*: Tuna Vilayeti) The Danube Province or Tuna Vilayeti (1864–77) was established as a model project for the application of the Ottoman Provincial Law Code of 1864, which introduced further centralization into provincial government complemented by some principles of decentralization. The project entailed a number of Western-inspired reforms including government restructuring to include greater local involvement, increased secularization of government institutions (especially courts and schools), and the improvement of regional infrastructure. The purpose of this project was to expand the implementation of the Tanzimat reforms, to eliminate local discontent, and to integrate non-Muslims into the administration.

The province included the *sancak*s (subprovinces) of Tulçea (in present-day Romania), Varna, Ruse (Rusçuk), Turnovo, Vidin, Sofia (detached at the beginning of the 1870s), all in present-day Bulgaria, and, until 1869, Nish (in present-day Serbia). The Danube Province also included the island of Adakale, today submerged in the waters of the Danube after the construction of the dam on the Iron Gate in the 1960s. Ruse, a major Ottoman port on the Danube, was chosen as the province's administrative center. In 1867 the town was visited by Sultan Abdülaziz (r. 1861–76) on his return from a European tour. This visit served as the starting point for an inspection of the empire's Balkan provinces, during which Abdülaziz also received Prince Charles of Romania (r. prince 1866/ king 1881–1914) in Ruse.

The first governor of the Danube Province, Midhat Pasha (1864–68), had broad authority over provincial affairs. He was assisted in his duties by an Administrative Assembly that included state officials appointed by and directly responsible to their superiors in the Ottoman capital of Istanbul and six representative members, three Muslims and three non-Muslims, elected from among the inhabitants of the province. Convened by the governor annually for no longer than 40 days, the Provincial General Assembly, composed of two Muslim members and two non-Muslim members elected by each *sancak*, was charged with working out the provincial budget, the construction and upkeep of roads and bridges, tax collection, improvement of agriculture, and the development of crafts and commerce. The decisions of the Provincial General Assembly were subject to the approval of the Sublime Porte (Ottoman government) and the sultan. Non-Muslims also participated in the provincial criminal and commercial courts that were based on a secular code of law and justice, and in the Court of Appeals.

Significant efforts were devoted to the modernization of the *vilayet*'s administrative center of Ruse. These efforts included paving streets, improving public hygiene, and constructing hospitals, hotels, and other public buildings. Improvements to the infrastructure and communications network in the province included the construction of new roads and bridges, and support for steamship lines on the Danube River. These steamship lines carried both private passengers and commercial cargo. In addition, the Ruse-Varna railroad was completed in 1866; in 1869, Emperor Francis Joseph of Austria-Hungary was one of the passengers who used this line to travel to Istanbul. Both the railway and steamship lines were supported by repair workshops.

Agriculture became one of the priorities of the provincial administration. Under the direct supervision of governor Midhat Pasha, a model farm was established near Ruse, where imported modern agricultural machines and technologies were tested and applied. As early as 1864, agricultural credit cooperatives were introduced to provide farmers and municipalities with low-interest loans. The government also encouraged industry by opening specialized schools to train workers and through a protectionist policy which obliged provincial administrative officers to wear clothes made of locally produced woolens. Tax incentives were also offered to encourage new industrial enterprises.

The administration took extra measures to improve internal security, providing special assistance in the resettlement of Circassians and Tatars displaced due to the frequent RUSSO-OTTOMAN WARS. In 1869, a new Second Army (Tuna Ordusu) was stationed in the city of Shumen, clearly establishing the importance of this border province for the Ottoman Empire. From this vantage point, the army could monitor political developments across the Danube.

The policy of the provincial administration was backed by the first official *vilayet* newspaper in the Ottoman Empire, *Tuna/Dunav* (1865–1877), which was published simultaneously in Ottoman Turkish and Bulgarian and had both Ottoman and Bulgarian editors. Among its editors in chief were Ismail Kemal and Ahmed Midhat Efendi. The former, an Albanian, after a long service to the Ottoman state and complex relations with the YOUNG TURKS, was in 1912 to declare Albanian independence. The latter was to become one of the leading Ottoman journalists and men of letters of the late 19th and early 20th centuries.

A staunch supporter of the ideas of OTTOMANISM, the provincial governor Midhat Pasha tried to promote cohesion between Muslims and non-Muslims and the formation of an Ottoman national identity. One of the major steps in this direction was the decision to establish mixed Bulgarian-Ottoman schools. However, this initiative was met with hostility. Local Muslims were reluctant to mix with non-Muslims and wanted an education intertwined with religion; ethnic Bulgarians suspected that these institutions were designed to promote their cultural assimilation and to deter the development of their own national educational and cultural institutions.

Administrative units modeled on the Danube Province were subsequently established elsewhere in the Ottoman Empire, and by the end of 1876 the new provincial system was in operation throughout the empire except in the Arabian peninsula and in autonomous provinces such as EGYPT. The main purpose of the reforms instituted in the Danube Province was to give the central government a better hold on the region; however, these changes also gave significant powers to the provincial governor, promoted the participation of the local population, including non-Muslims, developed the local economy, improved public infrastructure and education, and brought a better program of taxation. The Danube Province project contributed significantly to the extension of the reform outside the capital, including the modernization of the Ottoman Balkans and the introduction of the representative principle in Ottoman government. However, it failed in one of its most important goals: preventing the development of the Bulgarian national movement.

Rossitsa Gradeva

Further reading: Roderick Davison, "Midhat Pasha," in *Encyclopaedia of Islam*, 2nd ed., vol. 6, CD-ROM edition, edited by C. E. Bosworth, E. van Donzel, et al. (Leiden: Brill, 2001), 1031b–1034a; Bernard Lewis, "Ahmad Midhat," in *Encyclopaedia of Islam*, 2nd ed., vol. 1, CD-ROM edition, edited by H. A. R. Gibb et al. (Leiden: Brill, 2001), 289a; Bernard Lory, "Rusčuk," in *Encyclopaedia of Islam*, 2nd ed., vol. 8, CD-ROM edition, edited by C. E. Bosworth, E. van Donzel, et al. (Leiden: Brill, 2001), 633b–634b; Stanford Shaw and Ezel Kural Shaw, *History of the Ottoman Empire*, vol. 2: *Reform, Revolution, and Republic: The Rise of Modern Turkey, 1808–1975* (Cambridge: Cambridge University Press, 1977).

Danube River (*Bulg.*: **Dunav**; *Ger.*: **Donau**; *Hung.*: **Duna**; *Rom.*: **Dunarea**; *Russ.*: **Dunay**; *Turk.*: **Tuna**)   Originating in Germany's Black Forest, the Danube is Europe's second largest river after the Volga. Flowing mainly eastward for 1,771 miles (2,850 km) before emptying into the Black Sea, it connects most of central and eastern Europe. Its size and position defined it as an important boundary to several empires. The Roman Limes, or military frontier, followed the river for the most part, and the Lower Danube served as the Balkan peninsula's northern border for centuries. It marked the northern border of the BYZANTINE EMPIRE in the late fifth through the early seventh centuries as well as that of the hurriedly assembled empire of Sultan BAYEZID I (r. 1389–1402). Although the Ottomans lost most of their possessions in the Balkans after the BATTLE OF ANKARA and the ensuing civil war (1402–1413), by the mid-15th century the Danube was again the demarcation line between the expanding Ottoman Empire and the medieval Hungarian kingdom that ruled the Carpathian basin from 1000 through 1526.

In the face of the Ottoman threat, the Hungarians reorganized their southern border by building new fortresses or strengthening existing castles along the rivers Danube and Sava, which flows into the Danube at BELGRADE. This line stretched from Szörény (Turnu Severin) via Orsova (Orşova) and Nándorfehérvár (Belgrade) to Zimony (Zemun) and Szabács (Šabac), where it finally left the Sava and continued through Srebrenik, Jajce, and Knin up to Klis on the ADRIATIC SEA coast. The Ottomans also recognized the importance of the Danube as early as the late 14th century and occupied all strategically vital fortresses along the river during the next 150 years. These included the fortresses at Kilia (1484), Silistra (1388), Ruse (1388), Nikopol (1395), Vidin (1396), Szörény (1524), Orsova (1522), Golubac (1427, 1458), Hram (1483), Smederevo (1439, 1459), Belgrade (1521), Petrovaradin (1526), BUDA and Pest (1541), Vác (1543), Visegrád (1544), and Esztergom (1543).

Following their conquests, Belgrade and Buda became Ottoman administrative centers and were used as logistical bases during Ottoman campaigns against the Habsburgs. The Ottomans also established naval arsenals at Ruse (Rusçuk), Nikopol (Niğbolu), and Vidin, and smaller shipbuilding sites at Golubac (Güvercinlik), Smederevo (Semendire), Belgrade, Zvornik (İzvornik), Kruševac (Alacahisar), Pojega, Mohács, Buda, and Esztergom. Smederevo and Zvornik were each capable of constructing some 200–250 riverboats for Süleyman's campaigns in the 1540s and 1560s.

Most of the cannons, military equipment, food, and fodder during Ottoman campaigns against Hungary and the Habsburgs were also transported via the Danube. However, the river was not fully navigable, and the waterway was used only from Ruse or Belgrade up to Buda or Esztergom. Thus supplies shipped from Istanbul via the BLACK SEA to Varna were then transported overland on carts to Ruse (or Belgrade), where they were again loaded onto ships.

The Danube, together with the "imperial road" that ran along the right bank of the river, also functioned as a major trade route. In 1571, 437 boats reported at the Buda customs carrying mainly wheat and agricultural produce from the Balkans. Most of the boat captains were residents of the major ports along the Lower Danube or its tributaries (including Belgrade, Semendire,

Petrovaradin, Osijek, among other locales), though some did arrive from Vienna.

During the Holy League's war of 1684–99 against the Ottomans, the Danube—along with its tributaries to the west, the Drava and Sava rivers, and its tributaries to the north and northeast, the Tisza and Temes rivers—received much attention from Habsburg military planners, for the rivers and their extensive marshlands created major logistical problems. The 1690s also witnessed the first serious exploration of the river and its basin by the Italian Luigi Ferdinando Marsigli (1658–1730), a scientific polymath and military engineer in Habsburg service. Viennese authorities directed Marsigli to identify crossings for the Habsburg army, map the Danube's marshes, and, during the peace talks with the Ottomans that led to the TREATY OF KARLOWITZ in 1699, to delineate the new border between the defeated Ottomans and Habsburg Hungary. Using his notes, sketches, and maps from the 1690s, Marsigli later prepared a six-volume encyclopedia of the Danube, which appeared in 1726.

By the end of the 17th century, the Danube again became the northern border of the Ottoman Empire, the demarcation line between Ottoman and Habsburg lands, and a *cordon sanitaire* (line of containment) against the Ottomans. Yet the Danube, and the "imperial road" along the river, continued to facilitate trade, as it had done for centuries. Orthodox Christian merchants from the Ottoman Balkans and Habsburg Hungary championed this commerce. Between 1650 and 1850, some 1,500,000 "Greeks" (as these Balkan merchants were commonly known to contemporaries regardless of their ethnicities) were involved in this profitable trade, exporting mainly Ottoman textiles, garments, and other "oriental" goods from Ottoman territories to Habsburg lands.

The CRIMEAN WAR (1853–56) brought international recognition of the Danube's importance. The Congress of Paris (1856) that ended the war established the European Commission of the Danube, appointing it to clear the Danube delta of obstructions. In 1878 the lower Danube became a neutral waterway; however, by that time the Ottoman Empire had already lost the Danube due to the independence of SERBIA and Romania, the creation of an autonomous BULGARIA, and the occupation of BOSNIA AND HERZEGOVINA by Austria-Hungary.

Gábor Ágoston

dar al-harb In the political theory prevalent in Muslim lands before the 19th century, Muslim rulers were believed to be under an injunction from the Quran to wage holy war (GHAZA) against non-Muslim rulers until their territories were conquered or they acknowledged their vassalage to a Muslim overlord. For this reason, those parts of the world that were not under direct Muslim rule were termed by Muslim legal scholars as *dar al-harb*, meaning "house of war." During the Ottoman period, Sunni religious scholars at the sultan's court ruled that Shii rulers such as the Safavid shahs were also in the "house of war" as they had strayed from Muslim orthodoxy and had become *rafidi* (renegades) or *khariji* (Muslim extremists). The sultans therefore considered themselves justified in waging war against these groups until they returned to SUNNI ISLAM, the mainstream or conventional form of the faith.

According to Islamic legal theory, no true peace (*salam*) could be established between a Muslim state and one in the "house of war." But a truce (*sulh*), which was understood to be of limited duration, was permitted between the Ottoman sultan and a non-Muslim monarch. The territory of such a ruler was considered to be in the "house of truce" (*dar al-sulh)* and his subjects were allowed to visit, trade with, and even reside in the Ottoman Empire with a status known as *istiman* (trust or confidence). This legal status provided the framework for the CAPITULATIONS, which allowed European merchants to reside in the Empire and provided the framework for diplomatic relations between the Ottoman Empire and various European powers.

Bruce Masters

See also CAPITULATIONS.

dar al-Islam In Islamic legal theory as it was developed in the first centuries of Muslim rule, territories governed by Muslim rulers and where Islamic law is in force constitute one monolithic entity known as the "house of Islam" (*dar al-Islam*), as differences between secular Muslim rulers are not recognized as legally valid. This category invokes a historical time when there was a universal CALIPHATE that ruled all Muslims. A desire for its return is in implicit in the discussions of the *dar al-Islam* by Muslim legal scholars. This "house of Islam" is contrasted with the DAR AL-HARB, the "house of war," non-Muslim territories that are considered fair target for holy war, or jihad, unless their rulers have concluded peace treaties with a Muslim state. Even when such a treaty does exist, other Muslim states do not have to honor that treaty and the Muslim state that entered into the treaty can abrogate it at any time.

This stark dichotomy between two monolithic "houses" was undermined when Muslim rulers went to war against one another. For Ottoman jurists, a claim that a war against Shii rulers was justified under Islamic law seemed reasonable as they were willing to concede that some Shii doctrines were un-Islamic and those who believed them might be considered heretics. But when the Ottoman sultans went to war against Sunni rulers, such as the MAMLUK EMPIRE that ruled Egypt and Syria in the 16th century, or against the 18th-century Ira-

nian ruler NADIR SHAH, the legal justification for war was not as apparent because under that same law, war between Muslims was illegal. Nonetheless, in the capital, jurists generally issued legal justifications for such actions, whatever their personal views of the legality of the campaigns, that stated that the war was necessary to secure the Ottoman sultans' position as the protectors of the Holy Places in Arabia and to defend Islam against its non-Muslim enemies. Away from the capital, Muslim jurists were openly ambivalent about whether the sultans could transform regions that properly belonged in the *dar al-Islam* into arenas of the *dar al-harb*.

Bruce Masters

Further reading: Muhammad Shaybani, *The Islamic Law of Nations: Shaybani's Siyar,* translated and edited by Majid Khadduri (Baltimore, Md.: Johns Hopkins University Press, 1966).

Darülmuallim *See* EDUCATION.

Darülmuallimat *See* EDUCATION.

darülfünun The *darülfünun* (meaning "house of sciences") was the institution of higher EDUCATION developed by the Ottoman Empire in the 19th century to address the growing need for scientific and technical education, as opposed to the madrasas, or religiously based schools, that had hitherto been the foundation of Ottoman learning. The *darülfünun* continued its activities during the first decade of the Republic of Turkey and was superseded by the University of Istanbul in 1933.

The idea to establish a university or *darülfünun* was initially proposed in an education report prepared for Sultan ABDÜLMECID (r. 1839–61) in 1845. However, basic requirements such as buildings, teachers, and books had to be met in order for this institution to begin its work. Foundations for the university buildings were laid near the HAGIA SOPHIA Mosque under the supervision of Italian architect Gaspare Fossati, while future teachers were sent to Europe to prepare to become the new faculty of the school. A committee, the Encümen-i Daniş (Ottoman Academy of Sciences), was formed in 1851 to prepare the school's textbooks. The prime minister (*sadrazam*) of the era, FUAD PASHA (1815–69), realized that these preparations would take a great deal of time; beginning in 1863, he started lectures in the form of conferences in the completed parts of the building.

On January 13, 1863, chemist Derviş Pasha became the first to teach at the institution, lecturing on physics and chemistry. These conference lessons lasted until 1865, when they were moved to the Nuri Pasha mansion in the Çemberlitaş district of Istanbul. September 8, 1865 witnessed a major fire at Darülfünun, which destroyed the building and ended this first experiment in Ottoman higher education.

Establishing the *darülfünun* gathered momentum again in the Public Education Regulation (Maarif-i Umumiye Nizamnamesi) of early 1869. The second *darülfünun*, identified in regulations as Darülfünun-ı Osmani (Ottoman University), was to include divisions of literature, science, and law, and detailed curricula were prepared for each discipline. However, when the *darülfünun* reopened on February 20, 1870, the curricula of the three branches were indistinguishable, with all students taking the same courses. This failure to specialize may have resulted from the difficulties in providing instructors and textbooks. It is unknown whether any students graduated before the second *darülfünun* closed its doors in 1873.

After these two failed attempts, the Ottoman government decided to develop the *darülfünun* on the foundation of an existing educational institution. Beginning in 1874, some classes were given at the Galatasaray High School or University (Galatasaray Mekteb-i Sultanisi or Darülfünun-ı Sultani). The new institution consisted of schools of law, literature, and engineering (rather than science). In the first academic year, 21 students were enrolled in the school of law and 26 students were enrolled in the school of engineering. It is unknown whether courses began at the same time in the school of literature. Both the law and engineering schools were closed in 1877–78, reopened again in October 1878, and graduated their first classes in 1879–80. A second class graduated in 1880–81, but no information is available about the activities of this *darülfünun* after 1881.

The first university in the Ottoman Empire based on Western models was the Imperial University (Darülfünun-ı Şahane), founded 20 years after Darülfünun-ı Osmani. Opened on August 31, 1900 on the 25th anniversary of the enthronement of ABDÜLHAMID II (r. 1876–1909), this university had branches of science, literature, and theology, as well as schools of law and medicine, though these last two were not connected officially.

Degrees were awarded after three years of study in the schools of science and literature and after four years in the school of theology. The Imperial University overcame earlier logistical problems of Turkish universities, such as inadequate instructors or textbooks. However, it restricted the number of students admitted, and courses remained fairly theoretical. The Imperial University remained in operation until the declaration of the second constitution in 1908 (*see* CONSTITUTION/CONSTITUTIONAL PERIODS), when its name was changed to Istanbul Darülfünun or Istanbul University. The schools of medicine and law were also officially connected to the

University at this time. In 1909 the university was moved to the Zeynep Hanım mansion in the Vezneciler district of Istanbul.

In 1912, the university was reorganized: the schools of pharmacy and dentistry were connected to the school of medicine, and the school of medicine in the province of DAMASCUS was attached to the Istanbul *darülfünun*. Some changes were also made to the university's administrative structure, including rules regarding attendance and discipline. During WORLD WAR I, 20 German professors joined the university's faculty, further strengthening it. With the contributions of these professors, various research institutes, laboratories, and libraries were founded, and the number of publications increased. More buildings were added to accommodate the university's growth, and on September 12, 1914, a women's college, the Inas Darülfünun, was founded. It consisted of schools of literature, mathematics, and biology. Its first graduates completed their studies in 1917, but with the advent of coeducation at the university in 1921, the separate school for women was closed.

The end of World War I and the consequent end of the Ottoman-German alliance coincided with the beginning of the 1918–1919 academic year, causing an academic crisis when a number of the university's German professors returned home. This departure resulted in a shortage of faculty that was exacerbated by an increase in the number of students.

New administrative and scientific organizations were created on October 11, 1919 when the regulation of the Ottoman University (Darülfünun-ı Osmani Nizamnamesi) gave the institution scientific and administrative autonomy and faculty directors, as well as trustees.

Until the foundation of the Republic of Turkey on October 29, 1923, the *darülfünun* operated under the statutes provided by these regulations. With the formation of the Republic, the *darülfünun* was given legal status. After World War I, when British forces withdrew from the Ministry of Defense building (Harbiye Nezareti), it was donated to the university. It currently serves as the main building of the University of Istanbul.

A reform process at Istanbul Darülfünun began in 1929. The project used internal recommendations from individual schools within the university. The Ministry of Education, however, rejected the project, considering it inadequate. Additional reforms were undertaken in 1930, resulting ultimately in the closure of Darülfünun and the founding of Istanbul University. Albert Malche (1876–1956), professor of education at the University of Geneva, was invited to Turkey to prepare a report on Istanbul Darülfünun. Malche submitted his report on May 29, 1932, after a month of research and observation. He criticized various aspects of the university, especially its emphasis on theoretical rather than practical knowledge, and suggested substantial reforms. The Turkish cabinet approved the report. The Grand National Assembly of Turkey closed the *darülfünun* on July 31, 1933 and opened the University of Istanbul the following day, August 1, 1933. Reşit Galip, the minister of education, personally led the reform: 65 Darülfünun professors and scholars were appointed to posts in the new university while another 82 were discharged. The 1933 university reform represents a milestone in the history of Turkish higher education: Darülfünun, the first university of the Ottoman era, was replaced by the University of Istanbul, the new nucleus for later Turkish universities.

Sevtap Kadıoğlu

Further reading: Ekmeleddin İhsanoğlu, *Science, Technology and Learning in the Ottoman Empire: Western Influence, Local Institutions, and the Transfer of Knowledge* (Aldershot, UK: Ashgate–Variorum, 2004); Feza Günergun, "Science in the Ottoman World," in G. N. Vlahakis, I. M. Malaquias, N. M. Broots, F. Regourd, F. Gunergun, and D. Wright, *Imperialism and Science: Social Impact and Interaction* (Santa Barbara, Calif.: ABC-CLIO, 2006).

Davud Pasha (d. 1873) (r. 1861–1868) *mutasarrif of Lebanon*   Davud Pasha was the first to hold the office of administering the MUTASARRIFIYYA, a new administrative structure established by the Ottoman government in 1861 to appease European outrage at the excesses committed by DRUZES against Christians in the LEBANESE CIVIL WAR of 1860. Davud Pasha was a career Ottoman diplomat who was born into an Armenian Catholic family in Istanbul around 1816. He was educated in French and Ottoman schools and held Ottoman diplomatic posts in Berlin and Vienna. He was appointed as *mutasarrif* in 1861 for a term of three years and given the rank of vizier. He was reappointed for a five-year term in 1864. Davud Pasha faced the opposition of Lebanon's feudal lords, who resented their loss of power, especially the Maronite Yusuf Bek Karam. Nonetheless, Davud Pasha is generally credited with implementing his charge and establishing a precedent for fair and impartial rule. But Davud Pasha's ambitions led to trouble as the Ottoman Foreign Ministry worried about his establishing direct contacts with the European diplomats and merchants in Beirut rather than going through the provincial governor. In 1868, in an attempt to pressure Istanbul to give him more power, he resigned his position. To his surprise, his resignation was accepted. He returned to Istanbul where he was appointed minister of public works. He was later charged with corruption and went into exile to France where he died in 1873.

Bruce Masters

Dawud Pasha (d. 1851) (r. 1816–1831) *governor of Baghdad*   Dawud Pasha was the last MAMLUK governor of BAGHDAD. He started his career as a mamluk of BÜYÜK SÜLEYMAN PASHA and was about 50 years old when he became governor of Baghdad in 1816. Unlike most of his predecessors, he had an established reputation as a scholar of Islamic legal texts and Quran commentaries. While Christian chroniclers in Baghdad praised his patron and predecessor Büyük Süleyman for his tolerance, Muslim chroniclers praised Dawud for his piety and good works.

However, although Dawud Pasha was enshrined in the historical memory of Baghdad's Muslims as a just governor, he lacked his predecessor's military skills, leaving his territory vulnerable to attack. In 1821, Abbas Mirza, the son of the Iranian Qajar Shah Fath Ali (r. 1797–1834), invaded Iraq and defeated Dawud in a battle in SHAHRIZOR, but an outbreak of cholera decimated the Persian forces and Baghdad was saved. Sultan MAHMUD II (r. 1808–39)dissolved the JANISSARIES in the capital in 1826 and ordered his governors to do the same. When those orders reached Dawud, he called his Janissaries to the parade ground, read them the order, and then offered them places in his new army corps that was to be commanded by French officers. Most accepted and Baghdad avoided the violence that accompanied the dissolution of the Janissaries elsewhere. But even under new organization, the former Janissaries remained as incompetent as they had been before. Sultan Mahmud attempted to replace Dawud in 1829, but his emissary was assassinated en route. Not deterred, Mahmud sent an army to march on Baghdad. Before this army arrived at the city's walls, however, plague struck Baghdad, decimating the city's population and Dawud's new army. When the Ottoman forces arrived at the city gates in 1831, Baghdad immediately capitulated. Dawud was sent in chains to Istanbul, but was given a partial reprieve and allowed to go into exile in MEDINA, where he died 20 years later. Ali Rıza Pasha, having removed Dawud from the political scene in Baghdad, proceeded to execute all the remaining male members of the Mamluk household that had ruled Baghdad province from the early 18th century.

Bruce Masters

Further reading: Tom Niewenhuis, *Politics and Society in Early Modern Iraq: Mamluk Pashas, Tribal Shaykhs and Local Rule Between 1802 and 1831* (The Hague: Martinus Nijhoff, 1981).

death and funerary culture   Although death rituals and funerary practices in the Ottoman Empire were as diverse as the ethnic and religious cultures included within the empire, the dominant rituals and practices were those of Ottoman Muslims. And although these were Islamic in essence, Ottoman funerary culture had its own peculiarities that distinguished it from the tradition of non-Ottoman Muslim lands and even from the Arab provinces of the empire.

In the early centuries of Ottoman rule, as in most Islamic social and political formations in medieval Anatolia, funerary practices were borrowed directly from the Arab-Islamic tradition. The earliest examples of Ottoman cemeteries and tombstones, dating from the 15th century and located in the first Ottoman capital, Bursa, resembled the model dominant throughout the Islamic lands. Tombstones were carved with inscriptions in Arabic with purely religious content and provided very succinct information about the deceased: name, father's name, date of death. Cemeteries were generally located within the city, very often adjacent to a mosque. Ottoman dignitaries such as beys, viziers, and sultans were generally put in mausoleum-like structures known as *türbe*s.

Yet despite this consistency with other Islamic practice, early Ottoman funerary customs still diverged from the norms in other Islamic lands on some major points,

generally as a result of surviving pre-Islamic Turkic traditions. Some evidence suggests that the practice of letting bodies decompose before burying the bones was still sometimes observed. The early Ottomans also infringed on a number of Islamic injunctions, showing excessive grief in mourning, for instance, or bringing the horse of the deceased with its tail cut to the funeral. Such behavior, frequently observed until the 16th century, was gradually abandoned as the state shifted toward Islamic orthodoxy and began to impose a control over funerary practices. Nevertheless, certain customs persevered, especially in rural areas and in the heterodox circles of certain mystic or Sufi orders (*tarikat*). Horses following their deceased masters to the grave were observed in the 19th century, and professional wailing has survived in Anatolia to the present day.

In most respects, Ottoman death rituals were consistent with fundamental Islamic principles. The body of the deceased was washed before being placed in a seamless

The Muradiye tomb complex in the first Ottoman capital of Bursa was the ancestral burial ground of the Ottoman dynasty. *(Photo by Gábor Ágoston)*

shroud consisting of two or three pieces; the shrouded body was then carried in a coffin to a mosque where a funeral prayer was held in the presence of the entire community. The body was then carried to the grave where it was laid to rest without the coffin, in direct contact with the earth, lying on the left flank and facing the *qibla* (the direction of MECCA).

The Ottomans shared the faith of other Muslims in terms of the meaning of death and their idea of an afterlife. Islamic eschatology was simple. Death was not an end but rather the beginning of another form of life; the dead waited in the grave until the resurrection of Judgment Day when souls would be subjected to the final test and sent either to paradise or to hell. One important principle was that of total submission to death, seen as the irrevocable will of God.

The 16th century was marked by the emergence of a more characteristically Ottoman funerary culture. Three major elements constituted the core of this culture: the importance given to increasingly conspicuous monuments; the appearance of a carved representation of headgear as a distinguishing feature on gravestones; and the development of a peculiar textual format for the epitaph, where Arabic was gradually replaced by Turkish. Although not prohibited, conspicuousness in gravestones and funerary monuments was considered reprehensible in Islam. Death was supposed to level human beings in the face of God, eliminating worldly inequalities; therefore, showy monuments were considered a breach of this essential principle. Purists in Islam went so far as to claim that no recognizable trace whatsoever should be left over a grave. The Ottomans, on the contrary, soon developed a taste for durable and prominent monuments, such as mausoleums for the sultans and members of the elite, and heavily carved and inscribed marble stones for the well-to-do. The carving of headgear, generally turbans, to decorate the top of tombstones seemed to stem from the same concern for visibility. Some have claimed that this was a remnant of the pre-Islamic Turkic tradition of anthropomorphic (human-shaped) gravestones; it is more likely that the inspiration came from the tradition of placing the deceased's headgear on the coffin, and that the real aim was to give a visual clue to his status in life. Finally, the use of Turkish instead of Arabic also responded to a growing desire to identify or characterize the dead. Instead of bearing only uniform or repetitive Arabic religious verses, tombstones came to record more detailed and specific descriptions of the deceased, especially with respect to status, patronage, and family links. In short, tombstones began to look more like social markers.

The organization of Ottoman cemeteries clearly reflected this evolution. The larger cemeteries were located outside the city walls but were easily accessible and frequently visited. Inside the city, smaller graveyards were generally attached to a religious building, generally a mosque, and enclosed behind walls. However, these walls always had windows, ensuring that tombstones remained visible to passersby. The arrangement of tombs within cemeteries suggested the existence of a notion of "prime space" defined in terms of visibility or of proximity to a prominent figure. As for those who had been most powerful, they generally enjoyed the privilege of a mausoleum where they and their close relatives would be buried. The most striking example was that of the sultan, whose mausoleum, generally built close to his own mosque, could then house a number of members of the dynasty. Istanbul was thus studded with a large number of imperial mausoleums that left a significant dynastic imprint.

From the 18th century on, thanks in part to the greater availability of marble, tombstones grew in size and sophistication, adopting baroque styles, while epitaphs grew in length. Increasingly secular stock verses derived from a largely oral tradition came to be widely used throughout the empire, allowing for sentimental laments over the loss of loved ones, especially children. The popularity of the style was such that traces of it can be found in the decoration of Jewish graves or in the wording of epitaphs within the Turkish-speaking Greek and Armenian communities.

By the second half of the 19th century, especially in the capital, funerary art reached a modern climax, with the monumentalization of tombstones, the occasional use of figurative sculpture, and the spread of lengthy epitaphs signed by renowned poets. NATIONALISM was soon to follow, after the YOUNG TURK revolution, bringing in a political and ideological dimension that further reduced the religious character of monuments. By the end of the empire, Ottoman funerary culture had become a strange mix of traditions, most of which were wiped out with the advent of the modern Republic of Turkey in 1923 and with the government's formal shift to the Latin alphabet in 1928.

Edhem Eldem

Further reading: Werner Diem and Marco Schöller, *The Living and the Dead in Islam: Studies in Arabic Epitaphs* (Wiesbaden: Harrassowitz, 2004); Edhem Eldem, *Death in Istanbul: Death and Its Rituals in Ottoman-Islamic Culture* (Istanbul: Ottoman Bank Archives and Research Centre, 2005); Gülru Necipoğlu, "Dynastic Imprints on the Cityscape: The Collective Message of Imperial Funerary Mosque Complexes in Istanbul," in *Cimetières et traditions funéraires dans le monde islamique*, vol. 2, edited by J.-L. Bacqué-Grammont and A. Tibet (Ankara: Türk Tarih Kurumu, 1996), 23–36; Minna Rozen, *Hasköy Cemetery: Typology of Stones* (Tel Aviv: Tel Aviv University and University of Pennsylvania, 1994); Jane Idleman Smith and Yvonne

Yazbeck Haddad, *The Islamic Understanding of Death and Resurrection* (New York: Oxford University Press, 2002).

debt and the Public Debt Administration Although, in the Ottoman context, the origins of the concept of borrowing from international markets dates back to the second half of the 18th century, the first instance of Ottoman international borrowing occurred at the beginning of the second half of the 19th century. The main impetus for drawing on the international markets stemmed from disorder in Ottoman public finances. The origins of this disorder can be traced back to the late 16th century. The Ottoman government was traditionally reluctant to borrow from abroad. It chose instead to use domestic instruments such as internal borrowing and currency debasement to raise revenue. Currency debasement involved reducing the amount of gold and silver in coins. It was only when the limits of these fiscal resources were reached that the Ottoman state resorted to international markets. When the Ottoman state finally turned to these markets it encountered various problems in attracting interest in providing loans to the Ottoman Empire. The reluctance of international investors to extend loans to the empire stemmed from the continued disorderly state of Ottoman public finances and a lack of information available to potential foreign investors.

Motivated by a lack of funding in the face of spiraling war costs, Ottoman bureaucrats first proposed the idea of external borrowing during the Russian occupation of the Crimea in 1783. In various reports prepared on this issue, France, the Netherlands, Spain, and Morocco were identified as possible lender countries. However, in this instance, the Ottoman state opted against international borrowing. In 1787, at the start of war with the Habsburgs and the Russian Empire, external borrowing was again proposed to finance war expenses. It appears that, after these initial attempts, the idea of borrowing from abroad was postponed until the second half of the 19th century.

In this interim period, the Ottoman State again turned to internal resources in times of financial emergencies. Debasement of the currency (that is, reducing the silver content of coins thus issuing more currency to increase state revenues) was one of the most frequently employed methods of Ottoman financing. During the reign of Sultan MAHMUD II (r. 1808–39), the Ottoman currency was reportedly debased 37 times.

Toward the second half of the 19th century, the Ottoman state stepped up its modernization efforts in the areas of administration and finances. After the 1839 declaration of the Imperial Rescript of Gülhane (see TANZIMAT), external borrowing efforts were renewed in order to finance restructuring the administrative and fiscal apparatus of the state. In a memorandum presented to Sultan ABDÜLMECID (r. 1839–61) on August 22, 1850, the British ambassador in Istanbul, Lord Stradford Canning, forcefully warned the Ottoman government that to sustain its financing it would have to borrow from abroad. Aware of the condition of the Ottoman treasury, Canning advised the Ottoman government that, to ensure the success of international borrowing efforts, certain sources of revenue would have to be presented as collateral. Although the grand vizier MUSTAFA REŞID PASHA was in favor of this action, the sultan obstructed further negotiations on the topic of international borrowing. However, it was just a matter of time before the poor state of the Ottoman fiscal situation would dictate the necessity of borrowing from abroad.

In 1852, after it defaulted on its debt to the Bank of Constantinople, the Ottoman government made its first serious attempt to borrow from abroad. In that year, Ottoman representatives signed contracts with Bechet, Dethomas & Co. in Paris and Deveaux & Co. in London. Without waiting for the approval of the sultan, Ottoman bureaucrats sought a loan of 50 million French francs (the equivalent of $237.4 million today), with a term of 27 years. The first installment of this loan was paid to the agent of the Bank of Constantinople in London. However, the sultan did not endorse this deal, claiming that the Ottoman representatives exceeded their authority by agreeing to the terms of the loan. This failure shocked markets in London and Paris and left a negative impression of Ottoman credibility in international loan markets. In order to erase this negative impression, the first installment drawn from this loan was paid back by the Ottoman government with an indemnity of 2,200,000 French francs (the equivalent of $10.4 million today) after seven months.

This initial foray into the realm of international borrowing affected future attempts to borrow on the international market. After the outbreak of the CRIMEAN WAR (1854–56), the Ottoman government, in search of emergency funding, attempted to borrow from the London market. This attempt was unsuccessful due to the negative impression left by the 1852 fiasco. In 1854, even with the mediation of the influential banking house Rothschild & Sons, the Ottoman government was only able to raise a loan of £1,100,000 (the equivalent of $115.6 million today). This loan was not taken due to its small amount. Most interest in lending to the Ottomans came from speculators. The lack of credibility of the Ottoman state made it impossible to borrow in international markets without the support of the British and French governments. In another attempt in 1854, during the Crimean War and with the support of its allies Britain and France, the Ottoman state was able to borrow internationally by pledging the tribute of EGYPT as collateral. In 1855, again backed by guarantees from the British and French governments to cover interest payments to bondholders, the Ottoman government was able to secure an international loan. The 1854 loan, which was underwritten by Dent, Palmer & Co., raised £3,000,000 (the equivalent of $311.3 million today); and the 1855 loan, underwritten by Rothschild & Sons, raised £5,000,000 (the equivalent of $518.8 million today). The Ottomans not only pledged important revenue sources as collateral for these loans, they also agreed to allow British and French monitoring to ensure that the borrowed funds were spent on war expenses.

In the 19th century, Britain, fearing the rise of a strong state astride overland routes to its Indian possessions, pursued a foreign policy that focused on shoring up and ensuring the survival of the Ottoman Empire. This policy continued until the death of Lord Palmerston (d. 1865), who had been an active supporter of Britain's foreign policy objectives concerning the Ottoman Empire. Guarantees on interest payments of loans and other forms of support during the Crimean War were manifestations of this policy. Thus the British government unofficially supported the loan of £5,000,000 underwritten by Dent, Palmer & Co. in 1858, and a loan of £8,000,000 (the equivalent of $812 million today) underwritten by Deveaux & Co. in 1862. These loans were primarily used for financial reforms in the Ottoman Empire. In particular, they were spent on recalling *kaime* (paper money) from circulation. *Kaime* was a major source of disorder in the Ottoman money market at the time.

As with the loans of 1854 and 1855, British inspectors were employed to ensure that expenditures were in accord with international agreements. Moreover, bondholders were allowed to create a committee to monitor the resources that were provided as collateral. Due to the opposition of the Ottoman government, however, this committee never came into existence. In the following years, this opposition proved to be a source of discord between bondholders and the Ottoman government. Bondholders' appeals to the British government to intervene in disputes went unanswered.

Before the 1862 loan, the Ottoman government had difficulty in paying down internal and external debt, and appeals to the British and French governments for help in obtaining loans were turned down. Thus the Ottoman state was forced to contact Mires & Co., a speculator in the Paris market, to secure a loan of £16,000,000 (the equivalent of $1.7 billion today). To obtain this loan, the Ottoman government was forced to agree to very harsh terms. However, due to the arrest and imprisonment of Mires, this loan was never finalized.

From 1863 to 1875, the Ottoman government engaged in frequent and large-scale borrowings from international financial markets. These loans were mostly used for interest payments on existing debt, recalling of debased coins from circulation, financing budget deficits, and repay-

ment of internal debt liabilities. For these purposes the Ottoman government was able to obtain loans, in nominal terms, of £8,000,000 (the equivalent of $812 million today) and £6,000,000 (the equivalent of $593 million today) in 1863 and 1865; £22,222,000 (the equivalent of $2.2 billion today) in 1869; £5,700,000 (the equivalent of $574 million today) in 1871; £11,126,000 (the equivalent of $1.1 billion today) in 1872; £11,000,000 (the equivalent of $1 billion today) and £28,000,000 (the equivalent of $2.6 billion today) in 1873; and £40,000,000 (the equivalent of $3.8 billion today) in 1874.

Excluding the 1852 loan, between 1854 and 1875 the Ottoman Empire borrowed from European financial markets 15 times and raised a total of, £217 million (the equivalent of $21.4 billion today), of which £107 million (the equivalent of $10.6 billion today) was retained. A small portion of these loans (£12 million, the equivalent of $1.3 billion today) was spent on railroad construction. As a result of rapidly growing public debt coupled with increased budget deficits, the Ottoman Empire was unable to fulfill its debt servicing obligations and declared a moratorium on its debt payments. According to the Ramazan Decree (October 6, 1875), in which the moratorium was announced, the Ottoman government promised to pay back half of its accumulated interest and capital and half of its debts in five years and to issue bonds with a 5 percent interest rate to cover the rest of its obligations. After a short time, the Ottoman government found itself unable to keep the promises in the Ramazan Decree. As a result, complete default was declared. From 1875 to 1881, when the Public Debt Administration was established, only one new loan was obtained by the Ottoman Bank. Although it was classified as an external loan, this loan, in the amount of £5 million (the equivalent of $532 million today), was underwritten by the Imperial Ottoman Bank and used to help finance a war with Russia.

Negotiations between bondholders and the Ottoman government during this period focused on re-starting debt payments. These negotiations culminated in the Muharrem Decree of December 20, 1881. In this decree, the Ottoman government agreed to allow the formation of a financial control administration. Called the Public Debt Administration, this administration was composed of bondholders of Ottoman debt. The administration was housed in Istanbul and consisted of seven members representing British, Dutch, German, Austro-Hungarian, Italian, and Ottoman bondholders. The administration was empowered to collect directly from tax revenues allocated to the administration and to use these moneys to repay the debt of the Ottoman state. It had the authority to hire and fire its personnel independently of the Ottoman government.

The Ottoman government allocated to the Public Debt Administration all the revenues from eight indirect taxes. They included taxes on alcoholic beverages, stamps, fish, and silk, and the revenues from salt and tobacco monopolies. The Public Debt Administration was also entitled to draw revenues from the tribute from Bulgaria, the surplus of revenues from Cyprus and Eastern Rumelia (an Ottoman province in present-day Bulgaria), any surplus in customs revenues that might accrue from revisions of trade agreements and, generally, any other surplus from government revenues. The Ottoman state could substitute sources of revenue for any of the sources listed above, provided that the substitute would raise the same amount of revenue and that the board of the administration was in unanimous agreement on the substitutions. The loans of 1854, 1855, 1871, and 1877, in which tribute of Egypt was pledged as collateral, were excluded from the agreement. Bondholders agreed to a reduction in their claims, from £191 million (the equivalent of $20.8 billion today) to £97 million (the equivalent of $10.6 billion today). This amount was eventually fixed at £106 million (the equivalent of $11.6 billion today) to compensate for the period between 1875 and 1881. This amount was split into four groups: series A loans consisted of the 1858 and 1862 loans; series B loans consisted of the 1860, 1863–64, and 1872 loans; series C loans consisted of the 1865, 1869 and 1873 loans; and series D loans consisted of the 1865–74 general loans and the 1870–72 lottery loans. Railroad loans, which did not carry interest and were called "Lots Turcs," were excluded from the agreement. The maximum interest rate was set at 4 percent and the sinking fund (minimum) rate was fixed at 1 percent.

The foundation of the Ottoman Public Debt Administration signaled a new era in Ottoman financial history. Because of the authority vested in the administration, Ottoman debt was subject to restructuring as to improve term and interest rate structure. These restructures, which took place in 1890, 1891, 1893, 1894, 1903, and 1906, did not lead to the imposition of new financial burdens on the Ottoman government. Instead, they proved beneficial to the Ottoman government by generating a credit to the Ottoman treasury that was equivalent to the tribute from Egypt.

The sound governance of the Public Debt Administration improved the Ottoman Empire's credibility in European financial markets and increased the willingness of European capitalists to lend to the Ottoman government. The efficiency of the Public Debt Administration in collecting revenues and fulfilling the debt payments in accordance with the Muharrem Decree was the main factor in the Ottoman state's improved international credibility. Improved international credibility resulted in a reduction of borrowing costs. Before 1875, the cost of borrowing had been 10 percent; it now decreased to 5 percent.

Following the formation of the Public Debt Administration foreign borrowing by the Ottoman state increased rapidly. The government raised new loans, many of

which were secured by the Public Debt Administration. The Ottoman government was able to raise other loans by stipulating specific income sources as collateral. These loans, like the ones raised before 1875, were spent on activities such as financing budgetary deficits and military expenditures. The loans of 1904, 1910, and 1912, which were under the control of the Public Debt Administration, were used to construct the Baghdad railway.

After 1881, French and German capital had a dominant position in the Ottoman loan market. From 1903 to the start of WORLD WAR I, the share of German capital in the Ottoman state's overall debt portfolio increased rapidly. In 1881, the share of English capital was 30 percent of total Ottoman debt. By 1914, this ratio had decreased to 12 percent. During this same time frame, the French share in Ottoman debt increased from 40 percent to 60 percent, and the German share increased from 5 percent to 21 percent. The most important representatives of French and German capital in the Ottoman Empire were, respectively, the Imperial Ottoman Bank and Deutsche Bank. These two institutions cooperated on many large investments. At the outbreak of World War I, the total external debt of the Ottoman Empire, including the tribute of Egypt, was about 157,000,000 Ottoman liras (£T, the equivalent of $16.2 billion today).

Following the conclusion of the BALKAN WARS (1912–1913), the Ottoman Empire was in a poor financial state. The government was saved from insolvency thanks to a loan of £22,000,000 (the equivalent of $2.2 billion today) from the Imperial Ottoman Bank. With the outbreak of World War I, the Ottoman government was forced to issue *kaime* to finance government expenditures. During World War I, the Ottoman government issued paper money on seven different occasions, equivalent to £T 160,000,000 (the equivalent of $12.6 billion today). While the first issue was backed by German and Austrian gold, the other six issues were backed by German treasury bills. Additionally, a total of £T 74,000,000 (the equivalent of $5.8 billion today) was raised from donations from Germany and Austria. A further £T 18,000,000 (the equivalent of $1.4 billion today) was raised from internal loans.

During World War I, the English, Dutch, French, and Italian members of the Ottoman Public Debt Administration left Istanbul. Only German, Austro-Hungarian, and Ottoman members remained. In this period, payments to non-allied countries (Italy, Britain, and France) were suspended. After the ceasefire, the German and Austrian members of the administration were deported and a new committee was formed by English, French, Italian, and Turkish members. The victorious countries planned to impose full financial control over the Ottoman Empire. Provisions to this end were included in the terms of the 1920 TREATY OF SÈVRES. However, as the Ankara government did not recognize this treaty, Allied plans to impose full financial controls on the Ottoman Empire were never realized.

The collapse of the Ottoman Empire soon after the end of World War I resulted in the emergence of many new countries in the Near East, North Africa, and the Balkans. The Republic of Turkey, occupying the core Anatolian territories of the former Ottoman Empire, refused to assume responsibility for all the Ottoman debt and proposed to share this burden with other successor countries. Subsequent negotiations resulted in an agreement whereby the new Turkish Republic would be responsible for 65 percent of the total Ottoman debt of £T 129,385,000 (the equivalent of $7 billion today). Turkey's share thus amounted to £T 84,578,000 (the equivalent of $4.6 billion today), which required annual payments of £T 5,808,000 (the equivalent of $315 million today). The rest of the debt was apportioned to other successor countries, including 9 percent for GREECE, 8 percent for SYRIA and LEBANON, 5 percent for IRAQ, 4 percent for Yugoslavia, 3 percent for PALESTINE, and 6 percent apportioned collectively to BULGARIA, ALBANIA, the HEJAZ (in present-day Saudi Arabia), YEMEN, Transjordan (present-day Jordan), Italy, NAJD (in present-day Saudi Arabia), Maan (in present-day Jordan).

The mission of the Public Debt Administration ended with the collapse of the Ottoman Empire. By 1954, The Turkish Republic had fulfilled its share of the debt obligations it inherited from the Ottoman Empire. The resolution of this outstanding Ottoman debt marked the conclusion of the roughly 100-year history of Ottoman relations with international lending institutions.

Hüseyin Al

Further reading: Donald C. Blaisdell, *European Financial Control in the Ottoman Empire: A Study of the Establishment, Activities, Significance of the Administration of the Ottoman Public Debt*, 2nd ed. (New York: AMS Press, 1966); David Gillard, ed., *The Near and Middle East—The Ottoman Empire: Finance and Trade, 1860–1879*, British Documents on Foreign Affairs: Reports and Papers from the Foreign Office Confidential Print, pt. 1, series B, vol. 7, ser. eds. Kenneth Bourne and D. C. Watt (Frederick, Md., University Publications of America, 1984); Vincent Caillard, *"Turkish Finance,"* in *Encyclopaedia Britannica.* 11th ed. (Cambridge: Cambridge University Press, 1911); Christopher Clay, *Gold for the Sultan: Western Bankers and Ottoman Finance, 1856–1881* (New York: I.B. Tauris, 2000); William H. Wynne, *State Insolvency and Foreign Bondholders*, vol. 2, *Selected Case Histories of Governmental Foreign Bond Defaults and Debt Readjustments* (New Haven, Conn.: Yale University Press, 1951).

defterdar See ADMINISTRATION, CENTRAL.

demography *See* POPULATION.

dervish *See* BEKTAŞI ORDER; MEVLEVI ORDER; NAQSHBANDIYYA ORDER; RIFAIYYA ORDER; SHADHLIYYA ORDER; SUFISM.

devshirme *See* DEVŞIRME.

devşirme (devshirme) The Turkish word *devşirme*, or "collection," refers to the periodical forced levy of children from among the Christian subjects in the provinces in Europe and Asia Minor. The children taken replenished the ranks of the JANISSARIES, the sultan's elite infantry troops, and were also trained for positions as high-ranking government officials. In 1395 Isidore Glabas, metropolitan (bishop) of SALONIKA from 1380 to 1397, lamented "the seizure of the children by the decree of the emir" with these words: "What would a man not suffer were he to see a child, whom he had begotten and raised . . . carried off by the hands of foreigners, suddenly and by force, and forced to change over to alien customs and to become a vessel of barbaric, speech, impiety and other contaminations." An Italian source from 1397 stated that the Turks took boys aged 10 to 12 years old for their army. These sources suggest that by the late 1390s the *devşirme* was already an established practice.

Unlike other Muslim empires, who purchased their slave soldiers from outside the lands of Islam, the Ottoman sultans seized slaves from amongst their own Christian subjects, contradicting the SHARIA or Islamic law that forbade the enslavement of DHIMMIS or people of other revealed religions. It is possible that the *devşirme* originated in the Balkans, where Ottoman frontier warriors are reported as having taken, in the 1380s or earlier, "tribute children" in central Macedonia to fill the ranks of the Janissaries. In taking children for their own service, the Ottoman sultans might thus have been following a practice established by their frontier military commanders.

Under the Ottoman *devşirme* system Christian children between 8 and 20 years old—preferably between 12 and 14—were periodically taken, at varying rates. According to sources, including the memoirs of former Serbian Janissary Constantin Mihailović (1435–1501) and an early 16th-century Ottoman imperial decree, the recruiting officers seized one boy per 40 households. However, the sources are inconsistent regarding both the age of eligibility and the total numbers of boys taken per *devşirme*. These inconsistencies suggest that the rules of the levy varied greatly according to needs of the army, as did the intervals during which the *devşirme* was practiced. Sources indicate that the *devşirme* took place haphazardly in the 15th century and more regularly in the 16th century, when the frequent and prolonged wars often decimated the ranks of the Janissaries. By the end of that century however, the ranks of the Janissaries were filled from within the corps. As the Janissary corps ceased to be the elite force of the sultan, the *devşirme* was less valued. In the 17th century the levy was practiced only sporadically. English author and diplomat Sir Paul Rycaut (1629–1700), who stayed in Istanbul in the 1660s, claimed that by that time the *devşirme* was "in a great part grown out of use" and "wholly forgotten," though sources mention an attempt in 1705 to levy 1,000 boys in GREECE. Reports recording the number of youths taken during the levy also vary, from as low as 1,000 to as high as 12,000 per *devşirme*.

The regulations concerning the *devşirme* were extensive with regard to the physical and mental conditions of the children, as well as their social status. According to *The Laws of the Janissaries* (Kavanin-i Yeniçeriyan), written by a former Janissary in 1606, the officials charged with taking the boys could not take the only child of a family, for the head of the household needed his help in cultivating his land in order to pay his taxes. The same source noted that recruiting officers were not supposed to take the sons of the village headmen "as they belonged to the lower classes," the children of shepherds and herdsmen "as they had been brought up in the mountains so they were uneducated," the boys of craftsmen, townsmen in general, "since they did not fulfill their pledge for soldier's pay;" and married boys, because their "eyes had been opened, and those cannot become the slave of the sultan." The *Laws of the Janissaries* similarly excluded from the levy orphans, those who were considered in any way unhealthy or defective (e.g., cross-eyed boys); those who were too tall or too short, for they were considered stupid and trouble-makers, respectively, and those who had been to Istanbul (and the inhabitants of Istanbul, in general), "for they did not have a sense of shame." According to the same source certain ethnic groups were also ineligible, such as Hungarians and Croatians north of BELGRADE (who were considered unreliable by the Ottoman authorities), or those who lived in the regions between Karaman and Erzurum (because they were mixed with (Muslim) Turkomans and Kurds and (Christian but presumably untrustworthy) Georgians. Regions where the Christian population voluntarily acknowledged Ottoman rule were also exempted from the *devşirme*, as were those Christians who performed auxiliary military service, such as guarding bridges and mountain passes, working in mines, saltpeter works, and gunpowder works, or working as couriers. These exemptions also suggest that the levy was considered one of the many taxes Christian subjects owed to the sultan.

Turks and Muslims were excluded from the child levy to avoid a situation in which their relatives would demand tax exemptions. However, according to *The Laws of the Janissaries*, the Muslims of BOSNIA were subject to the *devşirme* because they requested and were granted this favor during their initial mass conversion to Islam after the conquest of the region in 1463. This shows that while many tried to escape the practice, others saw it as an opportunity for upward social mobility and access to the *askeri*, the privileged Ottoman military and bureaucratic class.

When a decree was issued to collect Christian boys from a specified region, the recruiting officers ordered all the boys, their fathers, and their priests to appear before them. Using baptismal registers, provided by the priests, the recruiting officers —aided by the local Ottoman district judge and the village's *sipahi* (Ottoman landlord) or his representative—inspected and selected the boys. For each group of 100–200 boys, designated "the flock," a detailed register was compiled. This listed the boy's name, the name of his father, the name of his *sipahi,* and the name of his village. It also gave a physical description of the boy so that if he escaped or disappeared, he could be found with the help of the register. The "flock" then traveled on foot to the capital, hundreds of miles away. Many died or ran away during the long journey. Others escaped service because their families bribed the recruiting officers.

Those who made it to the imperial capital were inspected, circumcised, and converted to Islam. Those who seemed smartest were sent for education in the elite PALACE SCHOOL or for service in the sultan's gardens, or were given to Ottoman dignitaries. These appointments were part of their grooming for later positions of trust and authority. Those designated for the Palace School were the most fortunate, for they were looked after and given the best education of the time and, in due course, could achieve the highest offices within the empire. The rest were hired out to Turkish farmers for seven to eight years, during which time they grew accustomed to hardship and learned the rudiments of the Turkish language and Islamic customs. All the boys were delivered by name and listed in registers so that the sultan could gather them when they were needed to fill vacancies in the Janissary corps. Government officials inspected the boys every year, and also collected an 80-akçe "inspection fee" (approximately equal to the price of three to four sheep) from the families on whose farm the youth worked. After seven or eight years of work in the fields the boys were recalled to Istanbul or Gallipoli. There they joined the ranks of Janissary novices or *acemi oğlans* and lived in their own barracks under strict military discipline. They also served as a cheap workforce for public works projects, carrying stones and earth, or manning the ships that transported snow from the BURSA mountains to the sultan's ice-houses or firewood to the palace. Others served in the sultan's gardens or in the imperial dockyards in Istanbul and Gallipoli, as blacksmiths, caulkers, carpenters, oar-makers, and so on. Others became apprentices in the Imperial Cannon Foundry or in the naval arsenal. Only after several years of such service did the novices become Janissaries or fill in vacancies in the corps of gunners, gun-carriage drivers, bombardiers, or armorers of the sultan's standing army.

The child levy and the system of military slavery created an extraordinarily strong and stable structure of support for the House of Osman, because the boys taken and raised by the state ultimately became its strongest supporters. In periods of crisis, the slaves of the sultan helped prevent the breakup of the state. In addition, the *devşirme* proved to be an effective means of conversion. The tribute children were Islamized and incorporated into the Ottoman military, while the inhabitants of some areas of the Balkans, especially Thrace and Macedonia, voluntarily converted to Islam in order to avoid the child levy.

Gábor Ágoston

See also ADMINISTRATION, CENTRAL.

Further reading: V. L. Ménage, "Devşirme," in *Encyclopaedia of Islam*, edited by P. Bearman, Th. Bianquis, C. E. Bosworth, E. van Donzel, and W. P. Heinrichs. Brill, 2007. Brill Online. Online edition (by subscription), viewed 14 March 2007: <http://www.brillonline.nl/subscriber/entry?entry=islam_SIM-1807>; Speros Vryonis, "Isidore Glabas and the Turkish Devshirme." *Speculum* 31, no. 3 (1956): 433–443; Speros Vryonis, "Seljuk Gulams and Ottoman Devshirme." *Der Islam* 41 (1965): 224–252; Vassilis Demetriades, "Some Thoughts on the Origins of the Devşirme," in *The Ottoman Emirate, 1300–1389,* edited by Elizabeth Zachariadou (Rethymnon: Crete University Press, 1993), 23–31; Colin Imber, *The Ottoman Empire, 1300–1650* (New York: Palgrave Macmillan, 2002), 134–142.

dhimmi (zimmi) *Dhimmi* was the Muslim term for a Christian or Jewish subject of a Muslim ruler. The term is derived from the Arabic expression *ahl al-dhimma,* "the people of the contract," and is translated as *zimmi* in Ottoman Turkish. The legal implications of this status, in terms of obligations and rights, were already established in Islamic law before the founding of the Ottoman Empire. The Prophet Muhammad set the precedent that Muslim authorities should recognize the rights of believers in the monotheistic faiths (*ahl al-kitab* or "the people of the book") to remain at peace within the Muslim state as long as they recognized Islam's political authority over them. This client status established the rights of these non-Muslims to property, livelihood, and freedom of worship, in exchange for paying an extra tax (the JIZYA) and promising not to help the Muslims' enemies. This rather rudimentary formula for political and religious coexistence was based on the realities of Arabia, where the vast majority of inhabitants had already at least nominally accepted Islam by the time of the Prophet's death in 632 C.E.

But as the first Arab-Islamic empire, the Umayyad Caliphate (661–750 C.E.), expanded its territory, millions of non-Muslims were incorporated into the new empire. As Islam became established as a mature political force, it became more legalistic, enshrining what might have been temporary historical expediencies as holy law. This was particularly true in its formulation of the conditions under which non-Muslims might enjoy Islam's protection. As Muslims gained ground numerically with large-scale conversions to Islam, the legal status of non-Muslims became more problematic. Social and political subordination to the people of Islam was given concrete legal form in a document known as the Pact of Umar. According to Muslim tradition, the caliph Umar ibn Khattab (634–644 C.E.) issued the Pact to the non-Muslims of Jerusalem following its fall to Muslim armies in the 630s. By the ninth century C.E., a written formulation of the agreement entered into Muslim legal texts as a standard formula, invariably ascribed to the caliph Umar. It was in this form that it came down to the legal scholars of the Ottoman Empire where it served as the foundation of laws governing both the freedoms of, and the limitations placed on, non-Muslims.

In return for being granted safe-conduct for their persons and property, *dhimmis* agreed to a number of conditions. These included the requirement to wear distinctive clothing to distinguish them from Muslims and prohibitions on riding horses or camels or having houses that could overlook those of Muslims. *Dhimmis* could not sell anything to Muslims that was forbidden to them by the Quran, such as pork or alcoholic beverages. They could not build new houses of worship or celebrate their religions publicly. There was to be no ringing of church bells. Non-Muslim men could not marry Muslim women, although Muslim men could marry *dhimmi* women.

The pact guaranteed that Muslims would not interfere in the personal affairs of non-Muslims. Islamic law would be applied to *dhimmi*s only when all parties involved in a legal case agreed to it, or in cases involving *dhimmi*s and Muslims in which Muslim law was the only option. In the latter case, *dhimmis* suffered a distinct disadvantage, as their testimony in Muslim courts was not accepted as valid in cases that might lead to the punishment of a Muslim. In effect, this meant that their testimonies were only accepted in commercial cases. No restrictions were placed on where *dhimmis* might live or what professions or trades they might enter. There were no religious ghettos mandated by law in the Muslim world, although the prohibition on building new houses of worship led both Christians and Jews to cluster near existing ones.

In the Ottoman Empire there was a tension between the theory of the place of *dhimmis* in the state and actual practice, as Islamic law sometimes conflicted with what the Ottoman authorities wanted. At times, invocation of the conditions established by the Pact of Umar could serve *dhimmi* interests. For example, during the campaigns against the KIZILBAŞ, those rebelling against the Ottomans in the name of Shah ISMAIL I (r. 1501–24), Sultan SELIM I (r. 1512–20) requested permission to kill or enslave Christians living in the territory where the rebellion was occurring. The chief judge of the empire responded that the KIZILBAŞ were heretics and therefore deserved no mercy, but the Christians were *dhimmis* and protected. They could only be executed or enslaved if they were found in actual rebellion. At other times, the Pact was used against *dhimmi* interests. For example, governors often threatened to implement the rules that *dhimmis* had to wear distinctive clothing in order to extract bribes from them. Similarly, the ban on new houses of worship could be imposed on communities in one location but ignored in another, depending on what the local authorities would allow.

The distinction between Muslims and *dhimmis* officially ended with the imperial decree (Hatt-i Hümayun) of 1856 that established equality between all the sultan's subjects, regardless of their religious community.

Bruce Masters

Further reading: Bruce Masters, *Christians and Jews in the Ottoman Arab World: The Roots of Sectarianism* (Cambridge: Cambridge University Press, 2001).

Dinshaway Incident   In June 1906 a group of British soldiers in EGYPT stopped to shoot pigeons for sport outside the village of Dinshaway. Pigeons were a major source of protein for Egyptian villagers, a fact of which the soldiers were apparently unaware. The villagers' anger at the soldiers' transgression increased to the point of riot when a stray bullet injured a local woman. Dinshaway residents surrounded the soldiers and two officers were injured in the melee that followed. The army opened fire on the villagers and beat a retreat. On their way back to camp, one of the officers died, probably of sunstroke.

The affair became widely known as the Dinshaway Incident after 52 villagers were arrested and put on trial. Egyptian Nationalists presented their trial in the popular press as proof of the injustice of British rule in Egypt since no British soldier was charged with any wrongdoing. Ultimately, four Egyptian men were sentenced to death, and the rest were sentenced to imprisonment or flogging. The anger of the Egyptian public at what was

viewed as an illegal outrage helped propel MUSTAFA KAMIL (d. 1908) to the forefront of the Egyptian Nationalist movement with his call for the return of national sovereignty to the Egyptians. The Egyptian judge who had presided over the trials, Butrus Ghali, was assassinated in 1910. Many Muslim Egyptians felt that it was a just reward for his collaboration with the British. For the largest sect of Egyptian Christians, the COPTS, however, the assassination of Ghali, the most politically prominent Copt in Egypt, seemed to be aimed at their community in general rather than being tied to his role in the Dinshaway Incident.

Bruce Masters

Divan   *See* ADMINISTRATION, CENTRAL.

Dolmabahçe Palace   Between the 17th and the 19th centuries, several mansions and outbuildings called *kiosks* were built by the Ottoman sultans along the coast of the Bosporus leading to the Sea of Marmara. The existing bays in this area were filled to widen and flatten the land and these mansions, extended with new additions, became known as the Beşiktaş coastal palaces. These were a favored retreat of Sultan MAHMUD II (r. 1808–39), who introduced a strong European influence into Ottoman institutions and architecture. These pleasure grounds became the site of the Dolmabahçe Palace, the empire's first modern, Western-style royal residence, when Mahmud's successor, Sultan ABDÜLMECID (r. 1839–61), demolished parts of the existing palaces and commissioned a new residence made entirely of stone. The adoption of many architectural changes and Western innovation reflected the changing circumstances and culture of the Ottoman state, weakened economically and thus more prone to European influences, and in the midst of the sweeping political and social reforms of the TANZIMAT. The sultan was ready to leave the old-fashioned TOPKAPI PALACE, which had been the Ottoman royal residence and the center of Ottoman administration for centuries. The new palace embraced a European architectural style in line with the empire's other changing structures, and its magnificence was intended in part as a demonstration of the weakened empire's remaining power.

Dolmabahçe Palace was designed in the European architectural style; however, the Baroque and Empire styles were blended with Turkish ornamental features. The palace was designed with two stories and three sections, with the basement and attic serving as service floors. Its style and structure and the lifestyle it was designed to accommodate bespoke a strong Eastern influence, but by incorporating Western features as well, the Dolmabahçe Palace became a monument with

Opened in 1856, the Dolmabahçe Palace was the first European-style palace in the empire and represented the westward-looking spirit of the Reform (Tanzimat) era. *(Photo by Alíz Ágoston)*

a uniquely Ottoman quality. The construction of the palace commenced in 1842, and it was opened in 1856. Abdülhalim Bey, Garabet Balyan, Nikogos Balyan, and Altunizade İsmail Zuhtu worked as architects in the construction of the palace. The interior decoration was completed by Charles Séchan, the decorator of the Paris Opera Hall. The palace, which stretched over a 110,000-square meter area, was used by the sultans until 1924 when the Ottoman dynasty was exiled.

Although most of the administrative functions were conducted from the Sublime Porte (Bab-ı Âli or "High Gate," also used to refer to the Ottoman government), the Dolmabahçe Palace also held a central role in the administration of the state. The sultans both worked and resided in the palace during the remainder of the Ottoman period. After the proclamation of the Turkish Republic, Kemal Atatürk used the Dolmabahçe Palace for both personal and state occasions until his death in 1938.

The main building has five gates from the sea side, nine gates from the land side, and a clock tower, which was added by Abdülhamid II (r. 1876–1909). The gate in the clock tower side is called the Gate of the Treasury and the gate on the road is called the Imperial Gate. The treasury and textile (*mefrusat*) departments are linked to the main building and stand in the Treasury entrance of the palace. The theatre hall and imperial tables, which no longer exist, were situated in the Cihangir section of the palace. The Beşiktaş section of the palace held the imperial kitchen and the private rooms of princes.

The three sections of the palace were the official part (*mabeyn-i hümayun*), the ceremonial hall (*muayede salonu*), and the residential area (HAREM). The official section was used for affairs of state and formal receptions. Statesmen and foreign ambassadors met the sultan here. The entrance hall (*medhal*) on the first floor and the ambassador hall (*sufera*) on the upper floor are spacious and impressive. Even more impressive are the glass ceiling and crystal staircase.

The second section, the ceremonial hall was used for large formal ceremonies. Situated between the *mabeyn-i hümayun* and the *harem*, the ceremonial hall is covered by a dome 120 feet (36 m) high and spanning 21,000 square feet (2,000 m²). The hall boasts a four-and-a-half-ton English chandelier, a gift from Queen Victoria.

The third section, the private residential area of the sultan and his family, occupies the largest area of the palace. This includes the sultan's personal rooms: a study, a relaxing room, a bedroom, and a reception room. The mother of the sultan (*valide sultan*), who helped administer the harem, also had private rooms for receiving, relaxing, and sleeping. Each of the princes, princesses, and wives of the sultan (*kadınefendiler*) also had his or her own three- or-four-room apartments in the palace, living separately with their own servants.

With its wooden parquet flooring and rich European furnishings, its ornamental carpets, curtains, and fabrics, its invaluable collections of paintings, vases, and clocks, the 19th-century Dolmabahçe Palace, both inside and out, reflects a moment in Ottoman history when Turkish taste was subject to the influence of 19th-century European style.

Zeynep Tarım-Ertuğ

Further reading: Nurhan Atasoy, *A Garden for the Sultan: Gardens and Flowers in the Ottoman Culture* (Istanbul: Aygaz, 2002); Çelik Gülersoy, *Dolmabahçe Palace and Its Environs* (Istanbul: İstanbul Kitaplığı, 1990).

dragoman (*tercüman*) A dragoman, known as a *tercüman* in Ottoman Turkish, was a translator for the European merchants and diplomats who resided in the Ottoman Empire. While these translators worked for the Europeans, they were typically subjects of the Ottoman sultans, as the Europeans rarely took the trouble to learn Ottoman Turkish or Arabic. The translators were non-Muslims, largely due to unwillingness on the part of Muslims to learn the languages of those they considered infidels. The role and privileges of the dragomans were first formalized by a commercial treaty between England and the Ottomans in 1675, by which Europeans were permitted to designate Ottoman subjects as translators. All subsequent treaties between the various European powers and the Ottoman Empire granted them similar privileges. While the practice of commercial translation was, of course, not new, these treaties explicitly gave rights to the translators comparable to those the Europeans enjoyed, even while asserting that they were to remain the sultan's subjects. These rights included exemptions from the JIZYA, the head tax on non-Muslim males, and the irregular taxes imposed on the dragoman's religious community by either the Ottoman central treasury or the local governors. The treaties established that individuals holding the *berats* (patents) of office as a dragoman would pay the same favorable customs duties as their European patrons; they could also avoid having their commercial disputes decided by local Muslim courts, being granted the advantage of heaving their cases heard in Istanbul in the presence of the consul of the country for which they worked.

Sephardic Jews and local Christians provided the majority of the dragomans working for the Europeans, although some were also the descendants of European merchants who married local women. The absence of Muslims in their ranks had two causes. Muslims were advised by their religious authorities not to learn the languages of the Franks (western Europeans), and the Europeans would have been wary of employing them even if they did. A Muslim employee could always demand that any dispute with the European merchants be heard in a Muslim court, and the Europeans were suspicious of Muslim justice. When trade involved parties who spoke different languages, it was usually conducted in Italian, known in the Mediterranean as the *lingua franca* ("language of the Franks"). As Catholic MISSIONARY SCHOOLS within the empire offered young Christian men the opportunity to learn both Italian and bookkeeping, their graduates were keenly sought after, even by merchants from Protestant nations. In many cases, the position of dragoman passed from father to son, sometimes over several generations.

The dragomans were in a privileged position, as they knew both the ways of the West and those of the Ottoman Empire. They also benefited from the various legal exemptions that their status provided. Many became wealthy, using their contacts and inside knowledge of both worlds. Although the treaties that established their rights as translators for the Europeans specifically stated that they should not engage in trade, as the Ottoman framers of the agreement recognized that the dragomans would have unfair advantages over their competitors, most did engage in trade. As one English merchant wrote in the 18th century, it would have been impossible to hire a competent translator if the Europeans did not allow them to trade so that they could make profits in addition to their salaries.

The representatives of the European trading companies were generally given the title of consul by their home governments and had diplomatic immunity and status. Each consul was in turn allowed to designate two men as dragomans and four more as "helpers." So in theory a country could have no more than six men employed as dragomans in any given city, all enjoying European diplomatic privilege that included favored legal status, special tax exemptions, and other trade advantages. Although the number of dragomans who were registered as working for the Europeans was well above the number stipulated in the various commercial treaties, in the 18th century they still only numbered in the hundreds. By the middle of the 19th century their number had risen to thousands. The issue of European powers' granting extraterritorial privileges to Ottoman subjects, claiming that they were translators, was a major point of diplomatic contention between Europeans and the Ottomans until the end of the empire.

Bruce Masters

See also CAPITULATIONS.

Further reading: Maurits van den Boogert, *The Capitulations and the Ottoman Legal System: Qadis, Consuls and Beraths in the 18th Century* (Leiden: Brill, 2005).

Drava River The source of the River Drava is in the Dolomite Alps in Italy. After passing through AUSTRIA and Slovenia, its right bank and some sections of the left bank lie in Croatia, while most of the left bank is in HUNGARY. It joins the DANUBE RIVER near Aljmas in eastern Croatia. It is navigable upstream as far as Barcs, in Hungary. Along with the River Sava, which runs parallel to it some 50–70 miles to the south, the Drava was important in that it separated Hungary from the Ottoman Empire's Balkan territories and facilitated the defense of Hungary. However, the Ottomans gained a foothold at the most important crossing at Osijek (Ösek, Eszék, in present-day Croatia) in the late 1520s, then made further conquests in 1543 and 1566. At Osijek the great bridge of Sultan SÜLEYMAN I (r. 1520–66) was built to facilitate the crossing of troops and commodities to Hungary, while a flotilla of some 50–60 vessels was built for military and commercial purposes. These facilities were exposed to damage by war and climate. The commander (*kapudan*) of the Ottoman Drava flotilla had his residence in Osijek.

The Ottoman conquest initiated the process of pushing back the southern border of Hungary. On the Drava crossings, customs dues were levied, and a law code from 1579 calls the left bank of the Drava the "Hungarian coast" (Engürüs yakası).

Nenad Moačanin

Further reading: Nenad Moačanin, *Town and Country on the Middle Danube, 1526–1690* (Leiden: Brill, 2006).

Druzes The Druzes are a sect that follows an esoteric teaching that broke away from Islam in the 11th century. Because this group does not accept converts and does not talk about its beliefs to outsiders, the faith has often been misunderstood and misrepresented by non-Druze neighbors. The Druzes identify the faith as originating with the Fatimid caliph al-Hakim bi-Amr-Allah, who ruled in CAIRO from 996 to 1021. The Fatimids were followers of the Ismaili sect of SHIA ISLAM and much of their theology was available only to those who were initiated into the mysteries of their faith. But without the support of the ruling elite, populist preachers from Cairo spread out through the Middle East saying that al-Hakim was the awaited imam of the Shia, who they believed would come at the end of days to restore the rule of justice. The movement gained popularity in what is today SYRIA and LEBANON until 1021, when al-Hakim disappeared.

Western historians suspect foul play on the part of the caliph's sister, Sitt al-Mulk. Christians in Egypt say that al-Hakim was overcome by the persecution that he had visited on them and that he joined a monastery in penance. Druze beliefs indicate that he had become the "hidden imam" who would return at the end of days. Whatever his fate, the movement he founded entered a period of persecution, for it was regarded as heretical by both Sunni and Shii authorities. Because it was an underground faith, early Druze history remains unclear, but by the Ottoman period, the Druze form of worship was well established among a significant minority in Syria in the JABAL AL-DRUZ, in Lebanon, and in the nearby hills of Galilee.

Druzes call themselves Muwahhidun, meaning "those who profess the unity of God," the same name, coincidentally, that is used by the WAHHABIS, or the followers of the 18th century reformer MUHAMMAD IBN ABD AL-WAHHAB, but any similarities between the two religious traditions end there. The Druzes hold that the Quran is sacred but that is an allegory to be interpreted by the wise men of the community, the sheikhs, who must go through years of study and preparation. After close scrutiny, if candidates are deemed worthy, they are admitted to the inner circle of the initiated, the *uqqal*, "those who know," as opposed to the rest of the community who are called the *juhhal*, "those in ignorance." In addition to the Quran, the Druzes have sacred writings of their own that they ascribe to al-Hakim.

The Druzes differ from other Muslims in a number of key areas. They do not pray five times a day, nor do they have noon prayer services on Fridays or build mosques. In place of mosques, the Druzes have a prayer hall where the main services are held on Thursday evenings and which men and women can attend in mixed company. The Druzes, like the ALAWIS, another offshoot of Islam, believe in reincarnation; they hold that all the souls that will ever be were created when God created the universe. The Druzes do not permit polygamy, and although women cannot enter the ranks of the *uqqal*, they are allowed to participate in religious services to a greater extent than is allowed in either the Shii or the Sunni tradition. Though the Druzes profess that they are Muslims, legal scholars in other Islamic traditions do not concede this point.

The Druze feudal lords (*muqtajis*) dominated the political life of LEBANON from the 16th through the 18th centuries. Although the Ottomans controlled the coastal cities of Lebanon, they could exert their control over the mountains that rise steeply behind the coast at only great cost in lives and treasure. In their mountains, which they shared with MARONITE Christians, the Druzes enjoyed virtual autonomy. The Ottoman authorities had an uneasy relationship with the Druzes. When they were compliant with Ottoman demands for taxation, the Ottoman authorities were content to accede to the fact that the Druzes were Muslim and the poll tax on non-Muslims (JIZYA) was never asked of them. But when they were in rebellion, those same authorities labeled them KIZILBAŞ, a term that had become a catchall phrase for "heretic" in Ottoman legal language.

Bruce Masters

Further reading: Robert Betts, *The Druze* (New Haven, Conn.: Yale University Press, 1988).

Duwayhi, Istifanus (b. 1629–d. 1704) *Maronite patriarch and historian*   Istifanus Duwayhi is considered by many to be the first modern historian of Lebanon. He was born into a Maronite Catholic family in the village of Ihdin, in the mountains of northern Lebanon. When he was 12 his uncle, who was a Maronite bishop, sent him to the Maronite College in Rome. He was ordained as a priest in 1655, and the office of the Propaganda Fide (propagation of the faith) sent him back to Lebanon to work as a missionary. He then served as a missionary among the various Eastern-rite Christians in the city of Aleppo. The Eastern-rite churches were those such as the Armenian Apostolic Church or the Nestorians who followed their own traditions rather than those of either the Roman Catholic or Orthodox churches. Duwayhi became Maronite bishop of Cyprus in 1668; in 1670, a council of Maronite clergy elected him patriarch. Pope Clement X confirmed him in that office two years later. Duwayhi served as patriarch until his death. During his long years of service as the patriarch he devoted much of his efforts to bringing the traditional practices and dogma of the Maronite Church into agreement with those of Rome.

Although Duwayhi wrote a number of theological texts, he is best remembered for his three histories: a history of the Maronite Church, a chronology of the Maronite patriarchs, and a general history of the region that comprises Lebanon and Syria from the time of the First Crusade in 1095 to his present. It is the last, entitled *Tarikh al-azmina* (A history of times), that is considered most significant.

As a historian, Duwayhi occupies a significant place in Middle Eastern scholarship. His *History of Times* serves as a bridge between the traditional Middle Eastern format, in which the author chronicles the events of the years in which he lived without analysis, and modern histories, which provide interpretation and use a variety of sources. Although Duwayhi was uncritical of his sources in a way that no modern historian would be, he acknowledges his sources, and pushes his narrative back to several centuries before his birth. Citing documents from his own time for his contemporary history, Duwayhi developed a historical methodology that would be followed by Maronite historians for the next two centuries.

Bruce Masters

Further reading: Kamal Salibi, *Maronite Historians of Medieval Lebanon* (Beirut: American University in Beirut, 1959).

E

Eastern Question First coined at the Congress of Vienna (1815) by the Russian delegates to describe the growing tensions between the Ottoman sultan and his Greek subjects, this phrase gained popularity during the 19th century as diplomats debated the fate of the declining Ottoman Empire. Simply put, the Eastern Question revolved around the question of how to eliminate the power vacuum in Eastern Europe, the Balkans, and the modern Middle East that emerged with the decline of the Ottoman Empire and the partitioning of the Polish-Lithuanian Commonwealth (POLAND) without harming the delicate balance of power in Europe.

There is no consensus among historians as to when the Eastern Question emerged, or when—or even if—it was resolved. The diplomatic circles of the 19th century understood it as a matter of contemporary politics and tried to find the best solution by improvising various reforms. However, the Great Powers of Europe were never in agreement about what to do with the Ottoman Empire, that is, whether to try to sustain it or let it die. Each power changed its position regarding the Sublime Porte based on that power's ambitions in the eastern Mediterranean.

Although it first came into use in 1815, the term Eastern Question is now used by historians to identify issues of imperial stability dating to the second siege of Vienna (1683), which ended Ottoman expansion in Europe; some historians even see the question as going back to the 14th century when "Turks" first set foot on the Balkan Peninsula. Conventional history now dates the issues of the Eastern Question in this sense as having been born out of the 1774 TREATY OF KÜÇÜK KAYNARCA, which marked the emergence of RUSSIA as a Great Power.

There is also significant controversy as to the final date of the resolution of the Eastern Question. Loaded as it is with imperialist ambitions, the Eastern Question was not resolved with the final dismemberment of the Ottoman Empire in 1918; rather, it paved the way for a new set of political problems in the Balkans and the Middle East that continue into the 21st century.

Acting to further their own strategic interests, the Great Powers all attempted to create their own zone of influence in the Ottoman Empire by claiming the status of protector of a particular Christian subject people and urging the Sublime Porte to undertake political reforms. The Ottomans, however, viewed all attempts to advance the rights of particular Christian subject peoples through such diplomatic pressures as an encroachment on the rights of their sovereignty. They viewed European intervention in internal Ottoman affairs as a smokescreen that hid the Great Powers' ambitions to dismantle the empire. Thus the Eastern Question has a legacy in shaping contemporary public opinion of some in modern Turkey toward the European Union (EU); they fear that EU demands that Turkey enhance the political and cultural rights of ethnic and religious minorities, and reconsider the Armenian deportation in 1915, might simply be a pretext to dismember Turkey.

The Eastern Question also became a code to cover a number of other "questions," including dissension and political unrest over the Romanian principalities (1774–1878); the Serbian revolt (1790s–1828); the French invasion of EGYPT (1799–1801); the GREEK REVOLT (1820s); the revolt of MEHMED ALI of Egypt (1830s); the problem of the straits on the Sea of Marmara (1830s); the problem of the Polish and Hungarian refugees (1848); the CRIMEAN WAR (1853–56); the Bulgarian revolt (1870s);

the Russo-Ottoman War (1877–78); the war with Greece (1897); the Armenian question (1878–1915), the question of Macedonia (1880s–1912); the War with Italy (1911); the BALKAN WARS (1912–13); and finally WORLD WAR I (1914–18). A glance at this list reveals that the Eastern Question has been stretched to its limits in an attempt to explain the entire history of the relations between Europe and the Ottoman Empire. Contemporary historians generally avoid the term, considering the "Eastern Question" to be a Eurocentric reduction of the Ottoman Empire and its peoples to passive recipients of the power politics of the Great Powers.

Kahraman Şakul

Further reading: Virginia Aksan, *Ottoman Wars 1700-1870: An Empire Besieged* (Longman, 2007); M. S. Anderson, *The Eastern Question, 1774–1923* (New York: St. Martin's, 1966); M. S. Anderson, ed., *The Great Powers and the Near East, 1774–1923* (New York: St. Martin's, 1970); Selim Deringil, *The Well-Protected Domains: Ideology and the Legitimation of Power in the Ottoman Empire, 1876–1909* (London: I.B. Tauris, 1998); Caroline Finkel, *Osman's Dream: The Story of the Ottoman Empire, 1300–1923* (London: John Murray, 2005); Donald Quataert, *The Ottoman Empire, 1700–1922* (Cambridge: Cambridge University Press, 2000); F. A. K. Yasamee, *Ottoman Diplomacy: Abdulhamid II and the Great Powers, 1878–1888* (Istanbul: Isis, 1997).

economy and economic policy Ottoman economic history can be divided into two main periods: the first, or classical, period from the beginning of the empire in the 14th to the end of the 18th century, which witnessed little change with regard to the basic institutions, values, objectives, and tenets; and the second period, characterized by modernization and REFORM, from the second half of the 19th century.

PRINCIPLES OF OTTOMAN ECONOMIC POLICY

Ottoman economics in the classical period was centered on the concept of need and was motivated by three main principles, provisionism, fiscalism, and traditionalism. Provisionism was the policy of maintaining a steady supply of goods and services, which had to be cheap, plentiful, and of good quality. Fiscalism was the policy of maximizing treasury income. Traditionalism was the tendency to preserve existing conditions and to look to past models when changes occurred. These three policies created the referential framework of the Ottoman economic system.

The first principle was that of provisionism. Because the early Ottoman economic atmosphere was characterized by low productivity and because it was difficult to increase productivity while transportation costs were high, the Ottomans built an extensive network of production and exchange facilities in the fields of AGRICULTURE,

artisanship, and TRADE. Family-run farms of between 60 and 150 acres were thought to be the most productive landholding pattern in agriculture, and the state, as the owner of the land, protected these units so that holdings would not be broken into smaller units through inheritance. While the state would allow the transfer of land between individuals to prevent potential setbacks in production, it restricted peasants from abandoning villages and leaving land untilled.

The basic economic, fiscal, and administrative unit in the empire at this time was the *kaza,* or judicial district, overseen by a KADI or judge with extensive powers. The *kaza* usually consisted of a town with a population of 3,000–20,000 and a number of villages varying from 20 to 200 with a total area of 200–1200 square miles. Small-scale artisanship was the norm in the *kaza* as was the small-scale landholding pattern in the village, and it was the responsibility of these small farmers to market their own agricultural produce in the town. Marketing of produce and goods out of the *kaza* was prohibited unless the demand within the town was already satisfied. Excess goods were offered first to the army and the palace, then to the city of ISTANBUL, followed by other regions. Export was an option only after domestic demands were satisfied.

Export was not an objective of provisionist Ottoman economic policy, which aimed at satisfying domestic demand. The state regularly intervened in export, forcing quotas and special customs taxes on export goods. Imports, by contrast, were fostered. This economic approach differs considerably from the export-oriented mercantilist policies pursued in Europe at that time. For this reason, Ottoman CAPITULATIONS, or trade privileges offered to foreigners who sold goods within the empire, were not restricted until the end of the classical period.

Although provisionist policy always took priority in this period, another economic policy followed during this era was fiscalism, which may be defined as the policy of maximizing treasury income and trying to prevent its level from falling. Like increases in production capacity, increases in treasury income were difficult and slow to achieve, especially when transportation costs were so high and gold and silver stocks were very limited. The reliance on provisionism was considered indispensable for social welfare, but this policy actually made any attempt to grow the economy both risky and costly, creating a situation in which any growth in revenues was difficult to achieve, which is evidenced by the BUDGETS or treasury balance sheets from the 1550s to the 1780s.

Also falling within this period, though not arising until provisionism and fiscalism had come into maturity by the mid-16th century, was the economic policy of traditionalism. This may be summarized as the tendency to preserve existing conditions, to look to past models instead of searching for a new equilibrium when changes occurred, and to maintain some institutions for the sake of traditionalism even when they had lost their functional value.

These three policies created the referential framework of the Ottoman economic system. Any difference in policies stemmed from the combination of the three principles in varying degrees. For instance, whenever provisionism prevailed, export was restricted and import was fostered; when fiscalism was favored, the opposite policy was followed.

STATE CONTROL OF PRODUCTION

Classical Ottoman economic policy coincided with the state's attempt to control all factors of production—including land, labor, and capital—with long-term consequences on the Ottoman economic and commercial structure. Of all factors of production, land was the most important. Agricultural land accounted for the largest portion of land use and, for the most part, was owned and controlled by the state. The landholding pattern prevalent in most of the Asian and European provinces was called *miri* (state-owned); it allocated small units of land for cultivation by families. Under this system, peasants paid taxes on the land they cultivated and consumed its produce as they saw fit, but they could not convert the land into a religious endowment (WAQF) or grant it to another party. If the land was left untilled for three years in a row without excuse, the plot would be given to another farmer. Furthermore, if a farmer moved to another area and abandoned his plot, he could be brought back by force in a decade unless he was registered in the land survey of the village he moved to or paid a specified penalty (*çift bozan resmi*). Family farms passed from generation to generation intact without inheritance taxes.

Given the inherent protections of this system for both the state and the peasantry, this ownership structure played a crucial role in the rapid expansion of Ottoman rule in the 14th century. Based on cadastral surveys of the 15th and 16th centuries, it seems that this structure enabled increases in both production and population.

Although this structure began to shift in the 17th century with the emergence of large farms, most of these new farms were located in previously vacant lands outside settled areas. Considering the spread of big farms both an economic and a cultural threat, the peasantry and the state reacted against this shift and prevented the big farms from expanding into the villages. Small landholders continued to constitute the basic unit of agricultural production, and statistics indicate that land distribution in Anatolia and Rumelia preserved its egalitarian character until the end of the empire in the early 20th century.

Ottoman control of labor during this period was secondary, important only for the state's control of the land; Ottoman subjects were not serfs or semi-slaves tied to the land. There was no law forcing the peasant to till the land but rather an obligation from which he could escape by paying a fine equivalent to 7–10 times his usual tax. This practice was valid not only for peasants but also for some urban industrial workers whose labor was indispensable to the state, and for workers in the mines owned by the state

State control of labor was also common in the case of several urban artisan groups, which were organized in accordance with the SHARIA, or religious law, and imperial decrees. All the members of each guild had to complete an apprenticeship, a means of building human capital in specialized fields. The guilds tended toward monopoly, each group coming to dominate a particular area of production, especially in Istanbul and other big cities. By the 17th century, the state began to issue guilds monopoly licenses (known as *gediks* or patents) stipulating that certain products or services could only be offered by members of specified guilds. This practice spread throughout the 18th century, enabling state control of the urban sector of artisans. Control of labor helped limit the mobility of labor in the pre-industrial age when insufficient production was chronic; it also enabled the government to protect both the structure and the volume of production, and promoted specialization, as evidenced by production successes in such fields as metal goods, jewelry, dyeing, and leather manufacturing.

While controlling both land and labor, the state also worked to control both financial and physical capital, with significant consequences. The policy of provisionism motivated the state to limit the rate of profit on consumer goods, setting a maximum of 5 to 15 percent profit for tradesmen and merchants from the 16th to the mid-19th centuries. The actual rate of profit was decided based on the kind of economic activity. In retail and wholesale trading the norm was 5 to 10 percent. The prices of the goods and services sold in the market, as well as the wages paid by guilds, were determined through the cooperation of the relevant guild with the *kadı*, the inspector of the marketplace (*muhtesib*). For example, in 1726, retail merchants selling Egyptian flax in Istanbul as raw material with minor processing were allowed a profit of 6.5 percent. Trades that required more complicated production—such as CERAMICS or nails—yielded profits as high as 20 percent.

Even when the state did not fix the prices, the complexities of the Ottoman guild system had a strong tendency to reduce profits, because each step in production was dominated by a particular guild. Any attempt by one group to increase its own profit would decrease that of others and thus artisans and tradesmen kept each other in check. When this system of internal balances failed to stabilize profit margins, the guilds would seek intervention and the state would impose a fixed average profit of

10 percent. Under the circumstances, it was very difficult for any group or individual to accumulate capital. State intervention led to the lack of capital in commerce and artisanship. Small-scale craftsmen could meet production costs, yet certain fields required substantial investment that only the state could undertake either directly or through pious foundations. These areas included the construction of covered bazaars; caravansaries; dyeing, printing, and finishing/polishing installations; oil, candle, and soap manufacturing; and tanneries. In these plants the state could charge rent equal to between 5 and 8 percent of the invested capital. In this manner, the state ensured necessary production by controlling physical capital, at the same time limiting the market in CONTRABAND goods.

The opportunity to accumulate capital was limited by the fact that interest rates on credit were higher than the 10 percent average permissible profit. Moreover, interest, a crucial factor for the formation and the outlet of capital, was only permitted in particular areas of the Ottoman economy and was required to comply with SHARIA, or Islamic law. An interest rate of approximately 20–25 percent was allowed to provide capital for the tax-farming sector in the 17th and 18th centuries. Money-changers, in their turn, were allowed to accept deposits at an interest rate of 15 percent in order to form the necessary capital for the tax-farming sector. The other two sectors in which free interest was applicable were operations concerning cash inheritance belonging to orphans and cash waqfs or endowments. While the upper limit for interest rates was between 12 and 29 percent with an average of 20 percent, the prevailing interest rates tended to be higher, limiting the flow of capital to those sectors working with a profit rate of approximately 10 percent. With such high interest rates, the main outlet for capital in the empire was tax farming.

PURPOSE AND CONSEQUENCES OF STATE CONTROL

During the classical period, the state usually did not actively engage in industry even when it owned the means of production. Except for goods and services consumed by the residents of the palace, the government left production to the market. Even in the military, the state ran only the arsenal (see TERSANE-I AMIRE), the gun foundry, and the gunpowder works. In other fields it only invested in the physical plant and passed management over to artisans and craftsmen, sometimes providing them with working capital.

State control changed depending on the industry. For instance, while the state legally possessed the land, it treated vineyards and vegetable gardens as private property. While the export of cotton was prohibited in the 16th and 17th centuries, this prohibition was lifted in the 18th century and its export was subjected to a new tariff, increasing both the volume of cotton exported and the customs revenue. This increase is all the more significant since domestic woven and printed cotton manufacture also expanded enormously. However, in accordance with the principle of provisionism, this growth in industrial crops did not take place at the expense of cereal cultivation. Likewise, dues from the export of silk began to yield more revenue in the 17th and 18th centuries. However, high domestic demand for silk increased prices, reducing foreign demand. Thus silk was mainly consumed domestically. After the domestic demand was satisfied, silk could be exported in small quantities. By the beginning of the 19th century, the increase in foreign demand increased silk prices to the detriment of domestic producers. The Ottoman authorities, in response, prohibited the export of silk. The export of any good was prohibited when it caused an increase in the price in the domestic market. During the classical period, the state always favored the domestic economy, and this policy played an important part in the vitality of the Ottoman economy for centuries.

As a rule, the Ottomans favored redistribution over accumulation and promoted general prosperity rather than progressivism or economic growth. Through its policies, the state aimed to prevent production from concentrating in private hands and sought to distribute these means of production equally among its subjects, an approach also used by Ottoman religious foundations, or waqfs, controlled by the state. The state kept earnings and savings low to prevent the accumulation of capital. By fostering this system it was thought that both the economy and the government would enjoy greater stability.

The economic policy of the state, however, was not always wholly consistent. The official Ottoman purchase regime (miri mübayaa), for instance, driven more by fiscalism than provisionism, worked to limit the costs of the state at the expense of its subjects. This policy imposed a tax-like levy to facilitate the provision of goods and services for the state at a price usually lower than the market prices (and sometimes even below production costs). During times of peace, this purchase regime had little affect on the people, but in times of war and during economic crises, larger-scale craftsmen and tradesmen would be vulnerable to the ever-increasing demands of the state. During the era of defensive wars from the mid-18th century to the 1830s, these groups were made especially vulnerable as the official purchase regime was applied frequently, damaging high-production workshops. As ongoing wars decreased revenues, the state increased its demand for goods and services at reduced prices, creating a situation in which those workshops that showed the most growth were hardest hit by the demands of the government. This situation, in turn, effectively favored small producers and reinforced the egalitarian tendencies of the Ottoman economy.

In keeping with the overall principle of egalitarianism, the state also undertook an unusual means of helping to fund its defensive wars during the period 1770–1812. This was the policy of confiscating the private inheritance money of those considered rich. Knowing that it had no legal right to pursue such a policy, the state presented these confiscations as compulsory loans, replaced confiscated funds with treasury bonds, and promised repayment in peacetime. Having already made it difficult for individuals to accumulate capital, this policy further hindered such accumulation by transferring the little available private capital into the war effort.

CHANGING THE CLASSICAL STRUCTURE

The process of investment liquidation that began with the period of defensive wars ultimately lasted 70 years, until 1839, the beginning of the TANZIMAT or Ottoman REFORM era. This coincided with the Industrial Revolution, which actually necessitated the fostering of capital accumulation. The preceding period of capital liquidation left the empire ill-prepared to meet the economic requirements of this new age, but radical economic changes were made nevertheless in an effort to rise to the demands of this new phase.

Because the civil sectors, the traditional providers of consumer goods, could not adequately meet increased demands at this point, the government undertook the production of goods and services by establishing state-run firms, although it did not push further its ever-expanding control of the capital. In addition to heavy investments for arms and ammunition production required by the new army, the state undertook the production of sailcloth, woolen fabrics, leather, garments, shoes, fezzes, paper, and other goods by setting up factories. It also entered into trade to finance the new army and these investments. The state monopolies that had started with a few goods at the beginning of the 19th century flourished with the inclusion of various new trade items, such as opium, wool, silk, olive oil, soap, and charcoal. In addition, the state assumed control of all trade in some regions, including SALONIKA and Antalya. These policies were without precedent in the classical system.

With the introduction of these policies, conventional Ottoman economic policy fell apart. Traditionalism was abandoned at the very beginning of the period of transition. Nevertheless, provisionism and fiscalism continued to prevail as motivating economic factors, and the means of the state began to play an active role in the economic life of the empire. The period of transition lasted until the beginning of the Tanzimat era and was replaced by a new trend of transformation in which the state abandoned both the principles of provisionism and fiscalism and its control over the mechanisms of production. Except for state control over the land, this process of economic transformation was completed within 25–30 years. Thus the classical paradigm effectively came to an end as a result of a long and contradictory period of transformation covering most of a century. From the mid-19th century on, the foundations of a modern economy were laid, but true economic growth began only with the demise of the empire.

Mehmet Genç

See also BANKS AND BANKING; CARAVAN; CARAVANSARY; CHARITY; DEBT AND THE PUBLIC DEBT ADMINISTRATION; *IHTISAB* AND *MUHTESIB*; MARKETS; MERCHANTS; MERCHANT COMMUNITIES.

Further reading: Fikret Adanır, "Tradition and Rural Change in Southeastern Europe During Ottoman Rule," in *The Origins of Backwardness in Eastern Europe: Economics and Politics from the Middle Ages until the Early Twentieth Century,* edited by Daniel Chirot (Berkeley: University of California Press, 1989), 131–177; Gábor Ágoston, *Guns for the Sultan: Military Power and the Weapons Industry in the Ottoman Empire* (Cambridge: Cambridge University Press, 2005); Engin Deniz Akarlı, "Gedik: A Bundle of Rights and Obligations for Istanbul Artisans and Traders, 1750–1840," in *Law, Anthropology and the Constitution of the Social,* edited by Alain Pottage and Martha Mundy (Cambridge: Cambridge University Press, 2004), 166–201; Giancarlo Casale, "The Ottoman Administration of the Spice Trade in the Sixteenth Century Red Sea and Persian Gulf," *Journal of the Economic and Social History of the Orient* 49, part 2 (2006): 170–198; Eunjeong Yi, *Guild Dynamics in Seventeenth Century İstanbul: Fluidity and Leverage* (Leiden: Brill, 2004); Haim Gerber, *Economy and Society in an Ottoman City: Bursa, 1600–1700* (Jerusalem: Hebrew University, 1988); Halil İnalcik and Donald Quataert, eds., *An Economic and Social History of the Ottoman Empire, 1300–1914* (Cambridge: Cambridge University Press, 1994); Charles Issawi, *The Economic History of Turkey, 1800–1914* (Chicago: University of Chicago Press, 1980); Bruce McGowan, *Economic Life in Ottoman Europe: Taxation, Trade, and the Struggle for Land, 1600–1800* (Cambridge: Cambridge University Press, 1981); Bruce Masters, *The Origins of Western Economic Dominance in the Middle East: Mercantilism and the Islamic Economy in Aleppo, 1600–1750* (New York: New York University Press, 1988); Linda Schatkowski Schilcher, *Families in Politics: Damascene Factions and Estates of the 18th and 19th Centuries* (Wiesbaden: F. Steiner, 1985); Benjamin Braude, "International Competition and Domestic Cloth in the Ottoman Empire, 1500–1650, a Study in Underdevelopment." *Review* 2 (1979): 437–54.

Ecumenical Patriarch of Constantinople *See* GREEK ORTHODOX CHURCH; *MILLET.*

Edirne (*Gk.:* **Adrianople;** *Lat.:* **Hadrianopolis**) The city of Edirne is at the junction of the Tundzha and

Maritsa rivers, near Turkey's border with GREECE and BULGARIA. As the city lies on the transit route between Europe and Asia Minor, migrations, invasions, trade, and cultural exchanges have shaped its history. The ancient city was probably first founded by Thracian tribes. At the beginning of the second century C.E. the Roman emperor Hadrianus rebuilt and enlarged the city, naming it after himself. The city soon grew into a military stronghold and commercial center of the Roman Empire, making it a desirable target for invaders. Goths attacked and captured the city in 378, Avars in 586, and Bulgars in 914. Edirne was plundered twice by the crusaders and fell to the Ottomans in 1361.

The Ottoman conquest of Edirne marks a turning point in Ottoman history, as the city served as the key staging area for further Ottoman expansion in Europe. Shortly after the conquest, Sultan MURAD I (r. 1362–89) renamed the city Edirne in the *fetihname* (declaration of conquest) and constructed its first Ottoman PALACE. The Ottoman advance through the Balkans after the conquest of Edirne led to the formation of a crusader army to stop the Ottomans. The Ottomans defeated the crusaders in the Maritsa River valley in the 1371 Battle of Çirmen, after which the Ottomans solidified their hold over the region. The city of Edirne acquired even greater importance during the interregnum period (1403–13) when three sons of Sultan BAYEZID I (r. 1389–1402) fought each other for the throne. During this time Bayezid's eldest son, Emir Süleyman Çelebi, moved the state treasury and archives from BURSA to Edirne and declared himself sultan, a claim that was challenged by Süleyman's brother, Musa Çelebi, and his half-brother, Mehmed Çelebi. In 1411 Musa Çelebi attacked the city, seized it, and minted coins in his own name, a sign that he, too, considered himself sultan. The interregnum period officially came to an end in 1413 when Mehmed, in alliance with the Byzantine Empire, took Edirne from Süleyman, reunited the state, and became Sultan MEHMED I (r. 1413–21).

Edirne enjoyed a further period of growth during the reign of Sultan MURAD II (r. 1421–1444; 1446–51), who was responsible for constructing the Muradiye Mosque in 1436, considered the most successful example of 15th-century Ottoman decorative art. Edirne's Üç Şerefeli Mosque, built by Murad in 1447, marks the transition between early and classical Ottoman ARCHITECTURE. Murad also began construction of the new Edirne Palace in 1450; it was completed by his son, MEHMED II (r. 1444–46; 1451–81), in 1452. Edirne became a center of magnificent celebrations, including those marking the circumcisions of Murad II's two sons, Alaaddin and Mehmed, in 1439, and of Mehmed's two sons, Bayezid and Mustafa, in 1457. Indeed, Edirne was the only city in the empire in which citywide celebrations were organized before the 16th century.

Mehmed II became the Ottoman sultan in 1451 in Edirne. The city served as his base of operations as he prepared for the 1453 CONQUEST OF CONSTANTINOPLE, also known as Istanbul. Following its conquest, Constantinople became the Ottoman capital, but Edirne continued to occupy a significant place in imperial strategy and cultural history. During the 16th century, the Ottoman advance westward was directed from Edirne. The sultans spent much of their time in the palace there, effectively making Edirne the seat of government for much of the century. Sultans BAYEZID II (r. 1481–1512) and SELIM II (r. 1566–74) built great mosques, building complexes (*külliyes*), and public buildings in the city. One of these is the *külliye* of Bayezid II, whose hospital and medical college became well known; another is the Selimiye Mosque, the largest of all Ottoman mosques, built between 1569 and 1575 by Sultan Selim's chief architect, Sinan.

In the 17th century Edirne regained its importance when Sultan AHMED I (r. 1603–17) chose the city as his place of residence. As the century progressed, sultans OSMAN II (r. 1618–22), MURAD IV (r. 1623–40), and MEHMED IV (r. 1648–87) organized magnificent hunting parties in the forests around the city, which was considered almost a second capital (after Istanbul); Mehmed IV also mounted military campaigns against VENICE and POLAND from Edirne. Other sultans who preferred to live in Edirne included SÜLEYMAN II (r. 1687–91), AHMED II (r. 1691–95), and MUSTAFA II (r. 1695–1703); Mustafa was deposed after an uprising in 1703, known as the Edirne Incident.

Edirne was devastated by a great fire in 1745 and by an earthquake in 1751. The city was also stricken by political turmoil; Ottoman notables in Edirne rebelled twice against SELIM III (r. 1789–1807) in 1801 and 1806. In 1829, for the first time in its history as an Ottoman city, Edirne was invaded by a foreign power when Russia took the city after a three-day siege; through the mediation of the Prussian ambassador, a treaty was signed, and the Russians withdrew. This withdrawal, however, did not prevent a mass exodus of Muslims from the city. Following this episode, Sultan MAHMUD II (r. 1808–39) visited the city in 1831, hoping to revive its former glory. A second invasion of Edirne by Russian forces during the RUSSO-OTTOMAN WAR of 1877–78 resulted in many casualties among the population and great destruction of the city's infrastructure and architecture. In 1913, during the First Balkan War (1912–13) (*see* BALKAN WARS), Bulgarian armies occupied Edirne for four months. Toward the end of the Ottoman period, at the close of WORLD WAR I, the city was invaded by Greece (1920–22). The Turkish army reentered Edirne in 1922 after the Mudanya Armistice. Finally, with the TREATY OF LAUSANNE in 1923, Edirne became a frontier city on the Turkish border with GREECE and BULGARIA.

The city of Edirne was the second capital of the Ottoman Empire. Its skyline is dominated by the 16th-century Selimiye mosque. *(Photo by Gábor Ágoston)*

The population of Edirne before the Ottoman conquest was about 10,000. Following the conquest, large numbers of Turks began to settle in Edirne, especially within the city walls. In the years after the conquest, the city's population exceeded 15,000, and people started building and living outside the city walls. According to 16th and 17th century Ottoman tax records, there were more than 150 quarters (*mahalles*) in Edirne where different demographic groups, including Muslims, Christians, and Jews lived together. The total population numbered between 20,000 and 30,000 people during those centuries. At the beginning of the 18th century, the population numbered between 35,000 and 45,000; most were Turks, with approximately 5,000 Christians (Greek and Armenian), 3,000 Jews, and 1,000 Roma, among others. After the conflagration of 1745 and the destructive earthquake of 1751, Edirne's population decreased dramatically. During the Russo-Ottoman War in 1828–29, the Muslim population largely abandoned the city; by the end of the 19th century, the population of 68,661 was predominantly Christian (48,546 Christians, 19,576 Muslims, and 539 Roma). After World War I and the Greek occupation of the 1920s, the population decreased by about half, to 34,528.

Because of its strategic location, Edirne was an important commercial center during the Ottoman period. During the 15th century revival of the eastern Mediterranean, Edirne's market grew. Several commercial buildings were constructed in Edirne to promote trade activities. These included a *bedestan* or covered market, 18 *hans* or inns, bazaars, and caravansaries. Many traders would buy locally produced goods or products from Asia in Edirne and travel to the Balkans to sell them. European products were also available in the Edirne markets from the 18th century onward.

Yunus Uğur

Further reading: Halil İnalcık, "The Conquest of Edirne (1361)." *Archivum Ottomanicum* 3 (1971): 185–210; F. Thomas Dijkema, *The Ottoman Historical Monumental Inscriptions in Edirne* (Leiden: Brill, 1977); Haim Gerber, "The Waqf Institution in Early Ottoman Edirne." *Asian and African Studies* 17 (1983): 29–45; Tayyip Gökbilgin, "Edirne," in *Encyclopaedia of Islam*, 2nd ed., vol. 2 (Leiden: Brill, 1960–), 683–686; Aptullah Kuran, "A Spatial Study of Three Ottoman Capitals: Bursa, Edirne, İstanbul." *Muqarnas* 13 (1996): 114–131; Godfrey Goodwin, *A Guide to Edirne* (Istanbul: A Turizm, 1995); Erol Haker, *Edirne, Its Jewish Community, and Alliance Schools, 1867–1937* (Istanbul: Isis, 2006).

Edirne, Treaty of (Adrianople, Treaty of) (1829)

The Treaty of Edirne, signed on September 14, 1829, concluded the Russo-Ottoman War of 1828-29 (*see* RUSSO-OTTOMAN WARS). Despite Russia's clear military supremacy in this conflict, Czar Nicholas I, fearing British and French intervention on the Ottoman Empire's behalf, was moderate in his territorial demands. In the Treaty of Edirne, signed by Russia's Alexei Orlov and the Ottoman Empire's Abdülkadir Bey, the Russians agreed to withdraw their troops from the Danubian principalities (WALLACHIA and MOLDAVIA), Dobruja, Ottoman Rumelia, Erzurum, Kars, and Bayazid. In return, RUSSIA acquired the entire DANUBE RIVER delta as well as the Armenian cities of Nakhichevan and Yerevan; Russia also gained Ottoman recognition of a Russian protectorate over all of Georgia. The Russian Empire was now in control of the entire northern BLACK SEA littoral from the Danube River to Poti in Georgia. Moreover, although Wallachia and Moldavia remained nominally Ottoman vassal states, an array of political, economic, and social provisions in the treaty effectively resulted in a Russian protectorate over the Danubian Principalities. For example, all Ottoman subjects were required to sell their land and leave the Danubian Principalities within 18 months, and the Ottomans lost exclusive rights over the trade in grain, cattle, and sheep in the Principalities.

Additional terms of the treaty included the unhindered passage of unarmed Russian commercial vessels through the straits of the Bosporus and Dardanelles; the dismantling of Ottoman fortresses on the Danube; the erection of quarantines along the Danubian border between the Ottoman and Russian empires; Ottoman acceptance of the terms of the Treaty of London (1827) concerning Greek autonomy; Serbian autonomy under Russian protection; the same commercial CAPITULATIONS for Russian subjects in the Ottoman Empire as those awarded previously to ENGLAND and FRANCE; and, most egregiously from the Ottoman perspective, the payment of an indemnity equal to twice the annual budget of the Ottoman Empire. The sum of the indemnity was subsequently reduced in exchange for increased territorial concessions to the autonomous Greek state. In general, the Treaty of Edirne continued a process, initiated with the TREATY OF KÜÇÜK KAYNARCA in 1774, of Russian territorial aggrandizement in the Black Sea region. This both increased Russian influence over Orthodox Christian subjects of the Ottoman Empire in the Balkans and heightened British and French awareness of the Russian threat to their interests in the Ottoman Empire.

Andrew Robarts

Further reading: Barbara Jelavich, *History of the Balkans,* vol. 1, *Eighteenth and Nineteenth Centuries* (Cambridge: Cambridge University Press, 1983); Paul Robert Magosci, *Historical Atlas of East Central Europe* (Seattle: University of Washington Press, 1993); Stanford J. Shaw and Ezel K. Shaw, *History of the Ottoman Empire and Modern Turkey,* vol. 2, *Reform, Revolution and the Republic: The Rise of Modern Turkey, 1808–1975* (Cambridge: Cambridge University Press, 1977).

education   For hundreds of years, education in the Ottoman world was carried out in both official and private institutions. One of the most important of these was the PALACE SCHOOL (Enderun Mektebi), an institution

As the first capital of the empire, Bursa had some of the most prestigious madrasas in the realm, including the Yeşil Madrasa, shown here. *(Photo by Gábor Ágoston)*

for the education of military and civilian administrators. The Palace School was located within the sultan's palace and was established to train individuals for elite positions within the imperial administrative structure. The curriculum included both traditional subjects and rational sciences: Quran, *hadith* (oral traditions of the Prophet), speech, calligraphy, Arabic, rhetoric, poetry, philosophy, history, mathematics, and geography. The major difference between the curriculum of the Palace School and other schools in the empire was that students were required to concentrate on military and administrative subjects. The most common educational institutions in the empire were religious schools known as madrasas (*medreses*). A free education similar to that found in the madrasas was also offered in mosques, in the libraries and mansions of prominent government officials, and by religious scholars called ULEMA. Education was also available within Sufi convents or lodges (*tekkes, zaviyes*). Education was not confined to formal institutional settings; the different levels of Ottoman bureaucracy often provided in-service training.

Primary schools (*sıbyan mektepleri*) established by the sultans, or by prominent statesmen or philanthropists, were generally located within the *külliye* (mosque complex), or in freestanding buildings in many villages and city quarters. These were established and operated through a charitable foundation or endowment system (*WAQF*) and might be co-educational or segregated by sex, according to the stipulation in the deed establishing the school. These schools had no official, formal curriculum; education simply followed an established tradition that might vary from place to place. Generally, children aged five or older could attend these schools. The teachers were selected from among those with madrasa education or simply from among those who were literate and judged by the community to be sufficiently knowledgeable. Often these were religious functionaries, such as the imam (prayer leader), the muezzin (person who calls the faithful to prayer), or the caretaker of the mosque. Women who had memorized the Quran were also eligible to teach in the schools for girls. The general objective of these schools was to teach children how to read, write, and perform the four basic arithmetic operations, and to have them to memorize passages from the Quran and the precepts of Islam. In their last years at school students would read dictionaries in Arabic and Persian, rendered in verse.

The madrasas associated with mosques typically provided the next phase for those who continued with their education. Although madrasa graduates were considered to be among the empire's elite, these schools drew from a broad spectrum of Muslim peoples of different origins, providing equal educational opportunities and the promise of social mobility to individuals from all social classes. They also served to create cultural uniformity and a common worldview among these different groups, forming an Ottoman Muslim elite with shared goals and values. When the Ottoman madrasas were first established, they drew on the educational traditions and models of existing schools in Anatolia established by the Seljuk Turks or the Turkic principalities who ruled Asia Minor before the Ottomans. The first madrasa teachers were either those born and raised in other parts of Anatolia outside the expanding Ottoman empire or those born in Anatolia and educated in ancient Islamic cultural centers such as those in EGYPT, IRAN, and Turkestan.

The primary objective of the madrasas, which had been established during the earlier Seljuk period and continued in the Ottoman period before the second ascension of Sultan MEHMED II (r. 1444–46; 1451–81), was to teach religious subjects and specifically to encourage the spread of Islamic jurisprudence. Despite this official focus, however, the fact that various Seljuk madrasas were built next to hospitals and sometimes included astronomical observatories attests to their founders' interest in the sciences of medicine and astronomy, as well as their devotion to religious teaching. Education in the early Ottoman madrasas was left to the initiative of the teachers, in accordance with the terms stipulated by the founders of the endowments or WAQFS. These terms included matters such as the choice of subjects to be studied, teacher qualifications, teaching hours, payment to be made to teachers, and student stipends.

The first Ottoman madrasa was established by ORHAN (r. 1324–62) in the early Ottoman capital city, Iznik, in 1331, approximately 30 years after the founding of the Ottoman state. A total of 84 madrasas were established between 1331 and 1451—about three every four years. After the 1453 CONQUEST OF CONSTANTINOPLE, Sultan Mehmed II began a program of urban redevelopment to give the capital city a new personality and make it a center of culture and learning. Central to that project was the construction of a magnificent monument, the FATIH MOSQUE COMPLEX (Fatih Külliyesi), a building complex named after Mehmed Fatih, "the Conqueror." According to the *waqf* deed establishing the Fatih Külliyesi, it was to be made up of eight upper-level madrasas, known as *sahn* (courtyard) madrasas, and eight preparatory madrasas, known as *tetimme* madrasas, where students were prepared for the *sahn* education; it was also to have a primary school and a library. The *külliye* also included a hospital, lodgings, and a soup kitchen that served the needy. The deeds of the Fatih madrasas stated that they were based on the principles of *hikmet* (science and wisdom), which included virtue, talent, religion, and SHARIA (canon law), and that they were dedicated to the development of human capacities and faculties. Unlike Ottoman madrasas before Mehmed II, whose deeds of establishment generally referred solely to the religious sciences, these deeds stipulated that their teachers would be selected from scholars who knew both the religious and the rational sciences such as logic, philosophy, mathematics and astronomy. Their curriculum was prepared by renowned scholars of the time including the Samarkand mathematician and astronomer ALI KUŞCU, who came from the scholarly circle of the famed TIMURID sultan and astronomer Ulug Bey (1394–1449). Ali Kuşcu's influence on the formulation of a new educational tradition within the framework of these madrasas was significant and provided the basis for the teaching of rational sciences along with religious sciences. This influence gradually increased after Mehmed II and culminated in the establishment of the Süleymaniye madrasas in the 16th century.

The Süleymaniye Külliye or building complex, named for SÜLEYMAN I (r. 1520–66), who ordered its construction, was built on the second prominent hill in Istanbul and marked the zenith of Ottoman culture and education. Its plan included schools, madrasas, a hospital, a public kitchen, a convalescence hospital, and a pharmacy, all built around the central mosque. Education was carried out at different levels in the complex and included two specialized madrasas, Darülhadis (the school where the traditions of the Prophet were taught) and Tarüttıb (the school of medicine). Darülhadis was considered the highest-ranking madrasa in the empire and its teachers were the most honored, as is evident from the high wages they received.

Of the 350 Ottoman madrasas constructed between the 14th and 16th centuries, 40 were built in the 14th century, 97 in the 15th century, and 189 in the 16th century. They were concentrated in different cities and towns throughout Anatolia and Rumelia (the empire's Asian and European provinces, respectively), primarily in Istanbul. In the Arab Ottoman provinces, by contrast, only three madrasas were established in SYRIA, six in HEJAZ, and one in YEMEN. On the other hand, a great number of madrasas were built in the territories that became Muslim after they were included in the Ottoman lands: 128 in Anatolia, 142 in Istanbul and 70 in Rumelia or the Ottoman Balkans. A total of 665 madrasas were established in Rumelia throughout the history of the Ottoman Empire. Although these figures are all approximate, they provide a rough outline of the pattern of investment and construction.

During the Second Meşrutiyet or constitutional period (1908–20), specialized madrasas were established for different positions of the Muslim clergy. These included schools to train imams and preachers and schools to teach religious science, calligraphy, and the related classical arts.

THE MODERN PERIOD

Beginning in the 18th century and continuing until the end of the imperial era, the Ottoman Empire went through a period of continuous change that often included radical reform. One of the most important aspects of this period was the introduction of modern institutions of education based on European models and developed to meet the changing needs of the empire. The educational reform movement began in the army, born out of the need to prevent further defeats on the battlefields and to regain Ottoman military superiority. Educational reforms were later extended to the civilian areas. In the 18th century, repeated defeats on the battlefields of Europe compelled the Ottomans to abandon their policy of conquest and instead focus on acquiring the cultural and technical skills of the Europeans. New methods and technology, as well as experts to teach them, were brought from Europe to modernize the Ottoman army. This modernization project focused initially on three areas: shipbuilding techniques, engineering, and modern medical education. Programs in these areas were instituted in the TERSANE-I AMIRE (Imperial Shipyard), reforming this existing institution to serve new needs.

MILITARY ENGINEERING EDUCATION

The first wholly new institution, established in 1735, was the Ulufeli Humbaracı Ocağı (Corps of Bombardiers), under the direction of Alexander Comte de Bonneval of France, in which recruits were taught practical lessons in geometry, trigonometry, ballistics, and technical drawing. In 1775 Baron de Tott, another Frenchman of Hungarian origin, was instrumental in establishing, the Hendesehane (Mathematical School) in the Imperial Shipyard, which was assigned exclusively to the task of teaching modern military technology. This school was later known as Tersane Mühendishanesi (Shipyard School of Engineering). Between 1783 and 1788, a great number of French experts taught at the School of Engineering. Upon their departure the courses that they had initiated were continued by Ottoman professors who had been trained in the traditional madrasas.

During the NIZAM-I CEDID (New Order) movement in 1793, the second military engineering school Mühendishane-i Cedide (The New School of Engineering) was established with the objective of providing education for bombardiers, mining specialists called sappers, and artillerymen. A new generation of Ottoman teachers of engineering, who had studied military engineering with the French experts at the Hendesehane, taught geometry, trigonometry, and the measurement of elevations for artillery. In 1806 this school acquired a formalized structure that was a blend of Ottoman and European traditions, and a new system of education composed of four classrooms and four teachers was initiated. Students were taught calligraphy, orthography, technical drawing, arithmetic, algebra, geometry, plane trigonometry, conic sections, differential calculations, integral calculations, Arabic, French, astronomy, geography, geodesy, military history, mechanics, applied explosive materials, military training, and military engineering.

With the transfer of the artillery and army engineering teachers to the New School of Engineering, the only courses still offered at the Shipyard Engineering School were shipbuilding, navigation, cartography, and geography. In 1806, it was re-named the Mühendishane-i Bahri-i Hümayun (Imperial School of Naval Engineering). After the French principal of the school returned to his homeland, Ottoman naval officers who were graduates of this school replaced him. It was later moved to one of the small islands near Istanbul where, as the Naval School, it continues to provide education.

With the establishment of other military and civil schools, interest in the Imperial School of Military Engineering decreased for some time. However, interest in this school revived in 1881. The traditional four-year period of education was increased by a year. An extra year was added to the traditional four-year period of education, with the name "distinguished class"; fifth-year students who knew foreign languages and wished to receive higher education were then accepted to the War School or Academy (Harbiye Mektebi).

IMPERIAL MILITARY ACADEMY

In 1826, Sultan MAHMUD II (r. 1808–1839) abolished the JANISSARIES and established a new army called the Asakir-i Mansure-i Muhammediye (Victorious Troops of Muhammad) in its place. Subsequently, in 1831, he opened Mekteb-i Harbiye-i Şahane (Imperial Military Academy), modeled on European military schools, with the objective of training scientifically skilled officers who would be able to use modern military methods and techniques. The principal was an Ottoman general who had been educated in Europe, and the curriculum was prepared by the teachers from the Army and Navy schools of engineering; the number of students to be accommodated was 400. A large number of Ottoman students were also sent to Europe to receive education in military and civilian areas.

CIVIL ENGINEERING EDUCATION

Graduates of the military engineering schools were also engaged in civil works such as surveying, preparing architectural plans, and directing public construction projects. From the second half of the 19th century onward, the construction of new industrial plants, small industrial enterprises, a TELEGRAPH system, RAILROADS, and highways increased the need for civil engineers. This need was met partly with Ottoman military engineers and partly with foreign experts or Ottomans who had been educated in Europe. But gradually specialized technical schools, such as the Telgraf Mektebi (School of Telegraphy) and Sanayi Mektebi (Technical School), were opened. In the

latter, students were offered a theoretical and practical education instead of the master-apprentice approach that was traditional in the empire. The school provided five years of education in subjects such as mechanics, casting, carpentry, bookbinding, architecture, blacksmithing, tailoring and dressmaking, and shoemaking.

Formal education in civil engineering began with the Mülkiye Mühendis Mektebi (Civil School of Engineering), which was opened in 1874–75 as a branch of the Darülfünun-ı Sultani (Imperial University of Galatasaray). Its four-year program was directed at educating engineers who would carry out the services required in public works, especially in the area of transportation. In 1909 the school was renamed the Mühendis Mektebi Alisi (Engineering School for Higher Education). In 1928, five years after the foundation of the Republic of Turkey, it was elevated to a university-level school with the name Yüksek Mühendis Mektebi (High Engineering School); in 1946 it became the present-day Istanbul Technical University.

MEDICAL EDUCATION

The first modern medical education began at the Tersane Tıbbiyesi (Shipyard Medical School) in 1806. The goal of the school was to make modern medical education available, thereby increasing the number of Muslim physicians in the empire. Previously, most physicians were drawn from the religious minorities. The school was closed in 1808 after Sultan SELIM III (r. 1789–1807) was deposed. Around the same time two famous Ottoman scholars—Mustafa Behçet Efendi, the court physician, and Şanizade Mehmed Ataullah Efendi—greatly influenced Ottoman medical education. Şanizade Mehmed Ataullah Efendi produced reference works on modern medicine and anatomy, while Mustafa Behçet Efendi founded a modern medical school, the Tıphane-i Amire (Imperial Medical School) in 1827. This was followed by the establishment of the Cerrahhane-i Amire (Imperial School of Surgery) in 1832, headed by a Frenchman, with some European physicians as teachers. In 1836 these two schools were merged under the name Mekteb-i Tıbbiye (Medical School). In 1839 that school was relocated and its name was changed to Mekteb-i Tıbbiye-i Adliye-i Şahane (Imperial School of Medicine) in honor of Sultan Mahmud II; it was headed by Karl Ambroise Bernard, an Austrian physician. In the same year, the school was opened to non-Muslim Ottoman citizens. Education was limited to five years, at the end of which graduates received a diploma.

Because the language of instruction at the Imperial Medical School was French, the system favored non-Muslims, many of whom had attended European-run private schools and thus were generally already familiar with the French language. To counteract this, a "distinguished class" was opened for talented Muslim students. Students in this class also received language courses in Turkish, Arabic, and Persian. Some of its graduates later, in 1866, founded the Mekteb-i Tibbiye-i Mülkiye (Civilian Medical School) under the Imperial Medical School, which provided medical education in Turkish. In 1905, a third medical school was established in Damascus. In 1909, the two medical schools based in Istanbul were merged into one, forming the medical faculty of the Istanbul University, while the Damascus school continued to function as its branch.

MODERN CIVILIAN EDUCATIONAL INSTITUTIONS

In the years following the implementation of the TANZIMAT or reforms (1839–76), the expected results did not materialize and it became apparent that the reforms should be based on education of the general population if they were take hold. The Provisional Council of Education undertook the organization of educational affairs, and many Ottoman scholars took part in preparing the basic principles and plans for the new educational policy and reforms that would produce a new educational system with three distinct levels: primary, secondary, and higher education.

SIBYAN MEKTEPLERİ (PRIMARY SCHOOLS)

Efforts to modernize primary education began under Mahmud II in 1824 and were accelerated during the Tanzimat in 1845. Radical changes were made by the Maarif-i Umumiye Nizamnamesi (Public Education Regulations) in 1869. These regulations, which reorganized the entire Ottoman educational system, created a standard curriculum and decreed that four-year schools be opened in villages and districts; attendance of boys between the ages of 7 and 11 years and girls between the ages of 6 and 10 years be mandatory at these schools; and teachers be required to be Ottoman subjects and graduates of the Darülmuallimin (Teachers Training Colleges). The reorganization of the primary education system was finally and successfully completed by the Constitution of 1876 and primary education became mandatory.

RÜŞTIYE MEKTEPLERİ (MIDDLE SCHOOLS)

The rüştiye mektepleri, which may be placed between the sibyan (elementary schools) and idadi (high schools),

The Harbiye Nezareti, built in 1898, was originally the Ministry of War, but was later incorporated into the campus of Istanbul University. *(Personal collection of Gábor Ágoston)*

were created as middle schools that would prepare students for higher education. After getting good results, the number of middle schools in Istanbul was increased, with the goal of eventually having one in every town with 500 households. The curriculum included an introduction to religious sciences, Ottoman grammar, composition, Arabic and Persian grammar, calligraphy, arithmetic, bookkeeping, introduction to geometry, world history, Ottoman history and geography, physical education, and local languages, depending on the region. French was an optional course in the regions where commerce was concentrated. By 1883 there were 460 middle schools in Ottoman territories, with 30,000 students.

GALATASARAY MEKTEB-I SULTANI (GALATASARAY HIGH SCHOOL)

Over time, it became apparent that the middle schools were not entirely adequate to prepare students for higher education. In 1868, therefore, in collaboration with the grand vizier, the Ottoman minister of foreign affairs, the French ambassador to Istanbul, and the French minister of education, FRANCE helped open a school to provide education in French at the level of European high schools, and promised all the necessary technical and financial support. The French assistant principal organized the establishment, which officially opened in 1868 as the Galatasaray Mekteb-i Sultani, or Imperial School of Galatasaray, at the former Military High School in Istanbul's Beyoğlu district. It was administered by two principals, one Turkish and one French. At first, the school had five grades for beginners and five college-level grades; this was later reduced to nine grades, with three primary, three secondary, and three college-level grades. The teachers were both Turkish and French. The school was renamed Galatasaray High School after the Republic of Turkey was proclaimed.

IDADI AND SULTANI (HIGH SCHOOL EDUCATION)

İdadis are schools that are higher than the rüşdiyes and lower than the sultanis. The Regulations of 1869 established the idadis as 3-year schools for Muslim and non-Muslim rüşdiye graduates. Set up in communities with a population of more than 1,000 households, the first idadi was opened in Istanbul in 1874. Under Abdülhamid II, the number of idadis in Istanbul and the provinces grew and the period of education was increased to 4 years; rüştiyes were merged with idadis in places where idadi were already present. The education programs were re-organized to ensure the transition between civil and military idadis. Towards the end of the Abdülhamid II period, the total number of idadis was more than 100. In 1880, an idadi for girls was also opened in Istanbul.

The Public Education Regulations of 1869 envisioned a sultaniye school for idadi graduates in every provincial center. However, prior to the Second Constitution of 1908 no sultani schools were opened. Later some of the idadis in provincial centers were converted into sultanis. The number of sultanis had reached 50 in 1918. In the years 1913-14, one Inas (Girls) Sultani was opened in Istanbul.

TEACHER TRAINING COLLEGES

The Darülmuallim (Teacher Training School for Boys) was established in 1848 to train teachers in conformity with the modernization policy. Their formal education lasted three years, and graduates worked as trainees before being appointed as teachers to middle schools. With the opening of modern primary schools (iptidai) in 1862, the Primary Teachers Training College was also opened to provide these schools with teachers.

As middle schools for girls were opened, the need for women teachers was felt, and the first Darülmuallimat (Teacher Training School for Girls) was opened in 1870. It had a principal, three male teachers, three female teachers, and 45 students. In the 1882–83 school year it was divided into a primary and middle school section. In the same year, the Darülameliyat (Applied Training School) was opened, with 24 students. During the 1910–1911 school year the Kız Sanayi Mektebi (Technical School for Girls) was established, which trained 737 teachers over the 39 years of its existence.

DARÜLFÜNUN (UNIVERSITY)

The idea of establishing a DARÜLFÜNUN or university for educating civil servants was proposed in the Tanzimat reform period, but early efforts to form one met repeatedly with insuperable obstacles. The first attempt to develop a darülfünun began in 1846 when a Swiss architect began work on a grand structure that continued for many years. While students and faculty waited for the completion of their new university building, public lectures in physics, chemistry, natural sciences, astronomy, and history were started in some of the completed rooms. When the building was finished, however, the authorities deemed it too large and grand for its intended purpose; the building was allocated instead to the Ministry of Finance, and lectures continued in the smaller Nuri Pasha Mansion in the Çemberlitaş district of Istanbul. Lectures were suspended when this building burned down in the fire of 1865.

A second effort to establish a darülfünun began in 1869, when new public education regulations reorganized the educational system and provided for a new university to resemble its European counterparts. This university was established under the name Darülfünun-ı Osmani (Ottoman University) and consisted of three schools: philosophy and literature, natural sciences and mathematics, and law. It also included a museum, a library, and laboratories. The departments of the first school of philosophy and literature included Arabic, Persian, French, Latin, and Greek. The department of law offered courses in Islamic and Roman law. But once again, conditions for the continuation of the university were unfavorable. Finances were limited, the number of teachers and books were insufficient, and this second attempt at a university also failed.

A third attempt to open a university was made in 1873. Established on the foundations of the Galatasaray Imperial School, which had been open since 1868, this university was called Darülfünun-ı Sultani (Imperial University of Galatasaray) and included schools of law, science, and humanities. Later the School of Law was affiliated with the Ministry of Justice and functioned independently until 1909 when it became a part of the university. The School of Science, which was transformed into the Civilian School of Engineering, was attached to the Ministry of Public Works. This formed the basis for the Istanbul Technical University.

The process of establishing the Ottoman university took so long because it lacked the necessary infrastructure (such as specialized faculty members, sufficient number of students educated in modern curricula, legal bylaws, and financial resources). The attempts that had started in 1846 ended in 1900 with the successful establishment of the Ottoman university under the name of Darülfünun-ı Şahane (Imperial University). In 1909 the Darülfünun became a full-fledged university under one central administration, marking the successful beginning of modern university education in the Ottoman Empire.

Ekmeleddin İhsanoğlu

Further reading: Ekmeleddin İhsanoğlu, *Science, Technology and Learning in the Ottoman Empire: Western Influence, Local Institutions and the Transfer of Knowledge* (Aldershot, UK: Variorum, 2004); Ekmeleddin İhsanoğlu, "The Genesis of Darulfunun: An Overview of Attempts to Establish the First Ottoman University," in *Histoire Économique et Sociale de l'Empire Ottoman et de la Turquie, 1326–1960*, edited by Daniel Panzac (Paris: Peeters 1995), 827–842; Ekmeleddin İhsanoğlu, "Ottoman Educational and Scholarly Scientific Institutions," in *History of the Ottoman State, Society, and Civilisation*, vol. 2, edited by E. İhsanoğlu (Istanbul: IRCICA, 2002), 357–515; Selçuk Akşın Somel, *The Modernization of Public Education in the Ottoman Empire: 1839–1908: Islamization, Autocracy and Discipline* (Leiden: Brill, 2001); Benjamin Fortna, *Imperial Classroom: Islam, the State, and Education in the Late Ottoman Empire* (Oxford: Oxford University Press, 2002).

Egypt (*anc.:* Aegyptus; *Ar.:* Misr; *Turk.:* Mısır) Thanks to its tremendous agricultural output, the result of a regular annual flooding of the Nile that provided renewed topsoil to its fields and water for irrigation, Egypt was the richest province of the Ottoman Empire. The Egyptian capital, CAIRO, also served as a major center of trade. But Egypt also had cultural and political traditions of its own, and these often came into conflict with those of the Ottoman capital. Egypt produced generations of legal scholars who contested the interpretations of Islamic law that were emanating from Istanbul. As a result, Egypt remained much less influenced by Ottoman norms than its neighbor SYRIA, in part, perhaps, because of the Egyptian tradition of forming MAMLUK households, founded by slaves and perpetuated not by conventional family succession but through the adoption and appointment of promising younger mamluks, or male slaves. The formation of households in this tradition led to the founding of the MAMLUK EMPIRE and did not end with the Ottoman conquest. Instead, these households provided an alternative structure of political power with national rather than imperial foundations.

The Ottoman Sultan SELIM I (r. 1512–20) conquered Egypt in 1517, but the arrival of the Ottomans did not signal a radical break with the country's Mamluk past. Rather than introducing the *timar* system, under which Ottoman cavalry officers (*sipahi*) would be assigned the revenues of agricultural lands on which they would live, the whole country was treated as one large tax farm: Revenue collection was turned over to the Ottoman governor in Cairo who would collect the taxes, pay a prearranged amount to the central treasury in Istanbul, and keep anything above that amount for himself. The governor then allocated the various sources of revenue to his subordinates and friends as smaller tax farms. This meant that direct Ottoman involvement in the day-to-day administration of the country through a state-trained bureaucracy was limited. Furthermore, the Ottomans made no attempt to limit the recruitment of new mamluks, into existing households, and many of the Ottoman governors established Mamluk households of their own.

The survival of the Mamluk system meant that there were two potential rivals to Ottoman authority in Egypt: the Mamluks, who could invoke a memory of a glorious political past that predated the Ottomans, and the Sunni religious intellectual class centered at AL-AZHAR, the famed Muslim university founded in 970 C.E., which provided a framework of religious law that often challenged the one imposed by Ottoman Istanbul. Despite these potential sources of opposition, Egypt remained politically quiet for the rest of the 16th century, enjoying a long period of peace and prosperity. In the 17th century, however, leaders of some of the Mamluk households, known locally as *emirs* (commanders), began to take on unofficial duties in the governance of the province. An Ottoman military commander remained as governor, but his authority was no longer absolute. The rivalry among the Mamluk beys, or military leaders, forestalled the collapse of Ottoman control in Egypt in the second half of 17th century, as the beys could not unite to make common cause against the Ottoman governor. Instead, broadly based confederations of smaller Mamluk households emerged; and within these broader coalitions, individual households might contend as much with each other as with rivals outside their confederation.

Within this shifting power balance in Cairo, a Mamluk household founded by Mustafa al-Qazdaghli, a member of the JANISSARIES who had himself been a client in a Mamluk household, emerged as the dominant political force by the middle of the 18th century. In 1760 the dominant Mamluk in the household, Ali, who would later be known as Bulutkapan (One who Grasps the Clouds), took the title SHAYKH AL-BALAD or "head of the town," a title that harked back to the days of Mamluk independence.

Ali entertained wider ambitions. In 1790 he replaced the Ottoman governor of JEDDAH with one of his own Mamluks, challenging the authority of Sultan MUSTAFA III (r. 1757–74) in his role as "Servant of the Two Noble Sanctuaries" (guardian of MECCA and MEDINA).Later in the same year, in an act of open rebellion against the sultan, Ali ordered his forces to invade Syria. Ali's Mamluk and lieutenant, Abu al-Dhahab, found a local ally in Yusuf al-Shihab (of the prominent SHIHAB FAMILY), who headed a coalition of Druze and Christian clans in Lebanon, and together they entered Damascus in 1771. Just when it looked as if Ottoman control of Syria might be at an end, Abu al-Dhahab turned against Ali Bey, his former owner and mentor, returning to Egypt with his army and forcing Ali to flee first to Upper Egypt and then to ACRE where ZAHIR AL-UMAR, the political strongman in Galilee, sheltered him. After a year in exile, Ali returned to Egypt to confront Abu al-Dhahab, confident that the other Mamluk households of Cairo would support him. They did not; Ali Bey was defeated, wounded on the battlefield, and taken prisoner by Abu al-Dhahab. He died a week later and Abu al-Dhahab himself assumed the title Shaykh al-Balad.

With Abu al-Dhahab's death in 1775, the Mamluk households in Egypt again reverted to factional fighting among themselves, with no single household able to dominate its rivals. The Ottoman army was dispatched to Egypt in 1786 in an attempt to bring the unruly province back under direct Ottoman control, but the Mamluk emirs simply retreated to Upper Egypt. There they waited until the Ottoman commander agreed to a truce as he could not defeat the Mamluks in their redoubts in the south and the war had become too costly to continue. But the two invasions of Syria mounted by the Mamluks had demonstrated that the sultan's suzerainty over Egypt existed in name only.

A blow to the continuation of the Mamluk system in Egypt came in 1798 when NAPOLEON BONAPARTE invaded the country. Mamluk cavalry skills proved no match for Napoleon's modern infantry and artillery tactics, and the French forces easily occupied the country. Napoleon pressed on into the Ottoman Empire but was stalled by CEZZAR AHMED PASHA, who had succeeded Zahir al-Umar as the military warlord in ACRE. Although Napoleon soon returned to France, French forces remained in Egypt until 1801, when they were withdrawn in the face of a combined British and Ottoman invasion. In the aftermath of the French withdrawal, the political situation in Cairo was in a flux for several years. Out of the turmoil MEHMED ALI, the commander sent by the sultan to restore Ottoman control in the province, emerged as the leading political player. Acknowledged by the local Muslim religious leadership as the best person to restore order to the country, he received the sultan's decree appointing him as governor in 1805.

With his authority to rule endorsed by the sultan, Mehmed Ali set about securing his position in Egypt. He did this first by killing all potential rivals and building a modern army. That army's effectiveness was proven in 1811 when the sultan called on him to rescue the holy cities of Mecca and Medina from the WAHHABIS, the radical followers of MUHAMMAD IBN ABD AL-WAHHAB who had seized the holy cities in 1804. The Egyptian forces captured Medina in 1812 and Mecca the following year. In a bid to enlist Mehmed Ali's new army to combat the GREEK WAR OF INDEPENDENCE, Sultan MAHMUD II (r. 1808–1839) also made him governor of CRETE in 1822 and of Morea (the Peloponnese) in 1824. The Egyptian troops under Mehmed Ali's son IBRAHIM PASHA proved to be too successful, however, and the British and French public clamored for their governments to intervene on the side of the Greeks. Fleets from those two countries destroyed the combined Ottoman-Egyptian fleet at the Battle of Navarino in 1827, which precipitated the withdrawal of the Egyptian forces from Greece.

Mehmed Ali next set his sights on the empire itself. In 1831 his son Ibrahim Pasha commanded the Egyptian army that drove into Syria. In December 1832 Ibrahim defeated an Ottoman army near Konya in central Anatolia, and the road to Istanbul was open. At that point, Mehmed Ali became cautious, and the army withdrew to Syria. Mahmud II reorganized the Ottoman army in response to the occupation of Syria; in 1839 the Ottomans moved to retake the region, but were again defeated. At this point the European powers intervened and forced an Egyptian withdrawal from Syria in 1840. In return, Sultan ABDÜLMECID (r. 1839–61) agreed to give Egypt to Mehmed Ali and his descendants as a hereditary governorship that could not be revoked by the sultan or any of his successors.

Mehmed Ali died in 1848 and was succeeded by Ibrahim Pasha, who died later that same year. Ibrahim was succeeded by ABBAS HILMI I, Mehmed Ali's grandson. Under Mehmed Ali's descendants, Egypt continued along the path he had envisioned for it. This included the modernization of the army and the redistribution of agricultural lands into the hands of a few men who were either in the royal family or closely connected to it. A boom in the cotton market during the American Civil War (1861–1865) propelled Egypt to the forefront of world cotton production. Foreign capital and foreign merchants, workers, and opportunists entered the country in increasing numbers, protected by CAPITULATIONS, treaties negotiated by the European powers that gave their citizens extraordinary legal and commercial protections and privileges.

Modernization projects, including the building of the SUEZ CANAL, took a heavy toll on Egypt's finances as the country's rulers borrowed from European banks to finance them. The banks put pressure on their governments to ensure that the moneys were properly expended, thus effectively establishing European control over Egypt's economy. KHEDIVE ISMAIL resisted European demands, but in 1879 the Europeans succeeded in getting the sultan to remove Ismail's patent of office and the leadership of Egypt passed to Ismail's son, KHEDIVE TAWFIQ. This was a symbolic act as the Ottomans had effectively lost political control of Egypt from the time of Mehmed Ali's governorship. Nevertheless, it preserved the outward appearance that Ismail's removal had been carried out by a Muslim ruler rather than by the Europeans. But the Egyptian public was not fooled, and the intervention of the Europeans fueled a growing anger among the Egyptian military, who saw the Europeans having colonial aspirations toward Egypt.

This military unrest broke out in 1881 and propelled Colonel Ahmad URABI to the forefront. Although the officers did not seek to topple Tawfiq, they demanded the return of the Assembly of Delegates, which had been suspended after Ismail's dismissal, an increase in the size of the army, and the dismissal of the unpopular Egyptian prime minister Uthman Pasha Rifqi. This led to a period of political instability that alarmed the Europeans, who began looking for an excuse to intervene in Egypt. The British and French sent their fleets into Alexandria Harbor in May 1882; this sparked anti-European riots in the city in June that, in turn, led to the shelling of the city by the British navy. The landing of British troops followed, and on September 13, 1882, these troops decisively defeated the Egyptian army, commanded by Colonel Urabi, at the Battle of Tel el-Kebir. Urabi was tried and sent into exile on Ceylon (Sri Lanka). Egypt was now securely in British hands.

The British did not seek to replace the khedive but simply to have him act as they wished. The façade of Egyptian autonomy was maintained, even though British troops remained in Egypt and the British consul in Cairo was the effective ruler of the country. The fiction that Egypt remained a province of the Ottoman Empire also continued, and the Ottoman sultan routinely issued a patent of office to each new khedive. This pretense only ended in 1914 when the Ottomans declared war on Great Britain; the British responded by announcing that Egypt was a self-governing sultanate, under their protection.

Bruce Masters

Further reading: Michael Winter, *Egyptian Society under Ottoman Rule, 1517–1798* (London: Routledge, 1992); Ehud Toledano, *State and Society in mid-Nineteenth-Century Egypt* (Cambridge: Cambridge University Press, 1990).

Enderun Mektebi   *See* EDUCATION.

engineering schools   *See* EDUCATION.

England   England's political relationship with the Ottoman Empire had its beginnings in the middle years of the reign of Queen Elizabeth I (1558–1603), less than a quarter of a century after the death of SÜLEYMAN I (r. 1520–66). From the founding of the English LEVANT COMPANY in 1581, through the granting of commercial and trading privileges known erroneously in the West as CAPITULATIONS, to the abolition of the Levant Company in 1825 and the abrogation of the capitulations in 1914, Anglo-Ottoman relations developed in a complicated and interwoven pattern of trade and diplomacy. There were, however, certain constants in this complex tapestry. These included: the primacy of the city of London in the Levant trade; the early entrepreneurial ebullience and the later timidity and conservatism of the Levant Company itself; and English diplomatic defense of Ottoman interests from Edward Barton's presence on the field of Mezőkeresztes in 1596 and Lord Paget's mediation at the Congress of Karlowitz in 1698–99, to the Congress of Berlin in 1878.

The English mercantile presence in the Ottoman Empire can be traced from the late 16th century with an English ambassador resident at the Ottoman capital, English consuls and expatriate merchants residing in major entrepots of the empire, including ALEPPO, Izmir, CYPRUS, and CAIRO), and a trade built around English exports, especially woolen cloth and munitions, and Ottoman exports such as silk, cotton, spices, and dyestuffs. This trading relationship would continue with little variation until the early 19th century.

During the later 17th century, the English Levant trade reached its highest point, but Britain did not pursue its advantage aggressively. In the 18th century the Levant Company's factors in Aleppo and elsewhere did not bid for provincial tax farms, as their contemporaries were doing in India, nor did Anglo-French rivalry at the Sublime Porte even begin to develop as it did in India. Instead, the history of English trade with the Ottoman Empire is one of slow, steady decline throughout the 18th century. In 1825 the Levant Company was formally wound up and its charter annulled; little more than a decade later, in 1838, the ANGLO-OTTOMAN CONVENTION of London opened up the Ottoman market to unrestricted free trade and to the inroads of 19th-century industrial capitalism.

It was this change in mercantile relations between Britain and the Ottoman Empire that provided the economic foundation for the diplomatic ascendancy of Britain at the Porte during the time of the 19th-century TANZIMAT reforms. That ascendancy, perhaps overvalued by British statesmen and publicists at the time, was embodied in the person of Stratford Canning, Britain's ambassador at the Porte for much of this period until the CRIMEAN WAR (1854–56). Canning envisaged leading the empire from what he regarded as an antiquated theocracy toward a modern capitalist economy. This vision points to a fundamental contradiction at the heart of Anglo-Ottoman relations: a desire to support and encourage a reformed Ottoman Empire, backing its claims against aggressive Russian expansion and the need to exploit the empire's economic resources in the interests of free trade. Because these competing desires were never capable of resolution, either by direct military action as in the Crimean War, or by diplomacy as at the 1878 Congress of Berlin, the British and Ottoman paths diverged.

At the Congress of Berlin, Britain secured CYPRUS as a forward base close to eastern Anatolia; three years later the British occupation of EGYPT and control of the SUEZ CANAL gave greater security to the British sea route to India than any earlier policy of friendly involvement with the Ottoman Empire. Moreover, during the despotic reign of Sultan ABDULHAMID II (1876–1908), the Porte came increasingly into the orbit of the Central Powers—GERMANY and Austria-Hungary—and Britain had little to offer in comparison. As England drifted into WORLD WAR I in 1914, it was not surprising that the Ottoman Empire allied itself with the Central Powers, taking arms not only against Russia, its traditional enemy, but also against Britain and France, hitherto its two oldest European allies and supporters. It was not until after the Ottoman Empire had ceased to exist that relations between Britain and Turkey could begin anew and on a very different basis.

Colin Heywood

Further reading: M. S. Anderson, *The Eastern Question, 1774–1923* (New York: St. Martin's, 1966); Sonia Anderson, *An English Consul in Turkey: Paul Rycaut in Smyrna, 1667–1678* (Oxford: Clarendon, 1989); Ralph Davis, *Aleppo and Devonshire Square: English Traders in the Levant in the 18th Century* (London: Macmillan & Company, 1967); Daniel Goffman, *Britons in the Ottoman Empire, 1642–1660* (Seattle: University of Washington Press, 1998); S. A. Skilliter, *William Harborne and the Trade with Turkey, 1578–1582* (London: Oxford University Press, 1977); A. C. Wood, *A History of the Levant Company* (Oxford: Oxford University Press, 1935).

enthronement and accession ceremony (*cülus*) In the Ottoman Empire, the term *cülus*, which means "to sit" in Arabic, was used to refer to a sultan's accession to the throne. Until the 19th century, the heir to the throne was not identified during the reign of his predecessor. All men who belonged to the dynasty through their father and who shared the title of prince had an equal right to the throne. A sultan governed the Ottoman Empire with the support of state dignitaries, the ULEMA (religious scholars), and military commanders, and gaining the support of these three powerful groups was thus fundamental for any prince to ascend to the throne. When a sultan died, the prince whom these groups considered most capable was invited to take the throne. Opposition from these groups could preclude a prince's ascension. According to a law code introduced by MEHMED II (r. 1444–46; 1451–81), a "prince who would succeed to the throne could kill his brothers for the integrity of the empire." Fratricide aided the stability and longevity of Ottoman hierarchical systems, as lands were not divided amongst sons. The Ottoman Empire witnessed several conflicts between brothers in the 15th and 16th centuries; fights for succession to the throne among Mehmed II's sons (BAYEZID II and Prince CEM), the sons of Bayezid II (r. 1481–1512), and the heirs of SÜLEYMAN I (r. 1520–66) caused various upheavals and severe turbulence.

Until the end of the 16th century, upon completing his initial EDUCATION in the Palace, each prince, together with his tutors and assistants, was installed in a different province of the empire as governor. Here the princes continued their education while also gaining practical experience. When a sultan passed away, the prince selected for ascension to the throne was informed of his imminent enthronement, for preparations were made simultaneously for both the enthronement and the funeral ceremony. On receiving the news of the death or abdication of a sultan, the prince and his escort came swiftly to the capital or place where the throne was left empty. If more than one prince survived his father, state dignitaries delayed sending news of the sultan's death to those princes who had been passed over. For instance, when Mehmed II died, Prince Cem was the assumed heir; however, state dignitaries prevented Cem from being informed and instead notified Prince Bayezid, thus securing his succession.

At the end of the 16th century, when MEHMED III (r. 1595–1603) succeeded to the throne, the Ottoman princes were no longer sent to the provinces but instead lived out their years in the confines of the palace. When AHMED I (r. 1603–17) died in 1617 he was followed by his brother, MUSTAFA I (r. 1617–18, 1622–23), the eldest living member of the Ottoman dynasty. With the enthronement of Mustafa I, the principle of seniority was introduced into Ottoman succession practices. In the 19th century, Ottoman princes began to live in their own palaces outside the sultan's court.

ENTHRONEMENT CEREMONY

The enthronement ceremony was always completed as soon as possible to ensure that a sultan reigned at all times. If the previous sultan died, the ceremony was held before the funeral; if the sultan was deposed, the ceremony was held within hours. A prince's ascension ceremony included state dignitaries, scholars, military commanders, and officials who, by escorting the prince, tacitly approved his succession. An ancient Turkish tradition, the *cülus* or enthronement ceremony began under the first rulers of the Ottoman Empire. It involved the swearing of oaths of allegiance to the sultan. The dignitary would approach the sultan and either kiss his hand or bend to the floor while taking his oath. The structure of the ceremony was of particular importance because without it, any prince could proclaim his succession individually.

For similar reasons, the ceremony was held where the throne was abdicated, preventing a prince from installing himself in a far-away province; this practice was regarded as essential to the integrity of the empire. For instance, after the defeat of BAYEZID I (r. 1389–1402) by Timur at the BATTLE OF ANKARA in 1402, many princes claimed the throne for themselves, leading to a turbulent interregnum period (1402–13). The throne accompanied the sultan on holidays or military expeditions, as state dignitaries accompanied the sultan and he continued to discharge his administrative duties. Accession ceremonies were thus held wherever the sultan passed away. SELIM II (r. 1566–74), for instance, came to the throne in BELGRADE in 1566 because Süleyman I died in Hungary. Apart from these special occasions, however, enthronement ceremonies were usually held in the TOPKAPI PALACE in ISTANBUL.

The sultans of the Ottoman Empire used the Topkapı Palace as their royal residence for 400 years beginning in the second half of the 15th century. The second courtyard of the palace, or Alay Meydanı (Ceremonial Square), was used for formal ceremonies. The throne was put in front of the third gate, the Babüssaade, or Gate of Felic-

ity; as the courtyard was suitable for crowded gatherings, people who were invited to the ceremony were welcomed there. When everyone had gathered, the new sultan was informed that everything was ready for the oath of allegiance and guests wearing ceremonial kaftans encircled the throne. Only the ŞEYHÜLISLAM (the head of the religious establishment) and members of the Imperial Council waited in the council hall to take their turn. The sultan then entered with the chief black eunuch (Darüssade Ağası) of the palace at his right hand and the Agha of the "Gate of Felicity" (Babüssaade Ağası), the head of all servants in the personal quarters of the Topkapı Palace, at his left. Before formally taking his seat on the throne, the sultan saluted three separate groups: to his right, the head gatekeeper; to his left, the palace elite group including sons of pashas, vassal lords, and the head tasters (çaşnegir); and facing him, the guardians (çavuş) of the Imperial Council, who applauded while offering short formal prayers such as "May you and your reign endure a thousand years."

At the beginning of the ceremony, the *nakibüleşraf* (head of the descendants of the Prophet Muhammad and one of the leading ulema in the Ottoman Empire) entered the sultan's presence and prayed. The new sultan then rose and received the kiss of the *nakibüleşraf* on his hand while the palace guards clapped. Following this the sultan returned to his throne and the *nakibüleşraf* returned to his seat in front of the treasury. During greetings, to prevent any confusion on the sultan's part, the guardians let him know when to stand and sit by saying "My Sultan, may you stand up" or "My Sultan, may you rest." One by one, the members of the court approached to take the oath of allegiance.

When the enthronement ceremony was held outside Istanbul, a throne was set between two *tuğs* (horsehair battle standards) in front of the imperial tent, and the allegiance ceremony was completed there. Bayezid I's enthronement ceremony was held in this manner, as was that of Selim II in Belgrade. The enthronement ceremonies of Mehmed II, AHMED II (r. 1691–95), MUSTAFA II (1695–1703), and AHMED III (r. 1703–30) were held in EDIRNE Palace.

As soon as the enthronement ceremony was over, a public crier was sent through the city to announce the new sultan's ascension to the throne. At the same time, cannons were fired from the Imperial Foundry and from naval ships. The enthronement ceremony, which was usually held two-and-a-half or three hours after sunrise, would be followed by a funeral ceremony held in the same place right after the midday prayer. After a few days, the new sultan welcomed greetings for the enthronement in the Chamber of Petitions. On the first Friday after the enthronement of the new sultan, the sultan visited one of his imperial mosques to pray. Immediately thereafter, the Friday sermon delivered in all mosques was read in the sultan's name. This custom, called *hutbe*, was as crucial as the oath of allegiance, and was one of the most important symbols of dynastic rule.

Another important aspect of the enthronement ceremony was the *cülus bahşişi* (accession bonus). This gratuity was promised to military officials, who cried out at the time of the oath of allegiance, "Your bonus and promotion will be accepted." The promised money was distributed immediately to prevent disturbances. The enthronement ceremony of Selim II was initially held in Istanbul, even though the viziers and military were in Szigetvár, Hungary. The ceremony was not acknowledged and a new ceremony in Belgrade was demanded. In Belgrade, since the sultan walked directly into the imperial tent without first giving the accession bonus, members of the standing army asked to be promised gratuity and promotion, but the new sultan did not take their demand seriously. As a result the army rioted while entering Istanbul, claiming that the enthronement ceremony had not been held. The practice of the *cülus* bonus often led to discord, particularly when sultans changed frequently, emptying the treasury. Apart from the gratuity and promotion given to the military, it was also customary to grant gifts to state dignitaries.

Zeynep Tarım-Ertuğ

Further reading: Zeynep Tarım Ertuğ, "Ceremony and Protocol at the Ottoman Court," in *A Cultural Atlas of the Turkish World: Ottoman Period,* vol. 1 (Istanbul: Turkish Cultural Service Foundation, 1999), 428–77; Gülru Necipoğlu, *Architecture, Ceremonial, and Power: The Topkapı Palace in the Fifteenth and Sixteenth Centuries* (Cambridge, Mass.: MIT Press, 1992).

Erdel *See* TRANSYLVANIA.

esham *See* TAX FARMING.

Euphrates River (*Ar.*: al-Firat; *Turk.*: Fırat Nehri) The Euphrates River rises in the Turkish highlands and flows 1,700 miles (2,700 km) before emptying into the Persian Gulf. The banks of the Euphrates served as the main overland route linking the Mediterranean and the port cities of the Persian Gulf for much of the Ottoman period. For much of its length, the river also served as the demarcation line between settled villages and the nomadic Arabic tribes of BEDOUINS.

In the 16th century, CARAVANS bringing trade goods from India and further east would arrive in BASRA, in southern IRAQ, and then be transported by camel across the desert to DAMASCUS or ALEPPO. In the 17th and 18th centuries, as more aggressive Bedouin con-

federations moved out of Arabia, the caravans became increasingly subject to being attacked and plundered by these groups, and the desert course was largely abandoned in favor of the safer route along the Euphrates which, besides providing water and forage for the camels, could be garrisoned. The valley of the Euphrates, in what is today SYRIA, is relatively fertile. At the start of the 16th century it was inhabited by peasants, but at the end of that century a combination of droughts and Bedouin raids led to its depopulation. This increased insecurity in the region and led more peasants to flee villages along the steppes that bordered the Syrian Desert to seek protection in cities or larger fortified villages, allowing the desert to expand, as without peasant cultivators to build barriers against drifting sand formerly arable land was covered in sand.

In a report sent to Sultan MAHMUD II (r. 1808–39) from the office of the tax collector of Aleppo in 1829, the derelict state of the Euphrates Valley was contrasted with its earlier flourishing state under the ABBASID CALIPHATE. The unnamed tax collector suggested that if only the sultan would commit the manpower to control the Bedouin tribes, the region could flourish again, producing revenues equal to the wealth the Europeans received from their colonies. Although no immediate action was taken in response, in 1870 the Ottomans established a province centered on the Euphrates town of Dayr al-Zor and opened the valley up to local notables to claim as their private property. The result was a small land grab that resulted in the reclamation of some of the formerly abandoned villages. Full restoration of the area's prosperity would await the 20th century, however, and the construction of dams along the river.

Bruce Masters

Evliya Çelebi (Mehmed Zılli) (b. 1611–d. 1683?) *Ottoman traveler and author* Evliya Çelebi was a famous Ottoman traveler who spent more than 40 years traveling all over the Ottoman Empire and beyond. His 10-volume travelogue is the most important single text of Ottoman literature. It is the largest work of its kind in Islamic literature, and perhaps in world literature, a literary source of unique richness. Born in Istanbul, Evliya spent several years in a madrasa, then trained as a page in the TOPKAPI PALACE. This education made him a perfect Ottoman gentleman, familiar with the Muslim religious traditions as well as poetry, calligraphy, and music. Known for his wit, his voice as a singer, and as a Quran reciter, Evliya became a boon companion to Sultan MURAD IV (r. 1623–40). Driven by an "insatiable wanderlust" (Dankoff 2006), after 1640 Evliya served several Ottoman dignitaries in different provinces; his various jobs included muezzin, secretary, entertainer, special envoy, and inspector, among others.

Due to the mobility of the Ottoman elite, this life took Evliya to almost every corner of the Ottoman Empire and into some adjacent territories. These included the southern Russian steppes, Vienna (accompanying an embassy in 1665), Sudan, and Abyssinia. In 1671–72 he went on the HAJJ, the pilgrimage to MECCA, and then settled in CAIRO, where he wrote his *Seyahatname* (Book of Travels). The *Seyahatname* is primarily based on what Evliya saw during his travels, although some sections clearly derive from sources written by other authors, and the authenticity of some other sections has been disputed. The text creates a vast panorama of the Ottoman Empire of the time from the point of view of the educated, cosmopolitan and pious Ottoman, much more comprehensive and colorful than the dry factual geography of his contemporary KATIB ÇELEBI. That is only fitting as the goal of the author was as least as much to entertain as to inform. Thus the work talks about cities, social and economic life, buildings, institutions, pious foundations (WAQFS), sanctuaries, pilgrimage sites, pleasure gardens, fountains, food, customs, local languages (with remarkably accurate examples), legends of saints and Sufis, dramatic or comical personal adventures, jokes, commentaries in poetry, and anecdotes about life at the court of the sultan or in his retinue.

Within a geographical arrangement and systematic fashion, all this is presented in a happily disorganized way, abounding with digression, in a language that playfully oscillates from the most complex ornate prose, to plain Turkish, to pun-filled slang, to dialect. The narrative shifts readily from persuasive to expository, from factual to ironic, building in tongue-in-cheek fables and even hoaxes. The distinction between reliable fact and Evliya's invention for the sake of entertainment is not always easy to make, and the work is thus a unique reflection of the oral aspect of Ottoman culture, the social gatherings in courts, in which such conversations took place. Judging from minor gaps and the presence of unedited portions in the manuscript, it appears that the book was never fully completed; since the latest events noted in the text occurred in 1683, scholars surmise that Evliya must have died at some point around or after this time, though the exact date and manner of his death are unknown.

Usually the strict canon of Ottoman literature seems to have prevented such narratives from being written down, and in this context, the *Seyahatname* has never been fully appreciated. Manuscripts are rare (due also to the size of the book), and references to it in contemporary works have not been found. The *Seyahatname* has also not yet seen a full critical edition, though several sections are available in transliteration and English translation in a series edited by Klaus Kreiser and Robert Dankoff.

Gottfried Hagen

Further reading: Robert Dankoff, *Evliya Çelebi: An Ottoman Mentality,* 2nd ed. (Leiden: Brill, 2006); Klaus Kreiser and Robert Dankoff, eds., *Evliya Çelebi's Book of Travels: Land and People of the Ottoman Empire in the Seventeenth Century: A Corpus of Partial Editions* (Leiden: Brill, 1988–).

F

fallah *Fallah* is the Arabic word for "peasant." In Ottoman-language sources it was only used in reference to peasants in the Arabic-speaking provinces, especially those of EGYPT. The word had a decidedly negative connotation. Ottoman officials considered peasants only a step above their field animals in terms of intelligence and moral qualities. Although peasants made up the overwhelming majority of the Ottoman Empire, the only attention the authorities usually paid them was to register them for taxation. These tax registers, known as *tahrir defterleri,* provide comprehensive information about life in the empire's thousands of villages in terms of production and ownership. Unfortunately for historians, such registers were only kept during the 15th and 16th centuries. After that, much of what historians know about peasant life before the middle of the 19th century has to be gleaned from European travelers' accounts or from court records in provincial towns in which peasants registered their debts.

From the historical record, we do know that peasants' lives were hard, short, and often touched by violence as armies passed through the countryside or bandits or tribesmen raided villages. Practices of land tenure varied across the empire, with some peasants owning their land outright while others worked land held in common by the whole village. By the end of the Ottoman period most peasants were sharecroppers, working land held by large landowners who were often physically distant from the villages.

Peasants often responded to the harsh conditions under which they lived by fleeing to the cities or to mountainous areas where they were safe from both tax collectors and raiders. The Ottoman authorities tried to limit peasant flight by ordering peasants to return to the lands from which they had fled or by requiring them to pay special taxes to compensate for the lost revenue from their villages. It is not clear how the KADI courts responded to these orders elsewhere in the empire, but in the Arab provinces, the religious authorities met such orders with contempt. They argued that such practices resembled chattel slavery and could not be imposed on freeborn Muslims. In their interpretation of Islam, peasants were free men and women who could go where they pleased.

Peasant flight meant that, after the 16th century, there was more tillable land than there were peasants to farm it in most parts of the Ottoman Empire. However, that did not necessarily lead to an improvement in peasant living standards. It did lessen the potential for large-scale rural famines, and most villages were self-sufficient in the production of food. Because of the high cost of transportation for agricultural commodities, peasants rarely sold their produce outside a range of 20 miles of their villages. As a result, most of what was grown in any region was consumed there. That isolation began to end toward the end of the 18th century when the Ottoman Empire became increasingly an exporter of agricultural products. The demand in western Europe for commodities such as dried fruit, cotton, raw silk, and tobacco led individuals to seek control of larger tracts of land that could be converted to the production of crops for export.

The commercialization of rural production was accelerated in Egypt with the rise of MEHMED ALI; although he was officially only an Ottoman governor, Mehmed Ali effectively ruled Egypt as an independent state from 1806 until his death in 1841. He appropriated much of the country's arable land, making it the private property of his family and connections. This led to a sharp decrease in the living standard of Egyptian peasants as they were forced to produce commodities for export rather than the grains and vegetables they had formerly produced to feed themselves and their families. Mehmed Ali also introduced a system of military conscription and unpaid labor for peasants, provoking a series of violent outbursts that the Ottomans quelled by force.

Reformers hoped that the introduction of a new land code in 1868 would improve peasants' lives by giving them title to the lands they worked. However, fearing that registration might lead to greater taxation and conscription of their sons, most peasants opted to have the land registered in the name of powerful men. This intended reform left most agricultural lands in the Ottoman Empire in the hands of a few locally prominent families, with peasants working as sharecroppers, a situation similar to that which had been imposed by force in Egypt.

Bruce Masters

Further reading: Henry Habib Ayrout, *The Egyptian Peasant* (Boston: Beacon, 1963); Kenneth Cuno, *The Pasha's Peasants: Land, Society, and Economy in Lower Egypt, 1740–1858* (Cambridge: Cambridge University Press, 1992).

family   In most traditional societies the family is the basic economic unit. In Ottoman society the predominant family type was the extended family. This extended family was embedded within a larger social unit in which three generations coexisted and which included the families of brothers and other close relatives. This was the case for both Muslim and non-Muslim Ottomans. According to the Ottoman revenue surveys (*tahrir defterleri*), the average household consisted of five persons. However, it would be erroneous to suppose that each household consisted of an independent family. More commonly, households belonging to three different generations of the same family lived as one socioeconomic unit in homes arranged around a courtyard, usually complemented by close relatives living in the same quarter. Because of this, a quarter in a typical Ottoman city was not just an administrative unit but also a close-knit community made up of relatives.

Together, the individual members of the extended family formed a unit of production. This was true for urban artisans as well as for the peasants who made up the vast majority of the population. Members of the family and near relatives formed the basic matrix of social relationships that surrounded the individual from birth to death. Security rested with the kinship group to which the individual was connected, and the individual lived for the family. As with most traditional societies, nepotism also defined the sum total of human relationships into

which Ottomans of all classes were born and in which they existed throughout their lives.

Thus the birth of a child was an event celebrated throughout the quarter as well as within the family. The new addition to the community was welcomed through a specific rite; another rite was employed when the small child started school. When the child successfully mastered reading he was paraded through the quarter and applauded. Weddings, becoming a parent, and all other major life events were occasions of great interest, first for the family, and then for the quarter. The extended family produced and consumed jointly. Nurturing multiple generations, women would sew together, prepare and store winter food in common, visit together, and entertain themselves as a group. The men of the family would buy food together and would build and do repairs for the extended family as a whole. Time and urbanization, of course, inevitably contributed to transforming this kind of family and relationships in Ottoman society as elsewhere. The Istanbul family of the 19th century, for example, as it is represented in literature, although still different from the modern family, clearly reflects a basic transformation of the old family structure.

Residential districts of Ottoman cities were demarcated and molded not along economic lines but along religious lines. Non-Muslims settled in a narrow belt on the fringes of the town would carry on their lives in much the same fashion within the framework of relationships structured by their own extended families and community. As in many other traditional societies, interdenominational marriages were very rare. Although religious law allowed Muslim men to marry non-Muslim women, it should be borne in mind that non-Muslim congregations also strove to prevent such marriages. In certain regions Muslim officials or merchants posted there did marry Christian women temporarily, but this also was quite uncommon. Contrary to what is usually supposed, polygamy was not very widespread in Ottoman society. Even some European travelers noticed as much. Salomon Schweigger, for example, a German Protestant minister who passed through the empire toward the end of the 16th century, noted that "Turks rule countries and their wives rule them. Turkish women go around and enjoy themselves much more than any others. Polygamy is absent. They must have tried it but then given it up because it leads to much trouble and expense. Divorce is rare, for then the man has to pay in money and goods and daughters are left with the mother."

MARRIAGE, DOWER, AND THE RIGHTS OF WOMEN

Given her role in reproduction, the woman is the most important member of the traditional family, but her status within the family and society as a whole was not commensurate with this importance. Her standing was nevertheless enhanced with age and increasing number of children. She also usually enjoyed financial security.

In Islamic law the dower or *mahr* was a payment made by the groom to the bride upon marriage and constituted the wife's economic security in case of divorce or widowhood. These payments have little to do with principles laid down in legal texts, however. In most traditional societies where women marry young into economic dependence, it is custom for the groom to make such a payment for his bride.

Before Islam, marriage customs that revolved around the payment of a bride price were already prevalent among Arabs in the region. Such traditions reflect a patriarchal, polygamous family structure. The pre-Islamic *mahr* was the purchase price for the woman. Islam, however, brought changes to this existing custom. Although these Islamic injunctions have not always been obeyed, they forbade the bride's father or other kin from appropriating the *mahr* and left it entirely in the hands of the woman to be given in marriage.

Islamic law requires that the *mahr* be paid in two parts, the first paid at the time of the wedding and the second out of the inheritance in case of divorce or if the husband dies. In order for the act of marriage to be formalized, the bride must have assented publicly that the *mahr* has been paid and this must have been duly recorded in the court register.

There is disagreement among Islamic jurists as to what the minimum *mahr* should be, but 10 dirhems (silver coins) seems to have been most common. Nevertheless, comparison of such injunctions of Islamic SHARIA or canon law with actual practice in Ottoman society does reveal certain conflicts between custom and the letter of the law. Many entries concerning marriage recorded in the *kadı* registers of 16th-century Ankara, Çankırı, Kayseri, and Konya (all in Anatolia, present-day Turkey), for example, do not fit the requirements of any of the four SUNNI ISLAM denominations on the subject, indicating that marriage practices in Anatolia in that period did not always accord with Islamic regulations.

In the district or province to which he was appointed and where he would remain for but a short time, the typical Ottoman *kadı* or judge refrained from strict implementation of standard legal rules and regulations. For him, it was better to conform to local traditions than to disrupt the local order. When it came to writing treatises concerning family relationships, Ottoman jurists did not go beyond loyally copying the works of classical Islamic jurists. However, they were not nearly so orthodox in actual practice. Thus, even though they were against the sharia, old Turkish traditions such as *başlık* and *kalın* were legally validated by courts in central Anatolia in the 16th and 17th centuries. *Başlık* and *kalın* were money paid by the bridegroom's family to his bride's family

independently of, and in addition to, the *mahr*. While the *mahr* was given directly to the bride as a financial safety net, the *başlık* and *kalın* were in effect bride prices paid for the economic loss a family incurred by giving away the bride.

Similarly, when it came to trying cases of adultery or divorce, Ottoman kadıs also proved more flexible than the strict clauses of classical Islam. Nevertheless, *kadı* registers record an equal number of cases conforming to and going against the Islamic principles on *mahr*. For example, in all places, marriage was recorded at the court register. Otherwise the man and woman concerned would be summoned to court for "cohabiting out of wedlock" and their illegitimate relationship would be recorded in the same registry.

The best examples of customs conflicting with the Islamic rules on marriage are to be found in 16th-century central Anatolia. On the basis of several entries in the Ankara court registers for that period, it would seem that a certain type of betrothal, called *namzedlik* (literally, "candidacy") was quite common. In this type of arrangement, the father would promise his daughter in marriage to someone while she was still very young and would accept money or goods in return. This sum would be used by the father; when his daughter came of age, he would hand her over to the man to whom she was betrothed.

The *kadı* registers also record the separation of a married couple or the fact that their joint existence has come to an end. Contrary to orthodox practice, in some places a wife who had left her husband's home was not required to return. Such a woman might instead forgo her rights to the second part of her *mahr* and to alimony. A woman stated to be "henceforth divorced" by her husband was required by canon law to wait at least two months before remarrying, and it seems that this particular injunction was commonly observed. Payment of alimony would be decided by the court on the woman's application, not only in cases of formal divorce but also in instances of abandonment or if the husband failed to provide for his family.

EXTRAMARITAL RELATIONSHIPS

As in most traditional societies, extramarital relationships and bearing children of uncertain fatherhood were severely frowned upon by 16th-century Ottomans. At the same time, Ottoman society had moved away from the much harsher punishments imposed by ancient eastern societies for such practices. According to Islamic law, for example, any adulteress upon proof of her "crime" was liable to be stoned in accordance with a provision adopted from old Judaic law, but even in the earliest period of Islam, provisos were added that must have made inflicting this punishment all but impossible. That adultery had in fact been committed had to be proved through the testimony of at least four male witnesses, and a woman accused by her husband of adultery could evade punishment by denying the allegation and basing her denial on a solemn oath.

This particular ruling was commonly adhered to in Ottoman jurisdiction where *kadıs* generally refrained from deciding that adultery had been formally proven. When residents of a quarter surprised a couple having an illegal affair and paraded and ridiculed them in the streets so as to bring them into court, the verdict would usually be one of "alleged adultery" and a prison term and/or condemnation to the galleys would be imposed. Throughout Ottoman history, there is only one recorded instance where stoning was decided upon and carried out. In 1680 a woman living in the Aksaray district of Istanbul whose husband was away at war was accused of having been caught in the act of adultery with a non-Muslim youth. The verdict of the court was stoning for the woman and death for the young man. The *kadıasker* or chief judge for Rumelia reluctantly assented, and the entire affair was much resented by the ULEMA. This happened in a period of extreme religious fanaticism, and encountered such opposition that the penalty was not repeated.

On the other hand, women who bore illegitimate children or cohabited out of wedlock were never regarded with tolerance, and urban security officers were empowered to keep an eye on them. In the provinces of the empire in the late 16th century, such women would be immediately placed in the custody of the *subaşı* (a kind of military police). In Ottoman cities, efforts were made to keep unmarried men out of residential districts. Even in Istanbul, the influx of single men looking for work would be channeled to special inns for bachelors (*bekar hanları*) in the central industrial district and quartered there under some sort of surveillance.

THE TRANSFORMATION OF FAMILY STRUCTURE

The last century of the Ottoman Empire is renowned as a period of reforms, and military reform especially; however, the statesmen of the 19th century were also aware of the need for a thorough modernization in the financial, judicial, and administrative spheres. These 19th-century reformers wanted a regime where the law was supreme. Thus European approaches gradually became the model not only for the Ottoman army, administration, and finances but also for its culture, literature, and daily life. The TANZIMAT or reform period (1839–76) was a time when a new type of Ottoman person began to emerge.

It was also a time when significant changes began to be felt in the life of Ottoman women. The traditional structure of the family in the rural countryside as well as in the larger cities came increasingly under the pressure of changes in agriculture, education, communications, and technology. At the same time, the issue of women's liberation began to occupy an increasingly important place. From the Islamic modernists to the newly founded political reform groups, most thinkers of the region advocated changes in the traditional family structure and in the social status of women.

The trend toward urbanization in this period was also a significant factor in the modernization of the Ottoman family structure. Throughout the Ottoman Empire, the introduction of mechanized production and the advent of a genuine world marketplace encouraged migration into cities and the settlement of previously nomadic peoples. Whereas previously only unmarried men would move to the big towns and at least some would stay there only on a seasonal basis, around this time entire families began to migrate; in Istanbul, close to the city walls, near the inlet to the Bosporus called the Golden Horn, the first squatters' quarters came into being. This increasing urbanization may be seen as the beginning of a transition to a nuclear family structure.

The sociocultural changes of the Tanzimat period constituted a golden age, which introduced women—at least those in the middle and upper class—to social life. While Islamic modernists came up with new interpretations of the sharia to justify abolishing or at least restricting polygamy, other thinkers and authors in both the Ottoman territories and other Near Eastern countries, as well as on the periphery of the Russian Empire, were directly campaigning against the traditional type of marriage and family structure. Thus Ibrahim Şinasi Bey somewhat naively satirized these antiquated customs in his 1859 play *Şair Evlenmesi* (The wedding of a poet), the first truly modern Turkish play. Mirza Fethali Ahundov, the founder of dramaturgy of Azerbaijan, and his followers also radically criticized in their works the sequestered existence of Muslim women, the patriarchal structure of the Ottoman family, and the ignorance to which female children were condemned. In the 1880s a group of women from among the Muslims of Russia started a women's journal called *Alem-i Nisvan* (Women's world) to spread feminist ideas. One of the most important undertakings of the Tanzimat in EDUCATION was to provide schooling for girls at the intermediate level. As the numbers of girls' schools increased and came to include high schools by the end of the century, a new professional group arose: female teachers. That the initial entry of women into working life in Turkey took place in the field of education rather than industry partially accounts for the relatively strong position of women in the Turkish bureaucracy to this day.

The new intelligentsia that emerged out of the intellectual ferment of the Tanzimat period included women of the upper class. Among the most significant was Fatma Aliye Hanım, the daughter of the famous Ottoman statesman and historian Ahmed Cevdet Pasha (1822–95).

In the larger cities women had broken out of the confines of the home and their visible presence in many types of social activity, ranging from moonlight excursions on the Bosporus to shopping in the Istanbul district of Pera, made a Tanzimat statesman such as Cevdet Pasha anxious about the increase in womanizing and immorality.

Despite the slowness of Ottoman industrialization and urbanization, Turkish women may be said to have entered a phase of moderate liberation in the 19th century. Statesmen of the Tanzimat period were aware that the existing family code and marriage customs were creating problems. Plans for legislation to cope with this date as far back as the attempt by Âlî Pasha to adopt the French Civil Code.

But since the level of social development had not permitted this, only certain decrees (*ferman*) and edicts (*tenbih*) to bring traditional marriage under some control could be produced. These decrees and edicts basically attempted to prohibit payment of *başlık* for marriage and to curtail great expenditures in general. Thus a *ferman* of May 1844 ordered that daughters of age must be allowed to marry of their own free will without any interference from their parents, and that payments such as *başlık* were illegal and could not be rendered to brides' parents.

Eighteen years later, in 1862, governmental edicts in connection with these *ferman* were issued. Ten articles in all, they prohibited extravagant weddings and the payment of *başlık* while setting the amounts of *mahr* at 100 kuruş for the poor, 500 kuruş for the middle class, and 1,000 kuruş for the wealthy. The very poor would pay nothing. All this was intended to make marriage easier. The edicts further abolished the custom of presentation of gifts by the groom to his bride's relatives after the wedding. Weddings were also classified as first, second, and third class, with the legal amount of expenditure for each category specified carefully.

In the Second Constitutional Period (1908–20), modernist ideological and political trends continued to focus on marriage and the family. There were polemics between administrators, lawyers, and thinkers on this subject, and novelists of the time elaborated on the problems of Turkish womanhood in a rhetorical and didactic manner. ZIYA GÖKALP, the master theoretician of the COMMITTEE OF UNION AND PROGRESS, was drawn to this question in his youth and even wrote a short story satirizing traditional marriage.

In this general climate, one would have expected the YOUNG TURKS to undertake certain innovations in the realm of family law and, in fact, the Turkish Hearths (Türk Ocakları) were a hotbed of feminist activity. But the Union and Progress government was unable to make radical moves in this direction in its dictatorial phase after the BALKAN WARS (1912 and 1913) and then again during WORLD WAR I (1914–18). In fact, a reactionary movement was even responsible for creating a commission to specify the length of the *çarşaf* (women's traditional outdoor overgarment) and standards for veils for women. For all these reasons, the Decree on Family Law of 1917 did not introduce any serious reforms. It was, however, considered binding for all Ottoman subjects regardless of religion, and in this respect it was the first standard legal text of its kind in any Islamic society. The decree lent women some protection against husband-initiated divorce and polygamy, practices inconsistent with contemporaneous European social norms, and it imposed state supervision of marriage for Ottomans of all religions.

İlber Ortaylı

See also LAW AND GENDER; SEX AND SEXUALITY.

Further reading: Marie Alexandrescu-Dersca, "Sur le Mariage entre Turcs Ottomans et Roumanies XVI–XIX siècles," *Interventions et Rapports,* XV Congrés Int. Des Etudes Historiques, Bucharest, 1980, 15–17; İlber Ortaylı, *Osmanlı Toplumunda Aile* [Family in Ottoman Society] (Istanbul: Pan, 2000).

Farhi family Farhi was the name of a Jewish family that came to prominence in Syria at the end of the 18th century as bankers (*sarraf*) to the various warlords who dominated the politics of southern Syria and Palestine. The Farhis were Sephardic Jews who probably came to DAMASCUS in the early 18th century from ALEPPO. The family's business interests in Damascus were aided by the fact that a collateral branch of the family in Istanbul acted as bankers and moneylenders to powerful men in the Ottoman government. They could buy influence at the sultan's court to help their cousins in Syria. The family's position was precarious, however, as they had few options for legal recourse should they run afoul of their patrons. An example of that came in 1820 when Haim Farhi, who served as chief financial adviser to various governors in ACRE from 1790 onward, was murdered by Abdullah Pasha. Abdullah was the son of a Mamluk in the household of Cezzar Ahmed Pasha, who had ruled Acre from 1775 until his death in 1804 and who had also occasionally used Haim's services. Abdullah himself had been raised in Haim's house as his ward and, through Haim's auspices, had been named governor of Acre. When Abdullah had Haim strangled and had his corpse thrown into the Mediterranean Sea, the Farhis sought retaliation, but the best they could accomplish was Abdullah's dismissal from his post.

John Bowring, an Englishman who reported to Parliament on Syria's economy in 1838, cited two members of the Farhi family, Nassim and Murad, as the richest merchants in Damascus at that time. Each had £15,000 (the equivalent at that time of $75,000) in capital, a considerable sum comparable to millions in current dollars.

However, the family's fortunes waned over the course of the 19th century as Christian merchants began to undercut them commercially and establish relationships with the Europeans. The antagonism between the Christian and Jewish communities in the region was part of the backdrop for the DAMASCUS AFFAIR in 1840. Later in the century, some members of the extended Farhi family settled in Cairo, while others went to New York. The family's history illustrates the success that a non-Muslim family could enjoy in the Ottoman Empire by pooling its resources. At the same time, it highlights the limitations they faced politically as non-Muslims, with little legal recourse when engaged in disputes with Muslims in Muslim courts of law.

Bruce Masters

Further reading: Thomas Philipp, "The Farhi Family and the Changing Position of the Jews in Syria, 1750–1860." *Middle Eastern Studies* 20 (1984): 37–52.

Fatih mosque complex (Fatih Külliyesi)   The Fatih, or "Conqueror," mosque complex was a religious and social building of unprecedented size and complexity built in Istanbul between 1463 and 1470 by the order of Sultan MEHMED II (r. 1444–46; 1451–81). It was the first monumental project in the Ottoman imperial architectural tradition. Displaying important influences from Byzantine, Italian, and Turkic architectural traditions, the *külliye* established the new imperial style of Ottoman architecture, marking the transition from state to empire and from provincial to global power.

The mosque complex was built by the royal architect Atik Sinan (Sinan the Elder). It was the largest *külliye* up to that time, covering an area of 3,400 square feet (320 square meters). Fatih Camii, or the Mosque of the Conqueror, was at the center of a complex that included eight madrasas and a porticoed courtyard. Eight buildings in front of the madrasas served as shops and as accommodations for travelers; revenue from these sources provided financial support for the complex. In addition to these buildings, there were two minarets, an *imaret* or soup kitchen, a CARAVANSARY, a library, a primary school, a hospice, a fountain, a kiosk, and an asylum, as well as the tombs of Mehmed II and his wife. The complex also included two large bazaars, a *saraçhane* or harness shop, and the largest BATHHOUSE (hammam) ever constructed, all of which belonged to the WAQF, or pious endowment, that founded the complex. It was often called "the Conqueror's complex" because it was constructed in part to commemorate the conquest of Constantinople (renamed ISTANBUL) in 1453.

The *külliye* articulated, renewed, and imperialized the earlier Ottoman architectural tradition in which the buildings were located throughout the city, as in EDIRNE and BURSA. In Istanbul, the buildings of the complex were arranged around a monumental mosque according to a rational, geometric, highly structured site plan. Although the mosque stood at its center, the complex was not limited solely to a religious function; it was an integral part of the social, political, and educational activities of the new Ottoman capital. Mehmed II put into place a repopulation policy that aimed to balance the non-Muslims in the city. As part of this policy, the first Muslim inhabitants of the city were encouraged, to settle in the Fatih district that came into being around the complex, which also served these newcomers.

The central mosque of the complex, Fatih Camii, was neither the first imperial mosque nor the first mosque in the city built by Ottomans. When construction began in 1463, there were already several small mosques in Istanbul. However, the Conqueror's mosque was built on a strategic site, on the crown of the third of the seven hills of Istanbul. Its monumental scale and hilltop location made it highly visible, and its silhouette gave the city's skyline a distinctive Muslim character. Moreover, it was located on the second most sacred Christian site in Constantinople; the Church of the Holy Apostles—the imperial burial place of the Byzantine emperors—stood on this site until its destruction in 1204 during the Fourth Crusade. By putting his own tomb on the same site, Mehmed II followed the Byzantine imperial funeral tradition. In doing so, he proclaimed himself both sultan and *kayser-i rum* (Caesar of Rome).

The Fatih complex was damaged by earthquakes in 1509 and 1766. BEYAZID II (r. 1447–1513) restored the complex after the first earthquake (1509). However, the second devastated the complex; the only elements that remained standing were the mihrab (a niche in the wall of a mosque that indicates the direction of MECCA), the bases of the minarets, and the walls of the courtyard remained standing.

Judging from contemporary engravings, miniatures, and memoirs, the first mosque had been influenced by other Turkoman mosques built in Anatolia and by the HAGIA SOPHIA, the ancient Byzantine imperial church. It was an experiment in the search for a new imperial architecture incorporating new and foreign forms. The plan for the mosque took some inspiration from classical Byzantine basilica plans. Its dome was 85 feet (26 meters) in diameter, a size only surpassed by the dome of Hagia Sophia. Unlike Hagia Sophia with its single central dome and two semi-domes of the same diameter, the first Fatih mosque had one central dome supported by a single semi-dome of the same diameter on the qibla (direction of Mecca) side and suspended on four arches. The second mosque, which was built (1771) by MUSTAFA III (r. 1757–74) after the 1766 earthquake, was built on a square plan. It has one central dome supported by four semi-domes.

The structure is unique among imperial mosques because of its internal fountain. The four madrasas, or religious colleges, on the northern side form the Karadeniz Medreseleri (Black Sea Colleges), while those on the southern side make up the Akdeniz Medreseleri (Mediterranean Colleges). The complex's medical systems (a hospital with 14 rooms and its own kitchen and an asylum) were staffed by Jewish doctors. Neither the madrasas nor the medical complex survived the 1766 earthquake. The bathhouse and harness shop that formed part of the *külliye* were destroyed in a fire in 1916.

Even though the *külliye* lost some of its component parts, the rest of the complex, including the tombs, madrasas, and primary schools, continued to be used, although for different purposes. The central building of the *külliye*, the mosque, remains one of the foremost monuments of Istanbul and continues to function as a public mosque with funeral services for important individuals in present-day Turkey.

Nuh Yılmaz

Further reading: Godfrey Goodwin, *A History of Ottoman Architecture* (Baltimore, Md: The Johns Hopkins University Press, 1971); Mehmed Agha-Oğlu, "The Fatih Mosque at Constantinople." *Art Bulletin* 12, no. 2. (1930): 179–195.

fatwa (*fetva*)   Fatwa is a term of Arabic origin (*fetva* in Ottoman Turkish) that refers to the issuing of a judicial ruling by a Muslim religious scholar. In theory, any Muslim scholar may issue a fatwa on a hypothetical question that has been put to him by a plaintiff, but in practice, a fatwa is only issued by those religious scholars recognized by their peers as legal authorities or appointed by the sultan to the post of mufti. A fatwa ruling is based on the scholar's understanding of Islamic law, although the author of the ruling may cite the sources he used to reach his ruling. In the Ottoman Empire the most important fatwas were those issued by the SEYHÜLISLAM, or chief justice of the empire. Such rulings were issued in response to specific legal queries that could be submitted by anyone in the Empire. Once a ruling had been delivered, it could be entered as evidence in a court case upon which it had bearing and could serve as a legal precedent for future cases.

Typically, a plaintiff would construct the question so as to elicit a favorable response. The judge at the court where the case was being heard did not have to accept the fatwa of the *şeyhülislam* as definitive, but it was a rare judge who would risk incurring the wrath of the chief justice by ignoring his opinion. This was especially true in regions that were within the effective control of the state and where the judges were graduates of the imperial madrasas. Further afield—in Syria, Palestine, and Egypt—the fatwas of the *şeyhülislam* in Istanbul were not given the same regard. However, in the provincial courts local muftis were equally important in shaping the character of the law as practiced. The fatwas issued by prominent jurists were frequently copied and could be found in the personal libraries of religious scholars and members of the Empire's judiciary.

Ebussuud Efendi (d. 1574), who served SÜLEYMAN I (the Magnificent) (r. 1520–66) and SELIM II (r. 1566–74) between 1545 and 1574, was undoubtedly the most notable *şeyhülislam*. Ebussuud's fame is partly due to the quality of his responses. It is also partly due to the fact that Süleyman's reign has been viewed by later generations as a halcyon age of Islamic justice, with Ebussuud regarded as the most judicious of men. For this reason, even centuries after his death, his fatwas continued to influence Ottoman jurisprudence and the collection of his rulings helped to establish definitive opinions for the Ottoman legal establishment.

Bruce Masters

See also SHARIA.

Further reading: Colin Imber, *Ebu's-su'ud: The Islamic Legal Tradition* (Stanford, Calif.: Stanford University Press, 1997).

finances and fiscal structure   The Ottoman fiscal structure had three phases: the classical period until the 1790s; the transitional period of 1793–1839; and the TANZIMAT or reform era beginning in 1839. The first period was characterized by the existence of a single central treasury, the imperial treasury (Hazine-i Amire). It was created with the aim of financing all the expenses of the central government while shaping the fiscal structure. The second period coincided with the beginning of Western-inspired reforms. The military reforms of SELIM III (r. 1789–1807) and MAHMUD II (r. 1808–39) necessitated the creation of additional treasuries to finance new, modernized armies. The creation of these new treasuries brought a period of transition in which the Ottoman fiscal system began to operate with multiple treasuries. The system then underwent a more fundamental change with the Tanzimat reforms in 1839 that signaled the modernization and replacement of traditional fiscal policies.

THE CLASSICAL PERIOD

The earliest documentary reference to a separate and relatively specialized office controlling revenues and expenses comes from the reign of BAYEZID I (r. 1389–1402), with the first survey registers and initial steps toward centralization of the bureaucracy. Unfortunately, not much is known about the structure and functioning of Ottoman fiscal institutions before the codification of Ottoman laws in the late 1470s. This law code—known as the Law Code of the Conqueror, referring to MEHMED

II (r. 1444–46; 1451–81)—puts the fiscal organization and its staff under the surveillance of the *baş defterdar* (keeper of the register), or director of finances. During Mehmed's reign there were two financial bureaus, one for Rumelia and one for Anatolia (the empire's European and Asian provinces, respectively).

Ottoman expansion into Arab lands from 1516 onward and into Hungary in the 1540s led to further changes in fiscal organization. Several additional financial bureaus began to function under the chief financial director. One new bureau had transprovincial responsibilities, controlling specific revenues from the Rumelian and Anatolian provinces as well as the tax farms in Istanbul. A separate bureau was set up to keep the financial registers of the Arab provinces. Toward the end of the 16th century a short-lived third branch was created to oversee the Danubian region.

Ottoman expansion also led to the emergence of provincial financial directorates and treasuries. They were in charge of overseeing provincial revenues earmarked for the central treasury. Although we lack exact information as to when and where such provincial treasuries were first established, Ottoman chroniclers of the late 16th century (Ibrahim Peçevi and Mustafa Ali) suggest that the financial directorates in ALEPPO and DAMASCUS, established after 1535, were probably the first. By the end of the 16th century there were some 20 provincial treasuries. They included Karaman and Sivas, initially tied to the Anatolian financial bureau in Istanbul, as well as treasuries in BAGHDAD, BUDA, BASRA, ALGIERS, Zulkadriye, Van, MOSUL, Maraş, and YEMEN. Control over local tax farms was transferred from the local KADIS to these financial bureaus. In provinces where there was no local financial bureau, the *kadıs* and governors continued to oversee the local tax farms throughout the 17th century. In the 1550s, with the establishment of local financial bureaus, the staff of the central financial bureau was cut in half. At the same time, subdivisions were set up that specialized in administering certain revenues such as poll-taxes, income from mines, and the sultan's *hases* or crown lands. There was no significant change to the bureaus responsible for keeping the registers of expenses.

THE TRANSITION PERIOD

In the second or transitional period, from 1793 to 1839, the Ottomans entered into a new fiscal phase. This phase was characterized by a number of independent treasuries set up to support the military reforms of Selim III and Mahmud II. Selim's Irad-ı Cedid treasury was abolished after the suppression of his NIZAM-I CEDID (New Order) troops, trained in the Western style. However, the treasury set up to finance the reformed navy lasted until 1839. The imperial treasury, which shaped the whole fiscal system, lost its importance after the JANISSARIES were abolished in 1826 and replaced by the new army, the Muallem Asakir-i Mansure-i Muhammediye (Trained Victorious Troops of Muhammad). Following the example set by his uncle Selim III, the new sultan, Mahmud II, created an additional treasury, the Mansure, to finance his new army. Although these reforms were significant from an organizational perspective, fiscal policies and measures during this period of transition did not differ substantially from those of the previous period.

THE TANZIMAT ERA

The Tanzimat era was a period of real change in Ottoman fiscal organization and policies. The central administration devised a new policy of transferring more revenue from the GNP to the state coffers. The office of the director of finances (*defterdar*) was replaced by the Ministry of Finance (Maliye Nezareti). All the separate treasuries were merged into a single treasury with authority over all the revenues and expenses of the empire, thus achieving one of the most significant fiscal goals of the Tanzimat. With this change, officials who had previously been paid from local revenues became salaried bureaucrats. Various tax exemptions and some taxes-in-kind were abolished, and the practice of TAX FARMING was formally eliminated. The state made use of the Ottoman Bank (*see* BANKS AND BANKING) to transfer the excess revenues of the provinces to the central treasury. It also set up a number of commissions to grapple with the financial complexities that arose after the abolition of the old system.

Erol Özvar

Further reading: Murat Çizakça, *A Comparative Evolution of Business Partnerships: The Islamic World and Europe, with Specific Reference to the Ottoman Archives* (Leiden, Netherlands: E.J. Brill, 1996); Linda T Darling, *Revenue-Raising and Legitimacy: Tax Collection and Finance Administration in the Ottoman Empire, 1560-1660* (Leiden, Netherlands: E.J. Brill, 1996); Halil İnalcık and Donald Quataert, eds., *An Economic and Social History of the Ottoman Empire, 1300–1914* (Cambridge: Cambridge University Press, 1994); Mehmet Genç and Erol Özvar, eds., *Osmanlı Maliyesi Kurumları ve Bütçeler*, 2 vols. (Istanbul: Osmanlı Bankası Arşiv ve Araştırma Merkezi, 2006).

firearms   The first true firearms appeared in China in the 12th century. These weapons probably arrived in the Ottoman Empire through the Balkans in the second half of the 14th century. Most early references to the use of firearms by the Ottomans are unreliable, as they appear in single sources by chroniclers who wrote several generations after the events they describe. However, several independent sources confirm that the Ottomans used firearms during the siege of Constantinople between 1394 and 1402.

By the 1390s the Ottoman government employed, on a permanent basis, gunners or *topçus* who manufactured and handled firearms. A separate corps of artillery-men was established under Sultan MURAD II (1421–44, 1446–51), well before artillery units became an integral part of European armies. Firearms in the Ottoman Empire gained tactical significance in the 1440s when the Ottomans fought several wars against the Hungarians, who had used various types of cannons for generations. These wars forced the sultan's soldiers to emulate their opponents' weaponry and tactics. It was also during these wars that the Ottomans became acquainted with the WAGON FORTRESS system, a defensive arrangement of war carts, chained together wheel to wheel, protected by heavy wooden shielding, and equipped with firearms.

Ottoman artillerymen were aided by the corps of gun carriage drivers or *top arabacıs*, established in the latter part of the 15th century. The gunners and gun carriage drivers, along with the armorers or *cebecis*, formed the Ottoman artillery corps that was part of the sultan's standing army. Numbering about 1,110 in 1514, the size of the corps almost doubled in the 1520s and reached 6,500 by the end of the 16th century. Although the numbers of the corps fluctuated in the 17th and 18th centuries, available figures suggest that the Ottomans maintained firepower superior to the Austrian and Russian artillery corps until about the mid-18th century. The Ottoman conquest of CONSTANTINOPLE in 1453 and the Ottomans' triumph against Hungarian and Habsburg fortresses in Hungary in the 16th century bear witness to the skills of Ottoman artillerymen. The superiority of Ottoman firepower in siege warfare remained unchallenged until the end of the 17th century both in the Middle East and in Europe.

The JANISSARIES, the sultan's elite foot soldiers, also started to use *tüfenks*, or handguns, under Murad II. However, it was not until around the mid-16th century that most Janissaries carried firearms. The Janissaries' firepower often proved fatal for the Ottomans' adversaries, as was the case for the Hungarians in the BATTLE OF MOHÁCS in 1526.

Like some of their European opponents in the 15th century, the Ottomans were capable of casting giant cannons, indeed some of the largest guns known to contemporaries. While these large bombards were clumsy, difficult to maneuver, had a very low rate of fire (a couple of shots per day), and were of questionable usefulness, the production of such monsters required unusual technical and organizational skills. Unlike most of their European adversaries, who had abandoned the production of such gargantuan cannons by the beginning of the 16th century, the Ottomans continued to use a handful of these oversized weapons. However, they also produced and employed all three main classes of guns used in early modern Europe: parabolic-trajectory mortars and howitzers; flat-trajectory large-caliber siege and fortress guns of the cannon class; and medium- and small-caliber pieces of the culverin type. Contrary to the common European theory that Ottoman ordnance was dominated by gigantic cannons, archival sources suggest that the overwhelming majority of the guns cast in Ottoman foundries and deployed in their battles consisted of small- and medium-caliber pieces. Indeed, large siege and fortress cannons made up only a small fraction of Ottoman ordnance.

Although large-scale military uniformity and technical standardization was not achieved anywhere in the early modern period, the Ottomans lagged behind the most advanced western European nations in terms of standardization. Ottoman armaments included a perplexing variety of artillery pieces, a deficiency that was shared by some of their adversaries, most notably VENICE and SPAIN.

Before Sultan MEHMED II (r. 1444–46; 1451–81) founded the Imperial Cannon Foundry, or Tophane, in ISTANBUL, the most important foundry was in EDIRNE, the Ottoman capital city before Istanbul. Most of the guns used during the 1453 siege of Constantinople were made there. The Ottomans also cast cannon in their provincial capitals and mining centers, as well as in foundries established during campaigns. Of these, the foundries of Vlorë and Preveza in the Adriatic; Rudnik, Smederevo, Škodra, Novo Brdo, Pravište (near Kavala) and BELGRADE in the Balkans; BUDA and Temesvár (Timişoara) in Hungary; Diyarbakır, Erzurum, Birecik, Mardin and Van in Asia Minor; BAGHDAD and BASRA in IRAQ; and CAIRO in EGYPT were among the most important. The production output of some of these foundries could easily match that of the Istanbul foundry, especially in the late 15th and early 16th centuries. However, the main function of these local foundries was to repair the guns deployed in provincial garrisons and to cast new cannons for the same forts. Occasionally, these provincial foundries were charged with casting guns for imperial campaigns. In such cases they could produce several dozen cannons of various calibers annually.

Despite the occasional importance of local foundries, Istanbul was the center of Ottoman cannon casting. During the 16th to 18th centuries, only about 50 to 60 cannon founders worked at the Imperial Cannon Foundry; however, if day laborers are counted, the total workforce numbered in the hundreds. With the help of these laborers, the Istanbul foundry was capable of casting hundreds of cannons annually, with a total weight of around 100 metric tons; during some extraordinary years, the weight of the newly cast pieces exceeded 200 and even 300 metric tons (220–330 short tons).

Although bronze guns were much more expensive than cast-iron pieces of the same caliber, they were considered much safer and of better quality. Since the empire had abundant quantities of copper, the most important constituent of bronze, the Ottomans cast their large and medium-sized pieces of bronze, unlike their European opponents who used cheaper iron guns. The Ottomans used iron to cast hundreds of small pieces that weighed only 25–100 pounds and fired projectiles of about 5 to 16 ounces in weight, usually for their river flotillas.

Archival records show that the proportions of copper and tin used in the composition of Ottoman bronze cannons was similar to those cast in Europe, suggesting that the weapons themselves were of good quality. On the other hand, some European contemporaries, especially the Venetians, expressed a less favorable opinion of Ottoman guns. While chemical analyses might eventually provide more precise figures, the very modest technical advances in weapon design and effectiveness before the industrial age meant that guns in 1800 were very similar to those made in 1500.

Janissary *tüfenks,* or handguns, resembled the muskets used by their Spanish and Venetian opponents. Well into the 17th century, the Janissaries used the matchlock musket, named for its firing mechanism. However, from the late 16th century on, more and more muskets with the more mechanically advanced flintlock firing system were manufactured in the Ottoman Empire. These often employed the Spanish *miquelet*-lock (a type of flintlock). Apart from the mechanism, the Janissaries used two different types of muskets. In field battles they used smaller and lighter weapons measuring 115 to 140 cm (3.8 to 4.6 feet) long and weighing 3 to 4.5 kg (6.6 to 9.9 pounds) with bore diameters of 11–16 mm (0.44–0.64 inches). In siege warfare or in defending fortresses, they used a heavy eight-sided or cylinder-barreled matchlock musket. These trench guns were 130–160 cm (4.3–5.3 feet) long and had bore diameters of 20–29 mm (0.8–1.16 inches). Alongside these guns, the Janissaries' traditional recurved bow remained an important and formidable weapon well into the 17th century, although the ratio of bows to muskets had changed significantly by the mid-1600s.

The Ottomans had a long-lasting superiority in making strong, reliable musket barrels, using flat sheets of steel similar to the materials used for the famous swords forged in DAMASCUS. These sheets were coiled into a spiral, producing great strength in the barrel and enabling it to withstand higher explosive pressure. Ottoman musket barrels were less likely to burst than European barrels, which were constructed with longitudinal seams. *Tüfenks* manufactured in private Ottoman workshops were apparently often of better quality than those manufactured in state plants. The large number of private arms manufacturers led to widespread availability of hand firearms, often illegally traded and privately owned, in Anatolia. The state's inability to disarm the Anatolian rebels known as Celalis was due partly to illegal private arms manufacturing and partly to large-scale arms smuggling.

Despite their impressive technical history, by the latter part of the 18th century, the Ottomans lagged behind their European adversaries, most importantly the Russians and the Austrians, in both the production and use of firearms. Modernization of the Ottoman weapons industry and army, especially under MAHMUD II (r. 1808–39) and in the TANZIMAT reform era of 1839–76, greatly improved the quality of Ottoman firearms as well as the skills of the soldiers who used them. However, by that time, Ottoman weapons production was no match for a European industry that had made enormous strides in weapons design and manufacturing techniques. Under ABDÜLHAMID II (r. 1876–1909), the Ottomans relied on GERMANY for weapons and military assistance. In the closing years of the empire, Ottoman cannons were manufactured by Krupp, and German Mauser rifles replaced the Ottomans' outdated carbines, a handgun similar to a musket, but shorter.

Gábor Ágoston

Further reading: Gábor Ágoston, *Guns for the Sultan: Military Power and the Weapons Industry in the Ottoman Empire* (Cambridge: Cambridge University Press, 2005); Kenneth Chase, *Firearms: A Global History to 1700* (Cambridge: Cambridge University Press, 2003); Avigdor Levy, "Military Reform and the Problem of Centralization in the Ottoman Empire in the 18th Century." *Middle Eastern Studies* 18 (1982): 227–248; Stanford J. Shaw and Ezel Kural Shaw, *History of the Ottoman Empire and Modern Turkey,* vol. 2, *Reform, Revolution, and Republic: The Rise of Modern Turkey, 1808–1975* (Cambridge: Cambridge University Press, 1997).

folk literature   *See* LITERATURE, FOLK.

Fondaco dei turchi   *Fondaco* is an Italian term for a trading complex with warehouses. In Venice the Fondaco dei turchi was the place where Ottoman Muslim merchants had their lodgings and kept their goods. In the first half of the 16th century an increasing number of Muslim Ottoman subjects, reached Venice to trade. They were usually housed in private homes or inns. After the crisis caused by the Ottoman-Venetian war over CYPRUS (1570–73), these traders began to look for a more secure place of their own, similar to Venice's existing Jewish Ghetto and the Fondaco dei tedeschi, or trading complex for Germans. In 1575 the first Fondaco dei turchi (Turkish inn) was established in the inn all'Angelo, near the Rialto market. The building had cisterns and a small hammam or Turkish bath as well as rooms to store goods. Ottoman Muslim merchants who lodged there came primarily from the Balkans. Christian Ottoman subjects, principally Greeks, Armenians, and Albanians, contin-

Opened in 1621, the Fondaco dei turchi hosted Muslim merchants trading and residing in Venice. *(Personal collection of Maria Pia Pedani)*

ued to live in the houses built by their individual nations near St. Mark's Cathedral.

Since the original Fondaco dei turchi could not host all the Muslims present in Venice, another building was chosen for that purpose. It was the ancient Palmieri Palace, on the Grand Canal, in the parish of San Giacomo dell'Orio, which then belonged to the Pesaro family. It was rented by the Venetian Republic, restored, and opened in 1621 as the new Fondaco dei turchi. Maintained and guarded by the Venetian Republic, the new Fondaco dei turchi had 24 rooms to store goods, 50 bedrooms that could accommodate four to six persons each, kitchens, courts, closets, and a bath and prayer hall. About 300 merchants could be sheltered there. Like the Jewish Ghetto, the Fondaco dei turchi was locked during the night. Christian boys and women could not visit it and the residents were not permitted to leave. However, during the day the merchants who lived there could go freely wherever they liked in the city.

Since Persian merchants were also Muslims, they were officially required to stay in the Fondaco dei turchi, together with the Muslim subjects of the sultan. However, they never agreed to move to the Fondaco. In 1662, when Venetian authorities tried to force them to do so, they left the Rialto market permanently. The last Ottoman subject was forced to leave the Fondaco in 1838, about 50 years after the fall of the Venetian Republic (1797) when the owners of the building, no longer obliged to rent it to the state, sold it. After many years it was restored and turned into a museum. Now it is the Museum of Natural History.

Maria Pia Pedani

Further reading: Cemal Kafadar, "A Death in Venice (1575): Anatolian Muslim Merchants Trading in the Serenissima." *Journal of Turkish Studies* 10 (1986): 191–217; Deborah Howard, *Venice & the East* (New Haven, Conn.: Yale University Press, 2000).

food   *See* CUISINE.

France   Relations between France and the Ottoman Empire fall into two different phases. The first period lasted from the late 15th century to the last years of the 18th century, and the second spanned from the very end of the 18th century to the early 20th century. France has often been considered the traditional ally of the Ottoman Empire during the first period. Even though direct military cooperation was rare and relations seemed to worsen at times, the Ottoman Empire and France considered each other useful for counterbalancing their common enemy, the Habsburgs. This first period came to a close in 1798 when NAPOLEON invaded EGYPT, which was then under Ottoman control. In the 19th century, France conducted a multifaceted policy with regard to the Ottoman Empire in which it tried to prevent the Ottoman Empire's fall, but only in order to keep RUSSIA and ENGLAND from enjoying a larger share of the spoils of the Ottoman Empire. It also started to interfere with the internal affairs of the Ottoman Empire by supporting the MARONITES and the rebellious governor of Egypt, MEHMED ALI, in an effort to increase its own influence. The final confrontation between the two empires came during WORLD WAR I, resulting in the fall of the Ottoman Empire and a victorious France laying claim to Ottoman territory in many provinces.

Mutual cultural influences constituted another element of the relationship between France and the Ottoman Empire. The Ottomans observed French culture as early as the 18th century. In the 19th century, French appeared as the language of modernization and of the intelligentsia in the Ottoman capital, and the westernization of the empire was modeled on the culture and administrative apparatus of France. Although less studied, the Ottoman culture seems to have also had an effect on French society, especially in the 18th century.

POLITICAL RELATIONS: 1482–1797

Relations between the Ottoman Empire and France were initiated by the former. After the death of MEHMED II (r. 1444–46; 1451–81) in 1481, a civil war started between two aspirants to the throne, CEM and BAYEZID II (r.

1481–1512). Bayezid II finally prevailed over his rival in 1482 and Cem was forced to seek refuge in RHODES, from where he was transported to France. There was no legal certainty in the accession to the Ottoman throne; any prince of royal blood could claim the throne. Thus the presence of an Ottoman prince in the hands of Christian rulers was a potential threat to the territorial integrity of the empire, and Cem's exile became an issue of international politics. Bayezid II's envoy paid two visits to France in 1483 and 1486 in order to arrange Cem's confinement there; however, Pope Innocent VIII (r. 1484–92), who wanted to recruit Cem for his crusade against the Ottomans, succeeded in having Cem transferred to Rome in 1489, despite the efforts of an Ottoman special envoy. Five years later, the intrepid French king Charles VIII (r. 1483–98), planning his own anti-Ottoman crusade, compelled the new pope to hand over Cem. This plan failed, however, when Cem died in 1495.

The tone of relations between France and the Ottoman Empire changed as a result of the emergence of the Habsburgs. In 1516 the young Habsburg prince Charles V (r. 1516–56, 1519–58) inherited a vast empire including Castile, Aragon, Navarre, Granada, Naples, Sicily, Sardinia, the Low Countries, and Spanish possessions in the Americas. In 1519 he was also elected as the emperor of the Holy Roman Empire, adding the Archduchy of Austria to his domains. This rise of Habsburg power in continental Europe disturbed the region's balance of power, and the threatened (and now encircled) French dynasty, the Valois, entered a half-century-long struggle with the Habsburgs in 1521. This struggle aided in the rapprochement of France and the Ottoman Empire.

When the French king, Francis I (r. 1515–47), was captured by the forces of Charles V after the Battle of Pavia in 1525, the king and his mother sent letters to the Ottoman sultan, SÜLEYMAN I (r. 1520–66), requesting his assistance. In 1526 the Ottomans began a campaign against HUNGARY, whose king was an ally of the Habsburgs. Thanks to Ottoman pressure against the Habsburgs in Hungary, Francis I was able to secure his freedom with the Treaty of Madrid, signed later in 1526. As soon as he was released he led an anti-Habsburg coalition that included the papacy and ENGLAND. At the same time, the Ottomans were undertaking vast military operations against the Habsburgs in Central Europe in 1529 and 1532. Still, a formal alliance was not formed until 1536, and even then it was kept secret. As a result of this alliance the French fleet assisted the Ottoman forces in 1537, besieging Venetian-controlled Corfu (then allied with the Habsburgs), while the head of the Ottoman navy, Hayreddin Barbarossa (*see* BARBAROSSA BROTHERS), wintered in Toulon and aided the French in their military operations against the Habsburgs in 1543–44. The French navy assisted the Ottomans in their naval operations against the Habsburg pos-

sessions in the Western Mediterranean in 1553, and the same year a formal treaty of alliance was made public.

The Ottoman Empire appreciated an ally that would keep Christian Europe divided, and even though France's reputation in the Christian world was jeopardized by an alliance with the "infidels," Francis I welcomed the support against the Habsburgs. The French also benefited economically: Apart from loans, France enjoyed the grant of trade CAPITULATIONS in 1569, which helped its trade flourish and facilitated its supersession of Venice's commercial supremacy in the eastern Mediterranean. The capitulations allowed French merchants to trade in the sultan's dominions free from Ottoman law and at reduced customs duties. Furthermore, trade vessels from other European states that did not enjoy similar privileges were required to fly the French flag in order to trade in the area; as a result, the French started to dominate the Levant trade.

However, in the second half of the 16th century, France's role diminished in the international scene. Henry II had chosen to abandon his father's anti-Habsburg policy after the Treaty of Cateau-Cambrésis in 1559, and therefore also abandoned France's infidel ally. The kingdom was financially exhausted. Moreover, a series of civil wars would weaken the kingdom until 1594. France could hardly save itself from Spanish Habsburg domination, let alone oppose it. Still, it did not participate in the Holy League of 1571 against the Ottomans, which included the Spanish Habsburgs, VENICE, the Papal States, and the KNIGHTS OF ST. JOHN of MALTA. In 1573, the Ottomans helped to establish the French candidate—Henry of Valois, future French King Henry III (r. 1573–1574, 1574–1589)—on the Polish throne, rather than the Habsburg contender. However, French diplomats were unable to keep the Ottoman government from granting trade capitulations to England in 1579 or from making a truce with Spain in 1580, which demonstrated that French influence was gradually decreasing. During the war of 1593–1606 between the Austrian Habsburgs and the Ottoman Empire, France remained neutral. For a while, amicable relations prevailed despite French Roman Catholic proselytizing missions in the eastern Mediterranean, piratical activities, and assistance to the Austrians during the 1662–64 war and to the Venetians during the CRETAN WAR (1645–69). In 1683 the French ambassador to Constantinople was able to convince the Ottoman government to declare war against the Habsburgs in Central Europe at a time when the Habsburgs, engaged in military confrontations against France in the west, would have preferred to refrain from an armed struggle. The war between the Ottomans and the Holy League of the Habsburgs, Venice, Poland, the Papal States, and Russia from 1683–99 coincided with France's struggle with the Habsburgs in the west, at least between 1688 and 1697, forcing the Austrians to fight on two fronts.

In the following century, France continued to exert its influence by playing an intermediary role among the Ottomans, Austrians, and Russians, even though the Ottomans began to rely increasingly on English and Dutch ambassadors. In 1724, France helped arrange a diplomatic treaty between Russia and the Ottoman Empire, and the French ambassador was again the main protagonist during the negotiations for the Treaty of Belgrade of 1739, which concluded another Ottoman war against the Austrians and Russia. France's efforts were appreciated in Istanbul to the extent that it was granted the 1740 capitulations.

During the RUSSO-OTTOMAN WAR OF 1768–74, France took a pro-Ottoman stand. Even though France provided no material help, it was the only Great Power on which the Sublime Porte could rely. The French were not able to render effective help against Russia in 1783, when the latter annexed the Crimea to the detriment of the Ottoman interests, nor did it interfere during the Russo-Ottoman War of 1787–92 (see RUSSO-OTTOMAN WARS) or the Austro-Ottoman War of 1787–91. Nonetheless, relations did not worsen immediately, even after the French Revolution. In fact, the Ottomans were one of the few powers who remained neutral with regard to the revolution. The revolution pushed France into a diplomatic isolation that suited the interests of the Ottoman Empire. Unlike other European governments, the Ottomans did not feel threatened by the decapitation of Louis XVI, since such events were not unprecedented in Ottoman history. In addition, they welcomed the revolution because of the chaos and diversion it created for their enemies. The immediate result was the possibility of concluding relatively advantageous peace treaties with the Austrians and Russians in 1791 and 1792. These treaties were valuable to the Ottomans who appreciated the chance to disengage at a time when they were about to undertake reforms.

POLITICAL RELATIONS BETWEEN 1798 AND 1922

The nature of Ottoman relations with France changed in 1798 when Napoleon attacked Ottoman-controlled Egypt. Relations were already tense, because the Ottomans were uncomfortable with French expansion in the Balkans and the Adriatic Sea as a result of the Treaty of Campo-Formio of 1797. However, it was only after the French invasion of Egypt that the two states confronted each other for the first time, leading the Ottomans to request help from England and Russia. In the short term, after the war was over, French influence in Istanbul rose again as the Ottomans became discontented with England's reluctance to evacuate Egypt.

Napoleon declared himself emperor of France in 1804; although the Ottomans were initially hesitant, they were eventually convinced by French victories to take a favorable stance toward Napoleon, recognizing his title of emperor in 1806. But this pro-French policy led to the Russo-Ottoman War of 1806–12, and in 1807 a British fleet appeared before the Ottoman capital threatening bombardment unless the pro-French policy was reversed. France could not help the Porte against the Russians, but French officers did at least help with the organization of Istanbul's defenses against the British fleet. The political difficulties suffered by the Ottomans as a result of their alliance with the French did not prevent Napoleon from concluding an agreement with the Russians in 1807 that left the Ottoman Empire exposed to the schemes of the Russian czar. Indeed, it seemed as though the Ottoman Empire was nothing but a pawn in Napoleon's plans. Fortunately for the Ottomans, the French emperor decided to attack Russia in 1812, and Russia had to ask for a hasty peace. It was a relief to the Ottomans in the aftermath of a serious defeat by Russian forces near Rusçuk (present-day Ruse, Bulgaria) in June 1811 and the surrender of Ottoman commander Ahmet Pasha to General Kutuzov in November of the same year.

The Ottoman Empire was not included in the European state system that was established at the Congress of Vienna in 1814–15 following Napoleon's abdication and exile. Thus its territorial integrity was not guaranteed by international law. The empire was considered a second-rate power whose imminent collapse would be perilous to the area since the resulting vacuum would upset the precarious balance of power that had been established with difficulty after the congress. Henceforth, France followed a multifaceted policy against the Ottomans and, as was the case with the other Great Powers of the 19th century, found itself playing the role of mediator in order to prevent the fall of the Ottoman Empire. The objective was to make sure that none of the rival Great Powers became too powerful to the detriment of French influence in the region, a common calculation for all the powers. Thus whenever a crisis occurred in the region, the European powers intervened in order to settle the issue among themselves in an effort to prolong the life of the Ottoman Empire.

France often acted as one of these powers. In 1827 France worked with England and Russia to keep the Ottomans from putting down the Greek Revolt (see GREEK WAR OF INDEPENDENCE) and to have them accept European arbitration; however, France's involvement was hesitant, and was largely because it was trying to improve relations with England. In the Egypt Crisis of the 1830s, when Mehmed Ali (r. 1805–49), the governor of Egypt, rebelled against the central government, and his forces under the command of his son Ibrahim were approaching the capital, France acted as a mediator, disturbed by the fact that the Ottomans had requested help from the Russian czar to defend the capital. On one hand, France ensured the territorial integrity of the Ottoman Empire, although not as enthusiastically as Britain did, while on the other, it established amicable relations with Mehmed Ali and later with his descendants.

In the CRIMEAN WAR of 1853–56 France fought alongside Britain and the Ottomans against Russia. The war ended in a humiliating defeat for Russia, now discontented with the concert of Europe established by the Congress of Vienna. The rise of Otto von Bismarck's Prussia in the 1860s as a major power, and the German unification that followed, further upset the balance of power. In this context, the French emperor Napoleon III (r. 1852–70), in an effort to revise the unfavorable balance of power established by the Congress of Vienna in 1815, sought a closer relationship with Russia. As a result of this, relations between the Ottoman Empire and France worsened.

By that time Ottoman rule was so tenuous that Christian powers began to exert their diplomatic weight in religious disputes between the subjects of the Ottoman Empire. Russia acted as the protector of the Orthodox Christians, while France did the same for the Catholics. France pressured the Ottoman government to improve conditions for Catholics in the region and supported the Catholic Maronites in the civil war that broke out in LEBANON to the extent that French contingents were sent to the region. France also expanded into NORTH AFRICA by invading ALGIERS in 1830 and TUNIS in 1881, both territories that were nominally under Ottoman suzerainty. Even though the Ottoman government resented these actions, it was helpless to stop them.

After France's defeat in the Franco-Prussian War of 1870, Bismarck ensured France's diplomatic isolation; France further lost interest in the preservation of the status quo in Europe, and thus in protecting the territorial integrity of the Ottoman Empire. Henceforth, the Ottoman Empire's fate was decided by the balance of power largely put in place by Bismarck, including the Triple Alliance of 1882 between Germany, Austria, and Italy, which rendered France unable to maneuver diplomatically in the region. After the fall of Bismarck in 1890 and as a result of the aggressive policies of the young Kaiser Wilhelm II (r. 1888–1918), Europe was divided into two camps: the Triple Entente, a military alliance formed in 1907 between France, Russia, and England; and the Central Powers, an alliance between Germany and the Austro-Hungarian Empire. Since France and England were allied with Russia, the pro-German Ottoman government decided that Russia's expansionist policies could only be checked by the Central Powers; thus it allied with Germany and Austria.

World War I resulted in the total collapse of the Ottoman Empire, while victorious France enjoyed favorable terms in the treaty by which it acquired Cilicia, southeastern Anatolia, and Syria, establishing joint control (with England) of the Ottoman capital. A new state

arose in Anatolia (*see* TURKEY) as a result of the War of National Liberation, and the last Ottoman emperor fled the capital in 1922. The new government in Ankara would eventually retrieve some of the territories ceded to France by the Ottomans as a result of the 1921 Treaty of Ankara.

MUTUAL CULTURAL INFLUENCES

The Ottoman Empire and France greatly influenced each other culturally. French cultural influence was evident in the Ottoman Empire as early as the first half of the 18th century. In this period of Ottoman history, known as the Tulip Era (1718–30), Ottoman interest in the Western world grew tremendously and France served as a model for the elites of the Ottoman Empire. In the popular travel accounts (*sefaretname*) of the Ottoman ambassadors to France, there were details not only about government, military, and technology, but also about the arts, culture, daily life, architecture, manners, and fashions of the French.

The Ottoman military reforms of the 18th and 19th centuries were dominated by French experts and French books were included in the curriculum of the newly established military schools, where French was taught as a foreign language. Students were sent to Paris to further improve their language skills. French influence further expanded with the establishment of the educational reform during which modern institutions of education on European—primarily French—models were introduced (*see* EDUCATION). French influence over this reform period was ubiquitous. No other European culture had as much impact in such diverse areas as government structure, the legal system, clothing, the press, the financial system, daily life, the arts, and culture.

French philosophers of the Enlightenment such as Jean-Jacques Rousseau and Charles de Secondat Montesquieu were influential in the formation of concepts such as liberty and democracy among Ottoman intellectuals. In fact, reformist Ottoman intellectuals often decided to settle in Paris after being exiled from their country; some of the young Ottomans even fought in the French army against the Prussians in 1870 and helped establish the revolutionary government called the Paris Commune during that war.

The large Ottoman community in France in turn influenced French culture. Christian and Jewish subjects of the sultan and Muslim galley slaves in French port cities, especially in Marseilles, also played an intermediary role in the transfer of culture. Furthermore, visits by Ottoman ambassadors created interest in Ottoman culture for the French public. The diplomatic visit of the Ottoman ambassador in 1669 started a fashion among the French elite for what they called *turquerie*, or things in the Turkish style. Lastly, the French themselves helped increase this cultural influence thanks to the large number of French visitors who made firsthand observations of the Ottoman Empire while there for diplomatic and commercial dealings, missionary activities, or as returning freed slaves. Many of these accounts were published and whetted the French reading public's appetite for learning more about Turkish culture.

Emrah Safa Gürkan

Further reading: Halil İnalcık, *Turkey and Europe in History* (İstanbul: Eren, 2006); Stanford J. Shaw and Ezel K. Shaw, *History of the Ottoman Empire and Modern Turkey*, 2 vols. (Cambridge: Cambridge University Press, 1976); M. S. Anderson, *The Eastern Question, 1774–1923* (New York: St. Martin's, 1966), Bernard Lewis, *The Emergence of Modern Turkey* (London: Oxford University Press, 1961); George F. Abbott, *Turkey, Greece and the Great Powers* (London: Robert Scott, 1916).

Fuad Pasha (Keçecizade Mehmed) (b. 1815–d. 1869) *Ottoman grand vizier* Born in Istanbul, the son of Hibetullah Hanım and the renowned poet Izzet Molla, Fuad Pasha was one of the most important statesmen of the Tanzimat or Ottoman reform era. He played an important role in the establishment of a new provincial organization, the Council of State (Şura-yı Devlet) and in legal arrangements that granted foreigners property rights in the empire. He served on the Council of Tanzimat (Meclis-i Tanzimat) and the Supreme Council for Judicial Ordinances (Meclis-i Vala-yı Ahkam-ı Adliye), supervising and determining the direction of reforms. Fuad Pasha and his closest colleague, Mehmed Emin Âlî Pasha, continued the Tanzimat reforms of Reşid Pasha and authored the Reform Decree of 1856. Fuad Pasha was also a member of the Ottoman Academy of Sciences (Encümen-i Daniş) and compiled, with Cevdet Pasha, a grammar book of Ottoman Turkish (*Kavaid-i Osmaniye*) and the Regulations of Şirket-i Hayriyye.

Fuad studied at a madrasa until the age of 14, when he was forced to quit because of his father's exile to Sivas in Central Anatolia. During his father's absence, Mehmed Fuad, financed by a small allowance, transferred to the Medical School to study French.

Upon graduation, Fuad entered the Ottoman military and served in Tripoli as a doctor with the rank of captain. After completing his service in 1837, Mehmed Fuad returned to Istanbul and, with the encouragement of Tanzimat reform pioneer Mustafa Reşid Pasha,

became an interpreter for the Sublime Porte in the Translation Bureau. Fuad became head interpreter in 1839. He subsequently served as first secretary of the London Embassy, temporary envoy on a special mission to Spain and Portugal, and interpreter of the Imperial Council (Divan-ı Hümayun). Then, in 1847, he was appointed to the highly prestigious post of *amedci,* one of the assistants of the Reisülküttab (head of the Ottoman chancery with responsibility for foreign affairs).

The question of the refugees, which emerged after the 1848 European revolution as thousands of Polish and Hungarian refugees fled to the Ottoman Empire, provided Mehmed Fuad with an opportunity to prove his diplomatic skills. He met with the czar of Russia on behalf of the Ottoman State and played a crucial role in solving the problem amicably. He was awarded the Order of Privilege (Nişan-ı Imtiyaz) for his role by the Ottoman sultan and appointed undersecretary of the grand vizier. After a special mission to Egypt in 1850, Mehmed Fuad was appointed foreign minister in 1852; he would serve in this post five times before his death. He also served twice as grand vizier and was named lieutenant of the grand vizier and commander-in-chief. He played an active role in all the important political, religious, and international events of his period: the "question of holy places" in Jerusalem, the Crimean War, the Reform Decree of 1856, the crisis of Lebanon, and the paper money crisis. He accompanied Sultan Abdülaziz (r. 1861–76) on visits to Egypt in 1863 and Europe in 1867. Fuad Pasha obtained the special favor of Sultan Abdülaziz and was the first recipient of the title of aide-de-camp to the sultan. He was also honored by the French government with a first-degree order of the Légion d'Honneur.

Fuad Pasha died on February 12, 1869 in Nice, France, where he had gone to rest on his doctor's advice after suffering from heart disease. His body was brought back to Istanbul for burial.

Fuad Pasha was one of the most brilliant statesmen of his age. Throughout his political life, he strove to preserve the empire through reform and diplomacy.

Ö. Faruk Bölükbaşı

See also Âlî Pasha, Mehmed Emin; Mustafa Reşid Pasha.

Further reading: Roderic H. Davison, *Reform in the Ottoman Empire, 1856–1876* (Princeton, N.J.: Princeton University Press, 1963); Roderic H. Davison, *Nineteenth Century Ottoman Diplomacy and Reforms* (Istanbul: Isis, 1999).

G

Galata (Pera; Sykai) Galata is a district located north of the city of Istanbul (formerly Constantinople), across the inlet of the Bosporus, called the Golden Horn. Known as Sykai (Greek "the figs") in the first century B.C.E., probably due to its rural character, the area was incorporated into the city of Constantinople in the fifth century C.E. and was renamed Justinianopolis under Emperor Justinian (r. 528–58). The name Galata is evident from the end of the sixth century with the construction, around 580, of the Castle of Galata. In the early eighth century a chain was drawn from the castle across the Golden Horn, protecting the harbor from potential attacks. There is no consensus as to the derivation of the name. Some link it to the Greek word *galaktos* (milk), due to the presence of dairy farms in the area; some argue that it derives from the Italian *calata* (stairs, steps), a possible reference to the steep hill on which Galata is set; yet another view claims that the name comes from the presence of the Galatians (Gauls), who stormed the city in 279 B.C.E. This district across the Golden Horn was also often referred to as Pera, from the Greek *peran* (across).

The development of Galata really started with its settlement by the Genoese, following the Venetian-led Fourth Crusade of 1204. In 1303 the Genoese obtained the privilege of building a wall around their thriving commercial colony, which they enlarged in successive steps until the mid-15th century. The walled Genoese city was crowned by the Tower of Christ (1348), which still stands today as the major landmark of the district. Dissociating themselves from the doomed capital of the Byzantine Empire, the Genoese surrendered the keys of their city to Sultan Mehmed II (r. 1444–46; 1451–81) upon the Ottoman conquest of Constantinople in 1453,

and were rewarded with a peaceful integration of Galata into the new Ottoman capital as one of its four districts.

The Galata tower was built as part of the 14th-century fortifications of Galata. It remained a landmark of the quarter under the Ottomans. *(Photo by Gábor Ágoston).*

Galata was founded as a Genoese trading colony on the northern shore of the Golden Horn opposite Byzantine Constantinople. In the Ottoman period it lost its specifically Genoese character but remained a preferred quarter for European residents of the city. *(Photo by Gábor Ágoston)*

Under Ottoman rule, Galata was viewed as having a Western character, a view confirmed by the gradual move of foreign embassies into the district, the settlement of foreign traders (including Venetians, French, English, and Dutch), the preservation of a number of Latin churches, and the dedication of its port to Western trade. But this appearance masked the fact that, since the conquest, a growing number of churches were converted into mosques, large numbers of Muslims were settling in the western and eastern quarters of the district, and neighborhoods were developing around Galata, near the arsenal and the cannon foundry. By the end of the 17th century, although both Western and local observers continued to stress its "infidel" or non-Muslim character, Galata had in fact become a rather typical Ottoman town. Feeling squeezed in overcrowded Galata, the richest among the foreign merchants started moving up the hill, toward Pera, forming the nucleus of what would become the westernized res-

idential district of Pera (Beyoğlu in Turkish) in the following centuries.

The second half of the 18th century, however, was marked by a reversal of this trend. As European—especially French—influence grew stronger, Galata and its northern neighborhood of Pera started to attract growing numbers of local non-Muslims seeking the protection and security of the embassies and the benefits of foreign CAPITULATIONS. By the mid-19th century, the whole area had started to take the lead in the process of westernization that swept the empire. A growing local non-Muslim bourgeoisie, primarily foreign diplomats and European traders, came to dominate the scene in this outpost of Western capitalism and culture. Innovations begun in the 19th century changed the outlook and organization of the district. These included bridges built across the Golden Horn in 1836 and 1845; the beginning of a stock exchange in 1852; the founding of the empire's first municipal organization in 1857; the tearing down of the medieval walls in 1864; and the introduction of streetcars (1871), an underground railroad (1875), and modern quays (1892). These completely transformed the area, turning it into a paragon of modernity.

The process of modernization brought about a division of labor between the two districts. Galata thrived on the activity of the port and on modern businesses, such as banks, insurance companies, lawyers, and the import/export trade, while Pera's high street, the Grand'rue de Péra, became the westernized residential and entertainment district of the city, with high-rise apartments, hotels, theaters, and bars. Along with these social and cultural changes, the demographic of the area changed as most remaining Muslim residents left, to be replaced by a growing concentration of Greeks, Armenians, JEWS, and other foreigners.

Edhem Eldem

Further reading: Halil İnalcık, "Ottoman Galata, 1453–1553," in *Première Rencontre Internationale sur l'Empire Ottoman et la Turquie Moderne,* edited by Edhem Eldem, (Istanbul and Paris: Isis, 1991), 17–105; L. Mitler, "The Genoese in Galata: 1453–1682." *International Journal of Middle East Studies* 10 (1979): 71–91; John Freely, *Galata: A Guide to Istanbul's Old Genoese Quarter* (Istanbul: Archaeology and Art Publications, 2000); Edhem Eldem, "The Ethnic Structure of Galata." *Biannual Istanbul* 1 (1993): 28–33.

Galatasaray Imperial Lycée   *See* EDUCATION.

Gaza (*Ar.*: Ghazza; *Heb.*: Gaza; *Turk.*: Gazze)   A port city located on the eastern shore of the Mediterranean Sea, Gaza was the chief port of the region that today comprises Israel and the Palestinian Territories. In the early centuries of Ottoman rule, it was a major commercial center, serving the overland CARAVAN route between SYRIA and EGYPT. It was also an important stopping place for the annual HAJJ caravan from Egypt. In times when BEDOUIN raids made the interior pilgrims' route from DAMASCUS, the Sultan's Road, impassable, pilgrims from Damascus would take a coastal route to Gaza; there they would meet up with pilgrims from Egypt and proceed together to MECCA.

For most of the Ottoman period, Gaza was the capital of a *sancak* (subprovince) under the authority of the governor in Damascus. Typically the *sancak* governor was from the MAMLUK household of Ridwan, which closely resembled the elite Mamluk households that were emerging in Egypt at this time. Members of the Ridwan household were also active in the politics of the neighboring district of JERUSALEM. Under their patronage, Gaza became a center for Islamic learning, attracting scholars from throughout Palestine and southern Syria.

The fortunes of Gaza began to decline in the 18th century as smaller towns, such as Jaffa and ACRE, grew into important ports. Although Gaza retained its importance as a way station for the caravans between Egypt and Syria, the weakening of the central state meant that the governors of Gaza had fewer resources at their disposal to halt the increasingly aggressive Bedouin raids. Gaza's population began to decline. Ottoman reports from the second half of the 18th century describe abandoned villages along the Mediterranean coastal plain of the province. While Gaza's role as a gateway to Syria helped it to flourish commercially, it also meant that it became a staging point for armies coming from Egypt that sought to conquer Syria. Muhammad Abu al-Dhahab (1770), NAPOLEON BONAPARTE (1799), and IBRAHIM PASHA (1831) all besieged Gaza on their way north. The last invader was the British General Allenby who, having tried unsuccessfully several times, finally captured the city in 1917 during Britain's campaign against the Ottoman Empire at the end of World War I.

Bruce Masters

Further reading: Amnon Cohen, *Palestine in the 18th Century: Patterns of Government and Administration* (Jerusalem: Magnes, 1973).

gazi   *See* GHAZA.

Germany   Germany only became a unified state in 1871, but relations between the Ottoman sultanate and various German principalities date back to the 15th century. German-Ottoman relations in the modern era took place primarily within the context of the Great Powers, a term coined in 1814 to identify the nations of western Europe and RUSSIA that dominated international politics with their strong militaries and expanding industrial economies. One of the most important early areas of contact between the Ottomans and Germans was through the Prussian military, and military ties were the most enduring aspect of German-Ottoman relations throughout most of the 19th century; however, by the early 20th century, increasing commercial penetration by German banking and trade complicated German-Ottoman relations.

EARLY CONTACT WITH THE PRUSSIAN MILITARY

It has been reported that Frederick II of Prussia offered the Ottomans a military alliance in 1760, but the first official military exchange took place in 1789, when SELIM III (r. 1789–1807) asked a Prussian officer to inspect the Ottoman army. By that time, there was already a long history of ex-soldiers and adventurers from Europe serving in the Ottoman military as mercenaries and technical advisors—some even rising to important positions. In the late 18th century, Ottoman officials began to see the importance of a complete reorganization of the army along European lines. In 1835, among the reforms that were being introduced by Sultan MAHMUD II (r. 1808–39), Prussia was again asked to lend military expertise, and Helmuth von Moltke, a young Prussian officer, was sent to act as an advisor to the Ottoman military. In 1836 the Ottomans requested and received an additional contingent of military advisors, but the mission was terminated in 1839 upon Mahmud's death. Nevertheless, this exchange established a precedent of active Prussian soldiers serving as military advisors to the Ottoman government. A handful of Prussian soldiers remained after 1839, although they were relieved of duty in the Prussian army.

The 1871 unification of German territories under Prussian leadership signaled a shift in the European balance of power that shaped future interactions between Germans and the Ottoman Empire. The defeat of the French army during the Franco-Prussian War (1870–71) created a powerful new nation in Imperial Germany, a federal state composed of many German principalities. The chancellor and foreign minister of this new Imperial Germany, Otto von Bismarck (in office 1871–90), pursued a conservative foreign policy that aimed at consolidation and at assuring other powers that Germany did not seek further territorial gains. This conservatism manifested itself in Bismarck's reluctance to alter the status quo in the Ottoman Empire, whose gradual loss of territorial integrity presented problems to the balance of power in Europe and created the so-called EASTERN QUESTION, as territory lost by the Ottomans created rivalries between European powers.

Germany sought to maintain, or at least minimize, changes to the territorial integrity of the Ottoman lands, because such changes would only benefit other states. In 1874 the German representative to the Ottoman government was raised to the rank of embassy, a move that signaled the importance of the Ottoman Empire and the Eastern Question to German foreign policy. The Congress of Berlin in 1878 symbolized Germany's self-perceived role as an "honest broker"; presided over by Bismarck, the Congress nullified many of Russia's gains during the Russo-Ottoman War and sought to balance the interests of Great Britain and Austria-Hungary.

The Russian victory in this war was a debacle for the Ottoman military and for reform in the empire. The Ottoman state almost collapsed as direct result of the war and was only able to survive because of British support. With the emergence of Imperial Germany, Sultan ABDÜLHAMID II (r. 1876–1909) began to see a possible ally in the young nation that had routed the French army and had sought relatively equitable terms for the Ottoman state at Berlin in 1878. Europe's leading army

was now the Prussian military combined with the royal contingents of smaller German states such as Bavaria, Saxony, and Württemberg. Bismarck was initially reluctant to provide direct assistance to the Ottomans, but he began to see the value of active support for the Ottoman Empire as the antagonism between Austria-Hungary and RUSSIA over the Balkans grew worse. A robust Ottoman army might deflect a Russian engagement with Austria-Hungary from the German border, an important consideration as Germany became increasingly tied to the maintenance of the Habsburg monarchy and the Austro-Hungarian Empire.

In 1880 Bismarck offered Prussian officers to the Ottoman government for the purpose of military reform, and in 1882 sent four officers to Istanbul. A year later Colmar von der Goltz, who became an important actor in both official and unofficial relations between Germany and the Ottoman Empire, came as a military instructor to the Ottoman military academy. Goltz was an accomplished theoretician and scholar of military affairs whose long service (1883–95) at the Sublime Porte and whose knowledge of the Turkish language gave him an unparalleled insight into Ottoman affairs. His role as an instructor brought him into contact with a younger generation of officers, who would later prove useful to Germany after the Young Turk Revolution of 1908 (see YOUNG TURKS). Throughout the 1890s and early 1900s, young Ottoman lieutenants were seconded to German regiments for training. A network of Ottoman officers with experience in Germany helped solidify military and commercial relations between the two countries, as the Ottomans increasingly bought military equipment and armaments from Germany.

The Ottoman interest in a German military mission must also be viewed against the backdrop of the Eastern Question and the Great Power rivalry for dominance over the Ottoman Empire. The encroachment of Western states into Ottoman affairs was a centuries-long process that had pitted European powers against one another. In the latter half of the 19th century this rivalry was largely between Great Britain and Russia as Britain attempted to maintain Ottoman rule, fearing Russian dominance of the BLACK SEA and the threat this would pose to British commercial interests. However, as the Ottoman state grew indebted to British and French financial aid and the British pressed for internal Ottoman reform, Britain's support became burdensome. The Ottomans grew weary of waning British support and were sensitive to the criticisms of their domestic policies. Germany was a logical choice as an ally, especially in light of French and British actions to take control of former Ottoman territory in NORTH AFRICA and EGYPT.

The German military mission of 1882, while an important aspect of the growing ties between Imperial

Germany and the Ottoman Empire, was only one component. A Prussian consulate opened in JERUSALEM in 1842 and soon became an important institution in PALESTINE for the local Jewish community and for the Templars, a group of German religious dissidents who settled in the Holy Land between 1868 and 1875. Christian missionaries, both Protestant and Catholic, established schools, orphanages, dispensaries, and hospitals in the Holy Land and in other parts of the empire. In the 1890s, the emergence of the Zionist movement among German-speaking Jews helped establish additional German organizations in the Holy Land, such as the World Zionist Organization and later the *Hilfsverein der deutschen Juden* (Aid Association of German Jews), which disseminated German language, culture, and propaganda, as well as assisting Jewish settlement.

German interests in trade and foreign investment also grew steadily in the last quarter of the 19th century. The foundation for German commercial relations with the Ottoman Empire was the 1862 treaty between the German *Zollverein* (Customs Union) and the Ottoman Empire, which was extended to the German Empire after 1871. This treaty regulated customs duties and was open to revision every seven years. The most important component of the German-Ottoman economic relationship in the 1870s and 1880s was the Ottoman bond market and the restructuring of the Ottoman debt. The Ottoman state amassed huge public debts to European investors after the CRIMEAN WAR (1853–56) and in 1875 defaulted on many of its loans. An 1882 agreement established the Ottoman Public Debt Administration (*see* DEBT AND PUBLIC DEBT ADMINISTRATION) and created a supervisory committee to the Ottoman Ministry of Finance, which was made up of delegates from the European creditor nations. German investment was only 5 percent of the total, but Germany was granted a representative on the committee in the spirit of the European balance of power. Germany also gained control of the Ottoman tobacco monopoly and access to its revenues. Both the debt administration and the tabacco monopoly were managed by Bismarck's personal banker, Gerson Bleichröder. However, this arrangement led to friction within the wider German banking community, as businessmen and bankers fought for influence on the financing and construction of railroads in Ottoman territory.

WILHELMINE GERMANY AND THE OTTOMAN EMPIRE

When German Emperor William II forced Bismarck to resign in 1890, Germany embarked on a new course, abandoning Bismarck's conservative policy and becoming more aggressive in claiming Germany's role as a world power. William II, who came to power in 1888, was personally fascinated by the Ottoman Empire, and

was more active in policy matters than his predecessors. He began his reign with a high-profile trip to Istanbul in 1889. A second trip to the Ottoman lands in 1898 earned him the suspicion of the European powers, since he proclaimed himself friend to the world's 300 million Muslims (many of whom were under British, Russian, or French rule) and since his trip closely followed the massacres of Armenian Christians in 1896. Beyond such gestures, German policy toward the Ottoman Empire consisted largely of protecting German investment and trade interests. German banks established branch offices in Ottoman territory, and the Deutsche Bank was one of the main agents financing the construction of RAILROADS in Anatolia. Concessions from the Ottoman state in 1888 helped a German-led syndicate build a railway from the Bosporus to Angora (present-day Ankara) in 1892 and a second line to Konya four years later. Under German management as the Société du Chemin de Fer Ottoman d'Anatolie, the syndicate obtained additional concessions in 1899 and 1903 to extend the Konya line through MOSUL to BAGHDAD. British protests kept the project from reaching the port of BASRA, which the British controlled. Most Anatolian railway projects also depended upon German equipment. The HEJAZ RAILROAD, between DAMASCUS and MEDINA, used German rolling stock exclusively. German engineers, technicians, and other experts were also helping modernize Ottoman agriculture and infrastructure through bridges, roads, canals, and ports.

The construction of railroads in Anatolia was the most controversial aspect of the growing ties between Germany and the Ottoman Empire. The rivalry for influence in the Ottoman Empire had long been dominated by FRANCE and ENGLAND, which were genuinely alarmed by Germany's growing economic strength and its penetration of Anatolia through the construction of railroads. Russia saw the modernization of Ottoman infrastructure primarily as a military threat, because a modern rail system in the Ottoman domains made mass mobilization of troops more effective. Despite these concerns, before WORLD WAR I, Germany's position in the Ottoman Empire was far from dominant. It lagged behind Great Britain, France, and Austria-Hungary in terms of trade, and German shipyards sold far fewer naval vessels to the Ottoman state than did the British or French.

Relations between Germany and the Ottoman Empire entered a period of uncertainty after the Young Turk Revolution of 1908, when a rebellion of young Ottoman military officers ousted the regime of Abdülhamid II. Kaiser William II had developed friendly relations with Abdülhamid II, whose approval was needed for railway concessions and armament contracts. This proximity to the sultan, whom the Young Turks held responsible for the empire's problems, and the Austrian annexation of Bosnia and Herzegovina led to mistrust between Germany and the empire's new rulers. Diplomatic maneuvering to support Ottoman interests in the Balkans, coupled with a counterrevolution and a new sultan, brought about a friendlier attitude toward Germany. In 1909, Colmar von der Goltz was invited back to Istanbul as an army inspector, and the reform of the Ottoman military was given greater priority.

The first Balkan War in 1912 (*see* Balkan wars) was a disaster for the Ottoman army and the German project of military reform. A coup in 1913 brought a more militant group of Young Turks to power who resumed hostilities in the Balkans but were soundly defeated. This resulted in the expulsion from southeastern Europe of the Ottomans and hundreds of thousands of Muslims. In the same year, a larger Germany military mission arrived, headed by General Liman von Sanders; it grew during World War I to several hundred men.

Despite high-ranking proponents of intervention such as Enver Pasha, the minister of defense, the Ottomans were reluctant to join the Central Powers at war. A secret alliance treaty between Germany and the Ottoman Empire was signed in August 1914, and the Ottoman Empire entered the war in October, albeit with reservations. The head of the German military mission was given influence over military planning, although Ottoman officials largely ignored German strategic advice throughout the war. The deportation and murder of Armenians was also carried out largely without German help. Cooperation took place only when the Ottoman command found it convenient or necessary. German officers in the field fared better, often commanding regiments or divisions and taking part in some important campaigns. Yet the Ottoman army was strained by material privations and a disorganized mobilization; German supplies began to arrive only at the end of 1915. Ottoman forces won some key battles, notably those of Gallipoli and Kut el Amara, but they lost the war. Defeat cost both Germany and the Ottomans dearly, as both empires collapsed in 1918. Political infighting among the successors to the Ottoman state and the occupation of Istanbul by the Allies severed formal ties between the two states until 1924.

German-Ottoman relations were beset by miscalculations on both sides. The Ottomans overestimated the value of a German partnership, which brought the country into World War I, while the Germans deceived themselves into thinking that the Ottoman Empire would be a pliant junior partner that could help it defeat Russia. In all events, relations between the Ottoman Empire and Imperial Germany were multifaceted and often contradictory. The Bismarckian policy of conservatism was itself full of contradiction as it sought to maintain the Ottoman order but was willing to sacrifice it to defeat Russia and placate Austria-Hungary. German disinclina-

tion to control Ottoman territory was at odds with the growing pressure from ultra-nationalists to make Germany an imperial or colonial power. By the same token, the Ottoman strategy of using limited German involvement to buffer the influence of the other Great Powers became increasingly difficult to square with the hope that, with more German support, the Ottomans could modernize their society on the German model. In the end, both empires succumbed to the destructive consequences of a devastating world war.

The common experiences during the World War I led the successor states of both empires to extended relations in the postwar period. The modern Turkish republic stayed out of World War II, but it became a haven for many German politicians and intellectuals fleeing Nazi persecution. In the post-1945 era, a significant aspect of the Turkish-German relationship has been the number of Turkish citizens who have emigrated to the German Federal Republic in search of employment opportunities. This has created a lasting dynamic that continues to influence the relations between the two countries.

Steven Chase Gummer

Further reading: Ulrich Trumpener, "Germany and the End of the Ottoman Empire," in *The Great Powers and the End of the Ottoman Empire,* edited by Marian Kent (London: G. Allen & Unwin, 1984); Edward Mead Earle, *Turkey, the Great Powers and the Baghdad Railway: A Study in Imperialism* (New York: Russell & Russell, 1966); Wolfgang G. Schwanitz, ed., *Germany and the Middle East, 1871–1945* (Princeton, N.J.: Markus Wiener, 2004).

ghaza (*gaza*)   In recent times, the word *ghaza* has been understood in the West as meaning "Holy War against the infidels" and as referring to religiously inspired military actions taken by the early Ottomans against their Christian neighbors. Despite being commonly used in this way, however, the meaning of this term has come to be widely contested by scholars. The early Ottoman military activity described as *ghaza* is now thought to have been a much more fluid undertaking, sometimes referring to actions that were nothing more than raids, sometimes meaning a deliberate holy war, but most often combining a mixture of these elements.

The terms *ghaza* and *ghazi* (*gazi*) were popularized in the West by historian and Turkologist Paul Wittek's seminal *The Rise of the Ottoman Empire* (1938), from which generations of students of the Ottoman Empire came to interpret the word *ghaza* as "Holy War" and *ghazi* as "Muslim warriors." Wittek's 20th-century reading of *ghaza* adopts the view of the late 14th-century Ottoman chronicler, Ahmedi. Ahmedi's *History of the Ottoman Kings* (1390) defined and explained *ghaza* according to the sharia (Islamic canon law) and transformed the early raiders, known in contemporary sources as *akıncıs* (raiders), into *ghazis*, or holy warriors, deploring all those who pursued *ghaza* for booty. By the reign of Sultan BAYEZID II (r. 1481–1512), Ahmedi's view had become the official version of the early Ottoman raids and campaigns.

Other Ottoman chroniclers present a rather different view of the terms. Aşıkpaşazade (1484) and Oruç (c. 1500), who in the latter part of the 15th century lived among the *akıncıs* or frontier warriors of Ottoman Europe, also portrayed the early Ottoman sultans as *ghazi*-heroes. However, in their works, the Arabic *ghaza* (holy war) and the Turkish *akın* (raid, without any religious connotation) appear as interchangeable terms. These texts not only reflect the reality along the empire's 15th century European frontiers, they are also closer to the nature of the early Ottoman military ventures which were often no more than pure raids without any religious motivation.

Recent scholarship also shows that many of the early *ghazas* of the Ottomans were in fact predatory raids, directed against both Muslim and non-Muslim neighbors. In these raids Muslims and Christians often joined forces and shared in the booty. Indeed, the history of conflicts in western Anatolia and the Balkans in the early decades of the 14th century offers numerous examples of temporary alliances and joint military undertakings between the various Muslim-Turkic principalities or *beyliks* (see ANATOLIAN EMIRATES) and their Christian adversaries (Catalans, Byzantines, and Genoese). Between 1303 and 1307 Catholic Catalan mercenaries, who originally arrived in Asia Minor to fight against various Turkic forces, fought both against and alongside Muslim Turks and habitually raided the frontier of the rival Orthodox Christian BYZANTINE EMPIRE. In fact it was in 1305 that Turks from Asia Minor first crossed to Europe as auxiliary forces in Catalan service. Also in 1305, a detachment of Catalan mercenaries joined the Ottomans.

Similarly, as has been pointed out by historian Heath Lowry, the closest comrades and fellow-fighters of the first two Ottoman rulers, OSMAN GHAZI (d. 1324) and ORHAN I (r. 1324–62), included several Orthodox Christian Greeks and recent Christian converts to Islam. Köse (the beardless) Mihal first fought at the side of Osman Ghazi as a Greek Christian, later converted to Islam, and in 1326, as an Ottoman commander, negotiated the surrender of Byzantine BURSA with the Byzantine emperor's chief minister, Saroz (who after the surrender also sided with the Ottomans). Ghazi Evrenos Bey, another famous Ottoman commander, was a converted Muslim of perhaps Aragonese or Catalan origin. The descendants of Köse Mihal and Ghazi Evrenos, the Mihaloğulları and Evrenosoğulları, represent the two best-known families of the 15th-century Ottoman frontier warrior nobility.

However, this does not mean that the Turks of western Anatolia did not go willingly to war against their Christian neighbors to seek booty and glory alike. A 14th-century text on the meaning and ways of *ghaza* (*Hikayet-i Gazi*), probably composed in the Karasi principality in northwestern Anatolia, demonstrates that the spirit of the holy war was very much alive on the Turco-Byzantine frontier. Located in the vicinity of Byzantium, the capital of the Byzantine Empire and the seat of eastern Christianity, the Ottoman Turks were strategically positioned to wage war against the Christian "infidels," and the Ottoman principality served as a magnet for the mighty warriors of the neighboring Turco-Muslim emirates. However, the nature of these early raids and campaigns was complex, and the ideology of the *ghaza* was only one factor.

The 14th century also witnessed Ottoman campaigns against fellow Turks and Muslims, as well as the subjugation and annexation of the neighboring Turkic emirates (Karasi, Saruhan, Germiyan, and Hamid) by the Ottomans. In accordance with their portrayal of the early Ottomans as *ghazi*-warriors, 15th-century Ottoman chroniclers often ignored these conflicts (along with the Ottomans' alliances with Christians), claiming that the Ottomans acquired the territories of the neighboring Turkic principalities through peaceful means (purchase and/or marriage). When they did mention the wars between the Ottomans and their Turkic and Muslim neighbors, Ottoman chroniclers tried to legitimize these conquests by claiming that the Ottomans either acted in self-defense or were forced to fight because the hostile policies of these Turkic principalities hindered the Ottomans' holy wars against the infidels.

Gábor Ágoston

Further reading: Pál Fodor, "Ahmedi's Dasitan as a Source of Early Ottoman History." *Acta Orientalia Academiae Scientiarum Hungaricae* 38 (1984): 41–54; Colin Imber, "What Does Ghazi Actually Mean?" in *The Balance of Truth: Essays in Honour of Professor Geoffrey Lewis*, edited by Çiğdem Balım and Colin Imber (Istanbul: Isis, 2000): 165–178; Cemal Kafadar, *Between Two Worlds: The Construction of the Ottoman State* (Berkeley and Los Angeles: University of California Press, 1995); Heath W. Lowry, *The Nature of the Early Ottoman State* (Albany: State University of New York Press, 2003); Orlin Sabev, "The Legend of Köse Mihal: Additional Notes." *Turcica* 34 (2002): 241–252; Kamal Sılay, "Ahmedi's History of the Ottoman Dynasty." *Journal of Turkish Studies* 16 (1992): 129–200; E. Zachariadou, ed., *The Ottoman Emirate, 1300–1389* (Rethymnon: Crete University Press, 1993).

ghazi See GHAZA.

Gökalp, Ziya (1876–1924) *Turkish sociologist and nationalist, prominent member of the Committee of Union* *and Progress* Ziya Gökalp was one of the most prominent Turkish political thinkers of the 20th century. He was born in Diyarbakır (in southeastern Anatolia, Turkey) on March 23, 1876. After graduating from the Askeri Rüştiye (Military Junior High School) in 1890, Gökalp entered the Mülki İdadiye (State Senior High School). His father blended in his son's education modern western and traditional Islamic values. His uncle taught him Arabic and Persian and acquainted him with the works of Islamic philosophers such as Ghazali, Avicenna, Farabi, Ibn Rushd, and the mystics Ibn al-Arabi and Mawlana Jalal al-Din Rumi. In this period, Gökalp was also introduced to Abdullah Cevdet, one of the founders of the COMMITTEE OF UNION AND PROGRESS (CUP), the reform-minded Ottoman political group that opposed the policies of Sultan ABDÜLHAMID II (r. 1876–1909). Cevdet also introduced him to the works of European organicist sociology (a philosophical direction that draws parallels between social institutions and organisms) and materialist philosophy (Herbert Spencer, Gustave Le Bon, Ernst Haeckel, and Ludwig Buechner).

Ziya moved to Istanbul in 1896 to study at the Baytar Mektebi (Veterinery College). He offically entered the CUP and accelerated his political efforts. But his revolutionary activities could not for long remain hidden from Abdülhamid II's efficent secret police. He was expelled from the college and was arrested (ca. 1898), and was sent back to Diyarbakır.

In 1908 Gökalp established the Diyarbakır office of the CUP and was elected to the CUP's central executive committee. In 1909 he went to Salonika where he organized various cultural activities and conferences. He established a library and, from 1910 to 1912, taught sociology in a secondary school there. In 1912, he returned to Istanbul. Exiled to Malta in 1919 by the British occupation, he returned to the newly forming Republic of Turkey in 1921. Under the new republican government, Gökalp was appointed chief of the Council of Compilation and Translation (Telif ve Tercüme Encümeni) and was elected as a member of parliament for Diyarbakır in 1923.

Gökalp was concerned in publishing in every period of his life, publishing local newspapers such as *Diyarbakı* and *Peyam* and magazines such as *Küçük Mecmua, Genç Kalemler, Yeni Felsefe Mecmuası,* and *Türk Yurdu.* Gökalp also wrote many articles and a number of influential books, including *Türkleşmek-İslamlaşmak-Muasırlaşmak* (*Turkification-Islamization-Modernization* 1912/1918), *Türkçülüğün Esasları* (*The Foundations of Turkism,* 1923), *Türk Medeniyeti Tarihi* (*The History of Turkish Civilisation,* 1926), and *Türk Töresi* (*Turkish Customary Law,* 1922).

Although he was active politically, it is perhaps as a sociologist that Gökalp made his most enduring mark. He was the first to introduce the study of sociology into the curriculum of the *darülfünun,* or Turkish university. He set up the first sociology institute (İçtimaiyyat Darul-Mesaisi) in 1915 and published the first sociology magazine, *İçtimaiyyat,* in 1917. Heavily influenced by French sociologist Emile Durkheim, Gökalp was an early proponent of Turkish nationalism, believing that the "nation" (MILLET) was a natural social and political unit. Gökalp proposed theoretical solutions to the practical challenges faced by the unraveling Ottoman Empire. He believed that modernization could rescue Ottoman society, but he was concerned that this modernization preserve basic social integrity and solidarity. Gökalp proposed a synthesis of Islam and Turkish ethnicity that he believed would form the basis of the Turkish society of the future. His famous statement "I'm from a Turkish nation, I'm from the Islamic community, and I'm from Western civilization" expresses the essence of his thought system that is known as the *Turkification-Islamization-Modernization* trilogy.

According to Gökalp, Turkish nationalism represented a cultural ideal and a philosophy of life that constituted the basis for social solidarity and unity. According to his model, a mystical interpretation of Islam, separate from its political ideals, provided the moral basis for social solidarity; modernization, which Gökalp regarded as synonymous with the scientific, technological, and industrial developments of European capitalism, formed the practical basis for a national revival program. Gökalp separated Western civilization's cultural aspects from its technological accomplishments and called this model *içtimai mefkurecilik* (social idealism). Gökalp's early pan-Turkism and nationalistic theories were important steps in trying to reconcile modernization with traditional Islam and Turkish culture.

Ziya Gökalp died in Istanbul in 1925.

Yücel Bulut

Further reading: Taha Parla, *The Social and Political Thought of Ziya Gökalp, 1876–1924* (Leiden: Brill, 1985); Niyazi Berkes, trans. and ed., *Turkish Nationalism and Western Civilization: Selected Essays of Ziya Gökalp* (New York: Columbia University Press, 1959); Uriel Heyd, *Foundations of Turkish Nationalism: The Life and Teachings of Ziya Gökalp* (London: Luzac, 1950).

government *See* ADMINISTRATION, CENTRAL; CONSTITUTION/CONSTITUTIONAL PERIODS; GRAND VIZIER.

Grand Bazaar One of the first structures Sultan MEHMED II (r. 1444–46; 1446–51) established in 1456 in the newly conquered Constantinople was the Inner Bedestan, a secure, compact stone marketplace that began as a small structure serving the city's commercial needs and ultimately grew to become the core of the Grand Bazaar.

As the population grew and the city, renamed Istanbul, expanded, so too did the Grand Bazaar, adding layers of shops and stalls in an outward spiral from the Bedestan Just as Istanbul became the center of the vast Ottoman empire, so did its Grand Bazaar become the center of the empire's trade network.

The structure of the grand bazaar as it exists today took centuries to produce. At the heart of the bazaar are two *bedestans* (domed market halls), strategically placed at the hub of the city's commercial center and arranged to promote the migration of merchants from trade centers throughout the empire—such as Edirne, Bursa, and Ankara—to a single nucleus of trade in Istanbul. The bedestans are compact, made of stone, with thick walls and lead-encased domes. This structure served to provide secure points for trade and banking. Security was so strict, that only with an imperial *ferman,* or edict, could one enter the *bedestan* after hours. The *bedestan* served numerous additional functions, including a storage facility for valuable merchandise, a base of operations for resident merchants, a safe-deposit facility for personal valuables, and a storage facility for items held in trust. Items held in deposit were under the supervision of the *bölükbaşı,* or head of security in the Old Bedestan.

The growth of the bazaar follows a simple pattern of construction, destruction, and reconstruction. At first, the *bedestan* made up the entire bazaar, with stalls for vendors selling valuable merchandise in its interior and along its exterior. The bazaar expanded, with stalls outside the *bedestan* forming a separate but connected structure of shops for less valuable goods. There were 9,000 such shops in the 17th century. Shops, or *çarşı,* were built opposite existing stalls in a pattern of growth that created a system of concentric shop-lined streets emanating from the *bedestan.* This complex as a whole is known as the *arasta.* At first the whole structure—streets and shops—was covered with canvas, but its repeated destruction by fire eventually necessitated stone vaulting. This vast network of covered shops radiating from the *bedestan* drew merchants and multiplied in size until it formed the empire's commercial core—an exchange of materials and services for craftsmen and a market of merchants for consumers. Merchants trading along routes through Anatolia and the Balkans could sell their wares in these secure arenas or could store them before continuing on their journeys. The construction of two *bedestans* in Istanbul and of caravansaries (lodges) to house traveling caravans of merchants, demonstrates the importance of commerce to the capital and the empire.

Mehmed II built the first of the two *bedestans,* the Inner or Old Bedestan, in 1456 to spark economic development in the newly acquired imperial capital. It was soon complemented by a second *bedestan,* the Silk or Sandal Bedestan. The two were differentiated by their

The Grand Bazaar was the principle marketplace of Ottoman Istanbul. It provided safe storage for goods and money as well as commercial space in the heart of the imperial city. *(Photo by Gábor Ágoston)*

respective functions and size: The Old Bedestan had 15 domes and dealt mainly with jewelry, furs, precious textiles, and arms, while the Sandal Bedestan had 20 domes and dealt mostly in silk. This specialization would later hurt the Sandal Bedestan as the Industrial Revolution of the 19th century led to an influx of cheap goods, especially European textiles, that flooded the Ottoman market.

Istanbul's *bedestans* composed part of the imperial WAQF, or pious foundation, donated by Sultan Mehmed II for the upkeep of Istanbul's HAGIA SOPHIA Mosque complex, which included a post office, railroad station, and madrasa, as well as civic, religious, and commercial centers. These structures ensured that Ottomans of all ages, professions, and social classes could be found in and around this area, making it a busy city center. The fees generated from the *bedestans* and surrounding Bazaar provided the revenue for the maintenance of these public structures. Rents were collected, varying in amount, depending upon the demand for shop space. The value of the right to occupancy could be sold for 3,500 gold pieces, and the cost to purchase a shop in the Sandal Bedestan was as high as 21,000 gold pieces. Although the Bazaar, as an imperial *waqf*, was ultimately under the control of the sultan, a council of 12 men and two palace-appointed officials oversaw its daily administration. The council oversaw the guilds and executives, the most important of which was the *kahya,* who was responsible for the proper behavior and conduct of shopkeepers.

Today's Grand Bazaar is alive with smells, sounds, and goods from throughout the world, just as it always has been. Walking through the curving streets as you are solicited from all sides to browse each shopkeeper's wares, this structure's history is palpable. Its history has molded its traditions and its practices, its construction, its shops' dimensions and winding streets, and its people and their culture. It is both a tourist beacon and a historic treasure, with an atmosphere that is simultaneously foreign and inviting. Mehmed's Bedestan was critical to his capital's growth and it still stands today, a fitting landmark to his conquest, his vision, his empire, and his people.

Jon Gryskiewicz

Further reading: Işık Aksulu, "The Ottoman Arasta: Definition, Classification, and Conservation Problems." *EJOS, Proceedings of the 11th International Congress of Turkish Art, Utrecht, the Netherlands* IV (2001): 1–17; Çelik Gülersoy, *Story of the Grand Bazaar* (Istanbul: Istanbul Kitaplığı, 1990); Halil İnalcik, "Istanbul," in *Encyclopaedia of Islam,* edited by P. Bearman, Th. Bianquis, C. E. Bosworth, E. van Donzel, and W. P. Heinrichs. Brill, 2007. Brill Online. Online edition (by subscription), viewed 12 Sept. 2005 http://www.brillonline.nl/subscriber/entry?entry=islam_COM-0393; Halil İnalcik, "The Hub of the City: The Bedestan of Istanbul." *International Journal of Turkish Studies* 1 (1980): 1–17; Aptullah Kuran, "A Spatial Study of Three Ottoman Capitals: Bursa, Edirne, and Istanbul." *Muqarnas* 13 (1996): 114–131; Marlia M. Mango, "The Commercial Map of Constantinople." *Dumbarton Oaks Papers* 54 (2000): 189–207; M. W. Wolfe, "The Bazaar at Istanbul." *Journal of the Society of Architectural Historians* 22 (1963): 24–28.

grand vizier The grand vizier was the highest-ranking administrative officer in the Ottoman Empire, the head of the government and the absolute deputy of the sultan. By the 19th century, the office of grand vizier had become comparable with that of a prime minister in Europe. Although subservient to the sultan, who appointed the vizier and ended his term in office at his pleasure, many grand viziers managed to amass power that rivaled and at times indeed surpassed that of the sultan. From the mid-17th century on, grand viziers often ruled the empire while the sultans reigned in name only. The viziers were certainly more important than the sultans in running the empire under the capable KÖPRÜLÜ FAMILY (1656–91) or during the TANZIMAT or reform era (1839–76), though ABDÜLHAMID II (r. 1876–1909) reasserted the power of the sultan.

ORIGINS

The institution of grand vizier has its origins in that of the *wazir* of the ABBASID CALIPHATE (750–1258) and of other Islamic empires. Although several scholars have posited Persian origins for the term, the word *wazir,* meaning "helper," occurs in the Quran, as well as in early Arabic poetry. Under the Abbasid caliphs the *wazir* was initially an influential counselor to the caliph but soon evolved into the most important office-holder, the chief administrative officer of the caliphate who was considered the caliph's deputy. *Wazirs* also headed the central organ of government in other Islamic empires, including that of the SELJUKS, who served as a model for the Ottomans.

EVOLUTION

As in other Islamic empires, the first Ottoman rulers (emirs or beys) delegated some of their authorities to their *vezirs* (Turkish form of *wazir*), known in English-language literature as *viziers.* Under ORHAN GAZI (r. 1324–62), there was probably only one vizier at a time. However, when the Ottoman state expanded, the sultans appointed second and third viziers, a practice that can be seen in the first decades of the 15th century. One of these viziers was then made "first vizier" and named *vezir-i azam* or, in later centuries, *sadr-i azam,* both meaning "grand vizier."

Until 1453, most viziers and grand viziers came from the Ottoman religious establishment, the ULEMA, whose expertise in both administration and Islamic law and jurisprudence was highly valued. As in other Islamic empires, some families managed to assert great influence over the institution. For example, from 1380 to 1453, several generations of the Çandarlı family held the position of vizier or grand vizier. Their influence led to their downfall when, following the CONQUEST OF CONSTANTINOPLE in 1453, MEHMED II (r. 1444–46; 1451–81) decided to get rid of his grand vizier, Çandarlı Halil Pasha, who had opposed the conquest in fear that it might trigger an anti-Ottoman crusade. The dismissal and execution of Çandarlı Halil Pasha marked a radical change in the history of the office of grand vizier. From 1453 onward, sultans chose their grand viziers from among the military men of *kul* or slave origin who had been trained for government service in the PALACE SCHOOL and in the royal household of the TOPKAPI PALACE. Of the 15 grand viziers who held the post between 1453 and 1516, only three were free-born Muslim Turks. The rest were either of DEVŞIRME origin, taken into Ottoman service through the child-levy system, or scions of Byzantine and Balkan ruling families and aristocracies. The presence of the latter among grand viziers under Mehmed II and BAYEZID II (r. 1481–1512) testifies to the still-precarious nature of Ottoman rule in the Balkans at that period and to the pragmatism of the sultans who assimilated the Balkan ruling families by appointing their scions to the highest office of the empire.

By the time of SÜLEYMAN I (r. 1520–66), however, the area of the Balkans was integrated into the empire and there was no longer a need for ties to Balkan aristocracies. From this period on, grand viziers were of *devşirme* origin and came from the sultan's household. This showed the power of the sultan, for it was he who made and unmade these men. The career of Ibrahim Pasha is a good example. Taken from a poor family in Parga (Greece), Ibrahim became the sultan's confidant and closest friend. In 1523 Süleyman made him grand vizier although he had no governmental experience, but executed him in 1536 when the sultan considered that his confidant exercised too much power.

Süleyman's reign brought other changes to the office. Starting in the latter part of his reign, Ottoman sultans gradually resigned from the day-to-day business of government and left this to their grand viziers. In the absence of the sultan, grand viziers headed the meetings of the Imperial Council. Beginning in the mid-17th century, the grand vizier's own council or *divan* replaced that of the Imperial Council as the center of government. From this time on the term Bab-ı Âli (Sublime Gate, or Sublime Porte in contemporary European usage) was used to refer to the grand vizier's office, which became the center of government.

By the time of MAHMUD II (r. 1808–39) the Sublime Porte had evolved into a governmental quarter housing all the main ministries. As part of his governmental reforms and his aim to reduce the grand vizier's power, Mahmud II abolished the office. However, it was restored after his death, along with the concept that the grand vizier was the absolute deputy of the sultan enjoying full freedom of action with regard to domestic, foreign, financial, and military affairs. The grand viziers of the Tanzimat era acted, indeed, as the sultan's alter ego, a formulation used in the 1856 Reform Decree, and played a leading role in reforming the Ottoman government, military, and economy. They also assumed a role similar to that of a prime minister or cabinet chief in Europe. Although the grand viziers had no formal right to choose their ministers, they usually insisted that the sultan consult with them regarding ministerial appointments. The grand vizier became prime minister in the modern sense, with the right to choose his ministers, only after the constitutional reforms of 1909 (*see* CONSTITUTION/CONSTITUTIONAL PERIODS).

See also ADMINISTRATION, CENTRAL.

Gábor Ágoston

Further reading: Carter V. Findley, *Bureaucratic Reform in the Ottoman Empire: The Sublime Porte, 1789–1922* (Princeton, N.J.: Princeton University Press, 1980); Colin Imber, *The Ottoman Empire, 1300–1650: The Structure of Power* (Houndmills, Basingstoke, UK: Palgrave Macmillan, 2002); Halil İnalcık, *The Ottoman Empire: The Classical Age, 1300–1600* (London: Weidenfeld & Nicolson, 1973); Leslie Peirce, *The Imperial Harem: Women and Sovereignty in the Ottoman Empire* (Oxford: Oxford University Press, 1993); Muhammad Qasim Zaman, Anne-Marie Eddé, A. Carmona, Ann K. S. Lambton, and Halil İnalcık, "Wazīr (a.)," in *Encyclopaedia of Islam*, edited by P. Bearman, Th. Bianquis, C. E. Bosworth, E. van Donzel, and W. P. Heinrichs. Brill, 2007. Brill Online. Online edition (by subscription), viewed 30 March 2007 http://www.brillonline.nl/subscriber/entry?entry=islam_COM-1346

Great Britain   *See* ENGLAND.

Greece (Hellas; *Gk.*: Ellada, Ellás; *Turk.*: Yunanistan) An independent Greek state was first recognized in 1832, as a result of the GREEK WAR OF INDEPENDENCE (1821–31). That state was initially established in the southern Balkan provinces (the Peloponnese or Morea and Sterea Ellada, or central Greece) and on some of the Aegean islands of the Ottoman Empire (Cyclades Islands), but continued to expand at the expense of the Ottoman Empire in the north and in the Aegean until 1923 (Thessaly and Arta in 1881, part of geographical Macedonia,

Epirus, Crete, and the majority of the Aegean islands in 1913, Western Thrace in 1920). Today Greece covers 50,942 square miles and has an estimated population of 10.7 million people.

Before 1832, Greece was not a specific geographical or political entity. The BYZANTINE EMPIRE, as the heir of the Roman Empire, had for centuries dominated the medieval northeastern Mediterranean world from its capital in Constantinople (ISTANBUL), without any political or administrative subdivision that could correspond to the ancient Greek lands or the modern Greek state. The Ottomans, who succeeded Byzantium in the early modern eastern Mediterranean world, followed, more or less, the same political and administrative patterns. In the second half of the 14th century Ottoman conquests in the Balkan Peninsula—called Rumelia (the land of the Rums, that is, the Byzantines) by the Ottomans—at the expense of the Byzantines and other medieval Balkan states, resulted in the establishment of Ottoman rule over vast territories inhabited by Orthodox Christians. The continuation of the Ottoman conquests in the Balkans during the 15th century (Salonika and Janina, 1430; Constantinople, 1453; SERBIA, 1459; the Peloponnese, 1458–60; BOSNIA AND HERZEGOVINA, 1463; Euboea, 1470) consolidated their rule over the Orthodox Christians of the area, which included all of what is today continental Greece. These Balkan territories were consolidated into the province of Rumelia. According to a list of 1526, the province was further subdivided into the districts of Paşa (Western Thrace and part of geographical Macedonia), Selanik (Salonika), Yanya (Janina, Epirus), Tırhala (Thessaly), Ağriboz (eastern Sterea Ellada), Karlıili (western Sterea Ellada), and Mora (Morea, the Peloponnese). Most of the islands of the Aegean Sea were conquered by the Ottomans in the 16th century (RHODES, 1522; Cyclades Islands, 1537 and 1538; Chios, 1566). Venetian CRETE was conquered only after a long war (1645–69) as late as in the 17th century and the islands in the Ionian Sea, held by Venice, never fell to the Ottomans. In all these cases, the Ottomans established an administration based on larger administrative (sancak) and smaller judicial (kaza) districts.

In the absence of detailed studies of both Ottoman and Greek primary sources, our knowledge of the history of the Greek provinces of the Ottoman Empire from the initial conquest by the Ottomans to the start of the 19th century is rather limited. In the first half of the 16th century, Athens was the largest town in southern Greece; the town was registered in the Ottoman defters as having 2,297 taxable households, 99.5 percent of which were Orthodox Christian. In Thessaly, Yenişehir-i Fener (Larisa) was registered with 768 taxable households, 90.2 percent of which were Muslim; in nearby Tırhala (Trikala), a larger town, Orthodox Christians made up

41.6 percent of the population, Muslims 36.5 percent, and Jews 21.9 percent. In the north, Selanik (SALONIKA) was the biggest city in the Ottoman Balkans, sheltering a large Jewish population, consisting mainly of exiles from the Iberian Peninsula. Selanik was registered with a total of 4,788 taxable households, 54.2 percent of which were Jewish, 25.8 percent Muslim, and 18.9 percent Orthodox Christian.

As in the other Balkan and Anatolian provinces inhabited by Orthodox Christians, the Ottoman state made use of the institutions of the Orthodox Church, including the many monasteries that played an important social, economic, and ideological role in the lives of Orthodox Christians, and the organization of urban and rural communities into confessional groups in order to consolidate its legitimacy with regard to the population. In the process of its expansion, the Ottoman Empire found a crucial ally in the Orthodox Church. Facing potential subordination to or forced union with the Roman Catholic Church, the Orthodox Church opted for its survival under the Muslim Ottoman sultans. For the Ottoman rulers, a tacit alliance with the ecclesiastical hierarchy of the Orthodox offered a great opportunity for legitimizing its rule in the eyes of its Orthodox subjects. In this vein, in 1454, Sultan MEHMED II appointed Gennadios Scholarios, a prominent figure of the anti-Catholic Byzantine faction, as patriarch of the Orthodox Church in the newly conquered Istanbul.

Under the Ottomans the "Great Church," based in Istanbul (see GREEK ORTHODOX CHURCH), controlled and imposed its own taxation on its faithful according to its own administrative subdivisions, located mostly in the Balkans and the Aegean islands. The subdivision into provincial confessional communities served to make tax collection possible, provide goods and services, and secure political and military control of those areas. In the 17th and, increasingly, in the 18th century, during the great transformation of the Ottoman state and society, a group of local notables, both Muslim and Christian, emerged and gained control of the local communities' fiscal and administrative affairs.

During the same period, the growth in the volume of commerce in the Ottoman Empire, following the expansion of European capitalism into the eastern Mediterranean, favored the rise of Greek merchants and shipowners who then sought their independence in regard to the traditional elites. This rising Greek bourgeoisie of the 18th century financed the establishment and development of Greek schools in the provinces of the Ottoman Empire—for example, in Janina and in Greek communities in western and central Europe—which promoted the new cultural orientations of Enlightenment Europe. At the same time, influenced by the French Revolution of 1789, a Greek national movement arose slowly, both inside and outside of the Ottoman Empire. That movement ultimately produced the Greek revolution of 1821, which broke out in the Peloponnese, Sterea Ellada, and on the Aegean islands, all areas inhabited mostly by Greek Orthodox, and ultimately led to the establishment of the Greek state.

Like other modern nations that once belonged to the Ottoman Empire, Greek historiography has typically viewed the centuries of Ottoman rule as an era of "catastrophe," "retardation," and "stagnation," blaming the Ottomans for the lack of modernization and westernization that occurred elsewhere. It is undeniable that the early modern Ottoman imperial economy grew more slowly than those of most other European countries, where a tremendous process of intellectual and political emancipation was undertaken in the same period; however, this was a relative decline, caused by the unequal development in the process of the rise of western European capitalism at the expense of eastern Europe, and not one inherent in the Ottoman development.

With the foundation of the Greek state in the first half of the 19th century, Greek scholars sought to legitimize the Greek nation-state in historical terms by outlining an anachronistic history of an Hellenic nation in the eastern Mediterranean stretching in unbroken continuity from antiquity to modern times; the Byzantine Empire was incorporated into this history of the Hellenic nation as a more or less wholly Hellenic polity. In contrast, the Ottoman conquest, especially the CONQUEST OF CONSTANTINOPLE in 1453 with its major symbolic value, was regarded as the start of a dark phase in the history of the Greek people, the beginning of foreign rule (*Tourkokratia*, "Turkish occupation," a term coined in 1834). This simplistic approach cannot describe the complex realities of Ottoman society, which was not composed along national identities as in the case of modern nation-states.

Consequently, the Ottoman centuries remain a relatively new field for Greek historiography that needs further exploration, especially the social and economic history of ordinary Greeks in the Ottoman Empire. At the same time, the formation of the Greek nation should be studied in the future, in light of the political, economic, social, and ideological realities of the late Ottoman centuries that influenced its birth. Thus, a comprehensive and balanced history of the social, economic, and cultural conditions of the Ottoman centuries is yet to be written in the case of the Greek lands.

Elias Kolovos

Further reading: John Alexander, *Toward a History of Post-Byzantine Greece: The Ottoman Kanunnames for the Greek Lands, circa 1500–circa 1600* (Athens: J.C. Alexander, 1985); Antonis Anastasopoulos and Elias Kolovos (eds), *Ottoman Rule and the Balkans, 1760–1850: Conflict, Transformation, Adaptation* (Rethymno: University of Crete, Department of History and Archaeology, 2007); Elias Kolovos, Phokion Kotzageorgis, Sophia Laiou and Marinos Sariyannis (eds), *The Ottoman Empire, the Balkans, the Greek Lands: Toward a Social and Economic History; Studies in Honor of John C. Alexander* (Istanbul: Isis Press, 2007); Nicolas Svoronos, *Histoire de la Grèce Moderne* (Paris: Presses Universitaires de France, 1972); Spyros I. Asdrachas et al., *Helleniki Oikonomiki Historia, IE–ITH aionas* [Greek Economic History, 15th–19th c.] (Athens: The Pireus Bank Group Cultural Foundation, 2008); Elizabeth A. Zachariadou, *Deka Tourkika Eggrapha gia tin Megali Ekklesia (1483–1567)* [Ten Turkish Documents Concerning the Great Church (1483–1567)] (Athens: EIE/IBE, 1996)

Greek Catholics   *See* MELKITE CATHOLICS.

Greek Orthodox Church   During most of the Ottoman period, the majority of the sultans' Christian subjects were under the spiritual leadership of the ecumenical patriarch of Constantinople, who headed the Orthodox Church in the former Byzantine Empire and claimed to be the spiritual head of all Orthodox Christians wherever they lived. These Christians were called

This recent mosaic in the Ecumenical Patriarchate of Istanbul commemorates an episode in which Mehmed II is believed to have presented Patriarch Gennadios Scholarios with a diploma confirming the privilege of the Greek Orthodox church within the empire. *(Photo by Gábor Ágoston)*

Greek Orthodox in western Europe but they viewed themselves simply as Orthodox Christians or, more commonly, Romoi (Romans). The Ottomans picked up the latter name and referred to the religious community as the Rum, a term that could create confusion as the Ottomans also used it to refer to Greeks as an ethnic group. Similarly, western European visitors to the empire routinely referred to Orthodox Christians as Greeks, regardless of which language they spoke.

The early Christian Church, in the first centuries after Constantine the Great (r. 324–37 C.E.) made it the official church of the Roman Empire, acknowledged that the pope in Rome was the spiritual head of all Christians. But as political power in the empire shifted to Constantinople, the Byzantine emperors who succeeded Constantine wanted a man of their own choosing to head the church in their empire. For that purpose they created the position of patriarch of Constantinople. This act led to increased political division, although the Church remained unified doctrinally. The political quarrels eventually led to the Great Schism of 1054 when the pope (in Rome) and the patriarch (in Constantinople) each excommunicated the other and the church separated in two groups, known today as the Roman Catholic Church and the Orthodox Church. The prestige and power of the Orthodox Church was tied directly to that of the Byzantine Empire; as that empire's political power shrank, so too did the ability of the patriarch to exercise religious authority over the Orthodox faithful and political control over the Church's clergy. In the vacuum, alternative centers of orthodoxy developed.

Soon after the fall of Constantinople in 1453, Sultan MEHMED II (r.1444–46; 1451–81) appointed the monk George Scholarios, who took the patriarchal name of Gennadios, as the head of the Orthodox Church in his new capital. It is not clear whether or not Mehmed meant Gennadios to have authority over all Orthodox Christians in his empire. Orthodox Church officials would later make the claim that he had and that Mehmed's elevation of Gennadios to patriarch founded the MILLET system. Future ecumenical patriarchs' claims to authority over the Orthodox faithful were strengthened by the continuing successes of the Ottoman armies on the battlefield. The conquests of Syria, Egypt, Cyprus, Crete, and the Balkans created a new reality in which most of the Orthodox Christians in the Mediterranean basin were subject to one political ruler and potentially to one spiritual authority as well.

After Mehmed, subsequent sultans seemed uninterested in the regulation of the spiritual lives of their Christian subjects as long as they continued to pay taxes and did not rebel. For example, in 1557, Sultan Süleyman I (r. 1520–66) confirmed the elevation of the cousin of his grand vizier Sokollu Mehmed Pasha as the Patriarch of Peć in present-day Kosovo, thereby establishing a Slavic Orthodox hierarchy outside the control of the ecumenical patriarch.

That nonchalance toward church politics changed, however, in the 17th century as Roman Catholic MISSIONARIES began operating in the Ottoman Empire. Because Ottoman law prohibited them from proselytizing among the sultan's Muslim subjects and the empire's Jews proved uninterested in their message, the missionaries concentrated their efforts among local Christians in an attempt to shift their spiritual allegiance from the patriarch to the pope in Rome. At first the Ottoman authorities did not object. But after local Catholics aided a Venetian attempt to seize the island of Chios from the Ottomans in 1695, the sultans sided with the Orthodox patriarch and issued stern orders that the missionaries could only minister to European merchants residing in the empire and not to the sultan's subjects. The representatives of the ecumenical patriarch had successfully linked religious heresy with treason against the state, and the political role of the patriarch's office in the lives of the empire's Orthodox Christian subjects would continue virtually unquestioned for more than a century.

With state support, the Orthodox patriarch of Constantinople moved against local churches that he viewed as straying into heresy. The first moves were against pro-Catholic clergy in the see of ANTIOCH, whose patriarch resided in DAMASCUS. After the Arab conquest of the region in the 7th century, the church hierarchy in Syria had been largely autonomous. Far removed from the court of the ecumenical patriarch, Orthodox clergy in Syria were carefully cultivated by Catholic missionaries, and many of the brightest young men were sent to the Maronite College in Rome for education. Recognizing the danger posed by this intimacy with Rome, the ecumenical patriarch intervened to end that autonomy in 1725. By choosing a new patriarch of Antioch, the ecumenical patriarch confirmed the split between the Catholic and Orthodox churches, leading to the development of the Melkite Catholic Church. In the Balkans, Catholic missionaries had enjoyed little success outside Bosnia and northern Albania. But the ecumenical patriarch's fears of a possible defection of the Orthodox faithful led the Orthodox Church in Istanbul to centralize its hierarchy throughout the empire. In the case of Crete and Cyprus, that meant simply replacing local clergy with appointees from the capital. But in the Slavic territories of the Ottoman Empire it often meant replacing clergy who were ethnic Slavs with men who were ethnic Greeks. In a culmination of the drive toward greater centralization in the Orthodox Church, the ecumenical patriarch succeeded in 1766 in getting an order from the sultan abolishing the independent patriarchate of Peć. Elsewhere in the Balkans, the sultan's grant of authority over the Orthodox faithful in Istanbul to Greek-speaking clergy sparked interest among Orthodox Bulgarians in their own history and led to the development of a standardized Bulgarian language. In WALLACHIA, local clergy fostered an awakening interest in history and the vernacular language. With a ripple effect, the centralization of Church authority pushed the peoples of the Balkans to found national churches that would minister to them in their own languages rather than in the Greek of the ecumenical patriarch.

By the late 18th century the parameters of the *millet* system had been fully articulated and the ecumenical patriarch of Constantinople was unquestionably the most powerful Christian in the Ottoman Empire. The prestige of the office was greatly undermined, however, by the GREEK WAR OF INDEPENDENCE that began in 1821. In response to rumors of Christian massacres of Muslims in the Balkans, a mob of Janissaries hung the patriarch and several of his bishops in front of the gates of the patriarchate in Istanbul. In the minds of many Muslims, the Ottoman use of the word Rum both for Greeks as an ethnic group and for the Orthodox Church blurred the distinction between the two. Angry at what they viewed as the disloyalty of the Greeks, they lashed out at the Church.

After the establishment of the Greek kingdom in 1833, relations between the sultan and the now independent ecumenical patriarch remained rocky, as the Ottomans viewed the patriarchate as an institution that might promote Greek national interests. Between 1833 and 1855, 11 men served in the post; the sultans removed seven of them on charges of treason against the Ottoman state. Furthermore, the relationship between the ecumenical patriarch and former subjects of the sultan was unclear. The patriarch recognized the independence of the Serbian Orthodox Church in 1832, but when the church in the Greek kingdom declared its independence in 1833, the ecumenical patriarch refused to recognize it until 1850, after Russian intervention. The Orthodox Patriarch of Moscow had established that his church was independent of the ecumenical patriarch after the fall of Constantinople in 1453, and the Russian government saw itself as the protector of the Ottoman Empire's Orthodox Christians. As such, the Russians also intervened to influence the sultan to grant independence to the Bulgarian Orthodox Church in 1872 and to effect the appointment of an ethnic Arab to fill the Orthodox patriarchate of Antioch in 1900.

Despite his diminished authority, the ecumenical patriarch remained the titular head of the Orthodox *millet* in the Ottoman Empire. The reforms instituted in the TANZIMAT era (1839–76) strengthened the control that churches could exercise over the lives of the faithful by granting governmental recognition to their local councils and school systems. In 1912, for example, schools main-tained by the patriarchate were educating 184,000 students, the largest number of students in any of the empire's autonomous school systems. In the last official Ottoman census conducted in 1914, the patriarch's community was recorded at over 1,700,000, the largest Christian community in the Empire, even though his jurisdiction had been eaten away by defections either to the various Catholic sects or to the Orthodox national churches.

Bruce Masters

Further reading: Richard Clogg, *Anatolica: Studies in the Greek East in the 18th and 19th Centuries* (Aldershot, UK: Variorum, 1996); Dimitri Gondicas and Charles Issawi, eds., *Ottoman Greeks in the Age of Nationalism* (Princeton, N.J.: Darwin, 1999).

Greek revolt   *See* GREEK WAR OF INDEPENDENCE.

Greek revolution   *See* GREEK WAR OF INDEPENDENCE.

Greek War of Independence   The Greek War of Independence, also referred to as the Greek Revolution, was a successful war for an independent Greek state directed against Ottoman authority that took place between 1821 and 1831. Its impetus, timing, unfolding, and outcome were dependent as much on internal social and political changes within the Ottoman Empire as they were on the broader tensions and constellations of European states in the Napoleonic Age and Age of Restoration. The war ended with the establishment of a republic in 1827–28. After the republic's collapse into civil war and further hostilities with the Ottoman Empire, a Hellenic kingdom (1832–33) was formed under the protection of the newly emerging Great Powers of Britain, Russia, and France, with Bavarian Prince Otto as its monarch.

THE OTTOMAN CONTEXT

With the use of the Ottoman *MILLET* system of political organization, religion rather than ethnicity was recognized as a legal and administrative division. Thus there was a category for Orthodox Christians, known as Rum, as distinct from Muslim, Jewish, and Armenian. The label Rum included groups recognized today as Greek, Bulgarian, Serbian, Vlach, and Albanian Christians. At the same time, the Greek language enjoyed primacy in the Orthodox Church, and thus implicit in the category of Rum was at least a linguistic association with things Greek. The emergence of "Greek" as a political and ethnic category was a long process of differentiation from other Christian groups in the empire, but it was strongly influenced by association with Orthodox Christianity.

There were Orthodox Christian populations in all corners of the Ottoman Empire. The largest concentrations were in the Balkans, the Aegean Islands, Istanbul, and Anatolia. The elite of Orthodox Christian society, known as PHANARIOTS, circulated between ISTANBUL, the Danubian principalities, MOLDAVIA, and WALLACHIA (in present-day Romania). These Phanariots and their lower-ranking associates cultivated connections between the Ottoman Imperial COURT, military, and bureaucracy, the ecclesiastical hierarchy of the Orthodox Church, provincial notables in Ottoman southeast Europe, and merchants and statesmen in Europe and Russia. The middle classes included merchants trading throughout the Balkans, Aegean Islands, and BLACK SEA area, as well as the Greek merchant marine. At the far end of the social spectrum were the peasants, many of whom had long taken to brigandage and piracy for survival.

In the 18th century many areas, such as the Peloponnese, were effectively ruled by armed clans who might come together in an alliance, fight each other, or band together with the Ottoman authorities at any time. There was also a range of Orthodox clergy—from the patriarch and Holy Synod in Istanbul all the way down to the humble local priests in the Peloponnese. Finally, there were middle-class merchants based outside the Ottoman realm in cities such as Vienna, Leipzig, Odessa, and Marseille, who transported ideas as well as goods into and out of Ottoman territory.

During the late 18th and early 19th centuries these groups began to evolve from being Albanian-, Romanian-, or Bulgarian-speaking Christians toward identifying linguistically, culturally, and politically as Greek. One reason was Russian Empress Catherine the Great's dream of a Greek revival in Ottoman lands, followed by her aborted attempt to foment uprisings against the Ottomans in the Peloponnese and Aegean islands A more influential cause was the TREATY OF KÜÇÜK KAYNARCA that ended the Russo-Ottoman War of 1768–74. The Russian Empire interpreted the treaty as granting them rights of protection over all Orthodox Christian populations of the Ottoman Empire, and by extension the right to intervene in the internal affairs of their political rival. One of the many consequences of this treaty was that Greek or Christian ships were thus able to sail under the Russian flag, increasing the involvement of Ottoman Christian subjects in the lucrative Black Sea trade.

In Europe the French Revolution and the Napoleonic Wars helped set the intellectual and political stage for Greek independence. In the intellectual sphere, the idea of national liberation and breaking free from ancien-régime monarchies made change seem possible. The Romantic movement also worked to glorify revivals of ancient peoples such as the Greeks. In the early 19th century the intricate and shifting alliances of the Napoleonic Age made elite Ottoman Christian Phanariots even more indispensable to Ottoman survival, as they were the interpreters and purveyors of strategic information regarding European international relations.

SEQUENCE OF EVENTS

A secret society known as PHILIKI HETAIRIA (Friendly Society) had been formed by merchants in Odessa in 1814 and had proliferated after 1818 amongst Ottoman Christian subjects. The goal of the Society was liberation from Ottoman rule. By the outbreak of hostilities in the winter of 1821, a coalition of social groups from several regions had formed. Thus when Alexander Hypsilantis crossed from Russian territory into Moldavia in early 1821 and the peasants of the area failed to support him, leading to his rapid defeat at the hands of Ottoman forces, other groups rose up in the Peloponnese within weeks, opening a second front against Ottoman military forces. The Peloponnese—more remote from the Ottoman center, and in close proximity to the empire within an empire of ALI PASHA OF JANINA, the Ottoman governor who supported the Greek rebels so as to strengthen his own position—proved the more lasting front, and the first independent Greek territory.

There were several turning points in the military struggle that unfolded between partisan guerrillas and Ottoman-aligned militias. What began as a deadlock in 1821 lasted until 1825, when the forces of MEHMED ALI and his son IBRAHIM PASHA were called in from Egypt to assist the Ottoman forces. Then in 1826 Ottoman Sultan MAHMUD II (r. 1808–39) abolished and massacred the JANISSARIES, thereby snuffing out his own nominal military force and leaving the empire dependent on the military prowess of vassal Mehmed Ali, based in Egypt. By the late 1820s it was unclear if the Ottoman sultanate would survive the many conflicts engulfing it.

EUROPEAN POLITICS OF RESTORATION

The Holy Alliance had been formed by Austria, Russia, and Prussia at the Congress of Vienna in 1815, reflecting a commitment to the status quo and against nationalist/separatist uprisings that could threaten the newly restored ancien régimes. In this climate of conservatism, newly emergent Great Power states such as Britain, France, and Russia were loath to support the Greek rebels' bids to topple Ottoman authority. It was predominantly through misunderstanding and a mutual suspicion of each other's motives that the three Great Powers got involved in the conflict on the side of the Greeks in 1827, resulting in the resounding defeat of the forces of Mehmed Ali and the Ottomans and a victory for the Greek partisans at the Battle of Navarino. From that point on, the Conference of London met several times to hash out a settlement, first for an autonomous Greek polity, then for a Hellenic republic, and ultimately, after the

Russo-Ottoman War of 1829 and the Treaty of Edirne, for an independent Greek state. Representatives of the Ottoman state were not involved in these negotiations until the Treaty of Edirne with Russia and the final stages of the multilateral Treaty of London in 1832–33.

As Great Powers stepped forward and took a more active role in the formation of an independent Greek kingdom, Greek politics grew into the divisions of European politics. Parties that were explicitly aligned with one or another foreign state took shape, with the British, French, and Napist (Russian) parties playing out factional, and social differences. Further complicating modern notions of national sovereignty, the Greek Kingdom featured a Bavarian monarch, French military advisors, and British administrators at the helm of government.

The original Greek kingdom had its capital not in Athens but in the Peloponnesian port of Nauplion. It included only the southern portion of present-day Greece, along with several nearby islands. Expansion of the Greek kingdom and consolidation of Greek-speaking, Orthodox Christian populations in the bounds of the Greek state would not happen for another century, with the 1922 Populations Exchange between Greece and Turkey as spelled out in the Treaty of Lausanne.

REPERCUSSIONS

The Greek War of Independence opened the proverbial Pandora's box in the Ottoman Empire. In the Balkans, the war and the historical-cultural justifications for secession would serve as a template for Balkan national movements and national historiographies. The Greek example set the precedent of Great Power guarantee and protection of fledgling Balkan states. The Greek War of Independence was important in the history of Egypt as well—the war set in motion Mehmed Ali's near-successful bid to overthrow the Ottoman sultanate in the 1830s, which led to the establishment of his dynasty in Egypt until the 1950s.

In the context of Ottoman imperial governance, the conflict started by Greek partisans contributed to a series of crises that prompted the Tanzimat reforms in 1839 and 1856. The Ottoman Empire only emerged from these crises because of its new relationship with European Great Power states, also a product of the 1820s. And finally, the establishment of an independent Greek kingdom created new and complex dynamics between the Ottoman state and the Orthodox Christian populations that remained Ottoman subjects, as the ethnic divide began an uncomfortable coexistence with the religious divide under the rubric of legal equality under the Tanzimat.

Christine Philliou

Further reading: Richard Clogg, *A Concise History of Greece* (Cambridge: Cambridge University Press, 2002); Nikiforos Diamandouros, ed., *Hellenism and the First Greek War of Liberation (1821–1830): Continuity and Change* (Thessaloniki, Greece: Institute for Balkan Studies, 1976); George Finlay, *History of the Greek Revolution* (London: Zeno, 1971); John Koliopoulos, *Brigands with a Cause: Brigandage and Irredentism in Modern Greece, 1821–1912* (Oxford: Clarendon, 1987).

Gregorian Church *See* Armenian Apostolic Church.

Gregorian Armenian Church *See* Armenian Apostolic Church.

Gregorian Orthodox Church *See* Armenian Apostolic Church.

Gülhane Imperial Rescript. *See* reform; Tanzimat.

H

Hagia Sophia (Ayasofya; Ayasofya Camii) One of the most hotly contested religious sites of all time, the Hagia Sophia (Church of Holy Wisdom) was built as an Orthodox Christian church in 532–37 under the auspices of Byzantine Emperor Justinian. Following the Fourth Crusade (1201–04), when the crusaders conquered Constantinople and established the Latin Empire of Constantinople (1204–61), the Hagia Sophia became a Catholic church. It recovered its Orthodox status in 1261, when the Byzantine emperor in exile in Nicaea reconquered the city. In the wake of the Ottoman conquest of the city in 1453 (*see* CONSTANTINOPLE, CONQUEST OF), the church was converted into a mosque by MEHMED II (r. 1444–46; 1451–81) and renamed Ayasofya Camii. In 1934 MUSTAFA KEMAL ATATÜRK had it transformed into a museum.

Although the structure has justifiably attracted the interest of architectural critics and scholars, it has also been the ongoing focus of political, mythical, and religious discussions. Over the course of almost 1,500 years the building has undergone many functional, aesthetic, cultural, political, and environmental transformations. It has served as a church, a site for imperial ceremony, a seat for the patriarchate, a seat of the CALIPHATE, a museum, a tourist attraction, and a source of architectural inspiration for many later mosques and churches.

The historiography of the Hagia Sophia has taken the form of many myths and stories that have served to justify the political and religious aspirations attached to it. These myths were widespread among both the Byzantines and the Ottomans. For instance, the Byzantines held that Emperor Justinian received the plan of the church from an archangel. Similarly, the Ottomans claimed that its shattered dome was repaired only after permission was granted by the Prophet Muhammad, thus endorsing the building's status as a mosque. Another Muslim myth narrated how the last ABBASID caliph passed the caliphate to SELIM I (r. 1512–20) under its dome, a myth that involves the building in the legitimation of Ottoman political power.

The church was built on the site of an earlier church that had been built by Emperor Constantine (d. 337 C.E.) to emphasize the city's transition from paganism to Christianity. When the Hagia Sophia was built on the site of that burned church in 537, it served as the last example in a long tradition of imperially sanctioned buildings in the Roman Empire. Emperor Justinian boasted about constructing a church whose dome surpassed that of Solomon's temple. But the first dome collapsed because of an architectural defect 17 years after its construction; the current dome is lower than the first one. One of the important renovations to the church was carried out in 1346 after its eastern arch and one-third of the dome collapsed during an earthquake.

The building went through several renovations that were not merely cosmetic but that deeply affected its identity. Following the CONQUEST OF CONSTANTINOPLE, Ottoman Sultan MEHMED II (r. 1444–46; 1451–81) ordered the church's conversion into a mosque. A wooden minaret replaced the cap of the turret of the west facade; a *minbar* (freestanding pulpit) and a mihrab (directional pointer niche) were added to the interior; the bell, relics, crosses, icons, and the cross on top of the dome were removed; the floor was covered with mats and carpets; and icons on the side of the *qibla* (direction of Mecca) were plastered over. The rest of the building

The Hagia Sophia was built in the 530s as the principle church of Byzantine Constantinople. After the Ottoman conquest in 1453 it was transformed into a mosque. In 1934 it was converted into a museum. *(Photo by Gábor Ágoston)*

remained untouched. The second large-scale renovation was undertaken in 1572–74 during the reign of SELIM II (r. 1566–74) by architect Mimar Sinan. The buttresses were repaired, the wooden minaret was replaced by a brick minaret, and two new minarets were added. In addition, the adjacent buildings were demolished, providing the structure with the courtyard characteristic of an imperial mosque. Selim II, who broke the Ottoman sultans' tradition of the funerary mosque complex, was buried in a tomb next to the building, thus giving the mosque imperial status. Another set of renovations was carried out in 1607–09 during the reign of AHMED I (r. 1603–1617); the flat panels were renewed, ceramic tiles were added to the interior, and most of the icons or figural mosaics were whitewashed over, having been interpreted as being contrary to Islam's ban on figurative art.

MAHMUD I (r. 1730–54) turned the mosque into a *külliye* (mosque complex) by adding a library, a fountain, an *imaret* (an inn or hospice), and a school for children.

The renovation of ABDÜLMECID I (r. 1839–61) in 1847–49 marks an important change in the perception of the building. Two Swiss architects, Gaspare and Guiseppe Fossati, were appointed to renovate the building. This structural renovation was in the neoclassical and neo-Byzantine style that carries traces of westernization. The figural mosaics of the mosque had been uncovered, but popular pressure against the sultan's decision led to their being whitewashed again. Only the images of the archangels on the pendentives were spared, provided that their faces were modified by being changed to stars. The last renovation project, directed by Thomas Whittemore, uncovered the mosaics in 1931. In 1934, under Mustafa Kemal Atatürk's orders, the mosque was converted into a museum.

The monument is steeped in symbolic value. Its construction represented the city's Christian character, and for a millennium afterward it was renowned as the seat of the patriarchate. Its conversion to a mosque at the hands of Mehmed II symbolized for many the transition from a Byzantine to an Ottoman era and the victory of Islam over Christianity. It was declared Istanbul's first royal mosque, and in 1517, it also came to serve as the seat of the caliphate. The conversion was part of the Islamization of the whole city. Since the church was the site of imperial ceremonies, the conversion was not only a religious act but also a military and political statement. The monument's importance as an emblem of sovereignty underlined the British attempt in the wake of WORLD WAR I to reconvert it into a church. Its eventual categorization as a museum in 1934 highlighted Republican Turkey's adoption of a secularist political model. The mosque's desanctification epitomized the attempt to distance the new Turkish Republic from its Ottoman past. Thus, for the first time in its entire history, the building was turned into an artifact of the past. Having served as an imperial mosque for 481 years, and as a seat of the caliphate, the building could not find a legitimate presence as a mosque in the new secular republic. Through this rupture, the Hagia Sophia became a site of memory instead of continuing as a symbol of lived religious experience. During the building's conversion to a museum, some features were removed, including rugs, racks for footwear, and a coffee shop in the courtyard.

From an aesthetic point of view, Hagia Sophia is a crucial witness to the transformation of Muslim attitudes against imagery. During the time of Mehmed II, only the images on the *qibla* side were seen as conflicting with Islam. Over time, other images were plastered over until, in the mid-17th century, almost all mosaics and figural images were either altered or whitewashed. In the second half of the 19th century, a process of westernization that valued the visual images in the structure led to their restoration. The formal secularization of the building by its transformation into a museum marked the culmination of this trend. In reflecting diverse approaches toward imagery, the Hagia Sophia is a living critique of the belief that Islam invariably takes an essentialist approach to figurative imagery.

As a splendid monument, the Hagia Sophia has been an object of desire, a source of inspiration, and a challenge to the Ottoman architectural tradition. A dome suspended on four arches and pendentives was not uncommon during the ancient times, but having two semidomes of the same diameter (102 feet; 31 m) was a novelty. Although the building was renowned throughout Christian Europe, it had little influence on the development of late medieval Christian architecture. Rather, it was Ottoman architects who regarded the structure as a technical challenge and who replicated the dome and window designs of the Hagia Sophia in other structures, finally managing to extend and exceed the technique. This led to the development of a universal mosque design that extended throughout the Muslim world. The revival of the popularity of the Hagia Sophia is thus closely related to the dome-based architectural tradition in Ottoman times.

Similarly, in the late 19th century, the Hagia Sophia became the universal example of Greek Orthodox churches around the world. This development should be understood in the context of the extended geographical reading of Europe, with the inclusion of the Byzantines into the European metanarrative. Before the 19th century, the Byzantine Empire was not perceived as an integral part of Europe but was associated with Eastern "corruption" and "despotism." But with the rise of 19th-century neoclassicism and historicism that imagined a direct ancestral line from the ancient Greeks and Romans, the genealogy of Europe was rewritten to include the Byzantines. This new perception of history coincided with Sultan Abdülmecid's promotion of the building in Europe following its 1847–49 renovations. To commemorate the event, Sultan Abdülmecid had a medal cast in Paris with his own TUGRA on one side and the Hagia Sophia's image on the other; he also had an album published that included lithographs of the Hagia Sophia. These events concluded a long process by which the Hagia Sophia complex replaced that of the Süleymaniye as the most important monument in Istanbul.

Starting with the 1847–49 renovations, when the area around the building was cleaned, gentrified, and opened like a European piazza, the character and experience of the building has changed dramatically. Since that time the Hagia Sophia has been experienced as an isolated tourist attraction rather than a building that is part of an active community. Therefore it must be understood that today's building is neither the Byzantine Hagia Sophia nor the Ottoman Ayasofya but a new space for tourism. The building is now open as a museum, and its status and identity continue to pose tantalizing questions of social and political significance.

Nuh Yılmaz

Further reading: Metin Ahunbay and Zeynep Ahunbay, "Structural Influence of Hagia Sophia on Ottoman Mosque," in *Hagia Sophia from the Age of Justinian to the Present*, edited by Robert Mark and Ahmed Ş. Çakmak (Cambridge: Cambridge University Press, 1992), 179–94; Cyril Mango, "Byzantine Writers on the Fabric of Hagia Sophia," in *Hagia Sophia from the Age of Justinian to the Present*, edited by Robert Mark and Ahmed Ş. Çakmak (Cambridge: Cambridge University Press, 1992), 41–56; Gülru Necipoğlu, "The Life of an Imperial Monument: Hagia Sophia after Byzantium," in *Hagia Sophia from the Age of Justinian to the Present*, edited by Robert Mark and Ahmed Ş. Çakmak (Cambridge: Cambridge University Press, 1992), 195–225; Robert S. Nelson, *Hagia Sophia, 1850–1950* (Chicago: University of Chicago Press, 2004).

hahambaşı *Hahambaşı* was the Ottoman Turkish title for the chief rabbi of the empire, a political office first assigned by the Ottomans in 1835. Unlike the various Christian sects, the JEWS avoided the creation of a MILLET and thus did not have an official in Istanbul responsible for the religious affairs of Jews throughout the empire. They preferred a decentralized rabbinate with local autonomy in each provincial center. The exception to this rule was Jerusalem in the 18th century. There, the wealthy community of Sephardic Jews in Istanbul took over the responsibility of the community's governance through the institution of the Istanbul Committee of Officials for Palestine, and it appointed the men who would represent the community locally. That situation was apparently unique to Palestine, with its diverse Jewish communities. Elsewhere, the Jews of BASRA elected a man to serve as *nasi*, or secular leader. The men holding the office might also be rabbis, but their primary function was to represent the secular interests of the community to the Muslim authorities. In BAGHDAD, the position of *nasi* was usually occupied by a prominent Jewish banker who had ties to the city's Muslim governors, apparently without the consent of those he governed. The office remained central in the administrative life of Baghdad's Jews until the Ottoman TANZIMAT reform period (1839–76), when the office of *nasi* was abolished and replaced by the office of *hahambaşı,* its holder chosen by the rabbis in the city as they reasserted their authority to govern and speak for their community.

Pressure on Jews to conform to the *millet* model followed by the Christian communities led to the official recognition of Jews as a community empirewide and to the creation of the office of *hahambaşı,* or chief rabbi in 1835. The man occupying that position would stand alongside the patriarchs of the Armenian, Greek Orthodox, and Catholic churches at state functions, and would represent his community's interests at the imperial court. At first, Jewish community leaders accepted the political function of the office but continued to select rabbis to serve the religious functions of the community. Gradually, however, as rabbis of unquestioned learning and scholarship were chosen as *hahambaşı,* the office gained spiritual authority as well. The office of provincial *hahambaşı* was created for Izmir and Salonika in the same year as the founding of the Jewish *millet,* and by 1841, there were also *hahambaşıs* assigned to Jerusalem, Sarajevo, and Baghdad. Ultimately every city that had a significant Jewish population had a similar office. The provincial chief rabbis did not bow to the religious authority of the chief rabbi in Istanbul. He simply represented them politically in the capital and theoretically recommended to the sultan the appointment of their replacements upon death or retirement. In reality, the local rabbis would agree upon a candidate and then send his name to the *hahambaşı* in Istanbul, who would then forward that name to the sultan for approval.

Bruce Masters

Further reading: Avigdor Levy, ed., *The Jews of the Ottoman Empire* (Princeton, N.J.: Darwin, 1994).

Haifa (Kaiffa, Khaifa; *Ar.:* Hayfa; *Turk.:* Hayfa) Haifa is today one of the leading port cities of Israel, but for most of the Ottoman period, it was overshadowed in size and importance by ACRE and Jaffa. European MISSIONARIES were partly responsible for drawing attention to Haifa's potential benefits as a port city. Roman Catholics established a monastery on nearby Mt. Carmel in the 1830s and the Templars, a German Christian group that sought to colonize the Holy Land, established an agricultural settlement outside the town in 1869. Both provided services to the local population and helped draw migrants to the town. A commitment to the aspirations of ZIONISM inspired European Jews to settle in the city, whose location seemed prime for development as the potential Jewish homeland's port city; unlike Jaffa and Acre, Haifa had no areas where the residents were traditionally Arabs, whom the Zionists viewed with mistrust. Bahai refugees, followers of a syncretic religious faith founded in 19th-century Iran, also settled in the town to be near the tomb of their prophet Bahaullah, who had been exiled to Haifa and died there in 1892. The city's future was made brighter still in 1905 when Haifa was connected to a spur of the HEJAZ RAILROAD. That development provided the city's merchants easier access to the agricultural produce of Galilee and southern SYRIA. By the start of WORLD WAR I, Haifa had grown significant enough to attract British colonial ambitions; it would become one of their chief objectives in the postwar settlement.

Bruce Masters

See also ACRE; SYKES-PICOT AGREEMENT.

Further reading: Mahmud Yazbak, *Haifa in the Late Ottoman Period, 1864–1914: A Muslim Town in Transition* (Leiden: Brill, 1998).

hajj All Muslims who have the means and the health are required to perform the hajj, or pilgrimage to MECCA, at least once in their lives. The annual pilgrimage brought prestige to the Ottoman sultans, one of whose titles was "Servant of the Two Noble Sanctuaries," Mecca and MEDINA; they not only ruled both of these cities, they also provided support and security for the annual hajj. Lacking an authentically Muslim lineage, that is, one that reached backed to the Prophet's family, the Ottoman sultans' legitimacy as Muslim rulers rested in no small part on how well the annual hajj went. In addition, the

This photo, taken around 1910, shows the pilgrims gathered at the Kaaba in Mecca for a part of the annual hajj ceremonies. The mosque in Mecca was refurbished by Sultan Murad IV. At that time, the Ottoman style minaret shown in this photo was added. *(Library of Congress)*

hajj generated revenue for the empire, as the thousands of pilgrims who descended on Mecca every year from all corners of the Muslim world used the occasion to buy and sell. For both these reasons, Ottoman officials were greatly concerned with the security of the caravans that set out yearly with pilgrims from CAIRO and DAMASCUS, and that were subject to frequent raids, especially within the empire's Arab provinces. No issue generated more correspondence between ISTANBUL and the provincial governors than the state of the infrastructure along the caravan routes, current political conditions among the BEDOUINS, and the smooth transit of pilgrims to and from the holy cities of Mecca and Medina. But despite the importance of the hajj in Ottoman foreign and domestic politics, no Ottoman sultan ever made the pilgrimage himself.

The Ottoman authorities required that all pilgrims coming overland to the HEJAZ assemble in either Damascus or Cairo, but pilgrims from South Asia usually arrived directly in JEDDAH by ship. Each year, the arrival of between 10,000 and 20,000 pilgrims from Anatolia, Iraq, and Iran in Damascus was accompanied by a frenzy of buying and selling in the city's markets. Damascus merchants also provided the gear for the arduous desert crossing that took 40 days on average. Other locals hired out animals for the journey, or hired themselves out as guides. On their return to Damascus after completing the hajj the pilgrims brought goods that they had acquired in Arabia, most notably COFFEE, but also Indian textiles, spices, and perfumes. The pilgrim trade was the leading engine of economic prosperity for the city, and in years when it was threatened, Damascus suffered profound economic slumps.

In the first century of Ottoman rule in Syria and Arabia, the pilgrim caravans went to and from Mecca unhindered. But in the 17th century, the dynamics of the politics of the desert began to change when Ottoman officials posted to the region became careless about cultivating the Bedouin tribes through whose territory the caravans passed. Compounding the problem, more aggressive Anaza and Shammar Bedouin tribal confederations were pushing out of Arabia into the Syrian Desert; they showed little compunction about attacking the caravans coming from Damascus. Raids on the caravans became increasingly frequent in the second half of the 17th century. In response, the Ottoman sultans shifted the responsibilities of the official designated to ensure the safety of the pilgrims (called the AMIR AL-HAJJ, or commander of the hajj) from a local military officer to the governor of Damascus, as it was felt a man with greater economic and military resources was needed. It was in that function as governor and commander of the hajj that the AL-AZM family rose to prominence in Damascus, the first local family to achieve political importance in the city for at least two centuries. Even so, the plan was not foolproof, as the Bedouin annihilated the hajj caravan in 1757, killing a reported 20,000 pilgrims.

An even more serious threat to Ottoman prestige came in 1803 when the WAHHABIS occupied Mecca. Inspired by a radically strict interpretation of Islam, this group seized Medina in 1804 and tore down the dome over the Prophet's tomb because they regarded this monument as violating the true worship of God. The Wahhabis allowed the pilgrimage to continue under their control but required the pilgrims to conform to what the Wahhabis considered proper Muslim dress and behavior. During the decade of Wahhabi occupation, it became difficult for Ottoman subjects to make the hajj, and impossible for adherents of SHIA ISLAM. With the rise of MEHMED ALI as governor of Egypt after 1805, Sultan MAHMUD II (r. 1808–39) asked him to restore the holy cities to Ottoman rule. In 1811, Mehmed Ali dispatched an army under the command of his son, Tosun. By 1812 he had taken Mecca; he took Medina the following year. Although the power of the ibn Saud family, who led the Wahhabi confederation, was not completely broken by the Egyptian expedition, the holy cities suffered no more military threats until WORLD WAR I.

New threats to the pilgrimage caravans emerged in the 1840s, but they were technological rather than tribal. With the introduction of steamships in the eastern Mediterranean and Red Sea, more and more pilgrims from the Balkans and Anatolia chose to go on the hajj by a sea route. With the opening of the SUEZ CANAL in 1869, even pilgrims from Iran preferred a sea journey that started in the Black Sea port of Trabzon in place of the traditional land route by caravan. By the 1870s, direct transportation to Jeddah was available from Iranian ports in the Persian Gulf, diminishing the flow of pilgrims by the traditional land route even further. With these innovations, the hajj caravans ceased to be practical, and the economy of Damascus suffered. Damascus's economy seemingly received a reprieve, however, when, in 1900, Sultan ABDÜLHAMID II (r. 1876–1909) announced plans for the HEJAZ RAILROAD that would connect Medina to the proposed Berlin-

Istanbul-Baghdad rail line, thus reviving hopes for the land route. The railroad was opened in 1908 but did not reverse the preference of most pilgrims who continued to make their way to Jeddah by steamer.

Bruce Masters

Further reading: Suraiya Faroqhi, *Pilgrims and Sultans: The Hajj under the Ottomans* (London: I.B. Tauris, 1994).

Hama (*bib.*: **Hamath**; *class.*: **Epiphania**) For thousands of years, there has been a city on the site in central Syria occupied today by Hama. Its location on a rise above the Orontes River provides the city with abundant water and protection, while the fertile plain that surrounds it offers incentive for human settlement. After the Ottoman conquest of SYRIA in 1516, the governors of TRIPOLI first administered Hama as a subprovince (*sancak*), but in 1725, that authority was shifted to the governor of DAMASCUS, some 120 miles to the city's south. In that year Ismail al-Azm (also known as Ismail Pasha) of the AL-AZM FAMILY was appointed governor of Damascus. This family had dominated the politics of Hama in the 17th century and Ismail's appointment meant that members of the family governed both cities. That connection meant that the political fortunes of Hama were linked to its southern neighbor for the next three-quarters of a century. Additionally, Hama served as an important stopping place for pilgrims on the HAJJ coming from Anatolia or Iran. The al-Azm family's link to the smooth functioning of the yearly pilgrimage, through their understanding of, and contact with, the BEDOUIN tribes who often obstructed the hajj, was undoubtedly also important in getting the district reassigned to them In the 19th century, although the al-Azm family no longer provided governors for Hama, they retained a position of authority in the city due to their extensive landholdings in the surrounding countryside.

Various European travelers' estimates put the population of Hama at about 30,000 inhabitants in the 19th century. The townspeople generally enjoyed good relations with the BEDOUIN of the neighboring Syrian steppes. Although the Bedouin would raid villages in the city's hinterlands at times when they perceived the power of the central government as weak, they did not attack Hama itself. In a reflection of the relative tranquility the city enjoyed, the walls that had existed in the period of the Egyptian MAMLUK EMPIRE (1260–1516) were allowed to decay and tumble down, and the city's citadel rarely had a garrison. Hama was primarily a market town for the Bedouin and the surrounding villagers, and most of what was produced there was sold locally. The workshops of ALEPPO and Damascus produced textiles that were more highly prized than those of Hama, but its artisans produced a plain white cotton cloth with block-print designs in black ink that found a market throughout Syria and was known as Hama cloth.

Bruce Masters

Further reading: James Reilly, *A Small Town in Syria: Ottoman Hama in the Eighteenth and Nineteenth Centuries* (Bern: Peter Lang, 2002); Dick Douwes, *The Ottomans in Syria: A History of Justice and Oppression* (London: I. B. Tauris, 2000).

Hamidiye   Hamidiye was the name given to tribal cavalry units established by Sultan Abdülhamid II (r. 1876–1909) in the 1880s. Modeled after the Cossack units in the imperial Russian army, they were meant to patrol the mountainous regions of the Ottoman Empire along the Russian border. Kurdish tribal chieftains were recruited as officers; they brought their tribesmen into the unit as their subordinates. The units were intended to counter any potential threat of Armenian nationalists seeking to separate eastern Anatolia from the Ottoman Empire to form an independent Armenian state, but they also served to bind the Kurdish tribes to the sultan, turning potential rebels into loyal subjects.

Although they were deployed against Kurds, Bedouins, and Yazidis whom the Ottoman sultan had judged to be in a state of rebellion, the Hamidiye gained notoriety in the West in 1894 when they went on a rampage against Armenian villagers in eastern Anatolia after the government claimed the villagers were in arrears paying their taxes. The attacks on Armenians continued until 1896 when protests from European ambassadors forced the Ottoman army to intervene to restore order. In the two years of the unrest, several thousand Armenians were killed. The resulting animosity between Armenians and Kurds helped fuel Kurdish participation in the Armenian Massacres of 1915.

Bruce Masters

Further reading: Hakan Özoğu, *Kurdish Notables and the Ottoman State: Evolving Identities, Competing Loyalties, and Shifting Boundaries* (Albany: State University of New York Press, 2004).

hammam   See BATHHOUSE.

harem   The term *harem* refers to the private quarters in a domestic residence and, by extension, to its female inhabitants. The royal harem at the Topkapı Palace was of particular importance because this institution was charged with the reproduction of the dynasty. Sex and reproduction were carefully regulated within the harem, and especially within the royal harem. Albertus Bobovius, a Polish slave serving in the Palace, compared the latter to a monastery, due to its rigid hierarchy and the enforced chastity of many of its residents. When we consider how crucial, and potentially dangerous, succession and succession politics could be, the significance of the harem becomes clear.

The word *harem* comes from an Arabic word meaning "forbidden" or "unlawful," but also "sacred" and "inviolable." At the most general level, it describes a space to which access is controlled or outright prohibited. Thus the private quarters in a domestic residence were referred to as a harem because of the Islamic practice of restricting access to these quarters. Similarly, the private quarters of the Ottoman royal family, within the larger structure of the Topkapı Palace, and the women living there, were also referred to as the harem. The royal harem, parts of which can still be viewed today, was a labyrinth of hallways, private apartments, mosques, libraries, dining rooms, and salons which was steadily added to over the years.

The population within the imperial harem also grew as a result of the dynasty's increasing preference for seclusion behind the walls of the palace complex, a trend that began in the 16th century. The Queen Mother, or *valide sultan*—the mother of the reigning sultan—stood at the apex of the harem hierarchy. Below her, the royal harem's population was divided into two groups: family members and harem administration. The family members included royal offspring—underage boys as well as young girls who had not yet entered puberty—royal consorts, and unmarried or widowed princesses.

High-ranking harem administrators—all of them women –received large stipends and enjoyed considerable prestige. They supervised the numerous servants who worked in the harem and managed the training of select young women who had been chosen for higher things, such as marriage to pashas and viziers or service to the sultan or the *valide sultan*. In short, the harem trained girls and women for service to the dynasty, just as the palace school trained young boys for the Janissaries. Servitude played an essential role in both cases. Like the boys being trained as Janissaries, the young girls who entered the harem were also slaves, although in their case they were usually captured beyond the borders of the empire, either in the course of war or in raids. Those who left the harem to marry a member of the Ottoman elite were manumitted before the marriage.

The harem's central task was the production of male heirs in order to ensure the continuation of the Ottoman dynasty. It was a peculiarity of the Ottomans that they relied exclusively on concubines for this; there were no wives in the harem. The concubinage system offered several advantages. First, because the sultan could have as many concubines as he chose, there was little danger of the dynasty remaining without a male heir, as happened so often with European royalty. Second, under Islamic law, a husband and a wife were bound to each other through

Although European Orientalist images of the harem depicted it as a sensual and erotically charged environment, it provided living quarters for the women and children of the imperial household and functioned as a school for the female members of the dynasty. The room pictured here is the reception hall of the Queen Mother. (*Photo by Gábor Ágoston*)

a number of rights and duties. This would have been an intolerable restriction on the sultan's absolute authority. There were powerful concubines, of course, but, like everyone else in the palace, their power came from their ability to play the political game rather than from any legal guarantees. An ambitious girl could have no higher goal than to bed the sultan and give birth to his son. Not only did this raise her far above the other concubines, it also put her in the running to become, some day, the *valide sultan*.

There was no more powerful woman in the empire than the mother of the sultan. At any one time it was likely that there were several mothers and several sons living within the confines of the harem; for this reason, palace politics revolved around the fierce struggle to secure the throne for one's offspring. This was not a matter of the harem alone; prominent men and women in the palace, and beyond, formed factions and threw their support behind one candidate or another. Factional struggles

took place in the shadows, but recent research has shown that the women of the dynasty also exercised their power in a more public fashion. The walls of the harem did not prevent Ottoman princesses, consorts, and others from endowing religious foundations (*WAQFS*), freeing slaves, and undertaking other acts of charity that were considered part of the requirements of high rank.

Like the men of the dynasty, Ottoman women were laid to rest in elaborate imperial tombs after being honored by imperial funerals. The death of the mother of Sultan SÜLEYMAN I (r. 1520–66) was met with an outpouring of public grief, which suggests that the women of the palace harem, despite their seclusion, were known to, and loved by, the general public.

Molly Greene

Further reading: Leslie Peirce, *The Imperial Harem: Women and Sovereignty in the Ottoman Empire* (New York: Oxford University Press, 1993).

al-Hashimi, Faysal ibn Husayn (b. 1883–d. 1933) (r. 1921–33) *king of Iraq, leader of the Arab Revolt* Faysal was the oldest of three sons of HUSAYN IBN ALI AL-HASHIMI, the SHARIF OF MECCA. Much of his youth was spent in ISTANBUL and he spoke Ottoman Turkish fluently. Many of his contemporaries wrote that his manners bore more of the imprint of Ottoman courtly society than of the BEDOUIN fighters that he would later lead. In 1914, as Faysal's father Emir Husayn was trying to decide what course to take in WORLD WAR I, which was pitting the Ottoman Empire against ENGLAND, Husayn's son Abdullah entered into negotiations with the British in CAIRO. Faysal went to Istanbul to gauge the political climate in that city. On his way back to MECCA in 1915, Faysal also met with representatives of the fledgling Arab nationalist movement in DAMASCUS. His discussions in both places led him to agree with his brother Abdullah that the Arabs should rise in revolt so that their father, Husayn, could claim an Arab kingdom in the aftermath of the war.

Husayn wisely did not want to raise the standard of revolt himself on the chance that the Ottomans might prevail. So it was his son Faysal, with Abdullah as his lieutenant, who began the rebellion on June 10, 1916. Rallying various Bedouin tribes to his father's standard, Faysal created the Arab army that proceeded to attack Ottoman garrisons along the desert frontier, pushing northward until they reached Damascus by October 1, 1918. In the war's aftermath, Faysal represented his father at the Paris Peace talks that decided the fate of the former Ottoman Empire. Faysal was deeply disappointed when he learned that the Allies were prepared to follow the SYKES-PICOT AGREEMENT. This agreement called for giving the British and the French control over Arab territories that had earlier been promised as part of a future Arab kingdom.

Feeling betrayed by Britain, Faysal returned to SYRIA, where he attempted to form an independent government. Arab delegates from what are now LEBANON, Israel, the Palestinian Territories, Jordan, and Syria met in Damascus in March 1920. They proclaimed Syria an independent country with Faysal as its king. The swift advance of the French army, which had already occupied Lebanon and coastal Syria since 1918, dashed their hopes. By the end of July, both Damascus and ALEPPO were under French occupation. Faysal fled to join his brother Abdullah in Jordan. To forestall a clash between the Arab army and the French, the British offered Faysal the newly formed kingdom of IRAQ. The British had faced wide-scale resistance to their occupation of that country and felt that someone with the status of Faysal might prove acceptable to the insurgents and quiet the country. In 1922, the British crowned Faysal as the first king of Iraq, and he ruled there until his death in 1933. Although Faysal was not as popular among the people of the newly

formed Iraq as he had been with the Syrians, the Iraqis accepted him as king, given his lineage as a member of the Prophet Muhammad's family.

Bruce Masters

Further reading: Malcolm Russell, *The First Modern Arab State: Syria under Faysal, 1918–1920* (Minneapolis, Minn.: Bibliotheca Islamica, 1985).

al-Hashimi, Husayn ibn Ali (b. 1856–d. 1931) (r. 1908–25) *Sharif of Mecca* In the Sunni political tradition, the notion of hereditary kingship is regarded with distaste, but Sunni legal scholars do consider the clan of the Prophet Muhammad, the Hashimis, to be "first among equals." As a result, Husayn ibn Ali, a member of the al-Hashimi family, was the closest thing to true royalty that Sunni Arabs recognize. Given this background, Husayn became the emir of MECCA in 1908, returning to the holy city from ISTANBUL after a coup brought the COMMITTEE OF UNION AND PROGRESS (CUP) to power. Once reestablished in Mecca, Husayn worked to undermine the secular CUP program, saying that the only law for Arabia was the Quran and the traditions of the Prophet. Despite his opposition to the CUP, he nevertheless remained loyal to the idea of the sultanate and he mobilized BEDOUIN tribesmen to support Ottoman military action against tribal rebels in the Asr region of southern Arabia in 1911. He did, however, protest against the Ottoman treatment of the Bedouin rebels that he thought was cruel and excessive.

As a result of his very open protests over the rebels' treatment, Arab nationalists living in EGYPT and western Europe began to put forward his name as a possible leader of an independent Arab kingdom. Faysal's lack of response to their entreaties to mount a rebellion led them to begin to consider other possible candidates, including candidates from other Arab families, the WAHHABIS and the Sanusis, who had established ruling dynasties in remote areas outside Ottoman control (*see* MUHAMMAD AL-SANUSI). Meanwhile Husayn's son, Abdullah, entered into discussions with British officials in CAIRO in 1914 after the CUP leadership attempted to remove his father from the position of emir. The Ottomans had joined Germany as an ally in what would become WORLD WAR I and the British were looking for possible allies against them. As the Ottomans planned their invasion of Egypt in January 1915, they requested Bedouin auxiliary troops from Husayn. Although he promised that he would raise the troops, they never materialized. Starting in July of 1915, there was an exchange of letters between Sir Henry McMahon, the British high commissioner in Cairo, with Husayn (*see* HUSAYN-MCMAHON CORRESPONDENCE) that sought to bring Husayn into the war as a British ally. Although Husayn also continued to negotiate with the

Ottomans, his son FAYSAL IBN HUSAYN AL-HASHIMI was preparing for a revolt against the Ottomans that began in June 1916.

After the war, the British recognized Husayn as king of the HEJAZ, but he felt that their support fell far short of what had been promised in the Husayn-Mcmahon correspondence. His position in the Hejaz became increasingly untenable as Abd al-Aziz ibn Saud, head of the Wahhabi confederation and future king of Saudi Arabia (1932–53), constructed a network of interlinking alliances with most of Arabia's tribes. In 1925 ibn Saud's forces took Mecca and Husayn went into exile, first to Jerusalem and later to Nicosia (Lefkosia) on CYPRUS, where the British kept a close watch over him, confining him to the island until his death in 1931.

Bruce Masters

See also ARAB REVOLT; FAYSAL IBN HUSAYN AL-HASHIMI; HUSAYN-MCMAHON CORRESPONDENCE.

hayduk (*hajdúk, haydud, haydut*) *Hayduk* was the general term for bandits in the Balkan provinces of the Ottoman Empire;, among the Balkan Christians, it was the term for the rebel bandits who resisted Ottoman rule. The word encompasses a range of meanings in a number of regional languages, establishing the *hayduks* as military irregulars of pastoral origins whose privileges had been curtailed by the Ottoman state, low noblemen of the pre-Ottoman Balkan states, or peasants who reacted to economic and religious oppression by taking to brigandage

The word is drawn from the Hungarian *hajdú* (pl. *hajdúk*), meaning "an armed soldier, professional landless mercenary," but the same word occurs with a similar meaning in Ukrainian, Polish, and Czech. For the Ottomans (*haydud*), Bulgarians (*haydut*), and Serbs (*hayduk*), the word meant "brigand," but for the southern Slavs the primary meaning of the term was "bandits who acted as protectors of Christians against Ottoman oppression." For Greeks, the term *klepht* defines a similar phenomenon. Often regarded as a synonym, the Serbian/Croatian word USKOKS combines all the above meanings of *hayduk*. For the Venetians and the Ottomans the *hayduks* were pirates and brigands, for the Habsburgs they formed part of the Military Frontier as paid soldiers and servicemen or soldiers of fortune, whereas in the folklore of the Christian population they were heroes who fought against the Ottomans.

The earliest Ottoman reference to *hayduks* dates back to the beginning of the 16th century. From the 17th century onward, *hayduks* became a constant feature of the Ottoman Balkans, and were most numerous in the mountainous areas. This expansion is related to the increased tax burden, the military defeats of the Otto-

mans in the wars against their Christian neighbors, and the general decline of security in the provinces. During the 19th century some of the *hayduks* joined the Balkan national liberation movements.

Rarely exceeding 100 men, each band of *hayduks* had a rigid hierarchy, with a leader who was responsible for all decisions. In larger bands, the second-in-command would be the standard-bearer. Both were elected by all members of the group for their personal qualities and experience. Christian folklore in particular speaks of *hayduks* as Christians only, but Ottoman documents mention religiously mixed and even exclusively Muslim bands. The *hayduk* bands operated independently of one another, mainly between the feast days of St. George (April 23 in the Julian calendar) and St. Demetrius (26 October). These are among the saints most respected by Balkan Orthodox Christians, and these saints' days are widely celebrated in the region. According to popular culture, these days frame the warm season favorable for various activities, including the banditry of the *hayduks* hiding in forest areas. The targets of their brigandage were representatives of Ottoman authority and rich people in general, mainly Muslims but also affluent Christians and Jews. Attacks were launched for plunder, to punish particularly oppressive Ottomans, or as acts of personal revenge.

Though the Ottomans may have regarded the *hayduks* as a manifestation of banditry that was common throughout contemporary Europe, folklore suggests that, at least in the imagination of Christians, *hayduk* activities went beyond pure brigandage. This other aspect of their activities—as heroes of the national, religious, and social struggle—has probably been overestimated in later nationalist and Marxist historiography, which interprets these groups as primitive national liberation guerrillas embodying a struggle against foreign domination and oppression. A more balanced view suggests that an element of the sectarian confrontation might have been mixed with class animosity, as Muslims were more often the rich and powerful. Thus religion is an important feature of the *hayduk* motivation that should not be overlooked. It is not surprising then that *hayduks* were often viewed with approval, even respect, and, despite their many acts of pure brigandage and destruction, were glorified in popular legends and folksongs of the Christian subjects of the sultans.

Rossitsa Gradeva

Further reading: John Koliopoulos, *Brigands with a Cause: Brigandage and Irrendentism in Modern Greece, 1821–1912* (Oxford: Clarendon, 1987); Eric Hobsbawm, *Bandits*, rev. ed. (New York: Pantheon, 1969); Catherine Wendy Bracewell, *The Uskoks of Senj: Piracy, Banditry, and Holy War in the Sixteenth-century Adriatic* (Ithaca, N.Y.: Cornell University Press, 1992); Peter Sugar, in *Southeastern*

Europe under Ottoman Rule, 1354–1804 (Seattle: University of Washington Press, 1977), 233–250.

Hayreddin Barbarossa See BARBAROSSA BROTHERS.

Hayreddin Pasha See BARBAROSSA BROTHERS.

Hejaz (Hedjaz; *Ar.***: al-Hijaz;** *Turk.***: Hecaz)** The region of Arabia that lies along the Red Sea is known as the Hejaz. Its principal cities are MECCA and MEDINA and their port cities, respectively JEDDAH and Yanbu. Lacking natural resources, the region nonetheless has great political and religious significance as the cradle of Islam and the Ottoman sultans viewed their sovereignty over the region as helping to legitimate their rule. Despite the region's importance to the sultanate, BEDOUIN tribes dominated the region and the Ottomans decided on a policy of indirect rule rather than confronting them. The sultans appointed Ottoman governors to Medina and Jeddah but allowed for local rule everywhere else, and only those two towns had permanent military garrisons. Subsidies provided by the state and charity (*zakat*) provided by individuals from throughout the Muslim world were the main source of income for the population of the two Holy Cities, but trade generated by the annual HAJJ was also an important source of revenue. During WORLD WAR I, the tribes of the Hejaz provided the main support for the ARAB REVOLT.

Bruce Masters

See also MECCA; MEDINA.

Further reading: William Ochsenwald, *Religion, Society and the State in Arabia: The Hijaz under Ottoman Control, 1840–1908* (Columbus: Ohio State University Press, 1984).

Hejaz Railroad (Hijaz Railroad, Hedjaz Railroad) Sultan ABDÜLHAMID II (r. 1876–1909) conceived the project of a railroad line to connect the Holy Cities of Arabia to the railroad that was being constructed from Berlin to Baghdad as one of great importance for the Ottoman Empire. It would enhance his position in the Muslim world by making the HAJJ more accessible and would also serve a military function. The Ottomans' ability to control YEMEN had been tenuous for centuries and the army commanders reasoned that a railroad that might eventually reach that troubled province would help secure it permanently. The biggest problem that the Ottomans faced in carrying out this plan was how to finance it. Europeans were constructing the other railroad lines in the Ottoman Empire. The Ottoman government obtained their cooperation by assigning future tax revenues to be generated by those railroads, as well as land rights along the tracks, to the companies financing the projects. Muslim sensibilities, however, would not accede to a railroad being built to the Holy Cities by non-Muslims. Sultan Abdülhamid II solved the problem by announcing in 1900 that the project would be financed entirely by the empire and through contributions from Muslims around the world. The railroad became a project of intense pride throughout the Ottoman Empire, with even schoolchildren contributing to the costs of its construction.

In 1900, construction of the line began in Damascus, heading south. In 1907 another crew started construction in MEDINA, heading north to meet the line coming south. The two lines met in 1908, completing the project. In addition to the main line, a secondary spur line connected the port of HAIFA to the Hejaz Railroad at Daraa, and plans were made to build additional connectors to JERUSALEM and GAZA. Religious sentiment among the conservative clergy in MECCA prevented extension of the railroad to that city and plans to extend the tracks to Yemen had to be shelved.

Conscript soldiers provided much of the physical labor of laying the tracks, and despite significant attempts to raise money outside the Ottoman Empire, especially in India, the Ottoman state paid most of the actual costs of construction in the end. However, once completed, the railroad did not produce significant income for the state. Most pilgrims continued to prefer to reach Mecca by steamship, as the overland journey from Medina to Mecca by camel remained arduous. Militarily, the railroad did serve Ottoman interests as it allowed them quickly to dispatch troops to JABAL AL-DRUZ, a mountainous region in southern Syria, to put down a rebellion in 1909 and again to the desert town of Karak, in present-day Jordan, in 1910. Furthermore, the railroad allowed the Ottomans to retain control of Medina by supplying its garrison during the ARAB REVOLT, although the trains and tracks of the line were frequent targets of attacks. The revolt forced the closure of the line to civilian traffic in 1917, but it continued to carry military transport until 1918. After WORLD WAR I, only the sections of the rail line in Syria and Jordan continued in use, although in the early 21st century negotiations began to reopen a line from Saudi Arabia to Jordan.

Bruce Masters

See also RAILROADS.

Further reading: William Ochsenwald, *The Hijaz Railroad* (Charlottesville: University Press of Virginia, 1980).

historiography Until the 16th century, Turkish historiography was written in the simple form of a story or epic based on folk language and thought. After the

16th century, and especially with writers Idris Bitlisi, Ali Çelebi, and Hoca Saadeddin, a new form of historiography began to emerge, shaped by Safavid historiography in neighboring Iran. In this new approach, historians sought to judge the causes and effects of events rather than simply relating a narrative. Nevertheless, the core of Ottoman historiography remained anchored in literal transmission, storytelling, and description. Although historians such as Katib Çelebi, Müneccimbaşı, and Naima used criticism in their histories, real change did not emerge until the 19th century, coinciding with the westernization process that occurred during the Tanzimat or Ottoman reform era (1839–76). The most significant aspect of this historiographical paradigm shift was the abandonment of a religious perspective in favor of a dynastic approach. One of the reasons for this shift was perhaps that this was seen as a means of establishing and preserving the unity of the Ottoman Empire in the face of increasingly aggressive secessionist demands on the part of Christian subjects of the empire.

The historical works of Ahmed Cevdet Pashas, especially his *Tarih-i Cevdet* (History of Cevdet), are the most representative products of Tanzimat historiography. Written as a continuation of German historian Joseph Freiherr von Hammer's 10-volume *Geschichte des osmanischen Reiches* (History of the Ottoman Empire), *Tarih-i Cevdet* was significantly different from classical-era Ottoman works of history in terms of its method and content. This introductory volume on historical sociology, inspired by Ibn Khaldun, offered a unique perspective on the rise and decline of world civilizations. Cevdet Pasha utilized travelogues, diplomatic documents, state memoranda, and archival documents in addition to earlier works on Ottoman history. Although this book was similar to earlier historiography in form, its content was radically different, for it noted developments in Europe and covered topics written by European historians. In many ways, Cevdet Pasha's work was a turning point in Ottoman historiography.

Nevertheless, some contemporary historians, such as Mükrimin Halil Yinanç, emphasize the Second Constitutional Period (1908–18), especially the publication of the Journal of the Society for Ottoman History, *Tarih-i Osmani Encümeni Mecmuası* (TOEM) in 1910, as the real turning point at which the Ottoman Empire began to produce more objective historical scholarship. With the publication of TOEM, leading historians of that era began to publish frequently. The society had the support of the sultan and initially aimed at producing a comprehensive history of the Ottoman state. The first volume of this work, written by Mehmed Arif and Necib Asım, discussed the history of Turks before the emergence of the Ottoman Empire. This was a new way of envisioning Ottoman history, as part of a greater history of Turkish people. Overall, the society was instrumental in producing and publishing various monographs, sultanic legislation, and chronicles, and thus in helping the next generation of historians by uncovering, disseminating, and preserving essential primary documents. Upon the establishment of the Turkish republic, the name of the society was changed to the Turkish Historical Association (Türk Tarih Encümeni); its journal, *Türk Tarih Encümeni Mecmuasi* (TTEM), continued publication until 1931.

Among the authors who wrote for TOEM, Ahmed Refik was undoubtedly the most influential. His work served as a bridge between traditional and modern historiography. As he was also a member of the Committee of Union and Progress, Ahmed Refik's historical writings were close to an official history. He followed developments in European historiography very closely and introduced German and French historians, such as Leopold von Ranke and Jules Michelet, to his readers. His popularizing style expanded his readership to include a broader literate public.

In Turkish historiography, the 1930s was a period when history was written under the influence of a nationalist approach. Institutional support was given to this history writing by both the 1933 university reform and the foundation of the Association of Turkish Historical Research. In this context, Mustafa Kemal Atatürk subsidized the translation of *The Outline of World History* by British author H. G. Wells in 1928.

Several other leading intellectuals and historians, such as Yusuf Akçura, Ziya Gökalp, Ahmed Refik, and Fuad Köprülü, also served as links between traditional Ottoman historiography and modern Turkish historiography. Köprülü, in particular, led the leap into modern Turkish historiography, including new perspectives and material evidence in writings such as his influential 1931 text, *The Review of Turkish Economic and Legal History*. Indeed, his works were so influential that the dominant school of historiography of the time, the Annales School, was supplanted by the Köprülü School.

There are two important points in Köprülü's approach: evaluating Ottoman history within the context of general Turkish history, and considering the economic, cultural, social, and judicial systems of Turkic states together. In accordance with this approach, Köprülü tries to explain the origins of the Ottoman Empire within the general framework of the Seljuk Empire's social, economic, and cultural history. In his opinion, the illumination of Turkish history is not the task of lawyers and philologists; rather, it is the business of historians who are able to see that economics and socioeconomic problems are the primary determining factors of social change.

The followers of the Köprülü School advanced further on the same path. Their works included Abdülkadir Inan's examination of the Shamanistic religion of the Turks that preceded their adoption of Islam; Faruk Sümer's research on the migrations and nomadic lives of the Turks; Abdülkadir Gölpınarlı's history of Turkish thought in the context of Sufism; Pertev Naili Boratav's anthropological and folkloric works about the Turks; Osman Turan's exploration of Seljuk history, Mustafa Akdağ's social and economic history of the Seljuks and the Ottomans; and, finally, Halil İnalcık's numerous works on the Ottomans.

Another important historian, Ömer Lütfi Barkan, cannot be included in the list, for although he benefited from the Köprülü approach and resources, he cannot be said to adhere to the Köprülü School. Indeed, Barkan's approach is itself novel, as he changed the method of historical research in Turkey through his research on, and publications of, social history and historical demography. Barkan even developed an independent economic history. Because of the work of such pioneers, Turkish historiography has gained an eminent position in the discipline of modern world historiography.

In the 1960s, Turkish historiography entered into the challenging social questions taken up by the nation's intelligentsia, such as how Turkey could be liberated from such problems as underdevelopment and political dependence. Historiography during this period was characterized by the study of economic history and there was an increasing tendency to explain current problems within the former Ottoman Empire through economics. Three major approaches have emerged as a result: the Asian Mode of Production, the Dependence Theory, and the Modern World System.

During the 1980s, the Ottoman archives were deregulated as political reasons such as the Ottoman-Armenian controversies pressured politicians. This opening initiated archival studies and led many specialists in the field to develop and produce documentary publications. Scholarship has benefited substantially from this activity as many new studies were launched in areas such as Armenian and Kurdish relations with the Ottomans and the Turkish minority issue in west Thrace. Scholarship in the arena of economic and social history, however, diminished significantly with this new movement.

Transformations in Ottoman Turkish historiography are reflective of transformations in the structure of Ottoman state and society itself, such as the modernization process of the Tanzimat period, the constitutional movements (see Constitution/Constitutional Period), and the foundation of the Turkish republic.

Çoşkun Çakır

See also Court Chroniclers.
Further reading: Halil Berktay, "The 'Other' Feudalism: A Critique of 20th-century Turkish Historiography and Its Particularization of Ottoman Society (Ph.D. diss., University of Birmingham, 1990); Bernard Lewis and P. M. Holt, *Historians of the Middle East (Historical Writing on the*

Peoples of Asia) (Oxford: Oxford University Press, 1962); Gabriel Piterberg, *An Ottoman Tragedy: History and Historiography at Play* (Berkeley: University of California Press, 2003).

Hungary (*Ger.:* **Ungarn;** *Hung.:* **Magyarország;** *Turk.:* **Macaristan**) Relations between the Ottomans and the Hungarians fall into three main periods. The first period started in 1375, with the earliest documented direct military conflict between Hungarian and Ottoman forces in Wallachia (present-day Romania) and lasted until the annihilation of the Hungarian army at the Battle of Mohács (1526) at the hands of Sultan Süleyman I (r. 1520–66). This first period was characterized by gradual Ottoman expansion in the Balkans, to the south of the medieval Kingdom of Hungary (1000–1526), as well as by Hungarian attempts to halt the Ottoman advance by extending Hungarian influence in the Balkans and by building an anti-Ottoman defense system along the southern borders of Hungary. With the collapse of this defense system by the early 1520s, the road to Hungary and central Europe was open for the Ottomans. The second phase of Hungarian-Ottoman relations started with the Battle of Mohács, which not only meant the end of the medieval Kingdom of Hungary in 1526 but also marked the beginning of a long period of Habsburg-Ottoman military confrontation in central Europe, for the Habsburgs ruled the remaining northern and western parts of Hungary from 1526 on. Unfortunately for Hungary, the country thus became the major battlefield for 150 years in the Habsburg-Ottoman rivalry in central Europe. In 1541, central Hungary was incorporated into the Ottoman Empire and was ruled as an Ottoman province until 1699, marking the end of the second period. In the third period, which lasted from 1699 until the collapse of the Ottoman and Austro-Hungarian Empires in World War I, the Ottomans lost Hungary to the Habsburgs and withdrew to the Balkans. During this time, Hungarian-Ottoman relations ran parallel with Austro-Ottoman relations (*see* Austria).

OTTOMAN-HUNGARIAN RELATIONS BEFORE THE OTTOMAN CONQUEST OF HUNGARY

The first ruler to face the Ottoman threat was King Sigismund of Luxembourg (r. 1387–1437; Holy Roman Emperor, 1433–1437). Unsuccessful in his campaigns against the Ottomans and defeated by them at the Battle of Nikopol 1396, King Sigismund reorganized his country's defense system and introduced thorough military reforms. The fortress system he had built along the country's southern borders using the Sava and Danube rivers was updated by his successors and successfully protected the country through the early 1520s.

In the 1440s János (John) Hunyadi, royal governor of TRANSYLVANIA, Hungary's eastern region, and governor of the entire kingdom between 1446 and 1452, led several victorious campaigns against the Ottomans, sustaining defeats on only two occasions: at the Battle of Varna (1444) and at the second Battle of Kosovo Polje ("the field of the blackbirds," 1448). In 1456 Hunyadi achieved his most important victory by defending BELGRADE, the key fortress of the southern Hungarian defense system, against Sultan MEHMED II (r. 1444–46; 1451–81). Due partly to the psychological effects of this Ottoman setback, partly to the military reforms of Hunyadi's son, King Matthias Corvinus (r. 1458–90), and partly to Ottoman military commitments in eastern Anatolia and EGYPT under sultans BAYEZID II (r. 1481–1512) and SELIM I (r. 1512–20), the Ottomans did not again launch a major campaign against Hungary until 1521.

However, in this year Sultan SÜLEYMAN I's (r. 1520–66) forces conquered Belgrade; in the course of the next three years, all the major Hungarian castles along the Danube as far as Belgrade fell into Ottoman hands. The Battle of Mohács (1526) marked a major turning point not only in the history of Hungarian-Ottoman relations but also in the history of central Europe.

HABSBURG-OTTOMAN RIVALRY AND THE OTTOMAN CONQUEST OF HUNGARY

Although Süleyman withdrew from Hungary by the autumn of 1526, his victory at Mohács, which killed the Hungarian king Louis II (r. 1516–26), led to a civil war in the country. The competing noble factions elected two kings: János (John) Szapolyai (r. 1526–1540), Hungary's richest aristocrat and royal governor of Transylvania, and Ferdinand of Habsburg (r. 1526–1564), archduke of Austria and younger bother of Holy Roman Emperor Charles V (r. 1519–56). With Ottoman military assistance, Szapolyai controlled the eastern parts of Hungary while Ferdinand ruled the country's northern and western parts. When Szapolyai's death in 1540 upset the military balance between the Habsburgs and the Ottomans, Sultan Süleyman occupied BUDA (1541), the medieval Hungarian capital. It became the center of a newly established Ottoman province, or *beylerbeylik*, which encompassed most of central Hungary. Since eastern Hungary lay outside the main military route leading from Belgrade through Buda to Habsburg Vienna, its occupation was not warranted. As an Ottoman *sancak*, this territory was left under the control of the guardians of Szapolyai's infant son, and was soon to become the principality of TRANSYLVANIA, an independent polity under Ottoman vassalage. However, due to its strategic location, the Ottomans occupied the area around Temesvár (Timişoara in present-day Romania) in 1552, and turned it into their

second Ottoman province in Hungary, the *beylerbeylik* of Temeşvar. Throughout the 16th and 17th centuries the Habsburgs, who remained on the Hungarian throne until 1918, had to content themselves with northern and western Hungary, known as Royal Hungary. Although the Ottomans launched seven campaigns against Hungary and the Habsburgs in the 16th and 17th centuries, and the two empires waged two exhausting wars on Hungarian soil (1593–1606 and 1683–99), the buffer-zone-turned-country saved Habsburg central Europe from further Ottoman conquests.

While successive Habsburg-Ottoman peace treaties (1547, 1568, 1606, 1627, 1642, and 1664) maintained the tripartite division of the country, the Hungarian elite did not accept this partition and wanted to unite the country. In the 16th century many sided with the Habsburgs and tried to expel the Ottomans. By the end of the century, however, the majority of Hungarians had converted to Protestantism. They were angered by Vienna's aggressive re-Catholization and hesitant policy toward the Ottomans. Beginning with the insurrection of István (Stephan) Bocskai (r. 1604–06), elected Prince of Hungary and Transylvania, the Hungarians launched several anti-Habsburg wars in the 17th century, led by the princes of Transylvania, who were considered by all Hungarians as the defenders of Hungarian sovereignty. However, these wars of liberation were often used by the Ottomans to enlarge their possessions in Hungary.

Ottoman conquests in the Long Hungarian War of 1593–1606 extended the area under their control in Hungary. Not counting the short-lived *beylerbeyliks* of Yanık (Győr) and Pápa, two new provinces were added to the existing *beylerbeyliks* of Budin and Temeşvar in the 16th century: Eğri (Eger in present-day northern Hungary) in 1596, and Kanije (Kanizsa in present-day southwestern Hungary) in 1600.

Further significant border changes took place in the 1660s under the KÖPRÜLÜ grand viziers' Hungarian wars, provoked by Prince György Rákóczi II's Polish campaign (1657) and Count Miklós Zrínyi's (Nikola Zrinski) anti-Turkish raids and campaigns. Prince György Rákóczi II launched his campaign against Poland with an eye on the Polish crown, without the consent of his overlord, the Ottoman sultan. The CRIMEAN TATARS, Istanbul's vassals, laid Transylvania waste. The Ottomans occupied Várad (present-day Oradea, Romania) in 1660 and organized a new *beylerbeylik* around it. Using as a pretext the construction of a new Hungarian fortress erected by Count Zrínyi, the *bán* or royal governor and commander of Croatia, Grand Vizier Köprülü Ahmed attacked Hungary again in 1663, conquering Érsekújvár (Nové Zámky in present-day Slovakia). Known in Ottoman documents as Uyvar, the fort and the new *beylerbeylik* around it, drove a wedge into the Hungarian defensive ring around

This memorial in the castle of Buda marks the site where Abdurrahman Arnavud Abdi Pasha, the last Ottoman governor of Buda, is believed to have fallen while defending the city on September 2, 1686. The writing honors Abdurrahman Pasha as a "brave enemy." *(Photo by Gábor Ágoston)*

Vienna and significantly increased the protection of Ottoman Budin, "the bulwark of Islam."

When Vienna conceded further Hungarian territories to the Ottomans at the Treaty of Vasvár (1664), despite Zrínyi's successful winter campaign and the Habsburg victory at the Battle of St. Gotthard, even the loyal Catholic magnates of Royal Hungary were outraged and many joined an anti-Habsburg conspiracy in 1670–71. The severe punishment of the members of this plot and Emperor Leopold's (r. 1658–1705) confessional absolutism triggered new waves of anti-Habsburg rebellions. Of these, the most serious was Imre Thököly's insurrection (1681–83). This led to the creation of yet another pro-Ottoman vassal state in Upper Hungary (Orta Macar or Middle Hungary) at a critical moment when the Ottomans' failed SIEGE OF VIENNA (1683) set off an international counteroffensive which, by 1699, had reconquered most of Hungary

from the Ottomans. Defeated in the war of 1683–99, the Ottomans ceded most of Hungary and Transylvania to the Habsburgs in the TREATY OF KARLOWITZ.

In the Ottoman-Habsburg War of 1716–17, the Habsburgs, led by Prince Eugene of Savoy (b. 1663–d. 1736), recaptured the remaining Hungarian territories, ending the 150-year-old Ottoman rule in Hungary.

OTTOMAN ADMINISTRATION IN HUNGARY

From an administrative point of view, Ottoman Hungary superficially resembled the core zones of the Ottoman Empire. Ottoman-held Hungary was divided into *beylerbeyliks* and *sancaks*; its resources were mapped and recorded during periodic land surveys (*tahrir*); and its inhabitants were taxed according to Ottoman provincial law codes (*kanunname*). Ottoman garrison towns in Hungary also looked a lot like those in the Balkans, with their mosques and minarets, covered and open bazaars, bathhouses, dervish lodges, and caravansaries, as well as with their wandering dervishes and their Muslim, Jewish, Greek, and Armenian merchants and craftsmen. However, Ottoman-held Hungary never was integrated into the Ottoman system like the core zones in the Balkans, and it retained its Hungarian and Christian identity throughout the Ottoman rule. The country was only partly conquered and, unlike in the Balkans, the defeated ruling elite and their institutions were not destroyed. The aristocrats and most of the nobility moved to Royal Hungary or Transylvania. From there, with the help of the Hungarian garrisons, they administered their estates in Ottoman Hungary, taxed their peasants, and delivered justice. The Ottomans, who considered these peasants Ottoman subjects, initially opposed these practices, but it proved impossible to seal the borders. In the peace treaty of 1547 Istanbul acknowledged the joint Hungarian-Ottoman rule or CONDOMINIUM. Henceforth the Ottomans shared administrative and judicial power, as well as the subjects' taxes, with Hungary's Habsburg kings, the Hungarian nobility, and the Catholic and Protestant churches.

DEMOGRAPHIC CONSEQUENCES OF THE OTTOMAN WARS AND RULE

Despite continuous skirmishes, raids, and wars, Hungary's population had increased from 3.1 million in the 1490s to 4 million by the early 1680s. This modest increase did not differ significantly from demographic trends in the region, which witnessed a population increase toward the end of the 16th century and stagnation or decrease in the 17th century. However, the increase in the population of Hungary was largely due to immigration, especially from the Balkans and the two Romanian principalities. While Magyars or ethnic Hungarians constituted some 75 to 80 percent of the kingdom's population before Ottoman rule, they had become a minority by the early 18th century. This had fateful consequences for the country in later centuries.

Gábor Ágoston

See also BUDIN; KARLOWITZ, TREATY OF; MOHÁCS, BATTLE OF; SÜLEYMAN I; TRANSYLVANIA.

Further reading: Géza Dávid and Pál Fodor, eds., *Ottomans, Hungarians and Habsburgs in Central Europe: The Military Confines in the Era of Ottoman Conquest* (Leiden: Brill, 2000); Béla Király and László Veszprémy, eds., *A Millennium of Hungarian Military History* (Boulder, Colo.: Atlantic Research and Publications, 2002); Béla Köpeczi, ed., *History of Transylvania* (Budapest: Akadémiai Kiadó, 1994); Peter F Sugar, ed., *A History of Hungary* (Bloomington: Indiana University Press, 1994); István György Tóth, ed., *A Concise History of Hungary* (Budapest: Corvina and Osiris, 2005).

Hünkar Iskelesi, Treaty of (Unkiar Skelessi, Treaty of) (1833)   This mutual defense treaty, signed between the Ottoman and Russian empires on July 8, 1833, was the direct result of the Egyptian invasion of the Ottoman Empire (1831–33). By December 1832 the Egyptians had driven deep into Ottoman Anatolia and were prepared to launch a strike against ISTANBUL. Neither the British nor the French were in a position to provide concrete military assistance to the Ottoman Empire. Therefore the Ottoman sultan MAHMUD II (r. 1808–39) appealed to the Russian czar Nicholas I to send troops to Istanbul to help counter the threat posed by IBRAHIM PASHA's Egyptian army. Sensing an opportunity to increase Russian influence in Istanbul at the expense of the British and French, and fearing the rise of a modernized Egyptian state in the Near East, Nicholas I welcomed Mahmud II's entreaty. In February 1833 Russian forces marched through the Danubian principalities of WALLACHIA and MOLDAVIA toward Istanbul; by March, 20,000 Russian soldiers were encamped in the environs of the Ottoman capital. Additionally, a Russian fleet sailed across the BLACK SEA toward Istanbul in preparation for military action against Ibrahim Pasha.

The Treaty of Hünkar Iskelesi, negotiated primarily by the able Russian diplomat A. F. Orlov, formalized the Russo-Ottoman military alliance that had resulted from the Egyptian invasion of the Ottoman Empire. This alliance signaled a stunning reversal in the traditionally antagonistic relationship between these two powers. In the treaty, the two empires agreed, for a period of eight years, to come to each other's defense in case either was attacked by a foreign power. In a secret article to the treaty, the Russians exempted the Ottomans from providing military assistance in return for an Ottoman agreement that upon the outbreak of hostilities between the Russian Empire and any foreign powers, the Ottoman Empire would close the strait of the Dardanelles to all non-Russian warships. This secret article, once it was uncovered by British and French agents in Istanbul, caused alarm in London and Paris and was interpreted to mean that the Ottomans had given the Russians free rein to send warships from the Black Sea into the Mediterranean. Additionally, it was clear to the British and the French that, for the time being, the Russian Empire had gained a dominant diplomatic position in Istanbul. This secret article of the treaty led to ongoing multilateral negotiations among RUSSIA, ENGLAND, FRANCE, AUSTRIA, and Prussia regarding access to the strait of the Bosporus and the Dardanelles. These negotiations, in turn, led to the signing of the London Straits Convention in 1841. This convention essentially barred all foreign warships from using the Straits and placed the Straits, for the first time, under international supervision. For these reasons—the issue of access to the Straits and the exposure of Russia's geostrategic ambitions in the Ottoman lands—the Treaty of Hünkar Iskelesi is generally analyzed within the context of the CRIMEAN WAR (1854–56).

Andrew Robarts

Further reading: Barbara Jelavich, *History of the Balkans,* vol. 1, *Eighteenth and Nineteenth Centuries* (Cambridge: Cambridge University Press, 1983); Paul Robert Magosci, *Historical Atlas of East Central Europe* (Seattle: University of Washington Press, 1993); Stanford J. Shaw, *History of the Ottoman Empire and Modern Turkey,* vol. 2, *Reform, Revolution and the Republic: The Rise of Modern Turkey, 1808–1975* (Cambridge: Cambridge University Press, 1977).

Husayn-McMahon correspondence   During WORLD WAR I, between July 1915 and March 1916, a series of letters between HUSAYN IBN ALI AL-HASHIMI and Sir Henry McMahon, the British high commissioner in CAIRO, set out British promises for an independent Arab kingdom in the postwar settlement if Husayn, the SHARIF OF MECCA, would declare a revolt against the Ottoman sultan. At the time the correspondence was initiated, the British campaign against the Ottoman Empire in World War I was going badly and British forces had suffered two significant defeats: he withdrawal of British Commonwealth forces (troops from Australia and New Zealand as well as Great Britain and Ireland) from Gallipoli, and the annihilation of the British expeditionary force in IRAQ. Additionally, a stubborn Ottoman defense in GAZA stalled the advance of British forces from EGYPT into PALESTINE. Britain needed another military front against the Ottomans, as well as a Muslim ally who could challenge both the Ottoman sultan's claim to the CALIPHATE and his declaration of holy war against ENGLAND and its allies.

In his initial correspondence, Husayn called for an Arab caliphate to include all of the Arabian Peninsula and the Asian portions of the Ottoman Empire that were south of the Taurus Mountains. That would include the territory that currently comprises Iraq, SYRIA, LEBANON, Jordan, Israel, and the Palestinian Territories, as well as Saudi Arabia and Yemen. McMahon replied that Britain would welcome a caliphate, led by an "Arab of true race." But because he was aware of British promises to France about the future of Syria, he was otherwise vague in his response. Pressed by Husayn, McMahon's letter of October 24, 1915 gave unconditional British political support for an Arab caliphate and the promise of British troops to defend the Holy Cities. He went on to say, however, that the Arabs would have to recognize that Britain had established interests in BAGHDAD and BASRA that would require "special administrative arrangements." But with these issues unclear, FAYSAL IBN HUSAYN AL-HASHIMI, Husayn's son, declared, the ARAB REVOLT in June 1916 in his father's name.

In the aftermath of World War I, the contents of the letters and what exactly was promised were hotly debated. The most controversial element of McMahon's letter was the following sentence: "The two districts of Mersina and Alexandretta and portions of Syria lying to the west of the districts of Damascus, Homs, Hama and Aleppo cannot said to be purely Arab, and should be excluded from the limits demanded." Although obviously written with French interests in Lebanon in mind, the exact parameters of the area described have been a subject of debate. Were these words intended to include Palestine as part of the territory promised to the future Arab kingdom? Winston Churchill argued at the Paris Peace Conference that they did not, but other historians have disagreed. They have also disagreed over whether the SYKES-PICOT AGREEMENT negated the promise made to Husayn about British support for an independent Arab caliphate even within diminished borders. Whatever the British felt they had promised to Emir Husayn, Arabs after the war, faced with the partition of the former Ottoman provinces into Palestine and Iraq, governed by the British, and Syria and Lebanon, governed by the French, felt that Emir Faysal had proclaimed his revolt in vain.

Bruce Masters

Further reading: Matthew Hughes, *Allenby and British Strategy in the Middle East, 1917–1919* (London: Frank Cass, 1999).

I

ibn Abd al-Wahhab, Muhammad (b. 1703–d. 1792) *Muslim reformer and scholar* Muhammad ibn Abd al-Wahhab was a radical Muslim reformer who, in the 18th century, founded a militant movement in the Arabian Peninsula that those outside the movement call WAHHABIS, after its founder. However, for those who follow his teachings, that name is as offensive as is the term "Muhammadanism" for Islam generally. Both terms seem to give precedence to a mortal over God and are unacceptable to the Muslim faithful. Those who follow the teachings of ibn Abd al-Wahhab prefer the Arabic term *Muwahhidun*, meaning "those who assert the absolute unity of God." This term is rejected by those who feel it implies that the faith of other Muslims is an inferior form. Whether identified as Wahhabi or Muwahhidun, the movement challenged the political legitimacy of the Ottoman Empire by asserting that the House of Osman had usurped political authority in the Muslim world and that their rule was therefore illegitimate. The movement had a profound effect that continues today as it created a new sect that views itself as the only legitimate form of Islam.

Muhammad ibn Abd al-Wahhab was born in the NAJD around 1703, the son of a respected religious scholar and judge. He studied in religious schools in BASRA, BAGHDAD, and MECCA before returning to his native town of al-Uyayna in the 1730s. Ibn Abd al-Wahhab was deeply influenced in his study by the writings of the 14th-century Muslim scholar ibn Taymiyya. Ibn Taymiyya had written that the Muslims of his day had strayed far from the path that the Quran and the Prophet's example had established. Ibn Abd al-Wahhab found a close parallel between the state of Islam in his time

and the world in which ibn Taymiyya had lived. Like ibn Taymiyya, ibn Abd al-Wahhab lashed out at what he saw as the saint-worship practiced within SUFISM, which he denounced as *shirk*, the sin of assigning partners to God. He was especially outraged by the practices of SHIA ISLAM that he encountered in Iraq, which included the veneration of the sanctified martyrs of Imam Ali's lineage. Ibn Abd al-Wahhab regarded this as a cultic practice. While his political ideology was not strongly developed, ibn Abd al-Wahhab particularly condemned those who—in his opinion, illegitimately—identified themselves as "shah." This was an attack on the Ottoman sultans, one of whose imperial titles was padishah. According to ibn Abd al-Wahhab, Muslim rulers had to conform strictly to Muslim law; if they failed to do so, they were no longer truly Muslims. In this he was again influenced by ibn Taymiyya who had elaborated the concept of TAKFIR, whereby Muslims could declare other Muslims "nonbelievers" if they failed to live up to the standards set by a strict adherence to Muslim law.

Ibn Abd al-Wahhab taught a literalist reading of the Quran and a healthy skepticism of Muslim traditions, known as the *sunna*. He believed that the *sunna* were the reflection of human intervention and, therefore, were not necessarily divinely inspired. He preferred to rely solely on the Quran, a work that all Muslims agreed was divine. In instances where the Quran offered no guidance, he allowed that Muslim scholars could make limited use of *ijtihad*, or judicial reasoning.

This was an open break with the SUNNI ISLAM legal traditions of the previous six centuries, which held that since Muslim scholars were far removed from the Prophet's generation, they did not fully understand the historical context of revelation. According to Sunni legal tradition, although earlier generations of scholars could form independent interpretations of the Quran, contemporary scholars must instead rely on the *sunna*, the legal traditions handed down to them. Muslim reformers of the late 19th century, such as MUHAMMAD ABDUH, would draw on ibn Abd al-Wahhab's sanction of the process of *ijtihad* to promote their own agenda in the SALAFIYYA, or reformist movement, as it would allow them to exercise independent judgment in advocating far-reaching reforms of their society. However, they did not necessarily adopt his other more radical readings of Islamic doctrine such as the use of *takfir*.

Ibn Abd al-Wahhab's attitudes toward tribal practices of the BEDOUINS—such as their methods of administering justice and their veneration of local saints, which he deemed un-Islamic—got him in trouble in Uyayna. He was forced to seek refuge in al-Diriyyah, near Riyadh, which was controlled by Muhammad ibn Saud. The two men formed an alliance, cemented by marriage, which their descendants would maintain down to the present. When Muhammad ibn Saud died in 1765 his son Abd al-Aziz, whom ibn Abd al-Wahhab had mentored, succeeded his father as the political head of the movement they called Muwahhidun, while ibn Abd al-Wahhab remained its spiritual authority. It was that separation of religious and political authority by the two clans that provided resiliency for the movement in times of political crisis.

Bruce Masters

See also IBN SAUD FAMILY.

Further reading: Aleksei Vasil'ev, *The History of Saudi Arabia* (New York: New York University Press, 2000).

ibn Saud family The ibn Saud family that rules the Kingdom of Saudi Arabia today also founded the dynasty to which the kingdom owes its name. The inception of this kingdom may be traced back to the relationship between Muhammad ibn Saud and the Muslim reformer MUHAMMAD IBN ABD AL-WAHHAB in the 18th century, when ibn Saud provided shelter to ibn Abd al-Wahhab. The two men formed an alliance in which the descendants of Muhammad ibn Saud would serve as the political leaders of a movement whose religious ideology would adhere to the teachings of Muhammad ibn Abd al-Wahhab; the movement, known as Muwahhidun, was more commonly called the WAHHABIS or Wahhabism by outsiders. With the death of Muhammad ibn Saud in 1765, the political leadership of the movement passed to his son, Abd al-Aziz. Abd al-Aziz captured Riyadh in 1773; he held all of the NAJD by 1785 and the entire Persian Gulf region of al-Ahsa by 1790. Having secured central and eastern Arabia, the Wahhabi warriors moved into IRAQ where they defeated the warriors of the SHAMMAR confederacy, the Bedouin tribal alliance that controlled the desert of what is today western Iraq. In 1798, alarmed by the success of the Wahhabis, BÜYÜK SÜLEYMAN, the governor of Baghdad, mounted a force of JANISSARIES and tribal allies to invade al-Ahsa; the expedition ended with a military stalemate and a truce. In 1801, in a dramatic break with that truce, Abd al-Aziz ordered his tribesmen to attack the Shii holy cities of NAJAF and KARBALA. Karbala was sacked, and many Shii civilians were massacred. In 1803, in retaliation for this attack, a Shii assassinated Abd al-Aziz. Abd al-Aziz was succeeded by his son, Saud, who pursued the campaign of Wahhabi military expansion, seizing both MECCA and MEDINA and raiding into Syria. Once in Mecca, the Wahhabis prevented Ottoman Muslims from performing the HAJJ, but allowed Muslims from other states to do so. Faced with the unraveling of Ottoman control along its desert frontier with Arabia and the loss of prestige that came with the disruption of the hajj by the Wahhabis, the Ottoman sultan MAHMUD II (r. 1808–39) requested the governor of Egypt, MEHMED ALI, to act. Mehmed Ali designated his son, Tosun, to take charge of the Egyptian force in 1811; he had recaptured Mecca by 1812. In 1816 Mehmed Ali removed Tosun for not pursuing his opponents into the Najd and replaced him with another son, IBRAHIM PASHA. In 1818 Ibrahim Pasha penetrated the Najd and took the Wahhabi capital of al-Diriyyah. Flush with victory, Ibrahim sent the captured Wahhabi leader, Abdullah, the son of Saud, to ISTANBUL, and destroyed the town of al-Diriyyah.

In 1824, when it looked as if the fortunes of the House of ibn Saud were in tatters, Turki, a cousin of Saud, seized the leadership of the clan and the Wahhabi movement, reviving the ideological motivation of the movement and capturing the oasis town of Riyadh that would henceforth serve as the dynasty's capital. Turki was able to restore Wahhabi rule to the entire Najd and al-Ahsa region, but he was unable to advance into the Hejaz. With Turki's death in 1865, rivalry within the clan weakened the Wahhabis' hold over their territories. Aware of the quarrels, the Ottomans sought to end the power of the ibn Saud dynasty. They landed an army on the Persian Gulf and were able to retake parts of al-Ahsa province in 1871. Another Bedouin clan, that of ibn Rashid, began to contest the monopoly of power held by the House of ibn Saud over the Arab tribes of the Najd and eventually dislodged the clan of ibn Saud from Riyadh.

The fortunes of the dynasty revived in 1902 when Abd al-Aziz ibn Saud, at the age of 20 and reportedly with only 40 men, retook Riyadh in a daring raid. Abd al-Aziz was able to rally some of the tribes that had formerly acknowledged the leadership of the House of Saud and wage a campaign against the House of ibn Rashid.

They, in turn, called on the Ottoman government for support. The Ottomans supplied ibn Rashid with a large force that initially broke the charge of the Wahhabi warriors in the summer of 1904. But the Wahhabi tribesmen rallied and in a second battle that same summer, they decisively defeated the expeditionary force.

Abd al-Aziz consolidated Wahhabi rule in the Najd but decided that, if the movement were to be successful, it would need a vanguard of ideologically committed warriors. In 1910 he set about establishing the Ikhwan, or Brethren. These were specially selected young men from various tribes. Once selected, the former nomads were settled in permanent sites in oases in the desert where they were taught both Wahhabi ideology and agriculture. The first of these settlements was established in 1912. By the outbreak of WORLD WAR I, the settlements included thousands of men who were ideologically committed to the Wahhabi movement. These formed the shock troops of the House of Saud. After the war, Abd al-Aziz would use them to conquer most of the Arabian Peninsula, formally establishing his kingdom in 1934.

Bruce Masters

Further reading: Leslie McLoughlin, *Ibn Saud: Founder of a Kingdom* (New York: St. Martin's Press, 1993); John Sabini, *Armies in the Sand: The Struggle for Mecca and Medina* (New York: Thames and Hudson, 1981).

Ibrahim I (b. 1615–d. 1648) (r. 1640–1648) *Ottoman sultan and caliph*   Ibrahim I was one of three sons of Sultan AHMED I (r. 1603–17) and his mother was Kösem Mahpeyker Sultan, Ahmed's favorite concubine. Ibrahim was born, raised, and educated in the imperial HAREM in ISTANBUL. His childhood and youth coincided with a period of multiple crises that shook the Ottoman dynasty and its imperial traditions. His mentally ill uncle, Sultan MUSTAFA I (r. 1617–18; 1622–23), was dethroned twice, first in 1618 and again in 1623. In between, Ibrahim witnessed the chaotic developments that resulted in the first regicide in Ottoman history as his older brother, Sultan OSMAN II (r. 1618–22), was murdered in 1622. Another older brother, MURAD IV (r. 1623–40), was enthroned in 1623, but Sultan Murad's early reign was marked by political turmoil and intense factionalism, both in the capital and in the countryside. After Murad IV managed to consolidate his power and declared his "personal rule" in 1632, he used severe and bloody measures to stabilize the politics of the empire until his death in 1640.

These events left deep marks on young Ibrahim, who remained in close confinement in the TOPKAPI PALACE. As Murad IV ordered the executions of his brothers, first Bayezid and Süleyman in 1632, then Kasım in 1637, Ibrahim became more and more concerned that he was next in line to be executed. This anxiety seems to have seriously disordered Ibrahim's health, both mentally and physically. As all Murad's sons died before adulthood, Ibrahim was the only other male member of the dynasty, but despite that, Ibrahim seems never to have anticipated the possibility of succeeding his brother who, by 1640, was terminally ill. When the grand vizier Kemankeş Kara Mustafa Pasha sent Ibrahim the news of Murad IV's death and invited him to the throne, Ibrahim did not believe him; rather, Ibrahim thought it was a trick to kill him like his unfortunate brothers. Only after being convinced by Mustafa Pasha and his mother, as well as personally examining his deceased brother's body, did he willingly sit on the throne.

For the first time since SÜLEYMAN I (r. 1520–66) succeeded his father SELIM I (r. 1512–20) in 1520, there was no rival prince who could claim the Ottoman throne. Although Ibrahim's succession was relatively smooth, he was now the only male in the royal household, but with no sons to guarantee the continuation of the dynasty. Luckily for the House of Osman, he did not fail to produce heirs, fathering nine sons, three of whom—MEHMED IV (r. 1648–87), SÜLEYMAN II (r. 1687–91), and AHMED II (r. 1691–95)—would eventually assume the sultanate. As Ibrahim prevented the dynasty's bloodline from becoming extinct, he has often been referred to as the "second founder of the Ottoman dynasty." Despite the apparent stability of Sultan Ibrahim's place on the throne, however, he could not escape the intrigues of factional politics that had plagued the sultanate since the time of SELIM II (r. 1566–74). In 1648 Ibrahim was dethroned and then murdered in the palace, the second Ottoman regicide in less than 30 years.

In retrospect, it can be seen that the first four years of Ibrahim's reign provided a stable administration for the empire, thanks to his decision to keep in office his brother's able grand vizier, Kemankeş Kara Mustafa Pasha, who continued the economic and political reforms begun under Murad IV. These provided economic relief to Istanbul and the provinces, which had suffered economically from the expensive campaigns mounted by the Ottomans against the Safavids of IRAN in the late 1630s. As part of these reforms Mustafa Pasha ordered a new tax survey, reduced the numbers of JANISSARIES and cavalrymen, stabilized the currency, and required that payments into and withdrawals from the treasury be made in coinage. He also issued a detailed price code (*narh defteri*) for the markets and restored the authority of the imperial government over disobedient provincial governors. Addressing the most intractable problem of the period, Mustafa Pasha significantly reduced the number of those who received salaries from the treasury without any service to the state.

Although Ibrahim left day-to-day matters in the hands of his ministers, he kept a close eye on politics and administration and regularly asked for written reports (*telhis*) from his grand vizier. Ibrahim's replies to these reports, in his own handwriting, show that, contrary to the popular understanding, Ibrahim had a good education and tried to keep a firm grip on the task of ruling the empire. He often traveled in disguise, inspecting the markets of the capital, and then ordered his grand vizier to correct the irregularities he observed. But like his father and brothers, Ibrahim was ready to listen to the entreaties of his royal favorites who had become indispensable actors in court politics as intermediaries for the sultan. With Ibrahim's enthronement, Kösem Sultan, as the queen mother (*valide sultan*) and supervisor of the imperial harem, began again to exercise the power that she had lost during Murad IV's rule.

Mustafa Pasha was well aware of these threats to his standing. At the beginning, the grand vizier managed to eliminate a favorite of Ibrahim, Silahdar Mustafa Pasha, by making the sultan appoint him to a distant province and then, upon some trumped-up charges, persuading Ibrahim to order his execution. This execution led to a deterioration in the relationship between the grand vizier and Kösem Sultan, who had been planning to marry her granddaughter, Kaya Sultan, to Silahdar. Also, the grand vizier's comprehensive reforms inevitably created some opposition, especially among the provincial governors whose fortunes were directly affected. The governor of ALEPPO, Nasuhpaşazade Hüseyin Pasha, revolted in 1642–43, but was soon defeated and killed by the powers in Istanbul.

However, by 1644, the grand vizier's standing was threatened by a much more powerful faction, which was effectively controlling all appointments and dismissals, enriching its members by bribes in the process. This party included Ibrahim's male favorites, Cinci Hoca, Silahdar Yusuf Agha, Sultanzade Mehmed Pasha, and his female favorite, Şekerpare Hatun, apparently with Kösem Sultan standing behind them. Although the grand vizier once again succeeded in appointing a potential rival, this time Sultanzade Mehmed Pasha, to the governorship of DAMASCUS, thus physically distancing him from the sultan, Mustafa Pasha failed to outmaneuver Cinci Hoca, who was a charlatan reputedly able to cure the sultan's ill health, and Yusuf Agha, who was both Ibrahim's sword-bearer and his son-in-law. In February 1644, Ibrahim ordered the execution of the grand vizier who had served him so well. Sultanzade Mehmed Pasha was then called back from Damascus to assume the position of grand vizier. After the death of Kara Mustafa Pasha, political instability and factionalism marked the remaining years of Ibrahim's reign.

In the summer of 1645, the war with Venice over Crete began. Ibrahim promoted his favorite Yusuf Agha to the rank of pasha and appointed him grand admiral of the Ottoman fleet. By the end of the summer, Yusuf Pasha captured the fortress of Candia (Iraklion), a quick victory that made the new grand vizier jealous and worried as his power was now challenged by the same faction that had toppled Kara Mustafa Pasha. Sultanzade Mehmed Pasha immediately tried to undermine Yusuf Pasha's position by criticizing the admiral for mishandling the siege and for bringing the sultan so little booty. Ibrahim first listened to the arguments presented by the two pashas, then removed Mehmed Pasha from the grand vizierate in December 1645. While Yusuf Pasha was favored in this conflict, he was soon to learn the bitter fact that Ibrahim's favor was not lasting: When he refused a sultanic order to lead another campaign on Crete, Ibrahim had him executed in January 1646 for disobedience.

Ibrahim was plagued by chronic headaches and physical exhaustion; his health became so unstable around this time that he chose to spend more time with his consorts in the harem and distanced himself from the business of ruling, giving his female favorites opportunities to manipulate him to their own advantage. Ibrahim elevated eight of his concubines to the favored position of *haseki* (royal consort), granting each a rich royal demesne. He legally married his concubine Telli Haseki, an almost unprecedented step. Ibrahim developed new habits of ostentatious consumption, such as an obsessive interest in sable fur, for the purchase of which he imposed heavy taxes on his ministers and provincial governors. Combined with a war economy and a Venetian blockade of the Dardanelles that created scarcities in the capital, Ibrahim's behavior fueled the growing unrest in the capital and the country.

By 1647 the grand vizier Salih Pasha, together with Kösem Sultan and the ŞEYHÜLİSLAM, Abdürrahim Efendi, plotted to dethrone the sultan and replace him with one of his sons, but their plot did not succeed. Salih Pasha was executed and Kösem Sultan faced a short exile from the harem. In the provinces a coalition of governors and subprovincial governors, led by Varvar Ali Pasha, the governor of Sivas, launched a major rebellion against the sultan and his corrupt new grand vizier, Hezarpare Ahmed Pasha. In May 1648 the rebel army was crushed near Ankara, and Ali Pasha was executed.

By the summer of 1648 all factions in Istanbul, including the sultan's elite soldiers, the Janissaries, were united against Ibrahim and his favorites. For them, the removal of the sultan was a necessity; after receiving a legal and religious approval for their decisions from the *şeyhülislam,* they took action. On August 8, 1648, Hezarpare Ahmed Pasha was killed. Ibrahim was deposed and locked in a room in the palace while his eldest son Mehmed, who was only seven years old, was enthroned. Ten days later, Ibrahim was strangled, as it was feared that his partisans might restore him to the throne. This second Ottoman regicide did not bring the tranquility desired by the empire. Factional politics and power struggles continued, as did the Ottoman crisis of the 17th century.

Günhan Börekçi

Further reading: Leslie Peirce, *The Imperial Harem: Women and Sovereignty in the Ottoman Empire* (Oxford: Oxford University Press, 1993); Colin Imber, *The Ottoman Empire, 1300–1650: The Structure of Power* (New York: Palgrave Macmillan, 2002); Caroline Finkel, *Osman's Dream: The Story of the Ottoman Empire, 1300–1923* (London: John Murray, 2005), 223–235; M. Tayyip Gökbilgin, "Ibrahim," in *Encyclopaedia of Islam*, 2nd ed., vol. 3 (Leiden: Brill, 1960–), 983.

Ibrahim Pasha (b. 1789–d. 1848) *Egyptian general* Ibrahim Pasha was the commander of the Egyptian army in Greece and Syria and the eldest son of Egypt's strongman MEHMED ALI. He was a teenager when his father brought him to CAIRO in 1805 and installed him as commander of the city's citadel. In 1807, he was promoted to the post of treasurer of the province of Egypt. After his brother Tosun died in 1816, Ibrahim took control of the Egyptian army and defeated the WAHHABIS, the militant followers of MUHAMMAD IBN ABD AL-WAHHAB in Arabia. He then supervised the transformation of the Egyptian army to one that was manned by conscripted peasants and trained by foreign military advisers. in 1824 that army was dispatched first to Crete and then to the Morea on the Greek mainland to support the Ottoman sultan's attempt to suppress the rebellion in GREECE. The success of the Egyptian army caused alarm in Great Britain and France, as the populations of both nations strongly supported the Greek insurgents, and their governments had decided that independence for Greece was in their national interests. They dispatched fleets to Greece, where they defeated the Ottoman-Egyptian fleet at Navarino in 1827. That victory led Mehmed Ali to call on Ibrahim to withdraw his troops and return to Egypt.

Mehmed Ali next ordered his son to invade Syria in November 1831, ostensibly to repatriate the thousands of Egyptian peasants who had fled there to avoid conscription. This was an open break with his former allies, the Ottomans, and signaled Mehmed Ali's ambitions to topple the Ottoman dynasty. Ibrahim laid siege to the formidable walled city of ACRE, which fell on May 27, 1832. Ibrahim then proceeded to occupy DAMASCUS. After defeating an Ottoman army that had been dispatched to stop him near the Syrian city of Homs, Ibrahim moved into Anatolia and delivered another decisive defeat to the Ottoman forces outside the city of Konya on July 29, 1832. With sure defeat facing him, Sultan MAHMUD II (r. 1808–39) agreed to a truce that recognized Ibrahim as the governor of the Syrian provinces.

During his eight years as governor in Syria, Ibrahim Pasha introduced a number of innovations that had already been tested by his father in Egypt. These included granting greater freedoms to the non-Muslim population of the region, establishing government monopolies, direct taxation, and military conscription. The Muslim population resented these innovations and, starting in 1834, rebellions broke out throughout the country. This led the Ottomans to believe that they could retake their lost provinces, and Mahmud sent a reorganized army toward Syria. Ibrahim once again demonstrated his tactical skills and destroyed the Ottoman army in the Battle of Nezip in June 1839.

Despite the victory the DRUZES and MARONITES, important Lebanese religious groups, rose in rebellion the following year. The revolt was partly a result of the efforts of Ottoman and British agents to foment an uprising, but it also arose out of a fear that conscription would soon be applied in Lebanon. British warships shelled Beirut and landed Ottoman troops there. Faced with a formidable alliance of both external and internal forces, the Egyptian occupation of Syria came to an abrupt end as Ibrahim surrendered to the British in 1840. In July 1848, when Mehmed Ali's advanced age left him unable to rule, Ibrahim succeeded him as governor of Egypt. He died soon after, however, and was succeeded by his nephew ABBAS HILMI.

Bruce Masters

Further reading: Khaled Fahmy, *All the Pasha's Men: Mehmed Ali, His Army, and the Making of Modern Egypt* (Cambridge: Cambridge University Press, 1997).

ihtisab and **muhtesib** (**ihtisap** and **muhtasip**) *Ihtisab* literally means "to call someone to account" or "to carry out responsibility." In Islamic legal theory, the role of *ihtisab* was to produce a set of controls, drawn from either customary law or religious law (SHARIA), that were intended to govern social, religious, and economic life and to reform those individuals who did not obey the rules through warnings and punishment. The principal enforcers of *ihtisab* were called *muhtesibs*.

The concept of *ihtisab* was first articulated during the lifetime of the Prophet Muhammad and was extensively applied in the Muslim states that succeeded him. Out of the theory emerged an institution that was charged with some of the duties that in other societies might be delegated to civil or religious authorities. As originally conceived, the office of *ihtisab* was a religious institution designed to promote social peace and order through the enforcement of decency and the prevention of evil. As a political institution, it developed and matured in the ABBASID CALIPHATE (750–1258).

The chief officials of this institution were the *muhtesibs*, often translated into English as "market inspector," who could be found in every major city of the empire. In general, the *muhtesib* was responsible for punishing and reforming those who acted against Islamic law. His duties varied widely. He ensured that Muslims attended Friday prayer; he could establish a Muslim community wherever there were more than 40 believers; and he was responsible for admonishing and punishing those who openly broke the fast during Ramadan, drank alcohol or played forbidden musical instruments, and widows who remarried before Islamic law allowed them to do so. As Ottoman government officials appointed by the sultan, the *muhtesib* inspected schools, warned or punished teachers who beat students without cause, banned the sale of strategic war materials and equipment to foreigners, and controlled the workings of the marketplace, including pricing and quality. In addition to observing markets and shops, he monitored ethical and religious behavior. These duties included ensuring that measuring and weighing equipment were accurate, that tradesmen were paying their debts, and that people were obeying the rules that banned gambling. He tested doctors' skills and imams' leadership during prayer, punished those who overburdened pack animals or dressed inappropriately, and made people provide for the needs of poor travelers in cities where there were no inns. Additionally, the *muhtesib* enforced building codes, maintained the order and cleanliness of streets, and collected some taxes.

Despite such broad authority, *muhtesibs* could not act arbitrarily for fear of being relieved of their duties and punished by their supervisors. A *muhtesib*'s qualifications were specific. He had to be a free adult Muslim male, wise, just, clever, and knowledgeable. In the Ottoman Empire, *muhtesibs* usually acquired their position by bidding on the post. The winner, provided he met the required conditions, was appointed as *muhtesib* for a year by the sultan. *Muhtesibs* chose their assistants from various professions. These assistants had to be meticulous in the performance of their duties and had to meet high standards for their personal behavior.

Salih Aynural

Further reading: Suraiya Faroqhi, *Towns and Townsmen of Ottoman Anatolia: Trade, Crafts and Food Production in an Urban Setting, 1520–1650* (Cambridge: Cambridge University Press, 1984).

illustrated manuscripts and miniature paintings
Miniature painting is a courtly art form in the Islamic world, developed to a high degree of sophistication among the late medieval Turco-Persian dynasties of IRAN, IRAQ, Central Asia, and Anatolia. In the court cultures of the Islamic world—particularly those who, like the Ottomans, drew their ideals of courtly culture from Persian models—miniature painting was used to illustrate and embellish manuscripts as luxury items for the sultan and other high-status patrons.

Miniature painting was one of a number of related artistic traditions known collectively as the "arts of the book." These traditional crafts included *hat* (CALLIGRAPHY—the most esteemed of the arts of the book), *nakş* (painting and ornamental design), *tezhip* (illumination), *ebru* (paper marbling), and *cilt* (bookbinding). The Ottomans learned the practice of maintaining an imperial scriptorium for the production of luxury books from the courts of the Islamic dynasties that preceded and rivaled them: the Ilkhanid Mongols, the Karakoyunlu (the "Black Sheep" Turkoman dynasty whose territory spanned western Iran, Iraq, and the CAUCASUS), the Akkoyunlu (the "White Sheep," a rival Turkoman dynasty to the Karakoyunlu centered in northwestern Iran and eastern Anatolia), the TIMURIDS (in Persia and Central Asia), and the MAMLUK EMPIRE (in the Arab world). Persia provided the model of courtly culture for the Ottoman sultans, and Persian influence was particularly strong in shaping the literary and artistic tastes of the Ottoman court. The Ottomans learned miniature painting and the arts of the book from contact with Persian and Turkoman dynasties, whose waning sent master miniaturists westward in search of employment in the Ottoman court.

Yet despite this strong Persian influence, the art of miniature painting developed in new directions under Ottoman patronage, producing distinctively Ottoman styles, themes, and preferences. Contact with artists and genres from Europe, the Balkans, and the Mediterranean resulted in uniquely Ottoman fusions of eastern and western traditions, particularly in the areas of portraiture and topographical representation. Ottoman miniature painting is also distinguished by its emphasis on historical realism. Whereas in the Persian tradition attention is lavished on legendary kings and heroes, mythical creatures, wonders of creation, paradisiacal gardens, and courtly entertainments, the Ottomans preferred documentary representations of their own imperial history. The finest Ottoman miniatures, produced in the mid- and late 16th century, illustrate historical narratives and represent real places, persons, and events.

THE *NAKKAŞHANE* AND METHODS OF PRODUCTION

The principal site of luxury manuscript production in the Ottoman Empire was the imperial scriptorium, or *nakkaşhane*, founded by MEHMED II (r. 1444–46; 1451–81) after the CONQUEST OF CONSTANTINOPLE and located just outside the walls of the TOPKAPI PALACE in ISTANBUL—although artists linked to the imperial *nakkaşhane* might also work out of smaller workshops located elsewhere in the city. Craftsmen linked to this workshop were trained in one or more of the arts of the book through a system of apprenticeship. Masters of *nakş* were called *nakkaş*, a term sometimes translated as "painter" or "miniaturist" although in fact the *nakkaş* could be called upon to produce sketches or designs for use in a wide variety of media, including geometrical, floral, and figural designs used in stone and wood carving, metalwork, ceramics, textiles, and the painting of interior architectural surfaces. Miniature paintings, however, were always produced in paint (normally made of pigment blended with albumen) on paper.

Not all the master painters of the Ottoman court were trained locally. From the time of the founding of the imperial scriptorium until well into the 16th century, the most influential masters were those who came to Istanbul—either voluntarily or by conscription—from the courts of Timurid Herat (Afghanistan) and Samarkand (Uzbekistan), the Turkoman courts of Shiraz (in northwestern Iran) and BAGHDAD (Iraq), or from Safavid Tabriz (western Iran). Masters seeking work also arrived from the Balkans, HUNGARY, Central Asia, and the Arab world. These masters trained new generations of Ottoman miniaturists, contributing to the emergence of an Ottoman synthesis of eastern and western styles and techniques in the second half of the 16th century.

Thanks to surviving payroll records, textual descriptions, and even depictions in Ottoman miniatures of the activities of the imperial scriptorium, the process by which luxury illustrated manuscripts were produced is well understood. Having won a commission, the author of the manuscript worked with the imperial scriptorium to assemble a team that would include a chief calligrapher, an illuminator, and a *nakkaş*. The author then worked closely with the chief *nakkaş* to design the illustration program for the project. The chief *nakkaş* took the lead in designing the miniatures, but the paintings themselves were almost always produced by a team of artists working under his direction. The Ottoman imperial *nakkaşhane* included painters who specialized in executing certain parts of the image, so one person might paint the landscape and vegetation, another the clothed figures, another the faces, and another the animals or architectural details of the scene. The collaborative nature of miniature painting in the Ottoman imperial scriptorium defies western European notions of artistic authorship, making it difficult to ascribe most Ottoman miniature paintings to the creative vision of a single artist. Nonetheless, the identities of some of the most important Ottoman miniaturists are known to us. The style of these masters is so distinctive, and the artistic collaboration they forged with their teams of illustrators so tight, that their artistic vision is revealed through the many hands executing it.

THE BEGINNINGS OF OTTOMAN MINIATURE PAINTING UNDER MEHMED II

Miniature painting began to gain importance in the Ottoman court toward the middle of the 15th century, during the reign of Mehmed II. Mehmed's interest in painting is well documented. This interest arose in part from a desire to emulate the courtly cultures of Persia, where the production of luxury manuscripts was an important dimension of royal patronage, but also from Mehmed's understanding of the visual arts as a means to reaffirm and perpetuate his own image as a world conqueror and imperial sovereign. Mehmed identified himself with the legendary conquerors of past eras, particularly Alexander the Great, and one of the earliest surviving examples of an illustrated Ottoman manuscript is an illustrated copy of the *Iskendername* (Book of Alexander)—a celebration of the conquests and feats of Alexander by the 14th-century Anatolian poet Ahmedi. Mehmed's *Iskendername* was produced in the middle of the 15th century in EDIRNE, the seat of Ottoman power prior to Mehmed's conquest of Istanbul in 1453. This and a small number of similar manuscripts provide evidence for the existence of a scriptorium in the Ottoman palace at Edirne.

After the conquest of Istanbul and the transfer of the seat of Ottoman power to that city, Mehmed founded a larger imperial scriptorium in the vicinity of the new Topkapı Palace complex. Patronage of the arts was an important part of Mehmed's imperial vision, as he sought to lay claim to Istanbul by making the city once again a center for artistic production and exchange. Artists, architects, and craftsmen were brought to Istanbul from all over the Ottoman Empire and beyond, including artists from Persia, Central Asia, the Balkans, ITALY, and northern Europe. Mehmed was keenly interested in European art; he was particularly drawn to the European tradition of commissioning medals and portraits, in which he saw a new way of perpetuating his own image. To this end, Mehmed invited renowned Italian artists to visit his court, where they executed works for him and shared their expertise with locally based painters and craftsmen. During a visit to Istanbul in 1477–78 the Venetian artist Costanzo da Ferrara designed a medal featuring a bust portrait of Mehmed. Shortly thereafter, in 1479–81, the Venetian painter Gentile Bellini took up residence at Mehmed's court, during which time he executed his famous portrait of the aging sultan.

The power of these images—together with the opportunity to study with Italian masters and, not least, Mehmed's active patronage—awakened an interest in portraiture among Ottoman miniaturists and their patrons. Soon portraits of the sultans began to be incorporated into the repertoire of the imperial *nakkaşhane*, and Ottoman miniaturists such as Nakkaş Sinan Bey and his student Ahmed Şiblizade began to specialize in this style of painting. In their portraits, these artists made use of such European techniques as shading and perspective learned from the Italian masters, thus introducing new techniques as well as new themes into Ottoman painting. Portraiture ultimately became an enduring feature of Ottoman miniature painting and even permeated more traditional miniature compositions, where the faces of individuals came to be far more individuated and expressive than in the older Persian tradition.

DEVELOPMENTS OF THE LATE 15TH AND EARLY 16TH CENTURIES

Mehmed's successors BAYEZID II (r. 1481–1512), SELIM I (r. 1512–20), and SÜLEYMAN I (r. 1520–66) witnessed the development and assimilation of his artistic legacy. In addition to the new interest in portraiture and physiognomy, Mehmed's enthusiasm for commemorating and glorifying the Ottoman dynasty through the art of painting persisted under Bayezid, Selim, and Süleyman, all of whom commissioned illustrated works of Ottoman history. No longer did the sultans turn to depictions of the fabulous exploits of Alexander the Great or other legendary heroes of the past when they wished to portray themselves as world conquerors. By now the Ottomans had emerged as a world-conquering force in their own right, and preferred to commemorate their own dynastic history. The role of painting in Ottoman historiography and self-representation became increasingly important in the 16th century, and the historiographical quality of Ottoman miniature painting eventually developed into one of its most important characteristics.

The reign of Selim witnessed a dramatic new development in the history of the Ottoman imperial *nakkaşhane*: an influx of Persian talent from Iran. In 1514 Selim defeated the Safavid army at Çaldıran, in eastern Anatolia, and occupied the Safavid capital at Tabriz, in western Iran. Although Selim was not ultimately able to hold Tabriz, he did manage to conscript a significant number of painters and artists there and bring them to Istanbul.

Persian painting had long been the principal influence on the Ottoman miniature tradition, and from the start the Ottoman *nakkaşhane* had included Persian-trained masters moving from one court to the next with the changing fortunes of dynasties. Masters trained in Timurid Herat and Samarkand, in the Karakoyunlu courts of Shiraz and Baghdad, and in the Akkoyunlu courts at Diyarbakır (southeastern Anatolia), Baghdad, and Mardin (southeastern Anatolia), had all made their way to Ottoman Istanbul, bringing with them various styles of Persian miniature painting. Nevertheless, the arrival of the masters from Tabriz was the single biggest influx of talent in the history of the Ottoman

nakkaşhane, and its impact would be felt for decades to come. These artists brought with them the highly decorative style of Tabriz, distinguished by its rich textures and intricately detailed treatment of surfaces. Western techniques of shading and perspective, introduced to the Ottoman *nakkaşhane* by European artists during the reign of Mehmed II, were absent from this tradition, in which space is represented two-dimensionally. The intermingling of these diverse traditions in the Ottoman *nakkaşhane* led to the emergence of distinctively Ottoman styles of painting in the mid- and late 16th century.

A further influence on Ottoman miniature painting during this period was connected to the rise of the Ottomans as a maritime power. Increased involvement in both seafaring trade and naval warfare in the Mediterranean brought the Ottomans into close contact with Mediterranean cartography, including portolan charts, nautical atlases, and gazetteers containing bird's-eye views of coastal cities and islands. The first evidence of Ottoman use of nautical maps and siege plans comes from this period, and although initially such images were produced for practical rather than decorative uses, they soon permeated the world of book art as the idea of producing luxury presentation copies of atlases (designed not for practical use but as collector's items) or illustrated histories took hold.

The two most important examples of the influence of cartography on Ottoman miniature painting were both produced during the early years of Süleyman's reign: the *Kitab-i bahriye* (Book of seafaring, 1521 and 1526) of Piri Reis and the *Beyan-i menazi-i sefer-i Irakeyn-i Sultan Süleyman han* (Description of the stages of the Iraqi campaign of Sultan Süleyman, hereafter *Beyan-i menazil*, 1537, Istanbul University Library T.5964) of Matrakçı Nasuh. The *Kitab-i bahriye*, produced in two versions in 1521 and 1526, was a nautical atlas designed as a presentation copy for Süleyman complete with painted views of cities and coastlines of the Mediterranean in the style of European gazetteers. The *Kitab-i bahriye* went on to become one of the most frequently reproduced books in the history of Ottoman luxury manuscript production, with over 30 copies being produced over the course of the 16th and 17th centuries. The idea of incorporating topographic imagery into the illustrated manuscript tradition was carried even farther by Matrakçı Nasuh who, upon the commission of Süleyman, produced the lavishly illustrated *Beyan-i menazil* in 1537 to commemorate Süleyman's 1534–35 campaign to the eastern frontier—a campaign that resulted in the extension of the Ottoman frontiers into Mesopotamia. The miniatures contained in the *Beyan-i menazil*, which were designed by Matrakçı Nasuh on the basis of firsthand observation and executed in collaboration with the imperial *nakkaşhane*, are figureless topographic paintings depicting the stages of the campaign along the route to the frontier and then along the newly extended frontier itself. They are clearly influenced by city views contained in contemporary European and Mediterranean atlases and gazetteers, and yet in both visual style and method of production they are very much a part of the miniature painting tradition. The use of such topographical imagery to illustrate a work of contemporary history clearly resonated with the Ottoman court: Supported by the patronage of Süleyman and his grand vizier Rüstem Pasha, Matrakçı Nasuh went on to produce at least three more similarly illustrated volumes describing the campaigns of Bayezid II, Selim I, and Süleyman I, and his style was widely imitated in historiographical miniature painting of the mid- and late 16th century.

Meanwhile, in the area of portraiture, a similarly innovative synthesis of eastern and western styles was being forged by a naval officer and amateur painter named Haydar Reis (d. 1572), who painted under the pseudonym of Nigari. Unusually, Nigari did not illustrate manuscripts but rather produced loose-leaf portraits, including both bust and full-length portraits. Nigari's portraits employ techniques of shading clearly learned from western European art, and his figures are always set against a dark background. The figures are posed in styles evocative of both the Islamic miniature painting tradition and western-style portraiture—and indeed, Nigari not only represented Ottoman figures but also Europeans, including bust portraits of Francis I of France and Holy Roman Emperor Charles V.

THE ZENITH OF OTTOMAN MINIATURE PAINTING

The period of Ottoman history spanned by the reigns of Süleyman I, SELIM II (r. 1566–74), and MURAD III (r. 1574–95) represents the zenith of Ottoman miniature painting. During this time, the influences of the late 15th and early 16th centuries—the encounters with western European portraiture, the growing emphasis on historiographical painting, the impact of Mediterranean nautical cartography, and the enduring influence of the Persian legacy—began to crystallize into distinctively Ottoman styles and genres. At the same time, the wealth brought by military conquest (during Süleyman's reign in particular) and political stability in Istanbul fueled a cultural efflorescence that extended to every area of the arts.

With regard to miniature painting, the most important development of the mid- and late 16th century was the creation of the post of şehnameci, or official court historian. The şehnameci was literally a "writer of şehnames," or "books of kings." The original Shah-nama (Book of kings) was a famous work by the Persian poet Firdawsi (933–1025) that narrated the lives of legendary Persian kings and heroes. In later centuries, illustrated copies of the Shah-nama of Firdawsi were frequently produced in court scriptoria of Iran and Central Asia. The Ottomans adapted this genre to their interest in contemporary history, using it to narrate the exploits not of legendary rulers of the past but of those of the Ottoman dynasty. The şehnameci was charged with authoring these histories—many of which, like Firdawsi's original, were composed in Persian verse—and collaborating with teams of master calligraphers, miniaturists, and illuminators from the imperial nakkaşhane to transform the resulting compositions into luxury manuscripts destined for the palace libraries. The three most important şehnamecis for the history of Ottoman miniature painting are Fethullah Arif Çelebi, or Arifi, who occupied the post between approximately 1540 and 1561; Seyyid Lokman, who served between 1569 and 1595; and Talikizade, who succeeded Lokman and served in the final years of the 16th century. The works of the historiographical studio of the şehnameci—most of which were produced as a single copy for the palace collections—are among the finest examples of Ottoman miniature painting and book art.

Some time around the year 1540 şehnameci Arifi was appointed and charged with producing a series of five illustrated histories of the Ottoman dynasty in Persian verse. Three of these manuscripts survive, the most important of which is the Süleymanname (Book of Süleyman), which was completed in 1558 and contains 69 full-folio miniatures (Topkapı Palace Library H. 1517). Although we do not know the names of the artists who worked on this manuscript, it is clearly a collaborative work of the highest quality from the imperial nakkaşhane. The contribution of miniaturists from a variety of different backgrounds is evident in the work. For example, architectural details are sometimes rendered in the two-dimensional style of Tabriz and sometimes in perspectival view, as was common among artists trained in the western Ottoman lands. On occasion both styles are found in the same composition. Similarly, some paintings render landscape in the Persian style, which bears traces of Chinese influence, while other landscapes hint at the influence of western European-style city views.

The most prolific Ottoman şehnameci was Seyyid Lokman, whose career spanned the reigns of Süleyman I, Selim II, and Murad III. Lokman's principal collaborator in the imperial nakkaşhane was Nakkaş Osman, whose career was as long and as prolific as Lokman's own and who is generally regarded as the greatest master of Ottoman miniature painting. Nakkaş Osman worked with Lokman to design the illustration programs for Lokman's histories of the Ottoman dynasty and oversaw their execution by a team of artists assembled from the imperial scriptorium. The manuscripts were lavishly illustrated, some containing over 200 illustrated folios and numerous double-folio images. Osman's control of the design and execution of the miniatures was such that even though the works were produced collaboratively his authorship is readily discernible to the trained eye. Osman's style eschewed the heavy ornamentation of the Persian tradition and focused instead on historical realism, with careful attention to detail in the representation of places and scenes. Landscape imagery in some of his works recalls the influence of maritime cartography and the city views of Matrakçı Nasuh—including instances of figureless city views. Osman's miniatures also testify to the assimilation of the art of portraiture into traditional miniatures. The faces of historical personages in his work (including in a few instances the artist himself) are not only readily identifiable but also remarkably expressive.

Lokman's early collaborations with Nakkaş Osman consisted of works relating the lives and exploits of recent Ottoman sultans: the *Zafername* (Book of victory, 1579, Chester Beatty Library, Dublin), relating the final years of the reign of Süleyman I; the *Şehname-i Selim han* (Book of kings of Sultan Selim, 1581, Topkapı Palace Museum Library H. 3595), concerning the reign of Selim II; the two-volume *Şehinşehname* (Book of the king of kings, 1581, Istanbul University Library F. 1404 and 1597, Topkapı Palace Museum Library B. 200), about the early years of the reign of Murad III; and the *Surname-i hümayun* (Book of imperial festivities, 1588, Topkapı Palace Museum Library H. 1344), describing the lavish public celebrations surrounding the circumcision of Murad III's son Mehmed.

In the 1580s, Seyyid Lokman and Nakkaş Osman took on two monumental commissions that offered overviews of Ottoman history: the *Zübdetü't-tevarih* (The cream of histories, 1583, Istanbul Museum of Turkish and Islamic Art MS. 1973) and the two-volume *Hünername* (Book of feats, 1585 and 1588, Topkapı Palace Museum Library H. 1523 and H. 1524). Because these commissions dealt with earlier eras of Ottoman history whose visual and material culture was less familiar to either the author or the miniaturist, Lokman and Nakkaş Osman undertook additional research into the dress and appearance of past Ottoman sultans. The results of this research were presented in 1579 in an illustrated manuscript that contains some of the finest examples of Ottoman portraiture, the *Kıyafet'ül'insaniyye fi şemail-i Osmaniyye* (General appearances and dispositions of the Ottomans). The *Kıyafet'ül'insaniyye* quickly became a popular manuscript in court circles, and numerous copies were produced in subsequent decades by Nakkaş Osman's assistants and students.

In the final years of the 16th century Sultan Mehmed III dismissed Lokman and appointed a new poet, Talikizade Mehmed, to the post of *şehnameci*. Talikizade lacked Lokman's skill and versatility as a poet, but he was able to recruit into his studio a distinguished master illustrator known as Nakkaş Hasan. Hasan was not a member of the palace scriptorium but is nonetheless regarded as one of the most important miniaturists of his day. His collaboration with Talikizade lasted only a few years but resulted in the production of several important works, including two describing events in the life of Sultan Mehmed III, the *Eğri fetihnamesi* (Book of victory at Eğri, 1596–97, Topkapı Palace Museum Library H. 1609) and the *Şehname-i Sultan Mehmed-i salis* (Book of kings of Mehmed III, Istanbul Museum of Turkish and Islamic Arts MS. 1965). Their final collaboration is an undated late 16th-century work about the lives of the Ottoman sultans that appears to be modeled on Lokman's *Hünername* (Topkapı Palace Library A. 3592). Nakkaş Hasan's work demonstrates some of the same hallmarks of Ottoman miniature painting as Nakkaş Osman's—mastery of historical realism, the use of city views, and an awareness of the art of portraiture—but with a distinctive color palette including vivid reds, greens, and yellows.

DEVELOPMENTS IN THE 17TH AND 18TH CENTURIES

The 17th century witnessed a shift away from illustrated works of court historiography. The office of the *şehnameci* was revived briefly under OSMAN II (r. 1618–22), whose court historian Nadiri collaborated with the most famous painter of the day, Ahmed Nakşi, to produce the *Şehname-i Nadiri* (Nadiri's book of kings, Topkapı Palace Library H. 1124). Nakşi also executed a masterful series of portraits for an illustrated translation of a famous biographical work of the previous century, Taşköprüzade's *Şaka'iku'n-numaniye fi ulema-i develeti'l-Osmaniyye* (The undying peonies of the Ottoman ulema), Topkapı Palace Library H. 1263). In addition to portraiture, Nakşi is known for his use of perspective and his vivid color palette.

However, as the age of great territorial conquests came to an end in the 17th century, so did the literary and painterly genre of the Ottoman *şehname*, which was largely premised on the commemoration and celebration of conquest. In the second half of the 16th century the focus of the imperial scriptorium (which, like the palace, moved for much of this period to Edirne) shifted toward the production of dynastic genealogies, or *silsilename*. These genealogies, illustrated with portraits, traced the Ottoman lineage back through the prophets as far as Adam. The most famous painter of this era was Musavvir Hüseyin, who created portraits for such genealogies.

The last great flourish of Ottoman miniature painting came in the early 18th century with the career of the painter Abdülcelil Çelebi (d. 1732–33), better known by his cognomen Levni, which means "the colorful." Levni created portraits for Ottoman genealogies and albums, but his most famous works by far are the paintings that illustrate the *Surname-i Vehbi* (Vehbi's book of festivities, Topkapı Palace A. 3593), authored by the poet Vehbi, which celebrates the public festivities held in connection with the circumcision of the sons of AHMED III (r. 1703–1730) in the year 1720. Levni, who is believed to have trained with Musavvir Hüseyin, uses pastel tones and emphasizes the human figures in his composition at the expense of scenery, reflecting his training in the art of portraiture. The *Surname-i Vehbi* was copied twice in the following decade, probably by artists in Levni's circle. It is the last example of an illustrated manuscript commissioned for the Ottoman imperial treasury. From the middle of the 18th century onward, the Ottomans came increasingly under the influence of western painting styles, and compositions on canvas designed for display overtook once and for all the older and more intimate tradition of miniature painting with its narrative emphasis on the lives and conquests of the sultans.

Kathryn Ebel

Further reading: Esin Atıl, *Levni and the Surname: The Story of an Eighteenth-Century Ottoman Festival* (Istanbul: Koçbank, 1999); Esin Atıl, *Süleymanname: The Illustrated History of Süleyman the Magnificent* (Washington: National Gallery of Art and New York: H.N. Abrams, 1986); Serpil Bağcı, Filiz Çağman, Günsel Renda, and Zeren Tanındı, *Osmanlı Resim Sanatı* (Ankara: Ministry of Culture and Tourism, 2006); Filiz Çağman, "Ottoman Miniature Painting," in *Ottoman Civilization*, vol. 2, edited by Halil İnalcık and Günsel Renda (Ankara: Ministry of Culture and Tourism, 2002), 893–931; Kathryn Ebel, "Representations of the Frontier in Ottoman Town Views of the Sixteenth Century." *Imago Mundi* 60, no. 1 (2008): 1–22; Selmin Kangal, ed., *The Sultan's Portrait: Picturing the House of Osman*, trans. Mary Priscilla Işın (Istanbul: İşbank, 2000); Svatopluk Soucek, *Piri Reis and Turkish Mapmaking after Columbus* (London: Nour Foundation in association with Azimuth and Oxford University Press, 1992); Hüseyin Yurdaydın, ed., *Beyan-i Menazil-i Sefer-i Irakeyn-i Sultan Süleyman Han, Nasuhü's-Silahi* (Matrakçı Nasuh) (Ankara: Türk Tarih Kurumu, 1976).

illustrated manuscripts in the Topkapı Palace Museum Manuscripts at the TOPKAPI PALACE Museum form one of the most important collections of Islamic art in the world. There are approximately 14,000 manuscripts, containing around 18,000 miniature paintings. The paintings represent the finest examples of a wide variety of schools and styles (*see* ILLUSTRATED MANUSCRIPTS AND MINIATURE PAINTING) originating from a vast geographical area and spanning many centuries. The books and albums illustrated with miniature paintings and drawings include works by SELJUK, Mongol (Ilkhanid), Timurid, Uzbek, Karakoyunlu ("Black Sheep") and Akkoyunlu ("White Sheep") Turkoman, Safavid, and Ottoman court artists, and form the most valuable part of the collection.

Approximately 600 books and albums contain miniatures illustrating scientific, historic, religious, and literary subjects. The collection includes 60 copies of the *Shah-nama* (The book of kings) by the Persian poet Firdawsi and 85 copies of the *Khamsa* (The book of five poems) by the Persian poet Nizami. This vast and diverse collection is a direct result of Ottoman military exploits. Various archival documents show that many of these artifacts entered the palace treasury as spoils of war following the capture of the Safavid capital, Tabriz, by the Ottoman Sultan SELIM I (r. 1512–20) in 1514 and of the Mamluk capital, CAIRO, in 1517. The collection of manuscripts acquired by the sultans over the centuries and kept in the palace treasury consists of the finest masterpieces of the Islamic world, illustrated by the most celebrated artists of their time. As a result, the Topkapı Palace Museum Library today possesses an unparalleled collection of Islamic miniatures.

SELJUK MANUSCRIPTS

The earliest manuscripts in the collection illustrated with miniatures are of Seljuk origin. These, for the most part, are from Seljuk states in IRAQ and Anatolia. Cities such as Konya and Diyarbakır in Anatolia and MOSUL and BAGHDAD in Iraq were major centers for the arts during this period. This group of manuscripts consists of scientific and literary works. The most important in terms of Seljuk figurative style is *Varka and Gülşah*, produced in Konya in the 13th century and illustrated by Abd al-Mumin of Hoy. Among the scientific works is an Arabic translation of *De materia medica*, a treatise on the pharmacological properties of plants by the Anatolian Greek physician Dioscorides. It was illustrated in 1228 by Abd al-Jabbar for the library of Abu al-Fadail Muhammed, ruler of Diyarbakır and Mosul. Another is *Kitab fi marifat al-hiyal al-handasiyya* (A book on the knowledge of tricks and engineering) by al-Jaziri, an engineer working at the Artukid court who wrote and illustrated the book in 1206 at the request of the Artukid emir Nasr al-Din Mahmud.

MONGOL (ILKHANID AND JALAYRID) MANUSCRIPTS

The Mongols took Baghdad in 1258, putting an end to the ABBASID CALIPHATE. This invasion laid the foundations for the western Mongol state of the Ilkhanids, who converted to Islam. Under the Mongols, works of history and religion as well as epic tales were illustrated with miniatures whose realistic approach derived from the pictorial traditions of Central Asia and East Asia. Of the three Mongol manuscripts in the Topkapı Palace collection, two are copies of a history of the world titled *Jami al-tawarikh* (A gathering of histories) written by a team of authors under the vizier Rashid al-Din on the orders of the Ilkhanid ruler Ghazan Khan (1271–1304), and the third is a copy of the *Garshafsnama* (The book of ancient princes).

With the collapse of the Mongol Empire in the mid-14th century, the Jalayrids, also of Mongol origin, took control of much of the empire and conquered western Iran and Iraq. Under them, the Tabriz (Iran) and Baghdad schools of illustration rose to the fore. In particular the reigns of Sultan Uways and Sultan Ahmed are notable for miniature painting. Shams al-Din, a student of 14th-century painter Ahmed Musa, worked at the court of Sultan Uways and illustrated the *Shah-nama* of Firdawsi. Another important painter of the period was Abd al-Hayy, a student of Shams al-Din. A miniature from this period collected in the album of Safavid prince Bahram Mirza, the brother of Shah Tahmasp I, bears a legend stating that it is the work of Abd al-Hayy, and this miniature has all the characteristics of the late Jalayrid and early Timurid court style.

TIMURID MANUSCRIPTS

When the famed warlord TIMUR invaded Iran at the end of the l4th century and captured famous centers of art including Tabriz, Shiraz (Iran), and Baghdad, his capital at Samarkand (Uzbekistan) developed into a major center for artistic activity. Following the death of Timur in 1405, miniature painting developed rapidly under the patronage of Timurid sultans in their capitals Herat (Afghanistan) and Shiraz. Today there are around 20 Timurid manuscripts in the Topkapı collection. Most of these are copies of the *Khamsa;* the others consist of various literary, religious, historical, and scientific works. These collections are illustrated with miniatures in the characteristic style of their respective periods.

Those from Herat include some beautiful historical and literary manuscripts illustrated with miniatures produced at studios employing celebrated calligraphers, writers, and painters during the reigns of Shahruh, Baysungur, and Husayn Baykara. Manuscripts such as *Kulliyat-i tarikh* (The complete history), *Kalila wa Dimna* (Tales of Kalila and Dimna), *Khamsa, Hasht bihesht* (Eight paradises), *Divan-i Husayni* (Collected works of Husayni), and *Humay u Humayun* (Prince Humay and Princess Humayun) are the most important works of the palace collection.

The finest work of the collection, however, was produced during the reign of Sultan Husayn Baykara at studios employing such famous artists and writers as the poet Jami, the calligrapher Sultan Ali Mashadi, and the miniature painters Agha Mirak, Qasım Ali, and, above all, Bihzad, the master artist in the Islamic world of this period.

TURKOMAN KARAKOYUNLU AND AKKOYUNLU MANUSCRIPTS

Approximately 50 manuscripts illustrated by Turkoman Karakoyunlu and Akkoyunlu painters form another important category in the collection. Most of these books are copies of the *Shah-nama* and *Khamsa* produced in Shiraz and Baghdad under the patronage of Sultan Pir Budak. The most important manuscripts illustrated by Karakoyunlu artists include the miniatures of the *Khamsa-i Nizami, Khamsa-i Husraw, Shah-nama-i Firdawsi,* and a geographical work, *Terjuma-i mesalik va'l-mamalik.* These miniatures are significant for reflecting not only Timurid Herat and Shiraz style but some motifs that foreshadow the Akkoyunlu style as well. Under the Akkoyunlu sultans Halil and Yakub miniature painting in Shiraz and Tabriz reached new heights.

SAFAVID MANUSCRIPTS

The Topkapı collection also contains around 200 illustrated Safavid manuscripts and albums on literature, religion, and history, although copies of the *Shah-nama* of Firdawsi and the *Khamsa* of Nizami outnumber all the rest. These are artifacts of the Safavid Empire (*see* IRAN), established by Shah ISMAIL I (r. 1501–24) when he defeated the Akkoyunlus in 1501 and took Tabriz, which lasted until the Afghan invasion of 1722. The extremely fine miniatures included in the Safavid manuscripts were produced in contemporary centers of art such as Shiraz, Isfahan, Tabriz, and Kazvin. When Shah Ismail conquered Herat, he brought the famous miniaturist Bihzad and other artists to Tabriz, resulting in an upsurge in quality from the Tabriz school, especially during the reign of his successor Shah Tahmasp I (r. 1524–76). Some of the most outstanding works of the period are the *Yusuf u Zulayha* (Joseph and Suleika), and the albums of Shah Tahmasp and Bahram Mirza, which represent the finest albums produced anywhere in the Islamic world.

From contemporary sources we learn that most of these manuscripts arrived in Istanbul during the Ottoman-Safavid wars, which commenced in 1578 and continued off and on until the early 17th century. Close friendships forged by military commanders, envoys, and statesmen with writers and poets of this time resulted in the transportation of many valuable books from Iran to the Ottoman capital. Various sources also note that envoys sent by Safavid rulers brought illustrated manuscripts as gifts for the Ottoman sultans SELIM II (r. 1566–74) and MURAD III (r. 1574–1595). It was also customary for Ottoman military commanders, state officials, and governors to present gifts to the sultan, and during the Ottoman-Safavid wars we find records of gifts of books that they had purchased or acquired as trophies. Another source of new books for the palace collection was the estates of high-ranking government officials, whose property devolved to the state upon their death if they had no heirs.

OTTOMAN MANUSCRIPTS

The hundreds of Ottoman manuscripts in the collection, on the other hand, were produced in the palace studios for the Ottoman sultans, who were almost all deeply interested in the arts. No Ottoman manuscripts predating the CONQUEST OF CONSTANTINOPLE in 1453 have survived, although sources reveal the existence of an art studio at the palace in EDIRNE. The collection contains a copy of the *Kulliyat-ı Katibi* (Complete works of Katibi) produced at Edirne Palace. The portraits of Sultan MEHMED II (r. 1444–46; 1451–81) made by local artists are also found in the palace collection.

Surviving manuscripts and written sources show that Sultan BAYEZID II (r. 1481–1512) was interested in the authors and poets of the Ottoman Empire and other Islamic states and acted as patron to many poets. The collection includes illustrated manuscripts such as the *Khamsa-i Hüsrev Dihlevi*, *Hüsrev u Şirin* (Khosrow and Shirin), and *Şehname-i Melik Ümmi*. A work entitled *Mantıku't-tayr* (Conference of the birds), produced at the court studio during the reign of Sultan SELIM I (r. 1512–20), is important because it reveals the stylistic influence exerted by artists the sultan brought from Tabriz after its conquest.

The collection contains items in the decorative style used mainly in literary works that developed under the influence of Islamic schools of miniature painting during the reign of SÜLEYMAN I (the Magnificent) (r. 1520–1566). These are copies of the *Divan-ı Nevai*, *Khamsa-i Nevai*, Arifi's *Guy u chawgan* (The ball and the polo stick), and *Selimname* (Book of Selim). This was a period of extensive innovations, among the most fascinating examples of which are the history books of Matrakçı Nasuh. Begun at the request of Süleyman I, the texts are illustrated by Nasuh in several parts with topographic representations of fortified towns. The illustrated manuscripts by Nasuh preserved in the Topkapı Palace collections include the *Tarih-i Sultan Bayezid* (History of Sultan Bayezid) and *Tarih-i feth-i Şikloş ve Estergon ve İstolni Belgrad* (History of the conquest of Siklós, Esztergom and Székesfehérvár). Another interesting group contains books describing the Muslim holy cities of MECCA and MEDINA and the customs and practices of the pilgrimage or HAJJ. The illustrations in these texts reveal a unique style from this period. One of the palace albums contains portraits of Süleyman the Magnificent, Selim II, and Hayreddin Pasha (see BARBAROSSA BROTHERS) by Haydar Reis, a portraitist who worked under the cognomen of Nigari. The most important work of the period, and indeed of the entire collection, however, is the *Süleymanname* (Book of Süleyman), written by court annalist Arifi.

THE CLASSICAL PERIOD

In the second half of the 16th century Turkish miniature painting emerged as an art in its own right, unencumbered by the traditions of other cultures. During this time, the Classical Period under the patronage of SELIM II (r. 1566–74) and MURAD III (r. 1574–95), Turkish miniature painting and the other arts of the book reached their zenith. Many of the works of this period in the palace collection belong to the genre represented notably by the *Hünername* (The book of feats) and *Şehinşehname* (The book of the king of kings). They depict victories of the Ottoman army, the justice of the sultan, diverse social activities, the sultan's skill at hunting, audiences given to ambassadors, and memorable events of the era. In many cases these were written by the famous court annalist Seyyid Lokman and illustrated by Nakkaş Osman.

The most important manuscript dating from the reign of Selim II is an account of the Szigetvár campaign, the last campaign of Süleyman I, who died of natural causes just before the successful siege of the town of Szigetvár on the Hungarian border in 1566. Of all the Ottoman sultans, Murad III stands out for his love of books and the arts of the book. During his reign, the celebrated painter Nakkaş Osman and his team painted miniatures in the palace design studio for numerous historical books, the *Şehname-i Selim han*, two volumes of the *Hünername*, and the *Zübdetü't-tevarih* (The cream of histories). Two other masterpieces of the same period also illustrated by Nakkaş Osman are the *Şemailname*, consisting of descriptions of all the Ottoman sultans from OSMAN I to MURAD III (r. 1574–1595), and the *Surname-i hümayun* (The book of imperial festivities) with its hundreds of miniatures, including some of the most outstanding examples of classical Ottoman painting. Other works prepared by the court artists of this period are *Nusretname* and *Kitab-i Genjine-i Feth-i Genje* (describing the Azerbaijan campaign of Ferhat Pasha in 1588).

The reign of MEHMED III (r. 1595–1603) saw an even greater output of miniature painting at the court studios where another famous painter, Nakkaş Hasan, and his assistants illustrated books about the sultan's victories, such as *Eğri fetihnamesi* (Book of victory at Eğri) and *Şehname-i Al-i Osman* (Book of kings of the house of Osman); books on religious subjects, such as *Siyer-i Nebi* (The life of the Prophet); and simple romances.

During the reign of AHMED I (r. 1603–17), Turkish miniatures appear in works of a different kind, notably books produced by Kalender Pasha, a vizier and master of the art of *vassale* (decoration using colored paper), such as his *Falname* (Book of fortunetelling) and the *Ahmed I* album illustrated with miniatures of single genre figures associated with the palace. Despite its brevity, the reign of OSMAN II (r. 1618–22) was the most prolific in terms of 17th-century Ottoman miniature painting. The miniatures in *Şehname-i Nadiri* (Nadiri's book of kings) and those in a biographical work called *Şaka'iku'n-numaniye fi ulema-i devleti'l-Osmaniyye* (The undying peonies of the Ottoman ulema) were completed by court artists, the most famous of whom was Nakşi.

The last flowering of Ottoman miniature painting occurred in the first half of the 18th century during the reign of AHMED III (r. 1703–30), with artists such as Levni and Abdullah Buhari leaving their mark on this period. Foremost among the paintings by Levni, whose work was extremely influential, are the 137 miniatures in the *Surname-i Vehbi* (Vehbi's book of festivities), an account of the celebrations for the sons of Ahmed III by the poet Vehbi. Other major works of the period were also illustrated by Levni, such as an album depicting men and women of the period in the dress of various classes and callings, and a genealogical album containing portraits of the Ottoman sultans. The pieces from this period follow the conventions of traditional Ottoman miniature painting and aspire to three-dimensional form through detail, while non-Muslim Ottoman artists of the period tended to follow Western aesthetic norms. Towards the second half of the century Western influence steadily increased throughout all the painters of the empire until Ottoman miniature painting was entirely superseded by works of a Western character.

Zeynep Atbaş

ilmiye *See* ULEMA.

iltizam *See* TAX FARMING.

imperial ideology The Ottoman state grew out of a small tribe without inheriting any major claim of imperial legitimacy. Rather, the imperial ideology of the Ottomans took shape through their own historical experience and interaction with a variety of political traditions. Founded at the frontier of the Islamic world and expanded toward both Muslim and Christian lands, the Ottoman Empire came to rule over a people embracing diverse faiths and ethnic communities. Ottoman imperial ideology formed out of, and reflected, this diverse heritage of the lands it ruled. Ottoman rulers viewed themselves as the rightful successors to past empires that once ruled the lands they conquered, including those of Alexander the Great, the Byzantines, the Abbasids, and even the kingdom of Solomon. Drawing on Byzantine, Iranian, Arab, and Turkic imperial traditions, they appropriated existing imperial titles such as caesar, padishah, sultan, khan, and caliph.

Much of what may be identified as imperial ideology in the 16th century was shaped by the experience of the Ottomans during their early history. The peculiar conditions of the Ottoman principality turned them into a major player with more power than their military strength should have warranted, a fact that profoundly affected their self-perception. Rising in the wake of the Mongol invasion that left few political structures intact the east of Nile, the Ottomans found themselves on practically equal footing with every other dynasty in the Islamic world. Concomitantly, their advances against the shrinking Byzantine territories, then known as the Roman Empire, gradually established the Ottomans as the rightful successors to the Romans. Furthermore, because of their location at the crossroads of maritime trade they were able to forge propitious relations with major powers of the Mediterranean basin such as Genoa and Venice. Thus their skills in state-building, helped by the favorable circumstances of location and timing, transformed their self-perception, leading them to percieve themselves as moral leaders of significant grandeur.

Bolstered by a steady stream of conquests, this sense of grandeur became an undistinguishable part of imperial Ottoman self-image that stayed in effect until the end of the empire. Accompanying this was a *ghazi* (*see* GHAZA) or Ottoman warrior ethos formed out of the Ottoman ruler's leadership in protecting and extending the realm of Islam against that of the infidels. Even when the conquests ended, Ottoman rulers retained the title *ghazi* (referring to their role as defenders and expanders of the realm of Islam) as their most praiseworthy honorific and were frequently reminded by religious reformers to act as such.

By the 16th century, the Ottoman dynasty had become a self-legitimating institution that manifested itself in a venerated genealogy and something verging on a cult of ancestors. As part of this genealogical obsession, the Ottomans sought to further legitimize their power by crafting a noble genealogy suitable to their imperial visions. The Ottomans lacked any connection to the two most prestigious lineages in the post-Mongolian Islamic world, those of the Prophet Muhammad and Genghis Khan (r. 1206–27, the founder of the Mongol Empire). To remedy this, Ottoman literati—especially in the 15th and early 16th centuries—busied themselves crafting impressive genealogical connections for their forbears. As a result the Oghuz genealogy came to be an official exposition of Ottoman lineage showing that the Ottoman rulers were the descendants of Oghuz Khan, who was also identified as the biblical Japhet or in some expositions as the Quranic Alexander the two-horned. Presenting Oghuz Khan as a believer who is praised in the Quran made the Ottoman genealogy superior to that of Genghis Khan. However, this genealogy gradually lost its appeal toward the end of the 16th century and was replaced by the self-justifying lineage of the Ottoman sultans starting with the founder of the principality, OSMAN I (d. 1324). With a sense of triumphalism, the Ottoman lineage itself came to be considered superior to any other contemporary noble lineage. Dynastic historians, geomancers, chancellors, mystics, political thinkers and apologetics of the 16th century gave imperial ideology a new and powerful twist, emphasizing the uniqueness of the Ottoman dynasty and the empire. By comparing the Ottoman dynasty to other great dynasties, historians accorded the crown title to the Ottomans in their grandeur and righteousness. With the claim of having materialized the most perfect form of political union promoted in Greco-Islamic political theory, the Ottoman ruler was declared to be a just ruler and his domains "virtuous cities." Further, certain Ottoman rulers were perceived as "ruler of both temporal and spiritual worlds," "renewer of religion" (*müceddid*), "pole of the universe" (*kutb*), and "the awaited savior" (*mehdi*). Esoteric interpretations showed the Ottoman lineage as the chosen one foretold in the Quran and by the Prophet.

As inherited from Turco-Mongolian steppe traditions, the right to rule was vested in the dynastic family where all members were equally qualified to succeed. The royal blood was considered sacred and shedding the blood of members of the dynastic family was strictly avoided. Thus when fratricide was practiced, Ottoman princes were strangled. Rulership was believed to be a grace from God and the ruler was considered to be God's choice. Conceptions of divine appointment inherited from three major imperial and religious traditions fused together in the Ottoman ideology and created a broad basis for the ruler's legitimacy. Accordingly, the Ottoman ruler was conceived to have received "fortune" (*kut*) as in the Turco-Mongolian tradition, "divine light" (*farr*) as in the Persian tradition, and "good turn of fortune" (*devlet*) as in the Islamic tradition. During the first three centuries of the Ottoman dynasty, almost all successions took place through violent struggles among the candidates, with the expectation that only the most competent and the recipient of God's favor would win. In later centuries, because of increasing public outcry and extensive institutionalization, fratricide was largely abandoned and the principle of primogeniture typically prevailed.

By the time Ottomans came into power in the early 14th century, the concept of the CALIPHATE had already lost its exclusive meaning as the universal leadership of the Muslim community. Although the Ottomans adopted the title of caliph from the beginnings of the 15th century, it was used more consciously after 1517 when the empire incorporated much of the Arabic-speaking Islamic world. By unifying the central lands of the Islamic world and becoming its largest and most powerful organization, the Ottomans found that they were the supreme rulers of, and spokespersons for, the entire Islamic world. A novel development resulting from this position was the fusion of the hitherto distinct juristic and mystical conceptions of the caliphate. The juristic conception of the caliphate referred to the successors of Muhammad in political terms as the universal leaders of the Muslim community, a concept that also embraced the historical caliphate institutionalized following the Prophet's death and continued through the Umayyad and Abbasid dynasties. The mystical conception of the caliphate regarded the reigning caliph as God's deputy on earth. Using the title with both associations, the Ottoman rulers viewed themselves both as God's deputies on earth and as successors to the Prophet Muhammad's political leadership. Akin to this authority and unique to Ottoman rulers was the jealously guarded title of Khadim al-Haramayn al-Sharifayn or "Servant of the Two Noble Sanctuaries," referring to their custodianship over the Islamic holy cities of MECCA and MEDINA. With their sovereignty extending also over Jerusalem, their control of the three principal pilgrimage sites of Islam gave the Ottoman rulers unsurpassed prestige over other Muslim dynasties as well as responsibility for the Muslim community in general. For unlike other religious or secular titles, which were subject to dispute and challenge because of their abstractness, the Ottoman protectorate over these holy cities made their rulership more tangible and therefore implied a superiority over, and loyalty from, all Muslims.

Although the early Ottoman ruling elite may have been somewhat eclectic in faith and more accommodating of different strands of Islam, as the state grew, they grew more conscious of Islamic orthodoxy. In line with the prescriptions of SUNNI ISLAM, upholding religion in public life and applying the SHARIA became primary objectives of the dynasty as well as the very foundation of its legitimacy. Stipulated by prevailing notions of legitimacy, in principle, all actions of the government had to be in conformity with the precepts of Islam. The ancient Iranian maxim, also attributed to the Prophet, that religion and state are twins, came to be a consensual and formulaic expression of this relationship. Because religion and government were inextricably intertwined, religious controversies had a tendency to turn into political problems, and vice versa. Thus the Ottoman ruler came to enjoy both political and religious power, a status best formulated in a statement from a 17th-century law book by jurist Hezarfen Hüseyin: "The leader of the religion alone is the grand mufti. The leader of the state alone is the grand vizier. The leader of both is the victorious ruler."

Political developments of the 16th century led the Ottoman ruling elite to further refine their religious identity and incorporate it into the imperial ideology. The rise of the Safavid dynasty in the east, with its claim of superiority, relentless propaganda in favor of Shia Islam, and ambitions to expand, challenged both the unity and the legitimacy of the Ottoman Empire. To counter this threat, the Ottomans considered themselves champions of Sunni Islam and redefined their rulership on the basis of a distinctly Sunni theory of government.

Amidst this complexity, it was justice that gained a prominent place in political discourse and became the single most important governing principle of Ottoman imperial ideology. In its official expositions, the empire's subjects were considered a trust from God and it was the sultan's foremost responsibility to protect them and dispense justice. Ottoman rulers thus believed that they needed to be harsher in their treatment of the ruling elite in order to protect the ruled from mistreatment. Both the continuity of the state and God's favor toward the sultan were thought to be dependent on the sultan's observance of justice. Injustice was the most frequently cited reason to dethrone sultans in the 17th and 18th centuries. Ottoman society was considered to have formed out of four main classes that comprised men of sword, men of pen, men of agriculture and husbandry, and men of crafts and trade. Keeping these classes in their respective spheres was thought to be the foundation of imperial justice.

As part of this overarching concept of just rule, the Ottoman state from its very beginnings seems to have been no stranger to the idea of ruling by law. According to the Turco-Mongolian legacy, the ruler had the right to issue laws and was expected to abide by them unless he abolished or replaced them. Ottoman chronicles and writers of advice literature often accorded the highest esteem to the rulers who passed just laws and observed the existing ones while severely criticizing outright violations of law. By the mid-16th century, the concept of "ancient law" (kanun-i kadim) came to enjoy a constitutional authority among the ruling elite. This ancient law referred to the body of promulgated laws or well-established customary practices that were deemed to have constituted the foundations of the Ottoman state. Secular laws formed the basis of universal justice throughout the empire, while religious communities were accorded the autonomy of applying their own laws. Corporate bodies, such as guilds, could have their internal regulations recognized as laws by the Ottoman ruler.

In the economic sphere, the Ottomans had three main principles: provisionalism, fiscalism, and traditionalism (see ECONOMY AND ECONOMIC POLICY). Provisionalism meant to make goods and services accessible, ample, and affordable for the empire's subjects. Under this principle prices were kept under state control, exports were discouraged, and imports were encouraged. Fiscalism meant maintaining or increasing the revenues for the treasury with the aim of bolstering the state's financial power. Traditionalism was the maintenance of ideal structures and balances in the economy that formed over time but had come to be thought of as immutable. Ottoman authorities, were uneasy with economic changes and consistently tried to achieve through reform a return to the economic status quo.

During the 17th and 18th centuries, the imperial ideology of state building and expansionism of previous centuries proved increasingly untenable. The governing idea of the imperial ideology in this period ruled that as long as laws, conventions, and institutions that were believed to be genuinely Ottoman were maintained, the empire would last forever. During this period the historical sultans—MEHMED II (r. 1444–46; 1451–81), SELIM I (r. 1512–20), and SÜLEYMAN I (r. 1520–66)—were perceived as the ultimate role models, and institutions and laws established during their reigns were regarded as genuinely Ottoman, to be preserved as benchmarks for later reforms. In the meantime, political power accorded to individual sultans decreased while bureaucratic institutions such as the military, the government administration, and religious functionaries impressed their own identities and visions onto the imperial ideology. The notion of "eternal state" (devlet-i ebed müddet), a laudatory phrase that conventionally referred to God's permanent grace for the ruler in political discourse, evolved to mean the continuation of the Ottoman Empire with its laws and institutions until the "end of days." Thus the sacredness of Ottoman institutions and traditions surpassed those of individual sultans who continued to receive their legitimacy from their noble lineage and the idea of divine appointment.

By the 19th century, traditional forms of legitimacy needed to be inflected to accommodate new developments in state and society. While religious and traditional components of imperial ideology were redefined and reinvented, modern political ideas and devices were integrated as well. Imperial ideology in this period, despite its radical turns at times, encompassed both tradition and modernity at the same time. With the advent of modern means of publicity, political symbolism gained a new emphasis to shape and promote imperial ideology. This symbolism was geared to enhance the sultan's image as well as the legitimacy of the Ottoman state. While such royal ceremonies as coronation and sword girding were reinvented to serve dynastic needs of legitimacy, such novel means as a national flag and coat of arms were introduced in order to give a sense of national unity in a newly emerging territorial state. Besides making Islamic doctrines a part of imperial ideology, the Ottoman leadership also adopted secular ideas from Europe to bolster and complement its legitimacy. As a result, the caliphate came to be dissociated from the sultanate. While the Ottoman ruler inculcated a new image as the universal leader of the Islamic world, he also promoted himself as the secular leader of all Ottoman subjects exercising his authority in both capacities. Thus while Islam was more politicized than it had been before, Ottoman government also grew more secular.

Toward the late 18th century reformism weighed in as the dominating component of imperial ideology. The sense of decline that pervaded the minds of the Ottoman elite from the late 16th century onward became more acute in the 19th century with closer interaction with Europe. Traditionally, every Ottoman sultan succeeded with a claim and expectation of a new era of justice. Sultans in this period attempted to turn their reigns into ages of reform. Most of these reforms were modernizing initiatives intended to update Ottoman law, government, and the military either to address contemporary needs or to make them comparable to the ones emerged in Europe. All these modernizing reforms were promulgated for public consumption with an appeal to returning to past ideals or applying Islamic principles.

As the state appeared to be the chief engine of modernization in the 19th century, one key aspect of this reformist ideology was centralization. But from the late 16th century onward, the Ottoman Empire was gradually decentralizing as imperial institutions turned into autonomous structures while provinces came to be ruled by provincial magnates. Ottoman rulers and the elite observed that this situation was not tenable and made incessant efforts to regain political power at the center. The question of who would control this power led to a series of crises between the sultan and ruling elite. Despite continuous demands from below to share power and initiate constitutionalism, the underlying imperial ideology was that political power should be wholly vested in the sultan. In the cases of MAHMUD II (r. 1808–39) and ABDÜLHAMID II (r. 1876–1909), this amounted somewhat to a cult of personality.

During the 16th century, the concept of the caliphate was to a large extent limited to domestic concerns of legitimacy. With the decline of other Muslim political powers and the advent of colonialism, however, the Ottoman state increasingly appeared to be the principal authority over Muslims around the world. With the contraction of Ottoman borders during the 18th and 19th centuries, the Ottoman ruler maintained his moral authority over the Muslim populations outside the physical boundaries of the empire. During the latter half of the 19th century, the caliphate became the core of PAN-ISLAMISM as official ideology. In response to demands from outside Muslim communities, and in order to counter colonial aggression by European powers, the Ottoman ruler fashioned a new image of himself as the supreme authority not only of Ottoman or former Muslim subjects but of all the Muslims in the world.

While Pan-Islamism governed foreign policy, in the domestic sphere, Ottomanism took shape as the defining component of imperial ideology in the 19th century. It was envisioned as a universally unifying identity among the diverse ethnic groups and religious communities in the empire. It centered on the dynasty and the sultanate rather than the caliphate and aimed to create one nation living in Ottoman territories. Although the society was organized around religious communities in the MILLET system, inequalities between Muslims and non-Muslims were removed to create Ottoman citizenship. The Ottoman dynasty and its history, which had been the basis of the legitimacy of the Ottoman state, now became part of a common identity of the newly envisioned Ottoman nation.

Hüseyin Yılmaz

Further reading: Selim Deringil, *The Well-Protected Domains: Ideology and the Legitimation of Power in the Ottoman Empire, 1876–1909* (London: I.B. Tauris, 1998); Cornell H. Fleischer, *Bureaucrat and Intellectual in the Ottoman Empire: The Historian Mustafa Âli, 1541–1600* (Princeton, N.J.: Princeton University Press, 1986); Colin Imber, *Ebu'ssu'ud: The Islamic Legal Tradition* (Stanford, Calif.: Stanford University Press, 1997); Halil İnalcık, *The Ottoman Empire: The Classical Age* (London: Phoenix, 1973); Kemal H. Karpat, T*he Politicization of Islam: Reconstructing Identity, State, Faith, and Community in the Late Ottoman State* (Oxford: Oxford University Press, 2001).

intelligence   Following the example of medieval Muslim states and their SELJUK predecessors in Asia Minor, the Ottoman government placed a great emphasis on the collection of information both at home and from abroad. Mustafa Ali, a prominent Ottoman intellectual and historian at the end of the 16th century, contended that "if a prospering monarch does not use spies secretly, if the sovereign of the realm does not investigate the conditions of the state and people, if he contents himself with only questioning and believing his ministers, if he only sporadically commands that his aghas, who are privy to his secrets, keep him informed, then he forfeits justice for himself, integrity for his ministers, awe and dread for his army, and peace of mind and comfort for his subjects."

Domestic intelligence was collected by, among others, the JANISSARIES, the elite soldiers of the sultan's standing infantry corps. They also acted as the military police and played an important role in domestic surveillance. Under the supervision of lower-rank Janissary officers, agents were sent out in plain clothes to patrol the markets, bazaars, COFFEEHOUSES, and taverns of ISTANBUL and other major cities, following which they prepared daily reports for the grand vizier. Similarly, central and local Ottoman authorities employed a large number of informers. The division of labor between the provincial and district governors (*beylerbeyis* and *sancakbeyis*) on the one hand, and the judges (*kadıs*) on the other, not only balanced the power of local Ottoman officials but also helped the central government verify the validity of incoming information. Incoming intelligence from the provinces covered a variety of issues that ranged from political issues (insubordination and rebellion of officials and garrisons, overtaxation, abuse of authority) to religious and moral ones (heresy, apostasy, religious sectarianism, adultery, prostitution). The range of issues dealt with in the imperial decrees preserved in the *mühimme* (important affairs) registers that contain the outgoing copies of sultanic decrees suggests a considerable degree of information-based surveillance on the part of the central government and its local agents.

The "mapping" of the empire's subprovinces through regular land surveys (*tahrirs*) in the 15th and 16th centuries afforded the Ottoman government and its provincial administrators a detailed and comprehensive database regarding the size, composition, and economic conditions of the population. The availability in Istanbul of land surveys, provincial law codes (*kanunname*) that summarized the main regulations regarding taxation and taxes, copies of imperial decrees, and a host of financial records provided the Istanbul government with "long institutional memory."

In addition to domestic data gathering and home intelligence, the Ottoman government also collected information about its neighbors and adversaries. Such intelligence concerned the enemies' military and economic strengths and weaknesses as well as their policy decisions. In the 16th century at least four levels of Ottoman information gathering may be discerned: central intelligence in Istanbul; information gathering by local Ottoman authorities, especially along the empire's frontiers; intelligence provided by Istanbul's client or vassal states; and espionage and counterespionage carried out by the Sublime Porte's spies and saboteurs in foreign countries.

Sources of Ottoman intelligence in Istanbul included the sultan's Jewish and Christian subjects, as well as European ambassadors residing in Istanbul. Regarding the first group, in the 16th century both Joseph Nasí (of the influential Mendes family, and a confidant of several grand viziers) and Don Alvaro Mendes, alias Solomon Abenaes or Ibn Yaish (the brother-in-law of Queen Elizabeth's physician) were suspected in Europe for spying for the Ottomans. Sultan SÜLEYMAN I (r. 1520–66) called Nasí, who had a vast commercial network in Europe and employed numerous agents there, "the true mirror, in which he saw all the developments in Christendom and from which he obtained information about all countries."

Despite the unilateral nature of European-Ottoman diplomacy and the lack of Ottoman permanent ambassadors in European capitals until the mid-1830s (following the first unsuccessful attempts at the end of the 18th century), the Ottomans still managed to use diplomacy and diplomats for collecting information, as the representatives of competing European governments often shared information concerning their rivals with the Ottomans. For instance, the Venetians and the French often informed the Porte about VIENNA's policy, while the English provided information on SPAIN. The Ottoman government—which knew that European ambassadors in Istanbul were also engaged in espionage—also tried to control the flow of information from Istanbul to the various European capitals. European ambassadors in Istanbul often had to submit their letters to Ottoman officials for prior reading, and their couriers were accompanied by Ottoman escorts and were under constant surveillance.

Ottoman officials in the frontier provinces gathered intelligence concerning the empire's neighbors. Governors and district governors in Ottoman-controlled HUNGARY, for instance, regularly sent information to Istanbul about Habsburg garrisons, troop concentrations, and military campaigns, as well as information about Vienna's foreign policy. This included information not only about their own territory but also about Vienna's policy with regard to the Porte's European vassals. These provincial Ottoman officials employed spies who regularly traveled into or resided in Habsburg Austria. They also collected intelligence from captured Christian soldiers serving in the Habsburg garrisons in Habsburg-controlled Hungary, to the north of the area under Ottoman rule. Ottoman governors and district governors in eastern Anatolia and IRAQ employed spies in Safavid Persia and also monitored the border to intercept spies and agents sent by the Safavids.

The client or vassal states of the Porte also provided Istanbul with information about neighboring territories. Ottoman intelligence could rely particularly upon RAGUSA, TRANSYLVANIA, and the Rumanian principalities of WALLACHIA and MOLDAVIA. Ragusa obtained information from Spanish, Venetian, and French agents residing in or passing through the town, as well as from its extensive commercial contacts in Europe; Ragusa relied on this network to provide Istanbul with information about Italy and about the Austrian and Spanish Habsburgs. Transylvania sent news about royal Hungary, ruled by the Habsburgs, and the Danubian Habsburg monarchy, informing Istanbul about Vienna's policy regarding Hungary and Transylvania, planned and actual Habsburg troop movements, and the conditions of Hungarian and Habsburg garrisons.

The central government in Istanbul also employed its own spies in Europe, who were usually Christians. Such Ottoman spies were active in Spain, VENICE, and the Austrian Habsburg lands. Although some of these spies were double agents, others remained loyal to the sultan even at the expense of their lives.

The Ottomans also paid special attention to military intelligence before and during campaigns. They employed local road guides (*kılavuz*), as well as auxiliary military forces such as the MARTOLOS and *voynuks* whose tasks, among other things, involved military intelligence. News, information, and orders between the Ottoman capital and its provinces were transmitted by an elaborate courier and communications network, called the *ulak* or MENZILHANE system.

While Ottoman information gathering did not reach the level of sophistication of the Venetian and Spanish intelligence services, it served Ottoman policymakers well. Contemporaries were often surprised by how well informed the Ottomans were both about major political and military events in Europe and about less important day-to-day policy decisions. For instance, the Ottomans were surprisingly quick to learn about the fire in the Venetian arsenal in September 1569 and about the defeat of the Spanish Armada in 1588. Ottoman intelligence regarding the arsenal fire was of particular importance in that the manipulation of this news proved crucial in launching the war against the Republic of Saint Mark, culminating in the Ottoman conquest of CYPRUS, which had been under Venetian rule. As a result of its information-gathering activities and its road and communications network, the Ottoman Empire of the 16th century remained an integral part of European politics and information flow. Juan de Vega, the viceroy of Sicily, stated in 1557 that the Ottomans were as quick as the Spanish government in receiving information about events in the Spanish and Italian Mediterranean.

The reorganization of Ottoman diplomacy at the end of the 18th century, an integral part of the modernization program of Sultan SELIM III (r. 1789–1807), known as the NIZAM-I CEDID, marked an important milestone in the history of Ottoman intelligence gathering. The transition from unilateral (or nonreciprocal) diplomacy to reciprocal diplomacy, that is to say, the establishment of permanent or resident embassies abroad at the end of the 18th century and especially from the early 1830s, greatly enhanced Ottoman information-gathering capabilities. Ottoman diplomats who served in Europe came primarily from the Translation Office (Terceme Odası), established in 1821 after the outbreak of the GREEK WAR OF INDEPENDENCE, when the Ottoman government lost its faith in the Phanariot Greek translators who had dominated the foreign relations offices since the early 1660s. Many of the officials who served in the translation office, such as MEHMED EMIN ÂLÎ PASHA and FUAD PASHA, had become leading politicians during the TANZIMAT reform era (1839–76) and placed great emphasis on information and intelligence, as did Sultan ABDÜLHAMID II (r. 1876–1909). Abdülhamid was known for his keen interest in news regarding world affairs. His domestic spy network was legendary, and rumor had it that he paid one half of his people to spy on the other half.

The first Ottoman secret police was founded under Sultan ABDÜLMECID (r. 1839–61) on the recommendation of the English ambassador Stratford Canning; it was established by MUSTAFA REŞID PASHA and was headed by Civinis Efendi, a foreign adventurer, perhaps of Greek origins. The first professional Ottoman intelligence service, the notorious Teşkilat-i Mahsusa (Special Organization), was established in 1913 by the members of the political group the COMMITTEE OF THE UNION AND PROGRESS. In addition to information gathering, the Special Organization also carried out military and paramilitary operations during WORLD WAR I in NORTH AFRICA, EGYPT, the CAUCASUS, and Central Asia. Dissolved at the end of the war, the organization and the "action groups" it organized and directed have been accused, especially by Armenians and Greeks, of committing atrocities and mass killings. Perhaps because of its reputed activities, the history of the organization remains understudied.

Gábor Ágoston

Further reading: Gábor Ágoston, "Information, Ideology, and Limits of Imperial Policy: Ottoman Grand Strategy in the Context of Ottoman-Habsburg Rivalry," in *The Early Modern Ottoman Empire: A Reinterpretation*, edited by Virginia Aksan and Daniel Goffman (Cambridge: Cambridge University Press, 2007); N. H. Biegman, "Ragusan Spying for the Ottoman Empire: Some 16th-century Documents from the State Archive at Dubrovnik." *Belleten* 27, no. 106 (1963): 237–55; V. L. Ménage, "The Mission of an Ottoman Secret Agent in France in 1486." *Journal of the Royal Asiatic Society* (1965): 112–132; Philip Hendrick Stoddard, "The Ottoman Government and the Arabs, 1911–1918: A Preliminary Study of the Teşkilat-i Mahsusa" (Ph.D. diss., Princeton University, 1963); A. Nuri Yurdusev, ed., *Ottoman Diplomacy: Conventional or Unconventional* (Basingstoke, UK: Palgrave Macmillan, 2004).

Iran (Islamic Republic of Iran, Persia)   Iran is one of the largest countries in southwest Asia bordering ARMENIA, Azerbaijan, Turkmenistan, and the Caspian Sea on the north; Afghanistan and Pakistan on the east; the Persian Gulf and the Gulf of Oman on the south; and TURKEY and IRAQ on the west. The country's name was changed from Persia to Iran in 1935 and to the Islamic Republic of Iran after the Islamic Revolution of 1979. The term *Persia* derives from the Hellenized name Parsa, or Persis, of one province (present-day Fars) in southwestern Iran, and of the Indo-European people by the same name who migrated to this region about 1000 B.C.E. The name was popularized by the ancient Greeks who met the Persians of the Achaemenian dynasty (sixth to fourth centuries B.C.E.). Locals, however, prefer the name Iran ("the Land of the Aryans"), and in 1935 the Iranian government requested that foreigners use the name Iran for the country instead of Persia. However, Persia had by that time become an established name, and the two names are used interchangeably, especially when referring to pre-20th-century Iran.

For the Ottomans, Iran was important for several reasons. First and foremost, under the Safavid dynasty (1501–1736), it was a major rival that challenged Ottoman rule in eastern Anatolia and Iraq. The clash between the Sunni Ottomans and Shii Safavids had significant political, territorial, and religious repercussions. Turkoman and Kurdish tribes managed to play the two empires against one another and establish themselves along the mountainous frontier regions with consequences that are felt even today. Ottoman-Safavid wars limited both empires' freedom of action against their other rivals—in the Ottomans' case against Habsburg SPAIN and AUSTRIA and their allies, in the case of the Safavids against the Uzbeks, Afghans, and Mughal India. Thus Ottoman-Safavid rivalry had significant impact on politics in Europe and Asia. The border between present-day TURKEY and Iran is also the result of the Ottoman-Safavid rivalry and goes back to the mid-16th century. Prior to the Safavids, the administrative and military practices of the various Persian and Turkish empires that ruled Iran, especially that of the Samanids (819–1005) and the Seljuk Turks (1038–1194), served as models for subsequent Islamic empires, including the Ottomans.

In the 19th century both the Ottoman Empire and Qajar Iran (1796–1925) faced challenges, including Russian expansion, the political and economic influence of the leading European empires, and the need for military, administrative, and economic reforms. Largely due to these pressing foreign and domestic problems, in the 19th century relations between the Ottomans and the Qajars were less hostile than under the Safavids, and there were no major wars (except for the 1820–23 war) or border changes.

BEFORE THE SAFAVIDS

The territory of present-day Iran was the site of ancient settlements that go back some 6,000 years. The province of Parsa was the cradle of two great Persian empires, the Achaemenid (559–331 B.C.E.), which in the sixth and fifth centuries B.C.E. extended from India to the Balkans and EGYPT, and the Sassanid (224–651 C.E.), which in the third century C.E. comprised territories from well beyond the Indus valley in the east to eastern Turkey and the Arabian Peninsula in the west.

In the mid-seventh century the Sassanid Empire was conquered by the Arabs and Islam was introduced into Persia. Both the Umayyad caliphs (661–750) and the rulers of the ABBASID CALIPHATE (750–1250) borrowed heavily from the Sassanids in terms of military organization, logistics, tactics, provincial and imperial administration, court culture, and manners. The Abbasid revolution that overthrew the Umayyads in 750 started in northeastern Persia (Khorasan). To counterbalance the Khorasani army upon which early Abbasid rule depended, the caliphs started to import Turkish slave soldiers (mamluks) as imperial guards. This decision had momentous consequences, for Turkish slave soldiers and the institution of MILITARY SLAVERY were to play major roles in the history of the Islamic Middle East for the next millennium. It also opened the way for the Turkic people who would dominate the history of Iran and the Islamic heartlands for centuries to come.

With the weakening of the Abbasid Caliphate, local Iranian dynasties ruled over much of Persia in the 9th and 10th centuries. Of these, the Samanids, whose original base was in Bukhara and Samarkand in present-day Uzbekistan, were the most important. Samanid administration, itself a blend of Sassanid, Islamic, and Central Asian administrative practices, served as a model for many future Islamic empires. In the mid-10th century the Persian Buyid dynasty, which followed the moderate Ismaili or Twelver persuasion of SHIA ISLAM, conquered the Abbasid capital BAGHDAD and soon extended its rule over western Persia, while in eastern Iran the Turkish Ghaznavids established themselves.

A century later, both were overthrown by the Seljuk Turks (see SELJUKS), who portrayed themselves as liberators of the Sunni Abbasid caliphs from the Shia Buyids. Although Seljuk rule gave impetus to the Turkification of Persia, one should note that the process had started earlier and would accelerate after the Seljuks. More important was the Seljuk legacy with regard to central and provincial government and the land tenure system that supported the Seljuk army and administration. This land regime was known as iqta, a land grant system through which the Seljuk government remunerated its administrators and troops. The institution would, under different names, survive in Persia into the Qajar era. It would also reappear, in the form of the timar system, in the empire of the Ottomans.

The Mongol invasion of Persia by Genghis Khan (r. 1206–27) after 1219 brought devastation to the country and caused the greatest upheaval in the history of Iran since the Arab conquest. Genghis Khan's successors, the Ilkhanid Mongols, ruled Persia from the mid-13th through the mid-14th centuries. While their rule was initially very destructive, later Ilkhanid rule benefited Persia. The Ilkhanids relied on Persian administrators in governing and, after Mahmud Ghazan's (r. 1295–1304) conversion to Islam, their capitals of Tabriz and Maragha in northwestern Iran became flourishing Islamic cultural centers.

By the late 13th century the empire of the Ilkhanids was divided into local states, and Iran was reunited again only by TIMUR (r. 1370–1405), founder of the Timurid Empire based in Transoxania (territories beyond the Oxus/Amu Darya River in Uzbekistan), who was of Mongol origin and Turkish in speech. He waged wars as far as India in the east and Ottoman Anatolia in the west, where he defeated the Ottoman sultan BAYEZID I (r. 1389–1402) at the BATTLE OF ANKARA, causing a temporary dissolution of the Ottoman state. Timur soon incorporated into his vast empire all the lands once under Ilkhanid rule.

Although his campaigns and plunders were as disastrous as those of Genghis Khan, certain Persian cities profited from his patronage, and architecture and decorative arts in Tabriz, Shiraz, and Herat (in present-day Afghanistan) flourished, as did Persian miniature painting. His empire survived for another century, but by the early 16th century it was absorbed into new emerging empires that would define the fate of Persia and its neighbors in the following two to three centuries. Timur's base in Transoxania was incorporated into the Shaybanid Uzbek Empire; his lands in Anatolia, SYRIA, and Iraq were conquered by the Ottomans; in Persia, the Safavid dynasty was established. One of Timur's descendants, Zahir al-Din Babur (r. 1483–1530), established the Indian Timurid, or Mughal, Empire that would rule most of India until 1858.

UNDER THE SAFAVIDS

The Safavid dynasty was established by Shah ISMAIL I (r. 1501–24); it ruled Persia from 1501 until 1736, when the last Safavid ruler, Shah Abbas III (r. 1732–36), was deposed, although effective Safavid rule ended in 1722 with the Afghan invasion of Persia. Shah Ismail's empire represented a serious challenge to the Ottomans. For the Turkomans and Kurds living in Ottoman Anatolia, the Safavid system of government, which resembled a nomadic tribal confederation, seemed more desirable than the centralized Ottoman rule that threatened the nomads' very way of life. Following Shah Ismail's decision to make Shia Islam Persia's official state religion, the shah's agents embarked on a major proselytization and propaganda campaign in Anatolia, winning many to their cause in the eastern provinces of the Ottoman Empire among the Turkoman nomads. The Ottomans called Shah Ismail's Turkoman followers in Anatolia by the same name they used for the Safavids: KIZILBAŞ (Redheads), after their red headgear. Pro-Safavid Kızılbaş rebellions in Anatolia in 1511–12 showed the seriousness of the Safavid threat.

Sultan SELIM I's (r. 1512–20) victory over Shah Ismail in 1514 at the Battle of Çaldıran in eastern Turkey and the subsequent Ottoman expansion into Azerbaijan and Iraq had major consequences, for it led to the readjustment of the Ottoman-Safavid frontier. At Çaldıran, the Safavids lost eastern Anatolia to the Ottomans, and in 1534 and 1548 Sultan SÜLEYMAN I (r. 1520–66) temporarily captured the Safavid capital Tabriz. In 1534 the sultan also conquered Baghdad, the most important city in

Iraq, which controlled the EUPHRATES and Tigris rivers and thus controlled regional and international trade. In the 1555 Treaty of Amasya Shah Tahmasp I (r. 1524–76) acknowledged recent Ottoman conquests in Iraq, and Baghdad remained in Ottoman hands until 1918 except for the short period of 1623–38, when the Safavids held the city. Following Sultan MURAD IV's (r. 1623–40) reconquest of Baghdad, the Treaty of Zuhab (1639) restored the 1555 borders, which were to remain essentially unchanged until WORLD WAR I.

After these Ottoman conquests, the Safavid court in Tabriz was dangerously close to the Ottomans. Thus in 1548 the Safavid capital was transferred first to Qazvin (south-southeast of Tabriz) and in 1598 further south to Isfahan. The transfer was a strategic decision but it also signaled the gradual evolution of the nascent Safavid state, which still resembled the pre-Safavid Turkoman states of Persia—above all the Akkoyunlu ("White Sheep") Empire of Shah Ismail's maternal grandfather, Uzun Hasan (r. 1453–78)—into a Persian empire whose capital now lay well within the borders of Persia.

Apart from the Ottomans, the Safavids repeatedly waged wars against the Shaybanid Uzbeks, who had replaced the TIMURIDS as rulers of Transoxania at the beginning of the 16th century. In 1510 Shah Ismail defeated and killed the founder of the Shaybanid state, Muhammad Shaybani (b. 1451–d. 1510), but the Uzbeks habitually invaded Persia's northeastern provinces when Safavid forces were occupied against the Ottomans at the opposite end of their empire. The Uzbek threat disappeared, albeit only temporarily, at the end of the 16th century, which coincided with the long reign of the last great Safavid ruler, Shah ABBAS I (r. 1587–1629), who restored Persia's international standing and reformed its government and military. After he recaptured his eastern provinces (Khorasan and Sistan) from the Uzbeks, in 1603 Abbas launched vigorous campaigns against the Ottomans, whose forces were fighting in HUNGARY against the Austrian Habsburgs. Abbas not only reconquered all the territories he had been forced to hand over to the Ottomans as a result of a humiliating treaty in 1590 (including Georgia, Azerbaijan, and Shirvan), he also captured Baghdad and Diyarbakır, albeit only temporarily. Abbas's military achievements notwithstanding, his dynastic policy proved harmful in the long run. It relegated the princes to long years of seclusion in the HAREM, depriving them of vital administrative and military skills that former princes had gained while serving as provincial governors. Still, the Safavid system produced some able ministers and one more remarkable ruler, Shah Abbas's namesake and great-grandson, Shah Abbas II (r. 1642–66).

Natural disasters, famine, and the anti-Sunni policy of the ineffective and oppressive late Safavid governments caused much unrest and rebellion, especially in Afghanistan, where the majority of the shah's subjects remained Sunnis. In 1722 the Sunni Afghans, led by the chief of the Ghalzai tribe based in Kandahar, captured the Safavid capital Isfahan and dethroned the inept Shah Husayn (r. 1694–1722), terminating effective Safavid rule in Persia.

THE TROUBLED 18TH CENTURY

The chaos created by the Afghan invasion of Persia presented the Ottomans and Russians a golden opportunity for territorial expansion at the expense of Iran. Under Peter the Great (r. 1689–1725), RUSSIA renewed its policy of seeking access to the Black and Caspian Seas and in 1722–23 occupied Derbend (in southeast Dagestan on the Caspian Sea) and Baku (capital of present-day Azerbaijan). Although the French volunteered to mediate between Russia and the Ottomans (so that the latter would be free to fight against FRANCE's rival, Austria, in Europe), the Ottomans decided that the most efficient way to stop the Russians was to occupy western Iran. When ISTANBUL declared war on Iran, Tahmasp Mirza, son of the deposed Safavid shah, sought help from Russia. In return for Russian military assistance, Persia ceded Derbend and Baku, along with the northern Persian provinces of Gilan, Mazandaran, and Astarabad (1723) to Russia. The Ottomans captured several of Iran's western provinces, and with French mediation St. Petersburg and Istanbul partitioned western and northern Iran in the 1724 Treaty of Istanbul. Russia kept the provinces ceded to it in 1723, while Istanbul received large territories in what is now Armenia and northwestern Iran (including Tabriz, the former Safavid capital). The death of Peter the Great in 1725, however, cut short

Map of Iran published in 1729 by İbrahim Müteferrika. (*Photo by Fikret Sarıcaoğlu*)

Russia's advance in Iran. The Ottomans proceeded with their conquests, and by 1730 they controlled Georgia, Armenia, Azerbaijan, Kermanshah, Hamadan, and parts of Dagestan.

The short-lived Afghan rule in Persia was ended in 1729 when Nadir Khan of the Turkoman Afshar tribe overthrew the second Afghan shah. As his adopted name, Tahmasp-Quli (the Slave of Tahmasp) indicated, Nadir Khan initially acted on behalf of the nominal Safavid shah, Tahmasp II (r. 1722–32). In 1736, however, he deposed the last Safavid ruler, the infant Shah Abbas III (r. 1732–36), and forced the notables of Persia to accept him as their new ruler under the name NADIR SHAH (r. 1736–47), thus inaugurating the rule of the Afsharid dynasty (1736–95) in Persia.

Ottoman expansion proved ephemeral as they lost the conquered lands to Nadir Khan in the early 1730s. The Ottoman-Persian treaty of 1736 restored the borders established by the 1639 Treaty of Zuhab. In the preceding year the Russians, whose forces by then were fighting in Poland and were preparing for a military conflict with the Ottomans (*see* RUSSO-OTTOMAN WARS), had returned to Nadir the lands they occupied. Having recaptured northern and western Iran, Nadir Shah turned against Persia's traditional enemy in the northeast, the Uzbeks, as well as against the Afghans and Mughal India.

Hostilities with the Ottomans were renewed in 1740 in the CAUCASUS and northern Iraq, but Nadir's conquests (Mosul and Kirkuk in Iraq) were short-lived, and he also had to abandon his demands that the Ottomans accept his moderate Shia Islam as the fifth school of Sunni Islam. In return, in the 1746 treaty, the Ottomans acknowledged Iran as a fellow Muslim empire, which was a radical departure from previous Ottoman policy that often branded Iran as a mortal enemy made up of Shia heretics.

Following the death of Nadir Shah in 1747 his successors lost control over much of Persia and pulled back to Khorasan, which they held until the end of the century. With the loss of central power, warlords and tribal chiefs emerged as local rulers, which is hardly surprising in a country where more than half the population was made up of nomad tribespeople as late as the early 19th century. One of these warlords, Muhammad Karim Khan of the Zand tribe, managed to extend his control over much of the country from his base in Shiraz (southern Persia). Although Karim Khan (r. 1750–79)—who never took the title of shah but ruled as *wakil* or regent of the nominal Safavid shah Ismail III— abstained from military ventures, he did take BASRA, the important port city in southern Iraq, from the Ottomans for a brief period (1776–79). Karim Khan's death was again followed by renewed power struggles within his family until the Zands were overthrown by the Qajars in 1796.

THE 19TH CENTURY AND BEYOND

According to some researchers the Turkoman Qajars entered Iran with Hülegü (r. 1256–65), grandson of Genghis Khan and founder of the Mongol Ilkhanid dynasty of Persia, while others maintain that they were part of the Turkomans who lived in Anatolia in the 15th century and migrated into Persia (Azerbaijan region) only at the end of that century. Under the Safavids the Qajars were one of the most important Kızılbaş tribes. Surviving the upheaval after the fall of the Safavids in their homeland in northwestern Persia, their leader Agha Muhammad Khan (r. 1779–97) defeated the last Zand ruler in 1796. Although Agha Muhammad Khan, who had transferred the capital to Tehran in 1786, was killed the next year, his successors gradually gained control over much of Persia and inaugurated a new epoch in Iranian history. The Qajar era was characterized by the struggle to defend Iran against foreign—primarily Russian and English—political and economic dominance, and by the military and administrative reforms designed to strengthen Iran in light of these foreign threats.

While Iran was less successful in these reforms than the Ottomans or MEHMED ALI in Egypt, unlike the Ottomans, Iran managed to preserve most of its former lands. However, after being defeated in two wars against Russia, Iran was forced to relinquish claims to the territories north of the Araks River, ceding what is now Armenia and Azerbaijan to Russia in the treaties of Gulistan (1813) and Turkmanchai (1828). The Araks river forms the present-day border between Iran on the one hand, and Armenia and Azerbaijan on the other. The Qajars were similarly unsuccessful in their attempts to reclaim Herat, a long-contested territory in western Afghanistan, which in 1857 became part of British-controlled Afghanistan.

As in the Ottoman Empire, the constitutional movement gained pace at the turn of the century, and Muzaffer al-Din Shah (r. 1896–1907) proclaimed the constitution in 1906. The next year Russia and Great Britain divided Iran into Russian and British spheres of influence, and despite Iran's declaration of neutrality in World War I, the two empires waged war on Iran's territory. After World War I Reza Shah Pahlavi, a leader of a Cossack brigade who, in 1925, seized power and founded Iran's last dynasty, the Pahlavis (1925–79), embarked on an ambitious project of westernization and modernization that had many similarities to those carried out by KEMAL ATATÜRK, founder of the Republic of Turkey.

Gábor Ágoston

See also ABBAS I.

Further reading: David Morgan, *Medieval Persia, 1040–1797* (London: Longman, 1988); Robert Olson, *The Siege of Mosul and Ottoman-Persian Relations, 1718–1743* (Bloomington: Indiana University Press, 1975); Roger Savory, *Iran under the Safavids* (Cambridge: Cambridge University Press, 1980).

Iraq (*Turk.:* **Irak**)   Iraq did not exist as a political entity during the Ottoman imperial period, although the same name was used to designate the central section of what is now Iraq. During the Ottoman era, the area that has become Iraq was divided into three provinces, each named for and centered in what are today the country's largest cities: BAGHDAD, BASRA, and MOSUL. There was also a fourth province, SHAHRIZOR, located in the mountains of Iraqi Kurdistan. Iraq had served as the heartland of the ABBASID CALIPHATE, which, from the ninth through the 11th centuries, ruled much of the Muslim world from Baghdad. With the destruction of Baghdad in 1258 and the end of the Abbasid Caliphate, Iraq's irrigation-based agriculture began to fall into disrepair, and in the centuries of political anarchy that followed, various tribal confederations of KURDS, Arabs, and Turkomans battled for dominance. Most of the area accrued to the Ottoman Empire during the reign of SÜLEYMAN I (r. 1520–66), although the Ottomans and their archrivals of the Safavid dynasty frequently struggled for control of the country and parts of the territory were sometimes under Safavid rule.

During the 19th century, two important social trends occurred in what would become Iraq that have had far-reaching effects on the country's present social and religious culture. The first was the rapid tribalization of the rural population. There had always been BEDOUINS on the desert fringes of the large plain watered by the Tigris and EUPHRATES rivers, but as scant resources limited the ability of the Ottoman governors to control the movement of the tribes, Bedouin tribesmen settled in the agricultural lands, either driving out the peasant cultivators or absorbing them into their tribes. The result was that by the beginning of the 19th century, almost the entire rural population maintained a tribal structure, with Arabs in the south and Kurds in the north. This framework was unique to Iraq; elsewhere in the Arab provinces of the empire, few peasants had tribal affiliations. When the Ottomans attempted land reform after 1868, the tribal sheikhs became the predominant landowners of the country as the peasants deferred to their authority and did not seek to register land in their own names. This strengthened the economic as well as political hold of the sheikhs over their tribesmen. The other important development was the shift of many of these tribesmen from SUNNI ISLAM to SHIA ISLAM. This was the result of a concerted missionary effort on the part of the Shii clergy in the holy cities of NAJAF and KARBALA who were faced with the threat of WAHHABI tribesmen, the militant followers of MUHAMMAD IBN ABD AL-WAHHAB who frequently attacked the Shia as "unbelievers." The missionary effort was thus designed to win the Wahhabi tribes as allies. The long-term effects of these two trends has been that the majority of the Arabic-speaking peasants in what would become Iraq are both tribally organized and practicing Shii Muslims.

Great Britain viewed southern Iraq with increasing interest after oil was discovered in neighboring Iran in 1908. In addition, they sought to protect the growing trade between the region and British colonial India, seeing this as vital to India's economy. British forces occupied the city of Basra in November 1914 after the outbreak of WORLD WAR I. A British expeditionary force moved toward Baghdad in October 1915 but was stalled by stiff Ottoman resistance. The British column surrendered on April 29, 1916 at Kut el Amara, a city on the bank of the Tigris River that today is known simply as al-Kut. The officers were taken to Istanbul to wait out the war, but the enlisted men simply disappeared, and no account has been given of their fate. A year later, a second British advance succeeded in taking Baghdad. The SYKES-PICOT AGREEMENT of 1916 awarded Britain direct control over Basra and Baghdad, as well as a "zone of influence" over most of the rest of southern and central Iraq. The status of the northern province of Mosul remained contested until after the war. Iraq was established as a kingdom under British protection in 1922, its borders drawn by an agreement between Great Britain and France. In 1932 the kingdom gained full independence and was admitted to the League of Nations.

Bruce Masters

Further reading: Stephen Longrigg, Four Centuries of Modern Iraq (Oxford: Clarendon, 1925); William Polk, *Understanding Iraq: The Whole Sweep of Iraqi History, from Genghis Khan's Mongol to the Ottoman Turks* (New York: Harper Collins, 2005).

Islam *See* SHIA ISLAM; SUFISM; SUNNI ISLAM.

Ismail, Khedive (b. 1830–d. 1895) (r. 1863–1879) *khedive of Egypt* Ismail ruled Egypt first as its governor (*vali*) and then as KHEDIVE from 1863 until he was deposed in 1879 in favor of his son, Muhammad TAWFIQ. The son of IBRAHIM PASHA and the grandson of MEHMED ALI, the military ruler of Egypt from 1805 until 1849, Ismail has been characterized by historians as a dynamic ruler who wanted to push Egypt along the path of modernization begun by his grandfather. The major challenge to Mehmed Ali's ambitions had been the Ottoman sultan. For Ismail, it was the French and the British, both of whom had ambitions for Egypt in their imperial schemes.

This photo of Ismail shows him wearing the Tanzimat era fez and frock coat and the medals he had received from the Ottoman sultans. Although he acted independently in his role of Egyptian head of state, this photo demonstrates that symbolically he was still a subject of the Ottoman sultan. *(Library of Congress)*

The most important modernization project of Ismail's reign was the opening of the SUEZ CANAL. Starting in 1854, Ferdinand de Lesseps, a Frenchman, had pushed a project to build a monumental canal at Suez that would link the Mediterranean to the Red Sea, thereby halving the sea voyage from western Europe to India. But the project was not realized until Ismail became governor of Egypt; he agreed to the plan, and construction of the canal began in 1866. It was finished in 1869, and to mark the occasion, Ismail made a grand tour of Europe's capitals. Upon his return, the opening of the canal was marked in Cairo by festivities that included the premier of Giuseppe Verdi's opera *Aida* in the grand Western-style Cairo Opera House that had been built for the occasion.

Ismail introduced a number of reforms as he hoped that modernizing the country's institutions and infrastructure would enable Egypt to effectively resist Western political domination. In 1866 he inaugurated an assembly of deputies made up of delegates indirectly elected by representatives from the country's main cities and also—more importantly—from its villages. Although this was solely a consultative body, it gave voice to popular politics for the first time in Egypt's history. Other reforms followed, including a law to grant peasants full ownership of their lands in 1872, which Ismail felt would improve the country's agricultural productivity. Ismail's plan for modernization also included a kind of Egyptian colonial expansion. At his orders, Egyptian forces pushed further into what is today Sudan, beyond the Arabic-speaking zone into the tropical African south of the country. This substantially increased the territories Ismail controlled but it also laid the foundation for future conflicts between northern and southern Sudan. Attempts to add Ethiopian territory to his domains were less successful.

But all Ismail's plans for modernization were expensive, and under his governance, Egypt became deeply indebted to foreign creditors, as the agreements to build the Suez Canal had invested Egyptian resources without guaranteeing the country a sufficient return of the profits that the canal generated. In 1876, faced with growing pressure to repay those debts, Ismail established a body whose membership represented Egypt's four largest creditor nations: Great Britain, France, Austria, and Italy. Its job was to organize the servicing of the national debt. This was not sufficient for the bondholders, however, and they insisted on the appointment of a British and French controller, known as the Dual Control, to supervise the collection of the state's revenues and all expenditures by the government of Egypt. With that, fiscal control of his country effectively slipped out of Ismail's hands. The pressure up to that point had come from private Western banks, but in 1878, the governments of Great Britain and France demanded reform and control over Egypt's financial affairs.

The European interventions were unpopular in Egypt, where the press reported each new development in bold headlines. In an attempt to gain public support at the expense of the Europeans, Ismail sought to broaden the powers of the assembly of delegates. This created a diplomatic standoff with the Europeans that Ismail could not possibly win. The British and the French pondered whether they should intervene militarily or seek to oust Ismail by appealing to the Ottoman sultan's nominal authority over Egypt. In the end, they chose the latter course. Their pressure brought an order from Istanbul deposing Ismail in June 1879. His son, Muhammad Tawfiq, took over as khedive; Ismail was exiled to Naples, where he lived until his death in 1895. The turmoil generated by the financial crisis in Egypt did not end, however, and three years later, Britain occupied the country.

Bruce Masters

Further reading: F. Robert Hunter, "Egypt under the Successors of Muhammad Ali," in *The Cambridge History of Modern Egypt*, vol. 2, edited by M. W. Daly (Cambridge: Cambridge University Press, 1998), 180–97.

Ismail I (Shah Ismail, Ismail Safavi) (b. 1487–d.1524) (r. 1501–1524) *shah and founder of the Safavid dynasty who restored Persia as a sovereign state and established Shia Islam as an official state religion* Ismail is known as the founder of the Safavid dynasty that ruled Persia, or IRAN, from 1501 through 1736. He is credited with restoring sovereignty over Persia's heartlands for the first time since the Arab conquest in the mid-seventh century. The other major change associated with Ismail is his decision to make the Imami or "Twelver" rite of SHIA ISLAM—the largest and most tolerant subdivision within that religion, whose followers believe that the 12th imam (Muhammad al-Mahdi) who went into occultation in the ninth century C.E. will return in the future—the official state religion of his country. By instituting Shiism as the state religion Ismail distinguished his country from Persia's neighbors and rivals, the Ottomans and the Shaybanid Uzbeks, who both followed SUNNI ISLAM. These fundamental changes provided the territorial and religious foundations of present-day Iran. In addition, the rivalry of Ismail and his successors with the Ottomans over eastern Anatolia, Azerbaijan, and parts of IRAQ had international ramifications because the Safavids often engaged Ottoman armies and resources, limiting ISTANBUL's ability to act against the Habsburgs in the Mediterranean and HUNGARY and thus altering power relations in Europe in the 16th and 17th centuries.

The basis of the Safavid dynasty and state was the Safaviyya religious order, a Sunni order based in Ardabil, northwestern Iran, which was named after the order's founder, Sheikh Safi al-Din Ishaq (1253–1334). In 1494 Ismail inherited the leadership of the order when Ali, his brother and the head of the order, was killed by the Akkoyunlu ("White Sheep") Turkomans. Originally a Turkoman tribal confederation that followed Sunni Islam and was based in Diyarbakır in eastern Turkey, the Akkoyunlus had offered refuge to the Safaviyya brotherhood against their common enemy, the Karakoyunlu ("Black Sheep") Turkomans who ruled in Azerbaijan and Iraq. By defeating the Karakoyunlus, the Akkoyunlu sultan Uzun Hasan (r. 1453–78) transformed his Turkoman confederation into an Islamic empire that controlled eastern Anatolia, Azerbaijan, Iraq, and western Iran from the capital Tabriz, and maintained amicable relations with the Safaviyya order. Uzun Hasan married his sister to Ismail's paternal grandfather, Sheikh Junayd (d. 1460), and married his daughter to Ismail's father, Sheikh Haydar (d. 1488). Uzun Hasan's son Yakub (r. 1478–90), however, perceived the militant Safaviyya order, which had tens of thousands of supporters among his Turkoman subjects, as a major threat to his rule; for this reason, he killed Ali.

After the death of his brother, Ismail was given asylum by the local Shii ruler of Gilan, on the Caspian coast.

Ismail thus spent his formative years in a Shia environment; the religious practice of his grandfather and father, a kind of popular Islam, also contained elements of Shiism. Sources credit Ismail's father, Haydar, with introducing the twelve-tasseled red hat (*taj*) that honored the 12 Shia leaders (imams), after which the Safavids and their Turkoman followers were called KIZILBAŞ, "Redheads" in Turkish.

By 1501, aided by his Kızılbaş followers, Ismail defeated the Akkoyunlus and captured Tabriz, which he made the capital of his nascent Safavid state. Ismail presented himself as both ruler (shah) and the long-awaited Mahdi, the prophesied savior of Islam. He had coins minted in his name in Tabriz, a common sign of sovereignty, and began the conversion of the majority Sunni population of Persia to Shia Islam. The forced conversion was carried out with resolve and often with brutality, and lasted for generations. Shah Ismail relied on leading Shia theologians from the areas of present-day Iraq and LEBANON and on those Sunni religious learned men (ULEMA) who were willing to change their religion for career advancement in the new state.

In 1503 Ismail defeated another Akkoyunlu army in western Persia, adding that region to his domains. In 1507 he extended his rule into the Akkoyunlu heartland in eastern Anatolia, capturing Diyarbakır. With this, his domains reached the Ottoman Empire's eastern frontiers. At this point Ismail appeared to be the heir to the Akkoyunlu Turkoman empire of his maternal grandfather, Uzun Hasan. From Tabriz, the traditional Turkoman capital on the western fringes of Persia proper, he coveted the loyalty of the Turkoman tribes of eastern Anatolia and Azerbaijan. The Turkoman tribes made up the bulk of his army, and the language of administration of his state was Turkish. However, regional rivalries with his two Sunni enemies, the Shaybanids in the east and northeast and the Ottoman Turks in the west, soon transformed Ismail's initially Turkoman state into a Persian empire.

The Shaybanids, or Shaybani Uzbeks (Özbeks), were descendant of Shiban (Shayban), grandson of Genghis Khan (d. 1227) and younger brother of Batu (d. 1255), the founder of the Golden Horde that ruled southern Russia until the 16th century. By 1500 Muhammad Shaybani (b. 1451–d. 1510), a descendant of Shiban, conquered Transoxania (present-day Uzbekistan, parts of Turkmenistan and Kazakhstan) from the TIMURIDS, who had ruled these lands from the 1370s, and established his court in the old Timurid capital, Samarkand. Muhammad Shaybani was now ready to challenge Shah Ismail's rule. He demanded that coins be minted and that the *hutbe* (Friday sermon) be read in his name, suggesting that Shah Ismail should accept him as his overlord. Muhammad Shaybani also insisted that the shah abandon his "false religion" (Shia Islam) and return to the faith of his forefathers (Sunni Islam). To bring these demands home, the Shaybanids raided territories under Safavid control as far as Kirman to the south of Tehran. Many persecuted Sunnis in Persia saw in Muhammad Shaybani their savior, which Shah Ismail could not ignore. After exchanging several heated letters, in which the opponents declared one another heretic, the two rulers met at the Battle of Merv (in Turkmenistan) in 1510, where Shah Ismail defeated and killed Muhammad Shaybani.

This Safavid victory had two major consequences. Although the Shaybanid Empire did not collapse immediately following Muhammad Shaybani's death—it lasted until the end of the 16th century, as did rivalries between the Safavids and the Shaybanids—the Uzbek-Safavid border was now settled along the Oxus (present-day Amu Darya) River, and the temporary respite of hostilities enabled Shah Ismail to turn against his Ottoman enemy. To signal his intentions, Shah Ismail had Muhammad Shaybani's skull made into a wine cup, covered with gold, and sent it to the Ottoman sultan BAYEZID II (r. 1481–1512). The other major consequence of Muhammad Shaybani's death was that Zahir al-Din Babur (r. 1483–1530), the last important Timurid ruler, tried to recover Transoxania from the Shaybanids. However, when he was defeated, he turned to the east, conquering northern India, where he and his successors established the Indian Mughal Empire that would rule most of India until 1858.

Shah Ismail's Safavid Empire represented a considerable challenge to the Ottomans. The Safavid system of government, which resembled that of a nomadic tribal confederation, appealed to the Turkoman and Kurdish tribes in eastern Anatolia. It seemed a desirable alternative to the more centralized Ottoman rule that jeopardized the nomads' very way of life, property, and social structure. Thus the Safavids threatened to deprive Istanbul of valuable territories, economic resources, and manpower. Shah Ismail also undermined the legitimacy of the House of Osman through his religious and political propaganda in eastern Anatolia. In 1501–02 Sultan Bayezid II tried to deal with Turkoman resistance against Ottoman bureaucracy and Sunni orthodoxy through the mass resettlement of Kızılbaş Turkomans into southern GREECE. However, the ineffectiveness of his methods can be seen in the large Turkoman uprising of 1511, led by a holy man known as Şahkulu (Slave of the Shah). Bayezid's inability to deal with the problem ultimately led to his deposition by his son SELIM I (r. 1512–20).

Sultan Selim's accession to the Ottoman throne in 1512 marked a radical change in Ottoman-Safavid relations. The new sultan made his political goals clear when he ordered the execution of thousands of those who had participated in the 1511 Şahkulu revolts or were suspected Kızılbaş. Selim also launched a full-scale campaign against Shah Ismail in 1514. The two armies met on August 23 at the Battle of Çaldıran (Chaldiran), northeast of Lake Van in eastern Turkey. The battle, which ended with an Ottoman victory, is usually presented in history books as an example of the effectiveness of firearms technology. Whereas the victorious Ottomans employed some 12,000 Janissary infantry musketeers and 500 cannon, the Safavids, who had previously used firearms, had none at this battle, the shah's army consisting mainly of light cavalry archers. While Ottoman firearms undoubtedly proved crucial, the fact that the Ottoman cannons were chained together, thus reducing the effect of the Safavid cavalry charges, and the Ottomans' numerical superiority (100,000 men versus 80,000 Safavid troops) also played important roles in the outcome. However, Selim was unable to exploit his victory. Although the sultan pursued Ismail as far as Tabriz, Ismail managed to escape. Moreover, Selim's troops refused to winter in Persia, forcing the sultan to return to Anatolia and abandon his plan to continue his anti-Safavid campaign in the Spring.

The Battle of Çaldıran resulted in a major readjustment of the Ottoman-Safavid frontier. Shah Ismail lost eastern Anatolia to the Ottomans, and with it the most important recruiting ground for his Turkoman army. Following Çaldıran, Ismail embarked on a major restructuring of his army, establishing artillery corps and musket-bearing infantry troops to counter both his Ottoman enemies and his own remaining Turkoman cavalry. With these changes Shah Ismail transformed his country from a Torkoman state into a Persian empire, whose heartland was now in Iran. Since the shah's court in Tebriz lay within the action-radius of his Ottoman enemy, it would be transferred to Qazvin in the middle of the century.

In the remaining 10 years of his rule after Çaldıran, Shah Ismail did not lead his army personally, and his claims of divinity was somewhat weakened by the defeat. However, he managed to lay the foundations of a new state that survived until the early decades of the 18th century, posing a threat for the Ottomans time and again.

Gábor Ágoston

Further reading: Mansura Haidar, *Central Asia in the Sixteenth Century* (New Delhi: Manohar, 2002); David Morgan, *Medieval Persia, 1040–1797* (London: Longman, 1988); Roger Savory, *Iran under the Safavids* (Cambridge: Cambridge University Press, 1980).

Istanbul (Byzantium; Constantinople) Istanbul, the capital of the Ottoman Empire after 1453, is today the largest city in Turkey (approximate population 12,000,000), located at the southeastern tip of Europe and set on both shores of the Bosporus Straits linking the Black Sea to the Sea of Marmara. Istanbul is one of the many names of the city. The word *Istanbul* is derived from the colloquial Greek *eis tin polin*, "to the city"; Originally, the name *Istanbul* referred only to the walled city and excluded all suburbs (including Galata, Üsküdar, Eyüp). To describe the whole city, the Ottomans continued using the Byzantine name Constantinople (Kostantiniyye), along with a number of metaphorical terms: Deraliyye (Sublime Gate), Dersaadet (Gate of Felicity), Asitane-i Saadet (Threshold of Felicity), or the short-lived Islambol (City of Islam or Plenty of Islam) in the 18th century. For the duration of Ottoman rule, western sources continued to refer to the city as Constantinople, reserving the name *Stamboul* for the walled city. With the collapse of the Ottoman Empire and the establishment of the Republic of Turkey, all previous names were abandoned and Istanbul came to designate the entire city. Today the use of the name Constantinople to describe the Ottoman capital, although historically accurate, is often deemed politically incorrect by Turkish historians and by most Turks.

Founded in the mid-seventh century B.C.E. as a Greek colony, Byzantium became the center of Roman imperial power in 324 C.E. when Emperor Constantine (r. 324–337) moved the capital of the empire from embattled Rome to Byzantium; the city was renamed after him in 330. The capital of the Eastern Roman or Byzantine Empire after 395, Constantinople reached its pinnacle under Justinian (r. 527–65). Subsequently the city successfully resisted a number of assaults — the Huns in 558, the Avars in 626, the Arabs in 673–77, 717–18, and 941, the Bulgars in 813 —but finally fell into the hands of the crusaders in 1204. Although the Byzantines were able to recapture the city in 1261, their empire had been weakened by the Great Schism of 1054 (the separation of the churches of Latin Rome and Greek Constantinople), the economic and commercial encroachment of Venice and Genoa, and the steady advance of Turkic Muslim power in Anatolia.

By the end of the 14th century Constantinople was facing the imminent threat of falling into the hands of the Ottomans, whose rapid territorial expansion in the Balkans and western Anatolia had completely encircled the few territories left to the Byzantine Empire. The Ottoman sultan Bayezid I (r. 1389–1402) blockaded the city in 1397 in preparation of a final siege, but was forced to abandon his plans when he was defeated by Timur in 1402. Bayezid's son Musa launched two unsuccessful assaults against the city in 1411 and 1412; Murad II (r. 1421–44; 1446–51) laid siege to Constantinople in 1422 but was forced to withdraw just as the city was on the brink of falling as a result of the revolt of one of his brothers in Anatolia. Unable to mobilize western support for the defense of his empire, Byzantine emperor John VIII (r. 1425–48) went as far as agreeing to the unification of the two churches under papal leadership in 1439, but refrained from officially proclaiming this union in Constantinople for fear of the consequences of anti-Latin feelings among his subjects.

THE CONQUEST OF CONSTANTINOPLE

The fate of Byzantine Constantinople was sealed by the young MEHMED II (r. 1444–46; 1451–81). Immediately upon his accession to the throne, Mehmed II started planning a siege, amassing troops, acquiring modern artillery to use against the formidable walls of the city, bringing together a fleet to support the army, building the fortress of Rumeli Hisarı on the Bosporus to organize the blockade of the city, and signing treaties with neighboring powers, including the Genoese colony of Galata (see CONQUEST OF CONSTANTINOPLE). By then Constantinople was reduced to a mere shadow of its past glory: in a half-deserted city of some 40,000 inhabitants, the emperor Constantine XI (r. 1448–53) could count on fewer than 10,000 men to oppose a well-equipped Ottoman army and navy of more than 60,000. The siege began in early April 1453, concentrating on the land walls northwest of the city. By mid-May the sultan had a number of ships hauled overland into the Golden Horn to assist his land forces. Following a call for surrender on May 23, rejected by the emperor, the final assault was launched on May 29. The city finally fell to the assailants and was subjected to the traditional three days of plunder.

Mehmed II, now dubbed Fatih (the Conqueror), entered Constantinople the following day and made it his first order of business to convert HAGIA SOPHIA, the symbol of Christianity in the East, into a mosque. His mind set on making Constantinople his new capital, he began planning for the reconstruction and revival of the moribund city. His strategy involved political, ideological, demographic, economic, and urban development. Politically he aimed at breaking the opposition of his own entourage to the transfer of power from EDIRNE —the center of the *ghazi*s or Ottoman warriors—to Constantinople, which was viewed as a symbol of autocratic and sedentary power in the tradition of imperial Rome. It took him about six years to realize this goal, which involved the purge of *ghazi* elements and their gradual replacement by a slave (*kul*) administration. By 1459 the administration had been transferred to the city, which had effectively become the capital of an imperial state. The abandonment of the first palace built in the center of the city in favor of the "New Palace" (today's TOPKAPI PALACE), built after 1462 on the site of the ancient Acropolis, symbolically completed the transition to a centralized structure.

The political process was coupled with an ideological thrust to legitimize the city as the capital of an Islamic empire while preserving a link to the Roman-Byzantine tradition. The "discovery" of, and erection of a shrine over, the alleged remains of Ayyub al-Ansari, a companion of the Prophet who fell during the Arab siege in the seventh century, was a typical example of this quest for legitimacy. Bayezid also systematically converted a number of churches into mosques. Yet at the same time, the sultan's imperial design involved the preservation or creation of a number of non-Muslim institutions, such as the Greek Orthodox Patriarchate (see GREEK ORTHODOX CHURCH), which was reinstated immediately after the conquest. This policy was consistent with efforts to demographically revive Constantinople, which had lost much of its population to massacres, enslavement, and flight. With this in mind, the sultan interrupted the traditional three-day plunder after only one day, freed his own share of captives, invited those who had fled the city to return and invited all his subjects to settle in Constantinople. Yet despite incentives, the response was insufficient, and the state resorted to forced migrations and deportations (*sürgün*) to repopulate the city with new settlers from the provinces.

Demographic revival was accompanied by a massive effort toward economic and urban development. The central area, up to the shores of the Golden Horn, became the commercial heart of the city, with a number of commercial buildings (*han*s), including the future GRAND BAZAAR, the foundations of which were laid in 1456. The sultan himself led the way, sponsoring much of the building activity, including the bazaar and a major mosque complex (*külliye*) bearing his name. Members of the ruling class were encouraged to follow his example, and the city soon boasted a number of religious and lay edifices symbolizing the new order. By the end of Mehmed II's reign, the city included more than 16,000 taxpaying households, corresponding to about 70,000–80,000 inhabitants, 40 percent of whom were non-Muslims. Clearly, the city had to a large extent recovered from the trauma of war and conquest.

During the following decades the city witnessed a boom, reflecting the growth of Ottoman power. The city had started to attract ever-increasing numbers of settlers from all over the empire and beyond, including JEWS expelled from Spain and Portugal. By the mid-16th century, at the height of Ottoman splendor under SÜLEYMAN I the Magnificent (r. 1520–66), Istanbul was considered the greatest city of Europe. Foreign travelers estimated its population at anywhere between 500,000 and one million, but it was probably closer to 250,000 inhabitants, already an impressive figure for the time. A showcase of imperial might, the city was largely used by the sultans, members of the dynasty, and the highest officials as a display of power and status. While supplying the population with much needed services, each new mosque, school, hospital, fountain, bath, water adduction system, and commercial building left the personal imprint of its patron on the texture and skyline of the city. Architects commissioned by the palace and grandees, such as the famed Sinan, contributed to the embellishment and development of the urban landscape.

Over time the social and economic structure of the capital became highly dependent on the state. The heavy concentration of state-sponsored industrial plants such as the arsenal and the cannon foundry, the presence of some of the elite corps of the army such as the JANISSARIES, the central role played by the palace and its bureaucracy, and the thriving activity of the Imperial Treasury, all contributed to this development. A parasitic city, Istanbul to a large extent lived off the state and depended on the state's capacity to organize, through economic intervention, the logistics of provisioning its oversized population with a steady flow of commodities from all over the empire. The heart of the empire fed on its periphery, greedily sucking on its resources; in return, it produced and distributed power in all its forms, political, social, cultural, economic, and financial.

THE 17TH AND 18TH CENTURIES

In the centuries that followed the Ottoman capital maintained much of its character but had to face growing difficulties due to crises and transformations within the empire. Being a showcase for the empire may have brought advantages to the city, but it also meant that it was extremely vulnerable to political, social, and economic instability. The 17th and 18th centuries were particularly replete with such occurrences: popular rebellions, palace coups, and Janissary insubordination and abuses were staple features of life in Istanbul well into the first decades of the 19th century. The fact that times were harder was also reflected in the drop in building activity: fewer and smaller constructions replaced the monumental projects of the 16th century. Nevertheless, the 18th century also witnessed the first signs of modernization, a result of both internal and external dynamics. A more hedonistic approach to life, a greater use of public space, experiments in new artistic and architectural styles, the growth of a non-Muslim bourgeoisie, greater visibility of court women and grandees, and an increased Western presence and influence were all signs of ongoing transformations of the city's social and cultural fabric.

THE 19TH CENTURY

A strong desire for westernization, combined with the growing ascendancy of Western powers, determined the

A tram at Bayezid square near the Grand Bazaar in historic Istanbul, 1930. *(Personal collection of Gábor Ágoston)*

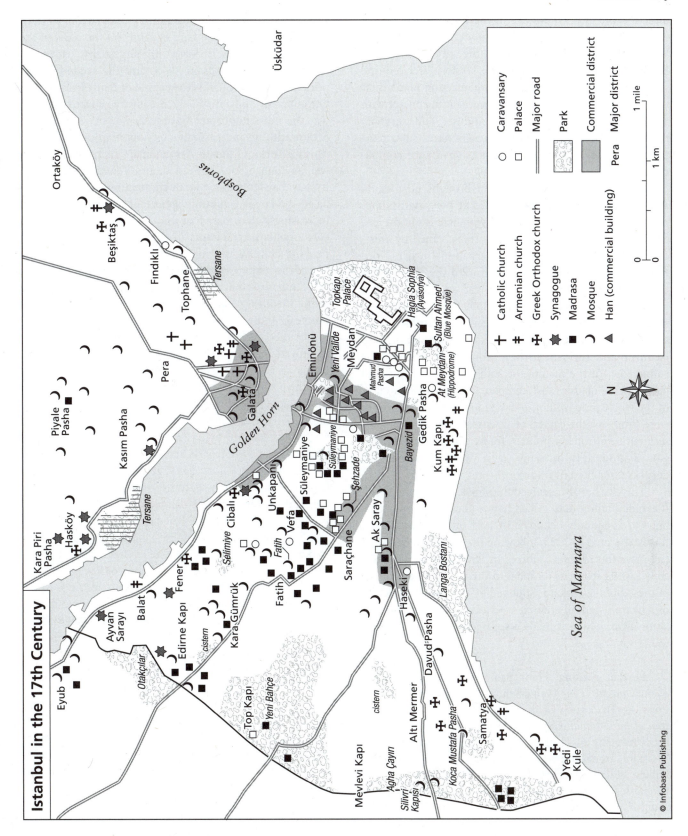

Istanbul in the 17th Century

Üsküdar

Bosphorus

Ortaköy

Beşiktaş

Fındıklı

Tersane

Tophane

Pera

Piyale Pasha

Kasım Pasha

Galata

Golden Horn

Eminönü

Tersane

Haskôy

Kara Piri Pasha

Tersane

Unkapanı

Cibali

Vefa

Fatih

Selimiye

Fener

Balat

Edirne Kapı

Ayvan Sarayı

cistern

Otakçılar

Eyub

Kara Gümrük

Top Kapı

Yeni Bahçe

Mevlevi Kapı

Agha Çayırı

Silivri Kapısı

Altı Mermer

Davud Pasha

Koca Mustafa Pasha

Samatya

Yedi Kule

cistern

Saraçhane

Süleymaniye

Süleymaniye

Şehzade

Ak Saray

Haseki

Langa Bostanı

Bayezid

Kum Kapı

Gedik Pasha

Mahmud Pasha

Yeni Valide

Meydan

Topkapı Palace

Hagia Sophia *(Ayasofya)*

Sultan Ahmed *(Blue Mosque)*

At Meydanı *(Hippodrome)*

Sea of Marmara

N

Legend

✝	Catholic church
✝	Armenian church
✝	Greek Orthodox church
★	Synagogue
■	Madrasa
︵	Mosque
◀	Han (commercial building)
○	Caravansary
□	Palace
═	Major road
	Park
	Commercial district
	Pera Major district

1 mile

1 km

0

© Infobase Publishing

direction the city would take in the 19th century. In the wake of the TANZIMAT reforms, modernization through Western norms came to be seen as the only viable model. By the second half of the century, Western architectural styles, urbanism, and municipal organization made their way into the city, while the public came into contact with new, and often imported, commodities and services: modern schools, newspapers, theaters, streetcars, photographers, department stores, banks, insurance companies, cafes, hotels, and street lighting.

Modernity and westernization brought new cleavages to the urban and social fabric of the city. Istanbul proper, the walled city, came to symbolize tradition and exoticism, while Galata and Pera, transformed by westernization, stood for the new international order. Non-Muslim elites gradually inclined toward the West, while the divide grew between modernist and traditionalist factions among the Muslim population. Nationalism started penetrating the masses, leading to revolts, massacres, and, eventually, to the shift from Ottomanism to Islamism and Turkism as the dominant ideologies of the ruling elite. At the turn of the 20th century, Istanbul had become one of the most complex and ambiguous cities of the world: one million inhabitants, only half of whom were Muslims; the capital of an empire, but entirely subservient to European politics, trade, and finance; a paragon of modernity in many ways, yet at the same time deeply entrenched in tradition.

The city hardly survived the shock of WORLD WAR I. It avoided falling into Allied hands during the war itself, but was eventually occupied in 1918 after the armistice. It was liberated in 1923, following the victory of Kemalist (see ATATÜRK, KEMAL) forces in Anatolia, but immediately lost its status as a capital to the new political center of the republic, Ankara. Snubbed by the nationalist elites of Ankara, Istanbul entered a period of oblivion and isolation from which it made a spectacular comeback after the 1950s.

Edhem Eldem

Further reading: Franz Babinger, *Mehmed the Conqueror and His Time* (Princeton, N.J.: Princeton University Press, 1992); Zeynep Çelik, *The Remaking of Istanbul: Portrait of an Ottoman City in the Nineteenth Century* (Berkeley: University of California Press, 1993); Edhem Eldem, "Istanbul from Imperial to Peripheralized Capital," in Edhem Eldem, Daniel Goffman, and Bruce Masters, *The Ottoman City between East and West: Aleppo, Izmir, and Istanbul* (Cambridge: Cambridge University Press, 1999), 135–206; Bernard Lewis, *Istanbul and the Civilization of the Ottoman Empire* (Norman: University of Oklahoma Press, 1963); Philip Mansel, *Constantinople: City of the World's Desire, 1453–1924* (London: John Murray, 1995); Steven Runciman, *The Fall of Constantinople* (Cambridge: Cambridge University Press, 1990).

Izmir (*Gk.*: Smyrna; *Turk.*: İzmir)   Located in western Turkey, at the tip of the Gulf of Izmir on the coast of the Aegean Sea, Izmir is Turkey's third largest city (with some 3.5 million inhabitants in 2005) and the second largest port, after ISTANBUL. It is the capital of Izmir Province. In Ottoman times, from the 17th century onward, the city was the most important trading center in western Asia Minor with an increasingly cosmopolitan population of Muslim Turks, Ottoman Armenians, Greeks, and Jews, as well as English, Dutch, French, and Venetian merchants. It played a significant role in connecting western Anatolia to the larger economic sphere of the Mediterranean, increasingly dominated by the French and English. Its cosmopolitan inhabitants in the 19th century created a thriving cultural life, and Izmir was rightly considered one of the major world centers for publishing.

Izmir was the site of the oldest human settlements in the Mediterranean world, going back to 4000 B.C.E. or even earlier. By 1500 B.C.E. the region was under the control of the central Anatolian Hittites, whose empire was destroyed in the 1200s B.C.E. Later, known as Smyrna, it was an important center in the Greek region of Ionia and the probable birthplace of Homer (before 700 B.C.E.). In the eighth century B.C.E. the city and its environs fell under Phrygian control. It was captured and destroyed by Alyates, king of Lydia (r. 610–560 B.C.E.), but rebuilt by Alexander the Great of Macedonia (r. 336–323 B.C.E.).

In the first century B.C.E. Izmir became part of the Roman Empire and was transformed into a major harbor and center of trade connecting Asia with Europe. It competed for the title "first city of Asia" with Ephesus and Pergamon (present-day Efes and Bergama in western Turkey). It is also the site for one of the "Seven Churches in Asia" mentioned in the biblical book of Revelation. Following the division of the Roman Empire into two under Emperor Constantine (r. 324–337 C.E.), Izmir and its surroundings became part of the Eastern Roman, later known as the Byzantine, Empire. The SELJUKS captured the city from the BYZANTINE EMPIRE in the 1070s but held it only briefly before the Byzantines recaptured it (1093).

During the Byzantine interregnum (1204–61), when the crusaders occupied Constantinople and forced the Byzantine emperor to move his government-in-exile to Nicea (Iznik), Smyrna flourished as the commercial center of the empire. In 1261 the Byzantines recaptured Constantinople but then neglected their defenses in Asia Minor, concentrating instead on their domains in the Balkans. As a consequence, much of their territory in Asia Minor was conquered by the Turkic principalities, or emirates, that emerged in the late 13th and early 14th centuries in the power vacuum caused by the decline of the Seljuks of Rum, the former lords of Anatolia. In about 1328, Smyrna fell to the Aydınoğulları maritime Turkish principality, based in Aydın (south-southeast of

Horse carriages in the waterfront district Izmir. *(Personal collection of Gábor Ágoston)*

Izmir), who used the city and its port as their base for naval raids.

The Ottomans first captured the city in 1389 but lost it in 1402 when TIMUR, the founder of the Timurid Empire, defeated the Ottoman sultan BAYEZID I (r. 1389–1402) at the BATTLE OF ANKARA and restored recently conquered Ottoman territories to their former lords—in Izmir's case, to the Aydınoğulları. It was not until 1425 that Sultan MURAD II (r. 1421–44; 1446–51) recaptured Izmir and made it the center of one of the *sancak*s (subprovinces) of Aydın province.

Unlike Ottoman Istanbul or ALEPPO, which were noteworthy symbols of the Ottomans' Byzantine and Islamic heritage and were also important hubs of international trade, Izmir had no such symbolic or economic significance for the Ottoman government. When Izmir emerged as a major international trading center by the 17th century, in the words of one researcher, it flourished despite, rather than because of, the policy of Istanbul. The Ottoman economic policy of provisionism, which focused on satisfying domestic demand (*see* ECONOMY AND ECONOMIC POLICY), assigned to western Asia Minor the role of securing foodstuffs for the bourgeoning Ottoman capital, Istanbul, and the region's commerce was

thus not encouraged. Izmir's development was largely due to local governments, the city's European merchants, and the merchants' local partners in Izmir's Greek Orthodox, Jewish, and Muslim communities.

In the 17th century all these players gained leverage with regard to the central government when a combination of international and domestic factors forced Istanbul to modify its economic policy. In the course of the century the military and economic prowess of the Ottoman Empire declined relative to those of their European opponents and rivals. As a consequence, the commercial agreements (CAPITULATIONS), which had in the past been dictated by a militarily much stronger Istanbul to the Ottomans' advantage, gradually became pacts from which western European nations profited more than the Ottomans. Of these, the English and Dutch gained prominence, and through their Indian Ocean spice trade via the Cape of Good Hope rendered ancient trading routes that crossed the Ottoman Empire less profitable, causing the (temporary) decline of such important Ottoman trading centers as BURSA, Aleppo, and ALEXANDRIA.

At the same time Istanbul also lost its leverage with regard to local Ottoman warlords and merchants. When these merchants and their European partners looked for alternative products to compensate for the lost spice trade, they found it in Ottoman and Persian silk and other local goods (such as grain, dried figs, raisins, cotton, and wool) in western Asia Minor. Istanbul, unlike in the 16th century, was no longer in the position to stop or substantially restrict such trade, and thus western Asia Minor, and most importantly Izmir, witnessed a remarkable economic revival and urban growth.

At the end of the 16th century Izmir was a modest settlement of some 2,000 people, but by 1640 it had developed into an important trade center with 35,000–40,000 inhabitants. Most of them were newcomers: Turkish Muslims from other towns of western Asia Minor (such as Manisa and Aydın); Armenians from Bursa, Aleppo, and even Safavid Isfahan; Greeks from the Aegean Islands and the Morea; Jews from Spain, Portugal, Italy, and from such Ottoman towns as Manisa or SALONIKA, despite opposition from Istanbul in the latter two cases; as well as Dutch, English, French, and Venetian merchants from Europe. The latter usually operated through their Armenian, Greek, Jewish, and Muslim brokers. By this time Izmir was the center of a surging commercial web in western Asia Minor that produced and collected food, wool, leather, silk, and other commodities for European merchants instead of the Ottoman capital as had been the case in the previous century.

By the 1660s Izmir was a cosmopolitan trading center in which Muslims constituted a slim majority of the inhabitants, some 60,000–70,000. The Ottoman government, directed by the experienced grand vizier Köprülü Mehmed Pasha (see KÖPRÜLÜ FAMILY) and at war with Venice over CRETE (1645–69), was now determined to reattach Izmir and western Asia Minor to Istanbul so that Izmir's wealth could be taken advantage of by the central treasury. To protect Izmir against a possible attack by the Venetians (who had captured and burned the town in 1472), Köprülü Mehmed Pasha in 1658–59 built a citadel (Sancakburnu) about halfway between the city and the Karaburnu peninsula to the west of the city.

In 1688 an earthquake, whose epicenter was beneath the newly built citadel, and the accompanying fire brought devastation to the city. Some 10,000 to 15,000 inhabitants perished, while goods, and several mosques, churches, and public buildings were destroyed. Thanks to the joint efforts of foreign merchants and their companies, Ottoman middlemen, wealthy Istanbul families who had religious endowments in Izmir, and Muslim notables in the region, Izmir was rebuilt within two years.

Despite the Ottoman Empire's military and economic problems in the 18th century, Izmir continued to thrive. While Istanbul was defeated by its old and new foes (AUSTRIA and RUSSIA) and lost much of its control in the provinces to local notables or AYANS, it also sought military and diplomatic assistance from western European powers, ENGLAND and FRANCE, which in turn resulted in significant redistribution of political and economic leverage among the major foreign and local players in the empire. The merchants of England and France enjoyed advantages compared to their rivals (the Dutch and Venetians) through the renegotiated capitulations. They were also able to find an effective working relationship with the *ayans* of western Anatolia, most importantly with the Karaosmanoğlus. Since the English and French usually traded through middlemen, their favored partners—Ottoman Armenians and Greeks—also gained influence with regard to their local rivals, Ottoman Jews and Muslims.

The predominance of the industrialized British economy in the Ottoman Mediterranean in the 19th century, combined with the TANZIMAT reforms of the Ottoman government that aimed at modernizing the empire's armed forces, government, and economy after 1839, brought further urban growth and resulted in a more cosmopolitan Izmir. The reforms and Istanbul's successful recentralization policy led to the decline of local notables. Their place was taken by Ottoman Armenians, Greeks, and Jews, who not only led the penetration of the western Anatolian market with European, mainly British, industrial goods, but also acted as Istanbul's proxies in the provinces, including carrying out and financing the reforms and collecting taxes.

The non-Muslims of Izmir profited greatly from both growing European trade in the area and the Ottoman reforms. The wealth thus accumulated was invested in new structures: schools, a state hospital (1851), a railroad station (1858), and a passport wharf (1880s). Streetcar lines and postal and telegraph services also opened. Although Izmir was overcrowded, not least because of the influx of tens of thousands of immigrants (many of whom had been expelled from the newly created nation-states in the Balkans), periodic fires created new spaces for new construction. The city's population had swelled to 200,000 by the 1890s, and to 300,000 after WORLD WAR I.

During World War I, the city was captured by Greek forces, and was given to GREECE by the TREATY OF SÈVRES (1920). However, the Turks rejected the treaty, and Izmir was recaptured by Mustafa Kemal (known later as KEMAL ATATÜRK) on September 9, 1922. Three days later it was destroyed by a fire, the origin of which is still debated (with Turks and Greeks accusing one another of causing the fire). The Treaty of Lausanne (1923) restored Izmir to Turkey. In a separate convention Greece and Turkey agreed on a massive population exchange, carried out under League of Nations supervision, as a result of which Izmir became predominantly a Turkish city.

Gábor Ágoston

Further reading: Elena Frangakis-Syrett, *The Commerce of Smyrna in the Eighteenth Century, 1700–1820* (Athens: Centre for Asia Minor Studies, 1992); Daniel Goffman, *Izmir and the Levantine World, 1550–1650* (Seattle: University of Washington Press, 1990); Daniel Goffman, "Izmir: From Village to Colonial Port City," in Edhem Eldem, Daniel Goffman, and Bruce Masters, *The Ottoman City between East and West: Aleppo, Izmir, and Istanbul* (Cambridge: Cambridge University Press, 1999).

J

Jabal al-Druz   Literally meaning the "Mountain of the DRUZES," the Jabal al-Druz is a formerly volcanic region in what is today southern Syria. Before the 19th century, the Ottomans frequently used the term to refer to LEBANON. The Syrian region, which has extremely fertile soil, has been settled since antiquity. It is not certain when they became the majority in the area, but many Druzes settled there after the civil unrest in Lebanon in 1860. Today, 90 percent of the region's population is Druze; most of the remainder are Christian. During the occupation of Syria in the 1830s by IBRAHIM PASHA, son of Egypt's military governor MEHMED ALI, the region became a center of armed resistance to Egyptian rule. The inhabitants of the region rebelled twice after the Ottomans regained control of Syria in 1841. The first rebellion came in 1896, after attempts to draft young men from the region into the Ottoman army. Faced with a fierce guerrilla war, the Ottomans finally agreed not to conscript Druzes. A longer rebellion in 1909–10 finally ended when the Ottomans tricked the Druze leaders into coming to Damascus for supposed peace talks, then executed them. That quelled the Druzes temporarily but did not win their loyalty for the Ottoman sultan. The region was later the center of Syria's revolt against French occupation in 1925.

Bruce Masters

al-Jabarti, Abd al-Rahman (d. 1825) *Egyptian historian*   Abd al-Rahman al-Jabarti was Ottoman Egypt's greatest historian. His principal work is a four-volume history that chronicles the history of 18th-century Egypt (the last century of Ottoman rule there), its occupation by the French (1798–1801), and the rise of MEHMED ALI, the military ruler of Egypt from 1805 until 1849. Little is known of al-Jabarti's life other than a few personal details found scattered in his history. Historians speculate that he was born in the early 1750s and died in 1825. Al-Jabarti was educated at AL-AZHAR and was a respected member of Cairo's religious scholar class, the ULEMA. His work is important for the details it provides concerning the politics of Mamluk households and his dispassionate description of the French occupation. Despite its importance, al-Jabarti's history was not published in its entirety in Egypt until 1880. The author's highly critical view of Mehmed Ali led publishers to fear that the full text might offend Mehmed Ali's descendants, the khedival family.

Bruce Masters

Further reading: Shmuel Moreh, trans. and ed., *Napoleon in Egypt: al-Jabarti's Chronicle of the French Occupation* (Princeton, N.J.: Markus Wiener, 1993).

Jacobites (Syrian Orthodox)   The origins of Jacobite Christians lie in the theological debates over the nature of Christ in the fifth century C.E. The dominant tradition in Christianity, embraced by the Roman Catholic and Orthodox churches, held that Christ was one person in two natures, that he was both human and divine at the same time. Many Christians in Syria, however, argued that the two natures were so commingled as to become only the divine. At the Council of Chalcedon in 451, the dominant churches condemned this belief as the Monophysite (one nature) heresy. The ruling of the council grouped the Jacobites with the ARMENIAN APOSTOLIC CHURCH excommunicating both groups as heretical.

Historians believe that the Church was named after Jacob Baraddai, a monk who helped revive the sect in the aftermath of the Chalcedon Council. In the 19th century, however, the hierarchy of the Jacobites claimed earlier origins for their name. Some said that it derived from Jacob the biblical patriarch, while others said it came from St. James the Great, one form of whose name in Syriac is Yaqub. In the Ottoman period, the community was generally referred to in both Ottoman and Arabic sources as "Suryani," or Syrian, and most European travelers to the region simply called them Syrians.

The Byzantines, as mainstream Orthodox Christian believers, persecuted the Jacobites as heretics. Most of the community was absorbed into the Arab Muslim state in the seventh and eighth centuries C.E. The Arab rulers tolerated the Jacobites and did not interfere in the Church's internal affairs. Jacobite Christians helped to translate classical Greek science and philosophy texts into Arabic. They enjoyed an intellectual flourishing of their own between the 9th and 13th centuries, which produced numerous theological and historical works written in the Syriac language. Like the NESTORIANS, the Jacobites allied themselves with the Mongols and to a lesser extent with the crusaders as both communities had suffered persecution under Muslim rule. As a consequence of those alliances, their Muslim neighbors retaliated against the Jacobites for what was seen as collaboration with the enemy.

By the start of the Ottoman period, the Jacobites were largely confined to an arc of territory stretching from Mosul north to Diyarbakir. Beyond the boundaries of that zone, they constituted significant minorities in cities such as ALEPPO and Urfa. They could even be found in DAMASCUS. But the official seat of their patriarch (the see) was in the remote monastery of Dayr Zafaran, outside of Mardin in present-day Turkey. It was an appropriate location as the true heartland of the Jacobites lay not in the cities but in the dozens of villages that dotted the mountains between Mardin and Midyat, known to the Jacobites as Tur Abdin, "the Mountain of the Faithful." Throughout this region the Jacobites lived as a minority amongst the larger Kurdish Muslim population.

With the arrival of Roman Catholic missionaries throughout the Ottoman Empire in the early 17th century, a number of Jacobite clergy in the city of Aleppo, which served as the main center of Roman Catholic missionary activity, became Catholic. The patriarchs of the Jacobite Church opposed their conversion to Catholicism and found allies in the Armenian patriarchs in ISTANBUL, who also faced the defection of Armenian clergy to Catholicism. The Armenian patriarchs appealed to the Ottoman sultans over the course of the second half of the 17th century. By the start of the 18th century, Ottoman governors in Aleppo routinely received orders forbidding the sultan's subjects from receiving the sacraments from Catholic clergy. But by that time the majority of the Jacobites in the city, approximately 5,000, had followed their clergy into communion with Rome.

The traditionalists were able to retain the loyalty of the rural Jacobites, although by the start of the 19th century Roman Catholic missions in the city of Mosul succeeded in converting some among the villagers in the plains surrounding the city. Most Christians in the city of Mosul itself, whether originally Jacobites or Nestorians, were also by that time Uniate Catholics, or members of Eastern-rite churches that came to accept the authority of the pope. Protestants from Britain and the United States also started missions in the Mosul region in the 19th century and managed to convert some Jacobite villagers to their own Christian sects. In the TANZIMAT reform period of the 19th century, the Ottoman government recognized the patriarch in Dayr Zafaran as the head of the "Ancient Syrians" and the Catholic patriarch in Aleppo as head of the Syrian Catholic community, thereby creating two separate MILLETs for the Jacobites.

Bruce Masters

Further reading: John Joseph, *Muslim-Christian Relations and Inter-Christian Rivalries in the Middle East: The Case of the Jacobites in an Age of Transition* (Albany: State University of New York Press, 1983).

Jamal al-Din al-Afghani   *See* AL-AFGHANI, JAMAL AL-DIN.

Janbulad Ali Pasha (d. 1610) *governor of Aleppo and Kurdish rebel*   Janbulad Ali Pasha was one of the leading rebels against the Ottoman Empire in the early 17th century, a period marked by numerous revolts that the Ottoman court historians labeled the CELALI REVOLTS. The JANBULAD FAMILY were the hereditary chieftains of the KURDS who lived in the Jabal Kurd.

Husayn, Ali's uncle, had risen to prominence as the defender of the city of ALEPPO against periodic forays by JANISSARIES stationed in DAMASCUS attempting to collect taxes to which they were not entitled. During these incursions the Janissaries—who acted as a law unto themselves—often pillaged villages in the region. In 1603 the governor of Aleppo, Nasuh Pasha, looked on ineffectively from the city's citadel as the Damascene Janissaries ransacked the town. Husayn rallied his kinsmen and retainers to defend Aleppo and its wealth. In gratitude for his service against this unauthorized tax-collecting on the part of the Janissaries, Sultan AHMED I (r. 1603–17) elevated Husayn to the governorship of the province, the first non-Ottoman to be so rewarded. Nasuh Pasha deeply resented the elevation of what he considered a non-Ottoman upstart and had to be physically removed from the city's citadel.

In 1605, however, the relationship between the sultan and the Janbulad clan soured when Husayn was called upon to deliver troops for a campaign against Iran.

He arrived late on the battlefield of Urmia, where the Ottomans had already been defeated. No excuse for his absence was found acceptable and he was executed for treason.

Ali raised the clan standard in revolt to avenge his uncle. Open warfare erupted in northern Syria and Lebanon as local chieftains decided whether to stay loyal to the sultan or to back the insurgents. In an attempt to stall this military opposition, Sultan Ahmed appointed Ali as Aleppo's governor while simultaneously raising an army to crush him. The armies met in 1607 and the Janbulad forces were defeated. Ali surrendered soon afterwards and was appointed to a post in remote Wallachia, present-day Romania. (It was a common Ottoman practice to buy off an opponent by offering him a post in a province far removed from his base of power until he could be dealt with.) Ali's turn came in 1610 when he was executed in Belgrade on trumped-up charges of treason. He remains a popular folk hero among the Kurds of Syria, with ballads commemorating his exploits.

Bruce Masters

Further reading: William Griswold, *The Great Anatolian Rebellion, 1000–1020/1591–1611* (Berlin: Klaus Schwarz, 1983).

Janbulad family (Jumblat family)   The Janbulad family were hereditary chieftains of the Kurds who lived in the Jabal Kurd, a hilly region straddling what is today the frontier between Syria and Turkey. With the defeat of Janbulad Ali Pasha, who had taken up arms against the Ottoman Sultan Ahmed I, some members of the Janbulad family sought refuge with the Druzes in Lebanon. The family ultimately rose to prominence in the Druze territory, becoming major landholders and playing a significant role in Lebanese politics.

In theory, the Druzes do not accept converts, but male members of Janbulad family married local women and became Druze. At the start of the 18th century, the Janbulads emerged as one of the leading families in the Shuf Mountains. There they led a political faction that was named after them, the Junblatis; their archrivals were members of the Yazbaki faction, led by the Imad family. The Janbulads and the Imads were often in conflict for control of the Shuf region in south-central Lebanon. Although the Janbulad family never attained the title of emir—the ultimate status in the politics of Lebanon—they often played a major role behind the scenes in determining who did receive the title. In the process they became one of the leading feudal landlords in the Druze country and remain a significant political force in Lebanon today.

Bruce Masters

Janissaries   By the reign of Murad I (r. 1362–89) the Ottoman sultans realized that they needed a reliable and loyal professional military force, independent of the Turkish warrior lords of the frontiers and their tribal levies. Such a force was provided by the Janissaries or "new soldiers" (*yeni çeri*). Established in the 1370s, the Janissary corps initially served as the sultan's bodyguard. However, the corps soon became one of the first standing armies in medieval Europe.

At first the sultan used prisoners of war to create his own independent military guard. In the 1380s the *devşirme*, or child levy system, was introduced to recruit new soldiers for the corps. Under this system, non-Muslim children from lands ruled by the Ottoman Empire were taken from their families. They were taught the language and culture of the Ottomans, converted to Islam, and were given rigorous military training. To avoid the development of a hereditary military aristocracy that could challenge the sultan, Muslims and Turks were excluded from the *devşirme*. The *devşirme* boys were subsequently trained as Janissaries and were known as the sultan's *kuls* or slaves. Despite this name, the Janissaries were not slaves in the conventional sense; they enjoyed many privileges and were paid for their services.

With the broadening of the pool of recruitment, the initial guard was soon transformed into the ruler's elite household infantry. By the Battle of Kosovo in 1389, the Janissary corps numbered some 2,000 men. By the mid-15th century, under Mehmed II (r. 1444–46; 1451–81), their number had increased to 5,000, and the sultan doubled the size of the corps by the end of his reign in 1481. By the middle of the 16th century there were some 12,000 Janissaries and 7,700 Janissary novices (*acemi oğlan*) whose salaries were paid from the central treasury. While the majority of soldiers were stationed in the Janissary barracks of Istanbul, substantial contingents also served in frontier provinces. For example, in the 1560s, some 3,400 Janissaries were stationed in the province of Buda, which faced the Ottomans' most serious enemy, Habsburg Austria.

Initially the Janissary corps was equipped with bows, crossbows, and javelins. Under Sultan Murad II (r. 1421–44, 1446–51), they began to use firearms, probably matchlock arquebuses. However, it was not until around the mid-16th century that most of the Janissaries carried firearms. While the Janissaries numbered 12,000 in the early 1520s, only 3,000 to 4,000 arms-bearing Janissaries participated in the 1523 campaign against the Egyptian rebels. Murad III (r. 1574–95) equipped all his Janissaries with a more advanced weapon, the matchlock musket, first introduced in the early 16th century by Spanish soldiers. Well into the 17th century the Janissaries used their matchlock muskets, although from the late 16th century on more and more flintlock muskets were manufactured in the empire with the Spanish *mique-*

let-lock. (*see* FIREARMS) In addition to their handguns, the Janissaries' traditional weapon, the recurved bow, remained an important and formidable weapon well into the 17th century, although the ratio of bows to muskets had changed significantly by the mid-1600s.

The Janissaries' firepower, especially in the early 16th century, often proved fatal for their adversaries. These elite troops could fire their weapons in a kneeling or standing position without the need for additional support or rest. In battle the Janissaries formed nine consecutive rows and fired their weapons row by row. They were so effective that most contemporary sources attribute the 1526 Ottoman success against the Hungarians at the BATTLE OF MOHÁCS to the firepower of the Janissaries rather than to the cannons, in sharp contrast to later historians who credited the victory to the Ottoman artillerymen.

Until the early 17th century the Janissaries maintained their firing skills by practicing regularly, usually twice a week. However, in 1606, the anonymous author of *The Laws of the Janissaries,* was already complaining about the decline of this practice, noting that the members of the corps were no longer given powder for the drills and that the soldiers used their allotted wick for their candles and not for their shooting drills.

By the long Hungarian War of 1593–1606, the Janissaries seemed to have lost their firepower superiority against their Hungarian and Habsburg opponents. Ottoman chroniclers noticed that the Janissaries could not withstand the Habsburg and Hungarian musketeers. In 1602, the grand vizier reported from the Hungarian front that "in the field or during a siege we are in a distressed position, because the greater part of the enemy forces are infantry armed with muskets, while the majority of our forces are horsemen, and we have very few specialists skilled in the musket."

To counter superior Habsburg firepower, the Ottomans increased the number of arms-bearing Janissaries. Whereas the Janissaries numbered 12,800 in the late 1560s, their number reached 37,600 by 1606 and fluctuated between 50,000 and 54,000 in the second half of the 17th century. These increases required widening the pool of recruitment, which now included Turks and other Muslims, who had previously been barred from the sultan's elite corps. It also led to a decline in military skill and put an additional burden on the treasury which already faced deficits from the early 1590s. To ease the burden on the treasury, in the 17th century, the Janissaries were allowed to engage in trade and craftsmanship. By the 18th century Janissary service had been radically transformed and most Janissaries had become craftsmen and shop-owners, privileged with tax-exempt status as a reward for their supposed military service, for which they continued to draw pay. In reality, only a small portion of the paid Janissaries participated in military campaigns, and their performance was usually poor.

The life of these Janissaries was far from the regime of rigid military discipline that characterized the corps in its early days. The Janissaries married and settled in cities, established relationships with the civil population, and were more interested in providing for their families than fighting the enemy. Nevertheless, the Janissaries jealously guarded their privileges and fiercely opposed all military reforms aimed at undermining their status. Apart from their diminished military value, they were also unable to execute the other vital functions they performed in the 15th and early 16th centuries, when Janissaries served in Istanbul and in major provincial capitals as military police, guards, night watchmen, and firefighters. By the latter part of the 16th century corruption was endemic; instead of protectors, the Janissaries had become the terror of the cities. During the 1588 Istanbul fire, for instance, instead of fighting the fire, Janissaries engaged in looting. They also went on rampages when their taverns or coffee shops were closed or their privileges otherwise threatened. The Janissaries had always occasionally mutinied, but in the 17th and 18th centuries these rebellions became frequent. Indeed, in one revolt, the Janissaries not only blocked the reforms of SELIM III (r. 1789–1807) but also murdered the sultan. By deposing and murdering sultans, the Janissaries ultimately became Ottoman society's kingmakers, confirmed in the habits of privilege and corruption.

Learning from Selim III's mistakes, MAHMUD II (r. 1808–39) carefully prepared his military reforms and made alliances within Ottoman religious and military establishments. In 1826, when the Janissaries revolted against his proclaimed reforms, the sultan was ready for them with a loyal modern artillery corps of some 12,000 men whose cannons destroyed and set aflame the Janissary barracks, killing some 6,000 Janissaries. Many more Janissaries were killed in the ensuing manhunt, while those living in provincial cities were killed by the local population that rose spontaneously against their tyranny. Known in Ottoman history as the AUSPICIOUS INCIDENT, the destruction of the Janissaries was regarded by the long-suffering Ottoman people as a form of liberation and it opened the way for substantive military reforms.

Gábor Ágoston

See also MILITARY SLAVERY.

Further reading: Gábor Ágoston, "Ottoman Warfare in Europe, 1453–1812," in *European Warfare, 1453–1815,* edited by Jeremy Black (London: Macmillan, 1999), 118–144; Godfrey Goodwin, *The Janissaries* (London: Saqi Books, 1997); Gyula Káldy-Nagy, "The First Centuries of the Ottoman Military Organization." *AOH* 31 (1977): 147–183; Rhoads Murphey, *Ottoman Warfare, 1500–1700* (New Brunswick, N.J.: Rutgers University Press, 1999).

Jassy, Treaty of (1792)   This treaty, signed in the Moldavian capital of Jassy (Iaşi) on January 9, 1792, ended the RUSSO-OTTOMAN WAR of 1787–92. The superiority of Russian military strength, both in the training of their soldiers and the quality of their officers, was clearly demonstrated during the course of the war and provided the Russian Empire with the upper hand during the treaty negotiations.

In the Treaty of Jassy, the Ottoman Empire confirmed the disastrous TREATY OF KÜÇÜK KAYNARCA (1774) and was forced to recognize Russian suzerainty over the Crimean Peninsula and its hinterland. The Ottoman Empire also recognized Georgia in the Caucasus as a protectorate of the Russian Empire. Under diplomatic pressure from the British and the Prussians, the Russians agreed to withdraw from their occupation of the Danubian principalities of WALLACHIA and MOLDAVIA. The Russians also ceded to the Ottoman Empire the key fortress town of Ismail in the Danubian estuary and Anapa on the eastern shore of the BLACK SEA. The Russian Empire retained its control over Özi. In the western Black Sea coastal area, the Russian-Ottoman boundary was moved southwestward from the Bug River to the Dniester River. As a result of the treaty, the Russian Empire came to border the Ottoman vassal state of Moldavia. In the east, the treaty fixed the Kuban' River as the boundary between the Russian and Ottoman empires in the Caucasus.

Other provisions of the Treaty of Jassy included a full exchange of prisoners of war (excluding those who had voluntarily accepted the citizenship or religion of their captors), Ottoman guarantees to provide increased autonomy in the form of political and fiscal privileges to the Hospodar rulers of the Danubian principalities, and Ottoman promises to protect Russian merchant vessels in the Mediterranean from North African piracy (*see* CORSAIRS AND PIRATES).

The long-term consequences of the Russo-Ottoman War of 1787–92 and the Treaty of Jassy were threefold. First, the clear inferiority of Ottoman military strength compared to the Russian military resulted in the first comprehensive and sustained Ottoman efforts, under Sultan SELIM III (r. 1789–1807), to REFORM the empire's military and affiliated support industries along Western lines. Second, the establishment of Russian political and military power on the northern shore of the Black Sea resulted in the buildup of Russian naval installations in the Black Sea region and an increase in the Russian Empire's ability to intervene, militarily and politically, in the Ottoman Balkans. Third, the British Empire, which had been a neutral observer of Russian-Ottoman confrontation for most of the 18th century, swung firmly behind the Ottoman Empire as a check against Russian aggression in the Balkans. This switch in the British Empire's strategic posture with regard to the Russian and

Ottoman Empires would be a key factor in the so-called EASTERN QUESTION of the 19th century.

Andrew Robarts

Further reading: Christopher Duffy, *Russia's Military Way to the West: Origins and Nature of Russian Military Power, 1700–1800* (London: Routledge & Kegan Paul, 1981); Alan W. Fisher, *The Russian Annexation of the Crimea, 1772–1783* (Cambridge: Cambridge University Press, 1970); Stanford J. Shaw, *Between Old and New: The Ottoman Empire under Sultan Selim III, 1789–1807* (Cambridge, Mass.: Harvard University Press, 1971).

Jeddah (Jedda; *Ar.*: Jidda; *Turk.*: Cedde)   During the Ottoman period, Jeddah, located on the Red Sea in what is today Saudi Arabia, was both the port city for MECCA and the main Ottoman administrative center for western Arabia. It also served as Arabia's main commercial port and was the only place on the Arabian peninsula where European merchants were allowed to reside. The city fell to the radical Islamic sect of the WAHHABIS in 1803 and to the Egyptian army in 1812. Direct Ottoman control of the city did not return until 1840 when an agreement between MEHMED ALI, the military governor of Egypt, and Sultan ABDÜLMECID (r. 1839–61) returned the cities of the HEJAZ, the western region of Saudi Arabia along the Red Sea, to Ottoman suzerainty.

The slave trade was important to Jeddah's economy throughout its history as the city served as a natural transit point between Africa and the Arabian Peninsula. The city's merchants thus opposed an Ottoman ban on the importation of slaves that was imposed in 1855 in response to British pressure on the sultan. The ban resulted in a major anti-Ottoman riot with slave dealers drawing their Bedouin allies into the fray. The deployment of Ottoman troops restored order to the city's streets, and the ban on the importation of new slaves remained.

After Jeddah was returned to Ottoman rule, the European commercial presence in the city increased. This led to another riot in 1858 when a mob attacked Europeans and those holding European passports in the city. Many Muslim residents viewed the European commercial presence as a threat to their economic position. They were also aware of the expansion of the British and French empires, which often came at the expense of Muslim territory and independence. With tensions building between local Muslims and Europeans, a dispute over the nationality of a ship anchored in Jeddah's harbor set off an explosion of anger directed at Europeans and those who had European protection. A mob formed on June 15, 1858 and 21 Europeans were killed in the fracas. The British naval commander on the scene felt that Jeddah's governor had not acted swiftly enough to apprehend those responsible for the death of British subjects;

in consequence, the British navy bombarded Jeddah on June 25, 1858. The crisis ended in 1859 with the execution of a number of men whom the Ottoman governor claimed were responsible for the murders.

In June 1916, not long after the proclamation of the ARAB REVOLT against the Ottoman Empire by Emir FAYSAL IBN HUSAYN AL-HASHIMI, Jeddah fell to the Arab army. It was thereafter used as the main British supply point for their Arab allies in WORLD WAR I.

Bruce Masters

Further reading: William Ochsenwald, "The Jidda Massacre of 1858." *Middle Eastern Studies* 13 (1977): 314–26.

Jerusalem (*Ar.*: al-Quds; *Heb.*: Yerushalayim; *Turk.*: Küdüs)   For most of the Ottoman period, the city of Jerusalem served as the district capital of a subdistrict (*sancak*) within the larger province of DAMASCUS. Until the 19th century the city's population was relatively small—between 10,000 and 20,000. However, Jerusalem's religious significance to Islam, Christianity, and Judaism meant that the city played a larger role in the minds of all the peoples of the Ottoman Empire than its size would warrant. For Sunni Muslims, Jerusalem was the third holiest site after MECCA and MEDINA as it housed the al-Aqsa Mosque and the Dome of the Rock, the site from which the Prophet Muhammad is said to have ascended to heaven on his Night Journey.

In the 1530s Sultan SÜLEYMAN I (r. 1520–66), in an acknowledgement of the city's religious importance, ordered a number of improvements to its infrastructure. These included the repair of the city's aqueducts, the installation of new fountains in various quarters, and the restoration of the city walls, which over the centuries had fallen into ruin. These walls still stand and encircle what is today known as the Old City. Süleyman was also responsible for refurbishing the city's most important mosque complex, the Dome of the Rock, thus signifying, in a very public way, the piety of the Ottoman royal house. Further adding to the dynasty's physical imprint on the holy city, Süleyman's consort, Hürrem Sultan, paid for the construction of a complex that included mosques, schools, hostels for pilgrims, stores, and soup kitchens for the city's poor. The complex was known as the Haseki Waqf and was financed by revenues from around Palestine, including the JIZYA (tax on adult male non-Muslims), and payments made by Christians from nearby Bethlehem and beyond.

In the late 16th and 17th centuries the political life of the city was dominated by three governing families: the Ridwans, Farrukhs, and Turabays. All three households were founded by military personnel stationed in the city. The Ridwans and Farrukhs were of MAMLUK, or military slave, origin, while the founder of the Turabay

house was a BEDOUIN. By the end of the 17th century, the three families had intermarried to the point where they merged into a single extended ruling family. Following the period of their ascendancy, the governorship of Jerusalem reverted to men appointed by either the Ottoman sultans or their representatives in Damascus. Without strong locally based military commanders, Jerusalem was subject to the AYAN or local notable families whose political influence was an aspect of many Arab provincial centers in the 18th century. In Jerusalem the authority of most of the *ayan* families, including the Husaynis and Khalidis, stemmed from their status as religious scholars (ULEMA) and their connections to the control of the pious foundations in the city (WAQF).

Although Jerusalem had a modest soap industry and revenue-producing villages in its surrounding region, its main source of income was tourism, specifically from Christian and Jewish pilgrims. For Ottoman Christians, the visit to Jerusalem was the equivalent of the HAJJ for Muslims. Balkan Christians who made the pilgrimage often added the honorific *hajji* (one who has made the pilgrimage) to their names. Arab Christians added *maqdasi*, "one who has been to the Holy Land," to their given names. Although Jews might also arrive in Jerusalem as pilgrims, they often stayed in Jerusalem for longer periods to study with the city's rabbis. It was also a common belief among Jews in the Middle Ages that those buried in Jerusalem would be resurrected first when the Messiah returned. Many of the Jews who came to Jerusalem were old or infirm. Their support through charity was a major concern for the Jewish community in Istanbul which took over the maintenance of charitable institutions for Jews in the city in the 18th century.

A particularly volatile issue was the control of the Church of the Holy Sepulcher, which holds the empty tomb in which Jesus is said to have been buried and which Catholic and Orthodox Christians believe stands on the site of his crucifixion and resurrection. Throughout the Ottoman period, various Christian sects battled one another for the right to maintain and refurbish the church, or to build chapels within it. That struggle only intensified as European powers began to exert pressure on behalf of one group or another. As the Ottomans did not want to appear to favor any one sect, officials in Jerusalem often had to balance one Christian group against another to maintain order. The ongoing dispute over the rights of access to the church was a significant contributing factor in the CRIMEAN WAR (1853–56).

At the start of the 19th century, Jerusalem consisted only of the land enclosed by the city walls that Sultan Süleyman had ordered built, what is today called the Old City. In 1840 the city's population was estimated to consist of 4,650 Muslims, 3,350 Christians, and 5,000 Jews. All of these groups lived within the confine of the Old

City, which had four main quarters defined by the community that lived within it: Muslim, Christian, Armenian, and Jewish. After the period of the Egyptian occupation, 1831–40, things began to change as the city returned to Ottoman rule. British Protestant MISSIONARIES established Jerusalem as their main mission station in the Ottoman Empire and started a church to the north of the city walls. The Russian government followed suit and built a large complex for its pilgrims to the northwest of the city walls. Jews coming from Europe built suburban neighborhoods to the west of the city. As the population within the city's wall grew, local Muslim and Christian families followed their example, building European-style neighborhoods to the northeast and southwest of the Old City.

During this period, the growing ZIONIST movement led to expanded Jewish immigration, which had a major impact on the city's demographic composition. By one European estimate, in 1890, the city's population included 9,000 Muslims, 8,000 Christians, and 20,000 Jews. This change was not lost on Jerusalem's Muslims. In the Ottoman Parliament of 1909, representatives of their leading families were among the first to protest this imbalance as a threat to their political position and status.

The issue of further Jewish settlement in the city was temporarily settled with the start of World War I. With the outbreak of fighting, the Ottoman government banned any new immigration into Palestine and ordered the arrest of those Jews who were Russian subjects as enemy aliens. On December 11, 1917, General Edmund Allenby, head of a British Expeditionary Force accepted the city's surrender without resistance. After World War I, the League of Nations awarded Palestine to the United Kingdom as a mandated territory with Jerusalem as its capital.

Bruce Masters

Further reading: Amnon Cohen, *Economic Life in Ottoman Jerusalem* (Cambridge: Cambridge University Press, 1989); Oded Peri, *Christianity under Islam in Jerusalem* (Leiden: Brill, 2001); Dror Ze'evi, *An Ottoman Century: The District of Jerusalem in the 1600s* (Albany: State University of New York Press, 1996).

Jesuits   *See* MISSIONARIES.

Jews   The Ottoman Empire was home to an important Jewish diaspora. Although they did not make up a large proportion of the population—probably no more than 1 percent of the total—there were well-established Jewish communities in most Ottoman cities. In some cities, such as JERUSALEM, BAGHDAD, and SALONIKA, Jews formed a sizeable minority, if not a majority, of the total population. Rural Jewish communities were rare, however, and could be found only in Kurdistan and a few villages in Galilee (present-day northern Israel).

Linguistically, the Jews of the Empire could be divided into four major groups: Romiotes, Sephardim, Ashkenazim, and Arabic-speaking Jews. There were also smaller Jewish communities in Kurdistan who spoke either Kurdish or Aramaic as well as some in North Africa who spoke Berber (Tamazight).

Romiotes were Greek-speaking descendants of the Jews who had lived in the former BYZANTINE EMPIRE. They formed the core Jewish population that the Ottomans encountered in the early centuries as they built their empire. Sultan MEHMED II (r. 1444–46; 1451–81) forcibly moved many Romiote Jews from towns in the Balkans and western Anatolia to populate his new capital in ISTANBUL after the city's conquest in 1453. The Sephardim and Ashkenazim were immigrants to the Ottoman Empire. The Sephardim, or Sephardic Jews, were those who had originally lived in either SPAIN or Portugal and spoke a dialect of Castilian Spanish, called locally either Ladino or Judezmo. The Ashkenazim, or Ashkenazi Jews, were from central and eastern Europe; most spoke either German or the Jewish dialect of medieval German known as Yiddish. Despite their different mother tongues, all educated Ottoman Jews would also know Hebrew, which served not only as the language of prayer but also as the language of intellectual life and, in some cases, of commercial correspondence.

JEWISH COMMUNITIES

Arabic-speaking Jewish communities existed in all the major urban centers of the Arab provinces, with those of CAIRO, ALEPPO, DAMASCUS, and BAGHDAD being the largest. Baghdad served as a place of refuge for Iranian Jews as SHIA ISLAM, which was the state religion of IRAN, was much less tolerant of non-Muslims than was the SUNNI ISLAM practiced in the Ottoman Empire. By the end of the Ottoman period, Jews constituted the largest single religious community in the city. During the Ottoman centuries, Baghdad was a major center of learning for Arabic-speaking Jews, much as Cairo served as the center of learning for Arabic-speaking Muslims. Rabbis trained in Baghdad were in demand in the cities of both Syria and Egypt. In the late 18th century, Jewish commercial families in Baghdad and BASRA began to establish ties with agents of the East India Company, the British joint stock company that had a monopoly on Britain's trade with Asia.

With the rise of Bombay as a trading center for the company, so many of these families moved their operations to Bombay that Arabic-speaking Jews in India came to be called "Baghdadis" regardless of their actual city of origin. The importance of the Arabic-speaking Jewish community in Bombay was greatly enhanced with the arrival of David Sassoon as a refugee from the rule of

This photo, taken in the 1870s, shows the courtyard of the house owned by the Jewish merchant family Liniado in Damascus. Locally, it was called the House of the Stambulis as the family had originally come from Istanbul. The children in the photograph are wearing a mixture of traditional and western dress that was typical among the urban inhabitants of the late Ottoman Empire. *(Photograph by Maison Bonfils, courtesy of the University of Pennsylvania Museum, Philadelphia)*

DAWUD PASHA, the governor of Baghdad (1817–31), who was much less tolerant of non-Muslims than his predecessors. Sassoon founded a merchant dynasty in Bombay that by the end of the 19th century extended to Calcutta, Singapore, Hong Kong, and Shanghai. Despite the wealth that some Baghdad Jewish families were able to acquire in the 19th century, British diplomats in Baghdad reported at the end of the century that most of the Jewish population was poor and indeed one put the percentage of Jews who were destitute or beggars at 65 percent.

JEWS IN PALESTINE

Contrasting with the cultural assimilation of most Jews in the empire's Arab provinces into the wider Arabic-speaking culture, the Jewish communities in PALESTINE had diverse ethnic origins and spoke in many tongues. In the 16th century, Safed, a center for the study of the Jewish mystical tradition of the Kabbalah, had separate quarters for Jews from Portugal, Cordoba, Castile, Aragon, HUNGARY, Apulia, Seville, and GERMANY. As the list suggests, Jews of Iberian origin (the Sephardim) increasingly found their way to Palestine and probably constituted the majority of Jews in Palestine in the 16th and 17th centuries.

Diverse Jewish immigration to Palestine continued in the 18th century with an influx of eastern European Hasidim (Jewish mystics) following the death in 1760 of revered mystic the Baal Shem Tov. Countless Jewish scholars came to find solace, freedom from persecution, and intellectual community in Palestine. Throughout the Ottoman period Jerusalem, Tiberias, and Safed served as places where Jewish intellectuals from throughout the diaspora could meet and exchange ideas in a cultural nexus parallel to that provided by Mecca and Medina for their Muslim contemporaries.

SEPHARDIC JEWS

Despite the diversity of the Jewish population in the Ottoman Empire, after the 15th century, the Ottoman sultans' contact with their subject Jewish communities was primarily through connections with the Sephardim. The Sephardic Jews were part of a general population movement of Jews from the Christian Mediterranean to the Ottoman lands in the aftermath of their expulsion from Spain in 1492. They were also the among the most economically dynamic groups to move into Ottoman cities in the 16th and 17th centuries. Some of the migrants had settled first in the port cities of Italy before moving on, and they retained valuable trade contacts with the larger Sephardic diaspora throughout the western Mediterranean and beyond, to Amsterdam and the New World. Many had been prosperous in their old homelands. No longer able to remain in their country of origin, they moved to other parts of the world, bringing with them their movable capital.

These migrants brought financial experience and skills and—perhaps most importantly for the Ottomans—an invaluable knowledge of European economic and political affairs. As non-Christians, the Sephardic Jews were viewed as potential allies, or at least as neutrals, by the Ottomans. The sultans, recognizing that this group would contribute to the empire's economic welfare, invited representatives of the community to settle in Ottoman lands and encouraged others to follow suit. Most settled in Izmir, Istanbul, and Salonika, although Sephardic Jews eventually made their way to Balkan cities such as Sarajevo and Sofia. Still others found their way to Aleppo, Damascus, and Cairo.

The welcome that the Ottoman sultans gave these Jewish immigrants is evident in the permissions granted to build new synagogues in the cities in which they settled. Islamic law explicitly forbade the building of new houses of worship by non-Muslims and similar exceptions were rarely extended to Ottoman Christian communities before the 19th-century TANZIMAT reforms. The impact of the Sephardic Jewish immigration on Ottoman urban life was most striking in the city of Salonika, where by the end of the 16th century Jews formed the majority of the city's population. Many Jewish males were employed in Salonika's woolen industry. Using techniques brought from Spain and Italy, they supplied most of the cloth used by the imperial army and palace. The city was also a center of Jewish learning and carried the nickname "Jerusalem of the East," even though the city of Jerusalem was itself a part of the Ottoman Empire.

The 16th century is usually considered the golden age of Ottoman Jewish history. Central to the period was the almost mythic career of Joseph Nasí, perhaps the century's most successful Jewish immigrant. Born in Portugal in the early 1520s, Nasí left for Antwerp as a teenager to join his aunt Gracia Nasí Mendes and to enter into the family business (the Mendes family was one of the great banking families of early modern Europe). In 1553, Nasí's aunt moved to Istanbul and he followed soon after. Both aunt and nephew shed their identity as Marranos (Jewish converts to Catholicism), openly embraced the practice of Judaism, and became important supporters of Jewish charities and scholarship. In Istanbul, Nasí quickly became invaluable to the Ottoman authorities for his knowledge of the West. In turn, he profited by receiving the right to collect taxes for the sultans in certain districts as well as trade monopolies over the export of specified commodities. Sultan SELIM II (r. 1566–74) awarded Nasí the governorship of Naxos and the Cyclades Islands. This political office carried with it the title of *sancakbeyi*, a title rarely bestowed on a non-Muslim. When he died in 1579, Joseph Nasí was probably one of the wealthiest men in the Ottoman Empire. Although Nasí's career was exceptional, his story is indicative of the ways in which Sephardic Jews were able to integrate themselves into their new environment and prosper there.

The willingness of the sultans to overlook Islamic law in earlier centuries was tempered in the 17th century by increasing Islamic conservatism at the court and Ottoman Jews suffered as a consequence. After the great fire of 1660, in which large swathes of Istanbul were destroyed, Jews in the city were not given permission to rebuild some synagogues as Muslim judges ruled that the permission they had originally received to build them was illegal. A stricter interpretation of Islamic law also played a role in the outcome of the case of SHABBATAI ZVI in which the self-proclaimed Jewish messiah was forced to convert to Islam or be sentenced to death for treason.

During most of the Ottoman period there was little friction between Ottoman Jews and their Muslim neighbors. Jewish visitors to the empire often remarked on Ottoman Jews' greater freedom to worship and earn a living compared to the restrictions in much of Christian Europe. Although Jews tended to cluster in neighborhoods where there was a synagogue, creating predominantly Jewish neighborhoods in most Ottoman cities, Ottoman Jews were not segregated into ghettos by law as they were in much of Europe. Within Jewish communities, rabbis who maintained both schools and religious courts to dispense Jewish law were the political leaders, and even wealthy merchant families tried to stay within the moral and legal boundaries they set. That did not mean that there were no disagreements but rather that the individual Jewish communities tried to manage conflict internally rather than seeking the mediation of Ottoman authorities. Furthermore, Ottoman Jews resisted attempts to create a religious hierarchy, as was occurring in the various Christian sects. Significantly, the office of HAHAMBAŞI, or chief rabbi of the empire, was only instituted in 1835 as a Jewish MILLET came into official existence.

Relations between Jews and Christians within the empire, however, were generally less amicable than those between Jews and Muslims, and many of the anti-Semitic outbursts that occurred in the empire were incited by Christians. One example of this was the DAMASCUS INCIDENT of 1840, when prominent Damascus Jews were arrested and tortured by the authorities after being accused by Christians of murdering a Roman Catholic priest.

The ties between the various Jewish communities and the Ottoman sultans grew stronger in the 19th century. As Christian minorities began to articulate nationalist alternatives to the Ottoman Empire, most Jews feared that any new states formed would be less liberal and tolerant than Ottoman imperial rule. For example, at the start of the GREEK WAR OF INDEPENDENCE in 1821, Greek Christian rebels indiscriminately killed both Muslim and Jewish civilians. The nationalist rhetoric put forward by many of the Balkan Christian peoples enshrined Orthodox Christianity as one of the essential elements of national definition and Jews were considered to be outsiders. At the same time, the schools set up by the ALLIANCE ISRAÉLITE UNIVERSELLE, a European Jewish philanthropic organization, provided a modern, secular education that promoted a cosmopolitan rather than a national outlook. As a result Ottoman Jews were not particularly interested in the Zionist project to establish a Jewish homeland in Palestine until the collapse of the Ottoman Empire. At that time, Ottoman Jews began to feel they had been left with few political alternatives.

Bruce Masters

See also ZIONISM.

Further reading: Avigdor Levy, ed., *The Jews of the Ottoman Empire* (Princeton, N.J.: Darwin, 1994); Esther Benbassa and Aron Rodrigue, *Sephardi Jewry: A History of the Judeo-Spanish Community, 14th–20th Centuries* (Berkeley: University of California Press, 2000).

jihad *See DAR AL-HARB.*

jizya *(cizye)* Under Islamic law, all non-Muslim men are required to pay an annual sum to the Muslim community as a symbol of their status as members of the *ahl al-dhimma*, "people of the contract." In Arabic, this tax was called the *jizya*. Under the Hanafi school (interpretation of the law based on the writings of Abu Hanifa, d. 767), as practiced in the Ottoman Empire, three levels of taxation were established, depending on the individual man's economic status and ability to pay. This was one of the few taxes in the Ottoman Empire that was assessed on an individual basis. The registers of *jizya* payers from

the periods when the tax was collected assiduously offer historians unique insight into the economic and demographic conditions of the Empire's Christians and Jews. Research has shown, however, that the Ottoman tax registers of the 18th century are unreliable, as the officers collecting the tax often simply recorded the same number of payers year after year.

The tax was not that onerous for individuals in the top two categories of ratepayers, but the amounts assessed for the poor could be a real hardship. Wealthy members of both Christian and Jewish communities established charitable trusts, or WAQFS, to help the poor of their communities pay the tax. Some non-Muslims sought creative ways to avoid paying the tax. The most common method was to seek employment from the resident European consuls, as such employment could exempt the employee from the tax. Because *jizya* payments represented an uninterrupted annual inflow of cash that was often needed for war expenditures, Ottoman officials sought to close any legal loopholes that freed non-Muslims from their obligations. This included careful scrutiny of the documents of non-Muslims who claimed exemption by virtue of their employment with the Europeans. The Ottomans also imposed a special travel tax, *yave cizye* in Ottoman Turkish or "the *jizya* on those who strayed," on those non-Muslims who claimed that they were not long-term residents, including even those who were subjects of the Iranian shahs. But by 1690 Iranian non-Muslim merchants in the Ottoman Empire were exempted from the tax.

During the TANZIMAT period, the Reform Edict (Hatt-i Hümayun) of 1856 abolished the *jizya* as discriminatory. At the same time, the edict made non-Muslims liable to military conscription, although it was possible to engage a substitute or purchase an exemption. The purchasing of exemptions was institutionalized in the following year in a tax called the *bedel-i askeriye* (substitute for military service), which was levied on all adult non-Muslim males, but this created discontent on all sides. Although they complained bitterly that it was simply the *jizya* with a new name, significantly, Christians did not ask to be drafted in lieu of payment. Muslims felt that their sons were unfairly carrying the burden of the defense of the empire, while Christians were permitted to stay at home and prosper. It was not until 1909 that the Ottoman parliament, dominated by the COMMITTEE OF UNION AND PROGRESS, abolished the *bedel* and made military service compulsory for all males, regardless of religion.

Bruce Masters

See also DHIMMI.

Further reading: Hidemitsu Kuroki, "Zimmis in Mid-Nineteenth Century Aleppo: An Analysis of *Cizye Defteris*," in *Essays on Ottoman Civilization* (Prague: Academy of Sciences of the Czech Republic, 1998), 205–48.

journalism *See NEWSPAPERS.*

K

kadı The term *kadı* is derived from the Arabic word *qada*, which means "to judge." *Kadıs* have existed since the earliest days of Islam. Muhammad himself both judged and delegated judicial decisions, and during his lifetime, judges' duties included both judicial and administrative tasks. This changed when the second caliph, Umar (r. 634–44), began assigning distinct positions for these two tasks, distinguishing them as two separate duties.

The judges of the Ottoman Empire—like judges in previous Islamic states—attended a MADRASA, or college. When they graduated they either entered judicial posts or became lecturers themselves. Those who chose to become judges worked in either Anatolia or Rumelia. A judge's first appointment was marked by a probationary period, or *mülazemet*, during which the new judge received firsthand training. Later appointments were based on seniority, with the judgeship of ISTANBUL the most senior and valued post.

Kadıs were not paid a regular salary but derived their incomes from court fees. Court fees were determined by imperial edict and were strictly enforced. In the 16th century, for every 1,000 households, a judge received 10 akçe (approximately one-fifth the value of a Venetian gold ducat) per day. A judgeship of the lowest degree had an income of 20 akçe, suggesting that such a court consisted of around 2,000 households with a probable population of 6,000–10,000. The judgeships with the highest income—500 akçe a day—were those of Istanbul, BURSA, and EDIRNE. *Kadıs* were responsible for paying themselves out of the fees they collected. They simply subtracted their income before forwarding excess moneys to the central government, thus saving time and bureaucratic processes. However, in periods of weak state control, this decentralized system was abused.

Kadıs were the only judges in the Ottoman legal system. Their decisions were based upon Ottoman law, a combination of dynastic and Islamic law, or SHARIA. Islamic jurists established legal regulations within the empire. These rules and laws were written in *fiqh* (Islamic law) books, and amounted to codified law. These texts included the *Mülteka*, which saw prominent use during the reign of Sultan SÜLEYMAN I (r. 1520–66). Judges often consulted these texts for legal guidance. However, these texts did not amount to a single legal code for the whole empire. To counteract this potentially confusing practice, the state periodically adopted juridical schools, signifying to judges which rules were to be applied. The state also prepared *kanunnames* (law codes) to address subjects and problems where Islamic law was not explicit. Judges applied these two distinct forms of law in legal conflicts throughout the empire.

Judges kept their proceedings in a register book, or *sicil*. These registers included the names of the defendant's and claimant's counsels, witness statements, investigatory information, and the court's judgment. Beginning in the 16th century, registers became standardized.

Kadıs' duties were not limited to judicial decisions. They also helped with city planning, registered matrimonial and other contracts, and supervised charitable foundations, or WAQFS. These tasks mirrored those of today's notary publics. *Kadıs* also had official assistants, which allowed judges to discharge their own duties more easily.

Beginning in the middle of the 19th century, *kadıs* no longer functioned as the sole judicial officers of the empire. New courts established during the TANZIMAT or

Reform Era (1839–76) restricted the activities of *kadıs*. The abolishment of the sharia courts in 1924 marked the end of the *kadıs*.

Mustafa Şentop

See also ADMINISTRATION, CENTRAL; *KADIASKER*; *KANUN*.

Further reading: Ronald C. Jennings, "Limitations of The Judicial Powers of The Kadı in 17th century Ottoman Kayseri." *Studia Islamica* 50 (1979): 151–84.

kadıasker (kazasker) The *kadıasker* was the top judicial official in the Ottoman Empire until the TANZIMAT reform period of the 19th century. The institution of *kadıasker*, though present in earlier Turkish-Islamic states, came into its own within the Ottoman Empire. In previous states, the *kadıasker's* jurisdiction was restricted to military affairs, but in the Ottoman period it expanded to include civil cases. Most historians agree that the first Ottoman *kadıasker* was appointed in the reign of Sultan MURAD I (r. 1362–89), though some believe there is evidence for an earlier date. In the last period of Sultan MEHMED II's reign (r. 1444–46; 1451–81), the institution was divided into two *kazaskerliks*, or judicial jurisdictions, so that two separate individuals served as *kadıaskers*, one assigned to Anatolia, the empire's eastern provinces, and the other assigned to Rumelia, or the empire's European provinces. A third *kazaskerlik* was established during the reign of Sultan SELIM I (r. 1512–20), but this office was short-lived.

Kadıaskers were selected from among the Muslim judges, or *kadıs*. With some notable exceptions, almost all *kadıaskers* served as the KADI of ISTANBUL before being appointed kadiasker.

As head of the Ottoman judiciary, the *kadıasker* oversaw the appointment of *kadıs* and made all *kadı* assignments, except those of the highest degree. The Anatolian *kadıasker* assigned *kadıs* in Anatolia and Arabia, while the *kadıasker* of Rumelia appointed judges in the European lands and the CRIMEA. The *kadıasker* was also allowed to change the places of the *kadıs*, audit them, discharge them if necessary, and to change the jurisdiction of regional judges. The *kadıasker's* responsibilities extended to madrasas, or colleges; he assigned professors to the madrasas, auditioned scholars, and discharged them if necessary. The *kadıasker* also represented the organization of scholars, of which he served as the head until the middle of the 16th century when the ŞEYHÜLISLAM, the chief mufti or jurisconsult, took on this role.

In the course of time, *şeyhülislams* began to influence the appointment of *kadıaskers*. In the Tanzimat period, after 1839, the Anatolian and Rumelian head judgeships were converted to justice departments and were officially connected to the *şeyhülislam*. The term of service for *kadıaskers* was initially unlimited, but by the end of the 16th century, though there were some exceptions, *kadıaskers* typically served a one-year term.

The most significant task of the *kadıasker* was to act as the state's supreme judicial officer. As such, he was a permanent member of the Divan-ı Hümayun (Ottoman Imperial Council), which also functioned as the empire's supreme court. He also participated in all meetings and discussions regarding the governance of the state. As a judge in the Imperial Council, the *kadıasker* had a number of responsibilities, including authorizing investigations of appeals. Even though the Imperial Council assembled as a committee, these rulings were made solely by the *kadıasker*. Some important lawsuits, particularly those involving statesmen, also took place in the Imperial Council.

The *kadıasker* also had an important role in bringing Islamic law and secular law into harmony. One of the tasks of the Imperial Council was to make secular legal regulations within the framework of Islamic law, or SHARIA. The body of regulations known as *örfi hukuk*, customary or secular law, was particularly concerned with tax law, land law, and the penal code. The regulations in these arenas were organized into written texts called *kanunname*, or law codes (*see KANUN*). It is important to understand that Ottoman secular law did not arise as a code separate from Islamic law but is bound up with and integrated into the sharia. Islamic law does not directly address issues that are considered potentially subject to change. Islam identifies this omission as a "conscious blank," because the rule of law in these areas is deliberately left to the legislator. The Ottomans sought to fill these blanks with the help of secular law in accordance with the general rules of Islamic law; it was the responsibility of the *kadıasker* to effect harmony between Islamic law and the rules of secular law. Beyond this central judicial work, the *kadıasker* worked as a member of the Imperial Council on issues including war and peace, taxation, land organization, and the penal code.

Kadıaskers also had their own divans (councils) and presided over certain lawsuits, though recent studies show that only the Rumelian head judge presided over cases in his court. Such cases involved public officials and can be classified as military trials. Officials had the right to appeal their judgments in the court of the *kadıasker*; their trials were held in Istanbul, no matter where the original trial took place.

The courts of the Anatolian and Rumelian *kadıaskers*, which were authorized after the Tanzimat era and attached to the *şeyhülislam*, functioned as supreme courts. In 1914 both of them united and became a single court.

Mustafa Şentop

See also ADMINISTRATION, CENTRAL.

Further reading: R. C. Repp, *The Mufti of Istanbul: A Study in the Development of the Ottoman Learned Hierarchy* (Atlantic Highlands, N.J.: Ithaca Press, 1986); Albert Howe Lybyer, *The Government of the Ottoman Empire in the Time of Suleiman the Magnificent* (Cambridge, Mass.: Harvard University Press, 1913).

Kamaniçe (*Pol. Kamieniec Podolski; Ukr. Kam'janec' Podil's'kyj*) Kamaniçe, as it was called in Turkish, was the medieval center of the province of Podolia, which was incorporated into Poland in 1430. Due to its strategic location, Kamaniçe soon became the main Polish bulwark against possible raids by the TATARS and Turks. The town, situated in an oxbow of the Smotryč River, was additionally protected from the west by an impressive castle, modernized in the 16th and early 17th century. While the rural population of Podolia was predominantly Ruthenian (a contemporary term for Ukrainian), the town itself was inhabited by Poles, Armenians, Ruthenians, and Jews (though the latter were officially prohibited to dwell within its walls). The Polish, Armenian, and Ruthenian communities enjoyed autonomous civil and religious institutions. A major trade center, Kamaniçe was regularly visited by Turkish, Greek, Bulgarian, Wallachian, and Moldavian merchants.

In 1672 the Ottoman army, led by Sultan MEHMED IV (r. 1648–87) and Grand Vizier KÖPRÜLÜ Ahmed Pasha, captured Kamaniçe after a short siege. According to the Buczacz Treaty (1672), Podolia was ceded to the Ottomans. Kamaniçe became the center of a new Ottoman *eyalet*, or province and the seat of the Ottoman governor. Although the Buczacz Treaty was rejected by the Polish Diet and war broke out anew, Polish troops were unable to retake the fortress. The truce of Żurawno (1676), confirmed by the Polish embassy to ISTANBUL (1678), left Podolia within Ottoman borders. A new Polish-Ottoman war broke out in 1683, following the Polish military participation in the rescue of VIENNA from besiegement by the Ottomans (*see* VIENNA, SIEGES OF). For the next 16 years, Ottoman rule in Podolia was limited to the blockaded fortress of Kamaniçe, held by a garrison numbering almost 6,000 soldiers. The fortress was restored to Poland as a result of the TREATY OF KARLOWITZ (1699).

During the 27 years of Ottoman rule in Podolia, Kamaniçe was administered by nine Ottoman pashas: Küstendilli Halil (1672–76 and 1677–80), Arnavut Ibrahim (1676–77), Defterdar Ahmed (1680–82), Arnavut Abdurrahman (1682–84), Tokatlı Mahmud (1684), the future grand vizier Bozoklu Mustafa (1685–86), Sarı Boşnak Hüseyin (1686–88), Yegen Ahmed (1688–89), and Kahraman Mustafa (1689–99). The *eyalet* was divided into four *sancaks* (Kamaniçe, Bar, Medžybiž, and Jazlivec'). A Muslim KADI resided in Kamaniçe, and the *timar* or prebendal land tenure system was introduced in Podolia.

The Ottomans built at least two new mosques and converted several churches into mosques; they also restored the castle and the bridge connecting it to the town, and founded a covered bazaar and two BATHHOUSES. But after the long siege and blockade by Polish troops in 1699, the city was ruined and severely depopulated. Ottoman chroniclers and poets devoted much attention to the conquest of Kamaniçe, such as Yusuf Nabi's poem *Fethname-i Kamaniçe*. As a result of the second partition of the Polish-Lithuanian Commonwealth in 1793, Kamaniçe was incorporated into Russia. Today it is a town in the Xmel'nyc'kyj District (oblast) of Ukraine.

Dariusz Kołodziejczyk

Further reading: Dariusz Kołodziejczyk, "Ottoman Podillja: The *Eyalet* of Kam"janec', 1672–1699." *Harvard Ukrainian Studies* 16, no. 1–2 (1992): 87–101; Dariusz Kołodziejczyk, *The Ottoman Survey Register of Podolia (ca. 1681): Defter-i Mufassal-i Eyalet-i Kamaniçe* (Cambridge, Mass.: Harvard University Press, 2004).

Kamieniec Podolski *See* KAMANIÇE.

Kam'janec' *See* KAMANIÇE.

kanun Derived from the Arabic word *qanun*, which itself derives from the Greek *kanôn*, meaning rule or measure of rule, the Turkish word *kanun* (pl. *kavanin*) was used in the Ottoman Empire to refer to a code of regulations and more generally to the state or secular law that supplemented the sacred Islamic law, or SHARIA. In theory, the latter regulates a Muslim's whole public and private life. The sharia was also the normative law regarding all cases involving Muslims and non-Muslims. However, in the multiethnic and multireligious Ottoman Empire, as in other Islamic polities, the sharia often had limited applications, especially with regard to land tenure, taxation, and criminal law. In these fields Muslim rulers, whose legislative authority with regard to matters not treated by the sharia is recognized by Islamic law, issued decrees. By the late 15th century Ottoman sultans also enacted laws based on custom and these laws or law codes, known as *kanun* or *kanunnames*, thus acquired a dual nature, their legitimacy lying in both custom and the sultan's authority as ruler.

One of the main subjects of Ottoman secular law was the legal distinction between the sultan's ordinary tax-paying subjects (*reaya*) and the *askeri*, those in roles attached to the sultan, which included members of the military class, the empire's bureaucrats, and the religious establishment (ULEMA). Members of the *askeri* did not pay taxes and, in return for their service, received regular salaries, either as cash from the imperial treasury or in the form of military fiefs or prebends (*timar*). Provincial law codes (*kanunname*s), attached as prefaces to cadastral surveys or tax registers, established the taxes and fines that the tax-paying subjects of a given administrative unit (*sancak* or subprovince) owed to their fief-holder landlords and the sultan. Since the basis of such taxes was local custom, modified by sultanic decrees, Ottoman laws often incorporated pre-Ottoman local customs, both Islamic and Christian. In the Hungarian provinces, for example, the *reaya* paid one gold coin to the sultan because they had paid the same amount of tax to the Hungarian kings before the Ottoman conquest of the region in 1541. On the other edge of the empire, in the subprovinces and districts of Ergani, Urfa, Mardin, Çimrik, Siverek, Erzincan, Kemah and Bayburt, the first law books were based in part on the laws of Uzun Hasan (r. 1453–75), sultan of the Akkoyunlu (White Sheep) Turkoman confederation who ruled the region before the Ottomans. All of these *kanunname*s, along with the special regulations regarding the Turkomans, preserved the pre-Ottoman tribal customs of these nomad tribes for generations.

Imperial decrees issued by the Ottoman sultans regarding state organization, land tenure, taxes, and criminal law created a growing corpus of state or secular law, independent of the sacred law. The idea of an Ottoman secular or state law emerged under Sultan BAYEZID II (r. 1481–1512), who ordered the compilation of all the *kanun*s of his empire. The *Kanun-i Osmani* (Law book) of 1499 contained the obligations of the *timar* holders and taxpayers. Attached to this are two criminal codes, one dating from about 1490 and one from the end of the 1490s. These penal statutes were incorporated into the general law book because the punishment of criminals was the responsibility of the members of the military class and thus formed an integral part of the main theme of the secular law, the relationship between the *reaya* and *askeri*. However, penal statutes often appear in the law codes haphazardly, making it difficult to understand the legal procedure from arrest through punishment.

In the 16th century, in order to eliminate inconsistencies between sacred and secular law, Kemalpaşazade (1525–34) and Ebussuud Efendi (1545–74), in their functions as the empire's chief muftis or jurisconsults (ŞEYHÜLISLAM), undertook to harmonize the sharia and the *kanun*. However, the dispute regarding the relationship between sharia and *kanun*, which in turn reflected the struggle between the religious establishment and the military-bureaucratic elite on the other, continued, and in 1696 the use of *kanun* side by side with the word sharia was forbidden by a sultanic decree. During the 19th-century TANZIMAT reform era, the enacting of secular laws independent of the sharia accelerated. Although these laws were often sanctioned by the written legal opinion (FATWA) of the chief mufti of the empire, they were either modeled upon or adapted without significant modification from European laws.

During this same period, an important segment of Ottoman society argued that laws could be altered according to the needs of the society through a national assembly. The first Ottoman CONSTITUTION (1876), known as *kanun-i esasi* (basic or fundamental law), and the constitutional movement were major steps in this direction. By the end of the empire the *kadı* courts were removed from the authority of the ŞEYHÜLISLAM and placed under the newly established Ministry of Justice. Whereas in several modern Muslim states the sharia retained its influence, these movements in the late Ottoman Empire gave way to the entirely secular legal system of the Republic of TURKEY, where the term *kanun* survives as the term for modern law.

Gábor Ágoston

See also KADIASKER; LAW AND GENDER.

Further reading: Haim Gerber, *State, Society, and Law in Islam: Ottoman Law in Comparative Perspective* (Albany: State University of New York Press, 1994); Halil İnalcık, "Ḳānūn," in *Encyclopaedia of Islam*, online edition (by subscription), edited by P. Bearman, Th. Bianquis, C. E. Bosworth, E. van Donzel, and W. P. Heinrichs. Brill, 2007. Brill Online. 8 May 2007 http://www.brillonline.nl/subscriber/entry?entry=islam_COM-0439; Colin Imber, *The Ottoman Empire, 1300–1650: The Structure of Power* (Basingstoke, UK: Palgrave Macmillan, 2002), 216–51.

kapıkulu *See* WARFARE.

kapudan *See* NAVY.

Karadjordje (Djordje Petrović; Kara George) (b. 1762–d. 1817) *founder of the Serbian Karadjordjević dynasty, military leader* Djordje Petrović, nicknamed Karadjordje or "Black George" because of his dark complexion, powerful build, and fiery temper, was an outstanding Serbian military leader and founder of the Karadjordjević dynasty. Born a poor peasant in Ottoman SERBIA, Karadjordje was forced to flee to the Austrian province of Srem in 1786 because he killed a Turk in a quarrel. Karadjordje took the Austrian side in the Austrian-Ottoman War of 1788–91, gaining invaluable military experience. Amnestied for his role in the war, Karadjordje returned to Serbia around 1794. When the Ottoman governor, Hacı Mustafa Pasha, decided to recruit and arm Serbian forces against rebel JANISSARIES, Karadjordje was appointed as one of the Serbian *bölükbaşıs* (captains). At the Serbian conference held in Orašac on February 2, 1804, Karadjordje, now a famed soldier, was appointed to lead an uprising against Janissary corruption and abuses in Serbia. The revolt against the Janissaries soon turned into a full-scale uprising against the Ottoman government. Although many Serbian leaders were opposed to his intentions, Karadjordje, a talented military leader of proven personal courage, managed to install himself as the hereditary ruler of rebel Serbia in 1808. When the rebellion was put down in the Ottoman offensive of 1813, Karadjordje first took refuge in Austrian Zemun and then in Russia. He joined PHILIKI HETAIRIA, a Greek revolutionary secret society founded in Odessa in 1814. Having been appointed the leader of an all-Balkans uprising, he secretly crossed into Serbia in 1817. Since this put the newly achieved results of the Second Serbian Uprising at risk, Serbian Prince Miloš Obrenović had Karadjordje killed.

He was the founder of the Karadjordjević dynasty, which ruled Serbia alternating with the Obrenovićs. His younger son, Aleksandar, became Serbian prince from 1842–58, and his grandson Petar was Serbian king from 1903–18.

Aleksandar Fotić

Karaites Deriving their name from the Hebrew word *qaraim*, "callers," as in "Callers to the True Faith," the Karaites were followers of a minority Jewish tradition that split off from what would become mainstream Judaism in the eighth century C.E. According to tradition, the schism between the two groups arose when Anan ben David was passed over as head of the Jewish community (Resh ha-Galut) in present-day IRAQ in favor of his younger brother. Anan then proclaimed that his interpretation of Judaism was closer both to the Torah, the scriptural law at the foundation of Judaism, and to Islam than was the Talmudic Judaism (based on rabbinical writing) that had evolved in Iraq and PALESTINE in the centuries following the destruction of the Temple in 70 C.E. Most of Anan's followers moved to Palestine (Eretz Yisrael) and in the 10th century they mounted a campaign to spread their version of Judaism to other Jewish communities. In the Ottoman Empire there were communities of Karaites in Palestine, EGYPT, and the CRIMEA.

The actual differences between the two forms of Judaism appear slight. The Karaites did not recognize Hanukkah as a holiday, and the holidays that other Jews celebrate on two days, Karaites celebrated on one. There were also minor differences in their respective calendars

and dietary laws. The most important difference was in the way each group defined consanguinity in marriage. The Karaites followed Muslim custom and permitted first cousins to marry, leading European rabbis to declare that the Karaites were illegitimate in their birth and forbidding other Jews to marry them. Rabbis of the Ottoman Empire, on the other hand, permitted Orthodox Jews to marry Karaites, provided that the children of such unions were raised in the Orthodox tradition. Intermarriage may explain why there were only a few thousand Karaites left in the Empire in the 19th century. The Ottoman state never officially recognized the Karaites as a MILLET, or religious community, but Ottoman KADIS, or judges, routinely ruled that Jews from one community could not interfere with the practices of the other.

Because most of the source material on the Karaites is written by Orthodox Jewish detractors, the information available is of questionable accuracy and objectivity.

Bruce Masters

Further reading: Amnon Cohen, *Jewish Life under Islam: Jerusalem in the Sixteenth Century* (Cambridge, Mass.: Harvard University Press, 1984).

Karaman *See* ANATOLIAN EMIRATES.

Karbala (*Turk.:* **Kerbela**) Located in central IRAQ, the city of Karbala is sacred to SHIA ISLAM as the site where the Imam Husayn, son of the Imam Ali, was martyred and buried in 680 C.E. Karbala is second only to NAJAF among the holy cities of Iraq for Shii Muslims. As such, it is the site of a major pilgrimage on the 10th day of the month of Muharram, Ashura, which commemorates the day on which Imam Husayn was killed. Many Shiis carry a small piece of baked clay from the city and place it on their prayer rugs so that when their head touches the carpet in prayer, it actually rests on the sacred soil of Karbala.

Historically, Karbala was surrounded by rich date groves, but these depended on water from the EUPHRATES RIVER brought by canals that had largely silted up by the time of the Ottoman conquest in 1534. To alleviate the water shortage, Sultan SÜLEYMAN I (r. 1520–66) ordered the building of the Husayniyya Canal to bring water to the city from the Euphrates.

The Ottoman governors of BAGHDAD controlled Karbala much more directly than Najaf. But even though these governors were always Sunnis, they made no attempt to interfere with Shii religious practices. In 1801 the militant followers of MUHAMMAD IBN ABD AL-WAHHAB overran the city, considering the reverence paid to Imam Husayn by the Shia as blasphemy. These Sunni Arab tribes massacred several thousand of the city's inhabitants as in their view the Shii Muslims were "unbelievers" and had therefore forfeited their right to life. The attack effectively ended Ottoman rule as the governors in Baghdad were too weak to extend their control over the city. In the absence of an Ottoman presence, Shii militias organized by their clergy governed the city. Local rule continued until 1843 when Necip Pasha, the newly appointed governor of Baghdad took the city by force and restored direct Ottoman administration. But even after that date, the Sunni Ottomans remained sensitive to the place the city played in the Shii religious imagination. The governors of Baghdad, therefore, allowed the Shii clergy to run the city's local government and treated its administration with care.

Bruce Masters

Further reading: Stephen Longrigg, *Four Centuries of Modern Iraq* (Oxford: Clarendon, 1925).

Karlofça *See* Karlowitz, Treaty of.

Karlowitz, Treaty of (1699) Signed on January 26, 1699, the Treaty of Karlowitz brought an end to the Long War of 1684–99 between the Ottomans and Habsburg Austria, with her allies Poland and Venice. Known in English-language literature by its German name, Karlowitz, the treaty was signed near the ruined town of Sremski Karlovci in northern Serbia. The Long War had initially broken out as a consequence of the Ottomans' second failed siege of Vienna in 1683. In 1684, following Vienna's successful defense, Austria, Poland, and Venice concluded an alliance known as the Holy League. Two years later Muscovy, as Russia was then known, also joined the league. The allies launched coordinated attacks against the Ottomans on four different fronts. Through the conflict, the Austrian Habsburgs recaptured most of Hungary, Venice regained the Morea (the Greek Peloponnese) and parts of Dalmatia, Poland retook Podolia, and Russia retook Azak.

Negotiations through English and Dutch intermediaries started as early as 1689 but were temporarily suspended due to Ottoman military victories in 1690–92. These were fought against a weakened Habsburg Austria, whose best troops had to be redeployed from Hungary and Serbia on the Ottoman front to the Rhine where the Habsburgs were fighting France in the War of the League of Augsburg (1689–97). The disastrous Ottoman defeat at Zenta on September 11, 1697 ultimately forced Istanbul to seek peace, especially since France was concluding its own treaty with the Habsburgs (September and October 1697), enabling the Habsburgs to redeploy their forces against the Ottomans.

Despite Istanbul's apparent military weakness and unfavorable diplomatic situation, the Ottoman peace delegation managed to conclude a treaty without further territorial sacrifice, reflecting simply the status quo. The Ottoman success can be attributed, at least partly, to the skills and steadfastness of the Ottoman mission, which was led by the chancery chief (Reisülküttab) and de facto foreign minister Rami Mehmed Efendi and the Sublime Porte's chief dragoman Iskerletzade Alexander (Mavracordato) of the famous Phanariot family of interpreters. Habsburg fears of further French conquests and possible Habsburg-French military confrontation over the Spanish crown, as well as the mediation offered by England and the Netherlands, were instrumental in concluding a treaty based on the principles of *uti possidetis* (literally, "as you possess"), a concept in international law that defines borders during a peace treaty so that all parties get what they possess at the time of the treaty.

Accordingly, the Ottomans were forced to surrender much of Hungary (including Transylvania), Croatia, and Slavonia to the Austrian Habsburgs, but kept the Banat of Temesvár (Timişoara), the historic region in southern Hungary between the River Tisza on the west and Transylvania and Wallachia on the east, south of the River Maros (Mureş). Podolia, with the dismantled fortress of Kamaniçe, was restored to Poland, but the Ottomans kept Moldavia. The Ottomans also secured either the evacuation or destruction of enemy-occupied strongholds along the border. Parts of Dalmatia and the Morea remained in Venetian hands, though the Ottomans recaptured the Morea in the war of 1715–18, and the Treaty of Passarowitz (1718) left it in Ottoman hands. Negotiations with Russia continued and peace was not reached until July 12, 1700 at Istanbul, when the sultan ceded Azak to Russia.

At Karlowitz the Ottomans suffered their first serious territorial losses after centuries of expansion. Moreover, the treaty marked the beginning of a new era in Ottoman-European relations. Unlike previous treaties that the Ottomans accepted as temporary terminations of hostilities, the treaties of Karlowitz and Istanbul established peace that was to last 25 years with the Habsburgs, 30 years with Muscovy, and indefinitely with Poland and Venice. More substantially, these treaties also marked the first time in the empire's history that Istanbul acknowledged the territorial integrity of its opponents by accepting the creation of well-defined borders. The details of the artificial boundaries were left to joint border commissions. Establishing clear demarcation lines proved to be an arduous task, and parts of the border were disputed as late as 1703. Nevertheless, due to the diligent work of the Habsburg border commission led by Luiggi Ferdinando Marsigli, the Croatian border was agreed upon by July 15, 1700, followed by the border of Bihać (July

20) and that of Temesvár (February 4, 1701). As a result, the border between Habsburg Austria and the Ottoman Empire had become, for the first time in their troubled history, distinctly demarcated and clearly marked with the erection of concrete landmarks. Moreover, the border was created by Marsigli in such a way that it served the Habsburgs' economic and military interests. Whenever it was possible the border followed navigable rivers so that strongholds alongside the rivers could be incorporated into the new Habsburg military frontier.

With the newly reconquered Hungarian territories, spanning some 60,000 square miles (160,000 km²) and that of the Banat of Temesvár, ceded by Istanbul to Vienna in the Treaty of Passarowitz (1718), the Austrian or Danubian Habsburg monarchy reached its largest extent and emerged as a dominant regional power. The Treaty of Karlowitz marked the end of European fear of the "Turkish menace," and the Ottomans were now perceived as a weakening empire.

Gábor Ágoston

Further reading: Rifaat A. Abou-El-Haj, "Ottoman Diplomacy at Karlowitz." *Journal of the American Oriental Society* 87, no. 4 (1967): 498–512; Rifaat A. Abou-El-Haj, "The Formal Closure of the Ottoman Frontier in Europe, 1699–1703." *Journal of the American Oriental Society* 89, no. 3 (1969): 467–75; Colin Heywood, "English Diplomatic Relations with Turkey, 1689–1698," Chap. 2 in *Writing Ottoman History: Documents and Interpretations* (Aldershot, UK: Ashgate/Variorum, 2002); John Stoye, *Marsigli's Europe, 1680–1730: The Life and Times of Luiggi Ferdinando Marsigli, Soldier and Virtuoso* (New Haven, Conn.: Yale University Press, 1994).

Katib Çelebi Mustafa b. Abdullah (Hacı Halife) (b. 1609–d. 1657) *historian, geographer, and encyclopedist* Although he had no regular education and earned his livelihood from a modest position in the state chancery, Katib Çelebi was one of the most prolific and influential intellectuals of his era, and continues to be universally admired as a scholar. One group of his works, partly in Turkish, partly in Arabic, is encyclopedic in nature: It includes a world history (*Fadhlakat aqwal al-akhyar*), a world geography (*Cihannüma*), a chronicle of the Ottoman Empire (*Fezleke*), a dictionary of famous men (*Sullam al-wusul*), and a bibliographical dictionary (*Kashf al-zunun*). In these works, Katib Çelebi aimed at compiling existing, but widely dispersed, knowledge to put it in the hands of an elite reading public, particularly the ruling class. He believed that ignorance and neglect of the lessons of history and current scientific findings were the major causes of the Ottoman political and military problems of his time, and his works were intended to revive the empire's fortunes.

Another group of his works consists of an intervention in the political and intellectual debates of his time. In a treatise on political reform (*Düstur al-amal*), Katib Çelebi compares the state to the human body, with each of the four bodily humors (blood, phlegm, yellow and black bile) representing one of the social classes; the government's task is to keep a healthy equilibrium between them. The only example in the genre of Ottoman reform treatises to provide such a philosophical framework, it concludes that, like the human body, the Ottoman state was aging, and only radical reform could rejuvenate it. In his history of the Ottoman NAVY (*Tuhfat al-kibar*) he reviews all of Ottoman maritime history in order to derive from it advice on how to defeat the superior Venetian navy that was blocking the straits of the Bosporus and the Dardanelles and threatened Istanbul in 1656.

Typically, Katib Çelebi advocated a return to the idealized practices of the past, not radical innovation. For example, his most popular work, *Mizan al-haqq*, deals with a conflict between the Sufi orders and a quasi-puritanical, literalist movement (similar to modern fundamentalism) that was criticizing and attacking the Sufis for practices allegedly contrary to Islamic scripture, such as singing, dancing, and visiting tombs. Other debated practices included smoking TOBACCO and drinking coffee. Although Katib Çelebi sympathized with a rationalist interpretation of scripture, which would prohibit those practices, he argued against forcing people to abandon beliefs and practices that were grounded in, and sanctioned by, history. This balancing of legal requirement and historical custom is an important example of Ottoman pragmatism, which was frequently practiced but rarely articulated.

Katib Çelebi's works also include treatises on sciences and astronomy, designed for teaching rather than providing new findings, and translations from European atlases and chronicles, prepared partly to form a basis for other works. Since Katib Çelebi did not know Latin and Italian, these translations were produced with the help of a European scholar who had converted to Islam. Katib Çelebi was not the first Ottoman scholar to use European sources, but he did so in a more systematic fashion than his predecessors. In particular, he was convinced that Europe's increasing military superiority and expansion in the Age of Discovery was rooted in the study of the sciences. Given this belief, he was eager to study and adopt those sciences, which he considered fully compatible with the Islamic tradition. Europeans of the 18th century Enlightenment period thus appreciated him as a kindred spirit. Several of Katib Çelebi's works were printed on the first Ottoman printing press by Ibrahim Müteferrika.

Gottfried Hagen

Further reading: Gottfried Hagen, "Katib Çelebi." *Historians of the Ottoman Empire.* http://www.ottomanhistorians.

com/database/html/katibcelebi_en.html; Eleazar Birnbaum, "The Questing Mind: Kātib Chelebi, 1609–1657: A Chapter in Ottoman Intellectual History," in *Corolla Torontonensis: Festschrift for Ronald Morton Smith*, edited by E. Robbins and Stella Sandahl (Toronto: University of Toronto, Center for Korean Studies, 1994), 133–158; Geoffrey Lewis, *The Balance of Truth by Katib Chelebi* (London: Luzac, 1957).

al-Kawakibi, Abd al-Rahman (b. 1849–d. 1902) *Arab journalist and nationalist* Abd al-Rahman al-Kawakibi was a prominent journalist in Syria in the late 19th century. He was born in the city of ALEPPO to a family that had produced many highly regarded Islamic scholars, including several muftis, or jurisconsults, in the Hanafi school of law. Al-Kawakibi received a traditional Muslim education that included studying Turkish and Persian, but unlike many of his generation and class, he knew no European languages. In 1878 he entered into a partnership with a merchant, Hashim al-Kharrat, to start a newspaper, *Halab al-Shahba* (Aleppo, the milky-white), in his native city. It soon ran into difficulties with the Ottoman censor in the city and was closed. A second try ended with the same result in 1880. In 1886 he was suspected of helping to plot the attempted assassination of the city's governor. He was not charged with the crime but some of his property was confiscated and his position in Aleppo became increasingly untenable. In 1899 Al-Kawakibi went into exile in Cairo where he wrote articles for Rashid Rida's *al-Manar* (Lighthouse) newspaper until his death in 1902.

Al-Kawakibi is most famous for his book *Umm al-Qurra* (Mother of villages, a nickname for Mecca) published in Cairo in 1899. Like other Arabs of his generation, he bemoaned the rise of Western imperialism and the decayed state of the Islam of his day. But unlike his contemporaries he placed the blame for the decline on Turks generally and Ottomans specifically. He thus became the first Arab Muslim, writing in Arabic, to call for the overthrow of the Ottoman sultanate and its replacement in the Arabic-speaking provinces of the CALIPHATE, a universal political state that would include all Muslims and would be headed by someone from the Prophet's tribe, the Quraysh. Although he named no candidate, it was apparent that he meant the clan of the Hashimis. Islam remained at the heart of his imagined future polity, but this polity was to be defined as ethnically Arab. This was a clear break from the future envisioned by those who followed AL-AFGHANI's desire for a pan-Islamic state. Scholars have argued that al-Kawakibi took his vision directly from the British writer William Blunt, whose *The Future of Islam* (1882) argued many of the same points and whose work was available in an Arabic translation in the 1890s.

Bruce Masters

Further reading: Joseph Rahme, "Abd al-Rahman al-Kawakibi's Reformist Ideology, Arab Pan-Islamism, and the Internal Other." *Journal of Islamic Studies* 10 (1999) 159–77.

khan See CARAVANSARY.

Khayr al-Din Pasha (Tunuslu Hayreddin) (d. 1889) *grand vizier of the Ottoman Empire and Tunisian political reformer* Known in Ottoman Turkish as Tunuslu (the Tunisian) Hayreddin, Khayr al-Din Pasha was a leading advocate of political reform in TUNIS and later in the Ottoman Empire. He was born in the 1820s into an Abkhaz family, part of an ethnic group living in the Caucasus region of RUSSIA. When his father was killed fighting the Russians, his mother sent him to be a MAMLUK in Istanbul. There he eventually entered the household of Ahmed Bey, the ruler of Tunis. Ahmed Bey gave Khayr al-Din a Western education and then sent his young protégé to Paris where he was involved in a protracted legal affair involving claims of a former Tunisian minister against Ahmed Bey. The four years Khayr al-Din spent in Paris proved formative; living in the West, he concluded that Muslim countries needed to modernize politically and economically if they were to retain their independence.

Upon his return to Tunis, Khayr al-Din was appointed by the bey to head the Ministry of the Navy. He also served on the board that promulgated Tunis's constitution in 1860 and was involved in diplomatic maneuvers in Istanbul, trying to convince the sultan to recognize the hereditary right of the Husayni line to the governorship of Tunis. In return, the bey of Tunis would acknowledge Ottoman sovereignty and pay a yearly tribute. But the sultan was not in a position to anger France, which had colonial designs on Tunis, and he demurred. Between 1873 and 1877, Khayr al-Din served as prime minister of Tunis and tried to implement civil and religious reforms. Muslim traditionalists and European interests succeeded in blocking most of his schemes, but Khayr al-Din did succeed in setting up a modern school where European languages and the sciences would be taught. That model would serve as the foundation of a modern school system for the entire country.

His brash style and zeal for reform, however, won him few friends at court. In 1877 the French consul in Tunis, Theodore Roustan, formed an alliance with Mustafa ibn Ismail, a close friend of Ahmed Bey, that succeeded in getting Khayr al-Din dismissed from office and his constitution suspended. Khayr al-Din then went to Istanbul and, in December 1878, was made grand vizier. He only lasted in that position a few months, however, before his push for wider reforms clashed with the vision of the future promoted by Sultan ABDÜLHAMID II (r. 1876–1909), and Khayr al-Din retired from public office.

Khayr al-Din is best remembered for his book *Aqwam al-masalik fi marifat al-ahwal al-mamalik* (The most sound paths to the knowledge of the conditions of political rule), published in Tunis in 1867 and later translated into French. Khayr al-Din set out the successes of various Western states in detail in his book. He then went on to outline the reasons for their success, which in his analysis were the rule of law and the practice of consultation between the ruler and the ruled. Khayr al-Din cited the works of European scholars to demonstrate that the glories of Islamic civilization in the past were universally acknowledged. He then argued that Islam as a civilization could be great again. The key to this transformation, he wrote, was the adaptation of Western ideas of constitutional government into an Islamic framework. He invoked the Islamic legal concept of *maslahat,* an exigency that is necessary for the public good, to explain that such a change was not only permissible according to Islamic law but also required by it. Khayr al-Din, having experienced the actual problems of trying to govern, sought to theorize the process of reform that he felt was required if Muslims were to remain independent of European control. His book was widely read by the Arab elite, and because it was also translated into Turkish, Khayr al-Din became the first political philosopher to put forward a practical agenda for reforming the Muslim world in a language accessible to its elite ruling classes.

Bruce Masters

Further reading: Khayr al-Din Tunisi, *The Surest Path: The Political Treatise of a Nineteenth-Century Muslim Statesman* (Cambridge, Mass.: Harvard University Press, 1967).

khedive (hidiv)   The title *khedive* was invented to distinguish the rulers of EGYPT in the line of MEHMED ALI from other provincial governors in the Ottoman Empire. It was used from 1867 until 1914. Until the mid-19th century, the rulers of Egypt were traditionally considered governors of an Ottoman province; thus all official correspondence from ISTANBUL refers to them simply by the title *vali,* or governor. This did not distinguish the governors of Egypt from those who were appointed by the sultan to other provincial capitals and who could be removed at his will. Starting with Mehmed Ali, Egyptian internal documents began to refer to the governor as khedive, or in the Turkish that served as the language of government in Egypt, *hidiv.* The word, meaning "king," was Persian in origin, but it was rarely used in contemporary Iranian or Ottoman documents. Therefore the title had symbolic meaning that conferred upon the bearer a status that exalted him above other provincial governors. At the same time, it made no explicit claim to sovereignty

that might offend the Ottoman sultan. After numerous gifts and the dispatch of Egyptian troops to help suppress a rebellion in CRETE, Sultan ABDÜLAZIZ (r. 1861–76) officially conferred the title of khedive on ISMAIL in 1867. Thereafter all his successors bore that title until 1914, when the British proclaimed Egypt an independent sultanate under their protection.

Bruce Masters

Kirkuk   *See* SHAHRIZOR.

Kızılbaş (Kızıl Baş)   Kızılbaş, or "Redhead," was the disparaging name that the Ottomans applied to the Turkoman tribesmen who followed Shah Ismail I (r. 1501–24) in a revolt against Ottoman control in eastern Anatolia at the end of the 15th century. The name came from the distinctive twelve-tasseled red hat they wore, a visible symbol of their belief that Shah Ismail was the promised 12th imam of SHIA ISLAM who had returned from his occultation, begun in the eighth century, to bring justice to the earth. Although the term originates specifically with this movement, after the 1511 rebellion, Ottoman jurists commonly applied the term Kızılbaş to any heterodox Muslim sect they believed to be in rebellion against the sultan's authority.

The Turkoman tribes had originally arrived in eastern Anatolia in the 11th century with the migration of Turkic peoples into what is today Turkey. Other tribes were pushed westward by Mongol expansion, and still others had ridden with the Mongols and settled with their herds in the region where they found kinsmen already present. The result was a volatile political mix; warfare among the various Turkoman tribes, and between the Turkomans and the indigenous Kurdish clans who claimed the same space, was common. In the 15th century many of the Turkoman tribes had coalesced around the leadership of Uzun Hasan of the Akkoyunlu confederation, a tribal confederation that controlled much of northern Iraq and eastern Turkey. But after Uzun Hasan's defeat at the hands of Sultan Fatih MEHMED II (r. 1444–46; 1451–81) in 1473, the sultan suppressed the tribes militarily and sought to subject them to direct rule from Istanbul, a move that included the routine payment of taxes.

It was within this political context that Shah Ismail Safavi took control of the lands once ruled by the Akkoyunlu in Azerbaijan and, in 1501, declared himself to be the long-awaited imam. Through the dervishes of his Sufi order, Shah Ismail had already established a propaganda network amidst the Turkomans under nominal Ottoman control. Under Shah Ismail's influence, these rose in rebellion in 1511 and initiated a path of destruction across Anatolia on their way to BURSA. Their seemingly unstoppable advance caused Prince Selim to move against his father, Sultan BAYEZID II (r. 1481–1512), and force his abdication as Selim felt his father's age rendered him incapable of mounting an adequate defense. Upon his assumption of the throne, Sultan SELIM I (r. 1512–20) mounted a campaign against the Kızılbaş that culminated in the Battle of Çaldiran on August 23, 1514, in which Selim defeated Shah Ismail's army. After the defeat, Shah Ismail retreated into Iran where he established Shia Islam as the state religion and his dynasty, the Safavids, as the ruling family of Iran for the next two centuries.

Despite this defeat, unrest in the shah's name continued to contest Ottoman control in eastern Anatolia for the next two centuries. The Ottomans' successful incorporation of the Turkomans' rivals, the Kurds, into provincial administration did much to weaken the possibility of another significant rebellion like the one in 1511. The so-called Kızılbaş movement lived on in eastern Anatolia in the form of the Alevis (see ALAWI) whose poetry venerated Shah Ismail and predicted his return to usher in a reign of justice.

Bruce Masters

Knights of St. John (Knights Hospitaller; Knights of Malta)   The Knights of St. John were a Christian military order with their roots in the First Crusade at the end of the 12th century. They were charged with the defense of Christian pilgrims traveling to the Holy Land. With the Muslim reconquest of Jerusalem in 1187, the Knights had to find a new home and, after several interim residences, ended up on the island of RHODES in the southeastern Aegean in 1309. With the Ottoman rise to power in the 14th century, their capture of Constantinople, the capital of the BYZANTINE EMPIRE, in 1453, and their slow extension of control over the islands of the Aegean, it was only a matter of time before the Ottoman rulers and the Knights of St. John came into conflict. At the beginning of the 16th century, there remained several important Latin (western Christian) enclaves that had held out against Ottoman imperial expansion. Ensconced in the well-fortified city of Rhodes, from which they sailed forth to do battle with the Ottoman fleet, the Knights of St. John were among the most formidable of these holdouts. An initial Ottoman attempt to take the island in 1480 failed and Sultan SÜLEYMAN I (r. 1520–66) was determined to rid his empire of this threatening Christian presence in the middle of what was otherwise Ottoman territory. He laid siege to the island in 1522, and this time the Ottomans were triumphant. Somewhat surprisingly, Süleyman allowed survivors to depart the island, in exchange for the promise that henceforth they would refrain from engaging in hostilities against the empire.

This was a promise that the Knights failed to keep. After seven years of wandering around the Mediterranean, they were settled on the small, stony island of MALTA by order of Pope Clement VIII and Charles V of Spain. The symbolic rent that they paid for this to the Viceroy of Sicily was, in fact, one Maltese falcon per year, a form of payment made famous by the 1941 film *The Maltese Falcon* starring Humphrey Bogart. Once installed on the island in 1530, the Knights resumed their attacks on the Ottoman Empire, fighting formal wars together with their perennial European allies SPAIN and the papacy, as well as conducting smaller-scale raids against Ottoman shipping in a practice known as the *corso* (see CORSAIRS AND PIRATES).

As the European fervor for crusade waned in the 16th century, the crusading order of the Knights, with their professed hostility toward all things Muslim, slowly became something of an anachronism. By the 17th century they were widely criticized for having abandoned the supposed Christian purity of earlier centuries; under the Knights, the Maltese capital of Valetta became a city of pleasure where young men newly appointed to the order spent as much time in brothels and in taverns as they did on ships, nominally engaged in battling the infidel but acting effectively as pirates. Nevertheless, financial donations continued to come in from across Catholic Europe, and the Knights of Malta, as they came to be called, still enjoyed substantial prestige, enough so that joining the order continued as a viable option for many younger sons of the aristocracy who could not hope to inherit their fathers' estates. Small and inhospitable as the island of Malta was, the Knights could not have survived without European support. They hung on until 1798, when NAPOLEON BONAPARTE occupied the island and formally abolished the order.

Molly Greene

Further reading: Peter Earle, *Corsairs of Malta and Barbary* (London: Sidgwick & Jackson, 1970); H. J. A. Sire, *The Knights of Malta* (New Haven, Conn.: Yale University Press, 1994).

Köprülü family   The Köprülüs were among the few vizieral households who played a central role in the Ottoman political establishment. Between 1656 and 1695, several members of the family served as grand viziers and successfully worked to solve some of the problems of the empire which had been experiencing interrelated dynastic, political, economic, and social crises since the 1640s.

KÖPRÜLÜ MEHMED PASHA

The name of the family stems from the association of its founder, Köprülü Mehmed Pasha (d. 1661), with the town of Köprü, then located in the province of Amasya in

The Köprülü Mosque was built by the founder of the most influential grand vizieral family of the Ottoman Empire, Köprülü Mehmed Pasha. *(Photo by Gábor Ágoston)*

Anatolia. Mehmed Pasha was originally from the village of Rudnik in ALBANIA. His first visit to Köprü appears to have taken place when he left his service in the TOPKAPI PALACE and served as a *sipahi*, or cavalry officer, in the town where he ultimately settled and established his household.

In his youth, Mehmed Pasha was recruited through the DEVŞIRME system, the Ottoman practice of child levy, and brought to ISTANBUL. He was educated in the PALACE SCHOOL (Enderun Mektebi) and passed through a number of positions in the sultan's service. By 1623, he was serving in the palace kitchens. Later, as sword-bearer of Sultan MURAD IV (r. 1623–40), he entered the ranks of the privy chamber. However, his quarrelsomeness and disobedience led to the termination of his palace service and he went out to the provinces as a member of the cavalry or *sipahi*. When he came to Köprü, Mehmed Pasha married Ayşe Hanım, the daughter of Yusuf Agha, the *voievod* (or mayor) of the town. When Mehmed Pasha's former patron Hüsrev Agha became the agha of the JANISSARIES, Köprülü reentered his service, becoming his treasurer when Hüsrev Pasha assumed the grand vizierate in 1628. Following Hüsrev Pasha's execution in 1632,

Mehmed Pasha served in various positions both in the capital and the provinces; he was elevated to the rank of vizier by 1645. In 1647, Mehmed Pasha was assigned to suppress a major rebellion led by the governor of Sivas (in central Anatolia). He fell prisoner to the rebel governor in 1648 as his army advanced toward Istanbul, but was rescued.

In the ensuing years, Köprülü Mehmed Pasha's career was affected by incessant factional struggles and favoritism in the capital. Köprülü was initially recommended as candidate for the grand vizierate by royal architect Kasım Agha, a fellow countryman of Köprülü. Kasım Agha's initiative resulted in Köprülü becoming a vizier of the imperial council, a position that could lead to the grand vizierate, but the reigning GRAND VIZIER, Gürcü Mehmed Pasha (1651–52), outmaneuvered Köprülü, banishing him to the provincial governorship of Kustendil in southwestern BULGARIA. Finally, in 1656, efforts made on his behalf resulted in Köprülü Mehmed Pasha being made grand vizier.

Köprülü's appointment to the grand vizierate marks a critical point in 17th-century Ottoman history. Although his career thus far had not been characterized by any resounding success, his actions as grand vizier proved his worth in this important office in a troubled age. Among his first actions was dealing with the Kadızadeliler, a puritanical sectarian group involved in factional politics since the reign of MURAD IV (1623–40). Köprülü Mehmed Pasha quickly managed to banish the group's ringleaders to CYPRUS and quieted the religious criticisms against the clerical establishment they had been provoking in Istanbul. He then secured permission from the sultan for the executions of certain individuals, such as Abaza Ahmed Pasha, accused of laxity in the war against VENICE (1645–69), and the patriarch of the Orthodox Church, Parthenius III, who was accused of seditious activities. Thanks to the authority delegated to him by the sultan, Mehmed Pasha also ordered the execution of many unruly officers and soldiers of the cavalry regiments. His bloody measures aimed to root out the troublemakers who had been part of the political turmoil since 1648, but these actions also caused widespread dissent in the provinces.

By 1657 Mehmed Pasha had recovered the islands of Bozcaada and Limnos which had been lost to the Venetians during his predecessor's time; this ended the Venetian blockage of the Strait of Dardanelles, which had been severely hindering Ottoman military campaigns in the CRETAN WAR of 1645–69. Mehmed Pasha then shifted his attention to the pressing problems in TRANSYLVANIA created by Prince George Rákóczi II (r. 1648–60), who was making a bid for independence. This Ottoman vassal was also marching against POLAND and inciting the neighboring Ottoman vassal states of WALLACHIA and MOLDAVIA to act with him. Istanbul defeated them in 1658, but before Mehmed Pasha was able to establish stability in this troubled area his plans were thwarted by a major revolt in Anatolia in which dozens of Ottoman officials under the leadership of ALEPPO governor Abaza Hasan Pasha rebelled against the heavy-handed rule of the grand vizier. The sultan's army, moved from the Balkans to Anatolia to suppress the rebellion, was initially defeated (in December 1658), but Murtaza Pasha, the commander of the sultan's army, later managed to deceive and execute the ringleaders in Aleppo in February 1659.

Following this success, Köprülü embarked on solving other interrelated internal problems with the goal of bringing further stability to the empire. He successfully dealt with revolts in DAMASCUS, CAIRO, and Antalya and sent Ismail Pasha, his proxy in Istanbul, to the eastern borderlands to seek out, seize, and punish any insubordinate person regardless of rank or status. Ismail Pasha restored order in the country and in his inspections confiscated 80,000 handguns found illegally in the possession of peasants. In the meantime, Köprülü Mehmed Pasha organized royal trips for the sultan in order to manifest his sovereign's majesty. He traveled with the sultan from Istanbul to BURSA, Çanakkale, and EDIRNE. On September 30, 1661, Mehmed Pasha died in Edirne, leaving behind a more stable, tranquil empire. He also left numerous endowments (see WAQF) in different parts of the empire, far more than were founded by members of the Ottoman dynasty during this period.

KÖPRÜLÜ FAZIL AHMED PASHA

The son and successor of Köprülü Mehmed Pasha, Fazıl Ahmed (b. 1635–d. 1676) was born in Köprü but at the age of seven he was brought by his father to Istanbul, where he studied under the leading scholars of the period. After this he quickly rose in the religious hierarchy in Istanbul, thanks to his father's influence. By 1657, he was teaching at the college of Süleymaniye, but was upset by rumors circulating among the ulema that he had achieved his position not by erudition but by favoritism and thus he left his learned profession to begin an administrative career. In 1659, at the request of his father, Fazıl Ahmed was appointed to the governorship of Erzurum with the rank of vizier. In 1660 he was transferred to DAMASCUS. There he won great popularity for lifting the taxes imposed on the local people by his predecessors, thus removing the cause of most brigandage in the region. Soon he was called to the capital to become the deputy grand vizier and hence to succeed his ailing father. Upon his father's death in 1661, Fazıl Ahmed assumed the grand vizierate as planned. For the first time in Ottoman history, a son succeeded his father as grand vizier.

Fazıl Ahmed Pasha's 15-year tenure in this post was marked by a number of military campaigns. He first decided to deal with unsettled issues in Transylvania. In January 1662, when the Transylvanian Prince János

Kemény (r. 1661–62) was killed in battle, the Ottomans installed Prince Mihály Apafi (r. 1661–90) in his place and established some measure of order in the region. The Habsburgs were uneasy with such Ottoman direct intervention in Transylvania, especially because Kemény had declined to accept the sultan as his overlord and had sided with the Habsburgs, but no conciliation was found between the two sides. The following year, Fazıl Ahmed's successful campaign against the Habsburgs resulted in the capture of Érsekújvár (present-day Nové Zámky in Slovakia), a fortress regarded by the Habsburgs as the last major obstacle to the Ottoman advance to the Habsburg capital of Vienna. This Ottoman success aroused great concern in Europe and led to the formation of a large Habsburg army commanded by Raimondo Montecuccoli and supported by the papacy, SPAIN, some German princes, and FRANCE. At the Battle of Szentgotthárd (western Hungary) on August 1, 1664, the Ottoman army under the command of Fazıl Ahmed Pasha was defeated, but the outcome was by no means decisive. Both parties suffered heavy losses and the Ottomans took a more defensive policy thereafter by concluding the Treaty of Vasvár on August 10, 1664, which left them in possession of Érsekújvár and assured their influence in Transylvania.

The next year Fazıl Ahmed undertook a major effort to capture Candia (present-day Iráklion) in CRETE. The costly Cretan War had been going on for more than two decades and the grand vizier wanted to see its end. In the autumn of 1669, after spending four years in military campaigning, Fazıl Ahmed succeeded in capturing Crete from the Venetians. He immediately took measures to revitalize the local economy and to complete the Ottomanization of the island.

By the summer of 1670 Fazıl Ahmed was back in Istanbul and two years later he joined forces with a group of Ukrainian COSSACKS to lead a campaign against the Commonwealth of Poland. The grand vizier, accompanied by sultan Mehmed IV (r. 1648–87) and Prince Mustafa, targeted the fortress of KAMANIÇE, which was quickly captured in August 1672. The Ottomans also annexed Podolia from Poland. When Poland rejected the terms of the treaty, Ottoman campaigns led by Fazıl Ahmed continued in 1673 and 1674. Also in 1674, the Ottoman army stopped Russian incursions and brought western UKRAINE under Ottoman suzerainty.

The 1675 and 1676 campaigns against Poland were left to others as Fazıl Ahmed suffered increasingly from the effects of his alcoholism. The grand vizier died on November 3, 1676 at the age of 41. His tenure was one of the longest in Ottoman history and saw the last major territorial expansion of the empire. Like his father, Fazıl Ahmed had established his own pious foundations, among which was a manuscript library near the covered BAZAAR in Istanbul, which is still functioning (*see* LIBRARIES).

FAZIL MUSTAFA PASHA

The younger brother of Fazıl Ahmed Pasha, Fazıl Mustafa Pasha (b. 1637–d. 1691) was born in Köprü. He began his education with his brother in Istanbul and in 1659 he entered the ranks of the sultan's guards in the palace. It seems that he had spent most of his time with his elder brother on military campaigns. In 1680, at the instigation of his brother-in-law, the grand vizier Merzifonlu Kara Mustafa Pasha, Fazıl Mustafa Pasha became the seventh vizier in the imperial council. Later he rose in the government ranks and by 1683 he had become the third vizier. Following the Vienna debacle (*see* VIENNA, SIEGES OF) and the death of Merzifonlu Kara Mustafa Pasha in 1683, the Köprülü family suffered from the enmity of the new grand vizier, Kara Ibrahim Pasha, who

banished Fazıl Mustafa Pasha from the center of politics in Istanbul and forced him to serve as commander of the fortresses on the Dardanelles.

Fazıl Mustafa's fortunes changed, however, in 1687 when a rebellious army made his brother-in-law Siyavuş Pasha grand vizier. The army forced Sultan Mehmed IV to abdicate the throne in favor of his son, Sultan SÜLEYMAN II (r. 1687–91). Unsympathetic to the former sultan, Fazıl Mustafa seems to have been closely involved in this dethronement; in the resulting change of government Fazıl Mustafa was summoned to Istanbul as second vizier and deputy to the grand vizier. Soon, however, he was exiled again, and was reappointed commander of the Dardanelles fortress. He was saved from an even worse fate thanks to the refusal of the ŞEYHÜLISLAM to sanction his execution. Until 1689, Fazıl Mustafa served as commander of Chania (Khania, Crete), then of Candia (Iráklion, Crete), and finally of Chios. At the instigation

The Köprülü Library in Istanbul was part of a foundation by the Köprülü family, who were patrons of education. *(Photo by Gábor Ágoston)*

of a faction in Istanbul, which was deeply concerned by the worsening position of the Ottomans before the armies of the Holy League on the European fronts, Fazıl Mustafa was called back to assume the grand vizierate in October 1689.

As a grand vizier, Fazıl Mustafa's first act was to lower the taxes that had been imposed to finance the continuing wars on multiple fronts. In July 1690 he personally led the army and, despite the lateness of the military campaign season and the opposition of his commander, he succeeded in recapturing BELGRADE from the Habsburgs who had conquered it two years earlier. In the winter of 1690–91 Fazıl Mustafa was occupied with internal problems such as suppressing the insurgency in EGYPT, instituting reforms in the JANISSARIES, and cutting expenses in the imperial treasury. In June 1691 Fazıl Mustafa once again took to the field and moved against the Austrians. In the Battle of Slankamen (northwest of Belgrade) on August 19, 1691, he was struck in the forehead by a bullet and killed.

Fazıl Mustafa Pasha was grand vizier for less than two years, but in this short time he proved himself an able commander and a strong reformer. Mindful of the factionalism in the court and government that undermined his authority, Fazıl Mustafa took steps to limit the number and the power of the viziers in the imperial council. He also lessened the tax obligations of the population. He established councils of notables in the provinces, modeled on the imperial government, to control the abuse of power by local magnates and bureaucrats. Furthermore, he ended the tradition of state officials giving gifts to the sultans during religious festivals. His reforms in the administration of the empire, some in response to the exigencies of the time, had far-reaching effects in the ensuing decades. Fazıl Mustafa Pasha was also a learned man, particularly in the fields of Islamic law and lexicography. He had three sons: Numan, Abdullah, and Esad.

Köprülü Numan Pasha served as grand vizier from 1710 to 1711, and other members of the Köprülü family continued to make a mark in political life down to the present day.

Günhan Börekçi

Further reading: Caroline Finkel, *Osman's Dream: The Story of the Ottoman Empire, 1300–1923* (London: John Murray, 2005), 253–328; M. T. Gökbilgin and R. C. Repp, "Köprülü," In *Encyclopaedia of Islam*, 2nd ed., vol. 5, edited by C. E. Bosworth, E. van Donzel, B. Lewis, and Ch. Pellat (Leiden: Brill, 1960–), 256–263; Metin Kunt, "The Waqf as an Instrument of Public Policy: Notes on the Köprülü Family Endowments, in *Studies in Ottoman History: In Honor of Professor V.L. Ménage*, edited by Colin Heywood and Colin Imber (Istanbul: ISIS, 1994), 189–198; Metin Kunt, "Naima, Köprülü and the Grand Vezirate." *Boğaziçi Üniversitesi Dergisi* 1 (1973), 57–62.

Kosovo, Battle of (1389) The Battle of Kosovo between the Serbian and Ottoman armies has great significance both as a military encounter and as a symbolic event for later Serbian historical consciousness. The battle is thought to have taken place on June 15, 1389, on the Plain of Kosovo, probably near Priština where the *türbe*, or mausoleum, of Sultan MURAD I (r. 1362–89) still stands. Led by Prince Lazar Hrebeljanović, the Serbian army was strengthened with squads sent by King Tvrtko of Bosnia. The Ottoman army, led by Murad I, included vassals from southern Europe as well as some Serbian nobility. The size of the armies, the course of the battle, and even its outcome are still contested by historians, but some crucial facts are undisputed: Both rulers were killed, and both sides suffered heavy losses. In particular, losses within the Serbian aristocracy were so great that SERBIA thereafter lost its military and economic resources for further warfare. Sources written soonest after the battle claim victory for the Christian Serbs and say that the Muslim Ottomans retreated immediately after the battle, but these were written by Christian authors and their objectivity must be questioned.

Despite the failure of reliable historical detail, the story of the battle has played a significant role in the Serbian historical imagination and has served as an important tool for national political propaganda. The Serbian oral tradition, especially after the 16th century, turned the unknown outcome of the battle into a defeat, creating a tale of a fateful Serbian-Ottoman battle that led to the downfall of the medieval Serbian state. This myth, disseminated through a rich epic tradition, was influenced by the centuries-long Ottoman occupation of the territory of the former Serbian state. In the 19th century and at the beginning of the 20th century, the myth was successfully used as a motivating factor in the wars of liberation against the Ottoman Empire.

Aleksandar Fotić

See also BAZEYID I; MURAD I.

Further reading: T. A. Emmert, *Serbian Golgotha: Kosovo, 1389* (New York: East European Monographs, 1990).

Küçük Kaynarca, Treaty of (Kuchuk Kainardji, Treaty of; Kücük Kaynardja, Treaty of) (1774) This peace treaty, signed at the village of the same name (in present-day northeastern Bulgaria) on July 21, 1774, brought to an end the RUSSO-OTTOMAN WAR of 1768–74. Containing 28 public articles and two secret ones, the treaty generated much controversy among contemporary diplomats and continued to generate controversy among historians regarding the interpretation of some of its articles and due to its long-term effects on the history of the Middle East.

By the formal terms of the treaty, the Ottomans granted independence to the Crimean Khanate, a concession that was actually a prelude to the Crimea's annexation by RUSSIA in 1783. This annexation led, in turn, to the RUSSO-OTTOMAN WAR of 1787–92.

According to article three of the treaty, the Ottoman sultan would maintain his religious authority as the caliph over an independent Crimea, creating a separation between the spiritual and secular authority of the Ottoman sultan for the first time in the Ottoman Empire's history. Russia gained a strong presence in the Black Sea through the acquisition of several fortresses in the region such as Kılburnu, Kerc, Yenikale, and AZAK, as well as the territories of the Greater and Lesser Kabarda steppes that lay to the north of the Caucasus Mountains. The treaty granted Russian merchants commercial privileges as well as unrestricted access to the BLACK SEA and the Mediterranean via sea and overland routes. The treaty also permitted Russia to open consulates in any place in the Ottoman Empire in addition to their permanent embassy in ISTANBUL.

MOLDAVIA and WALLACHIA remained under Ottoman suzerainty but Russia was accorded a special position in the affairs of these Romanian principalities that it used as a pretext to interfere with the internal affairs of the Ottoman Empire. In the treaty, the Ottomans also recognized the title of "empress or emperor of all the Russians," while Russia was to withdraw its troops from the Caucasus Mountains and hand over the islands it had occupied in the Aegean to the Ottomans. Finally, the Ottomans were obliged to pay a heavy war indemnity of 15.000 purses (7.5 million gurush/4.5 million rubles).

Articles 7 and 14 of the treaty later caused much trouble in international relations as their deliberate misinterpretation provided the pretext for future Russian pretensions of being the protector of Ottoman Orthodox Christians—ultimately one of the motivating factors for the CRIMEAN WAR (1853–56). Article 14 permitted Russia to establish a Russian Orthodox church, separate from the Russian embassy chapel, in the GALATA district of Istanbul for local Russian nationals; article 7 granted Russia the right to represent this church and its personnel. Actually, article 7 was intended to reinforce the protection of the Ottoman Sublime Porte over its Christian subjects by stating "the Sublime Porte promises a firm protection to the Christian religion and to its churches."

The contemporary Habsburg diplomat Franz Thugut's initial judgment of the treaty was that it signaled "Russian skill and Turkish imbecility." This assessment has had a great impact on how later historians viewed the treaty. Other contemporary observers, unaware that the official French translation of the treaty provided to them by the Russians was flawed, also cited article 14 to legitimize Russia's claim with regard to the Ottoman Orthodox Christians. This treaty is noted by later historians to have been crucial in the emergence of the so-called EASTERN QUESTION as well as creating ongoing problems for the Crimean TATARS that ultimately led to Joseph Stalin's "ethnic cleansing" of Crimean Tatars from their homeland during World War II. It also signifies the beginning of the Period of Dismemberment of the Ottoman Empire in modern Turkish historiography as it marked the first time that an Ottoman sultan was compelled to withdraw from a territory (the Crimea) whose inhabitants were primarily Muslims and not Christians.

Kahraman Şakul

Further reading: Virginia Aksan, *An Ottoman Statesman in War and Peace Ahmed Resmi Efendi, 1700–1783* (Leiden: Brill, 1995), 162-167; Virginia Aksan, *Ottoman Wars 1700-1870: An Empire Besieged* (Longman, 2007), 158-160; Roderic H. Davison, "Russian Skill and Turkish Imbecility: The Treaty of Kuchuk Kainardji Reconsidered." *Slavic Review* 35, no. 3 (1976): 463–483; Caroline Finkel, *Osman's Dream: The Story of the Ottoman Empire, 1300–1923* (London: John Murray, 2005), 377–381; Colin J. Heywood, "Küčük Kaynardja," in *Encyclopaedia of Islam*, 2nd ed., vol. 5 (Leiden: Brill, 1960–), 312–313; Ekmeleddin İhsanoğlu, ed., *History of the Ottoman State, Society, and Civilisation*, vol. 1 (Istanbul: Ircica, 2001), 61–64.

kul (slave)   *See* JANISSARIES; SLAVERY.

Kurdistan   *See* KURDS.

Kurds   The Kurds are a people who speak various dialects of a language related to Persian. During the early Ottoman period, any of the tribal peoples who were the indigenous Muslim inhabitants of the mountainous region known as Kurdistan were called Kurds. Although their neighbors identified them collectively as Kurds, this name was only adopted as a means of self-identification at the end of the Ottoman period. They were thereby distinguished from the Turkoman tribes who had settled more recently in the region. Over time, however, the definition of *Kurd* has shifted from one based in geography to one dependent on language. The sense that Islamic faith is a defining characteristic of Kurdish identity has persisted into the modern period, however, even after language became a key factor in determining who was a Kurd.

Many of the Christians and Jews who inhabited the mountains of Kurdistan also spoke Kurdish as their mother tongue, but these individuals were never called Kurds in Ottoman sources, nor did Muslim Kurds consider them to be Kurds until the late 20th century when the rhetoric of Kurdish nationalism became more inclusive. The fragmentation of the Kurdish people that slowed the emergence of a collective cultural identity was a product of three factors: their mountainous homeland; the fact that they spoke four largely mutually unintelligible dialects, none of which had established written forms; and their division into often mutually antagonistic tribes and clans. The last of the three was undoubtedly the most crucial, as feuds and open warfare between Kurdish tribes were commonplace into the 20th century.

The territory the Ottomans called Kurdistan stretched from what is today southeastern TURKEY across parts of SYRIA and northern IRAQ into northeastern IRAN. Strategically placed along the Ottoman Empire's borders with rival Iran, the Kurds were potential allies that the Ottomans sought to enlist to their side. Well-armed, possessing strongly developed martial traditions, and virtually inaccessible in their mountain redoubts, the Kurds were an ally that the Ottomans sought to control but whom they could not conquer. During his campaign against the rebel KIZILBAŞ in the early 16th century, the value of having the Kurds as on his side became apparent to Sultan SELIM I (r. 1512–20).

The Kurds also were looking for an ally. The Turkoman dynasty, the Ak-Koyunlu, had destroyed the power of the Kurdish tribal leaders, the *mirs*, in the 15th century and dominated Kurdistan, the country of the Kurds. Having experienced more than a century of abuse at the hands of the Turkoman tribes, the Kurds were eager to find help to regain control over their land. Sultan Selim became aware of the discontent in Kurdistan from his adviser Idris Bitlisi, a native of the region. He dispatched Idris to the region in advance of his army. Idris was able to convince many of the tribes to fight on the Ottoman side in an alliance that transcended tribal loyalties; Kurdish troops were thus present at the Battle of Çaldiran in 1514 and helped the Ottomans defeat their Persian rivals. When Selim withdrew from Kurdistan after his victory, Kurdish troops successfully defended the strategic town of Diyarbakır against a counterattack by Shah ISMAIL. Most of Kurdistan remained under Ottoman control from that point on. The only region of Kurdistan not under nominal Ottoman control was that controlled by the prince, or *mir*, of Ardalan, a dynasty that dominated much of western Iran from its seat of power in the present-day Iranian town of Sanandaj. The dynasty claimed to be vassals of the Iranian shahs and thus frequently waged war on those Kurds who were allies of the Ottomans.

Most of Ottoman-controlled Kurdistan was contained in three provinces: Diyarbakir, Van, and SHAHRIZOR. Throughout most of the 17th and 18th centuries, the first two had Ottoman military officers as governors while the governor of Shahrizor, with its capital in Kirkuk, was often a local Kurd of the BABAN family. In all three provinces, the Ottomans, following the advice of Idris Bitlisi, appointed *mir*s of various tribes at the district level (*sancak*), and Kurdish levies provided the military forces for the provinces. Local autonomy was the price for Kurdish loyalty to the sultans, and the Ottomans interfered in local politics only when tribal feuding threatened the security of the empire's borders or the trade routes that passed through the mountains of Kurdistan.

For most of the Ottoman period, the majority of the Kurds were shepherds who moved their herds of sheep and goats between summer and winter pasturage. In addition, they also farmed in the mountain valleys. There were few townsmen among them. Christian or Jewish craftsmen, many of whom spoke Aramaic rather than Kurdish as their first language, practiced most of the skilled trades in the towns of Kurdistan. Christian peasants, either NESTORIANS or JACOBITES, also did much of the farming for Kurdish landlords.

KURDISH LANGUAGE

Kurdish was not a written language until the very end of the Ottoman period; for example, in the 17th century, the Kurdish historian Sherefhan Bitlisi wrote his *Sharafnamah* (Book of honor), now recognized as the classic history of Kurdistan, in the Persian language. Other Kurdish intellectuals wrote in Arabic. But as Persian shares much vocabulary with Kurdish and has similar rules of grammar, it was the favorite literary language of the Kurds until the late 19th century when rules for writing Kurdish in Arabic script were first formulated. The popular Kurdish epic poem, *Mem-u Zin*, was part of a centuries-long oral tradition, but it was not written down until that time. But the attempt at standardizing Kurdish as a literary language was not a complete success as Kurdish has four distinct dialects: Kurmanji, Sorani, Gurani, and Zaza. Each dialect had proponents who put their dialect forward as the standard. In the 20th century, the quest for a standardized Kurdish was further plagued by those who preferred the Latin alphabet over the Arabic one.

With the exception of the speakers of the Zaza dialect of Kurdish who lived in what is today south-central Turkey and who were Alevis (see ALAWI), and the YAZIDIS of Jabal Sinjar in northern Iraq, most Kurds were Sunni Muslims who followed the Shafii tradition, one of the four Sunni legal schools, although the various Sufi orders were also extremely popular.

RELATIONS WITH THE OTTOMANS

The unofficial compact between the various Kurdish tribal leaders and the Ottoman government whereby the Kurds would be left to their own autonomy in return for their defense of the empire's borders began to break down in the 19th century. In part, this was due to schemes in Istanbul to strengthen the empire by centralizing political control of the provinces in the capital. But it was also due to a growing perception by Kurdish leaders that Ottoman power was waning. In addition, as American and British MISSIONARIES settled among them and opened schools and clinics, the Aramaic-speaking Christians who lived in Kurdistan and had served as vassals of the Kurdish *mirs* became more assertive of their rights.

It was the latter reason that motivated Bedirhan, the *mir* of Botan, a region in southeastern Anatolia, to attack Nestorian settlements in the 1840s. Christian missionaries protested his raids to the British ambassador in Istanbul who called upon the sultan to defend his subjects. This led to a military confrontation between Bedirhan and the Ottoman army in 1847. Bedirhan lost the battle and went into exile, although his descendants were prominent in the Kurdish national movement at the end of the 19th century.

A more serious challenge to Ottoman authority came from the Shemdinan family who also controlled territory in southeastern Anatolia. Unlike most Kurdish leaders who were hereditary *mirs* of their tribes, the Shemdinan family gained its prestige from their role as leaders in the NAQSHBANDI Order of SUFISM. For instance, during the Russo-Ottoman War of 1876–78, when a war-induced famine caused heavy mortality among the Kurds, many who turned to spiritual leaders for support found it in the charismatic Shemdinan family. The leader of the clan, Sayyid Ubaydallah, raised the standard of revolt against the Ottoman Empire in 1880, stating as his reason that after the Treaty of Berlin in 1878, the Armenians in eastern Anatolia would establish their own state. But he also proclaimed that he would restore order to the bandit-plagued region, claiming that neither Iran nor the Ottoman Empire was capable of doing so. In 1881 Sayyid Ubaydallah invaded Iran but was defeated. Upon his return to Ottoman territories he surrendered and went into exile. Contemporary European observers claimed that Ubaydallah had hoped to establish an independent Kurdistan, although it is not clear from Kurdish or Ottoman sources that such indeed was his intent.

In the aftermath of the revolt, Sultan ABDÜLHAMID II (r. 1876–1909) sought to co-opt any future Kurdish unrest by creating a Kurdish cavalry unit modeled on the Cossack regiments of Russia. This was called the HAMIDIYE, after the sultan. The sons of the *mirs* were recruited into units made up of their tribesmen, which the Ottoman sultan hoped would also be used against any outbreaks of nationalist agitation for an independent Armenia in eastern Anatolia. In 1893, after a tax revolt of Armenian peasants in the Sasun region, west of Lake Van, the Hamidiye went into action against Armenians throughout the Lake Van region, killing thousands in a series of massacres between 1894 and 1896. Abdülhamid had succeeded in winning the loyalty of the Kurdish tribes to his regime but it had come at the expense of fur-

ther polarizing existing tensions between Armenians and Kurds in southeastern Anatolia, thereby setting the stage for additional massacres in 1915.

With the revolution of 1908 that restored the Ottoman constitution, leading to wider political and cultural rights, Kurdish intellectuals in Istanbul began to create Kurdish cultural and political organizations. One such organization was the Society of Mutual Aid for Progress in Kurdistan. It was headed by Abd al-Qadir, a son of Ubaydallah of Shemdinan, but also included descendants of Bedirhan. The society sought to promote educational and economic progress in Kurdistan and to improve the deteriorating communal relations between Kurds and Armenians. Kurdish students in Istanbul founded a more overtly nationalist organization, Hivi-ya Kurd (Kurdish hope), in 1910. At first a secret society, Hivi-ya Kurd was legalized in 1912. With its newspaper *Roj-e Kurd* (Kurdish sun) the organization sought to standardize and promote written Kurdish and to instill Kurdish national sentiments in its readers. However, the nationalist sentiments that were developing among the Kurds in the capital and a few provincial centers such as MOSUL and Diyarbakir had little impact on the majority of Kurds who remained illiterate and tribal in their loyalties.

Bruce Masters

Further reading: Martin van Bruinessen, *Agha, Shaikh and State: The Social and Political Structures of Kurdistan* (London: Zed Books, 1992); Hakan Özoğlu, *Kurdish Notables and the Ottoman State* (Albany: State University of New York, 2004).

Kuwait (Kuweit, Koweit; *Turk.*: Küveyt) The emirate of Kuwait was a BEDOUIN principality under Ottoman protection. Although never independent of the Ottoman Empire, the emirs of Kuwait enjoyed a great deal of autonomy from the sultans until 1914 when British forces occupied the country at the start of WORLD WAR I. The origins of the principality lay in the mid-18th-century migration of the Utub Bedouin tribe from the NAJD in central Saudi Arabia to several places along the shores of the Persian Gulf. The Sabah clan of the tribe settled in Kuwait, literally "the little fort," while others settled in Bahrain and Qatar, establishing dynasties that would rule those two states until the present day. When Karim Khan ZAND, the military ruler of Iran, occupied the port city of BASRA in 1776, some of the trade that had passed through that city moved south to the tiny port of Kuwait. The port enjoyed a few years of prosperity before slumping back into virtual obscurity. Its main industry was pearl fishing, although it also served as a so-called free port, open to the commerce of all tribes as a neutral territory.

In the 19th century, the Sabah family learned to develop their diplomatic skills in order to preserve their autonomy. With the rise of the influence of the militant followers of MUHAMMAD IBN ABD AL-WAHHAB, led by the IBN SAUD FAMILY in the neighboring region of al-Ahsa (today the eastern province of Saudi Arabia), the Sabah family had to tread warily so as not to anger their powerful neighbors. At the same time, the leaders of the ibn Saud clan who dominated the tribes loyal to the teachings of ibn Abd al-Wahhab seemed to recognize the importance of Kuwait's role as a free port. The Kuwaitis developed a reputation as the best sailors in the Persian Gulf and their *dhows*, or sailing ships, visited both India and East Africa. As one British observer noted in 1854, the ruling family maintained its position by being "thrifty and inoffensive," acknowledging Ottoman suzerainty when it was necessary but otherwise sticking to trade and making profit.

That neutrality was threatened in 1871 when MIDHAT PASHA, as governor of Iraq, invaded al-Ahsa to support one claimant to head the House of Saud against another. In the process, he restored the province of al-Ahsa to Ottoman control. As part of the provincial reorganization that followed, the sultan recognized Sheikh Abdullah al-Sabah as the *kaymakam*, or acting governor, of Kuwait as a subprovince of al-Ahsa. This was the first formal acknowledgement by the Ottomans that Kuwait was a part of the Ottoman Empire and that the Sabah family was entitled to rule it. Sheikh Abdullah then served as an ally of the Ottomans in recruiting tribesmen from the Bedouin Muntafiq confederation to assist in the fight against ibn Saud followers raiding in Ottoman-controlled Iraq.

Despite that initial show of fealty to the Ottoman dynasty, the Sabah family proved skillful at sensing changes in the political power balance in their region. Sheikh Mubarak, Abdullah's successor, entered into secret negotiations with the British. He made the shrewd judgment that Britain, rather than the Ottoman sultan, was the best protector of his family's position in Kuwait in the face of a revived threat to his autonomy with the accession of Abd al-Aziz to head the house of Saud, as Abd al-Aziz's ambitions seemed to extend to all the territories comprising the Arabian Peninsula. With the outbreak of WORLD WAR I in 1914, British forces occupied Kuwait and proclaimed it a British protectorate.

Bruce Masters

Further reading: Frederick Anscombe, *The Ottoman Gulf: The Creation of Kuwait, Saudi Arabia, and Qatar* (New York: Columbia University Press, 1997).

L

land tenure system   *See* AGRICULTURE.

language and script   Ottoman Turkish belongs to the Oghuz or southwestern group of Turkic languages, of which Azerbaijanian and Türkmen are prominent members today. Ottoman Turkish was written with the Arabic script and is seen as having developed in three stages: Old Ottoman, or, in a context beyond the small early Ottoman state, Old Anatolian Turkish (OAT, 13th–14th/15th centuries), Middle Ottoman (15th/16th–17th/18th centuries), and New Ottoman (18th/19th century to 1928).

Ottoman Turkish contains elements of three languages: Turkish, Persian, and Arabic. Ottoman morphology was Turkic; the syntax was primarily Turkic with important Persian elements, especially regarding subordinate clauses. OAT emerged in the 13th century in the Turkish-ruled Anatolian principalities where Persian was the official language at the time. Based on the bilingual background of the Turkish-speaking immigrants to Anatolia the new rulers allowed the tradition of the Rum Seljuk Empire that preceded the principalities to continue and kept Persian as the official language. Persian itself had acquired a large number of Arabic borrowings following the Islamization of Persian-speaking lands and thus the Arabic elements entered the Ottoman language via Persian. This is why Ottoman vocabulary is largely based on Arabic and, to a lesser extent, on Persian. Both Persian and Ottoman continued to coin new words from Arabic roots according to Arabic rules of word formation.

SCRIPT AND SYNTAX

Ever since its first appearance in the 13th century, OAT was written with the Arabic script. Like modern Turkish, OAT had eight vowels (a, e, ı, i, o, ö, u, ü) plus a closed e (ė), which was lost in Middle Ottoman. The Arabic script, however, only has letters for three long vowels (ā, ī, ū) and additional vocalization signs for three short vowels (a, i, u). Since the short vowel/long vowel concept did not exist in OAT and Ottoman, the vowel letters and short vowel signs along with the signs for some back/front consonants (such as q/k) were used as indicators for the eight Ottoman vowels (for example *qal*, "stay!" and *kül*, "ashes").

Like all Turkic languages Ottoman is an agglutinative language, which means that suffixes are used to indicate case, plural, possession, and person. The word order in Ottoman Turkish is usually subject-object-verb. As in modern Turkish and all other Turkic languages, Ottoman Turkish strictly distinguishes between verbal and nominal stems, that is, stems that form verbs and those that form nouns, with some suffixes only applicable to verbal stems and some only applicable to nominal stems.

VOCABULARY AND LANGUAGE DEVELOPMENT

Usually it is thought that the establishment of Turkish as the official language in the Anatolian Karamanid principality marked a turning point in the development of OAT as a literary language. Karamanoğlu Mehmed, the leader of the principality, replaced Persian as the official language in 1277. Arabic and Persian, however, continued to be used by the educated for writing theoretical and religious treatises as well as poetry. Quotations from the Quran and other works, as well as Arabic, Persian, and Turkish poems, were liberally inserted into Ottoman prose texts. Book titles and chapter headings often were in Arabic or Persian. In Ottoman folk literature and folk poetry the foreign influence is much less evident, although a large number of Arabic and Persian words entered this linguistic layer as well. Aside from the Turkish words and forms no longer in use today, these texts are easier to understand for contemporary Turks.

In the Middle Ottoman and the early New Ottoman periods, which roughly coincide with the period of classical Ottoman literature, the amount of foreign elements reached a peak, resulting in a literary language that was increasingly difficult to comprehend for the lower classes of society. The reformers of the Tanzimat period (1839–76) sought to simplify the language in order to make it accessible to everybody and to promote literacy, which, as in all premodern societies, was low at the time. On the other hand, it was also necessary to develop a new vocabulary for new concepts introduced by the West. This was done mainly by applying the principles of Arabic word formation to Arabic roots and by introducing European loanwords.

In 1928, in the early days of the Turkish republic, the Arabic script was replaced by the Roman alphabet. Subsequent language reform attempted to "purify" the Turkish language by purging it of Arabic and Persian loanwords, an endeavor that is still ongoing.

Claudia Römer

Further reading: Lars Johanson, "The Indifference Stage of Turkish Suffix Vocalism," *Türk Dili Araştırmaları Yıllığı Belleten 1978–1979*, 151–156; Celia Kerslake, "Ottoman Turkish," *The Turkic Languages*, edited by Lars Johanson and Éva Ágnes Csató (London, New York: Routledge, 1998), 179–202; Mecdud Mansuroğlu, "The Rise and Development of Written Turkish in Anatolia." *Oriens* 7 (1954): 250–264; Wolfgang-E. Scharlipp, *Türkische Sprache, arabische Schrift: ein Beispiel schrifthistorischer Akkulturation* (Budapest: Akadémiai Kiadó, 1995).

Lausanne, Treaty of (1923) Signed in Lausanne, Switzerland on July 24, 1923, the Treaty of Lausanne formalized the terms of the peace between Turkey and the Allied Powers that fought in World War I and in the Turkish War of Independence. With the signing of the treaty, the 600-year-old Ottoman Empire came formally to an end.

The Treaty of Lausanne was the culmination of the Lausanne Near East Relations Conference, which lasted eight months and was organized in two sessions. The first session began on November 21, 1922 and ended on February 4, 1923; the second began on April 23, 1923, and ended with the signing of the treaty on July 24, 1923.

At the conference Turkey was represented by the newly established government in Ankara. The Allied Powers were represented by the United Kingdom, France, Italy, Greece, Japan, Romania, and Yugoslavia. At Turkey's insistence, the Soviet Union, Ukraine, and Georgia joined the Conference to negotiate problems concerning the zone of the straits of the Bosporus and the Dardanelles that connected the Black Sea and the Mediterranean. Bulgaria and the United States also sent observers to the conference. The aim of the U.S. delegation was to ensure that the territorial gains of the Allied Powers were based on a contract signed by Britain and France. Ismet Pasha, the head of the Turkish delegation, wanted to exploit the U.S. unfamiliarity with Europe's diplomacy tradition. Although the United States focused on American assistance organizations in Turkey, oil in Mosul, archeological excavations, and Armenian issues, the Turkish delegation wanted to ascertain American views on mandates, capitulations, and economical development.

Following the Mudanya Agreement of October 11, 1922, which ended the war between Turkey, Greece, and the Allied Powers, the peace process began with the Allies' invitation to the governments in both Istanbul and Ankara to send representatives to a peace conference. The Istanbul government represented the sultan, while Ankara represented a nationalist opposition government set up by Mustafa Kemal Pasha (*see* Kemal Atatürk). The leader of the Istanbul government, Grand Vizier Ahmed Tevfik Pasha, sent a telegram to the Turkish National Assembly asking for representatives from Ankara to join the Istanbul representatives. But Atatürk and his government refused to act in concert with the failing Istanbul government; on November 1, 1922, he responded formally by declaring the end of the sultanate in Turkey and the dissolution of the government in Istanbul. The Turkish National Assembly in Ankara then selected all the Turkish representatives for the conference, thereby solving the representation problem.

The Lausanne Peace Conference officially started on November 20, with negotiations getting underway on November 21. The head of the Turkish delegation was Ismet (İnönü) Pasha (1884–1973). Lord Curzon headed a large delegation from the United Kingdom. The goal of the Turkish delegation was to have the Allied Powers accept the conditions that had been declared by the last Ottoman Parliament on February 17, 1920. Before departing for the conference, the Turkish delegation received 14 principles from the Turkish National Assembly in Ankara, including a directive not to accept trade agreements unfavorable for Turkey (*see* capitulations) nor the foundation of an Armenian state in southern Anatolia. These were considered crucial for Turkey's political and economic independence. Also, it was feared

The Turkish delegation at the negotiations that would result in the Treaty of Lausanne in 1922-23 that recognized the territorial integrity of the new Turkish state. Note that most of the delegates are wearing the kalpak, the sheepskin hat, that was favored by Mustafa Kemal (Atatürk) and which had already become a symbol of Turkish nationalism. *(Library of Congress)*

that the Allied Powers intended to solve the historical EASTERN QUESTION to their own advantage.

The first period of negotiations was formidable, with especially contentious debates about the fate of the city of MOSUL and about capitulations. On January 31, 1923, as no agreement had been achieved, the Allied Powers gave the Turkish delegation a proposed peace treaty, asking them to accept it or reject it completely. Lord Curzon believed that it was the best treaty the Turkish government would get. However, Ismet Pasha rejected the proposed document, and the conference was suspended.

During the period of suspension, Ismet Pasha returned to Ankara and requested new instructions from the Turkish National Assembly. The assembly finally decided to leave territorial matters, such as the possession of Mosul, for resolution after the peace process, and empowered Ismet Pasha to sign a peace treaty as soon as possible.

On February 29, the Allied Powers sent a response to Turkey's rejection. When the government in Ankara sent a counter-proposal on March 8, a resumption of the negotiations was set, and the second period of the Conference began on April 23, 1923. In the negotiations, some disputes on financial and economic matters were raised. Turkey's demand of war reparations from Greece became a special problem. In the end, this demand was settled by Greece's ceding Karaagac Station to Turkey. Despite all efforts, however, the issues of the Turkey-Iraq border and the fate of Mosul could not be resolved and were postponed. Peace negotiations were completed on July 17, 1923. The Treaty of Lausanne was signed there on July 24, 1923 and approved by the Turkish National Assembly on August 23, 1923.

The Treaty of Lausanne was not a single document; the main contract was composed of four chapters and 143 clauses, with 17 different protocols and agreements as supplementary documents. Under the terms of the agreement, all Aegean islands except Gökceada and Bozcaada were assigned to Greece, and 12 islands were assigned to Italy. The Maritsa (Meriç) River was established as marking Turkey's western border. Turkey recovered eastern Thrace, a strip along the Syrian border, the IZMIR district, and the internationalized Zone of the Straits (Bosporus and Dardanelles), which was to remain demilitarized and subject to an international convention. Foreign zones of influence and capitulations were abolished. Other than the Zone of the Straits, no limitation was imposed on the Turkish military establishment and no reparations were exacted, although these were a typical feature of other treaties during this period. In return, Turkey renounced all claims on former Turkish territories outside its new boundaries and undertook to guarantee the rights of its ethnic and religious minorities. A separate agreement between Greece and Turkey provided for the compulsory exchange of minority populations. The treaty did not meet all the goals set forth in Turkey's National Pact—western Thrace and Mosul still lay outside the new republic's borders—but the recognition by European nations of the Republic of Turkey as an independent country, free and equal, was an important success. With the signing of the Treaty of Lausanne, the independence, borders, and full sovereignty of the new Republic of Turkey were accepted by nations of the new post–World War I world order.

Mustafa Budak

law *See* COURT OF LAW; *IHTISAB* AND *MUHTESIB*; LAW AND GENDER; FATWA; *KANUN*; MECELLE; SHARIA.

law and gender Islamic legal doctrines and institutions played a major part in the definition of gender, of what it meant to be a male or a female in the Ottoman Empire. The law assigned men and women distinct social roles, and made many rights and obligations contingent upon gender identity. Along with distinctions between free and slave, and between Muslim and non-Muslim, gender difference was one of the most significant distinctions of the Islamic legal system in the Ottoman Empire.

The Islamic legal system in the Ottoman period had a number of components. A *mahkama*, or Islamic COURT OF LAW, functioned in most of the cities and major towns of the empire. Both men and women appeared in these courts to do routine business, to press a variety of claims, and to lodge complaints. The voluminous extant records of the Islamic court system demonstrate that the courts were a familiar institution and one to which local inhabitants often resorted to order their daily lives—as members of families, businesspeople, neighbors, and subjects

of the empire. Women were just as likely as men to have business in court, although in some instances elite women sent authorized agents to appear in their place rather than appearing in public themselves. There is no question, however, that many women and men came to court to conduct their affairs and seek support for their legal rights from the judge, or KADI.

Jurisconsults or muftis also played an important role in the Ottoman Empire. Muftis were deeply learned and upright individuals who assumed their position either by state appointment or by popular acclaim. In either case, they issued nonbinding legal opinions (FATWAS) in response to questions posed to them by state officials, judges, or laypeople. It was the job of the mufti to apply the doctrine of his legal school to the issue raised by a petitioner and to offer guidance on the correct legal response to a particular situation. His opinion might form part of a court case, suggesting the best course of action to the presiding judge, or might allow the petitioners to avoid resorting to court and obtaining a formal judgment if they agreed to accept his guidance. The fatwas of prominent muftis were collected, often by their students, and came to serve as reference works on the broad range of legal issues they handled. Such collections offer insight into the legal approaches that were most significant for gender issues of the time.

The judges and the muftis were educated in the scholarly traditions (*fiqh*) of Islamic law, and they saw their task as applying the doctrines of that tradition to the problems of their age. Islamic law is not codified but requires jurists to draw on a broad range of texts to reach a proper understanding of the issue at hand (*see* SHARIA). Each jurist adhered to a particular school of legal thought. The Hanafi school, as the official school of the empire and the courts, was the most widespread, but the other three major schools of SUNNI ISLAM, the Shafii, Maliki, and Hanbali schools, also had followers among jurists and laypeople. There was mutual tolerance among the schools, and although the Hanafis had the most official clout, adherents of the other schools could be found acting as assistant judges or muftis. The differences among legal doctrines in the school sometimes proved important for gender issues in the Ottoman world, as they allowed for a certain measure of flexibility in interpretation.

The Ottoman state also developed a series of criminal codes, or KANUN, that incorporated many aspects of the sharia but also added further definition of crimes and a wide range of punishments for transgressions. These codes were intended to be the law of the land for the empire and to be enforced in the system of Islamic courts; they represented the state's interpretation and distillation of Islamic penal law, augmented by rules and punishments devised to further the state's purpose of bolstering public security and welfare. The kanuns must also be taken into consideration in any discussion of the law.

Many, if not most, of the issues handled by the courts and the muftis entailed considerations of rights and obligations connected to the gender of an individual. This is nowhere as true as in the case of marriage. Under Islamic law, marriage is a contract between the bride and groom. According to a 16th-century sultanic decree, all marriage contracts should be registered in court, but this regulation seems to have been observed only sporadically. In some Ottoman cities and towns it was commonplace to register marriage contracts, but elsewhere it seems to have been rare. But wherever we find Islamic marriage contracts, the basic formula is the same. The contract includes an offer and acceptance of marriage made by the groom and the bride, the specification of a dower (mahr) to be paid by the groom to the bride, and the record of witnesses to the contract. The dower was usually a significant sum of money, which became part of the bride's personal property; her relatives had no legal rights to it. In the Ottoman period it came to be standard practice to pay part of the dower at the time of the contract, reserving part to be paid when the marriage was dissolved by death or divorce. Under Hanafi law, a woman of legal age (having reached puberty) must freely give her consent to the contract and is empowered to arrange her own marriage if she wishes. In 1544, however, the Ottoman sultan, exercising his prerogative to interpret the sharia, issued a decree forbidding women to marry without the express permission of their guardians and instructing judges not to accept a marriage unless the bride's guardian had given his consent. Although this decree may have had some effect, most judges and muftis appear to have continued to hold the Hanafi position that women could arrange their own marriages.

Jurists viewed married couples as enjoying reciprocal, as opposed to symmetrical, rights. A husband owed his wife full support: All the costs of the marital domicile and his wife's personal expenses should be borne by him. Women were active in defending these rights to maintenance. In 18th-century SYRIA and PALESTINE, for example, women frequently came to court to ask the judge to assign them a fixed amount of maintenance from their husbands who, whether from absence or inability, were failing to support them properly. The judge typically calculated a payment to supply the necessary provisions based on a woman's status, imposed a requirement on the husband to pay, authorized the wife to borrow the money if her husband was not forthcoming, and held the husband responsible for any debts his wife so incurred. A wife, for her part, owed her husband obedience. A husband could restrict her freedom of movement by forbidding her to leave the house (except to visit her family) or he might insist that she accompany him on a journey.

The jurists of the time agreed that a wife owed her husband this obedience, particularly in regard to her presence in the marital home, and that her failure to remain or return home at his request rendered her disobedient (nashiza) and led to the forfeiture of maintenance payments.

Divorce was another legal option and was of three types: talaq, tafriq, and khul. Using the talaq type, a man could divorce his wife unilaterally and without going to court simply by pronouncing a formula of divorce. The talaq type of divorce was not open to Ottoman women, who were required to go to court and present grounds in order to obtain a court-ordered divorce (tafriq). Under Hanafi law, these grounds were extremely limited: a husband's impotence or insanity were among the few reasons a judge would accept for a judicial divorce. Some judges, however, were willing to allow the more flexible rulings of other legal schools to be applied in their courts: Many women obtained judicial divorces on the grounds of a husband's desertion, as permitted by the Shafii school of law. A woman could also negotiate a divorce known as khul with her husband by agreeing to forego payment of the balance of her dower or by absolving him of other financial responsibilities. All three types of divorce were known and practiced in the Ottoman period. In addition, a woman could obtain a divorce if she had inserted clauses into her marriage contract that gave her the right of divorce in the event that her husband did certain things; some contracts included contingencies about taking a second wife, changing residence against the wife's will, traveling more than once a year, moving permanently to a distant location, or beating the wife with enough force to leave marks.

Unless the khul divorce specified otherwise, a woman gained certain entitlements upon divorce: She should receive any balance owed on her dower, and material support for three months following the divorce. In addition, any underage children born of the marriage were entitled to full financial support from their father. Court records include many examples of litigation in which a divorced wife claims that her ex-husband failed to deliver what he owed, including the balance of her dower, the costs of her maintenance after divorce, or the outstanding amount of a loan she made to him or personal property she left behind. Many women sued for money and goods owed them by their former husbands, and they frequently met with success, particularly in their claims for payment of the balance of the dower.

Regardless of circumstances, the underage children of a marriage were, by law, placed under the guardianship of their father. A mother did have some rights to the temporary custody of young children, but after a certain age (seven years for boys and nine for girls in the Hanafi school), the father could assert his rights to custody. In the event of the death of a child's father, Ottoman courts routinely favored mothers as guardians over paternal uncles or older brothers, even though the law specified that guardianship devolved upon male relatives on the paternal side in the absence of any formal designation of a different guardian. These female guardians oversaw sales and purchases of property for their wards, collected the income owed to them from rents and endowment properties, and settled any debts they had inherited.

Such activities were very much in keeping with Islamic property law. Any adult of legal age, whether male or female, was a legal subject fully empowered to enter into contracts and exercise sole control over the property that he or she owned. Furthermore, marital status held no ramifications for legal capacity, and a husband had no right to manage or dispose of his wife's property. These rules stand in marked contrast to European legal systems of the same period that placed most women and their property under the legal authority of their husbands. Despite this equality of capacity in Islamic law, some of the ways in which women and men acquired property were affected by gender. Inheritance law, which specified the estate shares of surviving relatives, allotted females, in most instances, half the share of their male counterparts. In much of the Ottoman Empire, agricultural land was excluded from the jurisdiction of Islamic inheritance law, with the result that women in rural areas did not typically inherit any part of what constituted the bulk of family wealth. On the other hand, women did inherit their shares in other types of family property, including money, household and personal items, and urban real estate: Women are named as legitimate heirs to all these items in estate records. The evidence also shows that women often chose to sell off inherited shares of real estate or business equipment in order to acquire capital to be used for business investments or the purchase of luxury goods. Women may have chosen to convert their assets to money or personal items because these liquid forms of wealth were much easier for them to control and manipulate. Most surveys of women's estate records tend to confirm this trend, since women's estates, at least among the well-to-do, tended to include lots of elegant (gold and silver-embroidered) clothing, furs, jewelry, substantial household items such as weighty copper vessels, and money. Women did also own urban real estate, but not in the same proportions as their male kin. Overall, in both doctrine and practice, the law allowed for the free exercise of property rights by both males and female, although social context tended to circumscribe female activities.

A woman's freedom of movement could, of course, affect her ability to realize her full legal rights. If the law prevented women from moving freely in public space or allowed their families to confine them to their homes, then their ability to advocate for themselves would be severely curtailed. The jurists of the Ottoman period discussed the category of the secluded and veiled woman (Arabic *mukhaddara*, Ottoman Turkish *muhaddere*). It cropped up principally as a concern: How will the secluded woman be able to realize her rights in court? Will her business be properly conducted if she is not present? Ebussuud, the eminent 16th-century Ottoman mufti, addressed these issues and insisted that the witnesses to a secluded woman's appointment of an agent must see her face in order to ascertain her identity. Ebussuud thought of the *muhaddere* as a category of social custom—a woman who does not let herself be seen by people outside her household—rather than one of Islamic law. Although willing to discuss and define the category, Ebussuud never suggested that the sharia had legislated either the category or the behavior. Ottoman *kanun* did lend some official recognition to the *muhaddere* category. In the law book of Sultan Süleyman I (r. 1520–66), the punishments for women who brawl are differentiated based on whether they are secluded: A non-*muhaddere* woman is to be flogged and fined, while a *muhaddere* woman's punishment is visited upon her husband, who is to be scolded and fined. However, the *kanun* did not impose specific dress regulations, and public records indicate that many women attended Islamic courts with impunity, dressed in ways that made their female identity clear to both the judges and the witnesses, which suggests that fully secluded women were a rarity.

On the other hand, the Ottoman state did issue sartorial regulations from time to time that included prescriptions for female clothing. In 1726, for example, Grand Vizier Ibrahim Pasha decreed that women's outerwear should meet some exact specifications as to the sizes of collars, scarves, and headbands, prohibited some forms of headgear, and directed the police and Islamic courts to enforce these regulations. The motivation may not have been purely one of moral imperative. In part, these regulations were geared toward encouraging women to return to wearing traditional clothing of local manufacture in order to revive the local economy. There is little evidence, in any case, that these regulations were strictly enforced.

Another important area for legal regulation of gender relations in Ottoman society was that of sexual contact. Unlawful intercourse (*zina*) was defined in the sharia as all acts of all sexual penetration other than those between a married couple or a master and his female slave. *Zina* belonged to a particular category of crime, the punishment of which is considered to be a right of God, not of man. *Zina* is specifically mentioned in the Quran (4:15 and 24:1–2) as a crime that requires severe punishment; the sharia specified flogging or execution by stoning, depending on the status of the perpetrator. The Ottoman *kanun* tended to ameliorate the punishments for *zina* while expanding the scope of the crime. While the Ottoman *kanun* paid lip service to the penalties prescribed by the sharia, it also instituted a broad range of alternative penalties, primarily fines. The criminal code of Süleyman I, for example, listed a series of graduated fines incurred by perpetrators of *zina*, to be calibrated according to the status of the perpetrator, whether the perpetrator was a virgin or not, and by his or her assets. In the case of consensual *zina*, only a recurrent offender, such as a habitual prostitute, incurred stiffer penalties of flogging, ridiculing in public, or banishment. The law specified that a prostitute could have her face blackened or smeared with dirt and be led through the streets sitting backward on a donkey, holding its tail instead of its reins. In the case of abduction or rape, corporal penalties also applied: A man could be castrated, and a woman who ran off with a man could have her vulva branded. Although it was not specified in the criminal code, abduction of a minor came to be punished by indefinite servitude on Ottoman galleys. In brief, the Ottoman criminal codes effectively eliminated execution as a penalty for *zina*, prescribed only monetary fines for proscribed acts of consensual sexual intercourse, and reserved a range of nonlethal corporal punishments for those who were violent or habitual offenders.

Men were permitted more variety in licit sexual partners than were women. The law allowed a man to be married to as many as four wives at any one time and further sanctioned sexual intercourse with concubines, defined as female slaves personally owned by the man in question. A concubine, if she became pregnant, acquired some rights under the law. She could no longer be sold, she would automatically be freed upon her master's death, and any child of the union would be born free with full rights of inheritance in his or her father's property, just like a child of a legal marriage. The exercise of male rights to polygyny and the keeping of concubines appear to have been a feature only of very wealthy households. Most studies suggest that the rates of polygyny and concubinage were probably very low outside elite circles.

There were changes and adjustments in legal doctrine and practice in relation to gender throughout the history of the empire, but the most dramatic shift came with the legal reforms of 1917. At this time, criminal law (including the trial and punishment of sexual offenses) was removed altogether from the jurisdiction of the Islamic courts. Although these courts still held sway over matters related to family relations (marriage, divorce, child custody, and inheritance), they operated under a newly codified law, the Law of Family Rights of 1917, that swept aside former procedures and practices. The Islamic courts were now to apply the rules of a fixed legal code to the gendered issues that came before it. The law, still Islamic in inspiration, was thereby streamlined and standardized in ways that made it accessible to laypeople,

but much of the flexibility and diversity of legal opinion was lost. In 1924, after the end of the Ottoman Empire, the Islamic courts and codes were abolished in the newly formed Republic of Turkey, but the Law of Family Rights continued to be applied in successor Arab states in modified form.

Judith E. Tucker

See also FAMILY; HAREM; SHARIA; SLAVERY.

Further reading: Leslie Peirce, *Morality Tales: Law and Gender in the Ottoman Court of Aintab* (Berkeley: University of California Press, 2003); Amira Sonbol, ed., *Women, the Family, and Divorce Laws in Islamic History* (Syracuse, N.Y.: Syracuse University Press, 1996); Judith E. Tucker, *In the House of the Law: Gender and Islamic Law in Ottoman Syria and Palestine* (Berkeley: University of California Press, 1998); Madeline C. Zilfi, ed., *Women in the Ottoman Empire: Middle Eastern Women in the Early Modern Era* (Leiden: Brill, 1997).

Lawrence, T. E. (Lawrence of Arabia) (b. 1888–d. 1935) *British military officer, adventurer, and author* Thomas Edward Lawrence is better known by his nickname, Lawrence of Arabia, which he was given by American journalist Lowell Thomas. Lawrence was born in Wales in 1888. He studied archaeology at Oxford University and later served as an assistant for a British archaeological expedition in Iraq. Lawrence then traveled extensively in SYRIA, sketching crusader castles and practicing his Arabic. In 1914, at the start of WORLD WAR I, he was assigned to British Military Intelligence in CAIRO. From there he was sent to MECCA in 1916 to investigate reports about the ARAB REVOLT. Upon his return to Cairo Lawrence was assigned as a military liaison officer to Prince FAYSAL IBN HUSAYN AL-HASHIMI.

Historians continue to debate Lawrence's actual role in the revolt. He was not the only British officer to accompany the Arab Army, but journalist Lowell Thomas placed him at the head of the revolt in his dispatches from the field. After the war, Thomas became wealthy and established an international reputation by touring North America and Britain with a lecture and slide show that romanticized Lawrence's exploits, transforming "Lawrence of Arabia" into a household word in the English-speaking world. In Thomas's version of the events, Lawrence single-handedly molded a band of ill-trained Bedouin into an effective guerrilla force. Lawrence then led them to help defeat the Ottoman Empire as Britain's allies. In Lawrence's 1927 book *Seven Pillars of Wisdom: A Triumph*, the author also placed himself at the center of the action. Further adding to Lawrence's fame and to the myth surrounding him is David Lean's epic film *Lawrence of Arabia*, which won seven Academy Awards in 1962, including best picture and best actor. The film closely follows Lawrence's own account of his role in the Arab Revolt.

After the war, Lawrence was a part of the British delegation to the Paris peace talks that would decide the fate of the Ottoman Empire. Again, there is disagreement among historians as to whether he supported the claims of his erstwhile ally Faysal in pressing for the establishment of the Arab Kingdom. In 1922, Winston Churchill asked Lawrence to help the British restore order to Faysal's newly formed kingdom of Iraq, but Lawrence resigned after a short stay in Baghdad. He returned to England, disgusted by what he perceived to be British imperial plans for Iraq in the form of a continued British military presence in the country. Lawrence died in a motorcycle accident in 1935.

Bruce Masters

Further reading: T. E. Lawrence, *Seven Pillars of Wisdom: A Triumph* (London: J. Cape, 1935); Jeremy Wilson, *Lawrence of Arabia: The Authorized Biography of T. E. Lawrence* (New York: Atheneum, 1990).

Lebanese Civil War (1860)   The civil war in Lebanon in 1860 was sparked in the winter of 1858–59, when MARONITE Catholic peasants in the district of Mount Lebanon rose up against their overlord, a member of the Maronite Khazin family. Under the leadership of Tanyus Shahin the rebellion spread into the region of Kisrawan where Maronite peasants often worked lands held by DRUZE overlords; the Druze landlords responded by rallying Druze peasants to a holy war. In the spring of 1860, recalling the Maronite aggression in 1859 and fearing that the Maronites might attack again, the Druze lords rallied their retainers and peasants to launch an outright assault on villages and towns where there were mixed populations of Druzes and Maronites, or in the case of Dayr al-Qamar, where there was a pocket of Maronites surrounded by Druzes.

Although originally intended as preemptive strikes against the Maronite enemy, the Druze attacks quickly grew out of control. The unrest spread into the Bekaa Valley where the market town of Zahle was sacked, even though its inhabitants were MELKITE CATHOLICS, not Maronites. In some places, such as Zahle, the Christians put up a spirited defense, but generally they were simply overrun. Once a town had been taken, the Druzes executed the men and drove the women and children out, acts that would today be labeled ethnic cleansing.

The culmination of the conflict came in July 1860 with the DAMASCUS RIOTS, when Muslims in the city rose up against Christians, killing as many as several thousand. The arrival in Beirut of refugees from the slaughter prompted outrage in Europe and newspapers in both Great Britain and France called for action by their governments. In response, the French landed troops in Beirut in August 1860 and the Ottomans dispatched an army to Damascus to restore order. Christians demanded both the punishment of those involved and reparations for their loss of property. But in the end, as many of the Druze leaders had fled to JABAL AL-DRUZ (the Mountain of the Druzes) in Syria, few were tried for their offences. In 1861 the French withdrew and the Ottomans announced a new plan, the *MUTASARRIFIYYA*, to provide evenhanded representational government to Lebanon.

Bruce Masters

Further reading: Leila Fawaz, *An Occasion for War: Civil Conflict in Lebanon and Damascus in 1860* (Berkeley: University of California Press, 1994).

Lebanon (*Ar.:* Lubnan; *Fr.:* Liban; *Turk.:* Lübnan)   In the Ottoman period, the name Lebanon referred only to the mountainous region that forms the spine of today's Republic of Lebanon. MARONITE Catholic villagers inhabited the northern part of the mountain range, known simply as Mount Lebanon, while DRUZES initially dominated Kisrawan and Shuf, the central regions of the range. SHIA villagers inhabited the southern hills, known as the Jabal Amil, and the Bekaa Valley that lies between the Lebanon and the Anti-Lebanon Mountains. SUNNI Muslims and Orthodox Christians predominated in the coastal strip, whose largest towns at the start of the Ottoman period were TRIPOLI and SIDON.

The Ottomans added Lebanon to their empire in 1516, and established provinces in the coastal towns of Sidon and TRIPOLI by the middle of the 16th century. The mountains were a much bigger problem, as the terrain was rough and the well-armed villagers had access to the latest European weaponry from Venetian traders on Cyprus. Rather than enforce direct rule, the Ottoman governors on the coast allowed the local lords of the mountains to administer their territories autonomously as long as they paid taxes to the sultan and did not rise in rebellion. This allowed the lords in the region to exercise a great deal of power over the peasants who cultivated their lands. As a result a sociopolitical system emerged in the mountains that was similar to the feudal system of medieval Europe. Among the feudal lords were Druze families such as the al-Maanis and the JANBULAD FAMILY, Maronites such as the Khazin family, and the originally Sunni SHIHAB FAMILY. Although the various families might fight each other at times, differences in religion were ultimately less important than differences in class, and the families could easily close ranks in solidarity in the face of an outside challenge or a peasant uprising.

The Ottoman authorities recognized one individual as the emir, or prince, of the mountain, although the clans themselves determined who that person would be. From the end of the 16th century to the end of the 17th century, the emir was usually a representative of the house of Maan, FAKHR AL-DIN AL-MAANI being the most prominent of these. Throughout the 18th century and the first few decades of the 19th century, the emir was usually someone from the house of Shihab. This loose alliance between Druze and Maronite feudal lords began to break down in the 19th century as Christians increasingly became more politically assertive. Members of the Shihab family converted to Christianity, and Christians became prominent in the Shihab administration. Additionally, during this period, the Christian birthrate seems to have been higher than that of the Druzes, enabling Christian peasants to claim land in the Kisrawan that had formerly been Druze country. Lebanese Christians also benefited from education provided by Roman Catholic MISSIONARIES and the increasing wealth generated by the export of silk from Lebanon to France, as Christians had been instrumental in the production of silk since the start of the industry in the 18th century.

The occupation of Lebanon by Egyptian governor IBRAHIM PASHA in 1831 intensified rivalries between Druzes and Maronites that had been developing over both land and political power, as Ibrahim Pasha openly favored Christians in his administration and recruited them into his army. The Lebanese Druzes rose in rebellion against Ibrahim Pasha's policies of increased taxation, conscription, and forced disarmament of the clans. When Ottoman rule returned to Lebanon in 1841, the Druzes worked successfully to dislodge Bashir III al-Shihab, to whom the sultan had granted the title of emir. When Bashir III al-Shihab went into exile, the position of emir was undermined. In 1842 the Ottoman government introduced the double *qaimmaqamiyya*, or district governorship, whereby Mount Lebanon would be governed by a Maronite appointee and the more southerly regions of Kisrawan and Shuf would be governed by a Druze. Both districts would come under the indirect rule of the Ottoman governor of Sidon, who had transferred his actual residence to BEIRUT. However, this approach to administration proved largely unmanageable, and the Druzes began to force recent Maronite settlers out of territories that the Druzes considered rightfully theirs.

The tensions between Druzes and Maronites erupted in 1860 with wide-scale attacks by Druzes on all Christians, whether they were Maronites or not. Thousands of Christians were killed in massacres that lasted throughout the spring of 1860 and culminated with the DAMASCUS RIOTS of July 1860. The French landed troops in Beirut in August and called on the Ottomans to restore order. In the aftermath of the unrest, the power of the Druze families was broken, and many fled to the JABAL AL-DRUZ REGION in southern Syria. The Ottoman government abolished the unworkable system of the

qaimmaqamiyya and instituted in its place the MUTASARRIFIYYA, or autonomous governorate. It would enjoy a great deal of autonomy but would have one head, stipulated to be an Ottoman Catholic Christian from outside Lebanon. Under the *mutasarrif*, or autonomous governor, an administrative council of 12 men was to have proportional representation from the Maronites and Druzes, as well as representatives from Greek Orthodox, Greek Catholic, Sunni, and Shia communities. The idea of proportional sectarian representation in a "confessional" political system, that is one in which all political offices are allotted according to a quota for each religious sect, would outlast the Ottoman regime to survive in a slightly different form in the Republic of Lebanon.

The *mutasarrifiyya* ended the turmoil in Lebanon, and the region prospered in the last decades of the Ottoman Empire. Beirut grew to be the largest port between Izmir and Alexandria. Lebanese Christians, in particular, benefited from the educational facilities offered by the missionaries who established the first modern universities in the Arab world in Beirut. Although many Christian intellectuals participated in the NAHDA, or renaissance, of Arabic literature and culture, others, particularly among the Maronites, began to imagine an identity that was purely Lebanese and not Arab. French interests in the Levant, as the eastern Mediterranean was then called, further encouraged the Maronites to imagine Lebanon as a French protectorate in which they would dominate the political life.

With the expansion of the Lebanese silk industry, mulberry groves (required to feed the silk caterpillars) came to dot the countryside in areas that once provided the region with food. Lebanon became increasingly dependent on food imports from abroad, making the country extremely vulnerable to famine during WORLD WAR I. As part of its campaign to defeat the Ottoman Empire, British ships effectively cut off the import of food that had come to Beirut from Egypt and Anatolia; as a result, thousands of people in Lebanon's mountain villages starved to death. Adding to the country's hardships, the remittances of cash from those Lebanese who had already migrated to the Americas were cut off by the war. Money orders from across the Atlantic had become a major source of income for many, and people suffered as shortages caused the price of all foodstuffs to rise. In the aftermath of the war, Lebanon was given to the French as part of its Syrian mandate. France promptly divided Lebanon from Syria, giving it larger borders than it had known during the Ottoman period. While not all the inhabitants of this "greater Lebanon" welcomed the French, many among the Maronites saw the occupation as a necessary step to create an independent, and Christian, Lebanon.

When the country became independent in 1943, the Maronites emerged as the dominant religious community in the country, as the constitution guaranteed that the president would always be a Maronite. But as the Maronites were numerically a minority in the country as a whole, those religious communities left outside the political system were resentful of this power, a resentment that eventually erupted in civil war (1975–90). Although there was an attempt at the end of that war to divide political power more evenly, Lebanon continues to suffer from tensions between its various religious communities that first emerged in the 19th century when it was a part of the Ottoman Empire.

Bruce Masters

Further reading: Ussama Makdisi, *The Culture of Sectarianism: Community, History, and Violence in Nineteenth-Century Lebanon* (Berkeley: University of California Press, 2000); Akram Khater, *Inventing Home: Emigration, Gender and the Middle Class in Lebanon, 1870–1920* (Berkeley: University of California Press, 2001).

legal system   *See* COURT OF LAW; LAW AND GENDER; *KADI*; *KADIASKER*; *KANUN*; SHARIA.

Lepanto, Battle of   (1571)   Fought between the Ottoman NAVY and an alliance of Christian powers called the Holy League, the Battle of Lepanto took place on October 7, 1571, in the Gulf of Patras, currently recognized as part of Greece. Involving a diverse array of political and military powers, the battle arose out of a long and complex series of conflicts between Ottoman and Christian powers. The battle itself resulted in an overwhelming defeat for the Ottomans, but despite the devastation to their ships and crews, the empire was quickly able to rebuild, surprising and almost exciting the admiration of their opponents. It was also the last major battle in the Mediterranean between oar-powered fleets.

To set the stage for the battle, it is necessary first to understand that by the second half of the 16th century the Ottoman Empire had become a major power that controlled the BALKANS, the Middle East, the BLACK SEA, and the eastern Mediterranean. For Ottoman Grand Vizier Sokollu Mehmed Pasha (1556–78)—whose grand political designs included the unsuccessful Don-Volga canal project and a premature plan to construct a canal at Suez (1569) to encircle ISTANBUL's eastern rival, Safavid IRAN, and to counter Portuguese imperialism in the Red Sea and Indian Ocean— the conquest of CYPRUS seemed long overdue. The Venetian-held island was a nuisance in the otherwise Ottoman-controlled eastern Mediterranean, for it offered a safe haven to Christian CORSAIRS who preyed on Muslim merchant and pilgrim ships and who endangered Ottoman maritime activities between Istanbul and EGYPT, the richest province of the empire. The elimination of privateering by Christians would stem Ottoman economic losses, but it also seemed necessary to bolster Istanbul's legitimacy in the Islamic world. Furthermore, Cyprus was a tempting target for its own sake; it was known to be rich in land and taxes, and its proximity to Ottoman logistical bases was an important consideration, given the limited radius of operation of Ottoman warfleets.

The Ottomans thus mobilized some 208 to 360 vessels and at least 60,000 land forces in a 1570 campaign with the goal of eliminating Christian pirates from Cyprus. With the Ottoman campaign well underway, a number of European Christian powers gathered in Rome to form what became known as the Holy League of the Papacy. Proclaimed on May 25, 1571, the Holy League alliance included SPAIN, VENICE, Genoa, Tuscany, Savoy, Urbino, Parma, and the KNIGHTS OF ST. JOHN. The League committed itself to fighting a perpetual war against the Ottomans and the Muslims of NORTH AFRICA and specifically to the recapture of Cyprus and the Holy Land. For this purpose, the signatories agreed to combine their resources to provide 200 galleys, 100 ships, 50,000 infantrymen, and 4,500 light cavalry along with the necessary weaponry and supplies.

Nicosia, the capital of Cyprus, despite its up-to-date Italian bastion fortifications, had already fallen to the Ottomans on September 9, 1570, after a 46-day siege. Shorter Ottoman lines of supply and plenteous reinforcements enabled the Ottomans to maintain their six to one advantage against the besieged. Ottoman skills in siege warfare, the dismal performance of the Venetian relief fleet which was plagued by typhus and desertions, the incompetence of Nicosia's Venetian commander, and the support of local Cypriots who detested their Venetian overlords, all played a significant role in the conquest. The ferocity of the three-day sack of Nicosia persuaded the other Venetian forts to surrender, except for the eastern port garrison of Famagusta; it was finally captured on August 1, 1571, after withstanding seven general assaults and 74 days of heavy bombardment. Although the Ottomans initially agreed to generous terms of capitulation, the massacre of Muslim pilgrims in the Famagusta garrison provoked Ottoman retaliation. On August 5 the Venetian officers were beheaded. Governor-general Marcantonio Bragadin, who had ordered the killing of the Muslims, was skinned alive; his skin was then stuffed with straw and paraded along the Anatolian coast and Istanbul. Informed on October 4 of the fall of Famagusta and Bragadin's torture, the Holy League partners were quickly sparked to vengeance, giving the otherwise fragile alliance an unusual unity of purpose.

The Christian fleet, led by Don Juan de Austria, the 23-year-old half-brother of King Philip II of Spain (r. 1556–98), had already assembled in Messina in early September and reached Corfu on September 26. There they learned that the Ottoman NAVY, which had raided CRETE and Venice's Adriatic possessions during the summer, had returned to Lepanto, a harbor town on the northern side of the Gulf of Patras.

Equally well informed, Ottoman scouts told their commanders about the arrival of a Christian fleet off Caphalonia. At a war council held on October 4, Pertev Pasha, commander in chief of the entire 1571 campaign, and Uluç Ali Pasha, governor general (*beyelrbeyi*) of ALGIERS and an experienced Algerian corsair, aware that their navy was undermanned and exhausted, were of the opinion that the Ottomans should take a defensive position in the Gulf of Lepanto. However, Müezzinzade Ali Pasha, *kapudan* (admiral) of the navy, a land commander with no experience in naval warfare, prevailed. He ordered his fleet to attack the Christians.

The opposing navies clashed on October 7 in the Gulf of Patras. The Christians had 202–219 galleys and six galleasses (large galleys with auxiliary oars and substantial artillery), whereas the Ottomans had some 205 galleys and 35–68 galliots, or light galleys. These numbers are somewhat misleading, however, for they do not include the galliots in the Christian fleet or the *fustas*, smaller transport ships, in either navy. Estimated figures of soldiers and weaponry indicate that the Holy League slightly outnumbered the Ottomans in terms of combatants and auxiliaries—62,100 to 57,700—and had a substantial advantage in terms of firepower—1,334 guns to 741. Ottoman accounts also show that their fleet was undermanned due to losses during the 1571 campaign and because many of the soldiers aboard the coastal beys' ships had already left for the winter.

The battle started before eleven in the morning with the engagement of the inshore squadrons. Ottoman commander Mehmed Suluk, known to his Christian adversaries as Maometto Scirocco, almost outflanked the galleys of Agostino Barbarigo of Venice, commander of the left wing, maneuvering between the shoals and the Venetians. The Venetians lost several galleys and Barbarigo was mortally wounded. However, unengaged galleys of the Christian left wing and vessels from the rearguard sent in by another Holy League commander, Don Álvaro de Bazán, marquis of Santa Cruz, turned the defeat into victory, destroying the entire Ottoman right wing in two hours.

Meanwhile, a fierce mêlée developed between the Christian and Ottoman center, following a head-on clash of the two flagships, Don Juan's *Real* and Ali Pasha's *Sultana*. Ali Pasha planned to counter superior Christian firepower by using his reinforcements from the reserve until Mehmed Suluk and Uluç Ali outflanked the Christian wings. Despite losses from the cannons of the galleasses, Ottoman galleys penetrated the Christian ranks and Ali Pasha's men even boarded the *Real*. Soon, however, the Ottoman center was overwhelmed. When Ali Pasha was killed and his *Sultana* taken in tow by the *Real*, the Ottoman center collapsed. All the Ottoman ships in the center were sunk or taken and their crews massacred, almost to the last man.

The clash between the seaward squadrons started later. Uluç Ali and Gian Andrea Doria, the most skilled sea captains on either side, tried to outmaneuver each other. While the bulk of his galleys engaged Doria's right and center, Uluç Ali managed to inflict serious damage upon some 15 of Doria's galleys that had broken formation at the left flank. Uluç Ali proceeded to attack the Christian center's right flank in order to help the overwhelmed Ottoman center, but it was too late; Ali Pasha was already dead, and Bazán sent his remaining reserve against Uluç Ali. Realizing that he could not save the day, Uluç Ali escaped into the open sea with some 30 galleys. The Christian victory was complete. The Holy League fleet destroyed almost the entire Ottoman navy with its crew and ordnance.

To the surprise of the Christians, by next spring the Ottomans were said to have built 150 new vessels, complete with artillery and other necessary equipment. Reporting from Constantinople to Charles IX on May 8, 1572, seven months after the Battle of Lepanto, the French ambassador commented on the strength and prowess of the Ottomans: "Already their general is prepared to set out to sea at the end of this month with 200 galleys and 100 galliots, of corsairs and others. . . I should never have believed the greatness of this monarchy, had I not seen it with my own eyes." In the spring of 1572 it seemed as though Lepanto had done little to alter the balance of power. The Ottomans continued to hold Cyprus, and the Holy League collapsed as Venice concluded a treaty with Istanbul in 1573 and as Spanish resources were redirected to meet new challenges in the Netherlands. In 1574 the Ottomans retook Tunis, also capturing the Spanish garrison of La Goletta.

While the Ottomans appeared to have recovered quickly, the Christian victory at Lepanto did have some long-term impact, saving Venice and its remaining Mediterranean possessions (most notably CRETE) and the western Mediterranean from further Ottoman conquests. And while the Ottoman galleys were rebuilt by 1572, it took decades for Istanbul to replace the crews, especially the skilled Muslim marines, sailor-gunners, and naval archers. The new Ottoman commander, Uluç Ali, was too good a seaman to challenge the Christians with his green navy.

Gábor Ágoston

See also CORSAIRS AND PIRATES; KNIGHTS OF ST. JOHN; TERSANE-I AMIRE.

Further reading: Hugh Bicheno, *Crescent and Cross: The Battle of Lepanto, 1571* (London: Cassell, 2003); Niccolò Capponi, *Victory of the West: The Story of the Battle of Lepanto* (London: Macmillan, 2006); John Francis Guilmartin, *Galle-*

ons and Galleys (London: Cassell, 2002); Andrew Hess, "The Battle of Lepanto and Its Place in Mediterranean History." *Past and Present* 57 (1972): 53–73; Colin Imber, "The Reconstruction of the Ottoman Fleet after the Battle of Lepanto, 1571–1572," in *Studies in Ottoman History and Law* (Istanbul: Isis, 1996); Angus Konstam, *Lepanto 1571: The Greatest Naval Battle of the Renaissance* (Oxford: Osprey, 2003).

Levant Company Chartered by England's Queen Elizabeth I in 1581 and continuing to trade until its dissolution in 1825, the Levant Company was a joint-stock company that for almost two and a half centuries held a monopoly over the trade between England and the eastern Mediterranean, known in the 16th century as the Levant. The Levant Company was the first of many such companies that were formed in the period of European expansion, such as the Virginia Company and the highly successful East India Company. In these companies, merchants residing in England financed company operations and shared in the profits generated by agents, known as factors, who did the actual trading. In the case of the Levant Company, these factors were resident in the various ports and commercial centers of the Ottoman Empire. They typically used their own money to engage in commerce on the side in the hopes of raising enough capital to become company shareholders in their own right. It was not unusual for a factor to be stationed in an Ottoman port for more than 20 years, and many died before they could realize their dreams of financial independence. The height of the Levant Company's prosperity came in the 17th century when woolen broadcloth of English manufacture was a highly desired commodity in the Ottoman Empire and in IRAN. In return, the Levant Company factors purchased raw silk from Iran that was brought by CARAVAN to either ALEPPO or Izmir. They also purchased locally produced goods such as dried fruit (raisins, figs, and apricots), cotton yarn, carpets, and various products used for dyeing or processing cloth.

To handle local trade, the Levant Company established what was called a "factory" or station in the Ottoman cities in which it traded. In cities such as Izmir, the Company's commercial infrastructure could be substantial, but generally company factors found space for themselves in a CARAVANSARY. The head of the factory was the company consul who supervised the work of the factors and represented England's interests as well as those of the company, as the two were deemed synonymous by the English government. Thus, at least in the 16th century, the Levant Company's chief representative also served as England's ambassador in the Ottoman capital of ISTANBUL.

To conduct business with local merchants the Company factors usually relied on a DRAGOMAN, a local Christian or Jewish translator who knew the mixed Italian trade language, or *lingua franca* (literally, language of the Franks, or Europeans). Due to special rights and privileges accorded to these translators, many dragomans accumulated great wealth for themselves in the Levant Company's employ.

The company's factors, on the other hand, not knowing the local languages or customs, were often cut off from much contact with the local people and their letters home, preserved in the Company archive, indicate that their lives were often lonely. Some married local Christian women, but most remained bachelors. There were some exceptions to their general sense of isolation; Dr. Alexander Russell, for instance, who served as Company doctor in Aleppo in the 18th century, left an account of the people of that city that suggests that he was well integrated into the city's everyday life.

The fortunes of the Levant Company began to fade in the 18th century. Wars in Iran led to a sharp decline in the export of raw silk from that country at a time when English broadcloth, the staple of the Company's trade, was losing popularity among Ottoman consumers. French merchants had introduced lighter woolen cloth more suited to the Middle Eastern climate and dyed with brighter colors. In addition, British commercial interests were shifting to India, a region that overtook the Ottoman Empire as Britain's leading foreign trading partner at the start of the 18th century. The Company's presence dwindled everywhere in the Ottoman Empire but most notably in Aleppo where in 1800 there was only one factor, down from 20 a century before. During the Napoleonic Wars (1798–1815), Britain began to send professional diplomats to the Ottoman Empire, and the era of the Company representing the nation's interests was over. In 1825 the shareholders voted to dissolve the Company.

Bruce Masters

Further reading: Alfred Wood, *A History of the Levant Company* (London: Oxford University Press, 1935); Daniel Goffman, *Britons in the Ottoman Empire, 1642–1660* (Seattle: University of Washington Press, 1998).

libraries Ottoman libraries are best understood as falling within one of two groupings, those belonging to the traditional era and those belonging to the era of modernization. In the earlier traditional era only WAQF libraries were found; these institutions were founded and supported by an endowment or charitable trust system. The modern era saw the formation of many more libraries inspired by Western models, although there were still some *waqf*, or endowed institution, libraries.

TRADITIONAL *WAQF* LIBRARIES

Traditional *waqf* libraries, which were founded during the height of the Ottoman era in the 15th and 16th centuries, became an integral part of educational and cultural life. Almost 500 *waqf* libraries, spread throughout the vast Ottoman lands, were formed by sultans, sultans' mothers, government officials, scientists, and philanthropists who considered books and libraries essential. These libraries were the main centers that provided for the intellectual needs of scientists and citizens, and increased in number and in terms of the resources they contained. The three most library-rich cities of the Ottoman Empire were Istanbul, Bursa, and Edirne.

The foundation of a *waqf* library was documented by a *waqf* deed (*waqfiye*). Generally, originals of these deeds were kept by the foundation executives; approved copies were kept in government archives. *Waqf* deeds contained information such as where, when, by whom, and under what circumstances the library was founded, as well as the name(s) of the foundation executive(s). The number, salary, and qualifications of any staff were included in the deeds, along with rules about lending and other conditions of use. Information relating to donations of books sometimes included book lists, which could be considered as types of library catalogues. Information such as book names, quantities, and physical specifications can be found in *waqf* deeds organized in this manner. These libraries typically consisted of 15–20 manuscripts, although some independent libraries contained as many as 5,000 volumes. After the first Muslim-directed PRINTING house in the Ottoman Empire began operating in 1729, donations of printed books to libraries increased, although their numbers were still small compared to manuscript donations. Lending was a common practice in Ottoman *waqf* libraries. Information on to whom and under what conditions books were to be lent was stated in the *waqf* deeds. However, due to an increase in the number of books going missing, lending was stopped after the 18th and the 19th centuries. At the same time, the hours of operation were extended.

Libraries were managed by supervisors (*nazır*) who were responsible for daily operations and the appointment of staff, and foundation executives (*mütevelli*) who were responsible for the daily running of libraries and for supervising staff during book counting. The most senior library officers were the head librarians (*hafız-ı kütüb*). Payment of librarians depended on the size of the library they worked in. The main duties of librarians were maintenance, borrowing, and lending. In different eras they were given various duties during prayers and educational activities held in the library. Librarians were asked to serve the readers with a smiling face, to open and close the library on time, and to be honest and hardworking. It was clearly stated in the *waqf* deeds that librarians who did not obey such rules would be removed. Until the emergence of independent libraries in the 17th century, only one librarian was in charge at each institution. The

other library staff were the librarian's apprentice (*yamak*), the librarian's clerk (*katib-ı kütüb*), who kept recordings of borrowings and of new books, the bookbinder (*mücellid*), the gatekeeper (*bevvab*) and guards who opened and closed the library, and the servants (*ferraş*) who did the cleaning. Having all these staff working for a library was only possible in big libraries that had sufficient funds.

The construction of *waqf* libraries emerged with the formation of Ottoman madrasas that started after the establishment of political stability in the 15th century. Although there must have been a library within the first madrasa during the reign of Orhan Ghazi (r. 1324–62), there is no extant information on its foundation or specifications. Early Ottoman-era *waqf* libraries were mainly constructed in madrasas and mosques. The first known *waqf* libraries were in Edirne in the School of Islamic Tradition (1435) of Sultan Murad II (r. 1421–44; 1446–51), and the library built in the Umurbey Mosque (1440) of Bursa. Typically, madrasa and mosque libraries consisted only of a single bookshelf without staff to protect the books, or with only a low-paid librarian. As the empire expanded, however, growing in political and economic strength *waqf* libraries also grew both in number and in resources. There were approximately 50 libraries in the Ottoman Empire in the 14th century, rising to more than 80 in the 15th century, a growth that continued until the end of the 18th century.

After the CONQUEST OF CONSTANTINOPLE in 1453, the Ottomans began to construct a large number of libraries in their new capital, renamed Istanbul, with vast collections within madrasas, mosques, dervish lodges (*zaviye*), and *külliyes* (building complexes adjacent to mosques). Librarians assigned to work in such libraries started to receive salaries. In this period, outside Istanbul, construction of libraries also continued in other cities such as Edirne, Bursa, Afyon and Konya. During the reigns of Bayezid II (r. 1481–1512) and Selim I (r. 1512–20), developments taking place in science and the arts paved the way to the opening of many madrasa and mosque libraries in Anatolia and the Balkans.

In the second half of the 16th century, especially during the reign of Murad III (r. 1574–95), the empire began to witness a shift in library culture toward independent libraries. During this time, the typical madrasa library ceased to be the dominant variety, and specialized libraries were founded in Istanbul for the use of doctors in the palace and in the observatory. In this period, aside from the libraries that were constructed within madrasas, mosques, small mosques, schools, dervish lodges, and tombs, scientific scholars began to form libraries in their houses and *waqf* deeds of such libraries show that the books became the property of the *waqf*, giving priority of usage first to the family members of the endowment, then to neighborhood intellectuals, and then to those who would appreciate the importance of books.

Besides *waqf* libraries formed in the empire's major cities, the number of libraries in other areas also increased from the beginning of the 17th century onward with the widespread formation of madrasas. Many existing libraries were also enhanced with donations of new books. These newly emergent independent libraries generally consisted of a single square building. Precautions were taken against damp and fire, and the increasing use of windows created lighter spaces.

The library of the KÖPRÜLÜ FAMILY, founded in 1678 by Fazıl Ahmed Pasha following conditions in his father's will, is recognized as the first independent Ottoman *waqf* library, and it formed an example for independent libraries founded afterward. These libraries are distinguished from existing institutions in that they were founded in independent buildings, their staff was not allowed to work elsewhere, and they were paid higher salaries than their predecessors.

During the reign of MAHMUD I (r. 1730–54), the most important libraries founded in Istanbul were the library of the HAGIA SOFIA, the Asir Efendi Library, and the Atif Efendi Library, the last two named for a famed *ŞEYHÜLISLAM* and a widely respected *defterdar* (treasurer). One of the characteristics of the libraries of this era was that education within the library became more common and prayers in the library were considered essential.

MODERN OTTOMAN LIBRARIES

Among the administrative and military reforms that took place during the reign of MAHMUD II (r. 1808–39), *waqf* reforms were considered, and *waqf* libraries were examined. In this period, especially in Istanbul, the number of libraries increased within mosques, small mosques, and dervish lodges. As the 19th century progressed, the first union catalogues were prepared and library catalogues were printed. These were important operations that took place in *waqf* libraries of this time. However, with the political and economic decline of the Ottoman Empire, *waqf* libraries also went into a decline; no new libraries were built, and many existing institutions halted operations. The dissolution seen in all institutions of the state is reflected in *waqf* libraries. Libraries became less functional as their collections became less capable of meeting the changing needs of the era. With the decline of the *waqf* libraries, however, new, modern Ottoman libraries arose. These new types of libraries included libraries in schools, associations, official buildings, national libraries, and Ottoman public libraries.

As the *waqf* libraries became less adequate for the use of the public and researchers, a new type of library emerged: public libraries. The library founded in DAMASCUS in 1881 is one of the first examples of this type. Called Bayezit State Library today, the Ottoman Public Library (Kütüphane-i Umumi-i Osmani), was founded in Istanbul in 1884. This library was established because readers were unable to benefit from other libraries due to closures (for various reasons), and because these libraries had small collections spread among different locations. At the same time, a law was passed requiring publishers to donate a copy of each compilation or translation to the library. This indicates that the intention was to create a national library. However, lack of agreement regarding staff management and the library itself left the library unable to fulfill the purpose of its foundation.

During the 19th century, as well as reforming the classical educational institutions, the Ottoman administration also decided to form new schools based on Western models. Following these decisions, military and school libraries were founded. Besides books in Turkish, these new libraries also housed many books in other languages, especially in French. The Ottomans formed the first modern university, DARÜLFÜNUN, in 1845, and despite interruptions in its construction and course of study, the shelves of the university library were filled with 4,000–5,000 volumes. Unfortunately, the library's stock was destroyed in the fires of 1865 and 1907. When Darülfünun was restructured after the declaration of the Republic of Turkey in 1924, all existing literature, law, and science libraries were combined with the central library. In the same year, the Yıldız Palace Library was combined with the library at Darülfünun, bringing its resources to 200,000 volumes. The Ottoman Association of Scientists Library (*Cemiyet-i İlmiye-i Osmaniye*) was founded in 1861, and is accepted as one of the pioneers of modern libraries. This library was differentiated from the others in that it had a membership system in place and periodicals in French, English, Greek, and Arabic, as well as in Turkish, arrived at the library on a regular basis. It is known that there was a library of the first Ottoman Assembly, which started operations in 1876, but it was destroyed in a fire. A report dated 1917 that was prepared by Sasun Efendi, a member of the Ottoman Assembly, stated that the Assembly library had a collection of 2,277 volumes; it is understood that the library was catalogued in accordance with the principles of modern librarianship. It was the first Ottoman library to use a card catalogue system. The Bab-ı Âli Library, on the other hand, which opened in 1895, was founded as a place where civil servants could spend their spare time. During the construction of the buildings, precautions were taken against fire and dampness. It is known that these libraries later served the community as archives. The Committee of Ottoman History (Tarih-i Osmani Encümeni) was founded in 1909 with the aim of allowing a new and modern approach to Ottoman history writing. Its library's operation ended in 1932 and was transferred to the Turkish Historical Society with its collection of 3,000 volumes. In line with the Turkism doctrine of the COMMITTEE OF UNION AND

PROGRESS (Ittihat ve Terakki), libraries whose names contained the word "national" started to be built, particularly after 1911. These public libraries include the Izmir National Library, the Bursa National Library, and the Eskisehir National Library.

Libraries founded in the Ottoman Empire developed in parallel to the political, social, and economical state of the empire. After the foundation of the Republic, the training of modern librarians accelerated the modernization process that had started in the late Ottoman period. Valuable manuscript collections and books printed using the classical script therefore continue serving researchers in various libraries in Turkey, in accordance with the principles of modern librarianship.

Tûba Çavdar

See also ALI EMIRI EFENDI; EDUCATION.

Further reading: İsmail E. Erünsal, "A Brief Survey of the Development of Turkish Library Catalogues." *Libri* 51, no.1 (2001): 1–7; İsmail E. Erünsal, "Budgeting and Auditing in the Ottoman Libraries." *İÜEF Kütüphanecilik Dergisi: Belge, Bilgi, Kütüphane Araştırmaları,* 2 (1989): 91–99; İsmail E. Erünsal, "The Development of Ottoman Libraries from the Conquest of Istanbul (1453) to the Emergence of the Independent Library." *TTK Belleten* 60, no. 227 (Ankara 1996): 93–125; İsmail E. Erünsal, "Personnel Employed in Ottoman Libraries." *İslâm Araştırmaları Dergisi* 3 (Istanbul 1999): 91–123; İsmail E. Erünsal, "A Brief Survey of the Development of Turkish Library Catalogues," in *M. Uğur Derman 65. Yas Armağanı/65th Birthday Festschrift,* edited by Irvin Cemil Schick (Istanbul: Sabancı University, 2000), 271–282; İsmail E. Erünsal, "The Expansion and Reorganization of the Ottoman Library System: 1754–1839." *TTK Belleten* 62, no. 235 (Ankara 1999): 831–849.

Libya (Libia)   The territory that today constitutes the nation of Libya has long been divided between two coastal provinces: Tripolitania along the western seaboard of the country, with its capital in TRIPOLI, and Cyrenaica along the eastern shore, with Benghazi as its capital. The southern part of the country, known as Fazzan, is largely desert and was not administered by any outsiders until the 20th century. For most of the Ottoman period, the only military presence the Ottomans maintained in what would become Libya was in the port city of Tripoli and its surrounding countryside.

Pedro Navarro, a Spaniard, captured Tripoli in 1510 and established it as a base from which he could raid Muslim shipping and ports along the North African coast. It was later handed over to the KNIGHTS OF ST. JOHN OF MALTA. In 1535 the Ottoman naval commander, Hayreddin Barbarossa (*see* BARBAROSSA BROTHERS), established a base at Tajura, a town about 15 miles from Tripoli, with a plan to drive the Christians from that city. It was not until 1551 that the Ottomans captured the city, however, despite several attempted sieges. Under Ottoman control, which lasted until 1711, the city became a major center for Muslim CORSAIRS AND PIRATES who raided the Christian-held islands of the Mediterranean Sea and even at times the Italian mainland. The Ottoman navy administered the city from Istanbul.

At the start of the 18th century, Ottoman military strongmen rose against the sultanate and seized control in all the major North African ports. In 1711, Karamanlı Ahmed Bey seized control in Tripoli after massacring the Ottoman officers of the garrison. He was able to repulse an Ottoman counterattack the following year and thereafter remained in power by sending rich presents to the sultan. Basking in their autonomy, the dynasty established by Karamanlı Ahmed ruled Tripoli until 1835, with only one interruption (1793–95).

When the Ottomans reestablished direct control of Tripoli in 1835, they immediately removed the last of the Karamanlı dynasty, fearing, after the French conquest of Algeria in 1830, that the European powers might seek to add Tripoli to their growing empires. British and American forces had already occupied the city several times in the early 19th century in attempts to end piracy. Once Tripoli had been reclaimed for the empire, the Ottoman forces tried to subdue the BEDOUINS in the desert interior of the country. In order to maintain an Ottoman presence outside Tripoli, the governor established a number of military garrisons along the Mediterranean coast.

The major economic activity of the inhabitants of Libya, besides piracy, was as merchants engaged in the trans-Saharan trade in gold and slaves. Both piracy and the gold trade had largely stopped by 1835, but the trade of African slaves within the Ottoman Empire remained highly profitable. In 1857, British pressure on the Ottomans led them to abolish slavery in the province of Tripoli, although the empire itself did not abolish slavery until 1889. Nonetheless, illegal slave trading in Tripoli continued until the 1912 Italian occupation of the country.

After 1853, Ottoman rule in Tripoli was direct, but it was less so in the eastern region of Cyrenaica. The founder of the Sanusi Order of SUFISM, MUHAMMAD AL-SANUSI, viewed the Ottoman sultans as having illegally assumed the title of caliph as they were not descended from the clan of the Prophet Muhammad. At the same time, he also recognized that the Ottomans were the only Muslim military power that might prevent the Europeans from partitioning and assuming total political control of the Middle East and North Africa. Although their relationship was tenuous, the Ottomans nevertheless exempted the Sanusi Order from some taxes and the Sanusis, in turn, helped the Ottomans maintain order among the tribes and protect the flow of trade across the Sahara Desert.

The Ottomans continued to hold the region, but beginning in the late 19th century, the area increasingly became the center of competing French and Italian interests. Blocked from continued investment in neighboring Tunisia by France's 1881 occupation, Italian ambitions turned to Tripoli, where thousands of Italians had settled and Italian capitalists had made major investments. The relationship between the newly united Kingdom of Italy and the Ottoman administration started to deteriorate as the Italians living in Tripoli refused to accept Ottoman judicial sovereignty. In an age when a European nation's prestige rested on an overseas empire, the other European powers signaled to Italy that they would not oppose its imperial ambitions in Tripoli, but Germany, an Italian ally, was also trying to cultivate good relations with Sultan Abdülhamid II (r. 1876–1909) at this time; thus German diplomatic pressure worked to forestall any Italian aggression against the Ottoman province of Tripoli as long as Abdülhamid was sultan.

But the potential German-Ottoman relationship was jeopardized when the Ottoman government was confronted by the Young Turk revolution in 1908. Although it was no friend to German interests, the new government in Istanbul was also unwilling to forward Italian interests and actively resisted any further acquisition of land in Libya by Italian colonists. On September 23, 1911, the Italian government sent a formal protest to the Ottomans about the actions of the Young Turk party, the Committee of Union and Progress, in Tripoli, saying that it was harassing Italians living there. The Ottomans tried to placate the Italians by offering further economic concessions and guaranteeing the safety of Italians resident in Libya. But just in case diplomacy failed, the Ottoman government also sent weapons and troops to the province to strengthen its defenses. Receiving a diplomatic nod from the Germans, Italy responded by declaring war on the Ottoman Empire on September 29, 1911, and Italian forces quickly occupied the coastal towns.

The Ottomans had few troops in Libya to resist the Italians and these retreated inland. But their fortunes improved when the Sanusis joined the resistance. Preferring Muslim Ottoman to Christian Italian rulers, the Sanusis joined the Ottomans in the bloody and ruthless guerrilla war that followed. European papers were filled with stories of reputed Italian atrocities against the Arab population of the province. Despite growing public pressure at home to end the colonial adventure, the Italian government threatened to invade the Ottoman Empire as a means of stopping Ottoman support to the Libyan resistance The threat worked, and the Ottoman government concluded a secret agreement with the Italians in September 1912 to withdraw Ottoman forces from Libya and to confirm Italian sovereignty over the country. In return, the Italians recognized the Ottoman sultan as the spiritual leader of Libya's Muslims in his role as caliph. A public treaty was signed on October 17, 1912, and

the Ottoman forces withdrew. With the departure of the Ottoman forces, the Sanusis emerged as the legitimate rulers of Libya in the eyes of most Libyan Muslims. They continued their guerrilla war against the occupation off and on until the defeat of the Italians in World War II by Great Britain, whose forces occupied the country under United Nations sanction. In 1951, Libya became an independent kingdom with Idris al-Sanusi as its first king.

Bruce Masters

Further reading: Rachel Simon, *Libya Between Ottomanism and Nationalism: The Ottoman Involvement in Libya during the War with Italy, 1911–1919* (Berlin: Karl Schwarz, 1987).

literature, classical Ottoman (13th through 19th centuries) The literature that developed in the Ottoman territories between the 13th and 19th centuries stands as one of the richest and most significant links in what may be regarded as a greater chain of Islamic literature. Complex and symbolic, Ottoman literature encompasses nearly 700 years of writing. Its roots can be found in the pre-Islamic Turkish literary tradition of the Turkic groups who lived in the Central Asian steppes. From this eighth century culture comes a tradition of epic tales that these tribes brought with them when they later migrated from the steppe lands into Anatolia. In the 13th century, in its earliest phase, Ottoman literature consisted primarily of translations and adaptations from Arabic and Persian books, mainly about religion and ethics. In the 14th century literary production increased and textual language became more elaborate. By the 16th century, Ottoman literature is considered to have entered its golden age, and from this point until the close of the classical period in the 19th century, the artistry and invention of Ottoman writers grew and flourished. With the advent of the Tanzimat reform period (1839–76), ushering in a new set of political, social, and literary values, this classical Ottoman literary tradition began to be referred to as Edebiyat-ı kadime (old literature), old Turkish literature, classical Turkish literature, or most famously, divan literature, because the word *divan* means both a collection of poems and the meeting room of the sultans or Ottoman elite.

Ottoman literary artists are known for having combined previous Islamic literary traditions with their own in both form and content. After the 19th century Tanzimat reform period, Ottoman literature was sometimes accused of being "palace literature," "elite literature," or "court literature." However, it was produced and circulated not only within the court and the capital but also in the imperial periphery by poets from different social groups. While the sultans themselves composed poems using pen names (*mahlas*), even some illiterate (*ümmi*) people, such as the 16th-century poet Zati (d. 1546), made significant literary contributions. The literature produced in the last decades of the Ottoman Empire shows that it was embedded in the life of both the elite and ordinary people, and that it spread through many layers of Ottoman society from the court to the public.

The Ottoman language, Ottoman Turkish, is a mixture of Persian, Arabic, and Turkish words, and it is this richly mixed language that is the basis of Ottoman literature. In the 13th century, most Ottoman literary works were written in the dialect used in western Anatolia. Since its beginning, however, Ottoman literature has used words that came mainly from two languages, Persian and Arabic; great numbers of words from these languages were brought into the Ottoman Turkish language because traditional Turkish words did not lend themselves well to the system of Persian poetic meter that dominated classical Ottoman poetry.

Over time, two main literary traditions, Turki-i basit (plain Turkish) and Sebk-i Hindi (Indian style), came to dominate classical Ottoman literature. In Turki-i basit, the literary language is straightforward, Turkish words are in the majority, and clarity of expression is as important as meaning. In Sebk-i Hindi, which first appeared in the 17th century, the complex style and multiple layers of meaning are as important as the fundamental content. At the beginning of the classical period Ottoman literature consisted mostly of translations and adaptations from Arabic and Persian books that addressed mainly religious and ethical ideas and were written in aplain language. Many scholars agree that the literary style of this period was still largely undeveloped. After the 14th century, as the Ottoman civilization settled down and artistic patronage emerged, literary life and production increased, and language became more elaborate. The number of translated and adapted works increased, as well as original works; these works treated both secular and religious subjects. After the Karamanid Turkic principality was incorporated into the expanding Ottoman Empire in the latter part of the 15th century, Karamanoglu Mehmed Bey declared Turkish the official language, and Turkish literature became increasingly stylized. More and more, Ottoman literature addressed "classical" subjects—love, praise, and destiny—rather than the didactic, moral, epic, and religious topics of its earlier phase.

In the 16th century, considered the zenith, or golden age, of Ottoman literature, Turkish literary artists found their own authentic forms of expression in their own language, with their own style, and became more prolific. Also, after that time, Ottoman literary works became not only more elaborate and stylistic but also more distinctively Ottoman. The 18th century brought increasing novelty and generic diversity to Ottoman literature, poetry of the time being characterized as belonging to the Tulip Age (Lale Devri), while Ottoman prose of the time saw an increased interest in biographical works. The 19th century saw the transition between classical Ottoman literature and modern Turkish, or LATE OTTOMAN LITERATURE.

Classical Ottoman literature is divided into folk literature, mystical literature, and divan literature, and these, in turn, manifest themselves either in prose or in poetry. Of these, poetry plays a greater role in classical Ottoman literature than does prose.

POETRY

The basic structural unit in Ottoman poetry is the couplet (*beyit*). The basic characteristic of poetry is that poetical forms should be in meters called *aruz*, which is adopted from Persian literature. The vast majority of the divan poetry was lyric in nature, and the main genres in Ottoman poetry were *gazel* (love), *kaside* (panegyric), and *mesnevi* (romance). *Gazel* was the most common genre. *Kaside* was written for special occasions (birth, death, victory, enthronement, weddings, and so forth). *Kaside* could be named variously according to its beginning part. The poets used a richer, more textured language in *kasides*, and reserved a simpler one for *gazels*.

Ottoman divan poetry is also characterized by the recurrence of three central figures: the lover, the beloved, and the rival. Ottoman poetry is replete with symbolic relationships among these three. The lover may often be read as referring to the poet, whereas the beloved may be understood as referring to the sultan, a person in a higher position, or an actual beloved. The emotional situation of the lover was expressed with the use of metaphor and other literary devices such as simile.

Classical Ottoman poets often had other professions besides writing. According to classical Ottoman biographies of poets (*tezkire*), which cover the lives of 3,182 poets, these individuals belonged to 108 different professions, including members of the clergy, courtiers, sheiks, even sultans. Despite this illustrious listing, however, many Ottoman poets were not from the elite, or even from the literate classes, and classical Ottoman poetry was enriched by the widely respected work of oral poets. The best-known classical Ottoman poets are Mevlana, Dehhani, and Sultan Veled in the 13th century; Nesimi, Şeyyad Hamza, Ahmed Fakih in the 14th century; Ahmed Pasha, Necati, and Şeyhi in the 15th century; Fuzuli, Baki, and Hayali in the 16th century; Taşlıcalı Yahya, Nefi, and Nabi in the 17th century; and Nedim in the 18th century.

With the effects of westernization during and after the Tanzimat reform period, both the form and content of Ottoman poetry changed dramatically, introducing new subjects and concrete ideas, often nationalistic ones, and literary language became plainer and more direct.

This period also saw the rise of new literary forms and genres such as the novel, short story, and play. However, there were also some groups such as Encümen-i Şuara that worked to protect the classical tradition in literature. Enderunlu Vasıf, Leyla Hanım, and Şeyh Galip were eminent poets of the 19th century.

PROSE

Two kinds of prose writing styles were seen during the seven centuries of the Ottoman Empire: plain prose and stylistic (rhymed) prose that can also be called *inşa*. Ottoman prose was first seen in translated books in the 13th and 14th centuries. The first inşa (rhymed prose) samples emerged in the 15th century. In the 15th and 16th centuries religious, mystic, and epic books were written in plain language for the purpose of propaganda, whereas books on medicine, astronomy along with travel books and biographies of poets were written in stylistic prose (*inşa*). Writing history in prose began to develop in these centuries. In the 16th century, biographies of Turkish mystic sheiks, geographical works, and especially history books were written in rhymed prose.

Inşa is another important form of prose that developed in separate channels. *Inşa* means "the art of prose writing," and the *münşeat* is a work written in elegant style. It features a great deal of alliteration and rhymed words used with elaborate style. The first *inşa* samples go back to the 15th century. Several books were then written on the art of letter-writing, which was a novelty for Ottoman literature. Two of these books are *Teressül ile Menahicü'l-inşa* and *Gül-i Sadberg ve Gülşen-inşa*.

As with classical Ottoman poetry, the zenith of Ottoman prose literature coincided with the empire's political rise in the 16th century. In both prose and poetry, the numbers of writers and their works increased. In the 17th century, great writers such as Nergisi and Veysi gave the best examples of stylistic prose. Again, some history books, travel books, biographies of poets, and bibliographies were added to ambassadors' books and reports. In the 18th century the same style continued in various works without major change. In the 19th century, in parallel with westernization efforts, new prose genres were added to old ones, such as the novel, story, theatre, and newspapers. Prose gained many new features with the new genres. It grew closer to spoken language, thereby becoming plainer. Also, the Ottoman Translation Office, established in 1832, added new words from Western languages. As a result, prose became more didactic than artistic. The best-known Ottoman prose writers were Mustafa Darir and Celalüddin Hızır in the 14th century; Mesihi, Aşıkpaşazade, and Kaygusuz Abdal in the 15th century; Selaniki, Gelibolulu Mustafa Ali, Hoca Saadettin Efendi, and Taşköprülüzade in the 16th century; Sururi, Evliya Celebi, Katib Çelebi, Veysi, and Nergisi in the 17th century; and Esrar Dede in the 19th century.

Vildan Serdaroğlu

Further reading: Walter G. Andrews, *An Introduction to Ottoman Poetry* (Minneapolis, Minn.: Bibliotheca Islamica, 1976); Walter G. Andrews, *Poetry's Voice, Society's Song: Ottoman Lyric Poetry* (Seattle: University of Washington Press, 1985); Kemal Cicek, ed., *The Great Ottoman Turkish Civilization*, vol. 4 (Ankara: Yeni Türkiye, 2000); Elias John Wilkinson Gibb, *A History of Ottoman Poetry, 1319–1901,* edited by Edward Granville Browne (London: Lowe-Brydone, 1958).

literature, folk   There was a stark difference in the Ottoman Empire between the formal literature of the educated classes and the literature of the common people. The former was highly stylized and in a language that would have been largely incomprehensible to ordinary people. Although this was especially true for literature written in Ottoman Turkish, literature written in Arabic and Greek in the Ottoman Empire was also composed with a vocabulary and grammar taken from the classical languages. Thus these works would have seemed archaic, even incomprehensible, to uneducated speakers of either language. Another major difference between the two forms of literature is that folk literature was passed down from one generation to the next by an oral tradition. When scholars began to transcribe this oral folk literature in the 18th and 19th centuries, they found that different versions of a work with the same title could vary widely.

The forms of folk literature were most commonly poetry and long, interconnected stories. Poetry was often sung, while stories were the property of professional storytellers who would entertain in COFFEEHOUSES or perform for the wealthy at formal occasions such as weddings or circumcisions. There was also a third form, a kind of theater known as Karagöz (Black-eyed), after the name of the lead character. These were shadow puppet plays. The players would manipulate figures, made of brightly painted camel skin, behind a backlit screen while reciting the lines. The audience on the other side of the screen would only see the characters as they cavorted across the screen. The Karagöz plays were originally a Turkish art form, but Western travelers in the 18th century reported the performance of versions of the plays in Greek and Arabic, an indication of the popularity of the art form. The Karagöz shows were almost always coffeehouse entertainments and were often ribald. They were also often used as political and social satire. As a result, the coffeehouses offering them were frequently closed due to the ire of government officials who saw these shows as a potential disruption of the social order.

Folk poetry had two main genres, heroic and religious. In the Balkans, long epic poems were used to tell the adventures of heroes who were usually bandits and outlaws, the HAYDUKs of the Serbs and the *klephtes* of the Greeks. As Ottomans were the usual target of the robberies narrated, the bandit poems served to promote an early form of national consciousness among listeners, transforming outlaws into potential national heroes. Bosnian Muslims, on the other hand, recited poems in a language and style similar to that of their Christian neighbors, but theirs highlighted the role of Muslim Bosniak heroes fighting for the Ottomans. Heroic folk epics in poetry were less common among the Arabs and Turks, although the pre-Ottoman exploits told in the Turkoman tales of Dede Korkut remained popular among Turks in the Ottoman centuries, and the Arabs had poems extolling the heroes of the Muslim resistance to the crusaders. But more commonly, folk poetry popular with Turks and Arabs was either romantic or religious. Sufi orders, especially the BEKTAŞI ORDER of dervishes and the ALAWIS of Anatolia, used poetry set to music and composed in the Turkish vernacular of the peasants to spread their religious message.

For both Turks and Arabs, the most popular form of folk literature was a series of interconnected stories. An individual tale would be embedded in another, creating suspenseful narratives not unlike modern western forms of narrative serialization—episodic novels, multipart films, and television and radio serials—so that the listener would be sure to return on the following evening to hear what happened next. In Arabic, one of the most popular of these serial stories was the recounting of the exploits of the pre-Islamic Bedouin hero Antar and his beloved Abla. Scholars believe that the earliest manuscript version of these stories dates to the 13th century, but the oral tradition remained strong despite being committed to writing. The stories were still being told in coffee shops in Damascus even into the 20th century.

Perhaps more popular than the tales of heroes were those of ordinary people who found themselves in extraordinary circumstances. The two most famous of this genre are the Turkish tales known as the *Forty Viziers* (Kırk Vezirler) and the Arabic tales, *The Thousand and One Nights* (Alf Layla wa Layla). Both collections contain materials that predate the Ottoman period, but in their retelling over the centuries, they were continually modified by contemporary tastes. As was the case with the Karagöz plays, these stories were often ribald and also contained elements of social criticism. A French-language translation of some of the tales from *The Thousand and One Nights* appeared in 12 volumes between 1704 and 1717. The stories became immensely popular with European readers and various translation and editions followed. *The Thousand and One Nights* appeared

in several different English translations, by far the most familiar of which is the translation of British aristocrat Richard Burton, published to wide acclaim in 1885. The popularity of this text continues today, and it is probably the Middle Eastern literary work best-known to the English-speaking public, due in part to an unceasing succession of adaptations.

Bruce Masters

Further reading: *Tales from the Thousand and One Nights* trans. N. J. Dawood (New York: Penguin, 1973).

literature, late Ottoman (1860–1923)   Twenty years after the promulgation of the TANZIMAT, the Ottoman social and political reforms of 1839, which were launched with a view to drawing the empire closer to modern Western civilization, Ottoman literature saw a similar modernization movement. Ottoman intellectuals asserted that the centuries-old imperial literary styles were outdated and could not convey the modern Western values the Ottoman civilization wished to adopt. They criticized the old literature and began to develop a brand-new approach in terms of forms, topics, and language. From that time until the end of the imperial period and the advent of the Turkish Republic in 1923 Ottoman literary features were consistently transformed using models and ideas adopted from Western literature.

Late Ottoman literature is divided into the following periods, from the Tanzimat era to the Republic: Tanzimat Period Literature, 1860–95; Servet-i Fünun (Wealth of knowledge) Period Literature, 1895–1901; Fecr-i Ati (Dawn of the future) Literature, 1909–13; and National Literature, 1911–23.

TANZIMAT PERIOD (1860–1895)

Tanzimat period literature altered the abstract and aesthetical approaches of CLASSICAL OTTOMAN LITERATURE, also known as divan literature, which had been repeated for centuries in the same forms and topics. These were replaced by a new form of literature with a deliberate political agenda aimed at social progress. While they initially focused on introducing new ideas to the intellectual elite, writers of this period also strove to create a lucid and direct language with the hope of bringing these ideas to the general reader. The role model for these changes was Western literature, which the Tanzimat writers began to translate in 1858. Thanks to these translations, new literary forms such as short stories, drama, and the persuasive essay were introduced to the Ottoman consciousness, resulting in the immediate production of Ottoman works using similar forms. So, too, long-standing Ottoman literary forms such as poems were transformed along new lines, following new ideas, and showing a modern structure.

Tanzimat literature can be subdivided into two periods. In the first period, between 1860 and 1876, literature was used as a tool for reorienting an Ottoman society standing on the threshold of major social and political change. The founders of modern Ottoman literature were statesmen and journalists, intellectuals who, through their written work, put forward various reform suggestions aimed at rescuing the declining empire. The unique nature of the Tanzimat writers yielded a literature with a criticizing, exploring, guiding, and teaching quality.

The leading personality of this period was Ibrahim Şinasi (1826–71), who introduced myriad innovations in Ottoman literature. Şinasi translated various Western poems and published *Tercüme-i Manzume* (Translated poems) in 1858. The new poetic forms and topics in these translations became a model for the modernization of Ottoman poetry. In his own poems, inspired by Western literature, Şinasi combined political concepts such as justice, equality, and liberty with the visionary, abstract style of classical era poetry. Another remarkable aspect of these initial works is that they were written in a plain and lucid language. In this way, poems appealing to the elite class were for the first time written in a language intelligible to the public.

Journalism in this period also made a crucial contribution to the simplification of language and helped spread reformist ideas to the public. Again Şinasi played a leading role with the simplified language he employed in his articles in *Tercüman-ı Ahval* (State of affairs), the first independent Turkish newspaper, and in his play *Şair Evlenmesi* (Marriage of a poet), accepted as the first example of modern theater.

Şinasi's role in the foundation of modern Turkish literature was also significant due to his influence on NAMIK KEMAL (1888–1940), who would take the movement even further. Namık Kemal initially wrote his poems in the form of divan literature, then changed his literary approach when he became acquainted with and was influenced by Şinasi's style of poetry. Like Şinasi, Namık Kemal produced poems, theatrical plays, and novels that explored political content. He wrote newspaper articles that exhibited remarkable and influential ideas about the political and social issues of the period and took a leading role in the collapse of the divan literature. Working hard to create forms and techniques that could accurately express the new ideas and benefit the public, he became one of the most effective writers of the period.

Another notable personality in the first period of Tanzimat literature is ZIYA PASHA (1829–80), who favored the same political ideas and literary approach as Namık Kemal. Although he later deviated in part from his earlier opinions, he initially went a step further than Namık Kemal with his 1868 article "Şiir ve Inşa" (Poetry and prose). which asserted that the true root for Turkish literature was not the divan literature, which was heavily influenced by Arabic and Persian culture, but the FOLK LITERATURE that had been prevalent for centuries among the people.

The second period of Tanzimat literature commences with the enthronement of ABDÜLHAMID II (r. 1876–1909) in 1876 and continues until 1895 when the Servet-i Fünun literature, a real reformist period in Ottoman literature in terms of both content and form, starts. Acceding to the throne by promising to promulgate a constitution restricting the powers of the sultan, Abdülhamid II soon modified his policy and switched to a repressive rule that favored CENSORSHIP. Literary leaders who pondered and wrote on the country's problems were exiled. Those who stayed were forced to avoid the political content that had prevailed in the first period and to turn inward instead. Abdülhak Hamid Tarhan (1852–1937), Recaizade Mahmud Ekrem (1847–1914), and Samipaşazade Sezai (1860–1936) shared the social and political ideas of Namık Kemal, whom they revered as a master, but they could not explicitly express these ideas due to censorship. However, they continued to pursue his ideal to supplant the old literary approach with a new and modern one. Abdülhak Hamid's bold essays, which sharply criticize the aesthetics of the divan poetry in terms of form, and Recaizade's collection on the theory of the "new literature" in a book called *Talim-i Edebiyat* (Education of literature), stand out as the most effective efforts in this respect.

Furthermore, thanks to better and more widely available education, a generation grew up during this period that was better acquainted with Western languages, and closely followed and translated Western literature. Of this generation the most important writers were Nabizade Nazım, Mizancı Murad, Fatma Aliye, Nigar Hanım, and Beşir Fuad. At the same time, new periodicals sprang up dedicated to publishing translations. The intense and knowledgeable literary milieu fostered by this sort of literal periodical had a vital role in the rise of the Servet-i Fünun literature.

SERVET-İ FÜNUN PERIOD (1895–1901)

In 1895 a few young poets and writers, led by Tevfik Fikret (1867–1915), a student of Recaizade Mahmud Ekrem, came together to produce a literary periodical called *Servet-i Fünun* (Wealth of knowledge). Taking its name from the periodical, the Servet-i Fünun community became the first significant literary community of Turkish literature. Its members believed that literature was primarily an aesthetic form and thus they returned to the highly stylized forms and poetic language of the pre-Tanzimat literature. In terms of content the writers of the Servet-i Fünun community focused on human nature instead of abstract ideas, attaching importance to psychological analyses; mindful of the repressive nature of the government they continued to avoid political topics. Halid Ziya Uşaklıgil (1867–1945), considered one of the foremost personalities not only of that period but also of all Turkish literature, produced the first masterpieces of this literary tradition with novels and stories whose psychological insights attracted attention. His novels include *Aşk-ı Memnu* (*Forbidden Love*) and *Kırık Hayatlar* (*Broken Lives*). Other outstanding members of this community were Cenap Sahabeddin, Mehmed Rauf, and Hüseyin Cahid.

This period of Ottoman literature was characterized by a continual debate between supporters of the old and the new literary schools. While the "new literature" gradually took root, the "old literature" survived. "Old litterateurs, gathered around poet Muallim Naci (1850–93), who is known for his dictionary, critical essays, memoirs, and poems. His poems are easy to read. His poetry books include *Ateşpare* (1883), *Şerâre* (1884), and *Fürûzan* (1885). The group that gathered around him sought neither radical renovation nor blind loyalty to the past; spearheaded by Ahmed Mithat Efendi (1844–1913), Ahmed Rasim (1867–1932), and Hüseyin Rahmi Gürpınar (1864–1944), they were popular folk novelists.

NATIONAL LITERATURE (1911–1923) AND FECR-İ ATI LITERATURE (1909-1913)

Between 1901, when the Servet-i Fünun community dissolved, and 1908, when the Second Constitutional Monarchy restricting the sultan's power through constitutional rights for his subjects was promulgated, the seeds of social unrest were sown. The idea of liberty slowly gained traction and culminated in the termination of the repressive regime of Abdülhamid II in 1909. The relaxation of censorship under the Second Constitutional Monarchy led to the founding of an unprecedented number of newspapers and magazines and the expression of a variety of ideas, including Ottomanism, Islamism, and Turkism.

The 19th century had witnessed growing nationalist movements among the Balkan peoples, many of whom decided to now make a bid for political freedom. They rejected the idea of Ottomanism, which had, from the very beginning of the empire, aimed to gather all religious and cultural groups within the boundaries of the empire under the umbrella of an Ottoman identity. The national aspirations of the Balkan peoples in turn amplified nationalist sentiments among the Turks who formed the dominant ethnic group in the empire. Islamism was another influential intellectual trend during this time period; it aimed to strengthen the empire through religious unity and found its most striking representation in the poems of Mehmed Akif Ersoy (1873–1936).

With the end of the repressive regime in 1908, literature was again employed to serve intellectual trends and convey political ideas, as it had been during the Tanzimat Period. Numerous literary communities sprang up and dissolved again; among these the Fecr-i Ati (Dawn of the future) community (1909–13) stood out. It faded away shortly after the National Literature and New Language movements appeared in 1911 as reactions to this community. Adopting the slogan "literature is personal and estimable," the Fecr-i Ati community carried on the individualistic and aesthetic traditions of the Servet-i Fünun. With its notion of art for art's sake the movement's influence was short-lived, but it is famous for a group of young writers it produced who would gain lasting fame in later years. Among these writers Ahmed Haşim (1884–1933), Refik Halid Karay (1888–1965), and Yakup Kadri Karaosmanoğlu (1889–1974) are the most prominent. Ahmed Haşim became one of the most significant poets in Turkey, and Refik Halid and Yakup Kadri went on to become leading novelists.

Some of the young writers who opposed the idea of art for art's sake gathered around the *Genç Kalemler* (Young pens) magazine, founded in 1911, and initiated the National Literature and New Language movements. Their ideas favored a simplified language accessible to the general reader and purged of Arabic and Persian words; a return to Turkish traditions rather than Arabic, Persian, or Western influences; the use of themes originating in Turkish folk culture; and creating and maintaining a national literary tradition. The pioneer of the New Language movement was Ömer Seyfettin (1884–1920), renowned for his short stories. Ali Canib Yöntem (1887–1967) and ZIYA GÖKALP (1876–1924), the latter especially through his theoretical articles, made vital contributions to the establishment of the National Literature movement. An early representative of National Literature was Mehmed Emin Yurdakul (1869–1944). The poems he published during the time of the Ottoman-Greek War (1897) were written in pure Turkish, employed a syllabic meter that was based on Turkish rather than Arabic, and treated themes that praised Turkish identity.

One of the National Literature communities that emerged in the early 20th century was Beş Hececiler (Five poets of syllable), which took its name from its five members: Yusuf Ziya Ortaç (1895–1967), Orhan Seyfi Orhon (1890–1972), Enis Behiç Koryürek (1892–1949), Halid Fahri Ozansoy (1891–1971), and Faruk Nafiz Çamlıbel (1898–1973). It was a literary movement that aimed to replace the *aruz* meter (which was employed as the fundamental meter for centuries in divan poetry and functioned according to the logic of the Arabic language) with the syllabic meter, which is the original meter of the Turkish language.

The poet who would effect the most radical reform of Ottoman poetry was Yahya Kemal Beyatlı (1884–1958), who returned in 1912 from exile in Paris. Yahya

Kemal laid the foundation of modern Turkish poetry by applying the Poésie Pure approach of French poetry to traditional Ottoman divan poetry.

The National Literature movement itself did not yield many influential writers except for a few novelists. Among them the most significant writer was Halide Edib Adıvar (1884–1964), who is also considered the first important female novelist of Turkish literature. In her first novels, written in the final era of the Ottoman Empire, Halide Edib depicted the passionate love of female heroes, but later in her long and productive career switched to novels that focused on political and social reform. Yakup Kadri, who was initially a member of the Fecr-i Ati community but soon adopted his own path, wrote the last significant examples of Ottoman novels. Yet the true significance of the literary identities of Halide Edib and Yakup Kadri emerged only in the following period, the era of republican Turkey when both published novels that criticized the republic's new regime and its society model. Reşat Nuri Güntekin (1889–1956) and Peyami Safa (1899–1961), who published their first novels in 1922, turned out to be the most accomplished and popular writers of the republican period.

In sum, this final period of Ottoman literature was shaped by the same idea of westernization that heavily influenced the social and political policies of the republic. The fundamental reform that took place during this period was the fading away of divan literature, and with it the influences of Arabic and Persian culture and literature in terms of style, language, meter, and topics.

Handan İnci

Further reading: Emel Sönmez, *Turkish Women in Turkish Literature of the Nineteenth Century* (Leiden: Brill, 1969); Talat Sait Halman, "Poetry and Society: The Turkish Experience," in *Modern Near East: Literature and Society,* edited by C. Max Kortepeter (New York: Center for Near Eastern Studies, New York University, 1971), 35–72; Şerif Mardin, "Super Westernization in Urban Life in the Ottoman Empire in the Last Quarter of the Nineteenth Century" in *Turkey: Geographic and Social Perspectives,* edited by P. Benedict, E. Tümertekin, and F. Mansur (Leiden: Brill, 1974), 403–446; Carter V. Findley, "An Ottoman Occidentalist in Europe: Ahmed Midhat meets Madame Gülnar, 1889." *American Historical Review* 103, no. 1 (February 1998): 15–49.

M

al-Maani, Fakhr al-Din (d. 1635) *Druze warlord and rebel* Fakhr al-Din al-Maani was the Druze emir (ruler) of the mountainous region of the Shuf in LEBANON in the first half of the 17th century and a challenger to Ottoman authority. He is also considered by some Lebanese to be the founder of modern Lebanon as a political ideal. Throughout the 16th century, following the Ottoman conquest of Syria, the Druze country was rebellious. In 1585 IBRAHIM PASHA, governor of EGYPT, launched a major military operation into the Shuf that succeeded in temporarily disarming the DRUZES and compelled them to pay the back taxes they owed the sultan. In the aftermath of the campaign, Fakhr al-Din emerged as the leader of the al-Maani clan and the dominant political player in the clan-based politics of the Lebanese mountains.

While it is apparent from the historical record that he was adept at building coalitions between the Druze and MARONITE inhabitants of the mountains and in establishing relations with the Europeans, it is not at all clear that he had ambitions to found a nation. Significantly, he never claimed the title of sultan, being content with the traditional title of emir bestowed on the dominant Druze chieftain. Not daring to dream of independence, Fakhr al-Din sought to play various local competitors against one another while he deftly balanced the interests of the Ottoman state against those of various European parties were interested in gaining influence and trade in the eastern Mediterranean.

When JANBULAD ALI PASHA, governor of ALEPPO, rose in revolt in 1605, Fakhr al-Din sided with him, apparently as a way to eliminate his rival, Yusuf Sayfa, who was governor of TRIPOLI. But after Murad Pasha, the newly appointed governor of Aleppo crushed the rebellion in 1607, Fakhr al-Din was able to buy his way back into the sultan's good graces and his son, Ali, was appointed to head the district that included BEIRUT and Sidon. By 1614 Fakhr al-Din had again earned the sultan's displeasure and went into exile in Tuscany, where he stayed until 1618. Upon his return, he regained control over the Shuf Mountains and extended his authority into the Bekaa Valley in Lebanon and parts of northern Palestine. His hold over these districts lasted until the Ottomans went to war with Iran in 1633. In order to secure Syria from the possibility of a Druze rebellion, Ottoman troops moved against Fakhr al-Din, who was finally captured in 1635, sent as a prisoner to Istanbul, and executed there. Fakhr al-Din's death did not end the importance of his clan, which dominated Lebanese politics for the next 50 years, but no one after him would again threaten Ottoman hegemony over Lebanon.

Bruce Masters

Further reading: Abdul-Rahim Abu-Husayn, *Provincial Leaderships in Syria, 1575–1650* (Beirut: American University of Beirut, 1985).

madrasa *See* EDUCATION.

Maghrib *See* NORTH AFRICA.

mahkeme *See* COURT OF LAW.

Mahmud I (b. 1696–d. 1754) (r. 1730–1754) *Ottoman sultan and caliph* The son of MUSTAFA II and Saliha

344

of provincial disorders in Anatolia, DAMASCUS, and the Arabian peninsula (WAHHABIS), as well as those in Istanbul in 1740 and 1748, occupied the reign of Mahmud I.

During Mahmud's reign, Ibrahim Müteferrika wrote a treatise on the causes of the Ottoman military weakness in which he suggested the reforms of Russia's Peter the Great as a model for the Ottomans. His ideas signified the beginnings of Western-inspired military reforms. The French adventurer Claude-Alexandre Comte de Bonneval, known in the empire as Ahmed Pasha, was given the task of reforming the Corps of Bombardiers . For the first time, the curriculum of the corps included theoretical and applied mathematics as well as the modern arts of war. Mahmud's reign may be considered as the continuation of the preceding reign in terms of cultural activities and construction projects. The achievements of his reign include setting up a paper mill in Yalova, reestablishing the imperial school of Galatasaray, building the baroque-style Nuruosmaniye Mosque and the Tophane Fountain. The famous Taksim region in Istanbul was named after the cistern (*taksim*) he had constructed to solve the water problem in the Beyoğlu and Galata districts. He and his entourage founded numerous libraries in Istanbul, Belgrade, and Vidin, and continued with the passion for tulips, poetry, and music.

Kahraman Şakul

Further reading: Münir Aktepe, "Mahmud I," in *Encyclopaedia of Islam*, 2nd ed., vol. 6, edited by P.J. Bearman et. al. (Leiden: Brill, 1960–), 55–58; A. D. Alderson, *The Structure of the Ottoman Dynasty* (Oxford: Clarendon, 1956); Ekmeleddin İhsanoğlu, ed., *History of the Ottoman State, Society, and Civilisation*, vol. 2 (Istanbul: Ircica, 2001), 422–23. Caroline Finkel, *Osman's Dream: The Story of the Ottoman Empire, 1300–1923* (London: John Murray, 2005), 354-371.

Mahmud II (b. 1785–d. 1839) (r. 1808–1839) *Ottoman sultan and caliph, 29th in line of succession* Mahmud II was the son of ABDÜLHAMID I (r. 1774–89) and Nakşıdil Sultan, whom Western sources have sometimes confused with Aimée Dubuc de Rivery, a relative of Joséphine of Napoléon. Mahmud's enthronement came at a time of particularly violent struggle surrounding the throne. He succeeded his brother MUSTAFA IV (r. 1807–08), who had been become sultan after a coup that dethroned SELIM III (r. 1789–1807). When Mustafa IV himself was also deposed in a coup led by ALEMDAR MUSTAFA PASHA, also known as Bayrakdar, Mahmud II remained the only candidate for the throne, as Selim III had been executed in the turmoil. Often likened to Peter the Great, Mahmud II abolished the JANISSARIES and launched a series of social and administrative reforms that he deemed necessary for the survival of the empire. The third great progenitor of the dynasty after OSMAN

Built under Mahmud I, the Nuruosmaniye Mosque is the best example of baroque style in Ottoman architecture. *(Photo by Gábor Ágoston)*

Sultan of concubine origin, Mahmud I acceded to the throne in 1730. His accession and enthronement were the result of the forced abdication of his uncle Sultan AHMED III (r. 1703–30). His long reign was characterized by wars with RUSSIA, the Habsburgs, and IRAN, as well as the first Western-inspired military reforms.

The reign of Mahmud I began after the execution of the leaders of the Patrona Halil Rebellion that had led to his uncle's abdication. Suppressing minor uprisings the next year, Mahmud turned his attention to the ongoing war with Iran; that war ended in 1736 with an agreement that did not satisfy either side. A real accord with Iran's NADIR SHAH was only reached in 1746. War on the western front broke out with Russia (1736) and her ally the Habsburg Empire (1737) as a result of border disputes and a Russian attack on AZAK. Successive Ottoman victories convinced Russia and the Habsburgs to make peace with the Ottomans, as a result of which the Ottomans regained BELGRADE by the Treaty of Belgrade but left Azak to Russia (December 12, 1739). France, which had supported the Ottomans, received commercial privileges in 1740 and gained the upper hand in trade with the eastern Mediterranean. Thus the Ottomans entered into a long period of peace on the western front on advantageous terms avoiding participation in the Spanish War of Succession (the 1740s) and did not capitalize on the turmoil in Iran after the death of Nadir Shah. Suppression

I (d. 1324) and IBRAHIM I (r. 1640–1648), the last six Ottoman sultans were descended from him.

When Mahmud succeeded Mustafa IV, his empire was at war with ENGLAND and RUSSIA. The central government had little authority, with the AYAN, or local notables, holding the real power in the provinces. Bayrakdar Mustafa Pasha, the de facto grand vizier, invited the *ayan* to Istanbul for an assembly that resulted in a document known as the Deed of Agreement (Sened-i İttifak). This document sought to restrict the authority of the sultan while maintaining the interests of the *ayan* and reviving the NIZAM-I CEDID, the military and fiscal reforms introduced by Selim III. Signed on September 29, 1808, this document roused Mahmud's suspicions about the intentions of Bayrakdar Mustafa Pasha, who was also of *ayan* origin. Thus he turned a blind eye when the JANISSARIES mutinied in response to Bayrakdar's attempts to reform the military, bringing down his government in mid-November 1808. During the mutiny, Mahmud II ordered the execution of his predecessor, Mustafa IV, who had come to pose a real danger to Mahmud's position as sultan. With no male member left in the dynasty and Bayrakdar Mustafa Pasha eliminated, Mahmud reached an uneasy compromise with the rebellious Janissaries. He concluded peace with England (January 9, 1809) immediately, but war with Russia continued until the TREATY OF BUCHAREST (May 28, 1812), the terms of which returned MOLDAVIA and WALLACHIA to the Ottomans in return for Bessarabia and gave SERBIA autonomy.

In the first period of his reign, Mahmud concentrated centralizing the empire. Although he was ruthless in suppressing the *ayan*, he did not totally ignore the Deed of Agreement. He was able to subordinate most of the *ayan* by constantly reshuffling them in provincial administration throughout the empire. At the same time, he worked to eliminate the most powerful *ayan,* such as ALI PASHA OF JANINA, whom he had executed in February 1822.

MEHMED ALI PASHA of EGYPT escaped the fate of Ali Pasha of Janina, coming to an unofficial accord with the Sublime Porte according to which he kept the WAHHABIS in check in return for remaining the sole authority of his realm. When the Janissaries proved unable to suppress the GREEK WAR OF INDEPENDENCE that began in1823, Mahmud II enlisted the service of the Egyptian army in the Peloponnese in February 1825. In return, he gave the governorship of Crete and the Peloponnese to IBRAHIM PASHA, son of Mehmed Ali. The victory of Egypt's modern Muslim army helped convince public opinion in Istanbul that setting up a modern army on the Egyptian model would not contradict Islam.

Although it is unclear exactly when Mahmud II decided to dispense with the Janissaries once and for all, historians suggest 1812, 1823, and 1826 as possibilities. Regardless of the exact timing, the shift in public opinion surely encouraged him to introduce a series of military reforms. On June 15, 1826, when the Janissaries rose up in arms to protest these reforms, the sultan ruthlessly crushed the uprising. Two days later the sultan declared the Janissaries abolished. Known as the AUSPICIOUS INCIDENT (Vaka-ı Hayriye), this action paved the way for the westernizing TANZIMAT reform era. Mahmud established a new army called the Muallem Asakir-i Mansure-i Muhammediye (Trained Victorious Troops of Muhammad).

The suppression of the Greek revolt by the Egyptian forces brought about the active involvement of the European Great Powers, who sent a combined fleet of British, French, and Russian warships to the harbor of Navarino. The destruction of the joint Ottoman-Egyptian navy on October 20, 1827 by the allied fleet—without any declaration of war—coupled with European demands concerning the Greeks, drove Mahmud to declare war on Russia and to demand war indemnity from the three powers in compensation for his destroyed navy. The war with Russia (1828–1829) came to an abrupt end when a Russian detachment invaded EDIRNE (Adrianople), threatening to march on Istanbul. By the TREATY OF EDIRNE (September 14, 1829) the Ottomans lost the DANUBE delta and its territories in the CAUCASUS and paid a heavy war indemnity to Russia. Mahmud II finally had to accept the independence of Greece in 1832.

Provoked by the Ottoman refusal to confer on him the governorship of SYRIA in return for his service in the Greek Revolt, between 1831 and 1833, Mehmed Ali Pasha occupied the whole of Syria and a considerable portion of central Anatolia. With his capital under threat, Mahmud II accepted the anchoring of a Russian fleet at the Straits for the defense of Istanbul (February 1833) and the mediation of Britain and France. Preferring a weak Ottoman Empire to a strong Egypt, Britain, France, and Russia reconciled Mahmud and Mehmed Ali in the Convention of Kütahya (April 8, 1833), which left Syria and Adana to Egypt. By the conclusion of the TREATY OF HÜNKAR ISKELESI (July 8, 1833), the Ottomans secured the Russian military presence in the Straits. Unsatisfied by the Convention of Kütahya, Mahmud took over the initiative to recover Syria, but the Egyptian army once again emerged victorious in the Battle of Nizip on June 24, 1839; just a week later, Mahmud died of tuberculosis.

The 1830s was shaped as much by Mahmud's extensive reforms as by the Egyptian problem. Aware of the importance of public support, he was determined to eliminate the "Janissary mentality" along with the Janissaries. This was revealed by his suppression of the BEKTAŞI ORDER, the traditional ally of the Janissaries, as well as the establishment of an official newspaper, *Takvim-i Vekayi* (Calendar of affairs) (1831), in order to form a broad base of support. His readiness to dispense with the "old" is demonstrated by the imposition of dress codes, with Western-style uniforms required in the military and pants and jackets in the civil bureaucracy. Ignoring the popular view of him as the infidel sultan, he had his portrait placed on the walls of official buildings.

Mehmed's reforms included reinforcement of the permanent embassies, sending students to Western capitals, the creation of a quarantine system (1831) and of a modern postal service (1834), along with the opening of a military medical school and a cadet school. These and other reforms laid the groundwork for a modern, centralized, bureaucratic, and rational state. The creation of the Supreme Council of Judicial Ordinances (Meclis-i Vala-yı Ahkam-ı Adliye) in March 1838 and the abolition of the arbitrary practice of confiscation of the property of a deceased high functionary (müsadere) signaled the advent of the principle of guarantee of life, honor, and property in the Western sense. With the aim of enlisting the support of his non-Muslim subjects, Mahmud went on an official visit to Varna, where he stressed that his subjects would receive equal treatment, with no regard to their religious affiliations. Through conciliatory policies such as allowing the opening of new churches, he tried to secure the allegiance of his non-Muslim subjects. Mahmud's strong adherence to orthodox Islam was also a motivating source. Reconciling Islamic principles of law and justice with the Western principles of ideal state and society, he made every effort to secure the cooperation of the ULEMA in his reforms. At the same time, Mahmud's subjects, both Muslim and non-Muslim, suffered greatly because of his centralizing policies; hundreds of thousands of Turkish conscripts died of epidemics in the military barracks without firing a single shot, while thousands more died trying to suppress revolts in the Peloponnese, Serbia, Wallachia, Arabia, and Egypt. For all these reasons, Mahmud II is still a disputed historical figure in present-day Turkey.

Kahraman Şakul

Further reading: Virginia H. Aksan, *Ottoman Wars 1700-1870: An Empire Besieged* (Harlow, England: Longman/Pearson, 2007), 259-398; Caroline Finkel, *Osman's Dream: The Story of the Ottoman Empire, 1300–1923* (London: John Murray, 2005), 420–446; Butrus Abu-Manneh, "The Islamic Roots of the Gülhane Rescript," in *Studies on Islam and the Ottoman Empire in the 19th Century, 1826–1876* (Istanbul: Isis, 2001), 73–98; Uriel Heyd, "The Ottoman Ulema and Westernization in the Time of Selim III and Mahmud II," in *The Modern Middle East: A Reader,* edited by Albert Hourani, Philip S. Khoury, and Mary C. Wilson (Berkeley: University of California Press, 1994); Avigdor Levy, "The Ottoman Ulema and the Military Reforms of Sultan Mahmud II." *Asian and African Studies* 7 (1971): 13–39; Musa Çadırcı, "Tanzimat," in *The Great Ottoman Turkish Civilisation*, vol. 3, edited by Ercüment Kuran et al. (Ankara: Yeni Türkiye, 1999), 573–589; Stanford J. Shaw, "The Transition from Traditionalistic to Modern Reform in the Ottoman Empire: The Reigns of Sultan Selim III (1789–1807) and Sultan Mahmud II (1808–1839)," in *The Turks*, vol. 4, edited by Hasan Celal Guzel, C. Cem Oguz, and Osman Karatay (Ankara: Yeni Türkiye, 2002), 130–149.

malikane   See TAX FARMING.

Malta   The small, stony island of Malta—strategically located between Tunisia and Sicily in the narrow corridor that separates the eastern and western Mediterranean—was a major problem for the Ottoman Empire. This was because, in 1530, King Charles of SPAIN offered the island to the KNIGHTS OF ST. JOHN, an ancient crusading order with roots going back to the 12th century. The professed goal of the Knights was to pursue the struggle against the Muslim "infidels," wherever and whenever they might be found. Until 1522 the Knights had been based on the island of RHODES in the eastern Mediterranean, but in that year Sultan SÜLEYMAN I (r. 1520–66) took Rhodes from the Knights, allowing them to depart with the agreement that they would never again engage in hostilities against the Ottomans. This promise was not kept, and when King Charles of Spain, an implacable foe of the Ottomans, offered Malta to the Knights , they found a new base from which to resume their struggle against the Ottomans. In 1565 the Ottomans resolved to vanquish their enemy, once and for all, and they mounted a siege against the island that lasted from May to September. The epic struggle was famous for the large numbers of casualties on both sides—but particularly on that of the Ottomans—as well as for the brutality of the encounter. Having failed to take any of the Maltese fortresses by September, the sultan's navy gave up and sailed back to ISTANBUL. The Ottoman Empire never tried again to take Malta and the Knights continued to sail forth from their stony redoubt to terrorize the Muslim Mediterranean for many years to come. Although their presence in the eastern Mediterranean gradually wanted, they were active against North African shipping until 1798, when NAPOLEON BONAPARTE occupied the island.

Molly Greene

mamluk   The Arabic word *mamluk* originally meant a male slave. But beginning in the ABBASID CALIPHATE, it took on the more specialized meaning of a slave who been purchased for the express purpose of becoming a soldier. In the 9th and 10th centuries C.E. mamluk slaves were sought from the Turkic peoples of Central Asia who were thought by the more settled Persian- and Arabic-speaking peoples of the Middle East to have great martial qualities, as well as an almost inborn sense of loyalty to their masters. Some Turks apparently entered into the slave relationship with their masters voluntarily, in the hopes of gaining wealth, power, and prestige. As the Turkic peoples became Muslim they could no longer legally be enslaved, as Muslim law forbids the enslavement of Muslims. With that source no longer available, other tribal peoples living on the edges of Muslim-controlled territories were seen as a potential source for mamluks. Among the peoples who were valued for their martial abilities were the various peoples of the Caucasus such as the Circassians, Ingush, Chechens, and Georgians. Muslim states in North Africa and Egypt also enslaved Africans from south of the Sahara Desert to be military slaves. Once armed, mamluk soldiers could be a double-edged sword and could turn against their masters. The most successful examples were the mamluks of EGYPT who seized the sultanate in CAIRO in 1260 and ruled the country in the MAMLUK EMPIRE until 1517.

In the Ottoman period, the process of recruiting or enslaving mamluks was largely replaced by the DEVŞIRME, or child-levy, system, but the practice continued in Egypt from the time of the Ottoman conquest through the end of the 18th century and in BAGHDAD in the 18th century. In Egypt, individual mamluks who had been emancipated by their masters continued to serve the state and formed their own households through the purchase of slaves from the Caucasus region. As these slaves proved their loyalty to their masters, they were often given their freedom while remaining in their former master's household. But the Caucasus region became a poorer source of slaves when many of the mountain peoples converted to Islam and could therefore no longer be enslaved. As a result, the heads of mamluk households increasingly recruited Muslim freebooters from throughout the Ottoman Empire who had come to Egypt to seek wealth and fame. Typically, heads of households would cement alliances with younger men they had recruited by marrying their daughters to them. These younger men would in turn take the place of their patron and continue the household under its former name. The al-QAZDAGHLI HOUSEHOLD was the most successful Mamluk household in Egypt and its members, most notably Bulutkapan Ali Bey, dominated the politics of Egypt in the 18th century. The Mamluks continued to play an important role in Egypt following the French occupation of the country in 1798 until they were violently suppressed by MEHMED ALI in 1811.

Bruce Masters

Mamluk Empire   In 1250, mamluks, or soldiers of slave origin, seized control of the sultanate of EGYPT and established a form of dynastic succession different from any that had previously existed in the Muslim world. Although a few of the early sultans of the empire passed their office on to a biological son, increasingly, the sul-

tanate went not to a son of the former sultan but to one of his slaves. Master and slave usually shared the same ethnic origins, cementing bonds of loyalty that transcended the usual master-slave relationship. Further eroding the master-slave relationship, it was a common practice for masters to emancipate their slaves after mamluks had proven their loyalty. Many former slaves married the daughters of their former masters, further strengthening the bonds of loyalty between them. In the first period of Mamluk domination in Egypt, known as the Bahri, the slaves were of Qipchaq Turkish origin from the steppes of Russia; after 1390, in the period known as the Burji, most were Circassian, from the tribal peoples of the Caucasus Mountains. Despite ethnic and marriage ties, these households were extremely unstable, because individual Mamluks within a household competed with one another to become its head, and individual households competed with one another for the sultanate.

The Mamluks had secured their power by defeating the Mongol advance at Ayn Jalut, in present-day Israel, in 1260, thereby saving Egypt and Palestine from the ravages of the Mongol army. The Mamluk sultan Baybars welcomed Caliph al-Mustansir, one of the last survivors of the Abbasid family, to CAIRO in 1261, and the Mamluk regime distinguished itself by its loyalty to SUNNI ISLAM. That loyalty was confirmed by their conquest in 1291 of the city of ACRE, the last outpost of the crusader kingdom on the mainland; the crusader fortress on the island of Arwad, off the coast of the city Tartus in present-day Syria, held out until 1303. With the destruction of BAGHDAD by the Mongols, Cairo under the Mamluks became the primary center of Sunni learning in the Arabic-speaking world

Although the Mamluks were often despotic in their rule, Egypt prospered under them, in part because of the insecurity in much of the rest of the Middle East in the aftermath of the Mongol conquests. As a result, traffic carried by CARAVANS across the region diminished while the route to India via the Red Sea became increasingly profitable, making Cairo a natural meeting-place for merchants from the Italian city-states of Genoa and Venice and those coming from East Africa, Arabia, and India. Spices, pepper, gold, and slaves were all sought-after commodities available in the city's markets. After 1500, COFFEE from YEMEN started to arrive in the city, and European merchants were eager to capitalize on the popularity of the newfound drink in the West by buying coffee beans in Cairo. In addition, the Nile Delta provided abundant crops of indigo, rice, and sugar. For these reasons, Egypt undoubtedly seemed a tempting target for the increasingly powerful Ottoman Empire which, having taken Constantinople, was seeking to secure its borders on the east in southeastern Anatolia.

The rivalry between the Ottomans and Mamluks increased in the late 15th century when the Ottoman Sultan

BAYEZID II (r. 1481–1512) consolidated Ottoman rule over the Turkoman principalities of Karaman and Elbistan in southeastern Anatolia. These lay on the border of the Mamluk sultanate, and the rulers in Cairo considered the regions to be under their hegemony. The two sides managed a fragile truce that lasted until the reign of SELIM I (r. 1512–20), who moved into the contested territories with the excuse that he needed to secure them so as to wage war on his archrival Shah Ismail Safavi, who ruled Iran from 1502 to 1524. Having secured both Karaman and Elbistan by 1515, Selim turned his attention to the Mamluk territories to the south.

Selim moved on the Mamluks in 1516, claiming that although they were Sunnis the aid they had given to the "heretic" Shah Ismail legitimated their punishment. The two armies first met outside the city of ALEPPO in 1516 where the Ottoman cavalry, accompanied by artillery and infantry armed with muskets, obliterated the Mamluk cavalry on the field of Marj Dabiq. The Mamluk sultan Qansuh al-Ghawri apparently died of a heart attack during the battle and the remnants of his army fled the field, escaping first to DAMASCUS and then to Cairo. Selim's army followed them to Egypt and in 1517 delivered a second major defeat to the Mamluks at Raydaniyya, outside Cairo. With that defeat, the remaining Mamluks offered their surrender to Selim and the territories of the former Mamluk state were incorporated into the growing Ottoman Empire as the provinces of Aleppo, Damascus, and Egypt. That incorporation did not mean the end of the Mamluk system in Egypt, however, as Ottoman officials posted in Cairo began to create their own Mamluk-style households.

Bruce Masters

Further reading: Thomas Philipp and Ulrich Haarmann, eds., *The Mamluks in Egyptian Politics and Society* (Cambridge: Cambridge University Press, 1998); M. W. Daly, ed., *The Cambridge History of Egypt*, 2 vols. (Cambridge: Cambridge University Press, 1998).

markets Every Ottoman city had a market district, known in Arabic as *suq* and in Turkish as *çarşı*, where

The central market district, or *suq*, of Aleppo, which was one of the major trading cities of the empire. *(Photo by Gábor Ágoston)*

This photo, taken around 1890, shows rug merchants in the Khan al-Khalili market in Cairo. By the time this photo was taken, most of their customers would have been Western tourists as Cairo had emerged as a prominent stop on the "Grand Tour" for North Americans and Europeans in the Victorian era. *(Photo by Maison Bonfils. Courtesy of the University of Pennsylvania Museum, Philadelphia)*

both the manufacture and sale of goods were centralized. Large cities might also have other smaller market clusters, but even if they did, the sale of luxury goods would be confined to one centralized market. As in the case of modern shopping centers, the stores clustered together were often under one roof with different streets having shops catering to customers seeking particular products, such as the spice market, or the street of the gold sellers. The overall size of the central market, such as Istanbul's famous GRAND BAZAAR (Kapalı Çarşı) or Aleppo's Mdine (simply "the city"), could be as large as several dozen acres of interconnecting streets and alleyways. Most important markets also had an inner market, known as the *bedestan*, which could be closed off at night or in times of trouble. The *bedestan* housed the shops selling

the most precious commodities, and merchants would hire their own guards to protect their wares.

Although foreign visitors to the Ottoman Empire often described its markets as chaotic, as indeed Middle Eastern markets appear to many first-time visitors today, they were in fact carefully regulated by institutions of the Ottoman state. CARAVANS brought almost all the goods to a city's markets, with the exception of those arriving at the docks of a port city or locally produced commodities. Once a caravan arrived, it would halt outside a city until customs officials could register its merchants and merchandise. With the formalities over, drivers with donkeys or camels would then meet the merchants to transport the goods to a weighing station where the customs taxes would be assessed and paid. Once the taxes were paid, the merchants would hire porters to carry their goods to a CARAVANSARY (*khan*) where they would stay. The caravansaries were clustered around the central market for easy access to the shops where the commodities would be sold.

In Istanbul, the government maintained strict control over the prices at which goods could be sold. These were periodically posted in public and the city's judges (KADIS) would fine anyone found in violation of the prices set by the government. However, that degree of regulation does not seem to have been in force in the larger provincial cities of the empire. Rather, the merchants handling a particular commodity formed a guild. They collectively set both the wholesale price at which the product should be bought and the retail price the shopkeeper could ask from the customer. There was haggling between buyers and sellers, but if it came to the guild's attention that one of its members was trying to undercut prices or overcharge customers significantly, that person would be punished with the sanction of the *kadı*. In addition, a market usually had its own sheikh, or head. He was usually a merchant himself and was selected by prominent merchants and representatives of the guilds whose wares were sold in the market he was to supervise. The sheikh's job was to collect taxes that were levied by the governor on the market and to ensure that only authorized merchants were conducting business in the market under his supervision.

In addition to merchants and customers, markets usually included numerous people who acted as brokers and agents, helping to connect buyers and sellers. These too were organized into their own guilds. As was the case with all guilds, the members of the brokers' guild were not eager to admit new members, and places in the guild were often passed down from father to son. As most of the actual shops in a market belonged to a WAQF, or religious endowment, a merchant operating out of a shop had to secure a permit (*gedik*) from the *waqf*'s administrator to allow him to use the shop. The *gedik* itself was considered to be the property of the merchant and he was free to sell it to others or to pass it along to his heirs as a part of their inheritance.

As there was no metropolitan police force in Ottoman cities until the end of the 19th century, the merchants and guilds of a particular market would hire their own protection. These armed men were often ethnically distinct from the local population: North Africans in Syria, Kurds in Anatolia, and Albanians in the Balkans. The guards—who were also organized into guilds—were supposed, in theory, to arrest any lawbreakers and bring them before the *kadı* for judgment. But we know from European travelers' accounts that more typically they dispensed justice on the spot. This is supported by the fact that there are remarkably few records of trials involving theft or other crimes that occurred in the markets. The guards themselves could at times be the source of disorder, but in general, they provided the security for which the merchants paid.

Although the markets were largely a part of the male sphere of Ottoman society, women could be found there as well. Poor women and peasant women hawked produce they grew themselves or items they made, such as embroidered towels. As they were outside the guild structure, the guild chiefs frequently brought charges against women who were "illegally" selling in a market. Other women, most commonly Jews, acted as peddlers carrying wares in the upper-class neighborhoods, visiting the harems and offering goods to women who were barred by social custom from going to the public markets themselves. Among the wealthy classes, it was not unusual for women to own the *gediks* for shops or, in some cases, to own shops outright. It was also not uncommon for women to be the executor for a *waqf* that might include markets and caravansaries. In such cases, however, social custom did not allow the women to deal directly with men from outside their families. For these reasons, the actual daily running of the business was left to a male relative.

In the latter part of the 19th century, as many Ottoman cities began to acquire tramlines and street lights, merchants in the traditional market areas began to add Western innovations such as gas lighting and plate-glass windows. Western-style department stores also appeared in the newer modern suburbs growing up around Ottoman cities. This led to a division in the economy of markets whereby poorer people continued to use the old traditional markets while the Western-educated and prosperous upper classes preferred the new emporia. In many cases the old caravansaries that had surrounded the central markets were either torn down or allowed to become derelict. In the second half of the 20th century, recognition of the potential tourist value of the old markets has led to a restoration and revival of the surviving Ottoman markets in cities across the Middle East.

Bruce Masters

Further reading: Abraham Marcus, *The Middle East on the Eve of Modernity: Aleppo in the Eighteenth Century* (New York: Columbia University Press, 1989).

Maronites   The Maronites are Christians who take their name and trace the origins of their faith to Saint Marun, who died in the early fifth century. Saint Marun established a tradition of hermit monks who forsook worldly affairs to live away from temptations in the mountains or desert. Such monks formed the core of the Maronite clergy in the early centuries; they produced little in terms of theological works that might outline the tenets of their sect. The Maronite tradition holds that after the Council of Chalcedon in 451 C.E., the Maronite monks were among the few Christians in SYRIA to accept the officially approved definition of Christ's nature as being both wholly human and wholly God at the same time. Many others, whom the council described as monophysites (from *monophysis*, "one nature"), rejected this idea. The Council of Constantinople in 680 C.E. attempted to broker a compromise between Orthodox Christianity and the monophysite "heretics" by stating that Christ had two natures but one will (monotheletism). Some historians assert that the Maronites accepted this compromise, but Maronite scholars refute the claim that their church ever wavered from the statement of Christ's dual nature as expressed in the Nicene Creed, the universal confession used by both the Roman Catholic and Eastern Orthodox churches.

Although the Maronite community was originally found in northern Syria, over time most of the Maronites migrated to the safety of the Lebanese mountains where they formed the majority in some districts. During the crusading period in the 12th and 13th centuries, Maronites assisted the crusaders in their wars against the Muslims, and their clergy established direct contacts with the Roman Catholic Church. Those ties grew tenuous with the establishment of the MAMLUK EMPIRE, however, as the Mamluk sultans sought to prevent any contact between their subjects and the Christian West. But with the relative tolerance of Ottoman rule, Maronite clergy could once again travel to Rome.

In 1584, the Maronite College was established in Rome to train clergy with the aim of bringing Maronite beliefs and practices into line with those of the Catholic Church. Some clergy resisted the reduction of their received religious tradition into a Catholicism that was acceptable in Rome, and the transformation was gradual. It was not until 1736 that the clergy of the Maronites held a synod at Luwayza in the mountains of Lebanon in which they accepted Roman Catholic theology as their own and accepted the spiritual supremacy of the pope in Rome. They retained the right to maintain their own patriarch of Antioch and the East as the head of their church; he was vested with the rank of cardinal in the Roman Church. They also retained the rights to recite their liturgy in Syriac rather than in Church Latin, to use their own priestly vestments, and to permit marriage of their lay clergy. But in theological terms, they conformed with the Catholic Church in Rome.

Historically, the Maronites enjoyed good relations with the DRUZES with whom they shared the mountains of Lebanon. However, that partnership began to unravel with the Egyptian occupation of Syria in the 1830s. Emir Bashir II al-Shihabi, a convert to Maronite Christianity, had aligned his political fortunes with IBRAHIM PASHA, the son of MEHMED ALI and the military governor of Syria from 1831 to 1840, and ordered his retainers to support the Egyptian force militarily. In contrast, the Druzes

had soured on Egyptian rule, and by 1840 were openly resisting Egyptian occupation. After the withdrawal of the Egyptian army, Bashir II—who served as the prince of the mountain, as the political leader of Lebanon was called—was forced into exile. The SHIHAB FAMILY, which had dominated the post of the prince of the mountain for almost a century, attempted to recover under the leadership of Bashir III, but the leading Druze families challenged his leadership, and in 1842 he also went into exile. The political anarchy that accompanied the change of regimes witnessed major outbursts of fighting between Druzes and Maronites.

The Egyptians had armed the Maronites and given them a sense of empowerment. Maronite leadership thus felt that they could challenge the Druzes for the dominant political role in the Lebanese mountains. In addition, Lebanon was experiencing an economic boom through its export of silk to Europe, and Maronite merchants and growers were benefiting disproportionately from the trade. Further adding to sectarian tensions, the Ottoman sultan introduced a new administration in which some districts in Lebanon would have Christian administrators. All these developments created tensions with the Druzes, who felt they were losing ground to the Christians, both politically and economically.

Tensions were building between the two religious communities, but the spark that would ignite a religious war came from within the Maronite community itself. In 1848 Maronite peasants, chafing under a feudal regime in which most of the land and wealth was owned by a few families, rose in rebellion against their landlords. They succeeded in overthrowing the landed families, also Maronites, and established a peasant republic. When the rebellion threatened to spread into Druze territory, Druze leaders, in what they considered preemptive strikes, called their people to attack Christian villages and towns in April of 1860. They quickly routed the rebel Maronites and what had been started as a nominally defensive war quickly turned into a general massacre of Christians, in which thousands died. To end this LEBANESE CIVIL WAR, France landed troops in Beirut in August 1860.

From that point on, Maronite political leaders were in the ascendancy in Lebanon and they sought to draw the region into the political and cultural orbit of France. As the 19th century ended, some Maronite intellectuals began to envision an independent Lebanon that would be a Christian state in an otherwise Muslim Middle East. Ordinary Maronites experienced tremendous change in the years following the Lebanese Civil War as the silk industry drew them first into a wage-earning economy in the countryside and then, for many, to burgeoning Beirut. Tens of thousands of Maronites also left their country altogether to seek a life in the Americas. Due to the economic and political transformations the community experienced in the 19th century, by the end of the Ottoman Empire, the Maronites had become one of the religious communities most disillusioned with the prospect of continued Ottoman rule, and many looked forward to its collapse.

Bruce Masters

See also Druzes; Lebanese Civil War; Lebanon; Uniates.

Further reading: Matti Moosa, *The Maronites in History* (Syracuse, N.Y.: Syracuse University Press, 1986).

marriage *See* family; harem; law and gender; sex and sexuality.

martolos *Martolos* were the remnant of the militia of the Byzantine Empire, which the Ottomans gained control over around 1430 and which they maintained, in some form, into the early 19th century. The word *martolos* is derived from the Greek *armatolos*, meaning "armed man" or "militiaman." At the time of the full development of their organization under the Ottomans, the (mostly Christian) *martolos* served in many places in the provinces of Buda and Bosnia, as well as in western parts of Rumelia (the European part of the empire) down to Morea (the Peloponnese peninsula).

In fortresses and stockades, *martolos* were part of mobile troops and received a salary. Their commanders sometimes had *timars* (land grants). Over time most of the *martolos* converted to Islam. In the middle Danube area the *martolos* served as marines. Many had families and established town quarters. The time of their service could last from 10 to 20 years. In the Balkan countryside, *martolos* acted as police; they were unpaid, but were required to pay considerably less in taxes. One of the specific duties of the countryside *martolos* was to watch over land use, preventing ordinary peasants from neglecting their agricultural responsibilities and bringing new settlers into depopulated areas. Belonging to the same social and ethnic milieu as the peasants, they were experienced in local affairs. The duty of the *martolos* was inherited, usually passing from father to son.

Finally, since large groups of bellicose pastoralist Balkan Vlachs occasionally pursued "police intervention"—incursions aimed at capturing cattle and abducting people for ransom—into territories across Ottoman borders, mainly in Croatia, the designation *martolos* meaning "marauder" was attached to a technically non-*martolos* population.

In times of crisis in the 17th century the number of *martolos* began to decline. Fearing social debasement, that is, the status of ordinary taxpayers, some converted and joined the privileged Muslim *askeri* (military) class;

others revolted, became brigands, deserted, or chose to fight for the Habsburgs or Venice.

Nenad Moačanin

Further reading: Milan Vasić, *Martolosi u jugoslovenskim zemljama pod turskom vladavinom* (Sarajevo: Akademija nauka i umjetnosti Bosne i Hercegovine, 1967).

Mawali Bedouin Confederation The Mawali Bedouins were the dominant tribal confederation in the Syrian Desert when the Ottomans conquered Syria in 1516. The Egyptian Mamluk Empire that preceded Ottoman rule had chosen a policy of appeasement in dealing with the Mawali in the 15th century, including the payment of an annual sum in gold to the tribal sheikh or head of the confederation in return for his promise that the caravans that followed the Euphrates river route from Aleppo to Baghdad could pass through Bedouin-territory controlled in peace. The Ottomans brashly felt that they could dispense with the payments to the sheikh, whom European travelers dubbed "the prince of the Arabs," by using direct military force to control the Bedouins. After several campaigns failed to stop the raiding, the Ottoman government bestowed the title "lord of the desert" on the sheikh of the Mawali and agreed to pay him a yearly sum.

The first treaty, signed in 1574, recognized the hereditary right of the family of the current sheikh to serve as head of the tribal confederation. It also gave him a secondary title, Abu Risha (Arabic for "possessor of the plume"), as he was given a turban with a peacock feather to symbolize his authority. In return for a gift of 6,000 gold ducats a year, the sheikh agreed to protect peasants and travelers along the Euphrates route from Birecik to Ridwaniyya, which lay opposite Baghdad. In addition, the sheikh was free to make his own financial arrangements with European trading companies.

The peace held through the first quarter of the 18th century, although there were occasional lapses. In 1605, for example, there was a dynastic struggle within the ruling clan and order in the tribe broke down, leading to unauthorized raids. A misunderstanding over payment of the annual gift in 1644 led the tribe to massacre the Aleppo garrison. But generally, the caravans passed freely, and trade in both Damascus and Aleppo flourished. Unfortunately for travelers, the 18th century witnessed the migration of the Anaza Confederation of Bedouin into the Syrian Desert from the Arabian Peninsula; the Anaza sought to plunder any caravan that passed through their territory. This confederation defeated the Mawali in a number of battles and established themselves as the lords of the desert. The tribes of the Mawali Bedouin continued to inhabit the desert to the immediate south and east of the city of Aleppo and to work as guards for the caravans, but they were unable to mount a force large enough to reclaim their position as the paramount tribal confederation in the Syrian Desert.

Bruce Masters

Mecca (Mekka; *anc.*: Macoraba; *Ar.*: Makka) As the site of the Kaaba, Mecca is the holiest place in Muslim spiritual geography. The Kaaba is the structure that houses a black meteor that was sacred to the Arab tribes before the Prophet Muhammad. Muslim tradition sanctified it for the new faith by claiming it marked the spot where Abraham had offered to sacrifice his son Ishmael. According to Muslim tradition, God intervened and revealed the one true faith that is Islam to Abraham, making him the first prophet of God. To mark the spot where God had intervened, Abraham, with the help of the angels, constructed the cube-shaped structure known as the Kaaba to house the black rock. Muhammad established that the Kaaba marked the geographical center of Muslims' spiritual universe and was the point to which true believers should direct their prayers.

After gaining control of Mecca in 1517, the Ottoman dynasty sought to promote its prestige as the defender of Islam and the "Servant of the Two Noble Sanctuaries" (Mecca and MEDINA) by maintaining the HAJJ, or yearly pilgrimage to Mecca, and by providing services to the pilgrims once they reached the city. Although no Ottoman sultan ever visited the city, many contributed to the upkeep and refurbishing of the Great Mosque, Al-Masjid al-Haram, which has the Kaaba in its central courtyard, and the construction of further infrastructure for pilgrims. Sultan SÜLEYMAN I, who ruled the Ottoman Empire from 1520 to 1566, built a new madrasa that housed scholars representing all four Sunni legal traditions as well as a large soup kitchen to feed poor pilgrims that was named after his chief consort, Hürrem Sultan. But because of the sanctity of the place, even the sultans were reluctant to put their permanent mark on the physical appearance of the sacred shrine. In 1630, however, a freak flood inundated the Great Mosque and caused great structural damage to the Kaaba. This required the direct intervention of Sultan Murad IV (r. 1623–40), who sent workmen from Egypt to carefully restore the mosque.

The governance of the Holy City required a similar delicacy. The Ottoman sultan appointed the governor of the nearby port city of JEDDAH and the *kadı* of the Hanafi school, the interpretation of Islamic law favored by the Ottomans in Mecca. Both men were Ottomans from the capital. But the nominal head of Mecca was its emir, or commander, who was drawn from the Hashimi, or Hashimite clan (*see* Faysal ibn Husayn al-HASHIMI and Husayn ibn Ali al-HASHIMI). The Hashimis were the Prophet Muhammad's own clan, and male members of the clan were thus entitled to the honorific "sharif." The emirs, whose letters of appointment were issued by the sultan, generally worked closely with the governor of Jeddah and there were only a few instances in which an emir was dismissed from his post. The Ottoman sultans were careful to cultivate the Hashimi family and bestowed money and gifts upon its members. Over time, many of the family married women from prominent families in ISTANBUL and maintained summer residences there. At the same time, the emirs had to remain close to their Arab origins in order to maintain ties with the BEDOUIN tribes upon whose goodwill the hajj depended.

That goodwill was threatened by the rise of the Muwahhidun, better known as the WAHHABIS, at the end of the 18th century. The founder of the Muwahhidun, MUHAMMAD IBN ABD AL-WAHHAB, taught that Sufi beliefs and practices were un-Islamic. Because many of the people of Mecca belonged to one or the other of the Sufi orders, this group felt justified in attacking the city. In 1803 Mecca fell to the Wahhabis, who imposed their stricter interpretation of Islam on the city's inhabitants. The Wahhabis continued to hold the city until 1812 when an Egyptian army drove them out. From then until 1840, Mecca was controlled from CAIRO. During the last decade of Egyptian administration, the emirs were replaced by secular Egyptian officers. As a result, the local population viewed the return of Ottoman control of the city in 1840 as a return of the status quo, and welcomed it.

As methods of transportation improved in the 19th century, the number of pilgrims arriving in Mecca increased substantially. By the end of the century, it was not unusual for 200,000 pilgrims to show up in the city. By the beginning of the 20th century, almost half of these pilgrims traveled to Jeddah by steamship. The population of Mecca was about 80,000 at the end of the 19th century, and the arrival of the pilgrims put great stress on the city's infrastructure and facilities. Disease was a particular problem and the city was struck by several outbreaks of cholera, which was known in much of the Ottoman Empire as "hajj fever." This required the Ottoman authorities to undertake major sanitation projects at the end of the 19th century and to implement quarantines and other public health measures. The opening of the HEJAZ RAILROAD in 1908 also helped improve conditions for the pilgrims.

During the Ottoman centuries, Mecca served as one of the important centers of learning for Islam as pilgrims from across the Muslim world were constantly arriving in the city and many stayed for years. This fostered an exchange of ideas and a realization in the late 18th century of the growing threat to Muslim political independence presented by European imperial ambitions. The NAQSHBANDIYYA ORDER, proponents of the reformist Sufi movement, also frequently used the opportunity of the hajj to win new followers and share ideas. Mecca served as a major center from which the Sufi faithful could propagate and disseminate their ideas. The city's role as intellectual nexus of the Islamic world diminished as Muslims adopted new mass media at the end of the 19th century; printing presses, newspapers, and the telegraph spread new ideas, and new Muslim universities began to challenge the hegemony of a single intellectual center.

Bruce Masters

Further reading: William Ochsenwald, *Religion, Society and the State in Arabia: The Hijaz under Ottoman Control, 1840–1908* (Columbus: Ohio State University Press, 1984).

Mecelle (Medjelle) The Ottoman Civil Code, or Mecelle-i Ahkam-ı Adliyye (commonly referred to as the Mecelle), was an Ottoman legal code promulgated between 1869 and 1876. The product of the first-ever legal codification project in Islamic history and based on Islamic law, the Mecelle covered the areas of debt, property, personal status, and juridical law. It was abolished in 1926, three years after the new Turkish republic was founded.

Legal codification—especially in commercial and criminal law, which was part of the comprehensive Ottoman modernizing reforms (*see* TANZIMAT) that started in the second half of the 19th century—was a reflection of the political-historical conditions of the Ottoman Empire. The upsurge in trade with European countries as a result of new economic developments increased the need for codification in some areas covered by civil law; direct and indirect demands by European powers also created an important motive for codification in these areas. The reason for this was that European states sought security for both non-Muslim citizens of the empire and for European traders in their commercial transactions with the empire. Furthermore, France tried to impose the French civil code in order to increase its influence on the Ottoman Empire.

In addition, new regulations in juridical institutions, including the founding of the civil (Nizamiye) courts as well as the SHARIA courts, which created the need for a law that could be applied to non-Muslims as well as to Muslims, led to a debate on whether to adopt the French civil code or to make an original law based on Islamic jurisprudence, or *fiqh*. The Ottoman Council of Ministers eventually opted for the latter and decided to form a committee chaired by the minister of justice, AHMED CEVDET PASHA (1823–95), to codify the relevant rules of Islamic law.

The Mecelle consisted of an introduction and 16 books, which included 73 sections and 1,851 articles in all. The introduction consisted of 100 articles, the first of which defined the nature of Islamic law, the source of the code. The next 99 articles included general legal principles (*kavaid-i külliye*) derived from the Islamic legal tradition. Although these principles by themselves were not specifically laws, they constituted the background against which the rest of the rules included in the Mecelle could be understood and interpreted. The main function of these general principles was to justify the first-ever transition in Islamic history from a legal system based on the *fiqh* books to a modern one, for these principles had a significant place in the classical tradition. The next 16 books included articles on specific areas of law: sales (*buyu*); hire and lease (*icarat*); guaranty (*kefale*); transfer of debts (*havale*); pledge (*rehn*); deposit (*emanat*); gift (*hibe*); usurpation and property damage (*gasp ve itlaf*); interdiction, duress, and pre-emption (*hacr ve ikrah ve şuf'a*); partnership (*şirket*); agency (*vekalet*); settlement and full discharge (*sulh ve ibra*); acknowledgment (*ikrar*); lawsuit (*dava*); evidence and oaths (*beyyinat ve tahlif*); and courts and judgeship (*kaza*).

Although the Mecelle resembled Western legal codes in format, it did not cover all of the sections found in Western civil codes, such as family and inheritance laws. Furthermore, the last four books of the Mecelle included procedural provisions, which were not part of the civil law. This was because the Mecelle was prepared essentially for the newly established Nizamiye courts, which did not have regulations concerning civil procedure.

In terms of its internal structure, the Mecelle was based on the casuistic method, in accordance with the *fiqh* tradition. It did not classify the code into debts, personal status, family and inheritance laws, as in Western civil law. With few exceptions, it did not include general rules concerning debts and contracts; rather, it repeated individual principles for every kind of debt and contract. It also discussed examples for many articles that did not conform to the standard codification method. This was due to the fact that it was the first experience in codification and it was meant to create a specific legal norm for every known problem so that the practitioners of law could easily apply them in courts. For this reason, unlike the preexisting *kadı* system, the Mecelle did not leave much room for the discretion of judges. Furthermore, the fact that the Mecelle's method was close to the one found in the *fiqh* books made it easier for judges who were familiar with Islamic law and *fiqh* books to understand and apply it during the transition period. Moreover, the presentation of the Mecelle as the newest version of respected *fiqh* books that had been the main source of reference in Islamic jurisdiction greatly helped justify the idea of codifying the principles and rules of Islamic law as a modern legal code. Thus, when explaining in the justificatory memorandum (*Esbab-ı Mucibe Mazbatası*) the need for preparing the Mecelle, the authors referred to it as a collection (*mecelle*) or a book that gathers together rules selected, based on the new conditions of the time, from among the *fiqh* principles that had long been established within the Hanafi tradition, the official legal school in the empire.

The fact that the rules contained in the Mecelle were restricted only to the Hanafi school later brought frequent criticism. Although in general the Mecelle codified dominant views within the Hanafi tradition, sometimes it opted for minority opinions within the same tradition based on the idea that the latter would be more suitable for the new conditions of the time. During its preparation, the choices within the same *madhab* (school of law) made by the committee led to great debate, causing the delay of its preparation; given this fact, it was not possible at that time to make choices among the legal decisions of different *madhabs*, which was argued for by Islamic modernism in the 20th century. Furthermore, to criticize the Mecelle for being restricted to a certain tradition has made it difficult to notice its true significance: its modernizing effect on later attempts at codification in the Muslim world and on the overall structure of present-day Islamic law.

Among the important effects of the Mecelle and the literature around it is the fact that various aspects of the Islamic law started being discussed in light of contemporary problems. Thus such issues as the Islamic law's relation to social change, the relationship between codification and the Islamic law, the scope and limits of *ijtihad* (the process of deriving a legal decision from the principles of sharia) and so on came to the fore due to the Mecelle. Within this framework, some of the general principles that form the introductory part of the Mecelle have been the focus of discussions on Islamic law in the modern era. Although these general principles have received little scholarly attention, they were an important factor in codification projects in Muslim countries, which were intensified in the 20th century in general, and in the debates over civil law in particular. The general principles that form the introduction to the Mecelle have played an important role in the transformation of the classical theory of Islamic law in the modern era. Systemization of such principles was the first step in creating a modern legal code based on the Islamic *fiqh*. Therefore, these principles, expressed by the Mecelle as a binding code, contributed to the legitimization of a new legal ground for such concepts as the *örf* (mores), socio-legal change in time, and emerging necessity, all of which are connected to the idea of change.

Another significant impact of the Mecelle on contemporary Islamic law is that it helped justify the attempt to establish an eclectic approach replacing the idea of a legal unity limited to only one *madhab*, which had been the standard view in the classical *fiqh* tradition. Although it was strictly limited to dominant views within the Hanafi tradition, the Mecelle inspired many of the later codification projects with its modern form and structure that justify the political authority (*emir ül-müminin*) choosing one of many legal views (*ijtihads*) as the law, which is explicitly decreed by the Mecelle (art. 1801). Thus in EGYPT, where the Mecelle was not adopted by the government because there was concern that it would cause undue dependence on the Ottoman Empire, a legal code called Murshid al-Hayran, which was prepared as an alternative to the Mecelle but could not be put in effect, was similar in form and structure to the latter. Likewise, the Mecelle's effects can be seen in the Tunisian Law of Contracts and Debts, and in the Law of Debts in Morocco and IRAQ. In the Iraqi Civil Law, some of the general principles of the Mecelle were quoted directly. Finally, in contemporary Jordan, the Mecelle's rules are still applied in some areas not covered by the current civil law. All these examples indicate the Mecelle's continued significance.

The Mecelle was applied in all Ottoman courts, except in Egypt and the Arabian Peninsula. After the collapse of the Ottoman Empire, the Mecelle kept its official status partly or wholly until 1926 in TURKEY, 1932 in LEBANON, 1949 in SYRIA, 1953 in Iraq, 1977 in Jordan and 1980 in KUWAIT. In PALESTINE, most of its rules were in effect until 1948; when the Israeli state was founded, it kept its status there until the 1970s. Today the Mecelle is still the most important legal source for courts in Palestine. It also remained in partial effect in ALBANIA until 1928, in Bosnia until 1945, and in Cyprus until the 1960s. Finally, in Southeast Asia, the Mecelle was put in effect for some time in Jahore, a state in Malaysia.

In the 20th-century Ottoman Empire, the Mecelle was discussed and criticized for its incomprehensiveness, especially after 1908 during the empire's Second Constitutional Period (*see* CONSTITUTION/CONSTITUTIONAL PERIODS) even though this was approximately 40 years after the Mecelle was first promulgated. The Ministry of Justice formed several committees in 1916, 1923 and 1924 in order to revise the Mecelle according to the changing conditions of the time, but they could not achieve any significant success. The first of these committees tried to address existing criticism by declaring that it was permissible to adopt principles from other (non-Hanafi) *madhabs* and even from foreign (European) legal systems—provided they were in conformity with Islamic law. However, this recommended revision could be implemented only in the area of family law—not covered by the Mecelle—with the 1917 Decree of the Family Law (Hukuk-ı Aile Kararnamesi).

The Mecelle was translated into Arabic, English, and French shortly after it was introduced; there are many commentaries on it in Turkish and Arabic. Commentaries usually explain the text for those who are not familiar with legal terminology and Islamic law in general. Also, since the Mecelle selectively codifies just one of many views found in *fiqh* books, some commentaries aim to make it easier for judges and law students to interpret the text by discussing the Mecelle's sources and its rules in their wider context. These works provide not only alternative views within the Hanafi tradition but also views from other *madhabs*.

As the first text that codified some of the rules and principles of Islamic *fiqh*, the Mecelle has become a modern classic of Islamic law literature and has stood as an example for later codification projects. From its form and content, as well as from the commentaries and other literature that have emerged around it, the Mecelle has continued to influence modern interpretations of Islamic law and to affect various reforms in the areas of civil law in the 20th-century Muslim world.

Sami Erdem

Further reading: W. E. Grigsby, trans., *The Medjelle or Ottoman Civil Law* (London: Stevens and Sons, 1895); Sıddık Sami Onar, "The Majalla," in *Law in The Middle East*, vol. 1, edited by Majid Khadduri and Herbert Liebesny (Washington, D.C.: The Middle East Institute, 1955), 292–308; Şerif Arif Mardin, "Some Explanatory Notes on the Origins of the 'Mecelle' (Medjelle)." *The Muslim World* 51, no. 3 (1961): 189–96 and no. 4 (1961): 274–9; C. V. Findley, "Medjelle," in *Encyclopaedia of Islam*, 2nd ed., vol. 6 (Leiden: Brill, 1960–), 971–972.

medical education *See* EDUCATION.

medicine Early Ottoman medicine found its roots in the medical traditions of the medieval Islamic world as well as those of Central Asia and the Near East. Because of its central position straddling Europe and the East, and due to its extraordinarily diverse cultural components, the Ottoman Empire benefited from a varied set of medical information and practices. From the founding of the Ottoman imperial dynasty in the mid-14th century until the major Ottoman reform period of the 19th century, medical knowledge, education, and practice in the empire relied on Greek, Persian, and Turkic antecedents and the unique contributions of its many ethnic and religious groups. With the advent of the 19th century, especially during the mid-century period of sweeping reforms known as the TANZIMAT, the Ottomans largely abandoned their previous folk-influenced medical approaches in favor of the new Western model that relied on recently popularized clinical methods.

EARLY OTTOMAN MEDICINE

From the start of the Ottoman Empire, and for much of the subsequent 400 years, medicine was based on an understanding of the human body and human illness that was forwarded from the ancient Greeks primarily through Persian and Arabic renditions. Fundamental to this understanding was the notion, popularized by Hippocrates (460 B.C.E.–c. 370 B.C.E.), that the body was governed by four "humors," (*ahlat*) namely, blood, yellow bile, black bile, and phlegm. It was supposed that any disruption in the proper balance of these humors led to illness. In addition, the written work of Galenos (129–c. 200 or 216), an advanced anatomist and surgeon, was vital to classical Ottoman medical knowledge and practice.

Blood-letting or phlebotomy, cauterization, phytotherapy (the use of plant extracts for medicinal purposes), sinapism (the use of mustard plasters as a medical dressing), balneotherapy (the treatment of illness by bathing) and dieteties were the most common methods of treating illnesses. Bleeding (*fasd, hacamat*), cupping, and leeching were established practices. Blood-letting could be practiced prophylactically by incising a vein of the right arm or by applying a cutting device (*zemberek*) to other parts of the body to allow for the "renewal" of blood. Such minor surgeries were conducted in barber shops or at home. Cauterization (*dağlama*), employed by Central Asian Turks, was also popular in Anatolia. It found its nosological description in Avicenna's *Canon,* the classical text of medicine from the 11th century. Hot springs, spas, and Turkish baths were also frequently used for medical treatment. Ottoman rulers, like the Romans and SELJUKS of Asia Minor before them, built and restored hot springs frequented by the locals who sought remedies for almost any disease. Balneotherapy remained in practice, basically unaltered, well into the 20th century and also became popular throughout Europe. The BURSA and Yalova hot spring resorts were favored by the families of the sultans.

Treatment with herbal and animal products was common and widespread among the Ottoman populace. Some 600 herbal drugs were named in Ottoman medical books compiled during the 14th and 15th centuries. For their prescriptions, Ottoman physicians would refer to the formularies (*akrabadin*) and material medica of ancient and medieval physicians such as Dioscorides, Galenos, Ibn Sina (Avicenna), Ibn al-Baitar, and the Hippocratic corpus.

Early Ottoman physicians adhered to the classical medical teaching of Galenos, mostly edited in Arabic, but these physicians also referred to other textual sources, including Turkish translations of a 30-volume medical treatise by the famed Arab-Andalusian anatomist Abul Qasim al-Zahrawi (936–1013). This treatise, *al-Tasrif*, was a significant source of anatomical knowledge for the Ottoman physician; a translation of *al-Tasrif* by Sabuncuoğlu Şerefeddin (1385–1468), known as the *Cerrahiyetü'l-haniye* (Surgery for the khans, c. 1465) was particularly valued for its illustrations. In the 17th century, Shemseddin Itaqi's *Risale-i Teşrihü'l-ebdan* (Treatise on the anatomy of the human body) attempted to bring together the anatomical knowledge of 14th-century Persian scholar Mansur ibn Muhammad and that of Andreas Vesalius (1514–64) and other 16th-century European anatomists. A break with medieval Islamic anatomical knowledge came with the publication of *Mir'atü'l-ebdan fi teşrih-i azai'l-insan* (The mirror of the human body and the anatomy of human organs, 1826–28), the earliest comprehensive work on anatomy published in Turkish. The author, Şanizade Mehmed Ataullah Efendi (1771–1826), included 56 plates reproduced from European anatomy books and from the famed French *Encyclopédie* compiled by scholars Denis Diderot (1713–84) and Jean le Rond d'Alembert (1717–83).

Although many Ottoman medical texts had their origins in translations from the Greek classics, Ottoman physicians composed texts to include both medieval knowledge received from their predecessors and notes related to their personal experience. These compilations brought together information that had not previously been integrated and added significantly both to medical knowledge and to the wider dissemination of this knowledge. Other early Ottoman medical treatises included works on pharmacology and books dealing with the management of recognized diseases. Specialized treatises, for instance, those on eye diseases, were also produced in Turkish. One of the most referenced and reproduced Turkish medical texts was the mid-16th century *Menafi'ün-nas* (Benefit of mankind) by Dervish Nidai el-Ankaravi.

Ottoman medicine was also facilitated by the contributions of immigrants and other physicians invited to Ottoman centers. Ottoman sultans had in their entourage court physicians who were responsible for the well-being of the sultan, his family, and the household. The palace welcomed physicians from various cultures; at least four Iranian physicians served in the court of MEHMED II (r. 1444–1446, 1451–1481). The earliest mention of an official court physician, however, dates to the reign of BAYEZID II (r. 1481–1512). Bayezid's *hekimbaşı* or chief-physician was named Muhiddin Mehmed (d. 1504). As a general rule, the *hekimbaşı* acted as both the personal physician of the sultan and the head of the Ottoman health administration, in charge of supervision of medical affairs for the empire and its army. The preparation of medicines for the sultan, especially that of the mithridate (*nevruziye*, an antidote for poison) was among his responsibilities. Another of Bayezid's court physicians was Joseph Hamon, who had fled SPAIN to seek asylum in the Ottoman Empire; Hamon's son Moses (d. 1554) became the personal physician of SÜLEYMAN I (r. 1520–66). In fact, many Jewish physicians who fled persecution in Spain, Portugal, and Italy in the 15th and 16th centuries found asylum in Ottoman lands. They brought with them valuable medical knowledge and experience, having been schooled in Judeo-Arabic medical discourse in combination with early Renaissance medical ideas and practices.

CLASSICAL OTTOMAN MEDICAL EDUCATION

Medical training within the empire was acquired in a number of places, in colleges or madrasas, within the *darüşşifas* (clinics or hospitals), or through apprenticeship to a practicing physician, surgeon, or oculist. Graduation from a regular madrasa was a prerequisite for medical education, which remained in the context of a religious foundation. Medical education within the madrasa context was largely theoretical and focused on the study of medieval Islamic medical literature. The major Arabic medical texts preferred were Avicenna's *Canon* and its commentaries. The 13th century physician Ibn al-Nafis's commentary on the *Canon* was also central to the curriculum. However, education at the medical madrasa also included the study of the Turkish medical books and compendia which began to be compiled in the 14th century.

The Süleymaniye Medical Madrasa or Darüttıb, the first school exclusively devoted to the teaching of medical sciences, opened in ISTANBUL during the reign of Süleymant (r. 1520–66). Its objective was to train a qualified medical staff that would be entrusted with the administration of health-related institutions in the empire. These could be employed in the imperial court or as lecturers in the colleges.

The Ottoman hospital was known as the *darüşşifa* (house of health). In most places it was part of a complex including a mosque and a madrasa. The Ottoman *darüşşifa* resembled the pre-Ottoman Seljukid hospitals (*bimarhane*) in legal status: they were both WAQF or charity institutions providing free medical treatment for the poor. Structurally the *darüşşifa* resembled a CARAVAN-SARY, with cells or halls lining an inner courtyard. Medical and surgical practice was conducted in the hospital of Süleymaniye, located in the same complex (*külliye*). Following the opening of modern hospitals in the 19th century, many of the Ottoman *darüşşifa*s evolved into mental asylums (vulgarized as *tımarhane*s).

Another form of institutional medicine, and an important element of the history of medicine in the Ottoman Empire, is the practice of military medicine. The beginnings of Ottoman military medicine can be traced to the emergence of the state at the turn of the 14th century: the barracks had functions parallel to those of *darüşşifa*s serving the civilian population. The JANISSARIES were treated within their garrisons. During their frequent military campaigns, the armies were regularly staffed with surgeons, physicians, oculists, and phar-

The mosque complex of Bayezid II at Edirne included a hospital devoted to the care of mental patients and a madrasa that provided medical training to students. *(Photo by Gábor Ágoston)*

macists. The military recruited civil physicians trained in the *darüşşifas*, together with *frenk* (Frankish, that is, European) physicians from abroad.

THE BEGINNINGS OF MODERN MEDICINE

Although Ottoman medical systems and practices underwent a dramatic change in the 19th century, medical innovations as early as the 17th century anticipated the massive modernization efforts that would follow. Such innovations were perhaps most visible in the area of pharmacology. The use of minerals as remedies (iatrochemistry) was introduced in the Ottoman Empire in the late 17th century, but traditional herbal and animal pharmacological formulae remained in circulation even after ready-made drugs from Europe began to be imported into the Ottoman market in the mid-19th century.

In the 17th and 18th centuries, Ottoman physicians began editing books mentioning cures with mineral drugs. Iatrochemistry itself was referred to as "new

medicine" (*tıbb-ı cedid*), since it differed from traditional therapies based on herbal drugs. Ibn al-Baitar treatise on simple remedies had already been translated from Arabic into Turkish in 1488. The Ottoman court physician Ali Münşi Efendi from BURSA used the *Thesaurus & armamentarium medico-chymicum* of Adrian von Mynsicht (1603–38) as a source for his own book of pharmacopoeia (1731) and also prepared a medical formulary entitled *Kitab-ı Mynsicht Tercümesi* (Translation of Mynsicht's book). The *el-Kanun* (Canon) of Ibn Sina was translated into Turkish in 1766. The *Aphorisms* of Hermann Boerhaave (1668–1738) was also rendered into Turkish in 1771.

Thus, by the 18th century, Ottoman medical literature included texts both of respected European authors and of medieval authors from the Arabic tradition. Outstanding in this respect is the work of Abbas Vesim b. Abdurrahman Efendi (d. 1760), whose scholarship effectively combined Eastern and Western medical knowledge. Although the 17th and 18th centuries saw the gradual introduction of European medical literature and medical practices into Ottoman culture, this did not prevent Ottoman physicians from continuing to use and value their traditional medical texts.

OTTOMAN REFORM, MILITARY MEDICINE, AND MODERNIZATION

More far-reaching modernizations of Ottoman medicine were an outgrowth of a larger system of military, political, and social reforms which began at the turn of the 19th century with the reform of the Ottoman army. The formal process of modernization may be seen as beginning with the NIZAM-I CEDID reforms launched in 1792 during the reign of SELIM III (r. 1789–1807), which initiated the establishment of a Western-style army in the empire. The AUSPICIOUS INCIDENT on June 17, 1826, which brought about the formal abolition of the JANISSARIES, paved the way for the large-scale westernizing reforms of the Tanzimat era (1839–76). With these changes and especially with the establishment of the new army (Asakir-i Mansure-i Muhammediye) by Mahmud II (r. 1808–39), initiatives were taken to create modern military hospitals and a new medical school. Thus came the establishment of a series of modern military hospitals throughout the empire.

Among the first modern hospitals opened in Istanbul was the Maltepe Military Hospital (1827) close to the barracks of the new army in the Topkapı district. The Kuleli Military Hospital and the Haydarpaşa Military Hospital (both founded in 1845), located in Üsküdar (Scutari) and designed to meet the functional requirements of the newly formed Ottoman army, also made use of modern Western medicine.

With the modern military hospital as a model, other Ottoman healthcare facilities soon followed suit and many modern public hospitals opened from the mid-19th century onward. The majority of public hospitals in the various towns of the empire were opened during the reign of ABDÜLHAMID II (r. 1876–1909) and were named HAMIDIYE in his honor. The last charity (waqf) hospital to be endowed by a member of the nobility was the Bezm-i Alem Gureba-i Müslimin (Muslim poor). The Vakıf Gureba, as the hospital came to be known, was founded in 1845; it had a larger capacity than the average darüşşifa and was also one of the first health institutions to be called a hastane, a term used specifically to denote modern hospitals. Although in its early years the medical practice at the Vakıf Gureba hospital was still based on the principles of the traditional Ottoman hospital, it ultimately became a leader in the modernization and westernization of Ottoman medicine. Similar charity hospitals and healthcare institutions were formed by the non-Muslims of the Ottoman Empire. Hospitals for the Austro-Hungarian, French, German (Prussian-Swiss), British, and Italian (Sardinian) colonies in the capital were created prior to the CRIMEAN WAR (1853–56). The Greek, Armenian, and Jewish communities also had their own hospitals. During the Crimean War, many hospitals and dispensaries were established by the allies (France, Great Britain, and the Kingdom of Sardinia) in Turkey, including the British barrack-hospitals.

The earliest private hospital was founded as a charity (waqf) in 1875 by the Ottoman grand vizier Yusuf Kamil Pasha and his wife Princess Zeynep of EGYPT. The Zeynep-Kamil Hospital in the Asian quarter of Istanbul was instrumental particularly in the introduction of contemporary surgical technology, asepsis, and patient care. Whereas the trustees of the Zeynep-Kamil private charitable hospital could recruit their own staff, in the Vakıf Gureba and other trust hospitals endowed by members of the royal family, the personnel were appointed and remunerated by the government.

Demand for medical personnel for the new armed forces created by MAHMUD II (r. 1808–1839) led to a reform not only in medical care, but also in the teaching of medicine. The Kuleli Military School temporarily housed a college (idadi) for the medical faculty but a modern medical school (Tıphane-i Amire) and a school for surgery (Cerrahhane-i Mamure) opened in Istanbul in 1827. These schools were unified after the proclamation of the Tanzimat in 1839.

Again, the influence of Western medicine was vital. Austrian physicians were invited from Vienna to supervise the organization of the Imperial School of Medicine (Mekteb-i Tıbbiye-i Şahane) on the model of the Josephinum, the Viennese military academy of medicine and surgery, as an academic institution. At this school, teaching was conducted in French and based exclusively on European medical texts. The dean, Carl Ambroise Bernard (1808–44), published a pharmacopeiea to standardize the production of drugs in the army corps and to introduce new preparations. Pharmacists were trained in separate classes and the traditional formularies (akrabadins) of medieval Islamic therapists were kept as reference texts among graduate practitioners. Another important advance in medical education is that hitherto forbidden cadaver dissections, including post-mortem examinations and anatomical demonstrations, were sanctioned by the sultan and put into practice in the Imperial School of Medicine.

To promote modern medical education, the government sent physicians to Europe for specialization and, in 1867, founded a Civilian School of Medicine (Mekteb-i Tıbbiye-i Mülkiye) where classes were conducted in Turkish. Subsequently, the language of instruction at the Military Medical School was also changed to Turkish, leading to a rapid increase in the number of Muslim physicians and the publication of modern medical books in Turkish. The first French-Turkish medical dictionary *Lugat-ı Tıbbiye*, prepared by Turkish-speaking physicians who founded the Ottoman Medical Society (Cemiyet-i Tıbbiye-i Osmaniye), was published in 1863. The Turkish journal of military medicine (*Ceride-i Tıbbiye-i Askeriye*) was launched in 1871. Ottoman medicine followed European medicine very closely in this respect. Medical faculties were founded in DAMASCUS and BEIRUT, staffed by Turkish-speaking faculty.

And while it is not often regarded as having been a politically beneficial event, the Crimean War, too, made for important contributions to the contemporary medical infrastructure in Europe and the empire. Despite its grave consequences, the war was crucial to the introduction of new medical practices and institutions in the Ottoman Empire. One of these was the Medical Society of Constantinople (later, the Imperial Medical Society), founded in 1856 through the initiative of Peter Pincoffs (1815–72) and other physicians serving under the Allies. The society provided a continuous flow of knowledge from Europe and its journal, the *Gazette Médicale d'Orient* (est. 1857), published research articles, excerpts from European medical journals, and the minutes of the society's meetings where members presented and discussed case studies. The war years saw a surge in the number of European physicians practicing in the empire. It was in this period that legislation on medical and sanitary services was drafted. Missionary hospitals were established, mostly in the eastern provinces of the empire and in PALESTINE.

PUBLIC HEALTH

The first International Sanitary Conference was held in Istanbul in 1866. The Ottoman government, while reforming medical education, undertook the reorganization of the public health administration and here, too, the military influence was significant. Among the most important changes in public health policy was the 1837–38 establishment of a Sanitary Office (Daire-i Sıhhiye) within the Ministry of War to administer the medical issues of the military. At the same time, the Sanitary Board (Meclis-i Umur-i Sıhhiye) was authorized to deal with epidemics and enforce quarantine measures. The Sanitary Board established disinfection stations in the empire's municipalities and was otherwise instrumental in combating the cholera epidemics spreading from Asia during the 19th century. A Medical Board (Conseil des Affaires Médicales) founded within the Military Medical School was responsible for physicians' qualifications and the licensing of pharmacies within the Ottoman Empire. In addition to these other reforms, the authority and responsibilities of the *hekimbaşı* or chief physician of the court were transferred to councils in the sanitary administration. In 1850 the position of the *hekimbaşı* was abolished and thereafter court physicians acted merely as private physicians to the sultan.

A crucial advance in public health was the early development and widespread use of vaccines, especially against smallpox. Following Louis Pasteur's discovery of rabies vaccine in 1885, two professors from the Military Medical School and a veterinarian traveled to Paris in 1886 to present Pasteur with a *mecidiye* decoration from Sultan Abdülhamid II and a contribution to the Institut Pasteur. At the institute they learned about the preparation of the vaccine, its application, and recent developments in microbiology and virology. As a result, a rabies laboratory (Daü'l-kelb Ameliyathanesi) opened in the Military Medical School in 1887 under the direction of Alexander Zoeros Pasha (1842–1917) for the production of rabies vaccine.

The establishment of the Imperial Bacteriological Laboratory (Bakteriolojihane-i Şahane) in 1894 was also realized in collaboration with Institut Pasteur. André Chantemesse (1851–1919) and Maurice Nicolle (1862–1932), were commissioned from France to organize this institute in Istanbul, where early experiments on vaccines were conducted and an antiserum for diphtheria was produced for clinical use. A second bacteriological laboratory (Bakteriyolojihane-i Baytari) opened in the Veterinary School under the supervision of Mustafa Adil (1871–1904), who was trained at the Alfort Veterinary School; serums for diphtheria and rinderpest were produced there in 1897.

As an outgrowth of these activities, experiments were conducted in 1811 in Istanbul to prepare the smallpox vaccine from cattles infected with cowpox. By 1880 Giovanni Battista Violi (1849–1928) from Modena established his Institut Vaccinogène in Istanbul, successfully preparing smallpox vaccine derived from calves. By 1894, with the establishment of the Imperial Vaccine Institute (Telkihhane-i Şahane) and due to the efforts of its founder and director Dr.Hüseyin Remzi (1839–1896), ample smallpox vaccine was being produced and distributed to allow for the control of this disease in the empire.

20TH-CENTURY MEDICINE IN THE EMPIRE AND AFTER

By the turn of the 20th century, Ottoman medicine had undergone an incredible transformation in large part due to the open cooperation between Ottoman and European medical experts and public health advocates. Two modern training hospitals were established in Istanbul. The Gülhane military hospital opened in 1898 and was administered by a Prussian staff; the Hamidiye Etfal, which opened in 1899, was a benevolent children's hospital and an acclaimed research institution. The military and civilian medical schools were merged together in 1909, in the aftermath of the YOUNG TURK Revolution of 1908. A class for dentistry was initiated in this new school and pharmacy education was separated from that of medicine.

International collaboration was emphasized during the BALKAN WARS of 1912–13 and numerous medical missions from abroad (United States, Belgium, Egypt, India) arrived in the Ottoman capital to deal with increasing war casualties and to combat epidemics. During WORLD WAR I (1914–18), as the war raged on many fronts, troops and civilians were ravaged by the devastating effects of typhus, cholera, and influenza. In response to this suffering, the Ottomans entered into medical cooperation with Germany, conducting successful field research in the endemic diseases of the eastern Mediterranean.

The health policy of the Turkish Republic after 1923 was radically different from that of the Ottoman Empire in that the primary objective of the new government was to combat major communicable diseases such as malaria, tuberculosis, and trachoma, all of which were prevalent among the Anatolian population. With this focus on public health, the new Turkish Republic added to the number of physicians, nurses, and hospitals, made child health and social hygiene a priority, subsidized the national pharmaceutical industry, and established a central laboratory for vaccine production in the capital, Ankara.

Feza Günergun
Şeref Etker

Further reading: N. Varlık Akarsu, "Disease and Empire: A Study of Plague Epidemics in the Ottoman Empire (1453–1600)," (Ph.D. diss., University of Chicago, 2005); Feza Günergun, "Diseases in Turkey: A preliminary study for the second half of the 19th century," in *The Imagination of the Body and the History of Bodily Experience*, edited by S. Kuriyama (Kyoto: International Research Center for Japanese Studies, 2001), 169–191; Feza Günergun, "Science in the Ottoman World," in G. N. Vlahakis, I. M. Malaquias, N. M. Broots, F. Regourd, F. Gunergun, and D. Wright, *Imperialism and Science: Social Impact and Interaction* (Santa Barbara, Calif.: ABC-Clio, 2006), 71–118; Feza Günergun and Şeref Etker, "Waqf endowments and the emergence of modern charitable hospitals in the Ottoman Empire: the case of Zeynep-Kamil hospital in Istanbul," in *The Development of Modern Medicine in Non-Western Countries, Historical Perspectives*, edited by H. Ebrahimnejad (London: Routledge, in press); Rhoads Murphey, "Ottoman Medicine and Transculturalism from the sixteenth through eighteenth centuries." *Bulletin of the History of Medicine*, 66 (1992), 376–403; Gül A. Russel, "Physicians at the Ottoman Court." *Medical History* 34, no.3 (July 1990), 243–67.

Medina (Medinah; *Ar.*: al-Madina al-Munawwara) As the site of the mosque of the Prophet Muhammad's grave, Medina is considered by most Muslims to be sacred. Many Muslims include a visit to the city as part of the HAJJ to MECCA, which lies approximately 200 miles to the south of the city. As was the case with Mecca, the Ottomans used their control of Medina to advance the legitimacy of their rule. This required the restoration of the Mosque of the Prophet and annual subsidies to the city's residents. The Ottomans were sensitive to local suspicions about their intentions and usually appointed a local Bedouin leader to serve as the sheikh of the city. There was also, on occasion, an Ottoman governor assigned to the city, but at other times, a local tribal leader held both offices.

The fact that the main mosque in Medina was built around the Prophet Muhammad's grave seemed to the religiously conservative Muwahhidun, better known as WAHHABIS, as an affront to Islam. In their view, such veneration of a mere mortal, even the man chosen as the prophet of God, distracted the devotion of the believers that should be directed to God alone. In their crusade against what they considered to be a corrupted Islam, the Wahhabis seized Medina in 1804. They plundered the shrine and pulled down the dome over the Prophet's grave. Until their defeat at the hands of the Egyptian army in 1813, the Wahhabis prevented pilgrims from showing any reverence at the Prophet's grave. In a stunning reversal of their rejection of the legitimacy of the Ottoman sultan's right to rule, the political head of the movement, Muhammad ibn Saud, acceded to Ottoman sovereignty over Medina and Mecca in 1815 as he recognized he did not have the military resources to dislodge an army equipped with artillery. There was no further threat from this movement in the city as long as Ottoman control of the HEJAZ continued.

In 1908, the HEJAZ RAILROAD reached Medina. Besides offering easier access to pilgrims on the hajj, the railroad would greatly facilitate the movement of Ottomans troops to Arabia should the need arise. With the arrival of the railroad, Medina was transformed into a garrison town. In 1916, when FAYSAL IBN HUSAYN AL-HASHIMI proclaimed the ARAB REVOLT, the Ottoman governor of Medina was able to hold the town against attack from the Arab irregulars. The city only surrendered to the Arab army in January 1919, months after Faysal's men had entered DAMASCUS.

Bruce Masters

Mehmed I (Mehmed Çelebi [Prince Mehmed], Kırışçı [Young Lord]) (b. 1387?–d. 1421) (r. 1413–1421) *Ottoman sultan, second founder of the Ottoman state* Mehmed I, the son of BAYEZID I (r. 1389–1402) and Devlet Hatun (daughter of the emir of Germiyan, an Anatolian Turkoman principality), emerged victorious from the internecine wars of the interregnum (1402–13) that followed the Ottoman defeat at the hands of the central Asian conqueror TIMUR or Tamerlane at the BATTLE OF ANKARA in 1402. He is considered the second founder of the Ottoman state because he reunified the Ottoman realms after defeating his brothers in 1413, although at the time of his death in 1421 the territories of the Ottoman state were still smaller than those held by his father, Bayezid I, prior to the debacle at Ankara.

After the Battle of Ankara, Timur restored most of Anatolia to the Turkoman emirs or lords whose principalities had recently been absorbed into Sultan Bayezid I's expanding Ottoman state. What remained of the Ottoman realms became contested territory among Sultan Bayezid I's sons. Of the sultan's six sons still alive in 1402 (Süleyman, İsa, Kasım, Mustafa, Musa, and Mehmed), Prince Mustafa was taken to Timur's capital Samarkand (in present-day Uzbekistan), along with Bayezid himself. In the next decade or so, princes Süleyman, İsa, Mehmed, and Musa (whom Timur also captured at the battle but later released) fought against each other to attain sole control over the remaining Ottoman territories. Prince Kasım, who had been in BURSA at the time of the Battle of Ankara, was taken by his older brother Süleyman to the Balkans and then sent as hostage to the Byzantine Emperor Manuel II (r. 1391–1425); he remained in the Byzantine capital Constantinople until his death in 1417. Of the four remaining princes, Süleyman established himself in the Balkans, ruling over the Ottoman territories there, while Mehmed controlled the Tokat-Amasya region in north-central Asia Minor. From here, Mehmed moved to Bursa, capturing the city from his brother İsa. When İsa moved against Mehmed in alliance with the ruler of the BLACK SEA coastal emirate of Kastamonu, Mehmed defeated and killed him at Eskişehir in 1403–04. Soon, however, Prince Süleyman crossed into Anatolia and captured Bursa from Mehmed, who retreated to Tokat. At this point it seemed that Prince Süleyman would emerge as the sole ruler of the Ottoman territories on both sides of the Bosporus. Indeed, some historians accept him as sultan, and name him Süleyman I, numbering the much better known 16th-century Süleyman the Magnificent (r. 1520–66) incorrectly as Süleyman II. However, Prince Süleyman was never the sole ruler of the Ottoman lands; he soon lost control over his realms and was defeated and killed.

From his base in Tokat Mehmed now encouraged his brother Musa to challenge Süleyman. Musa appeared in the eastern Balkans in 1406, accepting the invitation of the *voievod* (governor) Mircea of WALLACHIA (part of present-day Romania), who tried to prevent the consolidation of Ottoman power in his region. He thus supported Musa, who married Mircea's daughter. By May 1410 Musa captured Süleyman's capital at EDIRNE and extended his rule through the Gallipoli peninsula. When Süleyman returned from Anatolia to reassert his rule in the Balkans, Musa defeated and killed him at Edirne in February 1411.

Musa's aggressive policy alienated the Ottomans' former Christian vassals in the Balkans who sided with Mehmed, considered at this point less powerful and thus less dangerous to them. Musa also besieged the Byzantine capital Constantinople, albeit unsuccessfully, for he feared that the Byzantines could use his brother Kasım or Prince Süleyman's son, Orhan, both residing in Constantinople as hostages, to instigate rebellion against him. The siege convinced Emperor Manuel that Musa was the bigger threat, and thus he also supported Prince Mehmed against Musa. With the help of SERBIA, Byzantium, the Turkish frontier lords in the Balkans, and several ANATOLIAN EMIRATES, Mehmed eventually managed to overcome Musa in July 1413 at a battle fought south of the present-day Bulgarian capital Sofia. Musa himself was killed when his horse stumbled.

Having emerged as victor from the decade-long internecine struggle for the Ottoman throne, Prince Mehmed, known from now onward as Sultan MEHMED I (r. 1413–21), set out to consolidate his rule over the Ottoman realms. The former Ottoman vassal or client states (including Wallachia, SERBIA, and Byzantium) acknowledged Mehmed's suzerainty and in turn received assurances that the new Ottoman sultan would pursue a peaceful policy in the Balkans. Reassured by these submissions, Mehmed I crossed to Asia Minor to subdue those Anatolian Turkoman emirs who had supported his rivals. The resistance of the emir of Karaman in central Turkey, and Cüneyd, the emir of Aydın based in IZMIR in western Turkey, was especially robust. Mehmed defeated Cüneyd in 1414 and turned his realm into an Ottoman subprovince or *sancak*, appointing Cüneyd as governor of Nikopol on the Danube in present-day Bulgaria. Although Mehmed defeated the Karamanids in 1415, their emirate proved to be a much stronger enemy, as Mehmed and his successors were soon to discover.

Mehmed's successes alarmed the Byzantine emperor Manuel. In a desperate move he released Prince Süleyman's son Orhan to Wallachia, whose voievod also opposed the consolidation of Ottoman power in the Balkans. However, Mehmed captured and blinded Orhan before he could reach Wallachia. The sultan's troubles were far from over. In 1415 Mehmed's brother Mustafa appeared first in Anatolia and then in Wallachia where he started negotiations with the Byzantines, Venetians, and Wallachians regarding a joint assault on Mehmed. Although Mehmed and later Ottoman chroniclers considered him an impostor and thus dubbed him "False Mustafa," it is plausible that he was indeed Mehmed's brother, released by Timur's son and successor Shah

Rukh (r. 1405–47), who also considered the consolidation of Ottoman power under Mehmed in Anatolia, in the vicinity of his Persian lands, undesirable. In any case, the trouble Mustafa and his allies (including the former rebel and newly appointed governor of Nikopol, Cüneyd) had caused proved short-lived, for they were defeated by Mehmed and found refuge in the Byzantine city of SALONIKA. By the autumn of 1416 Mehmed managed to secure an agreement with Emperor Manuel according to which Mustafa and Cüneyd were to be held in Byzantine custody for the duration of Mehmed's reign in exchange for an annual compensation of 10,000 gold ducats.

Mustafa was not the only threat to Sultan Mehmed in 1416. Southwest of the Danube delta in the Deli Orman or Wild Forest (in present-day southern Romania and northeastern Bulgaria) a dangerous rebellion erupted against Mehmed's rule, led by the charismatic Muslim judge (kadı) and mystic Sheikh Bedreddin. Bedreddin was born in 1358 in Simavna (Kyprinos in northeastern Greece), a son of the local Muslim judge and his converted Greek wife. Bedreddin studied with his father, then went to Konya (the center of the MEVLEVI ORDER of dervishes) to study logic and astronomy. In the early 1380s he studied in the Mamluk capital of CAIRO with famous theologians, lawyers, and physicians, and was appointed tutor of the future Mamluk Sultan Faraj (r. 1399–1412). Originally an enemy of SUFISM, in Cairo Bedreddin met the Sufi Sheikh Husayn Akhlati and under his influence he himself became a Sufi, perfecting his knowledge in Tabriz and Ardabil (the center of the Safaviyya mystical order and the later Safavid dynasty of IRAN) in the early 1400s. He later went to Asia Minor on a missionary journey, where he developed his ideas regarding common ownership and the "oneness of being" that sought to eliminate differences between religions as well as between rich and poor. Around 1410, Prince Musa appointed Bedreddin military judge in Edirne, but his tenure ended with the victory of Mehmed, who in 1413 banished him to Iznik. It was probably in Iznik that Bedreddin acquainted himself with a popular movement that by 1416 culminated in an uprising in Anatolia led by Torlak Kemal and Börklüce Mustafa. Sheikh Bedreddin, who appears to have been the ideological leader of the movement, crossed to the Balkans and instigated another rebellion southwest of the Danube Delta. He enjoyed the support of many marcher lords (rulers of borderlands) who opposed Mehmed because he had revoked the land grants given to them by Bedreddin in the name of Prince Musa. However, Mehmed's troops swiftly apprehended Bedreddin. He was accused of disturbing the order of the sultanate by advocating for communal ownership of property and the similarities between religions and their prophets. He was publicly hanged on December 18, 1416,

in the marketplace of Serres in Macedonia. Although Bedreddin was defeated, his ideas remained popular among the BEKTASHI ORDER of dervishes and their supporters, the JANISSARIES, the sultans' elite infantry.

After the suppression of these popular uprisings in Anatolia and the Balkans, Mehmed punished those who had supported the rebels. In 1419 the sultan defeated Mircea of Wallachia and forced him to accept Ottoman suzerainty. Mehmed also managed to impose vassalage upon the Karamanid Turkoman emirate. Weakened by poor health, the sultan's major concern in his last years was to secure the throne for his eldest son Murad. He concluded an agreement with Emperor Manuel that Murad would be acknowledged as Mehmed's successor, his son Mustafa would remain in Anatolia, and the two youngest sons, Yusuf and Mahmud, aged eight and seven, would be handed over to Manuel, who would keep them, in custody in Constantinople along with Mehmed I's brother Mustafa and would get an annual sum for their upkeep. When Mehmed I died on June 25, 1521, he was indeed succeeded by his eldest son MURAD II (r. 1421–44; 1446–51).

Gábor Ágoston

Further reading: Caroline Finkel, *Osman's Dream: The Story of the Ottoman Empire, 1300–1923* (New York: Basic Books, 2005), 22–36; Halil İnalcık, "Meḥemmed I," in *Encyclopaedia of Islam*, online edition (by subscription), edited by P. Bearman, Th. Bianquis, C. E. Bosworth, E. van Donzel, and W. P. Heinrichs. Brill, 2007. Brill Online. 21 May 2007 http:// www.brillonline.nl/subscriber/entry?entry=islam_COM-0728; H.J. Kissling, "Badr al-Dīn b. Ḳāḍī Samāwnā," in *Encyclopaedia of Islam*, online edition (by subscription), edited by P. Bearman, Th. Bianquis, C. E. Bosworth, E. van Donzel, and W. P. Heinrichs. Brill, 2007. Brill Online. 31 May 2007 http:// www.brillonline.nl/subscriber/entry?entry=islam_SIM-1017

Mehmed II (Mehmed Fatih; Mehmet II; Mehemmed II) (b. 1432–d. 1481) (r. 1444–1446; 1451–1481) *Ottoman sultan*   Mehmed II was the fourth son of MURAD II (r. 1421–44; 1446–51) and the seventh Ottoman ruler, whose first reign covered the period from 1444 to 1446 and whose second reign spanned three decades, from 1451 to 1481. Mehmed was born on March 30, 1432 in EDIRNE, which was then the Ottoman capital. The name and ethnicity of his mother have been the subject of much fruitless speculation but her identity remains unknown; she must in any case have been of non-Muslim slave origin. Mehmed's early years are equally obscure. According to some sources, in 1434 he was sent with his mother to Amasya, where Mehmed's half-brother Ahmed Çelebi (1420–37, the eldest son of Murad II) was governor, and where Murad's second son, Alaeddin Ali Çelebi (b. 1425?–43), also appears to have been in Mehmed's retinue. When Ahmed Çelebi died suddenly in 1437, the five-year-old Mehmed became the

Painted by the Venetian artist Gentile Bellini in 1480 during his stay in Istanbul, this portrait of Mehmed II depicts the sultan as a Renaissance prince and, according to the left plaque on the painting, a "world conqueror" (*Victor Orbis*). The distinctively western European style of the portrait, with its three-quarters profile, had an important impact on later Ottoman portraiture. *(Erich Lessing / Art Resource)*

provincial governor of Amasya and Alaeddin Ali Çelebi was sent to govern Manisa, in western Anatolia. Two years later, in 1439, both princes were brought to Edirne for their circumcision, after which Murad had his sons switch positions, sending Mehmed to Manisa and Alaeddin Ali to Amasya. It is widely believed that Alaeddin Ali, who participated with his father in a successful campaign against Ibrahim Bey, the ruler of Karaman, was the sultan's favorite, but in the spring of 1443, shortly after the campaign against Ibrahim Bey, Alaeddin Çelebi was assassinated. While the episode is shrouded in mystery, some historians believe the assassination was the result of an order from Murad; others suggest it was a consequence of political infighting among the sultan's leading men. Regardless of its cause, the death of Alaeddin Çelebi left nine-year-old Mehmed as the sole living heir of Murad II. In July 1443 Murad brought his son from Manisa to Edirne to reside at court and gain experience in affairs of state.

In the later months of 1443 a crusading army, which had left the Hungarian capital of BUDA, advanced deep into the Balkans and was finally halted by the Ottoman army in a bitter winter battle between Sofia (capital of present-day Bulgaria) and Edirne in December. Although hostilities were terminated in June 1444 by a 10-year truce signed by Murad at Edirne, to be ratified later by the king of HUNGARY, the truce was soon broken by Hungary under papal dispensation and an even larger crusading army was assembled and began its march toward Ottoman territory. Already engaged in another military campaign against Ibrahim Bey of Karaman in Anatolia, Murad II swiftly defeated the Karamanids, returned by forced march to Edirne, and went on with his army to confront and defeat the crusaders at the Battle of Varna (November 10, 1444).

In Edirne, the sultan had left the 12-year-old Mehmed as regent of the state's Balkan territories. At this time Mehmed was under the tutelage of his father's chief vizier, Çandarlı Halil Pasha, and his *kadıasker* (army judge), Molla Hüsrev. During this period the young regent was exposed to several crises, including the death of the leader of the radical Hurufiyya Sufi movement who gained many adherents as well as the protection of Prince Mehmed himself before being proscribed by the authorities and executed. During the same period, a Janissary revolt ended in the burning of the market quarter and the attempted destruction of one of Mehmed's special advisors, Şihabeddin Pasha, a man of the DEVŞIRME, or child levy. When Murad returned from fighting the crusaders in late November or early December 1444, he abdicated in favor of his young son, retiring to Manisa and leaving Mehmed to rule as sultan under the tutelage of Çandarlı Halil Pasha and Molla Hüsrev.

Mehmed's first reign as sultan was as troubled and difficult as had been his earlier regency; little more than 18 months after his ENTHRONMENT AND ACCESSION CEREMONY Mehmed was deposed and packed off to Manisa and Murad II resumed the sultanate. It is not clear why Murad was recalled to Edirne by Halil Pasha. It may have been that Mehmed was planning an offensive against Constantinople which would have been supported by men of the *devşirme* while being vehemently opposed by Çandarlı Halil Pasha; it may have been that the JANISSARIES were unhappy with Mehmed. Despite being deposed, Mehmed continued to work with his father, taking part with him in military campaigns in 1448 against a further Hungarian invasion (the second Battle of Kosovo, October 1448) and again in 1450 in ALBANIA. He seems to have ruled western Anatolia intermittently from Manisa as a virtual fiefdom, from which he undertook naval campaigns against Venetian possessions in the Aegean.

When Murad II died at Edirne in February 1451, Mehmed was once again in Manisa. His second reign began when he acceded to the throne in Edirne on February 18, 1451, confirming all his father's ministers in

Built just before the 1453 siege of Byzantine Constantinople, Rumeli Hisarı (the Rumelian castle) on the European shore of the Bophorus was used along with the Anadolu Hisarı (the Anatolian castle) to seal off the city from the straights and deny it any possible relief. *(Photo by Gábor Ágoston)*

their posts, including Çandarlı Halil as GRAND VIZIER, and ordering the judicial murder of the youngest son of Murad II, then an infant, in an act that historians have seen as the initiation of the so-called Ottoman "law of fratricide," although considerable doubt remains on this point. Mehmed was now 19, marked by the traumatic experiences of his childhood and youth, and determined to exercise absolute authority as sultan.

The first months of his reign were apparently tranquil: existing truces with SERBIA, VENICE, and lesser Aegean and Balkan entities were renewed, a three-year truce was negotiated with HUNGARY, and particular assurances of Mehmed's benevolence were accorded to the BYZANTINE EMPIRE, leaving Mehmed free to warn off Ibrahim Bey of Karaman from his pretensions to Ottoman territory in Anatolia. Soon, however, the situation changed and the determining features of Mehmed's reign began to manifest themselves: a sharp increase in state expenditure; lavish buildings works, including a vast new palace complex at Edirne; and an aggressive foreign policy, manifested first against the Byzantine Empire and signaled by the construction in 1452 of the fortress of Rumeli Hisarı on the European shore of the Bosporus, effectively blockading the Straits and isolating the Byzantine capital of Constantinople. Mehmed spent the

autumn of 1452 and spring of 1453 in Edirne planning the final CONQUEST OF CONSTANTINOPLE. He ordered the casting of huge siege guns, assembled land and sea forces, and moved a vast array of soldiers and equipment from Edirne to the land walls of the Byzantine capital.

Mehmed left Edirne late in March 1453 and began to besiege Constantinople on April 6. The siege lasted 54 days, the outcome remaining uncertain until the final storming of the city walls on May 29, after which Mehmed gave the city over to his soldiers for three days of pillaging. Mehmed entered the city later on May 29 and proceeded to the famed metropolitan church of HAGIA SOPHIA which he transformed into a Muslim mosque, called Aya Sofya. Most of the surviving population of the city were enslaved and deported. The Byzantine Empire was now effectively at an end, and Constantinople was renamed ISTANBUL. The conquest of Constantinople also marked the end of the old, paternalistic Ottoman state of Murad II. Within a brief time Çandarlı Halil Pasha, whose attitude toward the siege had been equivocal at best, was dismissed and later executed. He was replaced as grand vizier by Zaganos Pasha, a product of the *devşirme*, whose more aggressive attitudes would henceforth dominate the affairs of the sultanate.

By the conquest of Constantinople Mehmed had realized an Islamic ambition that dated back to the first sieges of the city by the Arabs in the mid-seventh century. The Ottoman state was now an empire, controlling the "two lands" (Anatolia and Rumelia) and the "two seas" (the BLACK SEA and the Aegean). Mehmed himself was henceforth known by the sobriquet "Fatih," or "the Conqueror," arrogating to himself not only the Muslim title of sultan, first claimed by BAYEZID I (r. 1389–1402), but two additional titles implying universal sovereignty, the old Turkish title of Khaqan and the Roman-Byzantine title of Qaysar (Caesar). It is in the light of his self-image as world-ruler and his ambitions for universal monarchy, contrasted with the practical limitations on the realization of that policy, that the complex record of Mehmed's activities during his almost 30-year reign can be best understood.

In the first place, Istanbul was rapidly restored to its historic position as a true imperial capital. The city was progressively redeveloped and was repopulated by successive waves of forced immigration from newly conquered areas. Moreover, Mehmed rebuilt the city through the development of new residential and mercantile quarters grouped around a mosque complex or a market. Edirne was quickly abandoned by Mehmed as an imperial residence in favor of new palaces built within the walls of Istanbul, the first being the so-called Old Palace and the second being the New Palace, better known as the TOPKAPI PALACE, built at the furthest extremity of the city, overlooking the confluence of the Bosporus, the Golden Horn, and the Sea of Marmara.

Secondly, the almost continuous WARFARE that marked Mehmed's reign can be seen as an attempt to expand Ottoman territory by the elimination or neutralization of all competing polities, Muslim as well as Christian, that stood in the way of the realization of his imperial ambitions. The remaining fragments of territory where Byzantine rule still endured were rapidly absorbed by Mehmed's burgeoning empire. Most of the Balkan states that still formed part of the Christian Orthodox world were also incorporated by a combination of warfare and diplomacy (Serbia, 1457; Bosnia, 1461–63), while Venetian possessions in the east came under sustained Ottoman attack with the Ottoman-Venetian war of 1463–79 and the capture of Negroponte in 1470. North of the DANUBE RIVER, the Ottomans were still not strong enough to take Belgrade (although they besieged it unsuccessfully in 1456) or to do more than ravage Hungarian territory by ceaseless razzias intended to preempt any hostile presence on the lower Danube. The Balkan territories of WALLACHIA and MOLDAVIA remained a military danger zone for the Ottoman armies and an area of abiding contention. Conversely, toward the end of his reign Mehmed was able to eradicate the Genoese trading

The Yedikule (or "Seven Towers") Fortress was built by Mehmed II using the existing Byzantine defensive walls. The fortress continued to be used as a treasury and a prison after it ceased to have any defensive purpose. *(Photo by Gábor Ágoston)*

colonies in the Crimea and to bring the Giray dynasty, the Crimean Khanate, into a vassal relationship (1478), thus controlling territories on all sides of the Black Sea, which for almost three centuries was given the sobriquet of the "Ottoman lake."

In Anatolia, Mehmed went on to control most of the remaining Muslim dynasties, employing a combination of strategies that included forced annexation and dynastic marriages. These dynasties were themselves largely of Turkoman origin, such as the Isfendiyarid in northern Anatolia, with its valuable Black Sea port of Sinop and its copper mines in the vicinity of Kastamonu. Karaman, long a thorn in the Ottomans' side, was neutralized in 1468 and re-annexed in 1474; the eastern Anatolian Turkoman confederacy of the Akkoyunlu (or "White Sheep" Turkomans), led by Uzun Hasan, proved more difficult to subdue, but the confederacy was much diminished by Mehmed's 1473 victory over Uzun Hasan in the Battle of Tercan (Otluk-beli).

In the latter years of Mehmed's reign, when he was already in poor health, the practical limitations of his policies became more apparent. Success had brought its own problems, including confrontations with the Egyptian MAMLUK EMPIRE and with Hungary, which would not be solved in the Ottomans' favor until the reign of Mehmed's grandson, SELIM I (r. 1512–20). There is no doubt also that Mehmed harbored a deep desire to conquer Italy and to bring Rome, as well as Constantinople, under his domination, but an expedition mounted against southern Italy in 1480 was a disastrous failure, and the Ottoman bridgehead at Otranto was abandoned the following year, after Mehmed's death. Likewise, a complex amphibious operation in the same year against the crusading KNIGHTS OF ST JOHN and their island fortress of RHODES was a costly failure.

While Mehmed Fatih is known primarily for his military successes, especially for the conquest of Constantinople, and for his impressive role in expanding the Ottoman Empire, there were other important aspects of his long reign. Mehmed's attempts to build up a unified and centralized empire strained the state's finances, forcing several devaluations of the Ottoman currency and requiring the extension of the state's monopolistic and unpopular tax-farming system. Through these measures, and despite vast and continuous military expenditure, the state treasury still contained some three and a half million ducats of ready money at the time of the sultan's death. At the same time, these actions and the frequent confiscation of private lands by the state alienated most of the old Ottoman landed families and society at large, creating strong social discontent.

Altogether, it is difficult to arrive at a balanced account of Mehmed's reign. His complex personality has been endlessly discussed but still defies satisfactory analysis. Mehmed seems to have been affected by both the perils and humiliations of his early years and possibly by the influence of what may be termed the "war party" at the outset of his reign. Attempts to describe him as a renaissance figure and a free thinker must be viewed with some misgivings in light of his preoccupation with enforcing strict religious orthodoxy. The darker aspects of his nature continue to defy analysis; although these are well documented, they stand in contrast to the historical picture we have of both his father, Murad II, and his son, Sultan BAYEZID II (r. 1481–1512).

Mehmed II died on May 3, 1481 while encamped with his army on the first stages of a campaign in Anatolia, possibly directed against Rhodes or the Mamluk Empire. There is substantial circumstantial evidence that Mehmed was poisoned, possibly at the behest of his eldest son and successor, Bayezid. Mehmed's death unleashed a short-lived but violent Janissary revolt and then a lengthy succession struggle between Bayezid and his brother CEM, who long contended for the throne. Although Bayezid immediately reversed many of his

father's fiscal and military policies, Mehmed's reign was one of undeniable achievement, the conquest of Constantinople and its subsequent transformation being foremost amongst his accomplishments.

Colin Heywood

Further reading: Franz Babinger, *Mehmed the Conqueror and His Time,* translated by Ralph Manheim, edited by William C. Hickman (Princeton, N.J.: Princeton University Press, 1978), a work to be used with caution, and read in conjunction with Halil İnalcık, "Mehmed the Conqueror (1432–1481) and His Time," *Speculum,* xxv (1960), 408–427, reprinted in Halil İnalcık, *Essays in Ottoman History* (Istanbul: Eren, 1998), 87–110; Michael Doukas, *The Decline and Fall of Byzantium to the Ottoman Turks,* trans. H. J. Magoulias (Detroit: Wayne State University Press, 1975); Colin Heywood, "Mehmed II and the Historians: The Reception of Babinger's *Mehmed der Eroberer* during Half a Century" (to appear in *Turcica,* 2009); Halil İnalcık, "The Policy of Mehmed II towards the Greek Population of Istanbul," *Dumbarton Oaks Papers,* 23–24 (1969–70), 231–249; Kritovoulos, *History of Mehmed the Conqueror,* trans. C. T. Riggs (Princeton, N.J.: Princeton University Press, 1954); Bernard Lewis et al., *The Fall of Constantinople: A Symposium Held at the School of Oriental and African Studies 29 May 1953* (London: School of Oriental and African Studies, 1955); Julian Raby, "A Sultan of Paradox: Mehmed the Conqueror as a Patron of the Arts." *The Oxford Art Journal,* 6, no. 1 (1982), 3–8; Steven Runciman, *The Fall of Constantinople* (Cambridge: Cambridge University Press, 1965); Tursun Beg, *The History of Mehmed the Conqueror,* edited and translated by Halil İnalcık and Rhoads Murphey (Minneapolis: Bibliotheka Islamica, 1978).

Mehmed III (b. 1566–d. 1603) (r. 1595–1603) *Ottoman sultan and caliph* Mehmed III was the son of MURAD III (r. 1574–95) and his Albanian-born concubine Safiyye Sultan. Mehmed's birth in May 1566 coincided with the last months of the reign of his great-grandfather SÜLEYMAN I (r. 1520–66), who gave him the name Mehmed in homage to the famous Sultan MEHMED II (r. 1444–46; 1451–81), the conqueror of CONSTANTINOPLE. In 1574, when his father succeeded to the throne, Mehmed also moved to ISTANBUL and began to live in the TOPKAPI PALACE. In 1582 his circumcision was celebrated with grandiose feasts and spectacles that occasioned an impressive dynastic propaganda. Two years after his circumcision, in the last days of December 1584, Mehmed III departed for Manisa to assume his post as prince-governor or *sancakbeyi* of the Saruhan subprovince or *sancak.* Four of his five sons were born during Mehmed's 11-year stay in Manisa, including the future AHMED I (r. 1603–1617) in 1590 and MUSTAFA I (r. 1617–18, 1622–23) in 1591. Upon the death of his father, Mehmed was invited to Istanbul, and acceded to the throne in 1595.

Mehmed III's reign coincided with serious social, economic, and political unrest. Aggravated financial problems, sociopolitical disturbances in Anatolia, and a costly war with the Habsburgs all added up to a crisis that was hard to manage. The Long Hungarian War with the Habsburgs (1593–1606), which had begun during the reign of Murad III and would continue after Mehmed III died, is very telling in terms of the position of the late 16th-century sultans in the business of rule and the possibilities of fulfilling the image of warrior sultan.

Beginning with the reign of SELIM II (r. 1566–74), Ottoman sultans began to abstain from participating in military campaigns. They became increasingly immobile within the close quarters of the Topkapı Palace. This immobility was not caused by a deficiency in their training or experience; rather, the emergence of the court culture as the central political arena required the constant presence of the sultans in the palace rather than on the battlefield. In the changing political setting of the late 16th century, Mehmed III, like any other power contender of the court, could not risk being an absentee in court politics. Thus in 1596, when Mehmed decided to lead his armies after 30 years of sultans' absence from battlefields, his decision was not made voluntarily. Like his father and grandfather, he would have preferred to stay in Istanbul and send field marshals to the ongoing war with the Habsburgs. The principal figure who convinced Mehmed III to lead the campaign was Grand Vizier Sinan Pasha. According to the argument of this tried statesman, who occupied the highest office of the empire five times, if the grand vizier was appointed as field marshal, the deputy vizier, in order to discredit the grand vizier, would avoid sending the necessary provisions. If one of the viziers became the field marshal then the grand vizier would consciously neglect the needs of the field marshal in order to ensure his failure. Thus Mehmed III had personally to lead the campaign in the style of his ancestor Sultan Süleyman the Magnificent.

Mehmed III, who had been troubled by the power struggles among his viziers, must have found Sinan Pasha's argument persuasive. When Mehmed III's participation in the campaign was also supported by his tutor Sadeddin Efendi, the sultan became a reluctant warrior. But when the Ottomans emerged victorious in the 1596 field battle (Haçova/Mezőkeresztes), the last example of which had been fought in 1526, Mehmed III earned the title "warrior."

Despite this victory, neither leading his armies in battle nor earning the title of warrior brought Mehmed III control over the business of rule in his remaining reign. Unlike his father Murad III, Mehmed seemed to fail in creating a favorite who would bring the business of rule to his immediate grasp. When he was not able to practice his sultanic authority his place was filled by the queen mother (*valide sultan*) Safiyye Sultan who acted almost as a regent. The empowerment of queen mothers was a direct result of the emergence of the court as the new center of power politics in the late 16th century. Like her predecessor Nur Banu, who had become a major power figure in Murad III's court until her death in 1583, Safiyye dominated court politics during the reign of Mehmed III through a network of allegiances that was composed of the power figures of both the bureaucracy and the palace.

However, Safiyye's dominance over the Ottoman court during the reign of her son Mehmed III also brought serious opposition from various groups. The JANISSARIES, the sultan's elite military corps, resisted the emergence of the court as the central political arena. In April 1600 Safiyye's Jewish *kira* or lady-in-waiting, Esperanza Malchi, was murdered by the standing cavalry (*sipahi*). Although the reason behind Esperanza Malchi's murder at first seemed to have been her mismanagement of a special tax farm, the *sipahis* accused her of interfering with the business of rule.

In January 1603 another *sipahi* uprising, which targeted the highest-ranking servants of the palace, revealed the networks of power and the complex framework that maintained Mehmed in his position as sultan. Inefficient handling of the revolts that plagued Anatolia after the 1596 Hungarian campaign contributed to fomenting this uprising. Outraged *sipahis* claimed that the *serdars* or field marshals sent to put down the CELALI REVOLTS in Anatolia were not chosen for their competence but were appointed through a bribery network. In order to present their complaints, the *sipahis* pressed hard to see the sultan in person. Seeing the sultan in person was a necessity, they argued, because the viziers and courtiers deliberately kept Mehmed III uninformed about the situation in Anatolia. The rebels demanded the execution of the two highest-ranking servants of the palace, Gazanfer Agha, the chief white eunuch, and Osman Agha, the chief black eunuch, as well as the former deputy vizier, Saatçi Hasan Pasha. During the meeting, Osman Agha and Gazanfer Agha—who had been one of the major power figures of the court since the reign of Selim II—were murdered. However, when Hasan Pasha showed the letters of Safiyye Sultan, which commanded him not to inform Mehmed III about anything, good or bad, he not only escaped execution but also justified the claims of the rebels.

Mehmed III—like his father Murad III and his grandfather Selim II—reigned in a political setting that was characterized by the rules of court politics. The emergence of the court as the central political arena required the presence of sultans in the court rather than in the battlefield. Therefore it was not his sedentary sultanate in the close quarters of the Topkapı Palace but rather his success in leading his armies in the Hungarian (Eger) campaign that should be considered as atypical for a sultan of the late 16th century. In terms of his success in the business of rule, Mehmed III seems to have been less successful than his father, mostly because of his inability to create court favorites who would be dependent on him.

Şefik Peksevgen

Further reading: Caroline Finkel, *Osman's Dream: The Story of the Ottoman Empire, 1300–1923* (London: John Murray, 2005), 152–195; Leslie Peirce, *The Imperial Harem: Women and Sovereignty in the Ottoman Empire* (New York: Oxford University Press, 1993).

Mehmed IV (Mehemmed IV; Mehmet IV; Avcı Mehmed) (b. 1642–d. 1693) (r. 1648–1687) *Ottoman sultan and caliph*   Son of Sultan IBRAHIM (r. 1640–48) and his concubine Hatice Turhan, Mehmed was born and raised in the imperial HAREM in ISTANBUL. In 1648, at the age of seven, he was placed on the throne following a coup that deposed his father, who was assassinated soon after. At the time, he was the youngest sultan ever to have succeeded to the throne, and his 39-year reign was surpassed in length only by that of Sultan SÜLEYMAN I (r. 1520–66). Mehmed's sobriquet Avcı or "Hunter" derives from his zeal for hunting, a pastime developed in childhood.

The first eight years of Mehmed's reign witnessed one of the severest and most turbulent periods of crisis in Ottoman history. He was represented during this time of his minority by two regents, the old Queen Mother (Valide Sultan), Kösem Mahpeyker Sultan, his grandmother, and the young Queen Mother, Turhan Sultan, his own mother, who was only in her early twenties. While acting as Mehmed's regents, both women ran their own rival factions, each supported by different segments in the military corps and the artisan guilds of the capital. In 1651, during the revolt of the JANISSARIES, who rose against the payment of their salaries in debased coins, Kösem Sultan was assassinated in the TOPKAPI PALACE while conspiring to dethrone Mehmed and replace him with his brother Süleyman. The death of Kösem resulted in the dissolution of her court faction and the elimination of the ringleaders of the Janissary uprising. With the death of Kösem Sultan, Turhan Sultan's partisans came to dominate court politics, led mainly by Süleyman Agha, the chief eunuch of the palace.

During this early period, the empire of Mehmed IV was characterized by incessant factionalism and rivalry in the capital, the direct involvement of the military corps in practical politics and power struggles, increasing and fluctuating prices, and extraordinary taxes levied to balance the budget deficit or to finance the ongoing war with VENICE over CRETE (1645–69). At the same time, the empire was troubled by plagues and poor harvests. Altogether, these factors created a highly unstable environment and led to major rebellions and tumults in Istanbul and the country. For instance, in these years, there were at least four major rebellions in the capital, and no fewer than 13 grand viziers were appointed.

In 1656 another bloody turmoil erupted, again instigated by the issue of debased coins. The major military rebellion lasted for weeks this time and forced Mehmed to sacrifice several of his favorites, including Süleyman Agha and other aghas and officials in the palace. Soon, however, with the appointment of Köprülü Mehmed Pasha as GRAND VIZIER, all unruly groups and alternative foci of power were subdued or eliminated by the iron-handed new grand vizier. Henceforth, until the end of Mehmed IV's reign, the KÖPRÜLÜ FAMILY and their clients occupied and dominated the key offices in the government and court. During this period the Köprülüs were able to establish a stable and comparatively reformist government that successfully ended the Cretan War in 1669 and conquered new lands in Europe, achievements due particularly to the management of Mehmed Pasha's son, Fazıl Ahmed Pasha.

With the Köprülü household guiding state affairs, Mehmed settled his court and household in EDIRNE, the former Ottoman capital, having acquired a distaste for Istanbul during his childhood and youth. By choosing the Edirne Palace as his chief residence, Mehmed initiated a pattern for his successors, and the city became the principal seat for the Ottoman dynasty and its court until 1703. Although Istanbul remained the official capital, Mehmed regarded the city as troubled and prone to rebellion, and he rarely returned to Istanbul, which was devastated by fire in 1660. Mehmed largely gave himself over to personal and domestic pleasures in Edirne. Among these were the grand imperial festivities of 1675. During this time Mehmed decreed a 15-day celebration for the circumcision of his sons, Mustafa (11) and Ahmed (2), and 18 days of festivities for the marriage of his daughter Hatice Sultan (17) to his favorite and second vizier, Musahib Mustafa Pasha. Mehmed IV also indulged in extended hunting trips, although he also used hunts for political purposes, preferring grounds in proximity to military campaign routes so that he could assess the progress of his armies and commanders. He also used the hunts as an opportunity to inspect the countryside, to hold audiences with his ministers, and to listen to the complaints of his subjects and personally dispense justice.

Mehmed IV was determined to portray himself as an active and able warrior-sultan. He personally led the Ottoman army during the campaign of 1672 against POLAND, taking with him his favorite concubine Rabia Gülnüş Emetullah and their son, Prince Mustafa. Mehmed used the occasion to teach his heir-apparent, rather than keeping him in seclusion in the palace, a practice that had been habitual since the early years of the century. Prince Mustafa would eventually follow his father's example, personally leading his own army soon after he became sultan in 1695.

Mehmed's reign ended with a coup similar to that of his father. In the years following the second unsuccessful siege of the Austrian capital Vienna in 1683 (*see* sieges of Vienna), the Ottomans were fighting against the armies of the Holy League, formed by the Austrian Habsburgs, Poland-Lithuania, Venice, and the papacy. Mehmed's armies were now required to operate on multiple fronts, and eventually the Ottomans suffered several defeats and experienced unprecedented territorial losses. By 1687 almost all Ottoman possessions in Hungary had been lost to the Habsburgs. The disgruntled Ottoman soldiers revolted and marched on the capital, demanding that Mehmed be replaced by his brother Süleyman. Mehmed was deposed by a joint decision of ministers and religious dignitaries in Istanbul, a decision he apparently accepted without protest. Retiring to Edirne, Mehmed died there in 1693 and was buried at the imperial tomb complex of his mother's mosque (Yeni Djami) in Istanbul.

Günhan Börekçi

Further reading: Caroline Finkel, *Osman's Dream* (London: John Murray, 2005), 253–328; M.T. Gökbilgin and R.C. Repp, "Köprülü," in *Encyclopedia of Islam*, 2nd ed., vol. 5, edited by C. E. Bosworth, E. van Donzel, B. Lewis, and Ch. Pellat (Leiden: Brill, 1960–), 256–263; Cemal Kafadar, "The City that Ralamb Visited: The Political and Cultural Climate of Istanbul in the 1650s," in *The Sultan's Procession: The Swedish Embassy to Sultan Mehmed IV in 1657–1658 and the Ralamb Paintings*, edited by Karin Adahl (Istanbul: Publication of Swedish Research Institute in Istanbul, 2006), 58–73; Metin Kunt, "Naima, Köprülü and the Grand Vezirate," *Boğaziçi Üniversitesi Dergisi* 1 (1973), 57–62.

Mehmed V (Reşad) (b. 1844–d. 1918) (r. 1909–1918) *Ottoman sultan and caliph* Mehmed V was the son of Sultan Abdülmecid I (1839–61) and Gülcemal Kadın Efendi. He was born on November 2, 1844, in Istanbul. He acceded the throne at the age of 65, on April 27, 1909, when Abdülhamid II (r. 1876–1909) was deposed by the Committee of Union and Progress (CUP) following the revolt of March 31, 1909. During his sultanate Mehmed acted within the limits of a constitutional monarch. The principal members of CUP, Talat Pasha and Enver Pasha, administered the empire.

The early months of his rule witnessed Armenian revolts in eastern Anatolia and in Cilicia (southern Anatolia). This was followed by a major Albanian insurrection in 1910. At the request of the CUP, Mehmed V made a trip to Salonika, Skopje, and to the Kosovo region in order to calm the Albanians.

In 1911 the Italians attacked the last directly governed North African province of Tripolitana (in present-day Libya). While the war in Libya continued, the Balkan neighbors (Bulgaria, Serbia, Montenegro, and Greece) formed an alliance and attacked the Ottoman Empire (*see* Balkan wars). As a result the Ottomans lost both Libya and nearly all of the Balkan provinces. Under these conditions, the CUP organized a coup d'état and terminated the multiparty regime (January 1913).

Under the military dictatorship of the CUP, Mehmed V acted as a symbolic head of state. When the Ottomans joined World War I on the side of the Central Powers (Germany, Austria-Hungary, and Bulgaria) in 1914, the CUP urged the sultan to use his authority as the caliph of world Muslims to declare jihad, or holy war, against the Allied Powers (France, Russia, Great Britain, and Italy).

Sultan Mehmed V ruled the Ottoman Empire for nine years and two months and died on July 3, 1918, shortly before World War I ended. Known as Sultan Reşad ("pursuer of the right path") among his people, Mehmed lived a comfortable life during the reign of his uncle, Sultan Abdülaziz (r. 1861–1876), but was imprisoned when his brother, Abdülhamid II, became sultan. He spent most of his time reading, was immersed in Islamic culture, was well versed in both Arabic and Persian, was a talented poet and calligrapher, and a devoted member of the Mevlevi Order of dervishes.

Selcuk Akşin Somel

Mehmed VI (Mehmed Vahdettin; Mehmed Vahideddin) (b. 1861–d. 1926) (r. 1918–1922) *last Ottoman sultan* Mehmed VI, son of Sultan Abdülmecid I (1839–61), acceded to the throne on July 3, 1918 upon the death of his brother, Sultan Mehmed V (r. 1909–1918), known as Reşad. At that time the Committee of Union and Progress (CUP) still controlled the state. When the Ottomans surrendered at the end of World War I on October 30, 1918, the leaders of the CUP fled the empire, leaving Mehmed VI with the opportunity to assume personal control over the government and reinforce his authority by appointing grand viziers loyal to him. Following the Ottoman Empire's loss to the Allied Powers, the sultan considered it in his best political interests to cooperate with them, especially with the British. As an enemy of the CUP, Mehmed punished former members of this party and ordered the dissolution of Parliament on November 23, 1918. When the Greeks occupied Izmir on May 15, 1919, Mehmed convened a consultative assembly (*saltanat şurası*) on May 26, 1919. Mehmed sent a young Ottoman officer, Mustafa Kemal Pasha (*see* Mustafa Kemal Atatürk) to pacify the Black Sea region. However, Mustafa Kemal instead worked to organize a national resistance in Anatolia against the

Allied Powers. The sultan regarded this movement as a continuation of CUP political activities and thus did everything to hamper the national resistance that ultimately gave rise to the modern Turkish republic. Since Mehmed VI considered it unrealistic to oppose the Allied Powers, he approved the TREATY OF SÈVRES (August 10, 1920), which stipulated the partitioning of Anatolia.

When the Anatolian resistance movement proved successful, Mehmed VI and his government tried to come to terms with the movement's leaders, based in Ankara. However, the empire's last sultan had already lost political legitimacy, and when the Allied Powers invited representatives from both Ankara (nationalist republicans led by Mustafa Kemal) and Istanbul (imperial government under Mehmed) to a major peace conference in LAUSANNE, the Turkish National Assembly of Ankara publicly declared the end of the imperial reign and officially dissolved the sultanate (November 1, 1922), thus implying that the republican government was the only legitimate Turkish political authority. This bold move paid off, as Mehmed VI subsequently fled the country aboard a British warship to MALTA. His later attempts to reinstate himself as caliph in the HEJAZ proved unsuccessful. He died on May 16, 1926, in San Remo, Italy. As the last Ottoman sultan, Mehmed VI has been a controversial figure. Turkish national historiography has regarded him as a traitor to the national cause.

Selcuk Akşin Somel

Mehmed Ali (*Ar. Muhammad Ali*) (d. 1849) (r. 1805–1849) *ruler of Egypt*   Mehmed Ali was an adventurer who rose to be the ruler of EGYPT and a formidable challenger to the Ottoman royal house's monopoly over the right to rule the Ottoman Empire. He was born in Kavala in northern GREECE; most historians assume that he was an Albanian because the unit he commanded when sent to Egypt was made up of Albanian irregular troops. But he may have been a Muslim of Greek or Slavic origin, and European visitors to his court reported that he spoke fluent Greek.

When the French expeditionary force that was initially commanded by NAPOLEON BONAPARTE and that had occupied Egypt in 1798 withdrew from Egypt in 1801, Ottoman Sultan SELIM III (r. 1789–1807) sent an Albanian unit to restore his sovereignty over the country. Mehmed Ali assumed command of the unit in 1803; in 1804 he succeeded in temporarily driving the remaining Egyptian MAMLUK elite out of CAIRO. By May 1805, however, the ULEMA of Cairo was growing increasingly fearful of the anarchy in the city and complained to the chief judge that the Ottoman governor, Hürşit Pasha, was not doing enough to control his troops. When he failed to act, the ulema appointed Mehmed Ali viceroy of Egypt. The government in Istanbul later confirmed that appointment. The Ottoman government was further distracted from affairs in Egypt by the coup that deposed Sultan Selim III (r. 1789–1807) in 1807. In the absence of direct Ottoman involvement in Egyptian politics, Mehmed Ali secured his position by eliminating his only possible local rivals, the Mamluks. This he accomplished in 1811 when he invited the Mamluks to a feast and then had them executed. The few who escaped the treachery fled to Upper Egypt. Once there, they no longer offered a threat to Mehmed Ali's ambitions.

Mehmed Ali was able to strengthen his position in Cairo by dispatching his son Tosun, at Istanbul's request, to Arabia in 1811 to free the Holy Cities from their Muwahhidun occupiers, better known as WAHHABIS. Tosun took MECCA in 1812 and MEDINA in the following year. Following the campaign in Arabia, Mehmed Ali enlarged his holdings by sending troops into what is today northern Sudan. His ambitions required a bigger and better army, so to meet the manpower needs, he authorized slave raids in Sudan to acquire mature males who might be molded into a modern army. Thousands of slaves were brought to Egypt, but most died from diseases and other causes.

Faced with the loss of thousands of men and the financial investment that had gone into procuring them, Mehmed Ali abandoned the experiment. He instituted conscription of peasants in its place. This was an unheard-of innovation in Islamic history and many of the peasants responded by either flight or armed rebellion. But Mehmed Ali persevered and by 1824 his army was impressive enough that Sultan MAHMUD II (r. 1808–39) requested his help against the insurgency in Greece. The success of an army commanded by Mehmed Ali's son, IBRAHIM PASHA, alarmed European powers, who sided overwhelmingly with the Greek rebels and attacked the imperial troops. The British and French fleets sank a combined Ottoman-Egyptian fleet at Navarino in 1827 and Ibrahim was forced to withdraw his troops from Greece.

In order to build and maintain his army, Mehmed Ali took control of much of the agricultural lands of Egypt to grow products such as sugar, indigo, and cotton that could either be used to make uniforms or that could be exported to Europe in exchange for weapons. He also sought to impose monopolies in many areas of production in order to start an Egyptian industrial base to supply his army with the weapons they otherwise had to import. For making all these radical changes, some historians have called Mehmed Ali the "Father of Modern Egypt," but it would seem that ruling Egypt was not his only ambition. In 1827 Mehmed Ali asked the sultan to grant him the governorship of SYRIA. When the sultan refused, Mehmed Ali ordered the Egyptian army into Syria in October 1831, saying that the Ottomans had given asylum to Egyptian peasants who had fled into the empire to avoid conscription.

Ibrahim Pasha, the commander of the Egyptian forces, enjoyed a number of quick successes. By December of 1832 he had reached the central Anatolian city of Konya, where he defeated an army led by the grand vizier. At that point, nothing stood in his way for a victorious march on the capital. Mehmed Ali claimed that he, as sultan, would restore the empire to its true glory; the Western powers were stunned. They applied pressure in both Istanbul and Cairo; the result was the Convention of Kütahya in May 1833 that recognized Ibrahim Pasha as governor of Syria and the southern Anatolian province of Adana. Ibrahim then implemented in Syria many of the same centralizing reforms that his father had imposed on Egypt. They proved to be as unpopular among the region's Muslim population as they were in Egypt and revolts against his rule began in 1834.

Encouraged by reports of revolts, the Ottomans attempted to retake Syria in 1839 but again received a resounding defeat at the hands of Ibrahim Pasha at the Battle of Nezip. But by 1840, much of Syria had risen in rebellion against Egyptian occupation, and British pressure led Ibrahim Pasha to withdraw. In return for the withdrawal, the sultan recognized Mehmed Ali as governor of Egypt for life and promised that, upon his death, the post would go to his sons. After the Syrian campaign, Mehmed Ali embarked on no further foreign adventures although his regime introduced programs for modernization, especially in education. By the end of his reign, Mehmed Ali had become incapacitated by senility, and Ibrahim governed in his place. Mehmed Ali died on August 2, 1849. Egypt continued to be ruled by his direct descendants until the revolution of 1952.

Bruce Masters

Further reading: Afaf Lutfi al-Sayyid Marsot, *Egypt in the Reign of Muhammad Ali* (Cambridge: Cambridge University Press, 1984).

Mehmed Pasha Köprülü *See* KÖPRÜLÜ FAMILY.

Mehmed Pasha Sokollu *See* SOKOLLU FAMILY.

mehter *See* MUSIC.

Melkite Catholics Melkite Catholics, or Greek Catholics as they are sometimes known, were the Orthodox Christians of Syria who chose to accept the spiritual authority of the Roman Catholic pope in the 18th century. The term *Melkite* derived from the common Semitic word for king (Syriac *melk*, Arabic *malik*). It was originally applied to Middle Eastern Christians who stayed loyal to the official teaching of the church of the BYZANTINE EMPIRE after the Council of Chalcedon in 451, when many of the region's Christians were accused of following a doctrine identified as heresy. As the Byzantine emperors—called simply "kings" in Arabic—promoted this version of Christianity, the Arab Muslim conquerors of SYRIA in the seventh century referred to those who followed the Byzantine rite as the "king's men." Although the name seems to have gone out of general use by the Ottoman period, when Roman Catholic MISSIONARIES in SYRIA began to court Orthodox Christian clergy with the possibility of their entering into communion with the pope in Rome, the name was revived as a convenient way to distinguish the Orthodox Christians of Syria from those of the rest of the Ottoman Empire.

Over the course of the 17th century, many of the men who held high ecclesiastical office in Syria (either as patriarch of Antioch, housed in DAMASCUS, or as metropolitans (bishops) in ALEPPO or in the Lebanese coastal towns of Sidon and TRIPOLI) hosted the missionaries and allowed them to open schools for Orthodox Christian boys. Promising young men from the community were sent to Rome where they attended the MARONITE College and were ordained as Catholic priests. In reaction, the Orthodox ecumenical patriarch in ISTANBUL sought to influence the process by which the patriarch of Antioch was chosen. Traditionally, a council of clergy and laity in Damascus had chosen the men who would hold that office, but in 1672 the ecumenical patriarch intervened to replace the candidate chosen by the council with one perceived as being more loyal to orthodoxy.

The political struggle between the Catholic and Orthodox factions led to a fracture in 1725 and the emergence of two claimants to the position of patriarch of Antioch, one supported by the ecumenical patriarch and the sultan and the other by the Catholic faction and eventually the Roman Catholic Church. From that point onward, the Catholic faction was called either the Melkite Catholic Church or the Greek Catholic Church, a name that is sometimes confusing to outsiders, as the members of the Church were typically Arab Christians and not ethnic Greeks. Throughout the 18th century, the Melkite Catholic Church functioned as an underground church in the empire in that it received no official recognition from the sultan and the Orthodox higher clergy could bring charges against anyone suspected of Catholic sentiments. From this time in 1725 until the GREEK WAR OF INDEPENDENCE almost a century later, the Ottoman Empire engaged in the systematic repression of Melkite Catholics in Damascus, while in Aleppo and the Lebanese port cities, Catholic merchants and French consular officials often had to bribe Ottoman authorities to ignore what were officially illegal religious services.

With the start of the Greek War for Independence in 1821, the Orthodox clergy in Istanbul came to be viewed as disloyal to the Ottoman sultan. Seizing the opportunity, the Melkite Catholics emphasized their own loyalty to the sultan and their separation from the ethnic Greek clerics in the capital. In these circumstances, the Melkite Catholics of Aleppo received imperial permission to practice their rites publicly without interference. Similar rights were extended to Melkite Catholics elsewhere in Syria, but the community did not receive recognition as an independent MILLET, or officially represented religious unit, until 1848.

On many levels, the creation of the Melkite Catholic Church represented no major break with the past other than switching allegiance from patriarch to pope. The interior of the Melkite Catholic Churches continued to resemble those of other Eastern Orthodox with icons instead of statues and the clergy wore vestments similar to those of their Orthodox counterparts. Melkite Catholic seminarians were allowed to marry before they took their final vows, although married priests, like those in the Orthodox Church, could not be elevated to higher ranks within the church.

The main difference between the Orthodox and Catholic factions in the see, or jurisdiction, of the patriarch of Antioch lay in the use of Arabic as the language of the Melkite Catholic Church. Although some prayers remained in Greek, the liturgy of the Church shifted increasingly to Arabic. Emphasizing the role of Arabic in the Melkite Catholic Church, Athanasios Dabbas, the metropolitan (bishop) of Aleppo, established the first printing press using the Arabic script in the Ottoman Empire in 1706. Additionally, Melkite artists produced a dazzling array of religious icons using Syrian themes and inscribed in Arabic rather than the traditional Greek. Citing those developments, some historians have sought to portray the emergence of the Melkite Catholic Church in Syria as an early triumph of Arab nationalism. But the driving force behind the discontent felt in the 18th century by formerly Orthodox Christians with regard to church hierarchy iseems to been driven by local concerns rather than national ones, and it was not until the late 19th century that spokesmen would refer to the Melkite Catholic Church as an Arab church.

Bruce Masters

Further reading: Robert Haddad, *Syrian Christians in Muslim Society: An Interpretation* (Princeton, N.J.: Princeton University Press, 1970); Bruce Masters, *Christians and Jews in the Ottoman Arab World* (Cambridge: Cambridge University Press, 2001).

menzil/menzilhane The terms *menzil* or *menzilhame* refer to a stage or halting place on the road, particularly, from the 15th to the early 19th century, a post and relay station of the Ottoman state courier system. The Ottomans, like most of the post-Mongol land empires of Eurasia, made use of a state post and courier system for communicating orders from the imperial center to provincial authorities and for the transmission of news from the provinces and frontiers of the empire. As an Ottoman institution, this courier system, the *ulaklık* (from Turkish *ulak*, *ulağ*, a term used for the state courier and for the institution itself) derives in its essentials from the *jam* (Persian *yam*), the empire-wide courier system of the Mongols in the 13th to 14th century, and not from comparable institutions in earlier Islamic polities, such as the Abbasid *barid*.

It is not certain exactly when the Ottoman *menzilhane* system emerged as a fully developed state institution. It is clear that in the early period of the state's history, in 1453 certainly and possibly up through the end of the 15th century, the *ulaklık* was an ad hoc institution. The couriers charged with the transmission of orders from the sultan or other high officials were empowered by their possession of a sultanic or vizirial courier order (known as *ulak hükmi*, "courier order," or *yol emri*, "road order") to requisition at will horses from travelers on the road. This unregulated courier system was, naturally, subject to considerable abuse, and by the time of SÜLEYMAN I (r. 1520–66) or even earlier, its reform had become a matter of some urgency. Lutfi Pasha, grand vizier in the middle years of Süleyman's reign, has traditionally—but on the basis of his own testimony—been credited with overseeing the construction of post and relay stations (*menzil*, *menzilhane*) along the major routes (*ulu yollar*) of the empire. In both Anatolia and Rumelia (the Asian and European parts of the empire, respectively), there were three principal routes, known as the route of the left (*sol kol*), the route of the middle (*orta kol*), and the route of the right (*sağ kol*), radiating (in Rumelia) from ISTANBUL or EDIRNE, or from Üsküdar (in Anatolia). The Rumelian *sağ kol* ran nominally from Istanbul (but administratively from Tekfur Tağı [Rodosto, Tekirdağ]) in Thrace, three stages (130 km) from the imperial capital, from whence it extended in 23 stages (850 km; 185 hours' riding time) to the *menzilhane* at Gördüs (Corinth), located at the entrance to the Morea (Greek Peloponnese). The Rumelian *orta* and *sağ kols* extended respectively to BELGRADE and from thence to BUDA and to Bender (Bendery, UKRAINE), then across the southern Ukrainian steppe to Taman on the Sea of Azov. These routes were much longer, as were the three routes across Anatolia leading respectively to ALEPPO, DAMASCUS, and CAIRO. Much information on the issuing of courier orders and the administration of the system from the mid-16th century onward is to be found in the *Mühimme Defterleri* (Registers of important affairs).

By the later 16th century and into the 18th century the Ottoman *ulaklık*, benefited substantially from the reforms of Grand Vizier Lutfi Pasha and those made by the Köprülü family. Each of the *menzilhanes*, or post stations, were established at distances ranging from 3 to 10 or more riding-miles (*yol saatı*) apart along the *ulu yollar*, or major routes. Branch lines diverged at intervals to serve administrative centers that lay at some distance from the major routes and to connect with other significant routes, for instance, the western end of the Rumelian *sol kol* with the middle Morava valley and Belgrade. Each *menzilhane* possessed an allocation of post-horses (*menzil bargiri*) and was in the charge of a postmaster (*menzilci*); under him was a staff of stable orderlies, smiths, and *sürücüs*, boys responsible for bringing back to the *menzilhane* the post-horses that the couriers had commandeered. The provision of horses was frequently made the responsibility of the Ottoman taxpaying subjects or *reaya* of particular villages in the vicinity of the *menzilhane*, the inhabitants of which were given tax exemptions in return for their services.

Supervision of the *menzilhanes* in a particular *kaza* or judicial district was the responsibility of the local KADI, who entered into his registers (*sicill*) details of the traffic passing through the *menzilhanes* under his jurisdiction. From the 1690s into the 18th century *kadıs* were responsible for drawing up separate detailed registers (*menzil defteri*) that gave a more or less full record of the operation of local *menzilhanes*. These registers were usually drawn up twice a year, ending on *Ruz-i Hızır* (April 23) and *Ruz-ı Kasım* (October 23), that is, on dates that mark the spring equinox (and the opening of the campaigning season for the Ottoman army and navy) and the traditional beginning of winter (and the end of the campaigning season), used for accounting purposes since the days of the Persian Empire. Existing in large numbers in the Turkish archives, these registers form a valuable source for the study of the operation of the system as it existed from the late 17th to the early 19th century.

A further development of the system also took place in the late 17th century. As a result of the pressure placed on the system, particularly in Rumelia, by the internecine wars of the late 17th century, steps were taken to abolish the existing system and to replace it with a fee-based (*ücret ile*) one in which the requisitioning of post-horses was placed on a franchised basis, with a variable fee charged depending on the length of the next stage and the number of horses taken. This reformed system appears to have survived into the 19th-century TANZIMAT reform era. At this point the Ottomans abandoned the term *beç ulağı*" (Vienna post courier) and introduced a new term with the same meaning, *Viyana kuriri*. At the same time, the introduction of a European-style public postal system and a TELEGRAPH system provided a modernized mode of communication for the resurgent state absolutism that characterized the reign of ABDÜLHAMID II (1876–1909)

Colin Heywood

Further reading: Colin Heywood, "The Ottoman Menzilhane and Ulak System in Rumeli in the Eighteenth Century" in *Türkiye'nin Sosyal ve Ekonomik Tarihi, 1071–1920*, edited by Osman Okyar and Halil İnalcık (Ankara: Meteksan, 1980), 179–186 (reprinted in Colin Heywood, *Writing Ottoman History: Documents and Interpretations* (Aldershot, UK: Variorum, 2002), item X); Colin Heywood, "The Via Egnatia in the Ottoman Period: The *Menzilhanes* of the *Sol Kol* in the Late 17th/Early 18th Century," in *The Via Egnatia under Ottoman Rule, 1380–1699*, edited by Elizabeth Zachariadou (Rethymnon: Crete University Press, 1996), 129–144 (reprinted in *Writing Ottoman History: Documents and Interpretations* (Aldershot, UK: Variorum, 2002), item XI); Colin Heywood, "Two Firmans of Mustafa II on the Reorganisation of the Ottoman Courier System (1108/1696) (Documents from the Thessaloniki Cadi *Sicills*)," *Acta Orientalia Hungarica*, liv/4 (Dec. 2001), 485–496; Colin Heywood, "Two Firmans of Mustafa II on the Reorganisation of the Ottoman Courier System (1108/1696) (Documents from the Thessaloniki Cadi *Sicills*), Appendix: Plates" (Wendover, UK: Dragomanate Press, 2002, [1]; 3 folding plates); Colin Heywood, "Ulak," in *Encyclopaedia of Islam*, 2nd. ed., vol. 10 (Leiden: Brill, 1960–), 800a–800b (with extensive further bibliography).

merchant communities Before the 19th century, long-distance trade in the Ottoman Empire was controlled by networks of MERCHANTS who were linked by ties of family and ethnicity. These proved remarkably resilient to changes in trade patterns, political upheavals, and foreign competition. Before the 17th century, Italian merchant communities from Genoa and VENICE had dominated the trade between the Ottoman Empire and Europe. These shared informal links similar to those of local Ottoman merchants in that they were not regulated or controlled by trading companies but functioned as individual merchant houses based on extended families. But by the end of the 16th century, the Italians were largely replaced by western European merchants who were agents for joint stock companies with headquarters in Marseille, Amsterdam, or London. The networks that handled trade to and from the port cities of the Mediterranean by CARAVAN continued to be dominated by local merchant communities well into the 19th century.

The most successful of these merchant communities were the Armenians of New Julfa in IRAN. Shah Ismail, ruler of Iran from 1502 to 1524, destroyed the original town of Julfa, which was located on the Araxes River, and moved its Armenian inhabitants to a suburb outside his capital of Isfahan. He then gave the Armenian merchants a monopoly over the export of Iran's silk to the West. These merchants made connections with fellow Armenians already scattered across the Ottoman Empire. By the end of the 16th century there was a network of Armenian traders that reached west as far as Amsterdam and east to the port cities of India. In the Ottoman Empire, the main hubs of commercial activity for these resident Armenian merchants were ALEPPO, IZMIR, and ISTANBUL.

With the decline of Iran's silk production in the 18th century, the network established by the Julfa Armenians collapsed. Local Ottoman Armenians established smaller networks of their own that dominated commerce in Anatolia and, to a lesser extent, BULGARIA. Syrian MELKITE CATHOLICS and Iraqi JEWS established similar trading networks in the 18th and 19th centuries, following the pattern established two centuries earlier by the Julfa Armenians. The Syrian Catholics controlled much of the trade of EGYPT while the Iraqi Jews moved to the colonial cities of British India and Southeast Asia, and eventually to Hong Kong and Shanghai.

Bruce Masters

Further reading: Philip Curtin, *Cross-Cultural Trade in World History* (Cambridge: Cambridge University Press, 1984).

merchants Although the Ottoman state itself played a major role in TRADE using its power of monopoly, the empire also embraced an extraordinarily diverse and idiosyncratic set of MERCHANT COMMUNITIES that included merchant groups and individuals such as wholesalers, retailers, urban businessmen, and rural area merchants who attended weekly bazaars and seasonal fairs. The organized merchant class played a significant role in Ottoman trade.

The Ottoman merchant class can be divided into three major merchant groups. The first group is foreign merchants, known as *mustemen* merchants; the second group is non-Muslim Ottoman citizens, called European merchants; and the final group is Muslim Ottoman citizens or *hayriye* merchants. European merchants and *hayriye* merchants were not institutionalized until the end of the 18th century.

Until the 19th century, foreign merchants dominated the Ottoman international trade, while Muslim and non-Muslim Ottoman merchants controlled the domestic trade. The predominance of Mustemen merchants in international trade was the result of trade privileges and conveniences granted them by CAPITULATIONS previously imposed on the Ottoman Empire. After the turn of the 19th century, both Muslim and non-Muslim Ottoman merchants became increasingly involved in foreign trade, whereas *mustemen* merchants started to be interested in Ottoman domestic trade.

Two terms were used for foreign merchants in Ottoman lands, *mustemen* and *harbi*. Even though it is unclear when exactly the term "*mustemen* merchant" was first used, state records show that it was sometime around 1740. With the exception of the limited trading done by European merchants, *mustemen* merchants led Ottoman foreign trade by the time of SELIM III (r. 1789–1807). The rights and responsibilities of *mustemen* merchants were determined by AHDNAME (privileged agreement). According to provisions of the *ahdname*, *mustemen* merchants and their commodities were protected by the empire while they sailed across Ottoman-controlled seas and traveled across Ottoman lands. They were exempt from all regular taxes, except customs taxes. *Mustemen* merchants could go to their countries' consulates for disputes among themselves. However, disputes between Ottoman citizens and foreign merchants were usually handled by local courts, although cases whose disputed amount exceeded 4,000 akçe were processed by the courts in ISTANBUL. Merchants who died had their assets and commodities protected and given to legal inheritors by the Ottoman state.

Customs rates for *mustemen* merchants were very close to those of Muslim merchants during the 18th century and sometimes even lower. By the 18th century, customs rates were 3 percent for Muslim merchants, 4 percent for non-Muslim merchants, and 5 percent for *mustemen* merchants. In the following years, however, customs duties for *mustemen* merchants were lowered to 3 percent, and additional exemptions were established. For instance, *mustemen* merchants did not have to pay transit tax (*bac*) and internal tax in Ottoman cities and towns.

Although foreign merchant classes had more trading advantages than other merchant groups, they sometimes violated Ottoman customs regulations. They also became enormously active in trading commodities that they themselves produced and marketed.

In spite of their comparatively weak position in foreign trade, Ottomans were still dominant in the domestic trade of the empire. Moreover, non-Muslim citizens played a role at the intersection between Muslim and foreign merchants. Gradually, Greek, Jewish, and Armenian merchants gained new privileges to trade with European countries. Later, the non-Muslim Ottoman merchants were recognized as European merchants.

Berat (a title of privilege) and *tercuman* (interpretership) were two critical elements in the first appearance of European merchants. The term *berat* described graduation or assignment orders given by the sultan to individuals appointed to different civil and public positions in the Ottoman Empire. At the beginning of the 18th century merchants under foreign protection participating in external and internal trade, such as *mustemen* merchants, were called *beratl* merchants (merchants with the title of privilege). Many argue that the term *beratl* merchants was also first used to also describe European merchants around the beginning of the 18th century.

A non-Muslim Ottoman citizen who wanted to be a European merchant had to apply in writing to the Divan-ı Hümayun (Imperial Council) to request a *berat*. He also had to designate two Istanbul merchants as his substitutes and pay a fee to the Ottoman state treasury. European merchants might also hire their own servants along with their two merchant substitutes. These servants were usually hired from big trading cities, such as Istanbul and Izmir, to organize and maintain European merchants' trade activities.

Muslim merchants began to raise objections to the trade privileges granted to European merchants under Selim III. Similar complaints charging unfair competition were also made to Mahmud II (r. 1808–39). Muslim merchants sought privileges and conveniences like those that European merchants enjoyed, including travel, customs, judicial, and tax-related benefits. In the following years the Bab-ı Âli (Sublime Porte) provided similar privileges to Muslim Ottoman merchants, expecting that the merchants would gain the same considerable profits previously reserved for European merchants. This positive development for Muslim merchants led to a newly named merchant class, the *hayriye* merchant.

Hayriye merchants had to follow similar procedures as European merchants to receive their *berat*. The only difference between the two was that *hayriye* merchants had to make smaller advance payments than European merchants. Like *mustemen* merchants, *hayriye* merchants were also able to trade commodities from Islamic countries domestically or internationally. To make sea trading more convenient for *hayriye* merchants, maritime trading was regulated by the Naval Arsenal (Tersane-i Amire). If a *hayriye* merchant who was engaged in maritime trade passed away, his eldest son would automatically be eligible to receive a new *berat* to continue his father's business.

Because of the *hayriye* merchants' affiliation with Muslim wholesalers and retailers in the Ottoman markets, their religious and ethical background received considerable attention. They and their employees were expected to be honest, religious, and righteous. Hayriye merchants had to obtain a letter of goodwill confirming their good reputation from local officials in the place where they resided and attach a power of attorney for two people to their *berat* applications.

Coşkun Çakır

See also dragoman; janissaries.

Further reading: Halil İnalcık and Donald Quataert, eds., *An Economic and Social History of the Ottoman Empire, 1300–1914,* (Cambridge: Cambridge University Press, 1994); Halil İnalcık, "Imtiyazat", *Encyclopaedia of Islam,* 2nd ed., vol. 3 (Leiden: Brill, 1960–), 1179–89; Bruce McGowan, *Economic Life in the Ottoman Empire: Taxation, Trade and the Struggle for Land, 1600–1800,* (Cambridge: Cambridge University Press, 1981); Bruce Masters, *The Origins of Western Economic Dominance in the Middle East, Mercantilism and the Islamic Economy in Aleppo, 1600–1750,* (Cambridge: Cambridge University Press, 1988).

Mevlevi Order (Mevlevi Order of dervishes)   The Mevlevi Order of dervishes claimed to have originated with the mystical Persian poet Jalal al-Din Rumi, who died in the city of Konya in 1273. His followers called him Mevlana, or "our teacher," and the order takes its name from that title of respect. Rumi left as part of his legacy a compendium of poems written in Persian known as the *Masnavi*. For many adherents of Sufism, the *Masnavi* is considered the most sacred Islamic text after the Quran. Besides his poetry, which has been translated into a number of languages, Rumi is best remembered for introducing music and dance into Sufi practice as he said that, through dancing, one could reach the union with God that Sufis sought. Rumi taught his disciples that, once that union was achieved, only poetry and music could convey the experience because simple language could not express the emotion that such a union could produce. His followers ritualized the dance with an elaborate choreography and were called "whirling dervishes" by Western visitors to the Ottoman Empire. The word *dervish* is derived from the Persian word *darvish* or "mystic."

Rumi's son, Bahauddin Walad, reputedly started the order and successive *pirs*, as the heads of the order were called, built a lodge (*tekke*) of dervish cells around the tomb of Rumi in Konya. The members of the order cultivated close relationships with men in political power and by the 15th century, the Mevlevi Order had become closely associated with the Ottoman ruling elite. The *pirs* of the order wielded a great deal of power due to the spiritual influence and wealth they derived from endowments made in the Mevlana's name. For these reasons the Ottoman sultans, while embracing the order spiritually, often came into conflict with individual *pirs* and removed them from their positions. But the leaders of the Mevlevi Order generally chose to avoid confrontation with the state and were rewarded by endowments to the order made by the royal family.

Since members of the order often taught music and calligraphy, the Mevlevi lodges became cultural centers in the towns where they could be found. Also, as the *Masnavi* was written in Persian and the order valued

One of the most important dervish orders in the Ottoman Empire, the Mevlevi dervishes are shown here in 1910 shortly before all dervish orders were banned in the early years of the Turkish Republic. *(Postcard, personal collection of Gábor Ágoston)*

collections of the works of other Persian mystical poets, the Mevlevi lodges were among the few places where aspiring Ottoman intellectuals could study Persian language and literature. The dervishes also translated many of the texts they valued into Ottoman Turkish, making them available to a wider audience. The Mevlevis were major contributors to what would become classical Ottoman poetry (*see* CLASSICAL OTTOMAN LITERATURE), music, and the art of book illustration, as most of the empire's artists were members of the order and learned their skills in the Mevlevi lodges.

Bruce Masters

Midhat Pasha (Ahmet Şefik Midhat Pasha, Ahmed Şefik Midhat Pasha) (b. 1822–d. 1884) *Ottoman reformer, governor, and prime minister* Ahmed Şefik Midhat Pasha, commonly known as Midhat Pasha, was one of the leading activists in the TANZIMAT reform period (1839–76) of the Ottoman Empire. He was born in ISTANBUL into a well-established family of Muslim scholars. He was given a traditional education, but he also served as an apprentice in the government bureaucracy. He took his work seriously and often clashed with those above him who he thought were derelict in their

duties. Unlike his more successful contemporaries, he did not establish patronage relationships (*intisab*) with more powerful men. He did, however, do his job exceedingly well and went on many fact-finding missions to the empire's provinces where he gained an insight into the realities of provincial life that was rare in the elite circles of power in Istanbul. Using that knowledge, Midhat helped to draft the new provincial law code of 1864 and was assigned to the post of governor to the newly formed DANUBE PROVINCE, in what is now BULGARIA. It was meant to be a model province and Midhat, by all accounts, did an admirable job. He was recalled to Istanbul in 1868, but soon clashed with the powerful Grand Vizier Ali Pasha, which led to his appointment as governor of the province of BAGHDAD in 1869.

Midhat's appointment to Baghdad, which was about as remote a posting as was possible, was clearly intended as an exile to punish his brashness. Undeterred, he threw himself enthusiastically into various projects that he hoped would push the province into modernity, including the destruction of Baghdad's city walls. During his brief tenure as governor, Midhat Pasha built a tramway, a hospital, schools, an orphanage, and factories to supply the local military garrison. In addition, Midhat sought to extend Ottoman sovereignty into eastern Arabia by re-establishing the Ottoman province of al-Ahsa along the Persian Gulf, in present-day Saudi Arabia. His most ambitious plan involved land reform, but here his lack of practical knowledge of Iraqi politics hurt his ambitions for reform. The peasants, fearing that registration of land in their names might lead to their sons' conscription, preferred that their land instead be registered in the names of their sheikhs. The land then passed legally into the hands of the tribal sheikhs, further impoverishing the peasantry Midhat had hoped to help. Despite that setback, the locals remembered him after he left IRAQ in 1872 as one of the few good governors the city had known.

Midhat returned to Istanbul with some success in Iraq to his credit, and Sultan ABDÜLAZIZ (r. 1861–76) appointed him to the position of grand vizier in 1873. But again, he found it difficult to work with his superior and was dismissed after two months. For the next three years, Midhat served on the Council of Ministers but his most important task was the drafting and implementation of a constitution. Sultan ABDÜLHAMID II (r. 1876–1909) promulgated the Ottoman CONSTITUTION in 1876 and Midhat was again appointed grand vizier in December 1876. However, Midhat ran afoul of Abdülhamid, who had not wanted the constitution in the first place. Dismissed from his post in February 1877 and sent into exile in Europe, Midhat was again appointed to an Ottoman governorship, this time through the intervention of the British. In 1878 he began a two-year term as governor of the newly reorganized and renamed province of SYRIA. As was the case in his tenure as governor of Baghdad, Midhat threw himself into the reform of the province. He founded a public library in DAMASCUS and greatly expanded the number of government schools in the province. Although Midhat faced DRUZE resistance to his centralizing policies, he was again genuinely popular, as he had been in Baghdad. He resigned his post in 1880 as he felt Istanbul was not giving him the support he needed to govern effectively. Midhat then served briefly as governor of Izmir but he was recalled in 1881 to Istanbul where he was tried and convicted for the murder of Sultan Abdülaziz, a charge that most historians believe was trumped up. British pressure prevented the sultan from imposing the death sentence upon him so he was imprisoned in YEMEN, which served as the Ottoman Empire's Siberia. He was assassinated there in his cell three years later.

Bruce Masters

Further reading: Shimon Shamir, "The Modernization of Syria: Problems and Solutions in the Early Period of AbdülHamit," in *Beginnings of Modernization in the Middle East: The Nineteenth Century*, edited by William Polk and Richard Chambers (Chicago: University of Chicago Press, 1968) 351–82.

military acculturation The term *acculturation* has been used widely in the social sciences and has acquired many definitions, with those associated with colonialism and imperialism being decidedly negative. The term is more widely used, however, to refer to the mutual borrowings between cultures such as those that occurred between the Ottomans and their European rivals in the areas of military knowledge, culture, and technology. Contrary to the usual understanding of the relationship between Europe and the Ottomans that posits uninterrupted and mutual hostilities, jihad and crusade were not the only ways in which these political powers engaged. While it is true that the Ottomans and their Christian adversaries devoted considerable resources to wars waged against one another, the rivalries between the European states and the constant shifting in the European balance of power often led to temporary European-Ottoman alliances. Equally importantly, Europeans and Ottomans learned about one another and, using this knowledge, they changed their policies and updated their military capabilities.

THE NATURE OF RELATIONS

Beginning with Venice in 1454, all major European powers stationed resident ambassadors in ISTANBUL, often shared information about their rivals with the Ottomans, and concluded peace and commercial treaties with the Ottoman government, known in Europe as the Sublime Porte. Despite prohibitions by the papacy and European monarchs, European merchant ships—especially those belonging to France in the mid-16th century and the Protestant states of England and the Dutch Republic in the 17th century—engaged in CONTRABAND trade, bringing weapons and ammunition, as well as other prohibited goods, to Istanbul and Ottoman port cities. In return, the Ottomans granted trade, legal, and religious privileges, known as CAPITULATIONS, to friendly European states, whose merchants supplied Istanbul with weapons and with such strategically important raw materials as tin and lead.

There was never any iron-curtain-like separation between the Ottomans and Europe. The two groups frequently came into contact with one another in direct military conflicts between Ottomans and their Christian adversaries in the Mediterranean, the Balkans, HUNGARY, and the BLACK SEA littoral, as well as in prohibited trade in weaponry and war materials, Christian captives, and in the passage of Christian renegades and adventurers who served in the Ottoman military. These were all channels by which the opposing parties learned effectively about their adversaries' weaponry and tactics.

CHANNELS OF ACCULTURATION: MILITARY TREATISES

Until the end of the 16th century the Ottomans were militarily superior to their Christian adversaries, and before the 1800s, they continued to represent a major military threat to Europe. Consequently, Europeans were careful to study the Ottomans' art of WARFARE. The hundreds of treatises written in Latin and other European languages that were published before 1600, in addition to the thousands of unpublished ambassadorial and consular reports preserved in the archives of VENICE, Paris, Marseilles, and Vienna, clearly demonstrate this interest. Italian, Spanish, German, and Hungarian military commanders and experts who fought against the Ottomans in the Mediterranean or in HUNGARY authored several valuable treatises on the Ottoman military. The works written by Lazarus Freiherr von Schwendi (Emperor Maximilian II's captain-general in Hungary in 1565–68), Giorgio Basta (Emperor Rudolf II's commander in Hungary and TRANSYLVANIA in 1596–1606), Raimondo Montecuccoli (field marshal and commander in chief of the Habsburg armies in 1664–80), and Miklós Zrínyi (Nikola Zrinski, a Hungarian/Croatian statesman and military leader, 1620–64) contain some of the best observations regarding the strengths and weaknesses of the Ottoman military and gave the Europeans useful advice on how to defeat the Ottomans. Luiggi Ferdinando Marsigli—a Bolognese military engineer and polyhistor who fought against the Ottomans in Habsburg service in the 1680s and 1690s—compiled the best concise description of the contemporary Ottoman army (*Stato militare dell'Imperio ottomano*, 1732).

Several military, scientific, and technical treatises in Europe were also inspired by the "Turkish peril" and aimed at strengthening Europe's military against the Ottomans. Italian mathematician Niccolò Tartaglia hesitated at first to publish his *Nova Scientia* and make public his discoveries regarding the path of cannon balls. However, he decided to print his work in 1537 and dedicated it to the Duke of Urbino so as to better prepare the duke's gunners in the face of a "Turkish threat."

Although linguistic and cultural barriers significantly limited the extent to which the Ottomans could profit from the thriving European literature on the art of war, some of the best works written in Europe reached the government in Istanbul. It is uncertain whether the printed copy of *De re militari* (1472) by Roberto Valturio (1413–1484), the first technical military treatise to appear in print, reached the Ottomans during the reign of Sultan MEHMED II (r. 1444–46; 1451–81), but it is known that a manuscript copy of the work was sent to him in 1461. It is possible that the printed treatise now in the Topkapı Palace Library was obtained only in 1526 during the reign of Sultan SÜLEYMAN I (r. 1520–66) from the library of the Hungarian king, Matthias Corvinus (r. 1458–90), when the Ottomans captured the medieval Hungarian capital of BUDA. However, Mehmed II acquired other works. A copy of one of the most influential 15th-century military trea-

tises, the *Tractatus* of Ser Mariano di Giacomo Vanni, ("il Taccola," 1381–ca. 1458) reached the sultan before the siege of CONSTANTINOPLE in 1453. Pietro Sardi's *L' Artiglieria* (Venice, 1621), one of the most celebrated books on cannon and siege warfare in 17th-century Europe, was translated into Ottoman Turkish and was used by the sultan's gunners. Muslims from Spain also played an important role in the transmission of knowledge regarding the art of war. The *Manual de Artilleria*, an Islamic treatise on artillery, was written by Andalusian sailor and master gunner Captain Ibrahim b. Ahmad (also known as al-Rais Ibrahim b. Ahmad al-Andalusi) in Tunis between 1630 and 1632 in the author's native Spanish but using Arabic script. Besides his own experience, the author relied heavily on Louis Collado's *Plática Manual de Artillería* (1592, Italian original from 1586), the most famous European treatise on gunnery in the late 16th and 17th century. In 1638, Captain Ibrahim found an able translator, the former interpreter of the sultan of Morocco and a fellow Morisco ("Little Moor," or former Spanish Muslim who became a baptized Christian), who, with his assistance, rendered the work into Arabic. Later the translator's son made several manuscript copies of the Arabic work, one of which was dedicated and sent to Sultan MURAD IV (r. 1623–40).

The systematic translation and publishing of Western military and technical books in the Ottoman Empire began in connection with the military reforms of sultans SELIM III (r. 1789–1807) and MAHMUD II (r. 1808–39) in the late 18th and early 19th centuries. The first among these, published in Ottoman Turkish in the early 1790s, were French military treatises and textbooks, often older ones such as the treatises on warfare, sieges, and mines by Sébastien le Prestre de Vauban (1633–1707). These texts were originally written between the 1680s and the early 1700s, though some were printed only in the 1730s. Many of these works were translated for students in the newly established military technical schools: the Imperial Naval Engineering School (Mühendishane-i Bahri-i Hümayun), the Artillery School (Topçu Mektebi), and the Imperial Land Engineering School (Mühendishane-i Berr-i Hümayun). In addition to these, lecture notes of French and other foreign teachers at the military and naval schools were also translated and printed in either the French Embassy's Istanbul press or in one of the newly established Ottoman printing houses.

CHANNELS OF ACCULTURATION: EXPERTS

While these and similar works may have played some role in the diffusion of European military technology to the Ottomans, the knowledge brought to Istanbul by European military experts was more significant. There were many ways by which European military experts came to the Ottoman Empire. Some—such as Master

Orban, a Hungarian by nationality and possibly German by birth, whose cannons played an important role in the capture of Constantinople in 1453—offered their services to the sultan hoping for a better salary and the possibility of social advancement. Others, like Jörg of Nuremberg, were captured in wars and raids; when their skills were discovered, the Ottomans forced them to use their skills for the benefit and glory of the sultan. Jörg was captured in 1460 in Bosnia and subsequently worked for the Ottomans for 20 years. Others arrived in Istanbul through a state-organized mass resettlement policy (*sürgün*) practiced mainly in the 15th and 16th centuries.

Foreign military experts—especially French and English—played an important role in the military reforms of the 18th and 19th centuries. The French renegade Claude-Alexandre Comte de Bonneval, known in the empire as Humbaracı Ahmed Pasha, established a new Corps of Bombardiers (Humbaracı Ocağı) in 1735. The bombardiers and their officers were, for the first time in the history of the corps, trained in military engineering, ballistics, and mathematics. Their instructor was another French renegade called Mühendis ("engineer") Selim, who had been educated in military engineering and fortress building in France. Although the corps faltered after its founder's death in 1747, it was revived under Selim III and Mahmud II. The corps proved to be an ideal environment for acculturation and the synthesis of European and Ottoman culture: an Ottoman engineer, Mehmed Said Efendi, who taught geometry at the corps, invented a new instrument for land surveying by combining the European telescope and the Ottoman quadrant.

Another well-known European in Ottoman service was Baron François de Tott, a French cavalryman of Hungarian origin, and France's consul in the Crimean Khanate in the late 1760s. Although Tott remained on France's payroll, between 1770 and 1775 the Ottomans occasionally contracted with him to help them rebuild the forts of the Dardanelles, cast cannons, and train artillerymen. As a former cavalryman in France's famous hussar regiment, Tott had only limited knowledge of fortress building, siege warfare, and cannon casting, and thus the value of his services to the Ottomans is uncertain. However, his *Memoirs*, in which he unashamedly exaggerated his role in Ottoman service, suited the tastes of his European readers and enjoyed unmatched popularity. His often superficial observations and inflated comments are partly responsible for perpetuating myths regarding the 18th-century Ottoman Empire and its military, such as the Ottomans' supposed preference for giant cannons and their alleged conservatism.

The great majority of European experts, however, were not known by name. Professional miners from Novo Brdo in Serbia were used by Mehmed II in 1453 to dig mines under the walls of Constantinople. Mehmed II also employed Christian artillerymen from Serbia, Bosnia, Germany, Hungary, and Italy. Ottoman pay registers from the latter part of the 15th century and the first half of the 16th century list Christian smiths, stone carvers, masons, caulkers, and shipbuilders in Ottoman Balkan fortresses. In the 16th century there were Marrano (or seciet Jews), Jewish, French, Venetian, Genoese, Spanish, Sicilian, English, German, Hungarian, and Slav experts working at the Ottoman cannon foundries. French and English military engineers aided the Ottomans in the 17th century. Some worked for the Ottomans voluntarily, others were captured during wars and raids and were forced to serve the sultan. In addition to Bonneval and Tott, some 300 French officers and engineers worked for the Ottomans in the 1780s.

With regard to the development of Ottoman nautical technology and naval warfare, European renegades and CORSAIRS of Christian origin were especially important. Italian artisans worked in the Ottoman shipyards, and many of the experts aboard Ottoman vessels were Italians and Greeks. The BARBARY STATES, too, were a rich source of expert sailors. Many of the admirals of the Ottoman navy came from there. Several of the corsairs started their careers as Christian converts to Islam, like the Algerian corsair-turned-admiral Uluç Ali Pasha, originally from Calabria; he was the most experienced Ottoman commander at the 1571 BATTLE OF LEPANTO and later became the grand admiral of the Ottoman NAVY. Such corsairs of Christian origin provided the Ottoman navy with vital information concerning the geography of the Italian and Spanish Mediterranean as well as the military and naval skills of Istanbul's Christian adversaries.

The employment of foreign military technicians and artisans was not unique to the Ottomans as it was also a well-established practice in Europe. Venice, the Ottomans' main adversary in the Mediterranean in the 15th century, also relied on foreign—mostly German—gunners. This changed only in the mid-16th century after the establishment of the Italian *scuole de' bombardieri* or training schools for gunners. Spain, Istanbul's main rival in the 16th-century Mediterranean, also lacked expert native ironworkers and employed Italian, German, and Flemish foundrymen. Employing foreign technicians from countries that were considered to be on the cutting edge was the major means throughout Europe to acquire new military technology. The Ottomans were very much a part of this transfer of early modern military technology.

What made the Ottoman case unique, however, was that Istanbul was ideally placed for technology diffusion. While experts from the mining centers of medieval Serbia, Bosnia, Greece, and Asia Minor brought their knowledge of metallurgy to Istanbul, Muslim blacksmiths contributed their knowledge of the metalworking techniques of the Islamic East that produced the world-renowned

Damascus blades. Istanbul, with its Turkish and Persian artisans and blacksmiths, Armenian and Greek miners and sappers, Bosnian, Serbian, Turkish, Italian, German, and later French, English, and Dutch gun makers and engineers, as well as its Venetian, Dalmatian, and Greek shipwrights and sailors, proved to be an ideal center for technological dialogue. All this was possible because of the pragmatism of the elite and the flexibility of the Ottoman system.

THE OTTOMANS' ROLE IN THE DIFFUSION OF MILITARY TECHNOLOGY

Another notable feature of European-Ottoman military acculturation is the Ottomans' role in the diffusion of gunpowder technology in the Middle East and Asia. Ottoman experts played roles of varying importance in the transmission of gunpowder technology to the khanates in Turkestan, the Crimean Khanate, Abyssinia, Gujerat in India, and the sultanate of Atche in Sumatra. Istanbul sent cannons and hand-held FIREARMS to the MAMLUK sultanate, Gujarat, Abyssinia, and YEMEN (before the latter two were incorporated into the empire). And Ottoman experts Ali Kulu, Rumi, and Mustafa played a significant role in the diffusion of firearms technology and Ottoman methods of warfare in Babur's Mughal India. Even Safavid IRAN, the Ottomans' main rival in the East, acquired Ottoman artillery and muskets when Prince Bayezid rebelled against his father Sultan SÜLEYMAN I (r. 1520–66) and escaped to Iran in 1559. Ottoman artillerymen, or *rumlu tofangchis* as they were known in Iran, were members of the Safavid army under Shah Tahmasp (r. 1524–76).

OTTOMAN IMPACT ON EUROPE

Perhaps the most significant legacy of Ottoman military culture, however, at least in terms of the development of modern Europe, is the influence of the Ottoman army's growth, development, and actions on the European art of war and military infrastructure. Ottoman expansion and military superiority, especially in the 16th century, played an important role in Habsburg military-fiscal modernization and in the creation of what became known as Habsburg central Europe. In order to match Ottoman firepower, Europeans took countermeasures. These included the modernization of fortress systems (the introduction of Italian bastioned fortifications that could withstand cannon sieges, known as *trace italienne*, into central and eastern Europe); an increase in the quality and production of the armaments industries; a change in the cavalry-infantry ratio; improvements in the training and tactics of field armies; and the modernization of the state's administration and finances. While all these were part of a larger phenomenon, often referred to as the European military revolution, and were undoubtedly

fostered by the frequency of interstate violence within Europe, it was Ottoman pressure and military superiority in central and eastern Europe that constituted the greatest challenge and required adequate countermeasures. Likewise, Ottoman methods of resource mobilization and warfare were taken into consideration during the reorganization of the Muscovite military under Ivan IV (Ivan the Terrible, grand prince of Moscow 1533–47; czar of Russia 1547–84), whose reforms were in turn influenced by the observations of the Ottoman military by Ivan Peresvetov, the early Russian social critic who presented his *Two Books* to Ivan the Terrible. Peresvetov regarded the Ottoman Empire and the armed forces of Sultan Mehmed II (r. 1444–46; 1451–81) as a model worthy of emulation. In the long run, the "Turkish threat" and Ottoman military superiority fostered widespread technological and scientific experimentation and military reforms in central and eastern Europe.

Gábor Ágoston

Further reading: Gábor Ágoston, "Behind the Turkish War Machine: Gunpowder, Technology and Munitions Industry in the Ottoman Empire, 1450–1700," in *The Heirs of Archimedes: Science and the Art of War through the Age of Enlightenment*, edited by Brett Steele and Tamera Dorland (Cambridge, Mass.: MIT Press, 2005), 101–133; Virginia Aksan, *Ottomans and Europeans: Contacts and Conflicts* (Istanbul: Isis, 2004); Ekmeleddin İhsanoğlu, *Science, Technology, and Learning in the Ottoman Empire: Western Influence, Local Institutions, and the Transfer of Knowledge* (Aldershot, UK: Ashgate, 2004); Rhoads Murphey, "The Ottoman Attitude towards the Adoption of Western Technology: The Role of the Efrencî Technicians in Civil and Military Applications" in *Contributions à l'histoire économique et sociale de l'Empire ottoman*, edited by Jean-Louis Bacqué-Grammont and Paul Dumont (Leuven: Peeters, 1983), 287–298.

military engineering schools   *See* EDUCATION; MÜHENDISHANE.

military organization   *See* WARFARE.

military slavery   Military slavery was a well-known practice in the Islamic world from the 830s, when the ABBASID CALIPHATE (750–1258) that ruled much of the Muslim world from BAGHDAD began to recruit Turkish-speaking bodyguards and later mounted archers from Central Asia, predominantly as slave soldiers (*ghulam, mamluk*). Though only few thousand in number, the *ghulams*' new military technique (mounted archery), tactics (feigned retreat), skills in horsemanship, and the endurance of their horses significantly enhanced the

Muslim armies' speed, maneuverability, and firepower. Soon, most armies of the Islamic heartlands had Turkish slave soldiers, and they often became key military figures. Since military and administrative careers were not separated, members of this caste also rose to become prominent in the administration and bureaucracy as viziers, generals, and governors.

The military slave system not only revolutionized Muslim warfare, it also had far-reaching political consequences. Recruited from among outsiders with no previous political allegiance and entirely dependent on the state for its subsistence, the slave army was a loyal and effective force in the hands of caliphs and other Muslim rulers. However, isolated from the rest of society, their main concern was to preserve their status by dominating the government and policy. This led to the weakening of the Abbasid Caliphate and the emergence of local dynasties and military dictatorships that engaged in bitter wars against one another.

Of the military regimes established by Turkish slave soldiers in the Middle East, the MAMLUK EMPIRE (1250–1517) of EGYPT and SYRIA was the most sophisticated, with a professional cavalry capable of mobilizing between 40,000 and 70,000 troops in the late 13th century. The Safavid dynasty that ruled IRAN from the early 16th century through the 1730s also employed military slaves in the army and administration. Recruited mainly from among Georgians, Armenians, and the peoples of the northern CAUCASUS, they were established to counterbalance the Ottoman JANISSARIES, the sultan's elite standing infantry whose members were also of slave origin. The Safavid slave army was also instrumental in strengthening the authority of the Safavid ruler against the Turkoman tribes of Persia, dominated by the KIZILBAŞ.

The Ottoman Janissaries differed from the slave soldiers of the Islamic heartlands in one important respect. Unlike the Abbasids or the Mamluks, who purchased their slave soldiers from outside the lands of Islam, the Ottoman sultans recruited their slave troops through the DEVŞIRME, or child levy system, from among the empire's Christian subjects. This practice continued despite the fact that Islamic law (SHARIA) forbade the enslavement of Christians and Jews who, as DHIMMIS or "people of the book," lived under the protection of a Muslim ruler.

The Ottomans believed that the enslaved, forcibly converted to Islam, became better soldiers than the Turks, because after their conversion they became zealous for their new religion and hostile to their former kin. This belief was only partly true. Sources indicate that the youths recruited for military and state service through the child levy system did not forget their native language, culture, or homeland. Many, especially those who attained high government offices in the empire, assisted their relatives and compatriots, such as Mehmed Pasha of the SOKOLLU FAMILY, who served as grand vizier from 1565 to 1579. Born into a Serbian family, educated in a monastery, and recruited through the *devşirme*, Mehmed Pasha, then serving as the empire's third in command after the grand vizier and the second vizier, played a crucial role in re-establishing the Serbian Patriarchate (1557) in Peć, whose first patriarch, Makariye, was either Mehmed Pasha's nephew or brother. From the mid-16th century onward, nepotism and favoritism among the sultan's slave administrators, as well as their ethnic-regional rivalry in the highest echelons of the Ottoman administration and army, did much to weaken the empire, as did the deterioration of the once elite Janissary corps.

Gábor Ágoston

Further reading: David Ayalon, *The Mamluk Military Society* (London: Variorum Reprints, 1979); David Ayalon, *Eunuchs, Caliphs and Sultans: A Study in Power Relationships* (Jerusalem: Magnes, 1999); Sussan Babaie, Kathryn Babayan, Ina Baghdiantz-McCabe, and Massumeh Farhad, *Slaves of the Shah: New Elites of Safavid Iran* (London: I.B. Tauris, 2004); Colin Imber, *The Ottoman Empire, 1300–1650* (New York: Palgrave Macmillan, 2002); Metin Kunt, "Ethnic-Regional (Cins) Solidarity in the Seventeenth-Century Ottoman Establishment." *International Journal of Middle East Studies* 5 (1974): 223–39.

millet The word *millet* comes from the Arabic word for nation, *milla*, but in the Ottoman Empire it came to mean a religious community, specifically, non-Muslim religious minorities represented within the empire by an official political leader. Official Ottoman correspondence dealing with the non-Muslims of the empire in the early 19th century consistently affirmed that non-Muslims were organized into three officially sanctioned *millets*: GREEK ORTHODOX, headed by the ecumenical patriarch, Armenians, headed by the Armenian patriarch of Istanbul, and JEWS, who after 1835 were headed by the *hahambaşı* in Istanbul. The bureaucrats further asserted that this had been the tradition since the reign of Sultan MEHMED I (r. 1413–21).

The *millets* as constituted in the 19th century were hierarchically organized religious bodies with a decidedly political function. Each was headed by a cleric (patriarch or chief rabbi, known in Ottoman Turkish as the *millet başı*) who was appointed by the sultan, usually from a list of candidates provided by the community's leaders, and resident in ISTANBUL. But beyond that, the *millet başı* was largely free to order the affairs of his community as long as he remained loyal to the sultan. More importantly, as an officially sanctioned bureaucracy, the *millet's* leadership could command the civil forces of empire, such as governors and KADIS, to implement its will over an errant flock.

Many historians have accepted the 19th century bureaucrats' claim at face value and have asserted that the *millet* system as it existed in the 19th century had been a part of Ottoman rule since the 15th century. Recent scholarship has shown it was, in fact, a relatively recent Ottoman political innovation, even if its workings were always cloaked in the rhetoric of an ageless tradition.

By the late 18th century, the Ottoman authorities were consistently intervening in disputes within and among the religious communities to support the established religious hierarchies against internal dissent. This was especially true within the Christian communities where there was conflict between Catholic and Orthodox Christian factions that eventually split every Christian *millet* into two competing bodies.

Unlike the Christian churches, the Jews of the empire did not have a pre-existing clerical hierarchy. In the place of patriarchs and bishops, their religious communities functioned autonomously in each of the Ottoman cities they inhabited. Although the Jews were recognized as a separate religious community by both Muslim legal scholars and Ottoman officials, the Jews did not seek formal status as a *millet* until 1835 when the Ottoman government, in its attempt to standardize the way it dealt with each of the minority religious communities, pushed the Jewish community leaders to name a chief rabbi (*hahambaşı*) for the empire.

After the start of the GREEK WAR OF INDEPENDENCE in 1821, the prestige of the Orthodox ecumenical patriarch in Istanbul plummeted and the special relationship that had existed between the Greek Orthodox Church and the sultan ended. Faced with pressure from the European Catholic powers, notably FRANCE and AUSTRIA, the Ottomans recognized the Catholics as a *millet* in 1830. Later, that *millet* would only include the Armenian Catholic community, as the various other UNIATE communities (those Christian sects that recognized the Roman Catholic pope as their spiritual head) pressed for recognition on their own behalf. By the end of the empire, the Ottoman officials recognized 12 separate Christian communities as *millets*.

During the TANZIMAT reform period of the mid-19th century, the Ottoman government pushed the *millets* to reform their internal governance, including school systems directed independently within each community. Reform was usually resisted by the clergy and advanced by the laity as a way of wresting some political authority away from the clerics. In 1863 the Armenians were the first community to write their own constitution governing the internal laws of their *millet*. This constitution transferred much of the community's governance to an elected body of laity and clergy. The Orthodox and Jewish communities soon followed, although their experimentation was much less democratic than that of the Armenians.

Some historians have seen this trend in local governance among the various religious communities as contributing to the rise of nationalist sentiments among the various Christian communities where religion and nationality could be conflated. The children of the communities were educated separately from Muslims and primarily in the language of their community. They were also taught the separate history of their community and its culture. It is this separate education that many believe inspired these groups to see themselves as separate peoples.

Bruce Masters

Further reading: Benjamin Braude and Bernard Lewis, eds., *Christians and Jews in the Ottoman Empire*, 2 vols. (New York: Holmes & Meier, 1982).

miniature painting *See* ILLUSTRATED MANUSCRIPTS AND MINIATURE PAINTINGS.

missionaries Christians in western Europe viewed the Ottoman Empire as a promising field for missionary activity. It seemed to them that its inhabitants were sunk in misery and ignorance, waiting to receive the spiritual truth they could provide. Both Roman Catholic and, later, Protestant missionaries were aware that any attempt to convert Muslims would result in the death of the missionary and the convert alike. Their efforts therefore were initially directed at the empire's JEWS. But as these remained stubbornly resistant, both Protestant and Catholic missionaries soon turned their spiritual attention to the sultan's Christian subjects.

CATHOLIC MISSIONARIES

Catholic missions to the Ottoman Empire began in the 17th century. The Catholic strategy, born out of the Counter-Reformation that followed the fracture of the Church in the 16th century, was to woo the higher clergy of the Orthodox Christian churches into communion with Rome, thereby securing them from the possibility of contagion by what Catholics viewed as the Protestant "heresy." In the process, Roman Catholics were content to overlook many existing doctrinal differences and allow the outward symbols of the faith—icons, clerical vestments, and titles—to remain as they had always been. Indeed, the Roman Catholic clergy usually donned the cassocks and turbans of their Eastern-rite counterparts while traveling in the Ottoman Empire. Their self-proclaimed spiritual mission had decidedly political overtones as it was ultimately designed to extend both the spiritual and the political authority of the pope by convincing the higher clergy of the churches of the East to accept the bishop of Rome as the first among equals. But local Christians had political goals of their own, and the process that led to the emergence in the Ottoman realms of the UNIATE churches—that is, churches that retained their own liturgies but recognized the spiritual authority of the pope—was often driven as much by those ambitions as by dreams of a "universal church" with the pope, or bishop of Rome, at its head.

Most European Catholic missionaries left the Ottoman Empire by the end of the 18th century, especially after the Jesuit order was disbanded. But their presence was increasingly unnecessary as local priests who had converted to Catholicism, many of whom had been educated in Rome, began to minister to their communities. Local seminaries were also established and at the start of the 19th century, what had begun as a missionary church had become a mature, local institution.

PROTESTANT MISSIONARIES

The Protestant missionaries arrived in the Ottoman Empire with the Second Great Awakening in the English-speaking world at the start of the 19th century. Born in part out of a reaction to an emerging secularism in their societies as elites in both ENGLAND and the United States embraced the ideas of Enlightenment writers, this movement stressed individual salvation and the necessity for evangelization of those not yet "saved" whether they were "pagans" or "nominal Christians." Accordingly, the Protestants placed a high premium on Bible literacy and sought the spiritual conversion of local Christians on an individual basis through Christian education. Despite the attention to the salvation of the souls of those to whom they ministered, the Protestant mission had unintended political results in that it aided the growth of nationalist sentiments among the empire's Christian populations. The missionaries made the conscious choice to emphasize their students' vernacular languages rather than teaching them in either the native English of most missionaries or in the state's official Ottoman Turkish, and that choice is seen by many historians as contributing to a nationalist consciousness among those the missionaries taught.

The American missionaries were drawn to the field of education as they felt that only when the peoples of the Ottoman Empire had been exposed to a "modern" education would they be intellectually and spiritually open to their religious mission. To further that goal of creating an intellectual elite, the Congregationalist AMERICAN BOARD OF COMMISSIONERS FOR FOREIGN MISSIONS established Robert College in ISTANBUL in 1863 and the Syrian Protestant College in BEIRUT in 1866. Both developed into major universities that trained students from all the religious communities in scientific and technological fields that were largely unavailable in government schools. These efforts did result in the conversion of some few to Protestantism. In 1914 there were about 65,000 Protestants in the Ottoman Empire out of a total of 18 million people. Most of those were Armenians who converted from the ARMENIAN APOSTOLIC CHURCH. In the same year there were approximately 250,000 Catholics, divided among five different groups. With relatively few converts, the more important lasting impact of the missionaries, both Protestant and Catholic, on the inhabitants of the Ottoman Empire was their introduction of Western-style education and the educational institutions they founded.

OTTOMAN RESPONSE TO MISSIONARIES

Although the Ottoman government never outlawed missionary activity, it showed concern about the presence of missionaries on Ottoman soil at several different times. In the 18th century, under pressure from the Orthodox Christian clergy, the Ottoman authorities forbade the Roman Catholic clergy from teaching Ottoman children, giving medical treatment to local people, or offering them the sacraments. In theory, the clergy's presence in the empire was to minister to Roman Catholic merchants from western Europe under terms established in the CAPITULATIONS. The stipulated limits of their activities were rarely enforced, however. During the reign of Sultan ABDÜLHAMID II (1876–1909), the concern was that Protestant missionaries would proselytize among groups that were either heterodox Muslim, such as the DRUZE and ALAWI, or not Muslim at all, as in the case of the YAZIDIS. Again, no move was made to forbid the missionaries from converting Christians, but the sultan warned his officials in the provinces to be vigilant to prevent non-Christians from converting to Christianity. In part, the government's attempt to bring a modern educational system to the provinces was propelled by fear that, without an Islamic alternative, Muslim students would attend the MISSIONARY SCHOOLS.

Bruce Masters

Further reading: Charles Frazee, *Catholics and Sultans: The Church and the Ottoman Empire, 1453–1923* (Cambridge: Cambridge University Press, 1983); Eleanor Tejirian and Reeva Spector Simon, eds., *Altruism and Imperialism: Western Cultural and Religious Missions in the Middle East* (New York: Columbia University Press, 2002).

missionary schools While missionary activities had started in the Ottoman territories as early as the 16th century, more organized American and European missionary endeavors began in the 19th century. These

The staff of Anatolia College, one of the colleges of the American Board of Commissioners for Foreign Missions in the Ottoman Empire, and their families in front of the main building of the college in Merzifon (a town in modern-day Amasya province, Turkey) *(Photograph © American Board Library, Istanbul)*

activities aimed both to bring Christianity to the peoples of the Ottoman Empire and to revitalize Eastern Christianity in the region. Missionaries to the Ottoman Empire were also attracted to the Holy Land. Christian missionaries were forbidden by imperial authorities from proselytizing among Ottoman Muslims. Therefore the Western missionaries concentrated primarily on the Jewish community and the many Christian minority groups in the Ottoman Empire, including Armenians, Greeks, Bulgarians, JACOBITES, NESTORIANS, Chaldeans, COPTS, and MARONITES.

The Roman Catholic Church had long been attempting to bring Orthodox Christians into communion with Rome. In 1622, the Sacred Congregation for the Propagation of the Faith (Propaganda Fide) was created by the pope in order to coordinate Catholic missionary activities. Protected by various European powers, particularly FRANCE, a number of Catholic orders and brotherhoods, including the Capuchins, Franciscans, Carmelites, Dominicans, Augustinians, and Jesuits, worked in the provinces of the Ottoman Empire. They established schools mainly for the Eastern Christians, but before the 19th century these were typically no better than the local schools.

The second half of the 18th century, when secularism and anti-clericalism were on the rise in Europe, was a period of decline in missionary activity. The European Catholic monarchies resented the Jesuits'

close connections with the papacy and Jesuit activities were greatly restricted in France, SPAIN, and Portugal, culminating in the suppression of the order by the papacy in 1773. All French missionary societies were suppressed by NAPOLEON BONAPARTE in 1809, ending French recruitment for a generation. However, the Catholic missionary enterprise gained momentum in the mid-19th century mainly because of the restoration of the Jesuits in 1814, the rivalry between Catholic and Protestant missionaries, and the TANZIMAT reform period in the Ottoman Empire. This momentum led to better Jesuit schools in ISTANBUL in the 1850s, offering a liberal education that included instruction in modern languages and fine arts.

The 19th century was marked by the rapid and widespread expansion of foreign missionary activities on the part of many Protestant churches in the United States and Europe, and by the late 19th century there had been a tremendous growth in the Catholic missionary enterprise. Thus in LEBANON and SYRIA, Catholic missionaries established schools to compete with growing Protestant missionary educational efforts. By 1914, French Catholic missionaries claimed to be teaching more than half of all the children enrolled in schools in Lebanon, PALESTINE, and Syria. By that same year the Jesuits, who had established the Université St. Joseph in BEIRUT in 1881, were running 150 schools in the cities and rural areas of Lebanon and Syria.

The Protestant missionary endeavor in the Ottoman Empire began in the early 19th century and was largely dominated by two organizations, the AMERICAN BOARD OF COMMISSIONERS FOR FOREIGN MISSIONS (ABCFM), based in Boston, and the Church Missionary Society, based in London. The ABCFM was born in 1810 in the midst of the Second Great Awakening, a diverse series of religious revivals that resulted in the foundation of several benevolent societies and missionary organizations in the United States. By the 19th century, the ABCFM had become the largest Protestant missionary organization in the world and the most substantial Protestant missionary organization in the Ottoman Empire. Levi Parsons and Pliny Fisk, the first American missionaries to the Holy Land sent by the ABCFM, set foot on Ottoman soil in 1820, to be followed by many others.

The ABCFM founded its first school in Beirut in 1824. In general the Tanzimat reform period, which began in 1839, provided a favorable environment for missionary activity. The ABCFM established an extensive network of schools at all levels in the hinterland of the mission stations, particularly in Anatolia. Education in the missionary schools was of good quality, and it was reported that 85 percent of Ottoman Protestants (mostly converted from Armenian Orthodoxy in Anatolia and from Greek or Syrian Orthodoxy in the Levant) could read and write by the 1870s. In 1870, the ABCFM decided to limit its activities to Anatolia, while another Protestant missionary organization, the Presbyterian Board of Foreign Missions continued to work in the Arab provinces. The number of the ABCFM's missionary schools for Eastern Christians, particularly Armenians, increased dramatically in the following years. In addition to opening kindergartens and primary and secondary schools in almost every city in the Ottoman heartland, several colleges were founded: the American College for Girls in Istanbul (1871), Central Turkey College in Antep (1876), Euphrates College in Harput (1878), Central Turkey Girls' College in Maraş (1880), Anatolia College in Merzifon (1886), and International College in Izmir (1898). Robert College (1863) and the Syrian Protestant College in Beirut (1866, later the American University of Beirut) were not under the direct control of the American missionaries, but were closely connected with them.

The annual reports of the ABCFM and Presbyterian Board of Foreign Missions in 1914 stated that the American missionaries in the Ottoman Empire directed 473 elementary, 54 secondary, and 4 theological schools, as well as 11 colleges, teaching a total of 32,252 students. Most of the colleges offered regular classes on history, literature, mathematics, science, economics, logic, and philosophy; religious instruction was also a part of the curriculum. American missionary schools offered students not only a Protestant education but also an opportunity to under-

stand the workings of the "Anglo-American mind." Language was always a major issue, and the ABCFM decided that instruction in its schools should be in the vernacular. Thus Arabic was used in Mardin, MOSUL, Syria, and the other Arab provinces; Armenian was used in eastern Anatolia; Turkish was employed in central Anatolia; and Greek, Armenian, Turkish, and Bulgarian were the preferred languages of instruction in western Anatolia and the Balkans.

Another important Protestant missionary organization was the Church Missionary Society (CMS), established in the period of British missionary revival in 1799. It began its operations in the Mediterranean in 1812. The CMS was strong in Palestine and Egypt and had 59 missionaries in Palestine by 1899. The CMS and the other British missionary societies had around 120 schools with nearly 10,000 students in the Ottoman Empire by 1905.

Many missionary societies of various sizes and different denominations from almost all Western countries sent missionaries to the Ottoman Empire. The variety of European and American missionary schools established in the Balkans, Anatolia, and the Arab provinces can be gauged from a few examples throughout the empire: the French Catholic Brothers of the Christian Schools' educational activities in Izmir; the Italian Salesian school in Antalya; the Russian Orthodox Imperial Pravoslavic Society's schools in Galilee; an Austrian Catholic girls' school in EDIRNE; the Prussian Protestant Kaiserswerth Deaconesses' school in Jerusalem; the Scottish Protestant schools for boys and girls in Beirut; the French Lazarist St. Benoit College in Istanbul; and the Quaker American Friends' schools in Ramallah.

According to the Protestant missionaries, the spread of the Bible required the establishment of "civilized Christian institutions," and literacy was a paramount requirement for gaining personal knowledge of the Bible and its teachings. Missionaries in the Ottoman Empire did not limit their educational activities to the establishment of schools for boys but, as is evident from the names of the schools, were also interested in educating girls as part of the general endeavor to reconstruct the society. In addition to educational and medical work (operating hospitals), the missions established printing presses to publish schoolbooks and copies of the Bible and other religious tracts in the vernacular, in order to reach those they referred to as the "nominal Christians" of the Eastern Churches.

As far as the Ottoman state was concerned, the missionary educational enterprise was a matter of concern for most of the 19th and early 20th centuries because the mission boards established their schools both with and without explicit permission from the Sublime Porte. Many Ottoman officials thought that the missionary schools constituted a threat to the empire and imple-

Music students of Anatolia College which opened its doors in 1886 and was closed in 1921. Students of the college were principally Armenian and Greek, and the college relocated in Thessaloniki, Greece in 1924. *(Photograph © American Board Library, Istanbul)*

mented measures to control and limit their activities. This distrust deepened when many graduates of Robert College went on to become leading members of the independent Bulgarian government.

One unintended consequence of the ubiquity and quality of these foreign missionary schools was that the Ottoman administration was motivated to combat the allure of these institutions by improving and modernizing its own educational system. Thus several new Ottoman schools for Muslim Turks were established in the 1880s in order to compete with the missionaries' efforts, and it is clear that the spread of missionary schools in the Ottoman Empire accelerated the state's adoption of Western educational models. During WORLD WAR I, shortly before the absolute demise of the empire, most missionary activities in the Ottoman Empire were either curtailed completely or severely restricted.

Mehmet Ali Doğan

Further reading: Heleen Murre-van den Berg, ed., *New Faith in Ancient Lands: Western Missions in the Middle East in the Nineteenth and Early Twentieth Centuries* (Leiden: Brill, 2006); Frank Andrews Stone, *Academies for Anatolia: A Study of the Rationale, Program and Impact of the Educational Institutions Sponsored by the American Board in Turkey, 1830–2005* (San Francisco: Caddo Gap Press, 2006); Martin Tamcke and Michael Marten, eds., *Christian Witness between Continuity and New Beginnings: Modern Historical Missions in the Middle East* (Berlin: Lit, 2006); Eleanor H. Tejirian and Reeva Spector Simon, eds., *Altruism and Imperialism: Western Cultural and Religious Missions in the Middle East* (New York: Middle East Institute, Columbia University, 2002); Selçuk Akşin Somel, "The Religious Community Schools and Foreign Missionary Schools," in *Ottoman Civilization*, edited by Halil İnalcık and Günsel Renda (Ankara: Ministry of Culture, 2003), 386–401.

Mitwallis   *See* SHIA ISLAM.

Mohács, Battle of   (1526)   Fought on August 29, 1526, south of the Hungarian town of Mohács—near the intersection of present-day HUNGARY, CROATIA, and Yugoslavia—this battle ended the independence of the medieval Kingdom of Hungary and led both to direct Ottoman-Habsburg confrontation in central Europe and to Hungary's Ottoman occupation.

The causes of the 1526 Ottoman campaign are hotly debated. Some historians claim that it was a response to the "provocations" of the Hungarian king Louis II (r. 1516–26), namely the king's refusal of Sultan SÜLEYMAN I's (r. 1520–66) peace offers and the Hungarians' interference in the sultan's two Romanian vassal principalities, especially in WALLACHIA, whose *voievod*, or lord, repeatedly rebelled against the Ottomans with Hungarian backing. Others maintain that these were mere pretexts and that the conquest of Hungary had been Süleyman's objective from the beginning of his reign and that he carried it out according to his plan of gradual conquest. Given Süleyman's pragmatic and often reactive policy, the empire's multiple commitments and constraints, the insufficiently understood nature of Ottoman ideology, propaganda, and decision-making, it is wise not to overstate the importance of religio-political imperatives with regard to Ottoman imperial planning.

In the 1526 campaign, the Ottoman army may have numbered some 60,000 provincial cavalry (Rumelian and Anatolian troops) and standing forces (JANISSARIES, cavalry, and artillery) and perhaps another 40,000 to 50,000 irregulars and auxiliaries. Due to the four-month march, rainy weather, and sieges, a number of these men had probably died before the army reached Hungary. Thus the estimate of Archbishop Pál Tomori, commander in chief of the Hungarian army, who put the whole fighting force of the sultan's army at about 70,000 men, seems more realistic than the inflated figures of 150,000 to 300,000 men suggested by some later historians. However, even this more modest estimate suggests considerable Ottoman numerical superiority, for the Hungarian army that met the Ottomans near Mohács numbered only about 25,000 to 30,000 men. A similar Ottoman superiority can be seen with regard to firepower: whereas the Ottomans deployed some 200 cannons, mainly small-caliber ones, the Hungarians had only about 80.

The battlefield was bordered by the marshes of the Danube to the east and by a plateau 80–90 feet (25 to 30 m) high to the west and south. The Hungarian command planned to charge against the much larger Ottoman army in increments as the Ottomans descended from the steep and slippery plateau. The Hungarians initiated the combat when only the Rumelian army was on the plain. Süleyman and his cavalry were still descending from the plateau, and the Anatolian troops of the right flank were further behind. The skirmishes of the light cavalry forces were already underway when the Hungarian artillery opened fire at the Rumelian army that was about to camp on the plain. This was followed by a cavalry charge of the Hungarian right flank that broke the resistance of the Rumelian cavalry. But instead of chasing the fleeing enemy, the Hungarians made the strategic error of setting out to loot. By then the Janissaries had arrived and inflicted major losses on the Hungarians with their volleys. Although the Hungarian infantry and left wing fought bravely, they were slaughtered by the Janissary volleys. Contrary to general belief, it was not the Ottoman cannons (which shot beyond the Hungarians), but the insurmountable wall of the Janissaries and their firepower that figured decisively in the Ottoman victory.

Such a severe defeat had not been inflicted on the Hungarian armed forces since the Battle of Muhi against the Mongols in 1241. King Louis II, most of the magnates and prelates, about 500 noblemen, 4,000 cavalry, and 10,000 infantrymen perished at Mohács. Hungary also lost its century-and-a-half-old struggle to contain the Ottoman advance into central Europe.

More importantly for Europe, the battle led to direct Habsburg-Ottoman military confrontation from the 1520s on, for in 1526 a group of Hungarian aristocrats elected Archduke Ferdinand of Habsburg, younger brother of Holy Roman Emperor Charles V, as their king. Ferdinand, who ruled as king of Hungary until his death in 1564, was able to control only the northwestern parts of Hungary, for the middle and eastern parts (including the medieval capital city, BUDA) were under the rule of János Szapolyai, also elected king of Hungary (r. 1526–1540), whose pro-Ottoman policy temporarily postponed the clash between the Habsburgs and Ottomans. Szapolyai's death in 1540 and Ferdinand's unsuccessful siege of Buda in the spring and summer of 1541 triggered the sultan's campaign that led to the Ottoman occupation of central Hungary, and turned the country into the major continental battleground between the Habsburgs and the Ottomans.

Gábor Ágoston

Further reading: Géza Perjés, *The Fall of the Medieval Kingdom of Hungary: Mohács 1526–Buda 1541* (Boulder, Colo.: East European Monographs, 1989).

Moldavia (*Ger.:* Moldau; *Rom.:* Moldova; *Turk.:* Kara Boğdan)   Moldavia, a territory located in what is now the northeastern region of Romania, became an independent state in 1359 under the *voievod* (governor) Bogdan I (r. 1359–65). As a voievodeship, Moldavia was usually under Hungarian control, but from time to time the state was held by POLAND. Prior to 1359 the region was a contested area, claimed or defended by the Hungarian kings Andreas II (r. 1205–35), Béla IV (r. 1235–70), and Louis the Great (r. 1342–82), but frequently attacked by Cumans (or Kipchak Turks) and Tatars or Mongols. Dragoş, a Romanian *knyaz* (military chief), was sent from HUNGARY to organize a defense zone in 1352–53. In 1359 Dragoş was expelled by Bogdan and Moldavia became independent for a while. The territory was particularly desirable (and thus highly vulnerable to military and political interference) due to its strategic location bordering present-day UKRAINE.

The Ottomans called the territory Boğdan, Boğdan Iflak, or Kara-Boğdan, all names deriving from that of the first *voievod*. Petru I Muşat (ca. 1374–92) was the first *voievod* to send taxes to the Ottoman Empire in 1377; in the eyes of the Ottomans his payments to Sultan MURAD I (r. 1360–89) denoted an acknowledgment of Ottoman suzerainity. Like other Balkan states, the Moldavians stood independent from the Ottomans during the Ottoman interregnum of 1402–13. Moldavia was first attacked by the Ottomans in 1420 when Ottoman troops besieged Akkerman (Belgorod- Dnestrovsky) without success; however, an archival source testifies to the fact that the Moldavian *voievod* Petru Aron (r. 1454–55, 1455–57) acknowledged Ottoman supremacy again in 1455 when he was compelled to pay a yearly tax of 2,000 golden coins to the much stronger Ottoman state under MEHMED II (r. 1444–46; 1451–81). In 1456 Sultan Mehmed II promised Petru Aron that merchants in the Moldavian city of Akkerman could trade in the Ottoman cities of ISTANBUL, BURSA, and EDIRNE without restriction.

Petru's successor, Stephen the Great (Ştefan cel Mare) (r. 1457–1504), was also considered an Ottoman vassal but he maintained close connections with the Polish kingdom in the first years of his reign. From the mid 1470s onward he established still closer ties with the Hungarian king, Matthias I Corvinus (r. 1458–90). Alarmed by what the Ottomans perceived as a challenge to Ottoman control, Ottoman troops invaded Moldavia under the leadership of Hadım Süleyman Pasha, *beylerbeyi* (governor) of Rumelia. The *voievod* defeated them in the Battle of Vaslui on January 10, 1475. When the Ottomans besieged CAFFA, held by the Genoese, in June 1475, the *voievod* was again hostile to the sultan's action. A year later, in 1476, Stephen the Great took an oath of allegiance to the Hungarian king Matthias I Corvinus.

In an attempt to restrain his rebel vassal, Sultan Mehmed II himself went to war against the Moldavians in 1476, defeating their troops at Valea Albă (Războieni) on July 26. The sultan ransacked the country, burned its capital, Suceava, and then left Moldavia with a large amount of plunder. Mehmed II then prepared an AHDNAME, or letter of contract, expressing his willingness to recognize the *voievod* as his subject again if the latter paid a tax of 6,000 golden coins instead of the former 3,000. This document is of importance because it is the only extant *ahdname* given to the Romanian *voievods* by an Ottoman ruler.

Soon war broke out again between Moldavia and the Ottoman Empire and in 1484 BAYEZID II (r. 1481–1512) captured Akkerman and Kilia, two important fortresses in the DANUBE delta. As a result the *voievod*, Stephen the Great, began paying regular tribute. The voievodeship submitted completely to Ottoman suzerainty and suffered further territorial losses in 1538 when Sultan SÜLEYMAN I (r. 1520–66) conducted a campaign against the Moldavian *voievod* Petru Rareş (r. 1527–38, 1541–46).

From the first half of the 16th century, the Moldavian *voievods* were confirmed in their position by the Ottoman sultans. From this time onward it is likely that they were given not *ahdnames* but *berat-i şerif* (documents of appointment), in which sultans gave orders about the form of rule, the extent of taxes, gifts to be given to viziers, and the security of the property of the Muslims residing in the voievodeship. The *voievods* of Moldavia were appointed to the throne either by the sultan or by a body consisting of boyars (high-ranking aristocrats) and the Orthodox clergy. It was the sultan who had, without exception, the right of enthronement.

Upon appointment, the insignia of appointment and the *berat-i şerif* were presented to the *voievod* by a dignitary from the Porte. The symbols of sovereignty, delivered to the new governor as symbols of the sultan's authority, included a flag as well as two horse-tails. *Voievods* were obliged to offer hostages from among their family members, usually their sons, who were kept in custody either at the Sublime Porte or in the interior of the empire.

SHARIA, the Islamic sacred law, was not in use on the territory of the voievodeship, which was dominated by Christian Orthodoxy, and the territory was thus subject to the JIZYA, an Ottoman tax on adult male non-Muslims. The *jizya* in Moldavia in the 15th century was 2,000 golden coins; from1527–28, 6,000 to 10,000 coins; in 1538, 15,000 coins; in 1551, 25,000 coins; in 1568, 40,000 coins; and from 1574 to 1575, 50,000 coins. The largest sum ever collected as *jizya* from Moldavia was 60,000 golden coins in 1591–92. This was reduced to 5,600,000 akçe (equivalent to 37,333 golden coins) around 1620.

Despite the difference in religious culture between the Ottomans and the Moldavians, the principality sometimes demonstrated its sympathy with Islam, as is illustrated by the conversion of Voievod Iliaş II Rareş (r. 1546–51) to Islam during an audience with Sultan SÜLEYMAN I on May 30, 1551. To reward his faith, the sultan appointed Iliaş II *sancakbeyi* or district governor of Silistra. Iliaş was succeeded by his brother Ştefan (r. 1551–52).

During the long Habsburg-Ottoman War of 1593–1606, Moldavia again seceded from the Ottoman Empire for a short time and concluded an alliance with Sigismund Báthory (r. 1581–97, 1598–99, 1601–02), Prince of TRANSYLVANIA, who sided with the Habsburgs. The *voievod* of the neigboring principality of WALLACHIA, Mihai Viteazul (r. 1593–1601), conquered Moldavia for a short while after also occupying Transylvania, but the Sublime Porte succeeded again in incorporating Moldavia into the empire during the second reign of Voievod Ieremia Movilă (r. 1600–06). In the 17th century Voievod Gheorghe Ştefan (r. 1653–58), in alliance with Prince György II Rákóczi of Transylvania (r. 1648–60), again tried to thwart Ottoman control of the principality in a confrontation with the troops of Grand Vizier Köprülü Mehmed Pasha (1656–61), but the *voievod* later fled. At the beginning of the 18th century Voievod Dimitrie Cantemir (r. 1710–11) attempted a similar tactic, changing his allegiance to the Russian czar, Peter the Great (r. 1682–1725), but when the Ottomans again conquered his forces at the river Prut in 1711, the defeated *voievod* went to live on his estates in Russia. After the fall of Voievod Dimitrie Cantemir the Porte enthroned *voievods* from among the reliable sons of wealthy Greek families from the Greek quarter of Istanbul called Phanar.

In 1775 the Habsburg Empire took possession of the northwestern part of Moldavia, called Bukovina, and in 1812 the Russian Empire seized Bessarabia, the territory in the south. In the first half of the 19th century Russian influence increased until 1859 when Western powers assisted in uniting the two Romanian voievodeships—Moldavia and Wallachia—under the name of Memleketeyn. This union, however, remained an Ottoman protectorate. The final secession of the principalities from the Ottoman Empire was declared by the Treaty of Berlin in 1878, which proclaimed Romania a sovereign state.

Sándor Papp

Further reading: Mihai Maxim, *Romano-Ottomanica: Essays and Documents from the Turkish Archives* (Istanbul: ISIS, 2001); Andrei Oțetea, ed., *The History of the Romanian People* (Bucharest: Scientific Publishing House, 1970); Sándor Papp, "Christian Vassals on the Northwest Border of the Ottoman Empire," in *The Turcs*. Vol. III. *Ottomans* (Ankara: Yeni Türkiye Publications, 2002), 719–30; Peter Sugar, *Southeastern Europe under Ottoman Rule, 1354–1804* (Seattle: University of Washington Press, 1977).

money and monetary systems Until the 16th century, Ottoman territories in Anatolia and the Balkans had a unified monetary system based on three coins: the silver akçe, the gold sultani, and the copper mangir or pul. The akçe was considered the basic unit of payment, and was commonly used in local transactions. While the silver value of the coin fluctuated with changes within the Ottoman government, the standards of the gold sultani originally remained identical to gold coins of other states around the Mediterranean, such as the Venetian ducat. This changed at the end of the 17th century when Ottoman expansion began unifying various territories.

When describing the Ottoman monetary regime, it is useful to adopt the same definitions of monometallism and bimetallism that were used in the 19th century. Accordingly, a monetary regime is characterized as monometallism if there is one standard commodity against which others are measured, even if the latter is composed of several metallic and paper elements. In the case of the Ottoman Empire, the silver akçe provided the standard for the gold sultani and the copper mangir.

The Ottoman governments originally adopted an interventionist policy, meaning they took an active role in controlling and regulating their economic affairs. This attitude peaked during the reign of the centralizing sultan MEHMED II (r. 1444–46; 1451–81). The state created detailed law codes (*kanunname*) covering different spheres of life during this period, and Mehmed II issued a large number of laws to regulate mint activity, the operation of mines producing gold and silver, and the circulation and transportation of specie (coin) in Ottoman lands. There are a number of reasons why these codes present a misleading picture of Ottoman practices with regard to monetary issues. For one thing, the reign of Mehmed II was exceptional in terms of its monetary conditions. The Ottoman lands, together with much of Europe, faced severe shortages of specie during the second half of the 15th century. These conditions allowed the Ottoman ruler to declare the aforementioned codes and practices, many of which are among the most interventionist in Ottoman history. Many of the codes dealing with monetary issues were rarely, if ever, enforced during subsequent periods.

Interventions in the economy also did not guarantee that the government would see the desired outcome. Premodern states did not have the capability to intervene in markets comprehensively and effectively, especially with short-term borrowing and lending within money markets. In comparison to goods markets and long-distance trade, it was more difficult for governments to control physical supplies of specie and regulate prices. Ottoman administrators were well aware that participants in the money markets, merchants, moneychangers, and financiers were able to evade state rules and regulations more easily than those in the commodity markets. After noting that interventionism did not guarantee success, government interference in money markets became more selective after the reign of Mehmed II, occurring mostly during periods of extreme monetary turbulence or war. On the whole, Ottoman monetary practices shifted to an attitude of flexibility and pragmatism after the 15th century.

One of the most telling examples of Ottoman pragmatism concerned the determination of exchange rates between different kinds of coinage. In an environment of frequently recurring shortages of specie, the Ottoman administrators knew that it was essential to attract into the Ottoman lands and maintain in circulation as much coinage and bullion as possible. Their monetary practices were guided more by this concern than by any other. They were also aware that the ratio between gold and silver as well as the value of different types of coins was subject to fluctuations. Under these conditions, a policy of fixed exchange rates between different coins would have driven the good or undervalued coins out of circulation. The government allowed local markets to determine not only the exchange rate for the sultani but that for all types of coins, Ottoman and foreign. Additionally, the government announced the official rates at which different coins, gold and silver, would be accepted as payment. Usually these rates did not diverge significantly from the prevailing market rates for the same coins.

As the Ottoman state expanded territorially to become a full-fledged empire, however, this simple system could not be continued. Newly conquered territories, each of which was subject to different economic forces and very different patterns of trade, already had well-established currency systems of their own. The Ottomans pursued a two-tiered approach to money and currency in these areas. They unified the gold coinage at the existing international standards but allowed the creation of multiple currency zones in silver to account for the sharply different commercial relations and needs of the new provinces.

In gold coinage, the sultani became the only Ottoman coin across the empire. This was due to both symbolic and economic reasons. With a single gold coin, the ultimate symbol of sovereignty, the Ottomans unified the empire from the Balkans to EGYPT and the Maghrib. The standards of the sultani, its weight and fineness, were kept identical to those of the Venetian ducat that had become the accepted standard of payment in long distance trade across the Mediterranean and beyond. Whether or not Ottoman gold coinage was issued in a given territory depended upon the territory's status—if it was part of the empire proper or was considered a province with some degree of autonomy. Thus the sultani was issued regularly in the controlled areas of Egypt, ALGIERS, TUNIS, as well as the Balkans and Anatolia, but it was never minted in the autonomous Danubian principalities of WALLACHIA and MOLDAVIA.

In terms of silver coinage, used in daily transactions and to some extent in long-distance trade, the central government chose to continue with the existing monetary units in the newly conquered territories with or without modifications. The most important reason for this preference was the wish to avoid economic disruption and possible popular unrest. It was also not clear whether the central government had the fiscal, administrative, and economic resources to unify the silver coinage of the empire. As a result, while the silver coinage minted in the new territories began to bear the name of the sultan, their designs and standards as well as the names of the currencies adhered to pre-Ottoman forms and usages in many instances. Earlier styles and types of copper coinage were also continued. In addition to the akçe in the Balkans and Anatolia, the para or medin became the Ottoman silver coin and unit of account in Egypt, the shahi in present-day Iraq and other areas neighboring Iran, and the square nasri in Tunis. These silver coins were issued by the local Ottoman mints. They were regularly exchanged against each other or against Ottoman gold coins at the market rates of exchange. The Ottoman governments also allowed and even encouraged the circulation of foreign coinage.

CHALLENGES FOR MONETARY POLICY

Even with pragmatism and flexibility, the Ottomans faced significant challenges. They dealt with problems common to all medieval and early modern states, such as maintaining a stable flow of coinage that depended on minting metals such as gold and silver. If a region experienced a trade deficit, specie flowed out and the money supply was adversely affected. Similarly, if citizens lacked confidence in the market or feared an unstable economy, they would often hoard these precious metals, which caused a decrease in money supply. Most of the medieval and early modern states were in fact subject to recurring shortages of specie, which had negative consequences on the economy. The Ottomans were no different.

The Ottomans also faced a number of other challenges arising from the size of the empire and its location at the crossroads of intercontinental trade. From the Balkans to EGYPT, from the CAUCASUS to the Maghrib, different regions of the empire were drawn into various commercial relations. The Balkans, for example, engaged in trade with central and eastern Europe and across the BLACK SEA. Egypt, on the other hand, was linked to the Indian Ocean and the trade of South and Southeast Asia. These far-reaching commercial linkages made it very difficult to control the movements of specie and maintain monetary stability.

In addition, the Ottoman Empire happened to be located on major trade routes between Asia and Europe. Ever since the discoveries of major silver deposits in Bohemia and HUNGARY in the 12th century, Europe tended to import more commodities from Asia such as spices, silk, textiles, and other goods, while Asia requested specie in return. Adding to this volume was the large amounts of gold and silver arriving from the newly "discovered" American continents. As the Ottomans began to establish control over the major trade routes in the eastern Mediterranean in the second half of the 15th century, they welcomed the arrival of specie from the West. At the same time, they could not prevent the outflow of specie to the East, and consequently felt pressure from the flux in the commodity and specie exchanges.

When the Ottoman Empire went into a state of decline in the 16th century, their monetary difficulties reflected their underlying economic and fiscal realities.

With the growing economic strength and commercial presence of Europe contrasting the Ottoman's loss of power, it was becoming increasingly difficult to control the large fluctuations in commodity and specie flows to maintain a stable monetary system. Ottoman difficulties were compounded by the recurrence of fiscal crises. In the face of these difficulties, the Ottoman governments had mixed success in their attempts to maintain monetary stability.

LATER CHANGES IN THE MONETARY REGIME

During the 17th century the local mints were closed down and the silver *akçe* ceased to exist as a means of exchange due to both global monetary disorder and Ottoman fiscal difficulties. In contrast, the 18th century until the 1780s was a period of commercial and economic expansion coupled with fiscal stability. These favorable conditions as well as the rising supplies of silver helped the Ottomans establish a new currency, the large gurush or piaster, as the leading unit of account and means of exchange. The emergence of the new unit was accompanied by centralization of mint activity in the core regions of the empire, from the Balkans to Anatolia, as well as SYRIA and Iraq. In contrast to the 17th century, when the ties between ISTANBUL and the currencies in different parts of the empire, Egypt, Tripoli, Tunis, and Algiers had weakened substantially if not dissolved altogether, these ties recovered and even strengthened during the 18th century.

For the Ottoman Empire the 19th century was a period of integration into world markets and rapid expansion in foreign trade, particularly with Europe. It was also characterized by major efforts at Western-style reform (*see* TANZIMAT) in administration, education, law, and justice as well as economic, fiscal, and monetary affairs. As part of these efforts, the Ottoman government adopted in 1844 the bimetallic standard as its new monetary regime. Under this system, the silver gurush or piaster and the new gold lira were both accepted as legal tender, freely convertible at the fixed rate of 100 gurush for one gold lira. In 1881, along with the re-settlement of its existing external debt, the Ottoman government abandoned the bimetallic standard and moved toward the gold standard but silver continued to play a significant role in the new system until WORLD WAR I.

DEBASEMENTS

Debasements, or the reduction of the specie content of the currency by the monetary authority, were the most contentious and controversial practices of the Ottoman government related to money. By far the most important motivation for the Ottoman debasements was the fiscal relief they provided to the state. Since the obligations of the state, to the soldiers, bureaucrats, and suppliers are expressed in terms of the monetary unit of account, a reduction in the silver content of the currency enabled the state to increase the amount it could mint from or the payments it could make with a given amount of silver. As a result, debasements were utilized as an alternative to additional taxation.

Prices almost always rose in the aftermath of debasements because a debasement typically increased the nominal value of coinage in circulation. Even if prices did not rise quickly because of the shortages of specie or some other reason, long-distance trade acted as the ultimate equalizer in the long term. If prices expressed in grams of silver in a given region became less expensive compared to neighboring areas, increased demand for the lower priced commodities attracted large quantities of silver, thus raising prices.

Debasements had an impact on virtually all groups in Ottoman society and in turn each group took a position on the matter. Most men and women at the time were clear about the consequences of different ways of dealing with the coinage, who gained and who lost. In general, those who had future obligations expressed in terms of the unit of account, most importantly borrowers and tenants paying fixed rents in cash, stood to gain from debasements. However, debasements generated powerful opposition among urban groups, especially in the capital city. One group that disliked debasements included guild members, shopkeepers, and small merchants as well as wage-earning artisans. Another group that stood to lose from debasements was made of those who were paid fixed salaries by the state, the bureaucracy, the ULEMA, and specially the JANISSARIES stationed permanently in the capital. There was a large overlap between the guild members and the Janissaries since the latter had begun to moonlight as artisans and shopkeepers. This broad opposition acted as a major deterrent against the more frequent use of debasements by the government not only in the capital but also in the provincial centers. The effectiveness of this urban opposition against debasements should not be measured in terms of the frequency of their rebellions, however. Ultimately, the threat of rebellions was just as effective. It ensured that the governments would refrain from debasements at least during periods of peace. The timing of Ottoman debasements confirms this picture. Most Ottoman debasements occurred during three distinct periods: the reign of the empire builder, Mehmed II, during the second half of the 15th century when debasements were undertaken methodically once every 10 years to finance military campaigns; during 1580 to 1650, a period of fiscal and monetary instability; and from 1788 to 1840, when the Ottomans had to deal with frequent wars and costs of military and other reform. The largest Ottoman debasements and highest rates of inflation occurred during this last period, especially after the abolition of the Janissaries in 1826. The silver content of Ottoman currency was quite stable in other periods.

Şevket Pamuk

See also BANKS AND BANKING; ECONOMY AND ECONOMIC POLICY; FINANCES AND FISCAL STRUCTURE.

Further reading: Sevket Pamuk, *A Monetary History of the Ottoman Empire* (Cambridge: Cambridge University Press, 2000); Halil Sahillioğlu, "The Role of International Monetary and Metal Movements in Ottoman Monetary History," in *Precious Metals in the Later Medieval and Early Modern Worlds*, edited by J. F. Richards (Durham, North Carolina: Carolina Academic Press, 1983), 269–304.

mosaic *See* CERAMICS.

mosque *See* ARCHITECTURE.

Mosul (*Ar.:* al-Mawsil; *Turk.:* Musul) Mosul, a city in present-day IRAQ, served in the Ottoman period as the capital of a province, also called Mosul. The province had a diverse population made up of SUNNI Arabs, Turkomans, KURDS, various Christian denominations, and JEWS. The city's economic importance lay in the agricultural produce of its hinterlands, a region known to the Arabs as the *jazira* (literally, "island") that consists of the fertile lands between the upper Tigris and EUPHRATES rivers. Mosul also served as a major trade center on the route that connected the Mediterranean to the Persian Gulf. The city was strategically important to the Ottomans both as a military outpost to control the Kurdish tribes to the north of the city and to defend the empire from its archrival, IRAN.

Mosul, like most of Iraq, came under the rule of the Iranian shah, Ismail Safavi, in the first decade of the 16th century. Sultan SELIM I moved against Shah Ismail in 1512 and defeated his army at the Battle of Çaldiran. That victory diminished the immediate threat that the shah posed to the sultan in Anatolia, but it was not until 1517 that Ottoman armies gained control of Mosul. Central and southern Iraq continued to be ruled by Iran, however, and Mosul remained a frontier garrison city until 1534, when Sultan SÜLEYMAN I (r. 1520–66) conquered BAGHDAD.

That victory did not secure Iraq for the Ottomans. In 1623 Persian armies again captured Baghdad and moved north to occupy Mosul. Although the Ottomans recovered Mosul in 1625, Baghdad remained in Persian hands until 1638. Once again Mosul became a garrison town with an estimated 3,000 JANISSARUES in resi-

dence during the 1631 campaign against the Persians. At the time, the city had no more than 20,000 civilian inhabitants.

In the 18th century, the Jalili family came to dominate the politics of the city and province of Mosul. The resilience of the family rested in part in its ability to secure Mosul from Iranian threats. Husayn Jalili, who had come from a humble merchant background, mounted a spirited defense of his native city against Nadir Khan, later NADIR SHAH, the military ruler of Iran, in 1733 and again in 1743. Jalili's son and grandson continued to hold the governorship of the city for most of the years between 1743 and 1807. The success of the family, ironically, led to its downfall. With few other competitors for political supremacy in Mosul, the family split into two contending factions by the middle of the 18th century. Whereas the city's population had once almost universally viewed the Jalilis as the champions of Mosul, with the emergence of this infighting, the family was increasingly seen as oppressive and corrupt. In 1826, riots in the city overthrew Yahya al-Jalili, who was then governor, and political unrest plagued the region until Ottoman control in the province was restored in 1834. Although no longer in political control, the Jalilis continued to remain one of the city's prominent land-owning families into the 20th century.

Mosul rarely impressed foreign visitors to the Ottoman Empire; Europeans invariably described it as a dirty and drab place, with few of the architectural wonders they noted in some of the empire's major cities. But they also remarked on the diverse population of the city, which included a significant minority of Christians. The majority of these had originally been NESTORIANS but this group split in the 17th century in a dispute over who was properly thereligious head of the community. Those in the Mosul area eventually accepted the pope in Rome as their spiritual head and took the name Chaldeans, while those who remained loyal to the traditional leadership called themselves Assyrians, after British archaeological teams in the Mosul region began to uncover the ruins of ancient Nineveh.

By the end of the Ottoman period in the early 20th century, the population of the city of Mosul had grown to about 90,000. After WORLD WAR I, the city and its hinterlands became hotly contested territory, with the French claiming they should belong to their Syrian mandate, while the British claimed the region for the newly established Kingdom of Iraq. The newly formed Turkish Republic also claimed the region as it said the population of the province, consisting as it did of Kurds, Turkomans, and others, did not have an Arab majority. That claim, however, was contested by Arab nationalists who said that the city itself and much of the hinterlands were occupied by Arabic-speaking Sunni Muslims and Christians. In 1924 the League of Nations ruled in favor of the Kingdom of Iraq.

Bruce Masters

Further reading: Dina Rizk Khoury, *State and Provincial Society in the Ottoman Empire: Mosul, 1540–1834* (Cambridge: Cambridge University Press, 1997); Sarah Shields, *Mosul Before Iraq: Like Bees Making Five-Sided Cells* (Albany: State University of New York Press, 2000).

Mount Lebanon *See* LEBANON.

mufti *See* ŞEYHÜLISLAM.

Muhammad Ali *See* MEHMED ALI.

Mühendishane Founded in the spring of 1775 as Hendesehane (Mathematical School) and renamed Mühendishane (Engineering School) in 1781, this institution served as the principal imperial military engineering school of the Ottomans until the mid-19th century, when the shifting social and political goals of the empire resulted in major restructuring of the EDUCATION system.

Many foreigners, particularly Frenchmen, served in the Ottoman army during this period. One of these, Baron de Tott, (1733–93) was influential in founding two schools teaching new artillery techniques: Topçu Mektebi (Artillery School), founded in 1772, and Sürat Topçuları Ocağı (Corps of Rapid-fire Artillerymen), founded in 1774.

The first Ottoman institution that offered instruction in mathematics and military engineering, Hendesehane, or the School of Mathematics, was founded on April 29, 1775 upon the request of Hasan Pasha, admiral of the navy, under the supervision of Baron de Tott. Here the French military engineer M. Kermovan, and Campbell Mustafa Agha, a Scottish convert to Islam, instructed students in groups of 10 in mathematics courses until October 1775. Seyyid Hasan, an Algerian who was second captain in the Ottoman NAVY, became the first non-European head teacher at Hendesehane.

Hendesehane was the nucleus of the military and civil engineering schools established by the Ottomans in the 18th century, adopting the new sciences that were then becoming prevalent in Europe as the mainstay of its curriculum. It became the first institution in the empire to provide a professional engineering education. Beginning in 1781, Hendesehane was renamed Mühendishane (Engineering School). Located in the TERSANE-I AMIRE (imperial shipyard), Mühendishane provided courses in both naval engineering and military engineering for min-

ers and bombardiers. In 1784, as a result of an alliance between the Ottoman Empire and FRANCE, two French engineers, André-Joseph Lafitte-Clavé and Joseph Bagriel Monnier, became instructors at Mühendishane, sent by the French government to Istanbul to strengthen the Ottoman military. In addition to these foreign instructors, madrasa teachers were also employed in Mühendishane as instructors. Until the end of 18th century the textbooks of Mühendishane—on mathematics, astronomy, engineering, weapons, war techniques, and navigation—mostly originated from Europe, and from France in particular. Upon the destruction of the Franco-Ottoman alliance in 1778, all foreign instructors left Istanbul and were replaced by Ottoman madrasa teachers.

After Sultan SELIM III (r. 1789–1807), who was known as a reformist sultan, came to the throne in 1789, naval and land engineering training was changed and the miner and bombardier corps were reformed. Mathematical and engineering instruction began at a new engineering school founded in 1793 named Mühendishane-i Cedide (New Engineering School) or Mühendishane-i Sultani (Imperial Engineering School), located next to the barracks in Istanbul. Courses began in 1794. The courses were generally taught by Ottoman graduates of the French-operated schools.

In 1795 construction began on a new school with classes, a library, and a printing house in Hasköy. When construction was completed in 1797, candidates selected from the Corps of Miners (Lağımcı Ocağı) and Corps of Bombardiers (Humbaracı Ocağı) resumed their engineering education in this new building. The same year, seven land engineers in the engineering school in the imperial shipyards were transferred to the New Engineering School in Hasköy, a quarter in the European part of Istanbul. The naval engineers in the shipyard institution continued their instruction in two branches, ship construction and navigation, under the supervision of French naval engineer Jacques B. Le Brun.

In 1801–02, upon the transfer of students from the Mimaran-ı Hassa Ocağı (State Architecture Corps) to the Corps of Miners and Corps of Bombardiers, all land engineers matriculated at the same institution. Studies took four years to complete and included courses in technical drawing, Arabic, geometry, calculus, integral equations, French, geography, trigonometry, algebra, mechanics, the history of war, and astronomy.

In 1806, at the command of Sultan Selim III, the engineering schools became independent of the Corps of Miners, Corps of Bombardiers, and the Imperial Arsenal Shipyard, beginning a new period in engineering education. The existing pedagogical and administrative structures were rearranged and a modern technical education order emerged. The engineering schools were renamed the Mühendishane-i Berr-i

Humayun (Imperial Military Engineering School) and the Mühendishane-i Bahri-i Humayun (Imperial Naval Engineering School).

With the establishment of the Bahriye Mektebi (Naval School) in 1828 and of the Mekteb-i Harbiye (School of War) in 1834 in Heybeliada (near Istanbul), the increasing need for educated military officers began to be met, leading to the gradual decrease in the significance of the old engineering schools. With the increasing need for engineering services for public works, civil engineering education began in Hendesehane-i Mülkiye (Civilian School of Engineering) as a part of Mühendishane-i Bahri-i Humayun in 1874. In 1881 Mühendishane-i Bahri-i Humayun was incorporated in the Topçu Mektebi (Artillery School) and integrated with the existing School of War. Thus the military side of the engineering schools became the nucleus of military education institutions such as the Land School of War and Naval School of War, and their civil side became the nucleus of the technical universities in present-day republican Turkey, mainly Istanbul Technical University, founded in July 1944.

Sevtap Kadıoğlu

Further reading: Kemal Beydilli, *Türk Bilim ve Matbaacılık Tarihinde Mühendishâne: Mühendishane Matbaası ve Kütüphanesi* (Mühendishane in Turkish Science and Printing History: Mühendishane Printhouse and Library) (1776–1826) (Istanbul: Eren, 1995); Mustafa Kaçar, "The Development in the Attitude of the Ottoman State Towards Science and Education and the Establishment of the Engineering Schools (Muhendishanes)," *Proceedings of the International Congress of History of Science (Liège, 20–26 July 1997)* vol. 6, *Science, Technology and Industry in the Ottoman World*, edited by E. İhsanoğlu, Ahmed Djebbar, and Feza Günergun (Turnhout, Belgium: Brepols Publisher, 2000), 81–90.

muhtasib* and *ihtisab *See* IHTISAB AND MUHTASIB.

***mukataa* (*muqataah, maktu*)** The term *mukataa* was used in the Ottoman financial administration for tax farms or renting contracts and for state revenues divided into smaller revenue portions whose collection was farmed out to individuals for a mutually agreed-upon price.. The practice of dividing state revenues into smaller revenue units (*mukataas*) and farming them out to tax farmers profited the state in more than one way. First, the state acquired large sums of cash paid by the tax farmers at the beginning of their terms. Second, the state was able to better calculate its revenues because the yearly sums that tax farmers had to pay into the state treasury were fixed in the contract concluded with the tax farmer.

And last but not least, by farming out the collection of revenues from designated *mukataas* to tax farmers, the state was able to reduce the number of state employees. On the other hand, the tax farmers acquired lucrative state revenue sources for a set period of time.

The revenue sources that could be turned into *mukataas* were wide-ranging, including economic activities such as customs, mints, and state-owned lands. In farming out a *mukataa* the payment schedule was first to be considered, but the nature of the revenues, the geographical features, and certain other aspects were also taken into account. *Mukataas* were usually lucrative economic enterprises, but *hans* (commercial buildings), shops, and public baths were also called *mukataa* once they were rented out. The process of tax collection in *mukataas* was carried out within the boundaries of the province where the *mukataa* was located and the collection was conducted in accordance with the stipulations of provincial regulations. The income obtained from *mukataas* was registered in the BUDGETS.

Mukataas were held with unrestricted freedom by private entrepreneurs and thus were legally secure from any interference by outsiders except for the representatives of the state. As a further upshot of this freedom, the *mukataa*-holders were authorized to collect such unrelated taxes as fines and traditional fees.

Baki Çakır

See also ECONOMY AND ECONOMIC POLICY; TAX FARMING.

Further reading: Halil İnalcık, *An Economic and Social History of the Ottoman Empire* (Cambridge: Cambridge University Press, 1994); Haim Gerber, "Mukataa," in *Encyclopaedia of Islam*, CD-ROM edition (Leiden: Brill, 1999), 508a.

mültezim *See* TAX FARMING.

Murad I (b. 1326?–d. 1389) (r. 1362–1389) *third ruler (emir and sultan) of the Ottoman state, conqueror of the Balkans* Murad, son of ORHAN (r. 1324–62), the second ruler of the House of Osman, and Nilüfer, the daughter of the Byzantine lord of Yarhisar in northwestern Anatolia, became the third ruler of the Ottoman principality in 1362. Although most Ottomanist historians would not regard him as sultan, or sovereign, the Ottoman chronicler Ahmedi, a contemporary of Murad, and a dedicatory inscription dated from 1388, mentioned Murad as sultan. He was the first Ottoman ruler with major conquests in the Balkans, called Rumelia by the Ottomans. By the time of his death in 1389 the Ottomans had more than tripled the territories under their direct rule, reaching some 100,000 square miles (as compared to 29,000 square miles under Orhan), evenly distributed in Europe and Asia Minor. In addition to these direct conquests, several Christian rulers and lords in the Balkans (the Byzantine emperors; the despot of Mistra; the Bulgarian czar of Turnovo; and, by 1389, Stephan Lazarević, the son and successor of the defeated and killed despot Lazar of SERBIA, among others) had become Ottoman vassals who had to pay tributes and provide troops to the Ottomans when called upon. Murad I's reign was also important regarding the evolution of conquest methods and military and governmental institutions.

METHODS OF CONQUEST

Later Ottoman chroniclers called Murad a *ghazi*, suggesting that he expanded the Ottoman principality by GHAZA, that is, by religiously inspired holy war against the Ottomans' Christian neighbors, although by the term *ghaza* contemporaries also meant predatory raids without any religious motive. Murad's successes were due as much to other techniques of conquest as to his military invasions. There were three particularly important methods of conquest.

The first was dynastic marriages concluded with Christian and Muslim lords of the Balkans and the Anatolian Turkoman principalities, by which the Ottomans acquired new territories and military assistance, and subjugated their allies into vassalages. The Bulgarian czardom of Turnovo, for instance, became a vassal following Murad's marriage to Thamar, the sister of Czar Shishman. Parts of the Turkoman principality of Germiyan in western Asia Minor (*see* ANATOLIAN EMIRATES) came with the dowry of the princess of Germiyan, married to Murad's son BAYEZID I (in ca. 1375 or 1381), although in both cases Ottoman military pressure also played a role.

The second method was spontaneous migration, as well as state-organized resettlements (*sürgün*) of Turkoman nomads from Asia Minor to the Balkans, by which Murad and his successors increased the number of their Turkic-speaking loyal Muslim subjects in a hostile, Slavic-speaking Christian environment.

The third method was granting Ottoman military fiefs (*timars*) to members of the Christian nobility in the Balkans, in return for their acceptance of Ottoman suzerainty. By this method the Ottomans gained supporters and collaborators, while the Balkan Christian lords preserved parts of their former lands.

INSTITUTIONAL DEVELOPMENTS

Murad I's reign also witnessed the establishment of several institutions that were crucial for the strengthening of the Ottoman military and administration. Ottoman chroniclers credit Murad's statesman Kara (Black) Halil Hayreddin Pasha (d. 1387), of the influential Çandarlı family with the establishment of the *yaya* (pedestrian)

infantry and later (in the 1370s, or perhaps earlier) that of the corps of the JANISSARIES, the ruler's bodyguard that soon evolved into a professional elite infantry, the first standing army in contemporary Europe. The child levy (DEVŞIRME) system, which was the recruiting method of the Janissaries and, increasingly, of state bureaucrats, was also introduced under Murad I, perhaps in the 1380s. Çandarlı Kara Halil Hayreddin Pasha was also the first to occupy the newly created post of *kadıasker*, or supreme judge. Since he was also a vizier he simultaneously oversaw the administration and the military and is rightly considered as the first *de facto* Ottoman grand vizier, that is, first minister and absolute deputy of the sultan. In connection with the Ottoman advance in the Balkans, Murad I also appointed his tutor (*lala*) and general Lala Şahin Pasha as the first *beylerbeyi*, or governor general, of Rumelia, thus establishing the first Ottoman governorship in the Balkans.

ACCESSION TO THE THRONE

Murad's older brother, Süleyman Pasha, was the heir presumptive. He had established the first Ottoman base in the Balkans by occupying the Byzantine fort of Tzympe, southwest of Gallipoli on the European shore of the Dardanelles in 1352. Using the opportunity of a devastating earthquake that demolished the walls of several Byzantine towns in the Gallipoli peninsula in 1354, he occupied Gallipoli, thus establishing an Ottoman bridgehead in Europe. However, his death in 1357 opened the way to the Ottoman throne for Murad. Following the death of his father in spring 1362, Murad acceded to the Ottoman throne in BURSA, winning the civil war against his younger brothers and their supporters, the Anatolian Turkoman emirs, or lords, of Karaman and Eretna.

ADVANCES IN ANATOLIA

Murad was fighting in Anatolia until about 1365 in order to stabilize his rule there. Ottoman chroniclers claim that he later (in about 1375 or 1381) acquired the territories of the neighboring Turkoman principalities of Germiyan and Hamid in western and southwestern Anatolia by marriage and purchase, respectively. However, other sources suggest that Ottoman campaigns preceded these events.

Murad's acquisitions brought him in contact with the Karamanids, the most powerful Turkoman emirate in Anatolia, who also claimed some of the territories recently annexed by Murad. The Karamanids' stance against Ottoman expansion in Asia Minor suggests that dynastic marriages, used extensively by the Ottomans to win over possible rival Turkoman emirs and to subjugate Balkan Christian rulers, did not always work. Murad I tried to win over Alaeddin (r. 1361–98) of Karaman by marrying his daughter, Nilüfer, to the Karaman ruler. The latter, however, challenged his father-in-law repeatedly, and Murad had to launch a campaign against him in 1386. The battle, fought in late 1386 near Ankara, the capital of present-day Turkey, proved the superiority of the highly organized Ottoman military over the more traditional nomad army of the Karamanids, and earned Murad's son Prince Bayezid the sobriquet Yıldırım (Thunderbolt) for his bravery as a fighter. Thanks to his Ottoman wife, Alaeddin of Karaman escaped the confrontation with minimal damage and loss of territory, ceding Beyşehir on the western border of Karaman to Murad. This in turn opened the passes of the Taurus Mountains for the Ottomans and enabled Murad to seize (in 1386 or 1388) the small Turkoman emirate of Teke, south of Hamid. By annexing these territories, Murad gained control over the lucrative trade routs connecting his capital Bursa with Antalya, the Mediterranean seaport in southwestern Anatolia.

CONQUESTS IN EUROPE

While Murad was fighting in Anatolia in his early years to stabilize his rule there, his generals Lala Şahin and Evrenos Bey captured several towns in the Balkans. By about 1369 the Ottomans had conquered northern and central Thrace, including such important cities as Adrianople (Edirne, European Turkey) in 1369 and Philippopolis (Filibe, Plovdiv in southern Bulgaria) either in late 1369 or in early 1370, although these early dates are often uncertain. Following later Ottoman chronicles, Turkish historians suggest that Adrianople was conquered in 1361 by Prince Murad and Lala Şahin Pasha, whereas European and Greek sources and historians suggest that it was not until 1369 that Murad captured the city. In any event, Edirne soon became the new capital and seat of government and the possession of the city at the confluence of the Maritsa and Tundzha Rivers gave the Ottomans access to Thrace and Bulgaria.

Ottoman advances in the Balkans alarmed Byzantium and the Balkan rulers. In August 1366 the allies of Byzantine emperor John V Palaiologos (r. 1341, 1354–91)—Amedeao of Savoy, the emperor's cousin, and Francesco Gattilusio, the Genoese ruler of the northeastern Aegean island of Lesbos and the emperor's brother-in-law—managed to reconquer Gallipoli from the Ottomans. This made crossing the Straits of the Dardanelles more difficult for Ottoman troops, although only temporarily, for Murad regained control over the city in 1376 during a Byzantine civil war.

The Serbian lords (despots) of Macedonia also challenged the Ottomans in 1371, perhaps recognizing the danger that the Ottoman conquest of Adrianople posed, but were defeated and killed at the battle of Çirmen on the Maritsa river. Their sons had to accept Ottoman suzerainty. The Ottoman victory in 1371 opened the way to western Thrace and the Macedonian lowlands, which

Murad's men conquered as far as Samakov (southeast of Sofia, Bulgaria) in the north by about 1375.

Murad masterfully exploited the civil war in Byzantium. This started in 1373 when Emperor John V's son Andronicus and Murad's son Savcı both rebelled against their fathers. They were defeated and blinded. However, in 1376, with Genoese and Ottoman help, Andronicus captured the Byzantine capital Constantinople, imprisoning his father and his younger brother and the future emperor Manuel. In return for Ottoman assistance, he ceded Gallipoli to Murad. Andronicus' reign did not last long. John V regained his throne and capital in 1379 with Ottoman help, and he too became Murad's vassal.

The troubles with Byzantium did not end there. In 1382 John V's younger son Manuel, who refused to accept Ottoman suzerainty, left Constantinople for SALONIKA, where he established an independent court and attacked the Ottomans. Led by Murad's vizier Çandarlı Kara Halil Hayreddin Pasha, the Ottomans laid siege to the city in 1383, which after several years of blockade surrendered in 1387.

By this time, much of southern Macedonia was in Ottoman hands. The Ottomans also advanced against Bulgaria and Serbia, where Murad conquered Sofia and Niš in 1385. This latter conquest opened the way to Prince Lazar's Serbia, which the Ottomans attacked repeatedly in the following years. However, in 1387 Lazar defeated them at Pločnik, near Niš. The next year the Ottomans suffered another setback when King Trvtko of Bosnia, whose territories between Serbia and the Adriatic the Ottomans had also raided, defeated the invaders. This in turn forced Murad to lead his armies in person against the Serbs in 1389. Although the BATTLE OF KOSOVO POLJE near present-day Priština (June 15, 1389) ended with Ottoman victory, both Murad and Lazar lost their lives. Murad's son BAYEZID I (r. 1389–1402), present in the battle, assumed power, whereas Stephan Lazarević, son of the dead Serbian ruler, became Bayezid's vassal.

To what extent Ottoman conquests and successes were due to Murad's personal skills and policy is difficult to tell. While his qualities as a military commander and ruler cannot be denied, it seems that the Turkish marcher (frontier) lords, especially Evrenos in Macedonia and the Mihaloğlus in Bulgaria, played crucial roles in pushing the borders of the expanding Ottoman state further and further. Similarly, Murad's generals Lala Şahin and Çandarlı Kara Halil Hayreddin Pasha and, after his death in 1387, his son Ali Pasha, were instrumental in Murad's military conquests. Their service in shaping the military and administrative institutions of the growing Ottoman state, whose administrative structure had become more complex and centralized by the end of Murad's reign, was also of great significance.

Gábor Ágoston

Further reading: Halil İnalcık, *"Ottoman Methods of Conquest" Studia Islamica* 2 (1954): 104–29, reprinted in Halil İnalcık, *The Ottoman Empire: Conquest, Organization and Economy: Collected Studies* (London: Variorum Reprints, 1978) with original pagination; Colin Imber, *The Ottoman Empire, 1300–1481* (Istanbul: Isis, 1990), 26–36; Cemal Kafadar, *Between Two Worlds: The Construction of the Ottoman State* (Berkeley: University of California Press, 1995); Heath W. Lowry, *The Nature of the Early Ottoman State* (Albany: State University of New York Press, 2003).

Murad II (b. 1404–d. 1451) (r. 1421–1444; 1446–1451) *Ottoman sultan* The son of MEHMED I (r. 1413–21) and one of his concubines, Murad was born in June 1404 in Amasya. At the beginning of his reign he had to deal with two pretenders to the throne ("False" Mustafa, that is, his uncle, and his own younger brother Prince Mustafa) supported by the BYZANTINE EMPIRE and VENICE. He also had to confront the ANATOLIAN EMIRATES of Germiyan, Karaman, Menteşe, and Isfendiyaroğulları, which all rejected Ottoman suzerainty and occupied Ottoman territories. The most dangerous threat, however, came from European crusaders led by the Hungarians who in the winter of 1443–44, in response to Ottoman encroachments in the previous years, invaded Murad's Balkan lands as far as Sofia, BULGARIA. After he had overcome these threats and concluded treaties with HUNGARY and Karaman (1444), in a hitherto unprecedented move Murad abdicated in favor of his 12-year-old son MEHMED II (r. 1444–46; 1451–81). However he was soon recalled by his trusted grand vizier Çandarlı Halil Pasha to command the Ottoman troops against the crusaders—who, despite the recently concluded truce, launched a new campaign in the autumn of 1444—and to quell the insurrection of the JANISSARIES, the sultan's elite infantry. Eventually Murad assumed the throne for a second time (1446). The crises of 1444–46 were as dangerous as those of the interregnum and civil war of 1402–13, and threatened the very existence of the Ottoman state. Using sheer military force and a variety of political tools (diplomacy, appeasement, vassalage, marriage contracts), Murad not only saved the Ottoman state from possible collapse but during his second reign (1446–51) he also consolidated Ottoman rule in the Balkans and Asia Minor. Murad II left a stable and strong state to his son Mehmed II, who during his second reign (1451–81) transformed it into a major regional empire.

ACCESSION AND POLITICAL TURMOIL

When he was 12 years of age, Murad was sent to Amasya as prince-governor to administer the province of Rum (north-central Turkey). He helped to consolidate his father's rule after the civil war (1402–13), and fought against the rebel Börklüce Mustafa. With his commanders he also conquered the Black Sea coastal town of Samsun from the Isfendiyaroğulları Turkish emirate. Murad was only 17 when his father died. Mehmed I's viziers concealed the sultan's death until Murad arrived in the old capital, BURSA, and was proclaimed sultan (June 1421).

Murad II's viziers refused to comply with the agreement Mehmed I had made with the Byzantine emperor Manuel II Palaiologos (r. 1391–1425). According to that agreement, upon Mehmed I's death Murad was to be acknowledged as Mehmed's successor and was to rule from the capital EDIRNE in the European part of the empire while his brother Mustafa was to remain in Anatolia. Their younger brothers (Yusuf and Mahmud, aged eight and seven) were to be handed over to Manuel. The emperor was to keep them (along with Mehmed I's brother Mustafa) in custody in Constantinople and receive an annual sum for their upkeep. Since the viziers refused to hand over princes Yusuf and Mahmud to the Byzantines, Emperor Manuel released from his custody Prince Mustafa (Mehmed's brother) and Cüneyd (the former emir of Aydın who had rebelled against Mehmed I). "False" Mustafa, as Ottoman chroniclers dubbed Murad II's uncle, soon defeated Murad II's troops and captured the Ottoman capital, Edirne, where he proclaimed himself sultan. He also enjoyed the support of the Rumelian frontier lords, including the Evrenosoğulları and Turahanoğulları, who viewed Ottoman centralization attempts in the Balkans as detrimental to their own freedom of action. In January 1422, at the head of his troops (some 12,000 cavalry and 5,000 infantry), Mustafa crossed to Anatolia through the Straits of Gallipoli. However, Murad II's troops stopped him before he could reach Bursa. Mustafa fled to the Balkans but was apprehended by Murad's men near Edirne and hanged as an impostor (winter 1422). In view of Murad II's strengthened position, the marcher-lords of the European provinces also acknowledged him.

Murad II's troubles were far from over. His 13-year-old younger brother Mustafa, called "Little" Mustafa by Ottoman chroniclers, was used by Byzantium and the Anatolian emirates to challenge Murad's rule. However, he too was defeated (due to the desertion of his vizier and troops) and executed (February 1423).

In the following years Murad II annexed the emirates of Aydın, Menteşe, Germiyan and Teke, thus reconstituting Ottoman rule in southwestern Asia Minor. While Murad was unable to subjugate Karaman, the most powerful Anatolian emirate, he exploited the unexpected death of the Karaman emir, Mehmed Bey (1423), and the ensuing power struggle. Mehmed Bey's son, Karamanoğlu Ibrahim Bey, surrendered the territories his father had occupied in 1421, including the lands of the former emirate of Hamid west of Karaman.

VENICE, BYZANTIUM, AND HUNGARY

After consolidating his rule in Anatolia, Murad's primary goal was to reestablish Ottoman rule in the Balkans by forcing the Balkan rulers to accept Ottoman vassalage and by capturing strategically important forts and towns. This, however, led to direct confrontation with VENICE and HUNGARY, two neighboring states with vital interests in the region.

Venice's commercial interests in the Balkans were guarded by the republic's colonies and port cities that dotted the Balkans' Adriatic coast from CROATIA in the north to ALBANIA and the Morea (the Peloponnese peninsula in southern Greece) in the south. In addition to its bases in the Morea, in 1423 Venice also acquired SALONIKA from its ruler, the Byzantine despot (lord) of the Morea. Ottoman recovery of Thessaly—a territory in present-day central Greece once conquered by BAYEZID I (r. 1389–1402) but ceded to the Byzantines by Prince Süleyman during the civil war of 1402–13—and the conquest of southern Albania by the early 1430s threatened the republic's commercial bases in the Adriatic. Murad never acknowledged Venice's possession of Salonika, which had been under Ottoman siege since 1422. The city succumbed to the Ottomans in 1430. Venice tried to block further Ottoman advance in the Balkans by supporting anti-Ottoman forces, whether in Albania or in Anatolia (such as the Karamanids). The republic also concluded treaties with Hungary and Byzantium against the Ottomans, both of which were now more eager than ever to confront the Ottomans.

After his defeat at the hands of the Ottomans at the Battle of Nikopol in 1396, the Hungarian king Sigismund of Luxembourg (r. 1387–1437, Holy Roman Emperor from 1433) developed a new defensive strategy to contain Ottoman expansion. He envisioned a multilayered defense system consisting of a ring of vassal or buffer states between Hungary and the Ottomans; a border defense line that relied on forts along the lower Danube; and a field army that could easily be mobilized.

Forcing the Balkan countries such as SERBIA, WALLACHIA, and BOSNIA to accept Hungarian overlordship inevitably led to confrontation with the Ottomans who also wanted to make these countries their vassals. Desperate, the Balkan states often changed sides or accepted double vassalage. SERBIA is a good example. Its ruler Stephen Lazarević (r. 1389–1427), known as Despot Lazarević by his Byzantine title, tried to be on good terms with Murad II. At the same time, he was Sigismund's vassal after 1403 and one of Hungary's greatest landlords after 1411. According to the Hungarian-Serbian Treaty concluded in May 1426 in Tata (present-day northwestern Hungary), Sigismund acknowledged Stephen's nephew George (Djuradj) Branković as his heir, who would also keep his uncle's possessions, except

for Belgrade and Golubac, key fortresses for Hungary's defense on the Danube River, which would pass to Sigismund. When Despot Stephen died in June 1427, Sigismund took possession of Belgrade, "the key to Hungary" in contemporary parlance. Golubac's captain, however, sold his fort to the Ottomans, causing a major gap in the Hungarian defense line. Sigismund tried in vain to capture the fort in late 1428. By 1433, the Ottomans had occupied most of the Serbian lands south of the Morava River. Despite the fact that Despot George Branković married his daughter, Mara, to Sultan Murad in 1435, and sent his two sons as hostages to the Ottoman court, he was considered an unreliable vassal. Taking advantage of the death of Sigismund (1437) and the ensuing collapse of the central authority in Hungary, by 1439 Murad had subjugated Serbia, capturing its capital Smederevo on the Danube. With the capture of Salonika, Golubac, and Smederevo, Murad had reestablished the Balkan possessions of his grandfather, BAYEZID I (r. 1389–1402).

Although Murad failed to capture Belgrade in 1440, his five-month siege forced Hungary and her allies to act more forcefully against the Ottoman advance. They also were urged to do so by Byzantium and the papacy, which had just concluded their historic agreement regarding the Union of the Catholic and Orthodox Churches (Council of Ferrara-Florence, 1437–39). The Byzantine emperor John VIII Palaiologos (r. 1425–48) signed the accord in 1439 in the hope that his acknowledgement of papal supremacy would result in Western military and financial assistance against the Ottomans.

Hungary, which suffered repeated Ottoman raids from 1438, led the anti-Ottoman coalition. The country's new hero, János (John) Hunyadi, royal governor of the Hungarian province of TRANSYLVANIA (1441–56) and commander of Belgrade, thwarted several Ottoman raids in the early 1440s, defeating the district governor (sancakbeyi) of Smederevo (1441) and the commander of the Ottoman forces in Europe, the *beylerbeyi* of Rumelia (September 1442).

ABDICATION AND THE CRUSADE OF VARNA

In October 1443 the Hungarian army led by King Wladislas (r. 1440–44) and Hunyadi invaded the Balkan provinces of the Ottoman Empire as far as Sofia. Although they did not conquer any territory, the campaign forced Murad II to seek peace. Through the mediation of Murad's Serbian wife Mara and his father-in-law George Branković, the Hungarian-Ottoman Treaty was concluded in the Ottoman capital Edirne on June 12, 1444, and was ratified by the Hungarians on August 15 the same year in Nagyvárad (Oredea, Transylvania).

Having concluded a truce with the Hungarians and the Karamanids, who had coordinated their attack on the Ottomans in Asia Minor with the Hungarian invasion, Murad abdicated in favor of his 12-year-old son Mehmed II and left for Bursa (August 1444). However, Hunyadi's victories prompted the papacy to forge a new anti-Ottoman Christian coalition with the aim of expelling the Ottomans from the Balkans. Despite the Hungarian-Ottoman truce, preparations for the Crusade went on, for the papal legate declared the peace made with the "infidels" void.

These were dangerous times for the Ottomans. In Albania, Iskender Bey (known in the West as Skanderbeg), alias Georg Kastriota—a local Christian who had been brought up a Muslim in Murad II's court and sent back to Albania to represent Ottoman authority there—rose up against the Ottomans in 1443. By spring 1444 the Byzantine despot of the Morea, Constantine, had rebuilt the Hexamilion (six-mile) wall that had defended the Corinth isthmus and thus the Peloponnese against attacks from the north since the early fifth century C.E.

In the summer of 1444, the Byzantine emperor released another pretender against Murad and, most dangerously, on September 22, 1444 the crusading army crossed the Ottoman border into the Balkans. At this critical moment, on the insistence of Çandarlı Halil Pasha, Murad was recalled from Bursa and, arriving in Edirne, assumed the command of the Ottoman troops, while his son Mehmed II remained sultan. The Ottomans met the crusading army at Varna on November 10, 1444. Outnumbered by 40,000 to 18,000, the crusaders were defeated; Hungarian king Wladislas died in battle; and Hunyadi, the hero of the Turkish wars, barely escaped with his life. Despot Branković remained neutral throughout the campaign, as the Ottomans had kept their end of the treaty of Edirne by returning Smederevo and all the other forts stipulated in the agreement on August 22.

MURAD'S SECOND REIGN

While the Ottomans were victorious at Varna, the 1444 campaign revealed the vulnerability of the Ottoman state that had been brought back from the brink of extinction just a generation ago. It also revealed the friction between the viziers of Murad II and Mehmed II. Murad's trusted grand vizier Halil Pasha, the scion of the famous Turkish Çandarlı family that had served the House of Osman since MURAD I (r. 1362–89) in the highest positions, wanted to avoid open confrontation with the Ottomans' European enemies. Mehmed II's Christian-born viziers belonged to a new cast of Ottoman statesmen who were either recent Muslim converts or recruited through the Ottoman child-levy (DEVŞIRME) system and pursued a more belligerent foreign policy. In order to avoid a possible disaster such aggressive policy might cause, Halil Pasha decided to recall Murad for the second time from

his retirement in Manisa, using as pretext the 1446 Janissary rebellion in Edirne, which erupted partly because of Mehmed's debasement of the Ottoman silver coinage in which the Janissaries received their salaries.

Upon assuming his throne for the second time, Murad returned to the Balkans. In a swift campaign in 1446, Ottoman troops breached the Hexamilion wall (December 1446). Other Ottoman troops were fighting, with limited results, against Skanderbeg in Albania. Murad achieved his last great victory at the second Battle of Kosovo Polje in Serbia (October 16–18, 1448) against another crusading army, again consisting primarily of Hungarians led by Hunyadi. When he died in 1451, his son Mehmed II, by then 19 years of age, was poised to revenge his humiliation and to assert his authority by pursuing an aggressive foreign policy against his Christian rivals.

Gábor Ágoston

Further reading: Caroline Finkel, *Osman's Dream: The Story of the Ottoman Empire, 1300–1923* (New York: Basic Books, 2005); Oskar Halecki, *The Crusade of Varna: A Discussion of Controversial Problems* (New York: Polish Institute of Arts and Sciences in America, 1943); Joseph Held, *Hunyadi: Legend and Reality* (Boulder, Co.: East European Monographs, 1985); Colin Imber, ed., *The Crusade of Varna, 1443–45* (Aldershot, UK: Ashgate, 2006); Camil Mureşanu, *John Hunyadi: Defender of Christendom* (Portland, Or.: Center for Romanian Studies, 2001).

Murad III (b. 1546–1595) (r. 1574–1595) *Ottoman sultan and caliph* Murad III was born during the reign of his grandfather Sultan SÜLEYMAN I (the Magnificent) (r. 1520–66) in Manisa where his father, the future SELIM II (r. 1566–74), was the princely governor. His mother was the Venetian-born Nur Banu Sultan. As his first princely seat Murad was appointed to Akşehir, a town in central Anatolia, in 1558. A year later, while he was still a teenager, Murad was actively involved in the succession struggle between his father Selim and his uncle Bayezid. After the defeat of his uncle, his father Selim was left sole heir to the Ottoman throne. In 1561 Murad stayed in ISTANBUL as the guest of his grandfather and a year later, when his father was appointed to Kütahya, a major administrative capital in central Anatolia, he was sent to Manisa, another prominent administrative seat for princes in central Anatolia, where he stayed until his ENTHRONEMENT in 1574.

The relatively long reign of Murad III saw two protracted wars. Conflicts with Safavid Persia on the eastern front of the empire culminated in the long Ottoman-Safavid war from 1578–90. The sultan did not personally participate in the conflict; Ottoman armies were led by various viziers sent from the capital. The other protracted war, the Long Hungarian War of 1593–1606, broke out in the closing years of Murad III's reign.

Beside the long and costly war with Persia, Murad III's reign also coincided with social disturbances and increasing imperial financial problems. Student revolts, caused by the tightening of the career lines in the religious bureaucracy, were also a serious social problem faced by Murad's administration during the 1570s and 1580s. The closing years of his reign saw the emergence of a more serious problem that ravaged the Anatolian countryside: military rebellions of provincial administrators and armed ex-soldiers known as the CELALI REVOLTS, which would be one of the major aggravations for Murad's successors.

Expenses of the long war with Persia and a general worsening in the economic conditions of the late 16th century, which affected the Mediterranean basin and beyond, put Murad's administration under severe financial strain. Eventually, financial burdens led to the devaluation of Ottoman coinage in 1585 and the problem of spurious coinage became the subject of various Janissary uprisings in the capital.

Murad III maintained the traditional sultanic position as patron of the arts. During his reign he favored many poets, writers, theologians, and scientists. He wrote mystic poems under the pseudonym Muradi and had a distinct interest in mysticism, associating himself with the Halveti Order of dervishes, one of the most popular Sufi orders in the empire.

In his 21-year reign, Murad III rarely left the palace or Istanbul. Like his father Selim II, he ruled the empire from the well-protected inner precincts of the palace. He was a sedentary sultan, unlike predecessors such as Süleyman I or SELIM I, whose reigns passed on the battlefields. Yet Murad III demonstrated a great ability to enforce sultanic authority. Along with his father, Selim II, and his son, MEHMED III (r. 1595–1603), Murad III was one of the first sultans whose reign was defined by the rules of court politics. The process of creating a permanent imperial seat, which had begun with the construction of the TOPKAPI PALACE under MEHMED II (r. 1444–46; 1451–81), came to completion when Süleyman I moved his household to the palace. This combining of the sultan's household with the business of governing made the court the center of Ottoman politics. Ironically, the new setting introduced a political paradox, for classical norms of statecraft dictated an omnipresent sultan while the norms of court life idealized a secluded sultan. Murad III. Murad III's long reign is distinguished by the advent of the formally immobile sultan.

Concurrent with the development of the court as the Ottoman political center was the increasing influence of the *valide sultan*, or queen mother, in the business of rule. After Murad III moved his mother, Nur Banu Sul-

tan, to the Topkapı Palace, the sultan's mother became a major power in court politics. Murad III's reign also saw the rise of favorites as a feature of court politics. The first five years of Murad III's reign coincided with the tenure of the all-powerful grand vizier Sokollu Mehmed Pasha, who had virtually ruled the empire from 1565. The death of Sokollu in 1579 marked a decisive moment in the power politics of the Ottoman court. In the remaining 16 years of Murad III's reign, the complex and ever-shifting dynamic of power in court politics did not allow any of Sokollu's successors to amass power and authority as he had during his 14 years in office.

From the very beginning of Murad III's reign the authority of his powerful grand vizier was challenged by an anti-Sokollu faction. One of the members of this faction was Şemsi Pasha. Şemsi Pasha was a retired palace servant who had also served Murad III's father, Selim II, and his grandfather, Süleyman I. His appointment as a favorite of Murad III was as a result of his unabated antagonism toward Sokollu and with the power he was given he tried hard to divert power back into the hands of the sultan. When Şemsi Pasha died in 1581, two years after Sokollu, Murad III needed a new favorite to broker his management of state affairs. The successor of Şemsi Pasha was Mehmed Pasha who was again a palace servant from the reign of Selim II. He had entered Selim II's service while he was governor-prince of Amasya and later became *agha* of the Janissaries. Thus the rise of Mehmed Pasha as favorite was a direct outcome of Murad III's search for an agent to act as his eyes and ears in government affairs. In 1584 an imperial decree was issued for Mehmed Pasha and he was given extraordinary privileges in order to guarantee his privacy with the sultan, including the right to enter the sultan's presence alone and to accompany the sultan during hunts. Mehmed Pasha's privileges bypassed the established patterns of the hierarchical order as well as the orbit of different offices of the bureaucracy. Not surprisingly, the power vested in Mehmed Pasha engendered opposition. In 1589, two years after he was made governor of Rumelia (the European part of the empire), Mehmed Pasha took charge of the debasement of Ottoman coinage. This was followed by an uprising of the cavalry troops of the Sublime Porte who demanded the execution of Mehmed Pasha as the sole actor responsible for the financial operation. Murad III had no choice but to surrender his most valuable asset to the enraged crowd, who murdered him.

The reign of Murad III marked the establishment of the COURT AND FAVORITES as defining features of Ottoman power politics. When his son, Mehmed III, put an end to the practice of princely governorships—placing the sultan's sons in positions of provincial authority to build their skills at governing—and his grandson AHMED I came to throne from the inner compounds of the palace, the position of the court in the Ottoman political system was irreversibly sealed.

Şefik Peksevgen

Further reading: A. H. de Groot, "Murad III," in *Encyclopaedia of Islam*, 2nd ed., vol. 7 (Leiden: Brill, 1960–), 595b; Leslie Peirce, *The Imperial Harem: Women and Sovereignty in the Ottoman Empire* (New York: Oxford University Press, 1993); Caroline Finkel, *Osman's Dream: The Story of the Ottoman Empire, 1300–1923* (London: John Murray, 2005), 152–195.

Murad IV (b. 1612–d. 1640) (r. 1623–1640) *Ottoman sultan and caliph*   Son of Sultan AHMED I (r. 1603–17) and his favorite concubine, Kösem Mahpeyker Sultan, Murad IV was born in ISTANBUL and grew up in the TOPKAPI PALACE. Together with his brothers, Süleyman, Kasım, Bayezid, and Ibrahim, Murad was confined in the HAREM apartments from early childhood. Although information from this period of his life is scant, Murad's reading knowledge of Arabic and Persian indicate that he received a fairly good education. Murad IV was an accomplished horseman and was especially fond of archery and javelin-throwing. His court was frequented by the leading men of letters and, being a talented calligrapher, poet, and composer himself, Murad also enjoyed intellectual and artistic debates. He fathered at least 16 children, but all of his five sons died before him, whereas three of his surviving daughters, Kaya Ismihan, Rukiyye, and Hafize, were married to high-ranking ministers during his reign.

The young Murad was enthroned in 1623 when his mentally disturbed uncle MUSTAFA I (r. 1617–18; 1622–23) was deposed. Because he was too young (at age 12) to rule, Murad's mother assumed the role of de facto regent, controlling the business of rule by her clique in the government. During the early years of his reign Murad IV was thus mainly a passive observer of events and was rarely involved in imperial politics personally. During this period, the empire-wide problems, mainly inherited from the turbulent years of OSMAN II (r. 1618–22) and Mustafa I, persisted: the war with the Safavids over BAGHDAD, the rebellion of governor-general Abaza Mehmed Pasha in Anatolia, and factional strife in Istanbul. Becoming increasingly uneasy with this state of instability, Murad IV, together with the chief eunuch of the harem, El-Hac Mustafa Agha, started to make tours of the capital in disguise to become acquainted with the true state of affairs.

In May 1632, after a bloody military rebellion that lasted for months, Murad managed to establish his personal rule and began to play a more active role in restoring the political, economic, and social health of his empire. Although he quickly eliminated the ringleaders of the military rebellion, Murad remained alert to possible treason and was suspicious of alternative foci of power. He thus did not hesitate to order the execution of several ministers in the government and some members of the religious hierarchy, including the ŞEYHÜLISLAM Ahizade Hüseyin Efendi in 1634. Overall, Murad IV pursued an iron-handed policy and resorted to harsh measures while his new GRAND VIZIER, Tabanıyassı Mehmed Pasha (1632–37, a protégé of El-Hac Mustafa Agha) brought the political situation under control and achieved stability..

During the four-and-a-half year incumbency (1632–37) of his new grand vizier, Murad kept himself informed regarding the breakdown of state and society and followed the presciptions of his advisors who emphasized the need for comprehensive administrative, military, and social reforms, including the reassessment of tax revenues, the reassignment of land-grants, the resettling of peasants who deserted their lands, and the subduing local power-holders. Murad also listened to a conservative-minded religious group that called for a moral regeneration of people and found its voice in the person of Kadızade Mehmed Efendi, a preacher of the HAGIA SOPHIA Mosque, who became one of Murad's advisors. In 1633, following Kadızade Mehmed's suggestion, Murad ordered the closing down and razing of all coffeehouses as well as renewing the prohibition on tobacco, which had first been issued in 1609 during the reign of his father.

Murad also emulated his forebears by playing the role of a warrior-sultan. He personally led two successful campaigns against the Safavids of IRAN, resulting in the recapture of Yerevan and BAGHDAD. But he helped to ensure the security of his reign while he was in the field by ordering the execution of his brothers Bayezid and Süleyman while on his first campaign in 1635 and of his brother Kasım prior to the campaign of 1638.

Although Murad was a man of tall stature and possessed extraordinary bodily strength, his health became unstable and often worsened during the long marches from the frontier. After the second campaign, Murad fell seriously ill, but managed to make a triumphal entry into the capital in June 1639 nevertheless. He recovered for a brief time, but his premature death, which was probably brought about by excessive drinking and other indulgences, came in February 1640. He was buried in his father's mausoleum in the complex of the Sultan Ahmed Mosque.

Günhan Börekçi

Further reading: Leslie Peirce, *The Imperial Harem: Women and Sovereignty in the Ottoman Empire* (Oxford: Oxford University Press, 1993), 91–112. Caroline Finkel, *Osman's Dream* (London: John Murray, 2005), 204–222; A.H. de Groot, "Murad IV," in *Encyclopaedia of Islam*, 2nd ed., vol. 7, edited by C. E. Bosworth, E. van Donzel, W. P. Heinrichs, and Ch. Pellat (Leiden: Brill, 1960–), 597–599.

Murad V (b. 1840–d. 1904) (r. 1876) *Ottoman sultan and caliph* Born on September 21, 1840, in ISTANBUL, the son of Sultan ABDÜLMECID I (r. 1839–61) and Sevketefza Valide Sultan, Murad V acceded to the throne on May 30, 1876, after the dethronement of his uncle, Sultan ABDÜLAZIZ (r. 1861–76). Murad had learned both French and Arabic. He ordered and read books and magazines from France and was influenced by French culture. He played the piano, composed Western-style music, and accompanied his uncle Sultan Abdülaziz on visits to Europe and Egypt. However, when Sultan Abdülaziz tried to change the succession system in favor of his own son Yusuf Izzeddin, Crown Prince Murad cooperated with the constitutionalist circles and took part in the deposition of Abdülaziz on May 30, 1876. Though Murad V successfully acceded to the throne, he was not capable of maintaining his place; his weak nerves, combined with alcoholism, led to a mental breakdown. MIDHAT PASHA, the leading statesman of the Ottoman TANZIMAT or reform era, and the Ottoman governing elite deposed him on August 31, 1876, and arranged the accession of his younger brother ABDÜLHAMID II (r. 1876–1909). Murad V was the shortest-reigning sultan of the Ottoman dynasty, ruling for just 93 days. He spent his remaining years in the Ciragan Palace in Istanbul, which Abdülhamid II did not allow him to leave. He died on August 29, 1904.

Selcuk Akşin Somel

music Music of the Ottoman empire flourished over the course of five centuries within a broader regional context of the Near East, Central Asia, and Persia. With its expanding and contracting borders, migrations of populations, and multitude of ethno-linguistic communities, the empire encompassed richly diverse musical cultures. The term "Ottoman music," however, frequently refers to a distinctive music of the imperial state and urban society: the classical (or art) music patronized by the palace and cultivated in a variety of urban settings, including the court, lodges of the MEVLEVI ORDER of Sufis, private homes, mosques, churches, and synagogues. Ottoman classical music can inform us about Ottoman COURT and religious culture, urban social entertainment, multiethnic artistic relations, and aesthetic change over time, particularly in the urban centers of the empire (ISTANBUL, BURSA, EDIRNE, IZMIR, and SALONIKA). Ottoman classical forms also came into contact with western European musical styles, thus reflecting cross-cultural interactions beyond the boundaries of the empire.

OTTOMAN CLASSICAL MUSIC

Important musical and social developments contributing to the formation of Ottoman classical music include the religious music of the Mevlevi Order of Sufis, known popularly as "whirling dervishes." Originating in Konya in the 13th century, the Mevlevi Order began in the 15th century to develop a distinctive musical form, the *ayın*, to accompany the religious choreography of the dervishes. After their first lodge or *tekke* was founded in Istanbul in 1494, followed later by lodges in other neighborhoods and urban centers, the Mevlevi gradually became the most prominent Sufi order connected to the sultan and the Ottoman ruling class. The order played a central role in classical musical culture through the presence of Mevlevi composers and musicians at the palace, the significant role of the Mevlevi lodge in classical music education, and the further development of *ayın* compositions as some of the most complex in Ottoman classical music.

Before and after the CONQUEST OF CONSTANTINOPLE in 1453, Ottoman courts interacted with the music of a

This picture shows the renowned Mevlevi *ney* player, Neyzen Emin Dede. *(Courtesy of Anders Hammarlund)*

broader, regional Arab-Persian art music. In the 16th century, after the Ottoman conquests of Tabriz, BAGH-DAD, and Arab territories, Persian musicians arrived at the court in Istanbul, contributing to a later Ottoman style through Persian compositional forms and musical modes. By the 17th century, a distinctive Ottoman classical style was taking shape. The "Ottomanness" of this music is reflected in its composers (musicians from Istanbul), poetic language (Ottoman Turkish rather than Arabic and Persian), and new musical forms and modes constituting an Ottoman suite (*fasıl*) distinct from Arab-

Persian predecessors. The classical Ottoman suite contained a specific sequence of pieces in a single mode, beginning and ending with an instrumental composition (the *peşrev* and *saz semaisi*, respectively) and presenting such distinctive genres as the *beste* and *kar*. In addition, the improvisational form (*taksim*) represents an important development within the Ottoman suite at this time. In contradistinction to the Mevlevi *ayın* ("serious sacred"), some scholars categorize the Ottoman court suite as "serious secular" classical music with related but distinctive arrangements, forms, and instrumentation.

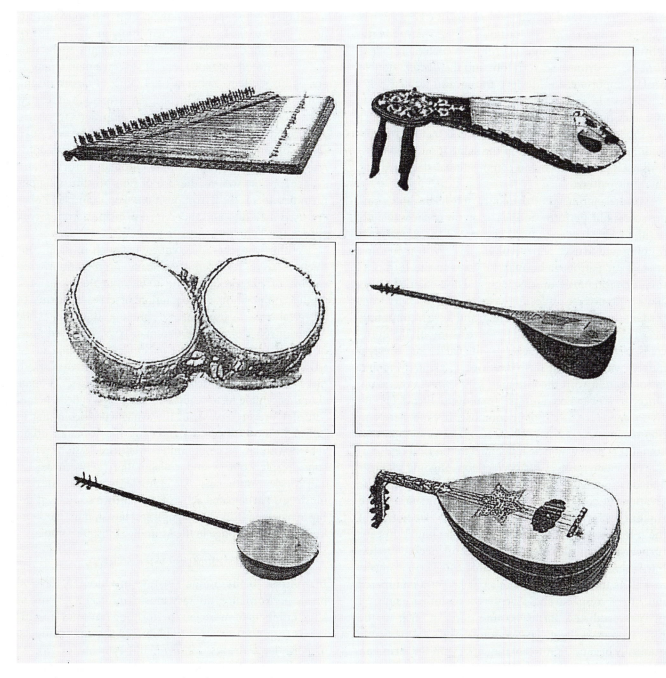

Musical instruments *(Courtesy of Anders Hammarlund)*

As a chamber music style, the classical Ottoman suite was performed in intimate settings by an ensemble of instrumentalists and singers. There is also some evidence of larger, outdoor ensembles. By the 1700s, classical groups began to showcase the *tanbur* (long-necked fretted lute) and Mevlevi *ney* (end-blown reed flute), instruments not included in antecedent suite traditions and thus reflective of a developing Ottoman distinctiveness, as well as Mevlevi influence.

The gradual attrition of such instruments as the *çenk* (small harp) and *miskal* (panpipes), used approximately until the end of the 18th century, exemplifies changing musical practices and tastes in Ottoman musical history. Among stringed and bowed instruments, the *kemençe* has a spherical body with two or three strings, played vertically with a bow. Rhythm instruments include the *bendir*, a frame drum held vertically, and the *kudüm*, double drums important in Mevlevi music and beaten with drumsticks by a seated musician. Not unlike the format of a Baroque suite or European concerto with distinct movements, the classical Ottoman suite included a collection of pieces composed in the same mode (*makam*), with each piece differing in compositional structure and rhythmic pattern.

Under patronage of the court, musicians and composers would perform and teach at the palace, including the HAREM, where music was part of the educational training and artistic activity of women. With increasing aristocratic patronage beyond the court in the 18th century, classical music-making included non-salaried musicians from diverse professions as well as composers from the GREEK ORTHODOX, Armenian, and Jewish communities. The Mevlevi continued to serve as important musicians, composers, and teachers at the palace and Mevlevi lodges, with the *ayın* form developing distinctively and in interaction with the Ottoman *fasıl*. Among the many Ottoman Mevlevi composers, Ismail Dede Efendi (1778–1846) stands out as a prolific composer of both *ayıns* and nonreligious pieces, as well as an important teacher of composers who would be influential in the 19th century.

Ottoman musical history reflects ongoing changes and developments over the centuries, for example the creation of new *makams*, *makam* combinations, and rhythm cycles (*usuls*), in addition to the elaboration of the instrumental and vocal *taksim*. By the mid-19th century, instruments such as the *ud*, a short-necked fretless lute historically important in Arabic and Persian music, as well as the *kanun* and *santur*, plucked and hammered dulcimers respectively, re-entered Ottoman musical practice, and new forms became popular, such as the song type *şarkı* (light classical song). The Ottoman suite gradually began to showcase the *şarkı*, with the term *fasıl* becoming associated with this song genre rather than with the classical court suite, especially when nightclubs (*gazinos*) took root as urban entertainment venues in the late 19th and 20th centuries. Hacı Arif Bey (1831–85), a palace singer and teacher at the harem, Selanikli Ahmet Bey (1870–1928), an *ud* player from Salonika, and Bimen Şen (1872–1943), a singer of Armenian heritage from Bursa, are among the prolific composers of this form, whose pieces are still performed today.

MULTIRELIGIOUS GENRES

Composers and musicians among the officially recognized non-Muslim religious communities in the empire (Greek Orthodox, Armenian, and Jewish) not only taught and performed at the palace but also made music in other venues, including their own religious institutions. Tanburi Isak (Isak Fresco Romano, 1745?–1814), a Jewish composer and *tanbur* player, taught at the palace and counted SELIM III, one of several sultan composers, as his student. Zaharya (d. 1740?), of Greek origin, and Nikoğos Agha (1836–85), of Armenian ancestry, were both examples of Ottoman composers who also performed as cantors in their respective churches. Such cross-communal interactions fostered a classical cantorial style and repertoire within Ottoman churches and synagogues, as well as the use of non-Muslim religious melodies in classical composition. For example, Zaharya used melodies and theoretical principles from Greek church music in his court compositions.

Within churches and synagogues such musical confluences were reflected specifically in the improvised singing of prayers according to *makam* theory as well as the composition or adaptation of classical forms to liturgical texts. A prominent example of the latter is the Maftirim repertoire of the Ottoman JEWS, a "sacred *fasıl*" of several pieces in a single *makam*, representing original compositions or adaptations from Ottoman Turkish pieces, with Hebrew scriptural texts as "lyrics." A male choral ensemble historically sang the *fasıl* a capella before Saturday prayer services in the synagogue. Beginning in Edirne in the 17th century and spreading to major urban centers with Jewish communities, Maftirim sessions reflect considerable contact and collaboration between Jewish and Mevlevi musicians. For example, in Edirne, Mevlevi musicians participated actively in Maftirim sessions at the Big Synagogue (Büyük Sinagog), and Jewish musicians visited the Mevlevi lodge in the Muradiye mosque complex.

OTHER MUSICAL GENRES

In contrast to the intimate nature of Ottoman classical music performance, military music (*mehter*) made use of large numbers of musicians performing on "loud" instruments (e.g., the *zurna*, or double-reed shawm, trumpets, or *boru*; large drums, or *davul*; and cymbals, or *zil*). As a highly symbolic music intended to represent the Ottoman state to outsiders, *mehter* military music was performed for ceremonies of state and in battle. The music represents a mix of classical and popular styles, forms, and instruments. For example, the *zurna* and *davul* are associated with folk music, while specific forms, such as the instrumental introduction (*peşrev*), reflect classical compositional genres. A related group, *mehter-i birun* (unofficial *mehter*), was performed for public festivals and was associated with Gypsy musicians and boy dancers (*köçekçe*).

In the 18th century, through gifts of *mehter* ensembles to European courts and *mehter* performances at Ottoman embassies in Europe, the music became associated there with Ottoman music as a whole, influencing European military music and introducing *mehter*-style percussion instruments into European orchestras. Particularly in the 18th century, the music generated an interest in "alla Turca" motifs among European composers, as reflected in rhythmic patterns and melodic intervals reminiscent of *mehter* in Mozart's *Rondo alla Turca* and Beethoven's Turkish March from *Ruins of Athens*. At the end of the 18th and beginning of the 19th century, European musical forms began to have an impact on Ottoman music as well, in part through the appointment of Giuseppe Donizetti, brother of the opera composer, at the court in 1828. However, Ottoman music historians disagree about the musical and social significance of these developments: whether they were the beginning of Europeanization and the decline of Ottoman classical music, or the integration of musical influences into the Golden Age of a well-established tradition.

The urban environment of Ottoman cities included other musical venues, such as the COFFEEHOUSE (*kahvehane*), associated with the performance of folk genres, and the hymns (*nefes*) of the BEKTAŞI ORDER of the JANISSARIES. After the dissolution of the Janissaries in 1826, the coffee house, (*semai kahvehanesi*) became popular for such events as poetic competitions and performances connected with the Muslim holiday of Ramadan. In addition, the drinking house (*meyhane*) was commonly connected with Greek folk music; Sufi lodges were connected with a variety of Sufi hymns and religious gatherings; and, beginning in the 19th century, the *gazino*, or nightclub, with increasingly "light" *fasıl* music. Depending on historical era and location, these spaces represent sites of varying multiethnic musical and social interaction, together with the more or less separate folk and popular music-making of diverse ethno-linguistic communities of the empire, whether indigenous or immigrant (for example, Sephardic Jewish, Armenian, Greek, Bulgarian, Albanian, Arab).

MUSICAL EDUCATION AND TRANSMISSION

Until the 20th century, Ottoman classical music primarily relied upon oral transmission for its survival, continu-

ity, and development. Within such venues as the palace music school, Mevlevi lodges, and private homes, master-pupil relationships took a central place in a teaching and learning method called *meşk*. In addition to instructional repetition of musical sections and technical challenges, the beating of the rhythm pattern on the knees served as a framework for linking up the melodic and poetic lines correctly, representing one of the memory arts involved in such learning. The song-text collection (*güfte mecmuası*), in manuscript and later printed form, typically provided the musician with song lyrics and composer/lyricist names, as well as minimal theoretical cues for the piece, such as the *makam* and *usul*. Such collections also served as mnemonic devices for triggering the memory of entire pieces learned through *meşk*.

In the course of Ottoman music history several systems of notation were developed, including those of Ali Ufki (Wojciech Bobowski, 1610?–75), Kantemiroğlu (Prince Demetrius Cantemir, 1673–1723), and Baba Hamparsum (Hamparsum Limonciyan, 1768–1839). However, despite their significance today as historic records, none of these systems were widely utilized by Ottoman composers, musicians, and teachers, with the exception of Hamparsum notation, which was used for the documentation of Armenian church music and numerous Ottoman compositions in the 19th century.

In a musical culture of oral transmission, a single Ottoman composition could have more than one version, whether instantiated at a single performance or legitimated by transmission from a recognized master. While composers' names and compositional skill were associated with individual pieces, such versioning nonetheless contrasts with the idea of the composer as sole authority and of performance as a precise reproduction of a notated score. Contemporary scholarship on Ottoman oral transmission and its performative implications reflects contrasting historiographical narratives representative of wider debates in Ottoman historical scholarship. For example, in recognition of the drawbacks of *meşk* (that is, musical losses), an evolutionary, Eurocentric perspective narrates Ottoman oral transmission as a gradual achievement of musical literacy through the development of a variety of notational systems, culminating in the establishment of European notation in the 20th century (Eugenia Popescu-Judetz). By contrast, recent research on *meşk* (Cem Behar) investigates, on its own terms, the musical culture surrounding such transmission practices, including the cultivation of social values, such as a master's generosity of time and knowledge and a pupil's loyalty, as well as the historical devaluing of notation as a deficient representation of the music. Given inevitable musical losses and changing musical tastes, such ethical values and textual judgments supported the more or less successful transmission of a large repertoire and musical technique through historical chains of masters and pupils.

OTTOMAN MUSICAL THEORY

The modal, or *makam*, system of Ottoman music developed within a wider regional and historical context of Near Eastern *makam* music. Simply put, a *makam* can be represented as a musical scale with a particular set of compositional rules and practices. For example, the character of a *makam* may be reflected in part through melodic conventions particular to that makam—a characteristic distinguishing *makams* from European musical scales, unattached to such compositional features. In the course of Ottoman musical history literally hundreds of *makams* were created and used, some going out of fashion and others continuing over time. Unlike European musical scales, a *makam's* intervallic relationships and compositional qualities can best be demonstrated through the performance of a composition or *taksim*. *Makams* became associated with "extra-musical" qualities of medical therapeutic value, contributing to the development of a theory of Ottoman music therapy, practiced most notably at the sanatorium for the mentally ill at the complex of Sultan BAYEZID II (est. 1488) in Edirne.

Like *makams*, the rhythmic cycles (*usuls*) of Ottoman music underwent development, change, attrition, and continuity. Unlike common rhythms of European classical music, Ottoman *usuls* include extremely long patterns across many measures (e.g., cycles of 32, 64, or 88), as well as odd-numbered beats (e.g., five, seven, nine). Out of hundreds of Ottoman *usuls*, earlier musical genres such as the *beste* vocal form employed some of the longest rhythmic cycles in tandem with long melodic lines, while other forms such as the later *şarkı* are characterized by shorter *usuls*.

SOURCES FOR OTTOMAN MUSIC HISTORY

Although notation never became established in the Ottoman musical world, the notated scores of Ali Ufkî and Kantemiroğlu survive as important sources for compositions, as well as evidence about style and repertoire preferences of a particular musical era. Treatises on music theory, both pre-Ottoman Arabic works as well as later works of al-Meragi (d. 1435) and Kantermiroğlu, provide valuable information on *makams* and *usuls*, even if theoretical texts do not necessarily inform us about actual performance practices of different periods. Recently, a number of scholars have made fruitful use of the under-researched song-text collections, or *güfte mecmuası*, for a number of research projects on *meşk*, musical change, and multi-religious genres. For example, Owen Wright's contrastive study of three Arab-Persian song-text collections and the collection of Hafız Post (1631–94) carves out the development of a unique

Ottoman style by the 17th century. Edwin Seroussi has examined a number of Ottoman Hebrew-language *güfte mecmuası* for evidence of classical adaptations (*contrafacta*), as well as original compositions, by Ottoman Jewish composers, thereby charting the gradual development of Hebrew-language art music and Maftirim *fasıl* in Ottoman synagogues.

In addition to the *güfte mecmuası*, numerous other sources provide rich detail or indirect clues about music-making in specific historical periods. For example, Ali Ufki's *Saray-ı Enderun* describes music-making and education in the palace in the 17th century; ŞEYHÜLİSLAM Esad Efendi's (d. 1753) biography of composers and musicians provides information on various classes of musicians in Istanbul including silk-weavers, street vendors, and stone masons, thus evidencing widespread nonprofessional urban music-making beyond the palace by the 18th century; and finally the multivolume travelogue by EVLIYA ÇELEBI (b. 1611–d. after 1683), a well-regarded musician himself, provides detailed information and statistics on instruments, instrument-

This picture reportedly shows Tanburi Isak (Isak Fresco Romano, 1745?–1814), a Jewish composer who was a famous player of *tanbur*, a long-necked fretted lute, and who taught at the palace. *(Courtesy of Yapı Kredi Koleksiyonu)*

makers, and musicians in the Istanbul of his day. Travel accounts, correspondence, miniatures, and other textual or visual sources can enrich both research on Ottoman music and scholarship on European views of the music and empire. In the 20th century, recordings of late Ottoman composers and musicians, such as Tanburi Cemil Bey (1873–1916) and *hazan* (cantor) Isak al-Gazi (1889–1950), represent aural sources not only for classical compositions and stylistic techniques influential in the 20th century, but also for information on the early recording industry and the impact of commercial recording on Ottoman and early Turkish Republican musical culture and historiography.

Maureen Jackson

Further reading: Cem Behar, *Aşk Olmayınca Meşk Olmaz*, 2nd. ed. (Istanbul: Yapı Kredi, 2003); Walter Feldman, *Music of the Ottoman Court: Makam, Composition and the Early Ottoman Instrumental Repertoire* (Berlin: Intercultural Music Studies, 1996); Edwin Seroussi, "From Court and Tarikat to Synagogue: Ottoman Art Music and Hebrew Sacred Songs," in *Sufism, Music and Society in Turkey and the Middle East*, edited by Anders Hammarlund et al. (Istanbul: Swedish Research Institute in Istanbul, 2001); Karl Signell, *Makam: Modal Practice in Turkish Art Music* (Seattle: University of Washington Asian Music Publications, 1977).

Further Listening: Lalezar, *Music of the Sultans, Sufis & Seraglio*: "Sultan Composers" (vol 1); "Music of the Dancing Boys" (vol 2); "Minority Composers" (vol 3); "Ottoman Suite" (vol 4) (Traditional Crossroads, 2000–2001). Detailed liner notes by Walter Feldman.

Mustafa I (b. ca. 1591–d. ca. 1639) (r. 1617–1618; 1622–1623) *Ottoman sultan and caliph* Son of Sultan MEHMED III and an Abkhazian royal concubine, whose name has not been determined, Mustafa I was born in Manisa when his father, as a prince, was governing the province of Saruhan. Following his father's enthronement in 1595, Mustafa and his siblings were taken to Istanbul. In 1603, Mehmed III ordered the execution of his oldest son, Mahmud, a decision that left Mustafa and his older brother Ahmed as the sole surviving males of the dynasty confined in the TOPKAPI PALACE. When Mehmed III died later that year, an inner court faction secured the succession for the 13-year-old Ahmed, who decided to keep his brother alive contrary to the established practice of royal fratricide, perhaps because that Mustafa was weak-minded and Ahmed had as yet no sons who could guarantee the male line of dynastic succession. However, even after AHMED I had fathered several sons he kept Mustafa alive. Although not finally established, the main factor behind Ahmed's decision may have been efforts by his favorite consort, Kösem Sultan, who seemingly worked to preempt the possibility of having Osman, Ahmed's firstborn son from another concubine, succeed to the throne, which would have led to the killing of her own sons. Until the death of his brother in 1617, Mustafa was thus confined to the palace, a situation that likely worsened his mental aberration and turned him into a paranoid man fearful of execution.

The death of Ahmed I thus led to an unprecedented situation in Ottoman history: several princes were eligible for the throne, all of whom resided within the Topkapı Palace. Eventually a court faction decided to enthrone Mustafa rather than Osman, thereby establishing the new principle of seniority in Ottoman succession practice as the deceased sultan was for the first time in centuries succeeded not by his son, but by his brother.

Mustafa I was soon deposed by the faction that opposed his succession and was replaced by OSMAN II (r. 1618–22). Mustafa was put in a HAREM chamber, with the door solidly sealed. Although Osman II ordered the execution of his younger brother Mehmed before departing for a military campaign in 1621, Mustafa's life was spared, probably due to his mental condition. Unexpectedly, after Osman II was murdered following a Janissary rebellion in 1622, Mustafa was taken by force from his chamber and then restored to the throne.

Mustafa I's second reign passed under the shadow of the turbulence Osman's regicide precipitated. Mustafa had neither the power nor the capacity to rule as a sultan; he was only a puppet in the hands of his mother and brother-in-law, the grand vizier Kara Davud Pasha. At the same time, the real masters in the capital were the Janissaries and the *sipahis* (cavalry), at whose pleasure several ministers were nominated, deposed, or executed. These elite regiments soon began a struggle for supremacy while people in the capital and the country held them accountable for the murder of Osman and pressured for those responsible to be punished. The political instability reached a climax when the governor-general of Erzurum, Abaza Mehmed Pasha, decided to advance on Istanbul to settle the score with the murderers of Osman II. Grand Vizier Kara Davud Pasha was chosen as the scapegoat and was executed in an attempt to mollify the discontent and preempt the rebellions that were building up in the empire, but to no avail: Mehmed Pasha, despite the offers made by the emissaries from the capital, continued his advance. Faced with an ever-deepening crises, clerics petitioned Mustafa's mother to agree to the deposition of her son in favor of 11-year-old Prince Murad, the oldest surviving son of Ahmed I. The Queen Mother concurred, only pleading that her son's life be spared. Accordingly, Mustafa I was dethroned and incarcerated again. Mustafa died in seclusion in 1639 and was buried in the courtyard of Ayasofya. He did not father any children nor establish any imperial foundation.

Günhan Börekçi

Further reading: Leslie Peirce, *The Imperial Harem: Women and Sovereignty in the Ottoman Empire* (Oxford: Oxford University Press, 1993), 97–112. Caroline Finkel, *Osman's Dream* (London: John Murray, 2005),196–205; J.H. Kramers, "Mustafa I," in *Encyclopedia of Islam*, 2nd ed., vol. 7, eds. C.E. Bosworth, E. van Donzel, W.P. Heinrichs and Ch. Pellat (Leiden: Brill, 1960–), 707. Baki Tezcan, "Searching for Osman: A Reassessment of the Deposition of The Ottoman Sultan Osman II (1618–1622)," (Ph.D. diss., Princeton University, 2001), 84–134.

Mustafa II (b. 1664–d. 1703) (r. 1695–1703) *Ottoman sultan and caliph* Son of Sultan MEHMED IV (r. 1648–87) and Rabia Emetullah Gülnuş Sultan, Mustafa was born in EDIRNE on June 5, 1664. Following the death of Sultan SÜLEYMAN II (r. 1687–91), certain court circles wanted to put him on the throne, but their plan was foiled by Grand Vizier Fazıl Mustafa Pasha (grand vizier in 1689–91) of the famous KÖRÜLÜ FAMILY, who supported Mustafa's uncle AHMED II (r. 1691–95). When Ahmed died, Mustafa ascended to the throne on February 6, 1695, even though the new grand vizier, Sürmeli Ali Pasha, supported Ahmed II's son, Prince Ibrahim.

Mustafa II's eight-and-a-half-year reign witnessed major military debacle (1697) and territorial losses (HUNGARY and the Morea), but it also heralded a new era of Ottoman foreign policy. The Holy League War (1684–99) that was triggered by the Ottomans' unsuccessful second siege of Vienna in 1683, had exhausted the empire's resources, led to revolts in the Arab provinces, and revealed the questionable loyalty to the dynasty of the Ottoman elite and provincial notables. To tackle these problems Mustafa's government experimented with new approaches to military recruitment and finances. The sultan's withdrawal to the old capital Edirne in the second half of his reign after 1699 and the nepotism of his tutor and chief political adviser, ŞEYHÜLISLAM Feyzullah Efendi, led to the revolt of the army in Istanbul and to the deposition of the sultan in 1703.

At the accession of Sultan Mustafa II, the Ottoman Empire was in the midst of the long Holy League War, fought against Habsburg AUSTRIA and her allies, VENICE, POLAND-Lithuania, the papacy and, from 1686, Muscovy, as RUSSIA was then known. The new sultan proclaimed a holy war against the empire's enemies, and despite opposition from the Imperial Council, decided to lead his army in battle in the hope that he would recover Hungary and other lost territories. His first campaign in 1695 brought some much-needed success. Ottoman troops led by the sultan recaptured Lippa (Lipova, Romania) on September 7, and at the battle fought near Lugos (Lugoj, Romania) on September 21 inflicted a disastrous defeat on Federico Ambrosio Veterani, the commander of the Habsburg troops in TRANSYLVANIA, who himself died in the fight. Mustafa then proceeded to capture Karánsebes (Caransebeş, Romania) before leaving the front for the winter. He entered ISTANBUL with the spoils of his successful campaign, including some 300 Christian captives, a rare occurrence in recent Ottoman history.

The 1696 campaign was less successful, and on August 7, 1696 Muscovy captured AZAK at the mouth of the River Don. Mustafa II suffered his most disastrous defeat on September 11, 1697 at the Battle of Zenta, near prsent-day Senta in northern SERBIA on the Tisza River. Despite the advice of the warden of Belgrade, Amcazade Hüseyin Pasha, who proposed to attack Habsburg-held Petrovaradin northwest of Belgrade on the DANUBE RIVER, Mustafa moved toward TRANSYLVANIA and consolidated Ottoman positions around Temesvár (Timişoara, Romania). The sultan and part of his army successfully crossed the Tisza River. The rest of the army, led by the grand vizier, was still in the process of crossing the river when Eugene of Savoy, commander in chief of the Habsburg forces in Hungary, who had followed the Ottomans from Petrovaradin, attacked them with his 50,000 men. After intense bombardment, Eugene charged his infantry and slaughtered half of the Ottoman army. Some 25,000 Ottomans, including the grand vizier, were reported to have lost their lives. A crowning victory for the Habsburgs, Zenta was a major disaster for the Ottomans, who, through English and Dutch mediation, sped up the peace negotiations that had started in 1688. The peace was concluded on January 26, 1699 at Karlowitz.

At the peace TREATY OF KARLOWITZ, the Ottomans surrendered much of HUNGARY, Transylvania (an Ottoman vassal principality ruled by pro-Istanbul Hungarian princes), CROATIA, and Slavonia to the Austrian Habsburgs, but kept the Banat Temesvár, the historic region in southern Hungary south of the Maros (Mureş) River. Podolia, with the dismantled fortress of KAMANIÇE, was restored to the Polish-Lithuanian Commonwealth, but the Ottomans kept MOLDAVIA (in present-day Romania). Parts of DALMATIA and the Morea (the Peloponnese) remained Venetian, though the Ottomans recaptured the Morea in the war of 1715–18, and the Treaty of Passarowitz (1718) left it in Ottoman hands. With Muscovy, negotiations continued, and peace was not reached until July 12, 1700 at Istanbul, when the sultan ceded Azak to the Russians.

Apart from these territorial losses, the Treaty of Karlowitz was a turning point in Ottoman history in that it heralded a new era in the way the Ottomans dealt with their rivals. Defeated and weakened, the Ottomans were forced to adhere, for the first time in their history, to European rules of international law and diplomacy. The peace treaties with the members of the Holy League were no mere temporary suspension of hostilities as previous treaties had usually been interpreted in Istanbul. Rather, they were concluded indefinitely (with Poland and Venice) or were to last for 25 and 30 years (those with Austria and Moscovy, respectively). Equally important, the Ottomans accepted the territorial integrity of their neighbors.

To deal with the pressing problems of manpower and war financing and the disloyalty of the ruling elite and the provincial notables, Mustafa's government experimented with new ways of raising troops and money for the war effort, including general mobilization from among the taxpaying subjects and an attempt to get rid of the militia-type troops (*sarica* and *levend*). Requiring viziers and wealthy statesmen to provide a set number of soldiers at their own expense was a novel way to raise troops and tap the wealth of an emerging affluent class, who acquired their assets partly from serving the state.

The most important financial reform was the introduction of life-long tax farms (*see* TAX FARMING). Although introduced under his predecessor Süleyman II in 1695, this approach was implemented under Mustafa II. Apart from raising much-needed money through the lump sums paid by the winners of the bid for these tax farms, the system also proved an effective tool to buy the loyalty of notables in faraway provinces, because they had access to state revenues only if they cooperated with Istanbul. The imperial treasury also confiscated the estates of dismissed viziers and other statesmen to raise money.

After the Treaty of Karlowitz Mustafa retired to Edirne, the old Ottoman capital. Karlowitz was perceived by many as a humiliation and the implementation of the treaty—including delineation of the new borders by the border commissions and curbing raids into enemy territory (traditionally a lucrative activity for the border garrisons)—adversely affected many in the Ottoman elite.

After the resignation of Grand Vizier Amcazade Hüseyin Pasha in 1702, Mustafa II's tutor and adviser, Feyzullah Efendi, was able to significantly increase his influence on the affairs of the state. He had also managed to secure many of the highest government posts (including the posts of chief justice of Anatolia and Rumelia, and judge of Bursa) for his sons and relatives. A new generation of statesmen began to plot against Feyzullah Efendi's nepotism and for regime change. When some 200 soldiers in Istanbul rebelled, demanding the salaries the treasury owed them, the uprising spread swiftly and the rebels, now demanding the deposition of Mustafa, marched toward Edirne. The opposing forces met halfway between Istanbul and Edirne on August 19. Mustafa's troops deserted and the sultan fled to Edirne, where he abdicated in favor of his brother Ahmed III (r. 1703–1730) on August 24. Five month later Mustafa II died in Edirne.

Gábor Ágoston

Further readings: Caroline Finkel, *Osman's Dream* (London: John Murray, 2005); Michael Hochendlinger, *Austria's Wars of Emergence: War, State and Society in the Habsburg Monarchy, 1683–1797* (London: Longman, 2003).

Mustafa III (b. 1717–d. 1774) (r. 1757–1774) *Ottoman sultan and caliph* Son of AHMED III (r. 1703–30) and Mihrişah Kadın of concubine origin, Mustafa III succeeded his cousin OSMAN III (r. 1754–57) at the age of 40 after spending 27 years in seclusion. Following two reigns without a royal birth (those of MAHMUD I (r. 1730–1754) and Osman III), Mustafa was a prolific father, siring eight daughters and two sons, including the great reformer SELIM III (r. 1789–1807). His reign is remembered for the RUSSO-OTTOMAN WAR OF 1768–1774, which resulted in the humiliating TREATY OF KÜÇÜK KAYNARCA (1774), and for the four successive earthquakes that occurred between May 1766 and January 1767, leaving ISTANBUL in ruins.

Mustafa III girded on the sword of Caliph Omar during his ENTHRONEMENT AND ACCESSION CEREMONY in order to demonstrate his special care for justice. He took a number of measures to increase prosperity in Istanbul including regulating coinage, building large grain stores, maintaining aqueducts, establishing a strict fiscal policy, and undertaking great construction projects, especially after the earthquakes in 1766–67. The Fatih (or "Conqueror") Mosque—that is, the Mosque of Sultan Mehmed II (r. 1444–46; 1451–81)—was rebuilt from the ground during Mustafa's reign, as were many other monumental buildings. In addition, he had the Laleli mosque complex built and the shore along Yenikapı filled to set up a new neighborhood. Although initial steps were taken in 1759 to link the gulf of IZNIK with the BLACK SEA to improve transportation of foodstuffs and fuel for Istanbul, this project was never realized. Mustafa was also said to have approved the plans for the construction of the SUEZ CANAL. In fact, the Suez Canal could only be opened in 1869.

Mustafa's celebrated grand vizier, Koca Ragıp Pasha, held the power from 1757 until his death in 1763. The sultan then returned to the traditional policy of rotation of the grand vizierate among his viziers for short periods for the remainder of his reign. In accordance with the policies of the peacefully minded sultan, Koca Ragıp Pasha pursued a noninterventionist policy in the Seven Years War (1756–63) and signed a treaty of friendship with Prussia in 1761. Renowned for his traditionalist mindset, Ragıp Pasha did not undertake any military REFORM of significance to keep the unruly JANISSARIES under control. However, this conservative policy resulted in the humiliation of the Ottoman Empire by RUSSIA and the loss of the Crimea in the war with Russia. After the defeats in Kagul (Kartal) and Çeşme in 1770, Mustafa III immediately initiated military reform with the help of Baron de Tott, the renown French artillery officer who organized the Ottoman field artillery marking the beginning of the decisive Western-inspired reforms that would culminate in the TANZIMAT or Ottoman reform period (1839–76). When Mustafa died in 1774, he left an empire struggling with economic and administrative problems. The extraordinary economic growth of the previous 60 years had come to an end, and the empire's authority in the provinces had collapsed as a result of the losses to Russia.

Kahraman Şakul

Further reading: Virginia Aksan, *An Ottoman Statesman in War and Peace: Ahmed Resmi Efendi, 1700–1783* (Leiden: Brill, 1995); A. D. Alderson, *The Structure of the Ottoman Dynasty* (Oxford: Clarendon, 1956); J. H. Kramers, "Mustafa III," in *Encyclopaedia of Islam*, 2nd ed., vol. 7 (Leiden: Brill, 1960–), 708–709; Caroline Finkel, *Osman's Dream: The Story of the Ottoman Empire, 1300–1923* (London: John Murray, 2005), 372–400; Ariel Salzmann, "An Ancien Regime Revisited: "Privatization" and Political Economy in the 18th Century Ottoman Empire." *Politics and Society* 21, no. 4 (1993): 393–423.

Mustafa IV (b. 1779–d. 1808) (r. 1807–1808) *Ottoman sultan and caliph*   Born on September 8, 1779, the son of Sultan ABDÜLHAMID I and Ayse Sineperver Valide Sultan, Mustafa IV succeeded Sultan SELIM III (r. 1789–1807), who had initiated a major reform program known as the NIZAM-I CEDID (New Order) aimed at modernizing the army and bereaucracy. Even before he acceded to the throne in 1807, Prince Mustafa was in contact with political circles who opposed the reformist policies of Selim III. On May 25–29, 1807, an anti-reformist revolt erupted, known as the Kabakçı Incident. Recruits from the BLACK SEA region, intended to be trained as Nizam-ı Cedid soldiers, rebelled against wearing a uniform, which they considered un-Islamic. This rebellion, led by Kabakçı Mustafa, received support from the JANISSARIES and resulted in the deposition of Selim III and Mustafa's accession (May 29, 1807). Selim III's Nizam-ı Cedid reforms were revoked, his new Western-style army was dissolved, most of the proponents of reform were killed, and the rest of them fled to Rusçuk (Ruse, northern BULGARIA), where they were protected by the powerful AYAN, or local notable, ALEMDAR MUSTAFA PASHA.

At that time the Ottoman-Russian War of 1806–12 (*see* RUSSO-OTTOMAN WARS) was still going on, and the Ottomans suffered defeats both on land and at sea. When an armistice was signed in 1808, Alemdar Mustafa Pasha, a partisan of the former sultan, Selim III, obtained the support of the grand vizier to depose Mustafa IV in

favor of his predecessor. On July 28, 1808 Alemdar Mustafa Pasha and his troops occupied Istanbul. Because his intention to depose the sultan became clear, Mustafa IV ordered the execution of Selim III and his own brother Prince Mahmud. However, Mahmud was able to escape, and acceded to the throne. Alemdar Mustafa Pasha, having established a military dictatorship in the capital, invited the *ayans* of Anatolia and the Balkans to Istanbul, where they accepted an agreement called Sened-i İttifak, or "Deed of Agreement" (October 7, 1808) that legitimized the political status of the *ayans* and imposed limitations on the absolute power of the sultan. He also founded a new military corps, the Sekban-ı Cedid (October 14, 1808). These measures angered both the sultan and the Janissaries. When the Janissaries launched a revolt against him, Mahmud II condoned the death of this grand vizier, while ordering the execution of Mustafa IV (November, 15, 1808).

Selcuk Akşin Somel

Further reading: Kemal Beydilli, "Mustafa IV," in *Türkiye Diyanet Vakfı İslâm Ansiklopedisi*, vol. 31 (Istanbul: TDV Yayınları, 2006), 283–285; J. H. Kramers, "Muṣṭafā IV," in *Encyclopaedia of Islam*, 2nd ed., vol. 7 (Leiden: Brill, 1960–).

Mustafa Kamil (b. 1874–1908) *Egyptian nationalist, journalist, and politician*   Mustafa Kamil is considered by some to be the founder of the Egyptian nationalist movement. He was born in CAIRO where he studied law in the newly established government law school. He later went on to earn a law degree at the University of Toulouse in France. Upon his return to EGYPT, he founded the National Party (al-Hizb al-Watani) in 1894. The primary goal of the party was to force an end of the British occupation of the country, through peaceful, constitutional means. To advance nationalist awareness among the Egyptian reading public, he started the newspaper *al-Liwa* (the banner) in 1900. Ever aware of the importance of European public opinion, Mustafa Kamil started English and French language editions of his paper in 1907.

Mustafa Kamil spent much of his time in Paris and ISTANBUL where he worked to win allies to promote his goal of ending British occupation of Egypt. Due to his eagerness to establish any ally against Britain, some historians have described him as an opportunist. For example, Mustafa Kamil was willing to recognize Sultan ABDÜLHAMID II (1876–1909) as the rightful caliph of the Sunnis if it meant gaining support for his cause. This was a step few other Arab Muslims were willing to take as the Ottoman sultans were not descended from the tribe of the Prophet Muhammad, the Quraysh, which was a requirement established by Islamic law for a candidate for the caliphate. The sultan, grateful for the acknowledgment, rewarded him with the title of pasha.

Mustafa Kamil received his chance to galvanize Egyptian popular opinion behind him with the DIN-SHAWAY INCIDENT in 1906, in which four Egyptian men were sentenced to death and a number of others were sentenced to imprisonment or flogging for the alleged murder of a British officer. The outrage at the treatment of the accused Egyptian peasants led to the formation of a united front among various political factions in Egypt. Mustafa Kamil called a national congress in December 1907 to give voice to nationalist demands. The delegates elected him president but his moment of glory was short-lived as he died of an undiagnosed illness on February 10, 1908.

Bruce Masters

Further reading: Jamal Ahmet, *The Intellectual Origins of Egyptian Nationalism* (London: Oxford University Press, 1960); Keith Wilson, *Imperialism and Nationalism in the Middle East: The Anglo-Egyptian Experience* (London: Mansell Publications, 1983).

Mustafa Reşid Pasha (b. 1800–d. 1858) *eminent diplomat and reformist statesman of the Tanzimat era* Mustafa Reşid Pasha was born in Istanbul on March 13, 1800 the son of a civil servant. When he lost his father in 1810, soon after graduating from madrasa, he was raised by Seyit Pasha, his brother-in-law, and became a clerk with his support. After serving in various positions in the Sublime Porte, Mustafa Reşid, by then a prominent diplomat, was appointed to Paris as ambassador in 1834. He sought to regain Algeria from the French who had invaded it in 1830. With his next appointment as ambassador to London in 1836 he further increased his influence on both domestic and foreign policy, leading to his subsequent appointment as minister of foreign affairs in 1837.

Mustafa Reşid endorsed the Balta Limanı Trade Treaty with Britain in 1838, which granted CAPITULATIONS to Britain that were intended to obtain their support in foreign policy, especially in the so-called Egyptian Question, which emerged in 1831 when MEHMED ALI Pasha, governor of Egypt, revolted against the Sublime Porte. In August 1838 Reşid Pasha was sent to London once more, this time as a special envoy to form a defensive alliance with Britain against Mehmed Ali Pasha in a possible war between Egypt and the Ottoman Empire.

Mustafa Reşid was instrumental in the political, social, and technical modernization of the empire and due to his persistent efforts and support for Sultan Mahmud II the Gülhane Edict, or TANZIMAT Decree, was promulgated on November 3, 1839. Mustafa Reşid's contribution to the Tanzimat Decree, a set of laws that sparked widespread reforms in all areas of government,

was significant and an important step toward establishing Western-style law in the empire. Foreign powers, especially the British, reacted favorably to the Tanzimat reforms, which helped resolve the Egyptian Question in the Ottomans' favor. The Treaty of London, signed on July 15, 1840, guaranteed support for the Ottomans against Egypt by all European states except France.

During his second term as ambassador to Paris, from 1841 to 1845, Mustafa Reşid helped resolve the Lebanon Question, an international dispute between MARONITES, a Christian group in LEBANON and DRUZES, an extremist Shia sect living mainly in SYRIA and Lebanon. After a brief second term as foreign minister starting in October 1845, he was promoted to the grand vizierate in September 1846.

During his term as grand vizier modern state archives were set up, educational reforms were initiated, and the Secular Trade Courts was established in 1847. In April 1848 Mustafa Reşidwas dismissed from his post on charges of promoting republicanism filed against him by Damat Sait Pasha, a conservative. However, he was soon cleared of the charges and restored to his post as grand vizier. In his second term as grand vizier, the domestic slave trade was prohibited and the Encümen-i Daniş, the Ottoman Academy of Sciences, was established in 1851 as a result of his efforts. In 1848 a series of revolts that began in France but soon spread all over Europe, created serious political problems in Europe and a refugee crisis in the Ottoman Empire when Hungarian and Wallachian refugees fled to the Ottoman Empire. After a short time RUSSIA insisted that the Ottomans hand over the refugees and threatened the Sublime Porte by war. Despite such pressure Reşid Pasha declined to expel the refugees from the empire and his determination contributed to favorable public opinion in Britain and France.

In 1853 a dispute emerged between Russia, representing Orthodox Christians, and France, representing Roman Catholics, over control of the holy places in JERUSALEM, which was on Ottoman territory. In the course of negotiations, Foreign Minister Reşid Pasha rejected Russian demands, giving in to pressure from the British ambassador, Stratford Canning. Immediately following that crisis and in accordance with alliance treaties signed in March 1854, Mustafa Reşid played a key role in getting his government to help defend British and French interests during the CRIMEAN WAR (1853–56). His success in this effort and the support of Ambassador Canning led to Mustafa Reşid's fourth appointment as grand vizier in November 1854. With his power at its zenith, Mustafa Reşid again put his weight behind the ongoing reform process, causing it once again to accelerate.

After the Crimean War European powers forced the Sublime Porte to issue the Islahat Fermanı (commonly known as Imperial Reform Edict) on February 28, 1856, which granted equal political rights to both Muslim and non-Muslim Ottoman citizens in the areas of education, justice, religion, and taxation. Mustafa Reşid Pasha strongly criticized this decree for being against Ottoman interests. In October 1857 Mustafa Reşid was appointed grand vizier again, but this final appointment was short-lived as Mustafa Reşid died on January 7, 1858 and was buried in Istanbul.

As the leader of the liberal reformist wing, Mustafa Reşid Pasha played a critical role in the Tanzimat reform process, but he cannot be considered the sole architect of these reforms. The Ottoman sultans of this period, MAHMUD II (r. 1808–1839) and ABDÜLMECID I (r. 1839–1861), as well as other statesmen, also made valuable contributions to this process and must not be ignored. Although he has sometimes been represented as the "prophet of civilization" and "the man who prepared the laws of individual freedoms which restricted the sultan's authority," these are exaggerated political slogans, created later by the YOUNG TURKS, members of a late 19th-century group that supported constitutionalism and modernization.

Mustafa Reşid's unique status as a symbol of modernity and reform in modern Turkish historiography is a politically and ideologically controversial issue, and not necessarily historical fact. Reşid Pasha thought that the Ottoman Empire could only survive with full British collaboration. This belief led to French and Russian resistance to his policies and caused intermittent dismissals from his diplomatic posts and his position as grand vizier. His opponents criticized him largely for his pro-British attitude and for the dismal economic consequences of the capitulations first granted to British merchants, then extended to include other European merchants. Although Reşid Pasha was the most prominent political figure of the Tanzimat era and an eminent statesman who led the process of Turkish westernization and modernization, his work and his personality had both positive and negative aspects and he should be appreciated as a complex and controversial figure.

Yüksel Çelik

Further reading: Roderic H. Davison, *Reform in the Ottoman Empire, 1856–1876* (New York: Gordian Press, 1973); Carther V. Findley, *Bureaucratic Reform in the Ottoman Empire: The Sublime Porte, 1789–1922* (Princeton, N.J.: Princeton University Press, 1980); C. V. Findley, *Ottoman Civil Officialdom: A Social History* (Princeton, N.J.: Princeton University Press, 1989); Şerif Mardin, *The Genesis of Young Ottoman Thought: A Study in the Modernization of Turkish Political Ideas* (Princeton, N.J.: Princeton University Press, 1962); Stanley Lane-Poole, *The Life of the Right Honorable Stratford Canning, Viscount Stratford de Redcliffe*, II (London: Longman, 1888).

mutasarrifiyya   In the aftermath of the LEBANESE CIVIL WAR in 1860, the Ottoman authorities imposed a new system of government for the mountain districts of LEBANON. Formerly, the region had been divided into two districts, one with a MARONITE Christian administrator and the other with a DRUZE. In place of this system, the Ottomans combined the two into a single district, known as the *mutasarrifiyya*. It was stipulated that the administrator of this region would always be an Ottoman Catholic, but one from outside Lebanon. The first was DAVUD PASHA, an Armenian Catholic from ISTANBUL. By 1864, an administrative council of 12 members was established to assess taxes and to control and advise the *mutasarrif*, or administrator, on matters of governance. The members of the council were allotted to the various religious communities so that there would always be four Maronites, three Druzes, two GREEK ORTHODOX members, and one member each from the Sunni, Shii, and Greek Catholic communities. The regulations of the *mutasarrafiyya* stipulated that all the inhabitants of the district were equal before the law, and ended all feudal privileges binding the peasants to the landlords as virtual serfs. There was some opposition from the feudal lords, but Davud Pasha was able to implement a smoothly running administration and his successors continued to provide excellent leadership. Some historians consider the *mutasarrifiyya* to have been the most successful experiment in Ottoman political reform, although its formula for representation on the administrative council established the principal of sectarian representation that continues to haunt Lebanon even into the present.

Bruce Masters

Further reading: Engin Akarlı, *The Long Peace: Ottoman Lebanon, 1861–1920* (Berkeley: University of California Press, 1993).

Muwahhidun   See DRUZES; WAHHABIS.

mysticism   See SUFISM.

al-Nabulusi, Abd al-Ghani (d. 1731) *Syrian jurist, intellectual, and Sufi* Abd al-Ghani al-Nabulusi was, for a time, mufti (chief jurist) of DAMASCUS, but he is best remembered for his writing, which was both prolific (between 200 and 250 manuscripts) and diverse, ranging from love poetry to a treatise on the proper care and propagation of olive trees. His most famous works were those about the great Sufi philosopher Muhiyy al-Din ibn al-Arabi (d. 1240), and his travel literature. The latter included *The Truth and the Marvel of a Journey in Syria, Egypt, and the Hejaz.* This was not an ordinary travelogue for it chronicled a voyage of interior discovery across the spiritual geography of the Middle East. Al-Nabulusi gave little space to the physical features of the lands he traversed but rather dwelt on the mystical links between the places he visited and the various Sufi saints, past and present, with whom they were associated. Al-Nabulusi also wrote at least two essays in defense of various Sufi masters who were under attack by orthodox Muslim critics for being lenient in their treatment of non-Muslims. Al-Nabulusi was particularly strong in his defense of 13th-century Muslim mystic Muhiyy al-Din ibn al-Arabi against charges that his concept of *wahdat al-wujud* (the unity of all existence) was heretical.

Al-Nabulusi stands as an outstanding example of the synthesis between Sunni legal scholarship and Sufi philosophy. That combination dominated Muslim intellectual life in much of the Ottoman Empire until the 18th century, with legal scholars and judges finding no apparent contradiction in composing mystical poetry or commentaries. But by the time of al-Nabulusi's death, Muslim scholars were already starting to challenge the Sufi philosophic tradition as being un-Islamic. Al-Nabulusi was

buried near the tomb of ibn al-Arabi in Damascus, as a sign of the respect that he had always demonstrated for the master while alive.

Bruce Masters

See also SUFISM.

Further reading: Elizabeth Sirriyeh, *Sufi Visionary of Ottoman Damascus: Abd al-Ghani al-Nabulusi, 1641–1731* (London: Routledge-Curzon, 2005).

Nadir Shah (b. 1688–d. 1747) (r. 1736–1747) *Iranian warlord and shah* Nadir Shah was a Turkoman from the Afshar tribe who seized the throne of IRAN. He was born about 1688 and attached himself to the service of Prince Tahmasp, a member of the Safavid dynasty that had ruled Iran since the early 16th century. In 1722, Afghan adventurers captured the royal capital of Isfahan and claimed the throne, as the remnants of the ruling family sought refuge in the tribally controlled areas of the country. The anarchy in Iran seemed a golden opportunity for the Ottomans and they invaded in 1723, capturing the city of Kermanshah. In the following year they pressed on to take Hamadan and most of western Iran. The Ottoman offensive bogged down in 1726, however, and they were defeated outside Isfahan. Tahmasp was able to regain Isfahan and his family's throne in 1729, thanks to Nadir, who was given the name Tahmasp Quli Shah, or the slave of Tahmasp.

Having secured central Iran, Nadir moved against the Afghan heartland, taking Herat in 1732. But while Nadir pursued conquests in the east, Shah Tahmasp reopened hostilities with the Ottomans in an effort to regain his lost territories. He was defeated and agreed to a treaty that restored Tabriz to Iranian control but left Kermanshah and Hamadan in Ottoman hands. Nadir was incensed at the treaty; he convinced the tribal warriors who formed the core of his army to depose Tahmasp in favor of the shah's infant son, for whom Nadir became regent, with the title *vekil-i dowle* or Agent of Sovereignty. He denounced the treaty with the Ottomans and laid siege to BAGHDAD. An Ottoman army, dispatched from Anatolia, broke the siege, and Nadir withdrew from IRAQ, returning to Iran to quell a rebellion.

Nadir took the title of shah for himself in 1736 and declared that the official religion of his state was SUNNI ISLAM. This began a period of persecution for the Shia, and many of their learned men sought refuge in Iraq. Despite his persecutions of the Shii clergy, Nadir Shah entered into negotiations with the Ottomans. He tried to convince their religious authorities to recognize a moderate form of SHIA ISLAM as a fifth legal school with the name of Jaafari, after Jaafar al-Sadiq, the sixth imam of the Shia and a noted legal scholar. That compromise was not accepted, however, either by Sunni clerics in the Ottoman Empire or by those of the Shia in Iran. Nonetheless, the Iranian frontier with the Ottomans quieted down as Nadir Shah moved east again, conquering Kabul and Lahore in 1740. With those victories and the wealth they provided, he began a new campaign against the Ottomans in 1741. The campaign again targeted Iraq, and Nadir Shah took Kirkuk in 1743. He then moved on MOSUL but the civilian population of the city was mobilized by the city's governor, Husayn Pasha al-Jalili; with the city's garrison, they were able to fend off the siege. Inconclusive fighting raged along the frontier in Kurdistan until 1746 when the two sides agreed to a peace treaty. The following year, Nadir Shah was killed by his own troops, and Iran descended once again into chaos.

Bruce Masters

Further reading: Robert Olson, *The Siege of Mosul and Ottoman-Persian Relations, 1718–1743* (Bloomington: Indiana University Press, 1975).

Nahda In the latter decades of the 19th century, Arabic-speaking intellectuals began to rediscover the classics of Arabic literature and to take pride in their Arab past. Arab scholars have labeled this period the Nahda, meaning "renaissance," or "rebirth." They view it as similar to the cultural awakening that occurred in early modern Europe when the classical era of Western culture was rediscovered. Led by intellectuals such as BUTRUS AL-BUSTANI, many of those involved in this period of discovery were Christians who had received what formal training they had in Classical Arabic from foreign MISSIONARIES. Muslims were also involved, taking the lead in editing and publishing secular classics of Islam's Golden Age in Cairo.

Before the 19th century, most Arab Christians had had little interest, and consequently little knowledge, of classical Arabic grammar and syntax, as is demonstrated by the loose colloquial style of extant written materials from before that time. This suggests that even educated Christians were unconcerned about the grammatical rules or vocabulary of *fusha* (the classical literary language). By the middle of the 19th century, however, some Arab Christians had begun to study and appreciate the classics of Arabic literature. In the process, they began to adopt its literary standards as their own. Their discovery of what they saw as largely secular classics of poetry, history, and science meant that they could establish connections with the wider Arabic-speaking Muslim world in which they lived. It is, however, doubtful that the Muslim authors of these classics would themselves have considered their works to be secular. With a newly acquired appreciation of Arabic culture, many in the Arab Christian elite started to define themselves culturally as Arabs with an acquired pride in the brilliant literary past they saw themselves as sharing with their Muslim neighbors.

The Nahda was not simply a movement by and for intellectuals. New Arabic-language newspapers and periodicals that dealt with all subjects, from the latest scientific discoveries to how to set a proper Western-style dinner table, were appearing in BEIRUT, CAIRO, Paris, and New York, and these helped shape the way the rapidly growing Arabic-reading public understood the West. Some scholars see the Nahda as the beginning of Arab NATIONALISM. While that might be an overstatement, the Nahda undoubtedly created an awareness of Arab culture and history that contributed to the growth of political nationalism. It also helped to create bonds of community across religious lines.

Bruce Masters

Further reading: Pierre Cacchia, *Arabic Literature: An Overview* (New York: Routledge Curzon, 2002).

Najaf (*Turk.*: Necef) After MECCA and MEDINA, Najaf, in present-day IRAQ, is the holiest city in the sacred geography of SHIA ISLAM as it contains the grave of the revered Imam Ali, whom the Shia believe was the rightful successor to the Prophet Muhammad. Many Shiis believe that burial next to Imam Ali will help them enter paradise and so seek to be buried there. Although Najaf is near the EUPHRATES RIVER, one of the city's challenges in its early centuries was a dependable supply of water, as the shrine complex itself is distant from the river. The city is connected to the Euphrates River by means of a canal but it silted in periodically and required major efforts to repair.

Sultan SÜLEYMAN I (r. 1520–66) visited the city in 1535 after his conquest of BAGHDAD and provided funds for the upkeep of the shrine of Imam Ali. Nevertheless, the city's population went into decline after that, due to chronic problems with the maintenance of the canal. The completion of the Hindiyya Canal in 1803 settled the water problem and the city grew tremendously, helped in part by donations from the Indian kingdom of Oudh, whose ruling dynasty were Shii Muslims. During the period of repression of the Shia by NADIR SHAH (r. 1736–47) in the 18th century, many clerics and scholars left Iran and settled in Najaf. By the 19th century, the city had become a rival to the city of Qum in Iran as a center of religious scholarship and education in the Shii world. At the beginning of the 19th century, the self-described Muwahhidun, or "those who proclaim the absolute unity of God," better known as the WAHHABIS, threatened the city several times, but never succeeded in taking it. By the end of the Ottoman period in the early 20th century, the city had an estimated 30,000 inhabitants and hosted tens of thousands of pilgrims every year; most of them came from neighboring Iran, but pilgrims from British India were also numerous. In 1915, the city's populace revolted against Ottoman rule, allowing the city to be occupied by British troops.

Bruce Masters

Najd (Nejd) Najd is the name for the large plateau in what is today central Saudi Arabia. It is harsh desert country that is broken by the presence of wells and natural springs. These provide the water for the maintenance of small agricultural areas, known as oases, where BEDOUIN tribesmen cultivate date palms and grain. It was a remote region in the Ottoman period, dominated by various Bedouin confederations, and never came under direct Ottoman rule. The region was also the birthplace and home of MUHAMMAD IBN ABD AL-WAHHAB, best known as the founder of the so-called WAHHABIS, and it was there in 1744 that he effected an alliance with Muhammad Ibn Saud of the IBN SAUD FAMILY. The Wahhabi movement that resulted from this alliance transformed tribal politics by providing an ideological and spiritual basis for the existing confederations. Not all the tribes of the Najd joined the Wahhabi cause, as tribal rivalries prevented the emergence of an all-embracing tribal confederation, but the ibn Saud family dominated the region politically from that point on and it remained their home base even after they conquered MECCA and MEDINA in the first decade of the 19th century. The Egyptian army retook these two holy cities by 1813 and drove deep into the deserts of the Najd. By 1818, the army had reached the oasis of Diriyya that served as the command center of the ibn Saud dynasty, and destroyed

it. But the family was able to regain power after the Egyptians left, establishing their base of operations in the oasis of Riyadh, today the capital of Saudi Arabia. That city remained their headquarters until the fall of the Ottoman Empire when they were able to extend their control over most of the Arabian Peninsula.

Bruce Masters

Nakşbendi *See* NAQSHBANDIYYA ORDER.

Namık Kemal (b. 1840–d. 1888) *writer, intellectual, reformer, and political theorist* Namık Kemal was a poet, playwright, and political essayist who espoused the cause of REFORM and the ideas of patriotism, OTTOMANISM, and PAN-ISLAMISM. A key member of the group known as the YOUNG OTTOMANS, Kemal both wrote for and published renowned opposition NEWSPAPERS, and coined the Turkish words for liberty (*hürriyet*) and fatherland (*vatan*). He was given the nickname Namık by the poet Ashraf, who read many of Kemal's works.

Kemal was born in Tekirdağ (in eastern Thrace, Turkey) on December 21, 1840. His mother, Fatma Zehra, was the daughter of Abdullatif Pasha, a tax collector; his father, Mustafa Asim Bey, was a chief astrologer in the sultan's palace. Kemal lost his mother when he was eight years old and came to Istanbul, where he attended secondary schools. In Istanbul, Kars (in eastern Anatolia, Turkey), and Sofia (Bulgaria), where he stayed because of his grandfather's official appointments, he took courses on SUFISM, literature, linguistics, logic, Arabic, and Persian from private teachers. It is here that he first seriously engaged with poetry. Kemal lived within the family circle of his grandfather Abdullatif Pasha for most of his youth (until he turned 19), but information about this period is incomplete, uncertain, and contradictory.

Namık Kemal began his career as a civil servant in the Customs Translation Bureau (1857–58) before entering the Translation Bureau of the Sublime Porte (1859). In this period, he was strongly influenced by Leskofçalı Galip, a supporter of classical LITERATURE who encouraged Kemal to join the Encümen-i Şuara, or the Society of Poets, which he did in 1861. When Leskofçalı Galip left for ISTANBUL later that year, however, this group of new-generation poets scattered, and Kemal became subject to new influences.

In 1862 Kemal joined the newly launched newspaper *Tasvir-i Efkar* (Herald of Ideas), founded by the western-educated Şinasi Efendi. Addressing political and social subjects and advocating the importance of public opinion in the day-to-day activities of government, this newspaper and its founding partners had a real impact on Kemal, changing the subjects of his poetry and drawing him into expository political writing. In Kemal's newspaper articles, he covered foreign policy and education, and touched on the situation of women in city life. As part of this more generalized political awakening, Namık Kemal joined the Ittifak-ı Hamiyet, or Union of Patriots, formed in 1864 for the purpose of promoting constitutional government (see CONSTITUTION).

In 1867 Kemal accepted the invitation of Mustafa Fazıl Pasha and traveled to Paris with Ziya Pasha to work on realizing the objectives mentioned in Mustafa Fazıl's open letter to Sultan ABDÜLAZIZ (r. 1861–76), which was published in *Nord* (a pro-Russian newspaper based in Brussels, Belgium) in 1866. In the letter, he noted that lack of liberty within the empire made reform efforts ineffectual and he emphasized that it was impossible to benefit from the institutions of education in the absence of liberty. He addressed his critiques mainly to MEHMED AMIN ÂLÎ PASHA and FUAD PASHA rather than to the sultan. Moreover, he accused Âlî Pasha and Fuad Pasha of hiding the real situation of the people and the country from the sultan and thus misguiding the ruler. He also expressed his opinions on financial reform, noting the deficiencies and irregularities of the tax system. He suggested that the sultan change the system of governance in order to save the state. Toward this end, he announced the establishment of a party called Jeune Turquie (Young Turkey) in Paris. The group referred to itself as the New Ottoman Society, or (as they are now more widely known) as the Young Ottoman Society.

In London, Kemal's Young Ottoman colleague Ali Suavi published a newpaper, *Muhbir* (Reporter), advocating the goals and values of the group. In 1868 Namık Kemal himself undertook the publication of another newspaper with similar aims, *Hürriyet* (Liberty).

Leaving the paper in 1869 after its 63rd issue, Kemal returned to Istanbul where he wrote for the newspapers *Diyojen* (named for the Greek cynic philosopher Diogenes, 412–323 B.C.E.) and *Hadika* (The garden), as well as forming his own intellectual newspaper in 1872, *Ibret* (Admonition), which covered social and national subjects.

In 1873, Kemal wrote and staged what may be his best-known work, *Vatan yahut Silistre* (Fatherland, or, Silistra). In the play Silistra, Bulgaria, is besieged by the Russians during the Crimean War (1853–56) and the play's hero, Ismail Bey, volunteers to fight against the invaders. The occasion is used by Namik Kemal to espouse his patriotic and heroic ideals. The play, however, caused his exile by Sultan Abdülaziz. He was forgiven by ABDÜLHAMID II (r. 1876–1909) in 1876 and returned to Istanbul, where the sultan appointed him to the Şura-yı Devlet (Council of State), and invited him to the commissioning of the new Ottoman constitution (Kanun-i Esasi). Namık Kemal died in 1888 while serving as an administrator in Mytilene.

Elements of Namık Kemal's political theory can be found in his writings in the newspapers *Hurriyet* and *Ibret*; his literary works also express his political ideas. His strong patriotic and heroic ideals are demonstrated in his play *Vatan yahut Silistre* and in his historical monographs on sultans MEHMED II (r. 1444–46; 1451–81) and SELIM I (r. 1512–20) and on Saladin (d. 1193), warrior of Islam and founder of the Ayyibid dynasty. A strong advocate of a constitutional and parliamentary political system, Kemal believed that an Ottoman representative assembly would serve as a powerful unifying force for the Ottoman lands. His political ideas are a mixture of traditional Islamic and European libertarian theories. He wrote that these two schools of thought must unite to defend themselves from assault. In the second phase of his writings, Kemal discussed the legitimacy problem of government. Kemal argued that the only type of government in which loyalty to the sovereign was legitimate was one that incorporated the institution of a *biat*, or oath of allegiance, with the annulling of the *biat* being society's rightful recourse against a corrupt or incompetent ruler. Kemal introduced political concepts that were new to Ottoman thought, such as "the people," the "interests of the people," and "public opinion."

Most of Kemal's articles were written to express the need to create what he called a constitutional monarchy in the empire. He believed that Ottoman Muslims—called by Namik Kemal *ummah*, a term that is used by others for the entire Muslim community—could only be free if individual and political rights were guaranteed by independent courts and by the principle of separation of powers. He also coined the Turkish words for liberty (*hürriyet*) and fatherland (*vatan*), writing articles on *vatan* that urged individuals to strengthen their own connection to their *vatan*. He considered all the citizens of the empire, regardless of ethnic or religious affiliation, as members of the Ottoman political entity. Toward the end of his life Kemal also began advocating Ittihad-i Islam, or Pan-Islamism, in politics.

Yücel Bulut

Further reading: Niyazi Berkes, *The Development of Secularism in Turkey* (Montreal: McGill University Press, 1964); Şerif Mardin, *The Genesis of Young Ottoman Thought* (Princeton, N.J.: Princeton University Press, 1962).

Napoleon Bonaparte (b. 1769–d. 1821) *French general under revolutionary government, later emperor of France*   Under the authority of the French revolutionary government, the Directory, General Napoleon Bonaparte landed French troops in EGYPT on July 1, 1798 as part of an expeditionary force. The purpose of the military action was to assault British trade routes to India in an effort to cripple the British enemy. In a bid to win Egyptian popular support for the invasion, Napoleon issued a proclamation that he was the friend of Sultan SELIM III (r. 1789–1807) and that he had come to liberate the Egyptians from the MAMLUK EMPIRE. Even more incredibly, he claimed that he and his men were Muslims. It seems highly unlikely that anyone in Egypt believed either claim. However, the French met with little resistance as they pressed on to Cairo, where on July 21, 1798, they decisively defeated the Mamluk forces in what the French promptly dubbed the Battle of the Pyramids.

This victory was checked, however, on August 1, when British Admiral Nelson destroyed the French fleet anchored at the Egyptian port of Abu Qir, thus stranding the French forces. Sultan Selim III declared war on the French in September, and in October Napoleon was faced with an urban uprising in Cairo. After it was brutally suppressed, Napoleon decided to advance against Syria where Ottoman governor CEZZAR AHMED PASHA was organizing resistance to the French occupation. In February 1799 the French army moved into Syria and took the town of Jaffa where, despite their surrender, the entire garrison was executed. Napoleon pressed on to ACRE but his army was decimated by an outbreak of the plague. When Cezzar Ahmed's garrison held firm, Napoleon decided on a strategic withdrawal. Napoleon left Egypt in August 1799, returning to France to participate in the coup d'état that made him the French head of state. The French military forces he left behind eventually surrendered to British and Ottoman forces in 1801.

Historians of Egypt often identify Napoleon's occupation of the country as a crucial watershed that ushered in the modern era in Egypt. In fact, the French occupation did little to change Egypt other than polarizing the Muslim community against the Christian minority and creating a political vacuum that made possible the rise of MEHMED ALI, the autonomous governor of Egypt between 1805 and 1849. But for Europeans, the occupation had a profound effect. First, it demonstrated the weakness of the Ottoman Empire and encouraged other colonial powers to seize Ottoman territories. Second, Napoleon brought with him scholars trained in the Enlightenment thinking of late 18th-century France, which stressed the need to approach knowledge in a scientific and rational way. These scholars produced the magnificent *Description de l'Égypte*, a multivolume study of Egypt's antiquities and of the society and culture of Egyptian people they encountered. Many historians consider this work to be the beginning of modern archaeology as well as of European Orientalism, the study of non-European cultures and languages that became part of the framework for controlling "colonialized" peoples.

Bruce Masters

Further reading: Irene Bierman, *Napoleon in Egypt* (Reading, UK: Ithaca Press, 2003); Dror Ze'evi, "Back to Napoleon? Thoughts on the Beginning of the Modern Era in the Middle East." *Mediterranean Historical Review* 19 (2004): 73–94; Edward Said, *Orientalism* (New York: Pantheon Books, 1978).

naqib al-ashraf See ASHRAF.

Naqshbandiyya-Khalidiyya See NAQSHBANDIYYA ORDER.

Naqshbandiyya Order The Naqshbandiyya Order was the most conservative and Sunni of the various Sufi traditions that flourished in the Ottoman Empire. It was also one of the most politicized orders, as Naqshbandis often took a leading role in organizing resistance to what they regarded as Western imperialist ventures in the Muslim world. The order was named after Baha al-Din Naqshband, who lived in Central Asia in the 14th century. However, the Naqshbandis claim that the founder of their order was in fact Caliph Abu Bakr, the immediate successor to the Prophet Muhammad. This claim stresses the order's identification with SUNNI ISLAM and distinguishes it from most of the other Sufi orders, many of which cite Ali, the Prophet's son-in-law, as their ultimate inspiration and see Abu Bakr as a usurper.

Another major difference between the Naqshbandiyya and the Sufi orders is that the Naqshbandis do not engage in any outward performance of their *dhikr*, the act by which Sufis meditate and seek a union with God. Rather, the Naqshbandis engage in what they call the silent *dhikr*, as they believe that the sort of physical exercise characteristic of other orders' practice of *dhikr* is a theatrical diversion from the true purpose of the act. The Naqshbandis also do not have a long process of spiritual internship that requires those seeking to join the order to pursue a series of stages under the guidance of a master before being judged worthy of admittance. They hold that a person will only approach the order for admittance if he has already reached a sufficient level of religious enlightenment internally and thus knows that he is ready. Influenced by al-Ghazali, the 11th-century Muslim jurist and scholar, the Naqshbandis hold that mysticism cannot negate anything that is taught by the Quran and the Sunna. At the same time, the mystical experience confirms for the believer the absolute knowledge that Islamic law is the divine path. Mysticism and Islamic law are seen, therefore, as not only compatible but also absolutely necessary to one another.

The Naqshbandi tradition received a major boost from the teaching and writings of Sheikh Diya al-Din

Khalid (d. 1827). Sheikh Khalid was a KURD from the SHAHRIZOR district in present-day Iraq. While on the HAJJ, he witnessed the WAHHABI conquest of Mecca. He remained in the city for several years, studying under masters who followed the tradition of Ahmad Sirhindi (d. 1624), an Indian scholar who had developed the ideology of the Naqshbandi Order into a much more coherent form than it had previously known. Sheikh Khalid rejected the anti-Sufi stance of the followers of ibn Abd al-Wahhab, who condemned all Sufis as heretics, but he also rejected what he believed to be the divergence from "true" Islam that most Sufi orders of his day represented. He saw his mission as nothing short of the revival of Sunni Islam in the Ottoman Empire through strict adherence to Islamic law, grounded in a certainty of purpose that could only come to the believer through the mystical experience.

Sheikh Khalid's movement soon gained many followers and so great was his influence on the order that some Western scholars have called the order the Naqshbandiyya-Khalidiyya after him. Sheikh Khalid's program of renewal enjoyed a great degree of popularity among Muslim intellectuals throughout the Ottoman Empire, gaining followers everywhere, but its main centers of activity were in Damascus and in Sheikh Khalid's native Kurdistan. The Naqshbandiyya offered an alternative to the more austere Wahhabi movement in that it preached the reform of Muslim institutions and practices but did not seek a break with the Ottoman sultanate. For this reason Ottoman officials were often strong supporters of the order and could be found in its ranks.

Bruce Masters

See also SUFISM.

Further reading: Butrus Abu-Manneh, "The Naqshbandiyya-Mujaddidiyya in the Ottoman Lands in the Early Nineteenth Century." *Die Welt des Islams* 22 (1982): 131–53.

nationalism   Nationalism describes the independent political, social, and cultural consciousness that flourished within the Ottoman Empire's member communities in the 19th century. It was instrumental in the ultimate demise of the empire in the early 20th century as specific groups broke away from the greater political structure and formed their own independent nations. Nationalism first arose in the second half of the 18th century among Orthodox Christians in the Balkan region. Muslims in the empire did not enter into a full experience of ethnic nationalism until around the time of the YOUNG TURK revolution of 1908.

The rise of nationalism in the Ottoman imperial state and the subsequent establishment of some 30 nation-states was influenced by many factors, including competitive and often divisive relationships between associated religious groups, or MILLETS; progressive REFORM of the Ottoman political structure, requiring the imposition of standards and central systems; the influence of Enlightenment philosophy and ideals; and the ever-looming peril of extra-Ottoman imperial interests, especially those of RUSSIA, FRANCE, and ENGLAND.

CHANGES IN OTTOMAN STATE POLITICAL STRUCTURE

The expansion of capitalism in the Ottoman state, which began in the Balkans early in the 18th century, undermined the classical statist system in favor of private property and entrepreneurship. As capitalism stimulated trade and gave rise to a new middle class, the urban Christian middle classes began to dominate that trade. Meanwhile, Muslims assumed control of agricultural production and became members of the municipal and provincial administrative bodies. After 1876 they took a similar role in the House of Deputies, in which non-Muslims were also well represented.

Early in the 19th century, the Ottoman government sought to cope with the new challenges through a series of reforms that centralized authority in the hands of a new bureaucracy and deprived the local elites of their administrative power and economic privileges. Those elites, both Muslim and non-Muslim, shorn of state support, eventually made the community the source of their power and, in the process, became defenders of the culture, language, and particular brand of religion of their respective communities.

THE ROLE OF THE RELIGIOUS *MILLET* IN THE RISE OF NATIONALISM

Although the empire had long been home to a wide variety of ethnic identities and although several forms of patriotism that centered on land or on opposition to the Ottoman imperial system began to emerge after the 1850s, the first true nationalist movements were founded in identity groups formed by the imperially defined religious community, or *millet*. Among these *millets* were specific groups of Orthodox Christians living mainly in the Balkans. Members of both the GREEK ORTHODOX and the Armenian *millets* were found throughout the area, the latter including the ancient Eastern Christians. JEWS, mainly Sephardim after the 15th century, accounted for about 3 percent of the empire's POPULATION and were found in all of its major urban centers. The patriarchate in ISTANBUL, representing the Orthodox Christian *millet*, created a formal union, while the Armenian *millet*, headed by its own patriarch, was more loosely defined.

Within the Orthodox Christian communities, intellectuals were especially attracted to the ideas of the Enlightenment, especially the notion, advocated by the

German poet and philosopher Johann Gottfried Herder (1744–1803), that language and literature are the distinct marks of a nation. Representatives of France in the Ottoman state, bringing with them the ideals of the French Revolution, which sanctified the idea of nation and turned it into a symbol of mythic value, aided these local Orthodox intellectuals, and fiercely attacked the old order, including institutionalized religion and the sultanate. When their efforts provoked sharp reaction among the established religious and social elite, Russia emerged from its victories against the Ottoman armies between 1768 and 1812 as the defender of Orthodox Christians. Shortly afterward, in the 1850s, it launched Panslavism as an ideology of unity and independence for all the Orthodox Slavs, many of whom were Ottoman subjects.

THE EMERGENCE OF NATIONALISMS IN THE BALKANS

Many scholars regard the Serbian revolt of KARAD-JORDJE (1768–1817), the founder of the Karadjordjević dynasty, as the first of the nationalist uprisings. However, a much more important development had already undermined the primacy and unifying effect of religion among Orthodox Christians and made ethnicity the source of their various national identities. Around 1767 the Orthodox Patriarchate of Istanbul, striving to revive Byzantium, put an end to the relative autonomy of the Serbian and Bulgarian churches and ordered them to use the Greek language and Greek priests in their services. Because the Ottoman government was unable to fathom the impact of this change among its Slavic-speaking subjects, it remained silent, and alienated many non-Greeks from the patriarchate. The Karadjordje "revolution" originated amidst those circumstances as a protest by Serbian peasants against the usurpation of their land by the sultan's JANISSARIES who were expected to guarantee their safety and property. Karadjordje, a former officer in the Austrian army, turned the social unrest of the Serbian peasants into a political movement, which was initially defeated. It was revived through the diplomatic ability of Miloš Obrenović (who replaced, then murdered, Karadjordje) and achieved a degree of autonomy in 1815. An Ottoman vassal, Miloš also managed to develop a written Serbian language, thanks to the efforts of Vuk Stefanović Karadžić (1787–1864), considered the father of the Serbian national revival. In 1834 SERBIA established its own national church and began to train a national clergy that joined the military and the intellectuals as the torchbearers of Serbian nationalism. By 1849 Serbia, still formally under Ottoman sovereignty, had devised an expansionist plan to revive the empire of Stefan Dushan, the 14th-century Serbian leader who is also revered as a saint, and had romanticized and glorified its nationalism.

THE GREEK UPRISING

The Byzantinist national movement that provoked the earliest Slavic response provides another striking example of the complex nature of nationalism in the Ottoman state. The Neobyzantinist revival started by the PHANARIOTS (upper-class Greeks in the Phanar district of Istanbul) relied heavily on the appeal of Orthodox Christianity and the patriarchate to spread throughout the empire. While imposing the use of the Greek language and clergy on Serbian and Bulgarian churches, the movement not only encountered the negative reaction of the Slavs but also had little mass appeal among Greeks, who favored a modern national Greek state over a dead empire.

The GREEK WAR OF INDEPENDENCE began in 1820–22 almost simultaneously in the Morea, or Peloponnese, among peasants led by village priests protesting usury and the appropriation of their land by Albanian merchants, and in Crimea under Alexander Ypsilanti, an officer in the czar's army. It was supported by both the British and the Russians. The British needed an intermediary group to serve their expanding trade with the Middle East and India. They also had something of a romantic attitude toward ancient Hellenic culture, which the modern Greek intellectuals (headed by Adamantious Korais) claimed as their cultural fountainhead. Russia's involvement stemmed from a combination of political and religious reasons.

In the resulting war the Sublime Porte (the Ottoman government) was defeated and forced to sign the TREATY OF EDIRNE, granting independence to GREECE in 1828–29. Opposed to the idea of secular nationalism, the patriarchate in Istanbul did not recognize the new government of independent Greece until 1847 at the urgings of the Ottoman government. Whether the source of Greek nationalism was the ancient Hellenes or the Christian Byzantines is still debated, but Greece became the first internationally recognized independent country to emerge from the Ottoman Empire.

INDEPENDENT NATIONS IN THE BALKANS

Russian intervention prevented the total collapse of the Bulgarian revolution begun by a handful of intellectuals in 1876, as it had prevented the collapse of the revolution in Serbia in 1875. After Russia defeated the Ottoman armies in the unprovoked war of 1877–78, the Berlin Treaty of 1878 recognized Serbia, ROMANIA, and Montenegro as independent nation-states and granted autonomy to BULGARIA. The Ottoman state retained control of Thrace, Thessaly, Macedonia, and ALBANIA, but its presence and power in the Balkans were greatly reduced.

Thus the first phase of Ottoman nationalism culminated in independence and nationhood for most of the Orthodox Christians in the Balkans.

Although the emergence of "national" states in the Balkans implied that the population of each consisted only of the ethnic group bearing its name, in reality practically all contained a variety of ethnic groups. Ignoring the different languages and cultures of those groups, the titular nations strove to create homogeneity by assimilating the minorities or forcing them to migrate. For instance, in 1877, the Bulgarians were a minority of the population in their own country, which had at least 17 ethnic groups, including Turks, Greeks, and Romanians. Romania, which had taken its ethnic name in 1858 after the union of MOLDAVIA and WALLACHIA, occupied Dobruja in 1878, but the Romanian ethnic group there constituted a minority of about 18 percent, the rest of the population being Turks, Bulgarians, Jews, Greeks, ARMENIANS, Russians, Germans, and so on. Today, ironically, the only relatively religiously homogeneous nations in the Balkans are TURKEY and Greece, the representatives of Muslims and Orthodox Christians.

THE FORMATION OF NATIONAL IDENTITY IN THE BALKANS

The first Christian nationalism in the Balkans stood on the foundations of language, ethno-religion, and history. Chosen usually from a variety of dialects—such as one of the seven major Hellenic dialects of Greece—the official "national" language typically was imposed on the population through government support, education, and textbooks while the popular dialects survived in a variety of ways. This "national" language was glorified as having maintained the national identity and consciousness and cultural continuity during Ottoman rule. However, in reality, the elites had often adopted or discarded their "national" language for social, economic, and personal reasons. For instance, the Vlach and Bulgarian elites often willingly adopted the Greek language in order to enhance their social and cultural status and thus became Hellenized. The Ottoman state promoted this trend by considering the Greeks representatives of the Orthodox Christians and according them positions in the government as DRAGOMANS (interpreters) until the revolution of 1821, when the Armenians replaced the Greeks as the government's trusted agents. Meanwhile, the once large contingent of Latin-speaking VLACHS barely survived as an ethnic group.

Ethno-religion, another source of national identity, derived from the inseparable bond between ethnicity and religion. This link persisted despite the fact that Ottoman emphasis on communal-religious identity had increased the strength of religion and achieved a degree of formal Orthodox unity enforced by the patriarchate of Istanbul before its ill-advised effort to impose the use of the Greek language in Slavic-speaking churches and schools. The split of the Ottoman Christians into Slavophile and Greekophile groups received a great boost after Russia launched Panslavism in an effort to gain the loyalty and support of the Balkan Slavs, mainly Serbians, Bulgarians, and Macedonians. At the same time, Panslavism pushed the non-Slavic Orthodox Christians away from Russia; the Romanians, who spoke a language derived from Latin, embraced the West, especially France, and the Greeks aligned themselves with England but remained friendly with Russia. Nationalism and nationhood thus gave ethnicity a secular meaning and placed it over religion even as each national state remained fiercely attached to its own "national" church, which supplemented ethnicity as a source of nationalism. All the new states in the former Ottoman territories, including Greece, established their own national churches in open defiance of the so-called Ecumenical Patriarchate in Istanbul.

The relationship between church and state in the independent Balkan nations differed from that in the Ottoman state. Catholicism, Islam, and Judaism had maintained a degree of independence from the Ottoman state while the Orthodox churches in the Balkan nations became political tools of the government, both immediately after independence and later during the communist era. While Christianity, Islam, and Judaism enjoyed almost total freedom of religion under Ottoman rule they lost that freedom under the "national" governments, including that of Turkey.

As for the Eastern Christians, the nationalism of the JACOBITES, NESTORIANS, MARONITES, Chaldeans, and COPTS living in the Middle East, unlike that of the Armenians, never acquired political-ideological dimensions. Rather, the main struggle there was between independent-minded religious autochthons and their counterparts who sought the protection of the Vatican by accepting its authority along with that of France, which could provide political and military backing.

The nationalism of the Balkan Orthodox Christians was also bolstered by the way these groups reconstructed their historical identities. Each national government in the Balkans wrote the history of its state from the perspective of the ethnic group in power. To foster national unity and gratify the national ego, historical events were sometimes distorted, magnified, or even falsified. Each nation described its pre-Ottoman existence as one of brilliant achievement and development that was ended by 500 years of "Turkish yoke." This nationalist identity went hand-in-hand with the view that Turks—which in the vocabulary of post-Treaty of Berlin nationalism meant "Muslim," particularly the Bosniaks and other converts to Islam—were interlopers or renegades and betrayers. The focus on ancestral "national" lands led the Balkan nation-states into conflict and wars unknown during those first Ottoman centuries now referred to as the Pax Ottomanica, or Ottoman peace. The disintegration of Yugoslavia, the Serbian attacks on Slovenia and BOSNIA, the ethnic cleansing, and the Serbian-Croatian wars of 1991–95 stand as the saddest enduring results of this aspect of nationalism in the post-Ottoman era.

NATIONALISM AMONG OTTOMAN MUSLIMS

The nationalism of the Ottoman Muslims followed a peculiar and rather unique course of its own. The Ottoman state viewed the Muslims as a single compact group, but the Muslims were divided into a variety of ethnic groups, including Turks, Arabs, Bosniaks, KURDS, Lazes, Georgians, Pomaks, and Vlachs. In contrast to the Christians, none of these groups, perhaps with the exception of the Bosniaks, had a separate national political existence as Muslim entities prior to joining the Ottoman state. Those who could claim any historical political existence would have had to acknowledge affinity with a Christian past rejected in the conversion to Islam. In other words, they would have had to follow the example of the Turkish-speaking Gagauzes of MOLDAVIA, who had converted from Islam to Christianity and rejected their SELJUK origin in favor of an invented earlier pagan Nordic origin as Göktürks.

Muslims in Europe and, to a good extent, in Anatolia, therefore, owed their identity and character as Muslims to Ottoman rule and had little, if any, connection to other Islamic states such as the Fatimids, Ayyubids, and MAMLUKS that ruled the Middle East and left memories of dynastic identities and loyalties. (The southeastern section of Turkey is somewhat different.) Yet scholars who claim that the Ottoman Turkish influence prevailed over the Middle East are only partially correct. Arabs on the peninsula always had a clear, even superior, sense of their Arabic identity and referred to the Ottomans as Turks (al-Atrak) and to Anatolia and the Balkans as Turkiyya, perceiving the Turks in ethnic terms, despite religious affinity. The tribes in the mountains, be they Arab, Kurd, or Turkoman, also maintained a strong sense of ethnic-tribal identity.

Nationalism among Muslims, however, did not begin as the result of residual historical or ethnic allegiance to an old identity, the claims by Kurds or Westerners sympathetic to contemporary Kurdish nationalism notwithstanding. Nor did it arise from the discontent of the propertied or intellectual elites, despite their deep resentment toward the government's centralization drive. Instead, modern Muslim nationalism was the by-product of the central government's desire to create a unified Ottoman nation—consisting of both Muslims and non-Muslims—by granting them all equality, common citizenship, and rights in the name of the sultan, the hoped-for rallying point of the "Ottoman" nation. This policy, known as Ottomanism, was quickly instituted when economic, educational, social, and cultural differences between Ottoman Muslims and non-Muslims rose rapidly in the wake of the Treaty of Paris and Edict of Reforms of 1856, which grossly favored the Christians.

Within a very short time, Muslims came to regard the treaty and the edict as instruments enabling France and England to interfere in Ottoman affairs. Indeed, the two powers not only championed Ottoman Christians against their own government but even attributed intellectual superiority to the Christians because of their shared faith with the West. The resulting defensiveness of the Muslims grew by leaps and bounds after England refused, in the name of neutrality, to provide weapons to the Ottoman army in the war with Russia in 1877–78. English efforts to rewrite the Treaty of Berlin in favor of the Ottoman government temporarily reversed the negative trend in Muslim feelings toward London until the policy of Benjamin Disraeli's government was drastically changed by William Gladstone. Gladstone's Liberal Party won the elections of 1880 after he accused Disraeli (a Jewish convert to Christianity) of having a friendly attitude toward Turks and indifference to the fate of Balkan Christians. During Gladstone's premiership, France occupied Tunisia in 1881, and Britain invaded EGYPT in 1882, reviving the Muslims' deep resentment. At the same time, after 1880, the Ottoman Empire and sultan ABDÜLHAMID II (1876–1909) pursued a silent and peaceful but determined resistance to European efforts to occupy Muslim lands.

Thus a range of international developments, including war and invasion, produced a sort of anti-colonialist, anti-imperialist Muslim nationalism represented by the Ottoman state and its sultan-caliph. Paradoxically, then, while the Ottoman state itself fought a variety of ethnic and religious nationalist groups seeking independence, there arose in NORTH AFRICA and Egypt (after 1830 and 1882) a local Muslim resistance to European occupation, which France and England believed to stem from Istanbul. Sultan Abdülhamid II attempted to reestablish the former good Ottoman relations with the British, only to be rebuffed by the prime minister, Lord Salisbury, who already had plans to partition the Ottoman Empire. Consequently Abdülhamid—unlike his predecessors, who emphasized their title as sultan, or secular ruler—used his title as caliph, or head of the Muslim community, to underscore Muslim unity and to intimidate Western powers. He threatened to call on Muslims worldwide to rebel if the French, Russians, and British attacked Ottoman lands, which included the holy cities of MECCA and MEDINA.

Accused of inciting hatred of the West and of its civilization and values, Abdülhamid II was branded as a reactionary Islamist. In reality Abdülhamid admired Western civilization, introducing a great number of reforms that included a universal educational system copied from the West, and he condemned bigotry of any kind. Nevertheless, the anti-Islamic frenzy of Europe was legitimized as the defense of civilization against the absolutism of Abdülhamid, who had suspended the CONSTITUTION and PARLIAMENT in 1878, and against his use of Islam to justify his absolutism. Eventually, the same "defense of civilization" was again invoked to legitimize Europe's occupation of the Middle East after the collapse of the Ottoman state in 1918.

THE YOUNG TURKS MOVEMENT AND THE BIRTH OF TURKISH NATIONALISM

The Ottoman struggle to remain independent in the face of the imperial designs of England, Russia, and France was the source of the first worldwide outburst of Muslim nationalism. It is interesting to note that this Muslim struggle to oppose foreign occupation had a national, rather than religious, source. In addition, nationalism in the Ottoman state was accompanied, and in many ways superseded, by modernism, which gave the nationalism a new content and scope. As the impact of the reforms in government institutions that began early in the 19th century spread to the intelligentsia, which was the pool for recruiting state bureaucrats, OTTOMANISM's idea of a political attachment to the land developed into the concept of *vatan* (fatherland). *Vatan* implied that the individual belonged to a given territory and had the sacred duty to defend it. Patriotism as a form of nationalism, thus defined as the greatest virtue of the Ottomans, was depicted in NAMIK KEMAL's famous play *Vatan yahut Silistre* (Fatherland, or, Silistre), which portrayed the heroic defense of a fortress on the Danube against the Russians.

At the same time the concept of a religious nation, or *millet*, acquired political connotations and became the focus of the intellectual discourse that took place in the expanding school system, modern press, and literature. Naqshbendism, a Sufi order that advocated the believers' involvement in the society's daily affairs, flourished after the 1850s (*see* NAQSHBANDIYYA ORDER).

Most schools, as well as the press and the literature, employed colloquial Turkish, intensifying its usage and broadening its scope. Although Turkish had always been the Ottoman state's language of communication, without any political or ethnic connotations, during the latter part of the 19th century the Turkish language became the distinguishing mark of the intelligentsia, the bureaucrats, and above all, the military, who were predominantly of Turkish ethnic origin. Some teachers in the military schools, such as Hüsnü Süleyman Pasha, were already using textbooks that discussed the Turks' ethnicity and central Asian origin in open contradiction to the official line placing the Turks and the Ottoman state within the framework of Islamic history. In fact, a number of lead-

ing Ottoman statesmen—such as Ahmed Vefik Pasha and AHMED CEVDET PASHA—and many other intellectuals stated openly that the Turks had founded the Ottoman state and were its true masters and loyal defenders.

Clearly, then, at the end of the 19th century a strong sense of Turkishness was widely shared by large groups of intellectuals even if it was buried under the euphemisms of "Muslim brotherhood" and "Ottoman unity." Turkishness at this stage, despite its deep roots in the Turks' original language and culture, applied politically to the relatively numerous intellectuals and government elites. By the time the Young Turks revolution occurred in 1908, these Turkish nationalists formed a substantial group, although few admitted their ideological preferences.

The second half of the 19th century was a period of profound demographic, cultural, economic, and social reconstruction in Ottoman history as millions of Muslims, driven out of their ancestral homes in the Caucasus, the Crimea, and the Balkans, settled in Anatolia. Throughout this period and into the 20th century, the Ottoman state's Muslim ethnic and linguistic groups were amalgamated into a new society that began to identify with cultural Turkishness just as the nationalism of the state's Orthodox Christians was in full and occasionally violent effervescence. The activities of the various Orthodox nationalists, in turn, galvanized Turkish nationalism, which was first formulated in the Balkans in Macedonia.

The numerous brewing Ottoman nationalisms, including the rising Turkish one, did not clash openly as long as all the groups were united against the absolutism of Sultan Abdülhamid. Because they believed sincerely that the sultan's autocracy was the source of all evil, including nationalist grievances, they expected all such ills to disappear if liberty—*hürriyet*—was restored. Indeed, by the time the Young Turks rebelled in 1908 and reinstated the Constitution and Parliament, freedom was viewed as a panacea that would cure every possible political and social malaise and restore peaceful multiethnic, multireligious coexistence, an idealized view of the Ottoman population that was shattered by the Young Turks.

Six months of relative peace among the various national groups was undermined by the new government's failure to meet the aspirations for independence of every national group. Bulgaria cast away its autonomy and declared independence, and predominantly Muslim Albania rebelled and declared its independence in 1912. Arab discontent burst into the open after Italy's occupation of LIBYA in 1911 proved the Ottoman government unable to defend the Arab lands and the Young Turks, showing brief interest in secularism, mandated the use of Turkish in schools in Arabic-speaking areas. Muslim unity had lost its practical usefulness but the Young Turks remained staunchly determined to preserve the territorial integrity and unity of the Ottoman state by adhering theoretically to Ottomanism, Islamism, modernism, and constitutionalism. Nevertheless, Turkish nationalists found in the era of the Young Turks (1908–18) a relative freedom to disseminate ideas that they had been prohibited to discuss under Abdülhamid.

Turkish nationalism was the last of the Ottoman nationalisms to emerge, not appearing openly until the final days of the state, despite its origin in the second half of the 19th century. Its formal expression occurred in the literary journal *Genç Kalemler* (Young pens), then took a more consistent political form in the review *Türk Yurdu* (Turkish homeland), which was also the name of an association dedicated to nationalist causes. The leading intellectual of this association was Yusuf Akçura (d. 1935), born in Russia, educated in Paris, and an advocate of Panturkism—that is, the unity of all Turks, but chiefly those in Russia. The real nationalist thinker, however, was ZIYA GÖKALP (d. 1924), whose book *The Principles of Turkism* (1923) is considered the catechism of Turkish nationalism. Actually, Gökalp's ideas were applied in the republic, with considerable revision. Specifically, the Turkish nationalism as developed in the Young Turks era embodies in spirit and form the political, cultural, and demographic legacy and the identity of the Ottoman state. Even today's Turkey represents the continuation of the Ottoman state, despite rejection of the Ottoman past and claims that the republic has built a new society and state.

The controversy within nationalist circles after 1908 began over the place of religion and ethnicity in defining Turkish identity. Yusuf Akçura viewed race and ethnicity or *soy* (lineage) as the essence of national identity, attributing only a secondary role to Islam as a supplement to identity and culture. He was thus a secularist in the sense of leaving religion outside the public sphere. Although Ziya Gökalp was an initial supporter of Panturkism, by 1916 Gökalp had distanced himself from international Turkism to favor a Turkish nationalism based on the culture of the Anatolian and Rumelian Turks. He condemned Ottoman rule for having prevented the Turks from developing their ethnic national culture and identity, which he believed the lower classes had preserved in pure and authentic form. But Gökalp never rejected Islam as incompatible with modernism, republicanism, or nationalism. He considered faith based on reason part of the folk culture, or *hars*, fully espoused by his own organization Türk Ocakları (Turkish Hearths). His motto, "Türkleşmek, Islamlaşmak, Muasırlaşmak" (Become Turkish, Muslim, and contemporary), summarizes his ideal of the Turk as a modern individual with a solid ethnic national identity and faith.

The nationalism implemented for a while in the republic based ethnicity on a rather hypothetical Turkish race and used secularism with a high dose of irreligiosity, termed "science," to cleanse the culture of its Islamic ingredient. After 1950, and especially after 1970, the reaction to this excess of nationalism was accompanied by a rising interest in the Ottoman legacy that produced a new cultural synthesis and possibly a new definition of Turkishness. Indeed, the Ottoman state appears to have been one of history's most successful multiethnic, multireligious states, preserving as it did during most of its existence a myriad of ethnic, religious, national, and tribal groups that grew and matured into the 30 some nations that ultimately put an end to its existence.

Kemal H. Karpat

See also PAN-ISLAMISM; YOUNG OTTOMANS.

Further reading: Benjamin Braude and Bernard Lewis, eds., *Christians and Jews in the Ottoman Empire: The Functioning of a Plural Society* (New York: Holmes & Meier, 1982); Ziya Gökalp, *Turkish Nationalism and Western Civilization: Selected Essays*, translated and edited by Niyazi Berkes (New York: Columbia University Press, 1959); Kemal Karpat, *An Inquiry into the Social Foundations of Nationalism in the Ottoman State: From Social Estates to Classes, from Millets to Nations* (Princeton, N.J.: Center of International Studies, Princeton University, 1973); Kemal Karpat, The Politicization of Islam: Reconstructing Identity, State, Faith, and Community in the Late Ottoman State (New York: Oxford University Press, 2001); David Kushner, T*he Rise of Turkish Nationalism, 1876–1908* (London: Cass, 1977); Taha Parla, *The Social and Political Thought of Ziya Gökalp, 1876–1924* (Leiden: Brill, 1985).

naval engineering school *See* EDUCATION.

navy The Ottoman navy reached its greatest strength during the early 16th century when the sheer number of vessels under its command and the ability of its officers and sailors had led to the empire's long-term control of the Black Sea, which contemporaries thus dubbed the "Ottoman lake." The extraordinary power of the empire's seaborne forces enabled it to control important sea routes for centuries, but this power was ultimately the result of long effort and experience, and of a substantial investment in maritime technology.

The Ottomans who reached the Marmara and Aegean shores by the beginning of the 14th century chose Gallipoli as their sea base and, after establishing their first navy, began to fight with the city-states of VENICE and Genoa, which had monopolized the Mediterranean Sea and Black Sea. In the 15th century, during the last years of MEHMED II (r. 1444–46; 1451–81), the sultan sent his navy to Otranto to conquer Italy; later, Sultan BAYEZID II (r. 1481–1512) acquired the castles on the southern edge of the Morea Peninsula (1499–1500).

By these means the Ottomans established footholds in the eastern Mediterranean.

Corsairs supported the Ottoman navy, striking Christian targets and sailing through the western Mediterranean to help the Muslims of Andalusia who were being forced by Spain to convert to Christianity. Venice and FRANCE were able to maintain their trade in the Mediterranean because of their efforts at establishing close relations with the Ottomans, which led to their obtaining contracts or AHDNAMES for safe navigation. By the end of the 16th century, after some unsuccessful attempts to repulse the Ottoman navy from the Mediterranean, Spain was forced to retreat. In this period, while turning the Black Sea into an "Ottoman lake," the Ottoman navy also dominated the Mediterranean, showing a strong presence in North Africa, and also ensured the safety of trade in the Indian Ocean by fighting Portugal in the Red Sea and Persian Gulf.

VARIETY OF SHIPS IN THE OTTOMAN NAVY

Ottoman shipbuilding went through three distinct periods. The first lasted from the empire's founding in the 14th century until the second half of the 17th century and was dominated by oar-rigged galleys. The second period, which lasted through the second half of the 19th century, witnessed the rise of the galleon, a sail-rigged ship, as the dominant naval ship. The third period, which lasted until the end of the empire in the early 20th century, employed steamships.

The Ottoman fleet was divided into two groups according to propulsion method: vessels that used oars, and those that used sails. In shipbuilding, Ottomans were faithful to these two types of vessels.

Among the oar-rigged ships that used sails as auxiliary propulsion methods were the bastard, galley, galliot, and frigate. The bastard was larger than a galley, with 26 to 36 rowing banks employing five to seven rowers for each oar. Galleys, the most utilized ship in the Ottoman navy, formed the striking force of the navy. Galleys were long, narrow, swift ships. The distance between the stem and the sternpost of a galley was about 42–43 meters (135–140 feet). There were three cannons in a galley, one on the front and two on either side. A galley had a crew of almost 330, including combatants, rowers, sailors, and officers. Galliots had an average length of 32–34 meters (105–110 feet) and 19–24 rowing banks, whereas frigates had from 10 to 17 rowing banks. Light coastal vessels, such as şaykas, were used in rivers. Ships that carried horses and guns were also employed in rivers and in the Black Sea.

The period of sail-rigged vessels began when the first galleon, the burtun, was completed in the middle of the 17th century. From the beginning of the CRETAN WAR in 1645, ships known as mahone (mavna) were also con-

structed and used. Although there were galleons in the Venetian fleet coming through the Dardanelles to blockade the supply line of the Ottoman navy, the Ottomans insisted on galleys. However, in 1648, Sultan MEHMED IV (r. 1648–87) himself attended a meeting at which the decision was made to begin the construction of galleons. In 1662 there was a temporary hiatus in galleon construction, but 20 years later Grand Vizier Kara Mustafa Pasha of Merzifon ordered the construction of ten galleons. Consequently, the galleon period in Ottoman navigation began anew. Four of those galleons were between 34 and 38 meters (110–125 feet) long, had three decks, and carried 80 cannons each. The remaining six galleons carried 60 cannons each. An average Ottoman galleon cost as much as three or four galleys. The galleon's size allowed for a large crew; 600 to 1,001 men crewed a three-decked flagship galleon.

In order to improve galleons and to reorganize Ottoman navigation, new arrangements were made through the drafting of the navy statute book in 1701. From then on, Ottoman navigation pursued the improvement of galleons and reemerged as a powerful presence on the seas. Thus, galleys faded away in the middle of the 18th century.

The Ottomans had plenty of resources for the construction and maintenance of a navy. None of the materials required for the Imperial Dockyard were imported; in fact, export of some materials was permitted.

MANAGEMENT OF THE OTTOMAN NAVY

The managers of the navy included high admirals and their subordinates. The highest military and administrative figure in the Ottoman navy was the kapudan pasha or grand admiral. Typically serving as governor of Gallipoli with the rank of sea captain, grand admirals would be promoted to the post of governor of the Aegean Island province, first established in 1534, when Hayreddin Pasha—known as Barbarossa because of his red beard (see BARBAROSSA BROTHERS)—joined the Ottoman navy. This office was raised to the rank of vizier toward the end of the 16th century.

When the Aegean Islands province (Cezayir-i Bahr-i Sefid) was formed, subprovinces, or sancaks, previously devoted to navigation were incorporated into this province. The islands of Gallipoli, Rhodes, Lesbos, Euboea, Karlıili, Lepanto, and Chios were included in the province. The chiefs of the sancaks in this province performed their military duty in sea expeditions as high admirals. Sea captains would join expeditions on their own galleys while also maintaining timarlı sipahis (cavalry at arms holding fiefs) in their sancaks. This reservist fleet was separate from the main fleet and operated defensively while the greater Ottoman navy was not on expeditions.

EARLY HISTORY OF THE OTTOMAN NAVY

Ottoman navigation depended on the western Anatolian maritime *gazi*, or warrior, tradition (*see* GHAZA) and dated to the beginning of the 14th century. Although the empire was first founded as a land principality, the Ottomans constantly sought knowledge of seafaring when their borders reached the coast. This search for knowledge led to a policy of using fleets and mariners from conquered maritime principalities. In the 14th century the ANATOLIAN EMIRATES made crucial contributions to the establishment of Ottoman navigation.

Dockyards constructed in Edincik, Gemlik, Karamürsel, and especially in Izmit created the nucleus of Ottoman sea power. By 1354, with the conquest of Gallipoli, which became the empire's first vital naval base, the Ottomans had devised new policies concerning the seas, while advancing toward the Balkans. Facing the threat of the imposing navies of Venice and Genoa, both of which had established important commercial colonies in the Black Sea and Aegean Sea regions, the Ottomans, under BAYEZID I (r. 1389–1402), opened a dockyard in Gallipoli in order to secure the Dardanelles and the coasts of the Sea of Marmara. The sultan recognized the strategic and economic importance of the Dardanelles.

During these early stages of Ottoman naval power, Venice and Genoa played substantial roles in ship construction and maritime personnel. Many of the hired crew in the Ottoman fleet during the Ottoman-Venetian War of 1416 were Genoese, and most dockyard and shipbuilding technology was Venetian in origin.

Preparations begun in Gallipoli by Sultan Mehmed II in 1452 aimed at the CONQUEST OF CONSTANTINOPLE, and included the construction of new ships and the repair of old ones by the Grand Admiral Baltaoğlu Süleyman Bey. In the spring of 1453, the Ottoman fleet consisted of 350–400 ships of various sizes and had a deterrent effect, although it did not play a serious role during the siege of Constantinople apart from forming a naval blockade. During the siege, some ships were transported overland to the Golden Horn (Haliç). This tactic was later repeated in 1456 during the siege of BELGRADE and again in 1470 at the siege of Euboea (Eğriboz) and has been a subject of scholarly interest for centuries.

BLACK SEA: AN INTERNAL SEA PROJECT

Upon the conquest of Constantinople (1453), Ottoman policies were directed toward the open seas. Mehmed II (the Conqueror) initially focused on the Black Sea. Aiming to seize the Anatolian coasts of the Black Sea, the Ottoman fleet, under the command of Grand Vizier Mahmud Pasha, took Amasra from the Genoese in 1459 and took Sinop and the adjacent territory from the Çandarids in 1461. That same year the Ottomans captured the

Trebizond-Rum Empire by besieging it from both land and sea. Mehmed constructed two fortresses on either side of the Dardanelles, the Kala-i Sultaniye and the Kilitbahir. The islands of Imroz, Thasos, Limni, Bozcaada, and Semadirek, all in dominant positions on the Straits and hitherto under Genoese rule, were also conquered. In 1475 Grand Vizier Gedik Ahmed Pasha, in charge of a strong fleet, captured CAFFA in the Crimea from Genoa, bringing the peninsula under Ottoman control.

The Ottoman-Venetian wars (1463–79), fought in the Aegean Sea and around the coastal cities of Venice, witnessed the fall of Euboea (1470) and the Ottoman conquest of essential parts of the Albanian shores. The Ottoman fleet later landed soldiers on the Pulya coasts of Italy under the command of Gedik Ahmed Pasha in 1480 and captured the region of Otranto, which belonged to the Kingdom of Naples. Another Ottoman fleet was sent to Rhodes under the command of Grand Vizier Mesih Pasha in 1480, but the siege was not successful. Mehmed later obtained the title "the sultan of land and sultan of seas." Upon Mehmed's death in 1481 and Gedik Ahmed Pasha's consequent recall to the capital, Otranto reverted to the Kingdom of Naples, having been under Ottoman rule for more than a year. Mehmed II had intended to invade the center of the Western Roman Empire from his position at the center of the former Eastern Roman Empire.

With the capture of Kilia and Akkerman, both the important commercial ports in the Black Sea during the reign of Bayezid II, all north-south trade in the region came under Ottoman rule (1484). Returning to the Mediterranean, the Ottoman fleet settled in the central Mediterranean by gaining LEPANTO, Modon, Coron, and Navarino (1499–1500) in Morea.

THE EMERGENCE OF SEABORNE VETERANS/ CORSAIRDOM

The advent of CORSAIRS in the 15th century also had a profound influence on Ottoman navigation. As a component of the *ghaza* and jihad values of Islam, Muslim raiders both on land and at sea regarded themselves as fighting for their beliefs in accordance with Islamic law, or SHARIA. Voluntary sea captains and pirate-like raiders called corsairs thus often operated as legitimate adjuncts to the official Ottoman navy. Such renowned sailors as Kemal Reis, Hayreddin Barbarossa, Turgut (known as Dragut in Italian sources), and Uluç Ali Pasha were indeed corsairs and later officially entered into state service.

NEW TARGETS IN THE SEAS

In the last quarter of the 15th century two new powers, SPAIN and the Ottoman Empire, emerged in the Mediterranean. At this stage, Spain had penetrated into the

Mediterranean, and the Ottomans had moved into the ADRIATIC SEA and NORTH AFRICA. The Ottomans sailed against Spain to help the Muslims and JEWS of Andalusia who were being massacred or forced to convert to Catholicism. They sailed against Portugal in order to aid the MAMLUK EMPIRE of Egypt. The Portuguese had reached the Indian Ocean and were threatening Muslim cities on the coasts of the Red Sea, especially the sacred cities of MECCA and MEDINA. Kemal Reis in the Mediterranean and Selman Reis in the Red Sea were famous Ottoman mariners of this time.

Troops in the Egyptian Mamluk fleet, which consisted of 19 ships under the command of Ottoman admiral Selman Reis, set off from Suez through the Red Sea in September 1515. The Ottoman contingent of the Mamluk fleet consisted mostly of JANISSARIES, the Ottomans' elite infantry, and hired Turks of Anatolia. The Ottomans took control of the eastern Mediterranean coast by conquering Syrian and Egyptian ports (1516–17), which had become trade centers in the region. This control compelled the Ottoman Empire to send a fleet against Portugal in the Red Sea and Indian Ocean.

SÜLEYMAN I (the Magnificent) (r. 1520–66) conquered Rhodes in 1522 and commissioned Hayreddin Barbarossa as the *beylerbeyi* (governor) of the newly established Cezayir-i Bahr-i Sefid (an Ottoman province made up of the Aegean islands) in 1534. Hayreddin Barbarossa's foremost achievement in the Mediterranean power struggle was at the Battle of Preveza (1538). Venice, the papacy, Genoa, Spain, Portugal, and MALTA united and formed an allied fleet against the Ottomans, with an accord signed in Rome in 1538. Andrea Doria, a mariner of Genoese origin serving Spain, was put in charge of this most powerful sea force of the time, constituting almost 300 battleships, some with sails. Under Ottoman commander Barbarossa were 122 oar-rigged ships. Well acquainted with the Mediterranean shores and climate, Barbarossa preferred galleys. Sail-rigged ships were not useful in the small bays and harbors because they were unable to move swiftly and their cannon ranges were short. The Ottoman fleet won the battle. With the Battle of Preveza the Christian West lost its domination in the Mediterranean. The resulting Ottoman control in the eastern Mediterranean subsequently made their expedition to Tripoli in 1551 possible.

During the reign of Süleyman the Magnificent there were also important developments against Portugal in the Indian Ocean, the second area of struggle for the Ottoman navy. Petty Islamic states in India and the Islamic Sultanate of Atjeh in Sumatra called for aid against Portugal; this led to Ottoman navigation across the Indian Ocean. Fleets prepared at the Suez and Basra dockyards arrived in India and the east Asia.

With the opening of this new front, the Ottomans faced struggles with the Portuguese in the Red Sea, the Gulf of Basra, and the Indian Ocean. The conquest of Egypt in 1517 had paved the way for the Ottoman conquest of the Red Sea. With the capture of BAGHDAD (1534) and BASRA (1546) the Ottoman fleet reached the Gulf of Basra and continued their fight on two fronts. Yemen Province, in the southeastern Arabian Peninsula, and Habeş (Abyssina) Province on the east coast of Africa were established to protect the Red Sea; the Ottoman provinces of Basra and Lahsa were formed to guard the Gulf of Basra.

Süleyman's reign saw four separate sea campaigns in the Indian Ocean between 1538 and 1554. The first Indian naval expedition was to aid Sultan Bahadır Shah of Gujarat, who had dispatched an envoy to Süleyman. An Ottoman fleet of 90 ships under the command of Hadım Süleyman Pasha, Governor of Egypt, set off from the Suez in 1538. Yemen and Aden were captured before the fleet arrived at the coast of Gujarat on the western shore of India. The second Indian expedition began with the promotion of Piri Reis, the author of *Kitab-ı Bahriye* (Book on Navigation), to commander of the Indian fleet. He seized Muscat but did not confront the Portuguese. He returned to Egypt with only two ships, leaving his squadron in the Gulf of Basra. In the third campaign, Seydi Ali Reis, the legendary mariner, set off from Basra with 15 ships. He confronted the Portuguese fleet but was driven to the coasts of Gujarat by a storm. He was forced to return to Istanbul on foot, as his fleet was destroyed.

FROM MALTA (1565) TO LEPANTO (1571)

The Christian corsair group the KNIGHTS OF ST. JOHN, removed from RHODES by Süleyman the Magnificent, were relocated to Malta, which then constituted the new defensive line in the Mediterranean. An Ottoman fleet of 240 ships under the command of Piyale Pasha surrounded Malta in 1565. But while the Fortress of St. Elmo was captured, the siege failed because the fortified towns of Birgu and St. Angelo could not be seized.

Upon the Ottoman conquest of the Venetian-held island of CYPRUS in 1570–71, another Christian Crusade was launched by the papacy, Venice, and Spain, which possessed vast armadas. The Ottoman fleet proceeded to LEPANTO. At the confrontation between the two armadas in the Gulf of Lepanto on October 7, 1571, many Ottoman sailors were killed, including the grand admiral, and the Ottoman armada was soundly defeated. Although the Battle of Lepanto was a resounding victory for the Christian allies, its effects were short-lived. The Christian fleet did not recapture Cyprus. By 1573 Venice established good relations with the Ottomans with an *ahdname*, or accord, and paid compensation for the Cyprus War.

Having lost a substantial portion of its fleet at the Battle of Lepanto, the Ottoman Empire, in the following winter, renewed shipbuilding activities in its all dockyards. And though Grand Admiral Kılıç Ali Pasha sailed again, no fleet materialized to fight against him. In the years that followed, the Ottoman armada appeared to recover its losses quickly and sailed across the Mediterranean where there was no fleet to compete with it. In 1574, the Ottoman fleet reconquered TUNIS.

THE CRETAN WAR AND CHANGE IN OTTOMAN SHIPBUILDING TECHNOLOGY

From the end of the 16th century, the Ottoman fleet served in a protective capacity, not sailing across the Mediterranean for large-scale campaigns. Although the fleet was taken to the Black Sea, it is not possible to compare this with the previous sea campaigns, which were on a more massive scale.

The Cretan War lasted almost 25 years (1645–69) and was a turning point for the Ottoman navy. The attitude toward oar-rigged galleys, hitherto the backbone of the Ottoman armada, was beginning to change, and the fame of the sail-rigged galleons rose. Although the Ottomans attempted to use galleons in their fleet during this war, galleys continued to be the core of the Ottoman fleet. In a short time British and Dutch sailing ships, entering the Mediterranean mostly for trade and piracy, had gained naval superiority. Venice, leasing ships from England and the Netherlands, tried to obstruct the Ottoman fleet surrounding CRETE and to blockade the Dardanelles to prevent the supply of troops and materials, changing the power balance in their own favor.

ÇEŞME CATASTROPHE IN 1770: THE ANNIHILATION OF THE OTTOMAN FLEET

Apart from the debacle at Lepanto in 1571, the second-worst defeat ever experienced by the Ottoman armada occurred in Çeşme in 1770. During the RUSSO-OTTOMAN WAR of 1768–74, a Russian fleet sailed through the Baltic and North seas and docked in Britain to acquire further personnel and weaponry there. Then the fleet went via the English Channel to the Mediterranean under the guidance of British officers. After the first clashes in the vicinity of the Koyun Islands, the Ottoman fleet receded to the Harbor of Çeşme, making a serious strategic mistake by anchoring its ships close to each as they came under a sudden offensive from the Russian fleet. During the artillery bombardment, ships of the Russian fleet secretly entered the harbor and set fire to the Ottoman fleet.

For the reconstruction of the fleet destroyed at Çeşme, French shipwrights were employed under the command of Grand Admiral Gazi Hasan Pasha. Afterward, French, English, and Swedish engineers continued to play an important role in Ottoman naval construction. The Ottoman Naval Engineering School opened in 1784, beginning a new chapter in the empire's shipbuilding technology. The most essential modernization in Ottoman navigation toward the end of the 18th century was the construction of a massive dry dock in Istanbul. With the assistance of Swedish and French expertise, the construction of the Great Dock was completed between the years 1797 and 1800.

NAVARINO RAID (1827)

The Greek revolt began in 1821 when Greeks in the Morea (Peloponnese), revolted, incited by Russia. Russia and England wanted an autonomous Greek state that would remain a taxpaying vassal of the Ottoman Empire. Over Ottoman objections, and with France's help, the European powers surrounded Morea. Navarino, where the Turkish and Egyptian fleets docked, came under attack and the Ottoman ships were sunk. In this raid, the Ottoman fleet lost 52 ships and 6,000 sailors.

Although the Ottoman navy was among the most powerful in the world during the reigns of ABDÜLMECID I (r. 1839–61) and ABDÜLAZIZ (r. 1861–76), the Ottoman Empire was in decline, losing land and power and coping with a deteriorating economy. Sultan ABDÜLHAMID II (r. 1876–1909) changed the navy in order to protect the coastlines, rather than contest the great powers of the time. Later the navy employed many British and German advisors both aboard ship and in the dockyard. The Ottoman navy saw its last use during WORLD WAR I.

İdris Bostan

Further reading: İdris Bostan, *Kürekli ve Yelkenli Osmanlı Gemileri* (Istanbul: Bilge, 2005); Palmira Brummet, *Ottoman Seapower and Levantine Diplomacy in the Age of Discovery* (Albany: State University of New York Press, 1994); J. F. Guilmartin, *Gunpowder and Galleys: Changing Technology and Mediterranean Warfare at Sea in the Sixteenth Century* (London: Cambridge University Press, 1974); A. Hess, "The Evolution of the Seaborne Empire in the Age of the Oceanic Discoveries 1453–1525)." *American Historical Review* 75, no. 7 (December 1970): 1892–1919; C. Imber, "The Navy of Süleyman the Magnificent." *Archivum Ottomanicum* 6 (1980): 211–282.

neomartyrs The term "neomartyr" means "new witness" in Greek. It is used to distinguish an individual martyred for his or her Christian beliefs in the era following the establishment of Christianity as one of the approved religions in the Roman Empire (313 C.E.) from the martyrs of the early Christian era (first through fourth centuries C.E.). In the Ottoman context, neomartyrs were Orthodox Christians who were persecuted by Ottoman authorities mostly because they had converted to Islam and subsequently returned to Christianity, or apostatized. According to Islamic law, or SHARIA, a suspected apostate would be given three chances to return to Islam. Upon the third refusal, a male apostate would be sentenced to death, while a female would be imprisoned for life. Situations leading to the accusation, trial in Ottoman courts, and subsequent execution were elaborately described in narratives called neomartyrologies.

The most famous compilation of neomartyrologies from the Ottoman period, the *New Martyrologion* (1794) by Nikodemos the Hagiorite of Mt. Athos, features two types of male martyrs—intentional (those willingly seeking to die as martyrs) and unintentional (those whose death was brought about by unforeseen circumstances, such as false accusation by a Muslim or fellow Christian). While male neomartyrs are depicted as either voluntary or involuntary converts to Islam, the few known female "witnesses," as these martyrs are sometimes called, are typically represented as unwilling converts who became victims of the scheming or sexual desire of Muslim men. Neomartyrologies depict a variety of situations that could induce people to convert voluntarily, such as love, rebelliousness against one's parents, the attempt to save one's life after committing a crime, or the effort to fit into a new working environment. These texts also demonstrate how the libel of apostasy made against Christians could be manipulated for widely differing personal ends by both Muslims and fellow Christians. For instance, many neomartyrs are represented as victims of the jealousy of their business partners or competitors.

For the most part, neomartyrologies accurately reflect the legal procedure prescribed by Islamic law. Although the number of apostasy trials suggested in neomartyrology compilations—over 150 cases during the entire Ottoman period—cannot be substantiated by records from the Ottoman courts, the few identified apostasy cases and their associated fatwas (legal opinions issued by the empire's leading Muslim jurists) confirm the credibility of the situations described in the neomartyrologies that could lead to conversion, apostasy, and death. For example, Nikola, a 16th-century neomartyr from Sofia, BULGARIA, is said to have converted to Islam while drunk; he was executed because he refused to stay Muslim after sobering up. Fatwas from the same period confirm the fact that conversion under the influence of alcohol was considered valid. Other examples of unintended conversions described in neomartyrologies and discussed in the fatwas as valid include being tricked into pronouncing the Muslim profession of faith (*shahada*), the donning of Muslim headgear (turban), and converting under coercion or as a consequence of being a child from a mixed marriage.

Intentional martyrs, whose numbers seem to increase in the 17th and 18th centuries, are particularly intriguing. Upon deciding to become martyrs, many fled to Mt. Athos, where they were trained by Athonite monks in the spiritual discipline necessary for undergoing martyrdom. When finally prepared, they would go to the place where they originally converted and publicly proclaim their rejection of Islam, provoking Ottoman authorities into taking harsh measures. This led some 19th-century Christian intellectuals to criticize Athonite monks for orchestrating a suicide movement.

Neomartyrs and neomartyrologies served an important function in the propaganda of the Orthodox Church. During the 17th century, conversions to Islam in the Ottoman European domains peaked, Protestant and Catholic missionaries appeared, and social distinctions between Muslims and non-Muslims in Ottoman society became blurred. The writing of neomartyrologies and the establishment of what might be considered training camps for aspiring martyrs at Mt. Athos during the 17th and 18th centuries were a part of the Orthodox establishment's conservative reaction to these developments and an attempt to re-educate the flock through the dissemination of texts that stressed the penitential, conscientious practice of Christianity. By describing the process of becoming a martyr step by step, neomartyrologies strove to provide models of ideal behavior and to discourage Christians from interacting with Muslims lest this interaction result in conversion to Islam.

Tijana Krstić

Further reading: Eleni Gara, "Neomartyr Without a Message." *Archivum Ottomanicum* 23 (2005/06): 155-176; Marinos Sariyanis, "Aspects of 'Neomartyrdom': Religious Contacts, 'Blasphemy' and 'Calumny' in 17th Century Istanbul." *Archivum Ottomanicum* 23 (2005/06): 249-262; Nomikos Vaporis, *Witnesses for Christ* (New York: St Vladimir's Seminary Press, 2000).

Nestorians Nestorian Christians are followers of a tradition that emphasizes the human nature of Christ over the divine one. Because of that belief, Nestorians were declared heretics by what would become mainstream Christianity in the Council of Ephesus in 431 C.E. Followers of the Nestorian tradition spread across the eastern Anatolian highlands, the mountains of Kurdistan, Iran, and into China in the centuries before the rise of Islam. With the rise of Islam, the Nestorians suffered a diminution of their numbers as many of their community converted to the new faith. During the Mongol period of the 13th and 14th centuries, the Nestorians enjoyed the royal favor of the Khans' court as many Mongol women of princely families converted to Nestorian Christianity, and these converts helped their coreligionists from less notable lineages. As a result of their identification with the Mongols, the Nestorians suffered from Muslim retaliatory attacks in the post-Mongol period.

During the Ottoman period, especially during the 16th through 18th centuries, Nestorian communities were located in the borderlands between Safavid IRAN and the Ottoman Empire, where they endured raids from both armies and many individuals from the community were enslaved. The Nestorians were a very isolated group in the Ottoman period. Unlike other Christian communities of the Empire, they had no merchant middle class. Rather, most Nestorians were peasants who continued to use Syriac as both their spoken language and their liturgical language.

The spiritual head of the community was the catholicos. At the start of the Ottoman period, the catholicos resided in Urmia on the Iranian side of the border. From the 15th century onward members of one family held the position, with authority passing from uncle to nephew, as a married priest was ineligible to head the community. The church split in the 17th century, however, over the elevation of a minor child to the rank of catholicos. Those in the vicinity of Mosul who rejected the youth sought support from the Roman Catholic MISSIONARIES active in that province and were acknowledged as a UNIATE Church by Rome. Not long after this schism, the traditionalist faction moved the see, or seat of office, of their catholicos to the village of Qudshanis, on the Ottoman side of the border, to be nearer the majority of his followers.

The pro-Catholic party took the name Chaldean, by which the Church had been known both in Arabic and Turkish, while the traditionalists continued to call themselves Suryani (Syrians). This created confusion for those outside the community as the larger Jacobite (Syrian Orthodox) Church also used that name. In the 19th century, as Western archaeologists excavated the ruins of the ancient Assyrian civilization at Nineveh near the city of Mosul, the traditionalists began to call themselves Assyrians, the name by which the community is known today.

During the ARMENIAN MASSACRES of WORLD WAR I, Muslim Turks and Kurds attacked Assyrian villages in eastern Anatolia as well as Armenian villages. Although the Assyrian villagers were often well armed and had established martial traditions, they were outnumbered by their opponents and lost most of their engagements. But because they were armed, they did not suffer the deportations of the Armenians, and a larger percentage of the Assyrians survived the war than did their less fortunate Armenian neighbors. In the aftermath of the war, most of the remnant of the community fled Turkey, going first to either Iraq or Iran. Although Assyrians can be found today in both Iraq and Iran, and a tiny community is found in Turkey, perhaps half of the community now resides in the West, primarily in the United States, Canada, Australia, and Sweden. The center for the numerically larger Chaldean community remains in Baghdad, with large communities also found in and around the city of Mosul.

Bruce Masters

Further reading: Aziz Atiya, *A History of Eastern Christianity* (Notre Dame, Ind.: University of Notre Dame, 1968).

newspapers Although printed matter began to be produced in the Ottoman Empire as early as 1493, the first newspaper to be published in the empire would not follow for more than 300 years with the advent of the French-language *Le Spectateur Oriental*, printed at IZMIR in 1821 and designed to meet the needs of French merchants for information relating to trade in the Mediterranean. The Greek independence movement that began immediately afterward was initially supported by the newspaper until the publishers realized that these activities disrupted trade. Led by its new editor, Alexandre Blacque, the newspaper quickly turned pro-Ottoman, launching polemics against the European press that gained the paper the support of the Sublime Porte. As a result, the Ottoman administration for the first time recognized the significance of a newspaper in creating public opinion, a realization that would ultimately have a profound influence on the implementation of CENSORSHIP in the empire.

The first Ottoman newspaper, *Vekayi-i Misriyye* (*Arab*: *Al-Waqai al-Misriyya*, The Egyptian bulletin), was published in CAIRO on December 3, 1828, by the governor of Egypt, MEHMED ALI. The first two pages were in Ottoman Turkish and the third and fourth pages were translations of the first two into Arabic. A total of 600 copies of the paper were printed, and were distributed to government officials only. The purpose of the newspaper was to communicate to the administrative staff the modernization that began within the Ottoman Empire through the TANZIMAT movement. This initiative affected the Sublime Porte and on January 1, 1831, the official paper of the Ottoman State, *Takvim-i Vekayi* (Calendar of occurrences), began publication. Some 5,000 copies of this paper were printed; other than government officials, it was sold to any others who wished to buy it. It was also printed in French, Persian, Greek, Armenian, and Bulgarian. Thus began the process of creating public opinion under the control of the state in accordance with the Ottoman social and economic structure. As a result, the first press controversy took place in 1831–33 between the state-owned newspaper and the newspaper belonging to Mehmed Ali Pasha, who had risen against Sublime Porte. Both sides were making modernization efforts, but each accused the other of breaking away from Islam.

The first privately owned Turkish newspaper was *Ceride-i Havadis* (Journal of news), published in 1840 by an Englishman named William N. Churchill. The content was unusually rich for its time, for it contained details of Western politics, financial news, material about controversial events such as the French Revolution, and items of cultural interest such as reports of new technology that had not yet been introduced into the Ottoman Empire. However, Churchill's paper did not appeal to the public and was able to survive only with state support. In fact, its writers were all members of the translation bureau of the Sublime Porte, who directed communication with foreign countries and followed the foreign press.

The most interesting attempts at informing the public through state-controlled opinion is seen in the provincial papers. This process of disseminating public information through state-implemented provincial printing houses began in 1860, under the guidance of the *mektupçus* or the deputies of provincial governors. Newspapers were printed both in Turkish and in the local language of a given region. Among the 37 provincial newspapers published until 1908, many were multilingual and could be found in cities and provinces throughout the empire, often taking their names from the place where they were published. Among these were newspapers published in Turkish-Arabic (in BEIRUT, DAMASCUS, TRIPOLI, ALEPPO, BAGHDAD, Yemen, Sanaa, JERUSALEM, and HEJAZ); in Turkish-Greek (in CRETE, EDIRNE, Yanina, Konya, Adana, and RHODES); in Turkish-Armenian (in Erzurum, Diyarbakir, and BURSA); in Turkish-Serbian (in Prizren, Herzegovina, and Skopje); in Turkish-Bulgarian (in Ruse); and in Turkish-Greek-Bulgarian-Hebrew (Ladino) (in SALONIKA). These newspapers were not limited to publishing official statements but were also vehicles for progressive reform. Articles appeared which claimed that advocating for the state without reflecting political and social realities was a kind of treason against the country. This indicates the fact that, in the Ottoman community, the state's administrators adopted the function assumed in Europe by the bourgeoisie, and Ottoman social change was initiated under their guidance. The 19th century was a period of sweeping social change in Europe as well as in the Ottoman Empire, and newspapers were an important vehicle for this change in both cultures. The role of the newspaper for effecting change in the empire was paramount, however, for pervasive censorship of books prevented the dissemination of progressive ideas through that medium. As a result, change in the Ottoman world at this time was dominated by newspaper culture.

As the society entered increasingly into a mode of political and social reform, due in part to the influence of these newspapers, the empire implemented new religious and cultural freedoms and the publication of newspapers in every language was also permitted. As a result of this, Istanbul became a unique cultural center, exerting a profound influence on both the Near and Middle East, and became home to numerous non-Turkish publications:

Arabic: The state-subsidized *Al Jawaib*, published in Istanbul, was the most influential among the Arabic-language newspapers. Editions in Beirut were later added, and circulation increased after 1908.

Armenian: The first newspaper in Armenian was *Liro Kir*, a translation of the official Ottoman newspaper, *Takvim-i Vekayi*. It is significant that newspapers published in Turkish with Armenian characters comprised one-third of all Armenian periodicals. Armenian publications pioneered primarily in the areas of humor and cartoons. Mostly based in Istanbul, the number of Armenian periodicals in Anatolia increased to 46 after 1908.

French: Between 1821 and 1908, a period when French was the primary cultural and political language in Europe, approximately 150 French-language newspapers and magazines were published in Istanbul. These involved not only political matters but also scientific subjects such as medicine.

Greek: The first newspapers in the Greek language were published in Izmir in 1831 and later concentrated in Istanbul. There were also periodicals printed in Turkish with Greek characters (*karamanlidika*). Greek-language newspapers ranked second in number behind French-language newspapers, with 109 publications.

Jewish/Ladino: Publications printed in the Ladino language by Jewish immigrants from Spain, mainly in Istanbul and Salonika, numbered 100.

Persian: Periodicals in Persian were limited in number, but in its 20 years of existence the newspaper *Ahter*, first published in Istanbul in 1876, played an important role in the modernization of Iran through supporting and promoting Ottoman Tanzimat reforms. Reformists who fled Iran also published newspapers in Istanbul.

European languages: The first English-language newspaper was the *Levant Herald* in 1858; the German-language newspaper *Osmanische Post* was printed in 1890. The first Italian newspaper appeared in 1838, and a more long-lasting one, *La Turchia*, appeared in 1909.

Other languages: There were 15 periodical publications in Bulgarian in the Ottoman Empire; there were also Serbian, Georgian, and Urdu-language publications, as well as publications in Albanian, Circassian, Kurdish, and Romani, whose alphabets were newly established.

Tercuman-i Ahval (Interpreter of events), the first independent Turkish newspaper, was published on October 21, 1860. The Western-educated owners Agah and Şinasi Efendis, in their editorial for the first edition, declared their objective as "existing without financial support from the state" and thus initiated the era of free press. By stating "freedom of expression is a part of human nature," they introduced the public to the Enlightenment principles espoused by the French Revolutionaries of 1789.

A truly dynamic newspaper was the *Tasvir-i Efkar* (Description of ideas), launched by Şinasi—who spent many years in Paris and became a member of the French Oriental Studies Institution—and later taken over by NAMIK KEMAL. The paper was first published on June 27, 1862, and became the unofficial mouthpiece of the YOUNG OTTOMANS, who added new dynamism to Ottoman modernization. In his article for the first issue, Şinasi stated, "we have to utilize the wisdom endowed upon us by God" and advocated an active public opinion. Further discussion on this topic considered the extent to which public opinion might control government administration, leading the government for the first time to institute press laws. In 1857 a press code was issued, and in 1858 articles on accusatory publication were added to the criminal law. A new press code, inspired by the French press law, was issued in 1864. A press bureau, which would act as preliminary censorship, was also established.

Also known as the New Ottomans, the Young Ottomans gained momentum in the press by openly addressing the concept of freedom, supported by the contributions of Ali Suavi's newspaper *Muhbir* (Informer). Ali Suavi was a revolutionary who ended his life while participating in a coup d'état in 1878. Disturbed by what they regarded as the revolutionary proposal of the *Meşveret* (Consultation), which may also be translated as "constitutional system," the government closed down all newspapers critical of their programs and policies and reassigned the government officials responsible for these inflammatory ideas to posts outside Istanbul. From this internal exile, writers such as ZIYA PASHA, Namik Kemal, and Ali Suavi fled to Europe in 1867 and continued their opposition to the Ottoman government by publishing the newspapers *Muhbir* and *Hurriyet* (Freedom) in Paris and London. Nor did the Kararname-i Ali, or high decree of the Ottoman grand vizier, function to restrain the press at home. On the contrary, the increase in Turkish periodical publications was greater than ever. In Istanbul, between 1860 and 1866, 17 new publications appeared; 113 new publications appeared between 1867 and 1878 as

government official-journalists were replaced by professionals. Basiretçi Ali and Ahmed Midhat are prominent names from this period. Meanwhile, the press expanded to include humor magazines (especially caricatures) and publications specializing in opinion and education. The empire began to see the introduction of humor magazines at the end of 1860s, reaching a peak in number and circulation during the early 1870s. They dealt mainly with local life as compared with the Western style that dominated Pera, the European quarter of Istanbul (*see* POLITICAL SATIRE). Among these publications were *Megu*, *Hayal*, *Çaylak*, and *Diyojen*. Important cartoonists of the period were Teodor Kasap (Greek), Nişan Berberyan (Armenian), and Ali Fuad (Turkish).

With the amnesty of 1870, those who led the opposition from Europe returned to Istanbul, and thus the press increased its critical attitude. Namik Kemal started a new campaign with his newspaper *Ibret* (Warning). The sale of 25,000 copies of its first issue, unprecedented in the history of Ottoman newspapers, indicates that society had become more dynamically opinionated. The government found this dangerous; the newspaper was shut down and Namik Kemal was exiled to Cyprus. However, the movement initiated by the New Ottomans also continued among the higher administrative tiers of the state. Sultan ABDÜLAZIZ (r. 1861–1876), who wished to return to the old, sultan-led administration, was dethroned by a military coup and was replaced by MURAD V (r. 1876) and later by ABDÜLHAMID II (r. 1876–1909), who accepted the parliamentarian regime. Thus the press proved that it had an active function in Ottoman society.

Between 1876 and 1908 the press continued to exist, but under strict restrictions. The Ottoman defeat at the end of the Russo-Ottoman War (1877–78) left no room for public criticism, either from parliament or from the press. Moreover, Sultan Abdülhamid's determination to be the sole decision-maker permitted no opportunity for freedom in this era. Humor magazines disappeared, and newspapers had to present their pages to the CENSORSHIP committee prior to printing, which functionally eliminated all opposition. Moreover, the sultan had developed a special reward system to silence both local and foreign press: All local publications received money for remaining loyal to the regime; correspondents of foreign newspapers and agencies were bribed as well. As a result, a strong Turkish opposition press, of which *Meşveret* (Consultation) was the leader, once more developed in Europe and Egypt.

In 1908 the YOUNG TURK Revolution forced Sultan Abdülhamid II to revalidate the CONSTITUTION, which he had suspended for 30 years, and which contained the clause "the press is independent by law." As a result, newspapers pursued publication without reference to censorship. The number of newspapers and magazines in circulation in the empire escalated from 120 to 730 in just seven months. Publishers wrote in total freedom about everything that had been banned. The non-Turkish press (Greek, Arabic, Armenian, and Albanian) found the opportunity to express their communities' patriotic yearnings. Although most of these publications were short-lived, 461 more publications were added by 1914. In this environment, the Islamic religious press, of which Abdülhamid had never been tolerant, also emerged. When one of these Islamic publications, *Volkan* (Volcano), advocated a return to the previous closed regime style of governance, this led to a clash. Conflicts of opinion led to the first assassination of a journalist in Ottoman history: A journalist opposed to the party in power, Ittihat and Terakki (the Committee of Union and Progress), was killed by the Young Turks. Muslim fundamentalists responded by attacking the Young Turk newspaper, *Tanin* (Resounding), and sought to kill its chief editor, Huseyin Cahid Yalçın. They mistakenly killed another editor instead, Hasan Fehmi, the commentator of the separatist paper *Serbesti* (Freedom) and, ironically, a fervent critic of Ittihat and Terakki. On April 14, 1909, these reactionary religious forces also raided the parliament hall and forced the government to resign. The upheaval was quickly suppressed by a Young Turk-controlled army from the Balkans. Although a new, more liberal press code was issued as a result, the desire for freedom of the press was so strong among intellectuals that they continued to oppose any code, however liberal.

Except for a short period in 1912, the Ottoman press remained under the control of the Ittihat and Terakki party until the Armistice of Mudros, which ended WORLD WAR I on October 30, 1918. This policy was strengthened with the loss of Ottoman territories in Libya and the Balkans. In 1913, all opposition journalists were either exiled or had fled the country. Among these was Ahmed Emin Yalman, who had been educated in journalism at Columbia University in New York City. Talented writers would usually start journalism through master-apprentice relations, but Ahmed Emin was the first to have received formal training. His dissertation, titled "The Development of Modern Turkey as Measured by its Press" and published by the university in 1914, was the first academic study of the Ottoman press.

During World War I, due to technical hardship and the newspapers' inability to truthfully deliver the news of failure on the frontiers, the press had become rather limited. However, after mid-1917, the peace treaty of Brest Litovsk, the steep decline of Ottoman political power, and the occupation of the empire from 1918 to 1922 resulted in a relatively unfettered press. It included several different components: separatist minority newspapers printed in the occupied cities of Izmir and Istanbul; Turkish publications demanding a rapid peace and that the seat of the caliphate stay in Istanbul; and those sup-

porting the national independence movement under the leadership of Mustafa Kemal (later, KEMAL ATATÜRK). The separatist newspapers, mainly Greek newspapers, advocated until 1922 for Greek sovereignty over Anatolia and Istanbul. The second group, Turkish publications, led by Ali Kemal's *Peyamı Sabah* (Morning news), openly supported the TREATY OF SÈVRES which would leave only one-fifth of Anatolia to the Turks. The third group, the pro-Turkish national movement press, began the influential "until independence" campaign under the leadership of the newspaper *Hakimiyet-i Milliye* (National sovereignty), which in 1920 was both founded and managed by the future leader of the Turkish Republic, Kemal Atatürk. At the same time, the Anatolian News Agency was established, and the mechanisms of independent broadcast journalism commenced. Eight out of ten of the country's most influential newspapers, including *Tasviri Efkar*, *Vakit*, and others, offered their support to the national movement based in Ankara. The era of the Ottoman press ended with the proclamation of the Republic of Turkey in 1923.

Orhan Koloğlu

Nizam-ı Cedid (1792–1807) By the reign of SELIM III (r. 1789–1807), the general term *nizam-ı cedid*, which the Ottomans had hitherto used to describe minor administrative and financial reforms, took on a new meaning: the opposite of *nizam-ı kadim*, an ambiguous term signifying the traditional Ottoman system. According to this newer meaning, Nizam-ı Cedid usually refers to the Western-inspired reforms undertaken by Selim in 1792 in the aftermath of the Russo-Ottoman War of 1787–92 that set the stage for the later groundbreaking TANZIMAT reforms as well as for the reforms of MEHMED ALI of Egypt. In its widest sense, Nizam-ı Cedid describes the transformation of the Ottoman Empire into a modern absolutist state. In its narrower sense, it refers to the establishment of the Western-style army with a separate treasury, Irad-ı Cedid (new revenues). Nizam-ı Cedid came to an abrupt end in May 1807 when Selim III was forced to abdicate by a Janissary-ulema coalition (Kabakçı Mustafa Revolt).

The formal Nizam-ı Cedid reform program instituted by Selim was carried out by a dedicated reform committee that worked to implement more than 20 reform proposals in all, the most influential of which was the report on the Habsburg Empire written by Ebubekir Ratıb Efendi, the Ottoman ambassador to Vienna. While the entire reform is said to have included 72 clauses on a variety of topics ranging from the military and judicial institutions to the central and provincial administration, the most tangible results of the Nizam-ı Cedid were seen in the spheres of the military and diplomacy.

The opening of new military technical schools and restructuring of the artillery corps were followed by the foundation of the Nizam-ı Cedid army in 1794 on the European model with Western-style uniforms, equipment, and—most significantly—military discipline. While the first recruits in this army included Russian and Habsburg fugitives and prisoners of war, recruitment later relied on the Turkish peasants and tribesmen of Anatolia. The Balkans were excluded as an area for recruitment since the strong power brokers (AYAN) of the region were opposed to the reform program. The new army was organized as a provincial militia force rather than a professional standing army in the Western sense; by 1807, it included more than 23,000 troops. The reorganization of the arsenal and the gunpowder works, the construction of the first modern military barracks on the outskirts of Istanbul, and the construction of about 45 state-of-the-art warships are among the successes of the reform program. Various works on military arts and sciences were translated from Western languages into Turkish to help lay the necessary infrastructure for the modern sciences; this signaled the coming of a new generation of engineers with Western-style thinking. In addition to the initial reform proposals, the advocates of reform penned many treatises, some in European languages, for propaganda purposes at home and "image-making" abroad.

Another sphere addressed by the reform program was diplomacy. Because Selim reigned in the Napoleonic age, his fate was directly affected by the instability in European politics. As the political and military power of the Ottoman Empire diminished, the Sublime Porte discovered that modern international diplomacy was an increasingly valuable tool. Thus the empire formally declared its neutrality in the First Coalition Wars (1793) between the revolutionary French regime and a coalition of European powers; it became a formal member of the European coalition in the Second Coalition Wars (1799–1801) in reaction to NAPOLEON BONAPARTE's invasion of Egypt. Entering a European coalition and declaring neutrality were novel experiences in Ottoman history, leading ultimately to the appointment of the empire's first permanent foreign ambassadors to London in 1793, to Berlin in 1795, to Vienna in 1795, and to Paris in 1795; no ambassador to St. Petersburg was appointed because relations between Russia and the Ottomans had soured in 1795. A new class of bureaucrats with a Western mentality rose from the ranks of these diplomats, and these would shape and carry out the Tanzimat reforms in the next period of Ottoman history.

The Nizam-ı Cedid reforms were not solely based on Western inspiration. A new Islamic discourse, partially shaped by the NAQSHBANDIYYA, MEVLEVI, and Halveti orders, was as influential in establishing and carrying forward these reforms as were the Western concepts of state and society. Unlike many in the West, Ottoman intellectuals did not automatically equate modernity with secularism; thus reinforcement of the traditional sumptuary laws, which continued to regulate moral conduct in the empire, went hand in hand with modern policies of industrialization and the establishment of a conscript army. In line with Ottoman pragmatism, the ruling elite incorporated Islamic laws (SHARIA) and values into the reform program, making every effort to justify the adoption of a Western model of the absolutist state by redefining conventional Islamic notions. Within this context, Ottoman reformers invited the population to understand the Western idea of civic duty within the more familiar Muslim framework of serving state and religion (din-ü-devlet) and submission to the ultimate state authority (ulu'l-emre ita'at). Likewise, the principle of due reciprocity (mukabele-i bi'l-misl), the Islamic formula justifying the adoption of Western military techniques, became a more general principle for the transfer of knowledge from Europe.

While the Nizam-ı Cedid reform program was successful and far-reaching, it was not, of course, without its critics. In the battle of narratives between supporters and opponents of reform, the pro-reform group presented the modern Nizam-ı Cedid troops as an effective guard against Russian attack, for during this period, the modernization of RUSSIA had become both a threat to the Ottomans and a model to emulate. Some Ottomans regarded Russian reforms as a danger to their own state, but others admired Russia's modern military or saw in the industrialization and progress of the Russian state and society an apt example for domestic change. The most significant internal conflict over the Nizam-ı Cedid reforms came not from any external force, however, but from an internal rebellion, the Kabakçı Mustafa Revolt of 1807, driven by religious scholars, or ulema, and the sultan's personal Janissary guard.

Often mischaracterized as the result of fanaticism, ignorance, and corruption that swept away all the westernizing reforms in bloodshed, the Kabakçı Mustafa Revolt was, in fact, the result of a political conspiracy carried out by a rival faction in the palace that, resenting the arrogance and corruption of the reform committee, made use of the discontented Janissaries, the ulema, and the strongmen of the Balkans whose vested interests were threatened by the reforms. In 1806, with the help of the masses who dreaded compulsory military service in the new army and resented heavy taxation, these combined forces managed to block the introduction of the Nizam-ı Cedid army the Balkans (the second Edirne incident). Selim's legitimacy was also undermined by other events and developments, including uprisings in the Balkans (Serbians) and Arabia (WAHHABIS), problems with Russia and Great Britain, the arrival of a hostile British fleet in the Bosporus, the extravagant life led by the court, the debasement of the currency, and periodic food shortages in Istanbul. Taking advantage of negative public opinion, the rival faction encouraged the guards deployed in fortresses along the Bosporus to refuse to wear the Nizam-ı Cedid uniforms and to mutiny. Unaware of the conspiracy, Selim did not send his new army to suppress the uprising, seeking to avoid a possible civil war while the empire was in the midst of yet another war with Russia. When the rebel group headed by Kabakçı Mustafa, the commander of the Rumeli fortress, entered the city and joined forces with the Janissaries, the mutiny became an open revolt approved by the discontented public. This group demanded the disbanding of the Nizam-ı Cedid army and the execution of the members of the reform committee. A demoralized Selim complied with all the rebels' demands but was still forced to abdicate on May 29, 1807. The members of the reform committee, 10 in total, were executed as part of the revolt, but this use of force has resulted in widespread misperception, causing students and historians to falsely romanticize the reign of Selim III as a struggle between religious reactionaries and the "luminous forces" of reform (teceddüd). In actuality, following the revolt, the technical schools and the printing house continued to operate, and the technical corps in the army was reinforced through new regulations by the succeeding sultans.

Kahraman Şakul

Further reading: Stanford J. Shaw, *Between Old and New: The Ottoman Empire Under Selim III, 1789–1807* (Cambridge, Mass.: Harvard University Press, 1971); Caroline Finkel, *Osman's Dream: The Story of the Ottoman Empire, 1300–1923* (London: John Murray, 2005), 383–412; Ekmeleddin İhsanoğlu, ed., *History of the Ottoman State, Society, and Civilisation*, vol. 1 (Istanbul: Ircica, 2001), 63–77; F. Babinger, "Nizam-I Djedid," in *Encyclopaedia of Islam*, 2nd ed., vol. 8 (Leiden: Brill, 1960–), 75–76; Virginia Aksan, "Selim III," in *Encyclopaedia of Islam*, 2nd ed., vol. 9 (Leiden: Brill, 1960–), 132–134; Butrus Abu-Manneh, *Studies on Islam and the Ottoman Empire in the 19th Century, 1826–1876* (Istanbul: Isis, 2001); M. Alaaddin Yalçınkaya, "Istanbul as an Important Centre of European Diplomacy (according to British Sources during the Period 1789–1798)," in *The Great Ottoman Turkish Civilisation*, vol. 1, edited by Ercüment Kuran et al. (Ankara: Yeni Türkiye, 1999) 523–537; V. Aksan, "Ottoman Political Writing (1768–1808)." *IJMES* 25 (1993): 53–69.

nomads Although a substantial number of Arab nomads became part of the Ottoman Empire after the conquest of the Arab lands in 1516–17, , in terms of the development of the empire, the most significant nomadic group was the Turkomans or Yürüks, who not only constituted an important part of the population of the Ottoman Empire from its beginning but was also the group out of which the Ottoman state arose. The terms *Turkoman* (Türkmen) and *Yürük* were used interchangeably within Ottoman documents to refer to the lifestyles of the same people. Other terms, such as *konar-göçer, göçer-evli, göçerler*, and *göçebe*, were also used when referring to nomadic people.

ORIGINS AND ORGANIZATION

Major nomadic groups called Oghuz or Turkoman came from Central Asia to Anatolia after the Battle of Manzikert (Malazgirt) in 1071. This migration wave reached its peak between the years 1221 and 1261 during the course of the Mongolian attacks. Among these migrants were Turkic tribes such as the Karluk, Khalac, and Kypchak. As a result of these population movements, significant changes occurred that affected the demographic, toponymic, and cultural structures of Anatolia. During the dominant periods of different Turkic states in Anatolia —including the first Turkic states (established in the region by Kutalmışoğlu Süleyman Shah and the Danişmends, Mengücüks, Artuks, Ahlatshahs, Saltuks and the Anatolian Seljuk State)—Turkic nomads began to know the region better. Many of the Turkic principalities in Anatolia were established by members of different dynasties belonging to the larger Turkoman clan. This played an important role in the occupation of the region by the Turks in such a short period of time.

Toponymical studies and place names provide us with geographic information about the areas in Anatolia in which the nomadic groups lived. Place names with Turkic origins are found in a vast area in the internal regions of the BLACK SEA and in the Taurus Mountains region stretching from west to east in the southern and northern parts of Anatolia, which were the areas settled by most of those nomadic groups. These names are more frequently found in Bolu, Kastamonu, Çorum, Tosya, Tokat, and the Ankara plains in the north, in the foothills of the north Anatolian mountains, in the central Anatolian steppes, Çukurova, and the lakes region in the south. In the west, it is evident that these nomadic groups settled in the vast plains of Menderes and Gediz. The nomadic people living in these regions used the wide plains and valleys near the coasts as their winter quarters (kışlak) and the plains located at higher altitudes in the internal parts of Anatolia as their summer pastures (yaylak). Geographically, the areas they lived in during the winter and summer were not a great distance apart. The tribes living in eastern and southeastern Anatolia had their summer pastures on the high plateaus in central and eastern Anatolia and spent the cold months in their winter quarters, which today border IRAQ and SYRIA.

The nomadic groups consisted of a number of *boys* or tribal groups. Each *boy* was like the trunk of a tree, with different groups growing out from the *boy* or tribe like branches. In other words, each *boy* consisted of several nomadic groups. In earlier periods, however, there were not so many nomadic groups in a *boy*. The number increased only after the Oghuz *boys* came to Anatolia, broke away from one another, and began living in smaller groups in different areas. Some groups that were previously members of the same *boy* came to be known by different names. Factors contributing to this process included the influence and pressure of the Mongols, who had formerly conquered and occupied the lands used by the Turkomans, and the population growth of the nomadic tribes living in Anatolia, which led to a lack of settlement areas. The incorporation of nomadic people into the administrative and economic structure of regional polities also played an important role in the division of tribes into minor structural groups.

During the Ottoman period, like the sedentary population, nomadic groups were involved in the administrative and economic structure of the empire. The major nomadic groups in the administrative and economic system were known as Bozulus, Yeniil, Aleppo, Damascus, Dulkadırlı, Danişmendli, Atçeken (Esbkeşan), Karaulus, Ulu Yörük, Ankara Yörüks, and Bolu Yörüks. These names were generally given to these groups by the bureaucrats of the central Ottoman administration. However, these names were not random or meaningless, but were derived from the geographic locations where the groups lived or from the Turkoman principalities under which they had lived before being subjected to the control of the Ottomans. Terms such as *il* and *ulus*, which reflect the traces of former nomadic administrative and social organization, also played an important role in these given names. Although several of the smaller nomadic groups were part of the *timar* system and were administered within the sub-provinces or *sancaks* in which they lived, some of these nomadic groups continued to live in accordance with the traditional tribal structure. Nevertheless, this traditional tribal structure started to lose influence as the *boys* were divided into smaller groups over time and as some minor groups emerged and began to be seen as more important than the original ones. Thousands, even tens of thousands, of nomadic groups or units that emerged from among the major *boys* are apparent in Ottoman archival documents. These groups, consisting of a set number of people, were referred to by such terms as *cemaat, oymak, mahalle, tîr, bölük, oba, tâbi,* and *taallukat*. Each of these nomadic groups or units had its own name, such as the "X Cemaati", "X Oymağı", or "X Mahallesi" (e.g., Abalu Cemaati, Sıdıklı Oymağı, and Kütüklü Mahallesi). These were often the names of original *boys* to which they belonged, such as Kayı, Bayat,

Döğer, Avşar, Beydili, or Eymir. Most of the groups were also known by the names of their leaders or ancestors, generally called *kethüda* and *boybeyi*, or distinguished persons such as the Ali Kocalu, Bayramlu, Beçilü, Cengizlü, Çakırlu, Gündüzlü, Güzel Hanlu, Ilyaslu, Ine Kocalu, Kara Isalu, Köpekli, Müslim Hacılu, Nusretlü, Pehlivanlu, Sarsallu, Süleymanlu, Yabanlu, and the Yunuslu peoples. Other groups were named after the fields they occupied or the region in which they lived.

Because each nomadic group consisted of closely related families, the members of the group knew each other very well. The number of families in each unit varied between five and 100; in some units, there could be even more. Each group was represented and governed by a leader known as *kethüda*, who was generally be chosen from among the most influential families of the unit. Although the title *kethüda* was passed from father to son, it was sometimes given to distinguished people who had influence and respectability. The candidate *kethüda* was chosen by the people and his name was reported to the Ottoman judge or KADI of the district. The *kadı* then submitted the candidate *kethüda*'s name to the central administration.

GEOGRAPHIC DISTRIBUTION

The geographical distribution of the most important nomadic organizations was already in place by the 1530s. Although there were slight changes in this distribution in the 16th century—when such major groups as the Yeniil, Aleppo, and Bozulus Turkomans moved from the east toward the west and when the Ottoman administration pursued different policies toward them—the overall structure and dispersal remained almost the same.

The nomads constituted an important part of the population in the areas in which they lived. According to Ö. L. Barkan's pioneering study on cadastral survey records (1957), in the lands that make up present-day Anatolia (including the provinces of Anatolia, Karaman, Dulkadır, and Rumelia) there were about 872,610 households in the 1520s and 1530s. Of these, 160,564 were nomads, while the remainder were sedentary groups. Of the four provinces, Anatolia had the largest nomadic population, 77,268 households. This number did not include about 52,000 households consisting of nomadic-origin *yaya-müsellems* (infantry and cavalry). Between 1570 and 1580, 220,217 households out of a total of 1,360,474 in these four provinces were nomadic; the province of Anatolia maintained the highest population of nomads with 116,219 households. Compared to earlier periods, the province of Anatolia during this period showed an abnormally large increase in the population. According to Ottomanist scholar Halil Inalcık, this was a result of population movements from the eastern provinces toward the west. The population in the provinces of Aleppo, Tripoli, Damascus, BAGHDAD, and BASRA also included a substantial nomadic population, including Turkoman and Yörük groups. Between 1570 and 1590, of 371,848 households in these provinces, 87,030 households were nomadic. Most of the summer pastures of nomadic groups in these five regions were in Anatolia.

SETTLEMENT PROGRAM

Most of the nomadic groups in Anatolia during the Ottoman period eventually adopted sedentary lives and established new settlement areas as a result of economic, social, and demographic conditions. It is understood that the systematic forced settlement of these people by the state in various regions began during the late 17th century. The main reason the Ottomans did not undertake this project earlier was that their attention was focused on continuous wars with neighboring states and on the CELALI REVOLTS. The Ottoman authorities launched plans to reopen settlements demolished by the Celali movements of the 17th century for agricultural production, and Istanbul intended to unite the nomadic people within the empire by providing them with efficient facilities for agricultural production.

One reason for the forced settlement program was that the Ottomans believed that a sedentary agricultural lifestyle would keep the nomads busy and prevent them from causing political trouble. This was especially urgent because the summer and winter lands had become insufficient for the nomads' traditional way of life. The Ottoman authorities chose various areas to settle the nomads. These included Afyonkarahisar (Karahisar-ı Sahib), Urfa, Adana, and Bozok in Anatolia, as well as Rakka and Aleppo. Of these settlement areas, Rakka was strategically important because it was considered a fortress that could resist possible Arab raids from the south. Whereas the Ottoman settlement policy during the expansion period that lasted until about the late 16th century was an external strategy, this settlement policy was a domestic strategy whose main objectives were to reopen devastated areas to agricultural production and to revive the economies of given regions. These settlement strategies seem to have worked well in some parts of Anatolia, but in such critical areas as Rakka, due to sociological, geographical, and climatic factors, they did not yield the expected results.

The settlement strategies of the central authorities of the late 17th century were continued into the 18th century, when nomadic groups were settled mostly in devastated areas or in their own summer and winter lands. Naturally, some groups preferred to establish their own settlements and adopted sedentary lives without state intervention. Additionally, as in the 17th century, other nomadic groups were settled and used as barriers, particularly along the southern border areas. This settlement policy was continued in the 19th century during the TANZIMAT period.

As a result of these settlement policies, nomadic groups within the Ottoman Empire adopted a sedentary life and established new settlements. This greatly contributed to the settlement and renovation of material and spiritual culture in Anatolia, and the establishment of an orderly settlement pattern.

İlhan Şahin

Further reading: Ömer Lütfi Barkan, "Essai sur les données statistiques des registres de recensement dans l'Empire Ottoman aux XVe et XVIe siècles." *Journal of the Economic and Social History of the Orient* 1 (1957): 9–36; Ömer Lütfi Barkan, "Research on the Ottoman Fiscal Surveys," in *Studies in the Economic History of the Middle East,* edited by Michael A. Cook (Oxford: Oxford University Press, 1970), 163–171; Halil İnalcık, "The Yürüks: Their Origins, Expansion and Economic Role," in *The Middle East and the Balkans under the Ottoman Empire* (Bloomington: Indiana University Press, 1993); Rudi Paul Lindner, *Nomads and Ottomans in Medieval Anatolia* (Bloomington: Indiana University Press, 1983); İlhan Şahin, *Osmanlı Döneminde Konar-Göçerler / Nomads in the Ottoman Empire* (Istanbul: Eren Yayıncılık, 2006).

North Africa   Ottoman interest in North Africa was prompted by a strategic aim to block Spanish expansion into the region. The fall of the Muslim kingdom of Granada in 1492 ended an Islamic political presence in Spain dating from 711 C.E. Inspired by that victory, Spanish fleets harried Muslim shipping in the western Mediterranean Sea while Spanish soldiers occupied Muslim ports in North Africa. The Ottoman response was to increase pressure on the Europeans through state sponsorship of Muslim CORSAIRS, who raided Christian shipping and launched slave raids on European coastal villages from Sicily to Ireland. To counter the Spanish, who were fortifying naval bases along the North African coast, the Ottomans needed their own ports. These were established by the mid-16th century in ALGIERS, TUNIS, and TRIPOLI. Although there would be other such ports, those three would serve to anchor the Ottoman political presence in North Africa.

There was a major difference between the Spanish settlements and those of the Ottomans. The Spanish faced hostile Muslim populations in the hinterlands beyond their fortified garrisons, while the Ottomans could appeal to a sense of Islamic solidarity to secure their own position. The Ottomans were unwilling, however, to commit a large number of ground troops to their North African outposts. As a result, the countryside remained largely under the control of Berber and Arab tribes who might ally themselves with the Ottomans but did not recognize their political suzerainty. As Ottoman control in the region relied heavily on the NAVY, the sultans' writ rarely extended beyond the narrow North African coastal plain.

The Berber clans in the mountains of Algeria effectively resisted any incorporation into the Ottoman Empire. Morocco, under first the Saadi and later the ALAWI dynasty of sultans, also repelled Ottoman incursions into its territory as vigorously as it did attacks by the Spanish. The Ottomans faced a special problem with the Alawis. As their dynastic name suggests, this group claimed descent from Ali, the son-in-law of the Prophet, and boasted a pedigree that was more exalted than that claimed by the Ottoman dynasty. North African jurists viewed the Alawi claim to SUNNI legitimacy to be stronger than that of the Ottoman ruling family. The practical result of the Alawi dynasty's claim was that the sultans of Morocco could rally Berber and Arab tribes into coalitions, based on religious devotion to the Prophet Muhammad's descendants, effectively resisting Ottoman attempts to expand their political control into Morocco.

The absence of a routine Ottoman military and bureaucratic presence in the North African ports engendered anarchy. Profiting from this power vacuum, the military in those cities created alliances with the local Muslim commercial elites and soon began to govern in place of Ottoman officials sent from Istanbul. At the start of the 18th century, military strongmen seized control in all the major North African ports. In 1705 Hüseyin Alioğlu established his rule in Tunis. His descendants, known as the Husaynis, would rule as beys—at least nominally—until 1957. In 1711 both Karamanlı Ahmed Bey in Tripoli and Sökeli Ali Bey in Algiers established their own dynasties. Although neither dynasty was as long-lived as that of the Husaynis, descendants of these two beys controlled their respective cities well into the 19th century. All three ports were in intense competition for control of the lucrative corsair or pirate enterprises, leading them to a continued reliance on Istanbul for legitimacy; reference to the sultan also allowed the beys to balance off their more immediate rivals—each other. Much of North Africa thus remained nominally in the Ottoman Empire despite the fairly passive role of the Ottoman sultans in asserting their sovereignty.

In the 19th century, North Africa's proximity to Europe made it an increasingly attractive target for colonization. The pirate industry, which had supported the economies of the port cities of North Africa for so long, went into sharp decline as western European and American naval forces focused on regulating the semi-criminal commercial activities that had hitherto thrived in the Mediterranean Sea. But while riches at sea were harder to come by, the region found a new niche in the larger Mediterranean economy. During the Napoleonic Wars (1798–1815), grain from North Africa, which had long been the breadbasket of the region, helped feed a France starved by Great Britain's continental blockade. As the economies of western Europe became increasingly dependent on food supplies from North Africa, European investors saw the remnants of the weakened Ottoman Empire as easy prey. In 1830 French forces occupied Algiers after the bey, or governor, hit the French ambassador in the face with a flyswatter. The war that followed placed Algeria under direct French colonial rule. In Tunis and Tripoli, the growth of European power came in the indirect form of European colonists and Western capital, the latter of which was used to develop the agricultural production of both provinces. Tunisia became a French protectorate in 1884; in 1911, Italy occupied Libya.

Bruce Masters

See also ALGIERS; TRIPOLI; TUNIS.
Further reading: Andrew Hess, *The Forgotten Frontier: A History of the Sixteenth-Century Ibero-African Frontier* (Chicago: University of Chicago Press, 1978).

notables *See* AYAN.

novel The novel was introduced into Ottoman literature in 1860 through translations from Western texts. Until that time, traditional folk stories, often narrating extraordinary loves, such as "Kerem and Aslı" and "Leyla and Mecnun," were the prevailing type of fiction in the Ottoman community. The novel was a form that Ottoman intellectuals were quick to adopt, recognizing in the new genre the possibility of introducing into Ottoman culture the modern Western values they admired.

The first Western novel translated into the Ottoman language was *The Adventures of Telemachus* by the French writer François Fénelon (1651–1715). Translated in ornate and powerful language by Yusuf Kamil Pasha (1808–76), an important Ottoman statesman of the period, *The Adventures of Telemachus* is a sort of advice book and resembles in this respect the Ottoman form of "advice to princes" already familiar to the Ottoman reading public. Later novels translated into Ottoman Turkish give a fuller sense of the genre and are generally stories of love and adventure. These include *Les Misérables* by Victor Hugo (1802–85), *Robinson Crusoe* (1719) by Daniel Defoe, *The Count of Monte Cristo* (1844) by Alexandre Dumas, and *Paul et Virginie* (Paul and Virginia) by Bernardin de Saint-Pierre (1737–1814). These early translations are awkward, however, often offering a mere summary of the novel, because the Ottoman translators of this period typically learned French either on their own or through private lessons. The more qualified translators of the next generation learned foreign languages in educational institutions and produced more fluid and accurate translations. Despite their failings, however, there was a real benefit to these initial translations in that they created a sympathy for the novel form.

Since the Ottoman novel did not arise out of a natural evolution as it did in the West but was rather imported as the product of a completely different culture, the initial examples of this literary form in the Ottoman world are imperfect. One reason for this was that Ottoman authors faced difficulties particular to their environment, for example, how to write a realistic romantic novel in a culture where women and men were not permitted to interact socially in public. This feature of Ottoman life led Ottoman authors to rely on extraordinary coincidences and other unnatural plot devices not characteristic of the emerging realism of the novel form in the West. Ottoman writers also faced the challenge of censorship, especially when depicting love relationships and domestic life.

The early Ottoman novel was characterized by its effort to serve as a tool to instruct or to effect REFORM. In this spirit, the most frequent topic is the adoption of a Western lifestyle, called "the European model," by individuals living within the empire, most often in ISTANBUL. Early novelists approached the subject mostly in a derisive style, looking critically at the impact of Western living on Ottoman culture. However, criticism of traditional lifestyles is also seen in these novels; for instance, the writers address the adverse impact of traditional Islamic marriages where young people are forced to wed unknown spouses selected by their parents, the problems faced by girls who were not allowed to go to school, and the status of the slaves who were indispensable members of wealthy Ottoman households.

An early Ottoman novel is *Taaşşuk-ı Talat ve Fitnat* (The romance of Talat and Fitnat) by Şemseddin Sami (1850–1904). While relying on some of conventions of earlier Ottoman literature, like the extraordinary coincidences that enable the love story, the novel is noteworthy for its introduction of topics new to Ottoman literature such as a critical reading of parental authority, the education of girls, and the troubles of women prevented from any involvement in a greater social life. This text is considered the starting point of the Ottoman novel. Written in Turkish using the Armenian alphabet, the *Akabi History* (1851) by Vartan Pasha is considered by some to be the first Ottoman novel. The story narrates a tale of love made tragic due to religious differences. Another early novel, written in Turkish using the Greek alphabet, *Temaşa-ı Dünya ve Cefakar ü Cefakeş* (1872) by Evangelinos Misilidis, an Ottoman Greek journalist, is another remarkable text of the period.

In many respects, however, these initial attempts at the novel form were false starts; with regard to the history of the Ottoman novels the first truly important writer is Ahmed Midhat Efendi (1844–1913), who introduced the novel form to the Ottoman community. His *Letaif-ı Rivayet* (Finest stories) series includes the long stories and short novels that he started to publish in 1870; he also published more than 30 additional novels. Acting as a journalist, Ahmed Midhat observed every aspect of the community he was living in, giving particular attention to the struggles that arose as part of the Westernization process. Ahmed Midhat's favorite topics included the superficially Westernized person, the education and labor problems of women, and slavery. Ahmed Midhat's success is keyed to the fact that he used literary techniques and language familiar to his Ottoman readership even as he adopted the relatively unfamiliar novel form. Like other novelists of this early period, Ahmed Midhat considered the novel a vehicle not only for entertainment, but also for instruction. Thus he pursued a popular style appealing to the masses. His most popular novel is *Felatun Bey ve Rakım Efendi* (Felatun Bey and Rakim Efendi) in which he compares two young persons, one of whom adopts Western ways without losing his own cultural heritage while the other merely imitates the West, becoming alienated from her own culture even as she takes up strange ways of dressing and relies on her slipshod knowledge of French.

Other novelists of this early era include Namık Kemal, who wrote *Intibah* (Vigilance); Recaizade Mahmut Ekrem, who wrote *Araba Sevdası* (Obsession with a carriage); Samipaşazade Sezai, who wrote *Sergüzeşt* (Adventure); and Nabizade Nazım, the author of *Zehra* (Zehra).

In 1895, when Ottoman literature of the westernization period was at the height of its maturity, a great transformation in the Ottoman novel took place. A new community of writers, called the Servet-i Fünun (Scientific wealth)—a group well acquainted with Western languages and literature and one that closely monitored literary movements in Europe—began to see a new purpose for the novel. This group argued that the novel need not be a mere tool with a social and didactic purpose, but that it should be primarily an art form governed by aesthetic concerns and dedicated to the representation of the human. The Servet-i Fünun writers were the first to break free from the traditional conventions of Ottoman narrative, a difficulty that writers from the initial period of the novel could not overcome. It is in the hands of the Servet-i Fünun writers that the Ottoman novel first attains the norms of the Western novel.

The first mature examples of the Ottoman novel were produced by Halid Ziya Uşaklıgil (1867–1945), the favorite writer of this community. *Aşk-ı Memnu* (Illicit love), published in 1900, is considered to be the first masterpiece written in Turkish. Another member of the community, Mehmet Rauf (1875–1931), was the first to write a psychological novel in Turkish, *Eylül* (September). The Servet-i Fünun writers took the Ottoman novel to new ground, traveling into the inside of the human mind. However, this interiority is due in some part to the intense policy of CENSORSHIP that prevailed under Sultan ABDÜLHAMID II (r. 1876–1909) and that restricted printed discussion of political matters.

Other Ottoman novelists were working at the same time as the Servet-i Fünun group yet deviated from their aesthetic. The most important of these writers were Ahmed Rasim and Hüseyin Rahmi Gürpınar, who focused on the folk novel. In his first novels, written during the last period of the empire, Hüseyin Rahmi was strongly influenced by his teacher, Ahmed Midhat. Hüseyin Rahmi's novels dealing with Westernization—*Şık* (Chic), *Şıpsevdi* (Always in love), and *Mürebbiye* (The governess)—are especially remarkable for their humorous style and piercing critique.

In addition to profoundly altering the social and political order of the empire, the advent of the Second Constitutional Monarchy (1908) had a deep impact on literature as well, putting an end to much of the successful experimentation that had been underway; during this time, the novel form showed no significant improvement. From this period, only Halide Edib Adıvar (1884–1964) came forward as a new and brilliant novelist, the first powerful female Ottoman novelist. While telling passionate love stories of influential, cultured female heroes in such novels as *Seviye Talib* (Seviye Talib) and *Handan* (Handan) early in her career, she later wrote novels discussing social topics; these include *Yeni Turan* (The New Turan), *Ateşten Gömlek* (The shirt of flame), and *Vurun Kahpeye* (Hit the whore).

While creating their most significant novels in the Republican era of Turkish literature (after 1923), Yakup Kadri Karaosmanoğlu (1889–1974), Reşat Nuri Güntekin (1889–1956) and Peyami Safa published their first novels in the closing years of the empire. Yakup Kadri depicted the collapse triggered in the aristocrat class in *Kiralık Konak* (Mansion for rent); in *Nur Baba* (Father Nur), he explored the critical role of the dissolution of religious denominations in social life. In *Sözde Kızlar* (So-called girls), Peyami Safa takes a critical look at what the writer sees as the degenerate way of living in the westernized sections of Istanbul during the War of Liberation. Reşat Nuri introduced an idealism that would have a strong influence on subsequent generations in her novel *Çalıkuşu* (The wren, about a well-educated young Istanbul woman sent to a rural territory of the empire to serve as a teacher.

Although the novel form was introduced in the empire as early as 1870, the genre underwent a long, slow maturation process of some 50 years before developing into a truly worthwhile literature; it was only with the emergence of the Turkish Republican period in the early 1920s that the novel form hit its stride and was thus one of the most significant art forms to rise out of the ashes of the dying Ottoman Empire.

Handan İnci

Further reading: Robert Finn, *The Early Turkish Novel* (Princeton, N.J.: Princeton University Press, 1978); Ahmet Evin, *Origins and Development of the Turkish Novel* (Minneapolis: Bibliotheca Islamica, 1983).

Nusayris *See* ALAWIS.

O

Orhan Gazi (1324–1362) *second ruler of the Ottoman dynasty* Orhan Gazi was the son of OSMAN I (?–1324?), the founder of the Ottoman imperial dynasty; Orhan's mother was the daughter of the sheikh Edebali. Orhan inherited the Ottoman emirate from his father in 1324 and expanded it to both Anatolia and the Balkans. Unlike his father's reign, the expansion and consolidation of Orhan's power is well documented. Orhan founded several mosques, dervish lodges, charitable institutions, and schools in the many important cities he conquered. In accordance with tradition, upon his ascendancy Orhan struck a silver coin, called an akçe, bearing his name. According to Turkish tradition, in 1299, Orhan married Nilüfer, the daughter of the Byzantine lord of Yarhisar (an unidentified fortress in the Sakarya River region in northwestern Asia Minor, Turkey). Their son, Süleyman Pasha, the conqueror of the Balkans, was the heir presumptive. However, his untimely death in 1357 resulted in the succession of Orhan's other son who became the first Ottoman sultan, MURAD I (r. 1362–89).

Byzantine authors such as Nikephoros Gregoras (1295–1359) and the Byzantine Emperor John Kantakouzenos (1341–54), both contemporaries of Orhan, provided vivid information about his reign, accounts that are invaluable since most accounts from Turkish sources were written more than a century after his death and are of legendary nature. The only exception among the Turkish sources is the chronicle of Yahşi Fakih, the son of Orhan's imam or prayer leader, but this is preserved only as part of a 15th-century chronicle.

Orhan participated in many raids organized by his father, whose troops controlled the littoral opposite Byzantine Constantinople. Orhan's first major success against the Byzantines came in 1326 with the conquest of the city of BURSA (Prousa), which then became the first Ottoman capital. This choice underlined Orhan's strategic interest against the neighboring BYZANTINE EMPIRE. His uninterrupted raids on Byzantine lands terrorized his Byzantine neighbors but also allowed him to amass great booty and to establish himself as a successful military leader in the eyes of wandering Turkoman tribes looking for employment. The Byzantine inability to react to this challenge is reflected in the defeat of the army headed by Emperor Andronikos III Palaiologos (r. 1328–41) in Pelekanon in 1329. The defeat demoralized the Byzantines and encouraged Orhan to concentrate his efforts on conquering the cities of Bithynia which had long been under siege. In 1331, Nicea (Iznik) surrendered, and although in 1333 the Byzantine Emperor was forced to pay a great sum per year for peace, in 1337 the port of Nicomedia (Izmit) also fell to the increasing might of the Ottomans.

This phase of animosity between the Byzantines and the Ottomans was replaced by a period of cautious alliance. During this time Orhan's involvement in the Byzantine civil war (1341–47) on the side of Byzantine Emperor John VI Kantakouzenos (r. 1347–54) was more beneficial to the Ottomans than to the Byzantines. Orhan's troops, led by his son Süleyman Pasha, complemented Kantakouzenos' lack of manpower, but came at a price. The dynastic marriage between Orhan and Kantakouzenos' daughter Theodora shocked the Byzantines but apparently did little to restrain Süleyman Pasha's brutal activities in the Balkans. Nikephoros Gregoras attacked Kantakouzenos' choice of allies, and the emperor's own chronicle apologizes for the havoc inflicted by

The mosque of Orhan Gazi in central Bursa. *(Photo by Gábor Ágoston)*

the Ottomans in Thrace, lamenting his subjects' loss of property and the enslavement of many who were involuntarily transferred to Ottoman territories in Anatolia. In 1352 Ottoman troops, now thoroughly familiar with the topography of Thrace, acquired Tzymbe, their first fortress in Europe, and in 1354, as a result of a devastating earthquake that destroyed the walls of several cities, the Ottomans were able to occupy the strategic fortress of Kallipoli (Gallipoli).

Thus the period of Byzantine civil war both brought Orhan valuable territorial gains and raised the international profile of the Ottoman emirate. In the 1350s Orhan concluded his first Genoese-Ottoman treaty and was negotiating a marriage alliance with the Serbian king Stefan Dushan. Aware that continued Ottoman expansion was dependent on the development of a NAVY and fleet, Orhan annexed the adjacent Turkoman emirate of Karasi around 1346, thus gaining access to the Aegean Sea. In 1361, Orhan's final conquest was of Didymoteichon, another important Thracian city. Orhan died in

1362, leaving as his legacy a formidable regional state with significant territories in both Anatolia and Europe.

The structure of the Ottoman emirate under Orhan remains an area of heated debate among scholars. Byzantine contemporary sources stress only the pastoral nature of Orhan's state and the rigor of his raids, but Orhan's conquests and the consolidation of his holdings began to bring about remarkable new cultural effects. Through mixed marriages, Byzantine Christians in Anatolia lost first their daughters, then their religion, and last their language, a shift lamented by Gregory Palamas, the bishop of SALONIKA, in letters written while he was in captivity in Orhan's territory in 1354. Palamas grieved over the number of conversions to Islam and described a society that was already producing bilingual members accustomed to the habits of the conquerors, and while his account does shed some light on Christian and Muslim inter-communal affairs under Orhan's rule, it is not sufficient to explain the policies of Orhan toward his Byzantine Christian subjects.

This complex cultural moment has resulted in vigorous debate among scholars as to the nature of administration in the early Ottoman emirate. Some focus on the tribal nature of Orhan's state and concentrate on the concept of jihad (holy war) as the major driving force of expansion. Yet this view is challenged by Byzantine and Turkish accounts which report the participation of local Christians in the Ottoman expansion. In response, some scholars suggest that the local society was brought together by shared ideas and values regarding valor and by the already diverse nature of Muslim culture. Other scholars propose that the commingling of converts together with the Turkish people resulted in a new "race" that became the driving force of early Ottoman society, a theory that has found few supporters. A revised version of this argument proposed that the early administrative apparatus had largely adopted the Seljuk tradition modified in accordance with the "accommodationist" policies of the rulers to include numerous practices inherited from the conquered states. Within Orhan's early Ottoman state, then, emirs clearly saw the need to adopt customs and other elements of the conquered peoples, resulting in a hybrid that enabled the continued expansion of the state and which would come to be a fundamental characteristic of the emerging Ottoman Empire.

Eugenia Kermeli

Further reading: Halil İnalcık, *The Ottoman Empire: The Classical Age, 1300–1600* (London: Phoenix, 1994); Cemal Kafadar, *Between Two Worlds: The Construction of the Ottoman State* (Berkeley: University of California Press, 1995); Heath W. Lowry, *The Nature of the Early Ottoman State* (Albany: State University of New York Press, 2003).

Osman I (Osman Gazi) (?–1324?) *founder of the Ottoman dynasty* Osman I, son of Ertoğrul and grandson of Süleyman Shah, is the acknowledged founder of the Ottoman (Osmanlı) imperial dynasty, also known as "the House of Osman." Reliable information regarding Osman is scarce. His birth date is unknown and his symbolic significance as the father of the dynasty has encouraged the development of mythic tales regarding the ruler's life and origins, however, historians agree that before 1300, Osman was simply one among a number of Turkoman tribal leaders operating in the Sakarya region. During the first decade of the 14th century, shrewd military tactics and good fortune enabled the ambitious Osman to conquer vulnerable but important territories from the Byzantine Empire and to accumulate these holdings into his own nascent empire. Osman is thought to have died shortly after the conquest of Prousa (Bursa, Turkey) on April 6, 1326. He was succeeded by his son Orhan Gazi (r. 1326–59).

The tomb of the eponymous founder of the Ottoman dynasty Osman Gazi in Bursa, as restored in the 19th century. *(Photo by Gábor Ágoston)*

Osman's success seems to have been founded on his contact with the settled peasant population of the Bithynian countryside which fostered a sympathetic relationship with the local Byzantine population. This group had long been disenchanted with Byzantine rule which had imposed heavy taxes and provided inadequate security in the wake of destructive wars with Rome and the West. Because this Anatolian region was under constant attack from tribal Turkoman groups, individual populations established local alliances to provide for their own security, creating the opportunity for Osman to establish his interest in the northern part of Bithynia (Sakarya region) to the detriment of Byzantine holdings. After an important victory over the Byzantine army at Bapheus, a district around Izmit (Nikomedia) in 1301, Osman assumed undisputed leadership of a large number of independent Turkoman tribes. And in cooperation with these tribes and local Christian agents, Osman then launched devastating looting raids against the countryside surrounding great Bithynian cities. Through this plan, the Bithynian cities were cut off from their countryside and the consequent economic "strangulation" paved the way for greater territorial gains for Osman. Luck also allowed

Osman's territories to avoid detrimental encounters with Mongols and the Catalan company sent by the Byzantine emperor, Andronikos II Palaiologos (r. 1282–1328), which attempted to secure the area in 1303. With the failure of these forces, the remaining former Byzantine peasants soon switched their allegiance.

Based on the meager information available, contemporary historians have attempted to reconstruct the nature of the early Ottoman emirate and its policies. The two most concrete sources of information are a silver coin stamped with Osman's name and a dedication document (*vakfiyye*) dated March 1324. The first confirms the Ottoman tradition that Osman had declared himself as an independent ruler and confirms as well the Turkish sources, beginning with the *Iskendername* of Ahmedi (ca. 1400), that unanimously identify Ertoğrul as Osman's father. The dedication document bears the names of Osman's children, including that of Orhan, the future ruler, and also bears the signature of Orhan, suggesting that the succession either took place during Osman's life or that Osman might have died in 1324.

Secondary sources regarding Osman, though somewhat more bountiful, are not perfectly reliable. These are Byzantine, Ottoman, and western narratives, the majority of which were written in the 15th century. Earlier sources include the chronicles of Nikephoros Gregoras (1295–1359), John Kantakouzenos (1341–54), and the Byzantine chronicle of George Pachymeres (1242–ca. 1310). Although the events recorded in his chronicle are rather confusing, this text records the first decisive victory of Osman over the Byzantine army at Bapheus, a district around Izmit (Nikomedia) in 1301. According to the Byzantine chronicler "this was the beginning of great trouble for the whole region". Although the exact sequence of events is unclear, it seems that in a second attempt to defeat Osman, the Byzantine Emperor Andronikos II Palaiologos (r. 1282–1328)sent another force which was defeated in a night attack near a fortress called Katoikia (an unidentified settlement in the Sakarya River region of northwestern Asia Minor, Turkey) which Osman had also occupied. Pachymeres then narrates the conquest of Belokome (Bileçik, in the Sakarya region) to be used as a fortress for the safekeeping of Osman's treasures. However, in a slightly earlier passage Pachymeres referred to the loss of Belokome together with that of Angelokome (Inegöl), Melangeia (possibly Yenişehir), Anagourdia, and Platanea. Pachymeres also mentions Osman's siege of Prousa and Pegai on the Marmara sea coast and an unsuccessful assault on Iznik (Nikaia) to indicate that there was no area around Nikaia, right down to the coast, which he did not control. Based on this chronicle, it appears that by 1308 the conquest of Belokome and neighboring fortresses in the Sakarya River valley enabled Osman to control the countryside west-ward as far as the Sea of Marmara. This is confirmed by the narrative of the *Iskendername* of Ahmedi and other non-Byzantine sources.

Apart from these chronicles, there are later sources that begin to establish Osman as a mythic figure. From the 16th century onward a number of dynastic myths are used by Ottoman and Western authors, endowing the founder of the dynasty with more exalted origins. Among these is recounted the famous "dream of Osman" which is supposed to have taken place while he was a guest in the house of a sheikh, Edebali. According to the dream, Osman saw a bright crescent rising from the chest of the aged sheikh and settling inside Osman. Then a great tree sprang from the body of Osman and its branches covered the whole world. Suddenly the leaves of the tree turned into swords aimed at Constantinople, which resembled a diamond set among rubies. As Osman tried to grasp the diamond he was awakened. This prophetic dream is supposed to have convinced the sheikh to marry his daughter to Osman because he seemed destined to become a great ruler. This highly symbolic narrative should be understood, however, as an example of eschatological mythology required by the subsequent success of the Ottoman emirate to surround the founder of the dynasty with supernatural vision, providential success, and an illustrious genealogy. Likewise, political considerations were behind the connection of Osman to the family of the Prophet Muhammad through marriage. This was the result of Ottoman efforts in the 16th century to convince the Islamic world that Sultan SELIM I (r. 1512–20) could legitimately use the title of caliph (*see* CALIPHATE). Similarly, the Byzantine author George Sphrantzes (1413–77) claimed that the House of Osman descended from the Byzantine Comnenoi dynasty, but this claim is dated after the CONQUEST OF CONSTANTINOPLE in 1453 in an effort to establish the rights of the Ottomans to inherit the Byzantine throne.

Contemporary Byzantine authors, travelers such as Ibn Battuta (1324–33), and early Western sources such as Nicolaos Euboicus (1496) offer no such extraordinary tales and were not aware of the dramatic mythology later developed by Ottoman writers. Rather, contemporary sources stressed the humble origins of Osman as a tribal nomadic leader settled in the border between the Byzantines and the SELJUKS.

Eugenia Kermeli

Further reading: Colin Imber, "The Legend of Osman Gazi," in *The Ottoman Emirate, 1300–1389*, edited by Elizabeth Zachariadou (Rethymnon: Crete University Press, 1993); Halil İnalcik, "Osman Ghazi's Siege of Nicaea and the Battle of Bapheus," in *The Ottoman Emirate, 1300–1389*, edited by Elizabeth Zachariadou (Rethymnon: Crete University Press, 1993); Cemal Kafadar, *Between Two Worlds: The Construction of the Ottoman State* (Berkeley: University of California Press,

1995); Heath W. Lowry, *The Nature of the Early Ottoman State* (Albany: State University of New York Press, 2003).

Orthodox Church See Bulgarian Orthodox Church; Greek Orthodox Church; Serbian Orthodox Church.

Osman II (b. 1604–d. 1622) (r. 1618–1622) *Ottoman sultan and caliph* Osman II was the first-born son of Sultan Ahmed I (r.1603–17) and his concubine Mahfiruz. Because his grandfather Mehmed III (r. 1595–1603) had put an end to the practice of sending Ottoman princes out as provincial governors as part of their political training, Osman, like his father, was raised within the private quarters of the Topkapi Palace. The early death of his mother, around 1610, left Osman without a genuine custodian and protective shield that had become essential to protect the interests of young princes in the treacherous setting of the Ottoman court. From early childhood Osman showed a great interest in riding, hunting, and the martial arts.

When Ahmed I died in 1617, Osman was only 13 years old. Because there were no rules in the Ottoman Empire requiring that the sultan's son succeed his father on the throne, the powers of the court fixed instead on Ahmed's brother Mustafa I (r. 1622–23) as the sultan's successor, an unprecedented decision. But when, only three months after Mustafa's enthronement, there were questions about his mental stability, the new sultan was deposed by a coup d'état masterminded by Mustafa Agha, the chief eunuch of the palace, and Osman II was enthroned in his uncle's place. The deposition of a sultan, also unprecedented, was an indication of the political setting in which Osman II would reign.

From the very beginning of his reign, Osman needed to assert himself. Mustafa Agha, who had engineered Mustafa's deposition, was exiled to Egypt soon after Osman's enthronement. Osman's first ally was Ali Pasha, the grand admiral of the Ottoman navy who was promoted to the grand vizierate in 1619. The promotion of Ali Pasha was closely related to his successful management of the treasury. In spite of his unusual methods of money-raising, such as confiscating the properties of rich statesmen and forcing European merchants to buy certain goods, Ali Pasha succeeded in providing funds both to the central treasury and to the private treasury of the sultan. Another person who had great influence on Osman was Ömer Efendi, his tutor since 1609 and a former preacher at the famous Hagia Sophia mosque.

Ali Pasha also brought the discipline with which he approached finance to Ottoman social life. For instance, soon after his enthronement, Osman issued orders to prohibit the cultivation, sale, and use of tobacco. This shying away from extravagance and pursuit of a modest life can also be seen in the Osman's approach to pomp and finery. He wore lighter and simpler clothes than his predecessors. He even contemplated closing down the palace harem and pursuing a simple life with his legal wives. While Osman's unconventional attitudes as sultan and his efforts to control the business of rule received serious opposition from various factions, the sultan looked to strengthen his position. One possibility for such strengthening was the opportunity to lead his armies personally, in the style of his warrior ancestors such as Mehmed II (r. 1444–45; 1451–81) and Süleyman I (r. 1520–66).

The very short reign of Osman II coincided with the beginning of what is known in European history as the Thirty Years War. The Ottomans were indirectly connected to these developments in Europe through their vassal states—Transylvania, Moldavia, and Wallachia—which constituted a buffer zone between the Ottomans and the Polish-Lithuanian commonwealth. The Ottomans and the commonwealth were in friendly relations during the late 16th century. However, this changed in 1620 when a Polish army marched into Moldavia. Although provincial Ottoman forces were able to repel the aggressors, Osman used the opportunity to declare war and lead his armies against Poland.

In order to prevent a power vacuum and a possible coup in his absence, Osman II requested an affirmative legal opinion (fatwa) from the state's chief mufti, Esad Efendi, to have his brother Mehmed executed. However, Esad Efendi denied the sultan's request, and Osman was forced to appeal to the chief judge of Rumelia (the European part of the empire), the second highest jurist of the religious hierarchy, from whom the sultan received affirmation for his request to execute his brother.

The Ottoman campaign began in May 1621, and Osman II became the youngest sultan to lead his armies in a military campaign. The confrontation between Ottoman and Polish forces at Hotin, in present-day Ukraine, was inconclusive. It brought only modest success to the Ottomans, including the recapture of Hotin, which had belonged to the principality of Moldavia, an Ottoman vassal state.

Soon after his return to Istanbul Osman II, who was dissatisfied with the performance of the army, announced his intention to go on the pilgrimage to Mecca. Prior to this, Ottoman sultans had not made the hajj or absented themselves from the capital other than for military campaigns and hunting. The rumor spread in Istanbul that Osman planned to recruit a new army from the eastern provinces under the guise of a pilgrimage and that he would take the treasury with him in order to finance the recruitment. The idea of a sultan's hajj was almost universally disliked. The chief mufti tried in vain to change Osman's mind.

On May 18, 1622, the imperial tents were carried to Üsküdar, which signaled the beginning of the trip. The troops of the central army who had gathered in the Hippodrome, the civic center of the Ottoman Istanbul, asked the sultan to cancel his pilgrimage. They also demanded the execution of the grand vizier Dilaver Pasha and the tutor Ömer Efendi, whom they considered a bad influence on the sultan. To prevent further mayhem, Osman cancelled the pilgrimage, but refused to execute his servants. The rebel soldiers were not satisfied with this answer and the following day entered the palace. In the third courtyard of the palace the frenzied crowd found Mustafa, who had been kept in the harem since his deposition four years before. After freeing him, the crowd declared Mustafa sultan and the jurists who were present were forced to swear allegiance to Mustafa. That night Osman II, who was unaware of Mustafa's enthronement, went in disguise to the barracks of the commander of the Janissaries, hoping to turn the tide by bribing the soldiers. However, the commander could not persuade the Janissaries and he also fell victim to the rage of the rebels. Osman was captured in the residence of the commander and imprisoned in the citadel of Seven Towers. On Saturday May 21, 1622, he was killed, becoming the first victim of regicide in the history of the Ottoman Empire.

Osman II's reign and his murder should be approached in the context of the evolution of the COURT AND FAVORITES that had been the primary elements of power politics in the empire since the late 16th century. The assertive yet untimely policies of Osman II, aimed at restoring the sultan's authority, were fiercely opposed by the other contenders for power within the court and resulted in regicide.

Şefik Peksevgen

Further reading: Caroline Finkel, *Osman's Dream: The Story of the Ottoman Empire, 1300–1923* (London: John Murray, 2005), 196–205; Baki Tezcan, "Searching for Osman: A Reassessment of the Deposition of the Ottoman Sultan Osman II (1618–1622)" (Ph.D. diss., Princeton University, 2001).

Osman III (b. 1699–d. 1757) (r. 1754–1757) *Ottoman sultan and caliph* The son of MUSTAFA II (r. 1695–1703) and Şehsuvar Kadın, Osman III succeeded his elder brother, Sultan MAHMUD I (r. 1730–54). When Osman acceded to the throne at the age of 55, he was the oldest sultan to be enthroned to date. Few details regarding Osman's early life are available since he spent most of his life in the seclusion of the palace. Regarded as an ill-tempered, nervous, and hesitant man, Osman changed grand viziers seven times in two years. During his reign, the period of peace that began with the Treaty of Belgrade in 1739 continued at the front; minor disorders that broke out in the provinces were suppressed with relative ease. The two most significant events of Osman's three-year reign were the freezing of the Golden Horn and of the Bosporus and the Cibali fire of July 4–5, 1756, one of the greatest ever to break out in ISTANBUL, which destroyed 3,851 buildings. Osman instituted limitations on women's dress and strictly enforced Ottoman sumptuary laws, causing resentment within the population of Istanbul.

The opening of the baroque-style Nuruosmaniye Mosque on December 5, 1755 was one of the achievements of his reign. Another important event was the appointment of Koca Ragıp Pasha as grand vizier in 1756. Ragıp Pasha would hold the post for six years (1757–63) and become one of the most celebrated grand viziers in Ottoman history. After the Cibali fire, Osman III undertook a major construction program that resulted in the building of the Ahırkapı Lighthouse, the fountain at the Nuruosmaniye Mosque, the Osman III Kiosk in the palace, and numerous buildings, some of which are still standing today.

Kahraman Şakul

Further reading: J. H. Kramers, "Osman III" in *Encyclopaedia of Islam*, 2nd ed., vol. 8 (Leiden: Brill, 1960–), 182–183; A. D. Alderson, *The Structure of the Ottoman Dynasty* (Oxford: Clarendon, 1956).

Osman Pazvantoğlu (Osman Passvan-Oglou; Osman Pasvanoglu; Osman Pasvanoğlu of Vidin; Osman Pazvan Oğlu) (ca. 1758/1762–1807) *quasi-independent ruler in northwestern Bulgaria and northeastern Serbia, pasha of Vidin, major opponent of Nizam-ı Cedid reforms* Osman Pazvantoğlu was an important political figure in the Balkans in the late 18th and early 19th century. A powerful opponent of the Ottoman Sublime Porte, insofar as it functioned to exploit his own region, and especially resolute in his resistance to the NIZAM-I CEDID reforms of SELIM III (r. 1789–1807) that threatened the historical power and privileges of the JANISSARIES, Osman Pazvantoğlu was successful in his military and political objects and left behind him a small territory nearly independent of Ottoman control. Osman Pazvantoğlu was born into an elite family in Vidin, a port town on the Danube in present-day northwestern Bulgaria. His father was a wealthy agha of a Janissary regiment in the local garrison, with a long record of opposition to the sultan's authority in the region; his mother was from a scholarly, or ULEMA, family. A devout Muslim, Pazvantoğlu's primary goal was the restoration of the former glory of the Ottoman Empire and of the Janissary corps as the embodiment of its power in the classical age. This he planned to achieve by reviving the principles of government from the time of Sultan SÜLEYMAN I (r. 1520–66) and blocking the introduction of governmental ideas inspired by Europe, especially the Nizam-ı Cedid.

Pazvantoğlu's rise to power began around 1791 or 1792 when he established an alliance with both the Janissaries banished from BELGRADE and the bands of brigands that riddled the core territories of Rumelia (the European part of the empire). Pazvantoğlu expanded his possessions several times, often attacking WALLACHIA. Well informed about the rapidly changing situation in Europe, Pazvantoğlu tried to establish direct diplomatic relations with FRANCE and RUSSIA and to obtain political recognition from them. His revolt against Sultan Selim was seen as particularly dangerous by the Ottoman central authority, which undertook three unsuccessful campaigns against Vidin in 1795–96, 1798, and 1800. After the siege of 1798, Selim granted Pazvantoğlu the title of vizier (the highest possible rank for a provincial governor) of Vidin. Around 1802 a balance of power emerged between Pazvantoğlu and Ismail Tırseniklioğlu of Ruse. The Vidin governor's expansion was also checked by the outbreak of the First Serbian Uprising (1804–13) to the west and by Austria and Russia from the north.

Unlike most of his contemporaries, Osman Pazvantoğlu declared his resistance to the Nizam-ı Cedid, or New Order, from the outset, upset by the establishment of new military detachments at the expense of the Janissary corps and the introduction of the taxes that supported it. This resistance made him popular among Muslims, especially the Janissaries.

Osman Pazvantoğlu had a special policy with regard to Christians, ordinary taxpaying subjects (reaya), merchants, and high clergy. Christians formed a significant part of his own military forces. They were among his most trusted spies, advisors, and agents in his diplomatic relations with the European powers most involved in the region—Russia, France, the Habsburg Empire—and participated in his administration. At the peak of his power in the 1790s, Pazvantoğlu also seems to have established contacts with the Greek revolutionary Rhigas Velestinlis. Within the territory he controlled, Pazvantoğlu succeeded in maintaining relative security and order. In keeping with Islamic principles, he fixed taxes at an affordable rate, allowed some religious freedom, and undertook, especially in Vidin, a number of projects related to the improvement of the commercial and communication infrastructure, such as development of the road system, paving and regulation of the streets in the town, and construction of inns and administrative buildings. While he introduced measures that improved the situation of ordinary taxpaying subjects, he never aimed at full equality of the faiths.

Pazvantoğlu died on February 5, 1807, probably of tuberculosis. He left behind great wealth in cash and landed property and a small, almost independent, territory whose reintegration into the empire was achieved only after the death of his successor in 1814. Long after his death, Pazvantoğlu's name continued to be associated with the firm entrenchment of the çiftlik (large landed estate) regime in the region that lasted until the 1850s.

Rossitsa Gradeva

Further reading: Stanford Shaw, *Between Old and New: The Ottoman Empire under Sultan Selim III, 1789–1807* (Cambridge, Mass.: Harvard University Press, 1971), 237–46, 298–327; Robert Zens, "Pasvanoğlu Osman Paşa and the Paşalık of Belgrade, 1791–1807." *International Journal of Turkish Studies* 8 (Spring 2002): 88–104; Rossitsa Gradeva, "Osman Pazvantoğlu of Vidin: Between Old and New," in *The Ottoman Balkans, 1750–1830*, edited by Frederick Anscombe (Princeton, N.J.: Markus Wiener Publishers, 2006), 115–161.

Ottomanism A counterpoint to the NATIONALISM that began to emerge in the early 19th century, Ottomanism was a state policy designed to unite the diverse cultural and ethnic components of the existing empire under the umbrella of a shared political identity. The idea of Ottomanism was that the state recognized and embraced the religious and ethnic differences of its people, but applied its laws and privileges universally, without discriminating on the basis of faith or national group. Coming to the fore during the reign of MAHMUD II (1808–39), Ottomanist thought was defined in part by the sultan, who according to Yusuf Akçura allegedly proclaimed that he wanted to see religious differences among his subjects only when they entered into their respective houses of worship. It was hoped that this policy of treating each group equally would create a center of loyalty above religious and ethnic differences, thus effectively consecrating the state and the sultan as its head. Ottomanist policies were also supposed to bring about a secular ideal of and love for vatan (the fatherland), creating a consecrated sense of the Ottoman land. By creating a universal "Ottoman" political identity and loyalty, above religious and ethnic differences, Ottomanism thus repositioned the state as a secular entity.

Ottomanism was pursued most eagerly in the late 19th century at a time when Serbian, Greek, and other nationalist movements pervaded and threatened the MILLET system that had been established to secure the mutual coexistence of various ethnic and religious communities. Although this suggests that Ottomanism was a continuation of an existing Ottoman administrative tradition, the idea of Ottomanism actually signified a significant rupture from the traditional ideology of the state. Above all, in this period, the categorization of subjects on the basis of religion (the millet system) was abandoned and all subjects—irrespective of their religious or ethnic origin—began to be acknowledged as legally equal citizens.

The idea of an Ottoman nation was most prominent in the 1850s when MEHMED AMIN ÂLÎ PASHA and FUAD PASHA served as grand vizier and foreign minister. It is believed that the term *citizen* was first used in official Ottoman documents at this time, most notably in the 1856 Islahat Fermani (reform edict), which stressed the equality of all subjects due to the justice of the sultan. The Islahat Fermani acted to strengthen the principles of the Tanzimat Fermani (imperial rescript): "the establishment of guarantees for the life, honor and property of the sultan's subjects," the "equality before the law of all subjects, whatever their religion," and the implementation of laws "prohibiting the use of any injurious or offensive term, either among private individuals or on the part of the authorities." In this document, the sultan further declares that "as all forms of religion are and shall be freely professed in my dominions, no subject of my Empire shall be in any way annoyed on this account and no one shall be forced to change his religion."

In order to fully realize the objectives of Ottomanism, the administrative and legal structure of the state had to be radically transformed. Efforts were made to establish a CONSTITUTION, to form periodical parliaments, to constitute a new public law, and to come up with legal text that would provide equality and inclusion for all Ottoman subjects and secure their common loyalty. These elements of transformation constituted the very basis of the new Ottoman constitution, or Kanun-ı Esasi, embraced both by Ottoman bureaucrats and by the opposition movements that emerged in this period. Marking the apex of Ottomanist policies pursued by Tanzimat reformers and Ahmed Midhat Pasha, the proclamation of Kanun-ı Esasi in 1876 included an official definition of Ottomanness: "All elements that are subject to the Ottoman State, without any exception based on religion or sect, are called Ottomans."

Despite these radical changes, the policy of Ottomanism was ultimately doomed, for it forced unpopular concessions on all sides. The new constitutional framework that restricted the power of the sultan was mostly guided by a practical concern to preclude secession from the empire by securing equality among Ottoman subjects and creating parliamentary representation, but these developments were little valued by the various population groups within the empire. Despite some exceptions, the policy did not find heartfelt supporters among its constituent elements. In fact, the sole defenders of Ottomanist policy were the Turkish elements, who believed that this was the only way to avert imperial collapse. Although Albanian, Kurdish, and Arab nationalists lent grudging support to the policy, this was only because they believed that present circumstances were not conducive to proclaim their nationalism. Among the reasons other ethnicities did not advocate the Ottomanist policies was the

belief that they would be represented in larger numbers in parliament if they continued to hold their privileges as defined *millet* groups; most groups thought that many more Turks would enter into parliament if all subjects became equal citizens and if all differences before the law were abolished. Obviously, this attitude was a significant obstacle to the diffusion and successful implementation of the policy of Ottomanism. Moreover, when it was understood that this policy would not be successful in precluding the independent nationalisms of other ethnicities, nationalist sentiments also strengthened among the Turkish intelligentsia.

The BALKAN WARS of 1912–13 and the January 1913 coup d'état by the COMMITTEE OF UNION AND PROGRESS (CUP) effected the total defeat and eradication of the policy of Ottomanism. The loss of territories in Europe as a result of the wars meant not only that the empire was shrinking geographically but also that it was losing its multiethnic character, hence nullifying the Ottomanist goal of collecting different religious and ethnic elements into a unified whole, leading in turn to the end of a century-old political ideal. At the same time, the increasingly centralist administration of the CUP ultimately put an end to those opposition political parties that had favored an Ottomanist policy: Hürriyet ve Itilaf Fırkası (Party of Freedom and Understanding), Osmanlı Ahrar Fırkası (Party of Ottoman Liberals), Osmanlı Demokrat Fırkası (Party of Ottoman Democrats), and Mutedil Hürriyetperveran Fırkası (Party of Moderate Liberals). Thus Turkish nationalism took the place of Ottomanism in the modern period.

Yücel Bulut

Further reading: Yusuf Akçura, *Üç Tarz-ı Siyaset* (Ankara: Türk Tarih Kurumu, 1991); Şerif Mardin, *The Genesis of Young Ottoman Thought* (Princeton, N.J.: Princeton University Press, 1962); Yusuf Akçura, "Three Types of Policies," in *Central Asia Reader: The Rediscovery of History*, edited by H. B. Paksoy (Armonk, N.Y.: M. E. Sharpe, 1994).

Özi (*Ott. and Tatar:* **Cankerman;** *Ott.:* **Özü;** *Ukr.:* **Ochakiv;** *Rus.:* **Ochakov;** *Pol.:* **Oczakow**) This town and fortress on the right bank of the Dnieper River (called Özi River in Ottoman) was originally constructed by the CRIMEAN TATARS in the 1490s and called Cankerman. It was taken over by the Ottomans during the reign of SÜLEYMAN I (r. 1520–66) in his Moldavian expedition of 1538. Özi's original strategic importance lay in its control of a major ford of the Dnieper, giving the Tatars access for slave raids into MOLDAVIA and the right bank of UKRAINE. Özi was also on the route used by the cavalry forces of the Crimean Tatars in their auxiliary service on Ottoman campaigns in central Europe. When the Ukrainian COSSACKS began their raids of the northern seaboard of the BLACK SEA shortly after the Ottoman takeover, Özi became a vital defensive outpost (and, for this reason, a prime target of Cossack raids). By the end of the 16th century, when the Cossacks began to descend southward along the western shores of the sea, and in the early 17th century, when they began attacking large towns such as CAFFA, Varna, Trabzon, and even the suburbs of ISTANBUL, Özi's strategic importance was heightened. This was because the best chance to protect the sea from the Cossacks was to block their entry into the sea or engage them on their return when they were laden down with booty. Accordingly, additional walls and even fortress constructions were built. The original fortress on a bluff overlooking the mouth of the Dnieper was extended all the way to the bank of the river. A separate fort was built downriver in order to be able to hit the Cossacks with cannon fire. On the other shore, opposite this point, the small fort of Kilburnu also had the capability to fire directly at the Cossacks. However, because of the width of the river mouth (ca. 2.5 miles; 4 km), it proved impossible to completely block Cossack entry to and return from the sea. Nonetheless, the expansion of the fortress complex meant that by the end of the 1620s, large Cossack flottillas of up to a few hundered boats could no longer enter the sea from the Dnieper with near impunity; as a consequence, in the 1630s, the proportion of raids mounted from the Don River increased.

In order to put the defense of the Ottoman Black Sea on a surer footing, in the 1590s a new *beylerbeyilik* or province, also named Özi, was created. As well as the area around of Özi and across the Dnieper (together known as the *sancak* of Kılburnu), this bulwark against the Cossacks included the northwestern shore of the sea and the southern bank of the lower DANUBE—the *sancak*s of Akkerman (Bilhorod-Dnistrovsky; at times it belonged to CAFFA), Vize, Kırk Kilise, Çirmen, Nigbolı, Silistra, and Vidin. This enabled the Ottomans to marshal the manpower, materiel, and financial resources of the region for its defense, leaving other sectors of the empire free for other undertakings.

During the struggle to maintain Ottoman control of the northern Black Sea against the encroachments of the Russian Empire, the Ottomans radically reconstructed the Özi fortress complex along the lines of artillery-resistant bastions developed in western Europe. Nonetheless, the fortress fell during the RUSSO-OTTOMAN WARS of 1736–39 and 1787–92. By the TREATY OF JASSY in 1792, Özi was formally ceded to RUSSIA.

Victor Ostapchuk

Further reading: Caroline Finkel, Victor Ostapchuk. "Outpost of Empire: An Appraisal of Ottoman Building Registers as Sources for the Archaeology and Construction History of the Black Sea Fortress of Özi." *Muqarnas: An Annual on the Visual Culture of the Islamic World* 22 (2005): 150–88.

P

palaces The Ottoman palace was at the heart of the empire since it was there that the government was administered, council meetings were held and the sultan—with his family and his close relatives, servants, and guards—lived. Thus the palace was both the center of the state and the residence of the sultan. In the 17th century, when the Imperial Council meetings and administrative units gradually moved to the grand vizier's palace, the function of the palace as the center of the state lessened, but the palace was never used solely as the sultan's residence. There were two kinds of sultan's palaces in Ottoman history. The first was the permanent center of the government; the second was a place for relaxing. As the Ottoman capital moved from one city to another in the 14th and 15th centuries, a new palace would be built, and the existing palace would be used for relaxation or for administrative purposes. From the 16th century to the mid-19th century, TOPKAPI PALACE was the main palace.

Bursa Palace was the first sultan's palace in Ottoman history. Residences mentioned as palaces before its construction were probably simply large houses. Bursa Palace was constructed in the inner part of BURSA after 1326; it was used until the 1360s, when the Ottoman capital was moved to EDIRNE. After that the Bursa Palace was used primarily for military and administrative purposes.

When Edirne was captured from the BYZANTINE EMPIRE in the 1360s, Sultan MURAD I (r. 1362–1389) moved the capital from Bursa to Edirne, built a palace around the place where the Selimiye Mosque was to be constructed in the 16th century, and moved his administrative center there. During the last years of the reign of MURAD II (r. 1421–44; 1445–51), the New Edirne Palace was constructed near Tunca. After a fire in 1457 Sultan MEHMED II (r. 1444–46; 1451–81), who restored the city, enlarged the palace. During these years the sultan continued to use Edirne Palace, although construction of the Old Palace at Istanbul had been completed.

Upon the CONQUEST OF CONSTANTINOPLE in 1453, Mehmed built the city's first Ottoman palace. Located in the center of the city and surrounded by an outer wall, this palace was plain but spacious. It had all the sections of a typical Ottoman palace. This first palace was occupied for only a short while. A new palace was soon built on the west side of Istanbul overlooking the Sea of Marmara, the east side of the city, and GALATA. Previously used as an olive grove, this site stretched over 700,000 square meters (840,000 square yards). Known as the Topkapı Sarayı or Topkapı Palace, it soon became the most important palace in Ottoman history.

The multisectioned buildings where the grand viziers, princes, and princesses lived were also called palaces. In the 15th and 16th centuries the palaces of the Ottoman princes were used as centers of provincial ADMINISTRATION. The palace in the city of Manisa was the largest of these. Between the 17th and 19th centuries, princesses were permitted to live outside the sultan's palace, and palaces were built for princesses in different parts of ISTANBUL. During this period the Ottoman princes were not allowed to leave the Topkapı Palace and live separately. It was only after the 19th century that princes were again allowed to live outside the palace, but the big houses in which they lived were not called palaces.

The palace residences of the grand viziers were, like the sultan's palace, used to conduct government business. After participating in meetings held in the sultan's palace four mornings a week, the grand vizier convened a meeting called *ikindi divanı* (afternoon council) in his own palace. After the 17th century, meetings in the sultan's palace ceased, and the grand vizier's palace became the center of government administration. In the 19th century the palace of the grand vizier became the official center of Ottoman governance and was given the name Bab-ı Âli (Sublime Porte); at this time, the grand vizier started to live in a separate mansion. The best-known example of a grand vizier's palace is Istanbul's Ibrahim Pasha Palace (today the Museum of Turkish-Islamic Works), constructed by Grand Vizier IBRAHIM PASHA in the reign of Sultan SÜLEYMAN I (r. 1520–66).

Zeynep Tarım Ertuğ

See also DOLMABAHÇE PALACE; PALACE SCHOOL.

Palace School (Enderun-i Hümayun Mektebi)

The Palace School (Enderun Mektebi) was the second essential educational institution in the empire, after the madrasas. This was a special type of institution that did not resemble any of the institutions in the pre-Ottoman Turkish state, other Islamic states, or Europe. Located in the inner section, or third court, of the Topkapı Palace, the Palace School was made up of officials in the sultan's personal service. It functioned as a formal school of government for Ottoman princes and others designated for important political positions within the empire. The Palace School was founded by Sultan MURAD II (r. 1421–44; 1446–51) in EDIRNE, but it was his successor, MEHMED II (the Conqueror) (r. 1444–46; 1451–81) who established the practice of using the Palace School to educate the future administrators of the empire. The children recruited from Christian families through the DEVŞIRME, or child-levy system, were first placed for training within Muslim Turkish families so that they could learn Turkish customs. Later the conscripted boys were educated at the Palace School and the military barracks. When the youths arrived in ISTANBUL the best of them were selected as *içoğlans* (pages) for the palace, with the sultan himself sometimes presiding at the selection.

The *içoğlans* then received special training at the Palace School in Istanbul and Edirne, the former Ottoman capital, whose palace was also used to educate future statesmen. Under the strict discipline of the aghas, the pages received instruction from the palace tutors for two to seven years. At the end of that period they underwent a second selection called *çıkma* (a graduation system, passing from the palace to the JANISSARIES) while those who did not join the Janissaries became members of the sultan's cavalry divisions. The pages normally received four years training in one of the chambers and then, after another selection, the most suitable went to the chambers reserved for the personal service of the sultan. Those who were unsuccessful, or who received disciplinary penalties, were sent to work outside Istanbul.

In the 16th century there were as many as 700 pages in Palace School. Each boy's temperament and capabilities were carefully considered. Those who showed an ability in the religious sciences were prepared for the religious profession; those who were proficient in the scribal arts prepared for a career in the bureaucracy. The sultans—particularly BAYEZID II (r. 1481–1512), who sometimes came to examine them personally—took a great interest in their education.

The subjects taught at the Palace School included the Quran, hadith, Islamic theology, CALLIGRAPHY, Arabic and Persian languages, poetry, philosophy, history, mathematics, and geography, subjects that were also taught at the conventional Ottoman madrasas or colleges. The main difference was that students at the Palace School studied and were trained in military and administrative fields, receiving instruction in horsemanship, archery, fencing, wrestling, and use of the *jeered* (javelin). Each page also studied the craft or fine art for which he showed an aptitude. The Palace School education was designed to produce warrior-statesmen and loyal Muslims, men of letters with eloquent speech and high morals. At the same time, the school aimed to instill complete obedience and loyalty to the sultan. All means were used to inculcate this ideal in the students of the Palace School who were destined to fill the highest offices of the empire. They were schooled in the idea that death in the sultan's service was the greatest blessing.

A great majority of the elite class, who held administrative positions in the empire, were educated at the Palace School. The first great change in the Palace School came about during the reign of MAHMUD II (r. 1808–39) when the AUSPICIOUS INCIDENT abolished the JANISSARIES in 1826. In 1830, the ministry of the Enderun-i Hümayun was established. After a time, the Palace School lost its previous stature; it was finally abolished with the reorganization arising out of the proclamation of the second CONSTITUTION on July 1, 1909.

Mustafa Kaçar

Further reading: Halil İnalcık, *The Ottoman Empire: The Classical Age, 1300–1600,* trans. Norman Itzkowitz and Colin Imber (London: Weidenfeld & Nicolson, 1973), 79–80; Ekmeleddin İhsanoğlu, "Ottoman Educational and Scholarly Scientific Institutions," in *History of the Ottoman State, Society and Civilization,* vol. 2, edited by Ekmeleddin İhsanoğlu (Istanbul: IRCICA, 2002), 357–515.

Palestine

Palestine did not exist in the geographical imagination of the Ottomans. But due to its biblical associations, Christians continued to use that name for the land that today comprises the state of Israel and the Palestinian territories. JEWS referred to the same territory as Eretz Yisrael, the land of Israel. Throughout the Ottoman period, pilgrims and clergy from both religious traditions visited what they considered the "Holy Land," following a route from the port of Jaffa to JERUSALEM. The Ottoman sultans were well aware of the importance of the region to the religious geography of both Jews and Christians. They sought to keep the pilgrims' route secure from BEDOUIN raiders and bandits, even while exacting profitable transit taxes from the pilgrims. Sultan SÜLEYMAN I (r. 1520–66) sought to enhance the Muslim religious claim to the territory by rebuilding the walls of Jerusalem and refurbishing the two most important Muslim sites in the city, the Dome of the Rock and the al-Aqsa Mosque, both located on the Haram al-Sharif, or Temple Mount.

For most of the Ottoman period, Jerusalem was the largest city in Palestine. But as the Bedouins increasingly mounted raids against settlers and travelers in the coastal plain, peasants fled the area for the relative safety of the hill towns of Nablus and Hebron. For most of the Ottoman period, Palestine was administered as a set of subprovinces (sancaks) of DAMASCUS; in the 16th and 17th centuries, Jerusalem, Nablus, Safed, and GAZA formed separate political districts. The governor of the province of Sidon, in present-day LEBANON, generally administered Galilee, the northern region of the territory. In the 18th century CEZZAR AHMED PASHA emerged as the strongman in that region. Although his title was governor of Sidon, he ruled his domain from the Palestinian seaport of ACRE. During his reign, Acre was probably the most populous city in Palestine. With the return of direct political control from Istanbul in the 19th century, the northern region of Palestine was placed under the provincial governor of BEIRUT.

Throughout the centuries of Ottoman rule in Palestine, Jews from Europe settled there. Many of these settlers were old or infirm and hoped that they might be buried in the Holy Land, but others came to study and teach. In addition to Jerusalem, the towns of Safed and Tiberias were noted centers of Jewish learning that attracted scholars and students from Europe, NORTH AFRICA, and the Ottoman Empire. Safed was especially noted as a center for the study of Kabbalah, or Jewish mysticism. That pattern of settlement started to change in the late 19th century as eastern European Jews, inspired by the Jewish nationalist ideology of ZIONISM, began to settle in Palestine.

By the outbreak of WORLD WAR I in 1914, although their numbers were still only in the tens of thousands, the Zionists had transformed the landscape of Palestine with the construction of agricultural settlements and a modern, wholly Jewish city, Tel Aviv. Muslim and Christian Arabs living in the region viewed the arrival of the Jewish settlers with some anxiety, as they feared that the Zionist settlements would eventually displace them. In response, the representatives of what would become Palestine in the Ottoman Parliament petitioned the Ottoman government in 1911 to restrict Jewish settlement in Palestine. Once World War I began, the Ottoman government arrested some of the Jewish settlers who were citizens of Russia, but it did not impose restrictions on Jewish settlement in Palestine. However, because of the economic hardship created by the British blockade of Ottoman seaports, many Jewish settlers did leave the region during the war. During the war, leaders of the Zionist movement actively sought British support for their cause of establishing a Jewish state in Palestine. In 1917 Foreign Secretary Alfred Balfour announced that the British government was in favor of the establishment of a Jewish homeland in Palestine after the war. In 1920 the League of Nations established a British mandate in the territory of Palestine. The question of which people—Jews or Arabs—had primary claim to the territory is still unresolved. Although the Ottoman government was largely indifferent to the conflicting claims of ownership of the land, it permitted the founding of the Zionist settlements in the territory that would become the nucleus of the State of Israel in 1948. The unresolved Palestine Question is, therefore, one of the legacies of the Ottoman Empire.

Bruce Masters

Further reading: Amnon Cohen, *Palestine in the 18th Century: Patterns of Government and Administration* (Jerusalem: Magnes, 1973); Beshara Doumani, *Rediscovering Palestine: Merchants and Peasants in Jabal Nablus, 1700–1900* (Berkeley: University of California Press, 1995); Neville Mandel, *The Arabs and Zionism before World War I* (Berkeley: University of California Press, 1976).

Pan-Islamism   Pan-Islamism was an idea, movement, and policy advocating unity of all Muslims inside and outside the empire, under the leadership of the Ottoman CALIPHATE; it emerged as a reaction against the European Great Powers' intervention in the Ottoman Empire and their colonialism in other parts of the Islamic world. There have always been conflicting and even contradictory notions about the origins, character, and definition of Pan-Islamism; nevertheless, as a religious doctrine, the unity of all Muslims or the Islamic world-community (ummah) across regional, national, and linguistic boundaries, has existed since the beginning of Islam.

Pan-Islamism emerged as a political idea in the Ottoman Empire during the second half of the 19th century. The term Ittihad-ı Islam (Union of Islam) was first used in its political sense by Ottoman intellectuals and journalists in the late 1860s. It was widely discussed and advocated in the Ottoman press and to some extent in official circles. The most representative examples can be found in the writings of NAMIK KEMAL, a leading member of the YOUNG OTTOMANS, and in the pages of the NEWSPAPER *Basiret*.

Pan-Islamism was primarily an indigenous reaction to European (including Russian) intervention and colonialism in the Islamic world. Following the example of Pan-Slavism and Pan-Germanism, it originated as a defensive policy, aimed at saving all Muslims, inside and outside the empire, by uniting them against foreign domination. The progress of Pan-Islamic sentiment and Muslim loyalty to the Ottoman sultan-caliph followed the spread of European colonialism in Islamic lands. The Sublime Porte increasingly fashioned a Pan-Islamic identity for the Ottoman Empire in response to appeals by foreign Muslims who were seeking help against European aggression and expansion.

Pan-Islamic ideas in the Ottoman Empire and the Islamic world had two sources. First, a growing interest emerged in Ottoman public opinion about the Muslims of RUSSIA, China, India, and Sumatra, along with a growing discontent and resentment toward the policies of the Great Powers, especially Russia and Britain. Second, as a result of European domination of formerly Muslim-ruled territories in NORTH AFRICA, Central Asia, South Asia, and Southeast Asia, non-Ottoman Muslims (those under foreign domination or foreign threat) turned to the Ottoman caliphate for help.

These new features of political Pan-Islamism were made possible by the emergence of public opinion in the Ottoman Empire as a result of the development of modern communications media and the press in the second half of the 19th century. The result was the development of a Pan-Islamic idea of Islamic unity or solidarity among Muslims worldwide against European domination of the Islamic lands. Articles and pamphlets in favor of this idea had begun to appear in the late 1860s, and some associations were formed to promote it. The Pan-Islamic ideas of the late 1860s and early 1870s blossomed into a full-fledged movement during the Great Eastern Crisis of 1875–78 and became a policy under ABDÜLHAMID II (r. 1876–1909). In the Abdülhamid period, three types of Pan-Islamism appeared: external political Pan-Islamism, internal political Pan-Islamism, and the Sunni-Shii unity movement.

EXTERNAL POLITICAL PAN-ISLAMISM

The external political type of Pan-Islamism refers to the foreign policy dimension upon which almost all literature in the West on Pan-Islamic movements since the late 19th century has concentrated. External Pan-Islamism called for the unity or solidarity of all Muslims worldwide under the political leadership of the Ottoman caliphate. It was largely a propaganda weapon based on

Sultan Abdülhamid's position as caliph of all Muslims, to be used against European colonial powers with a large number of Muslim subjects. It was not an actively and continuously implemented state policy that constituted a good part of the sultan's foreign policy as claimed by European sources; it was merely used at certain times as an element of potential threat, enabling the empire to take a firm stand against Russian Pan-Slavism and European colonialism.

For Abdülhamid, external Pan-Islamism was not an attempt to rebuild a unified, solitary Islamic state led by the caliph, but an attempt to realize a strong solidarity among Islamic people and countries concerned with their problems. For this purpose the sultan used influential religious notables, especially the sheikhs of various Sufi dervish orders (*tariqa*) and their networks, as well as the press, propaganda, education, and financial aid.

These officially sponsored *tariqa* networks, religious propaganda, and the growing pro-caliphate sentiments among colonial Muslims were seen as a serious political or military threat by the European chanceries. A substantial literature appeared in Western journals and newspapers around the myth of a Pan-Islamic threat. In fact, there were only a few examples of Pan-Islamic initiatives in the Abdülhamid period. These were prior to 1878 and included attempts to encourage the Muslims of Russia in the Caucasus and central Asia to rebel during the 1877–78 war between Russia and the Ottoman Empire.

INTERNAL POLITICAL PAN-ISLAMISM

The internal political dimension of Pan-Islamism focused on Muslim elements within the Ottoman Empire in an effort to establish a new axis for the state. For Abdülhamid, internal Pan-Islamism was a way to preserve of the state through unity of all Ottoman Muslims regardless of their ethnicity. Abdülhamid's reign witnessed a fundamental shift away from the TANZIMAT, or Ottoman reform, policies that had been initiated in the period between 1839 and 1876. Operating in support of the Tanzimat was the state policy of OTTOMANISM, which afforded equal rights to all subjects of the empire, regardless of their religious affiliation. The greatest challenge of the Tanzimat statesmen had been to integrate the empire's non-Muslim communities, who accounted for almost 40 percent of the population, into the imperial state, thus ensuring their loyalty. During the Tanzimat period, the already limited resources of the empire had thus been allocated primarily to the Balkans, whereas the Anatolian and Arab provinces had been neglected.

Because the empire lost its important Christian provinces with the Berlin Treaty of 1878, and received substantial Muslim immigration from the Balkans and the Caucasus, the non-Muslim ratio of the empire's population had decreased to around 20 percent. It was agreed that the policy of Ottomanism was of no use in preventing the rise of non-Muslim nationalism and the desire for independence among the non-Muslim population of the empire. However, not only did the Tanzimat and Ottomanist policies fail to satisfy the empire's non-Muslims, they also increased the frustration against the state, especially in the Arab and Albanian provinces where some sparks of nationalist feelings were being ignited.

Abdülhamid believed that, in order to survive, the Ottoman state needed a new common bond or a base of political identity for the unity and welfare of its Muslim subjects. This did not mean that Ottomanism was completely abandoned; it meant rather that the priority of the government changed to the bringing together of Muslims of different ethnic groups within the empire. The focus of attention shifted to the neglected Anatolian and Arab provinces. From then on, material, financial, social and cultural facilities were directed toward regions inhabited by Muslims, and investments were made in the infrastructure of those regions. Pan-Islamism in this sense was the adoption of a series of policies that gave priority to Muslim communities within the empire that demonstrated their loyalty to the state. This policy was applied in all areas, from education to transportation. All the Muslim groups in the empire, such as Turks, KURDS, Arabs, Albanians, and Circassians, benefited from this new policy in varying degrees. Traces of the policy were seen in a variety of venues, from symbolic gestures such as placing Arab provinces at the beginning of the state yearbooks (SALNAMES) to crucial investments in infrastructure such as the construction of the Baghdad and HEJAZ RAILROADS.

This new policy also had a long-term political and ideological dimension that could be called an attempt to create a Muslim nation through the unity of Muslims within the empire. After 1878, a clear Muslim majority dominated what was left of the empire, and the state adhered to a policy of prioritizing Muslim concerns. But there was no homogeneous Muslim element. It was necessary that these Muslim elements, which were socially and culturally heterogeneous, be unified into a proper and homogeneous group of subjects, that is, a Muslim nation within the Muslim state. This would arise with the development of a modern educational system with both religious and secular components. The new Muslim nation had to form around a common ideology and a common identity. The required cement was Islam. From this perspective, Islam was seen as an element of shared identity, a basis for social or national solidarity, a key factor in common citizenship, a point of reference in the relations between the state and its subjects, and a social catalyst to bring together the Muslim elements of the empire and guarantee their loyalty to the sultan above any nationalist or separatist tendencies.

Abdülhamid's greatest concern regarding the Arabs was the possibility of the establishment of an Arab caliphate centered in EGYPT or Hejaz and supported by the European powers, which could lead to the complete collapse of the empire. Particularly in such places as SYRIA, the Hejaz, Egypt, and the Sudan, Abdülhamid saw Muslim solidarity, expressed as a common loyalty to the caliphate, to be crucial to the empire's efforts to resist European imperialism and the separatist aspirations of his non-Muslim subjects. The sultan's concern was expressed in official deference to Islam and to religious leaders, and in officially sponsored religious propaganda, some of which assumed a Pan-Islamic form, appealing to the solidarity of Muslims both within and without the Ottoman Empire's borders.

PAN-ISLAMISM AND SHII-SUNNI UNITY

Pan-Islamism is also related to the promotion of Shii-Sunni unity or a rapprochement between SUNNI ISLAM and SHIA ISLAM, especially in the context of the Shii threat in Ottoman IRAQ and a potential Iranian threat. The Iraqi *vilayets* of BAGHDAD and BASRA were home to a substantial population of Arabic-speaking Shii Muslims. They constituted an absolute majority of the population in the two provinces. Furthermore, throughout the 19th century, the Shii population appeared to have increased through conversion, at the expense of the Sunnis. To the Ottoman authorities, the presence of a large and growing Shii population in Iraq represented a serious political problem. Shiis were regarded as potentially disloyal, and the growth of Shia Islam among the tribal population in Iraq alarmed the Abdülhamid regime and prompted the palace to embark upon a serious consideration of the Shii issue. Steps were taken to forestall the growth of Shia Islam. Several commissions were sent to the region; local officials were asked to write detailed reports on the subject; and some measures were taken in the field of education including the opening of Sunni madrasas in the region so that local people would not be attracted to the Shii ulema. However, these steps resulted in little change.

After a period of consideration and consultation, the sultan came to the conclusion that a policy of Sunni-Shii unity would be the best long-term solution to the "Shii problem" in Iraq, and decided to promote a radical program to secure a rapprochement between Shia and Sunni Islam. His chosen tool was JAMAL AL-DIN AL-AFGHANI, the Iranian-born political activist and philosopher, who arrived in Istanbul in the late summer of 1892. The implementation of the project for the creation of Islamic unity began in early 1894. A working group was set up under Afghani that sent hundreds of letters to prominent Shii ULEMA all over the Islamic world.

However, when Shah Nasir al-Din of Iran learned about the correspondence between Afghani's Istanbul circle and the Shii ulema, he quickly responded. Tehran demanded the deportation of Afghani and his disciples. The Iranian authorities also used this issue to bring the "Armenian question" to the fore, putting pressure on the Ottoman sultan by giving a free hand to Armenian revolutionaries, both inside IRAN and on the border. Under the pressure of the Armenian crises both in Anatolia and in ISTANBUL, and because of this Iranian support for Armenian revolutionaries in eastern Anatolia, Abdülhamid appears to have been forced to give up his scheme for Sunni-Shii unity. The project was abandoned, Afghani's relations with Abdülhamid deteriorated, and Afghani remained in Istanbul as a virtual prisoner until his death in 1897. During this period, the opposition of the Shii ulema to the Iranian government was partly expressed in Pan-Islamic ideas, in terms of Sunni-Shii rapprochement, and as open sympathy toward the Ottoman caliph. Abdülhamid's contacts with the Shii ulema both in Iraq and Iran continued, as did the Pan-Islamic ideas among the Iranian opposition in the early 20th century.

The COMMITTEE OF UNION AND PROGRESS that seized control of the government in 1908 took over all three of Abdülhamid's Pan-Islamic policies and used them at different times and in varying degrees. External Pan-Islamism was used especially during periods of war, such as the Tripolitanian War (1911–12), BALKAN WARS (1912–13), WORLD WAR I (1914–18), and to some extent, the Turkish War of Independence (1919–22). Internal political Pan-Islamism became a crucial policy after the Balkan Wars, when Ottomanism lost its credibility once again. Pan-Islamism in the context of Shii-Sunni unity also bore fruit for the Sublime Porte during World War I in the contexts of Iraq and Iran. However, the most fruitful results of Pan-Islamism were seen among Indian Muslims after the 1870s. Indian Muslims had always been receptive to Pan-Islamic ideas and propaganda, and eager to serve the movement and policy, during both the reign of Abdülhamid and YOUNG TURK regime (1908–18). The apex of Indian Pan-Islamism was the Indian Khilafat Movement of 1919–1924 that campaigned for the cause of the Ottoman caliphate against the British government. Pan-Islamism in the Ottoman Empire ended with the abolition of the caliphate in 1924.

Gökhan Çetinsaya

Further reading: Jacob M. Landau, *The Politics of Pan-Islam: Ideology and Organization* (Oxford: Clarendon, 1990); Azmi Özcan, *Indian Muslims, the Ottomans and Britain, 1877–1924* (Leiden: Brill, 1997); Gökhan Çetinsaya, "The Caliph and Mujtahids: Ottoman Policy towards the Shi'i Community of Iraq in the Late Nineteenth Century." *Middle Eastern Studies* 41 (July 2005): 561–574.

parliament   Although there was a localized parliamentary tradition in some Ottoman towns and provinces, the Ottoman parliament usually refers to the body that came together briefly during the Ottoman constitutional period under the reign of Sultan ABDÜLHAMID II (r. 1876–1909).

A tradition of partially representative councils existed in 18th-century Ottoman towns. The process of administrative modernization associated with the 19th-century TANZIMAT reform period included the foundation of semilegislative councils such as the Supreme Council for Judicial Ordinances (Meclis-i Vala-yı Ahkam-ı Adliye, 1838) and the Council of State (Şura-yı Devlet, 1868). Administrative councils with limited representative characteristics were also set up in the provinces in the 1840s. After 1856 non-Muslim communities transformed their religious assemblies into secular bodies. However, none of these amounted to a parliament in the sense of democratic representation and full legislative powers.

An Ottoman parliament was founded after the coup d'état of May 30, 1876, when—following the deposing of the sultans ABDÜLAZIZ (r. 1861–76) and MURAD V (r. 1876)—Abdülhamid II acceded to the throne. However, the liberal parliament, devised in the original CONSTITUTION of Grand Vizier MIDHAT PASHA, was redefined by Abdülhamid into an assembly with limited powers.

The Ottoman parliament was a bicameral body consisting of the Chamber of Deputies (Meclis-i Mebusan) and the Senate (Meclis-i Ayan). The members of the Senate were appointed by the sultan and were given a wide-ranging veto power on the laws proposed by the Chamber of Deputies. The parliament had the power to discuss law drafts only when they were proposed by the government or the sultan. During the constitutional period of 1877–78, the Chamber of Deputies consisted of 115 members (69 Muslims and 46 non-Muslims), and the Senate was composed of 36 members (25 Muslims and 11 non-Muslims). Despite limitations, the parliament of 1877–1878 was a politically dynamic institution, unexpectedly critical of the government and the sultan. Abdülhamid's authoritarian inclinations and the independent attitude of the deputies led to the dissolution of the first Ottoman parliament on February 13, 1878.

The parliament was reopened on December 17, 1908 following the YOUNG TURK Revolution, a military insurrection that ended Abdülhamid's reign. In its first period (December 1908–January 1912) the Chamber of Deputies consisted mainly of those elected from the lists of the COMMITTEE OF UNION AND PROGRESS (CUP), the revolutionary political organization of the Young Turks. Among the 288 deputies, there were 147 Turks, 60 Arabs, 27 Albanians, 26 Greeks, 14 Armenians, 10 Bulgarians, and 4 Jews. However, after 1909, an increasing number of liberal-minded deputies left the CUP and founded their own parliamentary groups and political parties. In 1911 all opposition groups came together and founded the Freedom and Friendship Party (Hürriyet ve İtilaf Fırkası).

In the elections of 1912, the CUP used physical violence to subdue the opposition and to regain absolute control over the parliament. Following the coup d'état of January 23, 1913, the Ottoman parliament became a body that rubber-stamped the decisions of the military regime. In the elections of winter 1913–14 the only party joining the elections was the CUP.

Following the collapse of the Ottoman Empire in WORLD WAR I, the leaders of the CUP left the country. On November 23, 1918, Sultan MEHMED VI (r. 1918–22) dissolved the parliament, which he considered to be loyal to the Young Turks. However, national resistance in Anatolia exerted pressure on the sultan's government, which was known to be loyal to the victorious Allied Powers (England, France, and Russia), thus forcing new elections. The last Ottoman parliament (January 12, 1920–March 18, 1920) was predominantly Turkish nationalist in membership. This parliament issued the National Pact (Misak-ı Milli) declaring the political indivisibility of Anatolia. The occupation of Istanbul by the Allie Powers led to the dissolution of this parliament.

Selçuk Akşin Somel

Further reading: Robert Devereux, *The First Ottoman Constitutional Period: A Study of the Midhat Constitution and Parliament* (Baltimore, Md.: Johns Hopkins Press, 1963); Stanford J. Shaw and Ezel K. Shaw, *History of the Ottoman Empire and Modern Turkey*, 2 vols. (Cambridge: Cambridge University Press, 1977).

Passarowitz, Treaty of *See* AUSTRIA; HUNGARY; KARLOWITZ, TREATY OF.

Persia *See* IRAN.

Phanariots (Fenerliler; Phanariotes) Phanariots is a term referring to the Greek (or Greek-identified) elite who held an influential political and social position in the Ottoman Empire from the 17th century until the GREEK WAR OF INDEPENDENCE in 1821. Associated with the Phanar (from the Greek *phanarion*, meaning lantern, and Turkish *fener*, meaning lighthouse) quarter of ISTANBUL where the Orthodox Patriarchate has been headquartered since 1586, this Orthodox Christian elite came traditionally to occupy four positions of major importance—grand DRAGOMAN (chief translator) of the COURT, dragoman of the fleet, and the *voievods* (lords) of Moldavia and Wallachia.

The Phanariots first came into a position of power in the late 16th and early 17th centuries as a small group of prominent Greek families that had remained in Istanbul after the Ottoman conquest in 1453, although the aristocratic Byzantine lineage they claimed for themselves was often not authentic. They retained earlier personal and commercial connections with Italian states, in particular with Genoa through the Istanbul quarter of GALATA and the Aegean island of Chios, which was held by the Genoese until the Ottoman conquest in 1566.

One outcome of these connections between early Phanariot families and the Italian states, aside from the accumulation of capital stemming from their engagement in commerce, was that the sons of such families were often sent to Italian cities, particularly Padua, Rome, and Milan, for schooling, especially medical school. Upon their return they engaged in commerce or became physicians at the Ottoman palace. Some Phanariots engaged in the long-distance commerce that was beginning to flourish (by sea in the Mediterranean and by land through the Balkans). Others entered the Ottoman court, finding employment as physicians or, thanks to their knowledge of European languages, as advisors and translators to members of the sultan's household, to viziers, or even to the sultan himself. The Phanariot physician Panagiotis Nikousios accompanied the Ottoman fleet to CRETE as they were battling the Venetians for that island in the mid-17th century. As a reward for his service and due to his close connections with the KÖPRÜLÜ dynasty of grand viziers, Nikousios was made grand dragoman, a position that commanded great influence at the Ottoman Court because of the dragoman's involvement in foreign relations and diplomacy.

A turning point for the Phanariots was the TREATY OF KARLOWITZ in 1699, negotiated by Reisülküttab (chief scribe) Rami Mehmed Efendi and Nicholas Mavrocordatos as grand dragoman. Although the treaty marked territorial losses for the empire, it was deemed by the Ottomans to have been successfully negotiated, and Mavrocordatos was granted the title minister of the secrets (ex aporiton), or official confidante of the sultan. In 1711 Dimitri Cantemir, the *voievod*, or prince, of MOLDAVIA (in present-day Romania), was accused of conspiring with the Ottomans' perennial enemy, Russia. As a result the Ottomans came to consider the local notables in Moldavia and WALLACHIA to be disloyal and decided to appoint Phanariots from Istanbul to the post of *voievod*, first of Moldavia, then of Wallachia. Nicholas Mavrocordatos was the first Phanariot *voievod* of Moldavia in 1711 and of Wallachia in 1716, establishing Phanariot rule in these Danubian principalities that would last until the Greek War of Independence.

In the 18th century the Phanariots began to take a more prominent position in church affairs (as archons) as well as entrenching their place in the Ottoman Court as grand dragoman, dragoman of the imperial fleet, and as the *voievods* of Moldavia and Wallachia. These positions gave them a foothold in the Ottoman court and divan or council, in foreign relations (and the commercial advantages that brought with it), in the provincial government of the Danubian principalities (an important source of grain for the Ottoman capital), and in the administration of the Aegean islands and the Anatolian coast (now under the authority of the kapudan pasha, or Ottoman admiral, whom the dragoman of the fleet would serve). They also became purveyors of meat and luxury items, such as furs, to the Ottoman palace.

Although there were only four "princely" positions available to Phanariots (grand dragoman and dragoman of the fleet, and the *voievods* of Moldavia and Wallachia), with the success of the Phanariots, the number of families that joined the retinues of these princes and their clients grew rapidly as the 18th century wore on. The families of the Rosettos, Cantacouzinos, and Mavrocordatos were joined at the upper echelons of power in the Phanar by the Kallimakis, Caradjas, Ghikas, Soutsos, Hantzeris, Mavroyenis, Aristarchis, and Hypsilantes. While the earlier families often claimed some connection to a Byzantine ancestor or claimed to have originated on the island of Chios, later families, such as the Ghikas, Soutsos, and Aristarchis, had risen from non-Greek origins and come to identify culturally as Greek in order to gain membership in the elite Phanariot circles; the Ghikas and Soutsos families were of Albanian origin, and the Aristarchis family was reportedly of Armenian origin in Anatolia before Helleniting.

As the geographic and political reach of Phanariot grandees expanded, so too did the phenomenon of Hellenization as a prerequisite to entrance into a Phanariot retinue. By the later 18th century it was not uncommon for Balkan and some Anatolian Christians to send their children to one of the academies founded by Phanariot princes in Bucharest (Wallachia) or Jassy (Moldavia) to learn Greek. The graduates of these schools took one of a number of possible paths. Some left Ottoman territory for medical school in Austria or elsewhere; others entered the retinue of a Phanariot or Ottoman military leader in Istanbul; some even entered the Orthodox Christian clergy in Istanbul. In this way the tiny group of individual Phanariot families of the late 17th century expanded and began to integrate Balkan Christians into the realm of Ottoman governance.

This expansion and integration of Phanariots into Ottoman foreign and domestic politics had wide repercussions, opening new possibilities for the relationships between Muslim rulers and Christian subjects at the dawn of the 19th century but also creating rising expectations that ultimately contributed to Phanariot involvement in the Greek rebellion. Following the Greek War of Independence, many Phanariots integrated themselves fully into the political and cultural life of the independent Greek kingdom. Others stayed in the Ottoman Empire, opting for a life of obscurity by dissociating from the Phanariot name or continuing the tradition of Phanariot involvement in Ottoman governance by remaining loyal servants to the sultan.

Christine Philliou

Further reading: Christine Philliou, "Worlds, Old and New: Phanariot Networks and the Remaking of Ottoman Governance, 1800–1850" (Ph.D. diss., Princeton University, 2004); Mihail-Dimitri Sturdza, *Dictionnaire historique et généalogique des grandes familles de Grèce, d'Albanie et de Constantinople* (Paris: M. D. Sturdza, 1983); *Symposium L'Époque phanariote, 21–25 octobre 1970: à la mémoire de Cléobule Tsourkas* (Thessaloniki: Institute for Balkan Studies, 1974).

Philiki Hetairia Philiki Hetairia, which means "Friendly Society," was a secret society founded in Russian Odessa in 1814 whose aim was to overthrow Ottoman rule in what is now Greece and the Balkans and to establish an independent state. Odessa, a Crimean port city, had only been founded a generation before by Catherine the Great, who invited groups such as Greeks to settle and trade there. Located on the BLACK SEA, Odessa was conveniently situated for Greek merchants who, since the TREATY OF KÜÇÜK KAYNARCA in 1774, had come to play a more prominent role in Black Sea trade between the Ottoman Empire and RUSSIA. As Greek merchants, they had also forged commercial ties to the agriculturally rich Danubian principalities (present-day Romania), which were run by the influential Greek Ottoman families known as PHANARIOTS.

A Greek-identified merchant middle class had developed in early 19th-century Odessa with connections not only in the Ottoman Empire but also throughout Russia and eastern Europe and in the Italian and French Mediterranean. Influenced by the Carbonari—secret societies, literally "charcoal burners," formed with the aim of obtaining a constitution by force in Italy—and the Freemason movement, another secret organization with older origins, three Greek merchants in Odessa came together in 1814 to form the Philiki Hetairia. Nicholas Skoufas, a 42-year-old native of Arta (in present-day southwestern Greece), 42-year-old Emmanuel Xanthos of the Aegean island of Patmos, and Athanasios Tsakalov, a 26-year-old from Epirus (in present-day northwestern Greece and southern Albania) formed the society. In the first two years, they brought in only about a dozen new initiates.

From Odessa, members attempted to recruit Greeks of Russia and the Ottoman Danubian principalities, with little success until 1818. In that year the society expanded dramatically in number and in geographic reach, recruiting throughout Greek communities in the Ottoman Empire as well as in Russia and Europe, reaching about 1,000 members by early 1821. At its height, the Philiki Hetairia included Phanariot grandees from the Hypsilantis and Kallimakis clans, brigand chieftains from Morea (Peloponnese) such as Theodoros Kolokotronis and Odysseas Androutsos, clerics of all ranks (such as Germanos, the bishop of Old Patras), and lay members of the Orthodox Patriarchate establishment (such as Lycourgos Logothetis, born Georgios Paplomatas, a secretary in the ISTANBUL Patriarchate and a native of the Aegean island of Samos).

The structure and lexicon of the Philiki Hetairia combined freemasonry with Orthodox Christian ecclesiastical terminology. The core entity was initially known as the Invisible Authority; after the 1818 expansion it became known as the Authority of the Twelve Apostles. When a member was initiated into the society he was given a *nom de guerre* that often combined Orthodox Christian-Byzantine and ancient Greek characters, such as Lycourgos Logothetis, referred to above: Lycourgos was the ancient lawgiver in Sparta, and Logothetis was a Byzantine-Orthodox title that was still in use in the Orthodox ecclesiastical hierarchy. Initiates then rose up through several degrees of membership, although they never knew the extent of the society's membership, as there was a pyramid structure so as to retain secrecy.

One of the benefits of this secrecy was that, to persuade others to join, members could claim (without having to give proof) that powerful figures were also members. Perhaps a reason for the sudden popularity of the society in 1818 (in addition to moving the headquarters from Odessa to Istanbul, the Ottoman capital) was members' claim that Czar Alexander I himself was a member and was promising military and financial support to the society. The society had also approached John Capodistrias, a native of the island of Kerkyra who had become Czar Alexander I's foreign minister, to be their leader, but Capodistrias flatly refused. In April 1821, Alexander Hypsilantis agreed to become the chief of the society. Less than a year later, a rebellion broke out in MOLDAVIA which, though abortive, marked the first in a string of uprisings that led to the Greek War of Independence in 1821.

Christine Philliou

Further reading: Richard Clogg, *A Concise History of Greece* (Cambridge: Cambridge University Press, 2002); George D. Frangos, "The Philike Etaireia, 1814–1821: A Social and Historical Analysis" (Ph.D. diss., Columbia University, 1971).

photography   From their earliest appearance, photography and photographic techniques found wide application in the Ottoman Empire and were used extensively by professionals and amateurs as an art form, a means of documentation and recording, an instrument of observation, and a tool for publicity. Photography arrived in ISTANBUL within two months of the introduction of the daguerreotype in Paris in August 1839. The oldest Ottoman document on the subject is a NEWSPAPER account from the October 28, 1839 issue of the *Takvim-i Vekayi* (Calendar of occurrences), the first official Ottoman paper, reporting Louis Daguerre's invention of the daguerreotype and giving technical specifications. On August 15, 1841, *Ceride-i Havadis* (Journal of news), the first privately owned Turkish newspaper, informed its readers that Daguerre's book introducing the daguerreotype (rendered literally as "Daguerre print") technique had arrived in Istanbul and had been translated. The same report coined the Turkish term for photograph, literally "fire print," a word that would not be used in the West for another ten years. On July 17, 1842, *Ceride-i Havadis* announced that an apprentice of Daguerre had arrived in Istanbul and, for a fee, would exhibit photographs, teach the art of photography, and take group or panoramic pictures. The first treatise on Ottoman photography in Turkish, Captain Hüsnü Bey's *Usul-i fotografya risalesi,* was printed in 1873 in Istanbul.

The palace saw photography as extremely important. Sultan MAHMUD II (r. 1808–39) presented medals that carried his pictures, and his portrait was exhibited at the Selimiye Barracks. Subsequent Ottoman sultans awarded titles of special merit—ressam-ı şehriyari, fotografi-i hazret-i şehriyari, ser-fotograf-i hazret-i şehriyari (designations meaning imperial photographer)—to the empire's most deserving photographers. The Ottoman princes took lessons in photography.

Although photography quickly became popular, the Ottomans never developed its potential uses for research and industry, the one exception being the technique for photoengraving by acid reduction realized by printer Ahmed Ihsan Tokgöz and photographer Teodor Vafiyadis in 1894. This technique was used for many years.

PHOTOGRAPHIC RECORDS OF THE OTTOMAN WORLD

The same week that news of Daguerre's invention was reported in *Takvim-i Vekayi*, Pierre Joly de Lotbinière was already taking pictures along the Nile, while PALESTINE, SYRIA, LEBANON and various locations in Anatolia were also being photographed by other early photographers. In the autumn of 1839, Noël Paymal Lerebours (1807–73) and his team went to EGYPT, Palestine, and BEIRUT and took panoramic pictures that were later published in an album called *Excursions daguerriennes: vues et monuments le plus remarquables du globe* (Daguerrien excursions: The most remarkable sights and monuments in the world). Such activities continued over the years and those pictures came to form an important part of the famous Yıldız Collection. Through the efforts of these enterprising people a significant cross section of 19th century Ottoman geography and life from various angles was recorded in photographs. One of those instrumental in creating this visual record was Joseph-Philibert Girault de Paraguey, who took more than 800 pictures of Istanbul and Anatolia between the years 1843 and 1845. In 1848 Maxime du Camp, editor of the *Revue de Paris* (Paris review), published pictures and travel notes of his visits to Egypt, Palestine, and Syria, then produced them in an album.

Because of the historical importance of the Ottoman lands, especially Istanbul, these places constituted a point of interest to many Western photographers and they made a habit of passing through Istanbul. British photographer James Robertson (1813–88) is among the best known of these. He came to the empire during the CRIMEAN WAR (1853–56) and wound up living in Istanbul until his death in 1881. The Irish archaeologist John Shaw Smith took photos of Istanbul in November 1851 that still survive. French photographer-architect Alfred Norman was in Istanbul in January 1852. Immediately afterward another Frenchman, Ernest de Caranja, pre-

sented an album comprising 55 pictures of Istanbul to Sultan ABDÜLMECID (r. 1839–61), who granted him the title fotografi-i hazret-i Şehriyari (imperial photographer). Jules Sandoz is also among the photographers who presented their albums to the palace. In 1863, Sultan ABDÜLAZIZ (r. 1861–76) sent his own photographic portrait to the Prussian Empress Augusta. Sultan ABDÜLHAMID II (r. 1876–1909) sent albums to promote the Ottoman state to several prominent people and institutions, among them the U.S. Library of Congress (1881).

PHOTOGRAPHY AND THE OTTOMAN MILITARY

Decades before the development of the daguerreotype, Ottoman engineers and military personnel were already recording images using the camera obscura, a pre-photographic technology. According to a document from 1805, two camera obscura devices were purchased from England and used in the school of engineering, or MÜHENDISHANE, graduates of which feature prominently among the pioneers of Ottoman photographic history. Ottoman military

This photo, taken by the Abdullah brothers circa 1890, shows the public square near the Dolmabahçe Palace (*Courtesy of IRCICA*)

This photo, taken by Emile Römler circa 1890, shows a typical Istanbul coffee house. *(Courtesy of IRCICA)*

institutions, including the Ministry of War and the NAVY and army commands, also played a role in introducing and spreading photography throughout the land. Indeed, military photography soon became its own specialty, and military academy graduates and engineers within the military organization were at the forefront of the technology. Captain Hüsnü Bey (1844–96), Servili Ahmet Emin Bey (1845–92), and Üsküdarlı Ali Rıza Pasha (d. 1907) are the first known Ottoman military photographers. The latter served as the head of the Department of Photography in the Ottoman War Ministry. The Crimean War was the first war to be photographed, and all the action at the 1879 Turco-Greek War was recorded by photographers officially appointed by the state.

THE ABDULLAH BROTHERS AND STUDIO PHOTOGRAPHY

In addition to giving rise to war photography, the Crimean War holds a special place in the history of Ottoman photography because it motivated many Western photographers to travel to Istanbul and produce new albums of Istanbul and Anatolia. Another important aspect of the war was the arrival of a chemist named Rabach, who

came to Istanbul with the troops of Helmuth Karl Bernhard Graf von Moltke (1800–91), the chief of staff of the Prussian army. Rabach established the empire's first professional photographic studio in 1856. Rabach's studio was instrumental in coaching local photographers. The Abdullah brothers (Abdullah biraderler, or frères Abdullah), owners of one of the most renowned firms in the history of photography, trained as apprentices in Rabach's studio and took it over when Rabach returned to GERMANY in 1858. These brothers, Wichen and Kevork (who later converted to Islam and took the name Abdullah Şükri), were painters before taking up photography, a fact that played a considerable part in their success as photographers. They improved Rabach's studio and played a significant role in the general spread and acceptance of photography. In addition to their work in the studio, they tried to capture the daily life and works of art in Istanbul, contributing ultimately to what would become the core of the Yıldız Collection. Their efforts were appreciated by Sultan Abdülaziz; in 1862 he appointed them as official photographers or ressam-ı hazret-i Şehriyari (literally, imperial painter), a title that was continued by the next sultan, Abdülhamid II. As a privilege, this title and the

TUĞRA or monogram of the sultan was stamped on back of all their photographs.

At the 1866 International Paris Exhibition, the Abdullah brothers' pictures were appreciated for their technique and aesthetic. They were recognized by the press and gained international fame. Among the other notable people photographed by them were King Edward VI of ENGLAND, King Frederick III of Germany, King Victor Emmanuel of Italy, Emperor Franz Joseph of Austria-Hungary, Nasruddin Shah of Iran, the Egyptian khedive, and the families of the Ottoman sultans.

Upon the invitation of the khedive in 1866, the Abdullah brothers opened a branch of their studio, in Egypt. Febus Efendi, an apprentice of the Abdullah brothers, replaced them as the palace photographer. Another Abdullah brothers apprentice, Aşil Samsun Apollon, who used photography to capture the constant bustle of everyday life in the empire, later became a palace photographer himself and established his own studio.

Other famous photographers of the late 19th century include Kargapulo, who photographed life in Istanbul, and Niclaides, Michailidis, and Vafiadis, who photographed and produced albums of existing buildings and those under construction. Another early photographer, Rahmizade Bahattin Bey (Baha Ediz), began his photographic career in Crete before moving on to Istanbul and opening studios in several other places.

With the dawn of the 20th century, Ottoman photography developed its most ambitious project yet, the World Archives started by Albert Kehn. Before Kehn's bankruptcy brought the project to a standstill, the four photographers involved had made 1,557 plates of Anatolia between 1912 and 1923. Stephanie Passet contributed 85 plates of Istanbul in 1912, Auguste Leon created 143 plates of Istanbul and Bursa in 1913 and 23 plates of Bursa in 1918, and Frédéric Gadmer produced 1,306 plates between the years 1922 and 1923.

Hidayet Y. Nuhoğlu

pilgrimage   See HAJJ.

pious foundations   See CHARITY; WAQF.

piracy   See CORSAIRS.

plague (*veba*; *waba*)   While not the only disaster that troubled the Ottoman Empire between the 16th and 20th centuries—floods, earthquakes, smallpox, drought, and famine all taking their toll—plague was the most frequent and deadly of all. Called *veba* in Turkish, from the Arabic *waba*, "to be contaminated," the lethal illness known simply as "plague" usually refers to bubonic plague, also known in the West as the Black Plague or the Black Death. Pandemic throughout the empire from the beginning of the 16th century to the middle of the 19th century, plague was caused by the bacillus *Yersinia pestis* and was usually transmitted by means of rodents infested with infected fleas, facts that have only come to light since the demise of the empire in the 1920s. Although the disease was endemic, meaning that it was both geographically widespread and constantly present at some level in the population, periodic epidemic outbreaks of great virulence frequently resulted in a 75 percent mortality rate among those affected. For this reason, plague was greatly feared both by Ottoman subjects and by the foreign travelers and traders who frequented the empire.

In its most serious outbreaks, the plague disrupted the Ottoman economy by interrupting harvests in the countryside and commercial activities and handicrafts in the cities. The plague therefore was a decisive factor at the root of the difficulties and weaknesses of the Ottoman Empire in the 18th century.

Without any modern understanding of germ theory, Ottoman doctors, like those in the West, hypothesized that plague was an airborne infection caused by miasmas (unpleasant or unhealthy air), carried by the wind. An alternative theory attributed the spread of plague to demons, or jinni.

TRADITIONAL RESPONSES TO THE PLAGUE

Plague was present even in the earliest centuries of Islam, the Prophet Muhammad having apparently issued commands indicating the proper behavior that must be adopted by Muslims during an epidemic; according to certain *hadith*, or traditions reporting the words and deeds of the Prophet, the faithful were instructed to remain where plague is raging, submitting themselves to God's will, which punishes nonbelievers; at the same time, they should not enter areas already affected by the plague. The behavior and convictions of Muslims with regard to plague epidemics were thus established very early. These were affirmed by scholars of the medieval period, especially by Ibn Hajar al-Askalani in the 15th century, who became an authority on the subject for the following centuries.

THE SPREAD OF PLAGUE AND MAJOR EPIDEMICS

It is mostly likely that the original source of plague in the Ottoman Empire was Iranian Kurdistan, in the Libyan Desert, and the territory of the Assyr Range between the HEJAZ and YEMEN. It was from these areas that the illness spread over vast territories by means of fleas and their rodent hosts, emerging with the most lethal impact, of course, in the more densely populated regions of the empire. In the 17th and 18th centuries the plague had thus entrenched itself in Albania, Epirus, MOLDAVIA, WALLACHIA, ISTANBUL, Anatolia, and Egypt. From these areas the plague continued to spread by land and by sea through the entire empire, aided by structures of trade and government that relied on travel: couriers, traders, pilgrims, sailors, nomads, the military, and fugitives.

While it is known that plague was firmly established in Europe in the 14th century, documentation of plague epidemics in the Ottoman Empire remain sketchy through the 16th century. There was a major Ottoman pandemic from 1572 to 1589, during which time, with few short interruptions, the plague was widespread from the Near East to Egypt, in Anatolia, and in the Balkans and NORTH AFRICA. In the 17th century records are more reliable and it is well documented, for instance, that ALGIERS suffered from major outbreaks of plague approximately every two years during the entire course of the century. In CAIRO seven major outbreaks of plague were recorded by chroniclers in the 17th century, covering some 18 years in total, though smaller outbreaks may have gone unrecorded.

The plague was equally frequent in the empire during the 18th century. During this time Istanbul was affected for 68 years, Aegean Anatolia for 57 years, Egypt for 44 years, ALBANIA-Epirus for 42 years, BOSNIA for 41 years, SYRIA for 33 years, BULGARIA for 18 years, the regency of Algiers for 45 years, and the regency of TUNIS for 19 years. The majority of these outbreaks were comparatively mild. The deadliest epidemics, responsible for killing between one-tenth and one-third of the population, and typically occurring in the larger cities—Istanbul, Salonika, and ALEPPO—arose about once every 20 years. There were two major plague epidemics in the empire at the beginning of the 19th century, in 1812–19 and in 1835–38, which ravaged almost the entirety of the empire. From 1840–44 the plague seems almost to have disappeared from the Ottoman Empire with the exception of limited outbreaks in Cyrenaica from 1856–59 and three episodes in IRAQ (1856–59, 1874–77, and 1891–92). The plague resurged again in 1894 and isolated incidents continued to affect the former Ottoman territories in Africa and Asia for more than half a century.

It is difficult to evaluate with precision the demographic effects of the plague on the empire. Nonetheless, the 16th century seems to have benefited from a seemingly long remission and is perhaps responsible for an upsurge in population growth in Anatolia and the Near East. This period came to an end in the 1580s; from then until about 1840, episodes of plague became more frequent, which may be responsible for the stagnation of Ottoman population growth.

MODERN RESPONSES TO EPIDEMIC

Things began to change at the beginning of the 19th century with the outbreak in the Near East in 1820 of a new epidemic illness, cholera, which originated in Bengal where it had already been pandemic for centuries. At this time, cholera spread out of its initial geographic area through two routes. The northern route went through Iran, then reached RUSSIA through the CAUCASUS and spread from there toward northern Europe and ultimately to the United States. The second route was over water, by the Red Sea and the Mediterranean Sea. Brought to MECCA by pilgrims from India, cholera contaminated pilgrims who had come from other parts of the Muslim world and who subsequently brought the disease back to their homelands.

Confronted by the combined forces of cholera and plague, especially in the 1830s, Muslim leaders began to approach epidemic outbreaks with an altered understanding. Looking at the importance of demographics in their military and the economy, these leaders adopted the methods of protection against the plague and cholera that had already been implemented in Europe. The traditional Muslim submission to the divine will was replaced, at least by the head of state, by an effort to reconcile Islamic law, or SHARIA, modern knowledge, and the welfare of the state. Since the 18th century, the Austrian Empire had been protecting itself from the frequent outbreaks of plague that contaminated its Ottoman neighbor with a cordon sanitaire, or buffer zone, which functioned effectively as the border between the two empires. This border region was patrolled by Austrian soldiers who forbade entry into their empire except where quarantines were possible. Beginning in the 1830s the Ottoman Empire, including the North African regions of Egypt, Tunisia, and Morocco, adopted a similar approach, giving way to the administration and regulation of sanitation and initiating a plan for lazarets (quarantine stations) to inspect travelers and protect the empire's borders, both land and water. These innovations, a part of the greater policies of the TANZIMAT modernization era, were aided by Westerners, both diplomats and doctors, who sought to expand their arena of influence. The speed of the positive results was remarkable. This was a result not only of the efforts of local sanitation institutions but also of the natural extinction of the breeding grounds for plague in the previous centuries. By the closing years of the 19th century, the occasional reappearances of the illness, often brought from the outside, were both rare and vigorously combated.

Daniel Panzac

Further reading: Daniel Panzac, *La peste dans l'Empire ottoman, 1700–1850* (Leuven: Éditions Peeters, 1985); Daniel Panzac, *Quarantaines et lazarets: l'Europe et la peste d'Orient, XVIIe–XXe siècles* (Aix-en-Provence: Édisud, 1986).

Poland Military confrontations with the Ottomans played a prominent role in shaping the national and Christian identity of Poland. In 1444, a Polish king was killed in the Battle of Varna. The 17th century brought two Ottoman-Polish wars of 1620–21 and 1672–78, and the spectacular relief of Habsburg Vienna (1683), besieged by the Ottoman army of Kara Mustafa Pasha, by the Polish troops led by King Jan Sobieski. Yet Ottoman-Polish relations were also characterized by long periods of peace and political cooperation, directed first against the Habsburgs and then against Russia. Oriental goods and fashion, imported through trade and war, deeply influenced the material culture of Polish nobility. In the 19th century numerous Polish political refugees found safe haven in the Ottoman Empire and participated in its modernization.

EARLY CONTACTS WITH THE OTTOMANS

Poland was first united under Duke Mieszko I from the Piast dynasty (r. ca. 960–992), who subjugated the various tribes of Western Slavs. Located on the eastern territories of Western Christendom, north of the Carpathian Mountains and south of the Baltic Sea, between 1340 and 1387 Poland extended its borders toward the Black Sea by annexing the Ruthenian principality of Halyč and forcing Moldavian rulers to acknowledge Polish suzerainty. The Polish-Lithuanian union (1385–86)—which was initially formed as an alliance against the Teutonic Knights but lasted long after the Teutonic threat had subsided—brought to the Polish throne the Jagiellonian dynasty, which held a long tradition of contact with the Muslim khans of the Golden Horde.

The first Polish embassy to the Ottoman court was sent in 1414. In the 15th century Polish-Ottoman relations were mostly peaceful while Ottoman expansion was directed against Hungary. Even when Ladislaus III (r. 1434–44) of Poland and Hungary, encouraged by the pope, set out for his fateful Crusade of Varna (1444), Poland officially stood outside the conflict, although many Polish volunteers perished along with the young king. In 1484 Bayezid II (r. 1481–1512) attacked the Polish vassal Moldavia, capturing two Moldavian ports at the mouth of the Danube and Dniester rivers. Poland did not react initially, even concluding a peace treaty with the Sublime Porte in 1489 (see AHDNAME); however, in 1497 the new king John I Albert (r. 1492–1501) led an expedition to Moldavia, resulting in a crushing defeat for the Polish forces.

The 16th century brought further Ottoman expansion against Hungary and the final subjugation of Moldavia. Although the last Jagiellonian king of Hungary, Louis II, perished in the Battle of Mohács (1526), the reaction of the Polish Jagiellonians was rather weak. In fact, the year 1533 brought an unprecedented treaty between Sigismund I (r. 1506–48) of Poland and Sultan Süleyman I (r. 1520–66) that protected Poland's southern provinces from invasion and was concluded for the lifetime of both rulers. In the following years, both sides tacitly cooperated against the Habsburgs and supported the anti-Habsburg candidate to the Hungarian throne, John Zápolya, who was married to a Polish princess. Along with France, Poland played a key role in the Ottoman European policy, directed against the Habsburgs. Friendly Polish-Ottoman relations continued during the reign of the last Jagiellonian king, Sigismund II Augustus (r. 1548–72).

OTTOMAN-POLISH RELATIONS IN THE 17TH CENTURY

Following the extinction of the Jagiellonian dynasty, the Porte supported anti-Habsburg candidates to the Polish throne. The subsequent elections of Henri de Valois (1573–74), Stephan Báthory (1576–86), and Sigismund III Vasa (1587–1632) were thus favorably received in Istanbul. However, the fierce Catholic policy of Sigismund III and his rapprochement with Vienna soon strained mutual relations. The rising activity of Ukrainian Cossacks raiding the Ottoman shores of the Black Sea, and the renewed Polish involvement in Moldavia, caused a further deterioration of relations between the two powers. In 1620 the Polish grand hetman, Stanisław Żółkiewski, led a preemptive campaign to Moldavia. Besieged and defeated at Țuțora (Cecora) by the Ottoman-Tatar army of Iskender Pasha, the Polish troops were routed and the hetman was killed. The following year, Sultan Osman II (r. 1618–22) led a major expedition against Poland-Lithuania. Due to an unprecedented mobilization of Polish-Lithuanian troops, supported by the Ukrainian Cossacks, the defenders were able to withstand a major siege in the fortified camp near Khotin (Chocim, present-day Xotyn, Ukraine). The truce of Khotin (1621), confirmed with a formal *ahdname* (1623), restored the peace.

The pro-Habsburg stance of the Polish court during the European Thirty Years' War (1618–1648) resulted in another short-term military conflict when the Ottoman commander Abaza Mehmed Pasha entered Podolia (1633). The crisis of Poland-Lithuania, resulting from a six-year uprising by the Cossacks that erupted in 1648 over the rights granted them by the Polish kings, and subsequent wars against Russia (1654–67) and Sweden (1655–60), caused the Porte to assist the Poles in order to maintain equilibrium in eastern Europe. The Crimean khans (see Crimean Tatars) were encouraged to conclude an alliance with Warsaw, and in 1657 the Ottoman governor of Özi was ordered to assist the Polish king.

The new active northern policy led by the Ottoman Köprülü viziers soon resulted in another crisis. The

Ukrainian Cossacks, disillusioned with both Warsaw and Moscow after the signing of a Polish-Russian treaty (1667), asked for Ottoman protection. The Porte, fearing a Polish rapprochement with Moscow and Vienna, acknowledged the Cossack leader Petro Dorošenko as its vassal (1669) and declared war on Poland. In 1672 the Ottoman army, led by Sultan MEHMED IV (r. 1648–87) and Grand Vizier Köprülü Ahmed Pasha, captured the key Polish fortress of KAMANIÇE (present-day Ukraine), center of the province of Podolia. According to the Buczacz Treaty (1672), the Polish king agreed to pay a tribute, Podolia was ceded to the Porte, and Cossack UKRAINE was mutually recognized as an Ottoman vassal. Although the Polish-Lithuanian Diet rejected the treaty and the grand hetman Jan Sobieski won a brilliant victory against the Ottomans at Khotin (1673), the subsequent war proved inconclusive and ended with the truce of Żurawno (1676), confirmed by the Polish embassy to Istanbul (1678).

In 1683, the Ottomans once again clashed with the Poles as Poland-Lithuania joined the Habsburg-Ottoman War and Jan Sobieski, now dignified as King John III, led a rescue expedition to help the Habsburgs defend Vienna. In 1684 Warsaw entered the anti-Ottoman Holy League along with Vienna and Venice, but only the TREATY OF KARLOWITZ (1699) restored Podolia to Poland.

During the 18th century, the Porte strove to preserve Polish sovereignty against the rising pressure of Russia. For instance, in 1711 Czar Peter I was forced to remove his troops from Poland-Lithuania. In 1768 the Porte, encouraged by Polish dissidents, declared war on Russia, demanding its disengagement from Polish internal affairs. The war, known in Turkish as Leh Seferi, or, the Polish War (see RUSSO-OTTOMAN WAR of 1768–74), ended with the first partition of Poland in 1772 and the TREATY OF KÜÇÜK KAYNARCA (1774), disastrous for the Ottomans. The Russian victory in the next RUSSO-OTTOMAN WAR of 1787–92 hastened the second (1793) and third (1795) partitions of Poland.

During the 19th century, numerous Polish refugees arrived in the Ottoman Empire. After the failed Polish uprising against Russian rule of 1830–31, a settlement for Polish refugees was founded on Ottoman soil in 1842. The settlement was named Adampol after its founder, Prince Adam Czartoryski, although its popular Turkish name became Polonezköy (Polish village). Another wave of Polish refugees, participants of the Hungarian uprising, arrived in 1849, including General Józef Bem, who adopted Islam along with the new name of Murad Pasha. Among the other prominent Polish immigrants who participated in the modernization of the empire were Michał Czajkowski (Sadık Pasha) and Konstanty Borzęcki (Mustafa Celaleddin).

Although Poland identified itself internally and externally as "the bulwark of Christianity" (antemu- rale Christianitatis), Polish-Ottoman relations remained peaceful most of the time. Mutual trade flourished and Ottoman fashion greatly influenced the Polish nobility, including men's clothing, tapestry, arms, armor, and horse trappings. Numerous Turkish loanwords, associated with horse riding and the imported habits of COFFEE drinking and pipe smoking, exist even today in the Polish vocabulary.

Dariusz Kołodziejczyk

See also AUSTRIA.

Further reading: Zygmunt Abrahamowicz, "Leh," in *Encyclopaedia of Islam*, 2nd ed., vol. 5 (Leiden: Brill, 1960–), 719–723; Norman Davies, *God's Playground: A History of Poland* (New York: Columbia University Press, 2005); Dariusz Kołodziejczyk, *Ottoman-Polish Diplomatic Relations (15th–18th Century): An Annotated Edition of 'Ahdnames and Other Documents* (Leiden: Brill, 2000); *War and Peace: Ottoman-Polish Relations in the 15th–19th Centuries* (exhibition catalogue) (Istanbul: Turkish Republic Ministry of Culture, 1999).

political satire   The Ottoman Empire had a rich tradition of humor and satire, embodied in poetry and in the sharp repartee of the shadow-puppet theater called Karagöz. Satirists writing in the late Ottoman era (1876–1920) drew from the multiple artistic and narrative traditions of ISTANBUL, a cosmopolitan city whose culture mingled Turkish, Persian, Arabic, Greek, Italian, French, and Armenian influences, among others. Satire appeared in the many languages of the Ottoman capital and in various forms, from one-man plays, to tea-house storytellers' tales, to broadsheets, to cartoons. In the mid-19th century the press became a primary venue for political, social, and cultural expression, including the work of satirists. Some Ottoman NEWSPAPERS, or gazettes, were entirely humorous or satirical. Others included elements of satire within their pages in the form of jokes, essays, editorials, and cartoons. In both cases satiric precedents were apparent in the use of dialogue, rhyming captions for cartoons, and Karagöz characters as mascots and spokespersons.

As in many other countries at this time, CENSORSHIP was prevalent, and the writers and artists of the Ottoman Empire were not free to publish anything they wanted. Autocratic rulers such as Sultan ABDÜLHAMID II (r. 1876–1909) were sensitive about the public image of their regimes and carefully monitored criticism, direct or implied, in the press. Publications could be edited or shut down if government censors found their content objectionable. Editors and satirists, however, were resourceful and found various ways to circumvent the censors, including smuggling in banned materials and printing offending newspapers under new titles. Nonetheless, the laws governing the content and tone of the press served to limit severely what could be presented to the Ottoman reading public. Forbidden topics included any critique of the sultan and any mention of challenges to monarchies abroad. Thus few lawful targets remained for the satirist's pen. That changed with the second constitutional revolution of July 1908.

The period 1908–09 is unique in the history of Ottoman satire and the press. In the aftermath of the revolution, government censorship was temporarily suspended as the form the new regime would take was contested. In the year after the revolution, more than 240 new Ottoman-language gazettes were published in Istanbul alone, among them an array of "funny papers" that ran the gamut from gentle humor to pointed and vehement satire. There was an explosion of satire in the newly liberated press that exuberantly scrutinized such themes as despotism, modernity, the transformation of GENDER roles, new technologies, and European imperialism.

That satire found its most dramatic form in a great outpouring of cartoons. Satirical gazettes (*mizah mecmuaları*), in the aftermath of the revolution expressed the desires and anxieties of the literate classes and of the public as a whole. Suddenly the sultan was the target of vehement criticism, accused of despotism, greed, and abuse of his subjects. Cartoons depicted him as a bloody tyrant, a buffoon, or a weakling. The new parliamentary deputies were portrayed as lazy, ineffectual, and unlikely to save the empire from the enemies that surrounded it.

Satirists were also preoccupied with the threat of European imperialism in its various forms (political, economic, and cultural). Cartoonists drew Britain as a greedy giant, leaning on the pyramids of Egypt or extorting riches from the Persian Gulf. France was a purveyor of immoral or frivolous fashions that tempted Ottoman elites to squander the resources of the empire. In the cartoon frame, the empire was envisioned as trapped between the old and the new, unable to attain the freedom associated with the French Revolution but unwilling to return to the absolutism of sultanic rule, a form of government that many in the press thought unlikely to survive. Abdülhamid was depicted as one among a caravan of monarchs (including the shah of Iran and the Russian czar) who were destined for extinction.

While politics was the primary area of concern in the satirical press, cartoonists also ranged widely over social and cultural topics. They targeted the demand for women's rights, spirit mediums, and new-style entertainments such as ice-skating and cafes. They also lampooned "old" styles of dress, EDUCATION, healing, and gender relations as obsolete, superstitious, or backward. Satirists viewed the Ottoman situation with a jaundiced eye; they were not persuaded that change was necessarily good or that

Satirist and cartoonist were preoccupied with the threat of European imperialism. In this image the cartoonist drew Britain as a greedy giant, leaning on the pyramids of Egypt whereas young Egyptians protest against the English occupation of Egypt. (*Personal collection of Palmira Brummett*)

new political and social regimes would eliminate the ills of the past.

Many characters populated the Ottoman cartoon frame, some real and some fictional. The sultan and government officials were the most prominent objects of cartoon scorn, as were individual viziers and government bureaucracy. Figures who were emblematic of their class, from wealthy socialites to maids and porters, were also commonly found on the cartoon pages. Extremely popular in the satirical press were the characters of shadow-puppet theater, especially the irrepressible everyman Karagöz (Black-Eye) and his sidekick Hacivat. Shadow-puppet theatre was a fast-paced, dialogue-rich, satirical theatrical form that translated very readily into the satirical press of the late Ottoman Empire. It lampooned gender relations, class conflicts, ethnic differences, and government authority in all its forms. Karagöz, like other cartoon figures, served as the man on the street who had little control over his own destiny but refused, nonetheless, to submit willingly to government regulations or standard social conventions. He was a perfect spokesman for the anxieties and ambiguities of the revolutionary era. A gazette entitled *Karagöz*, which included both pictorial and narrative satire, was published from August 1908 until 1928. The cartoon press of the empire thus survived the censorship that was reimposed after the abortive counterrevolution of 1909. Like that of the shadow-puppet theater, its satire changed to suit the political and social issues of the day, from the BALKAN WARS (1912–13) to WORLD WAR I (1914–18), and from Western-style fashions to female suffrage.

Although historical analysis of Ottoman cartoons has as yet been limited, there seem to have been at least two workshops of artists producing cartoons in Istanbul in the revolutionary period. Cartoons passed back and forth between gazettes in the capital and those in other cities, such as Izmir in western Anatolia. As in other forms of art, cartoons were referential, sharing and copying motifs not just from the Karagöz theatre but from Ottoman and foreign artists. The Ottoman press also reprinted cartoons from foreign gazettes such as the French *Rire* (Laughter). Cartoonists, like printers, might work for multiple publications at the same time, some innovating, others crafting images to suit the editorial policies of individual gazettes. Mehmed Fazlı, editor of the periodical *Lak lak* (Stork), penned his own cartoons. While many cartoonists signed their work, numerous others left their work unsigned, thus heightening the sense that cartoons were public property. Among those who did sign their work, the variety of styles and of ethnic names was a reflection of the cosmopolitan and multiethnic nature of Istanbul itself.

Palmira Brummett

Further reading: Metin And, *Karagöz: Turkish Shadow Theatre* (Istanbul: Dost Yayınları, 1987); Palmira Brummett, *Image and Imperialism in the Ottoman Revolutionary Press, 1908–1911* (Albany: State University of New York Press, 2000); Müge Goçek, ed., *Political Cartoons in the Middle East: Cultural Representation in the Middle East* (Princeton, N.J.: Markus Wiener, 1998); Şükrü Hanioğlu, *Preparation for a Revolution: The Young Turks, 1902–1908* (Oxford: Oxford University Press, 2001).

population In 1768, when the war against RUSSIA began, the Ottoman Empire was an enormous political structure that extended over 3,000 miles (5,000 km) from the Atlas Mountains in the west to the Persian Gulf in the east, and 1,800 miles (3,000 km) from the source of the Dniester River in the north to the rapids of the Assouan in the south, stretching across three continents. In considering the population of these vast territories, there are two main features to be considered: the great diversity of the people of the imperial territories, and the unusual pattern of population growth and migration that shaped the growing and changing empire. Thus both the composition of the population and the overall number of imperial subjects were affected by successive disruptions

including PLAGUE, WARFARE, and religiously motivated migrations, from the end of the RUSSO-TURKISH WAR in 1774 until the start of WORLD WAR I in 1914.

A GREAT DIVERSITY

The formation of the Ottoman Empire, which took place between the 14th and 17th centuries, consolidated many different groups of people under the power of the sultan, although the state never sought to restructure them all into one nation. As long as the sultan was revered, order was respected, taxes were paid, and the soldier levy (or conscription) was met, individuals were free to practice their religion, speak their language, and live in the private sphere of their religious community or *MILLET*—an institution recognized by the state—all while respecting the basic principles of Ottoman society. The Ottoman Empire was therefore an enormous conglomerate of both large and small communities of greater or less importance that coexisted without any real mixing.

It is practical to first distinguish between the NOMADS and the sedentary population. If the latter were greater in numbers, the former held a more important place within the empire, if only by the fact that the Turks, the original founders of the empire, were themselves a nomadic group that had come from Central Asia centuries earlier. In Ottoman culture, nomads—especially those of Turkoman ancestry—held a certain prestige. Apart from the Roma (more commonly known by the pejorative term "gypsy"), who were spread throughout the empire, nomads were typically found in certain areas of the Balkans, such as Mount Rhodope and Dobruja. They could also be found in central and eastern Anatolia. In the Near East there were the nomadic BEDOUINS of SYRIA, IRAQ, the Arabian Peninsula, NORTH AFRICA, EGYPT, on the coastal plain (Sahel) of Cyrenaica and Tripolitania (in present-day Libya), in Tunisia, and in the regency of ALGIERS. With the exception of the Roma, most of whom were Christians, the nomads were Muslims. Although they were likely to have been comparatively few, it was never possible to establish an exact number. These few traveled great distances and opposed the value of agricultural (fertile) lands set by the state, especially in Anatolia.

By comparison, with the exception of the Balkans, the sedentary population occupied the Asian and African regions of the empire very sparsely (in very limited areas) and were primarily settled in coastal regions such as western Anatolia and the shores of the Black Sea, or in Syria, Tripolitania, and northern Africa. They also populated the valleys of important rivers such as the Nile, the Tigris, and the EUPHRATES.

In regard to the sedentary population, the urban and rural populations must be distinguished. The great majority of the inhabitants of the Ottoman Empire lived in the countryside, but one of the characteristics of the population is the high number and significance of people in the cities, which created a dense and coherent urban network where governors, administrations, and garrisons were stationed and where the important economic activities took place. This urban setting was an essential element in the cohesion of the vast empire. Other than Istanbul, whose population was estimated to be approximately half a million inhabitants at this time—fewer inhabitants than London, comparable to Paris, and more populous than Vienna, Madrid, Berlin, or St. Petersburg—many other large cities (50,000–100,000 inhabitants) emerged within the empire by the end of the 18th century. They included port cities such as SALONIKA, IZMIR, TUNIS, and Algiers, and inland cities such as BURSA, ALEPPO, Sofia, BAGHDAD, Damascus, Sarajevo, and the second most important city of the empire, CAIRO, with 260,000 inhabitants..

A third important distinction within the population is between Muslims and non-Muslims. The former, whether Turks or Arabs, held a higher position within Ottoman society; for example, only Muslims could participate in administrative or military functions. Christians of various denominations and JEWS held a lower position but were protected by their status as DHIMMIS, or Peoples of the Book since it was considered that the Christian and Jewish bibles were precursors to the Quran and that Moses and Jesus were prophets who preceded Muhammad. The Balkans were mostly Christian in the 18th century and Muslims dominated Anatolia, the Near East, and northern Africa, yet there were substantial groups of different communities present in all the provinces of the empire, especially in the cities.

A DISORGANIZED DEVELOPMENT

The empire conducted property surveys (*tahrir defteri*) in the 15th and 16th centuries. Based on these surveys, the population of the empire in 1520 was estimated at approximately 12 to 13 million. By the 17th century, this figure may have reached 22 to 25 million, but these surveys were not renewed, and it was not until the 19th century that the state began to investigate the real numbers of its population.

The first inquiry, which only covered one part of the empire, dates from 1831. It included part of the Balkans, the western half of Anatolia, and the Aegean Islands. To complete the picture, however, there is the census of 1831 ordered by MEHMED ALI in Egypt and Syria. This census is particularly valuable because it was recorded at the end of an era characterized by high birth rates accompanied by high mortality rates. The latter were a result of natural disasters, notably the plague, aggravated by man-made disasters, such as foreign wars and internal revolts. In the 73 years from 1768 to 1841, the Ottoman Empire was involved in nine conflicts, totaling 35 years of war. Under such conditions, population growth was limited or nonexistent.

According to the combined information from these surveys, scholars have been able to determine that the Ottoman population at this time included approximately 25 million subjects. Despite the lack of precision, these statistics are important because they paint a picture of the population of the empire at the onset of fundamental changes that greatly affected the following decades. Beginning in the 1830s, the Ottoman lands began to diminish. In 1830 the Empire covered more than a million square miles (3 million square km) and included 25 million inhabitants, but that same year the empire lost control of GREECE, SERBIA, and the regency of Algiers. Beginning in the 1840s, the eradication of the plague and the return to peaceful times allowed for a modest, yet real, growth in the population of the empire. On the other hand, in 1856 the empire lost MOLDAVIA and WALLACHIA. Between 1878 and 1882 it lost Tunisia, Egypt, CYPRUS, Kars and Ardahan, BOSNIA, Thessaly, and BULGARIA; between 1911 and 1913 it lost ALBANIA, Macedonia, Western Thrace, CRETE, the Dodecanese, Tripolitania, and Cyrenaica. By 1914 the Ottoman Empire was reduced to about 500,000 square miles (1.3 million square km) and 21 million inhabitants. It had become essentially an Asian power.

Population growth played a role in the evolution of the Ottoman population in the years between 1830 and 1914, but another demographic phenomenon also had a great impact: migration. Emigration began in the 1860s and affected 80 percent of Christians. Some left for economic reasons, but for many, it was also a means of escape from the devastating ARMENIAN MASSACRES that took place in the 1890s and again between 1908 and 1910. In the years between 1860 and 1914, it is estimated that 1,200,000 Ottoman subjects departed for the United States, Argentina, and Australia, notably from Syria and LEBANON.

At the same time that other groups were leaving the empire, however, Muslims were relocating within the empire in ever greater numbers. Every time a province was lost, a part of its Muslim population relocated to the remaining parts of the empire. This was particularly true for the Balkans, where the ancient inhabitants of SERBIA and of Moldavia-Wallachia settled in Bulgaria in the 1850s. After 1880, a portion of the Bosnian and Bulgarian Muslims sought refuge in Macedonia. After the BALKAN WARS (1912–13), Istanbul welcomed nearly 200,000 persons fleeing Macedonia and Thrace. Yet a majority of these Muslim immigrants—about four million out of the five to six million who came to reside in the Ottoman Empire between 1783 and 1913—were from the Russian Empire. The first of these were the CRIMEAN TATARS who entered the empire between the end of the 18th century and the 1850s. It is estimated that they numbered

1,800,000 in 1922. The Circassians, two million or less, comprise the second ethnic group that arrived beginning in the 1860s. Like the Tatars, the Circassians first settled in the Balkans before relocating to Anatolia. The loss of the Balkan provinces and the migration movements—the replacement of the Christian population by the arrival of Muslims—reinforced the Muslim character of the Ottoman Empire in the second half of the 19th century. In 1830, Muslims accounted for 75 percent of the population; in 1914, they made up 81 percent.

Daniel Panzac

Further reading: Halil İnalcık and Donald Quataert, eds., *An Economic and Social History of the Ottoman Empire* (Cambridge: Cambridge University Press, 1994).

presidio Presidio is a Spanish term that originally referred to the fortresses established by the Spanish monarchs along the Mediterranean coastline and in the frontier areas of the Americas and the Philippines. Presidios emerged as fortified military complexes out of the need to exert control over and offer protection to areas located in otherwise unprotected or difficult geographic positions. In NORTH AFRICA, the presidio satisfied a defensive function (control of the coastline against COR-SAIR activities) while simultaneously offering important strategic support for launching military operations and protecting Spain's commercial interests in the Ottoman Empire.

The origins of the presidio go back to the establishment of military frontier posts along the North African coastline during the reign of the Catholic monarchs in the late 15th century. This network of presidios was designed to play an important part in the strategy of Spain, which wished to exert a limited control over the territory through a combination of military strength and a network of complex alliances with local Muslim authorities. Spanish presidios in Italy and North Africa played a key role in the development of new military tactics as well as the formation of a new type of soldier. Tactically, the presidio contributed to the inauguration of a new understanding of warfare in the early modern period (late 15th and early 16th centuries) through combining land-based operations with maritime ones. The transformations brought about by the military revolution of this period, such as the use of portable firing weapons, modern artillery, and new warfare techniques, affected the evolution of presidios. In addition, the North African presidios had to withstand the particular raiding and siege techniques employed by the Muslim groups in this area as well as the difficulty in supplying military equipment and water to the soldiers stationed there. The most important presidios in North Africa were the *presidios mayores* (major presidios) of Ceuta and Oran and

the *presidios menores* (minor presidios) of Melilla, Peñón de Vélez, and Alhucemas. During the 18th century the Bourbon monarchs, who ruled Spain from 1700 through 1808, ordered regular evaluations of the merit of maintaining the *presidios menores* and although several reports considered abandoning them, Spain retained sovereignty over them. The most important period of instability for the North African presidios occurred during the siege of Ceuta, between 1694 and 1727.

Presidios such as Ceuta also served as penitentiaries and became an important source of labor for the Spanish Empire. Spanish authorities in the 16th and 17th centuries sentenced criminal offenders to hard labor in the royal galleys or military presidios. Prisoners (*presidiarios*) performed maintenance tasks and contributed to the construction of fortifications and military facilities. In Oran and Ceuta, prisoners whose crimes were not considered heinous were allowed to be part of the garrison's military force, which offered them a chance at redemption. While their degree of freedom inside the presidio varied, prisoners were still subject to all conventional Spanish rules and regulations, being prosecuted, for instance, by the Spanish Inquisition well into the late 18th century. During the 18th century, the African presidios, most significantly Ceuta, harbored prisoners sent from the Americas.

Vanesa Casanova-Fernandez

Further reading: Ruth Pike, "Penal Servitude in the Spanish Empire: Presidio Labor in the Eighteenth Century." *Hispanic American Historical Review* 58 (1978): 21–40.

Prime Ministry's Ottoman Archives The Prime Ministry's Ottoman Archives or Başbakanlık Osmanlı Arşivi is the largest and richest source of Ottoman archival material in existence. Located in ISTANBUL, the archives belong to the Turkish Republic's Prime Ministry and include documents of the central governmental bureaus of the Ottoman Empire. However, it also includes documents related to some 40 present-day countries reflecting its territorial expansion and multiethnic nature. The archives are thus an international record office, and because of the extent and diversity of its collection, it is one of the most significant archive offices in the world.

HISTORY

Since its foundation, the Ottoman Empire attached great importance to keeping records. In the first capitals, BURSA and EDIRNE, authorities carefully kept documents and records related to the state. However, the records in Bursa were substantially damaged and depleted in 1402 during the invasions of TIMUR, the founder of the TIMURIDS in Transoxania (now Uzbekistan), who defeated the Ottomans in 1402 and in subsequent wars. Therefore, very few documents related to the foundation period of the Ottoman state have survived. In Edirne, records of the state were preserved in the royal court of the Edirne Palace.

After the conquest of CONSTANTINOPLE in 1453, documents were kept in the Seven Towers or Yedikule. The archives, which had been transported to the Sultanahmet district of Istanbul, were later placed in the Royal Treasury. Treasury documents were placed in the Old Tent JANISSARY Band Barracks at Sultanahmet. Because of a change in the structure of Ottoman bureaucracy in the middle of the 18th century, a new governing structure called the Sublime Porte (Bab-ı Âli) arose and in 1785 a building in the grand vizier's palace complex (today's governorship complex) was established to house government and political records. In 1794 a record office was established in the Engineer's Court for maps and plans for border castles.

The first steps for establishing a modern record office for the Ottoman Empire were taken in 1845 by Safveti Pasha, who was the minister of the treasury at that time. Due to his efforts, millions of documents that had been kept in the treasury of the TOPKAPI PALACE were placed in storehouses with an established system for recording provenance. The most significant preservation attempt was made by Grand Vizier MUSTAFA REŞID PASHA in 1846 when he ordered the building of a record office. This building was completed in 1848 by architect Gaspare T. Fossati, who was born in the Italian part of Switzerland, and named the Treasury of Documents (Hazine-i Evrak). At the same time, the office of Surveillance of Treasury of Documents was formed and Muhsin Efendi was appointed as its manager. For storage and sorting of documents, a council composed of Bab-ı Âli governors was formed and an ordinance regarding this council was prepared in 1849.

Due to this ordinance, the council sorted by subject the documents that had been kept prior to 1849. From 1850 onward, it adjusted which documents were to be preserved among the daily correspondence. A main storehouse and sub-storehouses were established, along with a catalogue for the documents to be kept in the treasury of documents. In 1892, during the period of Grand Vizier Cevad Pasha, a filing system was established in the Treasury of Documents and in other government offices. The first documents within this system were the ones related to EGYPT and BULGARIA.

The declaration of the second constitutional monarchy in 1908 precipitated the organization of record offices in the empire. The head of the Ottoman History Committee, Abdurrahman Şeref Bey, was appointed as the director of the council responsible for sorting the archives in the storehouses in the TOPKAPI PALACE and Sultanahmet. However, the council left its work unfinished in 1914. After the beginning of WORLD WAR I, Ottoman authorities noticed that the security of Istanbul was endangered and transported 208 chests of documents, foremost among them the imperial order documents, to Konya. After one year, these documents were brought back to Istanbul via ferries and military trains.

In 1923, when the Republic of Turkey was declared, the Department of Treasury of Documents was formed again as a unit bound to the Prime Ministry Private Office Department in order to protect and preserve Ottoman documents and possessions. The organization was named Management of Storage of Documents; in 1927 it became Submanagement of Treasury of Documents as a part of the Undersecretariat of the Prime Ministry.

This organization underwent some institutional modifications between 1927 and 1943 and was renamed Public Management of Archives, affiliated with the Undersecretariat of the Prime Ministry. Finally, on June 18, 1948, the government archives head office was formed and the Ottoman Record Office, or Prime Ministry's Ottoman Archives, was affiliated with it.

CONTENTS OF THE ARCHIVE

The Prime Ministry's Ottoman Record Office is largely composed of official documents of the Ottoman Empire that were related to the empire's CENTRAL ADMINISTRATION and PROVINCIAL ADMINISTRATION. Most documents are written using the Arabic alphabet in Ottoman Turkish. There are 95 million documents and 360,000 record books. Besides documents in Ottoman Turkish there are documents in Arabic, Persian, Greek, Armenian, and Russian. There are also some documents in French, since this was the formal international language of diplomacy during the late Ottoman period. In addition to written documents there are visual materials such as maps, photographs, and photo albums.

The Prime Ministry's Ottoman Record Office does not include many documents before the period of MEHMED II (the Conqueror) (r. 1444–46; 1451–81), and there are also relatively few documents related to the period between the reigns of Mehmed II and SÜLEYMAN I (r. 1520–66), with only a few hundred record books from that time remaining in the archives. However, a great number of documents are preserved from the period of Süleyman the Magnificent until the end of the empire.

The Prime Ministry's Ottoman Record Office has a rich variety of documents. There are documents related to cadastral surveys, population censuses, and tax registers; regulations concerning all provinces and subprovinces; records regarding the palace, military, NAVY, bureaucracy, civil servants, public works, CHARITY, religious foundations (WAQFS), education, and public health. In addition there are contracts and agreements with foreign states records about the non-Muslim subjects of the empire.

Records of the Ottoman state's central organization before the TANZIMAT period (administrative reforms after 1839) fall into two main groups. The first is the records of the Imperial Council or Divan-ı Hümayun, which issued political and legal rulings; the second is the records of the Bab-ı Defteri where official financial records were kept. The Imperial Council and court documents after the Tanzimat period are composed of the records of the ministries of religion, foreign affairs, internal affairs, and justice. Documents may also be found in the Ottoman archives relating to the Ministries of Treasury, Education, Commerce, and Agriculture, as well as *waqfs* and the military. The Yıldız Archives, named after the Yıldız Palace where ABDÜLHAMID II (r. 1876–1909) resided, which is composed of imperial documents issued during the reign of ABDÜLHAMID II (r. 1876-1909), are also kept in the Prime Ministry's Ottoman Archives.

Records from the various ministries were acquired by the Record Office at different times. The records of the Ministry of Treasury were acquired in 1934, those of the Ministry of Religious Endowments (*waqfs*) in 1947, the Foreign Ministry Department of General Security in 1963, Security Forces in 1972, Commerce and Public Works in 1972, Foreign Affairs in 1985, Communication and Education in the 1990s. Documents related to the Ottoman Empire previously kept in the archives of BULGARIA, HUNGARY, Macedonia, RUSSIA, Georgia, ALBANIA, and northern CYPRUS have also been added to the Prime Ministry's Ottoman Record Office in the form of photo-reproductions or microfilms; these are available to any individual with a research permit.

Some documents related to important historical and political figures of the more recent past—for example, Ali Fuad Türkgeldi (1867–1935), historian and chief secretary of the Chancery under Sultan MEHMED V (Reşad, r. 1909–1918)—have also been placed in the Prime Ministry's Ottoman Archive. Another recent example is the collection of documents of the *zaviye* (dervish convent or hospice) of Ali Baba of Sivas. This collection is composed of 804 records related to the *zaviye* from the years 1572 to 1916.

Microfilms have been used in the archives since 1998. Since 2002, 4 million documents have been transferred to a digital or microfilm format with four microfilm cameras and 10 digital cameras. Starting in 1976 and gaining momentum after 1987, the Prime Ministry's Ottoman Archives also began a major effort to save and restore damaged documents.

The archive also actively publishes works, both sources and monographs, relating to its collections. Between 1982 and 2006, 70 books were published, most about Armenian relations with Britain, France, Russia, and the United States.

Mustafa Budak

principalities *See* MOLDAVIA; WALLACHIA.

printing Despite widespread misconceptions that the Ottoman Empire lacked printing until the establishment of the first Arabic letter-printing house in 1727, new research indicates that the printing press has a rich history in the empire and that printing played an important role from the late 15th century onward in the religious and cultural life of the many denominations of this multireligious and multilingual empire, both in the provinces and in the capital of ISTANBUL.

EARLY OTTOMAN PRINTING: ISTANBUL AND THE PROVINCES

The earliest uses of printing technology in the Ottoman Empire occurred in urban centers such as Istanbul and SALONIKA. Printing in the Ottoman capital reflected the myriad languages and alphabets used by the diverse populations under Ottoman rule. The first book printed in the Ottoman Empire was published in 1493 in Istanbul by the brothers David and Samuel ibn Nahmias. It was a four-volume edition of the code of Jewish law in Hebrew. The Nahmias brothers were part of a wave of Jewish refugees that had been welcomed into the Ottoman Empire by Sultan BAYEZID II (r. 1481–1512) after their expulsion from the Iberian Peninsula in 1492. Other immigrants followed suit and, in the first decade of the 16th century, a copy of the Pentateuch (the first five books of the Hebrew bible) was printed in Salonika by Don Yehuda Gedalya, a Jewish refugee from Portugal. Having already experimented with the use of print in the Iberian Peninsula, these refugee communities probably brought their own presses and supplies with them, as well as the experience of editors, proofreaders, and compositors. Other residents of the capital also played an important role in early printing. From 1567 to 1569, for example, Agbar Tibir, an Armenian from Tokat (near the coastal town of Samsun in Anatolia) who had studied the art of printing in Rome, set up a printing press in the Church of Saint Nigogos in Istanbul. In general, these first books printed in Istanbul were religious in nature and were primarily intended for devotional or instructional use by small local communities.

The 17th century witnessed the first use of printing in the Arab provinces of the empire. In 1610, at the MARONITE monastery of Saint Anthony in Quzhayya, now northern LEBANON, an edition of the Book of Psalms was produced under the guidance of the Italian printer Pasquale Eli. The psalter was printed in Karshuni, the Arabic language using the Syriac alphabet. Despite these early ventures, the number of presses in operation, the output of printed titles, and the actual use of printed documents by Ottoman subjects remained quite limited well into the 17th century. This did not mean, however, that Istanbul residents were necessarily unfamiliar with the art of printing. In 1588 Sultan MURAD III (r. 1574–

95) authorized two Italian merchants, Branton and Orazio Bandini, to sell books printed in Arabic, Persian, and Turkish in Istanbul. These books were originally printed in Rome, and the merchants had met with opposition from local businessmen when they attempted to import and sell their books in the Istanbul BAZAAR. During his appointment as French ambassador to the Ottoman Empire from 1591 to 1605, Savary de Brèves claimed to have successfully procured a font of Arabic type from a local engraver in Istanbul, suggesting that artisans in the capital had sufficient skill to cast such a font. Printed books also made their appearance in the capital in the form of gifts. In 1668, a Dutch mission presented Sultan MEHMED IV (r. 1648–87) with a printed copy of a famous atlas published by Joan Blaeu, a prominent Dutch cartographer and member of the Dutch East India Company (*see* CARTOGRAPHY).

European social and political developments, such as the ongoing rivalry between Protestants and Catholics, also contributed to the output of printed matter in Istanbul. European MERCHANTS, diplomats, and other intermediaries could procure supplies, machine parts, and fonts that were otherwise difficult for Istanbul residents to acquire. In the early 17th century, Ottoman state officials were drawn into an incident sparked by the distribution of printed books among the Christians of Istanbul. The affair revolved around Cyril Lucaris, officially ecumenical patriarch of Constantinople but known at the time for his inclinations toward Protestant, and specifically Calvinist, thought. In 1620, Protestants in Europe printed an Arabic Bible and delivered copies of it to Lucaris via the Dutch ambassador in Istanbul. Lucaris reportedly passed these Bibles out freely. In 1627 Lucaris, this time with the help of a Greek printer named Metaxas and Thomas Roe, the English ambassador in Istanbul, established the first Greek printing press in the Ottoman Empire near the English and French embassies in the Pera neighborhood of Istanbul. Fearing the spread of Calvinist thought, Catholic partisans in Istanbul aimed to put an end to the spread of Lucaris's printed books. Intrigues and false accusations from the local Jesuits ultimately incited the sultan's personal troops, the JANISSARIES, to destroy the press, even though state officials later realized they had been duped. The affair illustrates the fact that Ottoman policies regarding printing were usually a response to specific circumstances of the moment, but it also reveals the presence of printed books in the capital.

Like many other states in the early modern period (between the medieval age and the Industrial Revolution), the Ottomans showed interest in the use of print by their subjects. Ottoman reactions to print during this period remain a subject of disagreement among historians. A 1584 travelogue written by the French traveler and cosmographer Andre Thevet specifically mentions that two edicts were declared by the Ottoman sultans (in 1485 and 1515) that threatened death for anyone caught printing. Although threats of similar punishments were pronounced at the same time in Europe, additional evidence is still needed to confirm that such edicts actually existed in the Ottoman world. In 1551 another French traveler, Nicolas de Nicolay, wrote that Jewish communities living in Istanbul had been permitted to print in Greek, Latin, Italian, Spanish, and Hebrew, but not in Arabic or Turkish. This may have been the result of a concern on the part of certain sectors of the Istanbul elite about the use of Arabic by non-Muslims, a concern dating to the early centuries of Islam. Given the use of printing by various communities in different parts of the empire, it is likely that state policies concerning the use of print were formed in specific social, political, and geopolitical contexts and not, as some historians have suggested, as blanket policies.

THE 18TH CENTURY: PRINT AND OTTOMAN ELITES

The 18th century marked the beginning of state-sponsored printing in the capital and the growth of printing in the provinces. In the capital, İbrahim Müteferrika, a Hungarian convert to Islam, founded a printing press with the help of state officials in 1727. This endeavor marked the start of Ottoman state involvement in printing as well as the first effort to print in Ottoman Turkish in the empire. Müteferrika was permitted to print books about SCIENCES, WARFARE, and history, but was forbidden to publish on matters of religion. The Müteferrika press published 17 titles including Turkish grammars, court histories of the empire, and military treatises on siege warfare. The operation of the press came to an end with the death of Müteferrika in 1745 and was renewed for a short time under Müteferrika's son.

In the Arab provinces, religious debate and polemic among Arab Christian communities contributed to a surge of printing. As with Lucaris in an earlier period, Christian, especially Catholic, MISSIONARIES maintained close links with a number of Arab monastic communities, providing them with supplies for the publication of religious texts. Such relationships resulted in the founding of a press in 1734 by Abdallah Zakhir, a MELKITE CATHOLIC priest, at the monastery of St John the Baptist at Shuwayr in Lebanon. As well as scriptural and devotional texts, the Shuwayr press published a series of Arabic translations of Catholic treatises first published in Italian and French during the Catholic Reformation in the early 17th century. The Melkite Catholic patriarch, Athanasius Dabbas, founded a press in ALEPPO in 1704 with the financial and technical support of Constantine Brancoveanu, the *voievod* of WALLACHIA, an Ottoman vassal state (in present-day Romania). Additional presses were later established in BEIRUT and other areas of the Levant.

Monasteries were also an important site for printing in the Danubian principalities of Wallachia and MOLDAVIA. Within the context of patronage for a revival of Greek culture, local elites supported the establishment of a number of printing presses. In the last decades of the 17th century Constantine Brancoveanu asked Anthim Ivireanul, the metropolitan (bishop) of Bucharest, to assist with the operation of a new printing press at Bucharest. Soon after, Ivireanul published a version of the Gospels in Romanian. In 1710 Ivireanul also founded the first Georgian printing press at Tbilisi (the capital of present-day Georgia), where a version of the Gospels was printed in Georgian for the first time in 1710. Thus printing in the Ottoman provinces, much like in the capital, was aimed at satisfying the devotional needs of local religious communities. But the 18th century marked the growing participation of elites in the sponsorship of printing, a trend that paved the way for the adoption of printing by Protestant and Catholic missionaries from Europe in their efforts to convert Eastern Orthodox Christians in the 19th century.

PRINT IN THE AGE OF REFORM AND NATIONALISM

In the 19th and 20th centuries, printing in the Ottoman world reflected the social and political developments taking place across the empire. Shifts in printing culture are distinguished by three important characteristics: increased output of printed material, growing diversity among printers, and a change in the content of what was being printed. In Istanbul, new presses established by the state published dictionaries and other texts related to language, history, and medicine. The age of NEWSPAPERS began in 1831 with the printing of the first official government newspaper of the empire, the *Takvimi Vekayi* (Calendar of occurrences). Many presses remained in continual operation from this time until the so-called alphabet revolution of 1928, when the new republican government of Turkey abandoned the use of Arabic script and adopted instead the Latin-based alphabet, ushering in a new era in the history of printing.

During the early 19th century, the major urban center of CAIRO also experienced an increase in printing. In the early 1820s, the establishment of a new printing press in the Cairo neighborhood of Bulaq was an important part of the strategies of military reform pursued by Governor MEHMED ALI OF EGYPT. Nicolas Masabiki, an Egyptian trained in typography in Italy, worked alongside Italian typographers to produce, first, an Italian dictionary, followed by a flood of legal texts, calendars, and other books in Arabic, Persian, and Turkish. From 1828 onward the Bulaq press produced an official gazette of government

affairs, *Vekayi-i Misriyye* (*Arab*: *Al-Waqai al-Misriyya*, The Egyptian bulletin), which mirrored the content of the publication produced by the central government in Istanbul. By the start of the 20th century, printing in Egypt was increasingly carried out by individuals outside the ruling elite. Because of a large missionary presence, a number of foreigners were engaged in printing, frequently using presses that had been brought from Europe.

Whereas early printing in the Ottoman world had been practiced only by limited groups, the 19th century witnessed an ever-increasing number of printers, many of whom published new types of material. In JERUSALEM, for example, the support and cooperation of various Christian missionary groups meant that books were being published in Arabic, Russian, Armenian, Greek, and Turkish. One crucial contribution to the enterprise of printing came from the body of self-proclaimed nationalists in the empire. These individuals played an important role in bringing local literature into print for the first time. In 1879 one such organization was founded in Istanbul, the Society for the Printing of Albanian Writings, which was dedicated to reviving Albanian works in a printed form. The printing press became an important medium for political campaigns and for the spread of NATIONALISM. At the same time, Muslim reformist thinkers also embraced the press as a means of engaging with larger theological debates about Islam, modernity, westernization, and the political organization of society.

Even more important, perhaps, than this emerging dialogue in print was the shift in the format of printed texts. Whereas earlier printing had been dominated by the production of multi-volume texts, increasingly the empire's printing presses were reserved for ephemeral periodical literature, especially NEWSPAPERS, as well as pamphlets and placards. Easy to produce and distribute to a mass audience, such printed matter played a vital role in the political changes that rocked the Ottoman Empire in the late 19th and early 20th centuries.

Historians have speculated about the reasons for the ebbs and flows in the use of print in the Ottoman Empire's long history. The difficulty of reading printed texts as opposed to manuscript ones, the existence of an organized and effective system for copying texts, and even the high costs and technical challenges of printing in Arabic script were probably important factors. Still, specific incidents of the use of print are best understood in light of the unique circumstances surrounding them. The experience of printing in other societies—for example, in early modern Europe or East Asia—suggests that it is not surprising that scribal production, or the copying of texts by hand, continued to play an important role in Ottoman society centuries after the discovery of Gutenberg's masterful invention. Similarly, the introduction of the printing press in the Ottoman Empire need not have ushered in a new era of the "print revolution." Rather, printing remained merely one medium for the spread of information in a complex and dynamic communications network, a world in which print interacted with other media such as manuscripts, visual signs, and, perhaps most importantly, the spoken word.

John-Paul Ghobrial

See also CENSORSHIP.

Further reading: Eva Hanebutt-Benz, Dagmar Glass, and Geoffrey Roper, *Middle Eastern Languages and the Print Revolution: A Cross-Cultural Encounter* (Westhofen: WVA-Verlag Skulima, 2002); Klaus Kreiser, ed., *The Beginnings of Printing in the Near and Middle East: Jews, Christians and Muslims* (Wiesbaden: Harrassowitz in Kommission, 2001).

prohibited goods   *See* CONTRABAND.

provincial administration   *See* ADMINISTRATION, PROVINCIAL.

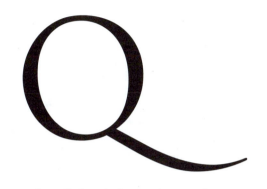

al-Qazdaghli household The al-Qazdaghli household, founded by Mustafa al-Qazdaghli at the end of the 17th century, was arguably one of the most successful MAMLUK households in Ottoman EGYPT. The political life of CAIRO in that century was dominated by the bloody competition between two great Mamluk households, the Faqariyya and the Qasimiyya. Mustafa, who was of obscure origins but may have been a freebooter from Anatolia, achieved the rank of *kahya* (literally, steward) of the Janissary forces stationed in the city and allied himself with the Faqariyya. When Mustafa died in 1704 the leadership of his household passed to Hasan Kahya, who had been recruited by Mustafa as a mamluk and who also commanded the JANISSARIES. The household continued to grow through steady recruitment of mamluks and Muslim adventurers, but its members were careful to cement their close relationships with the Janissary garrison stationed in Cairo. They also avoided engaging in the ongoing struggle among other Mamluk households for the *beylicate*, the unofficial administrative office held by a Mamluk, which often competed for control with the official Ottoman governor. Instead, the household concentrated on acquiring wealth through the control of TAX FARMING and various customs revenues, as well as by extorting money from the city's merchants.

This low political profile changed in 1736 when Ibrahim took control of both the Qazdaghli household and the *beylicate*. Ibrahim Bey, in turn, dominated Egypt's political life from 1748 to 1754, taking for himself the title of SHAYKH AL-BALAD. This term harked back to the earlier Mamluk Empire and reflected Ibrahim's actual control of Cairo, even while an Ottoman governor nominally ruled in the city. After Ibrahim's death one of his

Mamluks, Ali, later to be called Bulutkapan (One Who Grasps the Clouds) by his admirers and detractors alike, seized the position of Shaykh al-Balad twice, in 1760–6 and 1767–72.

Ali Bey broke with the tradition, established by the Qazdaghli household, of balancing the widening autonomy accruing to the Shaykh al-Balad by publicly offering fealty to ISTANBUL. In 1770 he replaced the Ottoman governor of JEDDAH with an Egyptian Mamluk, threatening the House of Osman's claim to be the guardian of the holy places. In 1771, in an act of open rebellion against the empire, he ordered his forces to invade SYRIA. But his commander of the invasion, Muhammad Abu al-Dhahab, returned to Egypt, having captured DAMASCUS but not wishing to press deeper into Ottoman territory. Abu al-Dhahab then broke with his former master, drove him into exile in Syria, and himself took the title of Shaykh al-Balad. Ali Bey attempted a return to Egypt in 1773 but was defeated and captured; he reportedly died later of his wounds in Cairo.

Abu al-Dhahab abandoned Ali Bey's policy of confrontation with the Ottomans. In 1775, in a move designed to reduce the autonomy of ZAHIR AL-UMAR, he invaded Syria a second time. He was initially victorious, but then died rather mysteriously outside ACRE. After Abu al-Dhahab's death the household broke into factions that battled for supremacy until a compromise established the joint leadership of two of Abu al-Dhahab's former Mamluks. The Ottomans attempted to wrest control of Egypt from the Qazdaghlis in 1786 but failed to unseat them. In the end, it was the French occupation of Egypt in 1798 that overturned the household's fortunes.

The Qazdaghli household demonstrates the strengths and weaknesses of the Mamluk household system in Egypt. Its flexibility in recruitment allowed the household to continually replenish its ranks with new talent, but the bonds that held members together were based solely on the self-interest of those individuals. As long as the household's main interests was the accumulation of wealth, individual members agreed to cooperate. But when the goal changed to the accumulation of political power, only one individual could ultimately triumph.

That led the others to conspire to overthrow him so as to achieve that prize for themselves.

Bruce Masters

Further reading: Jane Hathaway, *The Politics of Households in Ottoman Egypt: The Rise of the Qazdağlıs* (Cambridge: Cambridge University Press, 1997).

Qizilbash   *See* KIZILBAŞ.

R

Ragusa (Dubrovnik) The town of Ragusa (now known as Dubrovnik) is situated at the southernmost tip of the Republic of Croatia. The origins of the town, which eventually developed into a city-state, are said to lie in the early seventh century, when refugees from the destroyed Roman town of Epidaurus (Cavtat) established a settlement some 12 miles (20 km) to the northwest. Politically, Ragusa belonged first to Byzantine Dalmatia, then, after 1205, to Venice. In 1358 the already well-developed aristocratic republic accepted the suzerainty of Louis the Great, the Anjou king of Hungary (r. 1342–82), which effectively meant almost full independence. The basis of the republic's wealth was trade on land and sea, with a network of colonies all over the Balkans and consulates around the Mediterranean. Some Ragusa merchants may have received privileges from one of the early Ottoman rulers as early as the 14th century. The relationship between Ragusa and the Ottoman Empire is better documented, however, from the 15th century.

At this time, the Ottomans had conquered neighboring territories in Serbia and Bosnia, and Ragusa became a vassal state, paying, first a "gift," and then an annual tribute (*haraç*) continuously from 1458. Through this relationship, the republic had protection from Venetian aspirations and enjoyed a monopoly on trade between the Ottoman Balkans and Italy. Customs duties were set at the very low rate of 2 percent. In light of these many advantages, the tribute of 12,500 ducats paid to the Ottomans was moderate, but the Ragusans knew how to minimize even this burden. Ragusa was integrated into the Ottoman economic system. About 1580 it was a great mercantile power, the yearly turnover of its commercial activities totaling more than a million ducats, particularly in time of war, when Ragusan neutrality was advantageous.

After 1685 the *haraç* ceased to be paid annually, and Ragusa instead paid tribute in the form of information, informing the Ottomans about the plans of their enemies and providing some information of a purely formal nature. Of greater significance to Ragusa than any tribute formally due to the Ottomans were the military and economic pressures from the neighboring Ottoman officials in Bosnia, as well as from the everyday brigandage of Ottoman subjects.

The Ragusan fleet, highly active in trade, was among the largest in the Mediterranean, and the Ragusans were among the first states in the region to adopt Western innovations in banking and finance.

Ragusa's fortunes declined steeply in the 17th century, particularly after a major earthquake in 1667. Both the population and the commercial activity of Ragusa were halved and the fundamentals of success, much expanded in the "golden age" of Ottoman-Ragusan economic symbiosis, were shaken by the rise of Western merchants and the new traders from the Balkan hinterland. In the 18th century Ragusa profited from political and commercial changes in the Mediterranean, its fleet becoming very busy once again. The allegiance to the Ottoman Empire had altered dramatically from its original terms, yet because it continued to provide protection from Venice, North African pirates, and HAYDUKS, or brigands from the Ottoman hinterland of Ragusa, the formal relationship was maintained until the end of the republic on 26 May, 1806, when it was illegally occupied by Napoleonic troops who were taking over the Venetian possessions in Dalmatia from Austria. Ragusa's elite was

477

bitterly disappointed when AUSTRIA did not allow the reestablishment of the independent state after the Napoleonic episode (1806–13).

Nenad Moačanin

Further reading: Robin Harris, *Dubrovnik: A History* (London: Saqi, 2003); Bariša Krekić, *Dubrovnik: A Mediterranean Urban Society, 1300–1600* (Aldershot, U.K.: Variorum, 1997); Zdenko Zlatar, Between the Double Eagle and the Crescent: The Republic of Dubrovnik and the Origins of the Eastern Question (Boulder, Colo.: East European Monographs, 1992).

railroads   In the mid-1830s Britain began to experience a railroad boom, which soon gripped the rest of Europe and the United States. Within the next two decades, the railroad emerged as the ultimate symbol of Western industrial and economic power. Its tremendous visual impact and the public image it generated for the nations possessing it consolidated its strong association with modernity, progress, and growth.

The birth of railroads in Britain depended on the growing need to transport, cheaply and swiftly, large quantities of raw materials such as coal to large markets and industrial centers that were not served by waterways. In the sparsely populated Ottoman Empire of the early 19th century, where such large markets, industrial centers, and factories scarcely existed, this need was minimal. Wheeled vehicles were limited to a few big cities and paved roads were rare. Although relatively expensive, camels and other pack animals were still convenient and widely employed, and for centuries a network of camel CARAVANS had worked fairly well for the limited long-distance transportation of goods across and beyond the empire.

The initial incentive for railroads in the Ottoman Empire came from the government and European entrepreneurs. In the hope of becoming a railroad nation, the Ottomans, who lacked sufficient financial resources and technical know-how, put themselves in the hands of European capitalists to design, finance, and manage their railroads. Half a dozen European nations—ENGLAND, FRANCE, AUSTRIA, Belgium, Germany, Italy, and RUSSIA—vied with each other to exploit the opportunities for railroad construction created in the Ottoman Empire after the CRIMEAN WAR. Their competition should have spurred an Ottoman railroad boom, but that did not happen. Much of the contention, especially at the end of the century, was rarely genuinely entrepreneurial. Railroads often became tools for a nation's political maneuvering in Ottoman affairs. At a time of robust colonial expansion, railroads were not simply large industrial and business enterprises but also symbols of territorial influence, imperial grandeur, and power. Their investors intended that the railroads not only satisfy their financial expectations but also support the military, political, and territorial ambitions of their home countries. Furthermore, foreign railroads and other industrial undertakings were often intended to stake out the Ottoman territories with an eye to the potential future partitioning of the empire among the European powers. Russia's interest and involvement in Ottoman railroads in the northeastern part of what is now Turkey, for example, openly served its expansionist agenda and worked to keep other interlopers away.

Railroads promised political and military benefits such as the centralization of power and the ability to transfer troops rapidly to and from the far interior. When the sultans and their governments understood these capabilities, they became enthusiastic about railroads and offered generous incentives for their building. They also saw the railroad as a symbol and means of modernization. In 1867, in the first visit ever by an Ottoman sultan to western Europe, ABDÜLAZIZ (r. 1861–76) traveled almost exclusively by railroad, with Paris and London as his main stops, and became a keen railroad promoter. His infatuation with the new mode of transport helped attract railroad engineers and entrepreneurs to ISTANBUL in the 1870s. This railroad fervor did not mean, however, that the sultans and their officials were naïve about the territorial and political implications of foreign-built railroads. In fact, most Ottomans remained ambivalent about the foreign-financed railroads. Their suspicion grew as they witnessed Europeans extending their domination. Fearing that railroads might facilitate a sudden foreign invasion, ABDÜLHAMID II (r. 1876–1909), for example, was wary of connecting railroads directly with strategic ports.

On the whole, however, the Ottomans hoped to benefit from the European rivalry over the railroads, often by arranging a tactical balance among the contesting countries to Ottoman advantage. Having several major European powers build and operate lines across the empire ensured that none would be able to exercise too powerful an influence. It would also help to guarantee that a serious threat by one would be thwarted by the others, and thus Ottoman territorial integrity would be safeguarded. Railroad building in much of the late 19th century Ottoman Empire accordingly became an enterprise in which European ambitions were constantly moderated by the Ottoman effort to check the territorial and political designs they embodied. The Ottoman Empire at times came close to becoming an informal European railroad empire, coming increasingly under European financial control, especially with the formation in 1881 of the Ottoman Public Debt Administration (*see* DEBT) to oversee the collection of revenues, but through shrewd political management, it was able to rebuff the European colonial domination.

THE EUPHRATES VALLEY RAILWAY PROJECT

In the late 1830s, British politicians and entrepreneurs proposed a scheme to develop a shorter passage to India; this grand Victorian idea was to create a better passage for Britain by linking Europe to the Persian Gulf via Turkey. After the Crimean War, a company was set up in London to realize this idea, with its primary aim being to connect by rail the Mediterranean and the Persian Gulf by a route along the banks of the River EUPHRATES. Although suspicious of this huge project, the Ottoman government generally approved the scheme but wanted it to pass through ISTANBUL, the Ottoman capital—in fact, they sanctioned a similar line via Istanbul under the name of the Imperial Mecidiye-Ottoman Railway.

Although the Euphrates Valley Railway was never built, for four decades it generated public debate both inside and outside Britain. France was initially fiercely opposed to the scheme on the grounds that it would give Britain an unequal strategic position in the region. This opposition ebbed, however, when France became the sponsor of the SUEZ CANAL, opened in 1869. Thereafter, the Euphrates Valley Railway became the British rival to the largely French canal project. In 1871, the British Parliament appointed a Select Committee to investigate the whole matter, which reported in 1872 in favor of the railway. However, changing political circumstances altered Britain's interests in the railway. In 1875 Britain gained financial control of the Suez Canal, thereby effectively securing a route to India, and in 1882 Britain occupied Egypt, with the result that the building of the proposed railway lost its urgency and Britain finally gave up on the idea.

THE FIRST RAILROADS IN TURKEY

Beginning in the mid-1850s, the Ottoman government granted a large number of railroad concessions to European entrepreneurs. But the political rivalries and financial difficulties among the potential builders caused most to fail and delayed others. Buying and selling railroad concessions became a business in itself. A large amount of money was squandered. Nevertheless, by the late 19th century, several short lines had been built, linking seaports with the regions of rich agricultural production and valuable raw materials in the interior. The most prominent of these were the two lines, both built by British entrepreneurs, linking the major commercial port city of IZMIR on the Aegean Sea to its agriculturally rich and densely populated hinterland towns: the Izmir-Aydin and the Izmir-Kasaba (Turgutlu) lines.

The concession for the Izmir-Aydin line was granted in 1856 to a group of British investors. The company raised a substantial part of its capital in the Ottoman Empire; out of the initial 60,000 shares, the Ottoman government subscribed to 15,000 and Sultan ABDÜLMECID I (r. 1839–1861) himself subscribed to 500 shares as a sign of his personal support for the undertaking. The 10-mile section from Izmir to Seydiköy opened in October 1858, becoming the second railroad in the empire after the British-built Cairo-to-Alexandria railroad in the autonomous province of Egypt in 1856. However, the project did not go as planned. The projected completion date of 1860 saw only a short section of the line in operation; after further delays and additional expenditures, the 81.6-mile line to Aydin was completed in 1866.

Unlike the Izmir-Aydin line, the 58-mile line from Izmir to Kasaba was constructed more efficiently. In 1863 the Ottoman government granted a concession to Edward Price, a prominent British investor, to build this line, which was completed on time in 1866, and received praise from the Ottomans. Price's company, which operated under stricter Ottoman government control, received subsequent concessions to extend its line further inland, to Alaşehir in 1875 and to Afyon in 1890, where it later joined the Anatolian Railroads. In 1893 the company was taken over by a French-dominated syndicate. In 1912 its branch line from Manisa reached Bandırma on the Sea of Marmara.

With less generous concessions, meanwhile, the Izmir-Aydin Railway extended its line further inland, to Denizli in 1889 and Eğridir in 1912, but it was never allowed to join the Anatolian Railroads. Both these railroads proved profitable, with considerable passenger traffic and shipments of merchandise and agricultural products to carry.

Other lines connecting port cities to their hinterlands included the Mersin-Tarsus-Adana Railway (1886) on the Mediterranean, and the short line from Mudanya to Bursa on the Sea of Marmara. The 25-mile (41–km line) was "completed" in 1874 by the Ottoman government and its French contractors, but was not fully operational until Belgian entrepreneur Georges Nagelmackers took it over in 1891 and opened it to traffic in 1892 after laying it again as a narrow-gauge track) Several short lines terminating at Black Sea coastal towns such as Samsun, Eregli, Inebolu, and Trabzon were also projected before WORLD WAR I.

Most such railroads that were built did not form a network, and their engineering and machinery, which came from each builder's respective country, were sometimes incompatible. Furthermore, these companies did not have any financial or political incentives to link and extend their lines throughout the empire. A few of the lines (for example, those built by RUSSIA) used different gauges and were later either abandoned or rebuilt. But on the whole, the Ottoman system adopted a standard gauge, and thus avoided a gauge war.

RAILROADS IN THE OTTOMAN BALKANS

With the exception of the two lines built by British entrepreneurs on the Black Sea—the Küstenci (Constanta) to Boğazköy (Cernavoda) line in Romania (1860), and the Varna to Rusçuk (Ruse) line in BULGARIA (1867)—railroad building in the Ottoman Balkans followed a different pattern from that which prevailed in Anatolia, largely thanks to the financial schemes and managerial skills of Baron Maurice de Hirsch (1831–96), a German-born Austro-Hungarian financier. In 1870, Hirsch obtained from the Ottoman government an exclusive concession, originally granted to a Belgian company, to build an extensive network of railroads across the Ottoman parts of eastern Europe, with a trunk line linking Istanbul to western Europe at Doberlin on the Austrian border via EDIRNE, Sofia, Sarajevo, and Banja Luka. The concession is well-known for its extremely generous kilometric guarantee—2,500 km in all—that eventually made Hirsch immensely rich.

Hirsch's success largely depended on his effective methods of raising funds, mostly locally. By 1874, his Compagnie Générale pour l'Exploitation des Chemins de Fer de la Turquie d'Europe—which later became known as the Oriental Railways—connected Istanbul with Edirne, Plovdiv, and Burgas (Bulgaria), and connected the flourishing Ottoman city of SALONIKA with Skopje and Mitrovica (Kosovo), and its network continued to expand. Delayed considerably by uprisings and wars, the rail project finally linked Istanbul to Vienna in 1888, thus allowing rail travel to Istanbul from all Europe.

The relatively densely populated Balkans made railroads economically viable and generally profitable enterprises. But in 1890 Hirsch sold the company to a group of German banks led by the Deutsche Bank in a transaction probably influenced by Germany strategic consideration related to plans for a Berlin to Baghdad railway.

THE ORIENT EXPRESS

In 1872 the Belgian entrepreneur Georges Nagelmackers, inspired by the Pullman sleeping cars in the United States, founded the Compagnie Internationale des Wagons-Lits to provide a fast and luxurious train service with sleeping and dining cars for long-distance travel in Europe. He also had a keen interest, economic and otherwise, in Ottoman railroads.

In 1883 he started the famed Orient Express service, which at first ran from Paris to Giurgui in Romania via Munich and Vienna. A complete journey to Istanbul required further trips by train and ferry. In 1889, the Orient Express finally began to run directly to Istanbul. Its terminus there, Sirkeci Station, designed by the German architect and student of Ottoman ARCHITECTURE August Jachmund, opened in 1890 and is still in service. In 1892, the company built the now celebrated Pera Palace Hotel to serve its passengers arriving in Istanbul.

In addition to its company's advertisements, travelers and writers popularized the Orient Express and gave it a romantic glamour. Best known of the works commemorating the line are Agatha Christie's widely read mystery *Murder on the Orient Express* (1934), based on her trip in 1929, and Graham Greene's thriller *Stamboul Train* (1932), renamed *Orient Express* in its American edition. The popular fascination with the Orient Express continues to generate considerable literature today. Latter-day versions have sprung up and still run in several countries, including the American Orient Express, now called Grand Luxe Rail.

ON THE EASTERN SHORES OF THE BOSPORUS

Unlike the situation in the Balkans, building railroads from Istanbul's Asian shores to the interior of Anatolia proved to be a slow affair. The government considered this a particularly strategic part of the country and was initially reluctant to allow foreign companies to operate there. Nevertheless, in 1871, backed by French investors, construction was begun near the site of what was to become Haydarpaşa Station for a railroad eastward from that point, which was to be the western terminus of the line from Anatolia and Arabia. The line reached Gebze, 30 miles southeast of Istanbul, in 1872 and Izmit on the Sea of Marmara the following year. But financial and political problems made it impossible to extend the line until 1888, when it was taken over by the Anatolian Railroads, financed and operated by a German-led consortium.

TOWARD A RAILROAD EMPIRE

At the turn of the century, in the latter part of Abdülhamid's 33-year reign, an empire-wide railroad network began to materialize. The period was characterized by a German-Ottoman alliance that culminated in close political, economic, and military cooperation between the two powers. The sultan put his trust in Germany, the rising industrial and political power in Europe, to check the imperialist ambitions of Britain, France, and Russia. He and his officials also saw the financial, engineering, and entrepreneurial resources of Germany as essential for generating a substantial industrial and political drive that would keep the disintegrating empire united. A network of railroads across the empire would be essential to the effort. Starting in the late 1880s, Germany began to win all major new Ottoman railroad concessions and also began to take over the operation of several existing lines, while Britain's role in building and operating railroads began to shrink drastically.

Two very large railroad projects dominated this late Ottoman era: the Baghdad Railroad (1903–18) and the 800-mile (1,300-km) HEJAZ RAILROAD (1900–08). The Hejaz Railroad was a purely Ottoman undertaking connecting DAMASCUS and MEDINA. The sultan personally promoted the project and led the campaign to finance

Railroads, ca. 1914

it. Although in practical terms the railroad would only serve pilgrims going to MECCA, it was also a grand imperial undertaking, its primary purpose being the sultan's political agenda. The sultan hoped that it would facilitate Islamic unity and bring Arabia closer. The railroad also showed his Muslim subjects the sultan's determination to express his mastery over lands vital to the faith.

THE BERLIN TO BAGHDAD RAILWAY

A turning point in the history of railroads in the Ottoman Empire came in 1888 when the Société du Chemin de Fer Ottoman d'Anatolie, or Anatolian Railroads, dominated by the Deutsche Bank, not only obtained the operation rights of the strategically located Haydarpaşa-Izmit Railroad, but also won crucial concessions to extend it to Ankara and Konya in central Anatolia. The line reached Ankara in 1892 and Konya two years later, prompting discussions about planned branches to Iraq (Mesopotamia) and central Arabia. The long-dreamed-of railroad to Baghdad was becoming practicable.

Wilhelm von Pressel (1821–1902), a German railroad engineer in the Ottoman service since 1872 played

The arrival of Kaiser Wilhelm II at the railway station in Hereke, October 20, 1898 (*Historical Institute of Deutsche Bank*)

a considerable role in this project, as well in advancing the whole Ottoman-German railroad drive. The Ottoman government and the Anatolian Railroads intended to lay the track via Kayseri, Sivas, and Diyarbakır. However, because of Russian objections (the route would pass too close to its southern border, which was then in Kars), they decided to run the line via Konya, a much costlier alternative that required crossing the Taurus Mountains.

The scheme alarmed the European powers, Britain in particular, which viewed this revival of its Euphrates Valley Railway as a major threat to its interests in the region. The first visit of the German emperor, Wilhelm II, to Istanbul in 1898 gave the plan a final push. The following year, the Ottoman government granted the Deutsche Bank a concession for the 1,500-mile (2,400–km) railroad from Konya to Baghdad, plus 500 miles (800 km) of branch lines.

To reduce the financial burden of the project and ease political tension, the Deutsche Bank made overtures to Britain and France to participate in the undertaking, but failed to procure their full support. (Historians view the contest over this German-led project as a contributing factor to WORLD WAR I.)

Construction of the line began in 1903 and subsequently expanded to several sections simultaneously.

Almost 700 miles (1,100 km) of the line was completed by 1914, marking the halfway point between Konya and BASRA. Construction continued through World War I, but construction on the line was abandoned in 1918, still several hundred miles short of completion.

RAILROADS, MODERNIZATION, AND CHANGE

Like the TELEGRAPH, the railroad became a symbol of the social and industrial modernization of the empire. It also represented a new technological age, profoundly associated with Western Europe, which Ottomans aspired to join. The majestic images of trains in the mostly barren landscapes of southern Anatolia and Arabia became a source of romance and wonder. The architecture of railroad stations in particular conveyed a sense of modernism. Often designed by European architects, the stations generally blended European styles with Ottoman architectural features. The railroad station and the passenger railway car provided a form of new public space that encouraged interaction among the empire's diverse communities. Railroad works themselves, a great source of new employment, created an environment where Ottoman subjects mingled with non-Ottomans, creating an occasion for cultural exchange and learning.

The mobility facilitated by railroads stimulated travel and tourism domestically and internationally. At the same time, they allowed exploitation and smuggling, particularly of antiquities. Railroad construction itself was often motivated by its archaeological promise for its builders. Railroad companies, particularly in Anatolia and Arabia, enjoyed the exclusive rights and privileges over the lands along the routes, including that of archaeological excavations. Ottomans themselves used the new system intensively, with residents of the populous Balkan states taking a big lead, followed by those in Anatolia and Arabia. The railroads also stimulated economy and agriculture. They made it possible to transport grain to urban centers from the provinces and to export raw materials such as agricultural produce, widening the Ottoman market for manufactured European goods. At the same time, railroads increased exploitation and smuggling, particularly of antiquities.

Railroads introduced imperial grandeur and extended the political will of the sultan and his government. They enabled the rapid transfer of troops and material, which helped the central government suppress revolts and exercise control over distant provinces. In this way, railroads helped centralize political power. The railroad system also proved immensely helpful to the Ottoman war effort during World War I, enabling the Ottomans, for example, to stage an attack on the British-controlled Suez Canal in 1915. However, it is not easy to judge the extent to which the railways served the imperial ambitions of the sultan and his officials in their effort to reinforce political and territorial unity. World War I ended the empire before the full import of its new network of railroads could be realized.

After it became a republic in 1923, Turkey began to nationalize all the lines that remained within its new borders, about 2,500 miles (4,000 km) of track out of an approximate total of the 6,000 miles (10,000 km) built in Ottoman territories by 1918. But the skill and knowledge its engineers had gained made it possible for the new administration to launch a state railroad drive in the late 1920s, resulting in 2,000 miles (3,200 km) of new track by 1939.

Yakup Bektaş

Further reading: Yakup Bektas, "The Imperial Ottoman Izmir-to-Aydin Railway: The British Experimental Line in Asia Minor," in *Science, Technology and Industry in the*

The Haydarpasha railroad station and its adjacent quay, located proximate to the Kadıköy suburb of Istanbul, was the originating point for rail lines to Anatolia and the Arab provinces *(Historical Institute of Deutsche Bank)*

Ottoman World, edited by Ekmeleddin İhsanoğlu, Ahmed Djebbar, and Feza Günergun (Turnhout: Brepols, 2000), 139–152; Jonathan S. McMurray, *Distant Ties: Germany, the Ottoman Empire, and the Construction of the Baghdad Railway* (Wesport, Conn.: Praeger, 2001); Peter Mentzel, *Transportation Technology and Imperialism in the Ottoman Empire, 1800–1823* (Washington, D.C.: Society for the History of Technology and the American Historical Association, 2006).

Rashid Rida, Muhammad (b. 1865–d. 1935) *Islamic intellectual and reformer* Muhammad Rashid Rida was a student of Muhammad Abduh and a key figure in the Salafiyya movement to reform Islam at the end of the 19th and the start of the 20th century. Rashid Rida was born in a village outside the Lebanese city of Tripoli in 1865. His education was in both the traditional Quran schools and the new government schools where he studied science and learned French. Rashid Rida was unusual among the men of his generation in that he wrote a spiritual autobiography that detailed his intellectual passage through the various Islamic traditions. In the course of the journey that led him away from Sufism, he discovered the writings of ibn Taymiyya, a 14th-century Muslim theologian who called for radical reform of his society by a return to Islam as it was understood by the first generation of Muslims in the seventh century. Rashid Rida felt that there was a parallel between Islam in his age and that in ibn Taymiyya's time. That sense of spiritual decline convinced him of the need for a program of reform in the Ottoman Empire. After searching the writings of his contemporaries, Rashid Rida became convinced that the foundation for such a program lay in the writings of Abduh.

Rashid Rida went to Cairo in 1897 to be closer to Muhammad Abduh, and began publishing a periodical called *al-Manar* (The Lighthouse). The periodical became the major voice of the Salafiyya movement, and Rashid Rida would continue to publish it until his death in 1935. Rida also wrote an important biography of Abduh. Rashid Rida always considered himself to be the protector of Abduh's legacy and his chief interpreter. But political events in Egypt led him to develop an even deeper mistrust of the West than is reflected in any of the writings of his teacher.

In the aftermath of World War I, Rashid Rida was a strong opponent of the French occupation of Syria and an enthusiastic supporter of the new Saudi state in Arabia. Rather than seeing change as a benefit to Muslim societies and something that was in accordance with Muslim principles, Rashid Rida saw it simply as a necessity. Thus Rida was more reluctant than Abduh to accede to the modernization that frequently meant westerniza-

tion. Without modern technology and knowledge of science, Rida saw that the Muslim countries would remain weak, and that the West would continue to dominate them militarily and politically. Rashid Rida believed that Muslim nations should ultimately unite under one government. But in the absence of that union, Rida proposed that Muslim governments should work carefully with religious scholars so as not to enact any laws that were contrary to Islam.

Abduh viewed the prospect of reform of Muslim society with optimism, but for Rashid Rida, programs for reform were regarded with an uncertainty that bordered on pessimism. Islamic societies had to adapt to survive, he wrote, but at the same time individual Muslims had to constantly guard against the erosion of the moral order imposed by Islamic law. Abduh saw Islamic law as flexible and adaptable to change, but his student, Rashid Rida, believed that change and innovation were possible only if they were necessary for the Muslim community to survive and even then only if they did not contradict anything in the Quran.

Bruce Masters

See also Abduh, Muhammad; Salafiyya.
Further reading: Albert Hourani, *Arabic Thought in the Liberal Age, 1798–1939* (Cambridge: Cambridge University Press, 1983).

reform The idea and practice of reform existed among the members of the Ottoman elite from the 16th century. In fact, the Ottoman government underwent substantial and deliberate political and economic changes from that time until the late 18th century. From the late 18th century onward, however, Ottoman reforms began to be modeled primarily on European examples. Since the 1839 Gülhane Imperial Edict, which marked the beginning of the Tanzimat or Ottoman reform period (1839–76), the scope and goals of Ottoman reform not only became more comprehensive but also began to be self-consciously Eurocentric, relying on the notion of Western superiority.

Between the 16th and 18th centuries, a number of Ottoman bureaucrats and intellectuals, such as Mustafa Ali and Koçi Bey, argued for reform, urging for a return to the so-called "classical age" of Sultan Süleyman I (r. 1520–66), and writing about the perceived decline of the Ottoman classical system. Yet there is now an emerging consensus among scholars of Ottoman history that what several Ottoman bureaucrats considered a decline was rather a broader social and economic transformation of the empire due to external and internal pressures. Changes that occurred in the Ottoman state during this time, which included a degree of decentralization paralleled by an increasing specialization of administrative bureaucracy, was perceived as a decline, but this was due to the perspective of certain members of the Ottoman elite who had been negatively affected by these transformations.

The reforms in the taxation system, military technology, bureaucratic recruitment, and sultanic authority, especially under the leadership of sultans OSMAN II (r. 1618–22) and MURAD IV (r. 1623–40) or the KÖPRÜLÜ dynasty of grand viziers, helped maintain the Ottoman state during its many periods of crisis. With the enthronement of Sultan SELIM III (r. 1789–1807), however, the period of modern, Western reform began. Selim initiated a more systematic and ambitious program of reform, openly inquiring into and adopting European models, and focusing especially on technology, education, and the military. It was during this period that the opposition to some of the reforms by vested social and political interests, led by the JANISSARIES, led to the 1826 AUSPICIOUS INCIDENT, in which the Janissary corps was destroyed in a bloody domestic conflict under the reformist rule of Sultan MAHMUD II (r. 1808–39). With the abolition of the Janissaries, Sultan Mahmud II implemented an intense series of reforms, centralizing the government, restructuring the military and administration, establishing new educational institutions, and introducing European-style dress and head coverings.

The Gülhane Imperial Edict (Gülhane Hatt-ı Hümayun) of 1839 became a turning point in the history of Ottoman reforms in the sense that it declared European-modeled reforms as the primary goal of the bureaucracy. The Gülhane Edict initiated what is called the Tanzimat period, when a set of legal, administrative, and fiscal reforms were implemented in order to strengthen the Ottoman state and make it a member of the new European diplomatic order. There is a strong line of continuity of reform before and after the Gülhane Imperial Edict. The difference from the earlier reform efforts, however, lies in the way the Gülhane Edict was designed to enhance the central government's control by empowering the bureaucracy while changing and reshaping the relationship between the sultan and his subjects. The promised new legal system of the edict was intended to gradually reduce the arbitrary powers of the sultan and ensure full rights and equality to non-Muslims under the reinterpreted rule of Islamic law, or SHARIA. Moreover, by the Gülhane Edict, Ottoman bureaucrats declared a long-term commitment to "self-civilizing" reforms in harmony with the standards of Europe as a basis for peaceful relations with the European powers. It was hoped that the image of the Ottoman state as a reformed and civilized polity would enable the Ottomans to garner support from ENGLAND and FRANCE in the face of numerous external and internal pressures, among them Russia's attempts to influence or control Christian subjects within the Ottoman Empire and the Egyptian province's demands for autonomy.

Although the Gülhane Imperial Edict gave full legitimacy to the reformist bureaucrats and inspired further acts of reform, its implementation involved a gradual process during which the old institutions and customs were allowed to end naturally rather than being eradicated. Traditional Islamic courts or educational institutions were not abolished but were left to become the weaker part of a new two-pronged Ottoman legal and social structure. For example, while new European-style schools were established during the Tanzimat, the old madrasa schools continued to function, but with dramatic decreases in their social prestige and economic base. Meanwhile, although legal equality of all subjects was declared, different religious communities continued to have separate religious laws and privileges. More importantly, interventions by the European powers to protect the privileges of the Christian minorities prevented their assuming full political equality, since existing systems of privilege often gave them greater freedoms and powers than the empire's Muslim subjects. Thus the edict's implementation for the next three decades fell short of its intended goals.

By the end of the 19th century, reforms allowed the Ottoman state to have greater control over its own provinces with greater administrative efficiency, technological capability, and international legitimacy, even though many in Europe began to call the Ottoman state the "sick man of Europe." In fact, the Ottoman Empire managed to survive the 19th century as the only Muslim empire to also be part of the European balance of power system. The durability, diplomatic achievements, and centralized government of the Ottoman Empire were indicative of the successes of its reformist bureaucracy. Despite these reform achievements, however, the intensifying imperialist threat posed by the European powers, coupled with the inability of the Ottoman government to control its non-Muslim populations, led to a weakening of the Ottoman state in comparison to the European powers it sought to emulate. Ottoman reformists of the second half of the 19th century often complained that it was European interventions in the domestic affairs of the empire that prevented the success of their comprehensive programs to make the empire economically richer and militarily more powerful. While disillusioned by European interventions and imperialism, the Ottoman elite continued to call for more radicalized European-style reforms and the new generation of the elite, especially the YOUNG OTTOMANS and the YOUNG TURKS, called for a CONSTITUTION and other political reforms to save the Ottoman state from extinction.

While the call for reform remained strong, an intra-Ottoman conflict over the nature, vision, and scope of these European-inspired reforms also began to materialize. Symbolized by the disagreements between the Young Turks and the regime of Sultan ABDÜLHAMID II (r. 1876–1909), the Ottoman reform conflict may be understood in part by looking to the hotly debated questions of the reformers: Was the empire going to follow a British, French, or German model of reform? What were the real secrets of European progress and power? From the mid-19th century until the end of the empire in the 1920s, these questions were intensely debated among Ottoman intellectuals, leading to the proliferation of competing reform agendas, all advocating a more rapid program of change and sharper ideological justifications. Thus the ideological programs of change in the writings of NAMIK KEMAL and Ahmed Midhat Efendi led to more differentiated reform ideologies such as the Westernism of Abdullah Cevdet and the Islamism of Mehmed Akif Ersoy. The Westernist thread in the reformist tradition of the Ottoman Muslim elite continued into the early years of the Turkish Republic, which experimented with one of the most comprehensive westernization programs of the 20th century.

Cemil Aydın

Further reading: Roderick Davison, *Reform in the Ottoman Empire, 1856–1876* (Princeton, N.J.: Princeton University Press 1963); Stanford J. Shaw and Ezel K. Shaw, *History of the Ottoman Empire and Modern Turkey,* vol. 2 (Cambridge: Cambridge University Press, 1977); Suraiya Faroqhi et al., *An Economic and Social History of the Ottoman Empire,* vol. 2: 1600–1914 (Cambridge: Cambridge University Press, 1994).

reisülküttab   Also called *reis efendi*, the *reisülküttab* (literally "the head of the scribes") was the head of the chancery and record offices of the Imperial Divan or Council (Divan-ı Hümayun). However, foreign affairs of the state were also placed under his responsibility after the diplomatic success of Reisülküttab Rami Mehmed Efendi during the peace negotiations with AUSTRIA at Karlowitz in 1699. The *reisülküttab* probably existed from a much earlier period even though the first historical record regarding this position is found in the *Kanunname* or law book of Sultan MEHMED II (r. 1444–46, 1451–81), a compilation dating from the 1490s. According to this source, the *reisülküttab* was not a member of the Divan since he was considered a servant who worked under the command of the chancellor or *nişancı*. The latter was responsible for affixing the sultan's monogram or TUĞRA to documents and as such represented the chancery in the Divan.

However, the *reisülküttab* was present during Divan meetings, whispering quietly into the ear of the grand vizier if he had something to say and then returning to his place. In addition, until the end of the 6th century, the *reisülküttab* used to read petitions to the sultan and members of the Imperial Council. He was present at the Divan before the viziers came and left the meeting after them. The *reisülküttab* was not allowed to present a petition to the sultan; when promoted, he became either chancellor (*nişancı*) or chief treasurer (*defterdar*).

All the letters of appointment and award, administrative orders and codes written by clerks (*katib*) and checked by other officials, were eventually approved by the *reisülküttab* with his special imprint. Following this procedure, the letters were finally prepared with the command (*buyuruldu*) of the grand vizier and were sent to the *nişancı* if they needed the sultan's imperial seal or *tuğra*. The *reisülküttab* helped the *nişancı* in preparing the imperial edicts (*ferman*); he wrote confidential letters by himself and kept records of the sultan's decrees and treaties. All correspondence, except for military and financial affairs, was under his supervision. Moreover, it was part of his job to prepare the list of appointments (*tevcihat*).

A well-organized bureaucracy was needed to manage all these affairs. The *reisülküttab* thus supervised four offices (*kalem*): the *beylikçi, tahvil (nishan), ruus,* and *amedci.* The *beylikçi* served as the assistant to the *reisülküttab* and examined all writings prepared in various divan offices on his behalf. The *tahvil* arranged imperial rescripts of viziers, judges, and holders of *timar, ziamet,* and *has* prebends or fiefs. The *ruus* dispatched imperial commands with regard to religious institutions and foundations, clerks in state offices, and palace servants. And the *amedci* was a special scribe of the *reisülküttab*, who participated in meetings with foreign state representatives, took records of conversations, carried out correspondence with foreign state representatives, and collected monies for the *reisülküttab*.

The *reisülküttab* gained some importance after the 18th century, becoming clerk to the grand vizier and no longer working under the *nişancı*. This change occurred because state affairs were gradually transferred from the Imperial Council to the grand vizier's office (*babıali*). The clerks of the grand vizier naturally gained in importance and a special significance was attached to the *reisülküttab*, while the *nişancı* lost importance. In addition, the dramatic increase in foreign relations in this period made the *reisülküttab* position more important than in previous periods. At the same time, civil bureaucracy gained more gravity in state administration during the time of SELIM III (r. 1789–1807). In 1836, during the reign of MAHMUD II (r. 1808–39), an administrative decree transformed the position of *reisülküttab* into the position of minister of foreign affairs that fulfilled the same bureaucratic duties but with a new emphasis on foreign affairs.

Ali Akyıldız

Further reading: Carter V. Findley, "Origins of the Ottoman Foreign Ministry." *IJMES* 1, no. 1 (January 1970): 335–356; Carter. V. Findley, *Bureaucratic Reform in the Ottoman Empire: The Sublime Porte, 1789–1922* (Princeton, N.J.: Princeton University Press, 1980).

relazione The Italian word *relazione* means "report," and refers in particular to a report delivered by a public official of the Republic of VENICE. The origins of the Venetian *relazioni* may be found in the 13th century when, in 1268, Venetian ambassadors sent to foreign courts were ordered to deliver a report of their mission to Venice's head of state (doge) and his counselors. In 1425, another decree established that every diplomatic envoy had to deliver both a speech and a written text about his mission. In 1524, it ordered that every Venetian public official who had been sent either abroad or to subject lands had to compile a report.

The *relazioni* were eagerly sought by contemporaries interested in far-off countries. Thus they also became a genre of Venetian literature. Some officials even wrote two reports, one for the state about political affairs, and another for a larger public about curiosities, the life of high-ranking persons, and other matters of more general interest. The reports usually follow a precise scheme of composition. In the case of *relazioni* regarding the Ottoman Empire they start with introductory remarks, followed by information concerning the sultan and his family, the grand vizier and other viziers, the Ottoman bureaucracy, the army, the navy, and the staff of the Venetian embassy. Manuscripts of the *relazioni* can be found not only in the Venetian State Archives but also in other libraries and archives; the bulk of them were written between the 16th and 18th centuries. The *relazioni* give information about lands subject to the Venetian Republic (including Veneto, Friuli, Dalmatia, and the Greek islands) as well as about foreign countries.

At the beginning of the 19th century the *relazioni* became a relevant source for scholars interested in the history of many European countries. The Austrian historian and Orientalist Joseph von Hammer-Purgstall, for instance, used them to write his seminal history of the Ottoman Empire, *Geschichte des osmanischen Reiches* (History of the Ottoman Empire), complementing the *relazioni* with Ottoman chronicles and other Venetian papers.

Most of the *relazioni* were edited and published during the 19th century. The papers produced by Venetian officials sent to Istanbul were published at that time and reprinted in 1996 with additional reports. Other reports about the Ottoman lands were written by Venetian consuls in EGYPT and ALEPPO. The *relazioni* are still important for Ottomanists, even if many other sources are now available. They contain first-hand information about important events and gossip, which circulated but could not be written in Ottoman official documents.

Maria Pia Pedani

Further reading: Eric R. Dursteler, *Venetians in Constantinople: Nation, Identity, and Coexistence in the Early Modern Mediterranean* (Baltimore, Md.: Johns Hopkins University Press, 2006); Maria Pia Pedani, "Elenco degli inviati diplomatici veneziani presso i sovrani ottomani." *Electronic Journal for Oriental Studies,* 5, no. 4 (2002): 1–54; Maria Pia Pedani, *Reports of Venetian Consuls in Alexandria* (Cairo: IFAO, in press); Lucette Valensi, *The Birth of the Despot: Venice and the Sublime Porte,* trans. Arthur Denner (Ithaca: Cornell University Press, 1987).

religion *See* ARMENIAN APOSTOLIC CHURCH; BULGARIAN ORTHODOX CHURCH; BEKTAŞI ORDER; CONVERSION; COPTS; *DAR AL-HARB*; *DAR AL-ISLAM*; DRUZES; FATWA; GREEK ORTHODOX CHURCH; GREGORIAN ORTHODOX CHURCH; JACOBITES; JEWS; KARAITES; MARONITES; MELKITE CATHOLICS; MEVLEVI ORDER; *MILLET*; MISSIONARIES; NAQSHBANDIYYA ORDER; NESTORIANS; RIFAIYYA ORDER; SERBIAN ORTHODOX CHURCH; SHARIA; SHIA ISLAM; SUFISM; SUNNI ISLAM; UNIATES.

revolutionary press Although newspapers and magazines (both called "gazettes") were published in the Ottoman empire in the 19th century, it was not until 1908 that a press that could truly be called "revolutionary" due to its scope, critical vehemence, and political imagination, appeared in the Ottoman capital, ISTANBUL.

The history of the revolutionary press in the Ottoman Empire is closely bound with the movement toward constitutional government which, as elsewhere, was neither simple nor continuous. There were two constitutional revolutions in the empire, one in 1876 and one in 1908, marking the beginning and end of the long reign of Sultan ABDÜLHAMID II (r. 1876–1909). Each revolutionary movement was accompanied by activist writings in the press, both within the empire and abroad. It was the second revolution, however, that established a constitutional regime that endured until the empire was dismembered in the aftermath of WORLD WAR I.

The revolutionary press emerged in the context of a relatively bloodless political revolution and in an environment of heightened foreign intervention in Ottoman lands and affairs. This revolution began in July 1908, when Sultan Abdülhamid II was forced, under military pressure, to reinstate the constitution that had been promulgated in 1876 but that he had suspended shortly thereafter. In December of that same year Ahmed Rıza, the editor of *Meşveret* (Consultation), an expatriate newspaper of the YOUNG TURKS, was elected chairman of the newly constituted Chamber of Deputies. His election demonstrates the often intimate connection between the press (which was still more politically than commercially oriented) and opposition politics. The new parliamentary regime, which left considerable power in the hands of the sultan, was faced with addressing the dismal financial situation of the empire and the grave threats posed by European powers such as AUSTRIA (which had annexed Bosnia and Herzegovina outright), ENGLAND (which had occupied EGYPT since 1882), and RUSSIA (a chronic aggressor on the empire's northern frontiers). Internal affairs were further complicated when, in April 1909, Abdülhamid was implicated in an attempted counter-revolution and was deposed. How the empire would survive such threats constituted, not surprisingly, a primary theme in the revolutionary press, which highlighted the menace of European imperialism and pondered the proper role of monarchy in a constitutional regime.

The empire had a well-established press before the 1908 revolution, including an Ottoman-language official gazette, *Takvim-i Vekayi*, dating to 1831. In ISTANBUL and elsewhere in the empire, multiple newspapers were also published in a variety of languages including Greek, Armenian, Arabic, and French. The government, however, made vigorous efforts at control and censorship of the press, banning certain words and subjects, shutting down gazettes that became too outspoken, and confis-cating foreign publications. Under the Press Law, first implemented in 1865, all publications required government authorization. Despite such efforts at censorship, publishers were resilient, reintroducing newspapers that had been shut down, cleverly circumventing the censors, and smuggling in forbidden foreign literature. Overall, however, the Ottoman press, like other presses of the time, was distinctly limited by government restrictions. What made the press of 1908–09 "revolutionary" was that these restrictions were temporarily suspended in the open-ended political climate brought on by the constitutional revolution. The press thereby gained the potential to take an active role in defining a new political and social order. There was an immediate boom in Ottoman serial publication, with at least 240 new gazettes published in Istanbul alone in the 12 months beginning July 1908. POLITICAL SATIRE flourished. It seemed that writers, editors, and cartoonists were rushing to print everything they had been afraid or unable to print before. This freedom of the press did not last long. Once the new regime, with the COMMITTEE FOR UNION AND PROGRESS (CUP) in charge, had established itself, censorship was reintroduced, particularly in the aftermath of the

1909 counterrevolution. Nonetheless, the revolutionary press of 1908–09 expressed an unprecedented range of Ottoman voices; it illustrated the complexity of political, social, and cultural thought in the empire; and it set the tone for a new type of Ottoman press, one that was more ambitious, more wide-ranging, and more critical.

The press of this revolutionary era included a variety of literary and artistic forms expressing a wide range of viewpoints. Press output ranged from broadsheets through newspapers of four to 16 pages in length to illustrated magazines and yearbooks that carried a hefty price. Newspapers and magazines were sold to lists of subscribers, hawked in the streets, and delivered to commercial vendors such as bookshops. Reading rooms and COFFEEHOUSES also provided customers with newspapers to peruse while on the premises. Some newspapers were organs of specific political parties such as the CUP. Others represented the views of individuals, occupational groups, or religious communities. On any given day in the months after the 1908 revolution, consumers might read the daily paper *Ikdam* (Effort), which appeared from 1894 to 1928; the new satirical gazette *Boşboğaz* (Indiscreet); the short-lived women's gazette *Demet* (Bouquet); or the expensive illustrated journal *Kalem* (Pen), which was published in Ottoman and French and included articles on politics, culture, and society. There was no firm line between politics and the press; thus many publishers, editors, and writers were also government officials under the old or new regime, or both. The typical editor was politically active, more or less financially comfortable, and was often a member of the literati in his own right. Women participated in the writing, illustrating, and production of some Ottoman gazettes (and thus in the production of newspapers and magazines), but the Ottoman press was overwhelmingly male.

Some observers celebrated the newfound freedom of the press, but others were scandalized by what they considered license rather than freedom. The content and tone of certain articles or editorials could evoke strong feelings and even provoke violence as political positions were advanced, grievances were aired, insults were traded, and moral conventions were challenged. Fear of the power of the press led to the destruction of the offices of the pro-Unionist gazettes *Tanin* and *Şurayı Ümmet* during the abortive counterrevolution of April 13, 1909. Kıbrıslı Derviş Vahdeti, editor of the Islamic daily *Volkan* (Volcano), an active critic of the new parliamentary regime, was implicated in the counterrevolution. His paper was shut down and he was imprisoned and executed. Hasan Fehmi, editor of *Serbesti* (Freedom) and an outspoken critic of the CUP, was assassinated by an unknown assailant.

More commonly, the press engaged in an ongoing set of dialogues, hotly debating the social issues of the moment and publicly airing political concerns without bringing their battles to the point of physical violence. Such issues included the nature of the new regime, the condition of the Ottoman military, the obligations of citizens, imitation of the West, proper roles and dress for the modern female, and the adoption of new technologies. In general, the revolutionary press gave a wider voice to the literate Ottoman public. Readers expressed their views in letters columns, participated in contests sponsored by the various gazettes, and gained an increasing awareness of their fellow readers through ads, coupons, and promotions. The revolutionary era thus sparked the demand for a more wide-ranging, inclusive, and comprehensive coverage of Ottoman affairs, both domestic and foreign.

Palmira Brummett

Further reading: Feroz Ahmad, *The Making of Modern Turkey* (London: Routledge, 1993); Palmira Brummett, *Image and Imperialism in the Ottoman Revolutionary Press, 1908–1911* (Albany: State University of New York Press, 2000); Elizabeth Frierson, "Mirrors out, Mirrors in: Domestication and Rejection of the Foreign in Late-Ottoman Women's Magazines," in *Women, Patronage, and Self-Representation in Islamic Societies*, edited by D. Fairchild Ruggles (Albany: State University of New York Press, 2000), 177–201; Şükrü Hanioğlu, *Preparation for a Revolution: The Young Turks, 1902–1908* (Oxford: Oxford University Press, 2001); Bernard Lewis, *The Emergence of Modern Turkey*, 3rd ed. (Oxford: Oxford University Press, 2001).

Rhodes (Rodhos, Rhodos, Rhodus, Rodos) Rhodes is the easternmost of the major Aegean islands that are a part of present-day Greece. As such, Rhodes has always been a link between the Greek world and the Near East. The Ottoman capture of Rhodes in 1522 was a logical extension of Ottoman victories in Syria in 1516 and Egypt in 1517. By gaining control of the southern shores of the Mediterranean, the empire went a long way toward the re-creation of the old imperial unity of the eastern Mediterranean. As the 16th century began, Ottoman conquests had significantly shifted the political geography of the region. For the first time since the seventh century, Constantinople, now ISTANBUL, ruled over the Arab world, but this accomplishment brought with it the new challenge of guaranteeing the sea passage between the capital and the new provinces, a challenge made increasingly difficult by the belligerent crusading order of the KNIGHTS OF ST. JOHN, installed on the island of Rhodes since the early 14th century. Standing in the way of Ottoman security in the Aegean, the Knights were also an embarrassment for Sultan SÜLEYMAN I (r. 1520–66), given their militant anti-Islamic rhetoric, their naval prowess, and their penchant for enslaving Muslims. Determined to seize the island, a fleet of 300 Ottoman ships left Istanbul in May 1522, arriving in front of the walls of Rhodes the following month. The city of Rhodes boasted some of the strongest fortifications in the eastern Mediterranean and the siege dragged on for five months before the Grand Master of the Order of the Knights of St. John decided to surrender.

Ottoman chroniclers took great pride in the fact that the island was now an Ottoman possession. The long and violent history of the Knights, as well as the strength and even the beauty of the city's walls, had made Rhodes famous far beyond its rather modest size. Little is known of the island's history under the Ottomans, particularly in the earlier centuries after 1552. We do know, however, that it was a routine stop for ships sailing between Istanbul and ALEXANDRIA, thus playing a vital role in linking the northern and southern shores of the eastern Mediterranean.

Molly Greene

Rifaiyya Order The Rifaiyya Order of SUFISM was one of the more unconventional Sufi orders. Western travelers to the Ottoman Empire dubbed the order the "howling dervishes" due to the loud and boisterous *dhikr*, or prayer ceremony, they employed. Members of the Rifaiyya Order further drew attention with public displays of eating glass, dancing with snakes, and passing skewers through their cheeks. The order claimed Ahmad al-Rafai, a mystic who lived in IRAQ in the 12th century, as its founder. The order was very popular in EGYPT in the MAMLUK EMPIRE period, and after the Ottoman conquest of Egypt in 1517, Rifaiyya disciples spread the order to Anatolia. In the modern period, the Rifaiyya Order's practices included the public act of *dawsa*, or "trampling," wherein the sheikh of the order would ride his horse over the prostrate bodies of his followers. Such practices proved an embarrassment to modernizers in Egypt. MUHAMMAD ABDUH declared the order's practices un-Islamic and KHEDIVE TAWFIQ banned the order altogether. The Rifaiyya fared better in the Ottoman Empire, as ABU AL-HUDA AL-SAYYADI, the Syrian spiritual adviser to Sultan ABDÜLHAMID II (r. 1876–1909), was a member of the order and provided it with official patronage.

Bruce Masters

See also SUFISM.

Russia Russians, one of three Eastern Slavic peoples, emerged as a distinct ethnic group with the rise of the principality of Muscovy in the early 14th century, which subsequently evolved into the Russian Empire. By the 18th century, Russia had replaced Habsburg AUSTRIA as the main enemy of the Ottomans in central and southeastern Europe. Russia's expansion posed a major threat to the Ottoman Empire during the last three centuries of its existence and the 10 wars fought between the two empires had significant consequences for the history of the emerging nations in southeastern Europe.

EARLY ENCOUNTERS AND THE PROBLEM OF TERMINOLOGY

Russian-Ottoman relations at their earliest stages are difficult to follow because the historical use of the name Rus', commonly associated with Russians, changed over time. The term Rus' came to the Ottoman language from Arabic, where it initially referred both to the state of Rus', with its capital city of Kiev, and to its Slavic population. This term remained in use to designate all the Eastern Slavs and their lands despite the partitioning of Kievan Rus' in the aftermath of the Mongol conquest of 1237–41. Closer interactions with Eastern Slavs, most of whom were brought into the Ottoman realms as SLAVES or entered as MERCHANTS, made the Ottomans aware of various regional and political subdivisions among the Eastern Slavs and how they identified themselves. Those Eastern Slavs (ancestors of today's Ukrainians and Belarusians), who were incorporated into the Lithuanian, Polish, and Hungarian states and formed ethnic and religious minorities there, retained their old ethnic name of *Rus'* The Eastern Slavs in the northern and eastern parts of Rus', which became subject to the Mongol state of the Golden Horde, strengthened their regional identities and came to identify themselves by the name of their capital cities, such as Moscow (Moskvich), Tver (Tverich), and Novgorod (Novgorodets). Thus the term *Moskov* or *Moskovlu*, the Ottoman term for *Moskvich*, referred to the subjects of the prince of Moscow, and was one name for Russians. Even in official correspondence, the Ottoman chancellery addressed the Russian czars as "king/czar of Muscovy" (Moskov *kıralı/çarı*), disregarding the latter's claims (since the end of the 15th century) to all the territory of Rus'. Only when a separate name for UKRAINE (Turkish: Ukrayna, sometimes Ukranya) found acceptance at the end of the 17th century did it become possible for the Ottomans to use the name Rus' for Muscovy without confusion. However it was only after the renunciation of their claims to Ukraine in 1741 that the Ottomans agreed to recognize Elizabeth I (r. 1741–61) by the title "Empress of All the Russias" (*tamamen* Rusiya *imparatoriça*). *Rus'* became the term for Russian ethnicity later in the 18th century.

In view of this ambiguity in terminology, there is no reliable evidence of direct commercial relations between Russians and Ottomans prior to the end of the 15th century. While sources connect the Anatolian SELJUKS with Rus' merchants selling furs and slaves in the Crimea, it is uncertain which people the term refers to. The Seljuk sultan Kaykubad I (r. 1220–37) blamed the Rus' for the mistreatment of his merchants in the Crimean port of Soudak and sent out a naval expedition that conquered the city around the year 1223. In 1238 the Rus' were reported to have fled from the Mongols to Sinop (present-day Turkey), where a Seljuk ruler confiscated their property (presumably slaves) recovered from one ship, which was sinking by the shore due to a storm. In all probability these Rus' merchants represented Kiev, because as late as the 16th century all imports coming to eastern Europe from the Balkans and Anatolia through the Crimean ports passed through Kiev. Like any other branch of Muscovy's foreign trade, commerce with the BLACK SEA area was controlled by foreign merchants. They made up Moscow's richest merchant guild, called the Soudak merchants (*surozhane*).

MUSCOVY AND THE OTTOMANS

Up until the end of the 17th century the most important feature in the relations between the principality of Muscovy and the Ottoman Empire, which did not share a border, was long-distance trade. The exchange of products was important for both sides and dictated political behavior toward one another. In the mid-15th century the Ottomans grew to become the world's largest consumer of traditional east European commodities such as furs, birds of prey, and walrus tusks. Their interest in securing these commodities certainly motivated their conquest of the northern coast of the Black Sea, which included the port cities CAFFA, Soudak, AZAK (1475), Kilia, Akkerman (1484), and Özi (1538). At the same time, access to Ottoman silk and cash, traded in return for furs, paid for Muscovy's spectacular expansion after 1460. Muscovite princes gained control of this source of revenue by offering gifts and granting privileges to the international merchants, while prohibiting passage to neighboring states.

Diplomatic contacts, initiated in 1492 with the first Muscovite embassy in Constantinople, also focused on settling commercial disputes, in addition to carrying out the shopping orders of the two sovereigns and conducting merchant caravans into each other's country. Although Muscovy was interested in a political alliance with the Ottoman Empire, the Ottomans preferred to remain neutral in the area. They even left diplomatic relations with Muscovy, which included the exaction of an annual tribute, in the hands of the khans of the CRIMEAN TATARS, a Turkic-speaking Mongol group that had founded a khanate in the Crimea in the first half of the 15th century and that became Ottoman vassals in 1475. Muscovite ambassadors on their way to the Ottoman capital Constantinople were obliged to call on the capital of the Crimean Khanate. At the same time, the Ottomans refused to take responsibility for Crimean military expeditions against Muscovy, even though Ottoman troops occasionally took part in them. Such aloofness helped them avoid the political consequences of the slave hunt, an invariable feature of Crimean warfare and a much-appreciated source of slaves for the Ottomans. Tatar raiders procured about 100,000 Muscovite captives during the first half of the 17th century.

Yet relegating relations with Muscovy to the Crimean khans proved risky in the long run. In 1551 Khan Sahib Giray was deposed when he attempted to restore the rule of the Golden Horde, leading the Muscovite czar, Ivan IV (r. 1533–84), to conquer the Kazan Khanate (1552), an independent Tatar khanatewith its capital in Kazan on the Volga River (in the present-day Tatarstan Republic) and a powerful ally of the Crimean Khanate at that time.He subsequently subjugated Astrakhan (1556) and the Caucasus (1560). Ottoman sultan Selim II (r. 1566–74) attempted to conquer Astrakhan in 1569, but failed.

Muscovy at this stage proved more responsive to Ottoman customs and readily emulated court ceremonies, chancellery elements (including the Ottoman sultans' monogram, the *tuğra*), and system of government. At the same time, Orthodox clergy and artists who frequented Muscovy from the Ottoman realms in expectation of generous alms or royal patronage spread exaggerated stories about Christians' suffering at the hands of the Ottomans. They inspired the czars who believed that Muscovy's mission was to redeem Constantinople from the Muslims. The reality, however, did not favor the realization of such plans, and Czar Mikhail Feodorovich (r. 1613–1645) wisely decided not to take the Ottoman fortress Azak, offered by the Don Cossacks, who held it in 1637–42.

MUSCOVY, UKRAINE, AND THE OTTOMANS

The Cossack uprising in Ukraine against POLAND that began in 1648 presented Muscovy with a chance to get a foothold on the Ottoman northern frontier, along with a sizeable Cossack army experienced in steppe warfare. In 1654 Ukraine accepted a union with Muscovy in which the Cossacks would continue to exercise self-government. This move by Czar Alexis provoked a war with the Poles (1654–67) and the Crimean Tatars, as well as a civil war in Ukraine. The Ottomans were also dragged into this civil war by taking some Cossack factions under their protection, and they consequently occupied a part of Ukraine in 1672. Such conditions led the two powers into their first direct conflict, which broke out in 1676 over the possession of the Cossack capital, Chyhyryn. After the first aborted siege in 1677, the Ottomans took the city the following year, but soon evacuated. The peace talks of Bakhchisaray in 1681 resulted in an agreement that called for the creation of a broad buffer zone between Ottoman and Muscovite possessions in Ukraine through the depopulation of the territory on the right bank of the Dnieper River.

PETER THE GREAT AND THE OTTOMANS

The successes of the Holy League (Austria, Venice, the Papacy, and Poland) forces against the Ottomans in HUNGARY in the war of 1684–99 enticed Muscovy to join its ranks in 1686. Initially, though, its army, accompanied by Cossacks of Ukraine, unsuccessfully attempted to break into the Crimea on two occasions (1687, 1689). The campaigns of 1695 and 1696, this time led by Czar Peter I the Great (r. 1682–1725, reigned jointly with his half-brother through 1696 and alone thereafter) and Cossack Hetman Ivan Mazepa, ended with the conquest of Azak and several fortresses on the lower Dnieper. The peace agreement concluded in Constantinople in 1700 achieved all of the traditional strategic goals of Muscovy as it ended the tribute from Russia to the Crimean khans, established a Russian ambassador in Constantinople, and obligated the Porte to restrain Crimean khans from raids into Russian territory. Yet the annexation of Azak steered a new course in Russian-Ottoman relations. Indeed, by the time of this peace, Peter formulated his strategic goals against the Ottoman Empire. Excited by his military success and imbued with mercantilist ideas, he wanted to curb both the Tatars and Cossacks by surrounding them with fortresses, and he planned to force the Ottomans to open Constantinople and the Straits for trade and free passage to the Mediterranean with the help of a powerful navy. This became the blueprint for Russian policy in the Black Sea from that time forward. Ottoman-Russian relations entered a new phase whose main feature was Russian military expansion.

The war of 1710–13 is memorable for the Pruth campaign (1711). It was the first Russian attack inspired by the illusory hopes of an Orthodox Christian rebellion against the Ottomans. This time, however, Czar Peter did not have Ukrainian Cossacks on his side. He was surrounded and outnumbered in MOLDAVIA by Ottoman and Crimean troops and he therefore agreed to evacuate Azak and Poland. However, this turned out to be the last Ottoman success before the Russian advance.

RUSSO-OTTOMAN WARS

The Russo-Ottoman War of 1735–39, during which Russia allied with Austria, is usually ignored because of its lack of territorial exchanges, except for the recovery of Azak by the Russians. However, during this war a modernized Russian army, together with their Cossack allies, invaded the Crimea twice and proved to be effective against the Ottomans, both in taking fortresses and in the open field. Moreover, the Treaty of Belgrade, concluded in 1739 between the Holy Roman Empire and the Ottoman Empire, opened the Black Sea to Russian commercial activity. Russian trade with the Ottomans was primarily conducted through Greek merchants based either in Ottoman territory or in Ukraine. Extending a privilege to Russia that had been granted to the

Ukrainian Cossacks in the previous century (1648), Russian subjects were now allowed to trade in the Black Sea using Ottoman ships.

During the RUSSO-OTTOMAN WAR OF 1768–74, the Russians occupied the whole Crimean peninsula, including the Ottoman province, or *eyalet*, of Caffa on its southern shore in 1771, and won many decisive victories in Moldavia, WALLACHIA, and beyond the DANUBE RIVER. The Russian navy, sent from the Baltic Sea to the Greek archipelago, burned the Ottoman navy at Çeşme (1770), although this spectacular operation failed to stir a much anticipated Greek rebellion. With the TREATY OF KÜÇÜK KAYNARCA, Muscovy, known by now as the Russian Empire, received several ports and fortresses on the shores of the Black Sea along with the right of navigation in the Black Sea and free passage for merchant ships through the straits of the Bosporus and Dardanelles. The Crimean Khanate gained independence from the Porte.

This unprecedented success boosted Russian confidence. Empress Catherine II (r. 1762–96) consequently disbanded the Cossack host in Ukraine (1775) and ended Ukraine autonomy (1786); in 1783 she annexed the Crimean Khanate and established a protectorate in Georgia. A Russian navy was built and Sevastopol in southwestern Crimea was chosen as its base. All of these actions provoked the wars of 1787–91 and 1806–12 (*see* RUSSO-OTTOMAN WARS), which only resulted in more Russian victories over the Ottomans. Russia annexed Bessarabia (the eastern part of Moldavia) and the remaining parts of the Pontic Steppe.

In the 19th century the Russian Empire reoriented its territorial expansion toward the Caucasus and continued to support the nationalist movements of the Slavic and Greek coreligionists in the Balkans. The Russo-Ottoman wars of 1828–29 and 1877–78 were instrumental in creating the independent states in the Balkans. However, Russian influence in this area alarmed Britain (*see* ENGLAND) and FRANCE, and caused their joint military intervention in the Ottoman war against Russia in 1853–56 (the CRIMEAN WAR). Britain and Austria-Hungary arranged the revision of the Treaty of San Stefano that had concluded the 1877–78 war and that had envisioned an independent Greater Bulgaria under the influence of Russia. The revised Treaty of Berlin, signed on August 24, 1878, reduced the size of the Bulgarian territory to a third.

Due to intense military competition between the 17th and 20th centuries, the Russian and the Ottoman empires are justly known as enemies. Only a few treaties of alliance were concluded between Russia and the Ottomans (1799, 1805, 1833) and they were all prompted by dangerous circumstances for the Porte and were short-lived. The Russian efforts to bring the Straits under their control culminated in a secret agreement with Britain and France (1915) that envisioned the Russian annexa-

tion of the Straits after the victory of the Allied Powers (Britain, France, and Russia) in WORLD WAR I. However illogical this plan may have seemed, it remained on paper, even as both empires collapsed.

Oleksandr Halenko

Further reading: William McNeill, *Europe's Steppe Frontier, 1500–1800* (Chicago: University of Chicago Press, 1964); Alan Fisher, *The Russian Annexation of the Crimea, 1772–1783* (Cambridge: Cambridge University Press, 1970); *Mubadele: An Ottoman-Russian Exchange of Ambassadors*, annotated and translated by Norman Itzkowitz and Max Mote (Chicago: University of Chicago Press, 1970); Virginia H. Aksan, *An Ottoman Statesman in War and Peace: Ahmed Resmi Efendi, 1700–1783* (Leiden: Brill, 1995).

Russo-Ottoman War of 1768–1774   Although there were several military encounters between the Ottoman Empire and Muscovy, as RUSSIA was known until the late 18th century, the war that was fought between 1768 and 1774 significantly changed the balance of power in the Middle East in favor of Russia and testified to the growing Ottoman weakness in the international arena. The Ottoman Empire was concerned with the growing Russian hegemony in the Polish-Lithuanian Commonwealth (*see* POLAND). When a Russian army detachment entered Ottoman territory in pursuit of retreating Polish forces, the Ottomans found the necessary pretext to declare war on Russia without any military preparation (September 1768). Two decisive incidents in the course of the war were the naval disaster of Çeşme (Chesme), a natural harbor south of IZMIR, on July 6, 1770, and the Battle of Kartal (Kagul) on August 1, 1770.

In the summer of 1770, with the support of ENGLAND, the Russian Baltic fleet, under the command of Aleksi Orlov, appeared in the Aegean Sea. Despite the Ottoman victory in the first encounter between the two navies early in July 1770, a confusing maneuver by an Ottoman naval detachment resulted in the accidental retreat of the whole Ottoman navy into the harbor of Çeşme where, on the night of July 6, the Russians set fire to the collected Ottoman fleet, killing 9,000 Ottoman sailors and destroying 23 Ottoman ships.

A few weeks later, the Ottoman army hastily crossed the DANUBE on barges, determined to retake the fortress of Hotin (Khotin). In the resulting pitched battle, the Russian army, under the command of Field Marshal Rumiantsev, made excellent strategic use of light maneuverable field cannons and the newly invented bayonet attack, both of which had come into use during the recently concluded Seven Years War. Employing these new military developments, Rumiantsev easily defeated the Ottoman army, which was largely composed of irregular and undisciplined troops who had been pressed into military service. A total rout followed when, in the absence of a pontoon bridge, the retreating Ottoman field army was caught between the Russian forces and the Danube. One of the greatest military humiliations in Ottoman history, this battle cost the Ottomans tens of thousands of casualties. In fact, it was this defeat that spurred the Ottomans into making a series of Ottoman military REFORMS on the Western model, leading to the abolition of the unmanageable JANISSARIES in the AUSPICIOUS INCIDENT of 1826. By the year 1772, Russia occupied the western banks of the Danube.

Because the Ottoman grand vizier and commander in chief Muhsinzade Mehmed Pasha and the Russian field marshal Rumiantsev were inclined to make peace, the warring parties declared the armistice of Yergöğü (Giurgieu), which lasted through April and May of 1772. Peace talks broke down, however, in June 1772, when the Russian navy bombarded BEIRUT, thus aiding Zahir Ömer in SYRIA in his uprising against the Ottoman Empire. At the same time, the Russians carried out secret negotiations with the rebellious Egyptian Mamluk Buludkapan Ali Bey. By July, a truce had been declared between the two naval forces in the Mediterranean and peace talks at Fokşani in August 1772 opened with the Russian refusal of the mediation of the Habsburg ambassador Franz Thugut and the Prussian ambassador Johann Christoph Zegelin. The Russian delegates insisted on the independence of the Crimea, which had been under virtual Russian occupation since the beginning of the war, and demanded that the Ottomans cede the fortresses of Yenikale and Kerç in the Crimea to Russia. In addition to war indemnity, the Russians also demanded the granting of freedom of navigation and commercial privileges in the BLACK SEA and the Mediterranean.

The Sublime Porte was adamantly opposed to Russian control of the Crimea and its fortresses. However, with the intervention of Rumiantsev and Mehmed Pasha, the talks between the two powers continued in November 1772. The two sides eventually agreed on 10 articles, the most important of which were the granting of a general amnesty in the Romanian principalities, the cancellation of the Russo-Ottoman Treaty of Belgrade (a peace agreement signed in 1739 in which AUSTRIA, in alliance with Russia, had given up control of northern SERBIA and had given territory in WALLACHIA and Bosnia to the Ottomans), and the return of the CAUCASUS fortresses to the Ottomans. As for the Crimea, the Russian delegates complied with an Ottoman demand concerning the election of the Crimean khan by the Tatars and mentioning the name of the Ottoman sultan in Friday ceremonies, but rejected both the return of the Crimean fortresses to the Ottomans and dropping the matter of war indemnity.

This accord was not accepted by St. Petersburg, which instead put forward seven demands of its own:

The Crimea was to be independent under the protection of Russia; MOLDAVIA was to be granted full autonomy; the Sublime Porte was to grant freedom of navigation and commercial privileges to Russia in the Black Sea and the Mediterranean; Russia was to establish a permanent embassy in Istanbul; and the Sublime Porte was to recognize the official title of Empress/Emperor of all the Russias. Aware of their military weakness, the Ottoman military headquarters accepted these demands, but Istanbul, pressured by the ULEMA, or religious establishment, insisted on resuming the war. After the armistice ended in March 1773, the Ottomans achieved significant victories against the Russian army that besieged Silistra and Varna, while the Russian fleet continued to block maritime trade in the archipelago, to the detriment of Istanbul.

The last phase of the war began after the Ottoman rejection of the peace offer by Field Marshal Rumiantsev, who demanded that the Bucharest talks should constitute the frame of reference for any peace treaty. Acceding to the throne after the death of his brother on January 21, 1774, ABDÜLHAMID I (r. 1774–89) was unwilling to conclude peace before rescuing HIRSOVA, near Constanta, and the Romanian principalities. Russia had suffered overwhelming losses from a war-related outbreak of PLAGUE (which resulted in approximately 150,000 deaths), and these losses, combined with the exhaustion of the Russian Empire's financial resources, led to the Pugachev Revolt in the Russian countryside in 1773, the single most important COSSACK revolt in history. Under these pressing circumstances Rumiantsev was determined to launch a final offensive across the Danube to force peace on the Ottomans in the spring 1774. The defeat of the Ottoman army at Kozluca (Kozludja) on June 25, 1774 turned into a general rout that spread to the Ottoman military headquarters at Şumnu (Shumen/Shumla) (July 1, 1774) as a result of which Grand Vizier Muhsinzade Mehmed Pasha had to sue for peace on Russian terms.

The final outcome was the TREATY OF KÜÇÜK KAYNARCA, signed on July 21, 1774, with disastrous consequences for both the Ottomans and the Tatars. After 60 years of economic growth and reputable international standing, the long war and difficult peace with Russia now left the Ottoman Empire politically unstable, with an exhausted economy, an uncontrolled movement of decentralization in the provinces, and a devastating loss of face in the international arena.

Kahraman Şakul

Further reading: Virginia Aksan, *An Ottoman Statesman in War and Peace Ahmed Resmi Efendi, 1700–1783* (Leiden: Brill, 1995), 102-168; Virginia Aksan, *Ottoman Wars 1700-1870: An Empire Besieged* (Harlow, England: Longman/Pearson, 2007), 138-160; Caroline Finkel, *Osman's Dream: The Story of the Ottoman Empire, 1300–1923* (London: John

Murray, 2005), 372–412; Ekmeleddin Ihsanoğlu, ed., *History of the Ottoman State, Society & Civilisation*, vol. 1 (Istanbul: IRCICA, 2001), 63–66.

Russo-Ottoman Wars   (1787–1878)   Over the course of a century the Russian and Ottoman empires fought five wars (1787–1792, 1806–1812, 1828–1829, 1854–1856, and 1877–1878) for control over the BLACK SEA region. (For the 1854–1856 war, *see* CRIMEAN WAR.) While ideological factors (such as NATIONALISM and pan-Slavism) played a role in fomenting conflict between the Ottoman and Russian empires in the 19th century, the overarching geostrategic concern that drove Russo-Ottoman conflict during this period was the Russian Empire's military and economic goal of securing an outlet to the Mediterranean Sea. For RUSSIA, the achievement of this goal required, first, possession of ports on the BLACK SEA coast and, second, navigational rights through the straits of the Bosporus and the Dardanelles.

Starting in the 1770s with the acquisition of a small foothold on the northern Black Sea littoral, the Russian Empire, by 1878, had occupied a large portion of the Black Sea coast from the delta of the DANUBE RIVER in the west to the Georgian-Ottoman frontier in the east. In the late 18th and early 19th centuries, the Ottoman Empire was capable of mounting offensive military operations against the Russian Empire. However, by 1878, the Ottoman military generally found itself in a defensive posture and was reduced to countering Russian penetration into Ottoman territory. In the Balkans, Russian war plans generally focused on bridging the Danube River and striking toward ISTANBUL through Ottoman Rumelia. In eastern Anatolia, Russia's strategic goals centered on capturing key Ottoman cities in the region—Kars, Erzurum, and Trabzon.

RUSSO-OTTOMAN WAR OF 1787–92

On August 19, 1787, the Ottoman Empire declared war on the Russian Empire in an effort to regain territorial and political control over its long-standing vassals, the CRIMEAN TATARS. This war, following the RUSSO-OTTOMAN WAR OF 1768–1774, resulted in the Ottoman Empire's ultimate loss of the Crimean Khanate and the permanent establishment of a Russian political and military presence on the northern shore of the Black Sea.

The declaration of war against the Russian Empire was driven by a pro-war faction within the Ottoman government. Angered by the humiliating terms of the TREATY OF KÜÇÜK KAYNARCA (1774) and the lack of Ottoman response to the Russian annexation of the Crimea in 1783, this pro-war group included the religious establishment (ULEMA), exiled Crimean Tatar nobles, and Grand Vizier Hoca Yusuf Pasha.

For the Russians, renewed warfare with the Ottoman Empire provided an opportunity to realize long-standing imperial goals in the Black Sea region. In an ideologically driven plan known as the "Greek Project," Russian Empress Catherine II (Catherine the Great) envisaged the reestablishment of a Byzantine state on Ottoman territory with Constantinople (the ancient name of Istanbul) as its capital. More concretely, the Russian Empire sought to improve its military and political position in the Black Sea region and to fulfill its long-term geostrategic goal of gaining a commercial and naval outlet through the straits of the Bosporus and Dardanelles. The triumphal and highly public procession in 1786 by Catherine II (1762–96) to her new Crimean lands, coupled with the pro-Orthodox Christian activities of Russian consular officials posted in the Danubian principalities of WALLACHIA and MOLDAVIA, vassals of the Ottoman Empire, provoked this pro-war faction in Istanbul. These were the immediate causes of the Ottoman declaration of war in the summer of 1787.

The principal focus of the first armed clashes between the two empires was control over the key Ottoman fortress town of ÖZI, on the mouth of the Dniester River. In the spring of 1788, a combined force of over 100,000 Russian soldiers attacked Özi. Following a long siege, the Russians captured this fortress in December 1788, killing 9,500 Ottoman soldiers and taking 4,000 prisoners.

In 1789 the Ottoman army, under the command of Hasan Pasha, advanced north of the Danube River into the Danubian principality of Wallachia. Under the highly effective leadership of Russian General Alexander Suvorov, the Russian army beat the Ottoman army in two key battles in the open field at Foschani in July and on the Rimnik (Boza) River in September. Following these two losses, the Ottoman army, hampered by confusion at the command level and subject to heavy desertions, ceased to be an effective fighting force. The 1789 campaign season was one of the most disastrous in Ottoman history.

In 1790 Gazi Hasan Pasha replaced Hasan Pasha as commander of the Ottoman army in the Balkans. As a result of losses incurred during the war, the Ottoman army was now composed almost entirely of peasants and raw Anatolian recruits. The largest military encounter of the war occurred in December 1790 around the Ottoman fortress town of Ismail in the Danubian estuary. In one of the bloodiest battles of the 18th century, the Russian assault on Ismail resulted in the death of 26,000 Ottoman soldiers and civilians and the capture of 9,000 Ottoman soldiers. In that same year, the Russian Black Sea fleet forced the Ottoman NAVY to retreat to its ports in the Bosporus. In so doing, the Ottoman Empire effectively ceded naval control of the Black Sea to the Russians. In August 1791, on the eastern shores of the Black Sea, the Russian Empire gained control of Anapa, thereby defending its protectorate of Georgia and eliminating the Ottoman Empire's last stronghold in this region.

British and Prussian alarm at this demonstration of Russian military strength motivated these two European powers to support the Ottoman Empire as a bulwark against Russian aggression in the Balkans. In 1791, British diplomatic pressure, coupled with Prussian war preparations against the Russian Empire, brought the Russians to the negotiating table. Following protracted negotiations, the Ottoman and Russian empires signed the Treaty of Jassy on January 9, 1792, ending the Russo-Ottoman War of 1787–92.

RUSSO-OTTOMAN WAR OF 1806–12

The conflict between the Russians and the Ottomans that began just 14 years later must be understood within the context of the rise of Napoleonic France. Impressed with the military success of Napoleon, especially at Austerlitz in December 1805, the Ottoman Empire moved to improve its relations with France. Alarmed by developing Ottoman-French relations, the Russian Empire raised an army in southern Ukraine and resolved to occupy the Danubian principalities of Moldavia and Wallachia as a preventive measure against French influence in the Balkans.

The immediate cause of war between the Russian and Ottoman empires in November 1806 was the Ottoman removal of two pro-Russian rulers or *hospodars* in the Danubian principalities and their replacement with *hospodars* friendly to France. This unilateral action on the part of the Ottomans contravened agreements reached earlier between the Ottoman and Russian empires. On November 24, 1806, two Russian armies (one under General I. I. Michelson and one under General K. I. Meyendorff) moved across the Dneister River and occupied the Danubian principalities. In response, the Ottomans declared war on the Russian Empire. The only effective Ottoman resistance to this initial Russian incursion came from the Danubian notable (*see* Ayan) Alemdar Mustafa Pasha, who, commanding an army of 60,000, repulsed a Russian attack on the key fortress of Ismail on the Danubian estuary.

While the Danubian principalities and the Balkans constituted the principal theater of conflict in the Russo-Ottoman War of 1806–12, Russian and Ottoman forces also engaged in hostilities at sea in the northern Aegean and on land in the southern Caucasus and eastern Anatolia. Under the Ottoman-Russian defensive alliances of 1799 and 1805, the Russian navy had been allowed to sail through the straits of the Bosporus and Dardanelles. In July 1807 the Russian navy defeated the Ottoman navy off the north Aegean island of Lemnos and blockaded ships attempting to enter the trait of the Dardanelles. Additionally, in the spring of 1808, the Russians defeated

an Ottoman army of 30,000 commanded by Yusuf Ziya Pasha at Arpa Su in eastern Anatolia

In the spring of 1807, another Ottoman army of 30,000 soldiers crossed the Danube River with the objective of recapturing Bucharest and preventing a link between the Russian army and Serbian rebels. Succeeding in driving a wedge between the Russians and the Serbs, the Ottoman army laid siege to Bucharest in June 1807. The Ottomans were also able to repel a Russian attempt to cross the Danube at Giurgevo, located in present-day Romania across the Bulgarian port city of Ruse.

The Ottoman spring offensive of 1807 showed promise but was curtailed by two events, one external and one internal, which had a profound effect on the course and outcome of the war. On July 7, 1807, Napoleon and Czar Alexander I signed the Treaty of Tilsit. This treaty, which delineated Russian and French spheres of interest in the Balkans, made clear to the Sublime Porte that French material and diplomatic support for the Ottoman Empire, including assistance in reclaiming the Crimea, would not be forthcoming. A series of internal political crises in Istanbul from 1806–08 also severely hampered the Ottoman Empire's military capabilities in the Balkans and the Danubian principalities. On May 29, 1807 a conservative alliance of Janissaries and ulema, threatened by a series of reform measures, including the creation of a European-style army corps (*see* Nizam-i Cedid), imprisoned Sultan Selim III (r. 1789–1807) and forced him to abdicate the Ottoman throne. The reign of the new Ottoman sultan, Mustafa IV (r. 1807–08), was brief. In a struggle for power in the summer of 1808, Selim III's nephew ascended to the sultanate as Mahmud II (1808–39). These dynastic struggles, which occupied the attention of the regular Ottoman army and the armies commanded by the provincial notables in the Balkans, forced the Ottoman army to seek a defensive posture against the Russians and retreat behind its fortified Danubian line.

The Russian Empire's occupation of the Danubian principalities sapped the Russian army's war-making capabilities in the Balkans and, as a result, the Russians were unable to take advantage of these political crises in the Ottoman capital. Russian military doctrine of the early 19th century compelled armed forces to rely on local inhabitants for supply and provisioning. The severe socioeconomic dislocation caused by the presence of a Russian army of 80,000 in the Danubian principalities resulted in widespread looting in the countryside, outmigration of peasants, and a severe drop-off in agricultural production. Regular outbreaks of the plague also contributed to a reduction in the overall fitness of the Russian army in the Danubian principalities. Throughout the course of the war the Russian army lacked adequate supplies which, coupled with resistance offered by an Ottoman army encamped in Shumla at the base of the

Balkan mountain range, left it incapable of a sustained military effort beyond the Danube River. The Russians did succeed, however, in capturing Ismail in September 1809, Ibrail (Braila) in January 1810, and Silistra, on the Ottoman side of the Danube, in August 1810.

Fearing a French invasion of the Russian Empire, Alexander I's advisers in Saint Petersburg urged the czar to break the stalemate in the Balkans. In 1811 the Russians, seeking a speedy end to their hostilities with the Ottoman Empire, increased their military and diplomatic pressure on the Sublime Porte. Under General M. I. Kutuzov, the Russian army scored a series of military victories along the Danube at Vidin, Slobodzia, and Rusçuk (Ruse). Reducing their territorial demands from retention of the Danubian principalities to a slice of eastern Moldavia (subsequently known as Bessarabia), the Russians signed a peace agreement with the Ottomans, the Treaty of Bucharest, on May 28, 1812. By the time the treaty was ratified, Napoleon's armies were already deep into Russian territory.

RUSSO-OTTOMAN WAR OF 1828–29

The roots of the Russo-Ottoman War of 1828–29 war lay in the emerging national consciousness of the Orthodox Christian populations in the Ottoman Balkans and the imperial ambitions of the new Russian czar, Nicholas I, in the Black Sea region. Following the Greek War of Independence in 1822, Britain, France, and Russia signed the Treaty of London in 1827 calling for the creation of an autonomous Greek state. The Ottomans refused to agree to the formation of an independent Greek state and this, coupled with Russian demands for the restoration of its privileges in the Danubian principalities of Wallachia and Moldavia, resulted in a Russian declaration of war on the Ottoman Empire in April 1828. In declaring war at this time, Nicholas I (1825–55) sought to engage the Ottoman army before the extensive military reforms initiated by Sultan Mahmud II in 1826 could take effect. The Russian declaration of war was welcomed in Istanbul by some members of the political elite who viewed the war as an opportunity to reclaim territory lost to the Russian Empire in the Black Sea region during the preceding 60 years.

Upon the declaration of war, a Russian army of 100,000 mobilized rapidly, moving in three columns through the Danubian principalities toward Ottoman Rumelia south of the Danube River. In contrast, the Ottoman military was ill-prepared. The Janissary component of the army had been smashed by Mahmud II in the 1826 Auspicious Incident and the Ottoman navy had been virtually destroyed at the Battle of Navarino in October 1827. The Russian Empire enjoyed naval supremacy on the Black Sea and was able to avoid the supply problems that hampered its previous campaigns in the Balkans by opening up a supply route through the Bulgarian port of

Burgas. The Ottoman army that took the field in 1828 under the command of Agha Hüseyin Pasha was a ragtag army composed primarily of Crimean Tatars and other irregular forces.

Meeting little Ottoman resistance, the lead column of the Russian army occupied Bucharest and Craiova, took Ibrail on June 16, and, following battles in Kustenje and Mangalia, occupied Dobruja. The second column of the Russian army crossed the Danube in June and attacked the Ottoman fortress of Silistra on the southern side of the Danube River, while the third column laid siege to a series of Ottoman fortresses along the Danube. On October 11, the Russians captured the important Danubian port city of Vidin. Following the initial Russian onslaught the Ottoman army, toward the end of the 1828 fighting season, fell back on the natural defensive line of the Balkan mountain range, regrouped around Şumla under the command of the able Ottoman commander Hüsrev Pasha, and prepared to defend this key Balkan mountain pass against an expected Russian invasion in 1829.

In 1829 the Russians opened up a second front in the war in the eastern Black Sea region. By the spring of 1829 the Russians, under the command of General Paskievitch, had occupied the Georgian port of Poti and captured Ardahan, Kars, and Bayazid in eastern Anatolia. In July 1829 the Russian army occupied Gümüşhane and the key eastern Anatolian city of Erzurum. These gains were followed by the siege of the important Black Sea port of Trabzon.

At the start of the 1829 campaign season in the Balkans, the Russian army faced an Ottoman army composed of untrained irregulars. Additionally, the Ottoman army suffered from food shortages due to a Russian naval blockade of the trait of the Dardanelles. When the Russian army moved on Şumla the Ottoman army disintegrated, abandoned its artillery on the field, and fled into the Balkan Mountains. Rather than risk encountering the remnants of the Ottoman army in the Şumla Pass, the Russian commander, General Diebitsch, led his army on an arduous nine-day march through the Balkan Mountains and emerged south of the range in August. Encountering little effective resistance, the Russian army moved rapidly on Edirne, the capital of Ottoman Rumelia. Following a three-day siege, the Russians occupied Edirne on August 22 and were now only a few days march from Istanbul. Despite the effective collapse of the Ottoman army, however, the Russian army was not in a position to move in strength on the Ottoman capital. The overextension of its supply lines and the spread of disease had taken a severe toll on the Russian troops. Mahmud II and his advisers, however, were unaware of the diminished state of the Russian army, and after a Russian demonstration in the direction of Istanbul, the Ottoman government, following the advice of French and British diplomats in Istanbul, sued for peace. The Treaty of

EDIRNE, signed on September 14, 1829, concluded the Russian-Ottoman War of 1828–29.

CRIMEAN WAR 1854–56

In general, the Crimean War followed the broad 19th-century pattern of Ottoman-Russian geopolitical and ideological conflict for control over the Black Sea region and influence over Orthodox Slavic populations in the Balkan peninsula. The first phase of the war (1853) unfolded in a now familiar pattern: failed diplomatic negotiations between the Ottomans and the Russians; Russian military offensives into the Danubian principalities and eastern Anatolia; and Ottoman ability to slow the Russian advance coupled with a lack of military strength to seize the initiative. What distinguished the Crimean War from previous Ottoman-Russian conflicts, however, was the rapid internationalization of the war. While the British and French had exerted significant diplomatic pressure in Saint Petersburg and Istanbul during previous periods of Ottoman-Russian hostilities, in the Crimean War British and French troops were directly deployed in 1854 to protect the Ottoman Empire from Russian aggression. In this second phase of the war, the combined land and naval forces of the British and French allowed for forward operations on Russian soil (the Crimean peninsula). Ottoman military contributions in the second phase of the war were generally confined to support and supply operations. In the treaty that ended the war (the Treaty of Paris, signed on March 29, 1856), British and French support resulted in relatively advantageous peace terms for the Ottoman Empire.

RUSSO-OTTOMAN WAR OF 1877–78

The Treaty of Paris, which concluded the Crimean War (1854–56), had severely reduced the Russian Empire's influence, militarily and diplomatically, in the Black Sea region. After the introduction of sweeping domestic reforms in the 1860s, the Russian Empire, in the early 1870s, once again turned its attention to affairs in the Ottoman Balkans and the southern Caucasus. Influenced by a pan-Slavic ideology that, in its diplomatic and military worldview, envisioned Russian dominion over Orthodox populations in the Ottoman Balkans, the goals of Russian foreign policy in the early 1870s were focused on the reclamation of Russia's previously strong position in the Black Sea region. One of the prime architects of this pan-Slavic foreign policy was Count Nikolai Ignatiev, the Russian ambassador in Istanbul.

Against this background, the events that sparked another round of warfare between the Russian and Ottoman empires were uprisings in the mid-1870s in BOSNIA AND HERZEGOVINA, Serbia, Montenegro, and BULGARIA. While these uprisings are generally studied within the context of the rise of 19th-century European national-ism in the Ottoman Balkans, more mundane issues also animated the Ottoman Empire's Orthodox subjects in the Balkans. In the mid-1870s droughts, famine, and floods in Anatolia forced the Ottoman government to shift the weight of the empire's tax burden onto the empire's Balkan subjects. Increasingly onerous taxes, coupled with measures employed to raise revenues, promoted instability and provoked armed rebellion in the Balkans.

Events in Bulgaria in April 1876 internationalized these domestic Ottoman disturbances. Taking advantage of the rising discontent among the Bulgarian population of the Ottoman Empire the leaders of the Bulgarian national movement called for a mass uprising against Ottoman rule. While the uprising itself did not garner widespread support, in the ensuing intercommunal strife, Bulgarian rebels killed 1,000 Muslim Ottomans, including women and children. With most of their regular and professional forces involved in counter-insurgency operations in Serbia and Bosnia-Herzegovina, the Ottoman government relied on irregular troops (başıbozuks) and armed, ill-disciplined Circassian refugees to suppress the uprising in Bulgaria. The violent suppression of the April uprising resulted in the death of an estimated 10,000–12,000 Bulgarians, including women and children, at a time when political instability in Istanbul deflected central government attention away from affairs in the Balkans. In May 1876 Sultan ABDÜLAZIZ (r. 1861–76) was deposed; his successor, the mentally unstable MURAD V (r. 1876), was replaced by Sultan ABDÜLHAMID II (r. 1876–1909) three months later, in August 1876. The Sublime Porte was thus unprepared to cope with the public reaction in Great Britain and Russia to the violent suppression of the April uprising in Bulgaria (reported in the foreign press as the "Bulgarian atrocities"). Reports of these atrocities in British newspapers shocked and horrified the British public and resulted in a shift in British public opinion against the Ottoman Empire. This shift in public opinion tempered Britain's traditionally pro-Ottoman foreign policy. In Russia, the Bulgarian atrocities, resonating widely among the educated segment of Russian society, provoked calls for war against the Ottoman Empire and the liberation of the Ottoman Empire's Orthodox populations in the Balkans.

In an effort to defuse the growing crisis in the Balkans, European representatives assembled for diplomatic talks in Istanbul in December 1876. Pre-empting discussions focused on the socioeconomic condition of the Ottoman Empire's Christian populations, Sultan Abdülhamid II, during the course of the conference, issued a CONSTITUTION. The first of its kind in Ottoman history, the 1876 constitution called for the full equality of all Ottoman subjects regardless of religion. From the Ottoman perspective, the 1876 constitution satisfied demands made to the Sublime Porte concerning its Orthodox

Christian subjects in the Balkans. Therefore, all further demands made at the conference in reference to this population were rejected by the Ottomans.

In early 1878, the Russian Empire, believing that all avenues for a peaceful and diplomatic resolution to the Balkan crisis had been exhausted, initiated preparations for another round of war against the Ottoman Empire. These efforts included the negotiation of Austrian neutrality and the extraction of a Romanian guarantee for the safe passage of Russian troops through Romanian territory. Throughout the course of the ensuing Russo-Ottoman war, the French and Prussians would remain neutral. While British Prime Minister Benjamin Disraeli argued for British intervention on the side of the Ottomans, anti-Ottoman sentiment prevailed in the British Parliament. It was only toward the end of the war, with Russian troops threatening Istanbul, that the British threw their support behind the Ottomans.

On April 24, 1877 the Russian army, operating out of its recently established headquarters in Kishniev, Bessarabia, crossed the Pruth River into Romania and declared war on the Ottoman Empire. The military course of the war was very much a reprise of the Russo-Ottoman War of 1828–29. Expecting an easy victory, Russian war planning focused on sending the bulk of the Russian army across the central Balkan Mountains and, upon capturing Sofia, moving down the well-supplied Maritsa River valley to Edirne. In late June 1877 the Russian army bridged the Danube at Sistova. An advanced detachment, under the command of General Gurko, took Turnovo on July 7 and, despite heavy Ottoman resistance, secured the strategic Shipka Pass over the Balkan Mountains on July 19. The main Russian army, now joined by Bulgarian and Romanian fighters, moved south from the Danube toward the Shipka Pass. To remove a potential threat to Russian supply lines, the main Russian army attacked the Ottoman fortress town of Pleven, but here the Russian advance bogged down. Multiple Russian attacks on the fortress were repulsed by Ottoman troops under the capable command of Osman Pasha. The resistance at Pleven forced the Russian high command to alter its military plan and undertake a lengthy siege of the fortress. The siege of Pleven would last for five months and at its height involved 120,000 troops (84,000 Russian, 36,000 Ottoman).

In April 1877 the Russian army moved across the Ottoman-Russian border in eastern Anatolia. In May the Russians captured Ardahan and in June they took Bayazid. In November 1877, following a five-month siege, the key Ottoman city of Kars fell to the Russians, and in late January 1878 the Russians occupied Erzurum. The deterioration of Ottoman authority in eastern Anatolia resulted in a significant outbreak of intercommunal violence. As a result, during and after the fighting, 60,000–70,000 Muslim refugees left Russian territory in the southern Caucasus and resettled in the Ottoman Empire. Conversely, 25,000 Ottoman Armenians sought refuge in Russian territory.

In late November, 1877, Pleven fell to the Russians. Following up on this victory, the Russian army crossed the Balkan Mountains and took Sofia on January 4, 1878. Moving down the Maritsa River valley, the Russians captured Plovdiv on January 17 and Edirne on January 20. The Russian army was now in a position to seriously threaten Istanbul and a forward move by the Russians from Edirne toward the Ottoman capital provoked a British response in the form of a strong naval demonstration on the Sea of Marmara. Although exhausted, racked by disease, and as low on supplies as they had been in 1829, the Russian army, it was thought, might be in a position to challenge for Istanbul. The British presence around the Ottoman capital convinced the Russians instead to seek an armistice with the Ottomans. Conducted at the Russian encampment in San Stefano (Yeşilköy) and led by Count Ignatiev, the Russian-Ottoman armistice talks resulted in a bilateral treaty. Signed on March 3, 1878, this treaty, known as the Treaty of San Stefano, officially ended the Russo-Ottoman War of 1877–78. The provisions of the treaty, however, were later amended during the Congress of Berlin in 1878.

The terms imposed on the Ottoman Empire in the Treaty of San Stefano were harsh. The treaty called for the creation of an autonomous Greater Bulgaria under the protection of the Russian Empire. As it was envisioned, this Greater Bulgaria was to have stretched east-west from the Vardar and Morava river valleys in Macedonia and southern Serbia to the Black Sea coast and north-south from the Danube to the Aegean coast (except for Salonika). Bosnia-Herzegovina was granted autonomy. Romania, Serbia, and Montenegro were recognized as independent states and their borders were drawn to maximize Ottoman territorial losses. Bessarabia was returned to Russia. In eastern Anatolia, the Russian Empire took direct possession of Kars, Ardahan, Batumi, and Doğubayazit.

The terms of the Treaty of San Stefano elicited a swift reaction from Great Britain and the Austro-Hungarian Empire. Pre-war negotiations with the Russians had led the Austrians to believe that they would receive Bosnia-Herzegovina in return for their neutrality. The British were worried that the creation of a Greater Bulgaria as a Russian protectorate would result in the construction of a Russian navy in the north Aegean (most likely at the port of Kavalla). This could disrupt the balance of naval power in the eastern Mediterranean. Couching their protests in diplomatic terms, the British and Austrians argued that diplomatic protocol, in so far as the Treaty of San Stefano fundamentally altered the terms of the Treaty of Paris (1856), required further consultations with the European powers over the terms of the Russo-Ottoman armistice. In these demands, the British and Austrians were supported by the powerful and influential German Chancellor Otto von Bismarck. Able to defeat the Ottomans militarily, but unable to challenge Britain, Austria, and Germany diplomatically, the Russians agreed to participate in these consultations.

From June 13 to July 13, 1878, representatives of the major European powers convened in Berlin to renegotiate the Treaty of San Stefano. Despite working against the interests of the Russian Empire, the revised treaty, known as the Treaty of Berlin, severely reduced the Ottoman Empire's territorial possessions in the Balkans. The principal changes in the Treaty of Berlin concerned Bulgaria and Bosnia-Herzegovina. The idea of a Greater Bulgaria was dismissed and in its place Bulgaria was partitioned three ways. Northern Bulgaria—from the Balkan Mountains to the Danube River—was declared an autonomous principality. Central Bulgaria (Eastern Rumelia)—from the Balkan Mountains to the Rhodope Mountains—was given limited autonomy within the political framework of the Ottoman Empire. The southern parts of Rumelia—south of the Rhodope Mountains—remained an integral part of the Ottoman Empire. The autonomous Bulgarian principality (called "Berlin" Bulgaria) represented only 37.5 percent of the territory of Greater Bulgaria ("San Stefano" Bulgaria). Bosnia-Herzegovina was placed under the protection of the Austro-Hungarian Empire. The independence of Serbia, Romania, and Montenegro was recognized. Serbia was given possession of the Morava River valley (around Pirot and Vranya) in what had been part of Greater Bulgaria. Dobruja, around the Danubian estuary, was attached to independent Romania.

The territorial and political realignment of the Balkans that resulted from the Russo-Ottoman War of 1877–78 formed the basis for future irredentist claims on the part of newly independent Balkan states. Few of the newly constituted Balkan nation-states were wholly satisfied with postwar territorial arrangements and maintained designs, along ethnic-national lines, on territories outside their internationally recognized borders. Conflicts resulting from this irredentism would destabilize the Balkan Peninsula in the first and second decades of the 20th century.

In the Treaty of Berlin, the Russian Empire was given Southern Bessarabia and retained Batumi, Ardahan, and Kars. Additionally, Russia was awarded a large war indemnity. According to the Treaty of Berlin, the Ottomans were required to pay the Russians more than 800 million French francs ($340 million in current U.S. dollars) in war damages. Russian claims on Ottoman revenue in the ensuing years hampered Ottoman investments and reduced Ottoman economic prosperity. For the Ottomans, the Treaty of Berlin resulted in the loss of 8 percent of the empire's most productive territory and the loss of 20 percent of the empire's total POPULATION (or 4.5 million subjects). Additionally, the war and the territorial alterations imposed at the Treaty of Berlin resulted in an in-migration of an estimated 500,000–600,000 Muslim refugees from the Ottoman Empire's former Balkan possessions. The loss of the Orthodox Christian populations in the Balkans, coupled with the influx of Muslim refugees from the Balkans and the Russian Empire, significantly altered the demographics of the Ottoman Empire. By the early 1880s, Muslim subjects accounted for roughly 75 percent of the Ottoman Empire's population.

Andrew Robarts

Further reading: Caroline Finkel, *Osman's Dream: The Story of the Ottoman Empire* (New York: Basic Books, 2005); Charles and Barbara Jelavich, *The Establishment of the Balkan National States, 1804–1920* (Seattle: University of Washington Press, 1986); Barbara Jelavich, *History of the Balkans: Eighteenth and Nineteenth Centuries*, vol. 1 (Cambridge: Cambridge University Press, 1983); George Jewsbury, *The Russian Annexation of Bessarabia, 1774–1828* (New York: Columbia University Press, 1976); John P. LeDonne, *The Russian Empire and the World, 1700–1917: The Geopolitics of Expansion and Containment* (Oxford: Oxford University Press, 1997); Paul Robert Magosci, *Historical Atlas of East Central Europe* (Seattle: University of Washington Press, 1993); Justin McCarthy, *Death and Exile: The Ethnic Cleansing of Ottoman Muslims, 1821–1922* (Princeton, N.J.: Darwin, 1995); Stanford J. Shaw, *Between Old and New: The Ottoman Empire under Sultan Selim III, 1789–1807* (Cambridge, Mass.: Harvard University Press, 1971).

rüştiye mektepleri **(middle schools)**   *See* EDUCATION.

S

Sabbatai Sevi   *See* SHABBATAI ZVI.

Safavid dynasty   *See* IRAN.

Salafiyya   In the 21st century, Salafiyya is the name of an Islamic political ideology that seeks to impose a strict interpretation of Islamic law in Muslim societies and that views Western cultures with suspicion. But in its origins at the end of the 19th century, the movement sought to reform Islam so that Muslim societies could modernize by adopting the knowledge and institutions of the West. The reformers who spearheaded this movement, which included MUHAMMAD ABDUH and his students in CAIRO among others, felt that, over time, Islamic scholars had obscured the true spirit and meaning of the Quran and the Sunna, or traditions of the Prophet Muhammad, with superstition and irrelevancies. The reformers believed that Muslims needed to return to the sources of their religion and to understand them in the context of the society that had existed when the Prophet revealed God's message. The word in Arabic for "ancestors" is *salaf,* and the intellectual reformist movement took its name from that term as it sought to return Muslims to the practice of Islam its proponents felt their ancestors had known in the early centuries of Islam.

For the reformers, the key to the rebirth of Islam lay in the revival of the legal practice known as *ijtihad.* Early Muslim legal scholars had argued that the foundations of Islamic law, or SHARIA, were the Quran and the Sunna. Additionally, if the community as a whole agreed on a practice, known as *ijma* or consensus, then that too was binding on the believers. Beyond that, qualified scholars could apply their independent reasoning (*ijtihad*) to those two sources to interpret what Muslims should properly do in cases where there was no clear guidance. The principle behind the use of *ijtihad* is not unlike the one that guides members of the U.S. Supreme Court, who use the text of the U.S. Constitution as a guideline to deal with problems that are not directly addressed by it. For American constitutional scholars the central question is, "What did the original framers of the constitution mean?" The question for Muslim legal scholars is, "What was intended by a particular passage of the Quran?"

The use of *ijtihad* allowed for flexibility in framing laws that would govern the vast community into which Islam had grown in the centuries following the prophet's death in 632 C.E. But by the 13th century, Sunni Muslim legal scholars had become uneasy with what they felt were too liberal uses of independent reasoning by scholars and many called for the abandonment of the practice. The community of scholars gradually agreed with the dissenters and in the following centuries, Sunnis abandoned the use of *ijtihad* in making religious decisions. It remained an option, however, for Shii clergy with the rank of *mujtahid,* that is, a cleric recognized by his peers as having adequate training in sharia and its sources to allow him to exercise independent judicial reasoning in a specific case.

The reformers of the late 19th century were not the first to call for the return of *ijtihad.* The writings of Ahmad ibn Taymiyya, a Muslim religious scholar who died in prison in DAMASCUS in 1328, were the inspiration for many. Ibn Taymiyya had castigated SUFISM and the study of philosophy, both popular, as being un-Islamic.

He called upon the Muslim community to return to the spiritual purity it had known in the days of the original Muslims (*salaf*). If Muslims understood Islam as well as did those original Muslims, he reasoned, there would be no danger of error should their scholars use *ijtihad*.

Further inspiration for the Salafi reformers of the late 19th century was to be found in the writings of MUHAMMAD IBN ABD AL-WAHHAB. Deriving inspiration from ibn Taymiyya, ibn Abd al-Wahhab wrote in the 18th century that Islam had become a religion of superstition and unbelief, by which he meant that Muslims were practicing an Islam that was clearly not sanctioned by the Quran. As a corrective, he advocated a return to the Quran as the sole source for Islamic law. Although ibn Abd al-Wahhab was a literalist in that he held that the Quran's verses could not be interpreted by humans and must be accepted as they are, he did allow that the moral leaders of the community could make pronouncements on the legality of issues not prohibited by the Quran. To the reformers, this seemed to be sanctioning the return of *ijtihad*, and they eagerly studied the very works by ibn Abd al-Wahhab that Ottoman legal authorities had labeled "unlawful innovation (*bida*) and heresy" a century before.

Although the main center of the Salafiyya was in Cairo, Muslim scholars in Damascus and BAGHDAD had also rediscovered the writings of ibn Taymiyya and used them to formulate responses to the issues raised by the waning power of the Ottoman state in the face of Western imperialism. They also debated the role that Islam was to play in societies where political and social reformers were increasingly adopting Western ideas and institutions as models. As such, there was not one unified Salafi response. But in all cases, the Muslim scholars who were identified with the movement called for radical reform in the ways in which Islam was to be understood, even while they claimed that they were not introducing anything that was fundamentally new to the religion.

One of the issues on which most Salafi thinkers did agree was condemnation of Sufism as an un-Islamic practice. In contrast, there was a wide divergence of opinion on the compatibility of Islamic and Western values, whether applied in the public or private sphere. Muhammad Abduh was the scholar who probably felt most comfortable with Western models of government and education, but he also had limits beyond which he was not prepared to go. In 1899 one of Abduh's students, Qasim Amin, created a social outcry when he published *The Emancipation of Woman* (*Tahrir al-Mara*). In his book, Amin wrote that the Muslim world's decline could ascribed to the lowly status that Islamic law gave women, keeping them uneducated, veiled, and at home. He added that the Quran condoned none of these practices; in fact, he argued, Islam as it was originally revealed represented the liberation of women, hence the title of his book.

Abduh had argued that Islam did not require polygamy and that the Quran had provided women with far-reaching rights and responsibilities. But he was not prepared to back his student Amin in the bold assertion that contemporary Muslim society was a backward-looking patriarchate. Stunned by the rejection by his teacher and by the Muslim intellectual class in general, Amin published a second book in 1901, *The New Woman* (*al-Mara al-jadida*), in which he again stated that Muslim societies could never advance as long as they did not emancipate women. But he abandoned the Salafi approach of grounding his arguments in the Quran and Sunna. Instead he relied on rationalist arguments advanced by secular Western European thinkers.

From that point on, there was a division among Muslim reformers between those who believed a westernized modernity could be compatible with Islamic law and values and those who felt that it could be achieved only through a secularization of Muslim societies. A third option would later emerge; this group held that Muslim societies should not try to forge a compromise between modernity as defined by the West and Islamic law and traditions; rather, they should accept change—whether it was social, technological, or scientific—only if those developments were compatible with what they believed constituted Islamic values and were permissible according to Muslim law.

The question of how Islam as a belief system that encompasses spiritual, political, and social spheres should approach a rapidly changing world continued to be contested after the fall of the Ottoman Empire. For Abduh and his students, there was no question that Islam could adapt to change and that technologically progress would require Muslim societies to retain their faith in Islam as a moral certainty to guide them.

Bruce Masters

See also RASHID RIDA, MUHAMMAD.

Further reading: Aziz Al-Azmeh, *Islams and Modernities* (London: Verso, 1993); John Voll, *Islam: Continuity and Change in the Modern World* (Boulder, Colo.: Westview, 1982).

salname *Salname* is the name of the official governmental yearbooks or annual reports prepared by the government from the mid-19th century on to document the events and developments that occurred in the country in a given year. The word itself is a combination of two Persian nouns: *sal* meaning "year" and *name* meaning "letter" or "book." *Salnames* are akin to modern data banks. There were three types of *salnames*. The first type, known as *devlet salnamesi* (state annual yearbooks), were prepared every year and covered the entire empire. The first state annual yearbook was published in 1847. The second type, *vilayet salnamesi* (provincial annual yearbooks), included information on a single province. The first provincial annual yearbook in 1866. In addition to these two, there were *salnames* prepared by governmental and nongovernmental institutions such as firms and banks at the lower level.

The most common and important salnames were the provincial annual yearbooks. They included plans, maps, and photographs of cities, towns, and buildings. They gave detailed information about provinces, districts, and villages including topographic, demographic, commercial, social, political, juridical, and cultural conditions and history. They provided statistical tables related to mineral resources, agricultural production, industrial activities, population, roads, transportation, forests, religious foundations, schools, hospitals, libraries, mosques, churches, synagogues, fountains, stores, bakeries, towers, mills, and so on. They also contained information about the religious calendar and festivals of both Muslim and non-Muslim groups living in a given province.

Thanks to these *salnames*, the Ottoman central government could determine, in detail, the resources and conditions of its lands and population, from YEMEN to the CAUCASUS, from the Arab Peninsula to the Balkans.

Ahmet Zeki İzgöer

Further reading: Larsen Knud, *National Bibliographic Services: Their Creation and Operation* (Paris: UNESCO Publishing, 1955); Justin McCarty and D. Hyde, "Ottoman Imperial and Provincial Sâlnâmes." *Bulletin of the Middle Eastern Studies Association* 13, no. 2 (1979).

Salonika (Salonica, Thessalonica; *Gk.*: Thessaloniki; *Turk.*: Selanik)   The city of Salonika lies at the head of the Gulf of Therma, an inlet of the Aegean Sea, and is today the second largest city in GREECE, after Athens, in terms of population. But during the period in which the Ottomans ruled the city, 1430–1912, it was the most populous city in the territory that would become Greece and the largest city in the Ottoman Balkans. Salonika was important both as a port exporting the products of the Balkans to the rest of the empire and as a center of manufacturing. Given its vital economic role in the Ottoman period, the city drew migrants from throughout the empire and beyond, giving it an ethnically diverse population in which no single religious or ethnic group constituted the majority.

Salonika was founded in the fourth century B.C.E. and was named after Thessaloniki, a half-sister of Alexander the Great. The city flourished in the Roman period and after the empire's break-up in the fourth century C.E. Salonika was one of the largest cities of the BYZANTINE EMPIRE. But the city's economic position in the empire, and its population, began to decline in the sixth century

as Slavic-speaking tribesmen moved into the hinterlands of the city in Macedonia and Thrace. The newcomers eventually converted to Orthodox Christianity but their arrival marked a period of instability in the region. Crusaders from western Europe sacked Salonika in 1185. After the crusaders conquered Constantinople in 1204 they established the Latin Kingdom with Salonika as its capital. The Latin Kingdom lasted until 1224 when Byzantine rule was restored in the city.

In the middle of the 14th century, Ottoman armies began to raid in the hinterlands of Salonika. In 1387, as an Ottoman army approached Salonika, its people demanded that their governor, Manuel Palaiologos (later to be Byzantine emperor), surrender without resistance. Unwilling to comply with their demands, he fled the city, and its inhabitants opened the city gates to the Ottomans. As the city had surrendered without a fight, the Ottomans left its many churches and monasteries in the hands of the city's Orthodox Christians. Ottoman rule proved to be short-lived, however, as during the civil war that broke out among the sons of BAYEZID I (r. 1389–1402) following his defeat at the BATTLE OF ANKARA in 1402, Manuel Palaiologos, now emperor, was able to regain control of Salonika

Once Sultan MURAD II (r. 1421–44, 1444–46) had consolidated his control over the sultanate, he sought to regain the city his grandfather MURAD I (r. 1362–1389) had taken. The Ottoman army began a siege of Salonika in 1422. The inhabitants of the city responded to the siege by accepting Venetian protection in the form of troops and ships to break the Ottoman blockade of the harbor. But that aid only postponed the final assault on the city, which came on March 29, 1430. The Ottoman army quickly overcame Salonika's defenses and the city was pillaged, its churches and other religious buildings destroyed or converted into mosques, and its population enslaved. Once the city was sacked, Sultan Murad sought to revive it by ransoming some of its leading Orthodox Christian families from captivity and resettling them in their former homes. He also brought in numbers of Turkish-speaking Muslims to settle a city that had been largely abandoned by its inhabitants during the long siege. Murad and other members of the Ottoman royal family, as well as prominent Ottoman officials, established endowments (WAQFS) that built and supported mosques, caravansaries, and Islamic schools, and the construction of these institutions further aided in the city's reconstruction.

The biggest boost to Salonika's emergence as one of the empire's major commercial centers came in the reign of Sultan BAYEZID II (r. 1481–1512) when he invited the JEWS of SPAIN, who were expelled from that nation in 1492, to settle in the Ottoman Empire. In 1478, the year in which the earliest surviving Ottoman census was made, no Jews lived in Salonika, but by 1519 the Ottoman census showed 15,000 Jews living in a city whose population was estimated to have been between 30,000 and 40,000 people. Thereafter Jews were never the absolute majority of Salonika's population but they were always the largest single religious community in the city. Once Jews from Spain had settled there, the city also attracted Jewish immigrants from central and eastern Europe. The Jewish community in Salonika established the earliest printing press in the Ottoman Empire in 1510 to print books in both Hebrew and Ladino, a language based on the Spanish spoken by the original immigrants from Spain but written in Hebrew letters and with many borrowed words from Hebrew. The everyday language spoken by Salonika's Jews was known as Judezmo. It had fewer Hebrew words and more loanwords from Greek and Ottoman Turkish than did the literary language, Ladino. As the culture of Salonika's Jews became more secular in the 19th century, Judezmo was also used as a written language. After the city was attached to Greece in 1912, Greek gradually replaced Judezmo to become the dominant language spoken by Salonika's Jews.

The Jewish immigrants from Spain brought with them from their old country the technology for the production of woolen broadcloth known in Ottoman Turkish as çuka. They established dozens of workshops and Salonika became the center for the production of that cloth in the 16th century. Salonika's merchants enjoyed a monopoly of the supply of broadcloth to the imperial palace and the JANISSARIES and grew wealthy from the TRADE. Their wealth, in turn, was used to establish new synagogues in the city and to support Jewish education. The cloth industry created an economic boom in the city and its population climbed to an estimated 50,000 to 60,000 people by the end of the 16th century as migrants were drawn from the Balkans. These included Albanian Muslims and Orthodox Christians who spoke Slavic dialects. But Salonika's wool trade suffered from English and French woolen imports and the city's economy experienced a downturn in the 17th century as Ottoman consumers began to prefer cloth imported from Europe over the locally produced çuka.

That economic downturn may have prompted many of Salonika's Jews to look for a spiritual answer to their economic problems. They found it in the figure of SHABBATAI ZVI (1626–76) who proclaimed himself in 1648 to be the long-awaited messiah of the Jews. Jews throughout the Ottoman Empire heeded his call to hasten the reestablishment of the Kingdom of Israel by selling all their property to follow him. The cult following of Shabbatai Zvi was especially strong in Salonika where thousands of Jews embraced him as the messiah. The cult enjoyed an increased fervor and optimism among its adherents when Shabbatai Zvi announced in 1666 that the time had come when the sultanate would be overthrown and he would reign in its place. With that claim the Ottoman authorities took notice of the cult and Shabbatai Zvi was arrested and brought before Sultan MEHMED IV (r. 1648–87). He was given the choice of either converting to Islam or being executed for treason. Shabbatai Zvi chose the former, and hundreds of his followers followed him into the new faith.

The descendants of those converts to Islam were called dönme, "turncoats," by the Ottoman Turks as they did not believe the Jews' conversion was sincere. The converts called themselves the maminim, Hebrew for "faithful," and professed to be true Muslims. But they married only members of their own community and maintained their own mosques, separate from the rest of the Muslim community. These practices gave rise to suspicions among both Muslims and Christians that the maminim were still secretly practicing Jewish religious rites, although historians have found no evidence that this was true. The maminim could be found in various parts of the Ottoman Empire; their largest community was, however, in Salonika where they numbered about 10,000 in 1912. After the city's occupation by Greece in that year, the maminim, along with the remainder of the city's Muslim population, either departed the city as refugees for what was left of the Ottoman Empire after the BALKAN WARS (1912–13) or were expelled during the population exchange between Greece and Turkey in 1923–24.

In the 18th century, Salonika enjoyed a second economic boom that was fueled by the growth of the export of agricultural commodities such as wheat, cotton, and tobacco from the Ottoman Balkans to western Europe. As was the case with the wool trade of the 16th century, the majority of the merchants involved in this trade were drawn from the city's Jewish population. That supremacy was challenged by Greek merchants who were supported by Russian diplomatic efforts after the TREATY OF KÜÇÜK KAYNARCA in 1774. The Greek merchants suffered a major setback in March 1821, however, when their compatriots rose in rebellion against Ottoman rule. In response, the Ottoman authorities arrested several hundred prominent Greeks in Salonika; most of these were executed in retaliation for the rebellion that was occurring to the south in the Peloponnese. This was followed in May 1821 by a general riot, led by the JANISSARIES and Albanian military auxiliaries, in which over a thousand Greeks were killed. In the aftermath of the riot, perhaps several thousand of the city's Greek community fled the city, and Salonika entered into another period of economic decline.

In the 1860s, the Ottoman authorities destroyed the city's sea wall and the land walls on the eastern side of the city. The former action allowed for the modernization of the city's docks and the construction of warehouses to receive Balkan goods bound for export. The destruction of the land walls allowed the city's wealthy elite to build large houses in the European style in new suburbs outside the former city. This reflected a growing population in the city that had recovered from the trauma of the GREEK WAR OF INDEPENDENCE. In 1800 the population was estimated by foreign visitors to be between 50,000 and 60,000 people. It fell to perhaps 40,000 inhabitants in 1830 and only recovered its pre-war level by the mid-1840s. As the city once again recovered its crucial role as chief port of the Balkans in the second half of the 19th century, the population rose. In 1880, the population of Salonika was estimated to be 100,000 people, and 150,000 in 1909. In 1909 the population was roughly 30 percent Muslim, 30 percent Christian, and 40 percent Jewish.

The construction of railroads to Skopje in present-day Macedonia in 1888 and to ISTANBUL in 1896 encouraged investors in Salonika to construct factories for the curing and processing of tobacco and the production of cotton textiles. By 1900 Salonika was one of the most important centers of manufacturing and banking in the Ottoman Empire. It also had the largest industrial work force in the empire. The presence of so many workers in the city led to the formation in 1909 of the first socialist party in the Ottoman Empire. While Jewish workers were drawn to radical politics that stressed class differences, Christian workers were increasingly drawn to nationalist movements.

At the start of the 20th century, both Greece and BULGARIA coveted the port of Salonika. Greece saw it as the natural capital of the remaining Ottoman territory that the Greek nationalists claimed belonged to Greece. Bulgarian nationalists saw the city as Bulgaria's best chance to have a port on the Aegean Sea, allowing them to avoid having to ship goods through Istanbul. The governments of both Greece and Bulgaria clandestinely supported nationalist political groups and schools established among Greek-speaking and Slavic-speaking workers. With a newly formed patriotism to these two contending nation states, workers representing the two Christian nationalities frequently clashed with one another. Meanwhile, Muslims in the city were alarmed about what their fate would be if Salonika were annexed by either Greece or Bulgaria. Reflecting those fears, many of Salonika's Muslims supported the clandestine COMMITTEE OF UNION AND PROGRESS that was seeking to restore the Ottoman constitution. Salonika became one of the centers of revolutionary activity and its native son Mustafa Kemal (later KEMAL ATATÜRK) was one of the conspirators who helped engineer the revolution of 1908.

Muslim hopes for keeping Salonika a part of the Ottoman Empire quickly vanished in October 1912 when the armies of Greece, Bulgaria, SERBIA, and Mon-tenegro all invaded what was left of the Ottoman Empire in Europe. In the face of a land grab by the independent Balkan states, the Albanians declared their own country's independence. The Albanians, Greeks, Bulgarians, and Serbs all had ambitions for the city of Salonika and issued newly drawn maps that placed the city within their national boundaries. In the end, however, it was the Greek army that entered the city first on November 8, 1912. Greece's possession of the city was confirmed by the TREATY OF BUCHAREST in 1913 that ended the Second Balkan War, which had in turn started after the victorious Balkan states in the First Balkan War against the Ottoman Empire went to war with each other over the spoils. After WORLD WAR I, the Greek government settled many of the Greek Orthodox Christians (*see* GREEK ORTHODOX CHURCH) expelled from TURKEY under the terms of the Treaty of Lausanne in Salonika in the homes of Muslims who had either left or had been expelled. Some of the city's Jews left with the Muslims for Istanbul. Most of those who did not died during the Holocaust in World War II. By 1945, Salonika, which had been a multiethnic city under the Ottomans, was largely inhabited by Greek-speaking Orthodox Christians.

Bruce Masters

Further reading: Mark Mazower, *Salonica: City of Ghosts (Christians, Muslims and Jews 1430–1950)* (New York: Alfred A. Knopf, 2005); Eyal Ginio, "Migrants and Unskilled Local Workers in an Ottoman Port-City: Ottoman Salonica in the Eighteenth-Century," in *Outside In: On the Margins of the Modern Middle East,* edited by Eugene Rogan (London: Tauris, 2002), 126–148; Basil Gounaris, "Salonica." *Review* 16, no. 4 (1993): 499–518.

sancak See ADMINISTRATION, PROVINCIAL.

al-Sanusi, Muhammad (b. 1787–d. 1859) *Muslim scholar and reformer* Muhammad ibn Ali al-Sanusi was the founder of Sanusiyya, a reformist order of SUFISM that is named after him. Al-Sanusi was born in ALGERIA and studied with Ahmad al-Tijani in Fez, Morocco, where he established a reputation as a scholar and teacher of core Islamic texts. Al-Sanusi embraced the idea that Islam had become overly encrusted with tradition and that it needed radical REFORM to return to the purity of its roots, a view that was being increasingly voiced in the 18th century. He rejected many of the more extreme Sufi beliefs and practices and came into conflict with many established scholars as he advocated the return to the use of *ijtihad,* a practice whereby qualified scholars use their independent reasoning, with the guidance of the Quran, to interpret what Muslims should do in cases where there is no clear guidance. This practice would later be articulated by the scholars of the SALAFIYYA movement at the end of the 19th century.

Like most Muslim scholars, Muhammad al-Sanusi eventually ended up in MECCA, where he studied with Ahmad ibn Idris. Al-Sanusi left Mecca in 1841 and planned to return to Algeria. However, having reached Tunisia, he decided he could not live under French rule. Instead he moved first to TRIPOLI and then to the Jabal al-Akhdar region of Cyrenaica, in present-day LIBYA. There he established his first Sufi lodge (Ar: zawiyya) in 1843. Between 1846 and 1853 al-Sanusi was again in Mecca, where his order had already gained a following. Upon his return to Libya he moved deeper into the desert, establishing another Sufi lodge at an oasis called Jaghbub, as he wanted to live outside Ottoman-controlled territories. From there, al-Sanusi's order branched out, establishing other lodges along the trans-Sahara TRADE routes. He was considered by the BEDOUINS as a saint (sidi or wali) and they looked to him to dispense justice and to mediate in intertribal disputes. He also established schools to educate their sons. When he died in 1857, the leadership of the order and the mantle of sainthood passed to his son Sayyid al-Mahdi, who moved the headquarters of the movement further into the Sahara, eventually settling in Qiru, in present-day Chad.

Besides reform, Muhammad al-Sanusi believed very strongly that his order should engage in missionary work and his followers converted many people in central and western Africa to Islam. The ideology of the order was very literalist in its approach to the Quran. It was similar in approach to that which the WAHHABIS were preaching in Arabia, except that the Sanusiyya was organized as a Sufi order. Both, for example, forbade music. Along with their faith, the Sanusiyya engaged in commercial ventures, allowing MERCHANTS to stay in their lodges and collecting tolls from them, creating a socioeconomic network that stretched across the Sahara Desert.

As the Sanusiyya expanded into areas that the French were claiming as part of their growing empire in Africa in the late 19th century, the order developed a militancy that was directed against European colonial expansion into Africa and the Middle East. The bonds of membership in the Sufi order allowed for the unification of tribes that were historically antagonistic to one another, creating a fighting force that the Sanusi sheikh could direct against the Europeans. When the Italians invaded Libya in 1911, the Sanusiyya joined forces with the Ottomans. After the Ottomans withdrew, the Sanusiyya remained the core of anti-Italian resistance through the end of World War II. When Libya gained its independence in 1951, Idris al-Sanusi, a direct descendant of Muhammad, became its first and only king.

Bruce Masters

Further reading: Knut Vikor, *Sufi and Scholar of the Desert Edge: Muhammad b. Ali al-Sanusi and His Brotherhood* (Evanston, Ill.: Northwestern University Press, 1995).

al-Sayyadi, Abu al-Huda (d. 1909) *Syrian courtier and adviser*   Abu al-Huda al-Sayyadi was a member of the RIFAIYYA ORDER of SUFISM and an adviser to Sultan ABDÜLHAMID II (r. 1876–1909). Al-Sayyadi was born in a village outside ALEPPO, and many of the established families in that city considered him a peasant upstart. In Aleppo, he attached himself to the Rifaiyya Order, claiming that he was in fact a direct descendant of the order's founder, Ahmad al-Rifai. With that pedigree, he then added the honorific Sayyid to his name, although that title is permitted only to members of the ASHRAF, or descendants of the Prophet. To many in Aleppo, his claim to the prophet's lineage was preposterous, and they considered him an imposter and a fraud. Al-Sayyadi went to ISTANBUL shortly before the ENTHRONEMENT of Abdülhamid II, where he promoted his order and his belief that the Ottoman sultan was the only person who could save the Arabs from European imperialism. His brand of PAN-ISLAMISM, with the sultan as champion, was appealing to Abdülhamid, who brought al-Sayyadi into the imperial entourage at COURT.

In the palace, al-Sayyadi became the sultan's chief adviser for all things Arab, while remaining a constant promoter of the members of the Ottoman royal house as the natural leaders of the Islamic world. Through his self-promotion, and his attacks on Sufi orders other than his own as well as on the intellectuals of the SALAFIYYA movement, al-Sayyadi made many enemies, including JAMAL AL-DIN AL-AFGHANI, who was perhaps one of the most influential Muslim intellectuals of his time. Al-Sayyadi was also an enemy of the YOUNG TURKS, who demonized him as a "fanatical Arab" who sought to block the empire's path toward reform and progress. For his part, al-Sayyadi considered the Young Turks to be apostates. Given the level of polemic directed against him, it is often difficult to know how much influence al-Sayyadi had on the sultan, but he was clearly the most influential Arab at the sultan's court and a figure of controversy both then and now. With the Young Turk revolution of 1908, al-Sayyadi returned to Aleppo and the grand mansion he had built for his family there. He died the following year, and the members of the Rifaiyya Order maintain his grave in Aleppo as a shrine.

Bruce Masters

Further reading: Julia Gonnella, "As-Sayyid Abu'l-Huda al-Sayyadi in Aleppo," in *The Empire in the City: Arab Provincial Capitals in the Late Ottoman Empire*, edited by Jens Hanssen, Thomas Philipp, and Stefan Weber (Beirut: Orient-Institut, 2002), 297–310.

sciences The Ottoman conceptualization and classification of sciences (*ilm, ulum*) were not very different from those prevailing in the classical age of Islam. Science was either learned by studying the Quran or acquired by intellect. The knowledge transmitted from the Quran and the hadith (sayings of the Prophet Muhammad) was defined as *ulum-i nakliye,* that is, religious sciences. Knowledge acquired by the intellect and perceived through the five senses was known as the *ulum-i akliye,* that is, the rational or experimental sciences. Ottoman scholars adopted and elaborated this two-part classification that was first established by al-Farabi (d. 950 or 951) and later expanded by other Islamic scholars.

Taşköprülüzade Ahmed Efendi (d. 1561) in his *Miftahü's-Saadet* (Key to felicity) proposed a subdivision based on the usefulness of sciences. The religious sciences—that is, the interpretation of the Quran, the hadith, Muslim canonical jurisprudence (*fıqh*), Islamic theology (*kelam*), and Islamic mysticism (*tasavvuf*)—were regarded as the beneficial sciences. Intellectual or rational sciences such as MEDICINE, mathematics, astronomy, and agriculture were also worthy of study. He further grouped sciences into seven categories, the first five being the rational sciences and the last two being the most significant religious sciences, a classification emphasizing the relative importance of intellectual and religious knowledge. Taşköprülüzade's classification was influential on Ottoman scholars and constituted the basis of the curriculum of colleges (madrasas), the principal institutions of learning in the Ottoman classical age from the mid-15th century until the 18th century.

The study of sciences was initiated by reading and learning the Quran, followed by the study of Arabic grammar and syntax; logic; belles-lettres; theoretical philosophy, which included the study of philosophy and metaphysics; theology; Muslim canonical jurisprudence; the hadith and the interpretation of the Quran. Physics, geometry, arithmetic, and astronomy were taught both from theology books and from separate treatises devoted to these topics.

Until the 19th century, when the Ottomans began to primarily rely on Europe for the transfer of scientific and technical knowledge, Ottoman science was largely based on the scientific learning of classical Islam. Muslim scholars, who had endeavored to transmit Greek science—and to a certain extent Indian and Chinese science—beginning in the eighth and ninth centuries under the ABBASID CALIPHATE (750–1258), had interpreted the scientific knowledge they inherited, commented on it, and added valuable analyses of what it contained. They made original contributions in many fields over the following centuries.

When the Ottoman state was founded at the turn of the 14th century, Islamic scientific knowledge was being taught in the colleges created by the SELJUKS of Anatolia. The Ottoman elites soon established contact with the eastern centers of the Islamic scientific tradition of the Middle East and Central Asia. While Ottoman scholars set off for CAIRO, DAMASCUS, BAGHDAD, Tabriz, Herat, and Samarkand for scientific study, men of erudition who flourished in those cities came to settle in the Ottoman lands, and contributed their knowledge and expertise to the Ottoman intellectual milieu in late 15th and early 16th centuries.

While the Islamic scientific tradition was pursued in the Ottoman colleges, new information, mostly technical, gradually filtered into the empire from the 15th century on through its western frontiers. Ottoman military campaigns into central Europe and the naval expeditions in the Mediterranean Sea provided for the influx of new knowledge, mainly from Europe. Europeans trading or practicing various professions in Ottoman lands, as well as those recruited by the Ottoman government to work in military installations, were also influential in transferring information, techniques, and material (such as books, atlases, and astronomical tables) to the Ottoman world. Books and other printed materials were translated into Turkish by Ottoman bureaucrats, court officers, or army officers, either on the order of higher officials or through individual efforts.

Ottomans' contacts or alliances with western and central European countries in the military, political, and commercial fields broadened in the early decades of the 18th century. Ottoman court members became interested in European novelties, culture, and social life, especially after Yirmisekiz Mehmed Çelebi's (d. 1732) visit to Paris as Ottoman ambassador in 1720. Following his visit, his son Mehmed Said Efendi (d. 1761) and Ibrahim Müteferrika (1674–1747), a Hungarian convert, founded the first Arabic script printing press in ISTANBUL in 1726, producing books in Ottoman Turkish with Arabic characters (*see* PRINTING). Histories and dictionaries, as well as books on linguistics, geography, magnetism, and military reforms, were published.

In the early centuries of the Ottoman Empire the language for science was Arabic, which was the language of the Quran and the scientific language of the Islamic world. Ottoman scholars, however, had to learn Persian to complete their scientific studies. Since the Ottoman rulers, their administrators, and the Anatolian population spoke Turkish, scientific texts in Arabic and Persian were gradually translated into Ottoman Turkish, a version of Turkish full of Arabic and Persian words and written in Arabic script (*see* LANGUAGE AND SCRIPT). When the Ottomans began translating European texts in the 17th century, they were mostly rendered into Turkish. The textbooks for use in Ottoman modern schools during the 19th century were also compiled in Turkish, while Arabic continued to be used in the madrasas. The compilations and translations of European textbooks proved essential in the reception and elaboration of modern sciences in the 19th century. Besides Turkish translations, French books were also available in the empire, because learning French was popular among intellectuals and the language was part of the curriculum of the modern schools.

The 19th-century translators of European books on science often relied on Arabic to create a scientific terminology. Turkish books on medical sciences, botany, and chemistry thus include a large number of scientific terms derived from Arabic, as well as European and Turkish terms. Thus the Ottoman scientific nomenclature of the 19th century incorporated elements from the East and the West, making the Ottoman Empire the meeting place of different scientific traditions.

ASTRONOMY

Ottoman astronomers relied heavily on the discoveries and inventions of their Islamic predecessors. They wrote on theoretical astronomy, refined timekeeping and calendar computing methods, and manufactured astronomical instruments more precise than those known up to that time. Scholars affiliated with the Maraga and Samarkand observatories in central Asia had a deep impact on Ottoman astronomy. One prominent astronomer of the era was Nasir al-Din al-Tusi (1201–74), the founder of the Maragha observatory for the Ilkhanid khan Hulagu in the second half of the 13th century. Al-Tusi's commentary on Ptolemy's *Almagest*, together with his treatises on theoretical astronomy, calendar making, and astronomical devices were much favored by Ottoman astronomers. These works were introduced to Anatolia by al-Tusi's student Qutb al-Din al-Shirazi (1236–1311), who taught astronomy in the Seljukid madrasa at Sivas (present-day Turkey), before the Ottoman state was founded. The influence of the Maraga school of astronomy continued well into the 18th century.

Kadızade-i Rumi (d. after 1440) left Anatolia for Samarkand (present-day Uzbekistan) to study and work in the observatory founded by the Timurid ruler and astronomer Ulugh Beg (1394–1449), the grandson of TIMUR or Tamerlane. The commentary Kadızade-i Rumi wrote in 1412 on al-Chagmini's (fl. 13th century) compendium of astronomy became very popular among Ottoman students aspiring to learn astronomy. The astronomical works of ALI KUŞÇU (d. 1474), a distinguished member of the Samarkand school who taught in ISTANBUL upon Sultan MEHMED II's (r. 1444–46, 1451–81) invitation, were also much praised. The astronomical tables of Ulugh Beg, produced at Samarkand, were used by Ottoman astronomers until the late 18th century for calendar making.

The Ottoman conquest of SYRIA and EGYPT in the early 16th century intensified the exchange of scholarship between Istanbul, DAMASCUS, and CAIRO. The works of al-Mardini (d. 1506), the timekeeper of the AL-AZHAR mosque in Cairo and a learned astronomer-mathematician, became popular among Ottoman scholars. An observatory was established in Istanbul to improve the astronomical tables of Ulugh Beg. Its founder, TAKIYÜDDIN (1526–85), was a madrasa scholar trained in Damascus and Cairo. His calculations of solar parameters were as accurate as those calculated by his Danish contemporary Tycho Brahe (1546–1601). Takiyüddin proposed the creation of an observatory as soon as he was appointed chief astronomer (*müneccimbaşı*) in 1571. The construction of the building and the instruments started around 1573 or 1574. Besides the classical astronomical instruments such as astrolabes, quadrants, sundials, armillary spheres, and celestial globes, Takiyüddin used an instrument similar to the sextant and a device with a string to fix the position of the equinoxes. The demolition of the observatory in 1580 due to rumors aiming to depose Takiyüddin's mentor, Hoca Saadeddin Efendi, prevented Takiyüddin from completing his observations. He could only recalculate the tables for the Sun; his astronomical tables thus remained an incomplete version of the Ulugh Beg's tables.

The Ottomans switched to European astronomical tables in the late 18th century. Following the translation of *Tables Astronomiques* (1740) by Jacques Cassini (1677–1756) into Turkish, Sultan SELIM III (r. 1789–1807) ordered calendars to be calculated after Cassini's tables. In the early 19th century chief astronomer Hüseyin Hüsnü Efendi (d. 1840) translated the section on calendar-making of the *Tables Astronomiques* by Joseph-Jérôme de Lalande (1732–56) into Arabic and Turkish. From 1829 on, with the approval of Sultan MAHMUD II (r. 1808–39), calendars were computed according to Lalande's tables. Copies of the astronomical tables of Ulugh Beg were, however, still being made until the 19th century. Astronomy courses were included in the curriculum of the 19th-century modern schools, and textbooks were compiled based on French astronomy textbooks.

MATHEMATICS

Knowledge of mathematics was considered a basic requirement for graduates of Ottoman colleges—needed to solve common problems such as calculating inheritance payments in court, setting calendars, and keeping the accounts of state departments—and thus it was part of the standard Ottoman curriculum. Medieval Islamic mathematical knowledge was at the core of Ottoman mathematics. It incorporated Greek and Indian mathematics and was introduced to Anatolia in the 13th and14th centuries by scholars coming from Syria, Egypt, and Iran to teach at the Seljukid madrasas. In the 15th century the tradition of the Samarkand school was carried on by the Ottomans. Kadızade-i Rumi's commentary on Shams al-Din al-Samarkandi's (d. ca. 1310) short work that discussed Euclid's propositions became the most popular and studied geometry book in Ottoman madrasas. The book on arithmetic and algebra (*al-Muhammediya fil-Hisab*) by Ali Kuşçu from Samarkand was used in Ottoman madrasas until the 17th century. From then on, *Hulasatu'l-hisab,* composed by Bahauddin al-Amili (1546–1621), became the most widely used mathematics book in Ottoman madrasas. Commentaries on the works of Islamic mathematicians were also produced. Many mathematical treatises were written for practical purposes to meet the needs of tax collectors, land surveyors, accountants, and judges. Others dealt with more academic issues, such as the use of decimal fractions in trigonometry and astronomy, trisecting an angle, resolving algebraic problems, or discussing the properties of numbers.

Translation of European mathematical texts to Turkish started in the early decades of the 18th century. These were texts on applied mathematics and were used in calculations related to geodesy, mechanics, and ballistics. The opening of the Hendesehane (School of Geometry) in the Imperial Shipyard in 1775 to teach mathematics to officers from various military corps was a crucial step forward in the systematic teaching of mathematics. In the 19th century, professors of the school of engineering (Mühendishane) translated and compiled a number of mathematical textbooks from European languages for educational purposes. Gelenbevi Ismail (d. 1790) wrote on algebra and logarithms; Hüseyin Rıfkı and Selim Effendis translated the *Elements of Geometry* by the English mathematician John Bonnycastle (1750–1821); Ibrahim Edhem Pasha rendered A. M. Legendre's (1752–1833) geometry book into Turkish; Ishak Efendi devoted the first volume of his *Mecmua-i Ulum-i Riyaziye* (Compendium) to mathematics, in which he used Etienne Bézout's (1730–1783) works extensively; Mehmed Ruhiddin translated parts of Charles Bossut's (1710–1814) *Cours Complet de Mathématiques* (A Complete Course of Mathematics); Seyyid Ali Pasha wrote on conic sections using Apollonius' treatise together with contemporary French works; Emin Pasha, a graduate from Cambridge University and the director of the Mekteb-i Harbiye (Military academy) in Istanbul, wrote on both mathematics and engineering; Vidinli Hüseyin Tevfik Pasha's *Linear Algebra* (1882) introduced three-dimensional linear algebra and its applications to elementary geometry; Mehmet Nadir (1856–1927), obtained results of lasting value in number theory; and Salih Zeki (1864–1921), professor of mathematics at the Darülfünun (Ottoman University), by compiling numerous textbooks, contributed to the dissemination of mathematical knowledge in both higher and secondary education. Thus it was in the 19th century

that Turkish translations of European mathematical textbooks definitely replaced the works of medieval Islamic mathematicians.

PHYSICS

Physics taught in Ottoman madrasas was based on the philosophical and theological literature of medieval Islam. Texts discussing atoms, the void, space, form, motion, and time were included in philosophy books under chapters titled *tabiiyyat* (topics related to nature, physics) together with chapters on logic, cosmology, and metaphysics. A noteworthy example is the *Kitab al-Hidayah* of Umar al-Abhari (d. 1265), a Persian philosopher and mathematician from Abhar (Iran), which was the most studied of such books among the Ottomans. Treatises on optics/perspective and mechanics were also compiled. Those on mechanics dealt mostly with elevating heavy goods, the construction of war machines, and ballistics. In addition to his astronomical observations Takiyüddin is also known for his treatises that formed the basis for the construction of several mechanical devices including water pumps, gears, cranes, and mechanical clocks. The military factories and the dockyards were the key places for applied physics, and mechanics was learned there through training under a master.

The first printed book on physics, *Füyuzat-i Miknatisiye* (Properties of magnetism), was published in 1732. Translated from German, it described the properties of the lodestone and the work undertaken in Europe for determining latitude and longitude. Courses on mechanics were included in the curriculum of the Military Engineering School in the early 19th century. Physics (*ılm-i hikmet*) courses were also given in the medical schools and the Military Academy. The first comprehensive physics textbook in Turkish was Mehmed Emin Derviş Pasha's (1817–79) *Usul-i Hikmet-i Tabiiyye* (Elements of physics), published in Istanbul in 1865. Turkish translations of European textbooks, especially those of A. Ganot's (1804–87) book on experimental and applied physics, *Traité Élémentaire de Physique Expérimentale et Appliquée,* were largely used in the teaching of physics in the second half of the 19th century.

GEOGRAPHY

Knowledge of geography was essential for Ottoman administrators to effectively plan excursions and military operations. Medieval Islamic geography books were introduced to the Ottoman realm in the 15th century when Sultan Mehmed II ordered them to be copied for his imperial library. Between the 16th and 18th centuries almost all Ottoman works on geography were written in Turkish. They were either based on the work of Islamic geographers—including al-Masudi (d. 957), al-Idrisi (c. 1100–1165), al-Qazwini (d. 1283), and Abu

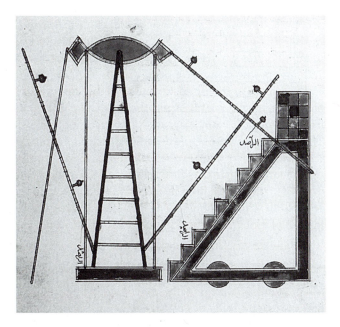

Parallactic instrument of Takiyüddin at Istanbul Observatory
(16th century) *(Courtesy of Istanbul University Library)*

al-Fida (d. 1331)—or on renowned European geographical texts. Eastern and European sources might be used comparatively. Although madrasa scholars compiled geography books, geography courses were not included in the madrasa's curriculum.

Ottoman seamen of the 16th century collected nautical and geographical information from far beyond the Mediterranean and BLACK SEA. Admiral Piri Reis (d. 1553), the author of *Kitab-ı Bahriye* (Book of seafaring, 1521, 1526), used nearly 20 maps, among them an Alexandrian map, eight Arab maps, four Portuguese maps, an Indochinese map, a Chinese map, as well as a map drawn by Christopher Columbus, to produce his Atlantic Ocean map (1513) depicting the shores of northwestern Africa, the Iberian Peninsula, and the eastern shores of Central and South America. His North Atlantic map (1528) presents in detail the shores running from Greenland to Florida. Seydi Ali Reis' (d. 1562 or 1623) *Muhit* (Ocean) was a portolan chart for seafaring in the Persian Gulf and the Indian Ocean.

The 17th-century campaigns to Crete stimulated KATIB ÇELEBI, a prominent Ottoman bureaucrat, to compose the *Cihannüma* (Cosmorama, 1654). The book is considered the first Ottoman geography that referred to both European works and Islamic geographies. A popular Latin version of Gerhard Mercator's *Atlas Minor* and Abraham Ortelius's catalogue of geographers appended to *Theatrum orbis terrarium* were among Katib Çelebi's western sources. Joan Blaeu's *Atlas major seu cosmographia,* the most spectacular atlas in 17th-century Europe, was also translated by Ebubekir b. Behram ed-Dimaşki (d. 1691) at Grand Vizier Köprülü Fazıl Ahmed Pasha's behest. The

printing of *Cihannüma* by İbrahim Müteferrika in 1729, almost a century after its compilation, also stimulated interest in European geography books. Books by Jacques Robbe (1643–1721), the engineer and geographer of Louis XIV; Dutch mathematician and geographer Bernhardus Varenius (1622–51); and others were translated at the request of Ottoman high officials. When geography was included in the curriculum of modern military schools in the 19th century, works by Adrien Balbi, Eugène Cortambert, Auguste Michelot, and Archibald Geikie were translated into Turkish, and many other geography books were published for secondary and higher education.

CHEMISTRY

Before the introduction of modern chemistry in the mid-19th century, the aspects of chemistry that interested the Ottomans were similar to those of the Middle Ages: the use of mineral drugs in therapy for providing longevity and to some extent for producing precious metals. Chemical knowledge was found in Ottoman materia medica giving detailed information on the properties and preparation of mineral, vegetal, and animal drugs, as well as in texts based on Islamic alchemical and chemical treatises accounting for the preparation of various chemical substances, the philosopher's stone, and the elixir of longevity. Jabir ibn Hayyan (d. ca. 777); al-Rhazi (ca. 865– ca. 925), known as Rhazes in medieval Europe; and Abul Qasim al-Iraqi (fl. 12th c.) were the authors cited most often. Iznikî Fazıl Ali wrote extensively on alchemy/chemistry in the 16th century. Translations made by Ottoman alchemists and physicians from iatrochemists such as Paracelsus (1493–1541), Adrien Mynsicht (1603–38), Jean Baptiste van Helmont (1577–1644), and Daniel Sennert (1572–1637) at the turn of the 18th century introduced both new therapies and new chemical substances.

The teaching of modern chemistry started in the 19th century in the engineering and medical schools and in the Military Academy, which were equipped with chemical laboratories. The earliest Turkish textbook on chemistry, *Usul-i Kimya* (Elements of chemistry, Istanbul, 1848), was composed by Mehmed Emin Derviş Pasha, a graduate of the Military Engineering School in Istanbul, based on the chemistry books he used during his studies in the École des Mines in Paris. His public lectures, which included chemical experiments, raised great interest in Istanbul. Laboratories were also set up in hospitals and state customhouses. The Yıldız Imperial Palace also had a private laboratory. C. Bonkowski Pasha (1841–1905) filled the position of sultan's chemist-in-chief. German chemists who taught at the Darülfünun (Ottoman University) during WORLD WAR I organized the teaching of chemistry within the faculty of sciences together with their European-trained Turkish colleagues. A multilingual chemical nomenclature was developed by Ottoman chemists over the course of the 19th century based on classical Islamic and European chemical literature.

NATURAL HISTORY

Ottomans were very interested in plants, their medicinal properties, and therapeutic use. The materia medica of physician, pharmacologist, and botanist Dioscorides (ca. 40–90 C.E.) of Anazarba in Asia Minor and that of the Arab physician and botanist Ibn al-Baitar (1190–1248) were among the most praised and popular books on medicinal plants.

Research on the flora of the Ottoman Empire started in the mid-16th century when western European naturalists began to explore the eastern Mediterranean region. P. Belon (1517–64), L. Rauwolff (1535–96), and J. P. de Tournefort (1656–1708) were among the naturalists who collected plant specimens and wrote travel books. G. A. Olivier (1756–1814) was an entomologist who collected insects as well.

Regular teaching of modern botany, zoology, and geology started in the Imperial School of Medicine in the context of its new curriculum of 1839, although a few texts related to natural sciences were published earlier. The first lecturer of botany was Dr. C. A. Bernard (1808–44), the Austrian medical director of the school. His *Elémens de Botanique* (Elements of botany, 1842) in French was the first textbook on medical botany published in Turkey. He also established a herbarium and a botanical garden in the grounds of the school. The teaching of botany was carried on by Dr. Salih Efendi (1816–95), who also contributed to the formation of Ottoman botanical nomenclature. In 1865 he translated into Turkish and published the zoology and botany sections of C. Arendts's (1815–81) *Eléments d'Histoire Naturelle* (natural history). Dr. Karl Eduard Hammerschmidt (also known as Abdullah Bey, 1801–74) was instrumental in the teaching of geology and mineralogy as well as in the organization of the Natural History Museum at the Medical School. The museum's collection included material he provided from Vienna and specimens from his private collection of minerals, fossils, insects, and plants. He published monographs on the geology and paleontology of the Ottoman Empire.

MEDICINE

Galenic humoral pathology, in which illnesses were believed to be caused by the imbalance of the four humors, provided the conceptual framework of Ottoman medical teaching and practice until the 19th century. Thus bleeding, cupping, leeching, cauterization, phytotherapy (herbal medicine), and balneotherapy (water-based treatments) were the most common methods of treating illnesses. The most authoritative medical book was the *el-Kanun fi't-Tibb* (Canon) of Ibn Sina (Avicenna, 980–1037). Medicine was mainly practiced and taught in the hospitals (*darüşşifas*) and in the Süleymaniye medical college (Süleymaniye Tıp Medresesi) founded in the mid-16th century in Istanbul. Physicians and healers who came to settle in the Ottoman Empire as early as the 15th century contributed to the introduction of various practices either from the East (Iran, Egypt) or from the West (Spain, Italy, and other parts of Europe). The necessity of training qualified physicians to maintain the healthcare services of the Ottoman army led to the opening of a military medical school in 1827 (fully reorganized in 1839), followed by a civilian medical school in 1866. Both schools contributed extensively to the dissemination of modern medical knowledge within the empire from the mid-19th century onward.

TECHNOLOGY

The Ottomans were mostly concerned with acquiring and developing military technologies indispensable for expanding Ottoman territories. Soon after taking over the western part of Asia Minor in the 14th century, they reached the Aegean coast, where they became involved in constructing ships. When Ottoman territories expanded to the Balkans in the 15th century, they met local craftsmen experienced in metalwork and collaborated with them in casting guns and manufacturing rifles. The guns produced in the Balkans were used in the siege of Constantinople. At first, cannons were cast on the battlefields, as the Ottomans had no permanent foundry. Following the CONQUEST OF CONSTANTINOPLE, a foundry (*tophane*) was built and together with the Istanbul dockyards (*tersane*), it soon became one of the main industrial centers for acquiring and advancing technical knowledge. The *enderun,* or inner circle, of the sultan's palace in Istanbul, served for centuries as a training center for high functionaries, as well as craftsmen, musicians, and architects. Work undertaken to reform and modernize the army in the 18th and 19th centuries largely determined the transfer of scientific and technical knowledge from Europe to the Ottoman Empire. The Military Engineering School (Mühendishane) and the Military Academy (Mekteb-i Harbiye) were created to train the staff needed by the Ottoman army. Both European and Ottoman experts and professors collaborated in their creation, organization, and instruction. The graduates of these modern schools, some of whom were then sent to European universities to improve their knowledge, contributed to the introduction of technical knowledge and to the teaching of modern sciences and techniques.

The Ottomans' adherence to Islamic culture, their central Asian origin, the multiethnic, multireligious, and multilingual character of their empire, and the acquisition of new knowledge and practices from western Europe characterized and shaped scholarly activities in the empire. Prior to the 19th century, science introduced from Europe was largely confined to the elites and did not prosper within the madrasa, the traditional educational institution, in which scholasticism prevailed. The modern schools of the 19th century also did not aim at scientific research. The emphasis was on catching up with European science through education, by translating European textbooks and hiring European technical personnel. The RUSSO-OTTOMAN WARS, CRIMEAN WAR, and nationalist and separatist movements, along with the gradual weakening of the central authority and the interventions of European Great Powers, proved further obstacles to scientific advances and developing the basic sciences fundamental to technological development.

Feza Günergun

Further reading: Feza Günergun, "Ottoman Encounters with European Science: Sixteenth and Seventeenth-century Translations into Turkish," in *Cultural Translation in Early Modern Europe,* edited by Peter Burke and R. Po-chia Hsia (Cambridge: Cambridge University Press, 2007); Feza Günergun, "Science in the Ottoman World," in George N. Vlahakis et al., *Imperialism and Science: Social Impact and Interaction* (Santa Barbara, Calif.: ABC-CLIO, 2006); Feza Günergun and Kuriyama Shigehisa, eds., *The Introduction of Modern Science and Technology to Turkey and Japan* (Kyoto: International Research Center for Japanese Studies, 1997).

Selcuks *See* SELJUKS.

Selim I (Yavuz Sultan Selim, Selim "the Grim") (b. 1470/1471–d. 1520) (r. 1512–1520) *Ottoman sultan who conquered eastern Asia Minor, Syria, and Egypt* Sultan Selim devoted most of his energies to fighting against the Shia Safavids of IRAN, who challenged Ottoman sovereignty in eastern Anatolia and Azerbaijan. He defeated the Safavids at the Battle of Çaldıran in 1514 and secured Ottoman rule over most of eastern and southeastern Asia Minor. In 1516–17, Selim waged a victorious war against the Sunni MAMLUKS, who had ruled EGYPT and SYRIA since 1258, conquering and incorporating Syria and Egypt into his empire. The SHARIF OF MECCA and YEMEN also acknowledged Selim's sovereignty.

The introduction of Ottoman rule in these Arab lands had major political and economic consequences. With his conquests, Selim became the master of the HEJAZ, that is, MECCA and MEDINA, "the cradle of Islam," as well as of DAMASCUS and CAIRO, former seats of the caliphs (successors to the Prophet Muhammad). Selim and his successors assumed the title of "Servant of the Two Noble Sanctuaries" (Khadim al-Haramayn al-Sharifayn), referring to Mecca and Medina, and with this the task of protecting and organizing the annual pilgrimage

(HAJJ) to Mecca, which gave the Ottomans unparalleled prestige and legitimacy in the Muslim world.

The conquest expanded the Ottoman Empire's territories from 341,100 square miles in 1512 to 576,900 square miles in 1520, an increase by almost 70 percent. More importantly, revenues from Syria and Egypt accounted for one third of the total revenue of the empire. The protection of the maritime lanes of communications between ISTANBUL and Cairo thus became vital and necessitated the further strengthening of the Ottoman NAVY. It also led to confrontation with the dominant Christian maritime powers of the Mediterranean: VENICE, SPAIN, and the KNIGHTS OF ST. JOHN, based on the Island of RHODES. Protecting the Hejaz against Portuguese encroachment into the Red Sea brought the Ottomans into conflict with the Portuguese. However, all these conflicts were left to Selim's successor, Sultan SÜLEYMAN I (r. 1520–66).

STRUGGLE FOR THE THRONE AND SURVIVAL

Selim, the youngest of Bayezid II's sons, had little chance to succeed his father, whose favorite was Ahmed, prince-governor in Amasya (northern Turkey). Selim was prince-governor of the faraway Black Sea coastal province of Trabzon (northeastern Turkey). Even their third brother, Korkud, prince-governor of Antalya (on the Mediterranean coast of southwestern Turkey), was closer to the capital than Selim. Proximity to Istanbul and the throne was crucial in the Ottoman Empire, where no particular rule governed the succession of sultans. The prince who first reached the capital, took hold of the treasury, and got the support of the army had the best chance to become the new sultan, while the fate of his bothers and their sons was execution.

Selim's rise to prominence was closely related to his father's failure to handle the Safavids, who regularly encroached on Ottoman territories and whose proselytizing policy among the Turkoman and Kurdish nomads challenged Ottoman sovereignty in eastern Anatolia. In 1507 the Safavids attacked the Dulkadırs, a Turkoman principality in southeastern Anatolia on the frontiers between the three major powers of the region: the Ottomans, Mamluks, and Safavids. Since the Dulkadır lord (emir) was Selim's father-in-law, Selim retaliated with his own raids into Safavid territory. In 1510 he defeated a Safavid army, led by Shah ISMAIL's brother, which threatened Trabzon, Selim's seat. Selim was disappointed when his firm stance against the Safavids was interpreted by his father, Bayezid II, as insubordination.

Bayezid was about 60 years old at the time and Selim was concerned about a possible succession fight with his two elder brothers; he decided to act preemptively. Since both Ahmed and Korkud were closer to Istanbul, Selim demanded a new governorship closer to the capital.

When a rumor spread that Bayezid was about to abdicate in favor of Ahmed, Selim traveled to CAFFA, which was governed by his own son, the future Süleyman I the Magnificent. Thence Selim crossed onto the Balkans and in March 1511 his army of 3,000 men reached the former Ottoman capital EDIRNE, where Bayezid had been residing since the 1509 Istanbul earthquake. In the meantime, a major Turkoman KIZILBAŞ revolt broke out in Teke in southwestern Anatolia, led by a holy man known in Ottoman sources as Şahkulu (Slave of the shah). When the rebels defeated the imperial forces sent against them under the command of Prince Korkud and were marching against BURSA, Bayezid yielded to Selim's demands and appointed him prince-governor of the Danubian province of Semendire (present-day Smederevo on the Danube in Serbia). However, Selim did not trust his father. When he learned that the grand vizier planned to bring Prince Ahmed to the throne after the defeat of Şahkulu, Selim decided to seize the throne. However, on August 3, 1511 he was defeated by Bayezid's army near Çorlu, between Edirne and Istanbul, and fled to Caffa.

When Prince Ahmed heard about the battle between Selim and their father, he went to Istanbul in the hope that Bayezid would abdicate in his favor. However, the sultan's elite infantry, the JANISSARIES, supported Selim and blocked Ahmed from entering the capital. Frustrated, Ahmed left for Anatolia, intending to return with his Anatolian supporters. In the meantime, yet another Kızılbaş rebellion broke out around Tokat in north-central Anatolia, and yielding to pressure from the Janissaries, Bayezid invited Selim to Istanbul, appointing him commander-in-chief of the army. Selim arrived in Istanbul in April 1512; with the support of the Janissaries he deposed his father and was proclaimed sultan on April 24. It was the first time that the Janissaries orchestrated the abdication of the reigning sultan. The deposed sultan died on June 10 on his way to Dimetoka, his birthplace in Thrace.

VICTORY OVER THE SAFAVIDS AND THE CONQUEST OF MAMLUK SYRIA AND EGYPT

Selim's accession to the Ottoman throne signaled a radical change in Ottoman-Safavid relations. He launched a full-scale campaign against Shah ISMAIL I (r. 1501–24) in 1514 and defeated his enemy at the battle of Çaldıran (August 23, 1514). As a result of his victory eastern Anatolia was attached to the Ottoman Empire, and Shah Ismail lost his recruiting ground for his Turkoman army.

Historians disagree as to whether Selim had planned the conquest of Mamluk Syria and Egypt. It seems that the Ottomans' renewed claims on Dulkadır territories led to the confrontation with the Mamluks, the Dulkadırs' nominal sovereign. When the Dulkadır ruler Alaüddevle took no notice of Ottoman demands of submission,

Selim defeated and killed him in 1515, installing Alaüddevle's nephew and rival as Istanbul's client and sending the dead ruler's head to the Mamluk Sultan Qansuh al-Ghawri (r. 1500–16) in Cairo. Ottoman chroniclers claim that when Selim was marching against the Safavids in 1514, his supply lines were attacked by Alaüddevle, and thus Selim was forced to make war against the Dulkadırs. Whatever the truth, Selim's victory over the Dulkadırs led to direct Ottoman-Mamluk confrontation.

To justify the war against the Shia Safavids, branded as heretics by Istanbul, was not a problem. However, the Mamluks followed SUNNI ISLAM, as did the Ottomans, and al-Mustansir, a descendant of the last Abbasid caliph, resided in Cairo. The Mamluk sultans were also the protectors of Mecca and Medina and guarantors of the hajj. To justify his attack against the Mamluks, Selim advanced several pretexts and secured a FATWA, or religious opinion, from the Ottoman religious establishment. This accused the Mamluks of oppressing Muslims and justified the war against them with an alleged Mamluk-Safavid alliance, declaring that "he who aids a heretic (that is, the Safavids) is a heretic himself."

The two armies met north of Aleppo at Marj Dabik on August 24, 1516. Ottoman firearms and desertion in the Mamluk camp, a result of intensive Ottoman propaganda in the previous months, sealed the fate of the Mamluks. When Mamluk sultan Qansuh al-Ghawri died, apparently of a heart attack, the remnants of his troops fled. Aleppo and Damascus both surrendered without a fight. Selim's name was incorporated into the *hutbe* (sermon) during the next Friday prayer performed in the great mosque of the Ummayyad caliphs in Damascus. The Ottomans followed the fleeing Mamluk army to Egypt and delivered a second crushing defeat to them on January 23, 1517 at Raydaniyya, outside Cairo. Although remnants of the Mamluk army offered stiff resistance in Cairo, the resistance collapsed when Sultan Tumanbay (r. 1516–17) was captured and killed. With him died the Mamluk sultanate that had ruled for more than 250 years in Egypt and Syria. Its territories were incorporated into Selim's empire as the new provinces of Aleppo, Damascus, and Egypt.

Selim was by now the most prominent Muslim ruler, having defeated the "heretic" Safavids and their Kızılbaş followers. He ruled over the holiest places of Islam, was protector of Mecca and Medina and guarantor of the hajj. His conquests were important to legitimize the House of Osman and brought substantial added revenue into the treasury. With the conquests of the Arab lands, however, the nature of the Ottoman Empire started to change considerably. The roles assumed by the sultan and the influence of the Arab religious establishment required fuller adoption of Islamic practices in governance and policy.

On the other hand, Selim's wars against Muslims and the lack of any major campaign against the Christian "infidels" seem to have presented a "legitimacy deficit" for the sultan. Later Ottoman chroniclers were at pains to emphasize Selim's raids, while still prince-governor in Trabzon, against the Georgians. Indeed, he might have contemplated a major campaign against Christendom. Venetian reports explained the large-scale shipbuilding activity in the Istanbul naval arsenal in 1518–19 with a planned overall Ottoman assault against Christian Europe, purportedly against Rhodes. It seemed probable, in light of the fact that Selim's navy acquired substantial added strength when in 1519 "the pirate of Algiers," Hayreddin Barbarossa (see BARBAROSSA BROTHERS), offered his services to the sultan. By appointing Hayreddin Barbarossa governor (beylerbeyi) of ALGIERS, Sultan Selim considerably strengthened the Ottoman navy and extended Ottoman influence as far as Algiers and TUNIS. Selim's premature death in September 1520, however, nullified all plans, whatever these might have been.

Gábor Ágoston

Further reading: Caroline Finkel, *Osman's Dream: The Story of the Ottoman Empire, 1300–1923* (London: John Murray, 2005); Halil İnalcık, "Selīm I," in *Encyclopaedia of Islam*, online edition (by subscription), edited by P. Bearman, Th. Bianquis, C. E. Bosworth, E. van Donzel, and W. P. Heinrichs. Brill, 2007. Brill Online. GEORGETOWN UNIVERSITY. 31 May 2007 http://www.brillonline.nl/subscriber/entry?entry=islam_COM-1015; Donald Edgar Pitcher, *An Historical Geography of the Ottoman Empire from the Earliest Times to the End of the Sixteenth Century* (Leiden: Brill, 1972).

Selim II (b. 1524–d. 1574) (r. 1566–1574) *Ottoman sultan and caliph* Selim was the third son of the famous Ottoman sultan SÜLEYMAN I (r. 1520–66); his mother was Süleyman's beloved concubine Hürrem Sultan (Roxalane). The history of sultanic succession in the empire was marked by fierce competition for the throne among the Ottoman princes. Although such competition was not missing from Selim's youth, by 1559 all of his brothers—and thus all possible rivals for the throne—were dead. (Prince Mehmed died in 1544, Princes Mustafa and Mehmed Bayezid were executed in 1553 and 1559, respectively.) (See SÜLEYMAN I.) However, in 1566, when Süleyman died in Hungary, Selim II's succession was not without complication. To protect the ENTHRONEMENT AND ACCESSION process, the brilliant grand vizier, SOKOLLU Mehmed Pasha, kept Süleyman's death secret until Selim reached the army in BELGRADE. Even then, Selim's accession was not immediately sanctioned by the JANISSARIES. When the army returned to ISTANBUL, the Janissaries did not allow Selim to enter the palace until he paid the *cülus* gratuity, a gift of money customarily paid by sultans to the military upon accession to the throne.

Perhaps the most significant aspect of Selim's reign was his near total reliance on Grand Vizier Sokollu Mehmed Pasha, one of the most powerful grand viziers in the history of the Ottoman Empire. Mehmed Pasha held the office of grand vizier uninterruptedly for 14 years, from 1565 to 1579, under three successive sultans: Süleyman I, Selim II, and MURAD III (r. 1574–95). The grand vizier was known for appointing family members and kinsmen to key posts in the empire, thus creating a reliable network made up of his protégés. According to contemporaries, during Selim's reign, the ruling the empire was altogether entrusted to Sokollu, who was a virtual sovereign. If Sokollu's overwhelming presence was one of the major reasons for Selim's abstaining from the business of rule, another significant reason was a dramatic shift in the political setting of the empire. The surfacing of the COURT AND FAVORITES system and the sedentarization of the sultanate coincided with the reign of Selim. In fact, these would become the defining features of the power struggles of Selim's successors.

In conventional terms, weighing the reigns of the sultans by the extent of their foreign conquests, Selim's reign was relatively uneventful, since no land campaigns took place during his reign. Selim II was the first sultan of the post-Süleymanic era whose reign passed in the court rather than on the battlefields. His absence from the battlefields and his reluctance to lead his armies cannot be attributed to a deficiency in his training. Like the other princes of the dynasty, he was given the training befitting a warrior sultan. Nor was he unfamiliar with armed conflicts. Even before he became sultan, Selim's competency in battle had been put to the test during the succession struggle with his brother Bayezid (1559). Instead, his absence from battlefields is due to the political circumstances in which he reigned that required a sultan actively involved in the careful planning of court politics, rather than on the battlefields.

Although Selim's reign was not characterized by significant land wars, there were naval campaigns in the Mediterranean during his time. In 1571 the Ottomans captured the island of CYPRUS from the Venetians; with the neighboring areas in mainland Anatolia, it was formed into a new province. At first the torrid climate of the island did not attract much migration, but with pressure from the state, a large number of Turkish people eventually settled there. Later in the same year the so-called Holy League—a joint force of the papal, Venetian, and Spanish fleets—avenged the taking of Cyprus, which was viewed as an important Christian stronghold in the eastern Mediterranean, in the devastating naval BATTLE OF LEPANTO, utterly destroying the Ottoman navy. Although the Ottoman fleet was completely rebuilt within one year, the state did not fully recover from the tremendous loss of skilled and seasoned naval personnel until after Selim's reign. The recovery of the fortress of Tunis from Spain in 1574, only months before Selim II's death, can be added to the naval successes of his reign.

While uncompleted, perhaps the most ambitious venture undertaken during Selim's reign was the building of a canal between the Don and Volga rivers. This large-scale project, which meant digging some 40 miles of uneven terrain, was especially supported by Grand Vizier Sokollu Mehmed Pasha. If completed, the channel would have served the Ottomans along the empire's northern frontiers by controlling Muscovy's advance and providing a base from which the Ottomans could attack Safavid Persia. However, the canal could not be finished because of bad weather and disorder among the soldiers who were sent to the region.

Selim II was represented by his contemporaries as a man of pleasure and was famed for his indulgences, most notably alcohol and hunting. He was also a genuine patron of the arts. Prominent Ottoman intellectual figures, such as the historian Mustafa Ali, the poet Baki, and the *şehnameci* (court chronicler) Lokman were among many who were supported by Selim II. One of the major social and cultural contributions of his reign was building the monumental Selimiye mosque complex, which was named after him. Selim II's preference of EDIRNE over Istanbul for the building site of this impressive mosque complex demonstrates his love for the former Ottoman capital which he enjoyed visiting, particularly during hunting sessions. The Selimiye mosque, with its masterful dome structure designed by the architect Sinan, represents a high point in Ottoman ARCHITECTURE.

Selim II died on December 12, 1574 leaving his son MURAD III (r. 1574–1595) to reign as sultan.

Şefik Peksevgen

Further reading: Leslie Peirce, *The Imperial Harem: Women and Sovereignty in the Ottoman Empire* (New York: Oxford University Press, 1993); Caroline Finkel, *Osman's Dream: The Story of the Ottoman Empire, 1300–1923* (London: John Murray, 2005), 152–195.

Selim III (b. 1761–d. 1808) (r. 1789–1807) *Ottoman sultan and caliph, reformer, and composer* Selim III was the son of Sultan MUSTAFA III (r. 1757–74) and Mihrişah Valide Sultan, a concubine of Georgian origin. Selim's birth was regarded as a fortuitous event since no prince had been born since 1725. Therefore he was given a careful, thorough education and was raised as the potential savior of the empire. His uncle Sultan ABDÜLHAMID I (r. 1774–89) granted him a degree of freedom in social interaction, whereas seclusion in the TOPKAPI PALACE had been the norm for Ottoman princes beginning in the 16th century. Given this freedom, the young prince

began forming his own circle of reformers and corresponded with Louis XVI of France concerning statecraft, social institutions, and military arts in Europe. His freedom of movement was restricted when his name was involved in the alleged plot of Grand Vizier Halil Hamid Pasha against Sultan Abdülhamid I in 1785. Acceding to the throne at the age of 28 after four sultans of advanced age, his reign meant for his subjects the beginning of a new era. With the imagination of a great reformer, Selim undertook the major reforms known as the NIZAM-I CEDID (New Order) with the aim of restructuring Ottoman politics and military institutions, reforms that ultimately had long-term repercussions in the political, social, and economic configuration of his empire.

The Ottoman Empire was caught up in wars with both RUSSIA and the Habsburg Empire as well as local uprisings, such as those of the WAHHABIS, throughout the Balkans and the Arabian Peninsula. The dramatic changes brought about in European continental politics by the French Revolution in 1789 made it possible for the Ottomans to conclude the TREATY OF SVISHTOV (August 4, 1791) with the Habsburg Empire with minimum loss of territory despite the military defeats. However, Russia fell on the exhausted Ottoman armies to gain the upper hand in negotiations that resulted in the TREATY OF JASSY (January 9, 1792) in which the Ottoman Empire reaffirmed the Russian annexation of the Crimea.

Peace provided the opportunity for Selim to introduce his Nizam-ı Cedid REFORM program, which was shaped by reform proposals submitted by several statesmen and intellectuals. The tangible results of the program were seen in the spheres of the military and diplomacy. The overwhelming costs of the new army (reaching 23,000 men in 1807) required setting up a separate treasury, the Irad-ı Cedid (New Revenues), which meant an increased tax burden on the already impoverished people.

The Ottoman alliances with Sweden (1789) and Prussia (1790) against Russia and the Habsburg Empire were followed by an Ottoman alliance with ENGLAND and Russia against FRANCE when France invaded EGYPT in 1799. Despite the strong pro-British leanings of the Ottoman reformers and the intense diplomatic pressure brought to bear on the empire during the First Coalition Wars (1793–95) declared on the revolutionary regime of France, the Sublime Porte declared neutrality for the first time in its history, determined to remain outside European political entanglements in order to carry forward its program of domestic reform. Given the weakened condition of the Ottoman state, Selim made use of political tools new to the Ottoman experience, most notably modern diplomacy. This resulted in the appointment of the first permanent ambassadors to London (1793), Berlin (1795), Vienna (1795), and Paris (1795); St. Petersburg was excluded because of rumors concerning Russian military preparation against the Ottoman Empire in 1795.

The first military action against France in the Second Coalition Wars (1799–1801) involved sending a joint Russo-Ottoman fleet against the French in the Ionian islands in the Adriatic. This made the Ottomans a party to a coalition for the first time in history. The second declaration of Ottoman neutrality during the Franco-British War in 1803 came under the pressure of its allies, Britain and Russia. However, successive French victories in Europe, especially the humiliation of the Habsburgs in the Battle of Austerlitz (1805), persuaded the Ottomans to pursue a pro-French diplomacy. The renewal of the Ottoman alliance with Russia in 1805 did not prevent Selim from recognizing NAPOLEON BONAPARTE as emperor of France in 1806. The Ottoman refusal to comply with Russian demands with regard to the Romanian principalities and to expel the French ambassador after 1805 resulted in a war with Britain and the Russo-Ottoman War of 1806–1812 (see RUSSO-OTTOMAN WARS). The British responded to the Ottoman recognition of Napoleon by sending a fleet to ISTANBUL in February 1807, a heavy political blow for pro-British Ottoman reformers, although the move was of little consequence in military terms.

Sultan Selim's internal opponents made use of the unsettled political conditions of the empire—the shifting international alliances and the ensuing revolts of the Wahhabis and the Serbians—to form a coalition composed of local Balkan power brokers, Istanbul-based ULEMA, and the JANISSARIES. When Sultan Selim attempted to introduce his reformed Nizam-ı Cedid troops in the Balkans in 1806, these opposing forces refused to admit the troops into EDIRNE in an episode that became known in Turkish historiography as the second Edirne Incident. The sultan's opponents in the palace transformed this political conspiracy into an open revolt that cost Sultan Selim III his throne and life.

The decisive incident took place in the fortresses along the Bosporus when troops there, encouraged by the sultan's opponents in the palace, refused to wear the European-style uniform of the Nizam-ı Cedid army. Unaware of the political conspiracy, Sultan Selim refrained from sending the Nizam-ı Cedid troops to suppress the uprising. The march of rebellious Ottoman troops to Istanbul on the secret invitation of the sultan's enemies created a snowball effect and the uprising turned into a revolt. The demoralized sultan complied with all the demands of the rebels, including disbanding his Nizam-ı Cedid army and executing his reform entourage, but he could not save his throne. Sultan Selim was assassinated the following year in an attempted counter-coup orchestrated by his supporters Alemdar (Bayraktar) MUSTAFA PASHA, the local power broker of Rusçuk (Ruse), and Grand Vizier Çelebi Mustafa.

Ebbs and flows of diplomacy notwithstanding, economic depredations, the extravagance of his court, and most importantly the lack of a broad base of support for his reform agenda sealed the fate of the first great reformist sultan of the Ottoman Empire.

Kahraman Şakul

Further reading: Virginia Aksan, "Selim III," in *Encyclopaedia of Islam,* 2nd ed., edited by P. J. Bearman et. al., vol. 9 (Leiden: Brill, 1960–), 132–134; Virginia Aksan, *Ottoman Wars 1700-1870: An Empire Besieged* (Harlow, England: Longman/Pearson, 2007), 180–258; Caroline Finkel, *Osman's Dream: The Story of the Ottoman Empire, 1300–1923* (London: John Murray, 2005), 383–412; Ekmeleddin İhsanoğlu, ed., *History of the Ottoman State, Society, and Civilisation,* vol. 1 (Istanbul: Ircica, 2001), 63–77; Stanford J. Shaw, *Between Old and New: The Ottoman Empire Under Selim III, 1789–1807* (Cambridge: Cambridge University Press, 1971); Stanford J. Shaw, "The Transition from Traditionalistic to Modern Reform in the Ottoman Empire: The Reigns of Sultan Selim III (1789–1807) and Sultan Mahmud II (1808–1839)," in *The Turks,* vol. 4, edited by Hasan Celal Guzel, C. Cem Oguz, and Osman Karatay (Ankara: Yeni Türkiye Yayınları, 2002), 130–149.

Seljuks (Selcuks, Selçuks) The Seljuk dynasty was one of the most important dynasties in Turko-Islamic history that ruled during the early medieval period over a vast area stretching from Central Asia to Anatolia. The Seljuks emerged in the beginning of the 11th century in Transoxania (present-day Uzbekistan). Until the early 14th century, they ruled over Khorasan, Khwarezm, IRAN, IRAQ, HEJAZ, SYRIA, and Anatolia. Although there were five states bearing the name Seljuk, the one called Great Seljuks by historians is the central one. The Great Seljuks, who conquered Anatolia from the Byzantine Empire, became the protectors of the Sunni Abbasid caliphs in BAGHDAD against the Shia Fatimids in EGYPT and Syria, and the Fatimids' Iranian allies in Iraq, the Buyids. Their state organization, based on central Asian, Iranian, and Islamic traditions, served as a model for many states, both contemporaneous and established later in history, including the Ottoman Empire, which succeeded the Seljuks in Anatolia.

THE GREAT SELJUKS (1038–1157)

Seljuk, after whom the dynasty was named, was the grandfather of Tughril (c. 990–1063), the first Seljuk sultan. Although there are differing views about the pronunciation and meaning of his name, Seljuk (Turkish Selcuk) can be translated as "Little flood" or "Contestant." Seljuk was the military commander of the Oghuz state in the upper regions of the Aral Sea during the second half of the 10th century. At some point, Seljuk and his people settled on the shores of the Syr Darya River, which bordered the Muslim Samanid state, and embraced Islam.

When Seljuk died his eldest son, Arslan Yabghu (d. 1032), became the head of the family. However, Arslan was taken captive by the ruler of another Turkic state, the Ghaznavids, and died in captivity. Although Musa Yabghu, the only surviving son of Seljuk, officially became the head of the family, in reality his nephews Chagrı (d. 1059) and Tughril held the power. Under their leadership the Seljuks routed the Ghaznavids and gained control of Khorasan, followed shortly by Khwarezm. Tughril Beg was enthroned as sultan and Nishabur was declared the capital, thus establishing the first Seljuk state. In 1048 Qawurd, son of Chaghrı, occupied Kirman and set up the state of the Kirman Seljuks, dependent on the Great Seljuks. During Tughril's rule, the local dynasties in Iran pledged allegiance to the Seljuks. Soon after some states in Azerbaijan and in eastern and southeastern Anatolia became vassals of the Seljuks. At the time of Tughril's death in 1063 the Great Seljuk Empire stretched from the River Oxus (Amu Darya) to the EUPHRATES.

Alp Arslan (r. 1063–72), son of Chagrı, who became sultan after crushing several insurrections, pressed the Seljuk expansion into Anatolia in 1071. Although Byzantine emperor Romanus IV Diogenes (r. 1068–71) gathered a huge army to repulse the Seljuk onslaught he suffered defeat at the Battle of Manzikert, near Lake Van, in 1071, which opened Anatolia to the advancing Seljuks.

Malikshah (r. 1072–1092), who succeeded his father Chagrı, further expanded the empire. Under his leadership JERUSALEM, DAMASCUS, ALEPPO, Mosul, Antioch in SYRIA, PALESTINE, Diyarbakir in southeastern Anatolia, al-Ahsa, Bahrain, HEJAZ, YEMEN came under Seljuk control. Turkish beys, or rulers, were appointed to administer each region. The Rum Seljuk state was established in Anatolia in c. 1075 by Sulayman Shah. Malikshah's brother Tutush established the Syrian Seljuk State in 1079. However, Malikshah died after the struggle for supremacy among the princes and rebellions by vassal emirates, and the empire began to disintegrate. Berkyaruk (d. 1104), the eldest son of Malikshah, was enthroned, but he was unable to stop the empire's collapse, and the commanders soon became autonomous rulers of their respective regions. The Iraq Seljuk state was established in 1119. Campaigns against the crusader armies were unsuccessful; the Ismailis gradually increased their power; and in 1141 Sanjar (d. 1157), the last sultan of the Great Seljuks, was defeated by the Qarakhitay, a central Asian people, and the Seljuks lost control of Transoxania. Sanjar could not revive the empire, and the Great Seljuks disintegrated after his death.

Other Seljuk states also soon disintegrated, including Syria and Palestine in 1117, Kirman, Iran, in 1186, and Iraq in 1194. Only the Seljuk state in Anatolia, called the Seljuks of Rum, survived and continued to fight the passage of the crusaders across their territory. However, after suffering a decisive defeat at Kösedagh in 1243, the Seljuk state was subjected to Mongol domination and lost its independence. The Rum Seljuk state is considered to have come to an end in 1308 with the death of Mesud III.

While the Seljuks disappeared as a ruling dynasty, various Turkoman dynasties established principalities in various parts of Anatolia. Known as ANATOLIAN EMIRATES or beyliks, the Karamanoğulları, Germiyanoğulları, Mentşeoğulları, Hamidoğulları, Candaroğulları, and the Ottomans founded their sovereignties on this Seljuk heritage.

POLITICAL SYSTEM

Dynastic succession in the Seljuk states followed Turkish tradition. Among the members of the ruling dynasty, the person who succeeded in imposing his supremacy over the rest of the family members became the sultan or ruler. The state was governed by the sultan and the princes who submitted to him. Every prince had the potential of becoming a sultan. The struggle for supremacy among the members of the dynasty continued throughout Seljuk history and caused considerable turmoil.

Because the Seljuks' transition from nomadism occurred shortly before their rise to power, they had no bureaucratic tradition of their own. Under these circumstances they benefited from the experience of the eastern Islamic states. The Seljuk civil service system was borrowed from the Ghaznavids, a Turkish state in Afghanistan and Iran. When the Seljuks entered the region, many bureaucrats and commanders in the service of the Ghaznavids came under Seljuk rule. The Seljuks continued the Ghaznavid tradition of selecting the palace staff, royal guard, khassa army (the private professional army under the command of the sultan), and senior bureaucrats of the government and provinces from among the educated ghulams, former slaves who had been bought from slave traders or taken prisoner in wars. Personnel received their salary quarterly. The finances of the state were based on a land grant system called iqta (ikta). Most land belonged to the state, and the tax revenue from the land was used to pay salaries to government staff and military personnel as well as to the vassal rulers. The system was administered by iqta holders, who in times of peace were responsible for administering the lands delivered to their custody and in times of war for recruiting soldiers within their region. Although feudalism was not part of the original system, in time the iqta holders, whose political and economic powers had increased, assumed quasi-feudal powers or became semi-independent.

The Seljuks were followers of SUNNI ISLAM and, out of the four schools of religious law, opted for that of the Hanafi. However, they tolerated followers of other religious schools and non-Muslim subjects. Under the Seljuks, Persian became the official and literary language while Arabic was preferred as the language of law, thus overshadowing the Turkish language.

The Seljuk government and bureaucracy reached its highest level under Nizam al-Mulk, vizier or chief minister for Alp Arslan and his son Malikshah for almost three decades. His treatise on government and politics, *Siyaset-name* (Book of government), served as a model for later Islamic treatises, including those written in the Ottoman Empire. Nizam al-Mulk also founded several madrasas or colleges, known as the Nizamiya madrasas, which served as models for later madrasas in successor Muslim states. Prominent scholars under the Seljuk dynasty included al-Ghazali (1058–1111), an outstanding theologian and philosopher and author of the *Intentions of Philosophers* and *The Incoherence of the Philosophers*, critical works of Neoplatonist philosophers; Omar Khayyam (ca. 1048–1122), the famed Persian poet, philosopher, mathematician, and astronomer, known in the West for his quatrains (*rubaiyat*); and the philosopher Fakhr al-Din al-Razi (1149–1209), who used new logical methods. Omar Khayyam and his fellow astronomers made a calendar called *Taqvim-i Malikshahi*. The influence of Jalal al-Din Rumi (1207–1273), the celebrated Sufi master and founder of the MEVLEVI ORDER of dervishes; Hajji Bektaş, another famous Sufi sheikh of the late 13th century and founder of the BEKTAŞI ORDER of dervishes, the order associated later with the Ottoman elite JANISSARIES, was especially important in the later Ottoman Empire. The Seljuks also set up innumerable madrasas, mosques, *zaviyes* (convents or lodges), hospitals (*dar al-shifa*), caravansaries, and bridges, and created WAQFS or religious endowments that supported them. Many of these institutions were used by and served as models for the Ottomans. Elements of the Seljuk governmental-bureaucratic system were later adopted by the Ottomans, as was the *iqta*, that is, the Seljuk land or revenues grant, which survived in the form of the Ottoman *timar* system (see AGRICULTURE).

Sadi S. Kucur

Further reading: C. E. Bosworth et al., "Saldjukids," in *Encyclopaedia of Islam*, 2nd ed., vol. 8 (Leiden: Brill, 1960–), 936–978; Cl. Cahen, *The Formation of Turkey: The Seljukid Sultanate of Rum—Eleventh to Fourteenth Century* (Harlow, U.K.: Longman, 2001); O. Turan, "Anatolia in the Period of the Seljuks and the Beyliks," in *The Cambridge History of Islam*, edited by P. M. Holt, Ann K. S. Lambton, and Bernard Lewis (Cambridge: Cambridge University Press, 1970), 231–50; Ann K. S. Lambton, *Continuity and Change in Medieval Persia: Aspects of Administrative, Economic and Social History, 11th–14th Century* (London: Tauris, 1988); A. Sevim and C. E. Bosworth, "The Seljuqs and the Khwarazm Shahs," in *History of Civilizations of Central Asia*, vol. 4, *The Age of Achievement: A.D. 750 to the End of the Fifteenth Century*—Part One: *The Historical, Social and Economic Setting*, edited by M. S. Asimov and C. E. Bosworth (Paris: Unesco, 1998).

Serbia (Servia; *Serb.*: Srbija; *Turk.*: Sirbistan) The medieval Balkan state of Serbia, built by the Nemanjić dynasty in the 12th century, reached its golden age during the rule of Czar Stefan Dushan (r. 1331–55). His state extended from the DANUBE River to Macedonia and Thessaly, incorporating present-day ALBANIA, Montenegro, parts of BOSNIA AND HERZEGOVINA on the west, and parts of BULGARIA on the east. During the second half of the 14th century Serbia was weakened and divided among local notables. After a long period of struggle and vassalage, the Serbian state was finally conquered by the Ottomans in 1459. Following an uprising at the beginning of the 19th century Serbs achieved autonomy for their future state in 1830, although they were not fully recognized as an independent state until 1878.

CONTACTS WITH THE TURKS

The first clashes between Serbs and Turks took place in 1344 in a battle with the troops of Omur, the leader, or bey, of the Anatolian Turkish principality of Aydın. Apparently the first contact with the Ottomans was diplomatic. In 1351 the ruler of Serbia, czar Stefan Dushan, offered the Ottoman ruler ORHAN (r. 1324–62) his daughter's hand in marriage, seeking to attract him to his side in the war against the Byzantine coregent, John VI (r. 1341–55). The alliance was not formed.

The first great battle between Serbia and the Ottoman Empire took place outside Serbian territory at the river Maritsa on September 26, 1371. Two Serbian despots (rulers) of Macedonia launched a preemptive strike to halt the Ottoman advance in the Balkans but suffered a crushing defeat and both lost their lives in the battle. The Serbian defeat opened the way for the Ottomans to the north and to the west. Although the BATTLE OF KOSOVO, which is thought to have taken place on June 15, 1389, seems to have been inconclusive, both the Ottoman sultan MURAD I (r. 1362–89) and the Serbian ruler Prince Lazar lost their lives in the battle, together with most of the Serbian aristocracy. After the battle, Lazar's sons became vassals of BAYEZID I (r. 1389–1402), which was confirmed by his marriage to Lazar's daughter Olivera. In the BATTLE OF ANKARA (1402) between the Ottomans and the troops of TIMUR, the Serbian troops and their rulers fought on the side of the Ottomans as their vassals. Soon after, the two most powerful Serbian families—the

Lazarevićs and the Brankovićs (see BRANKOVIĆ FAMILY)—began to fight for power, entering various short-lived alliances with the Ottomans, and also took part in the Ottoman civil war that followed the Ottoman defeat at Ankara and Sultan Bayezid's death in 1403 in Timur's captivity.

Despot Stefan Lazarević (r. 1389–1427) tried to avoid major conflicts with the Ottomans until about 1425. However, Serbian military buildup and open negotiations with Serbia's northern neighbor, HUNGARY, the strongest central European state and an Ottoman enemy, provided sufficient reason for MURAD II (1421–44, 1446–51) to launch a military campaign against Serbia. The Ottoman forces devastated parts of Serbia (including Niš, Leskovac, and Kruševac) and, at the beginning of 1427, laid an unsuccessful siege to the rich silver mines of Novo Brdo.

At that time the Ottoman-Hungarian conflict reached a crisis, often spreading into Serbian territory, while the new despot, Djuradj Branković (1427–56), failed to win the trust of the Ottomans. By 1433 all the territory south of the western Morava River and east of the Great Morava River had come into Ottoman possession. Despite the fact that he had married of his daughter to the sultan and had surrendered his sons Stefan and Grgur as hostages, Djuradj was considered unreliable as a vassal because he did not prevent Hungarian raids. For this reason, Murad II occupied the Serbian despotate in 1439, meeting little resistance apart from a somewhat protracted siege of Smederevo.

OTTOMAN CONQUEST OF SERBIA

The first Ottoman occupation of Serbia lasted until 1443 when they had to fall back before strong anti-Ottoman resistance led by János (John) Hunyadi (b. 1408?–d. 1456), governor of TRANSYLVANIA and commander in chief of the Hungarian army; the exiled Serbian despot Djuradj Branković also took part. Facing serious threats from both east and west, Murad II concluded a peace agreement with the Hungarians and the Serbian despot in EDIRNE in 1444. Serbia was restored to the Djuradj, but without the key strategic locations of Niš, Stalać, and Kruševac.

Despot Djuradj Branković did not participate in the Crusade, launched by the Hungarians, that ended in a crushing defeat at Varna in 1444. In spite of the obvious proofs of loyalty by Djuradj—exemplified by his capture of Hunyadi after the Ottomans defeated the Hungarians at Kosovo in 1448 and a complete break with Hungary, as well as his participation in the siege of Constantinople in 1453—the new sultan, MEHMED II (r. 1444–46, 1451–81), launched a military campaign against Serbia in 1454. He met strong resistance and it was not until the following year, 1455, that he finally managed to conquer the mining center Novo Brdo and extend Ottoman rule to the western Morava River. Despite the peace concluded at the beginning of 1456, in that same year Mehmed II again laid an unsuccessful siege to Smederevo and later to BELGRADE, then in Hungarian hands as the key fortress of the Hungarian defense system.

During the reign of Lazar Branković (r. 1456–58), the youngest son of Djuradj who became despot upon his father's death, Serbia enjoyed a short respite. Branković's older sons, Stefan and Grgur, had been blinded as hostages in Murad's court in 1441 at the time of the Ottoman-Hungarian War. The political situation grew tense when Stefan (r. 1458–59) was designated despot against the wishes of Mehmed, who supported Grgur. A strong pro-Ottoman faction in the despotate was headed by Mihailo Angelović, Grand Vizier Mahmud Pasha's brother. In 1458 Mahmud Pasha conquered several cities, the most important of which was the fortress Golubac on the Danube. The despotate fell into decline, reduced practically to Smederevo alone. The king of Hungary sought to resolve the situation by overthrowing Stefan and by declaring the son of the Bosnian king, Stefan Tomašević, despot in 1459. Lazar's daughter Jelena was married to Stefan Tomašević on April 1, and Stefan Branković was dethroned on April 8. However, Stefan Tomašević turned Smederevo over to Mehmed II on June 20 without a fight. This signaled the end of the Serbian medieval state.

OTTOMAN RULE IN SERBIA

Soon after this the subprovince (sancak) of Smederevo/Semendire was established. It kept its name even after the seat of its governor (sancakbeyi) was transferred to Belgrade following its capture in 1521. The first sancakbeyi of Smederevo was Mehmed Bey Minnetoğlu (r. 1459–63). Before that, the sancaks of Prizren, Vučitrn, and Kručevac (Alaca Hisar) had been set up. After the Ottoman conquest of Bosnia in 1463, around the year 1480, the sancak of Zvornik was founded, incorporating areas on both sides of the Drina River, a part of former western Serbia. A part of eastern Serbia had already been included in the sancak of Vidin.

The Serbian people had long inhabited many areas of southern Hungary, including Srem and Bačka. Scattered all over the central and western Balkans—including in Venetian Dalmatia and the Montenegrin coast and in the Habsburg monarchy—Serbs were brought together by a single institution, the SERBIAN ORTHODOX CHURCH. Its hierarchy was made up of the Serbian elite.

In all the wars fought in the Balkans (the Long War of 1593–1606, the war against the Holy League War of 1683–99, the Habsburg-Ottoman wars of 1716–18, 1736–39, 1788–91), the Serbs took an active part as opponents of the Ottomans, including organizing uprisings. They suffered severe consequences, while the areas in which they lived were devastated. During the war against the Holy League (*see* AUSTRIA) the patriarch, the head of about 60,000 members of the Serbian Orthodox Church mostly from Kosovo, was driven into exile in the Habsburg domain in Hungary. The mass emigration continued during subsequent wars.

The term *Serbia* appeared for the first time as the name of an administrative region in the newly conquered Habsburg area between the Sava, Danube, and western Morava (1718–36).

THE ROAD TO AUTONOMY

After 1793, Serbs in the *sancak* of Smederevo gained a certain level of autonomy, which mostly meant that local *knezes* (princes, headmen) had the right to collect taxes themselves. The situation in the *sancak* was tense due to an uprising against the Ottomans by the JANISSARIES. In 1804 the Janissaries took control of the area by killing the Ottoman governor in Belgrade and executing more than a hundred Serbian notables. This "felling of the *knezes*" led to a general uprising mounted on February 14, 1804 and led by Djordje Petrović, known as KARADJORDJE. Having succeeded in killing some Janissary officers, and carried away by their initial success, the Serbs refused to lay down their weapons to the regular Ottoman authorities. Encouraged by the Russian-Ottoman war, which began in 1807 and later led to the arrival of Russian troops (*see* RUSSO-OTTOMAN WARS), the Serbs refused all peace proposals and demanded full independence. The Russian-Ottoman TREATY AT BUCHAREST (1812) put an end to all hope of success and the rebellion was crushed the following year. Article 8 of the Bucharest agreement stipulated modest autonomy for the Serbs, but the Ottomans did not accept this provision.

The road to autonomy was not opened until April 23, 1815 when the Second Uprising was mounted under the leadership of Knez Miloš Obrenović. Miloš opened negotiations in the same year seeking to achieve autonomy gradually, without revolutionary demands. In the Russian-Ottoman Convention of Akkerman (1826), the Ottomans pledged to fulfill the rights guaranteed by the Bucharest treaty. Ottoman imperial rescripts (*hatt-i şerif*s) from 1829 and 1830, issued upon the conclusion of peace in EDIRNE (1829), granted Serbia autonomy and defined its borders, while Miloš was acknowledged as the hereditary prince. Serbia annexed six additional districts or *nahiye*s and became a de facto principality under Ottoman suzerainty while Russia was granted the status of protector. A fixed lump sum of taxes was paid once a year to Istanbul, the *sipahi* system was dismantled, and the military presence was limited to small garrisons in several fortresses. Only a few cities continued to have a Muslim population.

The Ottomans were forced to withdraw all military personnel from Serbia in 1867. The independence of Ser-

bia was not internationally recognized until the Congress of Berlin (1878). Bowing to public pressure, Serbia went to war with the Ottoman Empire, first in 1876 and then in 1877–78 following the uprising of the Serbs in BOSNIA AND HERZEGOVINA. Serbia conquered and annexed Niš, Pirot, Vranje, and Leskovac, later ratified by the Congress of Berlin. The final war between Serbia and the Ottoman Empire, the First BALKAN WAR, took place in 1912.

Aleksandar Fotić

Further reading: Colin Imber, *The Ottoman Empire, 1300–1481* (Istanbul: Isis, 1990); B. Jelavich, *History of the Balkans*, vol. 1, *Eighteenth and Nineteenthth Centuries* (Cambridge: Cambridge University Press, 1983); M. B. Petrovich, *A History of Modern Serbia*, 1804–1918 (New York and London: Harcourt Brace Jovanovich 1976).

Serbian Orthodox Church The Serbian Orthodox Church was established in 1219 as an autocephalous member of the Orthodox communion, meaning that the Serbian people followed the traditions of Orthodox Christianity but that their church was not subordinate to an external patriarch. Religious books were written in old Serbian-Slavonic, which was also the language of the service. In 1346 when Stefan Dushan (r. 1331–55) was crowned czar, the Serbian Orthodox Church was raised to the rank of patriarchate with its seat in Peć, Kosovo (for this reason also called the Peć Patriarchate), but the patriarch of Constantinople did not recognize the authority of the Serbian patriarch until 1375.

Following the Ottoman annexation of the BRANKOVIĆ lands in Kosovo (1455), the seat of the church was transferred to Smederevo, the capital of the Ottoman vassal state SERBIA. When the Serbian state came under direct Ottoman rule in 1459, the Serbian church organization did not disappear. However, little is known about its history until the mid-16th century. The Serbian autocephalous church, which comprised northern Serbia, Srem, parts of Bosnia, Herzegovina, and Montenegro, probably did not disintegrate until the 1520s. After the fall of the Serbian state, the church was weakened, and the well-organized neighboring autonomous Ohrid archbishopric wanted to take control of as many dioceses as possible. However, most of the Serbian clergy, led by Pavle, the bishop of Smederevo, did not accept the jurisdiction of the Ohrid archdiocese, which never managed to assume control of these territories.

The fact that the church hierarchy was ineffective in a larger part of the Serb-inhabited Balkans also meant that there was no proper state control. The Ottoman idea of controlling the empire's non-Muslim communities was based on firm and stable church organization, with leaders appointed by the sultan's decree. To resolve this problem the Peć Patriarchate was restored in 1557.

Sokollu Mehmed Pasha (see Sokollu family), who then occupied the position of third vizier, played an important part in the restoration of the patriarchate, and his cousin Makarije Sokolović was appointed as the first patriarch. The hierarchical organization of the Peć Patriarchate mirrored that of the Orthodox Patriarchate of Constantinople; it operated in the same way and had the same rights and duties. The only difference between the two churches was that services in the Peć Patriarchate were held in the Serbian language. The high clergy was made up of Serbs, although several patriarchs in the 18th century were of Greek descent.

The restored Peć Patriarchate covered a large territory, far beyond its original size: It stretched to the farthest Ottoman borders in Dalmatia, Croatia, and Hungary, and included Sofia (Bulgaria) in the east and territories south of Skopje (Macedonia). It also assumed control of dioceses outside the Ottoman Empire, including in Habsburg Croatia and along the Venetian Adriatic coast, which was certainly of great importance to the Porte. The extent of the territory was reflected in the patriarch's full title, "patriarch of Serbians, Bulgarians, maritime and northern parts." The Serbs controlled the patriarchate, but in concept it was a supranational organization created to encompass all newly conquered Ottoman territories and the entire population, regardless of national origins and whether or not they were followers of the Orthodox religion. Since the sultans did not want to officially allow the establishment of the Catholic Church, they issued berats (patents of office) granting the Peć patriarch the right to collect duties from the Catholic population but did not give it the right to interfere with the organization of the Catholic religious community and its spiritual work. This caused serious problems, especially in Ottoman Bosnia, which was densely populated by Catholics. The final solution to the problem was postponed for centuries. When Catholic complaints reached the Porte, Istanbul responded by issuing fermans (imperial decrees) demanding that the authorities honor an "ancient privilege," meaning that the Orthodox bishops had no right to interfere even with the collection of church taxes from Catholics.

The restoration of the patriarchate brought progress—new churches were built, diocese networks were established and strengthened, and religious art, especially painting, flourished. Books, primarily religious, were copied, and for a while some monastery printing shops were in operation.

Toward the end of the 17th century the position of the Peć Patriarchate weakened due to the patriarch's open collaboration with Austria during the Ottomans' war against the Holy League (1683–99) and the subsequent Austrian-Ottoman wars. When Ottoman attempts to regain control through the appointment of Greek patri-

archs failed, the Peć Patriarchate was brought under the Patriarchate of Constantinople in 1766. The key positions of the Orthodox religious hierarchy in lands inhabited by Serbs, including metropolitan and bishopric seats, were in the hands of Greeks from that time until the autonomous Serbian principality was proclaimed in 1830. Autocephaly was achieved in 1879, a year after Serbia was internationally recognized as an independent state in 1878.

Aleksandar Fotić

Further reading: L. Hadrovics, *Le peuple serbe et son Église sous la domination turque* (Paris: Presses universitaires de France, 1947).

Sèvres, Treaty of (1920)   Conceived in the wake of the Ottoman loss in World War I and signed at Sèvres, France on August 10, 1920, this treaty was designed to abolish the Ottoman Empire and to partition its territories. While much thought and discussion went into negotiating and framing its terms, however, the Treaty of Sèvres was never accepted by the Turkish national assembly and was thus unenforceable. Concluded between the Allied powers (France, Russia, England, Italy, and the United States) and the government of the Ottoman Empire, the treaty abolished the Ottoman Empire, obliged Turkey to renounce rights over its Arab lands in the Middle East and North Africa, and provided for an independent Armenia and Greek control over the Aegean islands commanding the Dardanelles. These provisions were rejected by the Turkish national assembly, and the Treaty of Sèvres was replaced in 1923 by the Treaty of Lausanne.

World War I ended on the Ottoman front on October 30, 1918 with the signing of the Armistice of Mondros. This agreement might have been an important step toward permanent peace for the Ottoman Empire. However, the Allies wanted the empires of all the defeated parties—Germany, Austria-Hungary, and the Ottoman Empire—to be dissolved. To that end the Allies organized a peace conference in Paris on January 18, 1919. The first item on the agenda at the conference was to force devastating terms on the defeated Germany, resulting in the signing of the notorious Versailles Treaty on June 28, 1919. Meanwhile, the Allies invited the leaders of the defeated Ottoman Empire to the Paris Peace Conference. The Ottoman delegation put forward a memorandum based on the four Wilsonian principles (an international security organization, reductions of national armaments, democracy, and the free flow of goods across national borders). This memorandum was rejected by the Allies. At the same time, a struggle against Allied forces in Anatolia took place under the leadership of Mustafa Kemal Pasha (see Kemal Atatürk).

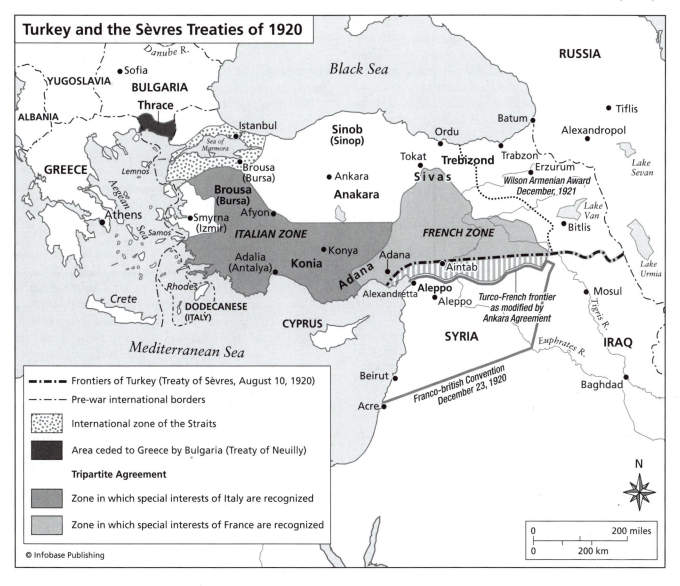

Turkey and the Sèvres Treaties of 1920

Legend:

— · ·— Frontiers of Turkey (Treaty of Sèvres, August 10, 1920)

— · — Pre-war international borders

International zone of the Straits

Area ceded to Greece by Bulgaria (Treaty of Neuilly)

Tripartite Agreement

Zone in which special interests of Italy are recognized

Zone in which special interests of France are recognized

© Infobase Publishing

The Allies discussed issues such as the future of the Ottoman Empire, the right to pass through the straits of the Bosporus and the Dardanelles, and control of ISTANBUL. From April 18–26, 1920, the prime ministers of France, Great Britain, and Italy, and representatives of Japan, GREECE, and Belgium held a meeting in San Remo, Italy, and prepared a draft of the peace treaty for the Ottoman Empire. The outline of this treaty was delivered to Grand Vizier Tevfik Pasha on May 11 in Paris. According to the draft, which later became known as the Treaty of Sèvres, Istanbul would be left to Turkey; Turkey's western borders would be marked by the province of Çatalca (today in Istanbul); IZMIR, the surrounding areas, eastern Thrace, including EDIRNE, and all the Aegean Islands, would be given to Greece; the straits of Istanbul and Çanakkale (Dardanelles) would be governed by an international commission; the Ottoman Empire's military power would be limited and the capitulations

increased. In Asia, Turkey would renounce sovereignty over IRAQ (Mesopotamia) and PALESTINE (including Trans-Jordan), which would become British mandates; Greater Syria (including Lebanon) and Cilicia (including Adana, Mersin) would become French mandates; and the kingdom Hejaz would come into existence. Also, an independent Armenian state would be founded in the territory that was left on the eastern side of the EUPHRATES RIVER; and the southern part of this region, where Kurds constituted the majority, would be granted autonomy under the name Kurdistan.

This treaty was unacceptable to Tevfik Pasha, who saw it as a means to destroy the Ottoman Empire. Together with two other members of the Ottoman delegation, Reşid Bey, the minister of Internal Affairs, and Cemil Pasha, the minister of Public Works, Tevfik Pasha prepared another peace treaty. He sent the new outline to the government headed by Damat Ferid Pasha in Istanbul. The government accepted the outline with minor changes, and Damat Ferid Pasha presented it to the Allies on June 25. However, the Allies initially did not respond to the outline, and after waiting in vain for a response, Damat Ferid Pasha returned to Istanbul on July 14. In the meantime the Spa Conference had been organized (July 7–16), at the end of which the Allies presented the Ottomans with an ultimatum.

Meanwhile, the Greeks had begun a military operation in Anatolia on June 12 to pressure the Ottoman Empire into accepting the Treaty of Sèvres. At the same time, a new Turkish national assembly founded in Ankara on April 23, 1920, promulgated a law on June 7, 1920 that declared any law introduced by the Ottoman government after March 16, 1920 not binding on the Turkish government. The Ottoman government called together the Imperial Council on July 22 to address the situation. Sultan MEHMED VI (r. 1918–22) and the highest Ottoman authorities came together and all but Rıza Pasha declared their approval of the peace treaty proposed by the Allies. As a consequence, the Ottoman delegation signed the Treaty of Sèvres with the Allies on August 10, 1920. On the same day, the Allies signed a tripartite accord that formalized the spheres of special interest in Anatolia for France and Italy. This accord was independent of the secret agreements of 1916 and the mandate system. By the terms of this agreement Italy was given parts of southwest Anatolia (including Antalya) and western Anatolia outside Izmir, while France obtained a zone that included Mersin, Adana, Maraş, Diyarbakir, Sivas, Malatya, and Harput.

For Mustafa Kemal Atatürk, the Treaty of Sèvres was a major setback. However, according to the Ottoman constitution of 1876, international agreements did not take effect until approved by parliament. As a result of the Turkish national independence movement the Treaty of Sèvres never took effect, because the Turkish parliament failed to ratify it.

Mustafa Budak

Further reading: Paul C. Helmreich, *From Paris to Sèvres: The Partition of the Ottoman Empire at the Peace Conference of 1919–1920* (Columbus: Ohio State University Press, 1974); Harry N. Howard, *The Partition of Turkey: A Diplomatic History, 1913–1923* (New York: H. Fertig, 1966); A. L. Macfie, *The End of the Ottoman Empire, 1908–1923* (London: Longman, 1998); Salahi Ramsdan Sonyel, *Turkish Diplomacy, 1918–1923: Mustafa Kemal and the Turkish National Movement* (London: Sage Publications, 1975); Harold William Vazeille Temperley, ed., *A History of the Peace Conference of Paris* (London: Oxford University Press, 1969).

sex and sexuality Stories of harems, odalisques, eunuchs, and sodomy seemed bizarre and intriguing to European travelers in the East starting in the 18th cen-

tury. Although concepts of sex and gender in the BYZANTINE EMPIRE, the Christian predecessor of the Ottoman Empire, were not dissimilar from those prevalent in the Ottoman world, by the late 15th and the early 16th centuries Europe had begun to evolve a new sexual morality. Thus when the Ottomans established their empire in the late 15th and early 16th centuries, European travelers, the main sources of information about the empire, were often preoccupied with issues of sexual morality and what they saw as debauchery. From this matrix—the rift between traditional and emergent Renaissance approaches to sex and sexuality, the perspective of the foreign traveler, and the demand for exotic tales in the European market—was born a European literature of desire in which the Ottomans became the imagined practicioners of a sexuality seen as different and corrupt.

This had several dire consequences for the image of Ottoman and Middle Eastern sexuality in early modern Europe. To the extent that such a unified image existed, it was biased in several ways. For one thing, it focused on the Ottoman elite, and mainly on the imperial COURT. Society at large was assumed to be either modeled on the court or subservient to its norms. From the 17th century on, such travel accounts also tended to exaggerate the depravity of Ottoman society in general and to link sexual "immorality" with political impotence. As European travel literature began to be translated into Ottoman Turkish and Arabic, and as Ottoman travelers visited Europe in ever greater numbers, such views found their way back to the Well-Protected Domains, as the Ottomans referred to their empire, and influenced the way they would hence fashion their sexual imagination. Ottoman misgivings about their traditional conceptions of sexuality, as well as the derision common in travel literature, were later taken at face value as descriptions of Ottoman sexual morality and influenced the way modern research reconstructed Ottoman sexuality.

At the height of the Ottoman Empire, its upper classes had a complex and balanced concept of sex and how it should be perceived. These ideas were voiced and elaborated in a set of separate but often overlapping spheres of discourse or scripts. Medicine, perhaps the leading discourse—certainly the most authoritative one—elaborated a concept of man and woman that was congruent with medical knowledge at the time. The law set down its rules based to some extent on these medical discourses; literature, poetry, and the performing arts offered a sophisticated and complex set of scripts; and local clerics, Sufis, and preachers contributed their points of view, usually more strict, but not necessarily in conflict with other approaches.

The medical profession's approach to sexuality was based on its conception of the body as a link in the chain of being, composed of four basic elements—air, fire, earth and water—as represented in four bodily fluids. In this conception of universal order, which was also shared by the European world, man and woman were virtually the same being, differing in the balance between the elements and in the degree of development. Rather than a separate sex, therefore, women were seen as an imperfect version of men, a form that did not reach its full development. The vagina, clitoris, and uterus were assumed to be an undeveloped version of the male penis and scrotum, and women were believed to be able to produce semen in their ovaries and thus contribute to the creation of the fetus. Because this science of the body implied that men and women were not inherently different sexually, present-day concepts of same-sex intercourse as radically different from heterosexual intercourse were not a part of Ottoman culture. Thus, while homosexual acts were forbidden by law, as were other forms of sexual activity such as incest and fornication, same-sex intercourse was not perceived as fundamentally unnatural or abnormal. Another consequence of these medical assumptions was that a person's sex was not perceived as immutable. Under certain circumstances women might become more masculine and men more feminine, and transgressions of sexual boundaries were believed to occur once in a while. Because the practice of religion and culture demanded a clear separation of sexes, in mosques, public baths, rituals, and the public sphere, unequivocal gender boundaries were required in order to safeguard indeterminate sexual ones. Sex was so fickle and liable to change that men and women were to be kept within their gender by clear markers such as dress codes, veils, beards and spatial segregation.

It could be claimed, in fact, that in most circles, same-sex love and intercourse (mainly, but not exclusively, between older and younger men) were perceived as more proper. Female same-sex intercourse was known and sometimes mentioned, but largely ignored by the men responsible for almost all writing in the empire until well into the 19th century. Records of private female sexual activity are, therefore, virtually nonexistent. This general preference for homoerotic ties was present most prominently in some mystical Sufi circles. In Sufi lore, love between an initiate and a young disciple, often referred to as "gazing upon an unbearded youth" (al-nazar ila al-amrad), was presented as one of the required steps in the Sufi path to God. By gazing upon the beauty of an amrad—the pinnacle of creation—the Sufi would fill his heart with the attributes of God's splendor and learn the virtues of unconditional love. Strict orthodox groups opposed this practice, not necessarily on grounds of sexual depravity but rather for fear of a distortion of the original divine message and law. In classical Islam, they claimed, nothing was said about love and admiration for young men, and the holy scriptures condemn

even lustful gazes. Claiming that this is an important part of religion is blasphemy. As Sufi brotherhoods became more popular and as such practices became prevalent in society during the 17th century, radical orthodox groups violently opposed this development and succeeded in curbing the trend. After the late 17th century, Sufis were wary of discussing nazar practices in public, although they continued clandestinely.

More libertine discursive spheres such as the very popular shadow theater (Karagöz) (see FOLK LITERATURE) continued to present sex as a ubiquitous and open practice until the mid-19th century. Shadow plays were for the most part very explicit about sex and sexual practices. Protagonists had sex on stage, story lines were habitually about the pursuit of sex in its myriad forms, and the language was unfettered. Paying scant lip service to common morality, such plays often made fun of religious hypocrisy. Spectators, from courtiers to the working class, found themselves identifying with the main characters, Karagöz and Hacivat, in their lewd sexual exploits. Nineteenth-century travelers to the Ottoman Empire were often dumbfounded by what they described as the pornographic and immoral nature of the shadow theater.

It is difficult to know what effect such discourses, from medicine to religion to theater, had on people's morality and on their sexual outlook in earlier centuries, but it seems that in the mid-19th century, probably as a result of Western derision, the Ottoman elite was irritated by the way their sex and sexuality were represented to the outside world. Shadow theater plays were excised and purified. Graphic sex on stage was forbidden, and explicit discussions of sex were censored. Sufis and their quasi-erotic practices were labeled a remnant of a primitive past and pushed deeper into the collective closet. Even medical treatises, previously unambiguous about sexual practice and tendencies, were now expurgated. Explicit references to intercourse in legal codes were replaced by various euphemisms, and homoerotic poetry and art were toned down to near extinction. This clearly had an effect on sexual practice. In a passage in his memoirs laced with irony, Cevdet Pasha, a famous 19th-century cleric, legal expert, and reformer, describes this confusion about sexual practices in the Ottoman elite. Until recently, he claims, pederasty was rife among the Ottoman elite, but now, as a result of foreign ridicule, all these boy-chasers, including the grand vizier and the sultan, have suddenly shunned the practice and now chase women instead.

Having by and large discarded their previous sexual culture, the Ottomans could not easily replace it with the one offered by Europe, which they viewed as artificial. They could no longer discuss same-sex intercourse and, perhaps as a reaction to European derision, rejected what they viewed as a monolithic heteroeroticism. Tradition was reinvented to present Ottoman-Islamic sexuality as orthodox and conservative. In the final years of the empire, sex and sexuality were engulfed in an awkward silence, which would continue to afflict many of its successor states in the Middle East for years to come.

Dror Ze'evi

See also HAREM; LAW AND GENDER.

Further reading: Walter Andrews and Mehmet Kalpaklı, *The Age of Beloveds: Love and the Beloved in Early Modern Ottoman and European Culture and Society* (Durham: Duke University Press, 2004); John Gagnon, *Human Sexualities* (Glenview, Ill.: Scott, Foresman, 1977); Leslie Peirce, *Morality Tales: Law and Gender in the Ottoman Court of Aintab* (Berkeley: University of California Press, 2003); Irvin Cemil Schick, *The Erotic Margin: Sexuality and Spatiality in Alteritist Discourse* (London: Vero, 1999); Khaled El-Rouayheb, *Before Homosexuality in the Arab-Islamic World* (Chicago: University of Chicago, 2005); Dror Ze'evi, *Producing Desire: Changing Sexual Discourse in the Ottoman Middle East, 1500–1900* (Berkeley: University of California Press, 2006); Dror Ze'evi, "Hiding Sexuality: The Disappearance of Sexual Discourse in the Late Ottoman Middle East." *Social Analysis* 49, no. 2 (Summer 2005): 34–53.

şeyhülislam **(shaykhulislam)** The term *şeyhülislam*, which emerged in the ABBASID CALIPHATE in the second half of the 10th century C.E., was a title of honor given to members of the religious establishment (ULEMA) who solved controversial legal problems arising among Islamic jurists. After the foundation of the Ottoman state around 1300, the title *şeyhülislam* continued to be used as an honorific similar to that of mufti, a jurisconsult authorized to issue a written legal opinion or FATWA, based on Islamic sacred law or SHARIA. While the Ottoman ulema performed the duty of issuing fatwa (Turkish, *fetva*) without an official affiliation to the state apparatus, the titles of mufti and *şeyhülislam* began to be used as official titles after the reign of Sultan MURAD II (r. 1421–44, 1446–51). Moreover, the mufti of the capital held the title of *şeyhülislam*, with authority over all other muftis in the empire.

In the first half of the 16th century, some other duties were also given to the *şeyhülislam*. He held a professorship in the madrasa of Sultan BAYEZID II (r. 1481–1512) and supervised the sultan's religious endowments, or WAQFS. In the late 16th century the *şeyhülislam* was also assigned to appoint and dismiss supreme judges (KADIASKERS), high ranking college professors (*müderris*), judges (KADIS), and heads of Sufi orders. In the times of prestigious *şeyhülislams* such as Zenbilli Ali Cemali Efendi (c. 1445–1526), Ibn-i Kemal (Kemalpaşazade) (1468–1533), and Ebussuud Efendi (c. 1491–1574), the

influence of the *şeyhülislam* and his office reached its peak, with the office of the *şeyhülislam* not only having authority over the ulema and their institutions but also widening its area of responsibility and employing a considerably increased staff.

Ottoman modernization efforts, which had started in the middle of the 18th century and accelerated during the reigns of Sultan SELIM III (r. 1789–1807) and Sultan MAHMUD II (r. 1808–39), required significant REFORM in the office of the *şeyhülislam*, as in many other state institutions. After the abolition of the JANISSARIES in the AUSPICIOUS INCIDENT of 1826, the Janissary headquarters, called Agha Kapısı, were allotted as a permanent residence for the *şeyhülislam* and it was renamed Fetwahane (building from where fatwas were issued). In 1836 the supreme judgeships of Anatolia and Rumelia and the Court of Istanbul (Istanbul Kadılığı) were also gathered in the same building. In 1838, the appeals court was moved there. Prior to these reorganizations, the court of appeal had taken place in the office of the grand vizier (Bab-ı Âli or Sublime Porte) in the presence of the grand vizier and the supreme judges of Anatolia and Rumelia, the judges of Istanbul, Eyüp, Üsküdar, and GALATA (the last three being districts of Istanbul). After this reorganization, the office of the *şeyhülislam* was the final step in the appeals procedure of the Ottoman justice system.

As the modern Ottoman bureaucracy was emerging during the Ottoman reform era, all departments related to Islamic law and all administrative offices dealing with the affairs of the Ottoman religious establishment came together in the office of the *şeyhülislam*. During the reorganization of the new Ottoman bureaucracy, the office also underwent a significant bureaucratization. In this process, there were some similarities between the offices of the *şeyhülislam* and that of the grand vizier. Although both institutions were structured like ministries, they were not named as such. The *şeyhülislam*, as minister responsible for religious affairs, became a member of the Council of Deputies (Meclis-i Vukela) and was equal in status to the grand vizier. The *ilmiye*, the Ottoman institution of learned men, became a fully developed bureaucratic department headed by the *şeyhülislam* and managing all religious affairs other than the WAQFS, or religious endowments, which were administered by several different state departments.

All these arrangements in the structure of the office of the *şeyhülislam* suggest that the Ottoman reforms in the 19th century included reform of religious institutions. This is important to emphasize, because the prevailing assumption among scholars is that Ottoman reformers struggled with the religious institutions in order to avoid potential resistance against their reforms. The *şeyhülislam* as the head of a vast institution and wielding enormous authority in Islamic law held an important position in the Ottoman decision-making process and in the Ottoman political sphere. Therefore he was a crucial figure in the Ottoman central bureaucracy. For 500 years, from the appointment of the first *şeyhülislam* Molla Şemseddin Fenari (c. 1350–c. 1430) in 1424, until its abolition in 1924, the office of the *şeyhülislam* was the core of the Ottoman learned or religious bureaucracy (*ilmiye*), constituting one of the three pillars of Ottoman rule, along with the civil bureaucracy (*kalemiye*) and the military bureaucracy (*seyfiye*).

İlhami Yurdakul

Further reading: Colin Imber, *Ebu's-Su'ud: The Islamic Legal Tradition* (Edinburgh: Edinburgh University Press, 1997); Madeline C. Zilfi, "Elite Circulation in the Ottoman Empire: Great Mollas of the Eighteenth Century." *Journal of Economic and Social History of the Orient* 26 (1983): 318–364; Madeline C. Zilfi, "Shaykh al-Islam," *EI2*, XIII, s. 229–230; Madeline C. Zilfi, *The Politics of Piety: The Ottoman Ulema in the Post Classical Age, 1600–1800* (Minneapolis: Bibliotheca Islamica, 1988); Norman Itzkowitz and Joel Shinder, "The Office of Sheyhulislam and the Tanzimat: A Prosopographic Enquiry." *Middle Eastern Studies* 8 (1972): 93–101; Richard C. Repp, *The Müfti of Istanbul: A Study in the Development of the Ottoman Learned Hierarchy* (Atlantic Highlands, N.J.: Ithaca Press, 1986).

Shabbatai Zvi (Sabatai Sevi, Sabbatai Zebi, Sabbetai Tzvi, Sabbetai Zvi, Sabetay Tzvi, Sabetay Zvi, Shabbatai Tzvi, Shabbethai Tzvi, Shabbethai Zvi, Shabbsai Tzvi, Shabbsai Zvi, Shabtai Tzvi, Shatz) (b. 1626–d. 1676) *Jewish mystic, alleged Messiah*   In the 17th century, Shabbatai Zvi became widely known in the Ottoman Empire as the self-declared Messiah of the Jewish people. Born into a Sephardic family in IZMIR in 1626, Tzevi outraged Izmir's rabbis when he declared in 1648 that he was the long-awaited Messiah who would redeem Israel. When the rabbis banished him from his native city, Tzevi began to wander throughout Jewish communities in the Ottoman Empire, preaching his message of impending cataclysmic change, but he gathered only a small band of followers. His fortunes improved in 1665 when a rabbi named Nathan in the town of GAZA in PALESTINE proclaimed him to be the true Messiah. This set off a wave of messianic fervor that spread throughout the Sephardic communities in the Ottoman Empire and beyond to Jewish communities in Europe.

Tzevi declared that 1666 would be the year that would see him depose the sultan and establish his rule in ISTANBUL. Many JEWS sold whatever they owned so that they would be unencumbered by material possessions at the time of the Messiah's enthronement. Before he could get to Istanbul, however, Tzevi was arrested and imprisoned. Nevertheless, the enthusiasm over his impending elevation did not cease, and Jewish pilgrims flocked to the prison to see him. Finally, Sultan MEHMED IV (r. 1648–87) gave him a simple choice, either to accept Islam or to be executed as a rebel. He chose the former, and until his death in 1676, he lived openly as a Muslim with the name Aziz Mehmed Efendi.

Some of Tzevi's followers also converted to Islam, calling themselves Maminim, or "the faithful" in Hebrew, and marrying only among their own. Many Turkish Muslims believed that the Maminim secretly practiced Jewish rites and only outwardly professed Islam; they thus called those who followed the would-be Messiah into Islam *dönme* or turncoats. While there is no evidence that the Maminim were not actually Muslim in their beliefs and practices, the charge that they were "secret Jews" was widely reported by Westerner travelers who were convinced that the Maminim were the Muslim equivalent of the Spanish Marranos, who had been converted to Catholicism under threat of death or exile but who remained practicing Jews in secret. British diplomats, in particular, seemed to be convinced that the Maminim secretly practiced Judaism and saw the Dönmes behind all kinds of conspiracies, including the YOUNG TURK revolution of 1908, which British diplomats reported as being organized by Freemasons and Dönmes. Under Ottoman rule, SALONIKA had the largest community of Maminim, but most of those left for Turkey when the city became a part of GREECE in 1912. After their migration to Turkey, the community ceased to maintain a separate identity as they became fully integrated into the larger Sunni Muslim population.

Bruce Masters

Further reading: Gershon Sholem, *Sabbatai Sevi: The Mystical Messiah, 1626–1676* (Princeton, N.J.: Princeton University Press, 1973).

Shadhliyya Order   The Shadhliyya Order of Sufis was often termed the Protestant Order by Western visitors to the Ottoman Empire because of the absence of any formal ritual associated with Shadhliyya practice. The order also avoided the elevation of individuals to sainthood and decried the visiting of Sufi shrines as an ostentatious display that detracted from true spiritual life. The Shadhliyya was an elite order that produced poets and commentators on religious texts, whose work had wide circulation in the Arabic-speaking provinces of the empire, yet it was also one of the most popular Sufi orders in Egypt throughout the Ottoman period. The founder of the order was Abu al-Hasan al-Shadhili, a 13th century Moroccan mystic. Al-Shadhili left his native Morocco and settled in ALEXANDRIA, where he died in 1258 C.E. The Shadhliyya, although not traditionally popular in Anatolia, came to wider attention toward the end of the Ottoman Empire when Sultan ABDÜLHAMID II (r. 1876–1909) joined the order.

Unlike some other Sufi orders, the Shadhliyya held that asceticism and poverty were not a requirement, as God intended his creatures to live in this world and to take pleasure from his creation. The order tolerated the music and dancing considered illicit by many orthodox Muslims, but otherwise kept its practice of the Sufi way within the boundaries set by conventional Islam. Nevertheless, by the 18th century, the Sunni religious establishment in CAIRO accused offshoots of the order of veering toward interpretations of the Sufi state of *hal*, or communion with God, which bordered on pantheism, and the order became suspect. In NORTH AFRICA and West Africa, the order was prominent in organizing Muslim opposition to Western colonialism.

Bruce Masters

Shahrizor   Shahrizor was a province of the Ottoman Empire that corresponded in location to present-day Iraqi Kurdistan. When the Ottomans conquered the region in 1554, they decided that it was better to leave the region governed by the Kurd leaders than to incorporate it directly into the empire's PROVINCIAL ADMINISTRATION, with governors and *KADIS*, or judges, sent from ISTANBUL. In part, this was a response to the presence of the powerful Kurdish beys of the Ardalan clan who were located on the Iranian side of the border in the town of Samandaj. The *mirs*, as the Kurds called their political leaders, of Ardalan claimed the territory of Shahrizor province and continued to exercise authority among some of the clans there. The Ottomans sought to set Kurd against Kurd as the best way of denying their Iranian enemies access to the cities on the Iraqi plain, and named as governors in Shahrizor members of Kurdish clans who were rivals of the Ardalan clan. The province remained contested for the next two centuries between the Ottomans and Iranians through their Kurdish proxies, but only rarely were there actual Ottoman garrisons in the province.

In the 18th century, the BABAN FAMILY dominated the province, first from the town of Kirkuk and later from Sulaymaniyya, which they built sometime after 1784 as their new capital. Although they sometimes got into trouble with both the governors in BAGHDAD and the sultans in Istanbul, members of the family headed the provincial government with some brief interruptions until 1850.

With the reorganization at the time of the TANZIMAT period of REFORM, the Ottoman state sought to impose direct rule on all of its provinces, eliminating the pockets of local autonomy that had sprung up in the absence of a strong centralized state. Chief among these was Kurdistan. The region was placed under the direct control of the governor of Baghdad in 1862 and later transferred to the province of MOSUL, although it still continued to carry its old name as a subprovince. In 1892 the former province of Shahrizor was divided into two subprovinces or *sancak*, Kirkuk and Sulaymaniyya, which were placed under the direct control of the governor of Mosul.

Bruce Masters

Shammar Bedouin   The Shammar were a confederation of BEDOUIN tribes that were pushed out of their original home in the NAJD in the mid-17th century. As the Shammar moved north they encountered the ANAZA CONFEDERATION. The two groups began to fight for primacy in the Syrian Desert in a series of wars that lasted more than a century. The Anaza were able to fend off the invaders and the tide of migration of the confederate tribes moved into the Iraqi provinces of the Ottoman Empire, where the Shammar defeated the local Bedouin tribes and established their supremacy. As was the case with the Anaza, the Shammar were less tractable in their relations with the Ottoman authorities than had been the MAWALI BEDOUIN CONFEDERATION that had previously controlled the desert CARAVAN routes. At times the Shammar could be bought off by gifts, but at other times they refused, in preference for what treasure they might gain by raiding.

Conflict with the the followers of of MUHAMMAD IBN ABD AL-WAHHAB in the Najd in the second half of the 18th century pushed more of the Shammar into IRAQ. The governors of BAGHDAD sought to enlist the Shammar against the WAHHABIS and it is reported that 20,000 Shammar tribesmen pledged their support to the governor of Baghdad in 1805. This gave them legal status in the Iraqi territories and they soon controlled most of what is now Iraq west of the EUPHRATES RIVER. Unlike some of the other Bedouin tribes who settled in Iraq to become peasant farmers in the 19th century and gradually came under the influence of preachers of SHIA ISLAM, the Shammar remained nomadic, content to control most of the overland caravan trade of the region in the 19th century. The majority of the tribesmen also remained at least nominally loyal to their SUNNI ISLAM tradition, although some of the sub-clans eventually became Shia.

Bruce Masters

Further reading: William Polk, *Understanding Iraq* (New York: HarperCollins, 2005).

sharia   Islamic law, or sharia (*şeriat* in Ottoman Turkish), does not consist of a code of rules that are immutable or even fully written down. Rather, it is an organic system that is grounded in two sources, the Quran and the *sunna*. The Quran is the primary scripture of Islam, which for Muslims is God's word unmediated by human intervention. As such, any rule that is explicitly articulated in the Quran is accepted by all schools of Muslim legal thought as binding on believers. The *sunna,* literally translated as "the path," refers to the reported tradition of the Prophet Muhammad's words and actions and serves as a model for other Muslims. In terms of sharia, however, the *sunna* is a more problematic source than the Quran, as some legal scholars held that it was the precedents of behavior, both religious and secular, set by the original Muslim community, while others held that the normative examples must be linked to the Prophet Muhammad himself. Either way, in the centuries following the Prophet's death in 632 C.E., Muslims collected sayings attributed to Muhammad and his close associates about various issues not covered by Quranic injunctions. The collected stories and sayings, or *hadith,* became the written embodiment of the *sunna.* Even so, there is no consensus as to which sayings are binding and which are not, or even as to which collection of such sayings is authentic. Rather, there is consensus within each Islamic school about the validity of certain sayings, leaving the interpretation of the finer points of the sharia to trained jurists, the *faqihs.*

Within SUNNI ISLAM, there are four principal schools of legal interpretation, each named after a leading jurist whose formulation of the law provides the basis of his school's approach to legal interpretation. These are the Shafii, Hanafi, Maliki, and Hanbali schools. All four were founded between the eighth and ninth centuries C.E. The differences between the schools are relatively slight, however, and adherents of all four recognize the others as valid ways to interpret the law. The founder of the school of law for SHIA ISLAM was Jaafar al-Sadiq and his school is called the Jaafari school. Generally, Sunni scholars do not accept it as a legitimate approach to the sharia, as it is heavily influenced by sayings attributed to Imam Ali, the son-in-law of the Prophet Muhammad and the father of the Prophets' only grandsons.

The official school of the Ottoman state was that of the Hanafi Sunni and all the judges appointed by the sultan to the courts in his provincial centers belonged to that school. Local judges representing the other schools were also present at court, however, in places where an alternate school of law was preferred. This was especially true in EGYPT and Kurdistan where local loyalties continued to lie with the Shafii school. At first, jurists in SYRIA also followed that school, but by the end of the 17th century most legal scholars there had switched their allegiance to the Hanafi interpretation of the law favored by the sultan.

As sharia is not a clearly established code written into a set of texts, the role of legal scholars was crucial for its articulation. Besides the judges who dealt with everyday cases, the system also included more senior scholars known as muftis who had the authority to issue FATWAS, or judicial rulings on theoretical questions. In the Ottoman Empire, there were official muftis who had received their training at the state-financed and state-monitored religious schools, the madrasas. These men were usually appointed to major provincial centers and were ultimately responsible to the chief mufti of the Ottoman Empire, the ŞEYHÜLISLAM. In addition, religious scholars in provincial centers away from the capital local might recognize local scholars as muftis and accept their rulings as valid. This was especially true in the Arabic-speaking provinces where local traditions sometimes clashed with interpretations of the sharia as articulated in ISTANBUL.

According to the sharia, non-Muslims did not have to use Muslim courts unless they were involved in cases with Muslims, or if all parties in a dispute agreed to approach a Muslim judge for his intervention. Nevertheless, the records of the sharia courts show that Christians and Jews frequently appealed to the Muslim courts for justice. Western Europeans living in the Ottoman Empire were initially required to use the Muslim courts. But as they perceived them to be unjust and biased against them as non-Muslims, they lobbied their governments to extend the CAPITULATIONS, or agreements governing the conditions under which Europeans could live and work in the Ottoman Empire, so that they were free from the jurisdiction of Muslim courts in most cases.

Bruce Masters

Further reading: Michael Cook, *Commanding the Right and Forbidding Wrong in Islamic Thought* (Cambridge: Cambridge University Press, 2000); Judith Tucker, *In the House of the Law: Gender and Islamic Law in Ottoman Syria and Palestine* (Berkeley: University of California Press, 1998).

Sharif of Mecca When the Ottomans established their hegemony over the Holy Cities of the HEJAZ, they decided to post their military governor in the port of JEDDAH, leaving the administration of MECCA in the hands of a prominent local BEDOUIN leader who was known as the Emir of Mecca. The person holding that office was always from the Banu Hashim tribe, commonly called the Hashimites in English. These were the descendants of the Prophet Muhammad's own clan and they were, according to the legal tradition of SUNNI ISLAM, the only persons eligible to head the Islamic CALIPHATE. A person of that lineage was entitled to use the honorific *Sharif* before his name, the plural of which in Arabic is ASHRAF.

The British poet, diplomat, and traveler Wilfrid Blunt drew attention to the potential importance of the office in his *Future of Islam,* published in 1882. He argued that the Ottoman dynasty, and the Turks in general, had become degenerate and that Islam could only be revived by a properly Arab caliphate led by one of the Prophet's lineage, as only such a person would receive universal respect from Muslims throughout the world. This was clearly meant to undermine the claim of Sultan ABDÜLHAMID II (r. 1876–1909) to the caliphate. According to Blunt, the obvious choice for caliph was the Emir of Mecca, whom he dubbed the "Sharif of Mecca," a rendering of the title that then entered into British political terminology and plans for a post-Ottoman Middle East. While the title "Sharif of Mecca" is commonplace, however, neither Arabic nor Ottoman Turkish-language documents used that title, settling on "Emir of Mecca" in both languages.

Bruce Masters

See also AL-HASHIMI, HUSAYN.

Shaykh al-Balad

Shaykh al-Balad *Shaykh al-Balad* is Arabic for "chief of the town." In the MAMLUK EMPIRE, it was an unofficial title for whichever Mamluk was the strongest in the ongoing battle for political control of CAIRO. The term passed out of usage after the Ottoman conquest of EGYPT in 1517, but in the early 18th century, Mamluk households again began to use the term unofficially, while nominally accepting the authority of the Ottoman governor in Cairo. This changed, however, in 1760 when Bulutkapan Ali Bey came to the fore in the internal politics of the Mamluk households in Cairo after capturing the leadership of the QAZDAGHLI HOUSEHOLD. He openly took the title of Shaykh al-Balad for himself as confirmation of his political supremacy, rather than seeking the approval of the sultan and the Ottoman title of governor. The revival of the title signified a shift in power away from ISTANBUL and back to the local strongmen who no longer acknowledged need of the Ottoman sultan's approval.

Bruce Masters

Shia Islam

Shia Islam The differences between SUNNI ISLAM and Shia Islam are largely products of historical developments. In terms of doctrinal belief and practice, there are few disagreements between these two dominant interpretations of Islam. The schism between the two arose over who should properly lead the community of believers. The Sunnis believe that a caliph should lead the Islamic community and that this CALIPHATE should have political authority as "Commander of the Faithful," but that religious authority should be left to the consensus of the community of religious scholars, or ULEMA. In contrast, the Shia believe that the head of the community is also rightly the imam, a leader with both religious and secular authority and to whom obedience is due. Sunnis accept that title as well, but by imam they mean that the caliph is the leader of the community in prayer and on the HAJJ, or annual pilgrimage. For the Shia, the imamate is more. They believe

it can only be held by a man descended from the Prophet Muhammad's lineage through his daughter Fatima and her husband Ali. For the Shia, the position of imam is more than a political office as they hold that he has the infallible ability to interpret religious doctrine as well.

Although Sunni Islam, as interpreted by the Hanafi School of law, was the state religion of the Ottoman Empire, there were sizeable Shii minorities in several of the Ottoman Arab provinces, most notably in what are today the countries of IRAQ, LEBANON, and YEMEN. In the first two, the Shia followed the Imami tradition. The dominant form of Islam in Iran today, the Imami tradition is known to some Western scholars as "Twelver Shiism" as its believers hold that the 12th imam, who vanished in the ninth century C.E., will return at some future time to institute a reign of absolute justice on earth. In Lebanon, the adherents of this community were known as the Mitwallis in the Ottoman period, although it is not a name they use today to refer to themselves. Both the Imami tradition and the Zaydi tradition followed by the Shia of Yemen trace the descent of their imams from the line of the sixth imam, Jaafar al-Sadiq (702–65), but the Imami trace their tradition through Sadiq's son Musa al-Kazim while the Zaydi trace their tradition through his son Muhammad. In addition, the ALAWIS of SYRIA and the Alevis of eastern Anatolia also claim to be Shia although the Shii clergy in Iran did not accept the Alawi claim until the 20th century.

Before the 16th century, the Ottomans were relatively uninterested in the differences between Shii and Sunni Islam. The Sufi orders (*see* SUFISM), which put Ali and the prophet's descendants at the center of their devotions, were much more popular in the early Ottoman Empire. But in 1501 Shah ISMAIL I (r. 1501–24) made Imami Shiism the religion of his court in Iran and began to persecute Sunni Muslims in his realm. In addition, the Turkoman tribes of eastern Anatolia rose in rebellion against the Ottomans, proclaiming Shah Ismail to be the long-awaited imam who would restore justice to the world. These rebels were known as the KIZILBAŞ in Ottoman texts and were ruled as heretics by the Ottoman Sunni legal establishment, making it legally permissible for the Ottoman army to kill them. The Shii rebellion against the Ottomans was temporarily ended by the Battle of Çaldiran in 1512. But the continued presence of a hostile Shii Iran played a significant role in bolstering the Ottoman attachment to Sunni Islam. With the hostile "heretic" Shia on their eastern borders and the ongoing anti-Muslim challenges from the Christian world, the Ottoman sultans were increasingly motivated to present themselves as the upholders and defenders of what they regarded as the true faith of Sunni Islam.

The embrace of Sunni orthodoxy by the Ottoman political and legal elite did not translate, however, into the persecution of those Shiis in the empire who accepted Ottoman rule peacefully, even if they held the view that such rule was illicit in the absence of the imam. This tolerance was especially manifested in the Ottoman treatment of the Shia of Iraq. When SÜLEYMAN I (r. 1520–66) conquered BAGHDAD in 1535, for instance, he endowed Shii shrines as well as Sunni ones and hosted Shii clergy along with their Sunni counterparts. Subsequent Ottoman governors extended this strategy of tolerance and even provided patronage to Shii shrines and clergy. In part, this was due to a realization that it was best not to alienate the Shii subjects of the sultan in Iraq. But it also seems to have arisen out of a more general cultural practice of tolerance that the sultans extended to both non-Sunnis and non-Muslims.

Ironically, despite the Ottoman dynasty's devotion to Sunni Islam, the Iraqi provinces of BAGHDAD and BASRA became much more dominated by Shia Islam during the centuries of Ottoman rule than they had been at the time of their conquest. The province of Baghdad contained many of Shia Islam's holiest sites: Ali's tomb is in NAJAF; his son Husayn was martyred and buried in KARBALA; and the seventh imam, Musa al-Kazim, is buried in Kazimiyya, to the north of Baghdad. Najaf and Karbala were established centers of Shii learning before the Ottoman period, but both centers grew substantially from 1732 to 1763, the period during which the Sunni NADIR SHAH ruled in Iran. Nadir Shah sought revenge on the Shii clergy for their persecution of his Sunni brethren during the rule of the Safavid shahs; as a result of this persecution many of the leading Shii clergy of traditionally Shii Iran fled to the relative safety of the Ottoman Empire. In addition, with the rise of the Shia-dominated principality of Oudh in northern India in the 18th century, students, pilgrims, and money from there arrived in the two Iraqi holy cities.

While the Ottomans practiced religious tolerance, however, many groups within the empire decried such an approach. Among these, the strictly Sunni WAHHABI movement in Arabia viewed the veneration of the imams' tombs as especially un-Islamic and in 1801, Wahhabi tribesmen captured the town of Karbala and destroyed the tomb of Imam Husayn. Regarded as an outrage by the Shii clerics in Najaf and Karbala, these religious leaders cultivated the BEDOUIN tribes of Iraq as a defense against future Wahhabi attacks, a policy that worked, since attacks against Najaf were thwarted in 1803 and again in 1806. As the Shii clergy increased their missionary work among the tribes, many of the Bedouins inhabiting Baghdad and Basra provinces declared their allegiance to the Shii interpretation of Islam. This led to a greater presence of Arabic-speakers in the religious schools of Iraq and these gradually displaced most of the Persians who had dominated Shii religious offices in the holy cities in the 18th century.

The success in winning the once nominally Sunni Bedouins to Shia Islam created a concern locally among Sunni clergy and Ottoman officials stationed in Iraq. But it was not until 1895 that the Ottoman government opened Sunni religious schools in Baghdad province in an attempt to train Sunni clergy who could counter the very active mission of the Shia. The fear of Shia Islam that startled the regime of ABDÜLHAMID II (r. 1876–1909) into this action seemingly dissipated after the YOUNG TURK revolution in 1908 as Sunni and Shii clergy in Iraq increasingly worked together to resist British colonial ambitions in Iraq.

In Lebanon, the Shii communities dominated the Jabal Amil region in what is today the south of the country and the Bekaa Valley in the east. In both regions, peasant farmers made up the majority of the Shii community, although those in Jabal Amil produced some religious scholars of note. Some of these scholars went to Iran in the 16th century to help guide the implementation of Shia Islam as the religion of state under the rule of the Safavid dynasty of shahs. The Shii Harfush clan controlled the political fate of the Bekaa Valley from the Ottoman conquest of the region in 1516 until the early 19th century, but elsewhere Shii clans were under the control of their more powerful DRUZE or Sunni neighbors and they had to seek political alliances with them.

With the dissolution of the Ottoman Empire in 1920, the Shii Muslims of Iraq came under British rule and those of Lebanon were governed by FRANCE. Both European nations used religion as a political category and assigned positions in the bureaucracies of their colonial governments based on a quota system for representatives of the various religious communities. This was a part of the "divide and rule" strategy used by colonial administrators who felt that the territories would be easier to govern if their populations were internally divided. When Lebanon became independent in 1945, sectarian religious identity was enshrined in the country's constitution and most political parties were formed along strictly sectarian lines in that they did not attract members from other religious sects. Iraq became independent in 1932 under a Sunni dynasty, the Hashimites, and Sunnis continued to dominate that country's military governments until the U.S. occupation of Iraq in 2003. The results of these developments in the post-Ottoman Middle East have politicized sectarian religious identity among Muslims and led to a greater polarization between Sunnis and Shiis than existed in the centuries in which the region was ruled by the Ottoman Empire.

Bruce Masters

Further reading: Yitzhak Nakash, *The Shi'is of Iraq* (Princeton, N.J.: Princeton University Press, 1995).

Shihab family   The Shihab family was one of the leading families of LEBANON and in the 18th and 19th centuries its members dominated the office of Emir of the Mountain, the title of the dominant warlord in the Lebanese mountains. The Shihab family was somewhat unusual in a region politically dominated by DRUZE dynasties, as they were nominally practitioners of SUNNI ISLAM. The descendants of Fakhr al-Din al-MAANI, who dominated much of what is today Lebanon in the first part of the 17th century, had held the office for most of the 17th century, despite attempts by the Ottomans to dislodge them. But when the last male descendant in the family line died in 1697, his vassals chose Haydar al-Shihab as emir. Although Haydar was a Sunni, his mother was a Druze from the Maan clan. He spent the next decade trying to win the support of various Druze and Shii clans in southern and central Lebanon. His rivals called in help from the Ottomans in 1711, but before the Ottoman expeditionary force could arrive, Haydar defeated his local rivals at the Battle of Andara and seized the former Maan capital of Dayr al-Qamar. Through intermarriage Haydar then effected an alliance with two powerful Druze groups, the Abu-Lamma family and the JANBULAD FAMILY. That alliance lasted for most of the 18th century.

When Haydar died in 1732 he was succeeded first by his son Mulhim and then by Mulhim's brothers. Mulhim's son Yusuf gained the title of emir in 1770. Throughout this period, the Lebanese mountains were relatively quiet, although simmering feuds between individual families frequently flared into violence. The status quo was shattered with the MAMLUK invasion of SYRIA in 1770. Yusuf al-Shihab aided the Mamluks and his troops even briefly occupied DAMASCUS. But in the aftermath of the Mamluk withdrawal, Sultan Mustafa III (r. 1757–1774) appointed CEZZAR AHMED PASHA to the governorship of Sidon. From his stronghold in ACRE, Cezzar Ahmed steadily acquired territories that had been held by vassals of the Shihab clan. In 1789, when there was an attempted coup against Cezzar Ahmed, he became convinced that Yusuf al-Shihab was behind it. In reprisal, he moved his army into Lebanon where he defeated the Shihabs in a battle in the Bekaa Valley.

In defeat, Yusuf abdicated, and his vassals then chose his cousin Bashir. It is not clear whether or not Yusuf had converted to Christianity as he participated in both Muslim and Christian religious services and visited Druze and Christian shrines, but Bashir openly acknowledged that he was a Christian. That fact marked a transition by which Maronite power began to eclipse that of the Druzes in the

Lebanese Mountains. The Abu-Lamma clan, who were close allies of the Shihabs, also became Christians around the same time. Bashir (usually referred to as Bashir II to distinguish him from Haydar's father, who had also been called Bashir) held the post of emir until 1841, making him the longest-reigning emir of the Lebanese mountains and the most powerful figure of the dynasty.

After the death of Cezzar Ahmed in 1804, Bashir II moved to destroy the feudal families his predecessors had relied upon as allies. When IBRAHIM PASHA moved his army into Syria in 1831, Bashir II offered his allegiance to the Egyptian forces and was granted extensive authority over much of Lebanon. He used his power to extract extra taxes and to impose military conscription, extremely unpopular measures that led to wide-scale revolts by Druze and Christian peasants. After the withdrawal of the Egyptian army in 1840, Bashir II surrendered to the British fleet anchored off BEIRUT and went into exile.

With the exile of Bashir II, the fortunes of the Shihab dynasty rapidly declined. The Ottoman sultan appointed Bashir III, Bashir II's distant cousin, as emir in 1841, but it was not a popular choice. Not long after his appointment the new emir called the principal Druze families to Dayr al-Qamar to discuss his tax policies. The families showed up armed and besieged him in his palace in October 1841. The stalemate ended when the sultan withdrew his appointment and Bashir III went into exile. With that, the reign of the Shihab dynasty collapsed. There were attempts to restore Bashir III as Emir of the Mountain after the civil unrest in Lebanon in 1860 but the era of the feudal emirs was over.

Bruce Masters

Further reading: William Polk, *The Opening of South Lebanon, 1788–1840* (Cambridge, Mass.: Harvard University Press, 1963).

shipbuilding   *See* TERSANE-I AMIRE.

sipahi   *See* MILITARY ORGANIZATION.

slavery   The age-old practice of slavery was widespread in the Ottoman Empire. It was a complex institution of many forms, combining elements of pre-Islamic, Islamic Near Eastern, and Mediterranean classical heritages with distinctive Ottoman conventions. Although the most intensive use of slaves occurred at the height of Ottoman power between the mid-15th and the late 17th centuries, slavery remained legal in imperial territories in the Balkans, the Middle East, and NORTH AFRICA until the end of the 19th century. When the Ottomans were in a position of military dominance, slaves were acquired through conquest in Europe, around the BLACK SEA, and on the Mediterranean. Tens of thousands of men, women, and children might be captured and brought to market in a single military campaign. A further source of captive labor, commercial raiding by professional drovers, was the principal mode used in the enslavement of sub-Saharan Africans, but it was also commonplace in the northern borderlands. In the later centuries commerce rather than warfare accounted for the bulk of slave imports.

The horsemen and merchants of the CRIMEAN TATARS were the principal suppliers and commercial agents for the Black Sea slave trade until around the mid-18th century. The African trade to the Middle East was historically more decentralized. Numerous towns and cities in Upper EGYPT, the Sudan, and coastal North Africa had regular markets to accommodate both regional demand and consignments for Mediterranean, Indian Ocean, and Persian Gulf buyers. ISTANBUL and CAIRO, the two largest cities in the empire, operated the most important end-destination markets dealing in slaves, although smaller centers like TUNIS, ALGIERS, and MECCA, among others, were also heavy consumers.

The importance of slavery is reflected in the empire's urban demography. In the 16th century, when Istanbul was the largest city in Europe and West Asia, slaves and former slaves made up about a fifth of its population. During BURSA's heyday as a silk-producing center in the 15th and 16th centuries, as many as half of its inhabitants, including many of its skilled weavers, were slaves and ex-slaves. Although such percentages declined in later centuries, slaves continued to be an important source of labor and a visible presence in major cities and ports. Throughout Ottoman history the ownership of slaves was one of the most consistent markers of high social standing.

Slave ownership was concentrated in the wealthier classes, especially among members of the ruling elites. Most slave owners, and the owners of the largest numbers of slaves, were Muslim and male. Women, overwhelmingly Muslim, also bought, sold, inherited, and bequeathed slaves, but they were a small percentage of all owners and their wealth in slaves did not approach that of male owners. Because of slaveholding's association with social status, non-Muslims were discouraged from slave ownership, the more so if slaves in their possession converted to Islam. Blanket prohibitions, however, were never consistently applied. Christian and Jewish slave owners, both native and foreign, could be found in the empire well into the 19th century.

Ottoman slavery was officially configured along religious and geographic lines. By law no Muslim, regardless of his or her country of origin, could be reduced to slave status. Captives who converted to Islam did not automatically gain their freedom, although many who converted did so hoping to improve their circumstances and has-

ten manumission. Slaves could be of virtually any origin, race, or ethnicity provided that they were not Ottoman subjects. The one programmatic exception to the geopolitical dictum occurred in the forcible recruitment of native Christians, usually sons of Balkan villagers, as elite imperial servitors, called *gulam, kul, or kapı kulu,* literally "slaves of the Porte." Ordinary war captives were also assigned to the elite ranks, but most *kul*s in the 15th and 16th centuries were products of the DEVŞIRME system, the periodic "levy of boys" carried out by the authorities in the Balkan provinces. Although they technically ought not to have been levied, since Christians within the empire were officially recognized as DHIMMI, or "people of the book," and were thus officially protected from enslavement, Ottoman pragmatism, cloaked in a dubious religio-political rationale, explained away the violation of the protective pact regulating state action with regard to religious minorities.

For most of the history of the empire, "white" captives of various ethnicities were arguably in greater demand than sub-Saharan Africans. In the early centuries, when eastern Europe and the Black Sea steppes lay open to Ottoman armies and their allies, Slavic, Germanic, and tribal Caucasian peoples constituted the majority of captives. The sale of sub-Saharan Africans dominated the market in the later centuries, although the ratio of African to non-African slaves always varied by locale, with a heavier concentration of white slaves in the capital and in the northern provinces generally.

The Ottoman practice of slavery, adhering to Islamic precepts, was also distinguished from many other slave-owning cultures by the imposition of legal restraints on slave owners' rights. Islamic law's recognition of the dual nature of slaves as human beings as well as property denied to owners life-and-death authority over their slaves and put strict limits on corporal punishment. The law, historical tradition, and the prestige value of magnanimity helped to protect Ottoman slaves from the excesses to which slaves were frequently subject in the Americas, and these factors encouraged, although they could not guarantee, an ethic of paternalism in master-slave relations. Thus, slave-owners often attended to their slaves' physical and material well-being as solicitous caretakers. A combination of paternalism and economic self-interest, resulting in more humane treatment in settled regions where community values and the legal system were strong. In areas destabilized by war, banditry, or paramilitary thuggery, protective mechanisms disappeared.

In terms of formal legal norms, the law empowered slaves to appeal to the courts in the event of egregious physical injury by a master or mistress, wrongful prolongation of servitude after a valid promise of emancipation, or other breach of the law. The surviving records of the

Islamic courts reveal a sprinkling of slaves' complaints regarding forsworn manumission vows and bodily harm. The absence of more such grievances may be attributable to a number of factors. Given the documented cruelties of galley slavery and other hard-labor occupations, slaves' lack of access to the legal system rather than extra-judicial conflict resolution or the mildness of slavery most probably accounts for the relative silence.

By far the most common complaint that reached the courts dealt with false enslavement of one sort or another. Ottoman subjects in remote or unstable rural areas were sometimes snatched and enslaved illegally. Women and children, both Christian and Muslim, were especially vulnerable to this sort of trafficking. The demand for nubile women and tractable children was usually high, and Ottoman Islamic rules of family privacy helped traffickers secrete their victims. Some who had been kidnapped were held for years before being restored to freedom. Others, of unknown number, never saw their homes again. Relatives and fellow villagers were crucial in establishing a victim's identity. Without them, a dealer's sworn denial was apt to outweigh a victim's unsupported protestations.

Male and female slaves served their owners in virtually every capacity—skilled and unskilled, indoors and out, admired and debased, intimate and remote—known to the early modern economy. They functioned as guards, servants, porters, field hands, miners, masons, concubines, weavers, secretaries, entertainers, and galley slaves, among other occupations. One of the distinctive features of Ottoman governance was its grooming of a special class of slaves to fill important military and administrative posts. Taken as boys, usually as part of the devşirme carried out in the Balkan regions, and forcibly converted to Islam, these "slaves of the Porte," including the famed JANISSARIES, were effectively the sultan's own bond-servants. Their imperial roles imparted a legal and social status superior to that of ordinary slaves (*abd, esir, rıkk, köle*). Despite their slave identity as the property of the sultan, as representatives of the sultan's authority, these individuals exercised rights and privileges superior to most free subjects whether serving as simple soldiers or grand viziers. While these elite contingents were a small and unrepresentative minority of the total slave population, the sultan's *kul*s and their remarkable social mobility have been taken to be hallmarks of the Ottoman system; certainly European visitors found their ascent most striking and foreign to the aristocratic governance of their own countries. Despite their elevated status, however, slaves of the Sublime Porte retained, in relation to their sovereign-master, the attributes of enslaved property. They were subjected to harsh discipline without recourse or redress during their apprenticeship. And even as powerful officeholders, many a slave-turned-grandee lost his estate and sometimes his life because of conduct displeasing to his autocratic master.

Most male and female slaves, whether gathered in commercial raids or in war, were employed in urban settings and in the myriad occupations of the domestic household. Most of the tasks performed by slaves for their wealthy owners were no different from those that fell to ordinary free householders. The Ottoman practice of slavery was not as severe a system of labor exploitation as the harsh agricultural slavery associated with plantation capitalism in the Americas and elsewhere. Another feature that distinguishes Ottoman slavery from the harsher conditions faced by most slaves in the Americas is the relative ease with which Ottoman slaves obtained their freedom. Most household slaves were freed by their owners either during the owner's lifetime or in testamentary declarations upon the owner's death. Although the length of bondage varied, in the 19th century it became customary to emancipate slaves after seven or nine years. Slave women who bore their master's child also customarily gained their freedom upon the master's death if not before. Moreover, a master's children born of his slave woman were not only free but became his legitimate heirs, entitled to the same share of his estate as offspring born to a legal wife.

The experience of former slaves as free Ottoman subjects varied as much as that of the freeborn. In general, freed Africans fared less well in terms of employment and opportunity than non-Africans. That is, dark-skinned, broad-featured male and female slaves were more likely than fine-featured, lighter-skinned slaves to remain clustered on the lower rungs of the social ladder. Nonetheless, many former Ottoman slaves of sub-Saharan origin attained wealth and position. Whether light- or dark-skinned, the opportunities for women who had formerly been slaves were quite constricted. Because there were few legal and respectable occupations for women, emancipated females typically continued a life of subordination and domestic service, whether as servant or wife, and there was often little material difference between these roles. Former slaves of every origin established social networks and cooperative ties with their co-nationals and co-ethnics. By law, freed slaves were entitled to the same rights and legal standing as the freeborn, and in general, no stigma attached to ex-slaves or their offspring.

Genuine assimilation depended to a great extent on the religious, ethnic, and linguistic affinities between ex-slaves and the larger community. The prospects for any emancipated slave were greatly enhanced if the former slave-owner continued in the role of patron or patroness. In any case, owners often eased the transition to freedom by supplying their freed men and women with "emancipation dowries" of household goods, clothing, and money. For others, suitable marriage partners were found, either with other former slaves or with freeborn individuals. Marriage between female slaves and their owners or other family members also sometimes occurred, but was not the norm. In order for marriage to take place between a master and his own slave, the slave had first to be emancipated. The more usual sexual relationship within slaveholding families was that of concubinage, with female slaves in the sexual and procreative employ of their masters. Once a female slave was emancipated, she could no longer legally be anyone's concubine, since by law a free woman could have sexual relations only within marriage.

Even though most female slaves were owned by men, not all were concubines or acquired for sexual purposes. Most functioned as maids, personal attendants, nannies, washerwomen, cooks, or had similar domestic responsibilities. Many female slaves were purchased by men to serve the women of the household. Despite the fact that most female slaves in the Ottoman Empire were domestic workers, however, slave women were particularly vulnerable to exploitation. Their sexuality was both a liability and, within the limits of bondage, an asset, a fact that colors the picture of all slave women's experience. Male slave owners were legally entitled to the sexual use of their female slaves. Although men were prohibited by law from sexual relations with slaves owned by others in the household or elsewhere, transgressions within the household appear to have been common, with penalties rare or inconsequential. Lacking the right of refusal in any case, it is not surprising that many slave women competed to attract the master's favor, a tactic that was a standard but often ruthless feature of life within the sultan's HAREM. Countless slave women gained status or otherwise improved their position within the household by bearing their owner's child, sometimes even becoming legal wives and earning the support and inheritance entitlements that legal marriage conferred.

Young male slaves were known to have been sexually exploited by slave traders and owners, although homosexuality and in particular the sexual exploitation of young males were illegal and widely condemned.

The regular passage of male and female former slaves into the Ottoman family system made for a porous boundary between slave and free. Paradoxically, it also hardened Ottoman attitudes against abolition. In response to European, principally British, efforts to end slavery in the 19th century, Ottoman apologists defended the Ottoman system as a uniquely benign and culturally imbedded practice. The tide was against them, however. The African slave trade was abolished in 1857 and slavery overall was sharply reduced by measures in the 1860s and 1870s, but slavery was still practiced sporadically in the empire until its dissolution.

Madeline C. Zilfi

See also SEX AND SEXUALITY.

Further reading: Y. H. Erdem, *Slavery in the Ottoman Empire and Its Demise, 1800–1909* (London: St. Martin's, 1996); Suraiya Faroqhi, "Quis Custodiet Custodes? Controlling Slave Identities and Slave Traders in Seventeenth- and Eighteenth-Century Istanbul," in Suraiya Faroqhi, *Stories of Ottoman Men and Women: Establishing Status, Establishing Control* (Istanbul: Eren, 2002); Halil İnalcık, "Servile Labor in the Ottoman Empire," in *The Mutual Effects of the Islamic and Judeo-Christian Worlds: The East European Pattern,* edited by A. Ascher et al. (New York: Columbia University Press, 1979); Ehud Toledano, *Slavery and Abolition in the Ottoman Middle East* (Seattle: University of Washington Press, 1998); Madeline C. Zilfi, "Servants, Slaves, and the Domestic Order in the Ottoman Middle East." *Hawwa* 2, no. 1 (2004): 1–33.

Sobieski, Jan (John III Sobieski) (b. 1629–d. 1696) (r. 1674–1696) *king of Poland, celebrated military commander in the wars against the Tatars and the Ottomans*   Born on August 17, 1629 into a powerful noble Polish family, Jan Sobieski studied politics, languages, and military art in Krakow and Western Europe. In the 17th century the once-powerful Poland was under threat from the Prussians and Swedes on its western borders and from the Russians, Turks, CRIMEAN TATARS, and Ukrainian COSSACKS to the south and east. During the period 1648–1653, Sobieski fought against the Cossack rebels and the Crimean Tatars, and in 1654, he participated in a Polish embassy to Constantinople. During the Swedish invasion of 1655, he initially sided with Charles X Gustav, the Swedish pretender to the Polish throne, reentering the service of King John Casimir in 1656. From 1656 to 1660, he fought successive wars against Sweden, the Transylvanian pretender George II Rákóczi (*see* TRANSYLVANIA), and RUSSIA.

His reconciliation with the royal court in 1656 coincided with his love affair with Marie Casimire d'Arquien, the French maid of honor and protégée of the powerful Polish queen, Marie Louise de Gonzaga. Though initially married to another man, Marie Casimire would become Sobieski's wife in 1665. The romance allowed the Polish court to win Sobieski's support for its plans to prepare a French candidacy for the future royal election and strengthen the monarch's role in POLAND. In the ensuing Polish civil war (the *rokosz* of Jerzy Lubomirski, 1665–66) that thwarted the royal plans, Sobieski fought on the side of the court.

After the abdication of John Casimir (1668), Sobieski headed the pro-French faction against a Habsburg candidacy to the Polish throne and then opposed the newly elected king, Michał Wiśniowiecki (1669–1673). As a commander of the Polish troops (field hetman since 1666, grand hetman since 1668), Sobieski fought against numerous Tatar incursions and yet another Cossack insurrection beginning in 1666. His military skills, demonstrated in the Battle of Podhajce (Pidhajci) (1667), made him increasingly popular. After the Ottomans decided to support the Cossacks and declared war on Poland, Sobieski was unable to prevent the loss of Podolia in 1672 (see KAMANIÇE). Yet his brilliant victory at Hotin (Khotin) over the Ottoman corps of Sarı Hüseyin Pasha (1673) ensured him the Polish throne in the following election. The inconclusive campaigns of 1674–76 against the Ottomans led Sobieski to conclude an armistice (the truce of Żurawno, 1676), followed by a formal peace with the Porte (1678).

Eager to cooperate with the French against the Prussians and the Habsburgs, he was soon disappointed by the insufficient support of King Louis XIV. This resulted in a reversal of his pro-French policy and his rapprochement with the Habsburgs. In accordance with a defensive treaty signed in 1683, Sobieski led a Polish rescue expedition to AUSTRIA and commanded the allied Christian troops in the Battle of Vienna (September 12, 1683), defeating the Ottoman grand vizier, Kara Mustafa Pasha. His further successes (e.g., the Battle of Párkány, 1683) and his popularity in HUNGARY led to renewed tensions with Vienna. In 1684 Poland became a member of the anti-Ottoman Holy League along with the Holy Roman Emperor, VENICE, and the pope. The last decade of Sobieski's reign was marked by his unsuccessful campaigns in MOLDAVIA (1684, 1686, 1691); his inability to reconquer the Podolian fortress of Kamieniec; and an unfavorable peace with Russia (1686), in which Poland resigned from the disputed Ukrainian territories, including Kiev, in order to draw the czar to the Holy League. Disenchanted with the rising opposition and the failure to secure the Polish throne for his sons, Sobieski died before the conclusion of the long war against the Ottomans, in whose beginnings he had played such a prominent role.

Sobieski's prominence in war and politics overshadowed his role as a writer (his erotic correspondence with Marie Casimire is a gem of the Polish baroque literature), a linguist (he even spoke pidgin Tatar-Turkish), and a patron of arts (he founded numerous churches and residences, including the palace in Wilanów near Warsaw; his Oriental art collections, including the spoils from Vienna, are partially preserved in Krakow, Dresden, and St. Petersburg).

See also VIENNA, SIEGES OF.

Dariusz Kołodziejczyk

Further reading: Otton Laskowski, *Sobieski: King of Poland* (Glasgow: Polish Library, 1944); John Stoye, *The Siege of Vienna* (London: Collins, 1964); Zbigniew Wojcik, "King John III of Poland and the Turkish Aspects of His Foreign Policy." *Belleten* XLIV, no. 176 (1980): 659–673.

Sokollu family The Sokollus were one of the most prominent families of Christian origin who emerged through the Ottoman child levy or DEVŞIRME system, attained numerous high-ranking posts in the Ottoman government and military, and built a powerful network of protégés. The name Sokollu has its root in the word *sokol*, meaning "falcon," and comes from the village Sokolovići near the town of Rudo in Bosnia. Although members of the Sokollu family served in various Ottoman administrative posts, the name Sokollu generally evokes one Ottoman statesman, Sokollu Mehmed Pasha (1505–79), who initiated the careers of many other family members. Yet the Sokollu family had more than one branch whose members advanced high in the Ottoman bureaucracy before Sokollu Mehmed Pasha's rise to power in the second half of the 16th century.

Among the best known of these is Hüsrev Pasha, who became the second vizier in 1543. Hüsrev Pasha, after receiving a traditional education in the PALACE SCHOOL, began his career as the commander of the imperial cavalry units in 1516. Later he served as governor (*beylerbeyi*) in different provinces of the empire and in 1535 became the governor of EGYPT. After serving in this position for two years he returned to ISTANBUL and was given the rank of vizier. When he died in 1544 as second vizier, he was at the height of his career.

While Hüsrev Pasha was approaching the end of his career in the early 1540s, Mehmed Pasha was in the process of creating a power network composed of his relatives and fellow countrymen. Sokollu Mehmed Pasha was levied by Ottoman officers from his village at a relatively late age, between 16 and 18, during the early years of SÜLEYMAN I (r. 1520–66). He was first brought to EDIRNE and received his education in the Edirne Palace. Later he was brought to the TOPKAPI PALACE and served in the privy chamber, which included the posts closest to the person of the sultan, such as the stirrup-holder, valet de chambre, and sword bearer. In 1541 he was made the head door-keeper and thus left the inner palace service. In 1549 he was appointed governor of Rumelia; two years later, as field marshal of the Rumelian troops, he commanded the campaign in TRANSYLVANIA. In 1554, during the campaign led by Süleyman against the Persian Safavid dynasty, Sokollu Mehmed Pasha distinguished himself with his Rumelian troops and was made the third vizier of the Imperial Council.

In the succession struggle among the sons of Süleyman in the closing years of the 1550s, Sokollu Mehmed Pasha played an important role. In 1558, he was sent by Süleyman to prince Selim with a message to persuade him to maintain the peace with his brother prince Bayezid. Although Sokollu succeeded in his mission and Selim (who would become his father-in-law in

An influential grand vizier for three sultans, Sokollu Mehmed Pasha endowed architecture and urban amenities all over the Ottoman Empire. This large complex was founded in Payas, a port that linked the Syrian trade routes with Cyprus. *(Photo by Gábor Ágoston)*

1562) complied with the sultan's request, prince Bayezid refused his father's request. In the ensuing civil war between Selim and Bayezid, Sokollu commanded the army sent by Süleyman to support Selim, playing a decisive role in Selim's victory over his brother. In 1565, following the deaths of two senior viziers, Rüstem Pasha in 1561 and Ali Pasha in 1565, Sokollu Mehmed Pasha was promoted to the grand vizierate, a position he would occupy uninterruptedly for 14 years and under three successive sultans.

One year after Sokollu Mehmed Pasha became grand vizier, Süleyman died during the Szigetvár campaign (1566) in southern HUNGARY, far away from Istanbul. In order to prevent chaos among the soldiers and to ensure the orderly ENTHRONEMENT AND ACCESSION of the next sultan, Sokollu Mehmed Pasha kept Süleyman's death secret for weeks until prince Selim reached the army in BELGRADE (northern Serbia). Sokollu's managerial skills and his control over this delicate political situation are indicative of his strategic skill and authority.

The power of Sokollu Mehmed Pasha rested on his vast network, mostly composed of family members, at key posts of the empire. Sokollu's strategy of appointing his kinsmen to important offices began before he became grand vizier. An early example of this was Sokollu's his cousin, the future Mustafa Pasha. He was first brought to Istanbul and enrolled as a page in the palace. Later in his career he became governor of BUDA for 12 years (1566–78). Later a younger brother of this cousin, Mehmed, was appointed tutor (*lala*) to a royal prince. Lala Mehmed also eventually became grand vizier. During Sokollu Mehmed Pasha's grand vizierate his eldest son, Hasan Pasha, became the governor of Diyarbakır (1570–71). Two other relatives, his cousin Ferhad Bey and his brother-in-law Sinan Bey, also attained high office in the provincial administration of the empire, the former as commander of Klis (Clissa) in 1570 and the latter as commander of Bosnia.

Sokollu Mehmed Pasha's network was composed not only of his relatives and fellow countrymen but also included trusted servants from both the central bureaucracy and the COURT. One of the most important of these confidants was his private secretary, Feridun Bey, described by contemporaries as Sokollu's seeing eyes and supporting hands. After having served Sokollu Mehmed Pasha as his most trusted aide, Feridun Bey became the head scribe of the imperial chancery in 1574. Although he was dismissed from that office as a result of the anti-Sokollu campaign during the first years of MURAD III's reign (1574–1595), after the death of Sokollu Mehmed Pasha Feridun Bey was reinstated in the same office in 1581 and was married to Ayşe Sultan, the daughter of Rüstem Pasha and granddaughter of Sultan Süleyman.

Another trusted favorite of Sokollu Mehmed Pasha was Cafer Pasha who, having received the traditional palace education, became the commander of the imperial cavalry during the reign of Süleyman. As the sultan's private secretary, Cafer Pasha was also in charge of writing letters and commands for Süleyman. In this capacity, Cafer Pasha played a vital role supporting Sokollu Mehmed Pasha in keeping Süleyman's death secret by continuing to write commands in the name of the deceased sultan. Later, Cafer Pasha was married to the daughter of Sokollu Mehmed Pahsa and became the commander of the JANISSARIES.

The power and authority of Sokollu Mehmed Pasha during his 14 years as grand vizier was constantly challenged in the delicate political balance of the emerging Ottoman court. However, especially during the reign of SELIM II (r. 1566–74), with the help of his own network of favorites, Sokollu Mehmed Pasha was able to counter any attack on his control over the business of rule. He skillfully managed to contain the aspirations of the favorites of Sultan Selim's court and was depicted by his contemporaries as virtual sovereign of the empire.

The accession of MURAD III (r. 1574–95), however, seriously challenged the power of Sokollu Mehmed Pasha. Although the new sultan felt deep respect for the old and experienced grand vizier who had successfully served both his father and grand father, the control of the court gradually shifted from the network of the grand vizier to Murad and his favorites. In this gradual takeover of the business of rule, the sultan's favorites targeted the protégé network of the grand vizier. The high-ranking bureaucrats of the Sokollu family and the most trusted servants of the grand vizier were dismissed from their posts and replaced by members of the anti-Sokollu faction of the court. Among those who fell from power were Sokollu Mustafa Pasha, the governor of Buda, who was executed in 1578, and Feridun Bey, who was dismissed from his office and exiled to Belgrade.

Some of the descendants of Sokollu Mehmed Pasha managed to maintain their offices until the end of the 16th century, including his son, Hasan Pash,a who became the fifth vizier in 1595. However, Sokollu Mehmed Pasha's death in 1579 marked the end of the great power and lucrative career opportunities of the Sokollu clan.

Şefik Peksevgen

Further reading: G. Veinstein, "Sokollu Mehmed Pasha," in *Encyclopaedia of Islam* 2nd ed., edited by H. A. R. Gibb et. al., vol. 9 (Leiden: Brill, 1960–), 706–11; Cornell H. Fleischer, *Bureaucrat and Intellectual in the Ottoman Empire: The Historian Mustafa Ali, 1541–1600* (Princeton, N.J.: Princeton University Press, 1986), 41–69.

Spain Following the conquest of Granada in 1492 by Queen Isabella of Castile and King Ferdinand of Aragon, the Mediterranean Sea became the center of a prolonged military conflict between the Iberian kingdoms and the Ottoman Empire. Despite Queen Isabella's mandate for her heirs to continue Castile's expansion in NORTH AFRICA, Spanish military action in the Mediterranean during the 16th and 17th centuries fell short of a full-scale conquest of the North African territories. Instead, Spanish policies aimed to control Ottoman expansion in the Mediterranean and combating the area's CORSAIRS AND PIRATES who operated with the thinly veiled approval of the Ottomans and whose activities destabilized and threatened Spanish imperial authority in frontier areas. Major military battles between Spain and the Ottomans occurred mostly during the 16th century, but protracted conflict between the two powers remained alive in the form of corsair activity until the mid-18th century. Throughout the 18th century, the Bourbon military reforms led to a reinforcement of the strategic role of Spain's PRESIDIOS, mainly as a defense against British intervention in the western Mediterranean. In 1782–83, negotiations between Charles III (r. 1759–88) of Spain and ABDÜLHAMID I (r. 1774–89) led to the signing of a peace agreement between Spain and the Ottoman Empire, thus putting an end to the hostilities that had characterized the previous centuries.

Both the Spanish and the Ottomans built their imperial ideologies in religious terms, each representing itself as the defender of its respective faith. However, as exemplified by the renegades and captives in the corsair North African port towns, these ideological differences were often underplayed and even subverted in frontier areas, where interaction led to social, economic, and cultural exchanges that frequently ignored rigid imperial doctrine. Within Spain itself, military conflict with the Ottoman Empire severely affected relations with the Morisco community, composed of former Muslims who had been forced to convert to Christianity in the early 16th century.

EARLY IMPERIAL CONQUEST

Inspired in part by the crusading spirit that had led to the unification of Christian kingdoms in the Iberian Peninsula, the Spanish conquest of North Africa followed in the footsteps of Portugal, whose expansion along the North African coastline began in 1415 with the conquest of Ceuta. In 1497, Castilian troops conquered the North African port town of Melilla, which has remained under Spanish sovereignty ever since. The Spanish conquest of the Algerian port of Mars al-Kabir (Mazalquivir) in 1505 served as the launching point for the conquest of the strategically important port city of Oran in an expedition led by Cardinal Cisneros and Pedro Navarro in 1509. (Oran, in present-day Algeria, remained in Castilian hands until 1708.) Peñón de Velez de la Gomera was conquered in 1508. The Treaty of Alcaçovas (1479) and the Treaty of Tordesillas (1494) delineated the limits of Portuguese and Castilian expansion in North Africa in a discussion that concluded with the Cintra Capitulation (1509), according to which the territories to the west of Ceuta were left for Portugal to occupy, and those to the east, to Spain. Spain subsequently took ALGIERS and TRIPOLI in 1511.

The reigns of Charles I of Spain (r. 1516–56, Holy Roman Emperor as Charles V, r. 1519–56) and SÜLEYMAN I (r. 1520–66) saw the consolidation of Spanish and Ottoman rule over the western and eastern Mediterranean respectively. Both monarchs, as well as their successors, relied on the power of propaganda to sustain their roles as defenders of the Catholic and Sunni Muslim faiths. The Ottoman conquests of RHODES (1522), Algiers (1529), and Tripoli (1551) under Süleyman, followed by the conquest of CYPRUS (1571) and TUNIS (1574) under SELIM II (r. 1566–74), consolidated Ottoman rule in the eastern Mediterranean. At the same time, Spain's grip over Ceuta, following the union with Portugal in 1580, and control over Oran reasserted Spanish influence over the western Mediterranean. Charles V's expedition to Tunis in 1535 led to the recapture of the city until 1574, when it again came under Ottoman control. Under the rule of Philip II of Spain (r. 1556–98), the Holy League attacked the Ottoman fleet at the BATTLE OF LEPANTO (1571). Although older historiographical approaches have interpreted this battle as the beginning of the so-called Ottoman military decline, recent interpretations have taken a different view. The Battle of Lepanto, while a spectacular military victory for Spain, nevertheless produced no substantial changes in the geostrategic position of the Mediterranean powers. Lepanto brought an end to the great military clashes that had characterized the 16th century, and inaugurated a new era dominated by small-scale warfare through the consolidation and perpetuation of corsair and privateer activities in the Mediterranean, particularly during the 17th century.

CORSAIRS, PRIVATEERS, AND THE REDEMPTION OF CAPTIVES

Privateers were independent vessel owners commissioned by states to attack enemy shipping. Unlike privateers, corsairs operated with government licenses, and both the Habsburg and Bourbon monarchs regularly issued strict regulations delimiting the scope of corsair activities. The term corsair had a religious connotation. The most notorious Christian corsairs were the KNIGHTS OF ST. JOHN on the island of MALTA and the most prominent Muslim corsairs operated out of three North African corsair states in ALGIERS, TRIPOLI, and TUNIS. The first corsair state was founded in Algiers in 1519 by Hayreddin Barbarossa, one of the famous BARBAROSSA BROTHERS. The corsair states were semi-autonomous entities formally dependent on the Ottoman authorities, whose economies were based on a combination of corsair and privateering activities and the ransoming of captives. The consolidation of corsair political entities along the North African coastline resulted in a new geostrategic situation, forcing the imperial centers to regulate their activities while simultaneously devoting significant efforts to their containment. The peculiar sociopolitical structure of frontier areas led to the emergence of a political structure dominated by armed JANISSARIES and corsair captains who acquired a significant level of political independence but whose actions remained tied to the imperial designs of the Mediterranean powers.

Renegades and captives were also important in the North African frontier. Renegades were free men who chose to cross borders, mainly for economic reasons, and embraced their former enemy's religion. They often specialized in maritime activities and had technical knowledge that could be put to use in frontier areas where corsairs played a strategic role in the conflict between empires.

Captives, on the other hand, had fallen prey to corsair and privateer activities, and the issue of their CONVERSION was a more complex matter. They were often employed in manual labor and lived in very harsh conditions, portrayed in the so-called "captive literature" genre (literatura de cautivos), whose most famous representative in Spain was Miguel de Cervantes Saavedra. Conversion often posed an important dilemma, since many of these captives were slaves whose legal status might be altered if their religious affiliation changed. Although the most well-known cases of converts are those who converted from Christianity to Islam, there were many requests to convert from enslaved Muslim men in the service of the kings of Spain, some of them Turks. Their requests to convert to Christianity, which are documented well into the 18th century, were not always granted. Spanish authorities often feared that the new Christian slaves might use their status to flee to Ottoman lands. The Spanish Inquisition punished individuals who had converted to Islam, although the degree of punishment varied considerably depending on a number of factors, including whether or not the convert had embraced Islam voluntarily.

For Christian captives, the most common path to returning to Christian lands was that of redemption, whether through general redemptive expeditions organized by religious orders, such as the Trinitarians and Mercedarians, or through individual requests. Captives played an essential economic role for both Spain and the Ottoman regencies: they were a cheap and specialized workforce whose economic value played a determinant role in the decision to redeem them.

RELIGIOUS PERSECUTION AND THE MORISCO PROBLEM

Military confrontation with the Ottoman Empire led to a significant increase in social tensions between old and new Christians in Iberia. Isabella and Ferdinand's decree of expulsion against JEWS in 1492 was followed by a massive exodus of Sephardic Jews to lands under Ottoman suzerainty. Important Sephardic communities settled in Ottomans lands, mainly SALONIKA, Cyprus, and ISTANBUL, playing a key economic role in the development of maritime commerce. Conflict with the Ottoman Empire also affected the Morisco population in Spain. Spanish court propagandists and members of the old Christian elite often expressed mistrust at the role of the Morisco population. Throughout the 16th century, Spanish Moriscos were often thought of as an Ottoman fifth column inside Spain, and the occasional alliance of some of their leaders with Algerian and Ottoman plans was one of the factors that led to their final expulsion from Spanish territory, beginning in 1609. The expulsion of the Moriscos was a controversial matter and its economic effects varied from one region to another, although some regions in the Spanish Levant were severely depopulated. Significant Morisco populations settled in North Africa, where they played an important role in the development of the North African regencies.

Vanesa Casanova-Fernandez

Further reading: Bartolomé Bennassar and Lucile Bennassar, *Les chrétiens d'Allah: l'histoire extraordinaire des renégats, XVIe et XVIIe siècles* (Paris: Perrin, 1989); Fernand Braudel, *The Mediterranean and the Mediterranean World in the Age of Philip II* (New York: Harper, 1972); Andrew C. Hess, *The Forgotten Frontier: A History of the Sixteenth-century Ibero-African Frontier* (Chicago: Chicago University Press, 1978); Geoffrey Parker, *The Grand Strategy of Philip II* (New Haven, Conn.: Yale University Press, 1998).

Suez Canal   The construction of the Suez Canal was a result of the intense competition between ENGLAND and

Opening of the Suez Canal as presented in Frank Leslie's illustrated newspaper, on January 8, 1870 *(Courtesy of the Library of Congress)*

FRANCE for economic dominance in EGYPT. The British initially sought to build a railroad that would link ALEXANDRIA to the Red Sea as a way of shortening the time required to transport goods to their colony in India. The French had a grander vision to construct a canal that would link the Mediterranean to the Red Sea, starting at the Egyptian port of Suez. The idea of a canal linking the two seas was not new, but the French recognized that it would cut in half the time needed for its Mediterranean-based fleet to reach Southeast Asia, a region of increasing interest to those who promoted French colonial expansion there as a counterbalance to the British in India.

In this contest between the two nations, the British won the first round with a contract from Khedive Abbas in 1851 to build their railroad. His successor, Khedive Said, however, was a good friend of the Frenchman Ferdinand de Lesseps, who convinced the khedive to support the construction of a canal. The initial agreement came in 1854, but further negotiations on the canal's construction and its financing ensued. It was not until 1858 that Said finally accepted the outline of the project. Said agreed to provide 20,000 Egyptian laborers to dig the canal and handed the development rights to the land on both sides of the canal to the French joint-stock company, headed by de Lesseps, that was formed to oversee the building of the canal. When only half the shares were purchased when the project went public in 1859, Said purchased the rest. The Egyptian government thereby committed a large amount of its own resources to a project by which it would benefit only indirectly.

De Lesseps' failure to acquire full financing for the project, British opposition, and Ottoman concerns about the project all conspired to delay the start of construction. Said's successor, Khedive ISMAIL, liked the project but not the arrangements that gave away so much to de Lesseps. After long and complicated negotiations, the various parties concerned reached a compromise and the sultan gave approval for construction of the canal to begin in 1866.

The construction of the canal was supervised by French engineers who established the route for the canal. As the land through which the canal was dug was relatively level, the canal did not require a system of elaborate locks. As a result, the technology required for the canal's construction was simple. The actual digging of the canal was done by hundreds of thousands of peasant laborers equipped with picks and shovels. It is not known how many of these perished in the process, as the Suez Canal Company kept no records of fatalities. But in Egyptian folk memory and popular opinion the numbers of those who died is reckoned to be in the tens of thousands. When the canal opened in 1869, Ismail organized festivities to mark the occasion. These included the first performance of Giuseppe Verdi's opera, *Aïda*, in the Cairo Opera House that was built especially for the occasion.

Although the Canal was not the only reason for Egypt's growing debt to European creditors, Egypt gained little financially from the deal struck between the khedival government and the Suez Canal Company, despite the fact that the canal had quickly become a very profitable enterprise. Stuck in a no-win situation, Ismail sold off his shares to the British government for 4 million pounds (20 million U.S. dollars). Although the British initially opposed the canal, British ships accounted for 80 percent of the traffic in the canal and Prime Minister Disraeli jumped at the chance to acquire the shares. Although Britain would not hold the canal outright, it had the majority of the members of the governing board and reaped large profits on its initial investment in the purchase of shares in the Suez Canal Company. The question of ownership of the canal would remain a thorny one between Great Britain and subsequent Egyptian governments until 1956 when Egyptian President Nasser nationalized the canal.

Bruce Masters

Further reading: Zachary Karabell, *Parting the Desert: The Creation of the Suez Canal* (New York: Knopf, 2003).

Sufism Western scholars refer to the mystical traditions in Islam, known in Arabic as *tasawwuf*, as Sufism. Both the Arabic and English terms are derived from the Arabic *sufi*, meaning "mystic." In Ottoman Turkish, the more commonly used word for a mystic was *derviş*, or dervish. A wide array of traditions come under the umbrella of Sufism, but they all agree on two basic tenets: to understand Islam requires an experiential relationship with God, and this can only be achieved through the guidance of a master who has already had such an experience. Simply put, religious truth cannot be learned by study alone; it has to be experienced.

There is much debate over the origins of Sufism. Western scholars have suggested that it represents either Indian influences or traditions arising from the Gnostic Christianity that existed in the Middle East at the time when Islam emerged as a new religion. Muslims cite the Quran as the source of Sufism, and many Sufi traditions attribute their traditions to Ali, the son-in-law of the Prophet Muhammad. Jesus, whom Muslims believe to have been a prophet, also figures in many Sufi traditions as an originator of the Sufi way.

In the earliest Sufi writings of the eighth century C.E., the emphasis was on turning away from worldly pleasures, living simply, and devoting oneself to prayer and contemplation. The Arabic word for wool is *suf*, and many Muslim scholars claim that the name for the movement comes from the simple woolen garments its early adherents wore. Many of the early Sufis were ascetics and some remained celibate, even though the Quran explicitly warns Muslims not to imitate the practices of Christian monks in that regard. By the tenth century C.E.,

This photo taken in the photographer's workshop in Damascus, around 1880, shows the traditional dress of the Mevlevi Sufis. The man seated is dressed as a *pir*, or master of the order, while the standing younger man is dressed as a novice. *(Photograph by Maison Bonfils, courtesy of the University of Pennsylvania Museum, Philadelphia)*

Sufis were beginning to profess that they could actually achieve a union with God wherein they lost any awareness of their own separate consciousness. They called this *fana* or "annihilation," and to experience it was to be in an altered state of consciousness, or *hal*. That experience of losing one's self-consciousness while in God's presence led some to make extreme claims that in those moments they had, in fact, become God. The Sufi saint al-Hallaj was executed in BAGHDAD in 922 for having said, "I am the Truth," which was one of God's names. Orthodox Muslim theologians condemned such claims and viewed most Sufis with suspicion.

Such attitudes began to change with the circulation of the spiritual autobiography of Muhammad al-Ghazzali, who died in 1111. Al-Ghazzali was a teacher at the prestigious Nizamiyya school in Baghdad and was acknowledged as one of the leading Muslim scholars of his time, but he suffered a crisis of faith and left teaching. Through the practice of Sufism, however, he came to believe that Islam was the true faith ordained by God and that the Quran was the word of God, and he returned to teaching. His spiritual autobiography represented a great synthesis of the legal and the mystical traditions. Al-Ghazzali stated that one could not know that the Quran and sharia were true without the inner certainty that one gains from the Sufi path. But once having gained that wisdom, one must follow the path of orthodoxy in Islam. After al-Ghazzali, most Muslim scholars accepted the principle that Sufism was permissible, and even desirable, for Muslims, as long as Sufi practices conformed outwardly to the letter of Muslim law.

In the centuries following al-Ghazzali, a number of individuals offered differing approaches to the goal of mystical union with God, and out of their teachings different Sufi orders emerged. Almost all of these had a program consisting of a linear path of specific steps that must be followed by the seeker, guided by a teacher. As such, the orders were called *tariqa*s, the Arabic word for "path" that is also a pun on the word for Islamic law, sharia, which also means "path" or "way." Some of the *tariqa*s were scrupulously orthodox, following the lead of al-Ghazzali. But others, taking as their guide the ecstatic approach of al-Hallaj, claimed that the knowledge they had gained through the Sufi quest negated the strict codes imposed by Islamic law.

These contrary Sufi traditions had already developed before the rise of the Ottomans in the 14th century and were present as alternative voices for the duration of the empire. The Turks were widely influenced by various strains of Sufi practice as Sufi missionaries converted their ancestors to Islam in Central Asia by blending Islamic beliefs and practices with the Turks' shamanism. Mystic poets such as Yunus Emre and Hajji Bektaş composed their work in the vernacular Turkish of those who were settling in Anatolia in the 13th century. They made Sufi beliefs accessible to large numbers of people in the form of songs that were passed from village to village by Sufi minstrel bards. Sufis also blended elements of Christianity into their practice, which appealed to Greek and Armenian peasants, thereby hastening their acceptance of Islam through the medium of the Turkish language and culture.

The early Ottoman sultans felt no apparent contradiction in practicing an Islam that contained both orthodox and heterodox elements. Indeed, the foundation myth of the empire had Osman Gazi being ordained as a world conqueror by a Sufi sheikh whose daughter he then married. Once they had established their empire, the Ottoman sultans had close relations to two Sufi groups, the MEVLEVI ORDER and the BEKTAŞI ORDER, although these two could not be more different in their religious outlook. The Mevlevi Order, founded by the son of the 13th century poet Rumi, was the order of Ottoman intellectuals and attracted poets, musicians, and calligraphers. The order established convents or hostels (*tekke*) in various Ottoman cities and these served as centers for the teaching of art and music as well as being places of spiritual retreat. The Bektaşi Order, by contrast, was the order of the JANISSARIES and its traditions were oral rather than literary. Although many of its practices were unorthodox, such as the drinking of wine, it too received official recognition from the sultans as a way of keeping the troops happy. The sultans and their families supported both orders financially by establishing some of their convents and bestowing lavish gifts on the orders' sheikhs.

Despite sultanic support of some Sufi orders, Sufis also sometimes challenged the sultans' authority by claiming they had access to a truth that could never be known by those who had not embarked on the path of mysticism. In the aftermath of the defeat of Sultan BAYEZID I (r. 1389–1402) at Ankara in 1402, the Sufi Sheikh Bedrettin preached in favor of a social movement that sought to tear down the differences between classes and religions. His movement gained great popularity among the ordinary people of all religions and his disciple, Börlüce Mustafa, started a revolt against the Ottoman in 1416. The rebels had some initial success but the Ottoman army was finally able to defeat them and Bedrettin and thousands of his followers were executed. The Ottomans also faced other revolts led by radical Sufis in the 15th and 16th centuries. Indeed, one of the greatest challenges to the Ottoman throne came from Shah Ismail, who headed an extremist Sufi order that believed him to be the long-awaited hidden imam.

Although Ottoman legal scholars condemned popular Sufi movements as heretical, they were generally tolerant of the intellectual Sufi orders that outwardly followed Islamic law. The exception to this was the Kadızadeli movement that emerged in the 17th century among the students of Birgivi Mehmed, a fundamentalist Muslim scholar and preacher, who died in 1573. This group condemned anything that it considered an innovation on the Islam practiced by the Prophet Muhammad and the first generation of Muslims, and it held that Sufism was such an innovation. In this, the Kadızadelis foreshadowed the WAHHABIS of the 18th century, a group that also refused to tolerate anything regarded as a deviation from the strictest adherence to foundational Islam.

In the second half of the 18th century, a more austere and rigorous Sufi order, the NAQSHBANDIYYA ORDER, answered some of the objections raised by the Muslim fundamentalists to Sufism. The Naqshbandis believe in a strict adherence to sharia and reject the notion of sainthood found in many other Sufi orders, but they still hold that the understanding of God that can only be gained from a mystical experience is a vital, necessary part of Islam. The sober interpretation of mysticism offered by the Naqshbandiyya Order was popular among intellectuals within the Ottoman Empire in the 18th and 19th centuries as it offered a compromise between mysticism and the interpretations of Islam that fundamentalists such as the Wahhabis were preaching. However, critics of Sufism still did not accept the Naqshbandiyya as being rooted in a proper understanding of Islam.

Despite the Kadızadeli movement's criticism of Sufi beliefs and practices, Sufism remained a vibrant part of Islam as it was practiced in the Ottoman Empire through WORLD WAR I. In the aftermath of the war, Mustafa Kemal, better known as ATATÜRK, opened an aggressive campaign against Sufism which he considered a superstition that impeded modernity and westernization. In 1925 Atatürk banned the Sufi orders, and their property in Turkey was confiscated. Sufism continued to be practiced in the former Arab provinces of the empire but it suffered attacks from the SALAFIYYA, another group that strictly interprets Islamic law, and from theologians influenced by the Wahhabi tradition.

Bruce Masters

See also SHADHLIYYA ORDER.

Further reading: Julian Baldick, *Mystical Islam* (New York: New York University Press, 1992); Annemarie Schimmel, *Mystical Dimensions of Islam* (Chapel Hill: University of North Carolina Press, 1975).

Süleyman I ("the Magnificent"; Kanuni, or "the Lawgiver") (1494–1566) (r. 1520–1566) *most famous and longest-reigning Ottoman sultan under whose rule the empire reached its zenith*   Born on November 6, 1494, in the Black Sea coastal town of Trabzon (eastern Turkey), where his father, the future Sultan SELIM I (r. 1512–20), was prince-governor, Süleyman I is regarded as one of the most important rulers of Islam and of the world

This 16th century painting shows the young Sultan Süleyman I, known as Magnificent to Europeans and as Lawgiver or Law abider to his subjects. Several paintings, of the young sultan, similar to this, are known from European museums. *(Erich Lessing/Art Resource)*

during his time. Süleyman's fame is due as much to his conquests in Europe as to the splendor of his court and the elaborate propaganda that publicized his triumphs. He led his armies on 13 campaigns, spending perhaps a quarter of his reign on campaigns. These brought IRAQ (1534–35) and HUNGARY (1526, 1541) under Ottoman rule, threatened the Habsburg capital Vienna twice (1529, 1532; *see* VIENNA, SIEGES OF); his victories at RHODES in the eastern Aegean (1522) and at Preveza in northwestern GREECE (1538) made the Ottomans masters of the eastern Mediterranean, leaving only MALTA and CYPRUS unconquered for the time being. The fact that he was a contemporary of Europe's most illustrious monarchs also assured Süleyman's reputation. Holy Roman Emperor Charles V (r. 1519–56) was Süleyman's chief antagonist with whom the sultan engaged in an epic and exhausting, yet ultimately futile, rivalry for world supremacy. Francis I of FRANCE (r. 1515–47), "the most Catholic king of France," was Charles V's archenemy and the sultan's reluctant ally. Süleyman's victories were commemorated by lavishly illustrated chronicles, poem-books, festivities, and by the many masterpieces of Ottoman architecture. Known to Europeans as "the Magnificent" for the grandeur of his court, to his subjects and to Muslims in general he was known as Kanuni (the Lawgiver), because it was under his rule that sultanic or secular laws (KANUN) were compiled, systematized, and harmonized with Islamic law (SHARIA). This sobriquet also reflects the sultan's self-image during the latter part of his reign, for he wanted to be remembered as a just ruler. The tradition that considers him Süleyman II is erroneous and is based on the presumption that Prince Süleyman—one of the sons of Bayezid I (r. 1389–1402) who ruled parts of the Ottoman lands during the civil war and interregnum (1402–13) that followed the Ottoman defeat at the BATTLE OF ANKARA in 1402—was Süleyman I.

The images of the Süleymanic "golden age" and that of a subsequent "Ottoman decline" both seem simplistic and inaccurate in light of recent research. These images—partly the results of the sophisticated propaganda of Süleyman's court that aimed at creating a favorable legacy for the sultan—not only exaggerate Süleyman's achievements and mask his failures, they also misrepresent later Ottoman transformations and adjustments in the fields of military, economic, fiscal, and organizational developments as "decline." The sultan's achievements were also the result of the talent, brilliance, and hard work of his statesmen, military leaders, and administrators who are often overshadowed by their master in narratives of Ottoman history; they include his grand viziers Ibrahim (1523–36), Rüstem (1544–53 and 1556–61), and SOKOLLU MEHMED PASHA (1565–79); his grand admiral Hayreddin Barbarossa (see BARBAROSSA BROTHERS); his chief jurisconsult (şeyhülislam) Ebussuud Efendi; and his chief chancellor (nişancı) and chronicler Celalzade Mustafa.

OTTOMAN-HABSBURG RIVALRY AND CONQUESTS IN EUROPE

Süleyman's accession to the throne in 1520 signaled a major shift in Ottoman policy. His father had devoted the empire's resources to fighting against Shah ISMAIL (r. 1501–24), the founder of Safavid IRAN, who challenged Ottoman rule in eastern Anatolia and Azerbaijan. Süleyman reoriented Ottoman strategy against the empire's Christian enemies. The reasons for this shift were mainly sociopolitical, economic, and military. By the time Süleyman ascended to the throne it had become clear that Selim's policy with regard to the Safavids could not be maintained. Warfare since 1511 had exhausted the eastern provinces and the imperial army was stretched too thin. Distance, inhospitable climate (early winters and snow), combined with Shah Ismail's tactic of avoiding battle and his use of a scorched-earth policy that destroyed crops and poisoned wells, caused serious problems for the otherwise well-organized Ottoman campaign logistics, rendering seasonal campaigning ineffective. The sultan's Asian troops also fought reluctantly against the shah's Anatolian KIZILBAŞ followers,

mainly Turkoman and Kurdish nomads, and they often deserted or allied with the enemy. They had had enough of the eastern wars and wanted instead to fight against the Hungarian "infidels," whom they considered weaker warriors. The sultan's troops in the Balkans likewise lobbied for the renewal of European campaigns from which they hoped to profit economically through spoils of war and new military fiefs.

In 1521 Süleyman marched against Hungary and conquered BELGRADE (August 29, 1521), the key fortress of the Hungarian border defense system along the lower DANUBE. The next year Süleyman's navy set sail against the island of RHODES, captured the fortress, and evicted the KNIGHTS OF ST. JOHN from the island to MALTA. These swift conquests in his early years, especially in light of previous Ottoman failures (Belgrade 1456, Rhodes 1480) under MEHMED II (r. 1444–46; 1451–81), the conqueror of Constantinople and the most formidable sultan Europeans had known hitherto, established Süleyman's image in Europe as a redoubtable adversary, and within the Islamic world as a warrior sultan and defender of Islam.

Süleyman achieved his greatest victory at the BATTLE OF MOHÁCS (August 29, 1526) in southern Hungary, where his armies crushed the Hungarians and killed their king, Louis II (r. 1516–26). The battle was related to the Habsburg-Valois rivalry between Charles V and Francis I. When Charles V defeated and captured Francis I at the Battle of Pavia in northern Italy (1525), the French king sought Süleyman's help. Süleyman chose to inflict harm on the Habsburgs (see AUSTRIA) through Hungary, whose king Louis II was the brother-in-law of Habsburg Ferdinand and Charles V. For Süleyman, Francis's plea for help served as pretext and opportunity to divide the Europeans; it was not the cause of the Hungarian campaign, which had already been decided upon in ISTANBUL. However, by killing King Louis II at Mohács, Süleyman miscalculated, because part of the Hungarian nobility elected then Habsburg Ferdinand king of Hungary (r. 1526–64). This made Habsburg-Ottoman military confrontation in central Europe inescapable. Since Süleyman was unable to capture the Habsburg capital Vienna in 1529 and 1532, he temporarily accepted the partition of Hungary between Ferdinand and Ferdinand's opponent, the Hungarian aristocrat János Szapolyai, also elected and crowned as king of Hungary (r. 1526–40), and supported the latter in the ensuing civil war.

Szapolyai's death in 1540 and Ferdinand's unsuccessful siege of BUDA, Hungary's capital, in 1541 triggered a new campaign, again led personally by Süleyman. This ended with his capture of Buda and the incorporation of central Hungary into the Ottoman Empire. Hungary's strategically less important eastern territories were left by the sultan in the hands of Szapolyai's widow and infant son; they later became the principality of TRANSYLVANIA, an Ottoman vassal state.

Süleyman's 1543 Hungarian campaign established a protective ring around Ottoman Buda, the center of the newly created province (*vilayet-i Budun*), especially by capturing Esztergom, the most important fortress northwest of Buda on the Danube that guarded the city from Hungarian and Habsburg attacks from the west. In the coming years local Ottoman forces expanded the territories under Istanbul's control and forced the Habsburgs to conclude a five-year peace treaty with Süleyman in 1547 that reflected the territorial status quo.

For the next couple of years the Hungarian frontier remained relatively quiet because the sultan was at war in eastern Anatolia and Iraq with the Safavids. However, troubles in Transylvania led to renewed military confrontation in Hungary. When Ferdinand's troops—following an agreement with the Transylvanians in 1549 regarding the transfer of that country to the Habsburgs—attempted to capture Transylvania in 1551, the Ottomans intervened. In 1551–52, Ottoman forces from Buda and the Balkans captured a series of strategically important forts in southeastern Hungary, including Temesvár (Timișoara in present-day Romania), which became the center of the Ottomans' second province in Hungary.

THE MEDITERRANEAN AND THE INDIAN OCEAN

In addition to the sultan's land campaigns, his fleet also battled the Habsburgs and their allies in the Mediterranean. The Ottoman navy was considerably strengthened after Süleyman appointed Hayreddin Barbarossa (*see* BARBAROSSA BROTHERS), an experienced corsair and governor of ALGIERS, as his grand admiral (*kapudan pasha*) in 1533. Hayreddin's conquest of TUNIS in 1533 proved short-lived, for Charles V retook the city two years later. However, the Ottoman admiral won a splendid victory at Preveza (1538) against the joint naval forces of SPAIN and VENICE, defeating his equally famous opponent, the Genoese admiral Andrea Doria, who had been in Spanish Habsburg service since 1528. In the long run, Preveza proved more important than Charles V's re-capture of Tunis, because it secured the eastern Mediterranean for the Ottomans. In 1551 Turgut Reis (Dragut in European sources), Süleyman's other admiral of corsair origin, took TRIPOLI (Libya) from the Knights of St. John of Malta.

Less successful were Süleyman's attempts to curb Portuguese expansion in the Indian Ocean, which threatened Muslim navigation, trade, and pilgrimage between India and Arabia. After Selim I's conquest of EGYPT (1517), the Ottomans reached the Red Sea, from where they managed to expel the Portuguese who threatened the holy cities of MECCA and MEDINA. In 1538 the governor of Egypt, Süleyman Pasha, set sail with 74 ships from Suez,

captured parts of YEMEN and the port city of Aden on the southwestern tip of the Arabian Peninsula, but failed to achieve his original aim, dislodging the Portuguese from their stronghold of Diu (Gujarat, western India). Another attempt from Suez in 1552 under the command of Piri Reis, the renowned Ottoman marine and cartographer, author of the famous naval manual *Kitab-i Bahriye* (Book of seafaring) and maker of the first Ottoman map of the New World, also ended in failure. After recapturing Aden in 1551 (lost in 1547), Piri Reis sailed from Suez in the spring of 1552 with 30 ships to evict the Portuguese from Hormuz. Although he temporarily captured Muscat (in present-day Oman), he failed to take Hormuz and withdrew to the Gulf of Basra. When a Portuguese fleet cut off his route back to Cairo, he left his fleet behind and fled with three vessels. By the time he reached CAIRO through Suez, the news of his humiliation had preceded him. He was executed for abandoning his fleet.

The next, equally unsuccessful, attempt was launched in 1554 from BASRA, in southern IRAQ. Following the Ottoman conquest of BAGHDAD in 1534, the commander of Basra accepted Ottoman suzerainty. However, it was not until the appointment of an Ottoman governor to Basra in 1546 that the Ottomans gained control over the city and the Persian Gulf. In 1554 Seydi (Sidi) Ali Reis launched his campaign from Basra but was defeated by the Portuguese near Muscat, losing nine of his small fleet of 15 ships. The disaster did not end there. A storm brought his remaining six ships to Diu, where the Portuguese stopped him. He sold his fleet and, returning from India to ISTANBUL overland, reached the Ottoman capital by May 1557.

OTTOMAN-SAFAVID RIVALRY AND CONQUESTS IN THE EAST

The other major rivalry of the 16th century involved the Ottomans and the Safavids of Iran. Although Shah Ismail's death in 1524 temporarily removed the Safavid threat, shifting loyalties of the commanders of various fortresses along the Safavid-Ottoman border made conflict unavoidable. When the commander of Bitlis in eastern Anatolia, west of Lake Van, sided with the Safavid Shah Tahmasp (r. 1524–76) in 1533, the sultan sent his trusted grand vizier Ibrahim Pasha against Bitlis and the Safavids. Since none of the empires of the 16th century was capable of waging wars continuously on more than one front, rivalries between various empires of the 16th century were often interconnected. In the case of the Ottomans, there was an attempt to avoid open war with the Safavids until a truce or peace could be made with the Habsburgs, and vice versa. Thus it is hardly surprising that Süleyman undertook his eastern campaigns in 1534–35 and 1548–49, after he had concluded an armistice (1533) and a peace treaty (1547) with the Habsburgs.

In 1533, Ibrahim Pasha not only retook Bitlis but also captured the Safavid capital Tabriz, abandoned by the shah. Süleyman joined his grand vizier in Tabriz in September 1534. At the end of November, the two captured Baghdad, the most important city in Iraq, which controlled the Euphrates and Tigris rivers and thus controlled regional and international trade. In Baghdad the sultan's "rediscovery" of the tomb of Abu Hanifa, the eighth-century Muslim jurist whose school of law the Ottomans favored, had symbolic importance and was used to further strengthen Süleyman's legitimacy within the Islamic world. Similarly, the first law code (*kanunname*) of the recently organized province of Baghdad, which, although similar to that of the Safavids, contained easier tax burdens, suggested to the newly conquered people that Süleyman would rule with moderation and justice. In 1535 the sultan returned to Anatolia through Tabriz. Unable to find the shah, he ended his campaign, which secured eastern Anatolia (Erzurum and Van) and Baghdad for the time being.

Back in Istanbul, Süleyman ordered the strangling of grand vizier Ibrahim Pasha, a faithful companion from childhood, skilled commander, and diplomat. Ottoman chroniclers claim that Süleyman got rid of his trusted statesman because the latter abused his power. However, it is plausible that Ibrahim Pasha was a victim of the intrigues of the sultan's beloved wife, Hurrem Sultan, known as Roxalane in the West, especially considering the grand vizier's support for Prince Mustafa, Süleyman's oldest living son, who would also be executed in 1553 on the grounds of planning to dethrone his father. With the execution of Ibrahim Pasha, Süleyman lost his chief ideologue and strategist who had carefully orchestrated Süleyman's image as *sahib-kiran*, the ruler of a new universal empire.

Confrontation with the Habsburgs in Hungary (campaigns of 1541 and 1543), and the Mediterranean (Preveza, 1538) temporarily diverted the sultan's attention from the eastern frontier. Returning here after the Habsburg-Ottoman peace treaty (1547), Süleyman wanted to seize the Van region from the Safavids who had retaken it after the main Ottoman forces returned home

The mosque of Rüstem Pasha in the main port district of Eminönü in Istanbul, is famous for its lavish Iznik ceramic decoration. Rüstem Pasha was a grand vizier of Süleyman I and the wife of Süleyman's daughter Mihrimah. *(Photo by Gábor Ágoston)*

from their last eastern campaign in 1534–35. The excuse for the campaign was provided by a plea from Elkas Mirza, Shah Tahmasp's brother, who had fled to Istanbul. In August 1548 Süleyman retook Van and fortified the frontier with Georgia. Since the planned insurrection against the shah by Elkas Mirza never materialized, late in 1549 Süleyman returned to Istanbul.

The sultan set off for another campaign against the Safavids in late August 1553. Almost 60 years old and in ill health, he initially declined to lead his army personally and wanted instead to send Rüstem Pasha (his grand vizier and son-in-law who had been married to Mihrimah, Süleyman's favorite daughter from Hurrem) as commander in chief to Iran. However, among rumors that Prince Mustafa—his eldest living son, child of his first concubine Mahidevran, and the heir to the sultanate preferred by the JANISSARIES—wanted to dethrone him, he changed his mind. On his way to ALEPPO in the province of Karaman the sultan summoned his son and ordered his execution (October 5, 1553). Contemporaries and later Ottoman chroniclers ascribed Mustafa's killing to the influence of Hurrem, who wanted to eliminate Mustafa so that one of her two sons, either Selim or Bayezid, could succeed the ailing Süleyman (her hunchbacked son Jihangir was not considered a potential heir because of his physical deformity). They also noticed that Hurrem acted in concert with Grand Vizier Rüstem Pasha and his wife Mihrimah. Contemporaries interpreted the dismissal of Rüstem Pasha from the grand vizierate on the day of Mustafa's execution as proof of Süleyman's remorse and a necessary temporary sacrifice to quiet down Mustafa's partisans. (Rüstem resumed his position within two years.) Traumatized by the execution of his half-brother, Jihangir died three weeks later, leaving only two of Hurrem's sons alive.

The campaign of 1553 achieved little, and with winter approaching the sultan moved to Aleppo. The campaign in 1554 brought Nakhichevan (in present-day Azerbaijan) and Yerevan (capital of present-day Armenia) under Ottoman rule. However, negotiations with Shah Tahmasp, who had carefully avoided open battle with Süleyman's forces, resulted in the peace treaty of Amasya (1555). The treaty left Iraq, parts of Kurdistan, and eastern ARMENIA in Ottoman hands, and returned Tabriz, Yerevan, and Nakhichevan to the shah. With the exception of a short period when Baghdad was in Safavid hands in the 17th century (1623–38), the border between the Ottoman Empire and Iran established by the Amasya treaty was to remain essentially unchanged through WORLD WAR I.

LAST CAMPAIGN AND LEGACY

The sultan's health started to deteriorate from the late 1540s when he was in his 50s. Saddened by the loss of Hurrem, his beloved companion for four decades (1558), and troubled by the succession fight among his two remaining sons, Süleyman's behavior and style of governance changed toward the end of his reign. He devoted most of his attention to just governing, law-making, and a pious life.

In May 1566, however, the 72-year-old sultan set off for what proved to be his last campaign against Hungary. Some speculated that it was to offset the failure at Malta (1565), others claimed that his target was again the Habsburg capital, Vienna. Whatever the reason, the sultan was hesitant as to his target. While in Belgrade he changed his mind twice. First he wanted to capture Szigetvár in southwestern Hungary, but altered his plan when flooding made crossing the Drava River impossible. Instead he decided to cross the Danube at Petrovaradin (northwest of Belgrade) and conquer Eger in northern Hungary, which the Ottomans had besieged in vain in 1552. However, when the Drava subsided enough to allow his troops to cross it, the sultan returned to his original plan. The ailing sultan now marched against Szigetvár, a fort close to Mohács, the site of his most splendid victory. He died in front of Szigetvár on September 6, two days before the castle surrendered. Grand Vizier Sokollu Mehmed Pasha concealed his master's death until his successor, Prince Selim, was enthroned in Istanbul and acclaimed by the returning army in Belgrade.

It is difficult to arrive at a balanced assessment of Süleyman's reign. Like all long reigns, it witnessed ups and downs as well as major policy changes. His conquests substantially expanded the empire's territories from 576,900 square miles in 1520 to 877,888 square miles in 1566, an increase of more than 50 percent. His most important conquests, central Hungary and Iraq, were seized from his two formidable opponents, the Habsburgs and Safavids. Up until the early 1540s Süleyman and Charles V fought in vain for world supremacy. In the later years of the sultan's reign just government, law and order, the well-being of his subjects, the economic and financial health of his empire, and religiousness and Muslim piety were given more attention.

These changes also reflected the policy of the sultan's statesmen and advisors, whose influence upon the sultan, although widely discussed in contemporary sources, still awaits satisfactory analysis. Ibrahim Pasha symbolized conquest, struggle for world supremacy, and lavish display of grandeur, and was also instrumental in formulating Ottoman strategy and Süleyman's image as world conqueror and defender of Islam. Rüstem Pasha's tenure as grand vizier (1544–53 and 1556–61) was important with regard to administrative and financial consolidation, legal codification, and greater emphasis on the Islamic character of the sultan's reign. It was an age of regular land and revenue surveys, but also of novel fiscal practices (such as using TAX FARMING rather than military

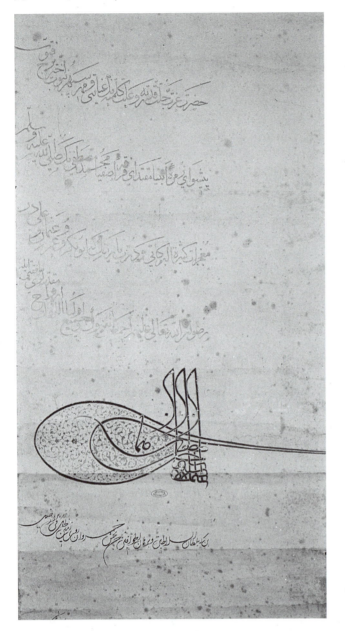

The *tuğra*, or sultanic monogram, of Süleyman was recognizable and proved the authenticity of the sultan's decree. *(Bridgeman-Giraudon / Art Resource).*

even more astonishing for contemporaries. It was a break with the "one concubine—one son" rule and with the practice by which the mothers of princes accompanied their sons to the provinces when these were appointed as prince-governors. The rivalry between Hurrem and Süleyman's first concubine, Mahidevran, initiated a troublesome process, known in Ottoman history as the "sultanate of women." The emergence of favorites, both among the women of the sultan's harem and among the *damad*s (sons-in-law, men married to princesses), also dates back to Süleyman's time. The two processes radically changed the way politics was done in Istanbul. Not surprisingly, Süleyman's reign also witnessed dynastic dramas such as the execution of Prince Mustafa and of Bayezid.

In the early years of Süleyman's reign Ibrahim Pasha consciously and masterfully propagated the sultan's image as the new world conqueror, the successor of Alexander the Great, his master's favorite historical hero. In his latter years the sultan viewed himself as the "Lawgiver," a just ruler in whose realm justice and order reigned. Justice was also associated with his growing religiousness and piety. Religion was an important part of Süleyman's legitimacy. He not only continued using the title "Servant of the Two Noble Sanctuaries" (Mecca and Medina), first introduced by his father Selim I, but from the 1540s he also adopted the title of caliph. In the formulation of his Grand Mufti Ebussud Efendi, this was to counterbalance the Safavid shah Tahmasp's assertions regarding sovereignty over Ottoman subjects living in eastern Anatolia and Azerbaijan, as well as Charles V's claims to universal Christian rulership.

The restoration of religious buildings (the tomb of Abu Hanifa, mosques in Jerusalem, Mecca, and Medina) was important for strengthening his legitimacy, while the great building projects in Istanbul and in the provinces all contributed to the image of the Süleymanic golden age. Of these, the Süleymaniye and Selimiye mosque complexes in Istanbul and EDIRNE are the most imposing, built by the sultan's chief architect, Sinan (*see* ARCHITECTURE), who in his long tenure (1538–88) allegedly built, designed, or supervised the construction of some 300 mosques and other public buildings. While Süleyman's conquered territories were lost in subsequent centuries, these buildings, along with the countless illustrated manuscripts and artifacts preserved in the Turkish libraries and museums, remind us of the wealth and splendor that the empire enjoyed at its zenith under his rule.

Gábor Ágoston

Further reading: Halil İnalcık and Cemal Kafadar, eds., *Süleyman the Second and His Time* (Istanbul: Isis, 1993); Metin Kunt and Christine Woodhead, eds., *Süleyman the Magnificent and His Age: The Ottoman Empire in the Early Modern World* (London: Longman, 1995); Gülru Necipoğlu,

fiefs as salaries for officials and soldiers), many of which were perceived as harmful; Rüstem was also accused of avarice and corruption.

Perhaps the most influential adviser was Süleyman's wife Hurrem. Whether ibecause of her beauty, charm, and other personal qualities extensively discussed by contemporaries, or because she gave birth to several potential heirs, Hurrem had exceptional influence on the sultan during their 40-year-long romance. Süleyman's marriage to his favorite concubine (*hasseki*) was itself unprecedented, but the fact that Hurrem had more than one son with the sultan and remained in the palace was

The Age of Sinan: Architectural Culture in the Ottoman Empire (Princeton, N.J.: Princeton University Press, 2005); Leslie P. Peirce, *The Imperial Harem: Women and Sovereignty in the Ottoman Empire* (Oxford: Oxford University Press, 1993) Donald Edgar Pitcher, *An Historical Geography of the Ottoman Empire from the Earliest Times to the End of the Sixteenth Century* (Leiden: Brill, 1972); Gilles Veinstein, "Süleymān," in *Encyclopaedia of Islam,* online edition (by subscription), edited by P. Bearman, Th. Bianquis, C. E. Bosworth, E. van Donzel, and W.P. Heinrichs. Brill, 2007. Brill Online. 31 May 2007 <http://www.brillonline.nl/subscriber/entry?entry=islam_COM-1114>; Gilles Veinstein, ed., *Soliman le Magnifique et son temps* (Paris: Documentation française, 1992); Galina Yermolenko, "Roxolana: The Greatest Empress of the East." *The Muslim World* 95, no. 2 (2005): 231–48.

Süleyman II (b. 1642—1691) (r. 1687–1691) *Ottoman sultan*   Born to Sultan IBRAHIM (r. 1640–48) and Saliha Dilasub, Süleyman II became ruler of the Ottoman Empire on November 8, 1687, following the deposition of his half-brother Sultan MEHMED IV (1648–87). Despite the turmoil at the beginning of his reign and the devastating military and financial situation he inherited, Süleyman managed to bring order into the military, administration, and state financing during his short reign. In 1690 his troops also recaptured BELGRADE (lost in 1688), and stabilized the empire's northern borders for the time being.

The military rebellion that forced the abdication of Mehmed IV lasted for several months. It was not until April 1688 that the new sultan and his frequently changing statesmen managed to quell the JANISSARIES and the other mutinous troops who brought havoc to ISTANBUL during their five-month rebellion. Once the sultans' elite infantry, the legendary military discipline of the Janissaries had given way to an unruly band of privileged troublemakers who habitually made and unmade sultans. In the 1680s the Janissaries were repeatedly defeated by the troops of the Holy League, an alliance of Habsburg AUSTRIA, VENICE, the Papacy, POLAND-Lithuania, and RUSSIA that was formed in 1684 after the unsuccessful Ottoman siege of the Austrian capital VIENNA (1683). Sultan Mehmed IV had suffered his most devastating defeat on August 12, 1687 at a battle in Nagyharsány, some 15 miles southwest of Mohács, the site of Sultan SÜLEYMAN I's (r. 1520–66) most splendid victory over the Hungarians in 1526 (*see* MOHÁCS, BATTLE OF). With the defeat at Nagyharsány, most of HUNGARY was lost. Abandoned by the sultan's main forces, several key Ottoman garrisons in Hungary surrendered, including Eger (December 17, 1687) and Lippa (June 20, 1688).

Desperate times required desperate measures. The new sultan dismissed several of his incapable viziers and advisors, melted down the gold and silver plates of the TOPKAPI PALACE to generate cash with which he paid his unruly troops, and co-opted one of the ringleaders of the rebellion, Yeğen Osman Pasha, by appointing him commander of the Hungarian front. However, he proved unable to halt the advance of the Holy League's troops and lost Belgrade (September 6, 1688), the key to Hungary and the most important Ottoman logistical center on the DANUBE. In a few months, he was made responsible for allowing the Habsburgs to march into the Ottoman Balkans, was declared a rebel, and killed.

With Belgrade gone, the way to the Ottoman Balkans was open. When the troops of the Holy League captured Vidin (October 14, 1689), it became obvious that the empire's dire situation required an experienced and capable statesman. On October 25 the sultan appointed Köprülüzade Fazil Mustafa Pasha as his grand vizier. Like his predecessors from this distinguished family of Ottoman grand viziers, the KÖPRÜLÜS, Fazil Mustafa Pasha brought order into the administration and the military by purging it of corrupt officials and incapable and ignorant officers and soldiers. He instituted strict roll calls to eliminate the widespread practice of soldiers collecting their deceased comrades' salaries, putting an extra burden on the treasury. He also proclaimed a general mobilization of the Muslim subjects of the empire and the conscription of Turkoman and Kurdish nomadic tribes, who had to send thousands of soldiers to the Balkan front. Other measures were aimed at winning over the population of the hinterland. The grand vizier reinstituted the custom by which the poll tax paid by the empire's non-Muslim subjects, was assessed on individual adults. In earlier years Istanbul had switched to collective assessment, which hurt communities whose population had dwindled, because the same (or increased) tax burden had to be paid by fewer people. It was especially unjust in wartime and in regions ravaged by war. Resettlement and repopulation were also encouraged by tax and other incentives, and permits to fix or rebuild Christian churches were issued more easily.

The 1690 campaign brought much-needed military success. The Ottomans recaptured Niš in September, and several key forts along the Danube River, such as Vidin, Smederevo, and Golubac. By the beginning of October 1690, Fazil Mustafa Pasha besieged Belgrade with his 40,000 infantry and 20,000 cavalry. On October 8, after a major explosion destroyed the defenders' armory, Belgrade's Habsburg commander capitulated. Although Fazil Mustafa Pasha had some three weeks before the traditional end (October 26) of the campaign season, heavy rains prevented him from continuing to fight.

Although his achievements are important, one should also remember that his success was partly due to the renewed Habsburg-French conflict (War of the League of Augsburg/Nine Years' War) that required the

Habsburgs to redeploy their best forces from Hungary to the Rhine front. However, not even a Köprülü could produce a miracle. In the 1691 campaign the Ottomans suffered a crushing defeat at Slankamen (August 19), north of Belgrade. They lost some 20,000 men, including Grand Vizier Fazil Mustafa Pasha. Sultan Süleyman had died on June 22 in Edirne and was succeeded by his brother AHMED II (r. 1691–1695).

Gábor Ágoston

Further reading: Caroline Finkel, *Osman's Dream* (London: John Murray, 2005); Ivan Parvev, *Habsburgs and Ottomans between Vienna and Belgrade, 1683–1739* (Boulder, Colo.: East European Monographs, 1995).

Sunni Islam All Muslims practice either Sunni or SHIA ISLAM. Approximately 85 percent of the world's Muslims are Sunni and the rest are Shiis. The origins of the two sects lie in the early division over who would lead the community after the death of the Prophet Muhammad in 632. Some felt that it should be Ali, the Prophet's cousin and son-in-law and the father of his only surviving grandchildren. But the majority chose Abu Bakr as the Prophet's successor or caliph. Abu Bakr was an early convert to Islam, a close confidant of the Prophet, and his father-in-law. He was also much older than Ali and the majority of the community felt that his maturity would be necessary to help steer the new community after the unexpected death of the Prophet. The rift caused by this decision was not healed, however, and when a group of disgruntled soldiers murdered the third caliph, Uthman, in 656, the rift opened into civil war. Following these hostilities, the majority of the community chose Ali as caliph but Uthman's kinsmen, the clan of the Banu Umayya (Umayyads), rejected Ali's leadership as they said his hands were stained with Uthman's blood.

The two sides prepared for battle in 661 but Ali, who did not want to plunge the community into further violence, agreed to arbitration of the dispute. A splinter group of his supporters, angry at his attempt at compromise, assassinated Ali in the same year and civil war ensued. In 680 the forces of the Banu Umayya slaughtered Ali's son Husayn at KARBALA, in present-day IRAQ. This action created the historical basis for the cleavage of the two sects of Islam, the Shia maintaining that the CALIPHATE rightly belonged to Ali's descendants while the Sunnis accepted the leadership of the Banu Umayya, under Caliph Yazid (d. 683) and later the ABBASID CALIPHATE (750–1258).

The name Sunni derives from the phrase *ahl al-sunna*, which refers to the people who follow the righteous path established by the Prophet Muhammad. In truth, there is very little doctrinal difference between the Sunni and the Shia. But over time, the Shia developed a hierarchy in the ranks of their clergy that was noticeably absent in the Sunni tradition until the Ottoman Empire. They also believed in the eventual return of the "hidden imam," the 12th imam who vanished in the ninth century but whose return will bring a reign of absolute justice. In contrast, the Sunnis emphasized the legal training of their clerics, creating a system wherein the quality of training and scholarship determined prestige. There was no single religious authority that all Sunni clergy were compelled to obey. While the Shia rejected the political authority of the caliphs after Ali, the Sunni clergy worked within the system as the caliph's advisers. This compromise was fully articulated during the Abbasid Caliphate when the caliphs agreed to let the Sunni clergy administer the law of their state in return for the clergy's acknowledgement of the caliphs' sovereignty over political affairs.

In the 11th century, Shia dynasties seemed on the verge of ruling most of the Muslim world as they seized political control of EGYPT, most of NORTH AFRICA, and IRAN. These were all areas that had previously been under the rule of the Sunni Abbasids. In BAGHDAD, however, the Turkish Seljuk family sponsored a revival of Sunni Islam through the establishment of religious schools and the sponsorship of religious scholars, thus establishing a link between Sunni Islam and the various Turkish dynasties that emerged in the Middle East from the 11th through the 14th centuries during the period of the Crusades. Although devotion to Ali and his descendants was strong among the Turks in Anatolia, almost all of them were nominally Sunni Muslims who followed the Hanafi school of legal interpretation. The Hanafi school was one of four in Sunni Islam; the others are the Shafii, Maliki, and the Hanbali. As the Hanafi school had developed in the caliph's court in Baghdad during the Abbasid period, it was particularly attuned to the political needs of a Muslim state.

THE HANAFI SCHOOL

Starting with Sultan ORHAN (r. 1324–62), Ottoman sultans promoted the Hanafi version of Sunni Islam, although they did not make it mandatory. In EGYPT, the Shafii school continued to dominate in nonofficial life, and the Maliki school persisted in NORTH AFRICA. However, the chief judges appointed to any of the Ottoman provincial capitals had to be graduates of the Ottoman legal schools, the madrasas, and administer the law according to Hanafi interpretations. The sultans lavishly supported the legal schools; after the CONQUEST OF CONSTANTINOPLE in 1453, they established an imperial hierarchy for the clergy. Direct state control over the training and licensing of the clergy was an Ottoman innovation, as no other Sunni state had attempted to enter so directly into their subjects' spiritual lives. The Ottoman state treasury also paid all the leading clergy's salaries. At the top of the clerical hierarchy was the ŞEYHÜLISLAM, or chief judge of the empire, who approved the appointments of the judges to the provincial centers and who, along with his immediate subordinates, the chief judge of Rumelia (European provinces) and the chief judge of Anatolia (Asian provinces), sat with the sultan when he conducted the Imperial Council (Divan-ı Hümayun).

THE OTTOMANS AND SUNNI ISLAM

The connection between the Ottoman ruling house and Sunni Islam intensified in the 16th century after the revolt of the Shia KIZILBAŞ. This group regarded Shah ISMAIL I (r. 1501–24) of Iran as the long-awaited imam who the Shia believed would restore justice to the world, and they supported his uprising against the Ottomans. For the next three centuries the Iranian shahs espoused Shia Islam as the state religion and did not permit other forms of worship in their territories, including that belonging to the Sunni tradition. While the Ottoman sultans promoted Sunni Islam as the empire's official faith, they did not retaliate against the Iranian shahs by taking any action against the peaceful Shia in their realm, whose freedom of worship was allowed to continue. At the same time, the Ottoman adherence to Sunni Islam became one of the legitimating factors for the regime in the eyes of the sultan's Sunni subjects.

In the 17th century, a Sunni reform movement known as the Kadızadeler gained strength in the empire. It promoted the teachings of Birgili Mehmed (d. 1573) and his disciple Kadızade Mehmed (d. 1635). Their doctrines were very strict and rigid, resembling those of the later WAHHABIS. In particular, the Kadızadeler movement opposed SUFISM and the prominent role that the Ottoman state played in training the Sunni clergy and providing them with salaries. In short, they saw as sinful anything they considered an innovation from the practice of the Muslim community at the time of the Prophet's death. Among the things they considered sins were singing, dancing, ILLUSTRATED MANUSCRIPTS AND MINIATURE PAINTINGS, the drinking of COFFEE, and the smoking of tobacco. Sultan MURAD IV (r. 1623–40) sought to placate the movement by banning alcohol, coffee, and tobacco in ISTANBUL, inaugurating an era of extreme religious purity. After his death, the movement lost much of its appeal in the inner circle of the sultan's palace, but it remained an intellectual current present in religious debates among the empire's Sunnis through the start of the 20th century.

SULTAN AS CALIPH

Sultan ABDÜLHAMID II (1876–1909) promoted the idea that the sultan of the Ottoman Empire was rightfully the caliph of all Sunni Muslims. Although some Muslim scholars challenged the legitimacy of that claim because the sultans were not descended from the family of the Prophet Muhammad, others, especially those in India and the Dutch East Indies (present-day Indonesia), saw that claim as a potential weapon against the Europeans who ruled their homelands. Jamal al-Din AL-AFGHANI, who was perhaps the most influential Muslim intellectual in the late 19th century, was an ardent promoter of this claim because it bolstered his belief that the Ottoman Empire remained the last hope of the Muslim world retaining its independence in the face of European imperial ambitions. When WORLD WAR I broke out in 1914, Ottoman sultan MEHMED V (r. 1909–1918), claiming to be caliph, called all the world's Muslims to holy war (jihad) against the western Allied Powers, but few Muslims outside the Ottoman Empire took the call seriously.

Bruce Masters

Further reading: John Esposito, *Islam: The Straight Path* (Oxford: Oxford University Press, 1998); Madeline Zilfi, *The Politics of Piety: The Ottoman Ulema in the Postclassical Age, 1600–1800* (Minneapolis: Bibliotheca Islamica, 1988).

suq (çarşı)   See MARKETS.

Svishtov, Treaty of (Ziştovi [tr.]; Zistovi; Zistow; Sistov; Sistovi)   Signed on August 4, 1791, in the village of Svishtov (on the right bank of the DANUBE in present-day Bulgaria), the Treaty of Svishtov concluded the 1787–91 Ottoman-Habsburg War, the last war to break out between the two powers. Except for ceding Old Orshova—the renowned gorge, also called the Iron Gate, forming part of the boundary between Romania and Serbia—to the Habsburg Empire and some minor changes made to the Croatian frontier in favor of the Habsburgs, this treaty restored the position that had been established by the 1739 Treaty of Belgrade.

The Ottoman declaration of war on RUSSIA in 1787, with the aim of recovering the CRIMEA, provided the pretext for Habsburg emperor Joseph II (r. 1765–90) to enter war in that same year on the side of his ally Catherine the Great (r. 1762–96) of Russia. The Habsburg's war aims concentrated on the conquest of BELGRADE while Russia sought to consolidate its previous gains by defeating the Ottomans. The two allies are also said to have contemplated the destruction of the Ottoman Empire in the 1780s. The Ottomans were unprepared to fight on two fronts, and in spite of early Ottoman victories on the Hungarian front, Belgrade fell to the Habsburgs, while a joint army of Habsburg and Russian troops occupied the Romanian principalities of WALLACHIA and MOLDAVIA by 1790.

The outbreak of the French Revolution (1789) and the death of King Joseph II of Germany (February 1790) coincided with the formation of an Ottoman-Prussian Alliance against the Habsburgs (January 31, 1790). All these developments, coupled with an important Ottoman victory over the Habsburgs at Yergöğü (Giurgiu, present-day Romania), forced the new Habsburg emperor,

Leopold II (r. 1790–92), to agree to a truce. After lengthy negotiations, the two powers signed the Treaty of Svishtov through the mediation of Prussia, ENGLAND, and the Netherlands. The treaty consisted of 14 articles and a special pact of seven clauses that stipulated the restoration of the prewar status except for the aforementioned changes in the border, and left the fortress of Hotin (Khotin) to the Habsburgs until the end of the war with Russia.

Kahraman Şakul

Further reading: Virginia Aksan, *Ottoman Wars 1700-1870: An Empire Besieged* (Harlow, England: Longman/Pearson, 2007), 160–180; Caroline Finkel, *Osman's Dream: The Story of the Ottoman Empire, 1300–1923* (London: John Murray, 2005), 383–89; Ekmeleddin İhsanoğlu, ed., *History of the Ottoman State, Society, and Civilisation*, vol. 1 (Istanbul: Ircica, 2001), 68–69; Virginia Aksan, "Selim III," in *Encyclopaedia of Islam.* 2nd ed., edited by P. J. Bearman et al., vol. 9 (Leiden: Brill, 1960–), 132–134.

Sykes-Picot Agreement   This was the name given to a secret agreement reached among Great Britain, FRANCE, Italy, and RUSSIA in 1916 to dispose of former Ottoman territories in the anticipated aftermath of WORLD WAR I, a war that the Allied Powers were confident of winning. The two principal framers of the document were Mark Sykes, a British diplomat who spent some time in the Ottoman Empire and had written a popular book about his travels, and François Georges Picot, who had served as France's consul in BEIRUT.

The original agreement was simply between Great Britain and France and was signed on January 3, 1916. It gave France direct control over LEBANON and the coast of SYRIA as well as a large parcel of what is today southern TURKEY. France also gained a recognized sphere of influence over any possible Arab state or states that might emerge in the Syrian interior after the war. Britain received direct control of BAGHDAD and BASRA, as well as the Palestinian ports of HAIFA and ACRE. The rest of PALESTINE was to be put under the control of an international consortium.

Russia soon became aware of the agreement and demanded a share of the territory. Britain and France agreed to Russia's inclusion in the secret pact, and in May 1916 the agreement was amended to grant Russia extensive territories in Ottoman Armenia and Kurdistan. Italy, which had joined the Allied Powers in 1915, also demanded a share of the spoils. To satisfy that demand, the three powers already in on the division agreed to Italy's occupation of Turkey's Mediterranean coast and its retention of the Dodecanese Islands in the Aegean Sea, which Italy had taken from the Ottomans in 1912 but which had not yet been granted to Italy officially and internationally.

After the Russian Revolution of 1917, the Bolsheviks leaked the contents of the hitherto secret agreement, causing outrage in the Arab provinces of the empire where the British had received Arab support in return for promises apparently contravened by the terms of the Sykes-Picot Agreement. Having offered, in the HUSAYN-MCMAHON CORRESPONDENCE, to support an Arab kingdom as recompense for Arab assistance in the war, the British were embarrassed by the untimely release of information from Russia, and British officers on the ground denied to their erstwhile Arab allies that any such agreement existed.

British historians have argued since that the terms of the secret agreement did not contradict the promises made to HUSAYN IBN ALI AL-HASHIMI, but in the negotiations in Paris that followed the end of the war, the resulting settlement closely followed the outlines provided by the Sykes-Picot Agreement. The Treaty of San Remo of 1920 established the French mandates over Lebanon and Syria and the British mandates in Palestine and Iraq; the boundaries drawn for those mandates were very similar to those drawn on a map of the region as an appendix of the Sykes-Picot Agreement.

Bruce Masters

Syria (*Ar.:* Bilad al-Sham, Suriyya; *Heb.:* Aram; *Turk.:* Arabistan, Suriye)   The nation of Syria did not exist in the Ottoman period. Most of the territory that makes up the present-day Syrian Arab Republic was divided between the provinces of DAMASCUS and ALEPPO. Europeans used the term Syria to mean the geographical region that was bordered by the Mediterranean Sea to the west, the Taurus Mountains to the north, and Syrian Desert to the south and east. That was the name by which the region had been known in the Classical Period, and western Europeans had used that term for the region from at least the time of the Crusades (1095–1291). In the 18th century, influenced by the Europeans, some Arab Christians also began to use the term Syria, *Suriyya* in Arabic, for their homeland. More commonly, however, they and their Muslim neighbors called it Bilad al-Sham (country of Damascus). At the same time, Arab authors in Aleppo or other parts of northern Syria never used that term, and presumably they would have chafed at the implication that they were somehow subordinate to Damascus. Although some Ottoman authors used the term ARABISTAN (land of the Arabs) for the region, more commonly they simply delineated it by listing its principal cities. The Ottoman authorities reorganized the boundaries of Damascus Province in 1864 to include much of what is today southern Syria, LEBANON, Jordan, Israel, and the Palestinian territories. They renamed the province Suriye, establishing the ancient name for the region in official Ottoman usage for the first time. After that, Arab nationalist writers began to use the Arabic form of Syria.

Bruce Masters

Syrian Orthodox Christians   *See* JACOBITES.

T

al-Tahtawi, Rifaat (b. 1801–d. 1873) *Egyptian religious scholar and educator* Rifaat al-Tahtawi was one of first intellectuals in the Arabic-speaking world to gain an appreciation of Western civilization and to seek to apply elements of it to improve conditions in his native EGYPT. Al-Tahtawi was born into a scholarly Muslim family in CAIRO and, like his ancestors, he studied at the famed AL-AZHAR university, the leading institution of higher study in the Arabic-speaking SUNNI world in the 17th and 18th centuries. But his career path diverged from that of the traditional Muslim cleric when he accepted the position of chaplain to the new army being created by MEHMED ALI, ruler of Egypt from 1805–49. After this, as chaplain to the Egyptian mission, al-Tahtawi lived in Paris from 1826 until 1831; there he learned excellent French and read widely in European history and philosophy. He was particularly interested in the Enlightenment philosophers Voltaire, Montesquieu, and Jean-Jacques Rousseau.

Upon his return to Cairo, al-Tahtawi wrote the first account of Parisian manners and customs to appear in Arabic. He did official translations of French texts into Arabic for the Ottoman government and, in 1836, he was placed in charge of a new school to train translators and officials in Western languages. Of his own accord, al-Tahtawi also translated a number of European works he considered important. Through his efforts, he made classic texts of Western history and philosophy available for the first time to an Arabic-reading public.

Al-Tahtawi was less successful in gaining the patronage of Mehmed Ali's successor, Abbas. In 1850, after Mehmed Ali's death, he was assigned a teaching position in Khartoum in Sudan and was not permitted to return to Cairo until 1854. He then worked in education and pursued his real passion, translating European works into Arabic.

Al-Tahtawi also played a major role in choosing which Arabic-language classics would be printed by the new government press in Bulaq. His work as an editor and publisher helped make the classics of Arab culture available to a growing middle class; these had previously been available only in manuscript form.

Al-Tahtawi also wrote some works of his own, including a description of Egyptian society and his recommendations for how it should be modernized. But it is for his work in educational reform that he is best remembered, and he is often called the "Father of Modern Egyptian Education." He was the first in Egypt to propose universal primary schooling for both boys and girls, and to propose universal secondary schooling for boys. Al-Tahtawi also worked to integrate the study of science into a model curriculum for the proposed schools and popularized the idea that Western science was not contradictory to Islamic principles. Although he did not see these proposals implemented in his lifetime, they provided the blueprint for the modern Egyptian educational system that emerged in the early 20th century

Bruce Masters

Further reading: Ibrahim Abu-Lughod, *Arab Rediscovery of Europe: A Study in Cultural Encounters* (Princeton, N.J.: Princeton University Press, 1963).

takfir *Takfir* is the act of declaring that a Muslim has, by his or her actions, become an infidel or unbeliever (*kafir*). This is an extreme step because historically, anyone within the Muslim community who has professed to be a Muslim remains one. All that is required to become a Muslim is to say, with a sound mind and under no compulsion, three times, in front of witnesses, "I testify that there is no god but God and Muhammad is the Prophet of God." Since admission to the community of believers is a matter of individual conscience, there has also traditionally been a reluctance on the part of the Muslim community to formally censure individuals for their beliefs, and the community typically leaves it to God to punish anyone who has sinned. This attitude emerged as a response to the murder of Ali in 661 C.E. by a member of a Muslim splinter group, called by their opponents the Kharijiyya, or "those who break away." Having broken away from the larger Muslim community, the Kharijiyya held that they could judge who was a good Muslim and claimed the right to kill anyone they judged to be an unbeliever for having strayed from the principles of Islam as they defined them. Because mainstream Muslims feared the result of this extremist position, there were very few cases in the first centuries of Islam in which people were punished for what they wrote or said.

This reluctance to condemn a fellow Muslim was challenged by Ahmad ibn Taymiyya, who lived in Damascus in the early 14th century. He affirmed that it was the duty of pious Muslims to identify those who by their actions did not uphold Islam and to declare them infidels. Because he stated that the rulers of the MAMLUK EMPIRE represented just this sort of "infidel," ibn Taymiyya became one of the few Muslims up to that time to be imprisoned for what he wrote. After his death in prison in 1327, the Muslim scholarly community largely ignored ibn Taymiyya's radical ideas. In the 18th century, however, another radical interpreter of Islam, Muhammad IBN ABD AL-WAHHAB, revived the practice of *takfir*. He wrote that Muslims who venerated Ali, worshipped Sufi saints, or claimed to be sultan but did not rule in strict accordance with Islamic law, were all to be considered infidels by believing Muslims. According to ibn Abd al-Wahhab, it was therefore legal for true Muslims, as defined by him, to kill the unfaithful. This principle became the legal justification for the devastating 1801 attack on the Shii shrine city of KARBALA by those who accepted the teaching of ibn Abd al-Wahhab, commonly called WAHHABIS. This group also justified their later occupation of MECCA and MEDINA based on the same principle.

Bruce Masters

Further reading: Gilles Kepel, *Jihad: The Trail of Political Islam* (Cambridge: Belknap Press, 2002).

Takiyüddin (Taqi al-Din; Taqi al-Din Abu Bakr Muhammad ibn Zayn al-Din Maruf al-Dimashqi al-Hanafi; Taqi al-Din Muhammad ibn Ma'ruf al-Shami al-Asadi) (b. 1526–d. 1585) *Ottoman mathematician,* *astronomer, scholar of optics and mechanics, founding director of the Istanbul Observatory*   Takiyüddin is best known as the founder of the Istanbul Observatory and is widely acknowledged for his activities there. An accomplished astronomer and physicist, Takiyüddin developed a number of new instruments and techniques, including the automatic mechanical clock. Takiyüddin's application of decimal fractions to trigonometry and astronomy stands as another important contribution to astronomy and mathematics. Although Takiyüddin was deeply involved in the intellectual world of ISTANBUL, he spent most of his adult life living and working in EGYPT.

Born in DAMASCUS in 1526, Takiyüddin began his studies according to the conventions of the period with the basic religious sciences and Arabic, going on to advanced mathematical study with scholars in Damascus and Egypt, including most significantly his father, Maruf Efendi. Takiyüddin taught for a short while at various colleges or madrasas in Damascus before accompanying his father to the Ottoman capital, Istanbul, around 1550. Although he remained in Istanbul only a short time, the associations Takiyüddin formed during this trip, including those with a number of prominent scholars, did much to serve him in later life. Among these associates was Grand Vizier Samiz Ali Pasha, whom Takiyüddin met on a brief trip back to Istanbul in the early 1550s, when Ali Pasha allowed Takiyüddin to use his private library and clock collection. When Ali Pasha was later appointed governor of Egypt, his influence helped Takiyüddin, who held positions as a teacher and judge (KADI). It was at this point that Takiyüddin was encouraged to continue his pursuits in mathematics and astronomy by a grandson of the famous astronomer ALI KUŞÇU. Armed with various observation instruments and books written by Ali Kuşçu and other important astronomers, Takiyüddin undertook a serious pursuit of astronomy and mathematics. While still serving as a judge in Tinnin, Egypt, Takiyüddin mounted an instrument in a well that was 85 feet (25 meters) deep to make astronomical observations.

Returning to Istanbul in 1570 with the knowledge gained from his further study and observations, Takiyüddin was appointed head astronomer (*müneccimbaşı*) by Sultan SELIM II (r. 1566–74) in 1571. As head astronomer, Takiyüddin conducted his observations in a building situated on a height overlooking the Imperial Cannon Foundry (Tophane) and in the Galata Tower in the GALATA district of Istanbul. Impressed with the data Takiyüddin thus gathered, several high state officials encouraged the construction of a formal observatory. This led to an imperial edict by Sultan MURAD III (r. 1574–95) in early 1579 to build an observatory in Istanbul, which was to be located on a hill overlooking the Tophane where the French Palace is located today. Vital astronomical books and instruments were collected there. ILLUSTRATED MANUSCRIPTS of the period offer magnificent depictions of the scholars at work and of the astronomical instruments in use. In addition to the observatory building, Takiyüddin also used a well to make observations. The observatory was demolished on January 22, 1580, due in large part to Takiyüddin's incorrectly interpreting the sighting of a comet as heralding a victory for the sultan's success in a military conflict.

Takiyüddin intended to correct and augment the uncompleted but seminal astronomical text written by the great TIMURID astronomer, mathematician, and sultan Ulugh Beg (1394–1449). As was usual in the Islamic astronomical tradition, Takiyüddin used trigonometric functions such as sine, cosine, tangent, and cotangent rather than chords. Following the work done at the Samarkand observatory, Takiyüddin developed a new method to find the exact value of Sin 1°, which Persian mathematician and astronomer Jamshid al-Kashi (1380–1429) had put into the form of an equation of third degree. In addition, Takiyüddin was the first to use the method of three observation points, which he used for calculating solar parameters. Apparently the eminent Danish astronomer Tycho Brahe (1546–1601), who was a contemporary, was aware of Takiyüddin's work, in part because Takiyüddin's technique for determining the longitudes and latitudes of fixed stars provided values that were more precise than those of either Brahe or the famed European astronomer Nicolaus Copernicus (1473–1543), thus evidencing the precision of Takiyüddin's methods of observation and calculation. Takiyüddin used Venus, Aldebaran, and Spica Virginis, which are near the ecliptic (rather than the moon), as reference stars. As a result of his observations, he found the eccentricity of the sun to be 2° 0' and the annual motion of apogee 63".

Takiyüddin's second most important work on astronomy is an astronomical/mathematical table or *zij* (entitled *Jaridat al-durar wa kharidat al-fikar*). In this work, decimal fractions in trigonometric functions are used for the first time. Takiyüddin also prepared tangent and cotangent tables. Moreover, in this *zij*, as in another of his observational tables, Takiyüddin gave the parts of degree of curves and angles in decimal fractions and carried out the calculations accordingly. Excluding the table of fixed stars, all the astronomical tables in this *zij* were prepared using decimal fractions.

Takiyüddin also wrote other astronomical works of secondary importance, including one about the projection of a sphere onto a plane as well as other topics in geometry. Another of his works deals with sundials drawn on marble surfaces and their features. In addition to his 20 books on astronomy Takiyüddin wrote one book on medicine and zoology, three works on physics and mechanics, and five on mathematics. He also wrote

a monograph on the specific gravity of substances and on Archimedes' hydrostatic experiments. All of his books are written in Arabic.

In his mathematical treatises Takiyüddin treats various aspects of trigonometry, geometry, algebra, and arithmetic, and his arithmetical work, in particular, carries on the work of Jamshid al-Kashi in developing the arithmetic of decimal fractions both theoretically and practically. Takiyüddin's works on physics and mechanics also have connections with astronomy. One concerns physics and optics and treats the structure of light, its diffusion and global refraction, and the relation between light and color. A number of others investigate various aspects of the mechanical clock. In 1559, while in Nablus, he wrote the first text to appear in the Islamic world on the subject of mechanical-automatic clocks (*al-Kawakib al-durriyya fi wad al-bankamat al-dawriyya*). In the foreword to this text Takiyüddin mentions that he benefited from using Samiz Ali Pasha's private library and his collection of European mechanical clocks. In this work Takiyüddin discusses various mechanical clocks from a geometrical-mechanical perspective. Another book on mechanics, written when he was 26, focuses on the geometrical-mechanical structure of clocks previously examined by other scholars.

Takiyüddin was a successor to the great school of Samarkand established by Ulugh Beg and the Timurids and, following the lead of Ali Kuşçu, he tended toward a more purely mathematical approach in his scientific work, anticipating the discrediting of Aristotelian physics and metaphysics.

İhsan Fazlıoğlu

See also SCIENCES.

Further reading: İhsan Fazlıoğlu, "Taqī al-Dīn," in *Biographical Encyclopaedia of Astronomers,* edited by Thomas Hockey (Springer/Kluwer forthcoming); Aydın Sayılı, *The Observatory in Islam* (Ankara: Turkish Historical Society, 1960), 289–305.

Tamerlane *See* TIMUR.

Tanzimat The word *tanzimat* means "reforms," "rearrangement," and "re-organization," and in Ottoman history, the Tanzimat period refers to a time of Westernizing reforms from 1839 until 1876. Although there had been periods of REFORM under earlier sultans, major reforms were begun with the *ferman*, or imperial mandate, issued by Sultan ABDÜLMECID (r. 1839–61) in November 1839, called the Gülhane Imperial Rescript (Gülhane Hatt-ı Hümayunu), in reference to the imperial rose garden where it was proclaimed. A second reform decree, the Imperial Rescript of Reforms (Islahat Ferman), was issued in 1856 following the CRIMEAN WAR (1853–56). Many scholars divide this era into the first Tanzimat period (1839–56) and the second Tanzimat period (1856–76). Throughout the Tanzimat period there was a movement toward a European-style governing structure through the establishment of councils and ministries. New reforms were implemented in local governing structures. Several journals and NEWSPAPERS began to be published and the press emerged as a distinct power within the Ottoman political and cultural structure. Interaction with Europeans and travel to Europe, mostly for education, increased, and the state became more open to the outside world.

The Tanzimat *ferman* was proclaimed in a huge, unprecedented ceremony in the Gülhane, or rose garden, near the imperial TOPKAPI PALACE. The *ferman* was read out by MUSTAFA REŞID PASHA and witnessed by Sultan Abdülmecid, the grand vizier, the ŞEYHÜLISLAM, officials of the palace, representatives of guilds, prominent statesman and religious leaders, the Armenian and Greek patriarchs, the chief rabbi of the empire, and foreign representatives. After the declaration, the Tanzimat *ferman* was published in the official state newspaper, *Takvim-i Vekayi* (The calendar of events), and French translations were sent to foreign embassies in ISTANBUL.

The Tanzimat reforms built on earlier edicts of the sultans, such as the NIZAM-I CEDID reforms of 1792–93, which wee largely associated with the military but which also initiated administrative and fiscal reforms. The Tanzimat *ferman* included a foreword that presented the reasons for the preparation of the imperial rescript, such as the escalating decline and weakness of the Ottoman state. The main body of the *ferman* addressed basic principles and issues: the right of all subjects to life, property, and honor regardless of their religion or sect; the TAX-FARMING system (*iltizam*); military conscription; the safety and security of all subjects in the empire; and the equality of all Ottoman subjects before the law. After setting out these basic principles, the planned implementation of the reforms was explained.

The Gülhane Imperial Rescript, which was intended to reform the administrative structure of the state, focused specifically on financial reforms. The first modern budget regulations were prepared during this time, the first foreign loans were undertaken, and a liberal economic policy was pursued. The Rescript identified three specific areas of financial reform: the implementation of a just tax collection and assessment system; the plan to abolish tax farms; and the development of BUDGETS for administrative expenditures. New regulations for the tax system were presented to realize these goals. Among these, the most important was the abolition of tax collection under multiple titles. All taxes were to be combined under a single title, and the people were to be taxed accordingly. Tax farms were abolished and instead a new *muhassillik* (tax collection) system was established. However, after three years, the old systems were re-established.

REACTIONS TO THE TANZIMAT REFORMS

The declaration of the Tanzimat initially received strong support from certain domestic factions and from European states. Nonetheless, the initial positive attitude toward the Tanzimat reforms was slowly eroded as different groups tried to interpret the *ferman* based on their own interests. Many Muslims complained because of the privileges given to non-Muslims. Muslim tax farmers who had been taking advantage of the *iltizam* system, bankers, and other intermediary groups criticized the new structure that arose as the tax farms were abolished because this resulted both in direct material losses and in anticipated future losses as their means of acquiring wealth were restricted. These Muslims often expressed their concerns by referring to the SHARIA, claiming that the new regulations and rights given to Christians were inconsistent with Islamic sacred law. These disgruntled factions began to spread rumors that the new regulations were fabricated by infidels (*kafirs*) for their own benefit.

At the same time, many non-Muslims perceived the planned reforms as inadequate to meet their needs. The absence of tax exemption for religious representatives and the continuation of the JIZYA or poll-tax system were harshly criticized. Greeks, in particular, were discontented with the reforms that stripped them of their pre-Tanzimat position as the most privileged non-Muslim group in the empire and as the pre-eminent group in the Ottoman Christian community. The Tanzimat reforms that proposed to treat Greeks, Armenians, Jews, and other discrete communities within the empire as equals were disadvantageous to many.

Internationally, four European powers were keenly interested in the Tanzimat *ferman* and closely monitored the reforms. Of these, ENGLAND and FRANCE, who were active in the preparation of the Gülhane Imperial Rescript, responded to the declaration quite positively. However, the two other great states, RUSSIA and AUSTRIA, responded negatively. Russia was concerned with the rise of British influence within the Ottoman government, or Sublime Porte, and the possible effects of Britain's anti-Russian policies. Austria declared its opposition directly through Prime Minister Prince Metternich.

OBSTACLES TO REFORM

One difficulty with the Tanzimat reforms was the lack of clear means and guidelines for implementing the program. For example, there was a crucial need for a current population and property census so that fair and reasonable reforms of Ottoman assessment and tax collection and assessment could be instituted, but there were not enough qualified staff to carry out this project. Furthermore, there were serious concerns among the empire's provincial elite (AYAN) that it would not be to their advantage for the government to have an accurate picture of their assets and economic power. For these and other reasons, the proposed reforms to the ECONOMY, the central and provincial ADMINISTRATION, and the military structure were implemented only in certain Ottoman provinces. These were selected quite carefully as the Tanzimat was applied only in provinces near the center and under the strict control of the state. At first, these included the provinces of BURSA, Ankara, Aydın, IZMIR, Konya, and Sivas. Trabzon was later added to the list. Provinces in which the programs of the Tanzimat were not implemented were defined as "exceptional districts" (mustesna mahalleler).

The Tanzimat period remains one of the most contested eras in modern Ottoman history and it has had its advocates and its opponents since it was first decreed. In fact, discussions regarding the meaning and importance of the Tanzimat era continue to influence the Turkish social, intellectual, and political climate as well as political positioning, and historians continue to debate and critique the Tanzimat ferman. One of the most significant aspects of this debate is whether the decree should be understood as a constitutional text or if it more nearly resembles a charter (carta), European documents that provide the basis for establishing constitutional government through legal and written recognition by the king of the rights of his subjects. This is why the ferman is called a "social contract" by some researchers. For others, it is merely a warrant that recognizes and guarantees the rights of the sultan's subjects. The ferman is also criticized as being inadequate in the protection and declaration of what are now regarded as basic human rights. Even today, the Tanzimat reforms continue to be one of the most heated subjects of discussion for Turkish intellectuals and scholars.

Coşkun Çakır

Further reading: Roderic Davison, *Reform in the Ottoman Empire, 1856–1876* (Princeton, N.J.: Princeton University Press, 1963); Carter V. Findley, *Bureaucratic Reform in the Ottoman Empire: The Sublime Porte, 1789–1922* (Princeton, N.J.: Princeton University Press, 1980); Donald Quataert, "The Age of Reforms, 1812–1914," in *An Economic and Social History of the Ottoman Empire*, edited by Halil İnalcık and Donald Quataert (Cambridge: Cambridge University Press, 1997); Stanford Shaw, *History of the Ottoman Empire and Modern Turkey*, vol. 2, *Reform, Revolution and Republic: The Rise of Modern Turkey, 1808–1975* (Cambridge: Cambridge University Press, 1977); Moshe Ma'oz, *Ottoman Reform in Syria and Palestine, 1840–1861: The Impact of The Tanzimat on Politics and Society* (Oxford: Oxford University Press, 1968).

Tatars *See* CRIMEAN TATARS.

Tawfiq, Khedive (b. 1852–d. 1892) (r. 1879–1892) *ruler of Egypt* Khedive Tawfiq came to power as the ruler of EGYPT in the late 19th century when a combination of French and British pressure led Sultan ABDÜLHAMID II (r. 1876–1909) to depose Tawfiq's father, KHEDIVE ISMAIL, after he refused to abdicate. The fact that it was European pressure that brought his father down did not bode well for the young Tawfiq, who was not particularly suited for the responsibilities he faced. Egyptian nationalist sentiment against foreign meddling in the country was growing and it coalesced around an Egyptian army officer, AHMAD PASHA URABI. Urabi organized a military demonstration outside Tawfiq's Abdin Palace in CAIRO on September 9, 1881, and demanded the dismissal of the prime minister, the recall of the Assembly of Delegates, which had been suspended, and an increase in the size of the army. Tawfiq met all three demands, but this capitulation demonstrated his political weakness, and a series of maneuvers followed that strengthened Urabi's political position while that of Tawfiq went into decline. The British and the French intervened in this emerging power struggle on January 8, 1882, with a joint note that supported Tawfiq. This enraged the Assembly, and they named Urabi Minister of War.

The crisis reached a boiling point in an anti-European riot that broke out in ALEXANDRIA on June 11, 1882. The British bombarded Alexandria on July 11; with the situation in Egypt sliding into chaos, Tawfiq fled to the British fleet off Alexandria and declared Urabi a rebel. The British then moved on Cairo and restored Tawfiq to his throne. From that point, Tawfiq had no support within the Egyptian nationalist camp or in the Egyptian army. As such, he was largely dependent on British advice and cooperated with the new British high commissioner, Evelyn Baring, later to be named Lord CROMER. Khedive Tawfiq died in 1892.

Bruce Masters

tax farming Tax farming was a widely used method by which the Ottoman state collected revenues. Rather than collecting taxes directly, sultans farmed out the collection of taxes to eligible applicants. The most widely practiced forms of tax farming were known as *iltizam* and *malikane*, but the latter was also associated with *esham*, a mechanism of domestic borrowing based on treasury issues.

THE *ILTIZAM* SYSTEM

In the *iltizam* system the sources of state revenue were farmed out to applicants by means of a public auction. An *iltizam* might consist of different sources of revenue including various state revenue sources (*mukataas*), the poll tax (*cizye*), and extraordinary levies (*avarız*). The holders of *iltizam* were called *mültezim*. The *mültezim* who undertook the collection of taxes from a group of revenue sources would have the revenues dealt with either through his own agents or would further farm out the enterprise to a third person. In the latter case, the sub-farming would be approved and registered by the state.

There was a certain amount of flexibility in a tax-farming unit. It could always be bolstered with additional sources of revenue, or altered by the transfer of revenue sources to another unit. It was also possible to form a new farming unit by grouping together revenue sources culled from other tax farm units.

The *mültezim* had to guarantee a predetermined sum of taxes from specific lands to the Imperial Treasury in order to be allowed to collect taxes from those regions for one to three years. The process was legalized by a contract between the Ottoman state and the *mültezim*, who was given a *kanunname*, or the legal regulation that listed and specified all the sources of state revenues from which he could collect taxes. The *mültezim* could undertake the enterprise either singly or jointly. The three-year span of operating the tax farms was called *tahvil*. A tax-farmer could undertake two or three of these *tahvil*s together, which meant the extension of the span to six or nine years. He would be able to make a profit if the amount he collected surpassed the predetermined sum; otherwise, he suffered losses.

The *iltizam* system did not require a military obligation and was strictly a financial arrangement for leasing the collection of taxes. The *mültezim* legally had to bring a guarantor before he could undertake tax collections. The guarantor was expected to assume responsibility in case of financial loss or in case of the *mültezim* deserting his duty. The *mültezim* had to make a payment (*kefalet bedeli*) fixed by a judge (*kadı*) who sanctioned the process. This was initially regarded as a deposit (*peşin*), but starting in 1632, was legalized as a down payment.

The presentation of financial accounts related to the business was another obligation of the *mültezim* and failure to maintain or present proper records could cost him his position. Settlement of accounts between the state and the *mültezim* was done annually and was not subject to the duration of the *iltizam* contract. The annual payment (*kıstelyevm*) was equal to the yearly amount that the *mültezim* pledged during the auction. The *mültezim* was typically accompanied to the annual presentation of his accounts by two subsidiary officials, a clerk and an accountant.

Throughout the period of the collection of state revenue by *mültezim*s, new bidders might emerge at the auctions to challenge the current tax farmer. The incumbent could only maintain his position by offering a higher price than his rival. The replacement of an existing *mültezim* by a new one, however, did not bring about a change in the term of computation or in the starting date of the collection period (*tahvil*). The *iltizam* system was often abused, with the positions becoming hereditary and *mültezim*s eventually developed into a separate class between the government and the peasants.

Another practice closely associated with *iltizam* was that of the *emanet* system (*emanet ber-vech-i iltizam*), which entailed the transfer of revenue administration to tax farmers with the status of *emins* (state agents) in return for a profit limit of 10 percent of the yearly total. Those who were assigned as *emins* were not liable for the accumulation of a specified yearly total.

THE *MALIKANE* SYSTEM

To eliminate the insecurity of the *iltizam*s, which changed hands too frequently, and to raise more cash for a state in financial crisis due to the protracted wars of the late 17th century, the Ottoman government introduced a new tax farming system in 1695 called *malikane*. The system of *malikane* initiated the practice of life-long tax farms. The *malikane* holders had to settle their accounts at the end of the year; otherwise the contract would be cancelled and the tax collector arrested. Holders of big estates (*has*) also could retain a *malikane* provided that they paid the requisite sum of the down payment (*muaccele*), which was fixed in auction, a transfer fee that did not generate income for the treasury. The holder of the *malikane* would either exploit the various state revenue sources himself or farm these out to a third person, which was also a legal practice. The *malikane* holders could reassign the revenue sources under their disposal to someone else as well. The *malikane* system remained in force through the TANZIMAT reform era (1839–76).

THE *ESHAM* SYSTEM

Between 1775 and 1870, as Ottoman state finances came under increasing pressure, the Sublime Porte developed a new type of tax farming, called *esham*, that was, in fact, a form of long-term domestic borrowing similar to a bond issue. In order to fill the imperial coffers, the sultan borrowed money from his subjects by estimating the income of a particular revenue source, dividing this into a large number of shares, called *faiz*, and selling these shares to the people. The sum paid for the *faiz* was generally between five and seven times greater than its annual value, but the *faiz* would continue to generate an annual income (similar to an annuity) for the holder's lifetime. The rises and falls in the annual profit rate of the *mukataa*, or revenue source, did not affect the annual sums paid by the state to the holders of *faiz*. The *esham* practice resembled the *malikane* system in many ways and was supposed to have been a continuation of it, although it aimed to eliminate the defects of the *iltizam* and *mukataa* systems.

Baki Çakır

See also AGRICULTURE; BANKS AND BANKING; ECONOMY; *JIZYA*; MONEY AND MONETARY SYSTEMS.

Further reading: Halil İnalcık, *An Economic and Social History of the Ottoman Empire* (Cambridge: Cambridge University Press, 1994); Sevket Pamuk, "The Evolution of Institutions of State Finance in the Ottoman Empire, 1500–1800" (paper presented at 14th International Economic History Congress, Helsinki, Finland, August 21–25, 2006).

technology *See* SCIENCE.

telegraph The excitement over the electric telegraph in Europe and America in the 1830s did not take long to reach the Ottoman Empire, which Western inventors, entrepreneurs, and travelers viewed as an exotic locale, favorable for introducing such a "magical" apparatus. Shortly after Samuel F. B. Morse exhibited a working model of his electric telegraph in Paris at the French Academy of Sciences in 1838, Mellen Chamberlain, a Vermont businessman who was present, made an agreement with Morse to sell the telegraph to a number of governments, including that of the Ottoman Empire. Chamberlain arrived in ISTANBUL in May 1839, but his set of Morse instruments was still crude and failed to produce good results; Chamberlain died before he was able to demonstrate the device to the sultan. In 1847 another American, John Lawrence Smith, an agricultural chemist and mineralogist in Ottoman employ, demonstrated the electric telegraph in an elaborate presentation to the young Sultan ABDÜLMECID (r. 1839–61) and his officials. The sultan, impressed, bestowed on Morse the prestigious Nishan-ı Iftihar, or Order of Glory of the empire, which was Morse's first official honor.

BUILDING THE OTTOMAN TELEGRAPH NETWORK

Although Smith's demonstration raised temporary enthusiasm for the telegraph, the first Ottoman telegraph line was not built until the CRIMEAN WAR (1853–56). Ottoman allies ENGLAND and FRANCE then cooperated in connecting Bucharest (the capital of present-day Romania), the eastern terminus of European telegraphs, with Varna on the BLACK SEA, and thence to the Crimea and to ISTANBUL by undersea cable, putting the Ottoman Empire in electric communication with Europe. At the beginning of the war, an Ottoman commission of high-ranking officers, which later became the Ottoman Tele-

graph Department, had been set up. Its first project was the construction of a telegraph line between EDIRNE and Istanbul. Built by French engineers, it was completed in time to relay the news of the end of the war.

After the war, the Ottoman desire to expand its telegraph network eastward coincided with the British push for a telegraph link with India via the Persian Gulf through Ottoman territories. Britain would have preferred an all-undersea cable, but the technology available for submarine telegraphy was not yet suitable for long distances. The British government offered its cooperation and allowed more than a dozen of its telegraph engineers to enter Ottoman service. Work on the line between Istanbul and the Persian Gulf began in August 1858, but progress on the line east of Diyarbakır was particularly slow, and a boundary dispute with Persia impeded its completion. Finally, in January 1865, the Ottoman overland telegraph reached Fao on the Persian Gulf, where it met the Indo-European submarine cable from Karachi, allowing telegraphic communication between Europe and India for the first time. While serving the Ottoman government, the line also carried most of the British electric communications with India until the 1870s when the more reliable undersea lines were finally established. At Fao, Britain maintained a large office, while the Ottoman government agreed to employ operators with a knowledge of English at the other main stations.

By the time the line to Fao was completed, major Ottoman cities and towns along the route were linked. The Ottoman telegraphic network thereafter continued to expand rapidly, far ahead of conventional roads or RAILROADS. By the time of the ENTHRONEMENT AND ACCESSION of ABDÜLHAMID II (r. 1876–1909) in 1876, the empire boasted one of the largest telegraph networks in the world. Abdülhamid II's reign saw it expand to the remote corners of the empire and become an efficient tool in running the empire.

The Ottoman government employed British and French experts to help build, operate and organize the system. Initially, French, the official foreign language, was used. As early as 1856, Ottoman operators at EDIRNE developed a Turkish version (then written in Arabic script) of Morse code, which became the basis of the official Turkish code. It took several years before this code became fully operational and the service in Turkish was established. Later, the Ottoman telegraph service could handle more than a dozen languages, led by French and English. As elsewhere, the telegraph had a profound impact on the way language was used and written, and perhaps gave a considerable momentum to the use of "simple" Turkish at the expense of the sophisticated Ottoman-Turkish.

All equipment, other than poles, was initially imported from Britain and France. In a matter of a decade, however, the Ottomans were able to produce locally most of its telegraph materials, including telegraph instruments. Its dependency on foreign experts also fell sharply. As early as 1861, an Ottoman telegraphic school was established, with a second following six years later. Prestigious colleges began to offer courses in telegraphy. The telegraph thus represents one of the few 19th-century technological innovations in which the Ottomans quickly achieved self-sufficiency.

SOCIAL AND POLITICAL BENEFITS

As in Europe and America, the telegraph became a huge apparatus for social and cultural experimentation. It facilitated the speedy and expansive circulation of new ideas and news, foreign and local, far and wide. It stimulated the study of foreign languages, as well as sciences related to electricity and magnetism. Although it was initially perceived as a military and state apparatus, it soon came to be widely used by the public and businesses. Telegraph offices became material symbols of modernity, standing as monuments of a new technological age. The incorporation of European architectural style in their design enhanced the up-to-date tone they created. The technology also offered new employment opportunities for the empire's many minorities, who came to be well represented in the telegraph service, from top officials down to operators. It provided a space where the empire's diverse ethnic and religious communities, which had previously kept themselves largely aloof, could interact with the general community. In 1871, the telegraph office merged with the postal service.

The telegraph separated communication from transportation and freed it from the restrictions of time, distance, and geography. This made it an ideal apparatus of control for the still huge Ottoman Empire, which spanned three continents, allowing it to consolidate its territorial boundaries as well as its political will at a time of frequent revolts and independence movements. Many Ottomans expected the telegraph to help keep the empire united. This expectation was to a great extent fulfilled. As the telegraph brought the distant regions within quick reach of the central government, it helped centralize political power. As early as 1874, an American missionary in Beirut wrote that the telegraph system enabled the Ottoman government "to move the whole empire like a machine." But it was not until the 32-year reign of Abdülhamid II that it attained its full power. The sultan had a telegraph office established at his Yıldız Palace, and his network of spies and secret agents relied on the device, sending their reports directly to this office. The sultan was able to have pashas, governors, and generals dismissed, replaced, or arrested in a matter of minutes, before they could organize any opposition. Private citizens in the remote hinterland also used the system widely to petition, protest, report disasters, and complain about officials. They often tried to telegram their political demands directly to the sultan.

The story of the electric telegraph in the Ottoman Empire concludes with a paradox. Although the telegraph played a crucial role in extending the authority of the sultan and his central rule, it also proved an effective tool for his opponents in undermining the sultanate and ultimately bringing it down. The formation of the YOUNG TURK movement and its revolution in 1908, which ended the long rule of Abdülhamid II and reduced him to a figurehead, owe much to the telegraph. A leading figure in the movement, Talat Pasha (1874–1921), who became minister of the interior and grand vizier, began his career as a telegraph clerk. The telegraph enabled him and other Young Turks to organize and spread the movement in spite of the sultan's spies and later to suppress any movement of the empire's minorities in Anatolia (Greeks, Armenians, Kurds) for social reforms and autonomy. The telegraph was also essential to the resistance movement after the Ottoman defeat in WORLD WAR I and contributed significantly to the success of KEMAL ATATÜRK, the founding father and first president of the Republic of Turkey.

Yakup Bektaş

Further reading: Yakup Bektaş, "The Sultan's Messenger: Cultural Constructions of Ottoman Telegraphy 1847–1880." *Technology and Culture* 41 (October 2000): 669–696; Yakup Bektaş, "Displaying the American Genius: The Electromagnetic Telegraph in the Wider World." *British Journal for the History of Science* 34 (2001): 199–232; Roderick H. Davison, *Essays in Ottoman and Turkish History, 1774–1923* (Austin, Tex.: University of Texas Press, 1990).

temettuat (income surveys)   The word *temettuat* is the plural form of *temettu*, which means "profit" or "income." However, *temettuat* is generally used to refer specifically to Ottoman income surveys (*temettuat tahrirleri*). These *temettuat* surveys were conducted immediately after the proclamation by Sultan ABDÜLMECID (r. 1839–61) of the TANZIMAT reform edict in 1839 They were planned, in large part, to gather economic and social data required for the implementation of reforms. The *temettuat* surveys had two main goals: to determine the economic conditions of the people in order to establish a fair tax system, and to increase state revenues. The information gathered in these surveys resulted in the compilation of detailed registers containing rich and useful data regarding real estate, land, animals, and income; the registers offer a wealth of information regarding Ottoman economic and social history.

There are 17,747 *temettuat* registers at the PRIME MINISTRY'S OTTOMAN ARCHIVES in ISTANBUL. These registers contain information about 543 *kaza* (districts or townships) of 15 provinces. In total, it is estimated that the registers include information about 1.1 million households. There are nine volumes of catalogues covering the registers. The first limited survey was conducted in 1840. A second was conducted in 1845 and included all the villages or towns where the government intended to implement reforms immediately. The surveys registered a variety of information, including the name of the head of the household, his title, lands, animals, other revenues, professions, the value of his belongings, his household income, taxes that had been paid, and taxes that would be paid. These data were highly detailed and included the types of land (such as field, vineyard, yard, mill, meadow) and animals (such as buffalo, ox, cow, calf, horse, mule, camel, donkey, sheep, goat, hen, beehives).

These *temettuat* registers contain information about the demographic, economic, fiscal, agricultural, and social structure of the area surveyed and provide valuable demographic information, including data regarding total population, household structures, and nomadic tribes (*göçebes*). In terms of economics, these records enable scholars to estimate sources of wealth and to identify trades and crafts practiced in particular areas. In terms of agriculture, they include important information about cultivated lands, crop distribution, and cultivation methods. The registers have even been used to aid in the practice of stock-breeding for they identify the variety and number of animals. In terms of fiscal policy, the information given in the registers is mainly related to taxes, especially agricultural taxes, including data about the regulation of special taxes (*vergiyi mahsusa*), tithe or produce tax (*aşar*), and the head tax (*JIZYA*) collected from non-Muslims.

Coşkun Çakır

Further reading: Hayashi Kayoko and Mahir Aydın, eds., *The Ottoman State and Societies in Change: A Study of the Nineteenth Century Temettuat Registers* (London: Kegan Paul, 2004); Halil İnalcık and Şevket Pamuk, eds., *Osmanlı devleti'nde bilgi ve istatistik/Data and Statistics in the Ottoman Empire* (Ankara: State Institute of Statistics, 2000).

Tepedelenli Ali Pasha   *See* ALI PASHA OF JANINA.

Tersane-i Amire   The Tersane-i Amire, or Tersane, was the Ottoman imperial naval arsenal, the administrative base and construction center for the Ottoman NAVY in Istanbul's Golden Horn (Haliç). The word *tersane* originally comes from the Arabic word *dar as-sinâa* (arsenal) and possibly comes into Turkish by way of the Italian *darsena*, a word found in various forms in contemporary European languages. The Ottoman naval arsenals were established on the foundation of existing naval arsenals

seized primarily from the Byzantines and Turkomans in the mid-15th century. This includes arsenals such as those in Nicomedia (Izmit), Gemlik, Edincik, Gallipoli (on the west shore of the Dardanelles), and the harbor of Kadırga in ISTANBUL, as well as the SELJUK arsenals in Sinop (on the BLACK SEA) and Alanya (on the Mediterranean in southern Anatolia).

The term *tershane,* or *dershane,* was used to designate ship construction yards as early as 1514, when it appears in the *Kitab-ı Bahriye* (Book of navigation) by renowned cartographer Piri Reis (d. 1553). Soon after, the term began to be used to refer to the naval construction center on the north shore of the Golden Horn in Istanbul, which finally attained the official name Tersane-i Amire (Imperial Arsenal) during the time of famed Ottoman navy commander Hayreddin Barbarossa (1534–46) (*see* BARBAROSSA BROTHERS). Although the Tersane remained the center of ship construction and naval administration throughout the Ottoman period, the arsenal served many other functions as well; it included all the social facilities required to accommodate its massive workforce, and it also became home to several important Ottoman educational institutions.

THE IMPERIAL ARSENAL OF ISTANBUL (TERSANE-I AMIRE)

The principal arsenal of the empire, in the Golden Horn, was founded by MEHMED II (r. 1444–46, 1451–81) at the time of the 1453 CONQUEST OF CONSTANTINOPLE and supplemented in the time of Sultan BAYEZID II (r. 1481–1512). During the reign of Sultan SELIM I (r. 1512–20) significant extensions were undertaken by Captain Cafer Agha (1516–20), after which the arsenal acquired its current size, stretching from the district of GALATA to the Kağıthane stream on the shore of the Golden Horn. The reorganization encouraged the government to shift shipbuilding activities from Gallipoli to Istanbul. In the middle of the 16th century, the number of docks within the arsenal had risen to 140, and on the land side a wall had been erected to encircle the arsenal and to conceal the resources and activities of the arsenal from outside observers. In addition, a number of subsidiary shipbuilding facilities—probably as many as 90—bound to the Tersane were located at strategic spots throughout the empire, in Suez and BASRA, on rivers such as the DANUBE and the EUPHRATES, and along the Mediterranean and Black Sea coasts. In fact, among its counterparts in the Mediterranean world in the 16th century, the Tersane was matched only by the Venetian arsenal.

Within the confines of the Tersane were located many industrial structures such as shipyards, drydocks, storehouses, a rope spinning factory, iron and anchor foundries, and social facilities such as a mosque, fountain, hospital, and prison. In 1800 the arsenal heralded the opening of its great dock to facilitate repair work

The shipyard of Alanya was built by the Seljuks in the 1220s and inherited by the Ottomans. Shipyards of this kind once dotted the shores of the eastern Mediterranean. *(Photo by Gábor Ágoston)*

on galleons. A naval engineering college (1775) and a medical school (1806), two institutions of great significance for both military and civil educational purposes, were also established within the walls of the arsenal. The Aynalıkavak pavilion in the Tersane, in front of which ships were constructed, and the Arsenal Garden served as resting residences for the sultan.

The Tersane, which remained the main naval base of the empire throughout its history, also helped to lead the Ottoman Empire in industrial change; as the center of an industrial district, it was at the forefront of industrial modernization, especially during the 19th century.

From the very beginning the Tersane served as a construction site for ships, both with oars and sails; as a supply center for naval equipment, and as a repair shop for ships. In time the arsenal came to expand over the entire coastline of the Golden Horn. While it is difficult to imagine the immensity of the work undertaken there, it should be noted that during the 17th century 317 new ships were built there and 808 ships were repaired.

STAFF OF THE IMPERIAL ARSENAL

The personnel at the Tersane, under the leadership of the grand admiral, was divided into two groups: the arsenal dignitaries and the arsenal corps. Arsenal dig-

nitaries were the high officials who held administrative posts within the shipyard and included the *tersane kethüdası* (chamberlain), the *tersane ağası* (majordomo), the *tersane emini* (paymaster general), the *tersane reisi* (warden), the *liman reisi* (harbormaster), and the *çavuş* (herald); the last three worked under the command of the *tersane emini*. During the age of sailing ships, the navy added three critical positions: a galleon *nazırı* (superintendent), a galleon *defterdarı* (treasurer), and a galleon *katibi* (scribe).

The arsenal corps consisted of various shipyard workers such as captains, *azabs* (marines), shipwrights, caulkers, oarmakers, ironsmiths, repairmen, spoolers, oakum workers, bomb makers, quarantine guardians, *gümis* (overseers), and guards. In the 1570s, the membership of the arsenal corps reached 2,650, whereas toward the end of the 17th century this figure fell to nearly 800, a reduction most probably linked with a change in the administrative structure of the Tersane.

The *tersane emini* was the state official who was responsible for the procurement of all necessary materials for shipbuilding. The Tersane produced or managed the transportation of supplies such as timber, masts, iron, nails, lead, tar, pitch, cod oil, tallow, wax, dyestuff, linen, oakum, oars, anchors, compasses, sailcloth, tents, broadcloth, and spools. During the period when the imperial navy mainly consisted of oared vessels, the *emin* was also obliged to provide the arsenal with sufficient numbers of oarsmen and hawsermen, a task of great importance. He also needed to ensure the delivery of oarsmen who had been conscripted from numerous designated districts, and was responsible for the overall supply of the arsenal with manpower for its vessels. Staff of the arsenal were also required to provide for the food and clothing requirements of crews and soldiers.

SHIPBUILDING AND SHIP TYPES

Ottoman shipbuilding in the Tersane may be understood as having passed through three phases. From the mid-15th to the mid-17th century, efforts focused on the construction of oared vessels; until the middle of the 19th century, the arsenal was devoted to the construction of sailing ships; and from the mid-19th century until the collapse of the empire, work was centered on the building of steam vessels.

There were numerous types of Ottoman oared vessels. Among the most significant were a variety of galleys including the *kadırga* (25 oar seats), *mavna* (26 oar seats), *baştarda* (26–36 oar seats), *kalyata* (19–26 oar seats), *pergendes* (18–19 oar seats), and *firkates* (10–17 oar seats). Other Ottoman oared vessels included the *karamürsel*, *şayka*, *üstü açık*, *çekeleve*, *kayık*, *kancabaş*, and similar types, which were named according to the size of the vessel and the number of oar seats. Ottoman shipbuilding was largely modeled on the successful engineering demonstrated by the Venetians, but Hayreddin Barbarossa nevertheless initiated certain novelties that mark the Turkish galley. Galleys continued to be in mainstream use and constituted the strike force among warships until the end of the 17th century, for galleys had an exceptional maneuverability and could easily enter narrow bays and harbors. Since the Mediterranean seas are typically calm and windless in summer, which is the naval campaign season, effective use of galleys was often a decisive factor in naval superiority.

While not so diverse in type as oared vessels, there was also a significant variety in the Ottoman inventory of sailing ships, which included the *kalyon* (galleon), *burtun*, *barça*, *ağribar*, *firkateyn* (frigate), *kapak*s, and *şalope*, among others. During the CRETAN WAR (1645–69) against the Venetian Republic, the Ottoman navy suffered from its lack of galleons, giving rise to a new era in Ottoman maritime history in which the Ottoman navy reformed its shipbuilding technology and introduced the construction of galleons. From this point forward, galleon construction prevailed, and by the end of the 17th century the construction of galleys had become extremely limited while the Tersane concentrated mainly on the production of galleon-type ships, including the three-deck galleon of the 18th century, used by all contemporary sea powers. As a result of the improvement in galleon construction, the Ottoman navy was able to maintain supremacy over the eastern Mediterranean until the disastrous defeat at Çeşme in Izmir in 1770. This defeat accelerated the reform attempts of Grand Admiral Küçük Hüseyin Pasha, who introduced new galleon construction techniques with the help of French naval engineer Jacque Balthasard Le Brun and his two assistants, Jean Baptiste Benoit and Toussauit Petit. They built a great number of galleons and frigates both in the Tersane and in provincial shipyards.

In the era in which the Ottoman fleet consisted of oared vessels and sailing ships, the numbers of craft in the fleet at any given time fluctuated greatly. For instance, during the great naval wars of the 16th and 17th centuries, Ottoman shipbuilding activities increased remarkably: approximately 300 Ottoman ships operated in the campaign of RHODES (1522), 120 ships in the Battle of Preveza (1538), 400 ships in the campaign of CYPRUS (1571), and 400 ships in the campaign of CRETE.

In peacetime, on the other hand, shipbuilding activities in the Tersane remained at a relatively limited scale. The office of Grand Admiral Kemankeş Kara Mustafa Pasha (1635–1638) ordinarily required the Tersane to maintain 40 galleys each year, an obligation extended in the Naval Regulation of 1701 to cover the number of galleons. During times of war, however, the arsenal was capable of incredible output. In the winter succeeding the devastating defeat at LEPANTO (1571), for instance, Ottoman shipyards produced more than 200 galleys to make up their severe losses.

İdris Bostan

Further reading: Henry Kahane, Renée Kahane, and Andreas Tietze, *The Lingua Franca in the Levant: Turkish Nautical Terms of Italian and Greek Origin* (Urbana: University of Illinois Press, 1958); İdris Bostan, *Osmanlı Bahriye Teşkilâtı: XVII. Tersane-i Amire* (Ankara: Tűrk Tarih Kurumu Basımevi, 1992); İdris Bostan, *Kürekli ve Yelkenli Osmanlı Gemileri* (Istanbul: Bilge, 2005); C. Imber, "The Navy of Süleyman the Magnificent." *Archivum Ottomanicum* VI (1980), 211–282; E. Zachariadou, ed., *The Kapudan Pasha, His Office and His Domain* (Rethymnon: Crete University Press, 2002).

Thessaloniki *See* SALONIKA.

Thousand and One Nights *See* LITERATURE, FOLK.

timar *See* AGRICULTURE; ECONOMY.

Timur (Amir Timur, Aqsaq Timur, Taimur, Tamburlaine, Tamerlane, Temür, Temur-e Lang, Timur bin Taraghay Barlas, Timur Lang; Timur Leng, Timur Lenk, Timur the Lame, Timur-i Leng) (b. 1336?–d. 1405) *founder of the Timurid dynasty* Renowned as a cruel but masterful military leader, Timur was the founder of the Timurid dynasty (*see* TIMURIDS), one of the great civilizations of Central Asia. Better known in the West as Timur the Lame, Tamerlane, or Tamburlaine, Timur's name combines elements of strength and weakness: Timur, from *temür*, a Turkic word meaning "iron," and Lang (or other variations), meaning "lame." Timur was an extraordinarily successful warrior, strategist, and political leader. Despite the destruction he caused throughout Asia and the Middle East, he valued scholarship and culture, and did perhaps as much to preserve and disseminate these as he did to destroy them. Timur's reputed lameness was authoritatively confirmed in 1941 by a Russian medical team that examined his skeleton and reported that it showed signs of tuberculosis in the bone. According to legend, however, Timur's disability arose from numerous wounds to his right hand and leg in a succession of battles.

Timur was born on April 8, 1336, in the Kish region (in Transoxania) of the empire, or *ulus* (nation), of Chaghatay. Ulus Chaghatay was comprised of two parts: Moghulistan in the north, occupied by Turkic and Mongol nomadic tribes around Lake Balkhash (in present-day Kazakhstan); and Transoxania in the south, between the Syr Darya and Amu Darya rivers, settled by Turkic-speaking, Persian-speaking (Tadjik), and Afghan-speaking communities living in richly cultured oasis towns (Samarkand, Bukhara, Khiva, and Kabul). During the first half of the 14th century, the descendents of the Chaghatayid khans lost control of the southern territories, where power was in the hands of local emirs, and it was from among these leaders that Timur emerged.

Timur's father, Taraghai, was a member of the Barlas or Barulas tribe, one of the more powerful ruling tribes, which was of Mongol origin but had been Turkicized by the time of Timur. The tribe was headed by Timur's uncle, Hajji Barlas. In the early 1360s, Tughluk Temür, khan of Moghulistan (r. 1360–64), made an attempt to regain power over the southern territories. This attack made it possible for Timur to assume leadership of the Barlas tribe, succeeding his uncle, who had fled. From then on, Timur gradually expanded his power with the support of his immediate relatives and his military escort (*nöker*). Timur also forged an alliance with Emir Hüseyin (Amir Husayn), a warlord from Transoxania. At first, Timur and Hüseyin extended their authority over the emirs in Transoxania and then, following the death of Tughluk Temür, over some of the tribal aristocracy in Moghulistan. The two allies, however, soon became ene-

mies. Timur had Hüseyin killed and enjoyed unlimited power in Ulus Chaghatay after 1370. As Timur was not of Genghisid lineage, he could not assume the title of khan. However, because of his Genghisid wife, he was able to take the title of *güregen*, meaning "royal son-in-law." As a ruler, Timur set up his headquarters in Samarkand and variously used the titles emir and sultan, ruling through the Genghisid puppet khan Soyurgatmish (r. 1370–1388) and his son Mahmud (r. 1388–1402).

Timur conducted a successful foreign policy, legitimizing his conquests by claiming to restore the *pax mongolica* (Mongol Peace) originally established by Genghis Khan. In the name of this peace, Timur led a military campaign in the 1380s against the small Persian royal families who had replaced the Mongol Ilkhanid dynasty. However, he came into conflict over Khorazm, once part of Ulus Chaghatay, with his neighbors to the north, the Blue Horde tribal confederation (which was the eastern constituent part of the realm of Jochi, first son of Ghenghis Khan). In an effort to weaken them, Timur supported certain pretenders, such as Toqtamish (Tokhtamysh), who became the khan of the Blue Horde with Timur's assistance. After 1380, Toqtamish extended his power west of the Ural River over the White Horde (or Golden Horde), which occupied the territories up to the Crimean peninsula, and reimposed the payment of tribute on RUSSIA and Lithuania. After this, Toqtamish came into conflict with his former patron regarding control over Derbent (in Dagestan on the Caspian Sea) and Tabriz (in IRAN), the two major hubs along the north-to-south TRADE route through the CAUCASUS. Timur defeated Toqtamish in three battles: by the River Terek (1385–86), by the River Kondurcha on the left bank of the Volga (1391), and again by the River Terek in 1395. Following this military campaign, Timur destroyed all the economically significant towns in Toqtamish's empire from the Crimean to Astrakhan, creating a power vacuum that would later be filled by the Russian state that evolved out of the Principality of Muscovy.

While waging war against Toqtamish, Timur also fought both the Muzaffarid and the Jalayirid rulers in western Persia. To escape Timur, Ahmed Jalayir went first to BAGHDAD and then to his ally, Sultan Barquq (r. 1382–89; 1390–99) of the Egyptian MAMLUK EMPIRE. In October 1393 Baghdad opened its gates to Timur's army. In 1398 Timur departed eastward against India, presenting himself as the defender of Islam against the Muslim sultanate of Delhi, which was tolerant of the Hindu faith.

Timur launched a new military campaign in 1399 in order to secure the western part of his empire against the danger posed by the newly emerging Ottoman dynasty. First, however, he attacked SYRIA again. He had Baghdad, DAMASCUS, and ALEPPO destroyed, and then turned against the Ottoman Sultan BAYEZID I (r. 1389–1402), winning a decisive victory at the BATTLE OF ANKARA (July 28, 1402), in which Bayezid was captured. Timur offered Bayezid the option of surrender, but the sultan refused. Timur divided the territory up among Bayezid's three sons, Isa, Musa, and Mehmed, who were willing to accept his supremacy. The Ottoman territories in the Balkans were given to the fourth son, Süleyman. The humiliated Sultan Bayezid died a year later, still in captivity. Timur's victory near Ankara caused a great stir in Europe. The Spanish king, Henry III of Castile, sent his ambassador Ruy de Clavijo to offer Timur an alliance against the Ottomans.

During the final years of his life, Timur was preparing to conquer China, but on February 18, 1405, he died at his camp in Otrar in present-day Kazakhstan. As two of his four sons had already died, Timur had appointed his grandson, Pir Muhammad, son of Jahangir, as his heir. However, the emirs of his army instead recognized his youngest son, Shah Rukh, as ruler. Shah Rukh (r. 1405–47) and his descendants no longer needed of the Genghisid puppet khans. Their father had successfully built an empire that legitimized their dynastic rule.

Timur's character integrated seemingly contradictory elements. He was both a cruel conqueror and an art-loving ruler. He considered himself a faithful Muslim, but razed a number of cultural centers of the Muslim world. From the booty he collected in his campaigns, Timur created a flourishing cultural and scholarly life in Central Asia. Through the skills of craftsmen captured from all over the world, monumental masterpieces of architecture were erected in and around the Timurid capital of Samarkand; the scholars whose lives Timur had spared in his campaigns became his servants and sources of Persian and Arabic learning for the Turkic population of Central Asia.

Mária Ivanics

Further reading: Gonzáles de Clavijo, Ruy. *Clavijo: Embassy to Tamerlane, 1403-1406,* transl. Guy Le Strange (London: G. Routledge, 1928); Beatrice Forbes Manz, *The Rise and Rule of Tamerlane* (Cambridge: Cambridge University Press, 1989).

Timurids The Timurids were a dynasty that ruled Central Asia, north Afghanistan, and Persia between 1370 and 1507, founded by TIMUR (r. 1370–1405), more commonly known in the West as Tamerlane. In his many wars, Timur is reputed to have terrorized and massacred Muslims and Christians alike, leaving in his wake a trail of devastation and disaster, but he is credited with having built up a huge empire with Samarkand (in eastern Uzbekistan) as its capital. Among his numerous military triumphs Timur conquered IRAN and the bordering area of Azerbaijan (then inhabited by Turkic tribes), India, SYRIA, east Anatolia, and Khorazm (in present-day Uzbekistan). In its entirety, this region encompassed the most important commercial routes between Central Asia and Astrakhan (on the Volga River) and the fertile Fergana Valley of western Central Asia. Timur established power in these conquered territories based on Genghisid (Mongol) traditions, with the exception of Persia, where he employed a form of Muslim administration. Once it had been centralized, the empire developed local administrative centers with Timurid rulers who kept a watchful eye on the indigenous populations.

While he was still alive, Timur divided his empire among his four sons, Umar Shaykh, Jahangir, Miranshah, and Shah Rukh, and named Jahangir's son Pir Muhammad as his successor. Nevertheless his commanders or emirs did not accept Timur's appointed successor, instead supporting his son Shah Rukh (r. 1405–47), who was then the governor of Khorasan. Shah Rukh reigned in Transoxania, Khorasan, and Persia, and made the city of Herat, in northwestern Afghanistan, his capital. He managed to reassert control over certain far provinces that had successfully rebelled against Timurid rule—Khorazm, eastern Anatolia, and Azerbaijan—but he could not keep the young empire completely united within the borders formed by his father. In particular, the Timurid supremacy over the Ottomans and the Delhi sultanate was purely nominal. While Shah Rukh continued to depend on Genghisid traditions in his army, Timurid imperial power came increasingly to rely on the importance of Muslim institutions, especially SHARIA, or Islamic sacred law. With this shift, Transoxania gradually ceased to be the center of the Timurid empire and has never since regained the importance it had in Timur's time.

One of the foremost figures of the Timurid Empire was Shah Rukh's son. Commonly known as Ulugh Beg (r. 1447–49), a designation that may be translated as "Great Ruler," this talented leader was sent by his father to Samarkand in 1409, at the age of 16, to guard against the ever-growing threat of Abul-Khayr (r. 1428–68), khan of the nomad Uzbeks. By 1411, Ulugh Beg's power had grown substantially, but despite his political and military responsibilities, he was a devoted scholar and, in particular, a gifted astronomer who made seminal contributions to this study. Ulugh Beg established Samarkand as a flourishing center of learning and culture. He was enthroned in 1447 but Shah Rukh had died without formally nominating a successor and several Timurid leaders became victims during the uprisings that broke out after his death, among them Ulugh Beg, who was killed by his own son in 1449.

Taking advantage of the discord, Jihan Shah (r. 1438–67), head of the Karakoyunlu Turkoman tribal confederation and a former Azerbaijan governor, seized Mesopotamia and the western Persian territories. At the same time, in the east, Abul-Khayr Khan again rose to the fore, interfering in the escalating conflicts among Timur's descendants. Abu Said (r. 1451–69), the grandson of Timur's son Miranshah, succeeded in driving his rival cousins, the descendents of Ulugh Beg, from Samarkand, and in occupying Herat, the capital. Abu Said also tried to retake Azerbaijan, but lost his life in the campaign. His sons managed to keep Transoxania and Fergana, but Herat fell into the hands of another Timurid, Husayn Bayqara (r. 1470–1506), the great-grandson of Umar Shaykh. With the help of Uzbek subsidiary forces, Husayn occupied huge territories, extending his power from Khorazm through Khorasan to Afghanistan.

Weakened in large part by this internecine fighting, the Timurid dynasty entered into a period of decline, and by the beginning of the 16th century two rising powers came to share the former Timurid territories. Azerbaijan and Persia fell into the hands of the Safavids, and Transoxania and Khorasan were conquered by an Uzbek, Muhammad Shaybani Khan. When in 1510 the Safavid shah ISMAIL I (r. 1501–24) defeated and killed Muhammad Shaybani, the last significant Timurid ruler, Zahir al-Din Babur (r.1526–30) briefly recovered Transoxania but found that he could not keep it. Settling in Kabul, Zahir turned his attention to the east and in 1526 conquered India, thus founding the Mughal dynasty that ruled India for the next 300 years.

The Timurid period is acknowledged as having brought about a golden age of science and culture in the region. Splendid palaces, mosques, madrasas, and gardens were built in the capitals Samarkand and Herat. Art patronage was common, and Persian literature, historiography, and ILLUSTRATED MANUSCRIPTS AND MINIATURE PAINTING flourished in the later Timurid courts. Timurid rulers not only promoted but were also themselves noted scientists and artists. While Ulugh Beg was an outstanding astronomer (his work was published in Latin in London in 1652), his brother Baysonghor demonstrated an equal interest in literature and is credited with having published *Shah-nama* (Book of kings), the renowned epic poem of Firdawsi, lauded as the pearl of Persian literature. Husayn Bayqara wrote poetry. Also working in Husayn's court in Herat was Mir Ali Shir Navai, known as the prince of poets of Chaghatay (a language also known as Turki, the middle Asian Turkic literary language). Zahir al-Din Babur was another Chaghatay poet; he also wrote memoirs, the *Babur-name*, which have become the most valued historical source of this age.

Mária Ivanics

Further reading: Wilhelm Barthold, *Four Studies on the History of Central Asia*, trans. V. Minorsky and T. Minorsky (Leiden: Brill, 1956–62); David Morgan, *Medieval Persia, 1040–1797* (London: Longman, 1988); David Morgan, *The Mongols* (Oxford: Blackwell, 1986); Wheeler M. Thackston, *The Baburnama: Memoirs of Babur, Prince and Emperor* (Washington, D.C.: The Smithsonian Institution, 1996). J. E. Woods, *The Timurid Dynasty. Papers on Central Asia no. 14.* (Bloomington: Indiana University, 1990).

tobacco The smoking of tobacco was widespread among Ottoman consumers after 1600 although its early use in the empire was surrounded by controversy. By 1914 tobacco was one of the Ottoman Empire's most important exports, and to the world's smokers, the phrase "Turkish tobacco" had become synonymous with a high-quality product. After the Ottoman Empire declared bankruptcy in 1875, the value of tobacco was such that the empire's European creditors were granted a monopoly over its sale both within the empire and as an export. This shift transformed tobacco into a highly politicized commodity and it became a symbol for western European influence in the empire's internal affairs and a source of significant anger for the Ottoman public.

Tobacco most probably entered the Ottoman Empire from either IRAN or the Arabian peninsula some time during the middle of the 16th century. There are reports by European travelers that tobacco was routinely smoked in pipes by the inhabitants of SYRIA and EGYPT in the 1590s, and tobacco had certainly reached ISTANBUL by 1600. It is thought that Portuguese sailors first introduced tobacco smoking in the Middle East, since they initially enjoyed a monopoly over the distribution and sale of tobacco, shipping it from the Americas to those who lived along the shores of the Persian Gulf and Red Sea. Farmers in IRAN were quick to adapt the new crop, however, and were growing their own tobacco by the middle of the 16th century. Iranian tobacco was most valued and commanded the highest price among Ottoman consumers through the end of the 19th century, even after farmers in the empire began to cultivate the crop.

Medical doctors in the Ottoman Empire extolled the medical value of tobacco in the 17th century, as did their contemporaries in western Europe. Ironically, given what we know today about its harmful effects, Ottoman doctors thought tobacco to be especially useful for the lungs and to calm smokers' nerves. But Muslim religious scholars were not certain that smoking tobacco was legal according to the SHARIA. It was, after all, an innovation in that it had not been known by the Prophet Muhammad or the early Muslims. Also, it was clearly an import from Christian Europe and was therefore suspect. Finally, it was deemed to be foul and offensive to non-smokers. Those arguments led Sultan AHMED I (r. 1604–17) to ban the smoking of tobacco sometime after 1611. Sultan MURAD IV (r. 1623–40) banned the growing of tobacco in the empire in 1627. After a fire destroyed much of Istanbul in 1633, his orders became more draconian, prescribing the death penalty for anyone caught smoking tobacco. Despite the objections of sultans and religious scholars, the smoking of tobacco in the empire continued, and later sultans made no attempt to ban the substance.

The prominent Syrian religious scholar, ABD AL-GHANI AL-NABULUSI (d. 1731), wrote a treatise on tobacco and its use in 1682 in which he extolled both the social and medical benefits of smoking. He was not alone. By 1700, tobacco had became an empire-wide addiction, with men, women, and even children reported by European travelers to be avid smokers. Initially, and for many of the same reasons, COFFEE drinking had also been opposed by Muslim scholars in Istanbul, although not by those in the Arab provinces; it represented an innovation in what had been the social customs of the Prophet Muhammad and the early Muslims and it was also believed that it encouraged users to engage in worse vices. By the end of the 17th century, faced with a wave of noncompliance by ordinary believers, most Muslim scholars in Istanbul dropped their opposition to the consumption of coffee and tobacco. Use of coffee and tobacco was seen as less harmful than that of alternative substances like wine and opium, which were clearly forbidden by sharia. The exceptions to this trend toward legalization were the followers of MUHAMMAD IBN ABD AL-WAHHAB, who continued to ban the smoking of tobacco, although they did permit the consumption of coffee.

With its popularity spreading in all levels of Ottoman society, tobacco production in the empire skyrocketed in the 18th century. Realizing the economic boom this might present for the state's treasury, the Ottoman authorities introduced new taxes on the production and sale of tobacco. From the registers of these tax receipts we know that the major production areas of the empire were in Macedonia and Thrace in Europe and in northern Syria, southeastern Anatolia, and the Black Sea coast in the empire's Asian provinces. Unlike western Europe, where tobacco smoking was seen as a masculine vice, in the Ottoman Empire women faced no opprobrium as a result of their smoking habits. Because social norms prevented women from entering the coffee shops where men usually consumed tobacco, public BATHHOUSES provided their female customers with both pipes and coffee.

A second wave in smoking's popularity came in the second half of the 18th century when the water pipe (hookah) was introduced from Iran. Known as a *nargile* in Ottoman Turkish and *arghile* or *shisha* in Arabic, the water pipe was viewed by Muslim scholars as an improvement over earlier pipes which consisted of a small bowl and a long stem because the waterpipe reduced both the smoke and the odor created by the burning tobacco. Water pipes were also viewed favorably by coffee-shop owners because the consumption of tobacco through a water pipe required the smoker to be sedentary and therefore likely to consume more coffee. The water pipe did not completely replace the older-style stem pipes whose prototypes had originally been introduced by the Portuguese. But stem pipes came to be associated with peasants, the urban lower classes, and most especially the JANISSARIES, who by the end of the 18th century were in ill repute among the empire's elite.

The glass bowls for water pipes became increasingly elaborate in their decoration and even spawned their own new industry. But those produced in Iran were considered by Ottoman consumers to be of the highest quality, and the Ottoman authorities sought to ban their import to promote local production. This was viewed by the Iranian authorities with alarm and it is significant that one of the clauses in the Ottoman-Iranian Treaty of 1823, drawn up to resolve outstanding differences between the two states, had a separate clause allowing Iranian merchants to sell glass waterpipes in Istanbul.

The production and consumption of tobacco became a highly charged political issue in the second half of the 19th century. One of the consequences of the Ottoman Empire's declaration of bankruptcy in 1875 was that an international body known as the Ottoman Public Debt Administration (see DEBT AND THE PUBLIC DEBT ADMINISTRATION) was created to find ways for the empire to repay its debts. One of the measures was to transfer the monopoly over the production and sale of tobacco in the empire, only established by the Ottoman state in 1874, to a syndicate of three foreign-owned banks known by the French name Société de la Régie cointéressée des tabacs de l'empire ottomane (Corporation for the collection of excise taxes on the tobacco of the Ottoman Empire) or simply the Régie, which came into being in 1884. The Régie was given a monopoly over the purchase of tobacco from Ottoman growers, which was then either made into cigarettes in factories owned and operated by the Régie or sold to foreign companies for export by Régie representatives. The Régie, in turn, paid a yearly fee to the Public Debt Administration and a fixed percentage of its profits to both the Administration and the Ottoman government.

From the inception of the Régie, both tobacco growers and employees of the Ottoman government opposed its broad powers, viewing it as a foreign intrusion into the Ottoman Empire's sovereignty. Growers responded by withholding part of their crop which they then smuggled to buyers outside the empire; factory workers smuggled thousands of cigarettes from the Régie-owned factories to sell on the black market; and Ottoman officials refused to enforce the monopoly. Muslim clerics again raised the issue of whether smoking tobacco was legal under the sharia and called for boycotts of tobacco by Ottoman consumers. By the mid-1880s, the Régie managers had to hire their own private police force to try to stem the losses they were suffering due to smuggling. But the presence of these foreign officers on Ottoman soil only increased the resentment of Ottoman subjects toward the Régie.

This standoff between the Ottoman government and the directors of the Régie continued until the YOUNG TURK Revolution in 1908. At the time of the revolution, the Ottoman Empire was beset by increased banditry in rural areas, and the government decided to join forces with the Régie's police to suppress the bandits who in many cases were also tobacco smugglers. In November 1914, with its entry into WORLD WAR I, the Ottoman Empire unilaterally declared that the Régie was abolished, disbanded its police, and sent its other foreign employees home. ENGLAND and FRANCE did not recognize the end of the Régie, however, until 1923, when the Treaty of Lausanne between the new Republic of Turkey and the Western powers ended the CAPITULATIONS and the Public Debt Administration.

Bruce Masters

See also COFFEE/COFFEEHOUSES.

Further reading: James Grehan, "Smoking and 'early modern' sociability: The great tobacco debate in the Ottoman Middle East (seventeenth to eighteenth centuries). *American Historical Review* 111/5 (2006): 1352–77; Donald Quataert, *Social Disintegration and Popular Resistance in the Ottoman Empire, 1881–1908* (New York: New York University Press, 1983).

Topkapı Palace (New Imperial Palace) Located in ISTANBUL, the capital city of the Ottoman Empire from the mid-15th century until the end of the empire, the Topkapı Palace was the most important royal palace of the Ottoman sultans. It is set on the Seraglio Point between the Golden Horn and the Sea of Marmara, its location offering the dual benefit of defensibility and beautiful views. Started in approximately 1465 under Sultan MEHMED II (r. 1444–46; 1451–81), known as Fatih, or "the Conqueror," the main part of the palace was constructed over four or five years, including the outer walls and the Imperial Gate (Bab-ı Hümayun). Over the next four centuries, Mehmed and his successors gradually added to the palace and its grounds, constructing a variety of chambers, kiosks, and other buildings, such as the Circumcision Chamber in the fourth courtyard, the Baghdad Pavilion, and the Mecidiye Pavilion. The Royal Gardens, which stretched down to the seaside, were planted with flowers and used as a place to relax and walk. One section in the garden was reserved for growing vegetables for the palace.

ORGANIZATION

The Topkapı Palace is constructed according to the conventions of other Ottoman palaces and thus consists of four main parts: a private living area, dominated by the HAREM or women's section; an area used for education, known as the Enderun, or inner section; an administrative center where the Imperial Council (Divan-ı hümayun) met; and an area for service and safety also known as the Birun, or outer section.

There are three monumental gates in the palace: the first or Imperial Gate (Bab-i Hümayun); the second or Middle Gate, known also as the Gate of Salutation (Bab-üs Selam); and the third gate, known as the Gate of Felicity (Bab-üs Saadet). The ramparts (left from the time of Byzantium) surrounding the palace, together with the main gates, were constructed in the early 15th century. The sea, on some sides of the palace, provided extra protection.

Between the first and second gates was a large open area to which the public had access. In this area were diverse facilities to meet the needs of the people including a hospital and a bakery. During the ENTHRONEMENT AND ACCESSION CEREMONY and on other holidays (*bayram*), military officials, as well as the public, gathered in this area.

Owing to their administrative duties, various officials, such as the head of the imperial kitchen and of the royal stables, doctors (such as the head surgeon and the eye doc-

The Bab-i Hümayun, or "Imperial Gate," was the second gate of the Topkapı Palace, leading into the area that was the center of governance for the empire. *(Photo by Gábor Ágoston)*

This photo, taken by the Abdullah brothers, shows the Topkapı Palace as seen from the Sarayburnu *(Library of Congress)*

tor), and the sultan's tutor and adviser went to the palace on a daily basis. The regular workers, however, in the imperial kitchen, the imperial stables, the arts and crafts studio (*nakkaşhane*), as well as tentmakers and the musicians of the imperial military band (*mehterhane*), were considered the people of the Birun, or outer section of the palace.

The Second Court (Alay Meydanı, also known as Divan Meydanı), between the second and the third gates, was the most important administrative center of the government. Meetings of the Imperial Council were held in the Divanhane or Council Hall, which was built in the second court. The Council Hall was rebuilt in the reign of SÜLEYMAN I (r. 1520–66). At the time of Mehmed II, the Imperial Council met every day of the week, but in ensuing years this changed and the council met only four times a week (*see* ADMINISTRATION, CENTRAL). Accession and holiday ceremonies were also held here. At the time of these ceremonies a throne was placed in front of the third gate (Bab-üs Saadet) and, with the participation of state dignitaries, scholars, and representatives from the military, the ceremony of the oath of allegiance to the new sultan took place. Through

the second gate on the right of the second court was the imperial kitchen, which was built in the 15th century. However, its distinctive silhouette in the palace today comes from later centuries.

INNER PALACE OR ENDERUN

Passing through the third or Middle Gate led to the Third Court called Enderun, or inner section. In the first part of the entrance of this rectangular courtyard was the square Chamber of Petitions (Arz odası), which was built in the 15th century. In this chamber the sultan received state dignitaries and foreign ambassadors; it was the only place in the palace used for receiving outsiders.

Another important building found in the third courtyard was the PALACE SCHOOL, also known as Enderun Mektebi. This was an imperial academy that educated both the Ottoman princes and the most promising boys of the child levy (*DEVŞIRME*) to prepare them to serve as governors and in other positions of state bureaucracy. Students attending Enderun Mektebi studied law, linguistics, religion, music, art, and fighting. In addition, one group of students, known as Falconers, were attached to a room called Doğancı Koğuşu (Şahinciler Koğuşu in the 15th century) where they were responsible for the training and care of the wild birds that were symbols of heroism for the warrior- and hunter-rulers. During their education students were given some duties and at same time they became officers in the palace. The Palace School educated numerous state dignitaries and important artists from its inception in the 15th century until the palace ceased to be used by the ruling sultans in the second half of the 19th century.

CHAMBERS IN THE INNER PALACE

Within the Enderun, in addition to the Palace School, there were also a number of rooms with specialized uses. Among these, the Privy Chamber (Has oda) was the most important section in the inner section of the palace and those assigned to the Privy Chamber were closest to the sultan. In the 15th century the staff of the Privy Chamber included 32 pages (iç oğlan), the custodian of the sultan's weapons, the sultan's stirrup-holder, the custodian of his outer garments, and the keeper of his linens. From these modest beginnings, the number of staff steadily increased. People working in the Treasury Chamber (Hazine odası) were responsible for the protection and maintenance of both the inner and outer treasuries and they regularly went on expeditions with the sultan. The Chief of the Treasury occupied the most important position here; when promoted, he became the head manager of the Abode of Felicity. Those assigned to the Commissary Chamber (Kilar odası) set the table for the sultan and helped in the preparation of jams and sherbets in the Imperial Kitchen. They also ensured the proper protection and preservation of foods.

HAREM

The imperial harem, adjacent to the right side of the second and the third courts, was a separate place. The word *harem* derives from the Turkish *haram*, or "forbidden," and refers to the private residence of the family. In the Topkapı Palace, the harem, called the Abode of Felicity (Darüssaade ağası), was the residence of the sultan's family, specifically his mother (the *valide sultan*), his wife or wives and their young children, his sisters, and their servants and slave girls (*cariye*). Like the favored boys from the *devşirme* who were selected to become students in the Enderun School, female slaves brought from different parts of the empire were considered fortunate to become palace servants. Many of them received an education in language, religion, music, embroidery, and art in the harem. Based on these acquirements, some were then given duties in the palace while others might be married to state dignitaries or might become concubines or even wives of the sultan himself. Each sultan approached these relationships differently;

some sultans had one or two wives while others had more than 10 wives. Typically, however, concubines needed to prove their fertility before they could become wives.

The head of the harem was responsible for the management of the harem, although the mother of the reigning sultan (*valide sultan*) was the harem's highest authority. The number of people residing in the harem increased as the empire aged. This was partly because the harem was a place unto itself, forbidden to most outsiders, and thus needed to provide for its own needs: education, entertainment, dressing, and eating.

In 1853, after almost four centuries as the official residence of the Ottoman sultans, the Topkapı Palace was superseded by the newly constructed Dolmabahçe Palace, the first Ottoman palace to be built in the European style. Today the Topkapı Palace is one of Istanbul's most visited museums.

Zeynep Tarım Ertuğ

Further reading: Gülru Necipoğlu, *Architecture, Ceremonial, and Power: The Topkapi Palace in the Fifteenth and Sixteenth Centuries* (New York: Architectural History Foundation, 1991).

trade   The Ottoman Empire was established along what were then the most significant trade routes of the world, the silk and spice routes. By controlling first the east-west trade route, and later the north-south route, the empire was able to maintain its trade supremacy for close to four hundred years. While maintaining the overland trade between Asia and Europe, the empire also built trade on the Mediterranean Sea and the BLACK SEA. Through its success managing and supporting this expansive trading network, the Ottoman Empire established itself not only as an entity of great commercial significance but also as a power of enormous political consequence.

COMMODITY TRADE

Trade in the Ottoman Empire may be understood as falling into two categories—internal and external. So-called internal trade involved the transportation of goods from one city in the empire to another, whether over land or by sea, and was subject to taxation, identified as internal custom tax. Customs were named depending on location: shore customs, land customs, or border customs. The trade that took place between countries, cities, or towns was wholesale trade and the MERCHANTS involved in this trade were foreigners, both Muslim and non-Muslim. CARAVANS and seaports were important mechanisms in this wholesale trade and *hans*, or warehouses, in big cities were used to store and distribute goods to retailers. Grain and meat constituted the two most basic consumer goods. Grain came primarily from the Balkans and the ports of WALLACHIA. The DANUBE RIVER and the Anatolian and Rumelian sides of the BLACK SEA were used to transport this grain. Meat usually came from both Thrace and Anatolia and consisted mainly of lamb and mutton. Rice and COFFEE came by sea from EGYPT. Vegetables came from towns around the city, while fruits were supplied from the Aegean region.

In cities, there were *çarşı* (bazaars) and *bedestan* (permanent markets) while rural areas had weekly markets and fairs. As the empire's capital city, ISTANBUL played a special role within this commercial system. It was a major city as well as the center of government; besides providing for the city's large population, trade in the capital had to meet the needs of the army and the palace. Moreover, the Istanbul markets were a venue for artisans to procure raw material for their work. Therefore, meeting Istanbul's need for essential commodities was a significant undertaking.

A POLICY OF SELF-SUFFICIENCY

During the 15th and 16th centuries, when the Ottomans emerged as a great power, the primary goal of trade was the self-sufficiency of the empire. In keeping with this goal, the Ottoman Empire established three essential trade policies: ensure adequate supplies of primary goods within the empire; store primary goods in preparation for times of famine and scarcity; and, finally, avoid economic scarcity during wartime. As a natural result of these policies, Ottoman trade focused on imports, and most exports were prohibited.

In the same period in Europe, a number of significant trade developments began to take place. The Portuguese, for instance, developed sea routes to India and China, establishing their primacy in the sea trade. The Spanish reached the Americas and thus introduced a new world order in which sea trade would take an indispensable role; with this new order, the world's politics and power balances were also radically changed and conflicts between nations shifted from rivalries on land to rivalries at sea. The new order also brought about a new trade policy in western Europe, called mercantilism, in which imports were discouraged while exports were encouraged. As a result of this policy, which was the opposite of the economic policy supported by the Ottomans, the axis of world trade slowly shifted to the West. Although this did not influence the Ottoman Empire right away, in the long run, it resulted in the empire losing its primacy in world trade.

The history of trade in western Europe and in the Ottoman Empire during the 16th, 17th, and 18th centuries, while intimately interconnected, followed two fundamentally different courses. While western Europe expanded its export markets and built its manufacturing and transportation technologies, the Ottomans pursued a more conservative approach, continuing to rely heavily on agricultural foundations and a policy of self-sufficiency, an orientation that provided substantial

economic security but that naturally resulted in much slower growth than in the West. This situation was only exacerbated in the 19th century with the advent of the Industrial Revolution in the West and the explosion of European factory manufacturing.

THE GROWTH OF FOREIGN TRADE

To facilitate foreign trade, the Ottoman sultans had early given privileges to the Genoese, the Venetians, and even to the Byzantines. But it is believed that the first such trade privilege (AHDNAME) was granted by Sultan MURAD I (r. 1362–89) to the merchants of RAGUZA (present-day Dubrovnik). These privileges were mostly legal, political, and commercial privileges. Commercial privileges included the right to unrestricted trade, the use of Ottoman ports, and the exemption from various taxes in the import and export of goods within the empire. The primacy of Venetians and Genoese in Ottoman foreign trade was overtaken by French merchants by the mid-16th century. By the early 19th century the majority of the Ottoman foreign trade was carried out by foreign merchants who had expanded their commercial privileges into a broad and complex trading network. During the same time internal trade was in the hands of Ottoman subjects, both Muslims and non-Muslims.

As part of the conservative approach to trade, much commerce was held or managed primarily by the state. Trade was regulated through commodity provision (*iaşe*), monopoly (*yed-i vahid*), and a system of internal trade permits (*tezkire*); high customs fees and export prohibitions discouraged foreign trade. Most of these obstacles to foreign trade were ended by the Balta Limanı Treaty signed between the Ottoman Empire and Great Britain in 1838 (*see* ANGLO-OTTOMAN CONVENTION), and the empire finally became an open market for Europe, a situation that put the Ottomans at a decided disadvantage, particularly in the case of manufactured goods. During the 19th century the majority of Ottoman exports were agricultural products. These included raw silk, angora, TOBACCO, grapes, figs, hazelnuts, opium, bonito, cotton, and olive oil. On the other hand, manufactured products constituted the bulk of imports. Among these, textile products made of cotton and wool comprised the greater part. Imported industrial goods included weapons and various machines. Sugar, tea, and coffee, which were not produced in the empire, were also imported from abroad.

Toward the middle of the 19th century it was found that traditional Ottoman industries could not compete with the more productive European ones, and many Ottoman industries started to collapse. During the 19th century, the empire's trade capacity increased 10 times, while it had only doubled during the 18th century; yet during this time the trade balance between the empire and Europe also clearly tipped in favor of European states.

In order to change these disadvantageous conditions, to enhance and develop commerce, and most important, to have a unity and coherency in the organization of trade, the Ottoman Ministry of Commerce was established in 1839. Furthermore, to support the organization of these activities, several different committees pertaining to commerce were introduced. For the purpose of developing and organizing commerce, the Code of Commerce was put into effect in 1850 and commercial courts were founded in 1860. Toward the end of the century, the Ottoman Chamber of Commerce was established (1880), and schools of commerce were launched in 1883. A free-trade policy was introduced and the Ottoman economy was opened to the world, thus creating an enormous upsurge in the Ottoman import and export markets. Finally, in accordance with a new economic paradigm that was dominant in the beginning of the century called the National Economic Policy, the Ottomans developed a national trade policy, which continued in effect when the Republic of TURKEY rose out of the disintegrated Ottoman Empire in the early 1920s.

Coşkun Çakır

See also CARAVANSARY; ECONOMY; GRAND BAZAAR; MONEY AND MONETARY SYSTEMS.

Further reading: Halil İnalcık and Donald Quataert, eds., *An Economic and Social History of the Ottoman Empire, 1300–1914,* (Cambridge: Cambridge University Press, 1994); Şevket Pamuk, *The Ottoman Empire and European Capitalism, 1820–1913* (Cambridge: Cambridge University Press, 1987); Suraiya Faroghi, *Towns and Townsmen of Ottoman Anatolia: Trade, Crafts and Food Production in an Urban Setting, 1520–1650* (Cambridge: Cambridge University Press, 1984); Bruce McGowan, *Economic Life in the Ottoman Empire: Taxation, Trade and the Struggle for Land, 1600–1800* (Cambridge: Cambridge University Press, 1981); Bruce Masters, *The Origins of Western Economic Dominance in the Middle East: Mercantilism and the Islamic Economy in Aleppo, 1600–1750* (Cambridge, New York: Cambridge University Press, 1988).

Transylvania (*Ger.*: **Siebenbürgen**; *Hung.*: **Erdély**; *Rom.*: **Ardeal, Transilvania**; *Turk.*: **Erdel**)   Transylvania is the western part of present-day Romania, bordered by the Carpathian mountains in the east. Part of medieval HUNGARY, Transylvania was a vassal principality of the Ottoman Empire between 1541 and 1690, when the Habsburgs seized it from the Ottomans. Although it was ruled by the Habsburg kings of Hungary, Transylvania was administered directly from Vienna and was again united with the rest of Hungary in 1867 as part of the Austro-Hungarian Compromise. Following the dissolution of the Austro-Hungarian Monarchy (1867–1918) at the end of WORLD WAR I, the Romanians of Transylvania declared their union with Romania, an announcement that Hungary was forced to accept at the Treaty of Trianon (1920). During World War II (1939–45), Hungary briefly annexed northern Transylvania (1940), but it was returned to Romania after the war. Hungarian, German, and Romanian inhabitants lived in medieval Transylvania, but Romanians are the most numerous ethnic group today.

After the defeat of the medieval Hungarian kingdom at the BATTLE OF MOHÁCS on August 29, 1526, the majority of the Hungarian nobility elected the royal governor (*vajda* or *voievod*) of Transylvania, János Szapolyai, king of Hungary (r. 1526–40). Another faction of the Hungarian nobility, however, elected Ferdinand of Habsburg, archduke of Austria, as king of Hungary (r. 1526–64). The Ottoman Empire intervened in the fight between the two rival kings, supporting John Szapolyai by force of arms. In 1529 Sultan SÜLEYMAN I (r. 1520–66) captured BUDA, the capital of Hungary, restored Szapolyai to the Hungarian throne, and made him a vassal. At the same time the *voievods* István Majlád and Imre Balassa of Transylvania, who had been appointed by King John, revolted against John. Majlád turned to the Ottoman government, the Sublime Porte, asking the sultan to appoint him *voievod* when King John died, promising in return to pay a yearly tax of 25,000 gold florins and a present of 1,000 gold florins to each of the sultan's viziers. The Porte negotiated with him but ultimately refused his offer when the Hungarian envoys protested. After the death of King John in 1540, the Hungarian nobility elected as king his infant son, John Sigismund Szapolyai (János Zsigmond Szapolyai, Istefan Kıral in Ottoman sources). Sultan Süleyman acknowledged the child's right of succession and confirmed him on the throne by means of an AHDNAME. The rival King Ferdinand responded with an armed action.

Ferdinand's military attack provided an opportunity for the Porte to intervene again in the conflict between the two rivals to the Hungarian throne. On the grounds that John Sigismund Szapolyai, who was then a year old, and his mother, Isabella of Jagiello, were unable to defend Hungary against Habsburg attacks, the Ottomans occupied Buda in 1541. The Porte allocated the part of the country east of the River Tisza to the Szapolyai family. This territory was referred to as Erdel (from Erdély, the Hungarian term for Transylvania) in Ottoman sources although it was twice as big as historic Transylvania. The sultan divided this territory into three *sancak*s or sub-provinces under Christian rule. The region east of the River Tisza was given to George Martinuzzi, the Bishop of Várad (Oradea), chancellor and administrator of John Sigismund; the province of Temesvár (Timişoara) was given to Péter Petrovics; and historic Transylvania was given to John Sigismund but it was governed by George Martinuzzi until the child reached legal age.

The peace treaty between the Habsburgs and the Ottomans in 1547 made it possible for King Ferdinand to peacefully take possession of the eastern parts of Hungary, including Transylvania. He promised to continue to pay to Istanbul the tax of 10,000 gold florins, which had been paid regularly from 1543, on behalf of the three *sancaks*. When the sultan refused this offer, the Habsburgs invaded. The Ottomans retaliated with a counterattack in 1551 and again in 1552, resulting in the Ottoman capture of castles along the River Tisza, and by establishing a new Ottoman province around Temesvár. The Szapolyai family, which had taken shelter in Poland, returned in 1556. John Sigismund reigned as elected king of Hungary until 1570. However, pursuant to an agreement concluded in 1571 with Maximillian II, the Holy Roman Emperor and King of Hungary, John Sigismund relinquished the title of king and started to use the title of prince of Transylvania for the first time in history. After his death, the estates in Transylvania and neighboring Partium (territory in eastern Hungary not under Habsburg rule) elected Stephen Báthory as their *voievod* (r. 1571–76) and prince (r. 1576–86). He was later elected King of Poland.

At the beginning of the Long War of 1593–1606 between the Habsburgs and Ottomans, Prince Sigismund Báthory broke off relations with Istanbul and entered into an alliance with Rudolph II, Holy Roman Emperor and King of Hungary. At the end of the war, a revolt against the Habsburgs began in Hungary and Transylvania under the leadership of Stephan Bocskai, who was acknowledged by Grand Vizier Lala Mehmed Pasha, on behalf of Sultan Ahmed I (r. 1603–17), as prince of Transylvania and King of Hungary in November 1604.

After the Treaty of Zsitvatorok in 1606, signed by the Habsburgs and the Ottoman Empire, the princes of Transylvania pursued an anti-Habsburg policy with Ottoman help on several occasions but this did not lead to the termination of the treaty between the two great powers. This period is considered the golden age of the Transylvanian principality. During this time, the reigning princes, Gábor Bethlen (r. 1613–29) and György Rákóczi I (r. 1630–48), participated in the Thirty Years' War joining on the side of the Protestant nobility and countries against the Catholic Habsburgs.

In 1657 the succeeding Transylvanian monarch, György Rákóczi II (r. 1648–57), without the permission of the Porte, started a military expedition in alliance with Sweden in order to obtain the Polish throne. Sultan Mehmed IV (r. 1648–87) sent the Crimean Tatars to fight him in Poland and later attacked Transylvania itself. In 1658 Grand Vizier Köprülü Mehmed (*see* Köprülü family) appointed Ákos Barcsay, one of the noblemen in the peace delegation that arrived at the camp, as prince of Transylvania. His formal appointment was drawn up as a *hüccet* issued by the chief military judge (kadiasker).

From this time on, the princes of Transylvania were not given AHDNAMEs as before but came into power through a formal written appointment (*berat-i hümayun*) from the sultan, similar to the appointments given to officials of the Ottoman Empire.

After the death of Michael Apafi I (r. 1660–90), the last ruling prince of Transylvania, the Habsburg Empire prevented his successor, Michael Apafi II, from taking the throne. Imre Thököly, the ruler of the Ottoman vassal principality in northern Hungary (r. 1682–85), seized power for a few months, but Habsburg military pressure forced him to leave 1690). From 1687, Habsburg military occupation of the principality became permanent. As a consequence, an agreement was reached between the three dominant Transylvanian political-ethnical groups (the Magyars or Hungarian nobility; the Székelys or Hungarians of eastern Transylvania; and the German Saxons) and the Ottoman Porte about a temporary suspension of tax payments. During the Hungarian anti-Habsburg revolt of Transylvanian monarch Ferenc Rákóczi II (r. 1703–11), the Hungarians hoped for Ottoman support and asked for an extension of the sultan's supremacy into Transylvania and Hungary, but without success.

Sándor Papp

Further reading: Béla Köpeczy and Zoltán Szász, eds., *History of Transylvania*. 3 vols. (Boulder, Colo.: Social Science Monographs, 2002); Sándor Papp, *Die Verleihungs-, Bekräftigungs- und Vertragsurkunden der Osmanen für Ungarn und Siebenbürgen: Eine quellenkritische Untersuchung* (Wien: Verlag der Österreichischen Akademie der Wissenschaften, 2003).

Tripoli (Lebanon) (*anc.*: **Tripolis**; *Ar.*: **Tarablus al-Sham**; *Turk.*: **Trablusşam**) At the start of Ottoman rule in Syria in 1516, Tripoli had the largest population of any city in the region. Located on the Mediterranean Sea and close to the olive-producing region of Akkar, the city was a major exporter of olive oil and olive oil based soap. The city was made the capital of a province with the same name around 1570. The first governor of Tripoli was Yusuf Sayfa, who was the head of a Turkoman clan that had settled in the region. The Ottomans feared the possibility of rebellion by the Druze and Maronite clans in the nearby mountains and felt that a Sunni Muslim outsider might serve the state's best interests, as their patronage would serve his. Yusuf thus took the field following the orders of Sultan Ahmed I (r. 1603–1617) in campaigns against Fakhr al-Din al-Maani, the Druze leader, and Janbulad Ali Pasha, the rebellious governor of Aleppo, but he fell out of favor with the government in Istanbul by 1610 and was removed from his office. Other members of the clan held the office of governor off and on until the 1630s.

Following the rule of Yusuf Sayfa and his family, no other individual or clan would dominate the politics of Tripoli and the city became subordinated to the ambitions of personalities elsewhere in LEBANON and Syria without a local strongman to advance its interests. Although the city had secure walls and a sizeable covered MARKET, its port facilities were meager. As a result, European merchants upon whom the TRADE of Ottoman port cities depended sought to establish themselves elsewhere. After the development of ALEXANDRETTE, they encouraged the CARAVANS that had come from Aleppo to the Mediterranean to go its new port facilities. Tripoli was soon overshadowed first by Sidon and then by BEIRUT as the leading port of Lebanon. In 1911, the population of Tripoli was only 32,000. While that was an increase over the 10,000 people who had lived there in the middle of the 19th century, it was well below the population of Beirut.

Bruce Masters

Further reading: John Gulick, *Tripoli: A Modern Arab City* (Cambridge, Mass.: Harvard University Press, 1967).

Tripoli (Libya) (*anc.*: Oea; *Ar.*: Tarablus al-Gharb; *Turk.*: Trablusgarp) The port city of Tripoli, today in LIBYA, was one of the great corsair strongholds of the Ottoman Empire. The Spanish seized the city in 1510 but turned it over in 1539 to an anti-Muslim group of CORSAIRS AND PIRATES of crusader origins, the KNIGHTS OF ST. JOHN, who had fled to the island of MALTA after the Ottoman conquest of their former headquarters on RHODES in 1522. The Knights then used Tripoli to raid Muslim shipping, provoking an Ottoman response. In 1551 the Ottomans dispatched a fleet to besiege the town, but its garrison capitulated without a frontal assault. Until 1911, the city remained nominally Ottoman, despite frequent attacks upon the empire from renegades based in the city.

The sultans' control of Tripoli was problematic almost from the start, however. The absence of a routine Ottoman presence in the North African ports tended to engender anarchy. Profiting from this power vacuum, members of the Ottoman garrison in Tripoli created alliances with the local Muslim elite and soon began their own unofficial government. The military was largely Turkish in origin, either JANISSARIES or, more commonly, freebooters from Anatolia and the Balkans. One of these, Karamanlı Ahmed Bey, seized control of Tripoli in 1711. Not trusting the Janissaries posted to the city, he built up his own militia consisting of Albanians and BEDOUINS. He also relied on Europeans who had been enslaved in acts of piracy on the high sea or in raids on the European mainland. These were freed upon their conversion to Islam and many joined the corsair fleets that had enslaved them. Ahmed Bey was also astute enough to secure his position with the European MERCHANTS in the city and the Bed-

ouin tribes in the surrounding desert. But it was not until 1722 that he was officially appointed by Sultan AHMED III (r. 1703–30) to the position of governor of the province, with the title of pasha. His descendants ruled Tripoli with only brief interruptions until 1835 when direct Ottoman rule was restored. During the intervening years, the sultan still reigned, in theory, in Tripoli, but he was only a titular head whose orders went unheeded.

The restoration of Ottoman authority saw little change in Tripoli, and the city remained a sleepy provincial backwater. By the end of the 19th century, however, capitalists in Italy began to view the plain to the east of the city as a prime location for investment and the settlement of European colonists. Increased tensions between the Ottomans and the Italian government generated by Italian colonial ambitions led Italy to declare war on the empire in 1911. The Italians occupied Tripoli in October 1911 with little opposition. They then proclaimed it the capital of their newly formed colony of Libya.

Bruce Masters

Further reading: Richard Parker, *Uncle Sam in Barbary: A Diplomatic History* (Gainesville: University of Florida Press, 2004).

tuğra (*alamet, nişan, tevki, tughra*) The *tuğra* was a monogram created for a specific individual of the ruling dynasty. Unique to each ruler, the *tuğra* was used to mark documents, coins, buildings, stamps, and the state insignia of the late Ottoman Empire. When it expressed a religious formula it was used only as a calligraphic ornament that carried no official implications. While the etymology of the word is unclear, it is first mentioned by

The *tuğra*, or sultanic monogram, of Süleyman I (r.1520–66). Such lavishly decorated and elaborated *tuğras* were usually used for copies of major international treaties or letters sent to foreign rulers. *(The Metropolitan Museum of Art/Art Resource)*

Mahmud al-Kashghari (11th century) as Oghuz *tughragh* (seal, signature). *Tuğra*s of other empires and dynastic houses, such as those of the MAMLUK EMPIRE, differ from the SELJUK type and those that developed in post-Seljuk Anatolian principalities around 1300.

The first known Ottoman *tuğra* is that of ORHAN GAZI (r. 1324–1362), which reads "Orhan, son of Osman." It already shows the basic shape of future *tuğra*s: the names form the bottom (*sere*), "son of" is a rounded line to the left (*beyze*, later elongated to the right, *kol*) and three upward shafts (*tuğ*). Gradually the *tuğra* came to take a constant form and text: "A son of B, Khan, always victorious." Sultans MAHMUD II (r. 1808–39), ABDÜLHAMID II (r. 1876–1909), and MEHMED V (r. 1909–18) added individual epithets to the upper right of each of their *tuğra*s. On important decrees, *tuğra*s were richly ornamented from the mid-15th century onward. In addition to the sultan, Ottoman princes, too, used individual *tuğra*s, especially in the 15th and 16th centuries, whereas viziers and other officials put their own *tuğra*-like shapes (*pençe*s) vertically to the text on the right margin of their documents.

The *nişanci*, a member of the Imperial divan, who was later assisted by viziers (*tuğrakeş vezir*), first verified that the document conformed to the law. Then the *tuğra* was drawn by him onto the upper part of the document as a means of corroboration. In the 16th and 17th centuries the grand vizier, viziers, and *beylerbeyis* issued documents in the sultan's name on sheets already bearing the *tuğra*, and after the TANZIMAT reform period of the 19th century, *tuğra*s were drawn by officials called *tuğrakeş*. Late Ottoman decrees were written on printed forms bearing the *tuğra*.

Claudia Römer

Further reading: Jan Reychman and Ananiasz Zajączkowski, *Handbook of Ottoman-Turkish diplomatics* (The Hague: Mouton, 1968) 141–44; Jan Reychman and Ananiasz Zajączkowski, "Diplomatic," in *Encyclopaedia of Islam*, 2nd ed., vol. 2, (Leiden: Brill, 1960–), 301–16, esp. 314; Jean Deny "Tughra," in: *Encyclopaedia of Islam*, 2nd ed., vol. 10, (Leiden: Brill, 1960–), 595–99.

Tunis (*Ar.*: Tunus) The city of Tunis is located on the Mediterranean Sea in western North Africa and is the capital of the Republic of Tunisia. The importance of Tunis for much of the Ottoman period lay not in the fertile plain that borders the city but rather in the city's central role in the ebb and flow of Mediterranean piracy. With the expansion of Spanish naval activity in the western Mediterranean after the fall of Granada in 1492, Sultan SÜLEYMAN I (1520–66) became acutely aware of the threat that the Spanish fleet posed to the Ottoman Empire and he sought to build a NAVY that could successfully counter the Spanish raids. In 1535 the Ottoman fleet, under the charge of Hayreddin (Khair ad Din) Barbarossa (*see* BARBAROSSA BROTHERS) took the city of Tunis from its Muslim Hafsid ruler, Mawlay Husayn, who seemed incapable of resisting the Spanish. But in the following year the forces of King Charles V (r. 1500–58) of Spain seized the city and handed it back to Husayn, who served as his vassal. A back-and-forth struggle followed during which the city changed hands several times until 1577 when it definitively became an Ottoman province.

Throughout the 17th century, Tunis had a governor appointed from ISTANBUL. It enjoyed an economic boom based on the produce of its agricultural hinterlands and the wealth that was coming into the city from the multitude of CORSAIRS AND PIRATES who plied their trade just off the coast. The population of Tunis grew quite substantially. Its Muslim population consisted largely of newcomers: Turks and Albanians from the Ottoman Empire, Muslims expelled from Spain, and European converts to Islam. The city also had a substantial Jewish population and resident European merchant colonies, leading European visitors to remark on the cosmopolitan flavor of the city. At the start of the 18th century, military strongmen seized control in all the major North African ports nominally ruled by the sultan. In 1705 Hüseyin Alioğlu, who had previously served as the head of the JANISSARIES in the city, established his rule in Tunis. His descendants, known as the Husaynids in English, would rule as beys until 1957, although after 1881 their authority was only nominal because the country was a French protectorate.

Piracy remained the mainstay of the economy of Tunis throughout the 18th century. Increasingly, however, corsairs had to confine their raids to the Italian mainland because central governments in the rest of Europe had the means of effective retaliation. Piracy enjoyed an upsurge during the French Revolution (1789–99) and the subsequent Napoleonic period when European navies were preoccupied. But after the French withdrawal from EGYPT in 1801, the British and American fleets threatened the beys of Tunis and the other North African ports, insisting that they desist from raiding. The death knell of piracy was sounded in pan-European agreements signed in 1815 and 1818 that outlawed piracy in the Mediterranean Sea and provided for military intervention to enforce the policy. No longer able to rely on piracy as a major source of income, the rulers of Tunis had to turn instead to the exploitation of their agricultural resources. To finance this, they invited European capitalists and settlers to transform the traditional subsistence agriculture of the city's hinterlands into a modern capitalist one, a transformation that led to increased borrowing and, ultimately, defaults on loans. Using the country's economic insolvency as an excuse, the French occupied Tunis in 1881, declaring a protectorate over a territory they named Tunisia.

Bruce Masters

See also ALGIERS; NAPOLEON BONAPARTE; NORTH AFRICA; TRIPOLI (LIBYA).

Further reading: Jamil Abun-Nasr, *A History of the Maghrib* (Cambridge: Cambridge University Press, 1975).

Turkey (*Turk.*: Türkiye) The peninsula that today makes up most of the Republic of Turkey was known as Anadolis, literally "the East," throughout the Greek-speaking world, both in antiquity and in the centuries during which the BYZANTINE EMPIRE (330–1453) flourished. That name entered the various languages of western Europe, including English, as Anatolia. With the victory of the Seljuk Turks over the Byzantines at the Battle of Manzikert in 1089, Turkish-speaking tribal peoples increasingly settled the region that had formerly been inhabited by Greek-speaking and Armenian-speaking Christians. The SELJUKS quickly established political control over most of the region; over time, many of the indigenous people living there converted to Islam and adopted the Turkish language.

Western Europeans traveled through Anatolia during the First Crusade (1095–99) on their way to JERUSALEM and those crusaders who wrote about their experience called the Muslims living in Anatolia "Turks" to distinguish them from Arabic-speaking Muslims, whom they called Saracens. By the end of the 12th century Europeans had begun to call the region Turchia or Turkey, "the land of the Turks." The name stuck, and as the Ottoman Empire began to emerge as a world power in the late 14th century, Europeans almost universally referred to it as Turkey and to all Ottoman Muslims as Turks, whether or not they actually spoke Turkish. An indication of the blending of the religious and ethnic meaning of the word "Turk" by the Europeans was the phrase, "to turn Turk," meaning "to convert to Islam," an expression used by English speakers from the 16th through the 19th centuries.

The Ottomans, however, retained the older Greek name for the peninsula, Anatolia, which they rendered as Anadolu. For them, the word "Türk" was reserved for the Turcoman tribal people or the Turkish-speaking peasants of Anatolia. Türk had a slightly negative connotation for the Ottoman elite, as the expression "Türk *kafa*" demonstrates; literally "Turk-head," it meant "blockhead." The Ottoman Arab subjects called the area we know today as Turkey "Rum," or the Roman Empire. That is what they had called the BYZANTINE EMPIRE before the Ottomans conquered the region and they simply extended the name to the successors of the Byzantines. Ottoman Arabs also used the word "Rumi," literally, "one coming from Anatolia," to mean an Ottoman. The Ottomans called themselves "Osmanlı," that is "belonging to the House of Osman."

In the 19th century, however, all of the various peoples of the Ottoman Empire began to adopt the relatively new European notion of NATIONALISM, that peoples should be distinguished by "nations," by which the Europeans generally meant those sharing a common language and sense of history. This was a revolutionary way of thinking for peoples in the Ottoman Empire as hitherto the primary social category had been groupings according to religion (MILLET). Nationalist identities were first articulated among intellectuals representing the various Christian peoples of the Balkans in the late 18th century. When the empire started to fracture as various peoples began to demand a political state that would correspond to their newly found sense of nation, Muslim intellectuals began to rethink the question of their own political identities. Those who spoke a form of Turkish as their mother tongue initially tried to create a national identity based on loyalty to the Ottoman dynasty. Historians identify this intellectual and political movement as OTTOMANISM. But because that ideology apparently failed to attract the loyalty of most non-Muslims, by the last decades of the 19th century, Turkish-speaking intellectuals replaced it with Turkish nationalism or Turkism.

In this ideological construction, all those speaking a form of Turkish constituted a "nation." With that shift in orientation, Anadolu or Anatolia no longer seemed an appropriate name for the country of the Turks. Initially, the Persian word "Türkistan," or "country of the Turks" was suggested as an alternative; other authors suggested yet another alternative, "Türkeli," which is simply the "country of the Turks" in Ottoman Turkish. By the start of WORLD WAR I in 1914, however, Ottoman Turkish intellectuals had gravitated toward the name "Türkiye," which was ultimately derived from the Italian name for the country first used at the end of the 13th century, "Turchia." Mustafa KEMAL ATATÜRK popularized that name in his struggle to overthrow the conditions imposed on the defeated Ottoman Empire by the Allied forces who occupied the region in 1918. With the emergence of a new republic in place of the disintegrated Ottoman Empire, Türkiye was enshrined as the new country's official name in the constitution of 1924.

Bruce Masters

See also YOUNG TURKS.

Further reading: Şerif Mardin, *The Genesis of Young Ottoman Thought: A Study in the Modernization of Turkish Political Ideas* (Princeton, N.J.: Princeton University Press, 1962); M. Şükrü Hanioğlu, *The Young Turks in Opposition* (Oxford: Oxford University Press, 1995); Eric Hobsbawm, *Nations and Nationalism Since 1780* (Cambridge: Cambridge University Press, 1990).

U

al-Ujaymi, Hindiyya (Hindiya the Nun) (b. 1720–98) *Christian nun and mystic, founder of the Sisters of the Sacred Heart of Jesus religious order* Hindiyya al-Ujaymi was born into a wealthy MARONITE Catholic merchant family in ALEPPO. Her brother, Niqula, became a Jesuit, and Hindiyya was drawn to the religious life early, reportedly reciting the prayers "Our Father" and the "Hail Mary" precociously at the age of three. As an adolescent, al-Ujaymi indulged in various acts of self-mortification and fasting. Then, sometime in her early twenties, she claimed to have experienced a mystical union with Christ. From the start of her mystical journey, al-Ujaymi had the support of the Maronite metropolitan of Aleppo, Jarmanus Saqr. When she was 28 she left Aleppo for the monastery of Ayntura in LEBANON. Two years later, in 1750, she started her own holy order, the Sisters of the Sacred Heart of Jesus, and established a convent in Bkirki in the mountains north of BEIRUT, where her open proclamations of her mystical experience soon became a matter of controversy. With al-Ujaymi's claim that Christ spoke directly through her and that she had been transformed by a shared physical presence with the Holy Trinity, her Jesuit advisers began to distance themselves from her, but she continued to receive strong support from the Maronite patriarch. Pope Benedict XIV, in an attempt to defuse the situation, appointed a committee headed by an Aleppine Franciscan monk in 1753. The committee found al-Ujaymi blameless. Realizing that conciliation was better than an open break with the Maronites, Pope Benedict recommended that al-Ujaymi's convent be constructed in the mountains, away from the distraction of the city.

Al-Ujaymi remained popular in her absence from Aleppo and received support from the hierarchies of the UNIATE MELKITE and Syrian Catholic churches in that city as well as from the sheiks of the influential KHAZIN FAMILY, some of whose female relatives joined al-Ujaymi's order. But controversy continued to surround al-Ujaymi both for her teachings and for her actions, including claims that she had performed miracles, including healing the blind and lepers, and the murder of one of her nuns that occurred at her convent. There was no proof that Hindiyya was directly involved in the crime but there were accusations that she tried to dispose of the body in secret. In 1780 a council consisting of Maronite clergy and laity and representatives of the pope met and abolished al-Ujaymi's order. From that point on, al-Ujaymi lived a quiet, secluded life in virtual imprisonment until her death in 1798.

Although al-Ujaymi's writings were proscribed by the Vatican in 1780, a manuscript copy of her work, with her seal, entitled *The Disclosure of the Hidden Secrets That I Saw in the Secret Treasury* and dated August 18, 1774, survives in the Vatican Library. In this narration of her mystical travels, al-Ujaymi describes how she became united with the eternal reality of Christ through the medium of the Sacred Heart. In that incarnation, she was able to travel back to the very creation of the universe, stopping along the way at the Garden of Eden. In her union with Christ, al-Ujaymi claims to have been able to share Jesus' experiences as a fetus growing in Mary's womb as well as the agony of His death. It was her claim of absolute union with Christ and ultimately with God "the Father," that led the Vatican to proscribe her work, although al-Ujaymi's writing remained popular in her native Aleppo for at least another generation after her death.

Bruce Masters

Further reading: Nabil Matar, "Christian Mysticism in the Ottoman Empire: The Case of Hindiya the Nun, 1720–1798." *The Muslim World* 95 (2005), 265–78.

Ukraine In geographic terms, *Ukraina* initially referred to the steppe borderland between the Grand Duchy of Lithuania (after 1569, the Kingdom of POLAND, as a consequence of the Union of Lublin when most Ukrainian territories were transferred from Lithuania to Poland) and the steppes to the south controlled by the purely nomadic Nogays and the semi-nomadic CRIMEAN TATARS. Ethnically, Ukraine included a much larger territory—including the lands of Kiev, Volhynia, Lviv, and Podolia, that is, the central and western lands of old Kievan Rus'. Although Ukraine had Polish, Jewish, Armenian, and other ethnic groups, the majority were Ruthenians, an early modern designation for Ukrainians. Politically, Ukraine was dominated by the old Ruthenian Orthodox and eventually by Lithuanian and Polish nobilities although starting in the 16th century the Ukrainian COSSACKS mounted a political and military challenge against these elites. Internationally, the fate of Ukraine was largely determined by three major powers: the Polish-Lithuanian Commonwealth, Muscovy, and the Ottoman Empire.

In terms of Ottoman influence, two major players affected the development of Ukraine: the Sublime Porte and its vassal, the Crimean Khanate. Subject to the same set of political demands and strategic motivations that governed Ottoman policy elsewhere in the region, Ukraine was affected by the long term Ottoman policy of attaining and then maintaining exclusive access to the BLACK SEA. In the second half of the 15th century, with the Ottoman-Crimean axis well established and their sole access to the Black Sea secured, the Ottomans were able to effectively lock the Commonwealth and Muscovy out of the Black Sea region for the next three centuries.

The Ukrainian lands of the Polish-Lithuanian Commonwealth were of importance for the Tatars and Ottomans thanks to their relative proximity, ease of accessibility, and, in the 16th and 17th centuries, robust population growth, which presented a ready resource for the Ottoman SLAVERY market. Ukrainian lands became the prime hunting grounds for Tatar and Nogay slavers, who were in turn prime suppliers of the Ottoman slave market.

The rise of militarized and independent frontiersmen known as Cossacks was due in large part to the dangerous conditions on the steppe frontier. The Ukrainian Cossack phenomenon grew throughout the 16th and early 17th centuries until by the second half of the 17th century it matured into a new polity that was known as the Hetmanate; dominated by the Cossacks it lasted until 1775. There were two main types of Ukrainian Cossacks: the Zaporozhians, who were based in the islands, waterways, and marshes of the lower Dnieper, downriver from a series of unnavigable cataracts to the north and just south of the Nogay and Tatar-controlled steppe; and the so-called town Cossacks, who garrisoned crown-held forts just north and west of the frontier.

Thanks to their use of FIREARMS, particularly in infantry and naval warfare, the Cossacks altered the balance of power in the northern Black Sea region as well as on the sea itself. It was most of all the constant Cossack reprisals against Tatar activity and their own incursions deep into Ottoman northern territories (including MOLDAVIA and virtually all coasts of the Black Sea) that led the Ottomans to depart from their traditional nonactive northern policy and engage in northern military adventures; one such northern expedition was the unsuccessful Hotin (Khotin) War of 1621 against the commonwealth, the outcome of which contributed to the unseating and execution of Sultan OSMAN II (r. 1618–22). While it was usually in the mutual interests of the Porte and the Commonwealth to remain at peace, the Tatars and the Cossacks often strained and even disrupted these relations; yet the Tatars and Cossacks also played an important role in bolstering the defense of their respective suzerains. For example, without the Cossacks, Poland-Lithuania would probably not have withstood Osman II's onslaught at Khotin.

Beginning with the 1648 uprising against the Polish-Lithuanian Commonwealth led by the Ukrainian Cossack Hetman Bohdan Khmelnytsky and continuing for much of the second half of the 17th century, Ottoman-Cossack relations took on a more positive nature. During his uprising Khmelnytsky several times accepted Ottoman suzerainty, which he maintained for a time even after his acceptance of Muscovite suzerainty in 1654 (Treaty of Pereiaslav). It is uncertain whether Khmelnytsky courted the Ottomans for tactical reasons or perhaps in pursuit of a more permanent arrangement for Ukraine, along the lines of the vassalages of Moldavia and WALLACHIA.

The partition of Ukraine between the Polish-Lithuanian Commonwealth and Muscovy in 1667 along the Dnieper River (Treaty of Andrusovo) led to a strong reaction in Ukraine against these powers and prompted the new acceptance of Ottoman suzerainty, now by Hetman Petro Doroshenko in 1668. In the following year, Doroshenko was given a sultanic patent (*berat* or *nişan*) and a horsetail and banner, making him an autonomous ruler akin to the *voievods* of Moldavia and Wallachia.

The acceptance of Ukraine under Ottoman overlordship led to wars with both the Polish-Lithuanian Commonwealth and Muscovy. In 1672 an Ottoman army led by Sultan MEHMED IV (r. 1648–87) took the fortress of Kamianets-Podilsk and established the province of KAMANIÇE in Podolia, which the Ottomans held until 1699. In 1678, after an unsuccessful campaign in the previous year, the Ottomans marched on south central Ukraine and captured the Muscovite-held fortress of Chyhyryn (Çehrin). However, for a variety of reasons, including the ongoing war over CRETE with Venice, mistrust of the Cossacks (once their most bitter foes in the region), and the difficulty of military operations at the frontier, the Ottomans effectively abandoned an active northern Black Sea policy when in 1683 they decided to return to their more traditional theatre of expansion in central Europe and besieged Vienna (see VIENNA, SIEGES OF).

In the 18th century the Cossacks of the Hetmanate, by then an autonomous region of the Russian Empire, played an important role in the Russian Empire's wars with the Ottomans. However, there were still periods of cooperation between groups of Ukrainian Cossacks and the Ottomans. For example, after the Battle of Poltava (1709), in which Czar Peter I's Russian forces defeated combined Swedish and Ukrainian forces, lead by Charles XII and Hetman Ivan Mazepa respectively, the latter and remnants of this army sought refuge in Ottoman Bender. His successor, Pylyp Orlyk, became hetman under Ottoman protection and, from Ottoman territory, sought to gain control of Right Bank Ukraine. Also worth noting is that after the destruction of the Zaporozhian Cossacks' Dnieper stronghold (known as the Sich) by Russian forces returning from war with the Ottomans in 1775, many of the Ukrainian Cossacks migrated to Ottoman territory (as had earlier Russian Don Cossacks, led by Ignat Nekrasov). There they established the so-called Danubian Sich near the mouth of the DANUBE RIVER, which lasted until 1828. During this period they became Ottoman subjects and were required to serve in military campaigns. Although eventually many of them returned to the Russian Empire, their descendants still live in the Danube delta.

Victor Ostapchuk

See also RUSSIA.

Further reading: Mykhailo Hrushevsky, *History of Ukraine-Rus'*, vol. 7–9 (Edmonton and Toronto: Canadian Institute of Ukrainian Studies Press, 1999–2008); Orest Subtelny, *The Mazepists: Ukrainian Separatism in the Early Eighteenth Century* (New York: East European Monographs, 1981).

ulak *See* MENZILHANE.

ulema The plural of the Arabic word *alim* ("man of knowledge"), in the Ottoman Empire the term *ulema* referred to those who were trained in the Islamic religious sciences (such as the Quran, the traditions of the Prophet Muhammad, and Islamic jurisprudence), and were members of the Ottoman religious establishment, the *ilmiye* hierarchy. The Ottomans divided their society into two main groups: the taxpaying subjects or *reaya*, and the privileged

askeri class. Within the latter, they distinguished the "men of the sword" (soldiers), the "men of the pen" (bureaucrats), and the "men of the *ilm*" (religious sciences/knowledge), that is, members of the religious establishment.

Religious sciences were taught in madrasas, or colleges. Between the 14th and 16th centuries the Ottomans established some 350 madrasas, more than half of them (189) in the 16th century. In addition, especially in the early period of the Ottoman state, the ulema of the empire were trained in the major centers of Islamic learning. Those who wanted to study Quranic exegesis (*tafsir*) or jurisprudence (*fiqh*), for example, went to EGYPT or IRAN.

The most important part of Islamic education was the teacher (*müderris*) and not the institution. It was his expertise that determined, in accordance with the founder's intent (expressed in the foundation document of the madrasa), the subjects and books that were taught in the madrasa. Nonetheless, there was a strict hierarchy of madrasas, the highest-ranking being those in the capital, ISTANBUL: the Fatih madrasas—that is, the colleges built by Fatih (the Conqueror) MEHMED II (r. 1444–46; 1451–81), also known as the Sahn-i Seman (Eight Courtyards) or Semaniye madrasas—and the Süleymaniye madrasas established by SÜLEYMAN I (r. 1520–66). While Islamic religious sciences (*tafsir, fiqh,* or *hadith,* that is, the traditions of the Prophet Muhammad) dominated the curriculum, medicine and astronomy also were taught. Upon mastering a given subject or text, the student received an *icazet* (*ijaza*), or certificate, from his teacher. This both confirmed the pupil's mastery of the specified text or subject and authorized him to teach it to others. In addition to the necessary training in the religious sciences, the patronage (*intisab*) of influential persons in and around the government was also essential for a career within the ulema.

The graduates of the main Istanbul madrasas had two career choices. They either pursued a life as professors or became judges (*kadı*) and jurisconsults (mufti), and thus members of the Ottoman administration. In the Ottoman Empire there was a firm hierarchy within the ulema and strict rules regulated promotion. Madrasa graduates seeking employment with the state either as teachers or as judges were registered in the government day-books of state appointees and waited until a position became available for which their education qualified them. For instance, a *müderrises* of lower-level madrasas and graduates of the Semaniye madrasas were eligible for judgeships in smaller towns, earning between 50 to 150 akçes per day in the mid-16th century. (The best paid *müderrises* earned 50 to 60 akçes per day, whereas the Janissaries earned 5 to 6 akçes per day). Holders of senior judgeships earned 300 akçes or more daily and could become *defterdars* (finance ministers) of the Imperial Council. The *müderrises* of the Semaniye madrasas could also become judges in Istanbul and, later, *KADIASKERS* (military or chief judges). This shows that the career paths to the secular bureaucracy were also open to the ulema, many of whom became viziers or even GRAND VIZIERS, that is, the sultans' deputies and heads of the government.

The head of the Ottoman ulema was the ŞEYHÜLISLAM or chief mufti of the capital, appointed by the sultan from among the most distinguished scholars of the religious sciences. Unlike the *kadıaskers*, the *şeyhülislam* was not a member of the Imperial Council. However, when the two *kadıaskers* of Anatolia and Rumelia, who represented the ulema in the Imperial Council, disagreed or sought a religious opinion, it was the *şeyhülislam's* written legal opinion (FATWA) that helped them decide the matter. His fatwas were also crucial in legitimizing disputed sultanic decisions, such as campaigns against Muslim neighbors. Since the *şeyhülislam* represented Islamic sacred law, the SHARIA, in principle, he was not part of the government. However when, under Sultan Süleyman I, he was given the right and obligation to appoint judges, who were arms of the executive branch of the government, the independence of the *şeyhülislam* ended. Indeed, the institutionalization of the Ottoman ulema and its close association with the government was unprecedented in other Islamic polities. In the long run, this significantly reduced their ability to act as mediators between the ruler and the ruled and as guardians of Islamic sacred law, functions that had traditionally been associated with the ulema.

In history books on the Ottomans, the Ottoman ulema from the mid-16th century on is often portrayed as a reactionary force that rejected the reforms needed to strengthen the empire in the face of Western encroachment. While it is true that the coalition of the ulema and the Janissaries opposed the military reforms of Sultan SELIM III (r. 1789–1807) and led to the sultan's deposition, the ulema of the 18th century was not homogeneous, and several members of the *ilmiye* hierarchy in fact supported the sultan to legitimize the reforms.

The TANZIMAT reforms (1839–76) seriously reduced the role and influence of the ulema, who by that time had become a rather closed class. With the introduction of secular schools and secular courts as part of the overhauling of the educational and judicial systems, the Ottoman ulema's traditional functions were substantially weakened. On the other hand, the *şeyhülislam's* right to appoint and supervise judges was left untouched, and his office was substantially enlarged and developed into a ministry in all but name. However, the establishment of the Ministry of Religious Foundations and its merger with the Imperial Mint considerably weakened the ulema's hold on these important assets. For the remainder of the 19th century the ulema coexisted, albeit somewhat uneasily, with these new structures, until their privileged existence was terminated with the abolition of the caliphate (March 1924) and the subsequent reforms introduced by the government of the Turkish Republic.

Gábor Ágoston

See also EDUCATION; KADIASKER; ŞEYHÜLISLAM.

Further reading: Uriel Heyd, "The Ottoman Ulema and Westernization in the time of Selim III and Mahmud II," in Uriel Heyd, ed., *Studies in Islamic History and Civilization (Scripta Hierosolymitana IX)* (Jerusalem: Magnes Press, Hebrew University, 1961); Halil İnalcık, *The Ottoman Empire: The Classical Age, 1300–1600* (London: Weidenfeld & Nicolson, 1973); Madeline C. Zilfi, *The Politics of Piety: The Ottoman Ulema in the Postclassical Age, 1600–1800* (Minneapolis, Minn.: Bibliotheca Islamica, 1988).

Uniates The Uniates were the formerly Orthodox Christians of the Ottoman Empire whose churches relinquished their communion with the Orthodox community and entered instead into communion with Rome when their leading clergy accepted the pope as their supreme spiritual authority, hence the term Uniate. Today their churches continue to have their own patriarchs who are subordinate to the pope and are given the rank of cardinal within the Roman Catholic hierarchy. Fear that the Eastern Church was too weak both institutionally and spiritually to resist Protestantism spurred the movement in the Roman Catholic Church for the unification of the Eastern-rite churches to Rome in the 17th century. Rather than seeking to convert individual Christians to Roman Catholicism, Catholic MISSIONARIES from the West concentrated their efforts on bringing the hierarchy of the various churches into communion with Rome. They were successful with the MARONITES, the historically dominant Christian sect in LEBANON, who accepted full papal authority in the 18th century. They were less successful with the other Eastern churches in the Ottoman Empire; in some, the missionaries succeeded only in creating schisms such as those that gave rise to the Melkite Catholics, the Chaldean Catholics, the Armenian Catholic Church, and the Syrian Catholics, all of whom broke with their traditional leadership in the 18th century.

Bruce Masters

See also GREEK ORTHODOX CHURCH; JACOBITES; MARONITES; MELKITES.

Further reading: Charles Frazee, *Catholics and Sultans: The Church and the Ottoman Empire, 1453–1923* (London: Cambridge University Press, 1983).

United Kingdom *See* ENGLAND.

Urabi, Ahmad Pasha (b. 1841–d. 1911) *Egyptian military officer and rebel* Ahmad Urabi is one of the great heroes in the nationalist version of Egyptian history. He was born into a peasant family in a village in the province of Zaqaziq in the Nile Delta and showed promise as a youth for religious education. He studied at AL-AZHAR, the leading Muslim school in EGYPT, but switched career paths when Egypt's military academy opened its doors to native Egyptians in 1854. This was a radical departure from past practice in which the sons of peasants were conscripted into the ranks of the army but were not allowed to rise above the rank of non-commissioned officers. Until this time, the officer class had been recruited from the Turco-Circassian ruling class among men whose origins lay outside Egypt and who were schooled in Ottoman rather than Arab culture. But even with this opening of the ranks of the officer class to Egyptians, there was still substantial discrimination against officers of Egyptian origin, and Urabi served as lieutenant colonel for more than 20 years without any further promotion.

Obviously disgruntled with his personal situation, Urabi caught the attention of the Egyptian authorities when he organized protests in the army against a proposal made by KHEDIVE TAWFIQ in 1880 to prohibit native Egyptians from becoming officers above the regimental rank. The proposal was fueled by the need to reduce the size of the army because the Egyptian state, saddled with foreign debt, could no longer maintain its former military strength. Rather than dismissing officers of the Turco-Circassian military elite, Tawfiq proposed instead to dismiss Egyptian officers who did not have influential friends. Faced with a potential mutiny, Tawfiq backed down in January 1881 as the troops rallied behind Urabi who had, quite unintentionally, become the focus of nationalist hopes and soon came to be regarded as the man who might stand up to the Europeans.

The disgruntled officers went on to press other demands. In particular, they sought the reinstatement of the popular Minister of War, Mahmud Sami Bey al-Barudi, who had been dismissed by Prime Minister Riyad Pasha on August 13, 1881 for being overly sympathetic to the complaints of the Egyptian officers. Urabi organized a large demonstration outside Tawfiq's Abdin Palace in September, demanding that al-Barudi be reinstated. The unrest continued until December 1881 when Riyad was dismissed and a new cabinet, with Urabi as Minister of War and al-Barudi as prime minister, was put in place. At that point, ENGLAND and FRANCE, fearing a collapse of the khedive's regime, issued a joint notice in his support. The Egyptian nationalist press saw this European support as yet another example of foreign meddling and propelled Urabi to the forefront of the nationalist cause. Urabi seemed to revel in the attention and made famous the slogan that would become the byword for the nationalist movement, "Egypt for the Egyptians."

On May 25, 1882, the Europeans demanded that Khedive Tawfiz dismiss Urabi. Giving in to European pressure, al-Barudi resigned, but Urabi refused to resign. In June 1882, anti-European riots broke out in ALEXANDRIA. The British fleet bombarded the city on July 11 in retaliation, and blamed Urabi's supporters for the unrest. In a panic, Tawfiq sought refuge with the British fleet and declared Urabi a rebel. That gave the British the justification they needed to move against Urabi, and a British expeditionary force landed in Alexandria in August. Urabi tried to rally the Egyptian people against the invasion, saying that Tawfiq had lost his mandate to rule by joining the "infidels." But the British troops quickly advanced on CAIRO; on September 13 they defeated the Egyptian army at Tell al-Kabir and entered Cairo. Urabi was tried, convicted, and sent into exile on the British colony of Ceylon (Sri Lanka). The British allowed him to return to Egypt in 1901. Taking no further part in his country's political life, Urabi died in 1911.

Urabi Pasha's revolt had given the British an excuse to occupy Egypt. Once British forces had secured the country, they did not leave. Egypt remained officially a province of the Ottoman Empire, with the khedive recognized by the Ottomans as an autonomous ruler; but in reality, Egypt was effectively ruled by Great Britain until 1922, when that country granted Egypt its independence.

Bruce Masters

Further reading: Juan Cole, *Colonialism and Revolution in the Middle East: Social and Cultural Origins of Egypt's 'Urabi Movement* (Princeton, N.J.: Princeton University Press, 1993).

Uskoks (Uskoci; Uscocchi; Uskoki) The term *uskok* comes from the Croatian word for "jump in," meaning refugee. It refers to people who left their homes in Ottoman territory in the Adriatic hinterland or in present-day western BOSNIA and settled in Habsburg Croatia, becoming members of the Habsburg borderland militia. Of Orthodox Christian or Roman Catholic background, they were largely from the Vlach population and came both individually and in small groups. Especially from 1537 on many became garrison members in Senj (Senia, Zengg) on the shores of the northern Adriatic. Living as a peasant borderland militia and conducting highly effective small-scale raids, the Uskoks harried the Ottoman territories and MERCHANTS trading there. Joined by former Venetian subjects (*venturini*) as well as Senj townsmen, Italians, and Albanians, the Uskok presence in Senj made the Military Border captaincy there the strongest and the most aggressive part of the Habsburg defense system. This was because most of the Uskoks, like most militias along the Habsburg Military Border, were not paid, and the town and its vicinity lacked arable land and pastures. As a consequence, with Vienna's tacit approval, the Uskoks plundered Ottoman lands in times of peace, and even attacked the Venetians. They also collected protection money from thousands of Ottoman subjects in the hinterland, down to the Neretva River.

The Ottomans never found a proper response to the constant and violent Uskok raids, which often left their defensive systems, communication networks, and economy in disarray. Skillfully using light boats, the Uskoks also plagued Venetian, Ragusan, and Jewish merchants, capturing valuable wares of "Ottoman" origin. Venice used her military to try to stop or curb these Uskok raids, but with little or no success. When Venice besieged key Habsburg strongholds in the area the Habsburg power itself was pushed into the conflict (the Uskok/Gradisca War fought in Istria and Friuli, 1615–1617). According to the stipulations of the Peace of Madrid (1617), the Uskoks were transferred from Senj to several small fortified places near the border, from where they continued with attacks on Ottoman territory, but with less serious consequences.

Nenad Moačanin

Further reading: Catherine Wendy Bracewell, *The Uskoks of Senj* (Ithaca, N.Y.: Cornell University Press, 1992).

V

vakanüvis *See* COURT CHRONICLES.

vakıf See *WAQF*.

Venice Ottoman-Venetian relations date back to the second half of the 14th century. The doge, the Venetian ruler, sent two ambassadors to congratulate MURAD I (r. 1362–89) for his conquest of Adrianople (EDIRNE). In 1384 the first Ottoman envoy reached Venice to discuss an improbable alliance against Genoa. A multitude of peace agreements followed; the earliest were concluded between the doge and Bayezid's sons, Prince Süleyman Çelebi (1403 and 1408), Prince Musa (1411), and in 1419 Sultan MEHMED I (r. 1413–21). Agreements with subsequent sultans included treaties after the Salonika war in 1430 and in 1454 after the CONQUEST OF CONSTANTINOPLE (1453); the renewal of earlier Venetian privileges in EGYPT in 1517; agreements after the CYPRUS war in 1573 and after the CRETAN WAR in 1670; the TREATY OF KARLOWITZ in 1699; and the treaty of Passarowitz in1718. The agreements were usually granted either at the ENTHRONEMENT AND ACCESSION of a new sultan or after a war.

Despite this extensive history of Ottoman-Venetian diplomacy, the two powers also had a history of military conflict. The first Ottoman-Venetian war was fought in 1416 at Gallipoli, where the Ottoman fleet was destroyed; from 1424 to 1430 the two powers fought for control of Salonika, and they came into conflict again in 1444 when the Venetians gave help to the crusader army. In 1453 the Venetians fought on the side of the losing BYZANTINE EMPIRE during the Ottoman siege of Constantinople. During conflicts from 1463–79 and 1499–1503, Ottoman *akıncı*, or raiding soldiers, attacked the Venetian land of Friuli, northeast of Italy. Five additional conflicts between the Venetians and the Ottomans were fought in the subsequent centuries (1538–40, 1570–73, 1644–69, 1684–99, 1714–18).

DIPLOMATIC RELATIONS

During their more than four centuries of contact, diplomatic relations between the powers were often strained. The Venetians had a residential diplomat (BAILO) in ISTANBUL and often sent ambassadors with particular missions. During the 16th century, diplomatic activity reached its peak, with almost one Ottoman envoy reaching Venice each year. Between the first diplomatic contact in 1384 and the final year of the Venetian Republic in 1797 about two hundred Ottoman envoys were sent to Venice, both by the central government and by provincial officials: some were ambassadors (*elçi*), others simple envoys (*çavuş, ulak*); some held the position of imperial interpreter. Some diplomatic missions were about the possibility of forming an alliance against common Christian foes. Most of these missions were not successful, but some resulted in meaningful alliances, as in the first half of the 17th century when the sultan, who desired to fight the Spaniards wherever possible, encouraged Ottoman volunteers to join the Venetian army.

The Venetians and the Ottomans also came into contact in the Balkans. In the second half of the 15th century the two states agreed on the creation of common borders, which they marked by heaps of stones or other devices. In 1479, for instance, a border was created in ALBANIA and in the Morea (Peloponnese). Beginning late in the 17th century, three borders were created in DALMATIA: the Nani in 1671; the Grimani in 1699–1700; and the Mocenigo in 1718–1720. With the TREATY OF KARLOWITZ, concluded in 1699 between the Habsburg Empire, Poland, and the Republic of Venice on one side and the Ottoman Empire on the other, the Ottomans recognized Venetian suzerainty over most of Dalmatia and Morea. The place where Habsburg, Venice, and the Ottoman Empire met was called Triplex Confinium. The point of contact was officially established on Debelo Brdo, a hill on Venetian land; however, the doge never accepted this decision and an unofficial "shepherds' border" remained in effect some miles away.

TRADE RELATIONS

While the Ottomans and Venetians were thoroughly engaged in both political and military terms, trade was nevertheless the most important link between Istanbul and Venice. Venetian merchants were present in the Levant, or the eastern Mediterranean, when it was still part of the BYZANTINE EMPIRE. In the beginning, Venetian cloth dominated Venetian exports and spices its imports, but as trade grew, Venetian merchants began to be more involved in the market for luxury goods. They exported falcons, dogs (large breeds at first, later replaced by lapdogs of the Bolognese breed), glass of all kinds (including slabs, spectacles, even glass feathers for turbans at the end of the 16th century), maps and printed Ottoman spelling-books, theriaca and other drugs, and gold and silver works. Likewise, Ottoman merchants found a lucrative market in Venice beginning largely at the start of the 16th century. In 1575 the Venetian government built a warehouse and lodging for the Ottoman merchants, the FONDACO DEI TURCHI; a larger one was created in 1621. Most Ottoman merchants trading in Venice came from the Balkans, but some, who sold cloth of camel's hair and Angora wool, came from central Anatolia. Members of the Ottoman elite found trade with Venice extraordinarily lucrative. Export of horses from the Ottoman Empire to Venice and export of weapons from Venice to the empire were forbidden, but smugglers enjoyed a flourishing trade in CONTRABAND nonetheless.

CULTURAL EXCHANGE

In addition to their formal political and military relationship and their trade ties, the Ottomans and Venetians were also connected by a number of influential Venetian subjects who developed careers in the Ottoman Empire. The Venetian jewel dealer Alvise (Lodovico) Gritti, for instance, was a friend of Sultan SÜLEYMAN I (r. 1520–66), to whom he sold a famous crown-helmet, and of Süleyman's grand vizier, Ibrahim Pasha. Gritti was sent by the sultan to serve as governor of HUNGARY (1530–34), where he was killed in 1534.

Although Gritti remained a Christian, other important Venetians in the Ottoman Empire converted to Islam. Among these were Venedikli Hasan Pasha (Andrea Celeste, d. 1591), governor or beylerbeyi of ALGIERS and kapudan pasha (grand admiral of the Ottoman navy), who was also the master of the renowned Spanish writer Miguel de Cervantes (1547–1616) when Cervantes was a slave. Another well-known convert was Gazanfer (d. 1603), of the Venetian Michiel family, who served as an Ottoman kapıağası, head of the servants of the inner palace, for about 30 years. The convert Mehmed Agha Frenkbeyoğlu (d. 1602), also known by his birth name, Marcantonio Querini, was the leader of the Ottoman sipahis (cavalry) during the 1600 rebellion; Gazanfer's nephew, Mehmed (Giacomo Bianchi), became one of the four favorite boon companions of MURAD IV (r. 1623–40).

Sometimes, however, Venetian involvement in Ottoman affairs is apocryphal; while there are rumors that Nur Banu (d. 1583), the mother of MURAD III (r. 1574–95), was born a member of the Venetian nobility, this story has no definite historical basis. The story of her noble birth circulated widely during her lifetime and was politically advantageous both for her and for the Venetian Republic. However, Nur Banu Sultan was probably of Greek origin and only a Venetian subject.

Culturally, the Ottomans provided a rich source of material for Venice. Its diplomats wrote reports, RELAZIONI, about their missions that ultimately became a literary genre unto itself; a famous Venetian painter, Gentile Bellini, went to Istanbul to make an official portrait of MEHMED II (r. 1444–46; 1451–81), and turbans and oriental dresses have always had a place in Venetian pictures. Books about the Turks were often printed in Venice, for instance, Francesco Sansovino's Gl'Annali Turcheschi in 1571, Giovanni Battista Donà's Della letteratura de Turchi in 1688, and Giovanni Battista Toderini's Letteratura turchesca in 1787. Recently an anonymous poem in honor of SELIM I (r. 1512–20) written in Veneto about 1518, has been discovered. Today Venetian place names serve as symbolic markers of these past relations, as for instance the Venetian Calle delle turchette, or street of little Turkish women.

The documents produced in the centuries of contact between these powers have been of great value to scholars interested in Ottoman history. The 19th-century historian Joseph von Hammer-Purgstall, for example, in his History of the Ottoman Empire (Geschichte des Osmanischen Reiches, Pest 1827–35) used Venetian sources at length. The greatest quantity of Ottoman documents in Europe is in the Venetian State Archives, and they remain an important source for historians.

Maria Pia Pedani

Further reading: Antonio Fabris, "From Adrianople to Constantinople: Venetian-Ottoman Diplomatic Missions, 1360–1453." *Mediterranean Historical Review* 7 no. 2 (Dec. 1992): 154–200; Suraiya Faroqhi, "The Venetian Presence in the Ottoman Empire (1600–1630)." *The Journal of European Economic History*, 15, no. 2 (1986): 345–384; Maria Pia Pedani, "The Ottoman Venetian Frontier," in *The Great Ottoman-Turkish Civilization*, vol. 1 (Ankara: Yeni Türkiye, 2000), 171–177; Hans Theunissen, "Ottoman-Venetian Diplomatics: the 'Ahd-names." *Electronic Journal of Oriental Studies* 1, no.2 (1998).

Vienna, sieges of (1529, 1683)   When, at the BATTLE OF MOHÁCS in 1526, the troops of Sultan SÜLEYMAN I (r. 1520–66) wiped out the Hungarian army and killed King Louis II of Jagiello (r. 1516–26), they cleared the way to the Hungarian throne for their main rival, the HABSBURGS. After Süleyman's protégé, John Szapolyai (r. 1526–40), was ousted from HUNGARY by his rival, Ferdinand I of Habsburg, also elected king of Hungary (r. 1526–64), Süleyman was eager to redress the unintended consequences of his victory at Mohács. The Ottoman army of 80,000 to 100,000 men retook Buda, Hungary's capital, from the Habsburgs in September 1529 and gave it back to their ally, King János. Süleyman, however, wanted to resolve the Habsburg-Ottoman rivalry in Central Europe by conquering Vienna, the capital of the Habsburgs' Danubian monarchy.

Vienna was defended by some 18,000 to 25,000 soldiers under the able leadership of Niklas Graf zu Salm and Wilhelm Freiherr von Roggendorf, who had had the city's obsolete medieval defenses substantially strengthened. The siege lasted for some two weeks from September 27 to October 15, 1529, but the Ottoman bombardment was not effective because the attackers had been forced to leave their siege artillery in Bulgaria and Hungary as a result of unusually rainy weather and muddy roads. The defenders discovered or disarmed most of the Ottoman mines, and when other Ottoman mines did succeed in opening large holes in the city's walls, the attackers were successfully repulsed by pikemen and arquebusiers. With winter approaching, and with it the traditional closing date of the campaign season (October 26), the Ottomans ended the siege.

After another failed attempt in 1532, when troops posted at the small Hungarian castle of Kőszeg (Güns) in western Hungary stopped Süleyman's army, the sultan and Ferdinand accepted the status quo in Hungary. Central Hungary was soon conquered (1541) and annexed to the Ottoman Empire. The northern and western parts of the country remained under Habsburg rule. By the 1570s the principality of TRANSYLVANIA, a semi-independent Ottoman client state, had emerged from the eastern ter-

ritories that lay outside the Ottomans' main route of conquest. Despite several wars between the Habsburgs and Ottomans in Hungary, the status quo changed little during the next 150 years until the early 1680s, when the Ottomans again decided to try to take Vienna.

In 1683 the Ottomans were again in front of the walls of the Habsburg capital. This represented a major change from the peaceful relations of the first half of the 17th century, which may be attributed to the Habsburg commitments in the Thirty Years' War (1618–48) and the protracted Ottoman-Venetian CRETAN WAR from 1645 to 1669. Hostilities broke out in the 1660s, a decade that saw a series of Ottoman conquests in Hungary (1660 and 1663), CRETE (1669), and POLAND-LITHUANIA (1672) under the remarkable leadership of KÖPRÜLÜ Mehmed Pasha (grand vizier 1656–61) and his son, Köprülüzade Fazil Ahmed Pasha (grand vizier 1661–76). Increased Ottoman military activity and capability were linked to the reforms introduced by the Köprülü grand viziers, which strengthened Istanbul's authority and improved its administrative and financial capabilities. The recent revival of Ottoman military fortunes and Vienna's conciliatory policy toward the Ottomans, exemplified by the Treaty of Vasvár (August 10, 1664), which acknowledged the latest Ottoman conquests in Hungary (Várad/Oradea in present-day Romania and Érsekújvár/Nové Zámky in present-day Slovakia), despite the decisive Habsburg victory at Szentgotthárd (August 1, 1664), were interpreted in ISTANBUL as signs of Habsburg weakness. Emperor Leopold's (r. 1658–1705) ineptness against Hungarian insurgents in the 1670s and, especially, Imre Thököly's successful insurrection (1681–83), which resulted in the establishment of yet another pro-Ottoman Hungarian client state, Thököly's Middle Hungarian Principality (1682–85) in Upper Hungary (present-day Slovakia) between the Habsburg-controlled Royal Hungary and Transylvania, an Ottoman client state, reinforced the Ottomans' perceptions of Habsburg vulnerability. The renewed Franco-Habsburg rivalry, caused by Louis XIV's (r. 1643–1715) policy of "reunions" and perceived Habsburg military weakness, persuaded Kara Mustafa Pasha (grand vizier 1676–83) that the time had come to challenge Vienna. As it turned out, his assessment of international politics and of Ottoman and Habsburg capabilities proved wrong.

Rumors of a possible Ottoman campaign against the Habsburgs circulated from the 1670s onward, but Kara Mustafa Pasha managed to secure the sultan's consent for his planned campaign only in August 1682. SULTAN MEHMED IV (r. 1648–87) and his army left EDIRNE, the former Ottoman capital, on April 1, 1683, and reached BELGRADE in early May, where the JANISSARIES, artillery, and the bulk of the provincial cavalry from Asia Minor and the Arab provinces joined the army. Sultan Mehmed decided to stay in Belgrade and appointed Grand Vizier Kara Mustafa Pasha commander in chief, who reached Vienna on July 14 with an army of about 90,000 men. Of the Ottoman vassals, only the CRIMEAN TATARS took part in the actual fighting.

Emperor Leopold and his court left Vienna on July 7 for Linz (in present-day Austria on the DANUBE RIVER) and Passau (in present-day Germany, on the Danube). The defenders of Vienna under Count Ernst Rüdiger von Starhemberg numbered some 16,000 men: 10,000 infantry and 6,000 cuirassiers. They were strengthened by 8,000 citizens and 700 university students fit for military service. The city's fortifications had been modernized in the 1670s and had been reinforced before the siege. Due to the indefatigable diplomatic maneuvers of Pope Innocent XI (1676–89), military assistance was also on its way from Poland, Bavaria, and Saxony.

After a failed preventive siege against Érsekújvár, the Habsburg forces, commanded by the talented Duke Charles of Lorraine (b. 1643–d. 1690), tried to secure the left bank of the Danube while waiting for the Polish allied troops. The latter were to join the relief army according to an "everlasting offensive and defensive alliance" signed in Kraków by the representatives of Emperor Leopold and Jan III SOBIESKI, king of Poland (r. 1674–96) on March 31, a day before the sultan left Edirne. The Habsburg and papal diplomacy also secured the participation of some 10,000 Bavarian troops and a like number of Saxon soldiers, led by the Elector of Bavaria, Maximilian II Emanuel (r. 1679–26) and the Elector of Saxony, Johann Georg III (r. 1680–91).

By July 15, Vienna had been encircled and cut off. On that day the siege began in earnest with heavy bombardment that lasted for the next two months. Throughout the siege, the Ottomans concentrated their attacks against the walls between the Burg Bastion and the Löbl Bastion. However, as in 1529, the Ottomans lacked heavy siege artillery; moreover, their 130 field guns and 19 medium-caliber cannons were insufficient against the defenders' 260 cannons and mortars. The defenders, however, lacked sufficient ammunition, explaining why only one to two shots per weapon were fired daily during the siege. Ottoman trench and mine attacks, in which the sultan's soldiers were expert, proved more effective than Ottoman bombardment. But the defenders stood firm, made frequent sorties, repaired the walls, and stopped the besiegers with hastily erected fortifications behind the breaches. It was not until September 2 that the besiegers were able take the Burg Ravelin, a defensive outwork in the moat. On September 6, another mine exploded under the Burg Bastion and the defenders, who had by this time lost about half their strength and were weakened by dysentery and a food shortage, expected a decisive final assault. Instead, Kara Mustafa paraded his army in front of the walls to force the surrender of the city. Had the grand vizier launched his final assault instead, he might have been able to take Vienna before the arrival of the relief army in early September.

The decisive battle took place on September 12 near Kahlenberg, at the edge of the Vienna Woods. The relief army of 75,000–80,000 men and 160 cannons was gathering northwest of Vienna. The troops from Bavaria, Saxony, Franconia, and Swabia numbered 35,000–40,000 and joined the imperial forces of 20,000 men under Lorraine. Arriving last, King Jan Sobieski's Polish troops numbered approximately 20,000 men.

Underestimating the strength of the relief army, Kara Mustafa Pasha left most of his Janissaries in the trenches and planned to destroy the allied Christian troops with a decisive cavalry charge. Although Ottoman chroniclers put the number of the Ottoman forces at Kahlengerg at 28,400 men, they must have reached some 50,000 men with the Tatar and other auxiliary troops. However, they were carrying only 60 field guns. Due to flawed INTELLIGENCE, Kara Mustafa expected the Christian attack on September 11 and ordered his soldiers to stay awake throughout that night, a fatal error.

Instead, the battle started at dawn on September 12 between the Ottoman advance forces and the Christian left wing under Lorraine near Nussberg. Lorraine's forces, strengthened by the Saxons, soon reached the Ottoman right wing. The Bavarians and Franconians also descended from the slopes further inland and joined the fight against the Ottoman right wing and the middle. Sobieski's Poles on the Christian right wing advanced slowly because of difficult terrain, but by early afternoon, the Polish vanguard had joined the fight. Although the Ottomans fought bravely, an overall Christian attack at around three o'clock decided the battle. The Ottoman left wing and the Tatars were unable to withstand the charge of the Polish cavalry and dragoons, who were the first to reach the Ottoman encampment from the west. By six in the evening, the Ottomans were defeated. Those who had not been slaughtered fled the battlefield, leaving ample booty for the Christians.

Vienna was saved by a coalition of Central European countries whose army proved to be tactically superior and, for the first time in the history of Ottoman-European confrontations, matched the Ottomans in terms of deployed manpower and weaponry, as well as in logistical support. Kara Mustafa's defeat led to his downfall and execution, soon followed by the dethronement of his master, Sultan Mehmed IV. More importantly, the 1683 campaign and the siege of Vienna provoked the creation of an anti-Ottoman coalition, the Holy League, established in the spring 1684 by Pope Innocent XI (pope 1876–89) and made up of the papacy, Poland, Austria, Venice, and (from 1686) RUSSIA. In the ensuing Long

War of 1684–99 between the Ottomans and the armies of the Holy League, the Ottomans lost Hungary, Sultan Süleyman's most prestigious conquest. Although the Ottomans were far from defeated, and the early 18th century saw Ottoman military resurgence and success as well as the limits of Habsburg military capabilities, the TREATY OF KARLOWITZ, which ended the Long War in 1699, signaled a new era in the history of Ottoman-European relations.

Gábor Ágoston

See also AUSTRIA; HUNGARY; MOHÁCS, BATTLE OF; SÜLEYMAN I.

Further reading: Thomas M. Barker, *Double Eagle and Crescent: Vienna's Second Turkish Siege and Its Historical Setting* (Albany, N.Y.: State University of New York Press, 1967); Michael Hochedlinger, *Austria's Wars of Emergence: War, State and Society in the Habsburg Monarchy, 1683–1797* (London: Longman, 2003); Ivan Parvev, *Habsburgs and Ottomans between Vienna and Belgrade, 1683–1739* (Boulder, Colo.: East European Monographs, 1995); John Stoye, *The Siege of Vienna*, 2nd ed. (Edinburgh: Birlinn, 2000).

vilaye See ADMINISTRATION, PROVINCIAL.

Vlachs (Eflak) The Vlach populations encountered by the Ottomans from about 1400 in the western Balkans were remnants of the inhabitants of the region from pre-Roman times. They made up the majority of the population of the northwestern parts of Bosnia, having migrated there between about 1530 and 1570 from present-day eastern Herzegovina, western Montenegro, and southwestern Serbia. They were mainly transhumant livestock breeders, organized in large families, clans and tribes. The Ottomans did not want the Vlachs to settle on the borderland, but there were no ordinary peasant colonists at the Ottoman state's disposal, so the Vlachs' occupation of the land was recognized by Istanbul in return for militia service and an annual tax. Until the late 16th century the Vlachs were mostly loyal to the Ottomans but later, when general conditions and their own status grew worse, many of them deserted to the Habsburs and Venetians, became brigands, or converted to Islam.

A pastoral group with a patriarchal social structure, the nomadic Vlachs had a strong influence on Ottoman borderland society in the northwestern regions of the empire. They were extensively recruited into the Ottoman military, typically in clan-like groups. Although they gradually integrated into surrounding cultures, primarily that of the south Slavic peoples, Vlach culture and family groupings gave rise to a number of other social and cultural groups within the empire, notably such auxiliary and military groups as the *voynuks* and

the MARTOLOS. The structure of the Vlach groups also helped shape the new systems of *kapudanlıks*, or captaincies, and the institution of *ocaklık timars* in the 17th century. The *kapudanlıks* were military and administrative districts that emerged in Bosnia around 1630 and gradually expanded in number until 1800. *Ocaklık timars* were semi-hereditary tenures of the provincial cavalry in Bosnia. The Vlachs' culture was also a source of many famous western Balkan epic songs.

The Vlachs were linguistically Romanized, but retained a distinct culture. By the early 15th century, the Vlachs appear to have set aside their indigenous language in favor of Slavic vernaculars and had started to merge with the south Slavic peoples. However, they held onto their own political traditions, elite groups, culture, and church. This process of merging was quite extended, depending on region, lasting from the 16th through the 19th century. The Vlach heritage has had a remarkable impact on modern Serbs, Croats, and Bosnians, who came to share the so-called "Balkan family pattern," a pattern visible in the wide area of the Vlach settlement, including the whole of present-day BOSNIA, Montenegro, ALBANIA, and Macedonia, most of Serbia, western BULGARIA, some parts of CROATIA, and parts of northwestern GREECE.

The transformation of the Vlachs was influenced and accelerated by the establishment of Ottoman rule in the region. Although the Vlachs served in the Ottoman military, until the first quarter of the 16th century, they entered this service in groups as military auxiliaries in rotation, rather than as individuals. This engagement en masse, in groups of about 30–40 called *cemaats*, or "combat units," has made it difficult to study the early history of the Vlachs as ethnic groups in the Ottoman Empire because early records deal almost exclusively with military units. Because such groups were bound to serve as auxiliaries or were still pure livestock breeders, and because Ottoman record makers, interested only in data related to the fiscal realm, seldom recorded ethnic or religious affiliations, only a small portion of the Vlach population was identified by this name (Eflakan) in Ottoman tax records and other documents. By the 18th century the *filori* tax (*filori* comes from *florin/forint* a gold coin used in the region and Hungary) was replaced almost everywhere by agricultural taxes, and the official designation *Eflak* had nearly died out. The authorities energetically opposed autonomous decision-making on levels higher than the village. The bulk of the Vlach population was thus hidden under the bureaucratic heading "one-ducat payers" (*filoriciyan*), their dues being mostly assigned to imperial domains. In addition to groups of "true" Vlach auxiliaries, many Vlach "one-ducat payers" joined in borderland warfare and raiding or in everyday plundering (cattle and captives were the main booty). Some moved to the Habsburg or Venetian side in order to obtain almost total tax exemption for serving as militias.

Unlike their policy toward nomads in Anatolia, the Ottomans did not try to force the Vlachs to form permanent settlements, because the Vlachs were already engaged in this process. Designations such as *Eflak reayası* (Vlach taxpaying subjects) and *Eflak keferesi* (Vlach infidels) appear after the early way of registration was abandoned, probably after *sipahi* (Ottoman provincial cavalry and landlord) pressure in the 1520s to prevent *reayas* from entering the military class. Ottoman sources often call Vlachs in general *Eflakan tayfası* (corps of Vlachs), which might convey the meaning of an order or corps. But Vlachs are never mentioned as *askeris*, that is, those who belonged to the privileged Ottoman classes and who did not pay taxes, as groups with similar duties would usually be categorized. It seems that they were simply too numerous to be included in the Ottoman *askeri* or military elite.

Nenad Moačanin

Further reading: Karl Kaser, *Familie und Verwandtschaft auf dem Balkan: Analyse einer untergehenden Kultur* (Wien-Köln-Weimar: Böhlau Verlag, 1995); Nenad Moačanin, "The Question of Vlach Autonomy Reconsidered," *Essays on Ottoman Civilization, Archív Orientální,* Supplementa VIII (1998), Praha 1998, 263–269 (Proceedings of the XIIth Congress of the CIEPO, Praha 1996).

W

wagon fortress (*Ger.: Wagenburg; Ottoman tabur;
Hung.: szekér tábor*) The wagon fortress or wagon
camp was a defensive arrangement of war carts chained
together, wheel to wheel, and protected by heavy wooden
shielding. Manned with bowmen and hand-gunners,
these late medieval "armored vehicles" protected against
cavalry assault. First used in the Bohemian civil war after
1419 by the Hussites (followers of the reforming theologian Jan Hus, 1369?–1415), the wagon fortress tactic was
introduced to the Ottomans by the Hungarians during
the 1443–44 Balkan campaign of the Hungarian national
hero János Hunyadi (1407?–1456). Hunyadi, then governor of Transylvania (then a frontier province in eastern
Hungary, now in Romania), employed some 600 wagons,
operated by Czech mercenaries, against the Ottoman
Turks. By the end of the conflict, the Ottomans knew
how to besiege the *tabur*, that is, the Christian wagon
camp, so called in Ottoman sources after the Hungarian usage, *szekér tábor*, or wagon camp. In the Battle of
Varna (November 10, 1444), the Ottomans defeated the
crusaders' army and captured the Christian war wagons
and weapons. While the speed with which the Ottomans
adapted their way of fighting to the tactic of their Christian adversaries is remarkable, it should not surprise
us, for the *wagenburg* tactic was not dissimilar from the
Turks' own fighting traditions. Moreover, the Turks of
western Anatolia also used fortified camps in the 14th
century. In 1313, for instance, a Turkish raiding party,
using the carts that transported the booty, erected such
a fortified camp against the Byzantines who had intercepted them.

Gábor Ágoston

Wahhabis (Muwahhidun) Wahhabis is the name that
outsiders give to followers of the radical Arabian Muslim
reformer Muhammad ibn Abd al-Wahhab, who began
preaching in the Najd in the 1740s, urging Muslims to
return to a strict and rigid practice of their faith. The
strength of the movement came from the skillful blending
of religious ideology and political aspirations represented
by the union between the family of ibn Abd al-Wahhab
and that of ibn Saud. When ibn Abd al-Wahhab incurred
the wrath of tribal leaders for his brand of austere Islam,
he found refuge with Muhammad ibn Saud in 1744 and,
together, they began to spread both a religious message
and the political power of ibn Saud. When Muhammad
ibn Saud died in 1765, the relationship between ibn Abd
al-Wahhab's radical Islam and Saudi political power continued, as ibn Saud was succeeded by his son Abd al-Aziz
as the political head of the movement.

In 1775 Wahhabi forces took the oasis village of
Riyadh, and most of the tribes of the Najd accepted the
House of Saud as the paramount chieftains of the region,
thereby establishing a tribal confederation under the
political leadership of the ibn Saud clan. Fresh from that
victory, they pressed on against the tribes of northern
Arabia and the al-Ahsa region, which borders the Persian
Gulf. The campaigns were successful and by 1788 most
of the tribes of northern and central Arabia had pledged
their fealty to Abd al-Aziz and to his son Saud after him,
further enlarging the tribal confederation.

Muhammad ibn Abd al-Wahhab died in 1793 and
the spiritual leadership of the movement passed to his
sons. Emboldened by the success of the Wahhabi warriors, Abd al-Aziz authorized raids against Basra in

1798 and in 1802 against the Shii holy cities of NAJAF and KARBALA, sending shock waves throughout Muslim world and resulting in the 1803 Shii assassination of Abd al-Aziz in revenge. The political leadership of the movement then passed to his son Saud. Seeking to turn a setback into victory, Saud ordered his men into the HEJAZ, taking the city of MECCA in 1803. MEDINA fell soon after. The Wahhabi occupation of the Holy Cities lasted until 1812 when they were driven out by an Egyptian expeditionary force led by Tosun Pasha. In 1814 Saud died and his son Abdallah succeeded him as the political leader of the movement. The Egyptian army, led by IBRAHIM PASHA, eventually pursued the Wahhabis into the Najd, finally taking their headquarters in the village of Diriyya in 1818. Abdallah was sent as prisoner to ISTANBUL where he was executed. But the Egyptian forces then withdrew from the Najd, allowing the Wahhabi movement to regroup and reassess its methods of proselytism.

In 1823 Turki ibn Abdullah, the cousin of Saud ibn Abd al-Aziz, assumed the leadership of the movement and was succeeded by his son Faysal on his death in 1834; Faysal, in turn, headed the movement until his death in 1865. Together, father and son recast the Wahhabi movement as one that was more ideological than political. They wrote extensively to Muslim scholars outside Arabia, describing and elaborating on the interpretations of Islam advanced by Muhammad ibn Abd al-Wahhab. They calculated that the first Wahhabi attempts at spreading their political control by force against those whom they considered to be apostate Muslims or infidels were unsuccessful in reforming Islam. Rather, they felt that it was time to articulate what they believed to be the correct interpretation of Islam and to convince other Muslims, through dialogue, to see the errors in their understanding of Islam's beliefs and practices.

With Faysal's death, however, political infighting in the ruling clan left the movement with a weak leader, and Faysal's son Abdullah was not able to hold together the coalition of tribes that his predecessor had been able control. Faysal's grandson, Abd al-Aziz, was able to regain some of his family's former prestige and in 1902 he reestablished the family's control over Riyadh and the central Najd. Abd al-Aziz was aware of the political instability inherent in relying on tribal warriors to advance political and religious aims. He embarked on a policy of forcing BEDOUIN tribesmen to settle in oases and become farmers. Those whom he settled were known as the Ikhwan, or brotherhood. The former nomads were provided with scholars to teach them the movement's message, and their sheikhs were required to study at a religious institute in Riyadh. At the same time, the tribes were given agricultural tools to encourage settlement.

Abd al-Aziz's vision was to create ties of loyalty to the movement based on religious faith which would transcend the tribal alliances that had formerly dominated the movement but had also kept it unstable. He took as his model the way that the Prophet Muhammad had used Islam to unite disparate tribes in his time. Abd al-Aziz imagined that the settlements would become the backbone of a resurgent political movement that would sweep Arabia, and that what he regarded as a corrupted form of Islam would be eliminated in the same way that the Prophet had destroyed pagan Arabia. From this socioreligious base, Abd al-Aziz emerged after WORLD WAR I to drive the Hashimite clan from the HEJAZ and establish the Kingdom of Saudi Arabia.

Although the term Wahhabi is typically used by outsiders to identify members of the group, those within the movement refer to themselves simply as Muslims, as they believe that they are practicing Islam as it was meant to be. Furthermore, they consider the name Wahhabi an affront to their beliefs because it honors their founder when they believe that all honor belongs solely to God and not to any mere mortal. Therefore the only acceptable name for them, in their view, is Muwahhidun, or "those who insist on the unity and uniqueness of God." They believe that it was God who laid down the path they follow through his Prophet Muhammad and that ibn Abd al-Wahhab simply reminded Muslims of where that true path lay.

Bruce Masters

See also IBN ABD AL-WAHHAB, MUHAMMAD.

Further reading: Madawi al-Rasheed, *A History of Saudi Arabia* (New York: Cambridge University Press, 2002).

Wallachia (Walachia; *Rom.*: Ţara Romanească; *Turk.*: Eflak)   Wallachia is a region in the southwestern part of present-day Romania, bordered by the Carpathian mountains to the north and the DANUBE RIVER to the south. Wallachia was a vassal voievodship or principality of the Ottoman Empire from 1394 through 1878, ruled first by *voievods* and later by princes. The inhabitants of Wallachia are Romanians. The formation of a Romanian state in Wallachia is mentioned for the first time in the gift-deed of Hungarian king Béla IV (r. 1235–70) in 1247 when he endowed the KNIGHTS OF ST. JOHN with the Banat of Szörény (Severin). The territory came under the control of the *voievod*, the territorial ruler, at the beginning of the 14th century. It declared its independence from HUNGARY in 1330 when the troops of Voievod Basarab (d. 1352), who was of Cumanian (Kipchak Turkic) origin, defeated the troops of the Hungarian king, Carol Robert of Anjou (r. 1307–42). Nevertheless, the vassal relationship with Hungary was soon reestablished and Wallachia itself confirmed Hungarian suzerainty when it felt threatened by Ottoman conquests along the DANUBE RIVER.

EARLY OTTOMAN-WALLACHIAN CONTACTS

The Wallachians first established contact with the Ottomans around 1365, when Voievod Vladislav Valicu (r. 1364–ca. 1377) turned against the Hungarian king, Louis the Great of Anjou (r. 1342–82), and allied himself with a ruler of one of the principalities of BULGARIA, Sraćimir, who fought against the Hungarians in alliance with the Ottomans. But the Ottoman advances in the Balkan alarmed local rulers. A considerable amount of booty was taken away by plundering Ottoman troops and the town of Silistra (present-day Bulgaria) was also lost. For a time, Wallachian Voievod Mircea cel Bătrîn (r. 1386–1418) successfully fought back Ottoman attacks. It was a rival voievod, Vlad (r. 1394–97), who first acknowledged Ottoman supremacy in 1394 and paid taxes to the Ottomans. In the Ottoman civil war of 1402–13 that followed Sultan BAYEZID I's (r. 1389–1402) defeat at the hand of TIMUR at the BATTLE OF ANKARA (1402), Voievod Mircea supported Prince Musa. However, when Sultan MEHMED I (r. 1413–21) emerged victorious and rebuilt the Ottoman polity, Mircea agreed to pay taxes again in 1415.

WALLACHIA BETWEEN EMPIRES, 15TH TO 17TH CENTURIES

The policy of Wallachia in the 15th century was defined by the fact that it was situated at the point where the authority of two competing military powers, the Hungarian Kingdom and the Ottoman Empire—both of them bigger and militarily stronger than Wallachia—clashed. Peace treaties between the Hungarian Kingdom and the Ottoman Empire from 1444 to 1519 mention both Wallachia and MOLDAVIA as vassal states, or areas under the jurisdiction of the larger polities that pay taxes to both parties. Escalating conflicts between the Hungarians and Ottomans resulted in fights for the throne in Wallachia, as both parties intended to put their candidates at the head of that country. Voievod Vlad Dracul (Devil) (r. 1436–46) fought against the Ottomans in the beginning but later recognized the sultan's authority. This in turn led to a Hungarian attack and caused the voievod's death. Vlad Tepeş (r. 1456–57, 1476) was supported by the Hungarian king, Matthias I Hunyadi (Corvinus, r. 1458–90), in his fight against MEHMED II (r. 1444–46, 1451–81), but later the Hungarian king imprisoned him. After his release, Vlad Tepeş recaptured his throne with Hungarian help, albeit only for a short time, as he was killed by a Romanian nobleman. Voievod Mihnea Turcitul (r. 1577–83, 1585–91) was replaced by another claimant to the post, Petru Cercel, in 1583 and was forced to live in exile first on the island of RHODES and then in TRIPOLI; he regained his position by promising larger taxes to the Ottomans in 1585. In 1591 he converted to Islam and was appointed head of the sancak (subprovince) of Niğbolu under the name Mehmed Bey.

The most outstanding voievod of Wallachia was Michael the Brave (Mihai Viteazul) (r. 1593–1601), who rose against Ottoman supremacy in alliance with a Christian league. He rendered homage to Sigismund Báthory (1581–1601), prince of TRANSYLVANIA (r. 1586–97, 1598–99, 1599–1061, 1601–02), and intruded into Ottoman Rumelia south of the Danube. In an alliance with Báthory he defeated Grand Vizier Koca Sinan Pasha at Giurgiu (October 29, 1595). Because of this victory, Wallachia avoided becoming an Ottoman province, although Saturcı Mehmed Pasha had already been appointed to the new province (vilayet) in April 1595 as governor-general. Michael the Brave occupied Transylvania and Moldavia in 1599 as the governor of the Habsburg emperor, Rudolf II. Alarmed by his growing power, Giorgio Basta, the general of the Habsburg emperor, drove him out of Transylvania; Michael was later pardoned by the emperor. Suspecting that he had offered his services to the Porte, General Basta had Michael killed in 1601.

Michael's pro-Habsburg policy was followed by Voievod Radu Şerban's (r. 1602–1611) similar policy. In the 17th century some voievods also made attempts to counteract the more powerful Ottoman influence, including Matei Basarab (r. 1633–54) and Şerban Cantacusino (r. 1678–88). In 1658 Constantin Şerban (r. 1654–58) joined forces with the prince of Transylvania, George II Rákóczi (r. 1648–60), and turned against the Ottoman army. Constantin Brâncoveanu (r. 1688–1714) profited from the relative passivity of the Ottomans and entered into relations with Vienna and later with the Russian czar, Peter I; for the latter relationship he was later executed in ISTANBUL.

To improve control over the two Romanian principalities, Wallachia and Moldavia, beginning in 1715 the Porte decided to appoint voievods from the PHANARIOTS, wealthy Greek families living in Istanbul's Phanar district. The Phanariots held influential positions in the Ottoman Empire, including that of rand DRAGOMAN (chief translator) of the court. Just as Muslim dignitaries at the Porte became heads of provinces and subprovinces as a reward for their services, Phanariots were appointed to the position of voievod in Romania for a couple of years. Romanian historiographers have traditionally viewed the Phanariot regime in negative terms; however, the Greek voievods—usually well educated at European universities—contributed significantly to the development of culture. The custom in Wallachia ended in 1821.

In the 18th century Wallachia was occupied by Habsburg and Russian troops on several occasions and its western part, called Oltenia, was under Habsburg jurisdiction between 1716 and 1739. After the Russo-Ottoman TREATY OF EDIRNE in 1829, Wallachia and Moldavia united under Russian control. Also stipulated in the agreement was that Wallachian merchants could now pursue their profession freely across the Balkans. In 1848 Ottoman and Russian troops suppressed a revolution that had aimed to achieve general civil rights and protested against Russian occupation. The Treaty of Paris in 1856 declared the union of the two Romanian states, the joint head of which became Alexandru Ioan Cuza in 1859. However, nominally it was still part of the Ottoman Empire. The last ties to the Ottoman Empire were cut by the Treaty of San Stefano in 1878 and later that year by the Treaty of Berlin, which declared Romania an independent country.

WALLACHIA UNDER OTTOMAN RULE

Wallachia was designated a *dar al-ahd* ("house of the treaty," or territory whose population is protected by the treaty) by the Ottomans and its subjects were DHIMMI, non-Muslims who enjoyed the protection of the Porte. Although archival sources are rather limited in this regard, it appears that until the beginning of the 16th century Wallachian *voievods* were given letters of contract by the sultan (AHDNAMES), similar to the ones given to the Moldavian *voievods*. Their vassal relationship and their tax burden were established in these letters of contract. Later, the *voievod* was chosen by the boyars (high-ranking members of the feudal aristocracy) and the Orthodox clergy and then confirmed by the sultan, who issued a formal written appointment (*berat-i humayun*). These documents specified the extent of the tax to be paid to the Ottoman treasury and contained the allowances to be paid to dignitaries at the Porte and to the grand vizier, without mentioning their amounts. The *berats* also declared that Muslims in Wallachia were not to be harassed and that in case of death their property was to be turned over to their families or to the Ottoman treasury, in case their family could not be located.

The extent of the tax changed according to the devaluation of the Ottoman silver coinage, the *akçe* (MONEY AND MONETARY SYSTEMS). In 1480 it was 14,000 golden coins; in 1564, 2,850,000 akçe (47,500 golden coins); in 1568/69: 5,850,000 akçe (83,500 golden coins); in 1574/75: 6,150,000 akçe (94,600 golden coins); whereas in 1583/84: 7,000,000 akçe (58,333 golden coins). The amount decreased gradually from the end of the 17th century. Besides their tax burden, the Wallachians were obliged to pay regular presents (*peşkeş*) and an unofficial bribery fee (*rüşvet*), the total sum of which was approximately as much as their taxes. Furthermore, the Wallachian economy was under complete Ottoman domination, depending mainly on the market conditions of Istanbul, although some cattle and sheep dealers made big fortunes.

The *voievod* himself was obliged to go to war along with the Ottoman troops if the sultan so ordered. Once every three years, the country's taxes were taken to the Porte by the *voievod* himself. Some of the *voievods'* sons or close relatives were held as hostages in Istanbul by the Porte. The *voievods* sent regular reports, written in Turkish, to Istanbul about European affairs, some of which are still extant. Wallachia's status as a Christian vassal state of the Ottoman Empire allowed it to play an important part in the survival and development of the Orthodox religion and culture in southeastern Europe.

Sándor Papp

Further reading: Mihai Maxim, *Romano-Ottomanica: Essays and Documents from the Turkish Archives* (Istanbul: Isis, 2001); Andrei Oţetea, ed., *The History of the Romanian People* (Bucharest: Scientific Publishing House, 1970); Peter Sugar, *Southeastern Europe under Ottoman Rule, 1354–1804* (Seattle: University of Washington Press, 1977); Sándor Papp, "Christian Vassals on the Northwest Border of the Ottoman Empire," in *The Turcs,* vol. 3, *Ottomans.* (Ankara: Yeni Türkiye, 2002) 719–730.

wall tiles   *See* CERAMICS.

waqf (**Turk.: vakıf**)   A *waqf* is an endowment under Islamic law, or SHARIA, that benefits a pious cause by setting aside a personal source of revenue to finance the charitable cause in perpetuity. Within the Ottoman Empire, the institutions endowed by *waqf* contracts included religious structures such as mosques, madrasas, and Sufi hostels. Some of the complexes established as *waqf* were quite extensive, such as the complex that Sultan SÜLEYMAN (r. 1520–66) endowed in Istanbul, the Süleymaniye. Designed by the architect Sinan and built between 1550 and 1557, the complex included a large mosque, several madrasas, a hospital, and markets that supplied the income to support these institutions. Other large complexes were endowed by members of the Ottoman royal family and by Ottoman governors in various provincial centers. In addition to religious functions, *waqf* endowments could support institutions that would benefit the community of Muslims at large, such as soup kitchens for the poor, hospitals, insane asylums, and CARAVANSARIES for travelers. Typically, the source of income that was alienated from the *waqf* donor's private property consisted of commercial properties: shops, factories for the production of textiles or soap, BATHHOUSES, even whole market complexes if the donor were rich and powerful. But private homes were also so designated by less wealthy Muslims, with their rent being used to help in the ongoing upkeep of the institution. Revenues from agricultural properties could also be alienated under *waqf* contracts and, in the Ottoman period, whole classes of tax revenue, such as the *jizya* paid by the Christians of Bethlehem, could also be designated to support the upkeep of *waqf* properties

For the donor, the benefit of establishing a *waqf* was two-fold. First, he or she (in the Ottoman Empire wealthy women were prominent in the establishment of *waqfs*) would gain merit from God and the prayers of the believers who used the facilities that they had endowed. Second, the property would be exempted from taxation, confiscation, or division among potentially multiple heirs at the time of the donor's death. In addition, each *waqf* contract could designate an administrator who was entitled to a salary. The administrator was often the endower or his or her descendants; a *waqf* could thus provide substantial income for the donor as well as for the charitable enterprise.

Under the terms of sharia as it was practiced in the Arab provinces, there were two acceptable forms of *waqf*. The first was the *waqf khayri* that established a pious cause, such as those already mentioned, as the object of the endowment. The second was the *waqf ahli* which also ultimately had a pious cause, but not until the founder and all his descendants had died. The latter type of *waqf* was the object of some controversy among legal scholars as some saw it as simply serving as a tax shelter and a way of cutting certain family members out of the inheritance schedule established by the Quran, which provided daughters with half the share of their father's inheritance that their brothers received. Typically, for example, many such contracts eliminated daughters as recipients of the income generated by the *waqf*. But there were also cases of women endowing a *waqf* and then naming a female descendant as the endowment's supervisor. Another controversy arose over the acceptability of establishing cash *waqfs*. In these cases, the *waqf* would consist solely of a sum of money, the principal of which would be lent out to creditors. The interest paid on the loans would go to support the charitable cause. Most Arab jurists saw this as allowing usury and rejected it as un-Islamic. Ottoman jurists in Istanbul, however, saw nothing wrong with the practice as long as the interest did not exceed 10 percent a year and the recipients of the charity were truly needy.

Waqfs of all sizes were an extremely popular investment choice, for both spiritual and material gain. They funded the construction of new mosques and marketplaces that gave an Ottoman architectural stamp to almost every city in the empire, as Ottoman governors in provincial centers constructed mosques in the style of the grand mosques built in the capital by the sultans. Without the institution, it is hard to imagine that the incredible building boom that the empire enjoyed in the 16th century would have occurred. Furthermore, *waqf*-funded charities provided support for the urban poor that the central government was usually unwilling to provide. Besides feeding the poor, there were *waqfs* to help bridegrooms with the customary bride price (*mahr*), to fund education for poor Muslims, to provide water to neigh-

borhoods, and even to feed street cats. Non-Muslims also established *waqfs*, although typically Muslim jurists would not permit them to fund non-Islamic religious institutions such as churches or synagogues. They could, however, fund charities for the community's poor and needy, and Muslim judges even allowed Christian *waqfs* to support the upkeep of indigent monks who devoted their lives to prayer.

Bruce Masters

See also CHARITY.

Further reading: Amy Singer, *Constructing Ottoman Beneficence: An Imperial Soup Kitchen in Jerusalem* (Albany: State University of New York Press, 2002); Richard van Leeuwen, *Waqfs and Urban Structures: The Case of Ottoman Damascus* (Leiden: Brill, 1999).

War Academy *See* EDUCATION.

warfare Historians have often argued that warfare was the Ottomans' raison d'être—their justification for the empire's existence. They consider the Ottomans' hundred-year-long expansion in the Balkans—which had started in 1352 with the establishment of the first Ottoman bridgehead on the Gallipoli peninsula—and the CONQUEST OF CONSTANTINOPLE in 1453, their first major success, as manifestations of Ottoman imperialism.

Before one goes too far with such claims, it is advisable to remember that the same years witnessed the Hundred Years' War (1337–1453) in Europe, waged for very similar goals—land and glory—between ENGLAND and FRANCE. More importantly, for most of the 600 years of the existence of the Ottoman Empire (1300–1923), wars were common and a normal part of life in both the Ottoman Empire and Europe. The early modern age, roughly 1450–1800, was especially bellicose. Apart from 25 years in the 16th century and seven years in the next century, European powers were constantly at war with each other in these two centuries. In the 17th century, Sweden and the Austrian Habsburgs waged wars for two out of every three years, while SPAIN fought for three out of every four years.

Wars also dragged on for long periods and involved several, and often all, major European powers. The Eighty Years' War, also known as the Dutch Revolt (1568–1648), the Thirty Years' War (1618–48), the War of the Spanish Succession (1701–14), the War of the Austrian Succession (1740–48), the Seven Years' War (1756–63), the French Revolutionary Wars (1792–1802), and the Napoleonic Wars (1804–15) were especially notable with ever-growing war casualties.

From about 1500 on, the impact of wars on the population was felt more than ever before, due to protracted conflicts and ever larger armies who not only had to be paid and fed, but who also habitually ravaged the countryside. In the 16th and 17th centuries, 20–30 percent death rates in armies were not uncommon. While estimates regarding the death toll of these European conflicts vary greatly, when one includes civilian deaths from famine and disease, even the lowest figures exceed several millions for such long conflicts as the Thirty Years' War or the Napoleonic Wars. Against this background, the Ottomans do not seem to have been particularly belligerent. The "Turkish wars," as these wars were known in Europe, and the destruction caused were not unique either.

From an Ottoman point of view, the 16th century was an era of rivalry with Habsburg Spain and AUSTRIA in the Mediterranean and in HUNGARY, and with Safavid IRAN in eastern Asia Minor, Azerbaijan and IRAQ. In the 16th century the Ottomans usually proved militarily superior to their rivals, at least on land, but the 17th century saw a change in Ottoman military fortunes and by the end of that century the Ottomans lost Hungary to the Habsburgs. The latter, however, were not strong enough to push further with their conquests in the Balkans and a new border between the Austrian Habsburg Monarchy and the Ottoman Empire was established along the DANUBE RIVER. On their eastern front, the Ottomans consolidated their conquests against Safavid Iran. Their common border, established in 1555 and modified in 1639, proved exceptionally stable until WORLD WAR I. The 18th century witnessed the emergence of a new rival, RUSSIA, which by the second half of the century humiliated the Ottoman military forces (RUSSO-OTTOMAN WAR OF 1768–74). The 19th century witnessed repeated Ottoman defeats at the hands of the Russians as well as Ottoman retreat from and Russian advance in the Balkans. Of course, all these events reflected major changes with regard to the military (and thus economic and administrative) capabilities of the Ottomans and their rivals; prompted major Ottoman military, economic, and administrative reforms; and had significant consequences on the inhabitants of the empire.

THE EARLY OTTOMAN MILITARY

In the early years of the Ottoman state, the main constituent elements of the Ottoman army were the ruler's military entourage or guard; the cavalry troops of Turkoman tribes who had joined forces with the Ottomans; and those peasants who had been called up as soldiers for military campaigns. The members of the military entourage, known as *kul* (slave) and *nöker* (companion, client, servant, retainer), were the forerunners of the sultans' salaried troops that by the 15th century had become the pillar of the Ottoman military organization. The troops of the Turkoman tribes that were in alliance with the Otto-

mans received a share of military booty and were granted the right to settle on conquered lands. In return, they had to provide men-at-arms in proportion to the amount of benefice in their possession. Later they became the fief-based provincial cavalry (*timar*-holding or *timariot sipahi*), whose remuneration was secured through military fiefs or prebends (*timar*).

Like the Seljuk *iqta* and the Byzantine *pronoia* fiefs, the main function of the Ottoman *timar* was to pay the troops and bureaucracy. The military fiefs were also used by the Ottomans to incorporate conquered peoples into the military-bureaucratic system of the empire. Ottoman revenue surveys (*tahrir*) from the 15th-century Balkans recorded large numbers of Christian *timariot*s who, by accepting the new order and by performing military and bureaucratic services for the Ottoman state, managed to preserve, at least partly, their former *pronoia*s (military fiefs) and *bashtina*s (small hereditary possessions) as well as their privileged status within the society. Many of these Balkan Christian *timariot*s and their sons were called *voynuk*s (Slavic for "fighting man" or "soldier"). These *voynuk*s were former members of the pre-Ottoman minor nobility who retained part of their *bashtina*s as *timar*s in exchange for military service. Established perhaps in the 1370s or 1380s, *voynuk*s were to be found in significant numbers in BULGARIA, SERBIA, Macedonia, Thessaly, and ALBANIA. In addition, large numbers of Christian nomads in the Balkans, called VLACHS, were also incorporated into the ranks of the *voynuk*s.

Since the salaried troops of *kul*s and the *timariot* cavalry proved too few in number to fulfill the needs of a growing state, young volunteer peasant boys were also taken on. These youths later formed the infantry *yaya* (foot soldier) and cavalry *müsellem* (exempt from taxes) units. During campaigns they were paid by the ruler, and at the conclusion of the campaign season they returned to their villages. The numerous campaigns and predatory raids soon required that this third component of the early Ottoman army be made permanent; the voluntary nature of the force was therefore abandoned and compulsory enlistment was introduced during campaigns.

THE STANDING ARMY

Sultan MURAD I (r. 1362–89) introduced numerous changes in the organization of the salaried troops, which did not affect the *timar*-holding *sipahi*s. The *müsellem*s were slowly replaced by the palace horsemen, who were also called *sipahi*s, and the *yaya*s' place was taken by the *azab*s—a kind of peasant militia of originally unmarried (*azab*) lads serving as foot soldiers in campaigns—and by the JANISSARIES. The infantry *azab*s received their military gear from a certain number of tax-paying subjects (*reaya*). As a result, by the mid-15th century the *yaya*s and *müsellem*s, along with the *voynuk*s, gradually became auxiliary forces, charged with the restoration of military roads and bridges and, after the spread of cannons, with the transportation of ordnance. While the *müsellems* were serving in both Anatolia and Rumelia, the *yayas'* task in Rumelia was carried out by the *yürüks*, nomadic Turks originally from Anatolia. Their resettlement from Anatolia into the Balkans was part of the Ottoman method of deportation (*sürgün*) which aimed at increasing the numbers of both the available Turkish fighters and of loyal subjects in the newly conquered peninsula.

The most important change in the 14th-century Ottoman military organization was the establishment of the Janissary corps (from the Turkish term *yeni çeri*, or "new army"), the sultans' salaried elite infantry. It was the first standing army in Europe and stood under the direct command of the sultan. The Janissaries and the salaried palace cavalrymen were known as the slaves of the Sublime Porte (*kapı kulu*), that is, the standing army of the ruler. The sultans thus could claim a monopoly over organized violence, in sharp contrast to their European counterparts who had to rely upon and negotiate with local power-holders when they wanted to deploy armies that were operationally effective. Although the standing army was important, until the beginning of the 16th century the leading force of the Ottoman military was the freelance light cavalry, the *akıncıs* (raiders), descendants of early raiders who fought in return for their share of the war booty.

Reliable estimates with regard to both resource potentials and actually deployed troops are hard to come by. However, it is certain that until the end of the 17th century the Ottomans outnumbered their opponents both in Europe and in the Middle East. With vassals, MEHMED II (r. 1444–46, 1451–81), SELIM I (r. 1512–20), and SÜLEYMAN I (r. 1520–66) could mobilize 70,000 to 80,000 men or more, whereas their neighbors were capable of mobilizing only a fraction of that force.

The Ottomans also showed genuine interest and great flexibility in adopting European weaponry and tactics. They not only adopted FIREARMS at an early stage of the development of their armed forces (in the latter part of the 14th century) but were also successful in integrating gunpowder weaponry into their military by establishing a separate artillery corps as part of the sultans' standing army in the early 15th century. In Europe, artillerymen remained a transitory category somewhere between soldiers and craftsmen well into the 17th century. When Ottoman technological receptivity was coupled with mass-production capabilities, self-sufficiency in the manufacturing of weapons and ammunition, and superior Ottoman logistics, the sultans' armies gained superiority over their European opponents by the mid-15th century, which they were able to maintain until about the end of the 17th century.

CONQUESTS AND IMPERIAL OVERSTRETCH

The 15th and 16th centuries were an era of spectacular conquests and territorial expansion. The area of the empire increased from 218,000 square miles in 1451 at the death of MURAD II (r. 1421–44, 1446–51) to 335,000 square miles by the death of Mehmed II in 1481. On August 23, 1514, at the Battle of Çaldıran (eastern Turkey), Selim I's artillery and Janissary musketeers routed the army of Safavid Iran. In 1516 the Ottomans annexed eastern Anatolia and annihilated the Mamluk army at Marj Dabik, north of ALEPPO. In 1517, at the Battle of Ridaniyya near CAIRO, Selim I defeated the last ruler of the MAMLUK EMPIRE, Tumanbay (r. 1516–17), and proceeded to establish his rule over EGYPT and SYRIA. By the end of his reign, Selim I ruled over an empire of 577,000 square miles. Süleyman's conquests added Hungary, Kurdistan, Iraq, and the greater part of ARMENIA; with these new conquests the area of the Ottoman Empire reached almost 978,000 square miles.

These conquests would have been unthinkable without the support of the Ottoman NAVY, whose size was already impressive under Mehmed II. He employed some 280 galleys and other ships in his naval expeditions against the Greek island of Euboea in the Aegean in 1470 (then known as Negroponte and in Venetian hands), and some 380 ships against the Genoese-administered Crimean port town of CAFFA (Ukrainian Feodosiya) in 1475. The conquest of Egypt (1517) and the fact that it thereafter provided about one-third of the empire's total revenues made it imperative that the Ottomans controlled the maritime lines of communication between Cairo and ISTANBUL and eliminated all hostile bases in the eastern Mediterranean. The conquest of RHODES (1522), the base of the belligerent KNIGHTS OF ST. JOHN, and later CYPRUS (1570, then in Venetian hands), were thus strategically necessary. Co-opting the corsairs of the BARBARY STATES of ALGIERS and TUNIS was a smart and economically efficient way to further strengthen the Ottoman navy. In 1533 Süleyman appointed Hayreddin Barbarossa (*see* BARBAROSSA BROTHERS), an experienced corsair and governor of Algiers, as his grand admiral (*kapudan pasha*); Hayreddin's successes helped the Ottomans become masters of the eastern Mediterranean.

However, by the late 16th century the Ottoman army reached the limits of its reach. Power relations on all fronts were more balanced, which made wars longer and increasingly exhausting. Of these, the Long Hungarian War (1593–1606); the war in TRANSYLVANIA (1658–60); the war against the Holy League (1683–99) on the Hungarian frontier; the Iranian wars (1570–92, 1603–11, and 1623–39) on the eastern frontier; and the CRETAN WAR (1645–69) in the Mediterranean required commitments in fighting men, weaponry, supplies, and money at scales previously unheard of. Since none of the frontier provinces were capable of defending themselves by using merely local revenues, the defense of the empire's extended borders also became more and more costly. From 1592 on, the imperial treasury ended almost every fiscal year with a deficit, which is hardly surprising in light of the fact that the Ottomans waged wars continuously from 1579 through 1611 (against Habsburg Austria, Safavid Iran, and the Anatolian rebels of the CELALI REVOLTS).

The 17th century also saw the eclipse of the *timariot sipahi* cavalry and the deterioration of the military skills of the once-formidable Janissaries. The DEVŞIRME or child levy, once the main method of Janissary recruitment, also lapsed. By the end of the 17th century, due to extensive military and related administrative and financial reforms in Europe, the Ottomans' European opponents established their own standing armies that were comparable in size to that of the Ottomans. In addition, these European troops were of higher quality, enjoyed an efficient supply system, better command, and a professional military bureaucracy. The loss of Hungary by 1699 was the first sign of major shifts in power.

RETREAT AND REFORM

Ottoman military history in the 18th and 19th centuries is dominated by the Russo-Ottoman wars, the slow but continuous loss of territory until the late 19th century, followed by the collapse of Ottoman rule in the Balkans at the end of that century, as well as repeated efforts to modernize the Ottoman armed forces and government.

The wars fought against the traditional enemies of the Ottomans (VENICE, Austria, and Iran) in the first half of the century brought mixed results, while the wars against the Russians in the second half of the century ended in a series of devastating defeats. In the first half of the century, failure on the battlefield led to domestic political unrest; there were two rebellions, resulting in the dethroning of two Ottoman sultans (MUSTAFA II (r. 1695–1703) in 1703 and AHMED III (r. 1703–1730) in 1730). In the second half of the century the price of failure was even higher: exploiting the absence of the army—which was weighed down on the Russian front—provincial notables (AYAN), whose power rested in part on their public function and in part on land ownership (*çiftlik*), acted independently of the central government. By the end of the century some of them, including ALI PASHA OF JANINA, OSMAN PAZVANTOĞLU of Vidin, and the Karaosmanoğlu family of western Anatolia, were in possession of their own private fiefdoms and armies and had even begun to pursue their own foreign policy. At the beginning of the 19th century, the central administration lost control of many of the empire's outer zones: the WAHHABIS, led by the Saudi emirs, took control of the HEJAZ (MECCA and MEDINA, 1803–14). Meanwhile

Ottoman power in Egypt was challenged by the Mamluk emirs and by the invasion of the French (1789–1802). Finally, in 1805, MEHMED ALI, an Albanian mercenary of the Sublime Porte, seized power in Egypt. Relying upon his European-style army, Mehmed Ali was to remain in power for 40 years. Even in the Ottoman core provinces, the Balkans and Anatolia, Istanbul's rule was under threat. The Serb uprising of 1804 marked the beginning of a series of wars of national liberation. By the late 1820s, SERBIA and GREECE, as well as Egypt, had become effectively independent.

The empire tried to respond to the situation by experimenting with other forms of recruitments and military systems ranging from militias to state contracted formations, leading to Sultan SELIM III's (r. 1789–1807) Nizam-i Cedid (New Order) army. Launched in the aftermath of the Russo-Ottoman War of 1787–92, the military (and associated financial and administrative) reforms of Selim III resulted in a new, disciplined, European-style army equipped with up-to-date weaponry and dressed in modern uniforms. Financed from an independent treasury (Irad-ı Cedid, "new revenues"), the new army was 23,000 strong by 1807, when opposition mounted by an alliance of the Janissaries and the religious establishment (ULEMA) forced Selim III to disband it and abdicate.

However, the RUSSO-OTTOMAN WARS in the 19th century (1806–1812, 1828–1829, 1854–1856, and 1877–1878), with which Russia tried to achieve its main geopolitical goal to secure access to the Mediterranean through the Black Sea and the Straits of the Bosporus and Dardanelles, proved time after time the inferiority of the Ottoman military. These military setbacks forced Istanbul to undertake more substantial military, governmental, and financial modernization, culminating in the TANZIMAT reforms (1839–76).

MAHMUD II (r. 1808–39) continued his deposed predecessor's reforms, and when he felt secure enough he disbanded the unruly Janissaries in 1826. Their dismal performance against the Greek guerrillas in the first phase (1821–26) of what later became known as the GREEK WAR OF INDEPENDENCE (1821–31) sealed the fate of the Janissaries. On June 15, 1826, when the Janissaries rose in rebellion against the sultan's project that aimed at reforming their corps, Mahmud II ordered his modernized artillery corps to bombard the Janissaries' Istanbul barracks. Most of the Janissaries were slaughtered (*see* AUSPICIOUS INCIDENT), and the next day the corps was officially disbanded. The sultan announced the formation of his new, European-style army, the Trained Victorious Troops of Muhammad (Muallem Asakir-i Mansure-i Muhammadiye). Recruited from volunteers and peasants from the provinces, the new army was trained and organized along European lines, and grew quickly from 1,500 to 27,000 men. Along with the Mansure army, Mahmud established a modern imperial guard, known as the Hassa (Special) army, numbering some 11,000 by the end of his reign. In 1834 the sultan also created a reserve army, known as the Victorious Reserve Soldiers (Asakir-i Redife-i Mansure), or Redif, whose number grew to 100,000 men in 1836. Stationed in the provinces, they were responsible for maintaining law and order.

The next crucial step in overhauling the Ottoman army was the introduction of universal conscription along European lines. The need to reform the old recruitment methods was first expressed in the Gülhane Imperial Edict (1839), the famous reform charter that introduced the wide-ranging Tanzimat reforms. This in turn led to the army regulations of 1843 that established the modern Nizamiye (Regular) army, using conscription. The first conscription took place in 1848. Because the army's strength was determined at 150,000 men and conscripts initially had to serve for five years, every year some 30,000 men had to be conscripted. The empire's armed forces were divided into five territorial armies (the Guard, Istanbul, the European Provinces, Anatolia, and the Arab provinces) each with its own Redif, or reserve. While there were further fine-tunings in the coming years, the structure of the Ottoman army remained basically the same until the BALKAN WARS in 1912–13.

Most of the soldiers were Muslim peasants from Anatolia, for non-Muslims were able to avoid military service by paying an exemption tax (bedel-i askeri, or military payment-in-lieu), despite the 1856 edict that gave equal rights to and demanded equal service from all the sultan's subjects, regardless of religion. This system remained unchanged until the YOUNG TURKS introduced universal conscription irrespective of religion in 1909.

Due to lack of comprehensive censuses, adequate administrative infrastructure, and privileges enjoyed not only by non-Muslims but also by Muslim town-dwellers and members of certain professions (e.g., civil servants, the religious establishment), the size of the Ottoman army was modest in comparison to that of its rivals. Its peacetime strength of 180,000–200,000 men on the eve of World War I was only half the size of the Austrian army, and perhaps one-fifth the size of the Russian armed forces.

More importantly, the Ottomans, once self-sufficient in the production of weaponry and ammunition and masters of campaign logistics, struggled to pay and supply their armies throughout the 19th century. Mobilization was slow and desertion high. Soldiers suffered from malnutrition, and more died of cholera or typhus than of wounds. The underdeveloped Ottoman industry and transportation infrastructure (railways, roads, and waterways) could not support the mass army the Ottomans managed to put together through modern means of conscription. It was these shortcomings— and not the fighting spirit and skills of the Ottomans, which was admired by their enemies as late as World War I—that were mainly responsible for the many defeats the Ottomans suffered in the 19th century.

Gábor Ágoston

See also CRIMEAN TATARS; CRIMEAN WAR; GHAZA; LEPANTO, BATTLE OF; MILITARY ACCULTURATION; MILITARY SLAVERY; TERSANE-I AMIRE.

Further readings: Gábor Ágoston, *Guns for the Sultan: Military Power and the Weapons Industry in the Ottoman Empire* (Cambridge: Cambridge University Press, 2005); Virginia H. Aksan, *Ottoman Wars 1700–1870: An Empire Besieged* (Harlow, England: Longman/Pearson, 2007); Rhoads Murphey, *Ottoman Warfare* (New Brunswick, N.J.: Rutgers University Press, 1999); Erik J. Zürcher, ed., *Arming the State: Military Conscription in the Middle East and Central Asia, 1775–1925* (London: I.B. Tauris, 1999).

weights and measures Before the rise of the Ottomans, a variety of weights and measures—the Central Asian Turkish, the Seljukid, the Byzantine, and the Ilkhanid-Iranian—were in use in Anatolia. The Ottoman imperial metrological system apparently owed its formation to a combination of Turkish, Islamic, and local traditions. Turks of Central Asia were already familiar with a measuring system based on the *arşın* (a unit of length) and the *batman* (a unit of mass), a system they brought along to Anatolia in the 11th century. The *Divan-ı Lugati't-Türk* (the 11th-century Turkish encyclopedic dictionary prepared by Mahmud of Kaşgar) refers to measures such as the *batman*, *kulaç* (fathom), and *karış* (span), which were later used by the Ottomans. Seljukid and Italian sources of the early 14th century indicate that the *batman*, *lidre*, *okka*, *kantar* and *kile* were the commonly used weights and measures in Seljukid Asia Minor before the rise of the Ottomans. In fact, the Seljuk weights *okka* (*ukiyya*) and *dirhem* were later reinstituted and used by the Ottomans. Byzantine measures were also introduced into Ottoman metrology: the Ottoman *lidre* of 100 dirhems was identical to the Byzantine *litra* or *ratl Rumi*. The Iranian-Ilkhanid weights and measures used by the chanceries of pre-Ottoman Anatolian states in keeping public records also became part of Ottoman metrology.

COMMON WEIGHTS AND MEASURES

Together with the Islamic weights and measures, the Ottomans inherited the duodecimal, or base 12, character of the Islamic measuring system, meaning that weights and measures were generally divisible by 12. This offered the most efficient and practical means in accounting and transactions since divisibility into fractions is highest in a duodecimal system, a structure also used extensively by the Roman, Byzantine, and Perso-Arabic cultures. Within this structure, Ottoman imperial and local metrologies followed a serial arrangement with 12 and its fractions or multiples established as follows: 1 *kadem* (foot) = 12 *parmak* (fingers) = 144 *hatt*. In addition, the *zira* (*arşın*) was the basic unit for length to measure land and in the construction of buildings. Imported textiles were measured in *çarşı arşını* while indigenous fabrics were measured in *endaze*. The measure of capacity, the *kile* (*mudd*), was used for cereals. Heavy goods were weighed in *çeki* (especially wood), *kantar*, *batman*, *kıyye*, or *lodra*. Fine goods such as silver, gold, and precious stones were weighed in *miskal*, *dirhem*, *kirat*, *buğday*, and *denk*.

METRIC EQUIVALENTS OF 19TH-CENTURY OTTOMAN WEIGHTS AND MEASURES

Length

1 *kadem* = 37.9 cm = 14.92 inches
1 *parmak* / *üsbü* = 3.2 cm = 1.26 inches
1 *hatt* = 0.26 cm = 0.1 inches
1 *nokta* = 0.02 cm = 0.01 inches
1 *zira* / *zira-ı mimari* / *bina arşını* / *mimar arşını* = 75.8 cm = 2.46 feet = 0.82 yards
1 *çarşı arşını* = 68 cm = 2.2 feet = 0.74 yards
1 *rub* (of *çarşı arşını*) = 8.5 cm = 3.35 inches
1 *kirah* (of *çarşı arşını*) = 4.25 cm = 1.67 inches
1 *endaze* = 45 cm = 1.46 feet = 0.49 yards
1 *rub* (of *endaze*) = 8.125 cm = 3.2 inches
1 *kirah* (of *endaze*) = 4.0625 cm = 1.6 inches
1 *merhale* = 45.480 km = 28.26 miles
1 *berid* = 22.740 km = 14.13 miles
1 *saat* / *fersah-ı kadim* / *fersah-ı adi* = 5.685 km = 3.53 miles
1 *mil-i adi* = 1.895 km = 1.18 miles
1 *kulaç* / *bağ* = 1.895 m = 6.217 feet
1 *çörek parmak* = 3.15 cm = 1.24 inches
1 *dönüm* = 1600 square *zira* = 919. 3025 sq.m = 1099.47 sq. yards
1 *evlek* = 229.8 sq.m = 274.83 sq. yards

Volume

1 *kile-i istanbuli* = 37 liter = 65 pints
1 *şinik* = 9.25 liter = 16.27 pints
1 *kutu* = 4.625 liter = 8.14 pints
1 *zarf* = 2.3125 liter = 4.07 pints

Weight

1 *çeki* = 225.8 kg = 497.79 pounds
1 *kantar* = 56. 450 kg = 124.45 pounds
1 *batman* = 7.697 kg = 16.97 pounds
1 *kıyye* (*okka*) = 1.282 kg = 2.82 pounds
1 *lodra* = 0.564. kg = 1.24 pounds
1 *miskal* = 4.811 g = 2.71 drams
1 *dirhem* = 3.207 g = 1.8 drams
1 denk = 0.801 g = 0.45 drams
1 *kirat* = 0.2 g = 3.08 grains

1 *buğday* = 0.05 g = 0.77 grains
1 *fitil* = 0.0125 g = 0.19 grains
1 *nakir* = 0.00625 g = 0.09 grains
1 *kıtmir* = 0.003125 g = 0.048 grains
1 *zerre* = 0.00156 g = 0.024 grains

INSPECTION AND INSPECTORS

Regulations required *kile*, *arşın*, and *dirhem* to be checked by the market inspector, or *muhtesib*, an official charged with touring the market places periodically to check the accuracy of weights and measures, to check the scales in use, to inspect market prices, and to punish fraudulent practices. Under his supervision, weights and measures in shops and markets were regularly checked by a *kileci* (inspector of bushels) and a *tamgacı* (stamper). The *kileci*'s job was to adjust the weights or measures according to the standards kept in the imperial treasury. The *tamgacı* would certify their accuracy and validity by imprinting them with the official stamp (*miri tamga*). The *kutucus* (bushel makers) had to bring the measures they produced to the *kileci* and *tamgacı* for adjustment and certification.

UNIFICATION ATTEMPTS

When new lands were acquired, the Ottomans avoided changing local laws and customs. As far as metrology was concerned, the pre-conquest terminology was generally replaced by Ottoman terms, but the measures themselves remained unchanged. as part of the *timar* system however, in which taxes were paid in the form of commodities, often grain, the central government used the Istanbul *kile* (*kile-i istanbuli*) and the Istanbul *okka* as standard measures. Unification of metrology within a *sancak* (subprovince) was carried out by extending the use of a typical local measure to the whole *sancak*. A revolutionary plan for unification was proposed following the Ottoman economic crisis around 1640, and the government was advised to extend the use of Istanbul weights and measures to the provinces of the empire. The proposal, however, was not favored.

THE STANDARD *ZIRA* OF 1840

Under Sultan SELIM III (r. 1789–1807), the standard for the *zira-i mimari* (or *zira*), made of ebony, was kept in the MÜHENDISHANE, the Military Engineering School in Istanbul. In the field, however, the *zira* measures used by architects, engineers, and craftsmen varied in length. In the mid 19th century, the difficulties encountered in the casting of cannons in the Tophane-i Amire, the Imperial Foundry, made it clear that a standard *zira* was needed. Although the calibers of cannonballs could be calculated theoretically, they could not be produced precisely enough because the *ziras* used varied in length. To solve this problem, the engineer Mehmed Emin Pasha created an "average *zira*" (*zira-i mimari*) of brass in 1840 and had it compared in 1841 to the standard meter in Paris. The *zira-i mimari* was found to be equal to 0.757 738 m. The length of this *zira* became accepted by an imperial rescript as the official unit of length of the Ottoman state. A similar standard for the *okka* was produced and kept for future comparisons. The metric equivalents of the *zira* (0.757 738 m) and *okka* (1.282 945 kg) were both accepted as the official metric equivalents after the adoption of the metric system by the Ottoman government in 1869, and were subsequently used in conversion tables.

OTTOMAN ENGINEERS AND EUROPEAN MEASURES

The 18th-century attempts to transfer and adopt European science and technology paved the way for a comparison between Ottoman and European measures. The equivalence between them was first calculated by the engineers of the Mühendishane. The collaboration between Ottoman and European military experts in the Mühendishane, and the translation of engineering textbooks into Ottoman Turkish, required that the relationship between Ottoman, French, and English measures be established. Thus comparisons and tables included in textbooks compiled by Mühendishane director Hüseyin Rıfkı Tamani at the end of the century set the standard for the relationship between European and Ottoman measures. Once the ratio between the Ottoman *üsbü* (literally "finger," a measure of length equaling 3.2 cm) and the French *pouce* had been established (6 *üsbü* = 7 *pouce*), the Ottoman equivalents of various European measures of length were calculated.

THE METRIC SYSTEM

Prior to their official adoption by the Ottomans in 1869, metric weights and measures were already being widely used within the empire. As metric weights and measures came to be included in early 19th-century European textbooks, Ottoman mathematicians and engineers became aware of this new system and introduced it in the textbooks they compiled from European sources. They also calculated the metric equivalents of Ottoman weights and measures and prepared conversion tables. Ishak Efendi's 1834 book on fortification, *Usul-i Istihkamat,* and Ibrahim Edhem Pasha's 1836 translation of Adrien-Marie Legendre's book on mathematics, *Usul-i Hendese,* are early examples. Tables of conversion were intended to help Mühendishane students easily put into practice the new technical knowledge coming from Europe.

A number of doctors, chemists, and pharmacists also used metric weights and measures in the analyses they carried out at the Mekteb-i Tıbbiye-i Şahane (The Military School of Medicine) and at the hospitals in Istanbul. Some analysis reports sent to state offices were drawn up using the metric system. The kilogram measure was already in use in ports such as ISTANBUL, IZMIR, Mersin, Antalya, Trabzon, and Samsun, especially for purchases from abroad and wholesale trading. In Bafra and other towns engaged in the TOBACCO trade, kilograms were commonly used in transactions involving La Régie du Tabac, while in BURSA they were employed in the purchase of silk. The metric ton was used in highly developed commercial centers including large business houses or mines.

LAWS CONCERNING THE NEW WEIGHTS AND MEASURES

The official adoption of the decimal metric system seems to have been closely connected with a need to unify and standardize the weights and measures used throughout the Ottoman realms. According to 19th-century Ottoman documents, different weights and measures were employed in different parts of the empire, and units had different values in different regions. Indeed, in some cases, the same unit of weight differed in value according to the material weighed. The steadily increasing volume of trade with European countries made a universal system of measures necessary. It was also hoped that the introduction of the new weights and measures would put an end to fraudulent practices in the market; in fact, however, those practices intensified with the adoption of the metric system. The atmosphere of modernization in other aspects of social and political life at this time seems to have influenced Ottoman officials in deciding to adopt this new system. The law introducing the metric weights and measures was issued on 27 September 1869, and the meter, gram, and liter became the official imperial units of length, weight, and volume. The law required that, as of March 1871, the new weights and measures must be used in all business transactions carried out in government offices and local administrations. The metric system was to be applied throughout the Ottoman lands as of March 1874.

NEW MEASURES AND THE GENERAL PUBLIC

Following the promulgation of the 1869 law, work was undertaken to facilitate the dissemination of the new system. A regulation concerning the use and control of the new measures was issued the same year to specify the production , stamping, and control of metric weights and measures. A booklet introducing the metric system was made compulsory reading in schools. Posters illustrating the new weights and measures were ordered from Paris, and conversion tables were printed and distributed. Terms to denote the new units (*zira-i aşari* for meter) were coined and symbols for metric units were created using Arabic letters. A decree issued in 1881 aimed to facilitate the dissemination of the metric system. The terminology and conversion tables it introduced were less sophisticated. It abolished the use of traditional weights and measures beginning in 1882.

However, the transition to the metric system was regularly postponed during the last 20 years of the 19th century. The consecutive wars of the early 20th century made the adoption of the metric system less of a priority for the government. Although the general public and shopkeepers kept using the old system in the market, government offices favored the metric system from 1871 on, as required by the 1869 law. Wholesale merchants trading with Europe also supported the use of the metric system. The delay in the switch was mostly due to the longstanding familiarity of the general public with the traditional system. The fraudulent practices of shopkeepers also played a role in creating hostility toward the new system. The decimal base of the new system, its new terminology with confusing prefixes such as *uşr-*(deci-), *uşeyr-*(deca-), and *mişar-*(centi-), the various psychological obstacles, and the astronomical basis of the metric system, which was seen as lacking any social, functional, or human dimension, also slowed its adoption. Ottoman society seems to have experienced difficulties similar to those of many other societies in moving from traditional to new systems of measurement. In France, the shift to the new system took almost 50 years, and its adoption was delayed for a number of reasons. The period beginning in 1869 initiated the familiarization of Ottomans with the decimal metric system and can be regarded as the precursor to its final adoption by republican Turkey in 1934.

Feza Günergun

Further reading: Halil Inalcık, "Introduction to Ottoman Metrology," *Turcica* 15 (1983): 331–348; Feza Günergun, "Metric System in Turkey: Transition Period (1881–1934)," Vol. 6, *Journal of the Japan-Netherlands Institute (Papers of the Third Conference on the Transfer of Science and Technology between Europe and Asia since Vasco da Gama, 1498–1998,* edited by W. G. J. Remmelink) 6 (1996): 243–256; Feza Günergun, "Standardization in Ottoman Turkey," in *Introduction of Modern Science and Technology to Turkey and Japan,* edited by F. Günergun and S. Kuriyama (Kyoto: International Research Center for Japanese Studies, 1998), 205–225.

Weizmann, Chaim (b. 1874–d. 1952) (r. 1948–1952) *Zionist leader, President of Israel* Chaim Weizmann was one of the fathers of the Zionist movement and the first president of the state of Israel, serving from 1948 until his death in 1952. He was born in a village near the town of Pinsk, today in Belarus but then in the Russian Empire. He left RUSSIA in 1895 to study in universities, first in Germany and then in Switzerland where he earned a Ph.D. in chemistry in 1900. Weizmann moved to ENG-LAND in 1904; he lived there until the establishment of Israel in 1948. Weizmann was ardently committed to the cause of ZIONISM and served as a delegate to the Second Zionist Congress in 1898. He also firmly believed that the Jewish state had to be constituted in PALESTINE (Eretz Yisrael) and opposed the compromise suggested by Theodor Herzl (d. 1904), founder of the World Zionist Congress, that it be established in Uganda.

Chaim Weizmann labored for British support for the Zionist enterprise, and he is credited as having played a major role in the process that led up to the Balfour Declaration. In 1918 he went to Palestine to advise the British army on implementation of its occupation and met with Emir FAYSAL AL-HASHIMI, leader of the ARAB REVOLT and future king of IRAQ, to discuss the Zionist plans for Palestine. They issued a joint statement on January 3, 1919 that stressed the "racial kinship and ancient bonds" between Jews and Arabs and recognized that Palestine would be separate from the Arab Kingdom that Faysal wanted to establish in DAMASCUS. Although Faysal later repudiated that declaration, some historians have cited it as an indication that Arab leadership was not ideologically opposed to the establishment of a Jewish homeland in Palestine. After WORLD WAR I ended, Weizmann went to Paris where he lobbied delegates at the conference held to determine the fate of the territories controlled by the Central Powers for a British mandate in Palestine. Given the fact that the British government had issued the Balfour Declaration in 1917, in which it said that it was sympathetic to a creation of a Jewish homeland in Palestine, Weizmann felt that the British would best serve the Zionist program for the territory, which included the eventual establishment of a Jewish state there. He was successful in his lobbying efforts and the Treaty of San Remo in 1920, promulgated by the League of Nations, established Great Britain as the mandatory power for Palestine.

Bruce Masters

Further reading: Jehuda Reinharz, *Chaim Weizmann, the Making of a Zionist Leader* (New York: Oxford University Press, 1985).

World War I As is true for many of the powers engaged in World War I, the war fundamentally changed the shape of the Ottoman Empire. Victorious states partitioned the empire, thus causing its end. During the war, separatist nationalist movements, such as those of the Arabs and Armenians, intensified their activities. In reaction to the foreign occupation of Ottoman lands and the burgeoning separatist movements, a Turkish national resistance movement emerged in 1919–1922 under the leadership of Mustafa KEMAL ATATÜRK that drove the occupation forces back, toppled the sultanate, and created the modern Turkish Republic.

OUTBREAK OF WORLD WAR I

Following the assassination of Archduke Franz Ferdinand of Austria-Hungary in June 1914 by a Serb nationalist in Sarajevo, Austria-Hungary demanded that SERBIA stop pro-Serbian separatist activity in BOSNIA AND HERZEGOVINA. Serbia's refusal to cooperate ignited the war in which five major European powers were soon involved. As a result of their prewar commitments and collective defense agreements, two sides were formed. On one side there were GERMANY and Austria-Hungary (Central Powers), and on the other were Britain (*see* ENGLAND), FRANCE, and RUSSIA (Entente Powers—the United States joined them in 1917). The Ottoman Empire initially stayed out of the war. But on August 2, 1914, Enver Pasha (1881–1922), minister of war and perhaps the strongest personality in the Committee for Union and Progress (CUP) government in ISTANBUL, signed a secret agreement with Germany that pledged that the Ottoman Empire would enter the war alongside the Central Powers.

The pretext needed for the Ottoman Empire to enter the war was given when two German warships, *Goeben* and *Breslau*, entered Ottoman waters on August 11, 1914 to escape the British Mediterranean fleet. British demands that the Ottomans either confiscate the ships and detain the crews or force them out of Ottoman waters were rebuffed by the Ottoman government. Istanbul announced that it had purchased the two ships and had renamed them *Yavuz* and *Midilli*. The crews were dressed in Ottoman uniforms and Admiral Wilhelm Souchon was appointed commander in chief of the Ottoman NAVY in the BLACK SEA. When Souchon, under direct orders from Enver, bombarded Russian bases along the Black Sea and sank Russian ships on October 29, the Ottomans had officially entered the war.

The Ottomans were forced to fight on several fronts during the war. Their meager resources, further decimated during the BALKAN WARS (1912–13), and poor infrastructure hampered efficient troop transfer from one side of the empire to the other. The Ottomans also had to fight the Russians in Europe (Galicia between July 1916 and August 1917, Romania between August 1916 and May 1918, and Macedonia between September 1916 and March 1917) on the side of the Germans, Austrians, and Bulgarians. Consequently, apart from victories in Gallipoli and Kut al-Amara, the Ottoman armies had very little to show in the battlefields. They were overrun by the Russian armies until a revolution broke out in Russia in 1917, and by the British forces until the end of the war.

GALLIPOLI

Even today the battle at Gallipoli is a great moment in Turkish popular memory and psychology. In Turkish historiography, it is considered the starting point of modern Turkish history. Not only was the victory of the Ottoman forces against the British and French one of the most notable during the entire war, it also produced a local hero who would subsequently become the founder of modern TURKEY, Mustafa Kemal Atatűrk.

In February and March 1915, the British and the French attacked Gallipoli, the gate to the Dardanelles, with the goal of capturing ISTANBUL. The original plan was to engage the Ottomans and relieve Russia, which was being attacked by German-Austrian armies in the west and Ottoman armies in the east. The initial naval operation failed on March 18. On April 25, however, the British and the ANZACS (Australia-New Zealand Army Corps) embarked upon an amphibious attack on the Gallipoli peninsula that led to a relentless and wearisome trench war lasting nine months. Finally, in January 1916, the British and the ANZACS were forced to withdraw.

MESOPOTAMIA

During the initial phases of the war, the British attacked the Ottoman positions in Fao (present-day Al-Faw, Iraq) and BASRA, which they captured in November 1914. They then launched a major offensive on Kut-al-Amara, further up the River Tigris on the way to BAGHDAD, simultaneously with their attack on Gallipoli. General Townshend captured the city in May 1915. He moved further northward in September, but was stopped eventually by the Ottoman forces under the command of Nureddin Pasha at Selmanpak. Townshend retreated to Kut in November, awaiting new reinforcements for another attack on Baghdad. However, the Ottoman forces in Mesopotamia, now under the command of Field Marshall von der Goltz who had replaced Nurettin Pasha, besieged Townshend's forces in January 1916. After a number of attempts by British forces to break the siege, Townshend capitulated on April 29, 1916. After the surrender of Townshend, the British appointed General Stanley Maude as the commander of the British forces in Mesopotamia. General Maude attacked Kut in December 1916 and captured the town on February 23. He continued with his advance northward and on March 11 he entered Baghdad. Fortunately for the Ottomans, Maude did not march on Mosul.

CAUCASUS AND EASTERN ANATOLIA

In the Caucasus, during the initial phases of the war, the Ottomans carried out an operation around the Ottoman town of Kars, close to the Georgian border. The plan was to march toward the Caucasus and incite Russian Muslims to rise up against the czar. However, the operation failed badly around the small and strategic town of Sarikamish. The Ottoman forces were deployed in difficult terrain in the middle of winter, costing the lives of some 70,000 soldiers in December 1914. After the military fiasco in Sarikamish, the entire eastern Anatolia was left open to Russian attacks.

Turkish historians argue that the Ottomans had to deal with an Armenian revolt in Van in April 1915, and that many Armenians in eastern Anatolia had been collaborating with the Russians, either providing them with intelligence or actually joining the ranks of the Russian military and Ottoman authorities had started a systematic campaign of arresting Armenians suspected of collaborating with the enemy. The Armenian uprising in Van impelled the Ottoman government to take further measures, and in May it ordered the relocation of the Armenians from the war zone to SYRIA and LEBANON. This proved to be a difficult task. The relocation was carried out at the height of the war, while the Ottomans were fighting the British, French, and the ANZACS in Gallipoli; the British in Mesopotamia; and the Russians in eastern Anatolia. Therefore, the Ottomans could not spare sufficient regular forces to supervise the relocation and provide the necessary security to the Armenians. Armenians were robbed, harassed, and killed by bandits and army deserters. Many Armenians, like the Ottoman soldiers who accompanied them, perished due to bad weather conditions, poor transportation means, and starvation. The number of people who lost their lives during this forced relocation is subject to heated debate between Turkish and Armenian historians. Turkish historians put the number as low as 200,000, while Armenian historians put it as high as 2,000,000. The Tehcir, or deportation, as it is known in Turkish historiography, with its various aspects—including the intent, the figures, and the consequences—is still in need of unbiased scholarship.

The Russians continued their advance and took control of eastern Anatolia by 1917, when they eventually withdrew, not because of Ottoman military successes but because of political turmoil in Russia. Once Russia's participation in the war ended in March 1918, the Ottomans were able to retake eastern Anatolia. The Ottomans abandoned their operations in the Caucasus only after the Mudros Armistice was signed in October 1918.

SINAI AND PALESTINE

In January 1915 Cemal Pasha (1872–1922), one of the three powerful leaders in the CUP government, carried out an operation in the Sinai that was aimed at cutting off the SUEZ CANAL and taking EGYPT from the British. As on the eastern front, this operation failed, and the Ottoman forces retreated to PALESTINE in February 1915. Cemal launched another offensive in Palestine in July 1916, but Cemal's forces were again defeated in August. In 1917 the British attacked; General Allenby's forces captured Gaza in November and entered Jerusalem on December 8. In the meantime, HUSAYN

AL-HASHIMI, the SHARIF OF MECCA, had come to an agreement with the British to prepare an uprising in June 1916. The Arab revolt continued until 1917. Even though the Arabs did not inflict major casualties on the Ottomans forces, they cut the communication and transportation lines, making the defense of Hejaz difficult for the Ottomans. In February 1918 Allenby marched on Jordan. On September 25 Allenby captured Nazareth and a week later he took DAMASCUS. Finally, on October 25, he conquered ALEPPO, thus ending his Syrian campaign. The Ottoman forces retreated to Adana and waited there until the Mudros Armistice was signed at the end of October.

END OF THE WAR AND THE DEMISE OF THE EMPIRE

Allenby's successes in Syria terrified the Ottoman government. However, it was British general Milne's march toward Istanbul following the defeat of Bulgaria that forced the Ottomans to seek an armistice. Finally, on October 30, the Ottomans and the Allies signed the Mudros Armistice that effectively ended World War I. Until a final settlement could be reached, the Ottoman territories, except for central Anatolia, were occupied by the victorious powers.

World War I was the last war that the Ottomans fought. The war exhausted almost all imperial resources. Even though the Ottoman forces were supplied with modern German military equipment and personnel, the lack of food, water, and clothing that they experienced proved almost as fatal as the enemy's bullets. Moreover, the lack of sufficient communication and transportation facilities hampered the Ottoman war effort to a considerable extent. Finally, desertions from the army were another problem that the government had to deal with. It not only decreased Ottoman manpower, it also caused social unrest in the countryside because a considerable number of deserters turned into bandits during the war.

After the war was lost, the CUP resigned and a new government was formed. The new government in Istanbul started negotiations with the occupying powers for a final agreement. Meanwhile, Mustafa Kemal left Istanbul and led a resistance against occupation in Anatolia. Kemalist forces fought the occupying powers for three years and in November 1922 a ceasefire between the warring parties was established. Eventually, an international conference was convened in Lausanne, and in July 1923, at last, an understanding was reached between Turkey (the sultanate was abolished by the Ankara government in November 1922) and the Entente powers (see LAUSANNE, TREATY OF). Accordingly, the Western powers recognized the new Turkish state and withdrew all their forces from Turkey. In October 1923, a republic was proclaimed in Turkey and a new state emerged from the ashes of the Ottoman Empire.

Bestami S. Bilgiç

Further reading: Erik J. Zürcher, *Turkey: A Modern History* (London: Tauris, 2004); Douglas A. Howard, *History of Turkey* (Westport, Conn.: Greenwood, 2001); Edward J. Erickson, *Ordered to Die: A History of the Ottoman Army in the First World War* (Westport, Conn.: Greenwood, 2001).

Y

Yazidis The Yazidis are a religious community found today in the Jabal Sinjar region in northern IRAQ. In the Ottoman period, Yazidis were more widely spread throughout Kurdistan. Ethnically KURDS, the Yazidis claim that their faith predates either Christianity or Islam, although elements of both are found in their beliefs, with both Muhammad and Jesus figuring prominently as moral and spiritual guides. Non-Yazidis have frequently spread the tale that the Yazidis worship the devil, but the Yazidis deny that charge, saying that they worship the same God as do Muslims, Christians, and Jews. Yazidis also worship the seven angels of God, the most important of which manifests itself as a peacock (*melek-i taus).* This is most probably where the charge of devil worship arises, as in many Middle Eastern traditions the peacock is associated with Iblis, or Satan.

Dealings between the Yazidis and the Ottomans were usually tense and frequently erupted into violence. This was in part because relations between Yazidis and Muslims were generally poor and Yazidis avoided contact with Muslims whenever possible. As the Yazidis do not claim to be Muslims, they were liable to pay the *jizya,* or the poll tax levied on non-Muslims in the Ottoman period. The reputation of the Yazidi community among followers of SUNNI ISLAM further suffered from the fact that the inhabitants of Jabal Sinjar in today's Iraq often raided the CARAVANS that passed along the nearby EUPHRATES RIVER route.

Isolated and despised by their neighbors, many Yazidis converted to either Islam or Christianity. In the late 19th century, both Protestant and Catholic MISSIONARIES viewed the community as fertile ground for conversion, and this aggressive missionary activity was initially permitted by the Ottomans since Islamic scholars did not consider the Yazidis to be Muslims. Missionary activity in the community led the Ottoman state, however, to reconsider its position. Starting in the 1880s, Ottoman officials began to impose the Hanafi legal school of Sunni Islam on the Yazidis by building schools and mosques in their villages, as they concluded that if the Yazidis could be open to missionary activity by foreign Christians, they might as well be exposed to missionary activity conducted by Ottoman Muslims. This was accompanied by violence, the confiscation of religious relics, and the forced conversion of the community's leaders to Islam. These measures were later rescinded, but relations between the community and the Ottoman state remained tense.

Bruce Masters

Further reading: Nelida Fuccaro, *The Other Kurds: Yazidis in Colonial Iraq* (London: I.B. Tauris, 1999).

Yemen Yemen, with its capital at Sanaa, was at times a province of the Ottoman Empire, with boundaries more or less corresponding to those of the present-day Republic of Yemen, without the region of the Hadhramawt (formerly The People's Republic of Yemen). The Ottomans came to Yemen to forestall Portuguese expansion in the Red Sea and to control the valuable export of COFFEE, the popularity of which was sweeping the empire. But nowhere in the empire was direct rule from ISTANBUL more contested than it was in Yemen. This was due in part to Yemen's distance from the capital, and in part to its very rugged terrain. But more importantly, the difficulties the Ottomans experienced in Yemen arose from the fact that they were not viewed as legitimate rulers. A majority of the inhabitants of the province were practitioners of the Zaydi school of SHIA ISLAM who owed allegiance to a family of imams who traced their lineage back to the Prophet Muhammad through Imam Muhammad, son of Jaafar al-Sadiq, and through Husayn, the son of Ali and Fatima, the prophet's daughter. Given the importance they placed on their own ancestry, the Zaydi viewed the Ottoman royal house as upstarts and usurpers without any legitimate claim to rule and represent the Islamic world. War against the sultan was, in their eyes, holy war, as they viewed the Sunni Ottomans as heretics.

The Ottomans became increasingly aware of Portuguese ambitions in the Red Sea after their conquest of EGYPT in 1517, and indeed some scholars have suggested that one of the motivations that pushed Sultan SELIM I (r. 1512–20) to invade the MAMLUK EMPIRE that controlled Egypt and SYRIA was his fear that the Mamluks were too weak to forestall European expansion into Egypt. In 1526 the Ottomans sent a fleet to secure the Red Sea; it seized the port city of Mocha. This was soon followed by the fall of the inland city of Zabid to an Ottoman army that had landed at Mocha. But within two years, squabbling among the Ottoman commanders led them to withdraw, and the Zaydi imam, Sharaf al-Din, was able to reassert his control even over the coast. In 1538 the Ottomans launched a land assault on the mountain strongholds of the imam; in 1539 they succeeded in seizing the town of Taizz. Sanaa held out until 1547. Sharaf al-Din's son, al-Mutahhar, refused to concede defeat, however, and the Ottomans faced a protracted guerrilla war that ebbed and flowed according to which tribes were willing to commit men to the fray.

The tribes of the highlands rose in rebellion against Ottoman rule in 1567, led by the Zaydi imam al-Mutahhar, and they again drove the Ottomans back to the coast. The Ottomans were able to reestablish control over Sanaa, the highland capital of the region, in 1570, but the tribes remained restive in a campaign they viewed as holy war. Under the imam al-Qasim, known in Yemeni chronicles as "al-Kabir" (the Great), the tribes' resistance grew stronger, and in 1629 the Zaydis retook Sanaa. By 1636, the Zaydi tribesmen had driven the Ottomans out of the country completely. Two centuries of relative peace under the rule of the descendants of al-Qasim followed, during which the imams reaped considerable wealth from the export of coffee. That prosperity came to an end, however, toward the end of the 18th century, when coffee from the Americas, produced by slave labor, became much cheaper than that produced by tribesmen in Yemen.

During the 19th century, several leading Zaydi families and their tribal allies increasingly struggled for the title of imam. In the chaos that ensued, the Ottoman sultan sought to restore his sovereignty over Yemen, the claim to which his ancestors had never relinquished. In 1872 the Ottoman army returned to Yemen and was able to conquer and garrison its major cities. But that did not mean the end to Zaydi resistance. Al-Hadi Sharaf al-Din claimed the title of imam in 1879 and led a jihad against the Ottomans until his death in 1890. Resistance continued under the leadership of al-Mansur Muhammad Hamid al-Din until his death in 1904, when it was carried on under his son Yahya. In 1905 the Ottomans were forced to concede Sanaa yet again to the imam. They were not to return until 1911 when, faced with wars in LIBYA and the Balkans, the Ottomans finally sought peace with the Zaydi imam. The result of these negotiations was the Treaty of Daan, which ceded the region to the north of the capital to the imam in return for his entering into alliance with the Ottoman sultan. With the surrender of the Ottomans to the Allies in 1918, Imam Yahya entered Sanaa and claimed the entire country, which he ruled until his death in 1948. His descendants continued to rule Yemen until a military revolution toppled the dynasty in 1962 and established a socialist republic allied with Egypt.

Bruce Masters

Further reading: Caesar Farah, *The Sultan's Yemen* (London: I.B. Tauris, 2002).

Young Ottomans (Yeni Osmanlılar) The Young Ottomans were a late 19th-century Ottoman political group comprised of young intellectuals educated in the empire's newly established Western-style institutions and sent to Europe either as students or as commissioned officials. Its membership was characterized by its dissatisfaction with the far-reaching Western-style changes undertaken as part of the empire's sweeping TANZIMAT reform effort just prior to this period. The Young Ottomans were also unhappy with the policies of the Tanzimat bureaucrats. After 1860, when debates over the Tanzimat reforms intensified with the rising power of NEWSPAPERS and other media, public dissatisfaction focused on the delay in implementing the social and economic policies that were to have started right after the Islahat Ferman of 1856 (Imperial Rescript of Reform). Other factors also contributed to this widespread dissatisfaction, especially among the Ottoman intellectual class. Among these factors were the independence of the Romanian principalities (WALLACHIA and MOLDAVIA) and the empire's severe financial crisis, especially in light of the corruption and extravagant lifestyle among the governing elite. Spearheading the reaction against these elites were the Yeni Osmanlılar, or Young Ottomans, the most serious and effective intellectual protest movement in the empire at the time.

The Young Ottomans were formed in 1867 by exiled Ottoman intellectuals who gathered in Paris, brought together by Prince Mustafa Fazil, a brother of the Egyptian KHEDIVE ISMAIL and a grandson of MEHMED ALI of EGYPT. The group initially called themselves Türkistanın Erbab-ı Şebabı (Turkistan Youth) and Ittifak-i Hamiyyet (Society of Zealots), later changing their name to The Young Ottomans. The prominent founders were Ali Suavi, NAMIK KEMAL, and ZIYA PASHA; Reşat Bey, Mehmed Bey, and Nuri Bey later joined the group. Mustafa Fazil kept in contact with exiled Ottoman intellectuals in various European cities and invited those whose newspapers were under the ban of CENSORSHIP by the Ottoman administration to publish their papers in Europe.

The Young Ottomans founded, and disseminated their thoughts through, various newspapers funded by Mustafa Fazıl Pasha. The first of these, *Muhbir* (Herald), was established in London by Ali Suavi on August 18, 1867. Roughly one year later, on June 29, 1868, Namık Kemal and Ziya Pasha founded another newspaper, *Hürriyet* (Freedom), which consisted of a summary of Young Ottoman thought and published various articles related to the issues of government reform. Other Young Ottoman newspapers included *Ulum* (Science), launched by Ali Suavi in Paris, and the Geneva-based *İnkılab* (Revolution). Upon their return from exile, the voice of the Young Ottomans was most clearly expressed in the newspaper *İbret* (Lesson).

During their exile in Europe, the Young Ottomans were organized around Mustafa Fazıl Pasha. Although the Young Ottomans saw his return to Istanbul to accept a ministerial post under Sultan ABDÜLAZIZ (r. 1861–76) as a success for their cause, this return actually began the breakup of the group, which never shared an established ideological consensus.

Namık Kemal was the first member to abandon the group and return to Istanbul in 1870. Ziya Pasha, who strongly disagreed with Namık Kemal, continued his publishing activities and moved to Geneva. Mehmed Bey and Hüseyin Vasfi Pasha, seen as extremist members of the group, founded another newspaper, while Ali Suavi and Rıfat Bey resigned from the group. The next year, following the death of their opponent Grand Vizier Mehmed Emin Âli Pasha in 1871, the other members of the group started to return. Most of them returned from exile during the reign of Sultan Abdülaziz. Ali Suavi, the last exile, returned to Istanbul during the reign of ABDÜLHAMID II (r. 1876–1909).

The Young Ottomans developed highly effective political, financial, and administrative critiques. On the one hand, they presented theoretical discussions on the subjects of constitutional monarchy, equality, and the rule of law; on the other hand, they criticized political and economic applications conducted by Tanzimat bureaucrats. The main target of their critiques was the Tanzimat and its bureaucrats. Another important target was foreign intervention. They also wrote and published articles criticizing Ottoman financial policies, foreign DEBT, and extravagance.

The Young Ottomans played a significant role in Turkish thought, both as role models for a new intellectual tradition and as pioneers of political dissent. The ways in which newspapers could be mobilized as a tool for political criticism, the emergence of the press as a political power, and its use as a political weapon against rivals owes much to the energy and invention of the Young Ottomans.

Coşkun Cakır

Further reading: Serif Mardin, *The Genesis of Young Ottoman Thought: A Study in the Modernization of Turkish Political Ideas* (Princeton, N.J.: Princeton University Press, 1962); Şerif Mardin, "Young Ottomans," in *The Oxford Encyclopedia of the Modern Islamic World*, vol. 4 (New York: Oxford University Press, 1995), 357.

Young Turks   There is some confusion regarding the use and meaning of the term *Young Turks*. In Ottoman and Turkish historiography the term is used to refer to the movement that opposed the regime of Abdülhamid II between February 1878, when he suspended the parliament, and the Constitutional Revolution of July 1908. Turkish historians (following the usage of Ottoman sources dating from that period) refer to the regime that followed Abdülhamid II as the COMMITTEE OF UNION AND PROGRESS. Some European historians, however, call it the Young Turk government. This usage is misleading, because in fact both regime and opposition after 1908 stemmed from former Young Turks.

Terminological confusion does not end here. The phrase *young Turks* was first used by British historian Charles MacFarlane in 1828 to refer to the younger Ottoman generation. Later, in 1855, French publicist and historian Jean-Henri-Abdolonyme Ubicini (1818–84) coined the phrases "jeune Turquie de Mahmoud"(young Turks of Mahmoud) and "jeune Turquie d'Abdul Medjid" (young Turks of Abdülmecid) in an attempt to describe the reforming Ottoman statesmen under sultans MAHMUD II (r. 1808–39) and ABDÜLMECID (r. 1839–61). Hippolyte Castile was the first author to use the expression "Young Turks" with the clear intention of grouping them together with Young Italy of Mazzini. In 1867 a number of leading Ottoman intellectuals, who had secretly formed the YOUNG OTTOMANS in 1865, fled the Ottoman capital to organize an opposition movement in Paris financed by the Egyptian prince Mustafa Fâzıl. The European press called them "Young Turks," a title that Mustafa Fâzıl himself adopted. In a famous letter to the sultan inviting him to carry out extensive reforms, Mustafa Fâzıl used the phrase "grand parti de la Jeune Turquie." When these dissidents called themselves "Jeune Turquie" they were distinguishing themselves from conservative statesmen, whom they dubbed "Vieux Turcs" (old Turks). In Turkish historiography this group (the first Ottoman opposition movement abroad) is called the Young Ottoman movement. Later on, British and French diplomatic correspondence used the terms "Young Turk" and "the Young Turkey party" to refer to those statesmen and bureaucrats who supported the movement for a constitution.

Following the end of the short-lived constitutional regime in 1878, both Ottomans and Europeans referred in general to the opponents of Sultan Abdülhamid II's regime as "the Young Turks." It was the Ottoman Freemasons who, in 1893, first formally named their political branch "the Committee of Young Turkey at Constantinople." Then, in 1895, the main opposition group, the Ottoman Committee of Union and Progress, advertised its French journal, *Mechveret Supplément Français*, as "Organe de la Jeune Turquie" (Periodical of the Young Turks).

From this point on, the phrase "Young Turks" was used among Ottoman subjects (of all religions) to denote opposition organizations dominated by specifically Muslim dissidents. In Europe, however, no such distinction was made, and the term was loosely applied to include Armenian, Macedonian, and other committees formed against the regime.

1878–1908: IDEAS AND POLICIES

During the reign of Abdülhamid II the Young Turk movement was located in Europe and British-ruled Egypt. Members of the movement founded a host of political parties, committees, and leagues seeking to topple the absolutist regime of Abdülhamid II and to replace it with a constitutional monarchy. Although their European contemporaries and many scholars commonly labeled the Young Turks "liberals" and "constitutionalists," such a program was promoted only by a small minority in the movement. Members of the major Young Turk organizations did not adopt liberal ideas, and viewed constitutionalism merely as a device to stave off intervention in the Ottoman Empire by the Great Powers.

The initial activities of the Young Turks did not go beyond the publication by dissidents of a few journals, such as *Gencine-i Hayal* (The treasure of imagination, published in Geneva) and *İstikbal* (Future, published in Naples) and their clandestine distribution within the empire. In 1889, what became the major Young Turk organization was established in the Royal Medical Academy in Istanbul, originally calling itself the Ottoman Union Committee. After protracted negotiations between the founders and Ahmed Rıza, this name was changed to the Ottoman Committee of Union and Progress (CUP). This new title reflected the staunch positivism of Ahmed Rıza, who had

unsuccessfully proposed naming the group "Order and Progress" after Auguste Comte's famous aphorism. This committee, which remained the most important Young Turk organization until the end of the movement, was a loose umbrella organization until 1902. While some branches supported the gradual reform program of the positivists (supporters of a theory that states that true knowledge is based only on natural phenomena as verified by the empirical sciences), others advocated revolution, while still others were dominated by the ULEMA.

In 1902 a schism developed in Paris at the First Congress of Ottoman Opposition Groups. The majority party, led by the sultan's brother-in-law Mahmud Celaleddin Pasha and his two sons Sabahaddin Bey and Lutfullah Bey, allied itself with members of Armenian and Albanian committees and Greek intellectuals. They promoted the idea of a coup d'état with British assistance. Their willingness to work with foreign powers sparked the opposition of the minority party, under the leadership of Ahmed Rıza. It adopted a Turkist policy, demanding a leadership role for the Turks, and categorically rejecting any foreign intervention in Ottoman politics. After its failure to carry out a coup in 1902-3, the majority party reorganized itself in 1905 under Sabahaddin Bey's leadership, and advocated decentralization and private initiative. In that year Sabahaddin Bey also founded the League of Private Initiative and Decentralization, and he worked toward creating a mutual understanding with the non-Muslim organizations.

Also in 1905, the minority party, under the leadership of Dr. Bahaeddin Şakir, reorganized itself under the new name of the Ottoman Committee of Progress and Union (CPU). In 1907 this new organization merged with the Ottoman Freedom Society, which had been established in 1906 by army officers and bureaucrats in SALONIKA. From this point on, the Young Turk movement spread among the Ottoman officer corps in European Turkey. In the meantime, the 1907 Congress of Ottoman Opposition, held in Paris in December, brought about an understanding between the two major Young Turk organizations (the CPU and the League of Private Initiative and Decentralization) and the Armenian Dashnaktsutiun committee. But the alliance realized at the congress played almost no role in the Young Turk Revolution of 1908.

Since all members of organizations dominated by the Muslim opponents of the sultan and their sympathizers in the Empire were called Young Turks, this phrase does not necessarily refer to individuals who shared similar ideas. Thus ULEMA and ardent positivists worked as members of various Young Turk organizations. In the early stages of the movement, many Young Turks, including the original founders of the CUP, were adherents of mid-19th-century German materialism and admirers of Ludwig Büchner, Ernst Haeckel, Jocob Moleschott, and

Karl Vogt. In addition, Social Darwinism deeply influenced many Young Turks. Positivism, too, was advanced by various Young Turk leaders, and the French organ of the Ottoman Committee of Union and Progress used the positivist calendar for a while. Interestingly enough, Gustave Le Bon and his theories of crowd psychology made a strong impact on almost all members of the movement. Le Bon's ideas shaped the elitism promoted by the Young Turks. But following the reorganization of the CPU these ideas receded to the background, and practical political ideas and an activist agenda took their place. For instance, a powerful proto-nationalism emerged. It called for a dominant role for ethnic Turks in the empire while resisting European economic penetration and political intervention. By 1908 the CPU had adopted a Turkist and anti-imperialist stand with the dream of making the Ottoman empire "the Japan of the Near East." For their part, Sabahaddin Bey and his followers were deeply influenced by the *Science sociale* movement, particularly by Edmond Demolins. They maintained that private initiative and decentralization, the main reasons for Anglo-Saxon superiority, would save the empire from collapse.

THE YOUNG TURK REVOLUTION

In July 1908 the CPU carried out the Young Turk Revolution, which marked the end of both Abdülhamid II's regime and the Young Turk movement. The so-called Young Turk Revolution was the product of a single organization; other Young Turk groups played almost no role in the momentous event. The revolution was not a popular uprising of Young Turks throughout the empire, nor was it a liberal reform movement, as was assumed by many at the time. Rather, it was a well-planned military insurrection, conceived and executed in Macedonia by the CPU. The aims of this organization were also very conservative: to seize control of the empire, save it from collapse, and to put an end to the practice whereby foreign powers intervened in Ottoman politics by demanding reforms on behalf of Christian Ottoman subjects. The ideology behind the revolution was conservative activism, and not a revolutionary agenda in any real sense of the word.

Following the merger between the CPU and the Ottoman Freedom Society, new internal regulations that mirrored the bylaws of major Armenian and Macedonian revolutionary organizations clearly demonstrated a marked shift to an activist program. This program created self-sacrificing volunteer (*fedai*) branches and literally authorized them to kill anybody they deemed "hazardous to the fatherland"; it turned the organization into a paramilitary committee. Many officers attracted by this program now joined the organization, which recruited some 2,000 members in the European provinces. Early in 1908 the CPU made detailed plans for initiating an uprising in the European provinces of the empire. Following protracted negotiations with organizations active in these provinces, and

especially in Macedonia, the CPU secured the support of Albanian notables, societies, and bands, together with the left wing of the Internal Macedonian Revolutionary Organization (IMRO); organizations and bands of the Kutzo-Vlach, an ethnic minority in Macedonia; and the leading figures of the Jewish community in Salonika. The CPU was also able to secure a promise of noninterference from the Greek and Serbian organizations and the right wing of IMRO and their military bands. In the meantime, the sultan had ordered a thorough investigation of the CPU's revolutionary activities in June 1908. The palace's attempt to crush the movement, coupled with rumors of an agreement for the partition of Macedonia reached between British king Edward VII (r. 1901–10) and Russian czar Nicholas II (r. 1894–1917) in Reval (present-day Tallinn), prompted the CPU to accelerate its revolutionary activity, which had been scheduled to start in fall. Military units called CPU National Battalions headed to the mountains (the first such unit, the Resen National Battalion, did so on July 3, 1908); the so-called CPU Gendarme Force composed of young officers carried out assassinations of palace spies and officers still loyal to the regime; and Albanian feudal lords put their armed militia at the service of the CPU. In the meantime, some 20,000 Albanian Gegs, who had gathered in Firzovik (present-day Ferizaj, Kosovo) to protest a school picnic organized by a foreign railway company, were persuaded by CPU members to take a solemn oath on the constitution; they requested the constitution's reinstatement by sending telegrams to the capital. All major Ottoman divisions in the region, as well as first-class Anatolian reservists sent there to quell the revolution, now joined the movement, and the CPU threatened the palace with a march on the capital. The desperate sultan attempted to thwart the revolution by creating a state of war with BULGARIA, ostensibly an Ottoman principality. Upon the Bulgarian prince's refusal to cooperate with the plan, the sultan finally yielded on July 23–24. He issued an imperial decree ordering the reinstatement of the Ottoman constitution, in abeyance since 1878, and the re-opening of the chamber of deputies.

The Young Turk Revolution of July 1908 inaugurated the Second Constitutional Period, which lasted until the 1918 Mudros Armistice that concluded Ottoman participation in WORLD WAR I. The revolution not only forced the sultan to restore the constitutional regime, but also made the CUP (the committee started using its old name after the revolution) the supreme force in Ottoman politics.

M. Şükrü Hanioğlu

Further reading: M. Şükrü Hanioğlu, *Preparation for a Revolution: The Young Turks, 1902-1908* (New York: Oxford University Press, 2001); M. Şükrü Hanioğlu, *The Young Turks in Opposition* (New York: Oxford University Press, 1995); Şerif Mardin, *The Genesis of Young Ottoman Thought: A Study in the Modernization of Turkish Political Ideas* (Princeton, N.J.: Princeton University Press, 1962).

Zahir al-Umar (d. 1775) *Palestinian warlord* Zahir al-Umar was a member of the large Zaydani clan, followers of SUNNI ISLAM who are presumed to have had BEDOUIN origins but who had settled in Galilee, in present-day Israel, by the end of the 17th century. His father and uncles had controlled tax farms in the region and Zahir al-Umar used that base to build alliances with various local groups by offering peasant cultivators protection from Bedouin raids. Among these were the clans of Jabal Amil in LEBANON, practitioners of SHIA ISLAM. By the middle of the 18th century, Zahir moved his base of power to the port city of ACRE, which he fortified. With most of northern PALESTINE and southern Lebanon effectively under his control, he entered into extensive trade relations with the French for the export of cotton, produced in Palestine, which enriched his coffers and allowed him to recruit mercenaries from NORTH AFRICA.

Zahir al-Umar's political position was tenuous, despite his growing wealth. His official status in the provincial hierarchy of the empire was as a vassal of the governor of Sidon, and he held no higher authority from the sultan. Realizing that the sultan could, in fact, move against him at any time, Zahir opted to align himself with Bulutkapan Ali Bey of EGYPT whose forces took GAZA and Jaffa in 1770 in act of rebellion against SULTAN MUSTAFA III (r. 1754–74), who was the legal sovereign of both Zahir and Ali. In the following spring, Abu al-Dhahab, Ali's MAMLUK and lieutenant, arrived with a second Egyptian force and defeated the troops raised by the governor of Damascus. Abu al-Dhahab then entered Damascus supported by the DRUZE and MARONITE retainers of Yusuf al-Shihab (*see* SHIHAB FAMILY) while

Zahir occupied Sidon. But just when it looked as if Ottoman control of SYRIA might be at an end, Abu al-Dhahab turned against his former mentor and returned to Egypt with his army.

This left Zahir al-Umar as a rebel against the sultan but with few remaining allies. He sought reconciliation with the sultan and in 1774 was surprisingly named as governor of Sidon. But that seems to have been simply a delaying tactic on the part of the new sultan, ABDÜLHAMID I (r. 1774–89), until he could conclude a peace treaty with RUSSIA and rebuild his forces to punish Zahir. Before he could do so, Abu al-Dhahab invaded Palestine again in 1775, taking the city of Jaffa by storm. This time Abu al-Dhahab falsely claimed to be acting at the sultan's request to remove Zahir from office. Zahir was forced to flee his stronghold at Acre, which was subsequently occupied by the Egyptian forces. The Egyptian invasion was stalled by Abu al-Dhahab's sudden death, however, and Zahir recovered his capital. But at 80 years of age, Zahir was no longer in a position of either physical or political strength and he offered only token resistance to an attack on Acre by the Ottoman NAVY which had finally been dispatched to remove him from office. During the brief siege of the city, he was killed. After his death, Sultan Abdülhamid I appointed CEZZAR AHMED PASHA as governor of Sidon. Cezzar Ahmed appropriated Acre, which was a much better fortified city than Sidon, as his base.

Bruce Masters

Further reading: Amnon Cohen, *Palestine in the 18th Century* (Jerusalem: Hebrew University Press, 1973).

Zand, Karim Khan (d. 1779) (r. 1765–1779) *Iranian tribal leader and warlord* After the 1747 murder of NADIR SHAH, who had seized the throne of IRAN in 1736, Iran descended into anarchy with different factions fighting for the throne in a very bloody contest. A chieftain of the Zand tribe, who may have been ethnically Luris (a people who speak an Indo-European language related to Kurdish and who inhabit the Zagros Mountains of western Iran) emerged victorious in 1765. Eschewing the traditional title of shah, this chieftain, Karim Khan, declared himself to be only the regent for a claimant to the throne of Iran from the Safavi line, the dynasty that had ruled Iran from 1501 until 1722. Despite his diffident approach to the Iranian throne, Karim Khan is remembered by his chroniclers as a just ruler, in sharp contrast to his predecessor, Nadir Shah. This is probably due in no small part to the fact that Karim Khan restored SHIA ISLAM as the state religion at his court, giving patronage in the form of gifts to the Shii clergy.

Karim Khan's relations with the Ottomans were never good, and they worsened as a result of complaints by Shii pilgrims of ill treatment by Ottoman officials at NAJAF and KARBALA. In the early 1770s, dynastic struggles among the BABAN family for control of SHAHRIZOR spilled across the border into the affairs of the Kurdish *mirs* (princes) of Ardalan in territories that were in theory loyal to Karim Khan. As a result, in 1774, Karim Khan dispatched his army into Kurdistan to restore to the house of Ardalan a claimant who was his vassal. However, the Persian army was defeated by an alliance of Ottoman forces from BAGHDAD and Kurdish tribesmen, and the war intensified. Instead of moving toward Baghdad or MOSUL as Nadir Shah had done in a similar situation, Karim Khan moved to encircle BASRA. After a long siege, the city fell in 1776, and Karim Khan returned to his capital in Shiraz. But he did not live long to enjoy his victory as he was already suffering from some illness, probably tuberculosis, and he died in 1778. With his death, Iran descended into another prolonged period of political anarchy until the rise of the Qajar dynasty in the 1790s.

Bruce Masters

Further reading: John Perry, *Karim Khan Zand: A History of Iran, 1747–1779* (Chicago: The University of Chicago Press, 1979).

Zaydis *See* SHIA ISLAM; YEMEN.

zimmi *See* DHIMMI.

Zionism Zionism is a Jewish nationalist ideology that emerged in Europe at the end of the 19th century. Its central tenet is that the Jewish people constitute their own nation and need their own state. The word *Zion* refers literally to a hill in Jerusalem that, even in Biblical times, had come to represent for Jews all of the Land of Israel. The late 19th century was a time when many of the peoples of Europe were beginning to define themselves collectively by their ethnicity and were forming nationalist movements to create new independent nation-states out of dead or waning empires. A common language typically provided the basis for deciding who belonged to a nation and who did not, but ethnicity could also be based on a shared religious identity and a sense of a common history. It was the latter two that Zionists would use to claim that the Jewish people constituted a separate nation in need of its own political state.

Although many Jews lived in eastern Europe and the Balkans, the emerging national identities there were decidedly Christian and Jews were regarded as outsiders. Further isolating Jews from inclusion in these incipient nations, many eastern European Jews spoke their own distinct language, Yiddish. In addition, the Jewish people had a clear sense of being a group apart, but also one that was historically dispersed, or in diaspora. Jewish religious tradition held that this people would not come together to form a political state until the advent of the Messiah who would restore the Kingdom of Israel, a belief that had given rise to several messianic movements, including that of the SHABBATAI ZVI, which had galvanized Jewish hopes for a political redemption in the mid-17th century.

In the 19th century, many Jews in western Europe had hoped that the rise of modern secular nation-states would eliminate much of the conventional anti-Jewish discrimination that they had faced for centuries. It was hoped that the rise of the secular state would promote the peaceful coexistence of those with different religious faiths. That confidence in an evenhanded secular modernity was shaken in 1894 by the infamous Dreyfus Affair, in which Alfred Dreyfus, a French army officer who also happened to be a Jew, was charged with treason. His trial produced a wave of anti-Semitic articles and cartoons. Dreyfus was found guilty, but was later proven to have been innocent of the charge. The fact that he was not given a fair trial, and the anti-Semitic media coverage of the trial, shocked many Jews out their complacency and sent a strong signal that they would never be accepted fully in a predominantly Christian Europe. Although Leo Pinsker, a Russian Jew, had earlier articulated this same conclusion in his pamphlet *Auto-Emancipation*, published anonymously in German in 1882, it had received scant attention. Rather, it was the Austrian Jewish journalist Theodor Herzl, writing in the aftermath of the Dreyfus Affair, to whom many turned with serious attention. Herzl covered the Dreyfus trial as a correspondent in Paris and came to the conclusion that however much the Jews of Europe might seek assimilation into European society, Christian Europe would not accept them. The solution, he argued in his *Der Judenstaat* (The Jewish State), published in 1896, was to found a Jewish state where Jews could exist as a modern nation alongside the other nations of the world.

Herzl did not seem to have any particular geographical location in mind. Rather, he believed that the movement for a Jewish state would require the help of European imperial powers and that they would decide its location. But for the majority of those Jews in Europe who agreed that such a state was necessary, there was no question that it could be any place but Palestine, which they continued to call Eretz Yisrael, the Land of Israel. There already existed in Russia a movement known as the Lovers of Zion which called for the revival of Hebrew as a spoken language and for the Jewish return to Zion as the Biblical homeland. When Herzl called his first international congress in 1897 in Basel, Switzerland, the movement he had helped start already called itself Zionism and proclaimed that its goal was create for the Jewish people a home in Palestine; to that end, it encouraged the immigration of Jews to Palestine (ALIYA).

Although Herzl still toyed with alternative possibilities for the location of the Jewish state, the World Zionist Congress set out to acquire funds to realize a Jewish homeland in Palestine. The Jewish National Fund was created in 1901 and the Palestine Land Development Company in 1908. Not all of those who supported the Zionist cause, however, accepted Herzl's vision of this Jewish state as secular. Asher Ginsburg, for example, who wrote under the name of Ahad Ha-Am (One of the People), argued that the Jewish state could not jettison its faith in God and the laws of Moses and still be Jewish. But both secular and religious Zionists agreed that the goal of achieving the state was primary and urgent and that questions as to the nature of the state could wait. It was that ability to focus on primary practical goals before ideological questions that proved crucial in Zionism's success.

Jews had been settling in Palestine for centuries, with an escalation in immigration since the 1880s, but in 1904 a movement known as the Second Aliya began with the goal of creating an agricultural Palestine. The men and women in this movement saw themselves as pioneers (Hebrew *chalutzim*) who would transform the land into an agricultural paradise by hard physical labor. They would also culturally transform the Jewish people through the revival of Hebrew as a spoken language and the production of a Jewish culture free from the influences of what they deemed "ghetto culture." Those who believed in this ideology were known as Labor Zionists and included David Ben-Gurion, a future prime minister of Israel, and most of the founders of the state of Israel. The Labor Zionists believed socialism must be at the core of this rebirth and they founded their first collective agricultural settlement (*kibbutz*) in Degania in 1909 to promote its application.

Approximately 40,000 Jewish immigrants arrived in Palestine before 1914, although many of these were driven less by hope for the new state than by the harsh conditions they encountered in their homelands before the outbreak of WORLD WAR I. The official Ottoman attitude toward the Zionist program was ambivalent. Sultan ABDÜLHAMID II (r. 1876–1909) felt that his empire would be strengthened by Jewish immigration into Palestine, which was then an Ottoman territory, but at the same time, his advisers worried that the Zionist movement might eventually seek the secession of Palestine.

Ottoman Jews were largely indifferent to the Zionist program, partly due to a reluctance to leave the places in which their ancestors had lived for centuries and partly due to the fact they had not suffered the persecution that their coreligionists had experienced in Europe. When Vladimir Jabotinsky (who would later found the Revisionist Zionist movement) visited the city of SALONIKA, Jewish leaders there told him they favored the establishment of Jewish colonies in the Ottoman Empire but they preferred that they be in Macedonia rather than Palestine. The Arab population of Palestine looked on with trepidation as Zionists began to acquire property and build settlements. They feared the Zionists might seek to detach the territory they were settling from the Ottoman Empire, and their representatives in the Ottoman Parliament sought to limit Jewish settlement after 1908, with no success.

During World War I, Turkish authorities imprisoned some Zionists who had not acquired Ottoman citizenship, and many Zionist settlers left the country. The Zionist hopes, however, received a major boost with the Balfour Declaration of November 2, 1917, which stated that the British looked with favor on the establishment in Palestine of a "national home for the Jewish people." Though not quite a commitment to a Jewish state, this support was an essential first step in the establishment of what would become, in 1948, the state of Israel.

Bruce Masters

Further reading: Arthur Hertzberg, *The Zionist Idea* (New York: Jewish Publication Society, 1959); Neville Mandel, *The Arabs and Zionism before World War I* (Berkeley: University of California Press, 1976).

Ziya Pasha (Abdülhamid Ziyaeddin) (b. 1825–d. 1880) *Ottoman poet, writer, and statesman of the Tanzimat era* A key figure in the YOUNG OTTOMAN movement of the mid-19th century, Ziya Pasha devoted much of his life to the public critique of the late Ottoman Empire, focusing especially on government corruption and mismanagement. As an exile in Europe, the ISTANBUL native founded several influential NEWSPAPERS, including *Hürriyet* (Liberty), and gathered around him a group of like-minded fellow exiles who together had a profound effect on the public attitude toward political criticism in the Ottoman Empire. Although he was an ardent proponent of modern ideas, Ziya Pasha's familiarity with the palace and his immersion in sultanic culture left a deep impression on his mind and attitudes; due in part to these influences, he is also seen as having frequently embraced the ideas of a cultural traditionalist.

Ziya Pasha was born in 1825 in Istanbul and graduated from Mekteb-i Edebiye (Literature School) in 1846. That same year, with the support of MUSTAFA REŞID PASHA, he received a civil service appointment. In 1862, following Resid's death, Grand Vizier FUAD PASHA dismissed Ziya Pasha from his service in the private apartments of the palace (Mabeyn-i Humayun) and sent him on various administrative assignments as a *mutasarrif* or tax collector in CYPRUS, in Canik (a town in the BLACK SEA region of Turkey), and in Amasya (a city in the Black Sea region of Turkey), and he was a member of the Supreme Council for Judicial Ordinances (Meclis-i Vala-yı Ahkam-ı Adliye) in different terms. In 1867, when he was *mutasarrif* of Amasya, Ziya Pasha left Turkey for Paris on the invitation of Mustafa Fazıl Pasha, a brother of the Egyptian khedive and a grandson of MEHMED ALI. In Paris, Ziya Pasha, NAMIK KEMAL, and other friends established an opposition intellectual movement, the Young Ottoman Society (*see* YOUNG OTTOMANS), and with the financial backing of Mustafa Fazıl Pasha, published journals in Paris (*Muhbir*, or Reporter, in 1867) and in London (*Hürriyet*, or Liberty, in 1868). Although Mustafa Fazıl Pasha compromised to guarantee his future and bureaucratic status with Sultan ABDÜLAZIZ (r. 1861–76) in 1867 and returned to Istanbul, he continued to finance these publications. In the following period, he insisted that the Society should be less oppositional, and when his demand was not taken into consideration he ceased financial support for Society activities. As a result, Namık Kemal ended his association with the paper, and from the 64th issue (September 13, 1869), *Hürriyet* was published by Ziya Pasha alone. When Âlî Pasha died in 1871, other members of the Young Ottoman group also began to turn back to the empire. Ziya Pasha continued to publish *Hürriyet* until its 100th issue in 1871, whereupon he, too, returned to Istanbul.

Back in Istanbul, Ziya Pasha held some official posts (including mabeyn başkatibliği, or chief scribe of the private apartment of the palace; terceme cemiyeti reisliği, or chief of the translation society; and maarif müsteşarlığı, or under-secretary of education) for short periods. In 1876, he was active with Midhat Pasha in an attempt to dethrone Sultan Abdülaziz.

Familiar with Arabic, Persian, and French, Ziya Pasha was distinguished not only by his learning and his intellect, but also by his long administrative experience. He is best known for his writings, most of which related to improving the empire's administration. In a series of articles published in *Hürriyet*, it is apparent that Ziya Pasha had a contradictory political theory vis-à-vis the current administrative system. His ideas were sometimes modern, but he sometimes seemed to be a cultural traditionalist. These articles clearly show the influence of 18th-century French Enlightenment philosophers, especially Rousseau. Committed at once to innovation and tradition, Ziya Pasha's writing embraces the Young Ottomans' notions of consultation and assembly, but rejects their idea of rebellion. The reason for this seemingly dual position was probably his close relationship with the Sublime Porte and his devotion to and respect for the sultan. In his booklet *Rüya* (Dream, published after his death in 1910), for instance, Ziya Pasha suggests the establishment of a national assembly; however, he also claims that the sultan's "legitimate independence" should by no means be restricted. Moreover, he advises that the emperor should engage more actively in state affairs, linking the decline of the Ottoman Empire to the sultan's retreat from state affairs.

Ziya Pasha was also an acclaimed poet. In 1859 he wrote a traditional book of poetry titled *Terci-i Bend* (a poem in which each stanza ends with the same couplet). The text is one of those mystical works often encountered in classical Ottoman LITERATURE in which God is being sought in works, life is envisaged as a process of preparation for eternal life, and the human being is portrayed as a passing imagination. However, the poem is still modern in the sense that it turns into a struggle between faith and reason. Published in 1870, *Terkib-i Bend* (a poem the stanzas of which are connected by a refrain) illustrates Ziya Pasha's struggle against the Porte, not the sultan. Although he never gives up the main ideas of *Terci-i Bend*, the speaker is shown as having achieved peace of mind, saying "there is no way to understand the secret of creation, therefore, let's look at our earth and, before all else, clear it from injustice." In *Zafername* (Book of Victory, 1868), which is a fairly severe satire, he depicts a man of struggle who bluntly makes fun of his enemy and benefits from all possible means to beat him. This book also includes poems about major political crises of the era such as Serbian castles, Romania, and Lebanon affairs and especially gossips concerning Crete. *Harabat* (Ruins) is a continuation of classical Ottoman poetry from one aspect, yet from another aspect it demonstrates completely new characteristics. With this work a philosophical uneasiness was introduced to literature.

Ziya Pasha also prepared translations of Louis Viardot's *Histoire des Arabes et des Maures d'Espagne* (History of the Moors of Spain), Joseph Lavallée's *Histoire des Inquisitions Religieuses d'Italie, d'Espagne et de Por-*

tugal (History of the Inquisition), Molière's *Le Tartuffe* (Riyanın Encamı, or End of Hypocrisy, in 1880) and Rousseau's *Emile*.

Although Ziya Pasha wrote only poetry in the last years of his life, he is best remembered for his early political and philosophical writings, especially his articles in *Hürriyet*.

Yücel Bulut

Further reading: Niyazi Berkes, *The Development of Secularism in Turkey* (Montreal: McGill University Press, 1964); Şerif Mardin, *The Genesis of Young Ottoman Thought* (Princeton, N.J.: Princeton University Press, 1962).

Zistovi, Treaty of   *See* SVISHTOV, TREATY OF.

CHRONOLOGY

1071	Seljuk Turks defeat the Byzantines at the Battle of Manzikert; Seljuks established in Asia Minor.
1204–61	Latin Empire of Constantinople founded by crusaders after the sack of the Byzantine capital, Constantinople.
1243	Mongols rout the Seljuks at the Battle of Kösedağ; Seljuk power in Asia Minor wanes.
1258	Mongols sack the Abbasid capital, Baghdad; end of the Abbasid Caliphate.
?–1324	**Reign of Osman I (Gazi), eponymous founder of the Ottoman dynasty.**
1301	Osman defeats the Byzantines at the Battle of Baphaeon.
c. 1324–62	**Reign of Orhan I (Gazi).**
1326	Ottomans capture Bursa (Prusa), which becomes Ottoman capital.
1326–27	Earliest known Ottoman coin.
1331	Ottomans capture Nicaea (Iznik).
1337	Ottomans capture Nicomedia (Izmit).
1345–46	Ottomans are allies of Byzantine emperor John VI Kantakouzenos; Kantakouzenos gives his daughter Theodora in marriage to Orhan.
c.1345	Ottomans annex Karasi Emirate.
1352	Ottomans cross over into Europe (Thrace), establish their first bridgehead in Tzympe on the Gallipoli peninsula.
1354	Gallipoli destroyed by an earthquake, captured by Orhan's eldest son, Süleyman; beginning of Ottoman advance into Thrace.
1361?–1369?	Ottomans capture Edirne (Adrianople) at the confluence of the Maritsa and Tundža rivers; Edirne becomes Ottoman capital.
1362–89	**Reign of Murad I.**
1371	Ottoman victory over Serbs at Chermanon (Çirmen, on the Maritsa River); conquest of Macedonia and neighboring areas.
1373	Byzantine Empire and the Balkan rules become tributaries of the Ottomans.
1385	Ottomans capture Sofia from the Bulgarians.
1386	Ottomans capture Niš from the Serbians.
1389	First Battle of Kosovo; Ottomans defeat a Balkan coalition led by the Serbian Prince Lazar; Lazar and Murad I both killed in battle; Serbia becomes Ottoman tributary.
1389–1402	**Reign of Bayezid I.**
1390	Ottomans capture Philadelphia, last Byzantine city in Asia Minor.
1390s	Ottomans annex west Anatolian emirates.
1393	Ottomans capture Trnovo, capital of Bulgarian ruler Šišman.
1394–1402	Unsuccessful siege and blockade of Constantinople.
1396	Battle of Nikopol; Bayezid I defeats a crusader army led by Sigismund, King of Hungary and Holy Roman Emperor.
1397–99	Conquest of large part of Asia Minor.
1402	Battle of Ankara; Bayezid I defeated and taken prisoner by Timur (Tamerlane); Anatolian Turkish emirates regain independence; Byzantine Empire ceases being tributary and recovers substantial territory.
1402–1413	Bayezid's sons struggle for throne; Mehmed I triumphs, supported by Byzantine Emperor Manuel II (r. 1391–1421) and by Serb princes; Mehmed I unifies Ottoman territories.
1413–21	**Reign of Mehmed I.**
1415	Ottoman expansion in western Anatolia; conflict with Venice.
1416	Sheikh Bedreddin uprising in the Balkans; Ottoman fleet destroyed by Venetians at Gallipoli.
1419–20	Campaign on lower Danube; Wallachia becomes tributary.
1421–44	**First reign of Murad II.**
1421–22	Revolt of "False Mustafa."
1422	Unsuccessful siege of Constantinople.
1423–30	Salonika (Thessaloniki) under Venetian control; Ottoman-Venetian War.
1424	Ottoman-Byzantine treaty; Byzantines again become Ottoman tributary.
1430	Final Ottoman capture of Salonika.
1439	Ottomans annex Serbia.

1440	Unsuccessful Ottoman attempt to take Belgrade from Hungarians.
1443	Hungarian campaign into the Balkans leads to Ottoman retreat from Serbia; rebellion of Skanderbeg (George Kastriota) in northern Albania.
1444	New Hungarian campaign into the Balkans defeated at Varna.
1444–46	**First reign of Mehmed II.**
1444	Debasement of Ottoman silver coinage.
1446–51	**Second reign of Murad II.**
1448	Second Battle of Kosovo; Ottomans defeat Hungarian army led by János Hunyadi.
1451–81	**Second reign of Mehmed II.**
1453	Conquest of Constantinople (Istanbul) ends Byzantine Empire.
1455	Moldavia becomes Ottoman tributary.
1456	Ottoman attempt to capture Belgrade defeated by János Hunyadi.
1457–58	Construction of the Seven Towers (Yedikule) fortress and Old Palace in Ottoman Constantinople.
1459	Final annexation of Serbia; construction of Topkapı Palace begins.
1460	Conquest of Duchy of Athens; conquest of Byzantine Despotate of Mistra.
1460–51	Construction of covered bazaar begins.
1461	Ottoman capture of Trebizond (Trabzon) ends last Byzantine state.
1463	Ottoman conquest of most of Bosnia and Herzegovina.
1463–79	Ottoman-Venetian War.
1468	Ottomans annex Karaman Emirate.
1469–74	Pacification of Karamanids.
1470	Ottomans capture Negroponte in Euboea from Venetians.
1473	Ottoman victory over Uzun Hasan of the Akkoyunlu Turkoman confederation; consolidation of Ottoman rule in Anatolia.
1475	Ottomans capture Genoese colonies in the Crimea; the Crimean Tatars become Ottoman vassals.
1480	Control of most of Albania regained; Ottomans capture Otranto, Italy; failed Ottoman siege of Rhodes.
1481–1512	**Reign of Bayezid II.**
1481	Ottoman surrender of Otranto; the Ottoman pretender Cem flees to Mamluk Egypt.
1482	Cem takes refuge first in Rhodes, then in France.
1483	Ottoman conquest of Herzegovina.
1484	Ottoman conquests of Kilia and Akkerman deprive Moldavia of access to Black Sea.
1485–91	Ottoman-Mamluk War.
1489	Cem is taken to Rome.
1492	Jews are expelled from Spain, offered new home in the Ottoman Empire.
1495	Ottoman pretender Cem dies.
1499–1503	Ottoman-Venetian War; Ottomans capture several Venetian strongholds in Greece and Albania including Lepanto.
1501	Shia Safavid state in Iran established by Shah Ismail I.
1510–12	Succession struggle among sons of Sultan Bayezid II.
1511	Shia partisans of Shah Ismail rebel in southeastern Anatolia.
1512	Selim forces his father, Bayezid II, to abdicate.
1512–20	**Reign of Selim I.**
1514	Battle of Çaldıran; Ottoman victory over Shah Ismail; eastern Anatolia incorporated into empire.
1516	Ottoman victory over the Mamluks at the Battle of Mardj Dabik; conquest of Syria.
1517	Ottoman victory over the Mamluks at the Battle of Raydaniyya; conquest of Egypt; fall of the Mamluk Sultanate; the Sharif of Mecca submits to Selim I.
1520–66	**Reign of Süleyman I.**
1520s	Ottoman-Portuguese rivalry in the Indian Ocean.
1521	Ottoman conquest of Belgrade.
1522	Ottoman conquest of Rhodes; end of the rule of Knights of St. John in Dodecanese.
1526	Battle of Mohács; victory over Hungary; Ottoman-Habsburg rivalry in Hungary.
1529	First failed Ottoman siege of Vienna.
1530s	Ottoman-Habsburg rivalry in North Africa.
1533	Hayreddin Barbarossa, governor of Algiers, appointed to command Ottoman navy.
1534	Ottoman conquest of Tabriz and Baghdad.
1538	Ottoman campaign in Moldavia; Ottomans annex northwestern Black Sea coast; Ottoman naval victory at Preveza over the allied fleet of the papacy, Venice, and the Habsburgs.
1541	Ottomans annex central Hungary (Buda province); Transylvania becomes a tributary principality.
1548	Süleyman's campaign against the Safavids of Iran.
1553–55	War with Safavid Iran.
1554	Süleyman's campaign in Iran; Ottoman conquest of Nakhichevan and Erivan; Muscovy conquers Astrakhan.
1555	Ottoman-Safavid peace at Amasya stabilizes the eastern frontier and Ottoman-Safavid border.
1565	Ottoman siege of Malta defeated by Knights of St. John.

1566–74 **Reign of Selim II.**

1569 Failed Ottoman attempt to dig a canal between the Don and Volga rivers in an attempt to ship Black Sea fleet into the Caspian Sea, contain Muscovy's advance, outflank the Safavids.

1570–71 Ottoman conquest of Cyprus from Venetians.

1571 Ottoman defeat by Holy League (papacy, Spain, Venice) at Battle of Lepanto.

1573 Peace with Venice; Cyprus remains in Ottoman hands.

1574–95 **Reign of Murad III.**

1578–90 War with Iran; Ottoman conquest of Azerbaijan; financial crisis and inflation.

1580 Ottoman-Habsburg truce in the Mediterranean.

1590s Start of Celali revolts in Anatolia.

1593–1606 Long War against the Habsburgs in Hungary.

1595–1603 **Reign of Mehmed III.**

1595 Rebellion of Romanian principalities.

1603–17 **Reign of Ahmed I.**

1603–12 Renewed war with Safavid Iran ends in first major loss, that of conquests made in war of 1578–90.

1606 Treaty of Zsitvatorok with Austrian Habsburgs; Ottomans keep most of Hungary.

1609 End of first phase of Celali revolts.

1613–35 Rebellion of Fahreddin Ma'noğlu.

1614–18 War with Safavid Iran.

1617–18 **First reign of Mustafa I.**

1618–22 **Reign of Osman II.**

1621–22 War with Poland-Lithuania.

1622–23 **Second reign of Mustafa I.**

1622–28 Revolt of Abaza Mehmed Pasha.

1623–40 **Reign of Murad IV.**

1623–39 War with Iran.

1639 Treaty of Zuhab with Iran restores frontiers of 1555 and 1612.

1640–48 **Reign of Ibrahim I.**

1645–69 War with Venice over Crete.

1648–87 **Reign of Mehmed IV.**

1656–61 Köprülü Mehmed Pasha grand vizier with full powers.

1657–58 Ottoman campaign against Transylvania to subdue Prince György Rákóczi II.

1660 Ottomans capture Várad (eastern Hungary); province of Varad created.

1661–76 Köprülüzade Fazil Ahmed Pasha grand vizier.

1663–64 War with Austrian Habsburgs.

1669 Ottomans conquer Crete.

1672–76 War with Poland-Lithuania ends in annexation of Podolia; maximum Ottoman expansion in Europe.

1676–83 Kara Mustafa Pasha grand vizier.

1677–81 War with Muscovy.

1683 Second Ottoman siege of Vienna; Ottomans defeated by Austrian-Polish army.

1684 Holy League (Austria, Poland-Lithuania, Venice, papacy) against Ottomans.

1686 Fall of Buda; Muscovy joins the Holy League.

1687 Ottomans defeated at Battle of Nagyharsány ("Second Mohács") by Holy League; Mehmed IV forced to abdicate.

1687–91 **Reign of Süleyman II.**

1688 Austrian Habsburgs capture Belgrade, occupy parts of Serbia; Serbs revolt in support of Habsburgs.

1690 Ottoman reconquest of Serbia and Belgrade; first great Serbian migration from Kosovo and southern Serbia to Slavonia and Hungary.

1691–95 **Reign of Ahmed II.**

1691 Ottomans defeated by Habsburgs at Battle of Slankamen.

1695 Introduction of lifelong tax farms; Azak captured by Czar Peter I.

1695–1703 **Reign of Mustafa II.**

1697 Ottomans defeated by the Holy League at the Battle of Zenta.

1699 Treaty of Karlowitz; Hungary, Slavonia, Croatia, and Transylvania ceded to Habsburgs; Morea, Lika, and lesser Dalmatian territories ceded to Venice; Podolia ceded to Poland; Ottomans retained Serbia, Moldavia.

1700 Treaty of Istanbul; Azak ceded to Muscovy.

1703 Revolt of the army (Edirne Incident); Mustafa II deposed.

1703–30 **Reign of Ahmed III.**

1710–11 War with Russia.

1711 Ottoman victory over Peter I (the Great) of Russia.

1713 Peace with Russia; Azak recovered.

1715–18 War with Venice; Morea recovered.

1716–18 War with Austria.

1718 Treaty of Passarowitz with Austria and Venice; Morea recovered; Banat, northern Serbia, and western Wallachia ceded.

1720s "Tulip Age."

1722 Fall of Safavids; Russian and Ottomans in northwestern Iran.

1724 Partition agreement of Iran with Russia.

1724–46 War with Iran.

1730 Patrona Halil rebellion; Ahmed III deposed.

1730–54 **Reign of Mahmud I.**

1736–39 War with Russia and Austria.

1739 Treaty of Belgrade; Ottomans recover Belgrade, northern Serbia, Wallachia.

1743–46 War with Iran under Nadir Shah.

1754–57 **Reign of Osman III.**

1757–74	**Reign of Mustafa III.**
1768–74	Russo-Ottoman War; Russians occupy Crimea, Moldavia, and Wallachia; Russian fleet defeats the Ottomans in the Aegean; Russians foster rebellions in Greece and in the Levant.
1774–89	**Reign of Abdülhamid I.**
1774	Treaty of Küçük Kaynarca; Crimea becomes independent of Ottomans; Russia acquires fortresses on the northern shores of the Black Sea, territories north of Caucasus Mountains; Russia becomes protector of the Orthodox subjects of the Ottoman Empire.
1783	Russia annexes the Crimea.
1787–92	War with Russia and Austria; severe Ottoman defeats; northwestern Moldavia ceded to Austria; the French Revolution and the Polish problem save the Ottoman Empire from further territorial losses.
1789–1807	**Reign of Selim III.**
1791	Treaty of Svishtov with Austria.
1792	Treaty of Jassy with Russia.
1793	First Ottoman resident ambassadors in Europe.
1793–94	Selim III's Nizam-ı Cedid (New order) army and treasury.
1798–99	French campaign in Egypt and Syria.
1804	Serbian revolt under Petrović Karadjorde.
1805–48	Muhammad Ali ruler of Egypt.
1806–12	War with Russia.
1807	Janissaries revolt against Selim III's military reforms; Selim III deposed.
1807–08	**Reign of Mustafa IV.**
1808	Selim III murdered.
1808–39	**Reign of Mahmud II.**
1810s	Wahabbis subdued by Mehmed Ali and his son Ibrahim Pasha.
1814	Serbian revolt under Miloš Obrenović; secret society Philiki Hetairia (Friendly society) founded to liberate Greeks from Ottomans.
1821–31	Greek War of Independence.
1826	Abolition of the Janissaries.
1827	Ottomans defeated by British, French, and Russian fleets at Navarino.
1828–29	Russo-Ottoman War.
1829	Treaty of Edirne; Russia takes control of Danube delta.
1832–33	Treaty of London; Greece becomes independent.
1833	Treaty of Hünkar İskelesi with Russia.
1838	Anglo-Ottoman (Balta Limanı) trade convention.
1839–61	**Reign of Abdülmecid I.**
1839	Gülhane (Rose garden) Edict inaugurates Tanzimat reform era.
1840	Mehmed Ali Pasha recognized as hereditary ruler of Egypt.
1851	Ottoman Academy of Sciences (Encümen-i Danış) opens.
1853–56	Crimean War.
1856	Imperial Reform Edict; Treaty of Paris.
1861–76	**Reign of Abdülaziz.**
1863	Ottoman Imperial Bank established.
1865	Patriotic Alliance (Young Ottomans) founded
1869	Suez Canal opens.
1875	Ottoman bankruptcy.
1876	First Ottoman Constitution; suppression of April uprising in Bulgaria ("Bulgarian atrocities").
1876–1909	**Reign of Abdülhamid II.**
1877–78	Russo-Ottoman War.
1878	Congress of Berlin; Treaty of Berlin; constitution suspended.
1881	Public Debt Administration; French occupy Tunis, declare protectorate of Tunisia.
1882	British occupy Egypt.
1894	Committee of Union and Progress (Young Turks) is created.
1885	Bulgaria occupies eastern Rumelia.
1896–97	Insurrection in Crete; war with Greece.
1897	Crete becomes autonomous.
1908	Young Turk Revolution; restoration of Constitution of 1876; reopening of Ottoman Parliament.
1909	Countercoup; Abdülhamid exiled to Salonika.
1909–18	**Reign of Mehmed V Reşad.**
1911	War with Italy.
1912–13	First Balkan War.
1913	Second Balkan War.
1914–18	World War I.
1915	Deportation of Armenians of eastern Anatolia; Armenian massacres.
1915–16	Ottoman victory over Allied forces at Gallipoli.
1916	Arab Revolt in Hejaz.
1918–22	**Reign of Mehmed VI.**
1918	Mudros Armistice; Allies occupy Istanbul.
1919	National liberation movement begins, led by Mustafa Kemal.
1920	Treaty of Sèvres; French mandates established over Syria and Lebanon; British mandates established over Iraq and Palestine.
1921–22	Turkish nationalists defeat Greek occupying forces in Anatolia; France and Italy withdraw from Anatolia.
1922	Mudanya Armistice; Grand National Assembly abolishes Ottoman sultanate.
1922–24	**Abdülmecid II (as caliph only).**
1923	Treaty of Lausanne; Allies evacuate Istanbul.
1923	Republic of Turkey proclaimed.
1924	Caliphate abolished; members of the Ottoman dynasty exiled.

GLOSSARY

In compiling this glossary, we relied mainly on our encyclopedia, which we supplemented with material found in various textbooks on Ottoman and Middle Eastern history used in the United States and material found in specialized historical dictionaries of the Ottoman Empire and Islam.

acemi oğlan A novice in the JANISSARIES.

agha (*ağa*) A title for a civil or military leader, such as the chief black eunuch (the head of the sultan's private household) or the commander in chief of the JANISSARIES.

ahd An Arabic word meaning contract, agreement, oath.

ahdname A letter of contract or treaty, often translated as "CAPITULATIONS"; from the Arabic *ahd* (contract, agreement, oath) and the Persian *name* (letter, document).

ahi (akhi) A member or leader of an urban men's fraternity who lived their lives according to a set of Islamic religious and social ideals and values (*futuwwa*), such as courage, honesty, loyalty, and nobility.

ahl An Arabic word meaning people, household, family.

ahl al-dhimma Literally, "people of the contract"; non-Muslims.

ahl al-kitab Literally, "the people of the book"; people who believe in one of the monotheistic faiths.

akçe A small Ottoman silver coin that also served as a unit of account.

Akkoyunlu Literally, "White Sheep"; originally a Turkoman tribal confederation based in eastern Turkey, it developed into a Sunni empire that controlled eastern ANATOLIA, Azerbaijan, Iraq, and western Iran and were the fiercest rivals of the Ottomans.

akıncı From the Turkish word *akın,* "raid"; the descendants of early raiders who fought in return for a share of the war booty and constituted the main body of the early Ottoman army as freelance light cavalry.

aliya From the Hebrew word for "ascent"; the immigration of Jews to Palestine.

Anatolia Asia Minor, roughly the territory of modern Turkey; an Ottoman province (Anadolu) in western Asia Minor.

ashraf The plural of SHARIF; descendants of the Prophet.

askeri Literally, "soldier," "military," referring to the Ottoman ruling, tax-exempt, elite of the military, administrative and religious establishment.

avarız A "costumary" tax, introduced as an extraordinary emergency tax and service especially during wartime, hence also translated as "extraordinary wartime tax."

ayan Provincial notables.

azab (azap) Literally, "unmarried"; a kind of peasant militia, originally made up of unmarried youths who served as foot soldiers in the early Ottoman army; infantryman serving in forts; seaman serving on galleys and shipyards.

Bab-ı Âli (Bab-i hümayun, Dergah-i ali) Literally, "Sublime Porte"; the seat of government; in the 15th–17th centuries the Topkapı Palace where the sultan and the Imperial Divan or Council resided; later it referred to the GRAND VIZIER's office; the Ottoman government.

Bab-i asafi Literally, "the Gate of Asaph"; the GRAND VIZIER's gate, named after Solomon's famous vizier Asaph.

bailo The representative of the Republic of Venice and head of a Venetian community abroad; the Venetian resident ambassador at the sultan's court.

Balkans The mountainous region and peninsula in southeastern Europe that includes present-day Romania, Bulgaria, Greece, European Turkey, Albania, and the countries of the former Yugoslavia.

bashtina Small hereditary possessions in the pre-Ottoman Balkans.

bedestan (bedesten) A covered bazaar or market building with a domed or vaulted hall and external shops.

Bedouin Arabic-speaking, tribally organized nomads.

berat A patent of office or letter of appointment.

bey (*beğ*) A military commander; prince, ruler of an EMIRATE or principality; Ottoman governor of a province or subprovince.

beylerbeyi (beğlerbeği) Literally, "BEY of the beys," commander of the SANCAKbey, that is, provincial governor and commander of the provincial army.

beylerbeylik (beğlerbeğilik) A province; large provincial administrative unit consisting of several SANCAKs or subprovinces or districts.

caliph The successor to Muhammad as head of the Muslim community; titular ruler of Muslims.

cami (jami) A congregational mosque.

capitulations Commercial agreements by which Muslim states granted extraterritorial immunity from local laws and taxes to subjects of Western countries.

cizye See JIZYA, HARAÇ.

dar al-harb Literally, "house of war"; those parts of the world not under Muslim rule.

dar al-Islam Literally, "house of Islam"; territories governed by Muslim rulers where Islamic law is in force.

dar al-sulh Literally, "house of truce"; territories of non-Muslim rulers who entered into a truce with the Ottoman sultan.

defter A register or record book or a single list of records. There were several types of *defters*, such as tax or revenue surveys (*tahrir*), registers of poll tax (sing. *cizye defteri*), soldiers' pay lists (sing. *mevacib defteri*).

defterdar Literally, "the keeper of the DEFTER"; a treasurer or Ottoman official similar to a finance minister in Europe; the head of provincial treasuries and finances.

dergah-i ali See BAB-I ÂLI.

dervish A member of an ascetic SUFI religious brotherhood.

despot A Byzantine court title meaning "lord"; also used in the successor states of the Byzantine Empire established after the Latin conquest of Constantinople in 1204 during the Fourth Crusade (Empire of Trebizond, Despotate of Morea), in the Latin Empire of Constantinople (1204–61), in Bulgaria, and in Serbia.

devşirme (devshirme) Literally, "collection"; the system by which Christian Ottoman boys were forcefully recruited into the Ottoman military and administration.

dhimmi (zimmi) A non-Muslim subject of a state governed by Islamic law.

Divan (divan-i hümayun, divan-i ali) The Imperial Council; the GRAND VIZIER's council, the central organ of Ottoman administration.

doge The elected leader of the Venetian state.

emirate A polity ruled by an emir; a principality such as the many Turkish emirates that were established in ANATOLIA after the collapse of the RUM Seljuk Empire there.

eyalet A province; from the late 16th century, the term used for the *beylerbeylik*, the largest provincial administrative unit in the empire.

faqih A specialist in Islamic law, jurist.

fatwa A written legal opinion issued by a qualified authority, usually the mufti or the chief mufti of the empire, also known as the ŞEYHÜLISLAM, in response to an impersonalized legal question.

ferman (firman) A sultanic edict.

filori A coin named after the European coin the fiorino, also used in the Ottoman Empire with a value of 50–66 akçes in the 16th century.

firman See FERMAN.

fiqh Islamic law, jurisprudence.

ghaza Warfare in the name of Islam; raid.

ghazi A fighting man, one who fights the GHAZA.

grand vizier The highest-ranking administrative officer in the Ottoman Empire, the head of the government and the absolute deputy of the sultan.

Habsburgs (Hapsburgs; House of Habsburg) An important European dynasty that ruled for centuries in Austria, Spain, and as Holy Roman Emperors.

hadith Reports about the sayings and actions of the Prophet and his companions. Collected and sifted for their authenticity some hadith collections attained religious authority second only to the Quran.

hajj The annual pilgrimage of Muslims to Mecca, one of the "five pillars" of Islam, to be performed at least once in a lifetime.

han (khan) A caravansary; a structure either in a city or placed along caravan routes where traveling merchants could stay.

hüküm An order or decree issued by the Imperial DIVAN or Council.

hammam (hamam) A bathhouse.

haraç Also known as *cizye* in the Ottoman Empire, the *haraç* was the capitation or poll tax to be paid by non-Muslims.

harem Literally, "forbidden," "sacred"; private quarter of the house and its female inhabitants; the sultan's household.

has (hass) Sultanic or crown lands or revenues; lands or revenues of BEYLERBEYS and SANCAKBEYS, usually (but not always) yielding an annual revenue of more than 100,000 AKÇES in the 16th century.

hatt-i hümayun An imperial decree; the Reform Edict of 1856, the second most important sultanic decree of the Ottoman reform or TANZIMAT era (1839–76).

hatt-i şerif Literally, "noble sultanic decree"; the Gülhane Decree of 1839 that introduced the Ottoman TANZIMAT or Reform era (1839–76).

hutbe (hutba)   Friday sermon in Islam in which the ruler's name is mentioned.

Ilkhanids   A Mongol dynasty established after the dissolution of the Great Mongol Empire of Ghengis Khan that ruled in Iran from the mid-13th through the mid-14th century.

iltizam   A tax farm, tax farming; Ottoman method of revenue collection by which sources of state revenues were farmed out to proper applicants by means of a public auction.

imam   In Sunni Islam, the leader of prayer in mosques; in Shia Islam, the divinely ordained leader of the Shia community.

imaret   A public building complex supported by a religious endowment or *waqf*; public kitchen; soup kitchen.

Janissaries   From the Turkish *yeni çeri*, "new army"; the sultan's elite infantry, originally made up of prisoners of war, later recruited through the *devşirme* system.

jihad   The struggle to defend and extend Islam; war to achieve these goals.

jizya (cizye)   An Islamic poll tax imposed on non-Muslim adult males.

kadı (qadi)   A Muslim judge.

kadıasker   The chief judge; the top judicial official in the Ottoman Empire after the *şeyhülislam* until the Tanzimat reform period of the 19th century.

kanun (qanun)   Secular or sultanic law, a body of law promulgated in the name of the reigning sultan, which supplemented the sacred Islamic law, or sharia.

kanunname   A collection of sultanic laws; a shorter law code, for instance those at the beginning of land surveys (*tahrir defteris*) that regulated taxation in a given district.

kapukulu (kapıkulu)   Literally, "slave of the Porte," who served in the military, administration, and palace and were in the early centuries of *devşirme* origin.

kapudan pasha (kapudan-i derya)   An admiral; commander in chief of the Ottoman navy.

khedive   A ruler of Egypt in the line of Mehmed Ali.

kızılbaş   Literally, "Redheads," followers of Shah Ismail, the Ottomans' main rival in the early 16th century, named after their twelve-tasseled red hat, a symbol of their belief that Ismail was the promised 12th imam of Shia Islam.

Levant   The eastern Mediterranean.

madhab (mezheb)   A schools of law in Sunni Islam. The preferred *madhab* in the Ottoman Empire was the Hanafi, although the three other major schools (Hanbali, Maliki, and the Shafii) were also tolerated.

madrasa (medrese)   A college or school whose primary aim was the teaching of Islamic religious sciences, although rational sciences, such as medicine, could also be taught.

Maghrib   North Africa, especially present-day Morocco, Algeria, and Tunisia.

mahkeme (mahkama)   A sharia court and its building.

malikane   A life-long tax farm.

mamluk   A military slave; a member of the Turkish cavalry forces who established their own sultanate, the Mamluk Empire of Egypt and Syria.

medrese   *See* madrasa.

mihrab   A niche or blind arch in the wall of a mosque indicating the direction of Mecca which Muslims should face when praying.

millet   A non-Muslim community in the Ottoman Empire represented by a clergyman appointed by the sultan.

miri   Lands and revenues belonging to the state.

Morea   The large peninsula in southern Greece, also known as the Peloponnese.

Muscovy   The Russian principality centered around Moscow that by the 18th century expanded to become the Russian Empire.

mukataa   The revenues from fiscal units administered as tax farms.

nişancı   The chancellor; head of the sultan's scribe service; member of the Imperial Council who was responsible for attaching the *tuğra* to official orders.

pasha (paşa)   The highest title given to military or civil officials in the empire.

Phanariots   Greek elite from Istanbul's Phanar district who held important political positions in the Ottoman Empire from the 17th century until the Greek War of Independence in 1821.

Pontic   An adjective referring to the territories around the Black Sea.

presidio   Spanish frontier forts along the Mediterranean coastline and the frontier areas in the Americas and the Philippines.

pronoia   A military fief in the Byzantine Empire, similar to the Ottoman *timar* system.

reaya   "Flock"; originally all taxpaying subjects of the sultan regardless of their religion as opposed to the *askeri* ruling elite; later the Christian subjects of the empire.

reisülküttab (reis efendi)   A title; literally, "head of the scribes," head of the chancery and record offices of the Imperial Council; in the 18th-century the title was change to "foreign minister."

Rum A geographical term in Islamic literature that refers to ANATOLIA (Asia Minor), the land of Rome, the Eastern Roman Empire, as in the name of the Rum Seljuks, the dynastic heirs of the Great Seljuks; also the Greek Orthodox Christian community.

Rumelia (Rumeli) The Balkans, the European provinces of the Ottoman Empire.

sadrazam (sadr-i azam) The GRAND VIZIER.

salname An official governmental yearbook or annual report in the 19th century Ottoman Empire; official provincial yearbook.

sancak (sanjak) A subdivision of a province (EYALET, VILAYET, BEYLERBEYILIK), translated as subprovince or district.

sancakbeyi The governor of a SANCAK.

şeyhülislam (shaykh al-islam) The head of the Ottoman religious establishment (ULEMA); the chief mufti of Istanbul and of the empire.

sharia (şeriat) Islamic law, derived from the Quran, HADITH, analogy, and consensus.

sharif *(plural: ashraf)* A descendant of the Prophet Muhammad.

sheikh (shaykh, şeyh) A title of respect for a learned man, the leader of a religious brotherhood or dervish order, or a tribal chief.

sicil (sijil) An Ottoman judicial court register in which the KADI kept track of proceedings.

sipahi (spahi) A cavalryman, remunerated through military fiefs or TIMARS, who was stationed in the provinces and formed part of the provincial cavalry of a given SANCAK; **sipahi of the Porte**: member of one of the six cavalry divisions of the Porte's standing army.

Straits The straits of the Bosporus and Dardanelles.

Sufi A Muslim mystic; a member of an Islamic religious order or TARIQA.

Sufism Mystical traditions in Islam, known in Arabic as *tasawwuf*.

sultan A ruler with supreme authority; ruler of the Ottoman Empire; a title used by princes and senior female members of the Ottoman dynasty.

sürgün Deportation or state-initiated and state-organized resettlement.

Tanzimat The Ottoman reform era of 1838–76.

tariqa (tarikat) Literally, the "path" or "route" of spiritual growth, hence Islamic mystic or SUFI order.

tekke A dervish lodge or SUFI convent, known in Arabic as ZAVIYE.

Tersane-i Amire The Ottoman imperial naval arsenal.

timar An Ottoman military or administrative fief or prebend given to soldiers and officials in return for their service, usually (but not always) with an annual value of less than 20,000 AKÇE in the 16th century.

Transoxania (*ma wara' Al-nahr*) A historic term referring to the region "beyond the river," that is, beyond the Oxus River (present-day Amu Darya) and Jaxartes River (present-day Syr Darya). It was the region ruled by the Timurid Empire (1370–1506) and became a major center of Islamic civilization during that time. It roughly corresponds to present-day Uzbekistan and parts of Turkmenistan and Kazakhstan.

tuğra The sultan's official monogram.

Turkomans (Turcomans, Türkmens) Turkish pastoralists living in ANATOLIA.

ulema *(sing. alim)* Persons trained in the Islamic religious sciences; the Ottoman religious establishment.

vakıf See WAQF.

vakfiye The deed of endowment for a WAQF, or charitable foundation.

valide sultan The queen mother, the mother of the ruling sultan.

vezir See VIZIER.

vilayet A province, the largest administrative division of the empire in the 16th century, headed by a governor or BEYLERBEYI.

vizier (*vezir*) The sultan's minister; a member of the Imperial Council.

voynuk The Slavic term for " soldier"; auxiliaries in the Balkans.

waqf A religious endowment that provided funds for mosques, schools, hospitals, and other religious, charitable, and educational institutions.

yaya A foot soldier; infantry forces in the early Ottoman Empire who later served as auxiliaries.

yeniçeri See JANISSARIES.

yürük TURKOMAN nomads who also served as military auxiliaries in the early Ottoman army.

zeamet (ziamet) An Ottoman military or administrative fief or prebend given to officers and officials in return for their service, usually (but not always) with an annual revenue of between 20,000 and 100,000 AKÇE in the 16th century.

zaviye (zawiya) A dervish lodge or SUFI convent.

zimmi See DHIMMI.

BIBLIOGRAPHY

GENERAL WORKS

Ahmad, Feroz. *The Making of Modern Turkey*. London: Routledge, 1993.

Alderson, Anthony Dolphin. *The Structure of the Ottoman Dynasty*. Oxford: Clarendon Press, 1956.

Cicek, Kemal, ed. *The Great Ottoman Turkish Civilization*. 4 vols. Ankara: Yeni Türkiye, 2000.

Cook, Michael, ed. *A History of the Ottoman Empire to 1730*. Cambridge: Cambridge University Press, 1976.

Faroqhi, Suraiya. *Approaching Ottoman History: An Introduction to the Sources*. New York: Cambridge University Press, 1999.

———. *The Ottoman Empire and the World Around It*. London: I.B. Tauris, 2004.

———. *The Ottoman Empire: A Short History*. Princeton, N.J.: Markus Wiener, 2008.

Finkel, Caroline. *Osman's Dream: The Story of the Ottoman Empire, 1300–1923*. New York: Basic Books, 2006.

Goffman, Daniel. *The Ottoman Empire and Early Modern Europe*. Cambridge: Cambridge University Press, 1992.

Hanioğlu, M. Şükrü. *A Brief History of the Late Ottoman Empire*. Princeton, N.J.: Princeton University Press, 2008.

İhsanoğlu, Ekmeleddin, ed. *History of the Ottoman State, Society and Civilisation*. 2 vols. Istanbul: IRCICA, 2002

Imber, Colin. *The Ottoman Empire, 1300–1481*. Istanbul: Isis, 1990.

———. *The Ottoman Empire, 1300–1650: The Structure of Power*. London: Palgrave Macmillan, 2002.

Inalcık, Halil. *The Ottoman Empire: The Classical Age, 1300–1600*. Translated by Norman Itzkowitz and Colin Imber. London: Weidenfeld & Nicolson, 1973.

Inalcık, Halil, and Donald Quataert, eds. *An Economic and Social History of the Ottoman Empire, 1300–1914*. Cambridge: Cambridge University Press, 1994.

Inalcık, Halil, and Günsel Renda. *Ottoman Civilization*. 2 vols. Istanbul: Republic of Turkey, Ministry of Culture and Tourism, 2004.

Itzkowitz, Norman. *Ottoman Empire and Islamic Tradition*. Chicago: University of Chicago Press, 1980 [1972].

Kreiser, Klaus. *Der Osmanische Staat, 1300–1922*. Munich: Oldenbourg, 2001.

Mantran, Robert, ed. *Histoire de l'Empire Ottoman*. Paris: Fayard, 1989.

McCarthy, Justin. *The Ottoman Turks: An Introductory History to 1923*. London: Longman, 1997.

———. *The Ottoman Peoples and the End of Empire*. London: Arnold, 2001.

Pamuk, Şevket. *A Monetary History of the Ottoman Empire*. New York: Cambridge University Press, 2000.

Pitcher, Donald Edgar. *An Historical Geography of the Ottoman Empire: From Earliest Times to the End of the Sixteenth Century*. Leiden: Brill, 1972, c1968

Quataert, Donald. *The Ottoman Empire, 1700–1922*. New York: Cambridge University Press, 2000.

Shaw, Stanford. J. *History of the Ottoman Empire and Modern Turkey*. 2 vols. Cambridge: Cambridge University Press, 1976–1977.

Somel, Selçuk Akşin. *Historical Dictionary of the Ottoman Empire*. Lanham, Md.: Scarecrow Press, 2003.

Sugar, Peter. *Southeastern Europe under Ottoman Rule, 1354–1804*. Seattle: University of Washington Press, 1977.

Zürcher, Erik J. *Turkey: A Modern History*. 3rd edition. London: I.B. Tauris, 2004.

MONOGRAPHS, EDITED VOLUMES

Abu-el-Haj, Rifa'at 'Ali. *Formation of the Modern State: The Ottoman Empire, Sixteenth to Eighteenth Centuries*. Second Edition. Syracuse, NY.: Syracuse University Press, 2005.

Abu Husayn, A. *Provincial Leaderships in Syria, 1575–1650*. Beirut: The American University, 1985.

Abu Husayn, A. *The View from Istanbul: Lebanon and the Druze Emirate in the Ottoman Chancery Documents, 1546–1711*. New York: I.B. Tauris, 2004.

Abu-Manneh, Butrus. *Studies on Islam and the Ottoman Empire in the 19th Century, 1826–1876*. Istanbul: Isis, 2001

Adanir, Fikret, and Suraiya Faroqhi, eds. *The Ottomans and the Balkans: A Discussion of Historiography*. Leiden: Brill, 2002

Ágoston, Gábor. *Guns for the Sultan: Military Power and the Weapons Industry in the Ottoman Empire*. Cambridge: Cambridge University Press, 2005.

Aksan, Virginia. *An Ottoman Statesman in War and Peace: Ahmed Resmi Efendi, 1700–1783*. Leiden: Brill, 1995.

———. *Ottoman Wars, 1700–1870: An Empire Besieged*. Harlow, England: Longman/Pearson, 2007.

Aksan, Virginia H., and Daniel Goffman, eds. *The Early Modern Ottomans: Remapping the Empire*. (Cambridge: Cambridge University Press, 2007).

Andrews, Walter G. *An Introduction to Ottoman Poetry.* Minneapolis: Bibliotheca Islamica, 1976.

Anscombe, Frederick. *The Ottoman Gulf: The Creation of Kuwait, Saudi Arabia, and Qatar.* New York: Columbia University Press, 1997.

Babinger, Franz. *Mehmed the Conqueror and His Time.* Translated by Ralph Manheim, edited by William C. Hickman. Princeton, N.J.: Princeton University Press, 1978

Bakhit, Muhammad Adnan. *The Ottoman Province of Damascus in the Sixteenth Century.* Beirut: Librairie du Liban, 1982.

Barbir, Karl. *Ottoman Rule in Damascus, 1708–1758.* Princeton, N.J.: Princeton University Press, 1980.

Barkey, Karen, and Mark von Hagen, eds. *After Empire: Multiethnic Societies and Nation-Building: The Soviet Union and the Russian, Ottoman, and Habsburg Empires.* Boulder, Colo.: Westview, 1997.

Benbassa, Esther, and Aron Rodrigue. *Sephardi Jewry: A History of the Judeo-Spanish Community, 14th–20th Centuries.* Berkeley: University of California Press, 2000.

Berkes, Niyazi. *The Development of Secularism in Turkey.* New York: Routledge, 1998.

Bisaha, Nancy. *Creating East and West: Renaissance Humanists and the Ottoman Turks.* Philadelphia: University of Pennsylvania Press, 2004.

Boogert, Maurits H. van den. *The Capitulations and the Ottoman Legal System: Qadis, Consuls and Beraths in the 18th Century.* Leiden: Brill, 2005.

Braude, Benjamin, and Bernard Lewis, eds. *Christians and Jews in the Ottoman Empire: The Functioning of a Plural Society.* New York: Holmes & Meier, 1982.

Brown, Carl, ed. *Imperial Legacy: The Ottoman Imprint on the Balkans and the Middle East.* New York: Columbia University Press, 1996.

Bruinessen, Martin van. *Agha, Shaikh and State: The Social and Political Structures of Kurdistan.* London: Zed Books, 1992.

Brummet, Palmire. *Ottoman Seapower and Levantine Diplomacy in the Age of Discovery.* Albany: State University of New York Press, 1994.

———. *Image and Imperialism in the Ottoman Revolutionary Press, 1908–1911.* Albany: State University of New York Press, 2000.

Çetinsaya, Gökhan. *Ottoman Administration of Iraq, 1890–1908.* London: Routledge, 2007.

Çizakça, Murat. *A Comparative Evolution of Business Partnerships: The Islamic World and Europe, with Specific Reference to the Ottoman Archives.* Leiden: Brill, 1996.

Cohen, Amnon. *Economic Life in Ottoman Jerusalem.* Cambridge: Cambridge University Press, 1989.

———. *The Guilds of Ottoman Jerusalem.* Leiden: Brill, 2001.

Darling, Linda. *Revenue-Raising and Legitimacy: Tax Collection and Finance Administration in the Ottoman Empire, 1560–1660.* Leiden: Brill, 1996.

Dávid, Géza, and Pál Fodor, eds. *Ottomans, Hungarians, and Habsburgs in Central Europe: The Military Confines in the Era of Ottoman Conquest.* Leiden: Brill, 2000.

———, eds. *Ransom Slavery along the Ottoman Borders.* Leiden: Brill, 2007.

Davison, Roderic H. *Reform in the Ottoman Empire, 1856–1876.* Princeton, N.J.: Princeton University Press, 1963.

Deringil, Selim. *The Well-Protected Domains: Ideology and the Legitimation of Power in the Ottoman Empire, 1876–1909.* London: I.B. Tauris, 1998.

Derman, M. Uğur. *Letters in Gold.* New York: Metropolitan Museum of Art, 1998.

Doumani, Beshara. *Rediscovering Palestine: Merchants and Peasants in Jabal Nablus, 1700–1900.* Berkeley: University of California Press, 1995.

Douwes, Dick. *The Ottomans in Syria: A History of Justice and Oppression.* London: I.B. Tauris, 2000.

Eldem, Edhem. *French Trade in Istanbul in the Eighteenth Century.* Leiden: Brill, 1999.

Eldem, Edhem, Daniel Goffmann, and Bruce Masters. *The Ottoman City Between East and West: Aleppo, Izmir, and Istanbul.* New York: Cambridge University Press, 1999.

Ergene, Boğac A. *Local Court, Provincial Society, and Justice in the Ottoman Empire: Legal Practice and Dispute Resolution in Çankiri and Kastamonu, 1652–1744.* Leiden: Brill, 2003.

Fahmy, Khaled. *All the Pasha's Men: Mehmed Ali, His Army, and the Making of Modern Egypt.* Cambridge: Cambridge University Press, 1997.

Faroqhi, Suraiya. *Towns and Townsmen of Ottoman Anatolia: Trade, Crafts and Food Production in an Urban Setting, 1520–1650.* Cambridge: Cambridge University Press, 1984.

———. *Men of Modest Substance: House Owners and House Property in Seventeenth-century Ankara and Kayseri.* New York: Cambridge University Press, 1987.

———. *Pilgrims and Sultans: The Hajj under the Ottomans.* (London: I.B. Tauris, 1994).

Fawaz, Leila. *An Occasion for War: Civil Conflict in Lebanon and Damascus in 1860.* Berkeley: University of California Press, 1994.

Findley, Carter. *Bureaucratic Reform in the Ottoman Empire.* Princeton, N.J.: Princeton University Press, 1980.

———. *Ottoman Civil Officialdom: A Social History.* Princeton, N.J.: Princeton University Press, 1989.

Finkel, Caroline. *The Administration of Warfare: The Ottoman Military Campaigns in Hungary, 1593–1606.* Vienna : Verlag des Verbandes der Wissenschaftlichen Gesellschaften Österreichs, 1988.

Fisher, Alan. *The Crimean Tatars.* Stanford, Calif.: Hoover Institution Press, 1978.

Fleet, Kate. *European and Islamic Trade in the Early Ottoman State: The Merchants of Genoa and Turkey.* Cambridge: Cambridge University Press, 1999.

Fleischer, Cornell H. *Bureaucrat and Intellectual in the Ottoman Empire: The Historian Mustafa Âli, 1541–1600.* Princeton, N.J.: Princeton University Press, 1986.

Fortna, Benjamin C. *Imperial Classroom: Islam, the State, and Education in the Late Ottoman Empire.* New York: Oxford University Press, 2002.

Frangakis-Syrett, Elena. *The Commerce of Smyrna in the Eighteenth Century, 1700–1820.* Athens: Centre for Asia Minor Studies, 1992.

Frazee, Charles A. *Catholics and Sultans: The Church and the Ottoman Empire, 1453–1923.* London: Cambridge University Press, 1983.

Gerber, Haim. *State, Society, and Law in Islam: Ottoman Law in Comparative Perspective.* Albany: State University of New York Press, 1994.

Göcek, Fatma Müge. *East Encounters West: France and the Ottoman Empire in the Eighteenth Century.* New York: Oxford University Press, 1987.

Goffman, Daniel. *Britons in the Ottoman Empire, 1642–1660.* Seattle: University of Washington Press, 1998.

———. *Izmir and the Levantine World, 1550–1650.* Seattle: University of Washington Press, 1990.

Goodwin, Godfrey. *A History of Ottoman Architecture.* London: Thames and Hudson, 1971.

Greene, Molly. *A Shared World: Christians and Muslims in the Early Modern Mediterranean.* Princeton, N.J.: Princeton University Press, 2000.

Griswold, William. *The Great Anatolian Rebellion 1000–1020/1591–1611.* Berlin: Klaus Schwarz, 1983

Hanna, Nelly. *Making Big Money in 1600: The Life and Times of Ismail Abu Taqiyya, Egyptian Merchant.* New York: Syracuse University Press, 1997.

Hanioğlu, M. Şükrü. *The Young Turks in Opposition.* New York: Oxford University Press, 1995.

———. *Preparation for a Revolution: The Young Turks, 1902–1908.* New York: Oxford University Press, 2001.

Hathaway, Jane. *The Politics of Households in Ottoman Egypt: The Rise of Qazdaglis.* Cambridge, UK: Cambridge University Press, 1997.

———. *A tale of Two Factions: Myth, Memory and Identity in Ottoman Egypt and Yemen.* Albany: State University of New York Press, 2003.

Hess, Andrew C. *The Forgotten Frontier: A History of the Sixteenth-Century Ibero-African Frontier.* Chicago, 1978.

Heywood, Colin. *Writing Ottoman History: Documents and Interpretations.* Aldershot, Hampshire, U.K.: Ashgate, 2002.

Imber, Colin. *Ebu's-su'ud and the Islamic Legal Tradition.* Stanford, Calif.: Stanford University Press, 1997.

İnalcık, Halil. *Turkey and Europe in History.* Istanbul: Eren, 2006.

İnalcık, Halil, and Cemal Kafadar, eds. *Süleyman the Second and His Time.* Istanbul: Isis, 1993.

Kafadar, Cemal. *Between Two Worlds: The Construction of the Ottoman State.* Berkeley and Los Angeles: University of California Press, 1995.

Karateke, Hakan T., and Maurus Reinkowski, eds. *Legitimizing the Order: The Ottoman Rhetoric of State Power.* Leiden: Brill, 2005.

Karpat, Kemal H. *An Inquiry into the Social Foundations of Nationalism in the Ottoman State: From Social Estates to Classes, from Millets to Nations.* Princeton, N.J.: Center of International Studies, Princeton University, 1973.

———. *The Politicization of Islam: Reconstructing Identity, State, Faith, and Community in the Late Ottoman State.* Oxford: Oxford University Press, 2001.

Kasaba, Reşat. *The Ottoman Empire and the World Economy: The Nineteenth Century.* Albany: State University of New York Press, 1988.

Kayalı, Hasan. *Arabs and Young Turks: Ottomanism, Arabism, and Islamism in the Ottoman Empire, 1908–1918.* Berkeley and Los Angeles: University of California Press, 1997.

Khoury, Dina Rizk. *State and Provincial Society in the Ottoman Empire: Mosul, 1540–1834.* Cambridge: Cambridge University Press, 1997.

Kolodziejczyk, Dariusz. *Ottoman-Polish Diplomatic Relations (15th–18th Century): An Annotated Edition of 'Ahdnames and Other Documents.* Leiden: Brill, 2000.

Köprülü, M. Fuad. *The Origins of the Ottoman Empire.* Translated and edited by Gary Leiser. Albany: State University of New York Press, 1992.

Kunt, Ibrahim Metin. *The Sultan's Servants: The Transformation of Ottoman Provincial Government, 1550–1650.* New York: Columbia University Press, 1983.

Kunt, Metin, and Christine Woodhead, eds. *Süleyman the Magnificent and His Age: The Ottoman Empire in the Early Modern World.* London: Longman, 1995.

Levy, Avigdor. *The Sephardim in the Ottoman Empire.* Princeton, N.J.: Darwin Press, 1992.

———, ed. *Jews, Turks, Ottomans: A Shared History, Fifteenth Through the Twentieth Century.* Syracuse, N.Y.: Syracuse University Press, 2002.

Lindner, Rudi Paul. *Nomads and Ottomans in Medieval Anatolia.* Bloomington, Ind.: Research Institute for Inner Asian Studies, 1983.

Lowry, Heath W. *The Nature of the Early Ottoman State.* Albany: State University of New York Press, 2003.

Makdisi, Ussama. *The Culture of Sectarianism: Community, History, and Violence in Nineteenth-Century Lebanon.* Berkeley: University of California Press, 2000.

Mango, Andrew. *Atatürk: The Biography of the Founder of Modern Turkey.* Woodstock, N.Y. : Overlook Press, 2000.

Mantran, Robert. *La vie quotidienne à Istanbul au siècle de Soliman le Magnifique.* Paris: Hachette, 1990.

Marcus, Abraham. *The Middle East on the Eve of Modernity: Aleppo in the Eighteenth Century.* New York: Columbia University Press, 1989.

Mardin, Şerif. *The Genesis of Young Ottoman Thought: A Study in the Modernization of Turkish Political Ideas.* Princeton, N.J.: Princeton University Press, 1962.

Masters, Bruce. *The Origins of Western Economic Dominance in the Middle East: Mercantilism and the Islamic Economy in Aleppo, 1600–1750.* New York: New York University Press, 1988.

———. *Christians and Jews in the Ottoman Arab World: The Roots of Sectarianism.* New York: Cambridge University Press, 2001.

Mazower, Mark. *Salonica, City of Ghosts: Christians, Muslims, and Jews, 1430–1950.* New York: Alfred A. Knopf, 2005.

McCarthy, Justin. *Death and Exile: The Ethnic Cleansing of Ottoman Muslims, 1821–1922.* Princeton, N.J.: Darwin, 1995.

McGowan, Bruce. *Economic Life in Ottoman Europe: Taxation, Trade and the Struggle for Land, 1600–1800.* Cambridge: Cambridge University Press, 1981.

Moačanin, Nenad. *Town and Country on the Middle Danube, 1526–1690.* Leiden: Brill, 2006.

Morgan, David. *Medieval Persia, 1040–1797.* Essex: Longman, 1988.

Murphey, Rhoads. *Ottoman Warfare, 1500–1700.* New Brunswick, N.J.: Rutgers University Press, 1999.

Necipoğlu, Gülru. *Architecture, Ceremonial, and Power: The Topkapi Palace in the Fifteenth and Sixteenth Centuries.* New York: Architectural History Foundation, 1991.

———. *The Age of Sinan: Architectural Culture in the Ottoman Empire.* Princeton, N.J.: Princeton University Press, 2005.

Özoğlu, Hakan. *Kurdish Notables and the Ottoman State.* Albany: State University of New York Press, 2004.

Panzac, Daniel. *La peste dans l'Empire ottoman, 1700–1850.* Leuven: Éditions Peeters, 1985.

———. *Quarantaines et lazarets: l'Europe et la peste d'Orient, XVIIe–XXe siècles.* Aix-en-Provence: Édisud, 1986.

———. *Barbary Corsairs: The End of a legend, 1800–1820.* Leiden: Brill, 2005.

Peirce, Leslie P. *The Imperial Harem: Women and Sovereignty in the Ottoman Empire.* New York: Oxford University Press, 1993.

———. *Morality Tales: Law and Gender in the Ottoman Court of Aintab.* Berkeley: University of California Press, 2003.

Philipp, Thomas. *Acre: The Rise and Fall of a Palestinian City, 1730–1831.* New York: Columbia University Press, 2001.

Piterberg, Gabriel. *An Ottoman Tragedy: History and Historiography at Play.* Berkeley: University of California Press, 2003.

Rafeq, Abdul-Karim. *The Province of Damascus, 1723–1782.* Beirut: Khayats, 1966.

Raymond, André. *Artisans et commerçants au Caire au XVIII siècle.* Damas: Institut Français de Damas, 1973–1974.

———. *La ville arabe, Alep, à l'époque ottomane, XVIe–XVIIIe siècles.* Damascus: Institut Français de Damas, 1998.

Reilly, James. *A Small Town in Syria: Ottoman Hama in the Eighteenth and Nineteenth Centuries.* New York: P. Land, 2002.

Salzmann, Ariel. *Tocqueville in the Ottoman Empire: Rival Paths to the Modern State.* Boston: Brill, 2004.

Shaw, Stanford J. *Between Old and New: The Ottoman Empire Under Selim III, 1789–1807.* Cambridge: Cambridge University Press, 1971.

———. *The Jews of the Ottoman Empire and the Turkish Republic.* New York: New York University Press, 1991.

Singer, Amy. *Palestinian Peasants and Ottoman Officials: Rural Administration Around Sixteenth-century Jerusalem.* New York: Cambridge University Press, 1994.

———. *Constructing Ottoman Beneficence: An Imperial Soup Kitchen in Jerusalem.* Albany: State University of New York Press, 2002.

Somel, Selçuk Akşin. *The Modernization of Public Education in the Ottoman Empire: 1839–1908: Islamization, Autocracy and Discipline.* Leiden: Brill; 2001.

Sonyel, Salâhi R. *Minorities and the Destruction of the Ottoman Empire.* Ankara: Turkish Historical Society Printing House, 1993.

Toledano, Ehud. *State and Society in Mid-Nineteenth-Century Egypt.* Cambridge: Cambridge University Press, 1990.

———. *Slavery and Abolition in the Ottoman Middle East.* Seattle: University of Washington Press, 1998.

Tucker, Judith E. *In the House of the Law: Gender and Islamic Law in Ottoman Syria and Palestine.* Berkeley: University of California Press, 1998.

Valensi, Lucette. *The Birth of the Despot: Venice and the Sublime Porte.* Ithaca, N.Y.: Cornell University Press, 1993.

Vaporis, Nomikos Michael. *Witnesses for Christ: Orthodox Christian Neomartyrs of the Ottoman Period, 1437–1860.* Crestwood, N.Y.: St. Vladimir's Seminary Press, 2000.

Vaughan, Dorothy M. *Europe and the Turk: A Pattern of Alliances, 1350–1700.* New York: AMS Press, 1976.

Veinstein, Gilles. *Les Ottomans et la mort: permanences et mutations.* Leiden: Brill, 1996.

———, ed. *Soliman le Magnifique et son temps.* Paris: Documentation française, 1992.

Vryonis, Speros, Jr. *The Decline of Medieval Hellenism in Asia Minor and the Process of Islamization from the Eleventh Through the Fifteenth Century.* Berkeley: University of California Press, 1971.

Watenpaugh, Heghnar Zeitlian. *The Image of an Ottoman City: Imperial Architecture and Urban Experience in Aleppo in the 16th and 17th Centuries.* Leiden: Brill, 2004.

Wittek, Paul. *The Rise of the Ottoman Empire.* London: The Royal Asiatic Society, 1938.

Yi, Eunjeong. *Guild Dynamics in Seventeenth-century Istanbul: Fluidity and Leverage.* Leiden: Brill, 2004.

Ze'evi, Dror. *An Ottoman Century: The District of Jerusalem in the 1600s.* New York: State University of New York Press, 1996.

———. *Producing Desire: Changing Sexual Discourse in the Ottoman Middle East, 1500–1900.* Berkeley: University of California Press, 2006.

Zilfi, Madeline C. *The Politics of Piety: The Ottoman Ulema in the Postclasscial Age, 1600–1800.* Minneapolis: Bibliotecha Islamica, 1988.

———, ed. *Women in the Ottoman Empire: Middle Eastern Women in the Early Modern Era.* Leiden: Brill, 1997.

INDEX